CORONAVIRUS AND THE LAW IN EUROPE

CORONAVIRUS AND THE LAW IN EUROPE

Edited by
Ewoud Hondius
Marta Santos Silva
Andrea Nicolussi
Pablo Salvador Coderch
Christiane Wendehorst
Fryderyk Zoll

INTERSENTIA
Cambridge – Antwerp – Chicago

Intersentia Ltd
8 Wellington Mews
Wellington Street | Cambridge
CB1 1HW | United Kingdom
Tel: +44 1223 736 170
Email: mail@intersentia.co.uk
www.intersentia.com | www.intersentia.co.uk

Distribution for the UK and
Rest of the World (incl. Eastern Europe)
NBN International
1 Deltic Avenue, Rooksley
Milton Keynes MK13 8LD
United Kingdom
Tel: +44 1752 202 301 | Fax: +44 1752 202 331
Email: orders@nbninternational.com

Distribution for Europe
Lefebvre Sarrut Belgium NV
Hoogstraat 139/6
1000 Brussels
Belgium
Tel: +32 (0)800 39 067
Email: mail@intersentia.be

Distribution for the USA and Canada
Independent Publishers Group
Order Department
814 North Franklin Street
Chicago, IL 60610
USA
Tel: +1 800 888 4741 (toll free) | Fax: +1 312 337 5985
Email: orders@ipgbook.com

ISBN 978-1-83970-082-8
D/2021/7849/80
NUR 820

British Library Cataloguing in Publication Data. A catalogue record for this book is available from the British Library.

PREFACE

In January 2020, a pandemic broke out. It brought death and havoc, and commercial and economic links were cut off. This coronavirus epidemic immediately became the subject of scientific research. How to find a vaccine to cure COVID-19? How to alleviate pain and suffering? But it was not only medical and pure scientific matters which were considered. Economic and ethical issues were explored as well, as were legal problems. This volume purports to explore the latter. The coronavirus has already led to a number of national publications from Belgium,[1] the Netherlands,[2] Switzerland,[3] the US,[4] and other jurisdictions.[5] A pan-European approach,[6] or even a global focus,[7] is quite evident. The current book enlists contributions from various European nations. The authors have mainly, but not exclusively, been selected from a group of scholars who, in the past, were engaged in European projects such as the Draft Common Frame of Reference and who still are in touch over issues such as Brexit.

I am very grateful to these authors, who have been so kind as to adhere to a very strict time limit, the idea being that in order to have any effect, a book should be on the market as soon as possible.

My gratitude also goes to the five eminent jurists who have been willing to take on the editorship of the volume. Travel restrictions brought about by

---

1 Eric Dirix, 'Corona en insolventierecht in België' {2020} Tijdschrift voor Insolventierecht 27.

2 Harriët Schelhaas, Jan Spanjaard, 'Contract en coronacrisis' {2020} Nederlands Juristenblad 881.

3 Pascal Pichonnaz, Ruth Arnet, Samantha Besson, Peter Isler, Vincent Martenet and Andreas Zünd (eds), *Pandemie und Recht: Beitrag des Rechts zur Bewältigung einer globalen Krise/ Pandémie et Droit: contribution du droit à la maîtrise d'une crise globale*, Zeitschrift für Schweizerisches Recht/Revue de droit suisse (Helbing Lichtenhahn 2020).

4 Katharina Pistor (ed), *Law in the time of Covid-19* (Columbia Law School 2020).

5 Richard Alderman, Alberto De Franceschi, Mark Giancaspro, Geraint Howells, Chen Lei, Javier Lete, Hans-W Micklitz, Emilia Miscenic, Tjakie Naude, Pascal Pichonnaz, Elise Poillot, Iain Ramsay, Evelyne Terryn, Christian Twigg-Flesner and Thomas Wilhelmsson, 'Consumer Law & Policy Relating to Change of Circumstances Due to the COVID-19 Pandemy {2020} *J Cons Policy* 43, 437-450.

6 European Law Institute, ELI Principles for the COVID-19 Crisis, Vienna, 2020.

7 André Janssen and Christian Johannes Wahnschaffe, "Der internationale Warenkauf in Zeiten der Pandemie" {2020} EuZW 10.

the coronavirus made a high-tech approach with Microsoft Teams and Zoom necessary. So, Marta Santos Silva, Andrea Nicolussi, Pablo Salvador Coderch, Christiane Wendehorst and Fryderyk Zoll, thank you so much.

We also wish to thank our publisher, Intersentia, for their cooperation. All contributions reflect the latest in COVID-19 emergency legislation as of at least July 2020.

Ewoud Hondius

CONTENTS

PART II. STATES AGAINST THE PANDEMIC

PART III. COMPENSATION FOR COVID-19 RELATED DAMAGE

LIST OF KEYWORDS

LIST OF CONTRIBUTORS

Ana Isabel da Costa Afonso
Catholic University of Portugal, Portugal

Antonio Albanese
Catholic University of Milan, Italy

Guido Alpa
University of Rome – La Sapienza, Italy

Christian Alunaru
Vasile Goldiş University Arad, Romania

Henrique Sousa Antunes
Catholic University of Portugal, Portugal

Wojciech Bańczyk
Jagiellonian University, Poland; University of Osnabrück, Germany

Hugh Beale
University of Warwick; Harris Manchester College and University of Oxford, England, UK

Lucian Bojin
West University Timişoara, Romania

Jean-Sébastien Borghetti
Université Paris II Panthéon-Assas, France

Christoph Busch
University of Osnabrück, Germany

Roberta Calvano
Unitelma Sapienza University, Italy

Angel Carrasco
University of Castilla-La Mancha, Spain

Jorge Morais Carvalho
NOVA School of Law, Portugal

António Menezes Cordeiro
University of Lisbon, Portugal

A. Barreto Menezes Cordeiro
University of Lisbon, Portugal

Luísa Cortat Simonetti Gonçalves
Academy of European Law (ERA) and Graduate Institute Geneva, Switzerland

Antonio Da Re
University of Padua, Italy

Eugenia Dacoronia
National and Kapodistrian University of Athens (EKPA), Greece

Gerhard Dannemann
Humboldt University of Berlin, Germany; University of Oxford, England, UK

Giacomo Delledonne
Scuola Superiore Sant'Anna, Italy

Ekaterina Dmitrikova
Saint-Petersburg State University, Russia

Gabriel Doménech-Pascual
University of Valencia, Spain

Merle Erikson
University of Tartu, Estonia

Sjef van Erp
Maastricht University, The Netherlands

Bénédicte Fauvarque-Cosson
Conseillère d'Etat, agrégée des facultés de droit, France

Andreas Furrer
University of Lucerne, Switzerland

Martina Gajdošová
Comenius University in Bratislava, Slovak Republic

Juan José Ganuza
Universitat Pompeu Fabra, Spain

Luca Giacomelli
University of Florence, Italy

Carlos Gómez-Ligüerre
Universitat Pompeu Fabra, Spain

Fernando Gómez Pomar
Universitat Pompeu Fabra, Spain

Mateusz Grochowski
Max Planck Institute for Comparative and International Private Law, Hamburg, Germany

Maria Raquel Guimarães
University of Porto, Portugal

Ewoud Hondius
Utrecht University, The Netherlands

Carmen Jerez
Autonomous University of Madrid, Spain

Miha Juhart
University of Ljubljana, Slovenia

María Kubica
Universidad Loyola Andalucía, Spain

Irene Kull
University of Tartu, Estonia

Elisabetta Lamarque
University of Milano-Bicocca, Italy

Angelika Layr
University of Lucerne, Switzerland

Álvaro Luna
Cuatrecasas, Spain

Hector L. MacQueen
University of Edinburgh, Scotland, UK

Marcello Maggiolo
University of Padua, Italy; Innsbruck University, Austria

Mikołaj Małecki
Jagiellonian University, Poland

Michele Massa
Catholic University of Milan, Italy

Svitlana Mazepa
West Ukrainian National University, Ukraine

Attila Menyhárd
Eötvös Loránd University, Hungary

Valentinas Mikelėnas
Vilnius University, Lithuania

Rosa Milà-Rafel
Universitat Pompeu Fabra, Spain

Luka Mišič
University of Ljubljana, Slovenia

Christina Möllnitz
University of Bayreuth, Germany

Andrea Nicolussi
Catholic University of Milan, Italy

Andrej Novikov
Saint-Petersburg State University, Russia

Carlo Padula
University of Padua, Italy

Sandra Passinhas
Universidade de Coimbra, Portugal

Denis Philippe
Université catholique de Louvain, Belgium; University of Paris, France

Katarzyna Południak-Gierz
Jagiellonian University, Poland; University of Osnabrück, Germany

Sonia Ramos González
Universitat Pompeu Fabra, Spain

Maria Regina Redinha
University of Porto, Portugal

Ewa Rott-Pietrzyk
University of Silesia, Katowice, Poland

Antoni Rubí-Puig
Universitat Pompeu Fabra, Spain

Albert Ruda
University of Girona, Spain

Anton Rudokvas
Saint-Petersburg State University, Russia

Pablo Salvador Coderch
Universitat Pompeu Fabra; Cuatrecasas, Spain

Marta Santos Silva
Maastricht University, The Netherlands; KU Leuven, Belgium

Martin Schmidt-Kessel
University of Bayreuth, Germany

Hans Schulte-Nölke
University of Osnabrück, Germany

Claudio Scognamiglio
Tor Vergata University, Italy

Ioannis Skandalis
National and Kapodistrian University of Athens (EKPA), Greece

Marek Sławiński
Jagiellonian University, Poland

Grega Strban
University of Ljubljana, Slovenia

Elena Sychenko
Saint-Petersburg State University, Russia

Dariusz Szostek
University of Opole, Poland

Verica Trstenjak
University of Ljubljana, Slovenia; Sigmund Freud Private University Vienna, Austria

Christian Twigg-Flesner
University of Warwick, England, UK

Antoni Vaquer
University of Lleida, Spain

Eduardo Vera-Cruz Pinto
University of Lisbon, Portugal

Jeremias Wartmann
University of Lucerne, Switzerland

Christiane Wendehorst
University of Vienna, Austria

Aneta Wiewiórowska-Domagalska
University of Osnabrück, Germany

Fryderyk Zoll
Jagiellonian University, Poland; University of Osnabrück, Germany

PART I

COVID-19 AND FUNDAMENTAL RIGHTS

THE CORONA CRISIS AND FUNDAMENTAL RIGHTS FROM THE POINT OF VIEW OF EU LAW

Verica TRSTENJAK*

* University of Ljubljana/Sigmund Freud Private University Vienna. I would like to thank Dr. Jorg Sladič and Dr. Petra Weingerl for their comments and assistance in the preparation of the English version of this contribution. The longer and amended version of this contribution will also be published in Slovenian legal journal Pravna Praksa.

> *"Human rights are not a privilege conferred by the government, they are every human being's entitlement by the virtue of his humanity."*
>
> *Mother Teresa*

In 2020, the world was surprised by the so-called Corona crisis, which has had adverse effects in several areas. Although initially it appeared only as a major public health emergency, it turned into a crisis of solidarity, economics and also a legal crisis. The Corona crisis also highlighted some other problems in the EU, in particular the issue of solidarity and the effectiveness of adoption of legal acts and decision-making. The issue of fundamental rights violations was often raised. The Member States have adopted specific measures, which have also restricted fundamental rights in certain cases. In practice, the protection of public health has almost always been balanced against all fundamental rights, which were at least partially restricted. There were restrictions based on considerations for public health such as: restriction of free movement, infringements of data protection, and restriction of free economic activities and enterprise (e.g. compulsory closure of shops). Against this background, this contribution provides an overview of the protection of fundamental rights in the EU, their possible limitations and restrictions, and discusses key Charter's fundamental rights during the Corona crisis.

1. INTRODUCTION

In 2020, the world was surprised by the so-called Corona crisis, which has had adverse effects in several areas. Although initially it appeared only as a major public health emergency, it turned into a crisis of solidarity, economics and also a legal crisis. When we talk about the latter, we are thinking mainly of the problems related to human rights at this time and their possible restrictions. The Corona crisis also highlighted some other problems in the EU, in particular the issue of solidarity and the effectiveness of adoption of legal acts and decision-making. The issue of fundamental rights violations was often raised. The Member States have adopted specific measures,[1] which have also restricted

[1] For example in Austria: Federal law on provisional measures to prevent the spread of COVID-19 (Act on COVID-19-Measures) (Bundesgesetz betreffend vorläufige Maßnahmen zur Verhinderung der Verbreitung von COVID-19 (COVID-19-Maßnahmengesetz)), Federal Official Journal of Austria, No. 12/2020; in Slovenia: the Law on Measures of Intervention to Contain the COVID-19 Epidemics and Mitigate its Consequences for Citizens and the Economy (Zakon o interventnih ukrepih za zajezitev epidemije COVID-19 in omilitev njenih posledic za državljane in gospodarstvo (ZIUZEOP)), Official Journal of the Republic of Slovenia, No. 49/2020.

fundamental rights in certain cases. Several essential legal issues appeared in this regard. Which rights are at stake and when do they apply in the Member States, when can they be restricted, and what are the solutions in the event of collision of several fundamental rights? In practice, the protection of public health has almost always been balanced against all fundamental rights, which were at least partially restricted. There were restrictions based on considerations for public health such as: restriction of free movement, infringements of data protection, and restriction of free economic activities and enterprise (e.g. compulsory closure of shops).

In this introductory part the terminological and historic difference between *human rights* and *fundamental rights* shall be highlighted. Some legal scholars consider that an important difference between these two terms lies in the fact that fundamental rights comprise human and civil rights.[2] However, in essence they also comprise so-called social rights. The EU, with 27 Member States, applies the term fundamental rights, while the Council of Europe, with 47 contracting states, applies the term human rights, which is also governed by the European Convention on Human Rights (Convention for the Protection of Human Rights and Fundamental Freedoms). The term human rights is also used by some other international acts such as the UN Universal Declaration of Human Rights adopted at the universal level.

Fundamental rights should not be confused with fundamental (economic) freedoms in the EU, such as free movement of persons, goods, services and capital, which are a part of the primary law of the EU governed by the Treaty on the Functioning of the European Union (TFEU).

Focusing on fundamental rights implications of the Corona crisis, the contribution will show that restrictions of fundamental rights are sometimes necessary. At the time of the Corona crisis, this applies to some of the rights discussed in this contribution.

2. FUNDAMENTAL RIGHTS IN THE EU

2.1. THE CHARTER

At the EU level, fundamental rights are governed by the Charter of Fundamental Rights of the European Union (henceforth: the Charter).[3] The Charter was adopted in 2000, but has been legally binding since 2009 and forms part of primary

2 See Gianluigi Palombella, From Human Rights to Fundamental Rights: Consequences of a conceptual distinction, *Archiv für Rechts- und Sozialphilosophie / Archives for Philosophy of Law and Social Philosophy*, vol 93, no 3 (2007) 396–426.

3 Charter of Fundamental Rights of the European Union, OJ EU C 326, 26.10.2012.

law under Article 6(1) of the Treaty on European Union. Though not called the constitution it is the highest legal act of the EU in the field of fundamental rights. Its content, the validity and legal value make it comparable to a constitution. The constitutional importance of the Charter has been recognised by the Court of Justice of the EU in Luxembourg.[4] We can even speak of a Magna Charta or the European Bible as far as fundamental rights are concerned. The Charter contains rights, freedoms and principles, although, generally the common term "fundamental rights" is applied when individual articles of the Charter are considered and discussed.

The Charter is a relatively short legal act with only 54 articles. However, its individual provisions are of extreme importance as the Charter comprises classic human rights (e.g. right to life in Art 2), as well as some other rights not belonging to classic human rights, e.g. in the field of worker's rights (e.g. Art 31 of the Charter), a provision on a high level of consumer protection in Article 38 and an extremely important provision on the Corona crisis in Article 35, namely on health care.

It shall also be stressed that most rights governed by the Charter (such as human dignity, prohibition of torture, etc.) are of general application and apply to all individuals, not only to citizens of the EU. In contrast, rights provided for in Chapter V of the Charter in principle either apply only to citizens of the EU (such as the right to vote in elections to the European Parliament) or to the citizens and to individuals residing or having its registered office in a Member State of the EU (e.g. the right of access to documents of the institutions, bodies, offices and agencies of the EU).

A special importance is to be given to the question of the *application of the Charter* in the EU as well as in Member States. Article 51 states that the provisions of the Charter are addressed to the institutions, bodies, offices and agencies of the Union with due regard for the principle of subsidiarity and to the Member States only when they are implementing Union law. The phrase "only when they are implementing Union law" generates many difficult issues in practice especially in the fields where EU law is not (predominantly) harmonised, such as criminal law and tax law. The Court of Justice of the EU has already had to interpret the applicability of the Charter, i.e. it had to assess if EU law is implemented in a particular case, as far as a certain directive is concerned.[5] Such questions should be assessed individually in consideration of concrete legal fields and concrete problems.

---

4 Opinion of the Court 1/17 [*CETA*- The Comprehensive Economic and Trade Agreement between Canada, of the one part, and the European Union and its Member States, of the other part, signed in Brussels on 30 October 2016 (OJ 2017 L 11, p. 23)], EU:C:2019:341, para 110.

5 See Case C-617/10 *Åkerberg Fransson* EU:C:2013:105.

2.2. RESTRICTIONS AND LIMITATIONS OF FUNDAMENTAL RIGHTS

2.2.1. Conditions under which rights may be restricted

The rights enshrined in the Charter (*mutatis mutandis* the same conclusion is to be applied to constitutions of Member States) are rights conferred on individuals. However, they are not absolute. Restrictions and limitations governed already by the Charter are quite often subjected to judicial interpretation in the case law of the Court of Justice of the EU.

The Charter contains provisions on limitations of fundamental rights in Article 52(1).[6] Any limitation on the exercise of the rights and freedoms is permissible only if certain conditions are met: the limitations must be provided by law and respect the essence of those rights and freedoms. Subject to the principle of proportionality, limitations may be made only if they are necessary and genuinely meet the objectives of general interest recognised by the Union or the need to protect the rights and freedoms of others.

In assessing limitations in a particular case, the timing must also be taken into account, as rights may only be limited (in many cases) for a certain period of time, which is especially important for the limitations introduced due to the Corona crisis.

The requirement that limitations must be "provided for by law" refers to legal acts of the EU as well as legal acts of Member States. As the Charter contains the term "law", the said term and its scope have to be interpreted according to the meaning given in each Member State or in EU law. It must be highlighted that the EU does not adopt "laws" as legal acts. Moreover, not all Member States consider the "law" as the only highest level legal act following the constitution. The Court of Justice of the EU ruled that the requirement that any limitation on the exercise of a right must be provided for by law implies that the legal basis for a specific limitation must define the scope of the limitation on the exercise of the right and it must afford a measure of legal protection against any arbitrary interferences.[7] For example, we can find special legal acts on proceedings and actions during the spread of contagious and infectious diseases.[8] During the Corona crisis almost

---

6 For an account on derogations under international human rights law, see Audrey Lebret, 'COVID-19 pandemic and derogation to human rights' (2020) 7(1) *Journal of Law and the Biosciences* 1–15.

7 See in this sense Case C-419/14 *WebMindLicenses* EU:C:2015:832, para 81.

8 See, e.g. on the basis of Article 7 of the Slovenian Communicable Diseases Act (Zakon o nalezljivih boleznih), OJ RS No. 65/95, in Austria the Law on Epidemics (Epidemiegesetz), Federal Official Journal of Austria, no 186/1950 as amended.

all Member States adopted special laws and other legal acts – not called laws.[9] Moreover, governments of Member States wanted a legislative endorsement in parliaments.[10] The majority of States allow for adoption of special laws and other legal acts based on the decisions declaring the pandemic.[11] National procedural specificities for adoption of such acts vary from one State to another.

The conditions that "the essence of rights and freedoms" is to be respected needs to be assessed on a case-by-case basis. The Court of Justice of the EU clarified the essence of rights under Articles 7 and 8 of the Charter in Opinion 1/15 on the draft agreement between Canada and the EU on the transfer and processing of passenger name record data.[12] Regarding the essence of Article 7 of the Charter (respect for private life), the Court of Justice of the EU held that even if PNR data (database of names of all air passengers) may, in some circumstances, reveal very specific information concerning the private life of a person, the nature of that information is limited to certain aspects of that private life, in particular, relating to air travel between Canada and the European Union. Regarding the essence of the right under Article 8 of the Charter (protection of personal data), the Court of Justice of the EU held that the envisaged agreement limits, in Article 3, the purposes for which PNR data may be processed, and lays down, in Article 9, rules intended to ensure, *inter alia*, the security, confidentiality and integrity of that data, and to protect it against unlawful access and processing.[13] Hence, the Court of Justice of the EU found that "the interferences which the envisaged agreement entails are capable of being justified by an objective of *general interest* of the European Union and are not liable adversely to affect the essence of the fundamental rights enshrined in Arts. 7 and 8 of the Charter".[14]

---

9 For the overview of the adopted acts, see, e.g. Democracy Reporting International, 'The Rule of Law Stress Test – EU Member States' Responses to Covid-19' (2020) https://democracy-reporting.org/dri_publications/the-rule-of-law-stress-test-eu-member-states-responses-to-covid-19/ accessed 31 July 2020.

10 Cf for example in Austria: Federal law on provisional measures to prevent the spread of COVID-19 (Act on COVID-19-Measures) (Bundesgesetz betreffend vorläufige Maßnahmen zur Verhinderung der Verbreitung von COVID-19 (COVID-19-Maßnahmengesetz)), Federal Official Journal of Austria, No. 12/2020.

11 For example in Austria specific law: Federal Law on Regulation of Higher Education and Special Provisions for the Promotion of Studies at Universities, Institutions of Higher Education for Teachers, Institutions Offering Courses of Applied Sciences and Technical Universities due to COVID-19 (Law on Higher Education and COVID-19 – C-HG)) (Bundesgesetz über hochschulrechtliche und studienförderungsrechtliche Sondervorschriften an Universitäten, Pädagogischen Hochschulen, Einrichtungen zur Durchführung von Fachhochschul-Studiengängen und Fachhochschulen aufgrund von COVID-19 (COVID-19-Hochschulgesetz – C-HG)), Federal Official Journal of Austria, No. 23/2020.

12 Opinion 1/15 on the draft agreement between Canada and the European Union on Transfer of Passenger Name Record data from the European Union to Canada, EU:C:2017:592.

13 Opinion 1/15 on the draft agreement between Canada and the European Union on Transfer of Passenger Name Record data from the European Union to Canada, EU:C:2017:592, para 150.

14 Opinion 1/15 on the draft agreement between Canada and the European Union on Transfer of Passenger Name Record data from the European Union to Canada, EU:C:2017:592, para 151. Emphasis added.

When examining Article 52(1) of the Charter, the Court of Justice of the EU also assesses "objectives of general interest". I have already mentioned the assessment undertaken by the Court in Opinion 1/15 on the agreement with Canada as far as Articles 7 and 8 of the Charter are concerned.[15] Another example is case C-283/11, *Sky Österreich*, where the Court of Justice of the EU had to interpret several rights under the Charter upon the preliminary reference of an Austrian court to interpret the Audiovisual Media Services Directive 2010/13: Article 11 (freedom of expression and information), Article 16 (freedom to conduct a business) and Article 17 (right to property).[16] The Court of Justice of the EU ruled that the safeguarding of the freedoms protected under Article 11 of the Charter undoubtedly constitutes a legitimate aim in the general interest, the importance of which must be stressed in particular in a democratic and pluralistic society.[17] In the remainder of the judgment, the Court of Justice of the EU assessed the proportionality as regards all the relevant rights in the said case.

The proportionality as a condition for limitations of fundamental rights under Article 52(1) of the Charter is an extremely important criterion of assessment. The Court of Justice of the EU recalled that, according to the settled case law, the principle of proportionality requires that measures adopted by EU institutions or Member States "do not exceed the limits of what is appropriate and necessary in order to attain the objectives legitimately pursued by the legislation in question; when there is a choice between several appropriate measures recourse must be had to the least onerous, and the disadvantages caused must not be disproportionate to the aims pursued."[18]

The Court of Justice of the EU assesses, in principle, two elements of proportionality: the appropriateness (in German: *die Geeignetheit*) and necessity (in German: *die Erforderlichkeit*) of the adopted measures. The opinions of Advocates General are sometimes even "broader", as they apply the standard of three steps of proportionality.[19] As a consequence, the test of proportionality

---

15 Opinion 1/15 on the draft agreement between Canada and the European Union on Transfer of Passenger Name Record data from the European Union to Canada, EU:C:2017:592.

16 The preliminary reference referred to the validity of Article 15(6) of the Directive 2010/13/EU of the European Parliament and of the Council of 10 March 2010 on the coordination of certain provisions laid down by law, regulation or administrative action in Member States concerning the provision of audiovisual media services (Audiovisual Media Services Directive) (OJ L 95, 15.4.2010, and corrigendum, OJ L 263, 6.10.2010).

17 Cf Case C-283/11 *Sky Österreich* EU:C:2013:28, para 52.

18 Cf Case C-283/11 *Sky Österreich* EU:C:2013:28, para 50; see also Case C-343/09 *Afton Chemical* EU:C:2010:419, para 45; Joined Cases C-581/10 and C-629/10 *Nelson and Others* EU:C:2012:657, para 71. Regarding Member States, see: Case C-2/10 *Azienda Agro-Zootecnica Franchini in Eolica di Altamura* EU:C:2011:502, para 73; Case C-28/05 *Dokter and Others* EU:C:2006:408, para 72; C-434/02 *Arnold André* EU:C:2004:800, para 45.

19 Cf Verica Trstenjak and Erwin Beysen, 'The Growing Overlap of Fundamental Freedoms and Fundamental Rights in the Case Law of the CJEU' (2013) 38(3) European Law Review 314; Verica Trstenjak and Erwin Beysen, 'Das Prinzip der Verhältnismäßigkeit in der Unionsrechtsordnun' (2012) 3 EuR 282–83.

comprises the appropriateness, necessity and the reasonableness[20] of interference, which can also be translated as the answer to the question whether the measures are reasonable (in German: *die Angemessenheit*).[21]

2.2.2. A case before the Court of Justice of the EU (proportionality)

Case C-293/12 in C-594/12, *Digital Rights Ireland and others*, can be considered as a case in which the Court of Justice of the EU applied an extensive assessment of proportionality.[22] The Court of Justice of the EU examined the interference with the right for private life (Art 7), protection of personal data (Art 8) and freedom of information (Art 11), and annulled Directive 2006/24 on the retention of data[23] as it enabled storage of personal data. The data which providers of publicly available electronic communications services or of public communications networks had to retain under Articles 3 and 5 of Directive 2006/24 included data necessary to trace and identify the source of a communication and its destination, the date, time, duration and type of a communication, users' communication equipment, and its location, data which consist, *inter alia*, of the name and address of the subscriber or registered user, the calling telephone number, the number called and an IP address for Internet services. Those data make it possible, in particular, to get to know the identity of the person with whom a subscriber or registered user has communicated and by what means, and to identify the time of the communication as well as the place from which that communication took place. It is possible to verify the frequency of the communications of the subscriber or registered user with certain persons during a given period. The Court of Justice of the EU ascertained that those data, taken as a whole, may allow very precise conclusions to be drawn concerning the private lives of the persons whose data has been retained, such as the habits of everyday life, permanent or temporary places of residence, daily or other

---

20 Slovenian language applies the term "sorazmernost v ožjem pomenu", the English language applies the term "reasonableness", the German language applies the term "Angemessenheit", and the French language applies the term "le caractère mesuré". Cf the relevant linguistic versions of the opinion of Advocate General Trstenjak in Case C-28/09 *Commission v Austria* EU:C:2010:770, para 118.

21 Cf Opinion of Advocate General Cruz Villalon in Case C-580/13 *Stadtsparkasse Magdeburg* EU:C:2015:243, para 43. See also Opinion of Advocate General Trstenjak in the Case C-28/09 *Commission v Austria* EU:C:2010:770 on sectoral traffic prohibition for lorries of more than 7.5 tonnes carrying certain goods in Austria (Tirol), where the question was rather the limitation of fundamental economic freedoms. Cf paras 93 and 118–132.

22 C-293/12 in C-594/12 *Digital Rights Ireland and others* EU:C:2014:238, para 68.

23 Directive 2006/24/EC of the European Parliament and of the Council of 15 March 2006 on the retention of data generated or processed in connection with the provision of publicly available electronic communications services or of public communications networks and amending Directive 2002/58/EC, OJ L 105, 13.4.2006.

movements, the activities carried out, the social relationships of those persons and the social environments frequented by them.[24]

The proportionality of measures played an important role in the assessment of interference with the mentioned fundamental rights. The Court of Justice of the EU ruled that the retention of data for the purpose of possible access to them by the competent national authorities may meet the objectives of general interest such as fighting against serious crime also in order to ensure public security. However, the Court of Justice of the EU considered that by adopting Directive 2006/24 on data retention the Union's legislator went beyond the limits required by the principle of proportionality.

Retention of personal data as required under Directive 2006/24 may be considered to be appropriate for attaining the objective pursued. The Court of Justice of the EU held that, having in regard the growing importance of means of electronic communication, data which must be retained pursuant to that directive allows the national authorities which are competent for criminal prosecutions to have additional opportunities to shed light on serious crime and, in this respect, they are therefore a valuable tool for criminal investigations. Consequently, the retention of such data may be considered to be *appropriate* for attaining the objective pursued by that directive.[25]

However, the Court of Justice of the EU stresses that a broad and very serious interference by the Directive 2006/24 with fundamental rights for respect for private life (Art 7) and protection of personal data (Art 8) is not limited enough. Thus, only necessary interference with fundamental rights would be allowed. Such an objective of general interest as derived from the facts of the case, however fundamental it may be, does not, in itself, justify a retention measure such as that established by Directive 2006/24 being considered to be necessary for the purpose of that right. The Court of Justice of the EU recalled that Directive 2006/24 covers, in a general manner, all persons and all means of electronic communication as well as all traffic data without any differentiation, limitation or exception being made in the light of the objective of fighting against serious crime. It does, however, not contain any objective criteria and the data retention period is also contentious as Article 6 of Directive 2006/24 requires that those data be retained for a period of at least six months, without any distinction being made between the categories of data on the basis of their possible usefulness for the purposes of the objective pursued or according to the persons concerned. It follows from the above that Directive 2006/24 does not lay down clear and precise rules governing the extent of the interference with the fundamental rights enshrined in Articles 7 and 8 of the Charter.

---

24 Cf Case C-293/12 in C-594/12 *Digital Rights Ireland and Others* EU:C:2014:238, paras 26 and 27.

25 Cf Case C-293/12 in C-594/12 *Digital Rights Ireland and Others* EU:C:2014:238, paras 46–49.

The Court of Justice found that the Directive entailed a wide-ranging and particularly serious interference with those fundamental rights in the legal order of the EU, without such an interference being precisely controlled to ensure that it is actually limited to what is *strictly necessary*. Thus, the EU legislature exceeded the limits imposed by the principle of proportionality in the light of Articles 7, 8 and 52(1) of the Charter.[26] Consequently, the Court of Justice of the EU ruled that the cited Directive is invalid (*ab initio*).

2.2.3. Collision of several fundamental rights

In the period of the Corona crisis, the key issue has been linked to the question when and under what conditions fundamental rights could be limited and what is the *fair balance* in a case of collision of several rights.

In practice, (public) health has almost always been applied as a reason or legitimate aim for a limitation to all the fundamental rights. Examples are the restriction of freedom of movement against protection of public health, interferences with privacy or protection of personal data due to public health, restriction of freedom to conduct a business (e.g. compulsory closures of shops) versus protection of public health, equality before the law restricted by public health protection, etc.

As regards the "collision" of several fundamental rights, the conditions under Article 52(1) of the Charter are important. Competent authorities and courts are called upon to decide on fair balance as often recalled in the case law of the Court of Justice of the EU.[27]

In case C-547/14, *Philip Morris*, the Court of Justice of the EU interpreted the provisions on health care in the Charter. The referring British court asked, *inter alia*, the Court of Justice of the EU whether Article 13(1) of Directive 2014/40 on tobacco products[28] must be interpreted as prohibiting the display on the labelling of unit packets and on the outside packaging, as well as on the tobacco product itself, of certain information, although that information is factually accurate. Moreover, if that is the case, the referring court asked whether that provision is invalid because it infringes Article 11 of the Charter (freedom of expression and information) and the principle of proportionality. The Court of Justice of the EU gave a statement of reasons referring to Article 35 of the Charter (health care) when assessing the proportionality of the interference. It underlined that the second sentence of Article 35 of the Charter and Articles 9, 114(3) and 168(1) TFEU require that a high level of human health protection

---

26 Cf Case C-293/12 in C-594/12 *Digital Rights Ireland and Others* EU:C:2014:238, paras 51–69.

27 See, e.g. Case C-131/12 *Google Spain SL and Google Inc.* EU:C:2014:317.

28 Directive 2014/40/EU of the European Parliament and of the Council of 3 April 2014 on the approximation of the laws, regulations and administrative provisions of the Member States concerning the manufacture, presentation and sale of tobacco and related products and repealing Directive 2001/37/EC, OJ L 127, 29.4.2014.

be ensured in the definition and implementation of all the Union's policies and activities. The Court of Justice of the EU recalled that the prohibition on the inclusion of the labelling of unit packets and on outside packaging, as well as on the tobacco product itself constitutes an interference with a business's freedom of expression and information. However, in accordance with Article 52(1) of the Charter, any limitation on the exercise of the rights and freedoms laid down by the Charter must be provided for by law and respect the essence of those rights and freedoms and, it must comply with the principle of proportionality, and it must actually meet objectives of general interest recognised by the EU or the need to protect the rights and freedoms of others.[29]

Further, the Court of Justice of the EU referred also to Article 35 of the Charter and recalled the importance of the fair balance in the exercise of rights. The Court of Justice of the EU found that "the discretion enjoyed by the EU legislature, in determining the balance to be struck, varies for each of the goals justifying restrictions on that freedom and depends on the nature of the activities in question. In the present case, the claimants in the main proceedings rely, in essence, under Article 11 of the Charter, on the freedom to disseminate information in pursuit of their commercial interests. It must, however, be stated that human health protection – in an area characterised by the proven harmfulness of tobacco consumption, by the addictive effects of tobacco and by the incidence of serious diseases caused by the compounds those products contain that are pharmacologically active, toxic, mutagenic and carcinogenic – outweighs the interests put forward by the claimants in the main proceedings".[30]

By having recourse to Article 35 of the Charter (health care), the Court of Justice of the EU found that the conditions set for limitations are met and the cited contentious provisions of the Directive shall remain valid as they do not infringe the provisions of the Charter and are justified in accordance with Article 52(1) of the Charter and other provisions of primary law as the fair balance between requirements of freedom of expression and information on the one hand and the requirements of public health of individuals on the other hand are met.

3. KEY CHARTER'S FUNDAMENTAL RIGHTS DURING THE CORONA CRISIS

3.1. HEALTH CARE (ART 35 OF THE CHARTER)

The first key provision is Article 35 of the Charter which refers to health care. According to this provision everyone has the right of access to preventive health

29 Cf C-547/14 *Philip Morris Brands and Others* EU:C:2016:325, paras 148–150.
30 Cf C-547/14 *Philip Morris Brands and Others* EU:C:2016:325, paras 155 and 156.

care and the right to benefit from medical treatment under the conditions established by national laws and practices. This last part of the rule is extremely important as there are quite significant differences between Member States in regard to health care. Moreover, the second sentence provides that a high level of human health protection shall be ensured when defining and implementing all the Union's policies and activities.

Human health protection is also referred to in other provisions of primary law, for example Article 168 TFEU.

However, Article 35 of the Charter does not directly confer rights on individuals, as this provision is to be realised on the EU level and by national laws and practices. During the Corona crisis this right was most frequently referred to when limitations were imposed on other rights.

3.2. RIGHT TO LIBERTY AND SECURITY (ART 6 OF THE CHARTER)

Article 6 of the Charter governing the right to liberty and security was often cited during the Corona crisis. It was referred to both by those who wanted more freedom of movement (right to liberty) as well as those who insisted on human health protection in the second part of the provision (security) referred to this article.

The said article regulates a right to physical free movement, and constitutes a protective mechanism against illicit interferences or limitations of that right. The text refers to two elements, i.e. liberty and security. Some legal scholars recall that these provisions are to be interpreted as a whole.[31]

The legal issues of that article raised by different interests were the subject-matter of an asylum case C-601/15 PPU, *J. N.*[32] The Court of Justice of the EU had to interpret two directives on asylum[33] in conjunction with the rights from the Charter, namely Article 18 (right to asylum) and Article 6 on the right to liberty and security in the light of Article 52(1) of the Charter on limitations of rights. The Court of Justice of the EU recalled that the protection of national security and public order also contributes to the protection of the rights and freedoms of others. Article 6 of the Charter states that everyone has the right not only to liberty but also to security of person. As regards the proportionality

31 See details in Schramm, in: Michael Holoubek and Georg Lienbacher (eds), *GRC-Kommentar: Charta der Grundrechte der Europäischen Union* (Manz 2014) 73.

32 Cf Case C-601/15 PPU *J. N.* EU:C:2016:84.

33 Directive 2008/115/EC of the European Parliament and of the Council of 16 December 2008 on common standards and procedures in Member States for returning illegally staying third-country nationals, OJ L 348, 24.12.2008; Directive 2013/33/EU of the European Parliament and of the Council of 26 June 2013 laying down standards for the reception of applicants for international protection, OJ L 180, 29.6.2013.

of the interference with the right to liberty that has been found to exist, the Court of Justice of the EU recalled that the principle of proportionality requires that measures adopted by the EU institutions do not exceed the limits of what is appropriate and necessary in order to attain the legitimate objectives pursued by the legislation in question, since the disadvantages caused by the legislation must not be disproportionate to the aims pursued.[34]

At the time of the Corona crisis this right, as already mentioned, was referred to by both sides, by those who attacked the limitations of this right (because of freedom of movement) as well as by those who wanted limitations (because of security). Possible violations were contended, especially regarding quarantine, and also regarding the ban on free movement between municipalities, etc. The proportionality of all these limitations will be assessed by courts. These violations were also claimed by young people on the basis of the provisions of the national constitutions, as their rights regarding free movement were limited due to the protection of the health of the elderly, an aim the German Constitutional Court ruled to be admissible and proportionate.[35]

3.3. PROTECTION OF PERSONAL DATA (ART 8 OF THE CHARTER)

During the Corona crisis, the right to protection of personal data was often referred to.[36] The reference was extremely relevant due to the processing of data of diseased persons and/or due to proposed possible ways and means of tracing the infected and the contacts of the infected. The said right refers to the protection of personal data concerning data subjects (individuals). According to Article 8(2) of the Charter, personal data must be processed fairly for specified purposes and on the basis of the consent of the person concerned or some other legitimate basis laid down by law and that everyone has the right of access to data which has been collected concerning him or her, and the right to have it

---

34 Cf Case C-601/15 PPU *J. N.* EU:C:2016:84, paras 52, 53 and 54.

35 In this sense, see also the decisions of the German Constitutional Court of 12 May 2020 and 13 May 2020, Case 1 BvR 1027/20 and 1 BvR 1021/20.

36 See, e.g. Commission, Communication from the Commission Guidance on Apps supporting the fight against COVID 19 pandemic in relation to data protection 2020/C 124 I/01, C/2020/2523, OJ C 124I, 17.4.2020, pp. 1–9; Council of Europe, 'COVID-19 and Data Protection' (2020) https://www.coe.int/en/web/data-protection/covid-19-data-protection accessed 31 July 2020; OECD, 'Ensuring data privacy as we battle COVID-19' (2020) http://www.oecd.org/coronavirus/policy-responses/ensuring-data-privacy-as-we-battle-covid-19-36c2f31e/ accessed 31 July 2020; DW News, 'Why tracking personal data to fight coronavirus could be problematic' (2020) https://www.dw.com/en/why-tracking-personal-data-to-fight-coronavirus-could-be-problematic/av-52962511 accessed 31 July 2020.

rectified. Compliance with Article 8 shall be subject to control by an independent authority.

This right is not an absolute right, but must be considered in accordance with the principle of proportionality in relation to its function in society and balanced against other fundamental rights.[37]

The right to protection of personal data is becoming more and more important in society especially after the entry into force of the Regulation (EU) 2016/679 of the European Parliament and of the Council of 27 April 2016 on the protection of natural persons with regard to the processing of personal data and on the free movement of such data (General Data Protection Regulation, GDPR).[38] During the Corona crisis, many politicians and affected persons also referred to the new regulation, although it is this regulation that sets out possible restrictions on personal data at the time of the epidemic.

Recital 46 to the GDPR provides that the processing of personal data should be regarded as lawful when it is necessary to protect an interest which is essential for the life of the data subject or that of another natural person. This recital provides further that "processing of personal data based on the vital interest of another natural person should in principle take place only where the processing cannot be manifestly based on another legal basis. Some types of processing may serve both important grounds of public interest and the vital interests of the data subject as for instance when processing is necessary for humanitarian purposes, including for *monitoring epidemics* and their spread or in situations of humanitarian emergencies, in particular in situations of natural and man-made disasters."[39]

Also Articles 6 and 9 of the GDPR contain several exceptions. The exception to the prohibition of data processing in Article 9(2)(i) applies where data processing is necessary for reasons of public interest in the area of public health, such as protecting against serious cross-border threats to health or ensuring high standards of quality and safety of health care and of medicinal products or medical devices, on the basis of Union or Member State law which provides for suitable and specific measures to safeguard the rights and freedoms of the data subject, in particular professional secrecy.

Various data gatherings, controls and data processing relating to the disease, several technological methods in the information society for tracing the infected as well as those in their vicinity, etc. were exposed as problematic. Legal experts

---

37 See in this sense the Joined Cases of the Court of Justice of the EU C-92/09 and C-93/09 *Volker und Markus Schecke and Eifert* EU:C:2010:662, para 48.

38 Regulation (EU) 2016/679 of the European Parliament and of the Council of 27 April 2016 on the protection of natural persons with regard to the processing of personal data and on the free movement of such data, and repealing Directive 95/46/EC (General Data Protection Regulation), OJ L 119, 4.5.2016.

39 Emphasis added.

took different views during several webinars during the Corona crisis in 2020, among them was also a very well-known data protection activist Maximilian Schrems.[40] The use of tracing applications will probably have to be based on consent in the light of high levels of the protection of personal data. The novel legal problem of the tracing applications and similar systems will be the qualification of the said application as a "medical device" which would allow broader interference with other rights. It would also be useful to consider a development of a uniform European application,[41] which would allow an equal level of protection of personal data across the EU.

In future, national courts will have to assess eventual illicit interferences in the right to protection of personal data and to consider all the before mentioned exceptions in the GDPR. National courts will have the possibility of preliminary references on the compatibility of national measures with EU law as well as the compatibility of the GDPR with the Charter much in the same way as the compatibility of the Directive on data retention was challenged in the case C-293/12 and C-594/12, *Digital Rights Ireland and others*.[42]

3.4. FREEDOM OF ASSEMBLY AND OF ASSOCIATION (ART 12 OF THE CHARTER)

The right to freedom of peaceful assembly and to freedom of association applies at all levels, in particular in political, trade union and civic matters, which implies, for instance, the right of everyone to form and to join trade unions for the protection of his or her interests. This right is not often a subject-matter of interpretation before the Court of Justice of the EU.

During the Corona crisis, this right was often mentioned as it was indeed limited, especially due to health protection. In some Member States, physical movement of people was completely restricted in March 2020, except for medical reasons and other emergency reasons (e.g. Italy, Spain).[43]

In other Member States, movement was restricted, for example, to two or four people, who had to reside at the same domicile. This can be understood as meaning that freedom of assembly could also be expressed under these

---

40 Maximilian Schrems, 'Datenschutz in Zeiten des Coronavirus' (2020) https://noyb.eu/de/datenschutz-zeiten-von-corona accessed 16 May 2020.

41 Luxembourg's Proposal in the Council of Ministers on 5 May 2020.

42 Cf Case C-293/12 in C-594/12 *Digital Rights Ireland and Others* EU:C:2014:238, para 68.

43 See, e.g. Guardian, 'Coronavirus: Italy bans any movement inside country as toll nears 5,500' (2020) https://www.theguardian.com/world/2020/mar/22/italian-pm-warns-of-worst-crisis-since-ww2-as-coronavirus-deaths-leap-by-almost-800 accessed 31 July 2020; The New York Times, 'Spain Imposes Nationwide Lockdown to Fight Coronavirus' (2020) https://www.nytimes.com/2020/03/14/world/europe/spain-coronavirus.html accessed 31 July 2020.

conditions. Everyone who exercises their rights must do so in a way that does not put others in danger or limit the rights of others.

3.5. EQUALITY BEFORE THE LAW (ART 20 OF THE CHARTER)

The right of equality before the law (providing that everyone is equal before the law) has also been mentioned several times during the Corona crisis. This provision is not linked to the citizenship of the EU, nor is it linked to sex or any other (special) circumstance.

As far as this provision in the Charter is concerned, special importance is to be given to laws concerning this right. The Court of Justice of the EU repeatedly recalled that a law has to treat citizens in an equal manner and must ensure that comparable situations must not be treated differently and that different situations must not be treated in the same way unless such treatment is objectively justified.[44] The principle of equality also implies the principle of equal treatment and is linked to Article 21(1) of the Charter on general prohibition of discrimination.

During the Corona crisis, there were also problems with equality before the law. Media emphasised problems faced by enterprises that had to remain closed because in some places only the opening of certain economic entities (e.g. with less than 400 m^2 surface) was allowed, inequality because some employees worked at home and others had to go to work, inequality regarding the accessibility of tests for COVID-19, which were not accessible to all and/or not under the same conditions,[45] as well as inequality regarding schooling when, e.g. not all students started lessons at the same time,[46] etc.

3.6. CONSUMER PROTECTION (ART 38 OF THE CHARTER)

The provision of Article 38 of the Charter provides for a high level of consumer protection. Due to the crisis, many problems have arisen in the area of consumer protection, especially with regard to non-refund of money for already paid trips and flights and offering vouchers or coupons, which would cause a problem if

---

44 See, e.g. Case C-356/12 *Glatzel* EU:C:2014:350, para 43. See also Case C-550/07 P *Akzo Nobel Chemicals and Akcros Chemicals* EU:C:2010:512, paras 54–55.

45 Thomas Straubhaar, 'Es kann solidarisch sein, Menschen ungleich zu behandeln' (2020) https://www.welt.de/wirtschaft/article206913185/Corona-Krise-Es-kann-solidarisch-sein-Menschen-ungleich-zu-behandeln.html accessed 16 May 2020.

46 FAZ, 'Corona und der Schulbetrieb: Gleichheit vor dem Gesetz' (2020) https://www.covid19-infos.de/2020/04/25/corona-und-der-schulbetrieb-gleichheit-vor-dem-gesetz/ accessed 16 May 2020.

companies go bankrupt.[47] Consumer organisations also warned of problems regarding withdrawal from distance contracts, unfair business practices, advertisements for "medina" masks and bogus "medicines" for the virus, excessive price increases for certain products (e.g. masks, disinfectants). Member States have made great efforts to protect their economies. For example, twelve Member States suggested that the EU adopts measures to ensure that airlines do not have to return already paid prices for airline tickets.[48] This area is regulated by the Directive (EU) 2015/2302 of the European Parliament and of the Council of 25 November 2015 on package travel and linked travel arrangements (Package Travel Directive)[49] and this national legislature lowers the consumer protection level below the minimum set by EU law, which is not permissible in the light of EU law.[50]

3.7. RESPECT FOR PRIVATE AND FAMILY LIFE (ART 7 OF THE CHARTER)

One of the most important rights of modern society is the right to respect for private and family life (Art 7 of the Charter) or so-called right to privacy, which includes the right to respect for one's private and family life, housing and communications. This right has become the subject of a number of proceedings specifically due to the development of the information society and is often assessed together with Article 8 of the Charter on the protection of personal data.

At the time of the Corona crisis, this right was mentioned in relation to employers' requirements for measurement of body temperature and also for wearing masks, etc.[51]

---

47 The coupons are mentioned by the Slovenian Law on Measures of Intervention to Contain the COVID-19 Epidemics and Mitigate its Consequences for Citizens and the Economy (Zakon o interventnih ukrepih za zajezitev epidemije COVID-19 in omilitev njenih posledic za državljane in gospodarstvo (ZIUZEOP)), Official Journal of the Republic of Slovenia, No. 49/2020, see Article 101a.

48 Coronavirus: 'Most EU states' want Brussels to suspend refunds for cancelled flights law, https://www.euronews.com/2020/04/29/a-dozen-eu-states-will-today-call-on-brussels-to-suspend-law-granting-refunds-for-cancelle accessed 31 July 2020.

49 Directive (EU) 2015/2302 of the European Parliament and of the Council of 25 November 2015 on package travel and linked travel arrangements, amending Regulation (EC) No 2006/2004 and Directive 2011/83/EU of the European Parliament and of the Council and repealing Council Directive 90/314/EEC, OJ L 326, 11.12.2015, pp. 1–33.

50 See, e.g. the Commission's Q&A, 'Passengers rights and package travel' (2020) https://ec.europa.eu/info/sites/info/files/faqs-travel-transportation.pdf accessed 31 July 2020.

51 See, e.g. BBC, 'Coronavirus: How much does your boss need to know about you?' (2020) https://www.bbc.com/news/business-53109207 accessed 31 July 2020.

3.8. OTHER FUNDAMENTAL RIGHTS LIMITED DURING THE CORONA CRISIS

Other rights codified in the Charter were also mentioned during the Corona crisis. For example, the right to life in Article 2 of the Charter,[52] the right to human dignity from Article 1 of the Charter, as well as some other rights which would *prima facie* not be mentioned.

The prohibition of discrimination (non-discrimination), which is extensively defined in Article 21(1) of the Charter, has been mentioned in various circumstances: regarding the restriction of the elderly to enter into shops, with regard to young people and the prohibition of visiting grandparents, etc. Some also referred to the limitations of Article 10 of the Charter (freedom of religion), in particular due to the closure of churches.[53] During the Corona crisis, there were also problems with Article 16 of the Charter (freedom to conduct a business) and to Article 17 of the Charter (rights to property). The Court of Justice of the EU has already ruled in this regard (also in regard to public health) in case C-544/10, *Deutsches Weintor*, that the freedom to conduct a business like the right to property are not an absolute right but must be considered in relation to their social function.[54]

The interference with the right to judicial remedy, i.e. the right to an effective remedy and to a fair trial under Article 47 of the Charter, was also often addressed during the Corona crisis. As the courts were in recess and no hearings were set, the length of procedures was extended. Certain Member States solved the problem of deadlines and statutes of limitations by special laws.[55] Individuals in proceedings had recourse to the said right in cases where they had to appear before a court (as there could be a risk for their health)[56] as well as in cases where no hearings were scheduled.[57] However, especially the industry and commerce warned of lack of protection of creditors and other problems due to interruption of proceedings.[58]

---

52 For a contribution focusing on the right to life, see Alessandra Spadaro, 'COVID-19: Testing the Limits of Human Rights', (2020) 11(2) European Journal of Risk Regulation 317–325.

53 See French and German case: Conseil d'État: https://www.conseil-etat.fr/actualites/actualites/rassemblements-dans-les-lieux-de-culte-le-conseil-d-etat-ordonne-au-premier-ministre-de-prendre-des-mesures-moins-contraignantes. German Federal Constitutional Court (Bundesverfassungsgericht) 1 BvQ 28/20.

54 See *C-544/10, Deutsches Weintor* ECLI:EU:C:2012:526, para 54.

55 In Slovenia, for example, Act on provisional measures for judicial, administrative and other public matters to cope with the spread of infectious disease SARS-CoV-2 (COVID-19), OJ RS No. 36/20 and 61/20.

56 See, e.g. in Germany a case before the Federal Constitutional Court (Bundesverfassungsgericht) 2 BvR 483/20.

57 See, e.g. in Germany a case before the Federal Constitutional Court (Bundesverfassungsgericht) 2 BvR 474/20.

58 Markus Bruckmüller, 'Slovenian courts in the times of Coronavirus: Have creditors been left with nothing?' (2020) https://www.wolftheiss.com/knowledge/client-alerts/detail/slovenian-courts-in-the-times-of-coronavirus-have-creditors-been-left-with-nothing/ accessed 16 May 2020.

During the Corona crisis, special attention was paid to freedom of expression and information, both in relation to individuals and in the media, as defined in Article 11 of the Charter. This provision shall include freedom to hold opinions and to receive and impart information and ideas without interference by public authority and regardless of frontiers. Furthermore, Article 11(2) of the Charter contains a very important provision that freedom and plurality of the media must be respected. Possible limitations mentioned in public were, for example, the instances of States in which the general public was informed about the measures undertaken only by the government and not by health agencies, problems experienced by relatives who wanted access to patient's information, limitations regarding press conferences (no presence of journalists), limitations on criticism of measures taken, limited access to libraries, etc.[59]

4. LIMITATIONS AND JUSTIFICATIONS FOR LIMITATIONS OF FUNDAMENTAL RIGHTS DURING THE CORONA CRISIS

4.1. PRACTICAL ISSUES

In many future legal proceedings national courts will have to assess possible interferences with fundamental rights under national law, taking into account EU law. At present, it is not possible to give definitive answers as to which rights have been justifiably or unjustifiably limited. The answers will depend on the circumstances of every situation and the facts of the case. It will also be necessary to take into account the aforementioned conditions for the limitations of fundamental rights (Art 52(1) of the Charter), in particular the principle of proportionality and fair balance between several fundamental rights.

Collisions of fundamental rights that will need to be addressed will involve conflicts between two or more fundamental rights. Examples are: health protection and protection of personal data, protection of health and freedom of movement, protection of health and freedom to conduct a business, protection of health and the principle of equality before the law, the right to liberty and security (e.g. freedom of movement) versus the right to liberty and security (security), the protection of health and the freedom to conduct a business.[60]

---

59 There has even been a special initiative "Ensuring the Public's Right to Know in the COVID-19 Pandemic" within the framework of Article 19. See www.article19.org accessed 16 May 2020.

60 Rubenstein and DeCamp warned that during the COVID-19 pandemic, misuse of emergency public health powers is also evident, such as lockdowns in prisons as a social distancing measure and restrictions on access to abortion in the United States. Leonard Rubenstein and Matthew DeCamp, 'Revisiting Restrictions of Rights After COVID-19' (2020) Health and Human Rights Journal, available at https://www.hhrjournal.org/2020/06/revisiting-restrictions-of-rights-after-covid-19/ accessed 21 September 2020.

4.2. LEGAL REMEDIES

4.2.1. EU level

Individuals and legal persons will have to make use of the legal remedies in the Member States. The path to the Court of Justice of the EU will only be possible in the context of the preliminary reference procedure under Article 267 TFEU. There will certainly be at least a few references dealing with this issue in the coming years. Individuals can access the Court of Justice of the EU only indirectly through the mentioned proceedings under Article 267 TFEU and in a rather limited way also directly via certain direct actions (action for annulment under Article 263 TFEU against EU legal acts). If individuals want to appear before the European Court of Human Rights (which is not an EU institution), where an individual access is possible, they will have to first exhaust all local remedies, i.e. legal remedies available in their home State.

As far as available legal remedies in the EU are concerned, the European Commission could also initiate infringement proceedings against Member States for non-compliance or breach of EU law under Articles 258 and 260(2) TFEU, where sanctions can be imposed on a country if it does not comply with a judgment of the Court of Justice of the EU.

4.2.2. Member States

There are several possibilities for initiating legal and judicial proceedings in Member States, and some have already been mentioned. Such proceedings may be of *civil nature*, e.g. claims for compensation, and even of *criminal nature*. As regards the issue in the Austrian town of Ischgl in Tirol, where several thousands of people later scattered across the EU were infected while skiing, several proceedings and remedies are possible. An Austrian lawyer, Dr. Kolba, who manages the (Austrian) Consumer Protection Association (*Verbraucherschutzverein VSV*), is gathering victims for a class action for compensation against the Land of Tirol and the liable persons.[61] By the end of April 2020 more than five thousand people had joined that class action.[62]

---

61 See, e.g. Nadine Schmidt, 'Authorities in Tyrol are accused of having reacted too late to the first signs of the coronavirus outbreak in Tyrol – particularly in Ischgl – contributing to the spread of the virus in Europe and beyond' (2020) https://edition.cnn.com/travel/article/austria-ski-resort-ischgl-coronavirus-intl/index.html accessed 16 May 2020.

62 The majority of persons having joined the class action come from Germany (roughly 70% according to available data), less from Austria and also two persons from Slovenia and two from the US, see https://www.verbraucherschutzverein.at/Corona-Virus-Tirol/ accessed 16 May 2020.

Many European and world media wrote extensively on the matter.[63] The media also mentioned possible criminal charges against those responsible, both the managers of tourist/catering establishments and holders of political power in Ischgl and in Tirol.[64]

Many of those infected in several countries were in nursing homes. If individuals or States have indeed been negligent as regards their duties, both criminal proceedings and lawsuits for compensation of damages could be initiated.

The problem of rapid spread of COVID-19 and lack of medical equipment (e.g. lack of medical devices, such as respirators and lack of hospital beds) may also be related to the lack of appropriate measures taken in due time. In this regard, both litigation for compensation and criminal proceedings at national or provincial level have been mentioned (e.g. Tirol in Austria).

Some numbers regarding the lawsuits from Italy[65] and Germany are already known. In Germany, the German Constitutional Court (*Bundesverfassunggericht*) has already dealt with more than 20 complaints by 10 May 2020, e.g. for closure of churches and freedom of religion, closure of gyms, closure of courts or hearings, prohibition of association, etc.[66]

Besides civil and criminal responsibility, the possibility of *political responsibility* should not be overlooked. Thus, in Ischgl, a question of motion of no-confidence against a provincial politician has already been raised.[67]

---

63 See in Germany, for example, Watson, '"Corona-Schleuder" Ischgl: Österreich droht teure Sammelklage' (2020) https://www.watson.de/international/coronavirus/575437490-corona-schleuder-ischgl-oesterreich-droht-teure-sammelklage accessed 16 May 2020; Nadine Schmidt, 'Austrian officials face lawsuit from 2,500 tourists over ski resort outbreak' (2020) https://edition.cnn.com/travel/article/austria-ski-resort-ischgl-coronavirus-intl/index.html accessed 16 May 2020; Derek Scally, 'Class-action lawsuit launched over Covid-19 ski resort' (2020) https://www.irishtimes.com/news/world/europe/class-action-lawsuit-launched-over-covid-19-ski-resort-1.4235393 accessed 16 May 2020.

64 See, e.g, Nadine Schmidt, 'The public prosecutor will have to examine whether something went wrong and if so, what exactly went wrong' (2020) https://edition.cnn.com/travel/article/austria-ski-resort-ischgl-coronavirus-intl/index.html accessed 16 May 2020.

65 See, e.g. Angela Giuffrida, 'Italians call for justice for relatives killed by coronavirus' (2020) https://www.theguardian.com/world/2020/apr/23/italians-call-for-justice-for-relatives-killed-by-coronavirus accessed 16 May 2020.

66 See website of the German Federal Constitutional Court https://www.bundesverfassungsgericht.de/SiteGlobals/Forms/Suche/Servicesuche_Formular.html;jsessionid=2E46564510710D24ACF79DC5C0D728E8.2_cid361?nn=5399998&resourceId=5402340&input_=5399998&pageLocale=de&templateQueryString=corona&sortOrder=score+desc&language_=de&submit.x=0&submit.y=0 accessed 16 May 2020.

67 See Die Presse, 'Causa Ischgl: Opposition stellt Misstrauensantrag gegen Landesrat Tilg' (2020) https://www.diepresse.com/5812108/causa-ischgl-opposition-stellt-misstrauensantrag-gegen-landesrat-tilg accessed 16 May 2020.

5. CONCLUSION

During the Corona crisis, the exercise of certain fundamental rights was limited. It remains to be seen whether all limitations of fundamental rights were justified and whether the limitations were proportionate. The courts will have the final say on these questions.

Although the highest possible level of protection of fundamental rights is to be advocated in the EU, it should also be emphasised that in some cases the protection of fundamental rights is guaranteed in such a way that interference with certain other fundamental rights is needed in order to ensure the protection of other rights considered as more important in given time. However, such limitations on fundamental rights must be imposed under strictly defined conditions and provided by the highest legal acts, i.e. in national constitutions and in the Charter at the EU level.

A GENERAL AND CONSTITUTIONAL OUTLINE OF ITALY'S EFFORTS AGAINST COVID-19

Michele MASSA*

During the COVID-19 pandemic, in Italy no aspect of individual and social life remained untouched, nor did the legal system. A special legislative model was enacted urgently, and this aroused several constitutional questions. Nevertheless, the contribution concludes that the Italian Constitution was generally able to

* Catholic University of Milan.

accommodate the necessary reactions, without forsaking its principles: emergency measures remained within the margins of intrinsic constitutional flexibility, considering the exceptional and transient situation which justifies – and limits – their scope. Some critical points are highlighted: above all, the marginalisation of Parliament and some weaknesses in official communications between science, government and public opinion. But these critical issues predate the pandemic and their correction does not require the introduction of new constitutional clauses on states of emergency.

1. OUTLINE OF THE CHAPTER

In the last days of February 2020, Italy unwittingly found itself at the forefront in the fight against the coronavirus disease (COVID-19) caused by the severe acute respiratory syndrome coronavirus 2 (SARS-CoV-2). The pandemic reached its peak in March. For most of that month, in the entire world only China had more confirmed cases. Deaths were counted in the tens of thousands. No aspect of individual and social life remained untouched, nor did the legal system.

This contribution surveys some of the unprecedented measures taken in this contingency and assesses their compatibility with constitutional principles. The focus is on national constitutional law,[1] but also considers the conceptual framework set out in recent comparative reports[2] and analysis.[3] Statutory law and regulations have been taken into account,[4] as well as case law[5] and a selection of legal commentaries.[6]

---

1 For a general introduction to Italian constitutional law, see Valerio Onida et al., *Constitutional law in Italy* (Wolters Kluwer 2013); Giuseppe Franco Ferrari (ed), *Introduction to Italian public law* (Giuffrè Francis Lefebvre 2018). For an introduction to the Constitutional Court (abbr. Corte cost) and its case law, see Vittoria Barsotti et al., *Italian constitutional justice in global context* (OUP 2016).

2 E.g. Venice Commission, 'Observatory of situations of emergency in Venice Commission member States' www.venice.coe.int/WebForms/pages/default.aspx?p=02_EmergencyPowersObservatory&lang=EN; EU Agency for Fundamental Rights, 'Coronavirus pandemic in the EU – Fundamental Rights Implications', Bulletins 1-5, https://fra.europa.eu/en/themes/covid-19. All the websites (quoted in this note, as well as in the subsequent ones) have been accessed 30 September 2020 unless otherwise stated.

3 Tom Ginsburg and Mila Versteeg, 'The Bound Executive: Emergency Powers During the Pandemic' (2020) Virginia Public Law and Legal Theory Research Paper No 2020-52, U of Chicago, Public Law Working Paper No 747 https://ssrn.com/abstract=3608974.

4 A collection of the national measures for the containment and management of the COVID-19 emergency is available at www.gazzettaufficiale.it/dettaglioArea/12.

5 Constitutional rulings are quoted from the official website www.cortecostituzionale.it/default.do, which also reports English translations of the most relevant judgments www.cortecostituzionale.it/actionJudgment.do. Administrative rulings are quoted from the dedicated section of the official website www.giustizia-amministrativa.it/covid19-focus.

6 E.g. Ermanno Calzolaio et al. (eds), *Il diritto nella pandemia* (eum – Edizioni Università di Macerata 2020) http://eum.unimc.it/img/cms/Full%20text_Il%20diritto%20nella%20

Only some general questions will be addressed. Many others, although constitutionally relevant, will be left aside: either because they are more specific (e.g. the impact of COVID-19 on prisons, protection of personal data, freedom of worship, disadvantaged sections of society); or because other chapters of this book deal with them.[7] This includes the questions raised by the extensive and complex measures taken to support families, workers and enterprises, as well as their interconnection with EU budget and social law and policy.[8]

2. OVERVIEW OF THE PANDEMIC

The first cases of COVID-19 (two Chinese tourists in Rome) were confirmed in Italy on 30 January 2020. On 22 and 25 January, the Health Minister had already ordered the monitoring of flight passengers arriving directly from areas with confirmed outbreaks, and then proceeded to block all flights from China. On 30 January, a national state of emergency was declared and the Head of the Department for Civil Protection, acting under direction from the President of the Council of Ministers, was empowered to take extraordinary measures, mostly focused on intensifying the procurement of resources for managing the expected health care crisis. For the same task, a special commissioner was appointed at a later point.

The first autochthonous case ("patient one") was confirmed on 21 February in Lombardy (Codogno, 60 km south-east of Milan). The chain of contagion and the national "patient zero" have never been identified. On the same day, the Health Minister ordered the first quarantines, with active medical surveillance (daily monitoring by medical professionals). In the following days, the lockdown started to be enacted. This phase began with decree-law (decreto-legge, dl) 23 February 2020 no 6, the first of its kind issued in this contingency. It mandated

---

pandemia_a%20cura%20di_Calzolaio_Meccarelli_Pollastrelli.pdf; Giovanna De Minico e Massimo Villone (eds), *Stato di diritto emergenza tecnologia* (Consulta Online 2020) www.giurcost.org/studi/index.html; Sandro Staiano (ed), *Nel ventesimo anno del terzo millennio* (Editoriale scientifica 2020) www.editorialescientifica.com/shop/catalogo/fuori-collana/edizioni-fuori-collana/nel-ventesimo-anno-del-terzo-millennio-detail.html; *Le fonti normative nella gestione dell'emergenza Covid-19*, special issue 2020 of *Osservatorio sulle fonti* www.osservatoriosullefonti.it/402-editoriale/3512-fascicolo-speciale-2020; Lucia Busatta and Marta Tomasi (eds), *Un diritto per la pandemia*, special issue 2020 of *BioLaw Journal* http://dx.doi.org/10.15168/2284-4503-20201S. See also the essays collected in *Quaderni costituzionali*, no 4/2020 (forthcoming). For a first glance see also Stefano Civitarese Matteucci, 'The Italian Response to Coronavirus and Constitutional Disagreement' (*UK Constitutional Law Association*, 30 April 2020) https://ukconstitutionallaw.org/2020/04/30/stefano-civitarese-matteucci-the-italian-response-to-coronavirus-and-constitutional-disagreement/.

7 See the contributions by Luca Giacomelli and Elisabetta Lamarque; Carlo Padula and Giacomo Delledonne; Roberta Calvano.

8 On European social law and policy see the contribution by Luka Mišič and Grega Strban.

"competent authorities" to adopt all the containment and management measures proper and proportionate to the evolving situation, including prohibition to leave or enter certain areas; suspension of work, meetings, events and teaching activities; closing of offices and shops. A long sequence of administrative orders and decrees-law was to follow soon, as the lockdown rapidly grew to encompass the entire nation and all its activities.

These measures have been gradually relaxed since May, in the so called "Phase 2" (coexistence with the virus, until a vaccination is available). With a first decree (decree of the President of the Council of Ministers, dPCm, 26 April 2020), entered into force on 4 May 2020, several activities could restart, including manufacturing and industrial production, building and wholesale distribution. Dl 16 May 2020 no 33, set out the general rules on "Phase 2", with effect from 18 May 2020. Subsequently both the state of emergency and the rules and limitations established by dl no 33/2020 have been extended.

The estimate of the economic impact is uncertain in its precise amount but is projected to be huge. According to the national institute of statistics, in the second quarter of 2020 the gross national product decreased by 13% from the preceding trimester, and by 18% from the second trimester of 2019.[9] Several measures – particularly in dl 17 March 2020 no 18 ("Cure Italy"), dl 8 April 2020 no 23 ("Liquidity"), dl 19 May 2020 no 34 ("Relaunch"), and dl 14 August 2020 no 104 – addressed the ensuing and ongoing economic and social crises, with packages of deficit-funded measures aimed at persons, families and enterprises.

3. LEGAL INSTRUMENTS

The emergency was tackled with a variety of legal tools, ranging from the national to the municipal level. Here it is impossible to summarise their content. Only their general legal types will be briefly described.

3.1. DECREES-LAW

A decree-law (Art 77 of the Italian Constitution (Const)) is a Government decree having force of law: it may amend ordinary laws, may be amended only by laws or equivalent acts, and only the Constitutional Court may annul it. A decree-law is adopted by the Government in extraordinary cases of necessity and urgency and issued by the President of the Republic. It may enter into force directly. The Government must introduce immediately to Parliament a bill

---

9 Istat, 'Conti economici trimestrali. Prodotto interno lordo, valore aggiunto, consumi, investimenti, domanda estera. II trimestre 2020' (2 October 2020) www.istat.it/en/archivio/246773 accessed 16 October 2020.

for the "conversion" of the decree into a law. The Parliament – following the ordinary legislative procedure, albeit with accelerated terms – examines the bill and, while doing so, may amend the decree: basically, this implies a re-evaluation of the situation of necessity and urgency, as well as of the measures adopted to manage it. If the law for the conversion is not approved (by both Houses of the Parliament) and promulgated by the President of the Republic within 60 days, the decree loses every legal effect from the beginning.

This peculiar legal scheme was reluctantly designed by the Framers of the 1948 Italian Constitution. On the one hand, they remembered and feared the extensive use of similar instruments made by the executive power under the Fascist rule, and indeed even before. On the other hand, they felt that it was better to set out precise provisions, as strict as possible, on emergency legislation, rather than let the matter remain undefined and leave it to political practice. Therefore, in theory, the decree-law has been conceived as an extraordinary tool, to be used only for specific and concrete emergencies. However, in practice, at least since the 1970s decrees-law have been used extensively as an alternative and more practical way for the Government to pursue its general legislative agenda.

Neither the President of the Republic, nor the Constitutional Court have ever been able to enforce a reading of the "extraordinary cases of necessity and urgency" as strictly, as the literal wording of the clause may suggest. Indeed, decrees-law always remained an ordinary legislative tool: e.g. there were 16 in 2018 and 24 in 2019. To date they have been 25 in 2020: an increase, but not out of range. Nor is it unusual for the Government to put pressure on Parliament and call for a confidence vote on the conversion:[10] usually, this happens with the decree-law as amended by the parliamentary committee, that has examined it in the chamber where it was first introduced for conversion.

As a matter of principle, a natural calamity such as a pandemic is precisely the kind of contingency which warrants the application of Article 77. Nonetheless, the use of decrees-law during the pandemic aroused novel and specific perplexities, e.g.:

- decrees-law are the only legislative instrument employed to tackle the emergency;[11]

---

[10] Also to overcome filibustering by the opposition: e.g. dl no 19/2020 was converted into law almost at the end of the 60-day time limit, although some amendments had been made to meet criticism by parliamentary minorities. See Ugo De Siervo, 'Emergenza Covid e sistema delle fonti: prime impressioni' in *Le fonti normative nella gestione dell'emergenza Covid-19*, special issue 2020 of *Osservatorio sulle fonti* www.osservatoriosullefonti.it/402-editoriale/3512-fascicolo-speciale-2020, 299, 307.

[11] Since March 2020, the only ordinary law passed – besides those converting decrees-law – concerned the ratification of international agreements and a couple of minor issues (a committee of inquiry into foster care communities, law 29 July 2020 no 107; primary chronic headache as a social illness, law 14 July 2020 no 81).

- some decrees-law were amended speedily (or had some of their provisions repealed) by subsequent decrees, before Parliament had completed the conversion procedure;[12]
- such was the haste, that Parliament employed a peculiar technique (dubbed 'the minotaur'): with a single law, it converted one decree and, at the same time, transplanted into it contents from another decree, while formally repealing the latter.[13]

Somehow paradoxically, Parliament did not assert the central role of ordinary laws in the legal system, but instead supported and encouraged the extensive use of decrees-law as the main way to ensure its own position in regulating liberties,[14] rather than leaving this issue to emergency administrative orders (see below) which elude direct parliamentary scrutiny. Nevertheless, by embracing the practice described above, the legislative power also shifted its control from the single provisions and decrees, to bundles of emergency measures, considered as unified sets:[15] a further step along the path from parliamentary legislation, towards mere parliamentary oversight of executive legislation.[16]

3.2. EMERGENCY ADMINISTRATIVE ORDERS

Even before the Constitution, the Italian legal system included a type of administrative act known as "ordinanze contingibili e urgenti": orders issued by administrative authorities to face specific contingencies, which urgently require extraordinary measures, i.e. measures which are different from those that the competent authorities may adopt ordinarily. Due to their function, these orders enjoy a special legal status: they may derogate the legislation currently in force, and their content is not legally predetermined (in this sense, they are atypical acts), as they may establish any prescription needed to face the contingency.

---

12 Emanuele Rossi, 'Appunti sull'abrogazione di decreti-legge in sede di conversione ad opera di successivi decreti-legge (nell'emergenza Coronavirus)' in *Le fonti normative nella gestione dell'emergenza Covid-19*, special issue 2020 of *Osservatorio sulle fonti* www.osservatoriosullefonti.it/402-editoriale/3512-fascicolo-speciale-2020, 641.

13 Salvatore Curreri, 'Il Parlamento nell'emergenza: resiliente o latitante?' (2020) forthcoming in *Quaderni costituzionali* no 4/2020, §5.

14 Camera dei deputati, mozione 1/00348 (19 May 2020) http://aic.camera.it/aic/scheda.html?core=aic&numero=1/00348&ramo=C&leg=18.

15 Gian Luca Conti, 'La crisi dello "Stato moderno" e l'emergenza pandemica: appunti sul ruolo delle Camere nella lotta contro il coronavirus' in *Le fonti normative nella gestione dell'emergenza Covid-19*, special issue 2020 of *Osservatorio sulle fonti* www.osservatoriosullefonti.it/402-editoriale/3512-fascicolo-speciale-2020, 517, 525.

16 Salvatore Curreri, 'Il Parlamento nell'emergenza: resiliente o latitante?' (2020) forthcoming in *Quaderni costituzionali* no 4/2020, §6.

Nevertheless, they are not sources of law, but discretionary administrative acts, subject to review by ordinary and administrative courts. They are also subject to some general limits: their duration must not be longer than urgency and necessity require; they must rely on an adequate motivation; when the adopted measures are not aimed at single persons, publication is mandatory; the general principles of the legal system, as well as the Constitution, must be respected.

Non-compliance with these orders, when they are legally adopted, is punished as a crime (Criminal code, Art 650) carrying a maximum sentence of three-month arrest and 206 euro fine, unless a more serious offence applies (e.g. causing an epidemic outbreak by voluntarily or involuntarily diffusing pathogens).

Several pieces of general legislation include emergency administrative powers, which have been vastly employed during the pandemic crisis. Some specific adjustments and additions have also been made through the decrees-law specifically adopted for the COVID-19 pandemic. Indeed, one of the main legal problems has been understanding both the links and the differences between two chains of administrative acts: those enacted by virtue of pre-existing pieces of legislation, starting with the declaration of a state of national emergency; and those based on the new decrees-law.

3.2.1. General provisions

Emergency powers for the protection of health are shared among three levels of government, according to Article 32 of law 23 December 1978 no 833 (the basic law on the national healthcare system):

- the Minister of Health may adopt emergency orders concerning public hygiene and health crises, as well as veterinary police, with effects on the entire national territory, or areas comprised in two or more regions;
- presidents of regions are competent when measures are to apply in the entire territory of a region, or in areas comprised in two or more municipalities;
- mayors are competent for measures applying only within municipal territory.

It is necessary to remember that, at least since 1992, the Italian healthcare system is essentially based on regions. The agencies managing the system and directly providing health services – also in cooperation with private clinics, laboratories and professionals – belong to the regional administrations and consume by far the largest portion of regional budgets. Regions also have legislative competence on health care, although the State retains the competence to set out the basic legislative principles in this area, as well as uniform levels of assistance to be guaranteed throughout the national territory. Municipalities are competent only for social, not for healthcare services, although mayors retain their traditional role of local health authority, particularly in case of emergencies (Art 50.4-5 of legislative decree, dlgs, 18 August 2000 no 267; see also Art 117 of dlgs 31 March 1998 no 112).

Further emergency powers are established in the legislation on civil protection (disaster relief), recently consolidated in dlgs 2 January 2018 no 1 (Code of civil protection). The task of national service of civil protection is to manage emergencies due to disasters, when they require extraordinary measures, particularly when they endanger the life and physical safety of the people, or other important public goods. This service too has a complex structure: the head national authority is the President of the Council of Ministers, through the Department for Civil Protection; regions and municipalities are part of the system, and take part, to some extent, also in the elaboration of general and contingency policies. Indeed, regions share legislative competence with the State also in this field, as in health care. But some essential powers are centralised: only the President of the Council of Ministers may mobilise the national system; only the Council of Ministers may declare a national emergency; only the President of the Council of Ministers has the power to adopt emergency orders, also through the Head of the Department for Civil Protection.

All these powers were employed during the pandemic emergency: e.g. the first orders were adopted under article of law no 833/1978; national emergency was declared under dlgs no 1/2018; to date, the main scientific and technical committee (Comitato tecnico-scientifico (CTS)), which has been established to cooperate with national authorities, finds its legal basis in an order issued by the Head of the Department for Civil Protection;[17] regional and local emergency powers continue to be widely employed.

3.2.2. *Special provisions*

The signature tool, so to say, of the Government's fight against COVID-19 were the decrees of the President of the Council of Ministers. Normally a generic format, which may hold any sort of administrative content (general rules, specific measures, etc.) delegated to them by ordinary law, dPCms were used to adopt the wide range of restrictive provisions which composed the national lockdown regime.

Dl no 6/2020 contained a list of possible limitations to individual and collective liberties (Art 1), as well as a general clause authorising further limitations whenever necessary (Art 2), and stipulated that said limitations would be applied through dPCms, adopted after hearing the competent ministers

---

17 Order 3 February 2020, Article 2.

and presidents of regions.[18] In the meantime, the same measures could also be anticipated through the emergency administrative powers established by other general provisions.

And so it was that a long chain of dPCms started, and that this legal instrument became very familiar to everyone in Italy and, in a sense, the true law of the land during the emergency, regulating limitations to mobility, assembly and economic activities.

A sort of consolidated and more precise text on lockdown powers was subsequently issued with dl 25 March 2020 no 19, as the first wave of measures had provoked legal uncertainties. Most importantly dl no 19/2020 (as converted into law 22 May 2020 no 35):

- recapitulates a long and detailed list of limitations and stipulates that – until a fixed date, already postponed several times – they may be established for 30 days, renewed and recalibrated, also differentiating among territories. The limitations may be imposed through dPCms, or temporarily by the Health Minister. All the administrative orders and decrees, previously adopted under dl no 6/2020 and law no 833/1978, are confirmed and their validity in time is regulated;
- still allows presidents of regions and mayors to enforce additional restrictions, but only:
  - in case of specific territorial emergencies;
  - within their legal competences, and without impacting on economic activities of national relevance;
  - with effect only until corresponding measures are adopted at the national level (mayors must respect regional measures also);
- sets out the default sanctions for violations (including those already committed) as follows (unless more severe provisions apply): (i) an administrative fine of 400-1.000 euro, increased by 1/3 if a vehicle has been employed; (ii) a 5 to 30-day closure for commercial and production activities.

After dl no 19/2020, more dPCms were issued: e.g. on 10 April (basically a restatement of the lockdown measures, with some variations) and on 26 April 2020, when "Phase 2" timidly started.

Dl no 33/2020 dropped the limitations to movement within regions (from 18 May 2020) and between them (from 3 June 2020), as well as the general prohibitions of events, meetings and public religious ceremonies. Said limitations may be maintained, or reinstated, in specific areas if necessary, with administrative orders according to dl no 19/2020.

18 See now dl no 19/2020, Article 2. DPCms may also be proposed by Presidents of regions, or by the President of the Conference of regions. They are subject to a preventive review of legality by the Corte dei conti (Court of Auditors), within an abbreviated deadline, but are immediately effective in the meantime (Art 2.4).

Also dl no 33/2020 was immediately complemented with a massive (127-page long) dPCm (issued on 17 May 2020 and amended on 18 May 2020) containing a vast array of rules, protocols and guidelines to ensure health and safety during "Phase 2". Many of the protocols and guidelines attached to the dPCm have been agreed with civil society (e.g. religious) organisations, social partners and regions.

Article 1.16 of dl no 33/2020 also mandates a regular monitoring of epidemiological trends by the regions, according to criteria and parameters uniformly established by the Health Minister after consultations also with technical and regional authorities.[19] The outcomes of the monitoring are shared with the Health Ministry and the CTS and may justify tightening up, or relaxing, rules and limitations currently in force under dl no 19/2020.

3.2.3. Analysis

Much has been written about dPCms, their legal basis and nature: do they rely only on the 2020 decrees-law, or also on the general provisions on civil protection emergencies?[20] Have they become proper sources of law or are they still just administrative measures, akin to traditional emergency orders? May they limit constitutional rights?

The third question will be considered below. Concerning the first two, the dPCms themselves – in their preambles – refer to the decrees-law as their specific legislative foundation, although in their turn both the decrees-law and the dPCms rely on the same material contingency, which has been declared as a national emergency under dlgs no 1 of 2018. Moreover, decree-law no 19 of 2020 clearly distinguishes between dPCms and other emergency orders, as the latter may be adopted only pending adoption of the former. This is not to deny – quite the contrary – that all these acts share a common legal nature: they all are administrative measures, not regulations, nor sources of law of any kind. It is true that, in the history of the Republic, never have emergency measures had such extensive and intense effects. But it is also true that these measures are, and have been, short-term, subject to continuous scientific and administrative monitoring, and clearly linked to a singular contingency. In legal scholarship, all these circumstances have been considered relevant for excluding the normative nature of administrative instruments enacted by national authorities.[21]

---

[19] See decree 30 April 2020 www.trovanorme.salute.gov.it/norme/renderNormsanPdf?anno=2020&codLeg=73981&parte=1%20&serie=null.

[20] Massimo Luciani, 'Il sistema delle fonti del diritto alla prova dell'emergenza', in Liber amicorum *per Pasquale Costanzo* (Consulta Online 2020) 12–13 www.giurcost.org/LIBERAMICORUM/INDICEliber.html.

[21] See Michele Massa, 'I regolamenti ministeriali' (2017) in *Federalismi.it*, special issue no 2 www.federalismi.it/nv14/articolo-documento.cfm?Artid=35214&content=I+regolamenti+ministeriali&content_author=%3Cb%3EMichele+Massa%3C/b%3E.

Was it indispensable to hastily develop a new, specific body of law for the administrative management of the pandemic? Were not traditional emergency powers already sufficient?

Some have argued that the framework for civil protection was adequate, as well as more clearly established in the legal and constitutional system and practice.[22] While the latter point is true, the former is highly disputable, due to the many peculiarities which distinguish a pandemic from other types of emergencies.[23] For sure, by opting for a special and transient set of rules and instruments, the Government and Parliament signalled that such a rigorous and all-encompassing lockdown regime goes well beyond what other emergencies may legitimately warrant. Drafting and coordination with pre-existing instruments could have been better, but the basic message is very significant, also from a constitutional viewpoint.

According to the taxonomy by Ferejohn and Pasquino,[24] emergency powers come in two models: constitutional or legislative, depending on the legal source authorising extraordinary executive action. It should be clear that, during the pandemic, Italy adopted a special legislative model, while at the constitutional level it relied only on the general provision of Article 77.

4. JUDICIAL REVIEW

Administrative measures adopted by national, regional and local authorities during the COVID-19 emergency have been subject to review by ordinary and administrative courts. Also emergency legislation has been subject to judicial scrutiny.

---

22 Andrea Cardone, 'Il baratro della necessità e la chimera della costituzionalizzazione: una lettura della crisi delle fonti del sistema di protezione civile contro le battaglie di retroguardia' in *Le fonti normative nella gestione dell'emergenza Covid-19*, special issue 2020 of *Osservatorio sulle fonti* www.osservatoriosullefonti.it/402-editoriale/3512-fascicolo-speciale-2020, 313.

23 See Ginsburg and Versteeg, 'The Bound Executive: Emergency Powers During the Pandemic' (2020) Virginia Public Law and Legal Theory Research Paper No 2020-52, U of Chicago, Public Law Working Paper No 747 https://ssrn.com/abstract=3608974, II.C. See also, from an Italian viewpoint, Antonio D'Aloia, 'Postilla. Costituzione ed emergenza: verso la fine del tunnel, con qualche speranza e (ancora) con qualche dubbio' in Busatta and Tomasi (eds), *Un diritto per la pandemia*, special issue 2020 of *BioLaw Journal* http://dx.doi.org/10.15168/2284-4503-2020lS, 13, 17; Cesare Pinelli, 'Il precario assetto delle fonti impiegate nell'emergenza sanitaria e gli squilibrati rapporti fra Stato e Regioni' (2020) in *ASTRID Rassegna* no 5/2020, 1, 6.

24 John Ferejohn and Pasquale Pasquino, 'The law of the exception: A typology of emergency powers' (2004) 2(2) *International Journal of Constitutional Law* 210. https://doi.org/10.1093/icon/2.2.210.

A detailed survey[25] highlighted numerous decisions by administrative courts (mostly interim) and concluded that overall the lockdown regime passed judicial scrutiny, with very limited exceptions. It also noted that, during the emergency, the appellate administrative court (Consiglio di Stato) exceptionally heard appeals against interim measures adopted by the lower courts, even in cases where the law, at face value, does not allow this.[26]

This is not to say that all judicial decisions were satisfied with every aspect of administrative management of the emergency. For example, after the Department of Civil Protection funded municipalities for the provision of shopping vouchers to poorer families, several Tribunals extended access to said vouchers to foreign nationals resident in Italy, although lacking residence permits, on the assumption that this was a basic guarantee of a primary need and of the right to food.[27]

Also, some controversies on the constitutional legitimacy of emergency law have been raised. For example:

- during the emergency, several convicts were released (e.g. to be put in home detention) due to personal vulnerability to the virus. Regarding convicts for organised crime, terrorism and drug trafficking, dl 10 May 2020 no 29 mandated immediate and frequent revisions of the release orders, which should cease as soon as adequate penitentiary placements are found. Several supervisory magistrates challenged this procedure, which allegedly did not guarantee the right to defence and due process. With a first decision, the Constitutional Court deferred judgment, as the relevant provisions had been extensively amended in the meantime,[28] but the question will be examined again in the next months;
- several courts[29] questioned Article 83 of dl no 19/2020 where it suspends the statute of limitations, in parallel with the postponement of public hearings and the suspension of procedural terms. Since in Italian law the statute of limitations is considered a part of substantive criminal law (the temporal dimension of criminal liability), its extension *ex post facto* is suspected of running counter to the "no punishment without law" principle.

---

25 Alfonso Vuolo, 'Il sindacato di legittimità sulle misure di contrasto alla pandemia' in Sandro Staiano (ed), *Nel ventesimo anno del terzo millennio* (Editoriale scientifica 2020) www.editorialescientifica.com/shop/catalogo/fuori-collana/edizioni-fuori-collana/nel-ventesimo-anno-del-terzo-millennio-detail.html, 305.

26 Ibid 319.

27 Tribunale (abbr. Trib) Roma, sezione diritti della persona e immigrazione civile, decree 21 April 2020; Trib Brescia, sezione immigrazione, protezione internazionale e libera circolazione dei cittadini dell'UE, decree 28 April 2020; Trib Ferrara order 30 April 2020; all in www.asgi.it/notizie/cittadini-stranieri-e-solidarieta-alimentare-al-tempo-del-coronavirus/. See also Tribunale amministrativo regionale per l'Abruzzo, sezione prima, decree 22 April 2020 no 79, on the provision of vouchers to homeless persons.

28 Corte cost 30 July 2020 no 185.

29 Starting with Trib Siena orders 21 May 2020 www.questionegiustizia.it/articolo/la-sospensione-del-corso-della-prescrizione-al-vaglio-della-consulta_26-05-2020.php.

5. CONSTITUTIONAL RIGHTS

5.1. ACCESS TO HEALTH CARE

The Italian Constitution recognises equal social dignity, and equality before the law, to all citizens, without distinction of personal and social conditions (Art 3), and safeguards health as a "fundamental" right of the individual, as well as a collective interest (Art 32). Accordingly, the Italian healthcare system follows a universalistic approach. Law no 833/1978 commits it to assisting the whole population, without individual and social distinctions, and to ensuring equality among citizens (Art 1).

According to a detailed report by the Corte dei conti (Court of auditors),[30] the Italian healthcare system is among both the most effective, and the most cost-efficient in the world. However, in recent years, while great efforts have been made to re-absorb imbalances in resources management, criticalities emerged: access to public services became more difficult; private expenditure grew; inequality – both territorial and socio-economic – increased. At the acme of the emergency, territorial services became critical and their weakness became manifest and decisive. Hospitals were put under severe strain. By pumping more resources into the system (1.4 billion euros) and concentrating all those already available, the number of intensive care units (ICUs) was increased by more than 50% in one month. Nevertheless, managing all the aspects of the pandemic (prevention, screening, tracing, etc.) remains a challenge for health administrations and facilities.

In the past, constitutional case law has frequently allowed the protection of health to be balanced against a variety of antagonistic interests, including financial and economic concerns. Lately, during the lockdown, it has been noted that the "fundamental" value of this individual right and general interest "took its revenge", by imposing itself albeit at a high price.[31] However, as it will become clear below, the whole emergency regime has been, and still is, above all, an exercise in balancing.

5.2. PERSONAL LIBERTY, RIGHT TO TRAVEL, FREEDOM OF ASSEMBLY

Under the lockdown regime, suddenly everyone found themselves prohibited from leaving their regions or municipalities, at first, and their homes,

---

30 Corte dei conti, sezioni riunite in sede di controllo, 'Rapporto 2020 sul coordinamento della finanza pubblica' (28 May 2020) www.corteconti.it/Home/Organizzazione/UfficiCentraliRegionali/UffSezRiuniteSedeControllo/RappCoord/RappCoord2020.

31 Donatella Morana, 'Sulla fondamentalità perduta (e forse ritrovata) del diritto e dell'interesse della collettività alla salute: metamorfosi di una garanzia costituzionale, dal caso Ilva ai tempi della pandemia' in Liber amicorum *per Pasquale Costanzo* (Consulta Online 2020) www.giurcost.org/LIBERAMICORUM/INDICEliber.html.

subsequently, unless under specific circumstances. Those testing positive for SARS-CoV-2 were, and still are, under an absolute obligation to stay at home.

Was this tantamount to a general suspension of habeas corpus? The question has been widely debated and different answers have been given,[32] although the most convincing one is in the negative.

The relevant provisions in the Italian Constitution are two. Under Article 13, no one may be detained, or otherwise subjected to restrictions of personal liberty, except by reasoned order of the judiciary (or by police measures, to be referred within 48 hours to the judiciary, which must decide whether to validate within further 48 hours) and only in such cases and in such manner as provided by the law. Under Article 16, every citizen has the right to travel freely in the country, except for such general limitations as may be established by law for reasons of health or security. Both constitutional provisions require ordinary law (or equivalent acts, including decrees-law, but excluding administrative orders and regulations) to set out limitations to personal liberty and right to travel ("riserva di legge", reserve to law); but only personal liberty has the additional guarantee, that every single limitation requires a previous or immediate scrutiny by the judiciary ("riserva di giurisdizione", reserve to the judiciary).

The exact legal boundaries between personal liberty and right to travel have always been somewhat uncertain: e.g. does the prohibition to leave a town impinge on the former or the latter? In constitutional case law, the issue has been debated mostly concerning crime prevention measures, as well as administrative detention of migrants. There are two leading criteria. Personal liberty is at stake when:

- individuals are legally degraded, i.e. the limitation downgrades their personal dignity and reputation, notably through a negative assessment of their morality or respectability;[33]
- at any rate when the interested person is physically subjected to direct coercion by others.[34]

In the light of these criteria, lockdown prohibitions fall within the scope of Article 16, not Article 13 Const:

- they do not imply judgments on anyone's morality or respectability;

32 E.g. see the diverging opinions recorded in Franco De Stefano, 'La pandemia aggredisce anche il diritto?' in (*Giustizia insieme*, 2 aprile 2020), with interviews to Corrado Caruso, Giorgio Lattanzi (former President of the Constitutional court), Gabriella Luccioli (former Section president of the Court of cassation) and Massimo Luciani (professor, former President of the Associazione italiana dei costituzionalisti) www.giustiziainsieme.it/it/diritto-dell-emergenza-covid-19/961-la-pandemia-aggredisce-anche-il-diritto.

33 For example, Corte cost 7 December 1994 no 419.

34 For example, Corte cost 10 April 2001 no 105.

- they are mandatory, but do not entail any direct coercion (violations are subject to criminal or administrative sanctions, but do not allow the immediate use of force to keep anyone at home, or to bring them back there);
- moreover – aside from certified COVID-19 patients and their immediate contacts – the prohibition to leave home (municipality, etc.) always had significant exceptions, making it far less intrusive than the condition of *Machtlosigkeit* that Article 13 aims at preventing, according to some scholarship.[35]

Therefore, "riserva di giurisdizione" does not apply, but limitations must still be established by law and justified by health reasons, as well as proportionate to them.

The lockdown regime also included a general prohibition of public events, organised meetings and casual gatherings of any kind; to this day, they may only take place in compliance with safety rules mostly established in dPCms and other administrative acts. Unquestionably this has an impact on freedom of assembly, as well as other collective constitutional rights, e.g. freedom of worship.

And yet:

- these are mostly indirect effects of limitations principally imposed on the right to travel;[36]
- in accordance with a rigorous and authoritative scholarly reading, the relevant constitutional provision on freedom of assembly (Art 17) allows such limitations if they are justified by documented concerns for public security or safety, and this is valid also for private meetings, notwithstanding the inviolability of personal domicile (Art 14), at least when crimes have been committed or there is a danger for health;[37]
- at any rate, the general doctrine of balance and proportionality also applies and may offer enough grounds for said limitations (see below).

5.3. LIMITATIONS TO RIGHTS AND PROPORTIONALITY

Concerning proportionality, the situation, especially at the pandemic's peak, was such – due to COVID-19's unexpected diffusivity and virulence, as well as to the

---

35 Roberto Cherchi and Andrea Deffenu, 'Fonti e provvedimenti dell'emergenza sanitaria Covid-19: prime riflessioni' in *Diritti regionali* no 1/2020. www.dirittiregionali.it/wp-content/uploads/2020/04/documento-integrale-50.pdf.

36 Edoardo C. Raffiotta, 'Sulla legittimità dei provvedimenti del Governo a contrasto dell'emergenza virale da coronavirus' in Busatta and Tomasi (eds), *Un diritto per la pandemia*, special issue 2020 of *BioLaw Journal* http://dx.doi.org/10.15168/2284-4503-20201S, 95, 102.

37 Alessandro Pace, 'Rapporti civili – art. 17' in Giuseppe Branca (ed), *Commentario della Costituzione* (Zanichelli-Il Foro italiano 1977) 145, 166.

uncertainties lingering regarding it and its treatment – to afford wide political discretion to the competent authorities, as long as their decisions were based on scientific evidence.

Constitutional case law has recently recapitulated the principles relevant to epidemiological prophylaxis in an articulate judgment concerning mandatory vaccinations:[38]

> legislative discretion in choosing the ways in which to ensure effective prevention of infectious diseases [...] must be exercised in light of the various health and epidemiological conditions, as ascertained by the responsible authorities [...], and of the constantly evolving discoveries of medical research, to which the legislator must turn for guidance in the exercise of its choices in this area.

Two critical aspects became manifest during the pandemic: the identification of the "authorities" responsible for assessing "health and epidemiological conditions", and the transparency of science-driven policymaking. The latter point shall be considered below. On the former, it is striking that – although the legislation on civil protection has established a national committee for major risks as scientific and technical consultative body – many specific committees were established for this emergency, including the CTS, whose composition was changed during the pandemic.[39] This has been considered a symptom of a lingering immaturity of the Italian system, when compared with other countries, concerning institutional channels of communications between science and government.[40]

Of course, scientific advice does not offer clear-cut directions for every choice and, at any rate, government responsibility belongs to politicians, not clinicians. Health risks must be balanced against a variety of different concerns and needs. Particularly after several months of lockdown, risk assessment is a complex exercise and must account for several factors, including political, social and economic.[41]

---

38 Corte cost 18 January 2018 no 5.

39 See Order 3 February 2020, Article 2. Currently the CTS includes officials from Ministries and public institutions competent for health care and prevention, as well as a representative of regions, and several experts. Order of the Head of the Department for Civil Protection 18 April 2020 no 663 www.gazzettaufficiale.it/eli/id/2020/04/22/20A02260/sg.

40 Antonio Iannuzzi, 'Leggi "science driven" e CoViD-19. Il rapporto fra politica e scienza nello stato di emergenza sanitaria' in Busatta and Tomasi (eds), *Un diritto per la pandemia*, special issue 2020 of *BioLaw Journal* http://dx.doi.org/10.15168/2284-4503-2020lS, 119, 125.

41 Antonio D'Aloia, 'Postilla. Costituzione ed emergenza: verso la fine del tunnel, con qualche speranza e (ancora) con qualche dubbio' in Busatta and Tomasi (eds), *Un diritto per la pandemia*, special issue 2020 of *BioLaw Journal* http://dx.doi.org/10.15168/2284-4503-2020lS. 13, 23.

In a famous ruling concerning the severe environmental and health repercussions of pollution around a colossal steel plant (Ilva) in Taranto,[42] the Constitutional Court clarified that:

> [a]ll fundamental rights protected by the Constitution are mutually related to one another and it is thus not possible to identify any one of them in isolation as prevailing absolutely over the others … For the reasons set out above, it is not possible to share the argument … that the adjective "fundamental" contained in Article 32 Const indicates a "predominant status" of the right to health over all other rights of the person … As is the case under other contemporary democratic and pluralist constitutions, the Italian Constitution requires that an ongoing reciprocal balance be struck between fundamental principles and rights, and that none of them may claim absolute status … Precisely because it is dynamic and not set in advance, the point of equilibrium must be assessed – by Parliament when enacting legislation and by the Constitutional Court upon review – according to the criteria of proportionality and reasonableness in such a manner as to ensure that their essential core is not sacrificed.

This is just a corollary of a general doctrine affirmed by the Constitutional court since its first ruling:[43] regulating the exercise of rights, in order to reconcile the pursuit of different aims by different people, does not amount to violating or denying rights; every regulation arguably entails a limitation, but nevertheless the notion of limitations is intrinsic to the notion of rights and in the legal system different spheres must necessarily limit each other, so that they can coexist in orderly civil cohabitation.

Summing up, if (cumulatively):

- scientific advice – to the extent that it is available – is duly taken into consideration;
- the prescribed limitations find reasonable grounds in it, i.e. they effectively serve a preventive purpose, which would be difficult to attain otherwise;
- at least the essential core of every constitutional right and principle is respected;
- there are no arbitrary discriminations amongst the sectors involved;

then, political decisions to enforce the lockdown regime should bear legal scrutiny.

---

42 Corte cost 9 May 2013 no 85.

43 Corte cost 14 June 1956 no 1.

Four other factors contribute to recommend a further degree of deference, in these circumstances:

1. first and foremost, all the measures are temporary,[44] many of them have been revised frequently and a constant monitoring is taking place;
2. especially in the first stages of the emergency and of each different phase, urgency justifies a more schematic ponderation of the myriad of relevant situations;
3. the uncertainty still concerning SARS-CoV-2 demands a precautionary approach, itself aiming at proportionate, non-discriminatory, transparent and coherent actions, subject to periodic review;
4. the objectives of immediate and widespread application, dissuasion of risky behaviours, as well as ease and promptness in enforcement, may weigh in favour of sweeping limitations, even when it would be possible, in abstract, to craft them in more complex, detailed or flexible ways.

Mutatis mutandis, a similar test of proportionality should apply on the decisions to relax the lockdown regime during "Phase 2": e.g. even as normal social and economic life restarts, health concerns cannot be disregarded and at least some essential precautionary measures must be maintained; greater caution and rigidity are more justified in the early stages of this phase.

Some have denounced a lack of proportionality for the non-selective character of many measures.[45] However, considering all the circumstances above, it seems understandable and correct that, at least until now, Italian courts have been mostly deferential towards scientific and political discretion.

Incidentally, this is in line with a general remark by John Roberts, Chief Justice of the Supreme Court of the United States of America:[46]

> [t]he precise question of when restrictions on particular social activities should be lifted during the pandemic is a dynamic and fact-intensive matter subject to reasonable disagreement. Our Constitution principally entrusts '[t]he safety and the health of the people' to the politically accountable officials of the States 'to guard and protect.' … When those officials 'undertake … to act in areas fraught with medical and scientific uncertainties,' their latitude 'must be especially broad.'

---

44 A detailed analysis in Carla Acocella, 'Spigolature sulle dimensioni del tempo nella stagione dell'emergenza da Covid-19' in Sandro Staiano (ed), *Nel ventesimo anno del terzo millennio* (Editoriale scientifica 2020) www.editorialescientifica.com/shop/catalogo/fuori-collana/edizioni-fuori-collana/nel-ventesimo-anno-del-terzo-millennio-detail.html, 185.

45 Giovanna De Minico, 'Costituzionalizziamo l'emergenza?' in Giovanna De Minico e Massimo Villone (eds), *Stato di diritto emergenza tecnologia* (Consulta Online 2020) www.giurcost.org/studi/index.html, 21 36–37.

46 *South Bay United Pentecostal Church, et al. v Gavin Newsom, Governor of California, et al.* 590 U.S. (2020). A majority of the court denied an application for injunctive relief seeking to enjoin enforcement of temporary numerical restrictions on public gatherings.

The link in the proportionality test between the scope and content of measures, on the one hand, and, on the other hand, the specific circumstances also guarantees that emergency limitations may not last longer than the exceptional situation justifying them.

5.4. LIMITATIONS TO RIGHTS AND SOURCES OF LAW

Lawyers – and particularly criminal lawyers – voiced concern for the type (sources) and quality (clarity and foreseeability in application) of the rules comprising the lockdown regime.

There is no denying that the clarity of lockdown rules was far from perfect: which were the "necessity reasons" required to circulate? How many people form a "gathering" exactly? Who are the "relations" that, at a point, it was again possible to visit? The number of circular letters, clarifying notes and "frequently asked questions" issued by the competent authorities are a telling symptom. But this was to be expected, given the situation and the very broad policies enacted to face it: some common sense in the construction and enforcement of open clauses was indispensable; means of legal protection were readily available when controversies arose. Moreover, particularly at the high point of the emergency, these policies fulfilled a basic, albeit sometimes overlooked, function of law:[47] serving as a guidance for individual and collective behaviour and fostering spontaneous cooperation, at a time when official policing in every single instance was practically impossible. From this perspective, the employment of open or non-technical clauses, as well as the gradual relaxation of sanctions, were only natural.

Indeed, a source of well-founded concern was the vagueness of the first decree-law (no 6/2020), particularly where it (Art 2) purportedly authorised dPCms to enact any necessary measure, without further specification. But subsequent dl no 19/2020 was more careful in listing, defining and authorising possible limitations, as well as validating previously adopted measures. Therefore, the limitations are now either enforced directly by an act equivalent to law, or by administrative orders which find in said act – and in the exceptional factual circumstances it contemplates, themselves a yardstick for judicial review[48] – the basis and limits to their legitimacy.

---

47 Angela Cossiri, 'Le norme di contrasto al contagio tra funzione sociale ed efficacia' in Calzolaio et al. (eds), *Il diritto nella pandemia* (eum – Edizioni Università di Macerata 2020) http://eum.unimc.it/img/cms/Full%20text_Il%20diritto%20nella%20pandemia_a%20cura%20di_Calzolaio_Meccarelli_Pollastrelli.pdf; 35.

48 Edoardo C. Raffiotta, 'Sulla legittimità dei provvedimenti del Governo a contrasto dell'emergenza virale da coronavirus' in Busatta and Tomasi (eds), *Un diritto per la pandemia*, special issue 2020 of *BioLaw Journal* http://dx.doi.org/10.15168/2284-4503-20201S, 99.

Under the Italian Constitution, laws or equivalent acts are needed as the basis for the limitation of most constitutional rights, as well as for imposing personal or financial obligations (Art 23). Limitation to certain rights – including personal liberty – must be entirely disciplined by law ("riserva di legge assoluta"), applied through judicial rulings, and not by administrative regulations or orders. It has been argued that this is not true for the right to travel, as Article 16 Const only requires law to set out a basic regulatory framework, leaving room for administrative regulation and discretion ("riserva di legge relativa").[49] At any rate, some constitutional case law states that a certain degree of administrative discretion in limiting this right is not incompatible with Article 16 Const, and may be also necessary to consider the ever-changing situations and to calibrate each specific limitation,[50] obviously without arbitrary discrimination among individuals and subject to judicial review.

From this perspective, the legal instruments employed during the emergency attracted criticism: e.g. Gaetano Silvestri (professor and former President of the Constitutional Court) complained that the clauses in decrees-law (particularly dl no 6/2020) were exceedingly vague and that – like in a domino effect – decrees-law were taking the place of ordinary laws, while at the same time administrative acts were being adopted with a wide discretion normally befitting decrees-law only.[51]

And yet the criminal indictment of COVID-19 patients who violate quarantine is clearly and directly established by the relevant decrees-law, so that even the higher requirements of Article 13 Const are met. As for the right to travel, assembly, etc., the case law mentioned above seems fitting: limitations find (now) a sufficiently precise legal basis in dl no 19/2020; in order to maintain them as adherent as possible to the situation (i.e. to the many and changing different situations contemplated), the definition of their exact extent (in scope and time) is left to administrative acts, adopted by the competent authorities, following scientific and medical advice and subject to constant monitoring and revision, as well as judicial review. Indeed, the rapid evolution of the situation, as well as its widespread effects, were such that, at one point, even hasty legislative tools such as decrees-law started to pile up, amending one another before their conversion, and leading Parliament to examine them in batches (see above). This is a tangible representation of the reasons that recommend leaving some leeway for administrative management of pandemic regulation.

---

49 Massimo Luciani, 'Il sistema delle fonti del diritto alla prova dell'emergenza', in Liber amicorum *per Pasquale Costanzo* (Consulta Online 2020) 13–14 www.giurcost.org/LIBERAMICORUM/INDICEliber.html.

50 E.g. Corte cost 28 May 1987 no 201.

51 Gaetano Silvestri, Covid-19 e Costituzione (19 April 2020) www.unicost.eu/covid-19-e-costituzione/.

6. DEMOCRATIC GOVERNMENT

6.1. STATE OF EXCEPTION?

The combination of the legal elements listed above – above all, the surge of decrees-law and administrative measures and the unprecedented limitations to constitutional rights – led many commentators to recognise critically a state of exception beyond law,[52] a kind of new constituent moment in conflict with the Constitution in force,[53] an "a-constitutional" action albeit necessary,[54] a "legitimising effectivity" prevailing on the legality – or lack thereof – of the enacted measures.[55] Many have recalled a celebrated essay by Santi Romano[56] – occasioned by another historical calamity – on necessity as an autonomous source of law.

However, while it is possible to question whether the measures comprising the lockdown regime found enough legal grounds in the Constitution and in primary legislation, democratic constitutionalism is hardly compatible with the idea that factual necessity may be a proper source of law.[57]

In particular, the Italian Constitution has no provision on any kind of state of emergency, besides the "state of war" (Art 78) that has never been declared and is irrelevant here. On the other hand, the principles reviewed above – including Article 77, political discretion in balancing rights, and the possibility to delegate some evaluations to the administration – give the constitutional framework all the elasticity that may be needed. Comparisons might be made with the "necessary powers" which the Parliament may vest into the Government under Article 78 (atypical in content and undetermined in duration): but only to point out the inevitable and mandatory differences.

---

52 Gaetano Azzariti, 'Editoriale. Il diritto costituzionale d'eccezione' in *Costituzionalismo.it* no 1/2020 www.costituzionalismo.it/wp-content/uploads/0.-Fasc.1-2020.-Azzariti.pdf.

53 Giovanna De Minico, 'Costituzionalizziamo l'emergenza?' in Giovanna De Minico and Massimo Villone (eds), *Stato di diritto emergenza tecnologia* (Consulta Online 2020) www.giurcost.org/studi/index.html, 30.

54 Antonio Ruggeri, 'Stato di diritto, emergenza, tecnologia' in Giovanna De Minico and Massimo Villone (eds), *Stato di diritto emergenza tecnologia* (Consulta Online 2020) www.giurcost.org/studi/index.html, 196, 198.

55 Enrico Grosso, 'Legalità ed effettività negli spazi e nei tempi del diritto costituzionale dell'emergenza. È proprio vero che "nulla potrà più essere come prima"?' in *Federalismi.it*, no 16/2020 www.federalismi.it/nv14/editoriale.cfm?eid=559.

56 Santi Romano, 'Sui decreti-legge e lo stato di assedio in occasione del terremoto di Messina e di Reggio-Calabria' (1909) in *Rivista di diritto pubblico*, pt. 1, 251. http://bpr.camera.it/bpr/allegati/show/13893_2272_t.

57 Alberto Lucarelli, 'Costituzione, fonti del diritto ed emergenza sanitaria' (2020) in *Rivista AIC* no 2/2020, 558. www.rivistaaic.it/images/rivista/pdf/2_2020_Lucarelli.pdf.

6.2. THE PRESIDENT OF THE REPUBLIC

Institutions such as the President of the Republic and the Constitutional Court (as well as the judiciary) remained operative, although with some difficulties and organisational adaptations.

At a time when the executive naturally takes centre stage, the role of the President of the Republic is especially relevant. In the Italian legal system, his constitutional attributions "do not imply the power to take decisions in relation to specific issues, but give him the means to induce other constitutional powers to fulfil their functions correctly"; to this aim, the President employs his many formal constitutional competences, and also makes

> a discrete use of what has been defined as the 'power of persuasion'; this power is essentially comprised of informal activities either before or after the adoption of specific measures by other constitutional bodies both to assess on a preventive basis whether they are appropriate on an institutional level and also to sound out at a later stage their impact on the system of relations between branches of state.[58]

At the peak of the emergency, the President of the Republic basically supported the Government in its request for a general effort in containing the outbreak and did not express any criticism towards the legal instruments employed. This has been considered an instance of conscious self-restraint and retreat before unprecedented (and questionable) executive action.[59] Moreover, while the President had the crucial role to oversee the content of decrees-law (both when they were brought to him to be issued, and informally during their drafting), he had no formal oversight on dPCms. And yet:

- the power of discrete persuasion should not be underestimated. For example, at a moment of high tensions between the national Government and some regional executives controlled by the national opposition, the President of the Republic solicited better cooperation between both political sides, whose leadership met to discuss their divergences;[60]
- formal acts of oversight resumed rapidly. For example, on 11 September 2020 the President promulgated a law converting a decree-law (on administrative

---

58 Corte cost 15 gennaio 2013 no 1.

59 Maria Cristina Grisolia, 'Rapporti tra i poteri ed emergenza' in De Minico and Villone (eds), *Stato di diritto emergenza tecnologia* (Consulta Online 2020) www.giurcost.org/studi/index.html, 51.

60 Monica Guerzoni, 'Coronavirus, la telefonata di Mattarella a Salvini dietro l'invito di Conte alle opposizioni' (*Corriere della sera*, 23 March 2020) www.corriere.it/politica/20_marzo_23/coronavirus-telefonata-mattarella-salvini-dietro-l-invito-conte-opposizioni-e156e66e-6d19-11ea-ba71-0c6303b9bf2d.shtml.

simplification) while at the same time publicly admonishing Parliament and Government that the (already voluminous) decree had been infused with important provisions (on road traffic) which were incoherent with its original aims, and that such an improper interweaving should have been avoided.[61]

Overall, the President has been an indispensable point of reference for the public opinion and all political actors, including oppositions, which could voice their concerns to him and count on his influence and non-partisan role as a guarantor of the Constitution.

6.3. THE FUNCTIONING OF PARLIAMENT

The pandemic put the functioning of the Chamber of deputies and the Senate of the Republic to a severe test.

Although the performance of parliamentary functions legally justified movement and travel also during the lockdown regime, health and safety concerns for the members remained and, especially at the outset, it was uncertain whether the two chambers would be able to meet with the necessary quorum. Besides obvious organisational measures (e.g. social distancing), some special accommodations had to be taken:

- activities were reduced and focused on the emergency;
- they were concentrated as much as possible in parliamentary committees;
- non-deliberative proceedings and activities were digitalised;
- plenary parliamentary votes were arranged in special fashions (e.g. staggered roll call);
- pairing arrangements were made, whereby majority and oppositions agreed that some of their members would be absent, reducing the total number without altering the overall proportions;
- absence due to COVID-19, or the ensuing difficulties in travel, were considered justified (members are considered as in leave for mission).

Nevertheless, these accommodations were limited and somewhat frail: e.g., at one point, one of the opposition parties defied the gentlemen's arrangement on pairing, forcing another party to summon more members.

61 Sergio Mattarella, lettera ai Presidenti del Senato della Repubblica, della Camera dei deputati e del Consiglio dei Ministri (11 September 2020) www.quirinale.it/elementi/50185.

Therefore, the question arose, if, how, and following which procedure ordinary rules and practices could be adapted in a more incisive fashion. No fully satisfactory solution was found. For example:[62]

- under the parliamentary regulations in force, the conversion of decrees-law may not be delegated to committees. The proposal to change this rule, possibly establishing a special or bicameral committee, met with no success;
- the question of distance participation and voting via the internet was raised. It is a novel issue for Italy, although distance participation has been allowed in some regional assemblies (consigli regionali: e.g. Friuli-Venezia Giulia, Toscana, Campania) and in municipalities.[63] The debate has been whether the literal references in the Constitution to the Parliament "meeting" (or being "convened", or to the "presence" of members) – and the general notion of political representation itself – require physical presence. At any rate, also this idea was rapidly discarded.

Such questions leave a broad margin to interpretation, which belongs primarily to the constitutionally entrenched autonomy of each chamber. Therefore, with a general parliamentary consensus, an evolutionary approach would be likely to settle down and resist hypothetical legal challenges, especially if it were strictly limited to the emergency.

In the end, Parliament was able to function, but only within certain limits.[64] On the one hand, from 23 February to 17 July 2020, 15 decrees-law were examined and converted into law. Eight hundred and sixty amendments were approved – largely in parliamentary committees – to the initial text enacted by the Government, with a significant portion of them being proposed (14.7%) or shared (14.2%) by the opposition. In converting dl no 19/2020, Parliament also expanded its own oversight on emergency administrative measures: the Government must anticipate them to the chambers, and consider their recommendations; if this is not possible due to urgency, the Government must still report every 15 days. Parliamentary assent was also necessary to authorise the borrowing of funds for emergency measures.

On the other hand, the role of Parliament seemed essentially subordinate to the Government. Besides what has already been reported above on decrees-law and dPCms, it is noteworthy that:

- the number of amendments does not necessarily disprove that the Parliament mostly ratified policy choices made by the executive;

---

62 Salvatore Curreri, 'Il Parlamento nell'emergenza: resiliente o latitante?' (2020) forthcoming in *Quaderni costituzionali* no 4/2020, §§3–4.

63 Dl 17 March 2020 no 18, Article 73.

64 Salvatore Curreri, 'Il Parlamento nell'emergenza: resiliente o latitante?' (2020) forthcoming in *Quaderni costituzionali* no 4/2020, §5.

- only on 25 and 26 March 2020 the President of the Council of Ministers appeared before the Parliament to report on the enacted measures;
- the Minister of Economy and Finance was enabled to shift budget funds directly among budget programs (belonging to the same mission) according to cash flows;
- obviously also the central role in negotiations with the European Union on the collective response to COVID-19 belongs to the Government.

Several commentators harshly concluded that, in substance, Parliament confined itself in a marginal position, very different from the one that it should have in political choices on legislation and budget.[65] However, constitutional scholarship largely opined that the pandemic was not the cause, but just an occasion for a further display of the ongoing decline of Parliament and political representation in Italy:[66] a situation too complex in its origins and development to be investigated here.

6.4. ACCOUNTABILITY OF PANDEMIC MANAGEMENT

One crucial issue has been – and still is, more so after the acme of the outbreak – the availability of scientific data underlying policy decisions,[67] to ensure the possibility of an effective scientific, political and legal debate on such decisions, and therefore increase their own legitimation, as well as public confidence in government action. Risk management is complex, as noted above. The strongest precautions against a danger, still uncertain in its precise extent, may cause immediate substitution risks on different fronts; regarding judicial review specifically, these choices are difficult to question directly; it is easier, and more reliable, to scrutinise the processes enacted to take them.[68]

---

65 Ibid §6. Maria Cristina Grisolia, 'Rapporti tra i poteri ed emergenza' in De Minico and Villone (eds), *Stato di diritto emergenza tecnologia* (Consulta Online 2020) www.giurcost.org/studi/index.html, 57–58.

66 Sando Staiano, 'Né modello, né sistema. La produzione del diritto al cospetto della pandemia' in Sandro Staiano (ed), *Nel ventesimo anno del terzo millennio* (Editoriale scientifica 2020) www.editorialescientifica.com/shop/catalogo/fuori-collana/edizioni-fuori-collana/nel-ventesimo-anno-del-terzo-millennio-detail.html, 11, 41; Gian Luca Conti, 'La crisi dello "Stato moderno" e l'emergenza pandemica: appunti sul ruolo delle Camere nella lotta contro il coronavirus' in *Le fonti normative nella gestione dell'emergenza Covid-19*, special issue 2020 of *Osservatorio sulle fonti* www.osservatoriosullefonti.it/402-editoriale/3512-fascicolo-speciale-2020, 519; Stefano Civitarese Matteucci, 'The Italian Response to Coronavirus and Constitutional Disagreement' (*UK Constitutional Law Association*, 30 April 2020) https://ukconstitutionallaw.org/2020/04/30/stefano-civitarese-matteucci-the-italian-response-to-coronavirus-and-constitutional-disagreement/.

67 Enrico Grosso, 'Legalità ed effettività negli spazi e nei tempi del diritto costituzionale dell'emergenza. È proprio vero che "nulla potrà più essere come prima"?' in *Federalismi.it*, no. 16/2020, www.federalismi.it/nv14/editoriale.cfm?eid=559, xiv.

68 Giovanni Pitruzzella, 'La società globale del rischio e i limiti alle libertà costituzionali. Brevi riflessioni a partire dal divieto di sport e attività motorie all'aperto' (*Giustizia insieme*;

Unfortunately, this issue has not been managed without some clumsiness, to the point that some legal commentators opined that crucial data were being subject to official secret.[69] In general, official information was not scarce: data on the outbreak were published regularly by government offices and agencies. However, for a relatively long time crucial documents were withheld from the public: most notably, the minutes of the CTS, which was the main consultative body on whose advice preventive measures were taken (see above). When some private actors tried to access the minutes, under the national equivalent of the "Freedom of information act",[70] their request was denied by the Department for Civil Protection (which reports to the President of the Council of Ministers); and when the competent administrative court ordered access to be granted,[71] the ruling was immediately challenged before the Council of State,[72] which suspended it. However, after a public outcry, the minutes were finally made available[73] and the administrative trial was abandoned. Currently, minutes are being regularly published within 45 days from each CTS meeting.

6.5. DELAYED ELECTIONS

Under Article 60 of the Italian Constitution, the Chamber of Deputies and the Senate are elected for a term of five years, which may not be extended save by law and only in the case of war. Therefore, not even a pandemic could delay the national elections, which are expected in 2023 (unless the Parliament is dissolved before due to political crisis).

On the other hand, other votes were delayed: parliamentary by-elections;[74] some municipal and regional elections;[75] the referendum to approve the constitutional law reducing the number of parliamentary seats.[76] A heated debate took place on how and when the votes – as well as the political campaigning necessarily preceding them – should take place, if this could happen during

24 March 2020) www.giustiziainsieme.it/it/diritto-dell-emergenza-covid-19/941-la-societa-globale-del-rischio-e-i-limiti-alle-liberta-costituzionali-brevi-riflessioni-a-partire-dal-divieto-di-sport-e-attivita-motorie-all-aperto.

69 Gian Luca Conti, 'La crisi dello "Stato moderno" e l'emergenza pandemica: appunti sul ruolo delle Camere nella lotta contro il coronavirus' in *Le fonti normative nella gestione dell'emergenza Covid-19*, special issue 2020 of *Osservatorio sulle fonti* www.osservatoriosullefonti.it/402-editoriale/3512-fascicolo-speciale-2020, 534.

70 Dlgs 25 May 2016 no 97.

71 Tribunale amministrativo regionale per il Lazio, Roma, judgment 22 July 2020 no 8615.

72 Consiglio di Stato, presidential decree 31 July 2020 no 4574.

73 See www.protezionecivile.gov.it/attivita-rischi/rischio-sanitario/emergenze/coronavirus/verbali-comitato-tecnico-scientifico-coronavirus.

74 Dl 20 April 2020 no 26, Article 1.

75 Ibid.

76 Decree of the President of the Republic 5 March 2020.

the summer, and whether different votes could be hold in the same day. In the end, the ballots were all cast on 20 and 21 September 2020, without particular problems. Voting by mail has never been seriously considered.

7. CONCLUSIONS

Since its very beginning, the COVID-19 pandemic has forced profound changes in social life, work and more generally social organisation: the final outcomes are far from settled, but it is now that the 20th century ends and the 21st begins.[77]

Was the Italian Constitution capable to accommodate the necessary reactions, without forsaking its principles? The analysis above suggests a generally positive answer.[78] Until now, emergency measures remained within the margins of intrinsic flexibility of the Constitution, considering the exceptional and transient situation which justifies – and limits – their scope. Some critical points have been noted: above all, the marginalisation of Parliament and the weaknesses in official communications between science, government and public opinion. But these criticalities predate the pandemic, which just catalysed and cast more light on them.

In line with some trends spotted from the comparative viewpoint,[79] pandemic governance in Italy was more "Madisonian" than "neo-Schmittian". The national executive took centre stage, but, at least until now:

- even the decisions adopted in dPCms were not purely monocratic, as they were shared to some extent with several Ministers, the CTS and Presidents of regions;

---

77 Alessandro Mangia, 'L'emergenza e le tre Grandi Cesure' in Giulio Sapelli, *2020. Pandemia e Resurrezione* (Guerini e associati 2020) 91.

78 For a generally positive assessment see Stefano Civitarese Matteucci, 'The Italian Response to Coronavirus and Constitutional Disagreement' (*UK Constitutional Law Association*, 30 April 2020) https://ukconstitutionallaw.org/2020/04/30/stefano-civitarese-matteucci-the-italian-response-to-coronavirus-and-constitutional-disagreement/; Massimo Luciani, 'Il sistema delle fonti del diritto alla prova dell'emergenza', in Liber amicorum *per Pasquale Costanzo* (Consulta Online 2020) 12–13 www.giurcost.org/LIBERAMICORUM/INDICEliber.html and Massimo Luciani (professor, former President of the Associazione italiana dei costituzionalisti) www.giustiziainsieme.it/it/diritto-dell-emergenza-covid-19/961-la-pandemia-aggredisce-anche-il-diritto; Ugo De Siervo, 'Emergenza Covid e sistema delle fonti: prime impressioni' in *Le fonti normative nella gestione dell'emergenza Covid-19*, special issue 2020 of *Osservatorio sulle fonti* www.osservatoriosullefonti.it/402-editoriale/3512-fascicolo-speciale-2020, 299, 307: Cesare Pinelli, 'Il precario assetto delle fonti impiegate nell'emergenza sanitaria e gli squilibrati rapporti fra Stato e Regioni' (2020) in *ASTRID Rassegna* no 5/2020, 1, 6; Sando Staiano, 'Né modello, né sistema. La produzione del diritto al cospetto della pandemia' in Sandro Staiano (ed), *Nel ventesimo anno del terzo millennio* (Editoriale scientifica 2020) www.editorialescientifica.com/shop/catalogo/fuori-collana/edizioni-fuori-collana/nel-ventesimo-anno-del-terzo-millennio-detail.html, 11, 41.

79 Ginsburg and Versteeg, 'The Bound Executive: Emergency Powers During the Pandemic' (2020) Virginia Public Law and Legal Theory Research Paper No 2020-52, U of Chicago, Public Law Working Paper No 747 https://ssrn.com/abstract=3608974.

- judicial checks remained in place: from the preventive review of legality by the Corte dei conti on executive acts, to judicial review of administrative and legislative decisions (e.g. it is precisely the concern for legality that led the Government to correct dl no 6/2020 with dl no 19/2020);
- no manifest breach of constitutional principles has been found on major issues;
- the President of the Republic remained vigilant;
- to some extent, oversight by the Parliament and public opinion also remained active, or at least possible, as the number of parliamentary amendments to decrees-law and the publication of the CTS minutes demonstrate.

A good summary has been offered on 28 April 2020 by the President of the Constitutional Court then in charge, Marta Cartabia, in her report on constitutional justice in the previous year. Due to the lockdown, the report was not presented in the usual public hearing and press conference. The President – who had recovered herself from COVID-19 only one week before – published it, and her personal remarks, in the Court's official website.

Looking to 2020, she concluded as follows:[80]

> [t]he new year opened with a truly unprecedented and unforeseeable happenstance, marked by a state of emergency and the urgent need to prioritize the protection of people's lives, health, and physical integrity, even at the cost of a necessary and temporary sacrifice of other rights. Our Constitution does not envisage a special form of law for states of emergency, and this was a conscious choice. The text of the Constitution does not contain clauses suspending fundamental rights, which can be triggered by exceptional circumstances, nor provisions that allow for changes to the power structures in times of crisis … Nevertheless, the Constitution is not insensitive to changing circumstances, or to the potential outbreak of emergency situations, crises, or extraordinary cases of necessity and urgency, as Article 77 of the Constitution puts it, on the topic of decree-laws. The Italian Republic has passed through various crises and emergencies – from the years of armed conflict to the more recent economic and financial crisis – all of which have been dealt with without ever suspending the constitutional system, but rather drawing from within it the tools it has needed to adjust constitutional principles to meet specific needs: necessity, proportionality, balancing, justiciability and transience are the criteria with which, according to constitutional case law, the 'systemic and not piecemeal' protection of the principles and fundamental rights enshrined in the Constitution must be implemented in every day and age.

---

80 Marta Cartabia, 'Summary of the report on the work of the Constitutional court in 2019', official English translation (28 April 2020) www.cortecostituzionale.it/documenti/relazione_cartabia/2_sintesi.pdf.

That the first major Western democracy to face the pandemic found adequate tools in its post-Second World War, 72-year-old Constitution, should be refreshing news for all those who still believe in contemporary constitutionalism.

Could the Constitution be amended to allow for a better pandemic management? Proposals have been made both in scholarship[81] and Parliament.[82] However, since the problems highlighted above have deep roots, action should be taken here, rather than with constitutional revisions aimed precisely at pandemics or comparable emergencies. If anything, it is the legislative model that could be adjusted, improved and consolidated, as in 2020 it was hastily cobbled together under the pressure of a fast-moving outbreak.

And what about the future? Will the Constitution hold, while the broader social, economic and political consequences of the pandemic unfold? No analytical forecast is possible here, just a hope: that it may not only hold, but thrive, particularly in its fundamental principles such as democracy, personalism, solidarity and openness to cooperation among nations to ensure peace and justice. These principles deserve to be supported and widely shared in a world that has never felt such a global, tangible and pressing need for general collaboration among people and social justice.

---

81 E.g. Antonio Ruggeri 'Stato di diritto, emergenza, tecnologia' in Giovanna De Minico and Massimo Villone (eds), *Stato di diritto emergenza tecnologia* (Consulta Online 2020) www.giurcost.org/studi/index.html, 202.

82 See Camera dei deputati, AC 2452, Proposta di legge costituzionale d'iniziativa dei deputati Ceccanti et al. 'Introduzione degli articoli 55-bis e 55-ter della Costituzione, concernenti la dichiarazione dello stato di emergenza e l'istituzione di una Commissione parlamentare speciale per l'esercizio delle funzioni delle Camere' (30 March 2020) www.camera.it/leg18/126?idDocumento=2452.
Under this proposal, the chambers, with a 2/3 majority, could declare a 2-month, renewable state of emergency; parliamentary functions (could be exercised at distance and) would be concentrated in an ad hoc committee (composed by 1/10 of the members of each chamber); the committee would be empowered to pass urgent laws, derogate to normal regional competences (with a 3/5 majority) and authorize borrowing, but not to pass constitutional and electoral laws (and any law requiring a special majority); all the acts approved by the committee would be re-examined, and possibly abrogated, by the Parliament in full within one year from the end of the emergency.

THE ITALIAN CONSTITUTIONAL COURT AND THE PANDEMIC

A National and Comparative Perspective

Luca GIACOMELLI and Elisabetta LAMARQUE*

Never before have the world's democracies simultaneously experienced such a major contraction of civil liberties as during the "new" coronavirus pandemic, producing massive debates about the role of government power during times of crisis. This contribution focuses on the response provided by constitutional courts to face the emergency. The attitude of the Italian court can be effectively summarised by the following keywords: continuity, loyal cooperation, autonomy, step-by-step approach, working methods. From a comparative perspective, the reaction of many other national and supranational courts was not so different and inspired by the same criteria.

* Luca Giacomelli, University of Florence; Elisabetta Lamarque, University of Milano-Bicocca.
The data reported in this contribution are updated to August 2020.

1. INTRODUCTION

Italy, well-known to be the first European country overwhelmed by the pandemic, found itself in the uncomfortable position of having to experiment with the tools and strategies – health-related, economic and legal – to tackle it.

In this situation, the very functioning of the constitutional bodies was severely tested. However, faced with the clear inevitable prevalence of government action in managing the emergency,[1] it was necessary to ensure above all that the supervisory bodies, both political (the President of the Republic) and jurisdictional (the Constitutional Court, with a typically counter-majoritarian vocation, and the whole judiciary), would not fail in their essential functions.

As an initial assessment of these difficult months – March/June 2020 –, it can be said that the Italian supervisory system, on the whole, acquitted itself very well.

In particular, the ways the Italian Constitutional Court (ItCC) handled the situation were effective and perfectly aligned with those adopted by other European constitutional courts and the two European courts of Luxembourg and Strasbourg. Although the President of the ItCC, Marta Cartabia, contracted the coronavirus, this did not affect her role, given that, even with the illness, she continued to fulfil all her responsibilities overseeing the body, including that of presiding over the college (remotely, of course) during strictly judicial activity.

This contribution will illustrate the functioning of Italian constitutional justice, first in normal times, then during the coronavirus emergency (sections 2–3), thereby placing the Italian situation in the comparative context (sections 4–6).

2. THE ItCC IN ORDINARY TIMES

It should first be said that with absolute fidelity to the Kelsenian court model, the ItCC is not part of the judiciary in the strict sense, though its functions are certainly jurisdictional.[2] The ItCC is rather a constitutional body on its own, which is provided by constitutional and legislative rules with significant guarantees of independence from other State powers, including judicial power.

---

1 See for example Edoardo C. Raffiotta, 'Sulla legittimità dei provvedimenti del governo a contrasto dell'emergenza virale da coronavirus' (2020) 2 BLJ https://www.biodiritto.org/content/download/3793/45322/version/1/file/21+Raffiotta.pdf accessed 31 July 2020; Francesco Torre, 'La costituzione sotto stress ai tempi del coronavirus' (2020) 2 BLJ https://www.biodiritto.org/content/download/3834/45465/version/1/file/51+Torre.pdf accessed 31 July 2020; Julinda Beqiraj, 'Italy's Coronavirus Legislative Response: Adjusting Along the Way' (*VerfBlog*, 8 April 2020), https://verfassungsblog.de/italys-coronavirus-legislative-response-adjusting-along-the-way/ accessed 31 July 2020.

2 On this point, Mauro Cappelletti, *Il controllo giudiziario di costituzionalità delle leggi nel diritto comparato* (Giuffrè 1968). More recently see also Maartje De Visser, *Constitutional review in Europe: A comparative analysis* (Bloomsbury 2013).

It is worth recalling that, as well as enjoying administrative and accounting autonomy, exempt from the controls generally in place for public expenditure, the ItCC establishes its organic plan and the statute of the people who work for it, and even has jurisdiction over any employment disputes concerning its employees.

Its regulatory autonomy is also particularly significant. With resolution by an absolute majority of its judges, in fact, the ItCC can regulate not only its internal organisation, but also the exercise of its jurisdictional functions (also with effects on third parties).[3]

It may also be useful to recall that around 45 law clerks[4] and 300 employees[5] work alongside the 15 judges at the seat of the ItCC in Rome. The judges meet in alternate weeks: during the work week in Rome, they are usually engaged in a public hearing and in some council chambers, while law clerks work alone or in small teams, and also attend a plenary meeting to discuss pending issues. In the so-called week "off", however, the judges each work alone or with their law clerks in their preferred location, dedicating themselves to drafting the sentences and orders for which they were rapporteurs and studying the cases to be dealt with the following work week. Currently, ItCC decides around 300 cases each year.

Having presented this overview, it is useful for our purposes to focus attention on the fact that the Italian system of constitutional justice provides for only two ways to challenge a law before the ItCC[6] and that, beside the judicial review power, the ItCC has very few other competences.[7] In this respect, the situation of Italy is unique within the European panorama.[8] Recently, a colleague of ours

---

3 At this regard, see the Supplementary Rules for proceedings before the Constitutional Court, 2008/261, available at https://www.cortecostituzionale.it/documenti/download/pdf/Norme_Integrative_per_i_giudizi2020.pdf accessed 9 June 2020.

4 Article 135, par. 1, It. Const.

5 All information can be found in the guide book *The Italian Constitutional Court*, written and updated several times by the constitutional judges themselves and available at https://www.cortecostituzionale.it/documenti/download/pdf/The_Italian_Constitutional_Court.pdf accessed 9 June 2020.

6 The "incidental method of judicial review" ("controllo di costituzionalità in via incidentale"), raised by the ordinary judge on his own motion or upon request of one of the parties during a judicial proceeding; and the "direct method of judicial review" ("controllo di costituzionalità in via principale"), when the national government and the regional government challenge, respectively, a regional or a national statute within 60 days of its publication. For further details, see Antonio Ruggeri, Antonio Spadaro, *Lineamenti di giustizia costituzionale* (Giappichelli 2004); Saulle Panizza, Roberto Romboli, *Giustizia costituzionale* (Giappichelli 2003).

7 For a general overview see Alessandro Pizzorusso, Vincenzo Vigoriti, Giuseppe L. Certoma, 'The Constitutional Review of Legislation in Italy' (1983) Tem. L.Q. 56, 503, and more recently Vittoria Barsotti, Paolo G. Carozza, Marta Cartabia, Andrea Simoncini, *Italian Constitutional Justice in Global Context* (OUP 2015).

8 Tania Groppi, 'The Constitutional Court of Italy: Towards a Multilevel System of Constitutional Review?' (2008) JCL 100 and Vittoria Barsotti, Paolo G. Carozza, Marta Cartabia, Andrea Simoncini, *Italian Constitutional Justice in Global Context* (OUP 2015) 49.

made-up the word "parchitudine" – we can translate it as "soberness", "frugality", or something like that – to describe the main feature of our constitutional review system.[9]

Nevertheless – or perhaps precisely for this reason? – the ItCC enjoys considerable authority both within our legal system, especially because it has cultivated an excellent collaborative partnership with the national judiciary over the years, and at European and international level, and not only thanks to its seniority (it held its first hearing back in 1956, making it one of the oldest constitutional courts in Europe after Austria's), but also for the content of some of its historic decisions.[10]

The manner itself in which the ItCC handled this challenging crisis confirms, on the internal front, its alignment with the Italian judiciary and, on the external front, its international standing.

3. THE ItCC IN THE COVID-19 EMERGENCY

The way the ItCC faced the emergency can be described with some key words: (1) continuity; (2) loyal cooperation; (3) autonomy; (4) step-by-step approach; (5) working methods.

3.1. CONTINUITY

The function of constitutional justice in Italy was not interrupted. In particular, during the emergency the judges never abandoned the collegiate work week, with all or some of them using a remote connection; the law clerks continued their individual research and discussion meetings (remotely) on a regular basis; the secretariats and administrative offices continued to operate (largely in online working mode); and the registry never closed, albeit observing a reduced timetable.[11]

There was only a slight slowdown in work, because while the council chambers were all held regularly, two public hearings in March were cancelled, and then postponed, and some cases set for a public hearing in April were postponed. Almost all the cases postponed, however, have been recovered thanks to summer work sessions (in July and September 2020) already scheduled in addition to the normal work calendar.

---

9 Tania Groppi, 'La Corte e 'la gente': uno sguardo 'dal basso' all'accesso incidentale alla giustizia costituzionale' (2019) 2 AIC 408.

10 On this point, Marta Cartabia, 'Of Bridges and Walls: The Italian Style of Constitutional Adjudication' (2016) 8 IJPL 37.

11 Except for the two days required for the sanitation of the offices.

In this regard, it is worth remembering that the Italian constitutional process requires the constitutional judges to decide all matters in the council chamber and in secrecy. The decision in the council chamber, however, is preceded in about half of cases by a public hearing, in which the parties' lawyers discuss the matter orally.[12] This only happens, of course, when there are private parties in that specific constitutional trial, and therefore always in constitutional proceedings that see the State and regions opposed. In contrast, in incidental constitutional proceedings, the public hearing is set only when the parties of the civil, criminal or administrative proceedings giving rise to the question of constitutionality have also chosen to appear before the ItCC.[13]

Therefore, given that no council chamber was postponed even in the most difficult period of the emergency (March and April 2020), all incidental cases where none of the private parties to the trial had yet appeared before the ItCC continued to be ruled upon regularly without any slowdown.

In short, it can be said that the ItCC is the only court in Italy without any backlog caused by the coronavirus emergency.

3.2. LOYAL COOPERATION

In the presentation of the work of the ItCC in 2019, at the end April 2020, its President Marta Cartabia pointed out that "in times like these, if there is one constitutional principle that deserves particular emphasis and attention, it is precisely that of 'loyal cooperation', the institutional side of solidarity. The Constitutional Court, for its part, will not tire of returning to this principle in its case law, so that the work and the energy of the entire national community will coherently converge and move toward a single, shared goal".[14] Likewise, the presidential decrees of 24 March and 20 April, containing measures to ensure the continuation of the constitutional proceedings during the COVID-19 emergency, had highlighted, in their preamble, "the need [of the ItCC] to operate in a spirit

---

12 In 2019, the ItCC held 27 public hearings, and the 53.61% of total decisions were issued after the public hearing.

13 And if the matter already appears, upon first summary examination, manifestly unfounded or inadmissible (rule obtained by interpretation from Article 26 of the law on the functioning of the ItCC No. 87 of 1953).

14 Summary of the Report on the Work of the Constitutional Court in 2019, 28 April 2020, at https://www.cortecostituzionale.it/documenti/relazione_cartabia/2_sintesi_eng.pdf accessed 9 June 2020. Similarly, see *COVID-19 emergency. Interview with the President of the Italian Constitutional Court, Marta Cartabia* (original interview by Roberto Conti and published on https://www.giustiziainsieme.it/it/dirittodell-emergenza-covid-19/950-la-corte-costituzionale-emergenza-covid; English version available at https://www.cortecostituzionale.it/documenti/download/pdf/article_cartabia-translated_20200407140303.pdf accessed 9 June 2020).

of loyal collaboration with the other institutions of the Republic, in the common efforts to address the current situation".

The ItCC cooperated with other institutional entities in various ways. First of all, the ItCC immediately adopted all measures to contain the contagion as announced over time by the government generally for each workplace, adapting them to the specific nature of its work. In particular, it closed the seat of the Court, Palazzo della Consulta, to the public (for example postponing all student visits, forbidding external access to the library and limiting access to the registry as much as possible); it ensured the safety of employees who had to keep going to the offices (sanitising the building, thermal scanner at the entrance); and above all, as mentioned, it reorganised the working methods for judges, law clerks and all its employees encouraging online working as much as possible. This last point is particularly significant for an institution like the ItCC, the work of which is based on interpersonal relation – in particular the constitutional judges and their law clerks, totalling about 60 – who for the most part do not live in Rome but in different parts of Italy.

Secondly, the President of the ItCC took care of the relationship with both private lawyers and the State Attorney's Office (and the regional attorney's offices). In fact, although updates on judicial activity procedures were always published in real time on the ItCC's official website, the President asked the registry to notify each party's lawyers individually, by phone, of any change in the programme of hearings, and informally also held a direct line with the President of the National Forensic Council and the State Attorney.

Thirdly, as will be covered under section 3.3 the ItCC reorganised its jurisdictional activity by taking into account the "specificity" of the constitutional proceedings (as stated in the decrees mentioned above), and the same specific features and aims of the constitutional justice, compared to the "common" jurisdictional function. *Nevertheless*, it did not forget the valuable collaborative partnership with the judiciary, and therefore chose to organise itself in ways, illustrated in section 3.4 below, fully *compatible* with those provided by government decrees for the "common" jurisdictional function.

In addition to this loyal cooperation attitude with the other powers of the State, during the months of pandemic the ItCC wanted to cultivate in a particular way the relationship with civil society and with the social media, considering them necessary means to never lose contact with the reality of the country and its citizens. In this regard, the choice, adopted by decree of the President of 8 June 2020 (see below section 3.4), as soon as the sanitary conditions allowed it, to reopen Palazzo della Consulta to the public and the press was emblematic. In this way it was again possible to allow the public and journalists to attend "live" public hearings held remotely (or, more precisely, with some of the judges physically present and others remotely connected). With this decision, the ItCC became the first Italian court to restore the principle of public hearings. This means that journalists were able to attend the hearing on 9 June, in which the

ItCC discussed an issue of considerable general importance and of particular interest for the category of journalists, i.e. the constitutional legitimacy of a prison sentence for the crime of defamation through the press.[15]

3.3. AUTONOMY

In perfect consonance with the *modus operandi* of other constitutional courts and of the European courts of Luxembourg and Strasbourg (see section 5), the ItCC took the necessary measures to ensure the continuity of the ItCC's jurisdictional activities and also to safeguard people's health, independently, i.e. without any legal obligation (or invitation to take action from the political bodies).

In particular, there was a sequence of five presidential decrees, which are measures adopted by the President of the ItCC by virtue of her powers to organise the ItCC's work and draw up the roll of cases.[16] It may be interesting to note that the last four decrees, given they concerned the procedures for carrying out work and the parties' rights of defence (see section 3.5 below), were undertaken by the President "in conformity with the opinion expressed by the Court". This is in homage to the marked collegiality of the Italian constitutional justice body in exercising its jurisdictional function and due to the delicacy of the extraordinary measures adopted, which reasonably are best shared by the 15 judges, rather than unilaterally being imposed by the President alone. It also complies with the rule of loyal collaboration that the constitutional justice body thus wished to express and practise throughout the emergency, not only with respect to the other State powers, but also within itself.

It is interesting to note that the first three decrees, on the one hand, expressly emphasise the constitutional body's autonomy in choosing the most appropriate measures to tackle the emergency, but on the other, still in that spirit of sharing and collaboration, recall the government decrees' choices regarding administrative justice,[17] stating the desire to be inspired by these in some way, though not considering themselves bound in any way. The connection of the constitutional

---

15 The Press Office has made it known that ItCC decided: that the solution of the issues requires a complex balancing operation between the freedom of expression and the protection of the reputation of the person; that the task of finding a balance between these rights, now urgent in the light of the indications of the ECtHR case law, lies primarily with the legislator; and that, in respect of loyal institutional cooperation, the discussion of the issues will be postponed to the public hearing of 22 June 2021 to allow time for Parliament to adopt a new legislation.

16 Articles 15, 18, 26, 34, 37 and 41 of the Law on the Functioning of the ItCC n. 87 of 1953; Articles 8, 9, 23, 24, and 25 of the Supplementary Rules for proceedings before the Constitutional Court (the rules on the functioning of the ItCC which are deliberated by the ItCC itself).

17 First with Article 3 of Law Decree no. 11 of 2020 and then with Article 84 of Law Decree no. 18 of 2020, both dedicated to urgent measures in the field of administrative justice.

process to the administrative one (and not to civil or criminal trials) is in fact textually suggested by the same law of 1953 on the ItCC's functioning, which establishes that "proceedings before the Constitutional Court … also observe, insofar as applicable, the rules of the regulation for the procedure before the Council of State in its jurisdiction function".[18]

3.4. STEP-BY-STEP APPROACH

The five presidential decrees tackle the situation gradually, taking into account developments in both the epidemiological situation and the rules on administrative justice. The sequence of decrees, however, seems to respond also and perhaps above all to the gradual emergence of specific requirements of the constitutional process. Such requirements are related to the need, mentioned above in section 3.1, to ensure the continuity of constitutional justice by adopting only those exceptional measures that are strictly necessary for that purpose. As we will say immediately below, in fact, with the last of her five decrees, of 23 June 2020, the President of the ItCC established to come back to the usual methods of work. But let us proceed in order.

The decree of 12 March concerns only the methods of filing deeds and briefs, temporarily allowing these documents to also be sent electronically.

The decree of 24 March establishes that the constitutional judges may meet in council via remote connection, and that the place from where they join the meeting remotely is to be considered part of the "chambers" for all legal purposes, and it also specifies that the remote connections may be used for all other meetings of the judges or of the internal bodies of the ItCC. This is a fundamental measure to ensure the functioning of the "machine", because the constitutional judges come from all over Italy – and three out of them, the President included, come from Lombardy, which is the Italian region most affected by the epidemic – not counting the law clerks at the ItCC, who live all around the country. In addition, the same decree provides the deferral of all the public hearings, starting from 7 April, except for the proceedings where all the parties request the ItCC to decide on the basis of the case file, without oral discussion.[19]

Unfortunately, almost none of the lawyers took advantage of this possibility, and consequently a lot of public hearings were postponed.

---

18 Article 22, Law no. 87/1953.

19 The Decree specifies that, in exceptionally serious and urgent cases, although, the President, after consulting the Court, can consider immediate discussion by means of a public hearing (in full compliance with the applicable safety and prevention requirements). See, in particular, https://www.cortecostituzionale.it/documenti/download/pdf/decreto_coronavirus_en_20200421131640.pdf accessed 9 June 2020.

So, in order to avoid a backlog, the ItCC changed its mind. The decree of 20 April revised (only) the rules concerning the public hearings (from 5 May to 30 June 2020, or, in any event, until further provision), ruling out every deferral. This third decree established that "proceedings for which a public hearing had already been scheduled would be decided in chambers directly, without an oral discussion, on the basis of the case file, allowing the parties to the proceedings to file brief notes". Nevertheless, if at least one of the parties to the proceedings requested, the relevant public hearing could be conducted remotely. In addition, the decree specified that, if public hearing was conducted remotely, the public would not have been able to attend and the publicity of hearings would be guaranteed, *inter alia*, also by providing for their audio-visual recording and publishing, at a later date, on the ItCC's institutional website.[20] Online hearings, however, do not seem to have attracted the parties and their lawyers: in fact, the requests for online hearings have not been as many as one might have expected.

Then, the already mentioned decree of 8 June 2020 allowed the public and the journalists to attend public hearings at Palazzo della Consulta[21] and, lastly, the decree of 23 June restored the ordinary way of lodging procedural documents and of celebrating public hearings, allowing the physical presence of constitutional judges and lawyers at the seat of the ItCC.[22]

3.5. WORKING METHODS

As noted, all the measures the ItCC took to deal with the coronavirus emergency concern the working methods of everyone (constitutional judges, as well law clerks and civil servants): online working, remote chambers and then remote public hearings, deferral (at first) or non deferral (subsequently) of the cases already scheduled at public hearings, and so on.

Unlike experiences in other countries (see section 4), no changes were made to the procedural deadlines for parties to proceedings and their lawyers to meet. Evidently, in exercising their autonomy, the constitutional judges decided there was no need to intervene on the terms of constitutional processes, which are all fairly broad. However, they wanted to provide greater flexibility to the most important deadline – the parties' initial deadline to file an entry of appearance which is set at 20 days from the publication of the introductory deeds of constitutional judgments in the Official Gazette of the Italian Republic

20 See, https://www.cortecostituzionale.it/documenti/download/pdf/20_04_decreto_en_20200421191939.pdf accessed 9 June 2020.

21 See, in particular, https://www.cortecostituzionale.it/documenti/comunicatistampa/decreto_presidente_20_aprile_up_telematica_20200420162017.pdf accessed 31 July 2020.

22 See, https://www.cortecostituzionale.it/documenti/comunicatistampa/CC_CS_20200623161403.pdf accessed 31 July 2020.

(first special series). Informally, the registry extended to the coronavirus emergency period the established practice of suspending publication of the introductory deeds of constitutional judgments in the summer, so the deadlines for the parties would not fall during the summer holidays.

4. COURTS' RESPONSES TO THE COVID-19 CRISIS: A COMPARATIVE OVERVIEW

Due to the particular circumstances linked to the COVID-19 pandemic, many countries have imposed emergency measures on its population such as self-isolation and restriction of movement and assembly, which are also directly affecting the functioning of their respective judicial systems.[23] The courts faced numerous challenges to remain operational due to lack of personnel, public hearings cancelled, and access to justice temporarily limited. As described previously, the ItCC did not stop during the epidemiological emergency but it adopted organisational measures to continue to operate safely "in the spirit of loyal cooperation with the other institutions of the republic, in a common effort to cope with the current situation".[24] In the vast majority of cases, the restrictive measures taken by the different countries to prevent the spread of the coronavirus were based on the two main aspects: the first was to protect the staff, including judges and prosecutors, from the disease; the second was to protect individuals (parties) from the unexpected results of these restrictions. In this context, all measures were set to prevent any result that causes deprivation of the rights of individuals in the balancing of the right to health.

---

23 For a general overview of States' responses to the epidemic, see Israel Waismel-Manor et Al., 'Covid-19 and Legislative Activity: A Cross-National Study' (2020) 20-12 Bar Ilan University Faculty of Law Research Paper https://papers.ssrn.com/sol3/papers.cfm?abstract_id=3641824 accessed 31 July 2020; Itta Bar-Siman-Tov, 'Covid-19 Meets Politics: The Novel Coronavirus as a Novel Challenge for Legislatures' (2020) 8 The Theory and Practice of Legislation https://papers.ssrn.com/sol3/papers.cfm?abstract_id=3603137 accessed 31 July 2020; Arianna Vedaschi, 'Il Covid-19, l'ultimo stress test per gli ordinamenti democratici: uno sguardo comparato' (2020) 2 DPCE http://www.dpceonline.it/index.php/dpceonline/article/view/1015/988 accessed 31 July 2020; Jan Petrov, 'The COVID-19 emergency in the age of executive aggrandizement: what role for legislative and judicial checks?' (2020) The Theory and Practice of Legislation https://www.tandfonline.com/doi/pdf/10.1080/20508840.2020.1788232?needAccess=true&; accessed 9 June 2020.

24 See the Summary of the Report on the Work of the Constitutional Court in 2019, 28th April 2020, at https://www.cortecostituzionale.it/documenti/relazione_cartabia/2_sintesi_eng.pdf accessed 9 June 2020. Similarly, see *COVID-19 emergency. Interview with the President of the Italian Constitutional Court, Marta Cartabia* (original interview by Roberto Conti and published on https://www.giustiziainsieme.it/it/dirittodell-emergenza-covid-19/950-la-corte-costituzionale-emergenza-covid; English version available at https://www.cortecostituzionale.it/documenti/download/pdf/article_cartabia-translated_20200407140303.pdf accessed 9 June 2020).

Although the measures were not uniform and consistent within the EU because each State has autonomously regulated the administration of judicial workload and the internal organisation of its judiciaries during the crisis, it is possible to identify some common trends which have somehow homogenised the management of the pandemic by the constitutional and supreme courts around the world. (1) Continuity, (2) Autonomy, (3) Flexibility and (4) Digitalization are the criteria that guided the response of most of the courts during the epidemiological crisis. The necessary measures to ensure the continuity of the jurisdictional activities and, together, to safeguard the health of people, were taken independently, without any legal obligation or invitation to take action by the political bodies. Furthermore, these were gradual and flexible measures to allow the organisation of judicial activities to be calibrated to the trend of the epidemiological curve. Information technologies and digital communication tools have been provided or reinforced, in order to facilitate the online working of judges, prosecutors, and other legal actors. Undoubtedly, some of these safety precautions substantially affect the work of courts, affecting the right to access to justice, in particular the right to an effective remedy and fair trial.[25]

In France, the "Emergency Law", that was adopted on 23 March to counter the spread of the coronavirus,[26] declared a "state of health emergency" for a two-month period.[27] This statute aims to give a specific legal framework, of legislative value, to the special measures taken previously and the forthcoming ones. As we know, physical and social distancing measures to limit the COVID-19 outbreak, including forms of quarantine, have been ordered. Such measures can affect many fundamental rights, including freedom of assembly and of

25 About the implications of the "Emergency Law" or "Disaster Law" on fundamental rights, see the interesting report prepared by the Fundamental Rights Agency, *Coronavirus pandemic in the EU – Fundamental rights implications* (2020), published on https://fra.europa.eu/sites/default/files/fra_uploads/fra-2020-coronavirus-pandemic-eu-bulletin_en.pdf accessed 9 June 2020. For further and more detailed information on the emergency measures adopted by the French government see: https://www.comparativecovidlaw.it/france/ accessed 9 June 2020.

26 See, in particular, Loi n° 2020-290 du 23 mars 2020 d'urgence pour faire face à l'épidémie de covid-19, available on https://www.legifrance.gouv.fr/eli/loi/2020/3/23/PRMX2007883L/jo/text accessed 9 June 2020. See, also, Décret n° 2020-293 du 23 mars 2020 prescrivant les mesures générales nécessaires pour faire face à l'épidémie de covid-19 dans le cadre de l'état d'urgence sanitaire. Text available on https://www.legifrance.gouv.fr/affichTexte.do?cidTexte=JORFTEXT000041746694&categorieLien=cid accessed 9 June 2020.

27 For an in-depth look at the French debate on coronavirus crisis management, see Maria Francesca de Tullio, Il mito dell'emergenza e le garanzie costituzionali. Insegnamenti dall'esperienza francese (2020) 3 AIC https://www.rivistaaic.it/images/rivista/pdf/3_2020_12_DeTullio.pdf accessed 31 July 2020; Claudia Sartoretti, 'La risposta francese all'emergenza sanitaria da Covid-19: Stato di diritto e Costituzione alla prova della pandemia' (2020) 2 DPCE http://www.dpceonline.it/index.php/dpceonline/article/view/975/949 accessed 31 July 2020; Jilles Paisant, 'Masques et mascarades; À propos de la crise de la covid-19' (2020) SJG https://drive.google.com/file/d/17SD-oSNR5i6yw-J7JQyHp2H84xzprqDV/view accessed 31 July 2020.

association, freedom of movement and of residence and also the right of access to justice. In particular, the Organic Law provided for the suspension of the terms relating to "priority preliminary rulings on the issue of constitutionality" (so-called QPCs). In proceedings before a court, an applicant can raise the question by way of a QPC as to whether a legislative provision violates the rights and freedoms guaranteed by the French Constitution. Under certain conditions, this question is then referred to the *Conseil d'État* or the *Cour de Cassation*, which may, within three months, refer it to the *Conseil Constitutionnel*, which, in turn, has three months to conduct its review and rule on the matter. In light of the present circumstances, which hinder the ability of these three courts to convene and consider the applications referred to them, the three-month review periods mentioned above would be suspended until 30 June 2020.

Basing its decision on the "particular circumstances" of the crisis,[28] the *Conseil Constitutionnel* dismissed the objections raised concerning, in particular, the incompatibility with the provisions of the Constitution governing the adoption of an organic law. Article 46, second paragraph, of the French Constitution prescribes indeed a period of 15 days between the filing of the draft organic law and its adoption by the first assembly.[29]

With regard to the ordinary and administrative courts,[30] the *Cour de Cassation* suspended all reception services to the public and postponed the conferences as well as the institutional meetings. With regard to the hearings, a continuity plan for the judicial activity has been implemented which allows guaranteeing the treatment, by the criminal chamber, of the proceedings regarding precautionary measures, European arrest warrant, extraditions, etc.; the *Conseil d'État* informed that all hearings are cancelled except for those scheduled under the *référés* procedures. In the latter case, however, attendance at the hearings was limited: the physical presence of the applicant was not mandatory and access to the public was severely restricted.

---

28 CC, Décision n° 2020-799 DC du 26 Mars 2020, available on https://www.conseil-constitutionnel.fr/decision/2020/2020799DC.htm accessed 9 June 2020.

29 On this point, see Par Olivier Dord, 'Covid19 et Constitution: la loi prorogeant l'état d'urgence sanitaire devant le Conseil constitutionnel' (*Le Club des Juristes*, 27 May 2020) https://www.leclubdesjuristes.com/blog-du-coronavirus/que-dit-le-droit/covid19-et-constitution-la-loi-prorogeant-letat-durgence-sanitaire-devant-le-conseil-constitutionnel/ accessed 9 June 2020.

30 See, in particular, Ordonnance n° 2020-304 du 25 mars 2020 portant adaptation des règles applicables aux juridictions de l'ordre judiciaire statuant en matière non pénale et aux contrats de syndic de copropriété, available on https://www.legifrance.gouv.fr/affichTexte.do?cidTexte=JORFTEXT000041755577&dateTexte=20200406 accessed 9 June 2020; Ordonnance n° 2020-306 du 25 mars 2020 relative à la prorogation des délais échus pendant la période d'urgence sanitaire et à l'adaptation des procédures pendant cette même période, available on https://www.legifrance.gouv.fr/affichTexte.do?cidTexte=JORFTEXT000041755644 accessed 9 June 2020.

In Spain,[31] the Constitution regulates three different emergency levels, ranging from a state of alarm, to a state of emergency and ultimately to a state of siege allowing for martial law: each of these requires different levels of parliamentary oversight and grants different levels of powers to the government.[32] Thus, while the details of emergency regimes vary, many constitutions seek to simultaneously enable and constrain emergency rule. The "state of alarm" was declared by the Spanish government on 14 March, upon publication in the Official State Gazette of the Royal Decree no. 463/2020,[33] and since then, social distancing measures were taken. The people's right to movement was limited and the legal procedural deadlines were suspended, among other economic and labour measures. With regard to the administration of justice, it was announced that proceedings would be suspended, and current deadlines would not be applied, while the courts would focus on essential services only. However, all courts remained open, unless otherwise ordered by health authorities. Some common rules were followed: preference for online working, guarantee of essential services (cases with prisoners, gender violence, fundamental rights, collective social conflicts, etc.) and postponement of public hearings.[34] The Constitutional Court and the Supreme Court suspended their face-to-face activity but they nevertheless remained operational. The provisions aimed to achieve three principal goals: (a) to suspend and postpone all non-essential procedural activities so as to reduce the possibility of infection; (b) to increase the use of digital communication tools and video and telephone conferences in proceedings; (c) to minimise the negative effects on the protection of the rights, due to the postponement of most procedural activity.

In full autonomy the Plenary of the *Tribunal Constitucional*, on the proposal of its President and in the exercise of the powers conferred to it by Article 10.1.n of the Organic Law no. 2/1979, met by video-conference and clarified how it would manage the emergency phase. The agreement concerning

---

31 For further and more detailed information on the emergency measures adopted by the Spanish government see: https://www.comparativecovidlaw.it/spagna/ accessed 9 June 2020.

32 See Oren Gross, Fionnuala Ní Aoláin, *Law in Times of Crisis: Emergency Powers in Theory and Practice* (1st edn, CUP 2006) https://doi.org/10.1017/CBO9780511493997 accessed 9 June 2020. See also Valeria Piergigli, 'L'emergenza Covid-19 in Spagna e la dichiarazione dell'estado de alarma. Ripercussioni sul sistemaistituzionale e sul regime dei diritti' (2020) 2 DPCE http://www.dpceonline.it/index.php/dpceonline/article/view/971/945 accessed 31 July 2020; Gerardo Ruiz-Rico Ruiz, 'Las dimensiones constitucionales de la crisis sanitaria en españa. Dudas e incertidumbres presentes y futuras' (2020) 2 DPCE http://www.dpceonline.it/index.php/dpceonline/article/view/970/944 accessed 31 July 2020.

33 Royal Decree no. 463/2020 declaring the state of alarm for the management of the health crisis situation caused by COVID-19. The text may be accessed at https://www.boe.es/buscar/doc.php?id=BOE-A-2020-3692 accessed 9 June 2020.

34 For an in-depth look at Spanish justice system's response to COVID-19 crisis, see Silvia Barona Vilar, 'Justicia civil post-coronavirus, de la crisis a algunas de las reformas que se avizoran' (2020) 2-*bis* Actualidad Jurídica Iberoamericana http://www.revista-aji.com/wp-content/uploads/2020/05/72._Silvia_Barona_pp._776-787.pdf accessed 31 July 2020.

the suspension of procedural and administrative deadlines during the validity of the Royal Decree no. 463/2020 was published in the *Boletín Oficial del Estado* on 16 March.[35] More specifically, the declaration of the "state of alarm" did not interrupt the functioning of the constitutional body.[36] In this sense, the Court has continued issuing any necessary resolutions and precautionary measures, at any constitutional proceedings that may so require, in order to guarantee the constitutional system and the fundamental rights as well as public liberties. In order to facilitate its activities, however, the time-limits to take any procedural or administrative actions before the Court have been suspended during the effective period of the "state of alarm" and, without prejudice to the suspension of the time-limit calculation, the filing of appeals and other documents affecting the various constitutional or administrative proceedings has been facilitated through the electronic Register on the Court's website.

In Germany,[37] on the basis of the Infectious Diseases Protection Act (*Infektionsschutzgesetz – IfSG*)[38] competent federal and State authorities are entitled to adopt different measures to prevent and control infectious diseases. This Act was amended by the Bundestag on 27 March, in order to provide special and emergency powers to the Federal Minister of Health only.[39] Concerning the legal basis for restrictions on the freedom of movement, the German Constitution (*Grundgesetz*) does not explicitly foresee a general curfew but allows fundamental rights to be limited through measures that are necessary and proportionate. Three steps have been adopted in order to fight the spread of the infection. First phase, prohibition of all large events for groups of more than 50 people. Second phase, closing services or activities such as libraries, museums, gyms, cinemas, restaurants, etc.). Third phase, quarantine.[40]

In particular, the Federal Constitutional Court (*Bundesverfassungsgericht* (*BverfG*)) remained fully functional in spite of various restrictions due to

---

35 The text is available online at https://www.boe.es/boe/dias/2020/03/17/pdfs/BOE-A-2020-3805.pdf accessed 9 June 2020.

36 The declaration of alarm, exception and siege state does not interrupt the normal functioning of the State's constitutional powers. The Organic Law no. 4/1981 can be found at https://www.boe.es/eli/es/lo/1981/06/01/4/con accessed 9 June 2020.

37 For further and more detailed information on the emergency measures adopted by the German government see: https://www.comparativecovidlaw.it/germany/ accessed 9 June 2020.

38 The IfSG law is available on https://www.gesetze-im-internet.de/ifsg/ accessed 9 June 2020.

39 On this point, see, for example, Sven Jürgensen and Frederik Orlowski, 'Critique and Crisis: The German Struggle with Pandemic Control Measures and the State of Emergency' (*VerfBlog*, 19 April 2020) https://verfassungsblog.de/critique-and-crisis-the-german-struggle-with-pandemic-control-measures-and-the-state-of-emergency/ accessed 9 June 2020.

40 See, among others, Jens Woelk, 'La gestione della pandemia da parte della Germania: "Wir schaffen das!"' (2020) 2 DPCE http://www.dpceonline.it/index.php/dpceonline/article/view/978/952 accessed 31 July 2020; Johannes Saurer, 'Covid-19 and Cooperative Administrative Federalism in Germany' (2020) The Regulatory Review https://drive.google.com/file/d/1QdyFPz5WxAQIziob9zfFGNJ1htWLRwvt/view accessed 31 July 2020.

the coronavirus.[41] As a precaution against potential cases of illness or quarantine, an alternating two-shift system that ensures the continued functioning of the Court was introduced in all areas of work from 19 March 2020 onwards. Additionally, external contact and the presence of staff at the Court remained restricted to a minimum. Oral hearings and pronouncements of judgments did not take place – except in urgent matters that could not have been postponed. The Court has also cancelled all trips to and visits from foreign courts. The Court building has been closed to the public. The handling of cases by the chambers, in particular preliminary injunction proceedings, has been maintained – particularly by means of IT equipment allowing the justices to work online.

This continuity is also reflected in the high number of decisions on matters relating to the COVID-19 pandemic published by the Federal Constitutional Court.[42] In most of them, the Court refused to grant interim measures for procedural reasons, e.g. for failure to exhaust legal remedies before administrative courts, or for substantive reasons (the BVerfG has supported the legitimacy of many of the restrictions, refusing to bypass the Government's appreciation and thus demonstrating a certain judicial restraint).[43]

The spread of the COVID-19 pandemic has an impact on justice at other levels as well. The Federal Supreme Court (BGH) has cancelled or postponed several non-essential hearings to reduce as far as possible the risks associated with the spread of contagion among people. What strikes most, in Germany, compared to the Italian and French situation, is that the specific legislation enacted to alleviate the effects of COVID-19 did not address any specific issue related to the functioning of civil proceedings during this period of crisis. It is

---

41 More detailed information is available on the Court's website: https://www.bundesverfassungsgericht.de/EN/Presse/Pressemitteilungen/pressemitteilungen_node.html accessed 9 June 2020.

42 See, e.g. BVerfG, Beschluss vom 15. April 2020 – 1 BvR 828/20; BVerfG Beschluss vom 17 April 2020 – 1 BvQ 37/20 (on the freedom of assembly); BVerfG, Beschluss vom 29. April 2020 – 1 BvQ 44/20 (on the freedom of religion). In essence, the Court's assessments have sought to affirm the need to avoid the blanket suspension of fundamental rights while granting a wide latitude to executive action to prevent the spread of the coronavirus. The decisions have forced local authorities to make contextualized assessments, and take responsibility for their decisions, ensuring a minimum level of protection of fundamental rights in areas that are particularly sensitive.

43 See, e.g. BVerfG, Beschluss vom 07. April 2020 – 1 BvR 755/20, §6; BVerfG, Beschluss vom 10 April 2020 – 1 BvQ 28/20, §14. The reasoning applied in these cases was the so-called "double hypothesis", by which the court compares the scenario in which a proportional and legitimate measure is instead declared illegitimate and suspended by the Court, with that in which the Court refuses the suspension of the same measure, but this is actually in violation of fundamental rights. See, *ex plurimis*, Irene Domenici, Tim Rohmann, 'Un'imposizione democratica. L'ordinamento costituzionale tedesco di fronte alla pandemia' (2020) 1 BioLaw Journal 697 http://rivista.biodiritto.org/ojs/index.php?journal=biolaw&page=article&op=view&path%5B%5D=628&path%5B%5D=537 accessed 9 June 2020.

for the respective courts and judges to decide what measures should be taken in each individual case.

Continuity of judicial activity, independence of the courts, flexibility of measures and online working are common trends that have also come to light in many common law experiences. From a comparative perspective, it is interesting to note that, despite the considerable differences from the civil law judicial systems, the responses provided by common law courts have not been so different and were inspired by the same criteria.

Both the United Kingdom and the United States Executive initially downplayed concerns arising from the spread of COVID-19 pandemic. Prime Minister Boris Johnson suggesting Britain should "take it on the chin", pursued a policy which introduced no significant measures.[44] On 23 March, the country entered lockdown through secondary legislation under the Public Health (Control of Disease) Act 1984 as amended in 2008 in light of the SARS outbreak.[45] A specific "Coronavirus Act"[46] was published on 19 March, and fast-tracked through Parliament to receive royal assent four parliamentary days later, on 25 March. The Act provides for several measures aiming to address the epidemic.[47] It is interesting to note that in contrast to concerns in other States as to the permanent changes to the law following the introduction of these emergency powers, the Coronavirus Act 2020 is not expected, or designed, to create any permanent change (the so-called "sunset clause").[48] With regard to the administration of justice, a number of changes have been made to allow the work of the UK Supreme Court (UKSC) and the Judicial Committee of the Privy Council (JCPC) to continue, following the latest advice from the Government. On 17 March the Supreme

---

44 BBC, 'Coronavirus: UK moving towards 'delay' phase of virus plan as cases hit 115' (*BBC*, 5 March 2020) https://www.bbc.com/news/uk-51749352 accessed 9 June 2020.

45 Tony Diver, 'London lockdown: are Tubes and buses still running – and can I travel out of the city?' (*The Telegraph*, 25 May 2020) https://www.telegraph.co.uk/news/2020/03/25/london-lockdown-coronavirus-tube-bus-leave/ accessed 9 June 2020.

46 The text is available on http://www.legislation.gov.uk/ukpga/2020/7/contents/enacted accessed 9 June 2020. For further and more detailed information on the emergency measures adopted by the UK see: https://www.comparativecovidlaw.it/united-kingdom/ accessed 9 June 2020.

47 On this point, see Ronan Cormacain, 'Keeping Covid-19 emergency legislation socially distant from ordinary legislation: principles for the structure of emergency legislation' (2020) The Theory and Practice of Legislation https://drive.google.com/file/d/195Ssji-2E0Pu2DzRq1WZRdPP1j4nuqVA/view accessed 31 July 2020; Giulia Caravale, 'Il Coronavirus Act 2020 e le misure adottate dal regno unito per affrontare l'emergenza Covid-19' (2020) 1 NOMOS https://drive.google.com/file/d/1lk1sCRuJtSgKazpuugFdm9PZ2BRCiKlG/view accessed 31 July 2020.

48 "Sunset clauses" are dispositions that determine the expiry of a law or regulation within a predetermined period. For instance, in the UK, The Terrorist Asset-Freezing (Temporary Provisions) Act 2010 stipulates that its provisions have effect for the period beginning when this Act comes into force and ending with 31 December 2010. See at this regard Sean Molloy, 'Covid-19, Emergency Legislation and Sunset Clauses' (*U.K. Const. L. Blog*, 8 April 2020) https://ukconstitutionallaw.org/ accessed 9 June 2020.

Court had already announced that it would give priority to judicial activities, i.e. the conduct of hearings relating to appeals submitted to the Supreme Court and the Judicial Committee, the delivery of judgments and the evaluation of requests for appeal. The judges, staff and defence lawyers involved in the proposed cases could continue to work at the Court's headquarters, but online work was encouraged as much as possible. Furthermore, the time-limits were applied in a "flexible" way. Subsequently, the Court prepared a real arrangement for the management of judicial activities during the pandemic.[49] In order to ensure the "openness" of the courts and the "continuity" of the judicial activity, courts have put in place arrangements to use telephone, video and other technology to continue as many hearings as possible remotely. Applying these measures was more complex for hearings involving a jury because it was not always possible to guarantee social distancing in court and in the court building.[50] For these reasons, all jury trials and many non-urgent cases were suspended during the lockdown but most of the higher civil courts – the Supreme Court, Court of Appeal, High Court and Family Court – conducted remote hearings via video links. Moreover, even before the coronavirus, the Supreme Court was already live-streaming its hearings, and some Court of Appeal hearings were also broadcasting live. The new jury trials will take place under special arrangements to maintain the safety of all participants, including jurors.

The containment of the pandemic in the United States has been very confusing.[51] In relation to the management of the crisis by the judiciary, a premise is necessary: the United States is a federal system, with a central federal government and individual governments for each of the 50 States. As with the other branches of government, each of the States has their own complete judicial system (State courts) as does the United States itself (federal courts).[52]

---

49 See the Court's guidelines on https://www.supremecourt.uk/docs/practice-note-on-arrangements-during%20the-coronavirus-pandemic.pdf accessed 9 June 2020.

50 A complete map of advice and guidance from the judiciary in relation to the coronavirus pandemic is available on https://www.judiciary.uk/coronavirus-covid-19-advice-and-guidance/# generalinfo accessed 9 June 2020.

51 See, for example, Alejandro E. Camacho and Robert L. Glicksman, 'The Trump Administration's Pandemic Response Is Structured to Fail' (2020) The Regulatory Review https://drive.google.com/file/d/1h-uefzYG5mKNLcyIBT42QgIQYkKN0V9p/view accessed 31 July 2020; Francesco Clementi, 'Gli Stati Uniti e la risposta al Covid-19, tra Federazione e Stati, nell'anno delle elezioni presidenziali' (2020) 2 DPCE http://www.dpceonline.it/index.php/dpceonline/article/view/986/960 accessed 31 July 2020; Maurizio Masi, 'Stati Uniti d'America e CoViD-19: alcune fasi della gestione di una pandemia annunciata' (2020) 1 BioLaw Journal 753 https://drive.google.com/file/d/10Lz5Rd4N5T0rkczoIaTxEZEjq50Ct0m5/view accessed 31 July 2020.

52 For a more detailed study see Richard Posner, *The Federal Judiciary. Strengths and Weaknesses* (HUP 2017); Mark Tushnet, *The Constitution of the United States of America: A Contextual Analysis* (Hart Publishing 2015); Robert A. Sedler, 'The Constitution and the American Federal System' (2009) 55 Wayne L. Rev. 1487 http://digitalcommons.wayne.edu/lawfrp/91 accessed 31 July 2020.

Thus far, court responses vary substantially across jurisdictions both at federal and at national level, with policies ranging from carrying on business as usual to closing courthouses entirely and suspending in-person proceedings indefinitely. Even within the same jurisdiction, different courthouses and judges often have wide discretion to determine which hearings must take place in person and who among the court staff must come to work.

The US Supreme Court announced that oral arguments that had been scheduled for the March and April 2020 argument sessions were postponed. Some of the cases that had been scheduled for March and April have been rescheduled for telephonic argument in May and the cases not heard have been rescheduled for the October 2020 term. The Justices and counsel attended the meeting remotely. The Court provided a live audio feed of these arguments to news media.[53] However, the Court failed to provide quick and transparent answers: for example, it was not clear from the start whether the Court would comply with the consolidated practice of deciding all pending cases before closing for the summer break, scheduled for late June, and even whether it would guarantee the carrying out of public hearings.[54] In fact, the Supreme Court's term usually runs from October to June, but given the large number of cases remaining on the docket, it exceptionally extended its term into July. Yet the Court gave little notice before announcing additional conference or decision days, sometimes informing the public only days beforehand.[55]

The Supreme Court's disorganised and opaque response to the pandemic is particularly alarming considering how much the stakes of cases in the Supreme Court register can affect the functioning of the government and public health during a pandemic.[56] For this reason, it is imperative that the Court continues

---

53 For the first time, the nation's highest court has opened a live audio feed as it hears arguments. See Adam Liptak, 'The Supreme Court Will Hear Arguments by Phone. The Public Can Listen In' (*The New York Times*, 13 April 2020) https://www.nytimes.com/2020/04/13/us/politics/supreme-court-phone-arguments-virus.html?smid=nytcore-ios-share accessed 9 June 2020. All updated information is available on the US Supreme Court's website: https://www.supremecourt.gov/publicinfo/press/pressreleases/pr_04-13-20 accessed 9 June 2020.

54 See Patrizia Magarò, 'La Corte Suprema degli Stati Uniti ai tempi del Covid-19 (Uno sguardo di insieme)' (2020) 1 GiurCost http://www.giurcost.org/studi/magaro.pdf accessed 31 July 2020.

55 In this regard, see, e.g. Stephanie Wylie, 'The Supreme Court's Failed Response to the Coronavirus Pandemic' (Center for American Progress, 7 August 2020) https://www.americanprogress.org/issues/democracy/news/2020/08/07/488938/supreme-courts-failed-response-coronavirus-pandemic/ accessed 21 September 2020.

56 These issues include cases regarding President Donald Trump's financial records and the Affordable Care Act's requirement that employer health plans cover birth control – both of which were heard remotely (see e.g. *Trump v. Mazars USA, LLP*, 591 U.S.___ (2020), *Trump v. Vance*, 591 U.S.___ (2020) and *Little Sisters of the Poor Saints Peter and Paul Home v. Pennsylvania*, 591 U.S.___ (2020)) or cases arising from the pandemic itself or on electoral matters. For example, it rejected a petition from a Nevada church arguing that State restrictions on church service attendance were unconstitutional (*Calvary Chapel Dayton Valley V. Steve Sisolak, Governor Of Nevada, Et Al.*, 591 U.S.____ (2020)) and decided cases

to operate efficiently during public health emergencies and ensure the public has continued access to live oral arguments. As noted, the Court began hearing remote oral arguments in May. This positive development should open the door for continued access to the Court remotely, even after the end of the pandemic.

Other federal courts have introduced different measures.[57] For example, in the Federal Circuit Court of Appeals, all cases scheduled for oral arguments during the April and May 2020 sitting have been conducted remotely by teleconference. In addition, no physical hearings have been held during this period, and rules have been changed so that parties were no longer obliged to file paper copies of documents that had been lodged electronically. Courts in most States have suspended/cancelled/postponed jury trials for safety reasons during the epidemiological crisis. A number of federal courthouses have closed, either because of infection of a particular staff member, or because they have been shut down pre-emptively by local judges on public health grounds. In general, each court acted independently, with great flexibility, coordinating with State and local health officials to obtain local information about the spread of the epidemic.

In this confused picture, however, it is interesting to highlight the existence of a plan of suggestions and measures to guarantee the continuity of judicial activity during times of crisis (terrorist attacks, natural disasters, pandemics). This guide, prepared by the National Center for State Courts with the assistance of a National Coalition of leaders from all sectors involved in business continuity planning for courts and supported by the US Department of Justice, Office of Justice Programs, Bureau of Justice Assistance, provides a step-by-step guide to help courts to develop and maintain a viable "continuity of operations" capability.[58] Courts are invited to draw up a "continuity of operations plan" to ensure the knowledge of how to face an emergency that threatens continuation of normal operations. The inclusion of pandemic planning within the guide recognises the critical need for courts to prepare for this type of emergency. Pandemic planning involves many of the same steps as "continuity of operations" planning for any emergency. However, there are some special considerations when preparing for a pandemic. The guide highlights many of these (e.g. limiting personal contact through social distancing; using informational technologies; online working) and links to currently available resources to address them.

---

concerning voting procedures during the pandemic in Wisconsin (*Republican National Committee v. Democratic National Committee*, 589 U.S.____ (2020)), as well as a Pennsylvania case examining the legality of the public health order issued by the Governor.

57 This site collects the updated guidelines from the judiciary (both federal and national level): https://www.uscourts.gov/news/2020/03/12/judiciary-preparedness-coronavirus-covid-19 accessed 9 June 2020.

58 National Center for State Courts, *Continuity Of Court Operations: Steps For Coop Planning* (2007), available on https://www.ncsc.org/__data/assets/pdf_file/0028/17389/toolkit.pdf accessed 9 June 2020.

5. EUROPEAN COURTS' RESPONSES TO THE COVID-19 CRISIS

The EU Member States' diverse responses to the WHO-declared pandemic have once again shown the insufficiency of national responses to global problems, and how the Union's construction remains stuck halfway between the tendency towards regional organisation of economic integration linked to the model of intergovernmental cooperation, and propulsion towards an effectively and politically integrated model.[59] As is known, the competence in the field of public health, based on the principles of attribution and subsidiarity, is limited to coordinating national competences: it is a support competence pursuant to Article 6 of the TFEU (therefore neither exclusive pursuant to Art 3, nor concurrent, if not to any residual extent, pursuant to Art 4), mainly focused on cross-border issues (understood as related to freedom of movement rather than to extension of the threat). The EU does not define health policies, nor the organisation and provision of health services and medical care. Instead, its actions serve to complement national policies and support cooperation between Member States in the field of public health.[60] On 28 January 2020, by decision of the Croatian Presidency, the *Integrated Political Crisis Response* (IPCR) was activated in the information-sharing mode. Also, by decision of the Presidency, from 3 March 2020 the Mechanism was in "full activation" mode.[61] In compliance with national competences, the worktables convened at EU level served to coordinate the actions of those actors present, with particular regard to responses at the political level (in fact we speak of "political response to crisis"). On 13 March 2020, the Commission published a Communication[62] which, as well as providing an initial analysis of the impact of the COVID-19 pandemic, made known its orientation regarding some particular problems and presented a series of its own decisions and proposals to tackle such problems. Albeit with

59 See, e.g. Alberto Alemanno, 'The European Response to COVID-19: From Regulatory Emulation to Regulatory Coordination?' (2020) 11 EJRR https://www.cambridge.org/core/services/aop-cambridge-core/content/view/F4CA8FEC38915D31EC0D680E29A71A8B/S1867299X20000446a.pdf/european_response_to_covid19_from_regulatory_emulation_to_regulatory_coordination.pdf accessed 31 July 2020; Tobias Tesche, 'The European Union's Response to the Coronavirus Emergency: An Early Assessment' (2020) 157 LSE 'Europe in Question' Discussion Paper Series https://papers.ssrn.com/sol3/papers.cfm?abstract_id=3624730 accessed 31 July 2020.

60 See, for example, https://eur-lex.europa.eu/summary/chapter/public_health.htmlroot_default=SUM_1_CODED%3D29&locale=it accessed 9 June 2020.

61 See the Conclusions of the President of the European Council at the end of the videoconference on COVID-19: https://www.consilium.europa.eu/it/press/press-releases/2020/03/10/statement-by-the-president-of-the-european-council-following-the-video-conference-on-covid-19/ accessed 9 June 2020.

62 Communication no. (2020)/112, https://eur-lex.europa.eu/legal-content/EN/TXT/?uri=CELEX%3A52020DC0112 accessed 9 June 2020.

some delay and uncertainty, the EU response to the pandemic arrived, mainly articulating four priorities: to limit the spread of the virus; ensure the supply of medical equipment; promote research into treatments and vaccines; and support employment, business and the economy.[63] The priorities were agreed by EU leaders, who met periodically via video-conference to identify the most effective (and shared) measures to be taken.[64]

Of course, the Court of Justice of the European Union (ECJ) also had to take exceptional measures to deal with the crisis and ensure continuity in its activities.[65] More specifically, with a joint press release from the Court of Justice and the EU General Court on 13 March 2020,[66] jurisdictional activities were partially suspended. In fact, the processing of all cases was suspended, except for those of an urgent nature (urgent, accelerated and summary proceedings for the Court of Justice; priority, accelerated and summary proceedings for the General Court). It was also specified that the terms of appeal and challenge were not suspended and had to be respected by the parties (except for the possible application of Art 45 of the Protocol on the Statute of the Court of Justice of the EU, which provides that "No right shall be prejudiced in consequence of the expiry of a time limit if the party concerned proves the existence of unforeseeable circumstances or of force majeure"[67]); while the time-limits on proceedings in progress (and until further notice those set by the registry from 17 March) were extended by one month. Oral hearings were, however, suspended and, in order not to delay cases' progress, the hearing initially scheduled for some of them was replaced by written questions addressed to the parties. Oral hearings in front of the General Court that had been scheduled up to 15 May 2020 were instead postponed. A progressive resumption of discussion hearings in the court hearing rooms was scheduled, starting from 25 May 2020, health conditions permitting.[68]

---

63 Detailed information on measures taken within the European institutions in response to the pandemic is available at https://ec.europa.eu/info/live-work-travel-eu/health/coronavirus-response_en and https://www.consilium.europa.eu/en/policies/covid-19-coronavirus-outbreak/timeline/ accessed 9 June 2020.

64 For further and more detailed information on the emergency measures adopted by the European Union see: https://www.comparativecovidlaw.it/unione-europea/#a4 accessed 9 June 2020.

65 On this point, see Michal Kianicka, 'Streaming of hearings. A tough call for the Court of Justice' (2020) EULawLive https://eulawlive.com/weekend-edition/weekend-edition-no13/; José Igreja Matos, 'Being a Judge in Times of Pandemic' (2020) EULawLive https://eulawlive.com/weekend-edition/weekend-edition-no12/. For further information see https://eulawlive.com/tag/news/ accessed 31 July 2020.

66 All updated information is available on https://curia.europa.eu/jcms/jcms/P_97552/en/ accessed 9 June 2020.

67 Article 45 of the Protocol on the Statute of the EU Court of Justice, available at https://eur-lex.europa.eu/resource.html?uri=cellar:07cc36e9-56a0-4008-ada4-08d640803855.0005.02/DOC_10&format=PDF accessed 9 June 2020.

68 See again https://curia.europa.eu/jcms/jcms/P_97552/en/ accessed 9 June 2020.

Meanwhile, within the Council of Europe and with particular reference to the European Court of Human Rights (ECtHR), a press release issued by the Court Registry on 16 March 2020[69] announced the Court's adoption of a series of exceptional measures to respond to the global health crisis.[70] Thus, only the Court's "essential activities" were maintained, in particular the examination of priority cases and requests for precautionary measures pursuant to Article 39 of the Court Rules. To ensure the continuity of its functions, the Court generally resorted to remote working procedures. The Court premises were closed to the public and hearings scheduled for March and April were cancelled pending subsequent decisions.

In particular, with a press release issued by the Court Registry on 9 April 2020,[71] the exceptional measures announced on 16 March 2020 were extended for a further two months. In this regard, the Court specified that:

- the six-month deadline for introducing appeals, pursuant to Article 35 of the European Convention on Human Rights, which had been exceptionally extended for one month from 16 March 2020, was further extended "for two months from 16 April 2020 up to and including 15 June 2020";[72]
- the deadlines assigned in the pending procedures, extended for one month from 16 March 2020, were further extended for two months from 16 April 2020, "except for the three-month deadline provided for by Article 43 of the Convention to submit any requests for referral to the Grand Chamber".[73] The Court also specified that, following the lockdown measures adopted by the host State and facilitating the use of remote work and electronic communication, it would continue to perform its essential activities, including the registration of new appeals and their assignment to the competent judicial bodies.

Although the intention of these measures, summarised above, is to ensure continuity in the Court's work, especially in light of its fundamental role as guarantor of fundamental rights, the following choices do not seem entirely "efficient": (i) general suspension of the six-month time limit for introducing

69 Press Release, Registrar of the Court, ECtHR 094 (2020), 16 March 2020, on https://hudoc.echr.coe.int/eng-press#{"itemid":["003-6666795-8866184 accessed 9 June 2020.

70 See, in particular, the Statement of the Consultative Council of European Judges, 'The role of judges during and in the aftermath of the COVID-19 pandemic: lessons and challenges' (*CCJE* 24 June 2020) https://drive.google.com/file/d/1X88QJfsH4Rx-rQZSDvsdlThuYlqE-5Je/view accessed 31 July 2020.

71 Press Release, Registrar of the Court, ECtHR 108 (2020), 9 April 2020, on https://hudoc.echr.coe.int/eng-press#{"itemid":["003-6675775-8879937 accessed 9 June 2020.

72 Ibid.

73 Ibid.

appeals pursuant to Article 35 Section 1 ECtHR, rather than allowing "case by case" assessment; (ii) freezing the publication of judgments that cannot be notified to the appellant through the *eComms* platform, considering that this electronic method was only recently introduced; (iii) generally suspending "communication" to defendant Governments of appeals (not "important and urgent") for the initiation of written exchanges between the parties.[74]

6. THE ROLE OF CONSTITUTIONAL JUSTICE IN TIMES OF EMERGENCY

Taking the context into account, the main concern is to identify what should be the role (if any) of constitutional justice and, when appropriate, of the international and supranational system for the protection of human rights during the pandemic. Answering these questions is particularly important in light of some common trends: (1) many States, especially in Latin America but also in Eastern Europe, have declared a national emergency giving the Heads of State such powers that they would not normally exercise in ordinary situations, such as suspension or limitation of fundamental rights;[75] and, (2) this global crisis does not affect everyone equally. There are people who are especially unprotected, such as medical, police, military personnel, imprisoned people, women, disabled people, poor families, homeless and the LGBTI population.[76]

The COVID-19 pandemic has prompted many countries to take extreme measures to protect lives including measures of social distancing, closure of schools, restriction of social gatherings and lockdowns of cities and entire States. Considering that more than half of the world's democracies have declared a state

---

74 See, e.g. Andrea Sacucci, 'Post Scriptum sulla sospensione dei termini processuali da parte della Corte Europea per l'emergenza Covid-19' (*SIDIBlog*, 20 April 2020) http://www.sidiblog.org/2020/04/20/post-scriptum-sulla-sospensione-dei-termini-processuali-da-parte-della-corte-europea-per-lemergenza-covid-19/ accessed 9 June 2020.

75 See, e.g. the case of Hungary: Andras Ràcz, 'A New Risk to the EU from Coronavirus: Viktor Orbàn's Hungary' (2020) DGAP Commentary https://dgap.org/sites/default/files/article_pdfs/dgap-commentary-2020-10-en.pdf accessed 9 June 2020; Laura Livingston, 'Understanding Hungary's Authoritarian Response to the Pandemic' (*Law Fare Blog*, 14 April 2020) https://www.lawfareblog.com/understanding-hungarys-authoritarian-response-pandemic accessed 9 June 2020.

76 See, among others, Carla Maria Reale, 'La dimensione costituzionale dell'emergenza: come l'epidemia moltiplica le disuguaglianze' (2020) 1 BioLaw Journal 269 https://drive.google.com/file/d/12gg2slGseiCslvz5yE2TKvGL7sKUTulM/view accessed 31 July 2020; Irene Dominici and Tim Rohmann, 'How to protect the Vulnerable? Legal Implications of Vulnerability in Times of COVID-19' (*VerfBlog*, 15 April 2020) https://verfassungsblog.de/how-to-protect-the-vulnerable/ accessed 31 July 2020; Ruqaiijah Yearby and Seema Mohapatra, 'Law, Structural Racism, and the COVID-19 Pandemic' (2020) Journal of Law and the Biosciences https://papers.ssrn.com/sol3/papers.cfm?abstract_id=3612824 accessed 31 July 2020.

of emergency,[77] the rule of law will be subject to a number of dangers during these months (and possibly later).[78] A state of emergency regularly implies that the government has the right to derogate from some basic rights – such as the freedom to assemble, to move freely, to practise one's religion, the right to privacy, etc. It also implies that the other two branches of power are weakened in contrast to the executive power. Many constitutions grant the executive the power to rule by decrees, i.e. to bypass the legislature, during the epidemiological crisis. Sometimes this happened even in the silence of the Constitution: for instance, differently from other Western European countries, Italy does not have a clearly articulated constitutional framework governing emergencies.[79] States of emergency, therefore, pose the most significant challenges to the rule of law and to safeguarding fundamental rights and civil liberties in various ways. Let us think about the strengthening of the executive power to the detriment of judicial authority and parliamentary oversight, the absence of effective domestic mechanisms of supervision of the executive power, the replacement of the judicial role with police operations, the absence of effective judicial review, etc.

The judiciary has been weakened in a very direct manner during the current wave of emergency declarations: many courts have simply been shut down, implying that it has become difficult or even outright impossible to challenge the legitimacy of government actions. However, despite the obvious difficulties, the lack of adequate resources and, in some cases, the technological backwardness

---

77 An overview of the measures taken by each country to combat the spread of the virus is available on https://www.theregreview.org/2020/04/20/comparing-nations-responses-covid-19/ accessed 9 June 2020.

78 On this point, see David Dyzenhaus, *The Constitution of Law. Legality in a Time of Emergency* (CUP 2006); Evan J. Criddle and Evan Fox-Decent, 'Human Rights, Emergencies, and the Rule of Law' (2012) 34 Human Rights Quarterly https://papers.ssrn.com/sol3/papers.cfm?abstract_id=1591970 accessed 31 July 2020; Olivier De Schutter, *International Human Rights Law: Cases, Materials, Commentary* (CUP 2014). More specifically, see, e.g. European Commission For Democracy Through Law (Venice Commission), *Opinion On The Protection Of Human Rights In Emergency Situations* (CDL-AD Opinion no. 359, 2006); Giovanni Di Cosimo, 'Sulle limitazioni ai diritti durante l'emergenza' in Ermanno Calzolaio, Massimo Meccarelli, Stefano Pollastrelli (eds), *Il diritto nella pandemia. Temi, problemi, domande* (EUM 2020); Michele Collazzo and Alexandra Tyan, 'Emergency Powers, COVID-19 and the New Challenge for Human Rights' (2020) 20/48 IAI Commentaries https://www.iai.it/sites/default/files/iaicom2048.pdf accessed 31 July 2020; Adina Ponta, 'Human Rights Law in the Time of the Coronavirus' (2020) 24/5 American Society of International Law https://www.asil.org/insights/volume/24/issue/5/human-rights-law-time-coronavirus accessed 31 July 2020.

79 See, e.g., Edoardo C. Raffiotta, 'Sulla legittimità dei provvedimenti del governo a contrasto dell'emergenza virale da coronavirus' (2020) 2 BLJ https://www.biodiritto.org/content/download/3793/45322/version/1/file/21+Raffiotta.pdf accessed 31 July 2020; Francesco Torre, 'La costituzione sotto stress ai tempi del coronavirus' (2020) 2 BLJ https://www.biodiritto.org/content/download/3834/45465/version/1/file/51+Torre.pdf accessed 31 July 2020; Julinda Beqiraj, 'Italy's Coronavirus Legislative Response: Adjusting Along the Way' (*VerfBlog*, 8 April 2020), https://verfassungsblog.de/italys-coronavirus-legislative-response-adjusting-along-the-way/ accessed 31 July 2020.

of the offices, the attitude of the courts – even in the great variety and diversity of legal contexts – has been of great responsiveness. The balance among the powers – the basis of modern constitutional democracies – proved to be resilient in the majority of cases.

First, courts have scrutinised whether proper procedures are followed and whether the emergency response is rooted in law.[80] Secondly, some courts have engaged in substantive rights review, with the goal of ensuring that the restrictions on rights are necessary, proportional and equally applied.[81] Thirdly, some courts have even demanded that the executive take action, especially in contexts where the governments failed to adequately respond to the pandemic.[82] Fourthly, we find that some courts have had to grapple with whether the pandemic allows for elections to be postponed.[83] Nonetheless, the fact that many courts have involved themselves in the pandemic response is a strong indication that executive power has not been entirely unbound during the current pandemic.

Undoubtedly, the judiciary has proven to have independence not only from an operational point of view (in most cases courts have had great autonomy in the measures to be taken to limit the spread of the epidemic) but also from a

---

80 See, e.g. Constitutional Review of Decision No. 01/15 of the Government of the Republic of Kosovo, of 23 March 2020, Case No. KO 54/20, https://gjk-ks.org/en/decision/vleresim-i-kushtetutshmerise-se-vendimit-nr-01-15-te-qeverise-serepublikes-se-kosoves-te-23-marsit-2020/ accessed 9 June 2020. In this case, the Court held that declaring a state of emergency was not necessary, but that limitation on rights had to be based in law. While the Court invalidated the government's lockdown measures, it left them in place until the legislature time had time to pass legislation. See also Yoav Dotan, 'Continuous Judicial Review in Coronavirus Times' (*The Regulatory Review*, 11 May 2020) https://www.theregreview.org/2020/05/11/dotan-continuous-judicial-review-coronavirus-times/ accessed 9 June 2020.

81 See, e.g. some decisions of the German Constitutional Court (See *supra* notes 30-31 and surrounding text). Another good example is the decision of the Sixth Circuit Court of Appeals which held that Kentucky could not prohibit religious gatherings when social distancing guidelines were observed (*Maryville Baptist Church, Inc. & Dr. Jack Roberts v. Andy Beshear*, 20-5427 (6th Cir. 2020). The text is available at http://lc.org/PDFs/Attachments2PRsLAs/2020/050220MaryvilleBaptistIPA.pdf accessed 9 June 2020.

82 See, e.g. 'Court Orders Zimbabwe to Protect Medics from the Coronavirus' *Eyewitness News* (Johannesburg, 15 April 2020), https://ewn.co.za/2020/04/15/court-orders-zimbabwe-to-protect-medics-from-the-coronavirus accessed 9 June 2020; Hardik Subedi, 'How Nepal's Supreme Court Upheld Dignity of Migrant Workers Without Diluting COVID Fight' (*THE WIRE* 28 April 2020) https://thewire.in/law/nepal-supreme-court-migrant-workers accessed 9 June 2020.

83 Some examples are: Anna Grzymala-Busse, 'Poland's Presidential Election Just Got More Complicated' *Wash. Post* (Washington, 18 May 2020) https://www.washingtonpost.com/politics/2020/05/08/polands-presidential-election-just-got-more-complicated/ accessed 9 June 2020; Green Muheya, Elijah Phompho, 'Malawi Electoral Commission Asks Court to Stop Voter Registration after Cabinet Directive' (*CONSTITUTIONNET*, 9 April 2020) http://constitutionnet.org/news/malawi-electoralcommission-asks-court-stop-voter-registration-after-cabinet-directive accessed 9 June 2020; Mark Joseph Stern, 'The Supreme Court's Wisconsin Election Decision is 2020's Bush v. Gore' (*SLATE.COM*, 7 April 2020) https://slate.com/news-and-politics/2020/04/wisconsin-election-dissents.html accessed 9 June 2020.

substantive point of view. At its most basic, courts can ensure the procedural integrity of emergency regimes, by ensuring that appropriate steps are taken as outlined in laws and constitutional provisions. Courts can also balance the lockdown measures with constitutional rights and freedoms (such as the right of access to justice), which are obviously limited by the measures.[84] On this last aspect, in many cases courts have done so with a great sense of responsibility and a loyal cooperation attitude (see section 3 above).

Therefore the active and independent role of the courts and, in particular, of the constitutional courts in times of crisis is essential. Constitutional courts can be "the forum to listen to experts, reduce the strongest forms of governmental inertia, coordinate the action between different levels of government and public entities, request explanations about the reason for their actions or omissions, and demand – while respecting margins of appreciation – that the fundamental rights of everyone be properly guaranteed",[85] especially of minorities and most vulnerable groups. Precisely for this reason it was so important to keep the courthouses open and operational in times of crisis.

---

84 See, amongst others, Cristie Ford, 'Rethinking Judicial Oversight in Time of Crisis' (*The Regulatory Review*, 5 May 2020) https://drive.google.com/file/d/1UfSczVnSj35Oz3ZKLX9UYfn13Dnt8pcJ/view accessed 31 July 2020; Romolo Donzelli, 'Emergenza pandemica e tutela giurisdizionale dei diritti' in Ermanno Calzolaio, Massimo Meccarelli, Stefano Pollastrelli (eds), *Il diritto nella pandemia. Temi, problemi, domande* (EUM 2020).

85 See, e.g. Lindsay F. Wiley and Stephen I. Vladeck, 'Coronavirus, Civil Liberties, and the Courts: The Case Against 'Suspending' Judicial Review' (2020) 133 Harv. L. Rev.; Andrés Cervantes, 'The Role of Constitutional Justice in Times of Crisis: The Case of Ecuador' (*Int'l J. Const. L. Blog*, 22 April 2020) http://www.iconnectblog.com/2020/04/the-role-of-constitutional-justice-in-times-of-crisis-the-case-of-ecuador/ accessed 9 June 2020. See, also, Rosalind Dixon, 'Creating dialogue about socioeconomic rights: Strong-form versus weak-form judicial review revisited' (2007) 5.3 IJCL 407.

HOW DID FRENCH ADMINISTRATIVE JUDGES HANDLE COVID-19?

Bénédicte Fauvarque-Cosson*

During the COVID-19 crisis, governments resorted to exceptional measures and restricted the fundamental rights of citizens in seeking to get control over the spread of the epidemic. Consequently, control over the governmental measures that were adopted during the Health State of Emergency was in great demand by citizens. In France, the existence of an administrative judiciary allows fast and efficient access to the judge (which is almost free) and ensures judicial control on public freedoms. French administrative courts, particularly the Conseil d'État, played a crucial role during this period. This was made possible thanks to efficient judicial practices which existed before the COVID-19 crisis, notably the accelerated procedure of "référés". This contribution analyses these practices over the first few months of the state of emergency in France (March–June 2020).

* Conseillère d'Etat, agrégée des facultés de droit, ancienne vice-présidente de l'ELI. I am grateful to Marc Clément, presiding judge at the administrative court of Lyon, Gaëlle Dumortier, conseillère d'Etat, Guillaume Halard, administrative judge, John Bell, professor (Cambridge) for their comments and reviews. This contribution is up to date as of July 2020.

1. INTRODUCTION

In May 2020, the European Law Institute (ELI) adopted Principles for the COVID-19 crisis,[1] a set of 15 principles, which are intended to guide European States, EU institutions and other bodies "with the object of ensuring that everything that is done accords with the rule of law and democratic values". Principle 5 is dedicated to the "*Justice system*" and its first paragraph provides:

> The judiciary should do all that is reasonably practicable to continue to conduct proceedings and trials, particularly through the use of secure video and other remote links where available to the courts. In any case, the judicial system should maintain a minimum level of operations to deal with urgent matters, safeguard the rule of law and provide proper remedies to litigants, provided that the right to a fair trial, including the right to defence, is not infringed. The restrictions on the operation of the judiciary must be immediately removed when the COVID-19 emergency permits.

On 18 June 2020, at an ELI webinar dedicated to the rule of law during and post COVID-19, the speakers were asked to concentrate on the judiciary and its independence and focus their attention upon the challenges in some Member States, especially on the Polish experience as it shows "how weaknesses in a judicial discipline system can be weaponised to seek to bend judges to a ruling party's political will". One participant suggested that many countries face similar situations to that of Poland whose constitution offers strong guarantees of judicial independence and that, consequently, the Polish experience can be a cautionary tale for other countries as well.[2] Although one can easily admit that risks are higher in times of crisis, from the perspective of Western jurisdictions, this sounded alarmist. Consequently, the purpose of this contribution is to show that, in France, in spite of the sanitary restrictions, the administrative judge, far from being prevented from exercising effective judicial review over the government's or local measures, became a key actor during the crisis.[3] The contribution also explains the specificity of its mission in summary proceedings (*référé*) and draw some lessons from this unprecedented period.

---

1 See their text here: https://www.europeanlawinstitute.eu/about-eli/covid-19-principles/ accessed 31 July 2020. It is to be hoped that these Principles will contribute to the development of a European vision of the judiciary's role in a democratic system (see especially Principle 5, titled "Justice system").

2 https://www.europeanlawinstitute.eu/newsevents/?tx_news_pi1%5B%40widget_0%5D%5BcurrentPage%5D=2&cHash=5ced4a0eb47f92f74f14d9ff2c632425 accessed 5 July 2020.

3 In countries, such as France, which separate administrative and "judicial" courts, judicial review over the decisions taken by authorities exercising executive powers is entrusted to the administrative judge.

2. THE FRENCH ADMINISTRATIVE JUDGE: A KEY ACTOR DURING THE CRISIS

2.1. AN OVERVIEW ON THE LEGAL FRAMEWORK

Under the terms of Article 11 of the Health State of Emergency Law, passed on 23 March 2020, the French Government was authorised to issue secondary legislation in order to regulate, anticipate and remedy issues linked to the crisis. Many pieces of secondary legislation have been issued, in a wide range of fields, such as labour law, education, etc. The Ordonnance No. 2020-305 of 25 March 2020, adapted the rules applicable before the administrative courts and contained provisions applicable to administrative courts.[4] As soon as the Health State of Emergency was adopted, the administrative courts activated the continuity plans they had previously adopted. In order to meet this task, and within the general framework of the procedure for urgent matters, called procedure of *référé*, the French administrative judge had to be flexible and innovative.

In France, administrative justice operates at three levels of court: the administrative tribunals, the administrative courts of appeal and the Conseil d'État. The French Conseil d'État has two main functions: it acts as an independent advisory body to the Government[5] and as the Supreme Court for administrative matters.[6] It is important to keep in mind that although it is a Supreme Court, the Conseil d'État, while it acts as an appeal court for the acts of entities that exercise delegated powers, is a first instance jurisdiction ("en premier ressort") when it exercises its judicial review upon administrative acts which have a national dimension (such as acts of the central administration). Claims related to hydroxychloroquine were thus brought to the Conseil d'État when they concerned national measures and to administrative tribunals when they related to actions to be taken by local authorities (such as the *agences régionales de santé*) or by a public hospital. Administrative tribunals, in their judicial review of the action of the prefects, regional health agencies, mayors, have rendered hundreds of *ordonnances* of *référé*.

---

4 In France, the word "ordonnance" is used to designate pieces of secondary legislation adopted by the government and also courts' decisions in summary proceedings.

5 During the COVID-19, the consultative sections examined 232 government's draft texts linked to the sanitary crisis, in very quick succession (their members met through videoconferences).

6 The Conseil d'État renders approximately 10,000 judgments. Around two-thirds of its docket are final appeals to the Supreme Court, challenging decisions by the administrative courts of appeal, decisions by specific courts ruling at last instance and certain judgments of the administrative courts ruling at first and last instance. During the COVID-19, hearings concerning these cases were postponed and judges continued to work remotely and through videoconferences.

One type of *référé*, called *référé suspension*, enables the judge to suspend an administrative act when there is a serious doubt about an administrative act's legality. Another, called *référé liberté*, enables the judge to order any measure necessary for safeguarding a fundamental freedom found seriously and manifestly illegally infringed by an administrative authority. Based on Article L. 521-2 *Code de justice administrative* (code of administrative justice), the *référé liberté* confers the judge a broad power of injunction. Its efficiency is reinforced by the fact that the judge's *ordonnance* is in principle rendered within 48 hours of the claim's introduction.

From 2000[7] to 2020, the number of ordonnances of *référé liberté* rendered by the Conseil d'État at first instance followed a decreasing trend: an average of 61 ordonnances were rendered annually from 2001–2010, against an average of 31 one from 2011–2019.[8] At the same time, due to the rise of ordonnances rendered by administrative tribunals (which increased from just under 800 in the first year to over 3,000 in 2010, to stabilise around this level until 2016, and started to rise again in the last three years), the activity of the Conseil d'État as a judge of summary proceedings, seized on appeal, reached around 200 ordonnances each year before the COVID-19 crisis.[9]

2.2. A SPECIFIC TASK FORCE WITHIN THE CONSEIL D'ÉTAT

In order to fulfil the formidable task it had to accomplish after the state of health emergency was created, the Conseil d'État constituted a task force of approximately 15 experienced judges (namely, the deputy presidents of the "section du contentieux", the presidents and some of the vice-presidents of each of its 10 chambers), under the authority of the president of the "section du contentieux".

From 13 March to 25 June 2020, 382 requests related to the COVID-19 crisis at the Conseil d'État, among which 230 were addressed to the *juge des référés*.[10] The vast majority of claimants opted for the *référé liberté* which gives the judge broad powers of injunction. They were individuals, businesses, associations, unions, etc. Some requests raised concrete problems (for instance, problems related to the organisation of hospitals, prisons, administrative detention centres).

The first *ordonnance* of the Conseil d'État, of 22 March 2020, set the general framework. It recalls that, under the specific procedure the *référé liberté*, the judge can "only order the emergency measures which appear to him likely to safeguard, within forty-eight hours, the fundamental freedom to which a severe

7 See Loi n° 2000-597 du 30 juin 2000 relative au référé devant les juridictions administratives.
8 Clément Malverti and Cyrille Beaufils, 'Le référé en liberté' (2020) AJDA 1154.
9 Clément Malverti and Cyrille Beaufils, 'Le référé en liberté' (2020) AJDA 1154.
10 Inconsistent applications were dismissed by a specific procedure.

and manifestly illegal infringement has been brought", and that "the manifestly illegal nature of the infringement must notably be assessed by taking into account the means available to the competent administrative authority and the measures it has, in this context, already taken".

While this *ordonnance* was issued by a collegiate panel of three judges, the others were rendered by a single judge. This does not mean that the judge was acting in isolation. In the exercise of his powers, the judge debated with colleagues on the points which necessitated greater consideration and relied on the acquis which had gradually been built up. Besides, public hearings have proved to be especially important in this crisis. It goes without saying that the hearings were organised in accordance with health requirements (on 22 March 2020, for the first time in its history, the Conseil d'État held its first videoconferences).

3. THE ROLE OF THE *JUGE DES RÉFÉRÉS* DURING THE COVID-19 CRISIS

3.1. A CONTEXTUAL APPROACH

In the procedure of *référé liberté*, the judge must verify whether a fundamental freedom has been manifestly and seriously infringed.[11] He/she must also establish that there is an urgency to rule and that the administration – by its actions or inaction – has seriously and manifestly unlawfully infringed a freedom which is fundamental. In doing so, the judge seeks to determine if the balance between liberties or fundamental rights is maintained, based on the existing context and the situation, at a given moment. In making his/her assessment of the situation, the judge thus takes into account the measures already adopted by the administration and the means it has effectively at its disposal.

The procedure of *référé* gives great importance to the public hearing where questions are posed to the parties in person (which is unusual in the French predominantly written procedure). Actually, during this period, the importance of those interactions was all the greater in that, having regard to the nature of the cases, the hearings most often led the administration to be challenged not by individuals, as is usually the case in a "référé liberté", but by associations,

---

[11] Baptiste Bonnet, 'Le Conseil d'Etat et le COVID 19. Quand le Conseil d'État porte l'État de droit sur ses épaules …' (2020) 22 JCPG 656. As well explained by Clément Malverti and Cyrille Beaufils, 'Le référé en liberté' (2020) AJDA 1154, in order to preserve the exceptional nature of this procedure, as the scope of interim measures was extended and the control of the *juge des référés* became stronger, the judge limited it to very urgent matters (with a strict interpretation of that condition) and only adopted the measures likely to be ordered in summary proceeding after having assessed, in consideration of the means available to the administration, whether there had been a serious and manifestly illegal violation of a fundamental freedom.

professional or union organisations, defending collective interests. French administrative law has wide rules on standing, such that many associations were able to bring actions for the interference with collective interests, rather than narrowly personal interests. The confrontation of the parties' views was crucial, and many questions were posed, notably to the administration. It also happened that the administration committed itself, during the hearing, to take certain measures (for example, to better track COVID-19 in prison) and that solutions were found there.

A specific difficulty the judge often encountered in that period was the various uncertainties it had to deal with: scientific uncertainties (for instance, the medical debates regarding the prescription of hydroxychloroquine), uncertainties on logistics (shortage of masks and tests) and, last but not least, uncertainties as to the evolution of the COVID-19 (should stricter or lighter measures be taken, in view of these evolutions?).

Facing all sorts of claims, the judge had to stay within his/her role. However, claimants and citizens asked the judge to endorse the role of politicians and parliamentarians.[12] This reached a point where the courtroom appeared "as the last forum of a democratic life partly suspended by the epidemic".[13] The judge's role is not that of a substitute for the government or legislator, nor is it that of a scientific expert – a role that in the midst of the scientific controversy on hydroxychloroquine, was also sometimes attributed by the claimants to the administrative judges.[14] In summary proceedings, the judge has wide powers and must therefore exercise them with great caution.

---

12 On the necessary safeguards to avoid such a confusion, see especially the developments of Clément Malverti and Cyril Beaufils, 'Le référé en liberté' (2020) AJDA 1154, in a paragraph entitled: "*Le prétoire ou le perchoir*?" and the solutions suggested by the authors.

13 Bernard Stirn, 'Le référé et le COVID' (2020) RFDA 634.

14 On 28 March 2020, in three distinct cases, the Conseil d'Etat rejected appeals requesting the State to produce, to requisite, to acquire or to widen the use of hydroxychloroquine (CE, 28 March 2020, *M. A.A. et autres, Mme A.A. et autres, Syndicat des Médecins Aix et Région et autres*, no 439765, no 439693, no 439726). On appeal of the hospital and the Minister of Solidarity and Health, the Conseil d'Etat (CE, 4 April 2020, *Centre hospitalier universitaire de la Guadeloupe et Ministre des solidarités et de la santé*, no 439904, no 439905) quashed a rather isolated decision of the administrative court of Guadeloupe which had ordered a hospital (CHU) and the *agence régionale de santé* (ARS) to order doses of hydroxychloroquine and azithromycin, as well as sufficient screening tests to cover the present and future needs of Guadeloupe. The Conseil d'Etat observed that the CHU had sufficient stock for the 20 or so patients already receiving this treatment, and that it had ordered sufficient doses of hydroxychloroquine and azythromycin to treat 200 to 400 potential new patients. It considered that the CHU and the ARS could not be criticised for not having ordered more of these treatments since they can only be administered to a limited number of patients and that several other molecules were undergoing clinical trials, the results of which were expected soon. In this "référé liberté", the Conseil d'Etat held that "if the administrative authority is entitled, when uncertainties remain as to the existence or scope of risks to human health, to take protective measures without having to wait until the reality and the seriousness of these risks are fully demonstrated, the existence of such uncertainties, in principle,

3.2. THE IMPACT OF THE EVOLUTION OF THE EPIDEMIC AND GOVERNMENTAL MEASURES ON THE DECISIONS RENDERED

From March to June 2020, two main phases can be identified. The first corresponds to the strict lockdown period and the second one to the progressive "*deconfinement*".

During the first phase (from the Health State of Emergency Law, from 23 March to mid-May), the epidemic was at its peak and strict measures were taken by the government.

The first claim brought before the Conseil d'État via a *référé liberté* was that of a Union of young doctors (*Syndicat des Jeunes Médecins*) which argued that the Prime Minister had showed a serious and manifestly illegal deficiency ("*carence*") by not deciding a "total lockdown" of the population throughout the territory.[15] It notably asked it to order the Prime Minister and the Minister of Health to adopt further restrictions so as to render such "total lockdown" possible, and to take measures capable of ensuring the production on an industrial scale of screening tests and of taking the regulatory measures suitable for ensuring the screening of medical staff. The Conseil d'État said that there was no such deficiency but enjoined the Prime Minister and the Minister of Health to "clarify, review or evaluate certain provisions of the decree of March 16, 2020 regulating movements of persons as part of the fight against the spread of the COVID-19 virus" (consequently, further restrictions were adopted to limit the practice of jogging). As regards the tests, it refused to order what had been requested. It referred to the statements of the Minister of Health and those made at the hearing and estimated that the authorities had made arrangements with all manufacturers in France and abroad to increase testing capacity and avoid delays. It decided that since the limitation of tests for health staff showing symptoms of the virus resulted from insufficient availability of materials, the request as regard this point could only be rejected having regard to the judge's powers in summary proceedings. Indeed, this ground of complaint was not one which a judge in summary proceedings could entertain since it concerns the exercise of discretionary power in the area of public health, rather than the direct infringement of fundamental rights.

This type of claim (requesting stricter lockdown measures) remained rather isolated since after the lockdown was decided by the French government, the great majority of claims requested the administrative judge to lift bans and restrictions on fundamental freedoms. From March to mid-May, when the risk of COVID-19 was very high, more than 150 claims were examined by the

prevents recognition of a serious and manifestly unlawful infringement of a fundamental freedom, justifying that the 'juge des référés' makes use of the powers which he derives from Article L 521-2 of the CJA" (non-official translation).

15 22 March 2020, *Syndicat Jeunes Médecins*, no 439674, B.

Conseil d'État (the most important decisions have been presented, in a simplified version, on its website[16]).

The Conseil d'État faced criticism for rejecting the vast majority of the claims during this period. Its unwillingness to challenge the government's measures and its refusal to use its powers to give injunctions to the government to take positive measures (for instance, when masks were still not available, it refused to give an injunction to deliver more masks to some professions that were particularly exposed) was sometimes perceived as a lack of independence from the government.[17] For a large part, criticism was based on a misunderstanding of the role of the judge in urgent summary proceedings. As the epidemic was declining in France, the first déconfinement measures were announced by the government on 11 May. Yet, many strict measures were maintained or put into place, among which some appeared inappropriate or disproportionate. Consequently, the Conseil d'État ordered the government to lift some bans or stop certain actions. Here are four examples.

- On 18 May 2020, the Conseil d'État enjoined the Prime Minister to modify, within eight days, the decree of 11 May 2020 by taking measures strictly proportionate to the health risks incurred and appropriate to the circumstances of time and place applicable at the beginning of *déconfinement*, so as to supervise gatherings and meetings in religious establishments. It recalled that freedom of worship, which is a fundamental freedom, also includes among its essential components the right to participate collectively in ceremonies, in particular in places of worship, provided this right is reconciled with the constitutional value of the protection of health and it found that this ban was incoherent since "common" meetings were tolerated with a maximum of 10 people.[18]
- On the same day (18 May 2020), the Conseil d'État ordered the Préfecture of Paris to immediately stop its use of drones to monitor whether health rules put in place during the lockdown were being respected. It considered that the conditions in which the drones were used amounted to processing of personal data and that the French privacy law (recently reformed) was

---

16 See: https://www.conseil-etat.fr/ accessed 2 October 2020.

17 This reached a point where the president of the *section du contentieux*, Jean-Denis Combrexelle, felt it necessary to explain to the citizens the role of the Conseil d'Etat, when it acts as a Supreme Court. In particular, he recalled that in order to ensure its essential missions, the administrative judge must preserve the balance between the necessity of safeguarding the general interest, especially public health and the protection of fundamental rights. See Jean-Denis Combrexelle, 'Les juges administratifs du Conseil d'Etat se situent loin des polémiques' *Le Monde* (12 April 2020) https://www.lemonde.fr/idees/article/2020/04/12/jean-denis-combrexelle-les-juges-administratifs-du-conseil-d-etat-se-situent-loin-des-polemiques_6036387_3232.html accessed 2 October 2020.

18 CE, 18 May 2020, *M. A F. et autres*, no 440366, no 440380, no 440410, no 440531, no 440550, no 440562, no 440563, no 440590.

not being respected. Consequently, it ordered the government to cease such surveillance as long as a decree had not been taken after the opinion of the CNIL (the French data protection authority), or until the drones are equipped with a device making it impossible to identify the people filmed.[19]

- On 13 June, after anti-racism marches took place in Paris, the Conseil d'État ordered the lifting of the ban on protests in public places of gatherings of more than 10 persons. The ordonnance recalls that "The freedom to protest is a fundamental right" and decided that "the ban on protests in public places is not justified by the health risks – except when physical distancing measures cannot be respected, or the event is likely to bring together more than 5,000 people".[20]
- On 26 June, the Conseil d'Etat considered that the use of thermal cameras by the municipality of Lisses was lawful within a building of the municipality and unlawful in schools.[21] The reasons for this distinction are that when entering the municipal building, a person was free to decide not to use the thermal camera and no data was registered, while pupils and staff could only enter the school after they had been controlled by the thermal camera. Besides, even though the data were not registered, a person, acting on behalf of the one which had decided the use of the camera, could take note of the data, to the effect that this constituted data processing within the meaning of the GDPR and manifestly infringed the right to respect for private life.

Taken as a whole, the decisions rendered by the Conseil d'État during the lockdown and *déconfinement* periods, far from weakening the rule of law, have reinforced it.[22] The Government focus on efficiency had to be balanced against fundamental rights in a proportionate way. The Conseil d'Etat did not restrict its intervention to ensuring the existence of the legal competence of the administration to act (*l'état de droit* in the narrow sense), but ensured proportionate respect for fundamental rights (the rule of law in the wide sense exhibited in the Delhi Declaration of 1959).

---

19 CE, 18 May 2020, *association "La Quadrature du Net" et la Ligue des droits de l'homme*, no 440442, no 440445.

20 CE, 13 June 2020, *Ligue des droits de l'homme, Confédération generale du travail et autres*, no 440846, no 440856, no 441015. The decree adopted immediately after by the government was still very restrictive, and a new request was brought to the Conseil d'Etat which suspended some provisions of the decree (CE 6 July 2020, Confédération générale du travail et autres, Association SOS Racisme, nos 441257, 441263, 441384).

21 CE, 26 June 2020, *Ligue des droits de l'homme*, no 441065.

22 As Lord Thomas pointed out while concluding an ELI webinar on "check and balances (Legislator/Judiciary)", "France has shown how courts can hold governments to account". See also, during this webinar, the presentation made by Bruno Lasserre, Vice-president of the Conseil d'État. https://www.europeanlawinstitute.eu/news-events/news-contd/news/eli-webinar-on-back-to-normal-checks-and-balances-legislatorjudiciary/?tx_news_pi1%5Bcontroller%5D=News&tx_news_pi1%5Baction%5D=detail&cHash=5ac6bc5259471637044b14fab5ad44a1 accessed 2 October 2020.

4. CONCLUSION

As of today, the political focus is on ensuring a quick post-pandemic recovery: Member States and the EU institutions will face new challenges for the application of the "rule of law". It is to be hoped that the epidemic will continue its decline and no more confinement measures will be needed.[23] However, return to normality does not simply mean return to the past. Evaluation is needed in order to draw lessons from this crisis, improve judicial practices, invest in more digital tools to enable all courts to continue their activities,[24] and improve the functioning of innovative measures that have proved efficient (such as distance hearings).

Judicial activity does not take place in a vacuum of legal norms (quite the contrary). However, we have experienced that, as detailed as they are, these norms can never provide for precise answers to all the practical questions that are posed, particularly when an epidemic surges so unexpectedly (for instance, there was no answer in the law as to the specific question on how to deal with a shortage of masks or tests). In such a crisis, the divide between politics and judicial activity is easily blurred. This is the reason why it is important to recall the distinctive features of judicial activity which are particularly prominent in the urgent summary procedures (*référé*) in France. A first feature is that judicial activity operates on a case-by-case basis and is, by nature, incremental and also more flexible, since it must adapt itself to a given situation, than governmental or legislative acts. A second feature is that judges listen to the parties and decide on the basis of information acquired in the course of the adversarial process (the hearing phase proved particularly important for the judges during this critical period). A third feature is that when applying the law, judges, who search for cohesion and proportionality, are prepared to intervene at a period when the normal political accountability of the administration is not operating, because of the exceptional suspension of political institutions. The separation of powers is not fixed but is flexible. Finally, one of the lessons that can be drawn from this crisis is how important it is to explain, generally, the limits of the judges' powers – particularly in a *procedure de référé* – and comment on such or such judicial decision by explaining not only the solution it adopted but its ways of reasoning (it is indeed difficult to understand the process that led to the decision by just looking at the final part of the decision, called *dispositif*). The rule of law can only flourish in a country whose citizens are conscious of the constraints and limits of the judges' role and feel collectively responsible for the implementation

23 See Article 15 of the ELI Principles for the COVID-19 Crisis.

24 Given the number of cases that could not be processed and the number of adjournments of hearings, the question of whether certain types of cases will need to be prioritised over others is now raised in some jurisdictions.

of the concept, making it an integral part of their own legal, political and social culture. As the fear is growing, within and beyond Europe, that governments use the sanitary threats to enforce measures which violate fundamental rights (for instance, contact-tracing applications that do not comply with the regulatory framework on privacy),[25] we need more citizens educated on the role of the judiciary.

---

[25] The French law on the use of *StopCOVID* application was examined not only by the French regulatory authority, but also by the Conseil d'État and by the Constitutional Court. See Ollia Horton, 'French MPs call for vote on StopCOVID mobile phone app over privacy concerns' *RFI* (21 April 2020) http://www.rfi.fr/en/france/20200421-france-coronavirus-smart-phone-app-tracking-technology-opposition-calls-for-vote-privacy accessed 5 July 2020.

THE REPRESSIVE NATURE OF SELECTED COVID-19 REGULATIONS IN THE POLISH LEGAL SYSTEM

The Question of Constitutionality

Mikołaj Małecki and Marek Sławiński*

The subject of this contribution is the question of the constitutionality of the sanctions for violation of restrictions and prohibitions introduced during the outbreak of the SARS-CoV-2 coronavirus epidemic in Poland. The starting point for our considerations is the distinction made by the Polish Constitution between extraordinary and ordinary measures in dealing with dangers. Extraordinary measures (which include, inter alia, *the state of natural disaster) allow for more severe limitations of constitutional rights and freedoms than is permitted by the ordinary ones. The state of epidemic introduced in Poland on 31 March 2020, is an ordinary measure. However, the comparison between sanctions used during this state, and sanctions that it is possible to impose during the extraordinary state of natural disaster shows that the former are more severe than the latter. This observation leads to the conclusion that the sanctions of the state of epidemic*

---

* Both authors, Jagiellonian University. This contribution is a result of the research project "Restrictions and Repressions of the State of Epidemic (Legal Aspects of Society's Functioning During and After Pandemic)" funded by Jagiellonian University as part of SocietyNow!#1 Research University Excellence Initiative.

are in breach of one of the basic rules that govern the limitation of constitutional rights and freedoms in the Polish Constitution, i.e. the proportionality rule.

1. INTRODUCTION

Shortly after the first appearance of SARS-CoV-2 coronavirus in Europe, Polish authorities undertook measures aimed at preventing the spread of the epidemic and minimising its negative impact. Among other things, a set of new legal provisions were adopted that have since been regulating the functioning of State institutions and various areas of social life. In many cases these regulations have a serious impact on everyday life, limiting the way in which even basic affairs, such as working, shopping, or simply moving from one area to another, can be performed. There is no doubt that these restrictions were introduced with good intentions in mind. Their main goal is to protect the public against the risk of contracting a dangerous and deadly virus. The practical realisation of this goal, however, did not avoid shortcomings, including serious ones that raise the question of their constitutionality.

One of the issues concerns legal sanctions that can be imposed on those individuals who violate new epidemic restrictions. Parliament chose the financial administrative responsibility in the form of administrative fines issued by the health inspectors. In this contribution, we will take a closer look at these fines by situating them within a broader, constitutional framework. In our opinion, their introduction for violation of epidemic restrictions does not meet the constitutional requirements of proportional limitation of rights and freedoms.

This contribution discusses the issue that arose within the Polish legal system. Despite this narrow approach, our considerations may still be of interest to a wider audience. We present how the Polish legislature faced the challenges posed by the coronavirus outbreak, especially the need to find a balance between the epidemic restrictions and the basic rights and freedoms of individuals. In this context, we offer the considerations concerning the role of the proportionality rule and its use. Although our discussion is not of a comparative legal nature, it provides material for such an approach.

2. STATE OF NATURAL DISASTER VERSUS STATE OF EPIDEMIC

The Constitution of the Republic of Poland of 2 April 1997 (the Polish Constitution)[1] provides that in the event of a certain type of danger it is possible

[1] Journal of Laws of 1997, No. 78, item 483, with subsequent amendments. English translation is available at the official website of Sejm (the lower house of Polish parliament) https://www.sejm.gov.pl/prawo/konst/angielski/kon1.htm accessed 9 July 2020.

to introduce extraordinary measures that allow the authorities to temporarily establish a special way of functioning of the State. According to Article 228 section 1 of the Polish Constitution: "In situations of a particular danger, if ordinary constitutional measures are inadequate, any of the following appropriate extraordinary measures may be introduced: martial law, a state of emergency or a state of natural disaster".[2] As we can see, the Polish Constitution distinguishes three extraordinary measures depending on the type of actual or impending danger. For the current situation of the coronavirus outbreak, the state of natural disaster is of the most relevance.

The constitutional provisions do not define what a natural disaster is, giving only two examples that can qualify as such an event. Article 232 of the Polish Constitution states: "In order to prevent or remove the consequences of a natural catastrophe or a technological accident exhibiting characteristics of a natural disaster, the Council of Ministers may introduce, for a definite period no longer than 30 days, a state of natural disaster in a part of or upon the whole territory of the State. An extension of a state of natural disaster may be made with the consent of the Sejm [i.e. the lower house of Polish parliament – M.M., M.S.]". From the Constitution's point of view, a natural disaster is something more than "an ordinary" natural catastrophe or technological accident. In other words, a natural disaster is an event characterised by such features that clearly distinguish it from typical dangerous or harmful situations caused by natural forces or technological defects.[3] This leads to the question of whether the current coronavirus outbreak could be considered a natural disaster in the constitutional sense.

In our opinion, the answer cannot be other than positive. As the scholars explain, a natural disaster mentioned in Article 232 of the Polish Constitution is an occurrence that has the following features.[4] First, it is a sudden and random event caused by the forces of nature. Second, this event poses a serious threat to important values such as life, health, property, natural environment, etc. Third, it is a widespread event, thus affecting (or having the ability to affect) a large number of people. The current coronavirus outbreak in Poland meets all of these conditions. The novelty of SARS-CoV-2 virus, its sudden appearance, high contagion rate and rapid spread throughout the country combined with the lack of known effective treatment pose a very serious threat to the safety and well-being of the Polish citizens.

---

2 For the translation of the Polish Constitution we use the translation from the official Sejm website https://www.sejm.gov.pl/prawo/konst/angielski/kon1.htm accessed 9 July 2020.

3 Because of the vagueness and brevity of the quoted article, the explanation of what exactly is this added value that constitutes a natural disaster rests solely on the law scholars and the judiciary.

4 See Piotr Tuleja in Piotr Tuleja (ed), *Konstytucja Rzeczypospolitej Polskiej. Komentarz* (Wolters Kluwer Polska 2019) 661–662, Sławomir Steinborn in Marek Safjan, Leszek Bosek (eds), *Konstytucja RP. Komentarz*, vol II (C.H.Beck 2016) 1625–1626.

Despite all these factors, the authorities decided not to introduce the extraordinary measure of the state of natural disaster. Instead, another solution was employed. The Act of 5 December 2008 on Preventing and Combating Infections and Infectious Diseases in Humans (the Act on Preventing Infections)[5] allows the authorities to introduce a state of epidemic. This state, according to Article 2 point 22 of the Act on Preventing Infections, is defined as: "the legal situation introduced in a given area in connection with an outbreak of an epidemic in order to take anti-epidemic and preventive measures specified in the Act to minimise the effects of an epidemic". On 31 March 2020, the Council of Ministers issued a Regulation that introduced the state of SARS-CoV-2 epidemic on the entire territory of Poland.[6]

If the authorities reacted to the spread of coronavirus by using one of the available solutions, where lies the problem? First, it must be emphasised that the state of epidemic referred to in the Act on Preventing Infections is not identical to the state of natural disaster referred to in the Polish Constitution. Both states are similar in function (they can be used to prevent or eliminate a dangerous situation such as virus outbreak) but differ in their legal status. To explain this, let us go back to Article 228 section 1 of the Polish Constitution. It states that extraordinary measures can only be applied "if ordinary constitutional measures are inadequate". Therefore, the Polish Constitution allows for the distinction between extraordinary and ordinary ways of reacting to danger. Moreover, Article 228 section 1 contains a closed list of measures that are considered to be extraordinary. This means that all other solutions aimed at managing dangerous events fall into the category of ordinary measures. As a result, on the basis of the conceptual framework of the Polish Constitution, the state of natural disaster is an *extraordinary measure* while the state of epidemic is an *ordinary* one.

One of the main differences between extraordinary and ordinary measures lies in the scope of restrictions that it is possible to impose upon individuals. The general rule for limitation of constitutional rights and freedoms is set out in Article 31 section 3 of the Polish Constitution. According to this provision: "Any limitation upon the exercise of constitutional freedoms and rights may be imposed only by statute, and only when necessary in a democratic State for the protection of its security or public order, or to protect the natural environment,

5 Consolidated text in Journal of Laws of 2019, item 1239, with subsequent amendments.

6 See Regulation of the Council of Ministers of 31 March 2020 on Introducing Restrictions, Orders, and Prohibitions in Relation to the Occurrence of a State of Epidemic (Journal of Laws of 2020, item 566, with subsequent amendments). It is worth mentioning that this Regulation has been subjected to many amendments since the date of its issuance. Currently in force (9 July 2020) is Regulation of the Council of Ministers of 19 June 2020 on Introducing Restrictions, Orders, and Prohibitions in Relation to the Occurrence of a State of Epidemic (Journal of Laws of 2020, item 1066, with subsequent amendments).

health or public morals, or the freedoms and rights of other persons. Such limitations shall not violate the essence of freedoms and rights". This provision is commonly called the proportionality rule. Because of its general character, this rule applies to the limitations of constitutional rights and freedoms imposed via ordinary measures. As for the extraordinary ones, the legal framework is a bit different. First of all, the Polish Constitution provides a version of proportionality rule specifically tailored for the cases in which extraordinary measures are employed. As stated in Article 228 section 5: "Actions undertaken as a result of the introduction of any extraordinary measure shall be proportionate to the degree of threat and shall be intended to achieve the swiftest restoration of conditions allowing for the normal functioning of the State". The quoted provision, due to the fact that it applies only to cases of extraordinary measures, is considered *lex specialis* to the general proportionality rule stated in Article 31 section 3 of the Polish Constitution.

For the sake of brevity let us call the latter "the ordinary proportionality rule", and the rule stated in Article 228 section 5 "the extraordinary proportionality rule". The fundamental differences between them can be summarised in three following points.

1. *Different context of proportionality assessment:* The ordinary proportionality rule requires that the limitation of constitutional rights and freedoms be evaluated in terms of its necessity in a democratic State, whereas the extraordinary proportionality rule requires this evaluation to be done in relation to the degree of an actual or impending threat.
2. *Different justification for the limitation of constitutional rights and freedoms*: The ordinary proportionality rule states that limitations can be justified by the need to protect at least one of the values explicitly mentioned in Article 31 section 3 of the Polish Constitution, namely, the security of the democratic State, public order, natural environment, health, public morals, freedoms or rights of other persons. The extraordinary proportionality rule mentions only one justificatory value: the restoration of the normal functioning of the State.
3. *Different scope of possible limitations*: The ordinary proportionality rule allows for limitation only to a certain degree. The limitations of constitutional rights and freedoms cannot violate "the essence of freedoms and rights". In other words, fundamental rights cannot be abolished or restricted in a way that would render them virtually ineffective. This clause is missing in Article 228 section 5 of the Polish Constitution. Therefore, during the application of extraordinary measures the constitutional rights and freedoms can be limited to a much greater degree, including their temporary abolishment. Of course, this does not mean that the authorities can act as they deem fit. In other words, the authorities can limit rights and freedoms to a higher degree during the application of

extraordinary measures but these limitations must always fall within the framework set by the constitutional provisions. Article 233 of the Polish Constitution provides a safeguard mechanism by imposing restrictions on the extraordinary proportionality rule. In the case of the state of natural disaster, which is our main point of interest in this contribution, section 3 of this Article precisely indicates constitutional rights and freedoms that can be limited using the extraordinary proportionality rule. This list is as follows:

a) freedom of economic activity (Art 22 of the Polish Constitution);
b) personal freedom (Art 41 sections 1, 3 and 5 of the Polish Constitution);
c) inviolability of the home (Art 50 of the Polish Constitution);
d) freedom of movement and sojourn on the territory of the Republic of Poland (Art 52 section 1 of the Polish Constitution);
e) the right to strike (Art 59 section 3 of the Polish Constitution);
f) the right of ownership (Art 64 of the Polish Constitution);
g) freedom to work (Art 65 section 1 of the Polish Constitution);
h) the right to safe and hygienic conditions of work (Art 66 section 1 of the Polish Constitution);
i) the right to rest (Art 66 section 2 of the Polish Constitution).

Any other constitutional right or freedom can be limited only in accordance with the proportionality rule stated in Article 31 section 3 of the Polish Constitution. Thus, we can clearly see the most important difference between the state of natural disaster and the state of epidemic. Because the latter is an ordinary solution, the authorities may limit rights and freedoms only according to the ordinary proportionality rule. The extraordinary proportionality rule from Article 228 section 5 of the Polish Constitution, as well as the enumeration from Article 233 section 3, do not apply here.

3. CHARACTERISTICS OF THE STATE OF EPIDEMIC

Let us now take a closer look at the restrictions implemented during the current state of epidemic. As we have mentioned earlier, this state was introduced in Poland on 31 March 2020. The Regulation issued by the Council of Ministers at that date contained a number of prohibitions and restrictions which have been the subject of many changes since then. It is not necessary to enlist them all or to outline precisely how they have changed in time. The presentation of chosen examples considered to be the most inconvenient and burdensome will be sufficient. Our main focus in this contribution is not on restrictions and prohibitions, but on sanctions that can be imposed for their violation. What follows is a list of various provisions that were introduced at the initial stage of the state of epidemic and were addressed to individuals.[7] Some of these are still in force, while others were repealed.

1. A prohibition on movement in public space except for conducting professional affairs, volunteering in affairs related to combating the epidemic, conducting religious affairs, or "satisfying the necessary needs associated with current matters of everyday life".[8]
2. A prohibition on the assembly and participation in any events, meetings, or gatherings regardless of their type except for meetings with relatives, persons living in the same household, or as a part of professional activity.[9]
3. A requirement to keep a distance of at least two metres between persons when in public space.[10]
4. A prohibition on the use of public green and leisure areas such as parks, promenades, boulevards, botanical or zoological gardens, or beaches.[11]
5. Limits on the maximum number of persons that can be at the same time in public transportation, shops, post offices, and marketplaces.[12]
6. A prohibition addressed to persons under 18 years of age on movement in public space without the supervision of a person exercising parental authority, legal guardian, or another adult.[13]

Along with these restrictions, sanctions for their violation were introduced in the form of the administrative fines imposed by sanitary inspectors. Two provisions are of importance here:

1. Article 15zzzn section 1 of the Act of 2 March 2020 on Special Solutions Concerning the Prevention, Counteraction and Combating COVID-19, Other Contagious Diseases and Crisis Situations Caused by Them (the Act on COVID-19)[14] which described the behaviour consisting in breach of the rules of hospitalisation, quarantine, or isolation.
2. Article 48a of the Act on Preventing Infections which described behaviour consisting in breach of restrictions introduced during the state of epidemic.[15]

---

[7] In this contribution, we leave aside restrictions and prohibitions addressed to business entities.

[8] Repealed.

[9] Partially in force at the date of writing (9 July 2020).

[10] In force at the date of writing (9 July 2020).

[11] Repealed.

[12] Partially in force at the date of writing (9 July 2020).

[13] Repealed.

[14] Journal of Laws of 2020, item 374, with subsequent amendments.

[15] It is worth emphasising that Article 48a was added only recently and entered into force on 1 April 2020. In its original wording, the Act on Preventing Infections did not have any provisions on the administrative fines.

In both cases, the default amount of fine that can be issued is up to PLN 30,000 with the lower limit ranging from PLN 5,000 to 10,000.[16] For example, in case of breaching the prohibition on movement in public space, the sanitary inspector may issue a fine from PLN 5,000 to 30,000.[17] In cases of violation of the prohibition on the use of public green areas the fine is even higher (from PLN 10,000 up to 30,000).[18] As a general rule, each violation is subject to a separate fine and their amount is added. Therefore, depending on the number of violated restrictions, a given individual may be subjected to fine even up to PLN 100,000 in total.[19]

This short exposition allows us to emphasise two important observations. First, the restrictions that accompany the state of epidemic are aimed at the basic activities of everyday life. Because of that, they are perceived as burdensome interference with individual rights and freedoms. Second, the violations of these restrictions are sanctioned by relatively high administrative fines which can easily amount to even higher quotas.[20]

4. THE QUESTION OF PROPORTIONALITY

After this brief presentation of restrictions and sanctions introduced during the state of epidemic, we can now move to the question of their constitutionality. We have stated above that the Polish Constitution distinguishes extraordinary measures from the ordinary ones. One of the key differences between them lies in the acceptable scope of limitation of constitutional rights and freedoms. In the case of ordinary measures, this scope is designated by the proportionality rule stated in Article 31 section 3 of the Polish Constitution (the ordinary proportionality rule, as we have called it). Therefore, the appropriate constitutional standard for the assessment of the administrative fines introduced during current state of epidemic is given by this rule. In our opinion, an important part of this assessment is the comparison between the sanctions in question and sanctions that can be imposed during the relevant extraordinary measure of the state of

---

16 According to the information published by the National Bank of Poland, the average exchange rate from EUR to PLN on 24 July 2020, was EUR 1 = PLN 4,4117. We will use this rate here. Therefore, the default amount of fine mentioned above equals EUR 6,810.36, and the lower limit equals from EUR 1,135.06 to 2,270.12.

17 EUR 1,135.06 to 6,810.36.

18 EUR 2,270.12 to 6,810.36.

19 EUR 2,2701.2.

20 This severity is clearly visible when we compare the upper limits of these fines to the average gross wage in Poland. In the first quarter of 2020 this wage was PLN 5,331.47 (= EUR 1,208.48). See Communicate of the President of Statistics Poland of 12 May 2020 on the average gross wage in first quarter 2020 (The Official Journal of the Republic of Poland "Monitor Polski" of 2020, item 412).

natural disaster. Without taking this comparative perspective into account, the proportionality evaluation will be incomplete. Since this issue plays a central role in our argument, we will discuss it in more detail.

As we have stated above, the Polish Constitution employs the distinction between extraordinary and ordinary measures. The rationale behind it lies in the recognition of a simple fact that dangerous situations may differ significantly from one another. Some of them will not be so significant, while others will pose a serious threat to the functioning of the State. For this reason, we can organise dangerous events, starting with those that are less harmful and ending with the most serious ones.

Of course, it is impossible to precisely predict in advance how dangerous a particular event will be. However, we do not need such a degree of accuracy. Even the basic layout of a general hierarchy of dangerous situations will be sufficient. This is exactly the role of the constitutional framework of extraordinary and ordinary measures. It helps to delineate two broad categories of harmful events. At the same time, this framework provides and distinguishes two types of measures that can be applied to corresponding types of danger as their countermeasures.

According to Article 228 section 1 of the Polish Constitution, the extraordinary measures can only be introduced if ordinary measures are inadequate. In other words, the former are to be applied when dangerous events cannot be sufficiently managed by the latter. This establishes the relation between the discussed measures. The ordinary measures are considered to be a standard response to dangerous events, whereas the extraordinary ones are treated as a last resort. Because of this, the extraordinary measures can be considered as a point of reference. There is nothing more extraordinary provided by the Polish Constitution than those measures, and they apply only to the events in which the degree of danger is far above what can be found in typical cases. To put it simply, they constitute the upper limit of the spectrum of possible responses to dangerous situations. Everything below this limit is an ordinary measure.

What consequences can we derive from this constitutional framework for the issue of proportionality of sanctions? As we already know from the comparison between Article 31 section 3 and Article 228 section 5 of the Polish Constitution, the extraordinary measures allow for a larger degree of limitation of the constitutional rights and freedoms than the ordinary ones. In other words, the maximum scope of limitation in the case of the ordinary proportionality rule is below the maximum scope of limitation in the case of the extraordinary proportionality rule. Therefore, in general, ordinary measures should not be more severe than their extraordinary counterparts. Because a legal sanction is a limitation of a particular right or freedom, we can formulate the above statement as follows: in general, the ordinary measures should not be equipped with more severe sanctions than the extraordinary measures. Let us consider the following example to better grasp this point.

Let us assume that we have the ordinary measure and the extraordinary one as a means of coping with a particular type of danger. Both measures introduce restrictions and limitations, violations of which are sanctioned. It happens that the ordinary measure employs more severe sanctions than the relevant extraordinary one. If this ordinary measure would prove to be inadequate in coping with danger, then the extraordinary solutions will apply. However, this would result in quite an unusual situation. On the one hand, the authorities admit that the degree of danger is high enough to introduce the extraordinary measure. On the other hand, the employed sanctions change from the more severe to the less severe ones. There are two possible ways to assess this situation:

1. The ordinary measure uses sanctions that are too severe for its purpose, which is for coping with a standard level of danger.
2. The extraordinary measure uses sanctions that are less severe than needed for its purpose, which is for coping with the levels of danger that cannot be sufficiently contained by the ordinary measure.

This comparison leads to the conclusion that either the extraordinary measure is not extraordinary as it is supposed to be, or the ordinary measure is more extraordinary than it should be. Because of the need to address this type of problem, the evaluation of proportionality of the ordinary measures must also take into account their relation to the relevant extraordinary measures. If the ordinary measure exhibits characteristics proper to the extraordinary one, then this is a strong indication that in this particular case the constitutional hierarchy of measures could have been reversed. In general, such a situation may prove to be a circumvention of the constitutional provisions concerning the extraordinary measures. In the case of a particular type of measures such as sanctions, this situation also raises the question of proportionality in terms of why a given ordinary measure uses a more severe solution than its extraordinary counterpart. The proportionality evaluation cannot be made in isolation. The Polish Constitution sets out a framework within which extraordinary and ordinary measures have their respective places. These measures differ in their characteristic features, one of which is the possible scope of limitation of constitutional rights and freedoms. Therefore, to properly assess the proportionality of a given measure it must be established that it is properly placed in this framework. In consequence, the following conclusion can be made. Limitations of constitutional rights and freedoms imposed via ordinary measures cannot be *more severe* than those which can be imposed via extraordinary measures. Any other situation raises serious doubts about the constitutionality of such sanctions.[21]

[21] For more on this matter, see the Judgment of the Polish Constitutional Tribunal of 21 April 2009, K 50/07 (OTK-A ZU 2009, No. 4, item 51).

To summarise this part, the assessment of the proportionality of sanctions introduced during the state of epidemic must take into account two factors: (1) the content of the provisions in question, and (2) their comparison with sanctions that it is possible to impose during the state of natural disaster.[22] In what follows, we will give an outline of such an assessment. First, we will briefly present the sanctions that it is possible to impose during the extraordinary state of natural disaster (section 5). Next, we will show similarities and differences between both types of sanctions (section 6), which will allow us to evaluate them according to the theoretical framework presented above (section 7).

5. SANCTIONS OF THE STATE OF NATURAL DISASTER

The constitutional provisions do not prescribe any specific legal sanctions that may be used during each of the extraordinary states. According to Article 228 section 3 of the Polish Constitution, this matter is left to be specified by the statute.[23] In the case of the state of natural disaster, the statute in question is the Act of 18 April 2002 on the State of Natural Disaster.[24] Its provisions give a general outline of what is considered by the authorities to be an adequate solution for coping with the danger posed by various natural catastrophes or technological accidents. Article 21 section 1 of this Act contains a list of restrictions and prohibitions that can be imposed during the state of natural disaster. It is worth mentioning that this is not a complete enumeration. Due to the dynamic and unpredictable nature of a natural disaster, it is impossible to accurately predict in advance what type of measures will be needed to prevent or to remove the consequences of such a disaster. Thus, it is also impossible to indicate what type of restrictions will be necessary. Because of that, the rule of the extraordinary proportionality from Article 228 section 5 of the Polish Constitution applies. During the application of the state of natural disaster any action can be undertaken by the authorities as long as it is proportionate to the impending or actual danger.

As we have already pointed out, the coronavirus outbreak could be considered a natural disaster in a constitutional sense. Therefore, all types of restrictions that are currently implemented under the state of epidemic could also be

22 As stated earlier, the state of natural disaster is the only extraordinary measure that can be taken into account when dealing with the coronavirus outbreak.

23 "The principles for activity by organs of public authority as well as the degree to which the freedoms and rights of persons and citizens may be subject to limitation for the duration of a period requiring any extraordinary measures shall be established by statute."

24 Consolidated text in Journal of Laws of 2017, item 1897.

imposed during the state of natural disaster, if they would be still considered adequate to the degree of danger.[25]

Violation of restrictions that can be introduced during the state of natural disaster is subject to sanctions. According to Article 27 section 1 of the Act on the State of Natural Disaster, such behaviour constitutes a petty offence. Because of that, the only sanctions that can currently be imposed are:

1. *the arrest* which consists of the deprivation of liberty from 5 to 30 days,
2. *fine* from PLN 20 to 5,000.[26]

6. SIMILARITIES AND DIFFERENCES BETWEEN THE SANCTIONS

Now we can move to the comparison between the sanctions introduced during the state of epidemic and those that can be imposed during the state of natural disaster. In general, three similarities and two differences can be pointed out. Let us begin with the former.

6.1. SIMILARITIES

First of all, both sanctions have an *identical purpose*. They are aimed at preventing individuals from violating given restrictions and serve as a form of punishment for violations that have already happened. It is worth emphasising that sanctions in question do not perform any other function, in particular they do not restore the state from before the violation or do not compensate for any damage caused by this violation.

Second, both sanctions are *imposed for the same type of behaviour*. If we look at these sanctions from a general perspective, then we can say that they are imposed for one type of behaviour, namely, violation of restrictions or prohibitions introduced during a given state (be it the state of epidemic or the state of natural disaster). There is no doubt that from this general point of view both sanctions are identical. Furthermore, if we go into detail to exactly determine particular types of sanctioned behaviour, then we will notice

25 It is also worth mentioning that list provided by Article 21 section 1 of the Act on the State of Natural Disaster explicitly mentions some of the restrictions that were introduced during the current state of an epidemic. For example, restrictions on movement, organization or participation in mass events, or staying in certain places or areas (see Article 21 section 1 points 13–15).

26 EUR 4.54 to 1,135.06.

another similarity. The restrictions that can be imposed during the state of epidemic and the state of natural disaster are to a great extent identical.

This observation leads us to the third similarity. The purpose of the introduction of restrictions and prohibitions during the state of epidemic and the state of natural disaster is to protect the important values, such as life, health, or well-being of the individuals. Therefore, the sanctions imposed for violation of these restrictions can be perceived as *protecting the same values*, although indirectly.

6.2. DIFFERENCES

Moving on to the differences between sanctions in question it should be noted that they are examples of two different types of legal responsibility. Sanctions of the state of natural disaster constitute *liability for petty offences* while sanctions of the state of epidemic constitute *financial administrative responsibility*. This distinction has very important and far-reaching consequences.

Liability for petty offences is governed by the same principles as criminal liability. In fact, the former is commonly considered a "softer" or "lighter" version of the latter.[27] As far as the Polish Constitution is concerned, liability for petty offences is regarded as a type of criminal liability.[28] Because of that, all constitutional provisions concerning the latter also apply to the former, especially the principle of legality (*nullum crimen, nulla poena sine lege*)[29] and the requirement of guilt.[30] The procedure in which liability in question is imposed closely resembles the criminal one with all its guarantees, such as the right of defence or presumption of innocence.[31] Because of the nature of petty offences, which are considered to be less harmful than crimes, there is a possibility to impose this liability via the penalty ticket issued by the police.

---

27 Provisions of the Polish Criminal Code (Act of 6 June 1997, Journal of Laws of 1997, No. 88, item 553, with subsequent amendments) and the Polish Code of Petty Offences (Act of 20 May 1971, Consolidated text in Journal of Laws of 2019, item 821, with subsequent amendments) are to a great extent similar.

28 See, e.g. the Judgment of the Polish Constitutional Tribunal of 8 July 2003, P 10/02 (OTK-A ZU 2003, No. 6, item 62). This view is commonly accepted by the legal scholars and the judiciary.

29 See Article 42 section 1 of the Polish Constitution: "Only a person who has committed an act prohibited by a statute in force at the moment of commission thereof, and which is subject to a penalty, shall be held criminally responsible."

30 See Article 42 section 3 of the Polish Constitution: "Everyone shall be presumed innocent of a charge until his guilt is determined by the final judgment of a court."

31 Again, the Polish Code of Criminal Procedure (Act of 6 June 1997, Consolidated text in Journal of Laws of 2020, item 30, with subsequent amendments) is very similar to the Polish Code of Petty Offences Procedure (Act of 17 October 2001, Consolidated text in Journal of Laws of 2020, item 729, with subsequent amendment).

However, the individual always has the right to refuse this ticket, and then the case is tried by the court. Therefore, the imposition of liability for petty offences is part of the administration of justice, as stated in Article 175 section 1 of the Polish Constitution.[32]

On the other hand, the status of *financial administrative responsibility* has been a subject of a dispute between Polish legal scholars and the judiciary for a long time.[33] Despite all the controversial issues, it is commonly accepted that this type of responsibility is something different from criminal liability or liability for petty offences.[34] In consequence, the principles and constitutional standards are also considered to be different.[35] First, the requirement of guilt is absent.[36] As a result, financial administrative responsibility is often construed as strict liability, based only on the fact of the violation of a particular legal norm. Second, there is no constitutional requirement of presumption of innocence. Therefore, the procedure in which financial administrative responsibility is imposed differs from the criminal one.[37] Third, the application of this responsibility does not fall

32 According to this article: "The administration of justice in the Republic of Poland shall be implemented by the Supreme Court, the common courts, administrative courts and military courts."

33 See Anna Błachnio-Parzych, *Zbieg odpowiedzialności karnej i administracyjno-karnej jako zbieg reżimów odpowiedzialności represyjnej* (Wolters Kluwer Polska 2016) 51–66; Mateusz Błachucki (ed), *Administracyjne kary pieniężne w demokratycznym państwie prawa* (Biuro Rzecznika Praw Obywatelskich 2015) 5–6; Marek Sławiński, 'Pojęcie tzw. przepisów o charakterze represyjnym – uwagi na tle dotychczasowego orzecznictwa Trybunału Konstytucyjnego' [2013] 118 Przegląd Sejmowy 5, 84–89; Małgorzata Stahl, 'Sankcje administracyjne – problemy węzłowe' in Małgorzata Stahl, Renata Lewicka, Marek Lewicki (eds), *Sankcje administracyjne* (Wolters Kluwer Polska 2011) 17–30.

34 However, the exact extent of their differences is another highly disputed issue. For more on that matter see Piotr Kardas, Marek Sławiński, 'Przenikanie się odpowiedzialności wykroczeniowej i administracyjnej – problem podwójnego karania' in Marta Matejczuk, Valeri Vachev (eds), *Węzłowe problemy prawa wykroczeń. Czy potrzebna jest reforma?* (Biuro Rzecznika Praw Obywatelskich 2016) 22–33.

35 For more on this highly disputed matter see Mirosław Wyrzykowski, Michał Ziółkowski in Roman Hauser, Zygmunt Niewiadomski, Andrzej Wróbel (eds), *System Prawa Administracyjnego*, vol. II (C.H. Beck 2012) 363–374.

36 More on this matter, especially on the different ways of understanding the requirement of guilt in criminal liability (and liability for petty offences) see Mikołaj Małecki, Marek Sławiński, 'Guilt in Criminal Law: Guilt in Us or in the Stars?' in Bartosz Brożek, Jaap Hage, Nicole A. Vincent (eds), *Law and Mind. A Survey of Law and the Cognitive Sciences* (Cambridge University Press 2021) 289–316.

37 Financial administrative responsibility is imposed in the administrative procedure which do not position its participants in the roles of suspects or accused. The main act governing it is the Act of 14 June 1960 – The Code of Administrative Procedure (Consolidated text in Journal of Laws of 2020, item 256, with subsequent amendment). It is worth mentioning that in 2017 a new chapter was added to this code that sets out the basic rules concerning the imposition of the administrative fines. Some of these rules closely resemble solutions used in criminal law. However, despite any similarities in this matter, these rules are still applied within the framework of administrative procedure.

into the scope of the administration of justice, as stated in Article 175 section 1 of the Polish Constitution.[38] This means that such cases do not have to be tried by the courts. In fact, financial administrative responsibility is imposed by the public administration authorities, which are part of the executive branch, not the judiciary.

To better summarise the discussed differences, we have listed them in Table 1 below.

Table 1. Differences between liability for petty offences and financial administrative responsibility

Liability for petty offences	Financial administrative responsibility
Regulated according to the same principles as criminal liability	Regulated according to its own set of principles, in many regards different than in the case of criminal liability
Considered to be a type of criminal liability by the Polish Constitution	Considered to be a different type of responsibility than a criminal liability by the Polish Constitution
Procedural regulation closely resembles the criminal procedure	Procedural regulation according to the administrative procedure
Imposed by courts or via penalty tickets by the police or other public authorities (however, penalty tickets can be refused, and the case is then tried by the court)	Imposed by the public administrative authorities. Court control is limited to the issues concerning the legality of the decision.
Falls into the administration of justice	Falls outside the administration of justice

Source: Compiled by the authors

The second difference between the sanctions in question lies in their *severity*. At first glance, it might seem that sanctions imposed during the state of natural disaster are more severe than those which can be imposed during the state of epidemic. The former are part of the liability for petty offences, which is considered by the Polish Constitution a type of criminal liability, while the latter

38 The imposition of financial administrative responsibility can be controlled by the courts, however, to a very narrow extent. It is done by the administrative courts whose function, according to Article 184 of the Polish Constitution, is to "control over the performance of public administration". This means that constitutional provisions set out a difference between the performance of public administration and its control. Because of that, administrative courts cannot make decisions in place of the public authorities. The control they exercise concerns only the legality of decisions and other activities of the public administration. If the decision is legal, then it is upheld, otherwise, it is reversed and referred back to the administrative authority for reconsideration. In cases of administrative fines discussed in this contribution, the administrative courts can check whether the sanitary inspectors observed all relevant provisions during the imposition of the fine, but cannot change its amount (for example, by lowering it).

are considered to be part of the administrative liability. However, the overall picture becomes more complicated if we compare the sanctions in question by taking into account the type of values they are limiting and the degree of this limitation. This comparison is illustrated in Table 2 below.

Table 2. Comparison of sanctions that can be imposed during the state of natural disaster and the state of epidemic

Sanctions imposed during the state of natural disaster	Sanctions imposed during the state of epidemic
Deprivation of liberty in the form of the arrest from 5 to 30 days	No equivalent
Pecuniary sanction in form of fine from PLN 20 to 5,000[39]	Pecuniary sanction in form of administrative fine from PLN 5,000 to 30,000[40]

Source: Compiled by the authors

As we can see, during the state of natural disaster two types of sanctions can be imposed, one aimed at the liberty of an individual, second at his or her assets. Only the latter type can be employed during the state of epidemic. Viewed from this perspective liability for petty offences is clearly more severe than financial administrative responsibility. However, if we look at the second type of sanction, the roles are reversed. The pecuniary sanction in the form of the administrative fine is much higher than its counterpart from the state of natural disaster. In fact, the highest possible fine that can be imposed during the state of natural disaster is the lowest possible administrative fine that can be imposed during the state of epidemic. Moreover, the upper limit of the latter sanction is six times the upper limit of the former. This leads to the conclusion that financial administrative responsibility is way more severe than liability for petty offences when it comes to the pecuniary sanctions.

To summarise this exposition of similarities and differences between sanctions in question it is worth emphasising the following conclusions. Both sanctions are of the same type, perform the same function, and protect the same values. They are a preventive and repressive measure and are imposed for violation of restrictions and prohibitions introduced during the respective State – of natural disaster or of epidemic – in order to warrant the protection of important values, such as life, health, and well-being of individuals. Despite this fact, they differ in their legal status. One of them is a part of liability for petty offences, the other is a part of financial administrative responsibility. Because of that, differences in their legal entourage follow. However, there is one factor

39 EUR 4.56 to 1,135.06.

40 EUR 1,135.06 to 6,810.36.

that clearly stands out and does not fit into this rationale, namely, the severity of the administrative fines. If the financial administrative responsibility is not considered to be a type of criminal liability by the Polish Constitution, then is it possible for pecuniary sanctions employed by this responsibility to be much higher than that used in similar circumstances by criminal liability? In our opinion, the shortest answer to this question is no. We will elaborate on this in the next and final part of this contribution.

7. THE PROBLEM OF CONSTITUTIONALITY

Now we can move on to the final part of our consideration, namely, to the assessment of the sanctions introduced during the current state of epidemic using the theoretical framework developed in previous sections. To begin with, it must be emphasised that our assessment here applies only to the sanctions in question. That is to say, we do not evaluate the constitutionality of the administrative fines or financial administrative responsibility in general. This would require broader and more comprehensive study. However, the presented discussion is more than enough for the evaluation of the administrative fines of the state of epidemic. Let us summarise the argument so far:

1. The state of epidemic, introduced on the basis of the Act on Preventing Infections, is considered to be an *ordinary measure* of dealing with danger by the Polish Constitution. There are only three extraordinary measures provided for by the Polish Constitution, and the state of epidemic is not one of them. From this perspective, the hierarchy is clear: the state of epidemic is an ordinary measure, whereas the state of natural disaster is an extraordinary one.[41]
2. Because of that, every limitation of the constitutional rights and freedoms imposed during the state of epidemic must be done in accordance with the proportionality rule stated in Article 31 section 3 of the Polish Constitution (*the ordinary proportionality rule*). None of the exceptions designed for extraordinary measures, such as the extraordinary proportionality rule from Article 228 section 5 of the Polish Constitution, apply.

---

41 It is also worth mentioning that in the opinion of the Polish Council of Ministers (which is the authority entitled to introduce the state of natural disaster) the coronavirus outbreak was not considered to be a situation that would require the use of the extraordinary measures (i.e. the state of natural disaster). Instead, an ordinary measure in the form of the state of epidemic was applied. See 'Dworczyk: W opinii rządu nie ma przesłanek żeby wprowadzić stan nadzwyczajny' *Dziennik Gazeta Prawna* 23.03.2020, https://www.gazetaprawna.pl/artykuly/1462755,dworczyk-pandemia-koronawirusa-rzad-stan-nadzwyczajny-przeslanki.html accessed 30 September 2020.

3. To assess this proportionality, one must take into account not only the content of the provisions in question but also their *relations* to the relevant extraordinary measures provided for by the Polish Constitution.

The last point is of special importance here. As stated above,[42] if a given legal solution falls into the category of ordinary measures, then it should not exhibit characteristics proper to the extraordinary ones. Otherwise, the distinction set out by the Polish Constitution between these two types of measures would be meaningless and its provisions in this matter could be easily circumvented. The extraordinary measures are designed to be applied only when ordinary solutions are inadequate. Therefore, if a given sanction, which is considered to be a part of the ordinary measure, is more severe than the sanction that can be imposed during the application of the relevant extraordinary measure, this is a strong indication that the standard of proportionality in the case of the former has not been met. This does not mean that the limitations of constitutional rights and freedoms must always be more intense during the application of extraordinary measures. It only means that if sanctions are considered to be part of the ordinary measure, then they should not be more severe than sanctions that can be imposed during the application of the relevant extraordinary measure.

Precisely this requirement is not met by the sanctions in question. As we have seen, the pecuniary sanctions of the state of epidemic turn out to be more severe than any similar sanctions that can currently be imposed during the state of natural disaster. To better capture this inconsistency, let us look at what would happen if the authorities decided that the state of epidemic is not sufficient to fight the coronavirus outbreak and thus introduced the state of natural disaster. Violations of the restrictions and prohibitions that are currently subject to the financial administrative responsibility would become subject to liability for petty offences. Instead of the administrative fines ranging from PLN 5,000 to 30,000[43] only a fine from PLN 20 to 5,000[44] could be imposed. Because of that, change from the state of epidemic – which is the ordinary measure – to the state of natural disaster – which is the extraordinary measure – would result in a noticeable reduction of sanctions. This leads us to the conclusion that the sanctions of the state of epidemic do not fit into the constitutional framework of ordinary and extraordinary measures of dealing with danger.

As stated above, there are two perspectives from which we can assess this situation: first, the case of overly excessive sanctions employed by the ordinary measure of the state of epidemic; second, the case of overly lenient sanctions employed by the extraordinary measure of the state of natural disaster. It is

---

42 See section 4.

43 EUR 1,135.06 to 6,810.36.

44 EUR 4.54 to 1,135.06.

important to notice that these assessments do not exclude each other. Therefore, it is viable to conclude that the sanctions of the state of epidemic are too severe and, at the same time, the sanctions of the state of natural disaster are too lenient. From the constitutional point of view, however, each perspective leads to different consequences.

The main problem posed by sanctions that are too lenient lies in the possibility of their ineffectiveness. In other words, there is a risk that they will not perform their function at all, or they will do so, although below the expected level of their effectiveness. This situation creates an obligation on the part of the authorities to adjust the means employed to the ends that are supposed to be achieved. The case of too severe sanctions is different. The severity of the sanctions could result in excessive limitation of constitutional rights and freedoms. In other words, the sanctions could be more burdensome than they need to be. Such a situation needs to be evaluated from the perspective of the proportionality rule.

As we can see, each of these two assessments leads to different problems. Therefore, even if we were to say that sanctions employed as a part of the extraordinary measure of the state of natural disaster are too lenient, it does not solve the problem posed by severe sanctions of the ordinary measure of the state of epidemic. Because the latter problem is our main concern here, let us now turn to the issue of proportionality. The ordinary proportionality rule is stated in Article 31 section 3 of the Polish Constitution: "Any limitation upon the exercise of constitutional freedoms and rights may be imposed only by statute, and only when necessary in a democratic State for the protection of its security or public order, or to protect the natural environment, health or public morals, or the freedoms and rights of other persons. Such limitations shall not violate the essence of freedoms and rights". According to the opinion of legal scholars and the judiciary, this provision sets out three requirements that limitation must pass in order to be deemed constitutional, namely *suitability*, *necessity* and *adequacy*.[45]

1. The limitation is considered *suitable* if it is useful in realising the goal for which it was introduced. This requirement simply assures that the limitation in question can serve its purpose.
2. The limitation is considered *necessary* if it is the only way to realise the goal for which it was introduced. That is to say, there are no other means

[45] For more on this matter see Anna Śledzińska-Simon, 'Proportionality Analysis by the Polish Constitutional Tribunal' in Mordechai Kremnitzer, Talya Steiner, Andrej Lang (eds), *Proportionality in Action. Comparative and Empirical Perspectives on the Judicial Practice* (Cambridge University Press 2020) 397–400; Marek Szydło in Marek Safjan, Leszek Bosek (eds), *Konstytucja RP*, vol. I (C.H. Beck 2016) 791–807; Joanna Zakolska, *Zasada proporcjonalności w orzecznictwie Trybunału Konstytucyjnego* (Wydawnictwo Sejmowe 2008) 9–31.

at our disposal than the limitation in question to reach the expected result. However, if the goal can be achieved by two or more means, the necessity requires choosing the least burdensome one.

3. The limitation is considered *adequate* if there is an acceptable proportion between the severity of imposed restrictions and the value of the goal that is achieved by the imposition of this limitation.

There is no doubt that the first requirement is met. The main goal of the sanctions in question is to warrant compliance with the restrictions and prohibitions of the state of epidemic, and by this, to protect the same values that are protected by these restrictions. Therefore, sanctions of the state of epidemic can be deemed suitable on the grounds of the proportionality rule. However, the same cannot be said of the next premise, that is the requirement of necessity.

The issue of necessity can be formulated as follows: Are there any other means besides the severe financial administrative responsibility to warrant the rules introduced during the state of epidemic? Based on our considerations so far, we can say that liability for petty offences presents itself as a viable option. This type of responsibility is used by the extraordinary measure of the state of natural disaster. In general, we have three possible answers to our question. The proper standard of necessity in the case discussed here is given (1) by financial administrative responsibility, or (2) by liability for petty offences, or (3) by neither of them. The first two are the most important because they indicate specific measures that can be evaluated on the grounds of the necessity requirement. The third one serves only a complementary role. If the other two possibilities were to be rejected, the third simply indicates that the answer must be sought elsewhere.

Which of the above answers meets the constitutional requirements and is best justified? In order to properly address this question, we must bear in mind the constitutional framework of ordinary and extraordinary measures presented so far.

First of all, it is worth emphasising that the Act on the State of Natural Disaster was passed in 2002. On that date, the legislature decided that liability for petty offences was the appropriate type of responsibility for violations of restrictions that could be introduced during the application of the extraordinary measure of the state of natural disaster. As stated earlier, the extraordinary measures can only be introduced if ordinary measures are inadequate. In other words, the danger must be of such a nature or degree as to justify the need for special solutions. Because of that, the extraordinary measures can be treated as a point of reference for the ordinary ones. The employment of liability for petty offences in the cases of violation of the rules introduced during the state of natural disaster is a part of this reference standard. By using the *argumentum a maiori ad minus* we can arrive at the following conclusion: if liability for petty offences is considered to be adequate for the extraordinary measures – that is during the situations that are characterized by the high levels of danger – then this type of liability is more than adequate for the ordinary measures – i.e. when the levels of danger are significantly lower.

Of course, it can be said that the decision to employ liability for petty offences in the case of the state of natural disaster was made in different circumstances than we are currently dealing with. In 2002, when the Act on the State of Natural Disaster was enacted, the global pandemic of a new and deadly virus may have presented itself as an unlikely event and thus may not have been taken into account at all. Regardless of what those who prepared this Act had in mind, the circumstances have changed. Therefore, it can be argued that the employment of liability for petty offences for the state of natural disaster no longer reflects the intentions of the authorities. In response to this deficiency, the administrative fines were introduced during the current coronavirus outbreak.

This line of reasoning may seem convincing, although, it has one major setback. The administrative fines were introduced as a part of the ordinary measure of the state of epidemic, not the extraordinary measure of the state of natural disaster. The use of liability for petty offences in the case of the state of natural disaster has not changed since 2002, when the statute concerning this state was first enacted. Even when it was finally understood that the coronavirus poses a serious threat of a global outbreak, the authorities still have not decided to change the type of liability provided for the state of natural disaster. Therefore, the decision to make no changes in this regard is just as important as the introduction of new sanctions as a part of the ordinary measure of the state of epidemic. Of course, such a choice is a part of the policy envisaged and implemented by the authorities. Nevertheless, it must remain within the boundaries set by the Polish Constitution, especially if this choice leads to the limitation of constitutional rights and freedoms. Even if liability for petty offences is considered to be a type of responsibility too lenient for the state of natural disaster, the authorities did nothing to change it. Instead, severe administrative sanctions were introduced as a part of the ordinary measure of the state of epidemic. Liability for petty offences in the case of the extraordinary measures and financial administrative responsibility in the case of the ordinary measures indicate two standards of necessity that contradict each other. The latter is more severe than the former, although the former is used in typical dangerous situations while the latter in ordinary ones. Precisely because of that it is hard to consider that sanctions of the state of the epidemic meet the necessity requirement of the ordinary proportionality rule.

8. CONCLUSIONS

There is no doubt that the coronavirus outbreak demands swift and firm actions from the authorities. One of the prominent features of the democratic state of the law is that all such actions, despite their specificity forced by current circumstances, must fall within the framework set out by the constitutional provisions. The authorities had the right to decide whether to introduce one of the extraordinary states – namely, the state of natural disaster – or to employ ordinary means. However, it is the Constitution that provides general rules with which the chosen solution must comply. Regardless of the degree of freedom that the authorities enjoy in exercising the legislative powers, the ordinary measure of the state of epidemic cannot take a form identical with, or even more severe than, the extraordinary measure of the state of natural disaster. This applies especially to the sanctions that can be introduced. Ordinary measures require ordinary sanctions, not extraordinary ones.[46]

[46] It is worth mentioning that at the date of preparing this contribution for publication most of the described legal solutions are still in force. The Polish authorities are still employing the ordinary measure of the state of epidemic that is accompanied by administrative financial responsibility.

COVID-19 AND ITS IMPACT ON UKRAINIAN CRIMINAL LAW

Svitlana Mazepa*

At the end of 2019 and the beginning of 2020, a new dangerous disease appeared in the world, which was named "COVID-19". Each country decided how to react and what steps should be taken as a first priority. The fact that national governments were taking exceptional measures to slow down the spread of the virus and to deal with the pandemic has implications not only for criminal proceedings that are already underway but also for future ones. In this scrutiny, the author highlights the legal response of Ukraine to the pandemic from the criminal law perspective. A number of restrictive measures and prohibitions were adopted, which were aimed at self-isolation. The focus in this contribution is on criminal law, as the pandemic has prompted changes to existing law, including criminal law and legislation. The immediate reaction of the Ukrainian parliament to the pandemic was to increase criminal liability and introduce administrative liability for violating quarantine. These changes have become the subject of this contribution. Also, a number of bills on amendments in the current Criminal Code in connection with the coronavirus are analysed.

1. INTRODUCTION

The COVID-19 pandemic, announced by the World Health Organization (WHO) on 11 March 2020, has had a major impact on all aspects of our lives.

* West Ukrainian National University.

Significant vulnerabilities were noted in various areas (primarily health and biosafety, cybersecurity, economics, etc.). Each State decided independently how to react and what steps to prioritise. Is it possible to overcome the pandemic by persuading citizens to take restrictive measures? Should the State ensure the fear of criminal liability?

According to the Centre for Public Health, as of 3 October 2020, 222,322 cases of COVID-19 were confirmed in Ukraine, of which 98,737 recovered and 4,353 passed away.[1] During the crisis in Ukraine, the situation was also complicated due to the warfare in the east of the country, the reform period and changes in the government. This contribution explores the impact of COVID-19 on some areas of Ukrainian criminal law. It shows that legal responses to the pandemic determine the severity of problems such as ineffectiveness of legislative changes, lack of criminalisation of some socially dangerous acts, overcriminalisation, and disproportionate punishments. In general, this applies to the establishment of criminal liability for violation of quarantine restrictions, pricing, resale and release through customs common goods for controlling and preventing the spread of epidemics.

First, hastily adopted criminal law changes were aimed solely at strengthening sanctions. The principles of criminal law, such as the principle of legality, principle of legal certainty and the principle of proportionality, were not respected. Secondly, the situation with COVID-19 showed gaps in the criminal law that need to be resolved. The mechanism of action of temporary criminal law was not created. Thirdly, overcriminalisation has only worsened during the pandemic. In this respect, overcriminalisation puts an excessive burden on the criminal justice system – criminal law and punishment have their place, but the current system of criminalisation has run amok.[2] Fourthly, when introducing or strengthening criminal liability for certain acts, the question of maintaining the balance and proportionality of the newly introduced penalties arises. The State at its discretion establishes criminal liability for certain acts, but the European Convention on Human Rights,[3] in the interpretation of the European Court of Human Rights, creates a certain framework for this. At the moment, Ukraine is implementing European standards into domestic legislation, carefully studying the case law of the European Court of Human Rights.

---

1 Ministry of Health of Ukraine official website https://moz.gov.ua/article/news/operativna-informacija-pro-poshirennja-koronavirusnoi-infekcii-2019-ncov2/ accessed 3 October 2020.

2 Benjamin Levin, 'The Consensus Myth in Criminal Justice Reform' (2018) 117 Mich. L. Rev. 259: https://scholar.law.colorado.edu/articles/1205 accessed 21 June 2020.

3 See its text here: https://www.echr.coe.int/Documents/Convention_ENG.pdf accessed 21 June 2020.

2. AN OVERVIEW OF LEGAL RESPONSES TO THE COVID-19 PANDEMIC

The COVID-19 pandemic has been a challenge for nations around the world. Ukraine as a State, in this difficult time, has a chance to assess the effectiveness of its main functions that include situation analysis, crisis management planning, the appropriate decision-making strategy, organisation of activities, and the control of responsible bodies and institutions.

The authorities' priority measures were aimed at isolating everyone as much as possible. Thus, on 11 March 2020, quarantine was introduced by adopting a resolution of the Cabinet of Ministers of Ukraine No 211 "On prevention of the spread of acute respiratory disease COVID-19 caused by coronavirus SARS-CoV-2" in Ukraine.[4] This resolution has been amended several times as the situation in the country has changed. Among the restrictive measures there were prohibitions to visit educational schools and universities by applicants. The activities of catering establishments, shopping and entertainment centres, other entertainment establishments, fitness centres, cultural institutions, trade and consumer services, parks and recreation areas were closed.

In addition, regular and irregular passenger transits in suburban, long-distance, intra-regional and inter-regional traffic were prohibited, as well as passenger flights. The authorities also made some decisions to restrict the operation of checkpoints and introduced new approaches and sanctions to prosecute individuals for violating quarantine measures. The quarantine meant the restriction of several human rights to free movement. Also, the Decision of the National Security and Defence Council of Ukraine dated 13 March 2020 "On urgent measures to ensure national security in the event of an outbreak of acute respiratory disease COVID-19 caused by coronavirus SARS-CoV-2" introduced a ban on inbound and outbound regular flights. Additionally, Ukraine has closed its borders to air, rail, and bus services.[5]

The above-mentioned resolution follows from the Law of Ukraine "On Protection of the Population from Infectious Diseases,[6] namely Article 29, entitled "Quarantine". The decision to establish quarantine shall specify, in particular, temporary restrictions on the rights of individuals and legal entities and additional obligations imposed on them. However, this article does not authorise the Cabinet of Ministers of Ukraine to impose any restrictions on

---

4 See its text here: https://www.kmu.gov.ua/npas/pro-zapobigannyaposhim110320rennyu-na-teritoriyi-ukrayini-koronavirusu-covid-19 accessed 21 June 2020.

5 See National Security and Defence Council of Ukraine official website https://www.rnbo.gov.ua/ua/Diialnist/4582.html accessed 21 June 2020.

6 See its text here: https://zakon.rada.gov.ua/laws/show/1645-14 accessed 21 June 2020.

the rights and freedoms of citizens, nor to impose additional responsibilities. Therefore, the question arises as to the constitutionality of the above restrictions. Is it possible to restrict people's rights through secondary legislation?

Overcoming the pandemic is a comprehensive measure, and Ukraine has decided that it is best to act on human behaviour in a pandemic by imposing prohibitions. This is based on the principle of proportionality (*ultima ratio*),[7] the essence of which is to take the necessary measures to achieve the goal. In other words, anything that goes beyond achieving the goal does not conform to this principle. The application of criminal law, where the situation can be settled by civil or administrative law, is a violation of the principle of proportionality. Also, this principle emphasises the repressive nature of criminal justice and positions it as the last measure of the legislator[8] or as the last resort.[9]

The Law of Ukraine dated 17 March 2020, No 530-IX "On Amendments to Certain Legislative Acts of Ukraine Aimed at Preventing the Occurrence and Spread of Coronavirus Disease (COVID-19)", introduced strengthening of liability for violation of a quarantine. In particular, the Code of Ukraine on Administrative Offences has been supplemented by Article 44-3 "Violation of the rules on quarantine of people". Also, a new version of Article 325 of the Criminal code of Ukraine was adopted. It provides responsibility for violation of sanitary rules and norms concerning the prevention of infectious diseases and mass poisonings.[10] I believe that it is advisable to also consider the administrative norms, as they are comparable to criminal ones.

3. THE IMPACT OF COVID-19 ON CRIMINAL LEGISLATION

During this unprecedented crisis, governments across Europe are intensifying their efforts to combat the global spread of the coronavirus by enacting various measures to support public health systems, safeguard the economy and ensure public order and safety.[11]

---

7 Neagu Norel, 'European (Criminal) Law v. National (Criminal) Law – a Two Way Street' (2015) II(2) Law. Review 46.

8 Sakari Melander, 'Ultima Ratio in European Criminal Law' (2013) 3 Oñati Socio-legal Series 42 http://ssrn.com/abstract=2200871 accessed 21 June 2020.

9 Douglas Husak, 'The criminal law as last resort' (2020) 24 Oxf J Leg Stud 207.

10 See the text of Law of Ukraine dated 17 March 2020, № 530-IX "On Amendments to Certain Legislative Acts of Ukraine Aimed at Preventing the Occurrence and Spread of Coronavirus Disease (COVID-19)", here: https://zakon.rada.gov.ua/laws/show/2341-14 accessed 21 June 2020.

11 Europol official website https://www.europol.europa.eu/newsroom/news/how-criminals-profit-covid-19-pandemic accessed 21 June 2020.

Below we will consider the changes that have already taken place in the current criminal legislation, as well as those bills that are currently under consideration in the Verkhovna Rada (Ukrainian parliament).

Before the introduction of the above changes and quarantine, under Article 325 of the Criminal Code, liability was imposed only for food poisoning. According to the official data of the Prosecutor General's Office of Ukraine, in 2019, 70 criminal proceedings were initiated. However, the situation has changed due to quarantine and after the introduction of changes. As a result, in 2020, during the quarantine alone (March–May), 179 criminal proceedings were registered.[12] Today, Article 325 of the Criminal Code imposes criminal liability for the violation of sanitary rules and regulations, the prevention of infectious diseases and mass poisoning, and if such acts have resulted in death or other serious consequences, the person is sentenced to eight years imprisonment.

Article 325, Violation of sanitary rules and norms concerning prevention of infectious diseases and mass poisonings, states:

> 1. Violation of the rules and regulations established for the prevention of epidemic and other infectious diseases, as well as mass non-communicable diseases (poisoning) and control of them, if such **actions** have caused or are known to cause the spread of these diseases, -
>
> shall be punishable by a fine of one thousand to three thousand tax-free minimum incomes, or arrest for a term up to six months, or restriction of liberty for a term up to three years, or imprisonment for the same term.
>
> 2. The same acts, if they have caused death or other serious consequences, -
>
> shall be punishable by imprisonment for a term of five to eight years.[13]

The established administrative responsibility is also rather strict. In particular, according to Article 44-3 of the Code of Administrative Offences liability included violation of rules concerning quarantine, sanitary-and-hygienic, sanitary-and-anti-epidemic rules and norms provided by the Law of Ukraine, entitled "About protection of the population against infectious diseases", other acts of the legislation, and also decisions of local governments concerning the fight against infectious diseases. Punishment for the above actions is a fine for citizens from one to two thousand tax-free minimum income and for officials from two to ten thousand tax-free minimum income[14] (Tax Code of Ukraine

12 Prosecutor General Office in Ukraine official website https://old.gp.gov.ua/ua/stst2011.html?dir_id=114138&libid=100820&c=edit&_c=fo# accessed 21 June 2020.

13 See the text of Criminal Code of Ukraine here: https://zakon.rada.gov.ua/laws/show/2341-14#Text accessed 3 October 2020.

14 See the text of Code of Administrative Offences of Ukraine here: https://zakon.rada.gov.ua/laws/show/80731-10 accessed 21 June 2020.

establishes tax-free minimum income for 17 hryvnias = 0.5 euro).[15] The amount of the fine in the criminal and administrative sanctions is almost the same. It should be stated that this administrative norm is of a criminal law nature.

The European Court of Human Rights in a number of its decisions on the application of Articles 6 and 7 of the Convention (see Articles 2 and 3 of Protocol No. 7) explicitly states that the term "criminal offence" is used in the practice of the ECHR in an autonomous sense. This means that, in each case, the ECHR determines at its discretion which offence is criminal under the Convention, based on established criteria.[16] The expediency of the autonomous concept of a criminal offence in the practice of the ECHR and the relevant criteria were substantiated in in the *Engel* case,[17] which stated: "If the Contracting States could, at their discretion, classify an offence as disciplinary instead of criminal, or prosecute the perpetrator of a 'mixed' offence at a disciplinary rather than a criminal level, then the effect of the basic provisions of Articles 6 and 7 would be subject to their sovereign will (§82, 83)."

Such an extension of power could have consequences that are incompatible with the goals and objectives of the Convention.[18] §§82–83 of the cited decision of the ECHR named the following criteria for classifying offences as criminal (the so-called Engel criteria): the assessment of the nature of the violation from the view of national law; the essence (nature) of the offence; the severity of the punishment that may be applied to the perpetrator.

We consider it necessary, first of all, to pay attention to the sanction. The amount of the fine in Article 44-3 of the Code of Administrative Offences (1,000–2,000 tax-free minimum incomes) almost corresponds to the amount of the fine under Part 1 of Article 325 of Criminal Code of Ukraine (1,000–3,000 tax-free minimum incomes). But if an official committed the offence, the amount of the fine for such an administrative offence is even greater than the potential amount of the fine for a crime, namely, the official in case of administrative liability under Article 44-3 of the Code of Administrative Offences is threatened with from 2,000 to 10,000 tax-free minimum incomes.

In connection with the above, both administrative and criminal laws must be considered. Part 1 of Article 325 of the Criminal Code imposes criminal prosecution for "the violation of rules and regulations enforced to prevent

---

15 See the text of Tax Code of Ukraine here: https://zakon.rada.gov.ua/laws/show/2755-17#Text accessed 21 June 2020.

16 Svitlana Khyliuk 'Zlochyn i kara" u Konventsii pro zakhyst prav liudyny i osnovopolozhnykh svobod' [Crime and punishment in European convention on human rights in Chasopys] (2015) Akademii advokatury Ukrainy 108, 110.

17 *Engel and Others v The Netherlands* (1976) Series A no 15.

18 Petro Rabinovych 'Fundamentalni poniattia kryminalnoho prava: interpretatsiia Strasburzkoho sudu' [Fundamental concept of criminal law: interpretation of Strasbourg court] (2011) 11 Yurydychna Ukraina 4.

epidemic and other infectious diseases, as well as mass non-communicable diseases (poisoning) and control them if such actions have caused or may have caused the spread of these diseases". With the help of a legal analysis of the crime, we propose to focus on the problems of the impact of this rule.

Article 325 of the Criminal Code has a blanket reference structure, which means a linkage to the array of legislation in other fields. The aim of the crime is a violation of the procedure for prevention of infectious diseases and poisonings,[19] which is contained in certain rules and regulations. In this case, there is a problem, because the citizen should be aware of only the rules and regulations which are reflected in the law.[20] Article 68 of Constitution of Ukraine[21] states that a person who is unaware of a law may not escape liability for violation of that law, but what if the rules and regulations are in the Resolution of the Cabinet of Ministers, which is not a law? Case law is an example of these contradictions. On 8 April 2020, there were registered criminal proceedings on the grounds of a crime under Part 1 of Article 325 of the Criminal Code of Ukraine.[22]

A clergyman of one of the Ukrainian churches, from 17 March 2020 to 27 March 2020, held a divine service with students and parishioners, violating the prohibitions contained in the resolution of the Cabinet of Ministers of 11 March 2020, No 211 (On the prevention on the territory of Ukraine of acute respiratory disease COVID-19 caused by coronavirus SARS-CoV-2), and from 12 March 2020 quarantine was established throughout Ukraine. As a result of violating the prohibitions, 21 people were confirmed to be infected with COVID-19. It is questionable whether the acts were properly qualified due to the lack of necessary rules in the law. It is not entirely clear what rules were violated.

It should also be recalled that these provisions contradict the principle of legal certainty enshrined in the decisions of the Article 7 of ECHR[23] "… besides, given the importance of personal liberty, it is essential that the applicable national law meets the standard of 'lawfulness' set by the Convention, which requires that all laws, whether written or unwritten, be sufficiently precise to allow the citizen – if need be, with appropriate advice – to foresee, to a degree

19 Mykola Melnyk, Mykola Khavroniuk, *Naukovo-praktychnyi komentar Kryminalnoho kodeksu Ukrainy* [Scientific and practical commentary of Criminal code of Ukraine] (Dakor 2019) [in Ukrainian].

20 Mykola Khavroniuk '"Protyinfektsiini" statti Kryminalnoho kodeksu Ukrainy ta kodeksu Ukrainy pro administratyvni pravoporushennia potrebuiut onovlennia' ["Anti-infective" articles of Criminal Code of Ukraine and Code of Administrative Offences need updating 291-301], Pravovi zasady epidemichnoi bezpeky: vyklyky ta perspektyvy: materialy internet-konferentsii (m. Poltava, 29 kvit. 2020 r.) (Pravo 2020) [in Ukrainian].

21 See the text https://zakon.rada.gov.ua/laws/show/254%D0%BA/96-%D0%B2%D1%80 accessed 21 June 2020.

22 Ukrainian State register of court decisions http://reyestr.court.gov.ua/Review/89234028 accessed 21 June 2020.

23 See, e.g. *Steel and Others v. United Kingdom* (1998) 28 EHRR 603, §54.

that is reasonable in the circumstances, the consequences which a given action may entail ..." according to which "the law must be accessible and predictable in terms of its consequences, i.e. expressed with sufficient precision to allow a person to regulate his conduct if necessary".[24] In particular, the ECHR recalls that "national law must define with sufficient clarity the limits and manner of exercising the relevant discretion conferred on public authorities to ensure that citizens have the minimum level of protection to which they are entitled under the rule of law in a democratic society".[25]

Another confirmation of the rather wide application of Article 325 of the Criminal Code in practice was when the Security Service of Ukraine initiated criminal proceedings under Part 1 of Article 325 of the Criminal Code regarding officials of a private medical clinic who did not inform the Ministry of Health of Ukraine and the Public Health Centre about the positive result of the coronavirus test.[26] This raises the question of the actus reus of the crime. According to Article 11 of the Criminal code of Ukraine, the crime is a socially dangerous guilty act (action or inaction), committed by the criminal offender. According to Part 1 of Article 325 of the Criminal Code, only action is punishable and lack of action is unpunishable.

The disposition of the article explicitly states that the violation of the rules and norms established for the prevention of epidemic and other infectious diseases, as well as mass non-communicable diseases (poisoning) and their control, is committed by action. As for the case with the medical staff of a private clinic, it is a matter of comission by omission. Because of this, the offence cannot be classified under Article 325 of the Criminal Code of Ukraine. Therefore, immediate changes should be introduced as soon as possible.

The subjective characteristics of the above-mentioned act should also be noted. According to most Ukrainian scientists, the criminal offender has to be an official – employees of certain institutions, organisations who are obliged to comply with certain rules and regulations established to prevent epidemic and other infectious diseases, as well as mass non-communicable diseases (poisoning) and to fight them. It is questionable how to deal with ordinary citizens who are infected with coronavirus, and whose non-compliance with quarantine measures has caused or could cause the spread of infectious disease. Depending on the consequences, it may be necessary to consider liability under Article 44-3 of the Code of Administrative Offences or Article 325 of the Criminal Code of Ukraine.

---

24 Tetiana Fulei 'Zastosuvannia praktyky Yevropeiskoho sudu z prav liudyny pry zdiisnenni pravosuddia' in *Naukovo-metodychnyi posibnyk dlia suddiv* [Application of the case law of ECHR in administering justice] (Kyiv 2015) [in Ukrainian].

25 Domenichini v Italy (1996) Reports 1996-V 33.

26 Security service of Ukraine official website https://ssu.gov.ua/ua/news/1/category/21/view/7389#.khDlZiUX.dpbs accessed 21 June 2020.

Another controversial issue regarding the considered norm is Law No 540-IX of 30 March 2020. Paragraphs 3, 4, 5, and 10 of Section I of this Law shall be valid for three months from the date of publication of the Law.[27] Thus, the strengthening of criminal liability is adopted for three months. In this case, criminal proceedings must take place at all stages of the investigation of the crime before the sentence is handed down, since the legislator did not take into account the principle of criminal law promptly.

According to Article 5 of the Criminal Code of Ukraine, the law on criminal liability, which abolishes the criminality of the act, mitigates criminal liability or otherwise improves the situation of a person, has retroactive effect and applies to persons who committed relevant acts before the entry into force of the law, including the application to sentenced persons or ones with a criminal record. On the contrary, the law on criminal liability which partially mitigates criminal liability or otherwise improves the situation of a person, and partially strengthens criminal liability or otherwise worsens the situation of a person, has retroactive effect only in the part that mitigates criminal liability or otherwise improves the position of the person. If a person has committed an offence and the penalty has since changed, the criminal law has retroactive effect only if the penalty has been reduced or if it has been abolished.

Thus, the wording of Article 325 of the Criminal Code, which was in force from 18 March 2020 to 17 June 2020, will amount to a stricter intermediate criminal law, and the original version that later replaced it (staff up to 100 tax free minimum incomes or arrest for up to six months, or restriction of liberty for up to three years), under Part 1 of Article 5 of the Criminal Code of Ukraine will have retroactive effect. Article 5 "Retroactive effect of the law on criminal liability in time" of Criminal Code of Ukraine states:

1. The law on criminal liability, which repeals the criminality of an act or lenifies criminal liability, shall be retroactive in time, that is, it shall apply to persons who had committed similar acts before that law entered into force, including the persons serving their sentence or those who have completed their sentence but have a conviction.
2. The law on criminal liability that criminalises an act or increases criminal liability shall not be retroactive in time.
3. The law on criminal liability, which partially lenifies and partially increases criminal liability, shall be retroactive in time only in the part which lenifies the liability.
4. If the law on criminal liability has been amended several times since a person committed an act stipulated by this Code, the law that abolishes criminality of an act or lenifies criminal liability shall be deemed as retroactive.

---

27 See its text here: https://zakon.rada.gov.ua/laws/show/540-20#n356 accessed 21 June 2020.

Thus, all efforts of the legislator to strengthen criminal liability for the crime provided by Part 1 Article 325 of the Criminal Code of Ukraine are useless without any urgent changes to the terms of the relevant law. It has already been mentioned above that 200 criminal proceedings have been underway without sentences since the commencement of the quarantine. This indicates that when the cases go to trial, the original version of the article will come into force and the sanctions will be significantly eased.

Today, Article 325 on the official website of the Ukrainian Parliament remains unchanged, despite the fact that the three-month period has passed. What sanction should be applied to the courts for this crime now?[28]

4. REVIEW OF BILLS ON AMENDMENTS TO THE CRIMINAL CODE OF UKRAINE IN CONNECTION WITH THE PANDEMIC

We also propose to consider the bills in the Ukrainian parliament on the introduction of other criminal law prohibitions in connection with the crisis related to the coronavirus. Panic of citizens encourages unscrupulous behaviour. The additions to the Criminal Code of Ukraine are given below. It matches the basic grounds for the criminalisation of socially dangerous acts. After all, combating the spread of COVID-19 infection is a priority for the country, but is limited to the availability of drugs, medical devices, personal protective equipment, laboratory, and medical equipment, etc.

The Draft Law of Ukraine "On Amendments to Certain Legislative Acts of Ukraine Concerning Liability for Violation of Pricing Legislation during the Legal Regime of Martial Law or State of Emergency or State of Emergency Regime"[29] is designed to introduce criminal liability for violating the legislation on price setting during the legal regime of martial law or state of emergency. The purpose of the bill is to improve the current legislation on criminal liability for violating the law on pricing during the operation of special legal regimes and the state of emergency. This goal is expected to be achieved by supplementing the Criminal Code of Ukraine with a new Article 199-1, which establishes criminal liability for violation of the legislation on pricing during the legal regime of martial law or state of emergency.

Thus, to establish the fact of committing the relevant socially dangerous act, it will be necessary to prove that (1) there was a resale of civil aids (medical devices and medicines) at a price that is twice or more times higher than the

---

28 See its text here: https://zakon.rada.gov.ua/laws/show/2341-14#Text accessed 3 October 2020.

29 See its text here: http://w1.c1.rada.gov.ua/pls/zweb2/webproc4_1?pf3511=68544 accessed 21 June 2020.

level of State-regulated price for such means, and the question of the need to prove the prior purchase of such funds; and (2) the resale of the relevant civil remedies were committed on a large or especially large scale.

In turn, the resale of civil protection in large or especially large amounts will take place if the amount from the resale of these means is one hundred or more times (large size) or two hundred and more times (especially large size) exceeds the tax-free minimum income (Paragraph 3 of the note to Article 199-1 of the Criminal Code in the draft version). The question arises if the sale of civil protection at a price not exceeding two or more times the level of the State-regulated price for such means and/or if such resale did not result in an amount that is one hundred times more than the tax-free minimum income, remains unpunished.

In this case, it is also necessary to propose amendments to the Code of Ukraine on Administrative Offences, which will establish administrative liability for similar actions of a smaller size.

Interestingly, buying and reselling are characteristic features of the concept of "speculation", which existed under socialism. Speculation was recognised not only as a "simple" criminal act, but also as a crime that directly undermines the existing model of economic development in that system, contradicting the existing moral dogmas of the "state of workers". The activity of buying and reselling goods and services for profit is officially recognised as one of the most prestigious and necessary activities under capitalism. The proclamation of democracy in capitalist countries, the consolidation of the basic postulates of the rule of law, and the development of a market model of the economy in such States do not create any grounds for doing business that is not controlled by the State at all. That is why criminal liability should be imposed for specific criminal manifestations of violation of the established economic law and order.[30]

The provisions of the draft law are covered by Ukraine's international legal obligations in the field of European integration, given in Chapter 5 Customs and trade facilitation, and Chapter 12 Transparency Title IV "Trade and Trade-related Matters".

Bills must comply with EU law. This bill meets the requirements of the EU-Ukraine Association Agreement. According to Article 76 of the "Legislation and procedures" of EU-Ukraine Association Agreement, the Parties[31] agree that their respective trade and customs legislation, as a matter of principle, shall be stable and comprehensive, and that provisions and procedures shall

---

30 Yevhen Streltsov 'Vidpovidalnist za spekuliatsiiu pry kapitalizmi: mif abo realnist?' [Ability for speculation under capitalism: myth or reality] (2016) Yurydychnyi Visnyk Ukrainy 12, 13.

31 See its text here: https://trade.ec.europa.eu/doclib/docs/2016/november/tradoc_155103.pdf accessed 21 June 2020.

be proportionate, transparent, predictable, non-discriminatory, impartial and applied uniformly and effectively. Additionally, they shall, *inter alia*:

(a) protect and facilitate legitimate trade through effective enforcement of, and compliance with legislative requirements;
(b) avoid unnecessary or discriminatory burdens on economic operators, prevent fraud and provide further facilitation for economic operators with a high level of compliance;
(c) apply a single administrative document for the purposes of customs declarations;
(d) lead to greater efficiency, transparency and simplification of customs procedures and practices at the border;
(e) apply modern customs techniques, including risk assessment, post clearance controls and company audit methods in order to simplify and facilitate the entry and release of goods;
(f) aim at reducing costs and increasing predictability for economic operators, including small and medium-sized companies;
(g) without prejudice to the application of objective risk-assessment criteria, ensure the non-discriminatory application of requirements and procedures applicable to imports, exports and goods in transit;
(h) apply the international instruments applicable in the field of customs and trade including those developed by the World Customs Organization (WCO) (Framework of Standards to Secure and Facilitate Global Trade of 2005, Istanbul Convention on temporary admission of 1990, HS Convention) of 1983, the WTO (e.g. on Valuation), the UN (TIR Convention of 1975, 1982 Convention on harmonisation of frontier controls of goods), as well as EC guidelines such as the Customs Blueprints;
(i) take the necessary measures to reflect and implement the provisions of the Revised Kyoto Convention on the Simplification and Harmonisation of Customs Procedures of 1973; 29.5.2014 Official EN Journal of the European Union L 161/37
(j) provide for advance binding rulings on tariff classification and rules of origin. The Parties ensure that a ruling may be revoked or annulled only after notification to the affected operator and without retroactive effect, unless the rulings have been made based on incorrect or incomplete information;
(k) introduce and apply simplified procedures for authorised traders according to objective and non-discriminatory criteria;
(l) set rules that ensure that any penalties imposed for the breach of customs regulations or procedural requirements are proportionate and non-discriminatory and, in their application, do not result in unwarranted and unjustified delays; and finally,
(m) apply transparent, non-discriminatory and proportionate rules in respect of the licensing of customs brokers.

Also, it is worth noting the sanction of the article in terms of confiscation of property, as the above crime is of medium gravity. It should be considered that confiscation of property as a form of punishment is established for serious and especially serious mercenary crimes, as well as for crimes against the national security of Ukraine and public safety, regardless of their severity and can be imposed only in cases specifically provided for in the Special Part of the Criminal Code (Part 2 of Art 59 of the Criminal Code).

The issue of the crime subject is also controversial, since the concept of "civil protection" about current legislation includes firefighting, rescue, and other special equipment, mechanisms, devices, tools, medical devices, medicines, collective and individual protection, which are designed and used for civil defence. This definition does not give an unambiguous answer as to medical masks and disinfectants as a means of civil protection. This bill needs to be finalised.

Also, in connection with the COVID-19 crisis, attention should be paid to the Draft Law 3271 of 27 March 2020 "On Amendments to Certain Legislative Acts of Ukraine on Criminalisation of Export (Shipment) Across the Customs Border of Ukraine of Anti-Epidemic Goods" in connection with recorded by Security Service of Ukraine numerous attempts to export anti-epidemiological protection goods.[32]

The purpose of the bill is to prevent the illegal export (shipment) across the customs border of Ukraine of anti-epidemic goods. To achieve this goal, the bill proposes: (1) to supplement the Criminal Code of Ukraine (the Criminal Code) with a new Article 201-2, which establishes criminal liability for the export (forwarding) of anti-epidemic goods across the customs border of Ukraine outside customs control or with concealment from customs control; (2) to include pre-trial investigation of the crime provided by Article 201-2 of the Criminal Code, to the competence of the investigative security bodies (Paragraph 1, Part 2 of Article 216 of the Criminal Procedure Code of Ukraine).

Significant damage should be understood as the damage that is two hundred times more than the tax-free minimum incomes, and a gross amount should be understood as an amount that is eight hundred times or more than the tax-free minimum incomes.

The explanatory note to the bill states that the establishment of criminal liability for export (shipment) across the customs border of Ukraine, outside customs control or with concealment from customs control of anti-epidemic goods, among other things, is based on resolution of the Cabinet of Ministers of Ukraine of No 214 from 11 March 2020, which amended the resolution No 1109 of the Cabinet of Ministers of Ukraine from 24 December 2019

32 Security service of Ukraine official website https://ssu.gov.ua/ua/news/1/category/2/view/7326#.sOgLKHYe.dpbs accessed 21 June 2020.

"On approval of lists of goods, export, and import of which are subject to licensing, and quotas for 2020". At the same time, Paragraph 2 of the Resolution of the Cabinet of Ministers No 214 states that "licensing the export of anti-epidemic goods necessary to prevent the introduction and spread of acute respiratory disease caused by coronavirus COVID-2019 in Ukraine is introduced until June 1, 2020." The disposition of Part 1 of Article 201-2 of the Criminal Code is formulated as a blanket and requires the appeal of law enforcement agencies, *inter alia*, to the relevant provisions of the Cabinet of Ministers Resolution No 214, proposed in the draft amendment to the Special Part of the Criminal Code which is designed to regulate the most important social relations in this area. The use of provisional rules in criminal legislation should be avoided.

Regarding the above-mentioned disposition of Part 1 of Article 201-2 of the Criminal Code, it would be worthwhile to indicate a certain period during which the relevant crime is committed (for example, when counteracting the spread of a particularly dangerous viral disease in Ukraine). Otherwise, even when no pandemic threats are officially recognised on the territory of Ukraine, the export (shipment) across the customs border of Ukraine, outside customs control or with concealment from customs control of (surgical) medical masks in a large amount, will still be classified as a severe crime and will entail criminal liability under the relevant part of Article 201-2 of the Criminal Code. Can this be considered appropriate?

Analysing the sanction of Article 201-2 of the Criminal Code, a penalty was initially proposed: a fine of eight to twelve thousand non-taxable minimum incomes of citizens with confiscation of these goods (Part 1); or, a fine of twenty to twenty-five thousand tax-free minimum incomes with confiscation of these goods (Part 2). After paying attention to the proportionality of punishment, the sanctions were reviewed and reduced and the relevant acts were classified as moderate crimes, as their commission without aggravating circumstances does not cause significant harm to the object of criminal protection of such serious crime.

After the next revision, the fine was raised from five thousand to ten thousand tax-free minimum incomes (Part 1), and in case of qualifying features, from ten thousand to twenty thousand tax-free minimum incomes.

It is worth mentioning that the laws of Ukraine, namely No 770-VIII of 10 November 2015 "On Amendments to the Criminal Code of Ukraine to improve the institution of special confiscation to eliminate corruption risks in its application" and No 1019-VIII of 18 February 2016 "On Amendments to the Criminal and Criminal Procedure Codes of Ukraine to Implement the Recommendations Contained in the Sixth Report of the European Commission on Ukraine's implementation of the Visa Liberalisation Action Plan for Ukraine on Improving the Procedure seizure of property and the institution of special confiscation", provisions on the application of the so-called special confiscation

(confiscation of objects, means, instruments of crime, etc.) were excluded from all sanctions of the Special Part of the Criminal Code.

In this case, due to the requirements of Articles 96-1 and 96-2 of the Criminal Code, special confiscation of anti-epidemic goods will be possible based on (1) court conviction; (2) court rulings on the release of a person from criminal liability; (3) court rulings on the application of coercive measures of medical nature; and (4) court rulings on the application of coercive measures of educational nature, etc. (see Parts 2 and 3 of Article 96-1 of the Criminal Code) in the manner prescribed by the current criminal procedure legislation of Ukraine. Based on the above, we believe that it is logical to exclude the phrase "with the confiscation of these goods" from the sanctions of the relevant parts of Article 201-2 CC. The Resolution of the Cabinet of Ministers of Ukraine of 11 March 2020, No 214, amended the Resolution of the Cabinet of Ministers of Ukraine "On approval of lists of goods, export, and import of which are subject to licensing, and quotas for 2020"[33] of 24 December 2019, No 1109, which provides additions to the list of goods, the export of which is subject to licensing with anti-epidemic goods, which are necessary to prevent the introduction and spread in Ukraine of acute respiratory disease caused by coronavirus COVID-19, introduced before 1 June 2020, extended until 1 July.[34]

5. CONCLUSION

Establishing responsibility for quarantine violations is an important step in overcoming the pandemic in Ukraine. However, the analysed norms need to be refined.

- Restrictions on human rights can only take place on the basis of law and not secondary legislation;
- Establish a clear list of prohibited acts with reference to specific laws;
- The formation of sanctions should take into account a number of factors, such as the level of income of citizens, the amount of fines for similar acts;
- The legislator needs to clarify the interim criminal law, as its form has not changed since the expiration of the temporary law;
- It is necessary to resort to other measures of legal influence, where possible, avoiding the criminal law instrument;
- The mentioned bills are still under consideration of parliament though the country's experience the second wave of a pandemic.

---

33 See its text here: https://zakon.rada.gov.ua/laws/show/214-2020-%D0%BF#n9 accessed 21 June 2020.

34 See its text here: https://zakon.rada.gov.ua/laws/show/423-2020-%D0%BF accessed 21 June 2020.

Criminal law is an important tool, albeit not the main one, for overcoming a pandemic. The level of legal awareness of the population is the main lever through which the authorities decide what measures to take to overcome crises. However, it is undoubtedly necessary to adhere to all the principles of law-making in the criminal sphere and to thoroughly study the practice of the ECHR on these issues. Only the analysis of problematic issues will make it possible to improve criminal law and control the situation in such difficult cases. Currently, the analysed norms need to be changed and are a valid topic for further research.

WHO "OWNS" THE DATA IN A CORONAVIRUS TRACING (AND/OR TRACKING) APP?

Sjef VAN ERP*

To combat the spread of the COVID-19 virus, e-health has taken a sudden leap forward. Already use cases were studied to see if by means of advanced IT tools, particularly e-health applications (apps), patients could be monitored from their homes so they did not need to visit a hospital for frequent checks. The Corona pandemic gave rise to the rapid development of tracing (and/or tracking) e-health apps, which allow quickly finding the source of an infection as well as others who might have been infected because they were in the close vicinity of someone who became ill. The development and widespread use of these apps makes it even more urgent than before to answer questions regarding to whom the data gathered through such apps belong and what belonging means. Can the owner of the mobile device be considered the "owner" of the data, what does "ownership" then mean, do other stakeholders (such as health care providers, public health authorities) also have a claim to "ownership"?

* Professor (em.) of Civil Law and European Private Law, Maastricht University.

1. INTRODUCTION: E-HEALTH AND CORONAVIRUS APPS

As might have been expected in a rapidly expanding hybrid world, in which physical reality integrates with digital and virtual reality, lockdowns and forced physical isolation to combat the COVID-19 virus have resulted in an incredibly fast changing use of Internet Technology. We suddenly find online meetings no longer a surrogate for "real" meetings and we get used to, whenever possible, working at and from home to avoid running the risk of being infected by leaving the place where you live. All at once, e-health gains momentum, as doctors experience difficulties getting in touch with their patients in hospitals. Studies have already been conducted about the use of mobile phone or tablet applications (apps) to monitor patients while at home, but these were for the most part so-called "use cases" meant to test the app and see if the results are at least comparable to actual physical meetings with a patient.[1] Sometimes these apps have already reached the stage of accepted tools in medical care, such as apps which allow you to take a picture of your skin, send it digitally to a health service provider whose servers, supported by Artificial Intelligence, perform an algorithm based check to see if, for example, there was a possibility of skin cancer. E-health uses all the possibilities offered by the Internet of Things which, by gathering data through sensors, makes data collection and data analysis possible where it would have been unthinkable before.[2] It does not, therefore, come as a surprise that in response to the COVID-19 pandemic the medical profession together with software developers began considering how e-health tools could be used during this pandemic. Regular patients were to stay at home as much as possible and there was an urgent need for monitoring them from a distance. Such distance monitoring was also considered to be a perfect tool for combatting the pandemic and the obvious technological response was to build a mobile phone application that would do just that. If persons infected with the

---

1 Cf, as examples, Paul Wicks et al., 'Innovations in e-health' (2014) 23 Qual Life Res 195; Lisa Abbott and Saxon Smith, 'Smartphone apps for skin cancer diagnosis: Implications for patients and practitioners' (2018) 59 Australasian Journal of Dermatology 168. It is interesting to note that Wicks et al. see the patient as the owner of the data. On p. 201 they write: "Privacy data protection and ownership is a major concern of any Internet-based application. The balance between the patient as the owner of data and the medical and academic profession's documentation and use of the data must be struck, with patient confidentiality always at the forefront without impeding the development of innovative solutions." Medical professionals seem quite aware of the problems regarding control over (access to) patient data.

2 See Martina Barbero et al., *Study on emerging issues of data ownership, interoperability, (re-)usability and access to data, and liability* (European Union 2017) Final Report, 347, a study prepared for the European Commission DG Communications Networks, Content & Technology by Deloitte, discussing Real-Time Location Services (RTLS) used for patient and asset tracking.

virus could be found quickly and if others who had been in contact with them sufficiently long enough to be also at risk could likewise be discovered fast, then this would be a powerful instrument in the fight against the virus. The result is the worldwide development and rapid introduction of coronavirus apps, which "follow" people possibly infected with the COVID-19 virus. Such "following" can mean monitoring on a real time basis, monitoring through analysis of a (potential) patient's data history (for example by looking at behavioural patterns) or a combination of both. As a consequence, e-health no longer is an area for medical specialists, e-health software developers and lawyers specialised in health law, but entered the world of essentially all of us; thus, bringing the hybrid world of e-health with its integrated digital and physical reality not only very close to our homes, but even into our homes, and not only for the younger generations within a population but for all of us.

Make no mistake. This new hybrid world (in the case of the coronavirus apps: the world of e-health apps) is just as real as the old physical world, but it demands a different mindset to actually see and fathom what its effects are on us and what its wider societal, economic and political consequences are. Of course, we will all accept that what happens on a physical screen is "real" (the screen is physically there, the images can be seen, sounds can be heard), but it is different from a painting where you can feel the actual image (and not a projection of that image) by physically touching the canvass. A painting is physical and static. However, a computer screen, although physical, is meant to create impressions on our mind, which we consider to be equal to an impression of, for example, a painting. But, although we can certainly touch the screen, the images as such cannot be touched; they are not made of paint but are the result of software which projects these images on our screen so we will accept them as "real". Computer images are virtual and dynamic. Our law, and my focus in this contribution is more specifically on property law, still takes this old physical and static perception of reality as its foundation. We expected to have time for reconsidering these old and established values, policy choices, principles, notions, concepts and ground rules, developed over several centuries, to see whether they would fit in this new virtual and dynamic world. If they would not fit, we expected to have time for considering either adaptation of existing rules or the development of new rules. The COVID-19 pandemic, by causing an incredibly fast rise of e-health in the form of coronavirus apps, shows, however, that time is running out, we need to give answers now. In this contribution, I will focus on the legal nature of the data gathered by the COVID-19 apps. More precisely, I will question whether these data can "belong" to (be "owned" by) anyone or are the data to be considered "*res nullius*", what does "belonging" ("owning") mean and, if data can belong to anyone, to whom do they belong. To put it differently: I will look both at the possible existence of a property entitlement concerning data gathered by coronavirus apps and, if such entitlement can be accepted, what its content is and to whom such entitlement should be allocated.

2. THE SO-CALLED "FOURTH INDUSTRIAL REVOLUTION" (INDUSTRY 4.0)

The rise of the digital economy with its virtual reality is the result of developments which are relatively recent. It took us quite some time to move from the era of mechanisation, the steam engine and water power to the rise of mass production and the widespread use of electricity, but it took less time to develop electronic and IT systems and automation. In today's world developments even go so fast that, if you do not follow changes very closely, "recent" innovations have already been overtaken by others. Those who saw the introduction of the fax machine, also witnessed its exit. In order to give a proper response to such changes, lawyers need to understand – at least at a technically superficial, but basic level – advances regarding cyber-physical systems, Distributed Ledger Technology (including so-called smart contracts), Artificial Intelligence and the Internet of Things. These are the stages from the First to the Fourth Industrial Revolution, as described by Schwab, where the latter stage is happening all around us and who knows where it will end?[3] This is all going on at such a pace that for many lawyers developments seem problematic to follow and difficult to comprehend, making it hard to learn how to live with it let alone start thinking about redesigning the law to adapt it for this new hybrid world. It seems as if either you belong to this new world, and then you depend on having access to the Internet and your attitude is to have a flexible mindset to understand what is going on, or you do not belong to this world, which cuts you off from the hybrid world that others join. Being an outsider to this new world not only may happen at a mental level but also – more than we in Europe sometimes tend to think – at a physical level. Third World countries have a far less developed IT structure than can be found in, for example, the European Union, North America and China. All of this echoes how we look at the use of IT and e-health as part of modern medicine. The COVID-19 pandemic has created (and still creates) havoc in countries all over the world and, pressed by an urgent need to react and prevent the spread of the disease against a background where, until now, no effective – preventive or curative – medication has been found, it is quite understandable that IT solutions are looked at. In order to stop the spread of the virus, it is of utmost importance to identify new infections and to trace back infection chains. Because spreading happens, as far as we know at present, primarily through human interaction, it is this interaction which needs to be monitored and regulated. Monitoring requires tracing and/or tracking. In the advancement of ideas about how people could be traced and/or tracked, so as to prevent them

---

3 See Klaus Schwab, *The Fourth Industrial Revolution* (Penguin Random House 2016); Klaus Schwab, Nicholas Davis, *Shaping the Future of the Fourth Industrial Revolution: A guide to building a better world* (Penguin Random House 2018).

from spreading the virus and make certain that they undergo medical treatment, IT technology is proving to be a prime facilitator.[4] Where societies have become or are in the process of becoming more affected by technological change and, consequently, develop into information societies, a large part of the population will most likely use a mobile phone. These phones can only work if they are connected to a wider network, which allows them to be followed. Localisation data is gathered by, among others, telephone providers and has turned out to be a very valuable source of information which can be used for various purposes. Thus, the idea to develop a mobile phone application ("coronavirus app"), which collects information about where a person was and with whom that person has been in relatively close contact, appears simply a logical step in a hybrid and data-driven society. However, the data which are collected by using these so-called coronavirus apps are not only a source of personal information about your private life (where you were, with whom you were in close contact) but also a source of information relevant from the perspective of public health and the dire need to do research about the virus in order to find curative medication. The gathered data are therefore as well as being primarily of a personal nature, also of non-personal (general interest: public health) nature. In other words: the use of coronavirus apps brings to the surface a deep conflict between, on the one hand, the need to protection of everyone's personhood by shielding people from having to give up their privacy regarding personal location and contact data, for they are part of how they live and who they are, and, on the other hand, the interest of public health and medical research, not to forget further societal and economic interests.

From a more traditional legal viewpoint, all of this is confusing. The law, particularly property law, leans towards revolving around what we can find in the physical world outside us and from that perspective property lawyers encountered grave difficulties when dealing with intangible things, such as monetary claims and the outcomes of human creativity. In some legal systems, monetary claims were not considered to be "things" and could for that reason not be owned, but as monetary claims represent considerable monetary value one could be "entitled" to the claim and the claim could be offered as security for a loan. Regarding the products of human creativity, it was also clear that such products represented considerable economic value and also could not be ignored. Because these products were even further away from the objects of traditional property law than monetary claims, the final outcome of the theoretical struggle was to consider the law that governs these products as a new, separate legal area

4 See 'BKC Policy Practice: Digital Pandemic Response Provides Practical Guidance, Expert Opinion for Decision Makers | Berkman Klein Center' (28 July 2020) https://cyber.harvard.edu/story/2020-07/bkc-policy-practice-digital-pandemic-response-provides-practical-guidance-expert accessed 10 August 2020.

with its own framework, although – very much as we saw with claims – not infrequently mimicking traditional property law.

In the case of the fundamental building blocks of the digital economy: data, questions about their legal status have become even more pressing than earlier problems caused by the growing economic importance of monetary claims and human creativity. All of the problems, which I mentioned earlier, triggered by the growing impact of IT on our lives, are coming together here. The world has become hybrid, with both real and digital aspects which, more and more, interact and even integrate. This hybrid world functions on the basis of technology, both physical (hardware) and non-physical (software), that results in data, which by their very technical nature can be copied, combined, shared, etc. in ways which until relatively recently were inconceivable in the real world. Data provides a meaning to us and about us, in other words: information, is now so readily available that it seems as if we as human beings are now also becoming hybrid personalities. We have a real life and a life in virtual environments, and these lives are also now merging and becoming hybrid. Our physical lives are reflected in our virtual lives to such a degree that data IT companies perhaps might know more about us than we do ourselves. As such, this requires that we are protected against the unlimited and unjustified use of data which affect us as a person (privacy and data protection), but it also cannot be denied that these very data are part of the present digital economy (and consequently the free flow of non-personal data) and might be of crucial importance from the perspective of public health.[5] The rapid development of coronavirus apps has brought these issues to the forefront and made them even more pressing than they already were and has resulted in an academic debate even more intense than it already was. From the perspective of coronavirus apps this results in the following two questions. What is the legal status of location and contact data? To whom, if

---

5 Only very recently, the Court of Justice of the European Union again made it crystal clear that privacy and data protection are fundamental human rights and that, for this reason, personal data only under the strictest conditions can be transferred from Europe to the United States. See CJEU Case C-311/18 *Facebook Ireland and Schrems*, www.curia.eu accessed 16 July 2020. The court states: "It follows that, since, first, a transfer of personal data, such as that at issue in the main proceedings, for commercial purposes by an economic operator established in one Member State to another economic operator established in a third country, falls, as is apparent from the answer to the first question, within the scope of the GDPR and, second, the purpose of that regulation is, inter alia, as is apparent from recital 10 thereof, to ensure a consistent and high level of protection of natural persons within the European Union and, to that end, to ensure a consistent and homogeneous application of the rules for the protection of the fundamental rights and freedoms of such natural persons with regard to the processing of personal data throughout the European Union, the level of protection of fundamental rights required by Article 46(1) of that regulation must be determined on the basis of the provisions of that regulation, read in the light of the fundamental rights enshrined in the Charter." The last reference is to the Charter of Fundamental Rights of the European Union [2012] OJ L326/1919.

any, do they belong? And if they can belong to someone, who, upon a balance of interests, is entitled to these location and contact data?

3. WHAT ARE "TRACING" AND "TRACKING" APPS?

Before I will embark upon an attempt, while concentrating on coronavirus apps, to offer a methodology towards answering questions about a possible framework for entitlements ("ownership") to data, first some clarification about the technical side of these apps must be given. There is a difference between a "tracing" and a "tracking" app, although apps at the same time could do both. If an app permits tracing, this means that it is possible, retroactively, to find out where a person, on whose phone the app is installed, has been and with whom that person was in contact. The latter can be done in several ways, but one way is using Bluetooth technology. The use of this technology requires that mobile phone users allow their phones to be connected via Bluetooth. Whenever the mobile phones come within one another's vicinity for a relatively long period of time, the phones store an anonymous code which links the two persons as having been present at a particular time in a particular spot. As soon as one of the persons reports in the app on his/her phone that (s)he has become ill, the phone will send a message to everyone stored on that phone who through the Bluetooth codes can be traced back as having been in close contact with that person. Technically the message that someone is ill might also be sent to a central server that then copies the various anonymous Bluetooth codes stored on the infected person's phone, which server will be checked regularly by other apps to find out whether "their" code is now in the database, warning that a risk of contamination exists. This whole process can be done without the persons involved knowing anything else about one another but for the risk of getting infected. Another possibility is that the data are not first only stored on your mobile phone but directly on a central government server. An advantage could be that the government, in the interest of public health, then also has the information about people falling ill, but at the same time, there is a clear privacy threat, as the government could find out which contacts a particular person had. Anonymity would no longer be guaranteed. A further step towards government involvement is when the app is not tracing, but actually tracking you. In that case, the mobile phone transmits location data to a central government server, which can follow everyone using the mobile phone with the app installed. That allows government authorities to contact persons directly who have been in touch with COVID-19 infected phone users. Apps can also do both: allow tracing, next to tracking.[6] A government could also, of course, demand direct access to the location data which are being

---

6 See Patrick Howell O'Neill, Tate Ryan-Mosley and Bobbie Johnson, 'A flood of coronavirus apps are tracking us. Now it's time to keep track of them', presenting an MIT Technology Review

stored by telecom providers, without an app having been installed, but from a European perspective that would be highly problematic considering the rigorous protection mechanism laid down in the General Data Protection Regulation (GDPR) and the law governing telecommunications providers.[7]

4. STAKEHOLDERS

Medical health apps are part of a rapidly developing medical technology or "medtech" market: the use of modern IT as part of diagnosing, preventing and curing disease.[8] Internet Technology is seen as both an effective and efficient tool in medical science. That these apps could turn out to be a valuable tool for medical care is, of course, primarily relevant for patients and healthcare providers, such as family doctors and medical specialists, but that these apps also could increase efficiency and become cost-cutting tools is very relevant for health insurers and governments.[9] Furthermore, these apps provide important information necessary for developing new medicines or new methods of treatment and, therefore, the pharmaceutical industry also has a stake. Next to the pharmaceutical industry, stakeholders can also be producers of medical equipment. Blood pressure measuring instruments can be built into smart watches which, being part of the Internet of Things, may send the information gathered to the developer of the smartwatch, the software developer or others

Covid Tracing Tracker, MIT Technology Review 7 May 2020 https://www.technologyreview.com/2020/05/07/1000961/launching-mittr-covid-tracing-tracker/ accessed 16 July 2020; cf also the various contributions on tracing and tracking apps as part of MIT's '*Privacy in the Pandemic*' series https://slate.com/tag/privacy-in-the-pandemic accessed 16 July 2020.

7 Regulation (EU) 2016/679 of the European Parliament and of the Council of 27 April 2016 on the protection of natural persons with regard to the processing of personal data and on the free movement of such data, and repealing Directive 95/46/EC (General Data Protection Regulation) [2016] OJ L119/1.

8 Cf Martina Barbero et al., *Study on emerging issues of data ownership, interoperability, (re-)usability and access to data, and liability* (European Union 2017) Final Report 345.

9 See e.g., Kimberly van den Bergen et al., *The future of the medical technology market. Addressing challenges and utilising opportunities* (Rotterdam 2018), a report prepared for the Dutch government and presented to the lower house ("Second Chamber") of the Netherlands Parliament. One of the tendencies signalled in the report is "patient ownership". On p. 16 the report states: "The position of patients/consumers is changing and driven by the digital transformation, personalised care, remote healthcare, regulation and the focus on prediction and prevention. Patients are no longer simply recipients of healthcare, but are self-managing emancipated participants, in combination with their social network. There is and will be an increased focus on patient centeredness and patient ownership: patients are seen as co-producers of data as they increasingly have health technologies available to actively measure certain (surrogate) outcomes and aspects which are meaningful for their daily lives, and which enable active engagement." It can be assumed that "ownership" here was not used in a legal sense, but to explain how a patient experiences the use of "his/her" data. Still, the fact that the term ownership is used expresses a wider feeling that data are not just there, they are not "*res nullius*" and do belong to someone.

with an interest in these data. So-called "health apps" are already used widely by, for example, long-distance runners and others who are interested in their personal health and well-being. The development of coronavirus apps was, considering this rapid expansion of medtech among the general public, as such only a logical next step. However, unlike health apps which you can download from Google Play or the App Store, checking your heart beat, the distance you walk in a day, etc., coronavirus apps are no longer purely about patient-centred care.[10] Stakeholders regarding access to data collected by coronavirus apps are, therefore, next to obviously the (potential) patients themselves, health care providers, health insurers, health authorities, governments, the pharmaceutical industry, producers of medical equipment, hardware and software developers. With regard to software developers, we see great interest from the global tech industry, such as Google and Apple. Their initiative is, of course, to be supported, as both companies are active players on global data markets and, because of their access to extremely large data, are, perhaps more than many of us, aware of the enormous worldwide impact which the COVID-19 pandemic is having. Also, they did not develop an app as such but, in their own words an "Exposure Notification system in service of privacy-preserving contact tracing".[11] However, both Google and Apple are US-based companies and in light of the growing tendency towards de-globalisation, economic disintegration as a result of growing nationalism, isolationism and a call for regaining sovereignty, there might come a moment where political and strategic concerns are given precedence over idealist interests. Political data analytics might then take over from national patient-centred care analytics. It is, therefore, not unthinkable that a patient's health data (hopefully at least in an anonymised or pseudonymised format) might flow across the world to be used for research purposes in a foreign jurisdiction only for its own internal strategic purposes.[12] Such a government is of course not a legitimate stakeholder, but even as an illegitimate interested party it should not be ignored. Finally, when looking at who the stakeholders are regarding coronavirus apps, we must take into account that the European Union is an internal market where freedom of establishment and free flow of non-personal data exists, and where within the Schengen area the freedom exists to cross borders without being checked. Although these freedoms have been curtailed as part of national lockdown measures, still people work, travel and go on holiday cross-border. Within such an area of free travel, it is crucial

---

10 Cf Lucienne Berenschot et al., *The role of medical technologies and devices for patient-centred care* (Ecorys 2018), a report prepared for the Dutch government submitted to the lower house ("Second Chamber") of the Netherlands Parliament. It seems as if the widespread use of tracing or tracking apps was not really on the minds of the drafters. A possible global pandemic was outside their vision.

11 See https://www.apple.com/covid19/contacttracing accessed 16 July 2020.

12 Leaving aside the possibility that through reverse engineering the data might be traced back to a particular person.

that national coronavirus apps also work outside the countries for which they were developed. This is why the European Commission has become very active in at least coordinating the efforts by Member States to develop coronavirus apps. Together with the Member States, the European Commission developed a European Union (EU) toolbox to promote common standards, gave guidance on data protection and as part of the European eHealth Network presented "Interoperability guidelines for approved contact tracing mobile applications in the EU".[13] Thus, we need to add the European Union itself as another stakeholder concerning the data which result from such apps. In certain respects also the World Health Organization (WHO) is a stakeholder, given the worldwide nature of the pandemic, but the WHO is largely dependent on the cooperation of States regarding the gathering of data.

The difficulty with coronavirus apps is that the various stakeholders at the same time have shared interests (preventing or curing a disease) and diverging interests, more specifically health, commercial and public (societal, economic) interests, next to the reality that the apps potentially or perhaps already even actually are of great political relevance.

We all agree that we are, directly and indirectly, affected by the COVID-19 pandemic; we all want to avoid becoming ill and, once infected, we do not want to harm others by spreading the disease. However, we seem to deeply disagree when it comes to being traced or even tracked, because contact and localisation data resulting from tracing and tracking apps can also very well serve different aims than medtech purposes considering the diverse and sometimes opposing interests of stakeholders. Although the collected data are raw facts which gain meaning and can only be made useful in light of the purpose for which these data are being analysed, perhaps after having been combined with other data, still control over these raw facts is of vital importance for all interested parties.

Given the diversity of stakeholders and considering the possibility that data, once collected, could easily be used for purposes other than purely medical, no longer with the interests of patients as the underlying aim, fundamental legal questions have to be asked. To my mind the first, and all-enveloping, question is: to whom belongs the data in the first place, or phrased differently: Who "owns" the data? What does "belonging to" and "owning" mean in this respect? These are

---

13 See Commission Recommendation (EU) 2020/518 of 8 April 2020 on a common Union toolbox for the use of technology and data to combat and exit from the COVID19 crisis, in particular concerning mobile applications and the use of anonymised mobility data [2020] OJ L114/7. In their own words the European Commission requires coronavirus apps to be tracing apps, which "must be voluntary, transparent, temporary, cybersecure, using temporary and pseudonymised data; they should rely on Bluetooth technology and approved by national health authorities, and be interoperable across borders as well as across operating systems." For more information on the other aspects of EU policy mentioned see: https://ec.europa.eu/digital-single-market/en/news/coronavirus-common-approach-safe-and-efficient-mobile-tracing-apps-across-eu accessed 16 July 2020.

questions about (a) what the object of ownership is; (b) who the subjects holding a right of ownership can be; (c) the content of an "ownership" right; and (d) the relationship with others who also perhaps hold rights in such an object. This is the crux of property law, although not what might be called "classical" property law dating back to an era where first copying texts in monasteries and then using the printing press was already a revolution in disseminating information.

5. DATA AS "*RES NULLIUS*" OR PART OF "*DOMINIUM EMINENS*"?

Although data flows across borders, EU Member States have been developing their own versions of COVID-19 apps. Defending public health was (and to a greater or lesser degree frequently still is) seen as, primarily, an area strictly for national policy. The result was, except for a shared debate on privacy and data protection, a tendency to move away from European integration and sometimes even international coordination towards returning to old-style public international law notions of sovereignty. In such a view data about a country's citizens are seen as somehow "belonging" to that territory and are, therefore, what the Australian government called with regard to criminal intelligence a "national asset".[14] It resembles arguing that data are part of a State's eminent domain or "*dominium eminens*": "The state's right to exercise sovereignty and direct control over its territory, or any part thereof."[15] It is interesting to see that

---

14 Australian Criminal Intelligence Commission, *Australian Criminal Intelligence Management Strategy 2017–20, Intelligence partnerships for a safer Australia* (Commonwealth of Australia 2017), for example on p. 3. See Lyria Bennett Moses, 'Who owns information? Law enforcement information sharing as a case study in conceptual confusion' (2020) 43(2) UNSW Law Journal 615, 618, 635. As to data generated by the Australian COVIDSafe app Section 94ZC of the Australian Privacy Amendment (Public Health Contact Information) Act 2020 now states beyond doubt that it is the Australian Commonwealth which "owns" the data. The section reads as follows: "COVID app data is the property of the Commonwealth, and remains the property of the Commonwealth even after it is disclosed to, or used by: (a) a State or Territory health authority; or (b) any other person or body (other than the Commonwealth or an authority of the Commonwealth)." Cf on data as "national property" also Jasper A. Bovenberg, *Property Rights in Blood, Genes and Data: Naturally Yours?* (Martinus Nijhoff Publishers 2006), who in ch 5 discusses ownership and commercialisation of national collections of blood, genes and data.
It seems that no one is arguing that data belong to no one and are "*res nullius*", although it has been argued that personal data might be qualified as existing outside the realm of commerce ("*res extra commercium*"), see Václav Janeček and Gianclaudio Malgieri, 'Commerce in Data and the Dynamically Limited Alienability Rule' in Sebastian Lohsse, Reiner Schulze and Dirk Staudenmayer (eds), *Data as Counter-Performance: Contract Law 2.0?* (Hart/Nomos 2020).

15 Definitions taken from Aaron Fellmeth and Maurice Horwitz, *Guide to Latin in international law* (OUP 2009, online 2011). On the history of the eminent domain doctrine see Katherine McFarland, 'Privacy and Property: Two Sides of the Same Coin: The Mandate for Stricter Scrutiny for Government Uses of Eminent Domain' (2004) 14 BU Pub Int LJ 142, 144.

Germany also seems to approach data ownership questions from the perspective of sovereignty, but then sovereignty from an individual perspective. In a discussion paper from the German Ministry for Traffic and Digital Infrastructure it is stated that a "*Digitale Souveränität*" exists.[16] The paper, however, does not use the term "sovereignty" in the public international law sense, but as meaning "*wirtschaftliche, positive Verwertungsmöglichkeit*" (an economic and positive opportunity to make data valuable).[17] But even if sovereignty is limited in the way as is done by this German government paper on digital sovereignty, such personal sovereignty can only be given and defended by a State acting under its public international law sovereignty. Data are then, consequently, "things" under the control of the State and the State can, as a consequence, limit their transfer cross-border and can take data from individual citizens in the public interest. This is clearly the idea underlying the control of data flows in countries which created or are creating digital firewalls around them, demanding that data which are created, processed, analysed and transferred must remain on servers within that State's territory. Depending on the political system and data content, the State in this view also has the right to control such content and intervene if deemed necessary in the interest of public policy, public morals or the political foundations upon which the State is built.[18] This all may sound like a State with hardly any political freedoms, but it should be realised that no State accepts data flows with objectionable (i.e. criminal) content. States do intervene to protect citizen's fundamental rights and freedoms if data contains abusive substance, criminal law enforcement agents are given access to data as part of a criminal investigation and civil law enforcement agents may access a person's

16 Bundesministerium für Verkehr und digitale Infrastruktur, *"Eigentumsordnung" für Mobilitätsdaten? Eine Studie aus technischer, ökonomischer und rechtlicher Perspektive* (Berlin 2017); cf Andreas Boerding et al., 'Data Ownership – A Property Rights Approach from a European Perspective' (2018) 11 J. Civ. L. Stud., available at: https://digitalcommons.law.lsu.edu/jcls/vol11/iss2/5 accessed 16 July 2020, 331.

17 *"Eigentumsordnung" für Mobilitätsdaten?*, 86. It seems as if in questions regarding data ownership the term "sovereignty" is becoming just as ambivalent as the term "ownership". See also on the confusing use of the term "sovereignty" Julia Pohle, 'Digitale Souveränität' in Tanja Klenk, Frank Nullmeier and Göttrik Wewer (eds), *Handbuch Digitalisierung in Staat und Verwaltung* (Springer VS forthcoming), also available electronically https://papers.ssrn.com/sol3/papers.cfm?abstract_id=3435017 accessed 16 July 2020.

18 I will leave aside here the economic debate about public goods, which are both non-excludable and non-rivalrous. This aspect is particularly relevant when we could also consider academic researchers to be stakeholders. Indirectly they certainly are, as national health authorities will need input from academic and clinical research. The difficulty with e-health data gathered by coronavirus apps is that, if the app is technically only a tracing app, the data on the phone may for the time being only have been shared with a specific group of other mobile phone users who also have their Bluetooth function switched on. In that case only a limited number of data copies exist, limiting and thus excluding access and securing privacy. Nevertheless are the data still of a non-rivalrous nature. Cf David Blumenthal, Characteristics of a public good and how they are applied to health care data, in Claudia Grossmann et al. (eds), *Clinical Data As the Basic Staple of Health Learning : Creating and Protecting a Public Good: Workshop Summary* (National Academies Press 2010) 139.

assets in judicial enforcement proceedings at the request of a creditor against his/her debtor(s). So to some degree we accept that the State has some form of eminent domain regarding data as expression of its sovereignty. In the European Union this implies that, as far as Member States transferred their sovereignty to the Union as part of its developing internal market, the EU may also, albeit to the extent limited by the European treaties, control data flows and in fact this is precisely what the EU does. I only need to refer to the ePrivacy Directive, General Data Protection Regulation (GDPR), the Regulation on the free flow of non-personal data and the Directive on Open Data and the Re-use of Public Sector Information.[19] It is within the framework of both these regulations that the EU is considering whether it can oblige governments and businesses to share information.[20]

6. "OWNERSHIP" OF DATA?

In academic debates about the legal status of data, using the term "ownership" seems to provoke immediate and deep conflicts of opinion between public lawyers, particularly public lawyers focusing on privacy and data protection,

---

19 Directive 2002/58/EC of the European Parliament and of the Council of 12 July 2002 concerning the processing of personal data and the protection of privacy in the electronic communications sector (Directive on privacy and electronic communications), [2002] OJ L201/37 (to be replaced by a Regulation on Privacy and Electronic Communications); Regulation (EU) 2016/679 of the European Parliament and of the Council of 27 April 2016 on the protection of natural persons with regard to the processing of personal data and on the free movement of such data, and repealing Directive 95/46/EC (General Data Protection Regulation) [2016] OJ L119/1, Regulation (EU) 2018/1807 of the European Parliament and of the Council of 14 November 2018 on a framework for the free flow of non-personal data in the European Union [2018] OJ L303/59 and Directive (EU) 2019/1024 of the European Parliament and of the Council of 20 June 2019 on open data and the re-use of public sector information (recast) [2019] OJ L172/56 (replacing, from 17 July 2021, Directive 2003/98/EC of the European Parliament and of the Council, OJ L345/90 and Directive 2013/37/EU of the European Parliament and of the Council, OJ L175/1). See also the Communication from the Commission to the European Parliament and the Council *Guidance on the Regulation on a framework for the free flow of non-personal data in the European Union* (COM(2019) 250 final).

20 Communication from the Commission to the European Parliament, the Council, the European Economic and Social Committee and the Committee of the Regions *Towards a common European data space* ({SWD(2018) 125 final}, COM(2018) 232 final); Communication from the Commission to the European Parliament, the Council, the European Economic and Social Committee and the Committee of the Regions *A European strategy for data* (COM(2020) 66 final). On p. 29 and 30 of the Communication on a European Strategy for Data, the European Commission proposes to create a "Common European health data space". Whether the "sharing" or "pooling" of data will always be beneficial has already been questioned. See the report published by the European Commission, Directorate-General for Competition: Jacques Crémer, Yves-Alexandre de Montjoye and Heike Schweitzer, *Competition Policy for the digital era*, Final report (Publications Office of the European Union 2019), where next to pro-competitive advantages also anti-competitive aspects are being considered.

and private lawyers.[21] Merely using the term "data ownership", even when it is argued that we need to find a balance between shielding a person's privacy and giving proper weight to the interests of market participants who are in fact dealing in data for commercial purposes, is seen by some privacy lawyers as coming close to a contention which is inherently objectionable. The argument is that when data are so connected with an individual that they can be seen as part of one's personhood and are, therefore, "personal data", a reference to marketability (this being equal to accepting data "ownership") by itself comes close to a violation of someone's human rights, and reduces a person from a subject to an object.[22] Next to this split between public and private lawyers, we can see a further divide, throwing the debate into even further upheaval, caused by a fundamentally dissimilar approach, so it seems, towards legal thinking resulting from differing legal traditions, especially Civil Law and Common Law. Civil lawyers are inclined, as they are trained to think in more theoretical and systematic terms, to look at the debate from the viewpoint of trying to reach a consistent terminological framework which fits with the needs of legal practice. Common lawyers, however, are trained to think more from the perspective of problem solving, which however needs to be done in a conclusive way to convince those involved that the outcome is based on solid arguments and not on haphazard thoughts. Still, even within the two traditions, another difference of approach can be found. Sometimes the arguments are highly formalistic and dogmatic, sometimes more flexible and open to changing times. Let me first give two examples of the rather formalistic approach, one from a Civil Law jurisdiction another one from a Common Law jurisdiction. The German Civil

---

21 Cf Nadezhda Purtova, *Property Rights in Personal Data: A European Perspective* (Oisterwijk 2011); Barbara J. Evans, 'Much Ado about Data Ownership' (2011) 25 Harv J L & Tech 69; Lennart Chrobak, 'Proprietary Rights in Digital Data? Normative Perspectives and Principles of Civil Law', in Mor Bakhoum et al. (eds), *Personal Data in Competition, Consumer Protection and Intellectual Property Law. Towards a Holistic Approach?* (Springer 2018) 253 ff. See for a more recent overview of the debate from the position of European Union and property law Andreas Boerding et al., 'Data Ownership – A Property Rights Approach from a European Perspective', (2018) 11 J. Civ. L. Stud., available at: https://digitalcommons.law.lsu.edu/jcls/vol11/iss2/5 accessed 16 July 2020. Cf also about the broadening (and potentially challenging) impact of privacy law on questions relating to data entitlement Nadezhda Purtova, 'The law of everything. Broad concept of personal data and future of EU data protection law', Law, Innovation and Technology, 10:1, 40-81, DOI: 10.1080/17579961.2018.1452176 accessed 24 September 2020.

22 It has been argued that the Internet is in a process of recreating a feudal society where an elite group governs others who must serve their economic interests. This is called the "feudal Internet". See Sascha D. Meinrath, James W. Losey and Victor W. Pickard, 'Digital feudalism, Enclosures and erasures from digital rights management to the digital divide', Commlaw Conspectus 2011, 423; Natalie M. Banta, 'Property Interests in Digital Assets: The Rise of Digital Feudalism' (2017) 38 Cardozo L. Rev. 1099. In relatively recent Western history, a most horrific example of dehumanisation and denial of personhood is the Dred Scott case, in which the US Supreme Court ruled that slaves had no standing in court, lacking US Citizenship, Dred Scott v. Sandford, 60 U.S. 393 (1856).

Code (BGB) states in §90: " Only corporeal objects are things as defined by law." §903 states: "The owner of a thing may, to the extent that a statute or third-party rights do not conflict with this, deal with the thing at his discretion and exclude others from every influence. The owner of an animal must, when exercising his powers, take into account the special provisions for the protection of animals." The question whether data can be an object of ownership, is to be answered in the negative. Data is not a "thing" according to §90 and can, in light of §903, not be owned. In spite of the elaborate discussions in German legal literature on this question, this to my mind is the essence of the dogmatic debate.[23] Interestingly enough, a comparable methodology can be found in recent Australian literature, but not from the perspective of private law but criminal law.[24] If the starting point for the analysis (including interviews with law enforcement agencies) is the suggestion that "rather than searching for a coherent conception of information ownership, what matters is clarity around the rules for allocating the power to make decisions with respect to information and allocating responsibilities for information",[25] then the final conclusion of the interviews and the following theoretical analysis is an almost given fact. Data ownership does not exist.

European Union law certainly agrees with the latter statement when it comes to existing EU law regarding data as such. Neither the ePrivacy Directive, the General Data Protection Regulation (GDPR), the Regulation on a Framework for the Free Flow of Nonpersonal Data, the EU's laws on intellectual property, nor the Trade Secrets Directive contain a framework for accepting ownership of data outside the protection of personal data, trade secrets and software.[26]

23 Cf Andreas Boerding et al., 'Data Ownership – A Property Rights Approach from a European Perspective', (2018) 11 J. Civ. L. Stud., available at: https://digitalcommons.law.lsu.edu/jcls/vol11/iss2/5 accessed 16 July 2020, 359.

24 See Lyria Bennett Moses, 'Who owns information? Law enforcement information sharing as a case study in conceptual confusion' (2020) 43(2) UNSW Law Journal 615.

25 Lyria Bennett Moses, 'Who owns information? Law enforcement information sharing as a case study in conceptual confusion' (2020) 43(2) UNSW Law Journal 615, 624: "The law enforcement community includes individuals with two different understandings of what 'ownership' of information might mean. Each of these two conceptions of ownership comes with common means of identifying the entity that 'owns' information and articulating the consequences of that ownership. In particular, ownership as an allocation of power or control over information generally suggests a single owner, whereas ownership as the allocation of responsibilities for information may involve multiple owners. This suggests that, rather than searching for a coherent conception of information ownership, what matters is clarity around the rules for allocating the power to make decisions with respect to information and allocating responsibilities for information."

26 For databases see Directive 96/9/EC of the European Parliament and of the Council of 11 March 1996 on the legal protection of databases [1996] OJ L77/20, for software see Directive 2019/790/EU of the European Parliament and of the Council of 17 April 2019 on copyright and related rights in the Digital Single Market and amending Directives 96/9/EC and 2001/29/EC, OJ 2019, L130/92 (effective 7 June 2021) and for trade secrets see Directive 2016/943/EU of the European Parliament and of the Council of 8 June 2016 on the protection of undisclosed know-how and business information (trade secrets) against their unlawful acquisition, use and disclosure [2016] OJ L157/1.

Several reports have been published on this, and they all come to the same conclusion, with which the European Commission now apparently agrees.[27] However, this leaves the question unanswered whether data as such can be owned and if the European Union still should not introduce such a notion. Given that, at least for the time being, no unambiguous EU law in this area exists, answers can only be given at the level of the Member States, resulting in the need for a comparative legal examination. Such a comparative exercise, in light of socio-economic reality, might lead to a badly needed flexible and open mind, which is not held captive – not excluding being inspired! – by past dogmatic thinking. In that respect the recently expressed view by the European Commission that stakeholders do not favour a "data ownership" type of right is remarkable, considering that it is immediately followed by admitting that we do need rules on access. To my mind, there is hardly any difference between ownership and access. What is, given the nature of data, ownership other than being in control of access, portability, transfer or erasure (including the desisting from control or processing of data)? What else, to put it differently, than the right to manage data in an environment where several people at the same time may have concurring or competing rights to access, portability, transfer and erasure?[28] In such an environment, ownership of data means management of access, and it seems as if the European Union is moving into that direction.

I must admit that the term "ownership" and particularly the use of that term in English has an inherently ambivalent meaning. In (particularly American) English you can "own" a management process next to "owning" your car. The meaning of the term in a legal sense is also not clear, to put it mildly, certainly not from a comparative viewpoint.[29] Whereas in Germany, ownership is limited

---

[27] Cf also, Martina Barbero et al., *Study on emerging issues of data ownership, interoperability, (re-) usability and access to data, and liability* (European Union 2017) Final Report; Benoit Van Asbroeck, Julien Debussche and Jasmien César, *Building the European Data Economy. Data Ownership.* White Paper (Bird & Bird 2017), *Data Ownership. A new EU right in data.* Supplementary Paper (Bird & Bird 2017).
See recently the view of the European Commission in their Communication *Towards a common European data space*, 9: "In general, stakeholders also do not favour a new 'data ownership' type of right, with a range of inputs indicating that the crucial question in business-to-business sharing is not so much about ownership, but about how access is organised."

[28] Martina Barbero et al., *Study on emerging issues of data ownership, interoperability, (re-) usability and access to data, and liability* (European Union 2017) Final Report 286, discussing the nexus between data ownership, access to and use of data, and the interoperability of services in Industry 4.0 in general.

[29] Cf Yaëll Emerich, *Droit commun des biens: perspective transsystématique* (Éditions Yvon Blais 2017) 241 ff. (discussing the "notion" – not the "concept" – of a thing ("bien"); Sabrina Praduroux, 'Objects of property rights: old and new' in Michele Graziadei and Lionel Smith (eds), *Comparative Property Law* (Edward Elgar 2017) 51 ff. Remarkably enough, although the book was published in 2017, Praduroux does not devote any attention to the enormously important role of data and the data economy.

to the most extensive right concerning physical things, in France, ownership can also be the most extensive right with respect to immaterial things, such as a claim. There is clearly a legal diversity from a comparative law perspective.[30] Nevertheless, without, on the one hand, becoming too elusive and, on the other hand, falling in the abyss of technicalities, my approach is to look for common thought patterns or, if you wish, stepping stones or signposts.

Property law is about legal relations between a subject and a considerable and relevant group of other subjects regarding an object. Property rights have a far greater effect than rights arising from contracts, tort or unjust enrichment. These latter rights are between two or more specific persons, where one person has a right which corresponds with an obligation resting on another person. Interestingly enough, the law regarding such personal rights does not seem to focus on the right itself but, more negatively, on the corresponding duty and is called the law of "obligations". The law of property is more positive, it focuses on what the holder of the right can do and is only negative when it regulates how others can be excluded, but even that appears to be a positive exclusion. In the law of property, the rights conferred on a person are against a group of other persons, in Civil Law terminology even the whole world ("*erga omnes*"). These other persons have a duty to accept such property right.[31] This makes a property right very strong and this is why it is given the qualification "absolute" to distinguish it from more personal rights, which are qualified as "relative". The terms "absolute" and "relative" express the strength of the right by delineating against whom it can be invoked. To put it differently: absolute rights are relative in the sense that a subject can only have rights against other subjects. Saying that a property right is a right in a thing is therefore an unfortunate expression. A property right concerns the legal position of a subject vis-à-vis other subjects regarding an object. Another question is, as we already saw, which objects the law recognises, in other words: which legal objects does the law accept? Can only physical things be legal objects, can monetary claims or the products of human creativity be a legal object too? And finally, also the subject who has such a property right concerning an object is defined by the law: only natural and legal persons can be a legal subject. Taken all of the above together, we see that legal systems, given the absolute nature of property rights, not only limit the number and content of these rights but also the number and content of legal objects and

30 Although Christian v. Bar, *Gemeineuropäisches Sachenrecht* (Volume I, C.H. Beck 2015, Volume II, C.H. Beck 2019) seems to imply that property law underlies an overall legal-dogmatic theory and system. For a brief overview of definitions of ownership in various legal systems see Christian v. Bar, Vol. I, 499. See also: Sjef van Erp and Bram Akkermans (eds), *Ius Commune Casebooks for the Common Law of Europe. Cases, Materials and Text on Property Law* (Hart Publishing 2012) 211.

31 Cf for a further analysis: Willem Loof, *Of trustees and beneficial owners. An inquiry into the proprietary aspects of trusts and trust-like devices from a European private law perspective* (Datawyse/Universitaire Pers Maastricht, 2016) 36.

the various categories of legal subjects. Traditionally, it is argued that limiting the number and content of property rights is at the heart of the doctrine of the "*numerus clausus*" of property rights. The law lays down in mandatory format which rights are possible as having absolute effect, what the content of these rights is and how these rights are created, transferred and extinguished. This *numerus clausus* doctrine, therefore, has both a substantive and a procedural side. However, what has been forgotten is that, when the law defines or describes – depending upon how the legal system approaches its basic concepts and terms – the number and content of absolute rights, the object of such right is part of the definition. By being an element of the definitional framework, the object qualifies what the right's content is, as the right only concerns that particular object. It could, therefore, be said that the object is a "qualifier" of the right, it gives shape to what the right means.[32] This is, furthermore, done against the background that only natural or legal persons can be holders of a right. A clear example is the Netherlands Civil Code. In Article 5:1 ownership is defined as the most complete right which a person can have regarding a thing. What a thing is can be found in Article 3:2, where it is defined as physical objects prone to human control. The definition of ownership is qualified by the object of the right with, furthermore, a reference to natural persons by demanding that human control be the yardstick. The qualification, and consequently limitation, of the right by including the type of object in its definition implies that different types of "most complete" rights can be created, depending on the object. This is, both from a historical and from a comparative point of view, nothing new.

Before the French Revolution, the Civil Law knew the distinction between "*dominium directum*" and "*dominium utile*". The *dominium directum* was the *superior*'s right to collect rent from the person actually using the land (*inferior*), a situation of *duplex dominium*. After the French Revolution a different type of ownership was introduced: *dominium plenum*, although the French *Cour de Cassation* decided in the famous *Caquelard v Lemoine* case that the definition of ownership in Article 544 of the French Civil Code was an expression of French common law ("*droit commun*"), but did not exclude other types of ownership, as pre-existed under the customary law of Normandy.[33] The *Cour de Cassation*

---

32 For a further analysis see Sjef van Erp, Ownership of data and the numerus clausus of legal objects, in Sandra Murphy and Padraic Kenna (eds), *eConveyancing and title registration in Ireland* (Clarus Press, 2019) 125–140.

33 *Caquelard c. Lemoine*, Req. 13 februari 1834, D. 1834, 1, 218, S. 34, 1, 205. The decision is very short and reads as follows: "Sur le premier moyen, tiré de la violation des articles 544, 546, 552 et 691 du Code civil, et 607 de la coutume de Normandie:

> Attendu, en fait, qu'après avoir, dans ses motifs, reconnu formellement à Caquelard et à Lemoine un droit de copropriété sur la berge ou chaussée dont il s'agit, et avoir expliqué la nature et les limites respectives de ce droit, d'après les faits et les circonstances particulières de la cause, et notamment l'origine commune des deux usines, la possession réciproque, l'intérêt commun à la conservation de la berge, la charge de l'entretenir, et l'appréciation

affirmed its approach in two more recent cases regarding the *Maison de Poésie*, introducing a new property right the "*droit réel de jouissance spéciale*" (property right of special use).[34] It is also interesting to note that in the recent Belgian property law reform also a more flexible and open approach towards the doctrine of *numerus clausus* can be found.[35] Article 3.3 new Belgian Civil Code on the one hand enumerates which property rights are recognised under Belgian law and that only the legislator can change this list but on the other hand, it is made clear in Article 3.1 new Belgian Civil Code that this provision is of a non-mandatory nature, allowing parties to deviate, except for the definitions and unless the legislative text provides otherwise. As I already indicated, the *numerus clausus* doctrine is inherently linked with the concept of ownership. It contains not only that the number and content of property rights is limited, but it also contains a limitation regarding the object of the right as well as the subject. There can only be one subject and not several, except in situations of, for example, co-ownership in which full ownership is shared. The policy choice behind the Civil Law *numerus clausus* doctrine is to prevent fragmentation of ownership. This becomes clear when looking at the definition of ownership in, for example, the new Belgian Civil Code. In Article 3.50 ownership is defined as the most complete right, given to a legal subject (the "owner") directly, to use, benefit and alienate the object of such right, although as limited by legislation and the rights of third parties.[36] What objects can be is defined in a rather indirect and somewhat complicated way; an expression of today's uncertainties as to what may constitute an object of property law. First of all, a distinction is made between legal objects and legal subjects. According to Article 3.38 things (in French: "*choses*") must be distinguished from animals, objects and animals must be distinguished from persons. Article 3.40 states that things ("*choses*") can

---

de certains actes, l'arrêt attaqué reconnaît et déclare de nouveau, dans son dispositif, le même concours de propriétaires et les limites respectives de leurs droits; ce qui écarte l'application des articles 691 du Code civil, et 607, coutume de Normandie;

Attendu, en droit, que les articles 544, 546 et 552 du Code civil, sont déclaratifs du droit commun relativement à la nature et aux effets de la propriété, mais ne sont pas prohibitifs;

Que ni ces articles, ni aucune autre loi, n'excluent les diverses modifications et décompositions dont le droit ordinaire de propriété est susceptible;"

34 *Maison de Poésie I*, Cass Civ 3ème 31 October 2012, no. 11-16304 and *Maison de Poésie II*, Cass. 3ème civ. 8 September 2016, n° 14-26.953.

35 The text of Book 3 new Belgian Civil Code, containing the new law of property can be found at http://www.ejustice.just.fgov.be/cgi_loi/change_lg.pl?language=nl&la=N&cn=2020020416&table_name=wet (Dutch version), http://www.ejustice.just.fgov.be/cgi_loi/change_lg.pl?language=fr&la=F&cn=2020020416&table_name=loi (French version) accessed 16 July 2020. The new law will enter into force on 1 September 2021.

36 The French version of Article 3.50 new Belgian Civil Code reads: "Le droit de propriété confère directement au propriétaire le droit d'user de ce qui fait l'objet de son droit, d'en avoir la jouissance et d'en disposer. Le propriétaire a la plénitude des prérogatives, sous réserve des restrictions imposées par les lois, les règlements ou par les droits de tiers."

be material and immaterial, to which Article 3.41 adds that objects (in French: "*biens*") in their widest sense can be anything that can be appropriated, including patrimonial rights.[37] Furthermore, the new code distinguishes public property ("*biens publics*") from private property ("*biens privés*") as separate legal objects by stating in Article 3.45 that public property belongs to the private domain, unless meant to be used in the public domain. A reference to who can be the owner of public property has deliberately not been given. This does not necessarily have to be a public legal person.[38] The Explanatory Memorandum further clarifies that the legislator was guided by the need to follow technical evolution and scientific progress combined with pragmatism.[39] Still, from the perspective of the question whether data can be owned, the new provisions do not result in an obvious reply. If personal data are considered to be part of someone's personality, does Article 3.38 then prevent the conclusion that data can be owned, even though the new Belgian Civil Code shows a very open, flexible and pragmatic approach as to what can be an object of ownership? Furthermore, defining ownership following the classical triangle "*usus, fructus, abusus*", qualified by a classical description of what can constitute a legal object, counterbalances the open *numerus clausus* approach. The new code does not really tell us whether ownership could also mean access, portability, transfer and erasure of data. The new legal framework could result in two completely contradictory approaches, depending upon how the judiciary would relatively value the classical definition of ownership in light of the explicitly open policy regarding the *numerus clausus*. It could mean that the content of what ownership is in fact results in undoing the flexibility earlier created regarding the *numerus clausus* doctrine. It could, however, also mean that the openness of the *numerus clausus* approach must have its beneficial impact also on the content of the right of ownership. As far as I can see, there is no clear answer yet. All of this shows how difficult it is for a legislator, bound – even with the awareness that flexibility is badly needed – by the format of setting rules, to create rules providing workable answers for our fast-developing hybrid society. It also raises the question whether perhaps in the area of data ownership case law should be preferred.

A look at the Common Law will immediately show that, if a property law system is primarily case-law based, it becomes very complicated, depending on a myriad of cases functioning against a plethora of separate statutes. Answers to

---

37 Article 3.39 makes clear that animals, although having a protected legal status, are not things.

38 *Wetsontwerp houdende invoeging van Boek 3 "Goederen" in het nieuw Burgerlijk Wetboek/Projet de Loi portant insertion du Livre 3 "Les biens" dans le nouveau Code civil*, Belgische Kamer van Volksvertegenwoordigers/Chambre de Représentants de Belgique, 31 October 2018, Doc 54 3348/001, 111. The full legislative file can be found under number 55K0173.

39 *Wetsontwerp houdende invoeging van Boek 3 "Goederen" in het nieuw Burgerlijk Wetboek/Projet de Loi portant insertion du Livre 3 "Les biens" dans le nouveau Code civil*, 102 and 104.

fundamental questions might take a very long time after a period of conflicting decisions and ensuing uncertainty. To avoid such overcomplication, an overall legislative framework seems unavoidable. The question, however, is how to formulate such a framework. The Common Law might not provide an adequate solution from a formal point of view, but it does provide possible answers from a substantive viewpoint. In the Common Law, no unifying and overall concept of "property" and "ownership" exists. The law is object dependent, and a distinction must be made as to land and personal property (next to, of course, intellectual property). In land law, at least in theory, ownership can only exist at the level of the Crown, but generally speaking rights in land are "held" by a subject. This is the direct result of the historical foundations of this part of the Common Law in feudalism, not unlike as can be found on the Continent of Europe before the French Revolution. Another layer, on top of this feudal origin, has been created by the development of equity, which supplements the older established common law in a strict sense. Since 1925, according to section 1 of the Law of Property Act 1925, in England and Wales, the common law estates in land are freehold and leasehold, next to which equity has created its own rights in land, the prime example of the coming together of common law and equity, of course, being the trust.[40] Also with regard to personal property, no unitary concept of ownership is recognised, except "title". Title is relative, it expresses that the entitlement of one subject is stronger than that of another. What we see is an object driven property law with right holders who have entitlements with varying degrees of (in Hohfeldian terminology) rights, powers, privileges and immunities.[41] There can be several "owners" with differing rights, sometimes in competition with one another, not unlike in pre-French Revolutionary law recognised in Continental legal systems with the acceptance of *duplex dominium* and in line with older French case law accepting that different types of fragmented ownership remained in existence next to the concept of ownership in the French Civil Code. The latter again shows that a classical Civil Law approach in which only the legislator can create property rights is running the risk that it turns a property law system into a straitjacket, thwarting future legal development. In today's world, we do not need a conservative and counter-progressive attitude towards property law, but we want pragmatism and flexibility against a background of recognised values, policy choices, principles, notions and concepts, and ground rules. Values such as stability and predictability; policy choices such as protecting fundamental human rights and promoting the development of commerce; principles such

40 Willem Loof, *Of trustees and beneficial owners. An inquiry into the proprietary aspects of trusts and trust-like devices from a European private law perspective* (Datawyse/Universitaire PersMaastricht, 2016) 54.

41 Wesley Newcomb Hohfeld, 'Some Fundamental Legal Conceptions as Applied in Judicial Reasoning' (1913) 23 Yale L J 16.

as *numerus clausus*, transparency and hierarchy; notions and concepts of core property rights; and ground rules such as that no one can transfer more rights than you have and that older rights have priority over younger rights. From a substantive viewpoint, the Common Law offers such a pragmatic and flexible approach by its historic focus on the objects of property law and its acceptance of a variation of property rights, which can co-exist and be in competition at the same time. A more pragmatic, functionalist approach, built on a case-based interest analysis, can also be found in Scandinavian legal systems.[42] So what would a possible framework regarding data "ownership", meaning a right to access, portability, transfer and erasure, look like?

7. UNBUNDLING "OWNERSHIP" AS ACCESS MANAGEMENT

Each and every property law system will be confronted with the following four basic questions: (a) What is the nature of a property entitlement (what distinguishes property rights from rights against one or more specific persons), (b) who can be a subject of property law (a "legal" subject), (c) what can be an object of property law (a "legal" object) and, in light of the foregoing, (d) which property rights does a legal system recognise? To give a very straightforward reply to the question what the nature of property rights is, it can be said that a property right protects the right holder against claims by a relevant and considerable group of other subjects. This includes both the traditional Civil Law and Common Law systematisation. The Civil Law considers the distinction between personal rights and real rights as essential, whereby real rights are rights "erga omnes", i.e. against the whole world. This might sound very principled, but it is in fact highly theoretical, because most of the world is not really interested in the objects around a subject. What matters are the subjects in your direct or indirect vicinity, which comes much closer to the Common Law's less absolutist and more relative approach.

The questions asked above, although they can be distinguished, are closely connected. If we take as our starting point for analysing the right of ownership,

42 Cf more generally about the position of Scandinavian law from the perspective of both the civil law and the common law tradition: Jacob W. F. Sundberg, 'Civil law, common law and the Scandinavians' 13 Scandinavian Studies in Law (Almqvist & Wiksell, 1969) 179. See also Claes Martinson, 'The Scandinavian Approach to Property Law, Described through Six Common Legal Concepts' (2014) 22 Juridica International Law Review, DOI: https://doi.org/10.12697/JI.2014.22.02 accessed 24 September 2020 and Karoline Rakneberg Haug, 'The historical development of the Scandinavian functional approach to transfer of ownership: a tale of change and continuity' (2017) 6 European Prop L J 236.

then defining it as the maximum of power over a physical asset, it inevitably becomes crucial to know if an asset is physical or not to find out whether you are the owner (or not). If, on the contrary, we take the object as our point of departure, we could then look at who are involved as stakeholders and, considering the nature of the object and who the stakeholders are, consider any rights which the legal system may confer while accepting this object as a "legal" object and the relevant stakeholders as "legal" subjects. It is the latter, object based, approach which I would advocate regarding data or, to put it more precisely, at least regarding digital assets: a cluster of data sufficiently separate from other data to be considered an individual object to fulfil the leading property law principle of transparency, more particularly specificity, as it must be clear as to which object a property right exists. If a sufficiently described object is absent, claiming that a subject has "ownership" of such an object is meaningless and without any effect. The question "I own", demands a reply to the question: "What do you own?". In my view data on a mobile phone, created by a corona app, are sufficiently limited in size and content that they can be considered, and hence qualify, to be at least a digital asset and hence a possible object of property law. Regarding who can be legal subjects, we must look at the various categories of stakeholders, considering the interests which they represent. The most important stakeholder is, first and foremost, the person on whose mobile phone the app has been installed and activated. The data concern such a person directly and immediately. Other stakeholders are third persons having been close enough to an infected person that they are now running the risk of becoming ill themselves. Stakeholders are also health authorities who need to know about how the disease is spreading, otherwise, they cannot react in the interest of public health. Closely linked to national health authorities are health providers who must be aware of the fact that a particular person has been in contact with an infected person and, consequently, might also be ill. Finally, it could also be argued that, by accepting that health authorities are stakeholders and, therefore, entitled to some right in the data, this likewise applies to a national government in the interest of public health. Furthermore, the pharmaceutical industry should not be ignored. Without their research laboratories, production facilities and manufacturing capacity, no vaccine can be created and mass-produced. From that perspective, commercial interests at least to some degree run parallel to, although they are not equal to, public health interests.

The overview of stakeholders makes clear that an overall framework for a right creating a property entitlement in data, more specifically a digital asset, that is enforceable against a relevant and considerable group of third persons cannot be an absolute and exclusive right for only one stakeholder. The same conclusion must be drawn from the perspective of the object. The intangible, fluid, non-rivalrous nature of data entails that it can be copied easily without the original holder of the data losing his/her own set of data. Whenever data are becoming mixed, already because of the combination itself, several stakeholders may be involved. Some because they pool data (for example by together using an online platform), others because together they co-generate enhanced data (for example by analysing raw data sets with other data sets, thus creating value added data).[43]

Considering the above arguments about legal objects and legal subjects of a possible ownership right in data gathered by a coronavirus app, the entitlement itself cannot be absolute in the classical sense of the legal term as understood in the Civil Law tradition, but must be relative in nature. We need to look at this from the perspective of each category of stakeholders. Let me, as the obvious example, focus on the person whose mobile phone collected data by using a coronavirus app, which, with the user's permission, were later sent to a central server which could be checked by other phone users who also installed such an app. Following a timeline, various types of interests in the data may be distinguished. At first, the interest is strictly personal, and the right attached can be full control over the data ("ownership"). After allowing the data to be transmitted to a central server, they become non-personal and consequently, competing rights can be attached. The latter type of rights can be of two kinds: of a public or of a commercial character and in some cases of a mixed nature. Given the character of the object (intangible, a cluster of data, e-health data relevant for third parties and for public health authorities), a flexible and open approach as to the content of the right must be sought which must include a time factor. As long as the data are on the user's phone, only the user is "owner", allowing only the user access, portability, transfer and erasure. Afterwards, ownership is fragmented over relevant third parties, such as health authorities and health providers. This process of fragmentation, or in European law terminology "unbundling", demands a management structure of data "ownership" whereby it could be argued that at the end it all comes down to time management of access, because portability, transfer and erasure (including the desisting from control or processing of data) are essentially all different aspects of giving, not-giving or ending access, with degrees of access varying over time.[44]

Access management based on unbundling of ownership is not only a legal but also a strategic tool and as such it can contribute to a balanced distribution and allocation of rights. Following that methodology is nothing new from the perspective of EU law. It is a frequently used instrument to open up markets and break monopolies. Examples can be found with regard to public transport (rail),

---

43 Nicholas Terry, 'Legal issues relating to data access, pooling and use' in Claudia Grossmann et al. (eds), *Clinical Data As the Basic Staple of Health Learning : Creating and Protecting a Public Good: Workshop Summary* (National Academies Press 2010) 151.

44 For a further elaboration of my views regarding management as data ownership see Sjef van Erp, 'Management as Ownership of Data' in Sebastian Lohsse, Reiner Schulze and Dirk Staudenmayer (eds), *Data as Counter-Performance: Contract Law 2.0?* (Hart/Nomos 2020).

gas and electricity markets and telecommunications.[45] The starting point for unbundling is that no one single stakeholder or market participant should have full control over data. This can be done by splitting up a market, services or service providers to create competition. Such unbundling can be done in several ways through legal, operational, informational and ownership unbundling. Legal and ownership unbundling can go hand in hand and is intended to divide control over several market participants. Operational unbundling implies splitting up operations over several independent legal entities, and informational unbundling implies making information accessible to other market participants. The latter approach can be found in recent policy papers by the European Commission to create European common data spaces and promote, perhaps even oblige, data sharing between business and governments, and among businesses.[46] One of these common data spaces should be in the area of health data. Such informational unbundling can be done by giving access to others than those who create data. At the same time, by giving access ownership unbundling has also been achieved. However, a clear and workable legal framework regarding time management of access rights must then be in place.

8. CONCLUSION

We must turn away from a negative approach towards data "ownership". Instead, we should start thinking about how to protect rights in data from the perspective of all those having personal, public or commercial interests. The law would then again become a realistic tool in a fair and equitable allocation of rights in data. By taking the model of ownership unbundling as part of a wider effort towards distributing data ownership rights over the various stakeholders, we can build a clear and workable framework within which data can be created and processed.

With regard to data gathered by the use of coronavirus apps, it is evident that the subject whose mobile phone is collecting contact data by using Bluetooth technology must be seen as originator of the data and therefore the prime person entitled to access, transfer, portability and erasure. However, it should not be forgotten that the purpose for which the data are gathered is of a public health nature. When analysing who could also be entitled to the gathered data we

---

45 For public transport see the "Fourth railway package" https://ec.europa.eu/transport/modes/rail/packages/2013_en, for gas and electricity see the so-called "Third energy package": https://ec.europa.eu/energy/topics/markets-and-consumers/market-legislation/third-energy-package_en and for telecommunications see https://ec.europa.eu/competition/sectors/telecommunications/overview_en.html accessed 16 July 2020.

46 See the Communication *Towards a common European data space* ([SWD(2018) 125 final], COM(2018) 232 final) and the Communication *A European strategy for data* (COM(2020) 66 final).

must take into account (a) all interests (private, public, commercial) involved, (b) the nature (personal or non-personal) of the collected data, (c) the purpose for which these data are collected (protecting public health) and how these purposes fit within both (d) the rule of law protecting our privacy and (e) our market-based economies. Finally, we should not deny the crucial role which governments have to play when societies become socially and economically disrupted because of a pandemic as we experience today. In such a situation, markets might fail and begin to disfunction (for example because of hoarding) and academic researchers, together with the pharmaceutical industry, will have to find adequate solutions at the shortest possible notice. It is then in the interest of all that governments through their health authorities become important stakeholders in the data collected by tracing (and/or tracking) apps. From that perspective it can be argued that such data are a "national asset" and that digital sovereignty not only means that an individual should have control over its "own" data but that also the State claims sovereignty over such data. That could, as a final consequence, result in an approach under which the State would be allowed to "expropriate" collected data in the general interest, subjects being safeguarded against unjust interference with their data through the general principles governing expropriation. Such expropriation could take place against individual citizens but also against anyone else having access to data, including commercial parties. Forced sharing of data, as discussed in EU documents, might prevent such a situation.

We urgently need a Data Act with a positive approach towards "ownership" of data, laying down clear rules on access management, portability, transfer and erasure, protecting individual's personal data, but also structuring the development of data markets and laying the foundations to justify State interference and consequently a State's right to obtain data access in the interests of public health. This Data Act must also provide a solid framework for a fair and equal allocation of data. That framework should, however, be flexible, accepting that "ownership" of data is not the same as ownership of physical assets, that several subjects can have differing rights in data, varying over time and that such rights may coincide. A classical 19th century, post-French Revolutionary, property law approach will not work anymore. The Civil Law will need a return to a fragmented notion of ownership in line with the Common Law.[47]

---

[47] Cf also Sjef van Erp, 'Fluidity of ownership and the tragedy of hierarchy. A sign of a revolutionary evolution?', (2015) 4 European Prop L J 56. Inspiration could perhaps be found in developments regarding Digital Rights Management (DRM) creating technologically controlled access to digital assets protected by copyright. See on DRM Christopher May, *Digital Rights Management: The Problem of Expanding Ownership Rights* (Chandos Publishing 2007), especially ch 3, discussing various types of DRM.

COVID-19 APPS AND DATA PROTECTION

Christiane WENDEHORST*

---

* University of Vienna.

In the fight against the pandemic the use of so-called COVID-19 apps has triggered a lively debate. This contribution analyses different types of COVID-19 apps and their legal implications, focusing in particular on aspects of data protection law. It demonstrates why – at least with regard to proximity tracing and fully decentralised designs such as the DP-3T design – the public uproar is completely unfounded and irrational, rejecting a measure that is so privacy-friendly that it may not even get into the scope of the GDPR, at the price of forcing public and private parties to use much more intrusive methods of contract tracing. The contribution closes by explaining why, paradoxically, it may precisely be the privacy-friendliness of the app and the voluntariness of its use that makes it rather ineffective as a means to fight the pandemic, which in turn has implications for its assessment, as remaining dangers of "function creep" suddenly seem to prevail.

1. INTRODUCTION

The COVID-19 pandemic has led to a digital boost for Europe. Almost everything that used to require physical presence is suddenly being done remotely and with digital means, ranging from school teaching to conferences to court trials. It does therefore not come as a surprise that the fight against the pandemic itself is being fought with digital means. Among these digital means, the use of so-called COVID-19 apps – i.e. mobile applications to be used by the broad population – has triggered a lively debate. The debate has not just been lively, but surprisingly emotional. While hardly anyone seems to worry about the many thousands of mobile applications used for collecting our data, accessing our cameras, microphones and messages, and possibly disclosing the most sensitive data or any inferences to unknown third parties, COVID-19 apps caused a public uproar in some places. In Austria, for example, a range of political parties agreed to some overdue and innocuous clarifications in the Epidemic Law only under the condition that the use of contact tracing technologies was explicitly prohibited.[1] For some experts, this does still not go far enough, and they are calling for a new law that forever guarantees absolute voluntariness of contact tracing apps.[2] So are contact tracing apps now the

1 Austrian Epidemic Law, s 15 (3), as amended by BGBl. I Nr. 33/2021, with certain exceptions for particular sectors added later.

2 Nikolaus Forgó, 'Einige Bemerkungen zu datenschutzrechtlichen Rahmenbedingungen des Einsatzes von Tracing Apps zur Bekämpfung der COVID-19-Krise' Version 1.0 (2020) 34 https://id.univie.ac.at/fileadmin/user_upload/i_id/Website_Header_IDLaw/Gutachten13.pdf accessed 16 July 2020.

decisive step into George Orwell's 1984, which data protection lawyers must put a halt to?

2. OVERVIEW OF COVID-19 APPS

At a closer look, there is not just one type of COVID-19 app, but rather a panoply of different types of COVID-19 apps that serve different purposes and feature different functionalities and designs.[3]

2.1. INFORMATION APPS

Information apps provide COVID-19-related information, for example, about the current restrictions applicable at a particular location or for a particular institution, or about the density of people at a particular location. They become all the more important as restrictions vary all the time, individuals start travelling again, and many States have changed their strategies from national to regional or local, i.e. there are many different COVID-19 regimes within the territory of the same State. Versions that are more sophisticated would be queue management apps[4] that help regulate the number of visitors at a sight, for example. From a data protection point of view, such information apps are not different from the many apps that provide information about nearby restaurants or public transport facilities, so everything depends on the design and on whether personal data – such as geolocation data – not strictly required for providing the service are processed and maybe used for different purposes. If either is the case, the free, specific and informed consent[5] of the data subject within the meaning of Articles 4(11), 6(1)(a) and 7 of the GDPR[6] is normally required. If this is not the case, the legal basis is Article 6(1)(b) as the processing is required for fulfilling

---

3 Lists with an overview of different apps are available at 'GNSS for Crisis' (4 September 2020) https://www.gsa.europa.eu/gnss4crisis; 'COVID-19 Digital Rights Tracker' https://www.top10vpn.com/research/investigations/covid-19-digital-rights-tracker/ accessed 16 July 2020.

4 'GNSS for Crisis' (4 September 2020) https://www.gsa.europa.eu/gnss4crisis accessed 16 July 2020.

5 European Data Protection Board (EDPB), 'Guidelines 05/2020 on consent under Regulation 2016/679' (Version 1.1, 4 May 2020) 6 ff https://edpb.europa.eu/sites/edpb/files/files/file1/edpb_guidelines_202005_consent_en.pdf accessed 16 July 2020.

6 Regulation (EU) 2016/679 of the European Parliament and of the Council of 27 April 2016 on the protection of natural persons with regard to the processing of personal data and on the free movement of such data and repealing Directive 95/46/EC [2016] OJ L 119/1 (General Data Protection Regulation).

obligations under a contract.[7] Only very exceptionally will Article 6(1)(e) or (f) provide the legal basis.

2.2. SYMPTOM CHECK APPS

Symptom check apps make it easier for people with certain combinations of symptoms to detect a possible COVID-19 infection and to have themselves isolated and tested at an early stage. They are just COVID-19 specific variants of the many health recommender apps around, where individuals tick boxes and answer questions in order to receive, ultimately, a score indicating the probability that they are COVID-19 positive and/or a recommendation on how to react. Such health apps always operate in a grey zone between the Medical Device Regulation[8] and unregulated lifestyle products,[9] the majority of providers making efforts to stay within the unregulated zone. From a data protection perspective, these COVID-19 apps have the same status as other health apps. Given that the data they process qualify as special categories of data within the meaning of Article 9 GDPR, they usually rely on explicit consent within the meaning of Article 9(2)(a).

2.3. DATA DONATION APPS

Data donation apps are used for the disclosure of mobility data and similar data for pandemic research and public planning purposes. For example, the German Robert-Koch-Institute first developed and advertised a "COVID data donation app" the sole purpose of which was the collection of data, while it was explicitly not foreseen to provide any warning to individuals even where the data disclosed that individuals had been close to a COVID-19 positive person.[10] In terms of

---

7 EDPB, 'Guidelines 2/2019 on the processing of personal data under Article 6(1)(b) GDPR in the context of the provision of online services to data subjects' (8 October 2019) https://edpb.europa.eu/sites/edpb/files/files/file1/edpb_guidelines-art_6-1-b-adopted_after_public_consultation_en.pdf accessed 17 July 2020; Friedrich Graf von Westphalen and Christiane Wendehorst, 'Der Entwurf neuer Leitlinien des Europäischen Datenschutzausschusses 2/2019 betreffend die Auslegung von Art. 6 Abs. 1 lit. b DSGVO' (2019) 41 ZIP, 1937.

8 Council Regulation (EU) 2017/745 of 5 April 2017 on medical devices, amending Directive 2001/83/EC, Regulation (EC) No 178/2002 and Regulation (EC) No 1223/2009 and repealing Council Directives 90/385/EEC and 93/42/EEC [2017] OJ L 117/1 (Medical Device Regulation).

9 Medical Device Regulation, Recital 19.

10 Robert Koch Institut, 'Coronavirus SARS-CoV-2 – Blog zur wissenschaftlichen Auswertung der Corona-Datenspende-App' (6 May 2020) https://www.rki.de/DE/Content/InfAZ/N/Neuartiges_Coronavirus/Corona-Datenspende.html accessed 16 July 2020; id. 'Corona Datenspende – Blog' (10 July 2020) https://corona-datenspende.de/science/ accessed 16 July 2020.

data protection, these apps are the paradigm case of free consent within the meaning of Articles 6(1)(a) and 9(2)(a) GDPR, consent not even being tied to the provision of any kind of benefit.

2.4. IMMUNITY APPS

A lively debate has also arisen around immunity apps, which are not really apps at all but should more appropriately be called digital immunity passports.[11] They are used to record and prove the immunity status of individuals for situations where freedom of movement or access to certain places or services is dependent on immunity. The main arguments against immunity apps were, first, that the sight of individuals disregarding restrictions is likely to demoralise others, and that it is still rather unclear from a medical-scientific point for how long an individual is immune after an infection. Nevertheless, there have been voices, for example in Germany, where the view was held that it is disproportionate and thus unconstitutional to subject immune individuals to the same restrictions as others and that therefore such means of immunity proof are required.[12]

The idea of immunity apps has also recently received greater attention in the context of vaccination.[13] The Austrian Bioethics Commission argues in favour of liberating vaccinated persons from specific measures used to control the COVID-19 pandemic. From a fundamental rights perspective, maintaining the full level of restrictions also for persons who have received vaccination may no longer be justifiable, provided vaccination not only protects the individual who has been vaccinated but also prevents that individual from spreading the disease.[14] The European Commission published, on 17 March 2021, a strategy for a common path to Europe's safe re-opening, which includes, *inter alia*, the basis for a Europe-wide Digital Green Certificate.[15]

---

11 Govind Persad and Ezekiel J. Emanuel, 'The Ethics of COVID-19 Immunity-Based Licenses ("Immunity Passports")' (2020) 323 JAMA 2241; Natalie Kofler and Françoise Baylis, 'Ten Reasons Why Immunity Passports Are a Bad Idea' (2020) 581 Nature 379.

12 Kirsten Sucker-Sket, 'Spahn verteidigt Pläne für generellen Corona-Immunitätsnachweis' (4 May 2020) https://www.deutsche-apotheker-zeitung.de/news/artikel/2020/05/04/spahn-verteidigt-plaene-fuer-generellen-corona-immunitaetsnachweis accessed 16 July 2020.

13 Robert Jaeger, '"Stopp Corona"-App als Impf-Nachweis für Reisen?' (Die Presse 11 December 2020) https://www.diepresse.com/5935815/stopp-corona-app-als-impf-nachweis-fur-reisen accessed 11 March 2021.

14 Bioethikkommission (Austria), 'Opinion of the Bioethics Commission on Ethical questions about vaccination against COVID-19' (2020) 18 https://www.bundeskanzleramt.gv.at/en/topics/bioethics-commission/publications-bioethics.html accessed 15 March 2021.

15 European Commission, https://ec.europa.eu/info/live-work-travel-eu/coronavirus-response/safe-covid-19-vaccines-europeans/covid-19-digital-green-certificates_en, accessed 17 March 2021. But see also the rather hesitant position taken by the German Ethics Council, Deutscher Ethikrat, 'Special Rules for Vaccinated People?' (2021) 5 https://www.ethikrat.org/fileadmin/Publikationen/Ad-hoc-Empfehlungen/englisch/recommendation-special-rules-for-vaccinated-people.pdf accessed 15 March 2021.

From a data protection point of view, immunity apps do not pose significant extra problems, in particular as use of the app occurs on the initiative and in the sole interest of the data subject. As in all other cases, immunity apps may pose problems in terms of data protection once the data (in this case health data) are processed for additional purposes not inherent in the original function of the app.

2.5. QUARANTINE AND CONTAINMENT APPS

Quarantine apps monitor compliance with quarantine regulations by persons who are required to self-isolate. They can work in a very similar manner as "electronic ankle tags" and more or less rely on the assumption that an individual would rather comply with quarantine requirements than leave home without his/her regular smartphone, which is an interesting point from a sociological point of view. In a broader sense, and much more effectively, containment apps can be used for issuing electronic permits to leave the home, for example to go shopping and enter a particular supermarket, as we have seen in countries like China or Russia. Needless to say, such apps, in particular when personal compliance data are collected and processed by the authorities, are highly problematic from a data protection and a general fundamental rights perspective. Depending on the concrete design, they may create a situation that comes close to total surveillance, and would arguably not be acceptable in EU countries. Milder versions of such apps are being used, for example at some EU borders, by requesting tourists to answer questionnaires and get an electronic permit to enter the country if their risk score is sufficiently low.[16]

2.6. CONTACT TRACING APPS

The type of COVID-19 app that is usually associated in the very first place with the term "COVID-19 app" is that of contact tracing apps,[17] i.e. apps that facilitate the identification of persons with whom an individual that has tested COVID-19 positive has been together under circumstances that would have allowed for

16 E.g. the Spain Travel Health portal https://www.spth.gob.es/ accessed 17 July 2020.

17 Nationale Ethikkommission (NEK Schweiz), 'Contact Tracing als Instrument der Pandemiebekämpfung' (2020) https://doi.emh.ch/saez.2019.17681 accessed 17 July 2020; Jeffrey Kahn, 'Digital Contact Tracing for Pandemic Response' (Johns Hopkins Univ Press 2020) https://muse.jhu.edu/book/75831 accessed 17 July 2020; WHO, 'Ethical Considerations to Guide the Use of Digital Proximity Tracking Technologies for COVID-19 Contact Tracing' (2020) https://www.who.int/publications-detail-redirect/WHO-2019-nCoV-Ethics_Contact_tracing_apps-2020.1 accessed 17 July 2020.

an infection. They are also often called track-and-trace apps or – after there had been a data protection debate and people were increasingly critical – also "exposure tracing apps". Strictly speaking, a distinction needs to be made between "tracking" and "tracing".[18] The former refers to the proactive collection of data, only few of which will ultimately turn out to be COVID-19 relevant. The latter refers to the retrospective identification of possible infection paths. However, the term "contact tracing" has more and more often been used to describe both aspects. Contact tracing is usually either proximity-based or event-based, or a combination of both. Proximity tracing would lead to individuals who have been physically close to the COVID-19 positive individual for a defined minimum duration. Event tracing would lead to individuals who have taken part in a particular event, for example who have been sitting at a particular table in a particular restaurant during a particular period of time, more or less functioning as "digital visitors' book".

3. PROXIMITY TRACING VIA COVID-19 APPS

The most common type of contact tracing app, which is held to be also the most promising one with regard to its potential contribution to combating the pandemic, is proximity tracing. Contact tracing based on proximity tracing involves a broad-based reconstruction of physical contacts of a certain minimum duration and spatial proximity that is not limited to specific groups of people or situations.

3.1. DIFFERENT DESIGNS OF PROXIMITY TRACING

Most proximity tracing apps use Bluetooth signals that indicate which mobile devices have been in the immediate vicinity of another device.[19] In addition, there are approaches based on the use of location data (such as GPS coordinates obtained via mobile phone or WLAN networks)[20] or combining these with Bluetooth-supported proximity tracing. The aim of contact tracing apps is the

---

18 Österreichische Bioethikkommission, 'Stellungnahme der Bioethikkommission zu Contact Tracing in der COVID-19-Pandemie' (2020) 5 https://www.bundeskanzleramt.gv.at/themen/bioethikkommission/publikationen-bioethik.html accessed 17 July 2020.

19 Luca Ferretti and others, 'Quantifying SARS-CoV-2 Transmission Suggests Epidemic Control with Digital Contact Tracing' (2020) 368 Science Fig. 4 https://science.sciencemag.org/content/368/6491/eabb6936 accessed 17 July 2020.

20 OECD, 'Tracking and Tracing COVID: Protecting Privacy and Data While Using Apps and Biometrics' (2020) http://www.oecd.org/coronavirus/policy-responses/tracking-and-tracing-covid-protecting-privacy-and-data-while-using-apps-and-biometrics-8f394636/ accessed 17 July 2020.

digital tracing of possible chains of infection with the aim of notifying and isolating affected persons.[21]

Even within proximity tracing apps, there exists a wide range of differently designed apps.[22] Differences are first of all in the definition of an infection-relevant contact (duration of contact, distance, time span covered) and in the technology used to detect it (precise GPS localisation of all app users or communication between the terminals via "digital handshakes"). There are also significant differences with regard to the way in which data is processed, depending on whether the app follows a decentralised or a centralised approach, i.e. whether data is stored in the respective terminal device of the end user or in some cloud space. Differences also depend on the location of execution of certain key features.[23] There are also differences in the authentication of the users during the installation of the app (no authentication, IP address, strong authentication), and in the conditions under which a COVID-19 infection is detected via the app (mandatory or voluntary, confirmed by health personnel or not).

Another difference is between apps that automatically inform the contacts of positively tested persons recorded via the app network about their risk of infection and the obligation to isolate or test themselves, and those that do not. Apps in the latter group lead to "enhanced manual tracing" by giving health authorities access to the proximity protocols of the apps of people who have tested positive, but leaving it up to the health authorities to manually track the infection chains and contact possible further infected persons. From a data protection perspective, the latter models are the more problematic as they lead to the direct identification of contact persons by the authorities.

3.2. DATA PROTECTION BEST PRACTICE: FULLY DECENTRALISED APPROACH

After some uncertainty as to the preferred approach in terms of privacy, and after some weeks of struggle between competing architectures promoted by different groups of developers – in particular the more centralised PEPP-PT[24] initiative

---

21 WHO, 'Contact tracing in the context of COVID-19' (2021) 7 https://www.who.int/publications/i/item/contact-tracing-in-the-context-of-covid-19 accessed 11 March 2021.

22 WHO, 'Digital tools for COVID-19 contact tracing' (2020) 1 https://www.who.int/publications/i/item/WHO-2019-nCoV-Contact_Tracing-Tools_Annex-2020.1 accessed 11 March 2021.

23 Matteo Ciucci and Frédéric Gouardères, 'National COVID-19 contact tracing apps' (2020) 2 https://www.europarl.europa.eu/RegData/etudes/BRIE/2020/652711/IPOL_BRI(2020)652711_EN.pdf accessed 11 March 2021.

24 Friedhelm Greis, 'Neuer Standard für Corona-Warnungen vorgestellt' (Golem 1 April 2020) https://www.golem.de/news/pepp-pt-neuer-standard-fuer-infektionswarnungen-vorgestellt-2004-147645.html accessed 11 March 2021; 'pepp-pt-documentation' (GitHub 2020) https://github.com/pepp-pt/pepp-pt-documentation accessed 11 March 2021.

and the fully decentralised DP-3T[25] approach – it was the decentralised DP-3T approach that arguably won the EU-wide race in terms of best privacy practice in Europe.[26] While some national solutions, such as the French StopCovid app (TousAntiCovid), are still based on a centralised architecture,[27] other national apps, such as the Austrian StoppCorona app, preferred a decentralised architecture as soon as it was available,[28] and countries like Germany changed horses in the very last moment and went for the decentralised option after all.[29] In April 2020, the tech giants Google and Apple announced their engagement in the development of a Bluetooth-based contact tracing technology, which led to the adoption of their so-called Exposure Notification application programming interface (API).[30] The Google/Apple API is also based on a decentralised architecture and was implemented by numerous COVID-19 contact tracing apps.[31]

Under the decentralised architecture, and taking the Austrian app as an example, each smartphone on which an app is installed sends a periodically (about every 15 minutes) changing code, which is received and recorded by other smartphones that are running the app and which have been for at least about 15 minutes in close proximity. These data are only stored locally on the respective terminal devices.

---

25 Carmela Troncoso and others, 'Decentralized Privacy-Preserving Proximity Tracing' (2020) arXiv:2005.12273 http://arxiv.org/abs/2005.12273 accessed 17 July 2020; 'DP-3T/Documents' (GitHub 2020) https://github.com/DP-3T/documents accessed 16 July 2020; any reference to a decentralized approach has been removed from the PEPP-PT project website Hanno Böck and Christiane Schulzki-Haddouti, 'PEPP-PT: Streit beim Corona-App-Projekt' (Golem 16 April 2020) https://www.golem.de/news/pepp-pt-streit-beim-corona-app-projekt-2004-147925.html accessed 17 July 2020.

26 This is also shown by the fact that the Pepp-PT website (www.pepp-pt.org/) is no longer available online.

27 Claude Castellucia and others, 'ROBERT: Robust and Privacy-Preserving Proximity Tracing' (Privatics 2020) https://hal.inria.fr/hal-02611265 accessed 17 July 2020.

28 The ÖRK confirmed to prefer a decentralized approach and agreed to implement a solution with DP-3T as soon as this architecture approach reaches practical maturity, Ulrich Bayer and others, 'Technische und Rechtliche Analyse der Stopp Corona App des Österreichischen Roten Kreuzes' (2020) 6.

29 See therefore the first approach based on PEPP-PT, 'Data Protection and Information Security Architecture – Illustrated on German Implementation' (GitHub 20 April 2020) https://github.com/pepp-pt/pepp-pt-documentation/blob/master/10-data-protection/PEPP-PT-data-protection-information-security-architecture-Germany.pdf accessed 17 July 2020; eventually leading to the final app based on decentralised architecture 'Open-Source-Projekt für Corona-Warn-App' with further references https://www.coronawarn.app/de/ accessed 17 July 2020; Marlene Delventhal, 'Anforderungen an Corona-Apps – Diskussion und aktueller Stand in Deutschland' (2020) 10, ZD-Aktuell 07140.

30 'Privacy-Preserving Contact Tracing' https://covid19.apple.com/contacttracing accessed 11 March 2021.

31 'Here are the countries using Google and Apple's COVID-19 Contact Tracing API' https://www.xda-developers.com/google-apple-covid-19-contact-tracing-exposure-notifications-api-app-list-countries/ accessed 15 March 2021.

If a person receives the information that he/she has tested positive for COVID-19 or has been in contact with a person who has tested positive, he/she is advised to send an alert which triggers the uploading of the codes sent by his/her smartphone within a certain period of time to a (non state-operated) central server on which the app is run. For this purpose, the person usually needs his/her own unique activation code, which is generated by an entirely separate, state-operated server when a corresponding entry is made in the register of notifiable diseases according to the epidemic law. The only purpose of this further step is to avoid false alerts from non-COVID-19 positive persons, but no data from smartphones whatsoever are transmitted to the state-operated server.

All smartphones with an app synchronise regularly with the first, non state-operated server running the app and receive all codes from positively tested persons' smartphones (but never any hint whatsoever as to these persons' identity). This enables a comparison with the codes stored locally on the smartphone, i.e. it is the smartphones of the many not (yet) positively tested individuals that "request" data to be sent to them from the app server, not the smartphones sending any user data to the server. If a code retrieved from the server matches a locally stored code, the relevant user receives an alert message that he/she had spent some time in close proximity to a person who tested positive in the relevant period. No information allowing identification of the COVID-19 positive person is shared whatsoever. It should be stressed that the data on positive tests stored in the register are only required to generate the activation code and are not connected to the app server.

4. DECENTRALISED APPROACHES FROM A DATA PROTECTION PERSPECTIVE

Under decentralised approaches, such as the DP-3T design (as under most other designs), three types of data processing are to be distinguished: (1) the processing of health data of a COVID-19 positive tested person in case of a notification; (2) the processing of health-relevant data of that person's contact persons; and (3) the precautionary storage of contact data of all app users for a possible later reconstruction of a chain of infection.

4.1. PSEUDONYMISED DATA

According to the DP-3T model, only pseudonymised data are exchanged and stored locally on the respective smartphones. Pseudonymised data are data which can be attributed to a natural person by the use of additional information, such as a key, even where that key is not held by the controller him/herself but by a third party.[32] Where data are pseudonymised it is difficult, but not impossible, to identify the data subject, and the data therefore qualify as personal data within the meaning of the GDPR. To determine whether a natural person is identifiable, account should be taken of all the means reasonably likely to be used, such as singling out, either by the controller or by another person, to identify the natural person directly or indirectly.[33] To ascertain whether means are reasonably likely to be used to identify the natural person, account should be taken of all objective factors, such as the costs of and the amount of time required for identification, taking into consideration the available technology at the time of the processing and technological developments.[34] Where this is not the case, the information qualifies as anonymous and is no longer subject to the GDPR.

The Court of Justice has caused some debate and confusion with the *Breyer*[35] judgment that qualified a dynamic IP address as personal data. While German law (as the law applicable in the *Breyer* case) did not allow the internet service provider to transmit directly to the online media services provider the additional data necessary for the identification of the data subject, legal channels for identification existed via the competent authority in the event of cyberattacks or similar extraordinary circumstances. The existence of these legal channels was sufficient to make the data personal data. Conversely, this can be read as saying that where these legal channels do not exist the data count as anonymised. If this were the case, it would mean that by merely changing (national) law and

32 General Data Protection Regulation, Article 4 (5); Achim Klabunde, 'Art. 4 DS-GVO' in Eugen Ehmann and Martin Selmayr (eds), *Datenschutzgrundverordnung* (C.H. Beck 2018) 177; Elisabeth Hödl, 'Art. 4 DSGVO' in Rainer Knyrim (eds), *Der DatKomm Praxiskommentar zum Datenschutzrecht – DSGVO und DSG* (Manz 2018) para 60; Gerald Spindler and Lukas Dalby, 'Art. 4 DS-GVO' in Gerald Spindler and Fabian Schuster (eds), *Recht der elektronischen Medien* (4th edn, C.H. Beck 2019) para 13 ff; Hermann Schild, 'Art. 4 DS-GVO' in Heinrich Amadeus Wolff and Stefan Brink (eds), *BeckOK Datenschutzrecht* (33rd edn, C.H. Beck 2020) para 68 ff; Marit Hansen, 'Art. 4 Nr. 5 DS-GVO' in Spiros Simitis and others (eds), *Datenschutzrecht* (Nomos 2019) 318; Reto Mantz and Johannes Marosi, 'Vorgaben der Datenschutz Grundverordnung' in Louisa Specht and Reto Mantz (eds), *Handbuch Europäisches und deutsches Datenschutzrecht* (C.H. Beck 2019) 43; Rolf Schwartmann and Robin Mühlenbeck, 'Art. 4 Nr. 5 DS-GVO' in Rolf Schwartmann and others (eds), *DS-GVO/BDSG* (2nd edn, C.F. Müller 2020) 63 f; Stefan Ernst, 'Art. 4 DS-GV' in Boris P. Paal and Daniel A. Pauly (eds), *DS-GVO BDSG* (2nd edn, C.H. Beck 2018) para 42 f.

33 General Data Protection Regulation, Recital 26; Marit Hansen, 'Art. 4 Nr. 5 DS-GVO' in Spiros Simitis and others (eds), *Datenschutzrecht* (Nomos 2019) 320 f; Reto Mantz and Johannes Marosi, 'Vorgaben der Datenschutz Grundverordnung' in Louisa Specht and Reto Mantz (eds), *Handbuch Europäisches und deutsches Datenschutzrecht* (C.H. Beck 2019) 43; Rolf Schwartmann and Robin Mühlenbeck, 'Art. 4 Nr. 5 DS-GVO' in Rolf Schwartmann and others (eds), *DS-GVO/BDSG* (C.F. Müller 2020) 61 ff.

34 EDPB, 'Guidelines 04/2020 on the use of location data and contact tracing tools in the context of the COVID-19 outbreak' (21 April 2020), paras 14 ff https://edpb.europa.eu/sites/edpb/files/files/file1/edpb_guidelines_20200420_contact_tracing_covid_with_annex_en.pdf accessed 17 July 2020; Rolf Schwartmann and Robin Mühlenbeck, 'Art. 4 Nr. 5' in Rolf Schwartmann and others (eds), *DS-GVO/BDSG* (C.F. Müller 2020) 66.

35 Case C-582/14 *Breyer* [2016] ECLI:EU:C:2016:779.

prohibiting re-identification of data subjects for pseudonymised data under any circumstances, including investigation into cyber attacks and similar extreme situations, the bulk of data that had so far counted as personal data would be outside the scope of data protection law. To the author's knowledge, no Member State has so far considered doing this, probably because the price of not being able to investigate even in cases of terrorism, child pornography and similar serious threats would seem much too high compared with the burden of having to struggle with the GDPR. In any case, the *Breyer* interpretation (which still referred to Directive 95/46/EC) seems not to be the understanding of the European Data Protection Board (EDPB)[36] and other relevant players, so for the time being, we have to assume that the signals emitted by the smartphones of app users under a decentralised model qualify as personal data.

This means, *inter alia*, that processing of these data by a controller requires a legal basis.[37] The legal basis for data processing is to be found in Article 9 GDPR for health data, which qualify as "special categories of data",[38] and in Article 6 GDPR for general data (non-health-related mobility data, etc.). In all cases, data processing must comply with the general principles of data processing expressed in Article 5 GDPR, including the requirement of data minimisation, purpose limitation, storage limitation and the guarantee of the best possible data security.[39] In addition, telecommunications law may be applicable in implementation of the ePrivacy Directive[40] when accessing data already stored in the terminal equipment.

4.2. HEALTH DATA OF A COVID-19 POSITIVE PERSON

The processing of data on the person identified as infected clearly qualifies as processing of health data, i.e. of a special category of data which is particularly sensitive.[41] The legal basis therefore needs to be found in Article 9(2) GDPR.

---

36 EDPB, *Guidelines 04/2020*, paras 14 ff.

37 See a list of national controllers and privacy policies with the respective legal basis for data processing https://ec.europa.eu/health/sites/health/files/ehealth/docs/gateway_jointcontrollers_en.pdf accessed 11 March 2021.

38 EDPB, 'Guidelines 03/2020 on the processing of data concerning health for the purpose of scientific research in the context of the COVID-19 outbreak' (21 April 2020), para 15 https://edpb.europa.eu/sites/edpb/files/files/file1/edpb_guidelines_202003_healthdatascientificresearchcovid19_en.pdf accessed 17 July 2020.

39 See Commission Recommendation (EU) 2020/518 of 8 April 2020 on a common Union toolbox for the use of technology and data to combat and exit from the COVID19 crisis, in particular concerning mobile applications and the use of anonymised mobility data [2020] OJ L 114/7, Recital 25.

40 Council Directive 2002/58/EC of 12 July 2002 concerning the processing of personal data and the protection of privacy in the electronic communications sector (Directive on privacy and electronic communications) [2002] OJ L 201/37.

41 Andreas Jaspers, Rolf Schwartmann and Robin Mühlenbeck, 'Art. 9 DS-GVO' in Rolf Schwartmann and others (eds), *DS-GVO/BDSG* (C.F. Müller 2020) 349.

At first sight, this seems to be a clear-cut case of consent, i.e. where "the data subject has given explicit consent to the processing of those personal data for one or more specified purposes" within the meaning of Article 9(2)(a).[42] While it is certainly possible to rely on this ground, it may not be the most advisable thing for an operator of the app system to do. The downside of consent as a ground of justification is, in the first place, that the requirements are very strict, in particular as far as concerns the requirement that consent is "freely given".[43] Imagine a situation where a person has tested COVID-19 positive and is, when the doctor or health authority announces the test result, interrogated under national epidemic law as to that person's contacts and whether that person runs a contact tracing app (maybe even telling the person that it is required under epidemic law to tell the truth and that any false statements may be subject to severe penalties) it is difficult to conceive consent to the uploading of the positive test result as "freely given" in all cases. Besides, consent may, under Article 7 GDPR, be withdrawn at any time without giving a reason, and the withdrawal of consent must be as simple as the granting of consent, so the app would have to provide for such a feature.[44] At the end of the day, relying on the data subject's consent would cause nothing but complications.

This is also why the European Data Protection Board (EDPB) primarily advises relying on one of the statutory grounds for processing health data.[45] The first ground that would lend itself is Article 9(2)(h) in conjunction with Article 9(3) GDPR, i.e. that "processing is necessary for the purposes of preventive ... medicine, for ... medical diagnosis, the provision of health or social care or treatment or the management of health or social care systems and services on the basis of Union or Member State law ..." provided that "those data are processed by or under the responsibility of a professional subject to the obligation of professional secrecy under Union or Member State law or rules established by national competent bodies ...". Maybe even more convincing as a legal basis would be Article 9(2)(i), i.e. that "processing is necessary for reasons

42 Gerald Spindler and Lukas Dalby, 'Art. 9 DS-GVO' in Gerald Spindler and Fabian Schuster (eds), Recht der elektronischen Medien (4th edn, C.H. Beck 2019) para 7; Andreas Jaspers, Rolf Schwartmann and Robin Mühlenbeck, 'Art. 9 DS-GVO' in Rolf Schwartmann and others (eds), *DS-GVO/BDSG* (C.F. Müller 2020) 356 ff; Marion Albers and Raoul-Darius Veit, 'Art. 9 DS-GVO' in Heinrich Amadeus Wolff and Stefan Brink (eds), *BeckOK Datenschutzrecht* (33rd edn, C.H. Beck 2020) para 49 ff; Markus Kastelitz, Walter Hötzendorfer and Christof Tschohl, 'Art 9 DSGVO' in Rainer Knyrim (eds), *Der DatKomm Praxiskommentar zum Datenschutzrecht – DSGVO und DSG* (Manz 2020), para 31 ff; Michael Frenzl, 'Art. 9 DS-GVO' in Boris P. Paal and Daniel A. Pauly (eds), *DS-GVO BDSG* (2nd edn, C.H. Beck 2018) para 21 ff.

43 General Data Protection Regulation, Recital 43; EDPB, *Guidelines 03/2020*, para 18; Darko Samardzic and Thomas Becker, 'Die Grenzen des Datenschutzes – Der beschränkte Schutz durch Freiwilligkeit und Einwilligung bei Corona-Apps' (2020) 15 EuZW 646, 651.

44 EDPB, *Guidelines 03/2020*, para 22.

45 EDPB, *Guidelines 03/2020*, paras 23 ff, 69 ff; EDPB, *Guidelines 04/2020*, para 33.

of public interest in the area of public health, such as protecting against serious cross-border threats to health or ensuring high standards of quality and safety of health care … on the basis of Union or Member State law which provides for suitable and specific measures to safeguard the rights and freedoms of the data subject, in particular professional secrecy". These grounds would arguably be more specific and easier to defend than the ground of "substantial public interest" under Article 9(2)(g).

Both Article 9(2)(h) and (i) require a further basis in Union or Member State law that fulfils the specific minimum requirements mentioned. In the case of (h) this would be legal provisions applicable to health care in general, as will probably exist in all Member States, be it rules regulating the medical profession or the running of hospitals or rules about social security and on the recording and exchange of health data. It will depend on how exactly these rules are phrased whether or not they provide a full basis for the uploading of the health data of the COVID-19 positive person onto the system. In the case of (i) the further basis would be legal provisions typically found in epidemic laws, in laws dealing with catastrophes and states of emergency, or national data protection law. In Austria, for example, the legal basis would be both the rules on contact tracing in the Austrian Epidemic Law[46] and Article 10(2) Austrian Data Protection Law,[47] which creates an obligation for anyone holding data that are relevant in a state of emergency to share these data upon request.[48]

4.3. HEALTH-RELEVANT DATA OF CONTACT PERSONS

Once an individual has tested COVID-19 positive and the data indicating this fact have been uploaded onto the system, there immediately emerges a group of contact persons who have, according to the technical settings of the relevant app, been close to the infected person in some way that has potentially led to an infection. These data are somewhat in a grey zone between general data and health data because they are not strictly about the health of these persons, i.e. they do not directly indicate those persons' health status, but are rather about those persons' location during the past 48 (or more) hours. However, the data are clearly health-relevant, i.e. they indicate a probability that the contact

46 Austrian Epidemic Law, s 5.

47 Austrian Data Protection Act, s 10 (2) as amended by BGBl. I Nr. 14/2019.

48 EDPB, *Guidelines 04/2020*, para 33, Annex: Contact tracing applications analysis guide https://edpb.europa.eu/sites/edpb/files/files/file1/edpb_guidelines_20200420_contact_tracing_covid_with_annex_en.pdf accessed 17 July 2020; implicitly critical of the "exposure" of COVID-19 patients without their consent Forgó, 'Einige Bemerkungen zu datenschutzrechtlichen Rahmenbedingungen des Einsatzes von Tracing Apps' Version 1.0 (2020) 10 https://id.univie.ac.at/fileadmin/user_upload/i_id/Website_Header_IDLaw/Gutachten13.pdf accessed 16 July 2020.

persons have a particular health status (risk score). Where it is not clear from the nature of data as such, i.e. their context and semantics, that the data qualifies as health data it is the purpose of data processing that should be decisive.[49] In this case, one could say that already the context is health-related, but definitely the purpose of data processing is clearly a health purpose. So, the processing of the personal data of contact persons would have to be justified by Article 9 GDPR. By and large the same grounds of justification in Article 9(2)(h) or (i) would apply as already apply for the processing of health data relating to the COVID-19 positive individual (see *supra* section 4.2).

However, this argument might apply to centralised systems. With decentralised systems it is already doubtful whether the GDPR becomes relevant at all, given that the data indicating that this person has been a contact person of the COVID-19 positive individual are only stored locally on the relevant person's terminal device. So it is only the relevant person him/herself who has access to the data and can determine the purposes and means of their processing, i.e. the data subject seems to be identical with the controller.[50] Unless upon the initiative of the data subject (or hacking of the device), the contact protocol data cannot be accessed by any other party. Should the data subject suddenly want to stop data processing, the data subject is free to de-install the app and delete all contact protocols at any time. Put bluntly, storing the contact data on the terminal device can be compared with writing the sentence "I might be COVID-19 positive" into a Word document on one's computer and storing it on the hard disk drive – nobody ever discussed whether this amounts to processing of personal health data and what should be the ground of justification.

The sole reason why we keep discussing data protection concerns even under decentralised approaches is that there is this uneasiness about third parties possibly being able to access the app without our knowledge, much in the same way as there are concerns about Microsoft or Apple or any other third party being able to access documents we have stored on our hard disk drives. But really, what we are speaking about in this context seems to be a general worry about cyber-risks and complexity of our brave new digital world, and a fundamental feeling of distrust against anything digital which the user does not understand,

---

49 Alexander Schiff, 'Art. 9' in Eugen Ehmann and Martin Selmayr (eds), *Datenschutz-Grundverordnung* (2nd edn, C.H. Beck 2018) para 2; Markus Kastelitz, Walter Hötzendorfer and Christof Tschohl, 'Art 9 DSGVO' in Rainer Knyrim (eds), *Der DatKomm Praxiskommentar zum Datenschutzrecht – DSGVO und DSG* (Manz 2020), para 20; Michael Frenzl, 'Art. 9 DS-GVO' in Boris P. Paal and Daniel A. Pauly (eds), *DS-GVO BDSG* (2nd edn, C.H. Beck 2018) para 9; Rolf Schwartmann and Robin Mühlenbeck, 'Art. 4 Nr. 15 DS-GVO' in Rolf Schwartmann and others (eds), *DS-GVO/BDSG* (C.F. Müller 2020) 118.

50 See for an in-depth analysis on the definition of a controller EDPB, 'Guidelines 07/2020 on the concepts of controller and processor in the GDPR' (Version 1.0, 2 September 2020) 9 ff https://edpb.europa.eu/sites/edpb/files/consultation/edpb_guidelines_202007_controllerprocessor_en.pdf accessed 11 March 2021.

but has a feeling big players and bad people may find ways to exploit, rather than any proven threat. So what seems to be at stake is a subjectively perceived risk of data processing rather than any real processing of personal data taking place.

4.4. DATA OF APP USERS BEFORE A RELEVANT CONTACT

As far as the precautionary storage of contact data is concerned, before any positive COVID-19 test is uploaded onto the system, the data arguably qualify as general data because any health-related purpose of their processing is so remote that justification under Article 6 GDPR is sufficient. This could be contested, but seems to be the view also taken by the EDPB.[51] These data are not only stored on the terminal device of the respective app user, but also on the terminal devices of other app users, which is why the situation is different from the situation just discussed (*supra* section 4.3) where an alert is received. The EDPB considers Article 6(1)(e) in conjunction with Article 6(3) GDPR as the most appropriate legal basis where processing occurs by public authorities based on a mandate assigned by and in line with requirements laid down by law.[52] In the case of private actors, Article 6(1)(c) GDPR would be available instead of Article 6(1)(e).[53] If the initiative is taken by the data subject him/herself by voluntarily using the app in order to help contain the pandemic, the processing can regularly be based on the data subject's free and informed consent within the meaning of Article 6(1)(a) GDPR.[54]

However, it is again not clear whether the GDPR really applies at all. According to its Article 2(2)(c) the GDPR does not apply to the processing of personal data by a natural person in the course of a purely personal or household activity. Other app users would store contact data on their mobile devices exclusively for personal reasons, i.e. to prevent becoming spreaders of the disease, so arguably the effect in terms of data protection would be about as data protection relevant as where an individual we have met mentions the meeting in his/her diary. Again it is not so much what is really happening from a technical point of view and the legal evaluation that seems to be influencing public perception of COVID-19 apps, but rather the vague feeling that whenever digital means are involved, and in particular where these digital means have been developed or facilitated by big

51 EDPB, *Guidelines 04/2020*, para 24–32; Jürgen Kühling and Roman Schildbach, 'Corona-Apps – Daten- und Grundrechtsschutz in Krisenzeiten' (2020) 22 NJW 1545, 1549.

52 EDPB, *Guidelines 04/2020*, para 29, 30 f.

53 In the case of the Austrian "Stopp-Corona" app the controller would rather be a private actor, cf. Nicole Gosch and Antonia Kühberger, 'Veranstaltungsbericht: Grazer Datenschutz-Gespräche – "Datenschutz in der Corona-Krise (?)" – ONLINE' (2020) 4 jusIT 168, 170.

54 EDPB, *Guidelines 04/2020*, para 32.

players in the tech industry and are supported by the State, these players will somehow find ways to access and abuse the data.[55]

4.5. INTEROPERABILITY

Finally, national borders – especially within the Schengen area or within the European Union – have been gradually reopening since May 2020, even though we have seen some borders closing again in late 2020 and early 2021. Originally, the functioning of contact tracing apps was limited to national territories. The European Union soon identified the need for interoperability and for citizens to be able to use the technology while travelling across borders.[56]

Following the early initiatives, the European Commission created an EU-wide system for the interoperability of different coronavirus warning apps in Europe.[57] The so-called European Federation Gateway Service (EFGS) is a network gateway operated by the Commission that receives, stores and makes available a minimum set of personal data between Member States' backend servers for the purpose of ensuring the interoperability of national contact tracing and warning mobile applications.[58] The EFGS, in other words, facilitates the secure exchange of diagnostic keys between EU Member States to allow for contact tracing and the identification of infected persons across various apps. The decentralised system used by most of the participating apps is linked with the gateway services. The EFGS is compatible in any case with the Google/Apple Exposure Notification API and the DP-3T approach.[59] Solutions to also include applications based on a centralised architecture are currently being analysed.[60]

---

55 Regarding the mistrust towards state and private surveillance Johannes Müller, 'Nutzung von Mobildaten zur Eindämmung der Pandemie' (2020) 6 MMR 355, 356; Darko Samardzic and Thomas Becker, 'Die Grenzen des Datenschutzes – Der beschränkte Schutz durch Freiwilligkeit und Einwilligung bei Corona-Apps' (2020) 15 EuZW 646, 647.

56 'Mobile applications to support contact tracing in the EU's fight against COVID-19: Common EU Toolbox for Member States' (15 April 2020) https://ec.europa.eu/health/sites/health/files/ehealth/docs/COVID-19_apps_en.pdf accessed 17 July 2020; 'Interoperability guidelines for approved contact tracing mobile applications in the EU' (13 May 2020) https://ec.europa.eu/health/sites/health/files/ehealth/docs/contacttracing_mobileapps_guidelines_en.pdf accessed 17 July 2020.

57 Commission Implementing Decision (EU) 2020/1023 of 15 July 2020 amending Implementing Decision (EU) 2019/1765 as regards the cross-border exchange of data between national contact tracing and warning mobile applications with regard to combatting the COVID-19 pandemic [2020] OJ L 227 I/ 1–9.

58 Commission Implementing Decision (EU) 2020/1023, Article 1 (1) (j).

59 'European Proximity Tracing: An Interoperability Architecture for contact tracing and warning apps' (2 September 2020) 13, 52 https://ec.europa.eu/health/sites/health/files/ehealth/docs/mobileapps_interop_architecture_en.pdf accessed 11 March 2021.

60 See for an overview of the countries connected to the European gateway server https://ec.europa.eu/health/sites/health/files/ehealth/docs/gateway_jointcontrollers_en.pdf

The exchange of personal data through the Federation Gateway is limited to the purposes of facilitating the interoperability of national contact tracing and therefore all information exchanged is fully pseudonymised, encrypted and limited to the essential.[61] The communication of user devices continues to take place only with the corresponding national backend. The participating Member States are treated as joint controllers,[62] while the Commission, as the provider of technical and organisational solutions for the Federation Gateway, is the respective processor.[63]

5. THE DEBATE AROUND VOLUNTARINESS

It is this vague gut feeling that has already been mentioned, and a general atmosphere of distrust, that has also sparked an emotional debate around voluntariness, with more or less all players unanimously insisting that the use of the app must remain entirely voluntary.[64] Although this question is closely linked to that of the legal basis under data protection law, it is by no means identical.[65] Even if data processing is based on a statutory ground and not on the consent of the data subject, it may still be necessary to make the use of an app purely voluntary because any obligation to use an app that is imposed by the State constitutes an encroachment on fundamental rights.[66] This applies even if no personal data leaves the user's terminal device at all, since the very activity of the app on the terminal device itself constitutes an encroachment (burden of download, Bluetooth connection, battery consumption, storage space), if not the

accessed 11 March 2021; 'France's Covid-19 tracing app hard to link to others, EU official says' https://www.france24.com/en/20200617-france-s-covid-19-tracing-app-hard-to-link-to-others-eu-official-says accessed 11 March 2021.

61 Commission Implementing Decision (EU) 2020/1023, Article 1(5).

62 See on the definition of joint controllers EDPB, *Guidelines 07/2020*, 16 ff.

63 Commission Implementing Decision (EU) 2020/1023, Recital 10, 11.

64 Council of Europe, 'Joint Statement on Digital Contact Tracing' (28 April 2020) 4 https://rm.coe.int/covid19-joint-statement-28-april/16809e3fd7 accessed 17 July 2020; EDPB, *Guidelines 04/2020*, para 8; European Commission 'Guidance on Apps supporting the fight against COVID 19 pandemic in relation to data protection' (C(2020) 2523 final) 3 https://ec.europa.eu/info/sites/info/files/5_en_act_part1_v3.pdf accessed 17 July 2020. European Union Agency for Fundamental Rights, 'Coronavirus pandemic in the EU – Fundamental Rights implications: With a focus on contact-tracing apps' (2020) 5 https://fra.europa.eu/sites/default/files/fra_uploads/fra-2020-coronavirus-pandemic-eu-bulletin-may_en.pdf accessed 17 July 2020; WHO, 'Ethical Considerations to Guide the Use of Digital Proximity Tracking Technologies for COVID-19 Contact Tracing' (2020) 3 https://www.who.int/publications-detail-redirect/WHO-2019-nCoV-Ethics_Contact_tracing_apps-2020.1 accessed 9 March 2021.

65 Darko Samardzic and Thomas Becker, 'Die Grenzen des Datenschutzes – Der beschränkte Schutz durch Freiwilligkeit und Einwilligung bei Corona-Apps' (2020) 15 EuZW 646, 649; EDPB, *Guidelines 04/2020*, para 29.

66 See Anna Gamper, 'Verpflichtende Corona-Trac(k)ing-Apps: von der "demokratischen Zumutung" zum "Rand der Demokratie"' (2020) 3 NLMR 155, 159 ff.

causing of (though unfounded) anxiety as such. The immediate consequence of this insight is that any such obligation must strictly comply with the principle of proportionality.

5.1. STATE-IMPOSED REQUIREMENTS

A temporary obligation to use such apps in times of epidemics can be justified from a fundamental rights perspective in particular if the alternative could only be the complete prohibition of many activities and a more drastic encroachment on freedom of movement, freedom of assembly, freedom of employment, freedom of religious practice, freedom of art and other fundamental rights. It can also be justified where the alternative would be a much more privacy-intrusive method of contact tracing (e.g. recording of all personal details and contact data in the context of use of a facility), bearing in mind that "manual" contact tracing is apt to reveal even the most sensitive data to public authorities, such as illegal employment relationships and extramarital love affairs. If this is the case, use of an app would ultimately be the more lenient remedy and preferable from a fundamental rights point of view.[67]

In order to exclude possible effects of discrimination, alternatives (e.g. forms of conventional registration) would have to be found for persons who do not own a smartphone or whose operating system is not compatible with an app for any reason,[68] and special solutions would have to be found for facilities required for basic supplies (i.e. supermarkets, pharmacies, hospitals, public transport or similar).

5.2. REQUIREMENTS IMPOSED BY PRIVATE ACTORS

As every operator of a facility, every host of an event, etc. is required to develop a COVID-19 policy for the facility or event (if not directly under a statutory obligation then certainly in order to ward off possible claims for damages or to avoid a loss of reputation) one of the most obvious components of such a COVID-19 policy is to prescribe digital contact tracing, because it is particularly easy and inexpensive to implement for the operator or host.

If private actors (e.g. supermarkets, restaurants) make the conclusion of a contract dependent on the fulfilment of certain conditions, non-discrimination

67 Österreichische Bioethikkommission, 'Stellungnahme der Bioethikkommission zu Contact Tracing in der COVID-19-Pandemie' (2020) 18 https://www.bundeskanzleramt.gv.at/themen/bioethikkommission/publikationen-bioethik.html accessed 17 July 2020.

68 Österreichische Bioethikkommission, 'Stellungnahme der Bioethikkommission zu Contact Tracing in der COVID-19-Pandemie' (2020) 16 https://www.bundeskanzleramt.gv.at/themen/bioethikkommission/publikationen-bioethik.html accessed 17 July 2020.

law must be taken into account in the case of mass transactions. In Member States with a narrow implementation of Directive 2004/113/EC on equal treatment for men and women in the access to and supply of goods and services private actors are unlikely to get into conflict with these provisions. This may be different in Member States that have extended the provisions to age, as making the conclusion of a contract dependent on the use of smartphones and apps amounts to indirect age discrimination.[69]

Concerning basic supplies, there is often national legislation creating an obligation for traders to conclude a contract with anyone who needs these supplies and is prepared to pay the price.[70] Apart from that, the general principles concerning obligations to contract must be taken into account, which are often based on tort and/or competition law. Even beyond an obligation to contract, any discriminatory exclusion from the use of a service must be avoided with a view to avoid infringement of personality rights and/or violation of public policy. Careful balancing of the freedom of contract of the supplier and the interests of others is required[71] in order to find out whether the refusal to conclude a contract with a customer without an app would be objectively justified.

6. BARRIERS TO THE EFFECTIVENESS OF DECENTRALISED PROXIMITY TRACING

The analysis of decentralised contact tracing apps under a data protection perspective has revealed that this type of contact tracing app is extremely privacy-friendly. This leaves the question of whether it is also an effective, or at least useful, tool for combating the pandemic. Unfortunately, the effectiveness of contact tracing apps is diminished by a number of factors.

6.1. INSUFFICIENT COVERAGE

Given the mantra of full voluntariness the density of individuals with an active app is usually not high enough to ensure sufficient coverage. According to some calculations, at least 60% of the population need to use the app for it to have any effect in the fight against the pandemic,[72] a figure that is difficult to reach under

69 See as an example for a narrow implementation the Austrian Equal Treatment Act as amended by BGBl. I Nr. 16/2020; see for extensive implementation the German General Equal Treatment Act as amended by BGBl. I S. 610.

70 Austrian Local Supply Act as amended by BGBl. I Nr. 56/2017.

71 For example, OGH 10.07.1991, 3 Ob 548/91.

72 Robert Hinch and others, 'Effective Configurations of a Digital Contact Tracing App: A report to NHSX' (16 April 2020) https://www.research.ox.ac.uk/Article/2020-04-16-digital-contact-tracing-can-slow-or-even-stop-coronavirus-transmission-and-ease-us-out-of-lockdown

conditions of full voluntariness and where not even private parties make use of the app as a requirement if people want to have access to particular services. Given that there will always be many persons who have failed to charge their batteries or to keep the app activated, whose Bluetooth connection fails or who have changed their device, the number of downloads even needs to significantly exceed the threshold of 60%. Previous experience with a number of COVID-19 apps in this regard is not very encouraging[73] and even though some apps may have quite decent download figures, the number of active users is still far from the required 60%, which are required to enable effectiveness.[74]

6.2. FALSE NEGATIVES

Apps working on the basis of a decentralised approach also have a number of reasons for false negative results, i.e. COVID-19 cases that the app cannot detect. Taking the example of the Austrian app, this could occur where a COVID-19 positive person does not have her mobile phone on her at the time of the infectious contact or has Bluetooth deactivated. It could equally occur where the infectious contact is too short to be registered by the app, where it took place earlier than 54 hours before the notification of illness (e.g. because symptoms were interpreted correctly late), or where COVID-19 was transmitted other than by close physical contact (e.g. through aerosol infection). Also, a COVID-19 positive person might be asymptomatic and never get tested or fail to report their test result via the app.

False-negative results are particularly harmful if the app causes a "reverse placebo effect", i.e. people who have false confidence that they are protected by using the app or that they are doing their part to contain the virus, refrain from taking preventive measures against infection (distance, mechanical protection).

accessed 17 July 2020; dissenting opinion Patrick Howell O'Neill, 'No, coronavirus apps don't need 60% adoption to be effective' (*MIT Technology Review*, 5 June 2020) https://www.technologyreview.com/2020/06/05/1002775/covid-apps-effective-at-less-than-60-percent-download/ accessed 17 July 2020.

73 For example, there are reports in the media that despite 6 million downloads in over four weeks, the Australian COVID-19 Safe app has only led to the identification of a single infected person and that the experience in Singapore also seems sobering 'Warum Australiens Tracing-App ein Flop ist' (4 June 2020) https://www.tagesschau.de/ausland/australien-coronavirus-app-103.html/ accessed 17 July 2020.

74 'Anzahl der Downloads der Corona-Warn-App über den Apple App Store und den Google Play Store in Deutschland von Juni 2020 bis Februar 2021' (23 February 2021) https://de.statista.com/statistik/daten/studie/1125951/umfrage/downloads-der-corona-warn-app/#professional accessed 11 March 2021.

6.3. ABSENCE OF ENFORCEMENT

Data protection-friendliness comes at a price. The immediate purpose of contact tracing apps should be the rapid isolation and testing of potentially infected persons. However, even if testing capacities have significantly improved, you still have to wait before you get a result and are told to isolate yourself and cancel all meetings with others in the meantime. So given that there is no way users who received an alert (and failed to respond) can be identified, users who do indeed receive an alert often think twice and then refrain from testing for fear of stigmatisation and hassle.

6.4. ABSENCE OF DATA FOR PLANNING AND RESEARCH

In the absence of any possibility to monitor compliance, or even to get an idea about how many alerts there have been (given that it is not the central server that sends the alerts, but the individual terminal device that matches signals and creates the alert), and in what areas, there is no way the app can be used for planning in the fight against the pandemic, allocating health care resources and understanding better how the disease tends to spread. Given that no data are stored and made available (except for the pseudonymised data of the COVID-19 positive, but their full identity is in the official record anyway), not even in aggregated and anonymised form, there is no benefit whatsoever for research.

7. CONCLUSION: A NEW PRIVACY PARADOX

Every COVID-19 app is different, even among the class of so-called contact tracing apps. This makes it difficult to give a general data protection assessment of COVID-19 apps. Generally speaking, the relationship between effectiveness to combat the pandemic on the one hand and data protection on the other seems to be one of indirect proportionality – the best practice model in terms of data protection, which relies on (1) voluntary use; (2) voluntary reporting of a positive test; (3) storage of contact protocol data only on the end user's device without any central traceability; (4) no hints as to the identity of the COVID-19 positive individual whatsoever; and (5) voluntary response to alerts, is so privacy-friendly that one can even argue whether data processing falls within the scope of the GDPR at all (given that some data may be considered anonymised, that the data subject him/herself may be the controller and that data only get onto devices of individuals acting in their private capacity).

The downside of this extreme privacy-friendliness is a degree of effectiveness so low that one may doubt whether it is at all a significant contribution to the fight against COVID-19, and of course the app does not yield any data whatsoever, not even in anonymised form, that is so badly needed for COVID-19 related research and planning.

Paradoxically, it may thus be the extreme privacy-friendliness itself, and the lack of effectiveness that comes with it, that renders COVID-19 apps doubtful in the light of human rights concerns. Because what always remains on the "con side" is peoples' subjective feelings of uneasiness with the technology, however unfounded it may be from a scientific point of view. What also remains is the danger of "function creep", i.e. that people who have – under the somewhat special circumstances of the pandemic – agreed to use COVID-19 apps get accustomed to surveillance technology and that this technology is, step by step, and starting in countries with authoritarian tendencies, developed into something really oppressive. In the absence of any concrete indications that such oppressive use might result, these cons might easily be outweighed by arguments on the "pro side" if COVID-19 apps were an effective tool against the pandemic. However, if they are, in order to calm data protection concerns, watered down to something completely ineffective, the "con side" may suddenly prevail.

PART II

STATES AGAINST THE PANDEMIC

CORONAVIRUS AND THE LAW IN ROMANIA

Christian ALUNARU and Lucian BOJIN*

Romanian authorities reacted to the COVID-19 pandemic with various legal instruments, applying in numerous fields of law. Some measures were implemented in order to control the spread of the disease and to ensure the maximum capacity of the healthcare service providers to deal with the situation. Other measures addressed (and tried to mitigate) the economic consequences of the pandemic and

* Christian Alunaru, Vasile Goldiş University Arad, Law Faculty; Lucian Bojin, West University Timişoara, Law Faculty.

of the measures from the first category. Both types of measures involved certain serious limitations on the exercise of certain fundamental rights, which would not have been compliant with the constitutional provisions governing Romania in normal times. Because of this, the state of emergency was declared (and was in force for 60 days) in order to allow authorities to adopt the proposed measures. These measures applied in various fields, among them: health care, public order, public administration, labour and social security, performance of agreements, dispute resolution, education.

1. INTRODUCTION: THE CONSTITUTIONAL AND LEGAL FRAMEWORK OF REGULATION DURING EXCEPTIONAL SITUATIONS IN ROMANIA

The emergence of COVID-19, following the example of many other countries, was swiftly qualified in Romania as an "exceptional situation", one that required exceptional legislative and regulative measures. Such measures usually entail restrictions on rights. However, human rights are protected by the Romanian Constitution. Therefore, the adoption of such legislative and regulative measures must observe the constitutional mechanism put in place for these exceptional circumstances.

The Romanian Constitution provides for the protection of an extensive catalogue of human rights in Articles 28–51, backed by an acknowledgement of the primacy of international instruments protecting human rights (including the European Convention of Human Rights) over the domestic provisions. According to Article 53 of the Romanian Constitution, the exercise of rights and freedoms may be restricted only by law (therefore not through administrative acts or decisions) and only for certain purposes, such as protection of national security, public order, health or morality, protection of other rights and freedoms, etc. Moreover, according to the same constitutional provision, the restrictions must be proportional to the "situation that generated it", must be "necessary in a democratic society", must not be discriminatory and must not annihilate the essence of the right or freedom whose exercise is restricted.

The Constitution also provides for the "exceptional circumstances" in which both rights limitations and derogations from the regular decision-making processes may be applied. Article 93 of the Romanian Constitution provides for two such exceptional situations: the state of siege and the state of emergency. Each is instituted through presidential decree which must be approved by the Parliament within five days. As the constitutional provisions on the state of emergency, as on the state of siege as well, are rather laconic, an implementation law was necessary to elaborate on the institutional and normative framework during such circumstances. To this effect the Emergency Ordinance (EOG) no 1/1999 was issued by the Romanian Government.[1] The EOG no 1/1999 was approved by the Parliament through Law no 453/2004.

According to the definitions provided by the EOG no 1/1999, the "state of siege" refers to the exceptional measures (of political, military, economic, social or other nature) adopted in order to adapt the defence capacity of the country to the actual or imminent dangers threatening the sovereignty, independence, unity or territorial integrity of the State. In contrast, the "state of emergency" refers to measures (of political, economic or public order nature only) that may be adopted in two specific situations: the existence of serious dangers (actual or imminent) for the national security or for the functioning of the constitutional democracy or the necessity to prevent, limit or clear the consequences of a disaster. The state of emergency may be instituted for a period of a maximum of 30 days which may be renewed.

Following the characterisation of COVID-19 as a "pandemic" by the World Health Organization on 11 March 2020, the President of Romania issued the Decree no 195 of 16 March 2020[2] by which it instituted a state of emergency over the entire Romanian territory for a period of 30 days. Eventually, the state of emergency would be renewed by Decree no 240 of 14 April 2020[3] for another 30 days. Both decrees were approved by Parliament. After the expiry of the second decree, the state of emergency ended. However, specific measures continued to apply, as a "state of alert" was declared by Government Decision no 398 of 18 May 2020.[4] The main difference between "state of alert"[5] and "state of emergency" is that the former does not allow for restrictions of the rights enshrined in the Romanian Constitution, but merely provides the framework for swift action on the part of the public authorities, without however affecting fundamental rights.

Concerning the legal framework applicable during the state of emergency, according to Article 4 of the EOG no 1/1999, the exercise of some fundamental

---

1 The historical circumstances of the adoption of the Emergency Ordinance no. 1/1999 are interesting. The currently in force Constitution of Romania was adopted in 1991 and provided (as today) only the general idea of a state of emergency and state of siege, but without any more detailed guidelines as to how legal order applies during these circumstances. In January 1999, a great number of miners (over 15,000), enraged by the low wages and the closure of mines deemed unprofitable, marched to Bucharest threatening the fall of the government. On their way, they confronted the police and special operations forces in a couple of violent encounters. Consequently, during the night of 21–22 January 1999, the Romanian Government adopted the emergency ordinance that would regulate the state of siege and state of emergency, in order to have a framework in which to adopt the exceptional measures required by the given situation.

2 Published in the Official Journal (*Monitorul Oficial*) no. 212 of 16 March 2020.

3 Published in the Official Journal (*Monitorul Oficial*) no. 311 of 14 April 2020.

4 Published in the Official Journal (*Monitorul Oficial*) no. 410 of 18 May 2020.

5 The legal definition of the "state of alert" is provided by Emergency Ordinance no. 21/2004 concerning the National System of Management of the Emergency Situation (Art 4).

rights and freedoms may be restricted, but such restrictions must meet the criteria provided by Article 53 of the Constitution and mentioned herein before. Moreover, according to Article 3(2) of the EOG no 1/1999, the following restrictions are prohibited in any case during the state of emergency: the limitation of the right to life, torture or inhuman or degrading treatments, exceptions from *nulla crimen sine lege*, and restriction of the right to access to justice. According to Article 14 of the same EOG, the presidential decree instituting the state of emergency must list the fundamental rights and freedoms whose exercise is restricted. During the state of emergency, the governing activity is realised through specific acts that are not applicable during regular periods, namely military ordinances and orders, issued by the Ministry of Internal Affairs (Arts 23 and 23^1 of the EOG no 1/1999).

The inobservance of the measures taken during the state of emergency triggers, according to the particular case, civil liability, criminal responsibility, fines or disciplinary sanctions for employees and public servants. Particularly high fines were attached to the inobservance of the measures taken during the state of emergency. Thus, Article 28 of the EOG no 1/1999 stipulated that inobservance of the measures contained in the EOG no 1/1999, in the related acts and the acts issued on its basis (military ordinances and orders), are punished with a fine from RON 2,000 to 20,000 (ca. EUR 400 to 4,000) for natural persons and from RON 10,000 to 70,000 for corporate persons (ca. EUR 2,000 to 14,000).

However, by its Decision no 152 of 6 May 2020, the Constitutional Court declared unconstitutional the above-mentioned article of the EOG no 1/1999. The decision has not yet been published in its entirety. According to the press release issued by the Constitutional Court,[6] the essential reason underlying its decision was that "provisions of Article 28 of the EOG no 1/1999 … do not meet the requirements of clarity, precision and predictability and are, thus, incompatible with the fundamental principle of the supremacy of the laws and Constitution, provided by Article 1(5) of the Constitution and with the principle of proportional restriction of the exercise of fundamental rights and freedoms, provided by Article 53(2) of the Constitution". It appears from the press release that the Court reached this conclusion mainly because the law stipulated the fine for "any inobservance" of "any of the measures" provided by all relevant acts (EOG, military ordinances, orders, etc.), without clearly describing the acts or omissions that would be punishable with the fine. Consequently, the Court considered that too much discretion is left to the sanctioning authority to qualify the facts for which the fines were applied.

---

6 https://www.ccr.ro/download/comunicate_de_presa/Comunicat-de-presa-6-mai-2020.pdf accessed 7 June 2020.

The Decree no 195/2020 (the Decree) instituting the state of emergency lists the rights[7] that are affected during the state of emergency, duly mentioning (according to Article 53 of the Constitution) that the restrictions must not annihilate the substance of the rights, but must pursue a legitimate purpose, be necessary for a democratic society and be proportional with their purpose.[8] The Decree expressly mentions that restrictions to rights are motivated by the necessity to prevent the spread of COVID-19 and to manage the consequences of such spread. Article 4(4) of the Decree lists the criteria to be considered when instituting restrictions to the above-mentioned rights.[9]

The measures adopted by the Decree or based on it, by subsequent acts, are divided into two main categories, that will be addressed each hereunder: (1) directly and immediately applicable measures; and (2) gradually applicable measures (both categories were qualified however as "prime emergency measures"). Both types of measures applied in various fields of the political, administrative, social, and economic life and some of them evidently affected some fundamental rights and freedoms in an exceptional and temporary manner.

2. DIRECTLY AND IMMEDIATELY APPLICABLE MEASURES

2.1. PUBLIC ADMINISTRATION AND PUBLIC ORDER

One of the measures adopted in this field concerned a temporary exceptional subordination of some bodies to other authorities that coordinated them under normal circumstances. As such, local police and local services of persons' records (normally under the control of the municipalities) were subordinated to the Ministry of Internal Affairs, while firemen and health ambulance services (also normally under the control of the municipalities) were subordinated to the national agency for emergency situations.

Another exceptional measure was the possibility for public bodies in the field of defence, public order and national security to hire people without a public

7 According to Article 2 of the Decree, the affected rights were the following: freedom of movement, right to private and family life, inviolability of the domicile, right to education, freedom of gathering, right of property, right to strike, economic freedom.

8 Preamble of the Decree no. 195/2020.

9 These criteria are the following: the intensity of the spread of COVID-19, the frequency of cases in certain geographical areas, the number of patients in a critical state as compared with the health system capacity, the need to ensure the public utilities, the capacity of authorities to maintain public order and safety, measures taken by other States impacting the Romanian population or economic situation, the capacity to ensure the quarantine measures, the possible occurrence of other emergency situations.

competition (as prescribed by law under normal circumstances) for a period of maximum six months.

2.2. ECONOMICS

Contrary to the principle of non-intervention of the State in the market economy, it was recognised the right of the government to grant subsidies to undertakings operating in the fields affected by COVID-19. In order to obtain such subsidies, the undertaking must apply and obtain a so-called "certificate of emergency situation" issued by the Ministry of Economy, Energy and Business Environment.

Moreover, the public entities, as well as State-owned and State-controlled companies, were granted the right to buy directly from the market materials and equipment necessary in order to fight the epidemic, without needing to resort to public procurement procedures, which are otherwise mandatory for such entities.

Another exceptional measure was the possibility to cap prices, during the period of state of emergency, for medicines, medical equipment, basic food, public utility services, at the average price for each item of the last three months before the declaration of the state of emergency.

The Decree also allows for the suspension of the financing agreements related to EU funds. The suspension is not automatic, however, as in the case of force majeure, for example. The Decree merely allows the parties to consensually suspend the performance of the agreements, which otherwise would not have been possible.

The Decree also created the possibility of requisitions (only for facilities of production of materials and equipment necessary to fight the pandemic), an exceptional measure affecting the right to property, which is not allowed during normal circumstances. To our knowledge, no such requisitions have been effectively performed.

2.3. HEALTH CARE

Many of the measures in the field of health care are cases of specific applications of the exceptional measures adopted in the economic and public administration field. Thus, the healthcare facilities and social assistance public services have been exempted from organising public competitions for hiring medical professionals, pharmacists, nurses and other auxiliary personnel. Such employment may be made only for a limited period of six months. Another measure was the automatic renewal of regulations (usually, of annual validity) concerning the supply of medical services and medicines, that would have expired on 30 March 2020.

Other exceptional measures referred to the status of public healthcare servants. According to the Decree, during the state of emergency, the heads of healthcare facilities, as well as heads of public authorities in the field of health care and social assistance can be suspended without following the regular procedure provided to this effect. Finally, healthcare facilities and medical institutions were allowed to purchase directly, without public procurement procedures, materials and equipment needed to combat COVID-19.

Two other specific provisions applied during the state of emergency. The first concerned the suspension of the applicability of healthcare cards. Medical services provided for free to the population by family physicians are available only to those possessing a healthcare card, proving that contributions to the healthcare system were regularly paid by the owner of the card. However, during the state of emergency, such services were available to everybody, irrespective of whether he/she possessed a valid healthcare card.

The second measure concerned the clawback tax for medicine producers, which is established on a quarterly basis by the State. The clawback tax for the first quarter of 2020 was limited to the amount that was due for the fourth quarter of 2019.

2.4. EMPLOYMENT AND SOCIAL SECURITY

The Decree established the possibility of specific measures and regulations during the state of emergency period, which were then decided upon through various acts issued by the authorities. However, some specific immediate measures have also been taken. For example, the possibility of a unilateral decision by the employer to have the employees work from home (which, under normal circumstances, would have required the agreement of both parties). Another immediate measure was the suspension of inspections from the labour law authorities at the employers' premises, except for cases related to COVID-19 or work incidents or work-related offences or crimes. The collective employment agreements, which are negotiated on an annual basis, have been automatically renewed, without carrying the collective bargains, for the period of the state of emergency. Finally, the right to strike was suspended during this period.

2.5. JUSTICE ACTIVITY

Several provisions that derogate from the ordinary rules have been adopted in this field. They can be classified into three categories: specific provisions for civil cases, specific provisions for criminal cases, specific provisions for the Trade Registry.

2.5.1. *Specific provisions for civil cases*

A very important measure was adopted concerning the statutory time limitation periods. According to Article 41 of the Decree, no limitation period starts to run during the state of emergency, while the limitation periods that started to run previously are suspended. This is by way of derogation from the default provisions in the Romanian Civil Code.

The adjudication activity of the civil courts during the state of emergency was limited to cases that are "extremely urgent". The adjudication of all other civil cases was suspended during the same period (to be resumed within 10 days after the end of the state of emergency). Deciding which cases qualify as "extremely urgent" was left to the direction board of the High Court of Cassation and Justice and to the boards of the courts of appeal, under the guidance of the Superior Council of Magistracy. The Superior Council of Magistracy adopted Decision no 192 of 12 March 2020,[10] by which it indicated as a general criterion of urgency the cases "whose postponement would be susceptible to affect fundamental rights and freedoms or to seriously endanger the public order or the safety of citizens". Each court communicated on its own website, as well as by electronic mail to the Bar Association and to the Prosecutor's offices, the list of such cases during the entire period of state of emergency. Examples of civil "urgent cases" (including private law and administrative law cases) that were deemed as such by courts are the following: urgent summary proceedings (*ordonanțe președințiale*, the equivalent of the French *référé* proceedings), provisional sequesters, tutorship cases, temporary delegation of parental authority, provisional suspension of the enforcement procedures (in the field of general private law and family law); provisional sequester and suspension of enforcement procedures (in the field of commercial law); public procurement cases, provisional measures, suspension of effects of administrative acts, suspension of competitions for public servants (in the field of administrative law litigation); appeals against dismissals of employees (in the field of labour law).

The adjudication of urgent cases that were not suspended had to be managed considering the specific threats of COVID-19 spreading. In particular, social distancing measures may be ordered by judges, as well as online hearings, while the summoning could be made not only through regular mail but also through electronic mail. Another important practical novelty, which hopefully will also be maintained after the cessation of the state of emergency, concerns the requirement that for each case a commencement time be assigned, instead of having a list of all cases starting at a certain hour, but without indication for the time of commencement for the hearing of each case (or group of cases) on

10 https://www.csm1909.ro/ViewFile.ashx?guid=add2eba7-d079-4010-960c-880490ad2832|InfoCSM accessed 9 July 2020.

the list. Moreover, the commencement time for each case needed to take into account a short break after the previous one, in order to perform disinfection activities in the courtroom.

In the ongoing civil proceedings where a judgment was rendered but is not final, the periods for appealing or requesting the review of the judgment were also suspended during the state of emergency.

2.5.2. Specific provisions for criminal cases

The criminal prosecution activity was limited to cases where preventive measures (such as arrests, etc.) were proposed, to cases with sanitary preventive measures (e.g. medical confinement, mandatory healthcare assistance), cases where minors are victims of crimes and offences, cases related to the purposes of the state of emergency, cases in which there is a risk of loss of evidence or escape of the presumed offender, and other cases deemed urgent by prosecutors on a case-by-case basis, depending on the concrete circumstances of the case.[11]

As a rule, as for civil cases, the ongoing criminal cases in courts were suspended during the state of emergency. Several exceptions applied as well, where the criminal trials continued: cases related to the purposes of the state of emergency, cases where preventive measures were ordered, cases concerning *in flagrante delicto* crimes, appeals against provisional measures, cases concerning judicial cooperation in the criminal field, cases concerning crimes against national security, crimes of terrorism or money laundering, other cases deemed urgent by the judges. As for civil cases, the ongoing criminal cases suspended during the state of emergency are to be resumed within 10 days after the end of this period.

The procedural periods of time for communicating judicial documents or for appealing were interrupted during the state of emergency (instead of merely suspended, as in civil cases) and will start to run again at the end of the state of emergency.

According to Article 153 of the Romanian Criminal Code, the expiry of the time limitation period prevents the triggering of criminal responsibility. However, during the state of exception, a time limitation period is suspended in cases where either the prosecution or the court trial is suspended.

Several exceptional rules were also adopted concerning the execution of the criminal sentences (both in confinement and not).

Concerning the execution of sentences outside of confinement, the main activities due by the convicted were suspended, such as the duty to periodically

---

11 The doctrine discussed the concept of "urgent acts" in the criminal procedure. See, e.g. Ionuț Nefliu, 'Noțiunea de acte urgente în procedura penală', Universul Juridic, 8 May 2020 https://www.universuljuridic.ro/notiunea-de-acte-urgente-in-procedura-penala/ accessed 11 June 2020.

present at the probation service, the visits of the probation officer, the duty to perform work for the community, to follow training courses, etc. The probation period was not suspended though. Consequently, if the probation period ends during the state of emergency it is considered over, with the mention in the final report that during the state of emergency the execution was objectively impossible.

Concerning the execution of criminal sentences in confinement, some rights of the inmates have been restricted. Thus, the rights to receive visits, to receive goods from outside and to be granted permission to temporarily leave the confinement were suspended. The justification of such measures was the protection of the confined persons and of those who would have met them. However, to somehow compensate these restrictions, other rights of the inmates were extended, such as the extension of the frequency and duration of discussions with the supporting physician, as well as the extension of the right to have online discussions with the relatives outside.

2.5.3. *The activity of the National Trade Registry*

The National Trade Registry is the institution realising the publicity of the activity of commercial undertakings (by-laws, managers, etc.). The rule in this field was the continuity of the ongoing activities (registration of mandatory mentions, release of certified copies, etc.). However, both requests addressed to the National Trade Registry and replies from the latter were to be made in electronic form.

2.6. FOREIGN AFFAIRS

Some exceptional measures have also been adopted in the field of foreign relations. Thus, the representation of Romania in the meetings of the international bodies, in particular, of the European Union, Council of Europe, NATO and United Nations, was to be realised through the permanent missions of Romania to these international organisations, irrespective of the field concerned by the reunions (normally, at least for some meetings, Romania is represented by delegates other than the members of the permanent missions).

2.7. EDUCATION

Because of the pandemic, this field was radically reformed. During the state of emergency, classes were suspended for all education institutions (from pre-school to higher education institutions, both public and private). This did not mean that the educational system ceased to function, but all educational activities moved online. Classes and examinations were all made online. This rule was also maintained for the period after the state of emergency, until the end of the scholastic year.

2.8. OTHER MEASURES

The last chapter of Annex 1 of the Decree provides for other various exceptional measures, some of which deserve some short comments. For example, all authorities and bodies of public interest (including the bar association, the chamber of public notaries or the chamber of public enforcers) were under a duty to take all measures to ensure that their activity complies with the rules of sanitary discipline issued during the state of emergency. Article 52 of Annex 1 contains a provision that interferes with personal freedom by allowing the Ministry of Internal Affairs to order natural persons to perform works in the public interest. Although this is a clear interference with personal freedom and the right to work, it is not *per se* a violation of these rights. Article 42 of the Romanian Constitution forbids forced labour; however, according to paragraph (2)(c) of the same article, the performance of works required in times of calamities or other danger do not qualify as forced labour. To our knowledge, the Government did not resort in practice to such orders.

An exceptional and exceptionally serious measure was the possibility to block access to electronic communication networks. This would certainly qualify as an interference with the right to information and with the freedom of expression. However, as none of these rights is absolute, restrictions are permitted even during normal periods. Article 54(3) of Annex 1 of the Decree provides that "upon motivated decision of the National Authority for Administration and Regulation of Communications and in parallel with informing the users, suppliers of services of hosting and suppliers of content are under a duty to immediately interrupt the transmission in an electronic communications network or hosting the content, by eliminating it at source, if the respective content promotes fake news concerning the evolution of COVID-19 or concerning the of the protection and prevention measures". The following paragraph (4) continues: "If elimination at source of the content … is not feasible, upon motivated decision of the National Authority for Administration and Regulation of, suppliers of electronic communications networks available to the public are under a duty to immediately block the access to the respective content and to inform users". If the content is hosted by a network outside Romanian jurisdiction, according to paragraph (5), "upon motivated decision of the National Authority for Administration and Regulation of Communications, suppliers of electronic communications networks available to the public are under a duty to immediately block the access of users from Romania to the content that promotes fake news concerning the evolution of COVID-19 or concerning the of the protection and prevention measures".

3. GRADUALLY APPLICABLE MEASURES

This category of measures is contemplated in Annex 2 of the Decree as measures whose practical applicability was to be decided, based on the Decree, by subsequent acts of the Government. The generic list of these measures is to be found in Annex 2 of the Decree:

1. Isolation and quarantine of the persons arriving from risk-designated areas and of persons which enter contact with them; quarantine over buildings, villages, towns or cities or entire geographical areas;
2. Gradual closing of the border checkpoints;
3. Restricting or prohibiting the movement of vehicle or persons from/towards certain areas, or between certain hours, as well as the exit from those respective areas;
4. Gradual prohibition of transportations, on roads, railways, sea, rivers, underground or aerial, on certain lines;
5. Temporary lockdown of restaurants, hotels, cafés, clubs, casinos, associations headquarters and other public spaces;
6. Ensuring the security of water, gas and energy supply facilities, and of the undertakings possessing national strategic importance facilities;
7. Finding and requisition of stocks and of production and distribution facilities of protection equipment, disinfectants, and medicines that could be used in treating COVID-19;
8. Limiting the activity of public hospitals to emergency cases, in this order: first degree emergencies – patients that might lose their life within the next 24 hours; second degree emergencies – patients that once diagnosed need to be treated internally; and third degree emergencies – patients infected or diagnosed with COVID-19.

These measures were implemented in practice to variable degrees by means of the 12 military ordinances that were issued during the state of emergency. In the first instance, many of these measures were adopted under the form of "recommendation", rather than mandatory measures. For example, in Article 4 of the Military Ordinance no 2 of 21 March 2020,[12] a number of recommendations were issued by the Ministry of Internal Affairs. It was "recommended" that during 06.00–22.00 the movement of persons outside their homes should be made for a limited number of reasons expressly enumerated in the ordinance, such as going to work (when work was essential and could not be done from home), procuring necessary goods, medical assistance, child care, relatives' care or funerals, individual physical activity or getting pets out. The authorities

[12] Published in the Official Journal (*Monitorul Oficial*) no. 232 of 21 March 2020.

explained that the purpose of this "recommendation" method was to prepare the population for the prohibitions that were to be issued with the military ordinances that were to follow. We should, however, underline that such recommendations, without legal sanctions, therefore without the coercive means of the State to be applied when the duties were not observed, did not involve proper legal duties. This principle was clearly underlined by the Romanian legal literature.[13] Only the military ordinances that instituted limitations and restrictions of certain rights and freedoms, attaching sanctions to the breach of these provisions, created legal duties.

4. OTHER MEASURES DURING THE STATE OF EMERGENCY

During the state of emergency caused by the COVID-19, the Romanian government issued not only military ordinances, but also acts that are usual during the government activity, despite being named Emergency Ordinances. According to Article 115(4) of the Romanian Constitution, "The Government may adopt emergency ordinances only in extraordinary situations whose regulation cannot be postponed, and the emergency must be motivated within the ordinance". The emergency ordinance enters into force when submitted to the Parliament for review and is in force until approved, rejected or modified by a law issued by the Parliament. Emergency ordinances became, over time, quite usual in Romania. In any case, they fit very well the emergency created by the COVID-19 pandemic.

Some of these ordinances were EOG nos 29/18 March 2020,[14] 30/18 March 2020,[15] 32/26 March 2020,[16] 33/26 March 2020,[17] 37/30 March 2020[18] and 53/21 April 2020.[19]

4.1. SPECIAL RULES ON FORCE MAJEURE IN THE PERFORMANCE OF THE AGREEMENTS

The EOG no 29/2020 contains very important provisions that derogate from the general rules applicable to the force majeure. According to Article 1351 of

13 Tudor Popescu and Petre Anca, *Teoria generală a obligațiilor* (Editura Științifică 1968) 12, Liviu Pop, Ionuț-Florian Popa and Stelian Ioan Vidu, *Tratat elementar de drept civil. Obligațiile conform noului Cod civil* (Universul Juridic 2012) 18.

14 Published in the Official Journal (*Monitorul Oficial*) no. 230 of 21 March 2020.

15 Published in the Official Journal (*Monitorul Oficial*) no. 231 of 21 March 2020.

16 Published in the Official Journal (*Monitorul Oficial*) no. 260 of 30 March 2020.

17 Published in the Official Journal (*Monitorul Oficial*) no. 260 of 30 March 2020.

18 Published in the Official Journal (*Monitorul Oficial*) no. 261 of 30 March 2020.

19 Published in the Official Journal (*Monitorul Oficial*) no. 325 of 21 April 2020.

the Civil Code, the force majeure precludes liability: "If the law does not state otherwise or the parties did not agree otherwise, the liability is precluded when the damage is caused by force majeure or by a fortuitous situation". The definition of force majeure is contained in the second paragraph of the same article: "Every event which is external, unpredictable, absolutely invincible and unavoidable constitutes force majeure".

This approach to force majeure is taken from the French private law, which exercised an important influence over the Romanian law. In a comparative view, we can note that although §1447 of the ABGB (Austrian Civil code) mentions *Zufall* (fortuitous event) as a cause precluding liability, the Austrian legal literature defines the force majeure in similar terms to the ones used in the Romanian law.[20] This is not surprising since even for the classical Romanian legal literature, the force majeure and the fortuitous event were synonymous.[21] Only the contemporary legal literature in Romania distinguishes between fortuitous event and force majeure[22] and considers that only the latter precludes liability, because it is an external event, absolutely unpredictable, invincible and unavoidable. Also, the German BGB (*Bürgerliches Gesetzbuch*) speaks about *Zufall* (fortuitous event) in §§287 and 848, but the German legal literature deals with force majeure (*Höhere Gewalt*) by underlying that the similar French concept and English concept (*Act of God*) do not exactly overlap with the German one.[23] The exceptional rules concerning the force majeure in Romania during this period also give rise to interesting conceptual problems for the general theory of private law.

The preamble of the EOG no 29/2020 mentions notions that are specific to Romanian contract law, such as "solidarity of the business environment, contractual loyalty and the availability to adapt the business relations to the challenges brought by this sanitary crisis without precedent in modern history". These notions are discussed by Romanian legal literature[24] which cites, as usual, the French literature.[25]

Article X paragraph (2) of the EOG no 29/2020 represents, as is explicitly acknowledged, a manifest exception from the principles of the force majeure established in the Civil Code. It provides that "as an exception from other legal rules,

20 Rudolf Welser, *Fachwörterbuch* (Manz 2005) 245.

21 Dimitrie Alexandresco, *Explicaţiunea teoretică şi practică a Dreptului civil român in comparaţiune cu legile vechi si cu principalele legislaţiuni străine*, vol 5 (Socec 1898) 186, Matei B. Cantacuzino, *Elementele dreptului civil* (Cartea Românească 1921) 442, Tudor Popescu and Petre Anca, *Teoria generală a obligaţiilor* (Editura Ştiinţifică 1968) 239.

22 Liviu Pop, *Teoria generală a obligaţiilor* (Lumina Lex 1998) 92.

23 Johann Georg Helm, *Handelsgesetzbuch: Großkommentar* (DeGruyter 2002), 255.

24 Liviu Pop, *Tratat de drept civil. Contractul* (Universul Juridic 2009) 55–75 (the theory of the contractual solidarism), 513–515 (good faith and loyalty), 517–521 (the duty to cooperate).

25 Denis Mazeaud, *Loyauté, solidarité, fraternité: la nouvelle devise contractuel?* in *L'avenir du droit. Mélanges en hommage à François Terré* (Dalloz - PUF - Éditions du juris-classeur 1999) 603–634, Yves Picod, *Le devoir de loyauté dans l'exécution du contrat* (LGDJ 1989) 144–156.

in ongoing agreements, concluded by small and medium-sized enterprises ..., the force majeure may be relied upon against them only after attempting, evidenced with documents communicated between parties by any means, including electronic mail, to renegotiate the agreement, in order to adapt the latter by considering the exceptional circumstances generated by the state of emergency". Therefore, force majeure ceases to be a simple cause precluding liability, but a previous requirement is introduced, i.e. the attempt to renegotiate the agreement.

Moreover, paragraph (3) of Article X introduces a presumption that is not provided by the Civil Code: "It is presumed to represent a case of force majeure, for the purposes of the present EOG, the unpredictable circumstance, absolutely invincible and unavoidable referred to by Article 1351 (2) of the Civil Code, resulting from an act of authorities issued to implement the measures of prevention and struggle against the pandemic caused by COVID-19, which affected the activity of the small or medium sized enterprise, as evidenced by the certificate of state of emergency". This is a relative presumption, as "the presumption may be overcome by the interested party by any means of proof". The text also mentions that "the unpredictable character is to be assessed against the moment when the agreement was concluded. The measures taken by the authorities based on the act instituting the state of emergency are not per se unpredictable".

In practice, these provisions mean that the relative presumption of force majeure is triggered only based on the certificate of the state of emergency issued by the Ministry of Economy, Energy and Business Environment. The certificate of state of emergency is meant to attest that the activity of the undertaking was affected and is issued by the Ministry after evaluating if the industry to which the undertaking belongs was indeed affected by the measures taken during the state of emergency. Such is the case, manifestly, for hotels, restaurants, commercial centres, etc.

A natural consequence of the force majeure, as a cause precluding liability, is that the "delay penalties provided for late performance of duties resulting from agreements concluded by the small and medium-sized enterprises with public authorities are not due for the period of the state of emergency". Although Article X only refers to penalties in agreements concluded between private parties and public authorities, it is manifest that, if force majeure is to be applied also to an agreement concluded between private persons, the debtor will not be under a duty to pay delay penalties for this period either.

4.2. MEASURES SUPPORTING SMALL AND MEDIUM-SIZED ENTERPRISES

Besides the special provisions in the field of force majeure, the same Article X of the EOG no 29/2020 also provided for certain supporting measures for small and medium-sized enterprises during the state of emergency. If these undertakings interrupted, entirely or in part, their activity following the measures adopted by the authorities (and the interruption is evidenced with the certificate of state of emergency), they are entitled to postpone payments for utilities (gas, electricity, phone and internet) as well as the rent for the immovable they use as headquarters or branches, until the end of the period of the state of emergency.

According to paragraph (5) of Article X, these provisions are also applicable for the following professions that provide services of public interest: public notaries, lawyers and public enforcers, family physicians and dentists, sports federations and sport clubs, whose activity is directly affected by measures combating COVID-19. Liberal professions (such as lawyers), together with self-employed people, were granted also other benefits. The most important of these was receiving from the State a monthly revenue up to 75% of the gross national average wage (Article XV of EOG no 29/2020). This revenue was granted to all self-employed persons who interrupted their activity during the state of emergency, based on a self-certification declaration. Lawyers benefited as well from this facility, provided that their monthly income during this period was at least 25% less than their monthly average for 2019 and less than the gross national average wage.

4.3. SPECIAL SUPPORT MEASURES IN THE FIELD OF LABOUR LAW

Monthly revenue was also paid by the State to other categories of persons. Such is the case of employees for which the labour agreement was suspended by the employer. The EOG no 32/2020 allowed employers whose activity was affected by COVID-19 to suspend the labour agreements of their employees (the so-called "technical unemployment").[26] These employees, in turn, were entitled to receive from the State the monthly revenue equal up to 75% of their gross monthly wage before the suspension of the contract, but no more than 75% of the gross national average wage. These measures were applicable during the state of emergency.

Another category of people benefiting from similar measures were the parents who needed to stay home to supervise their children following the lockdown of schools. As previously mentioned, all educational institutions carried out their education activities only by means of online platforms.

[26] According to the numbers communicated by the Ministry of Labour and Social Security, at 28 May 2020 there were a total number of 595,672 suspended labour agreements and 429,585 dismissals of employees in the entire country: https://www.libertatea.ro/opinii/somajul-creste-locurile-de-munca-dispar-ce-solutii-le-ofera-statul-roman-celor-ramasi-pe-drumuri-3023070 accessed 10 June 2020.

That implied that, in most families, one of the parents needed to stay home with their children. To that effect, Law no 19/2020[27] allowed one of the parents (or the parent in the one-parent families) to opt in for this legal possibility. The right to opt in was granted to families with at least one child under 12 years old (or under 18 years old for the case of children with disabilities) registered in an educational institution. The parent that opted in was entitled to unpaid holidays from the employer for the entire period of school lockdown (therefore even after the end of the state of emergency). That parent had to provide a self-certificated declaration from the other parent that he/she did not opt in for the same measure. To compensate for the loss of wages during the holiday period, the supervising parent was entitled to a monthly income up to 75% of their gross monthly wage, but no more than 75% of the gross national average wage.

4.4. SPECIAL RULES IN THE FIELD OF TAXATION

Some facilities were also provided in the field of taxation. Article VII of the EOG no 29/2020 provides that, during the state of emergency and the 30 days following to its end, unpaid taxes that would normally be due are not considered outstanding debts and do not trigger the duty to pay interest and delay penalties. The same article also provides that all tax payment enforcement procedures are suspended, except for procedures for recovery of taxes based on criminal sentences.

4.5. SPECIAL RULES IN THE FIELD OF BANKING FINANCE FACILITIES

EOG no 57/2020 provides important rules exceptionally applicable to the bank financing agreements, leasing agreements or financing from non-banking institutions. In all these categories of agreements, the debtors whose "incomes were directly or indirectly affected by the serious situation generated by COVID-19 pandemic" are entitled to request a suspension of the reimbursement payment for a period up to nine months. The creditors are under a duty to grant such suspension if the debtor proves that his/her income were directly or indirectly affected by the COVID-19 situation. However, only debtors who paid their reimbursement instalments for the period prior to the state of emergency are entitled to benefit from this facility. Up to 18 May 2020, 317,000 requests for suspension of the reimbursement payments have been made.[28]

---

27 Published in Official Journal (*Monitorul Oficial*) no. 209 of 14 March 2020.

28 https://www.digi24.ro/stiri/economie/bancile-din-romania-au-solutionat-83-dintre-cele-317-000-de-cereri-de-suspendare-a-ratelor-1308821 accessed 7 June 2020.

A LITHUANIAN EXPERIENCE OF CORONAVIRUS AND THE LAW

Valentinas Mikelėnas*

As in many other countries of the world, the pandemic of the coronavirus came to Lithuania unexpectedly, both for society as a whole and the public authorities, as well as for the country's health system and business. Although the Government decided quickly enough to introduce quarantine, discussions have arisen upon the Government's powers to introduce quarantine. The introduction of quarantine has raised not only the problem of the distribution of competence between Parliament and the Government but also many other issues in both public and private law. The pandemic has shown that many pieces of legislation do not provide for the specificities of legal regulation in quarantine or other extreme situations. As a result, both Parliament and the Government have had to adopt a number of new laws and other legal acts or amend legislation already in force during the pandemic. The pandemic has also shown weak support from the European Union and its institutions and as a result of this, the Member States have, in practice, dealt with pandemic problems on their own rather than centrally. For this reason, trust in the European Union could be further weakened.

---

* Vilnius University.

1. INTRODUCTION

As of 9 March 2021, Lithuania, with an estimated population of approximately 3 million inhabitants, recorded 202,900 people with coronavirus disease and 3,341 deaths due to coronavirus.[1] The Government responded to the impending threat of coronavirus by introducing a state-level of extreme situation by its Decree No. 152 of 26 February 2020.[2] By Prime Ministerial decree, the Head of State Operations of State-level Extreme Situation was appointed Minister of the Health Protection.[3] The Law on Civil Safety[4] was the legal basis of the state of extreme situation. The Government declared the Republic of Lithuania in quarantine and approved the quarantine regime by the Decree of the Government No. 207 of 14 March 2020,[5] in accordance with the Law on Civil Safety and the Law on Human Communicable Diseases Prevention and Control.[6] The quarantine regime has been relaxed several times since March and was lifted on 17 June 2020.[7] However, the state-level extreme situation remains in force. However, due to the increase in the number of infections, a new quarantine was introduced by the Decree of the Government No. 1226 of 4 November 2020[8] and remains valid until now.

The introduction of quarantine has caused several legal problems in all areas of law. Parliament, the Government, the ministries (especially the Ministry of Health Protection) responded to the threats of the pandemic by adopting a number of legal acts. A total of about 1,105 different legal acts (most of them adopted by the Government, individual ministries and various State agencies, and only a few by the Parliament) were adopted between 26 February and 22 September 2020.[9] Most of this legislation will only be in force during the state-level extreme situation. However, some changes will also be valid after the abolishment of the state-level extreme situation. For example, changes to the Labour Code on the remote way of working, as well as the establishment of downtime in the event of an extreme situation or quarantine, will also be valid if the extreme situation or quarantine is declared for other reasons. This can be seen as a positive result of a pandemic, because the legislator has realised that in

1 Information of the Ministry of Health http://sam.lrv.lt/lt/naujienos/koronavirusas accessed 9 March 2021.

2 TAR, 2020-02-26, no 2020-04023 (In Lithuania, all laws, decrees of the Government and other legal acts are published in a special public registry named TAR (Registry of Legal Acts). Internet access https://www.e-tar.lt/portal/lt/legalActSearch).

3 TAR, 2020-02-27, no 2020-04234.

4 TAR, 2018, no 2018-20879.

5 TAR, 2020-03-14, no 2020-05466; 2020-05-27, no 2020-11175.

6 TAR, 2019, no 2019-09854.

7 TAR, 2020-06-11, no 2020-12723.

8 TAR, 2020-11-05, no 2020-23062

9 Data of Infolex https://www.infolex.lt/teise/Tag.aspx?ZymesId=2893&VerifierId=0&Verified=&type=3 accessed 22 September 2020.

real life can be extraordinary situations and there must be special legal norms in law that govern legal relations in such extraordinary situations.

The main changes and amendments are discussed briefly below.

2. PUBLIC LAW

2.1. ISSUES OF CONSTITUTIONAL LAW

The Decree of the Government on the quarantine regime provided for numerous restrictions and prohibitions. For example, foreigners were banned from entering the Republic of Lithuania, except for drivers and crew members in the context of commercial and/or international cargo transportation. The departure of Lithuanian citizens from the Republic of Lithuania was also prohibited, except for return to their place of residence or place of work. For persons who have returned from foreign countries, a mandatory 14-day isolation was established. Entertainment, sports facilities and all services related to physical contact were banned, as well as all events and gatherings organised in open and enclosed spaces. Sanatoriums, recreation centres, catering facilities, restaurants, cafes, bars, nightclubs and other entertainment venues were closed, except where a takeaway service could be provided for meals. Services in shops and/or entertainment centres, with the exception of selling food and veterinary, medicinal and optic goods, were limited (but this prohibition did not apply to online sales), as was the provision of beauty services. It should be noted that each Member State of the European Union has applied different quarantine measures, and the European Union's institutions are not even today able to harmonise the actions taken by States in this area to impose uniform restrictive measures. This inaction by the institutions of the European Union is therefore rightly criticised.[10]

Therefore, the quarantine regime established by the Government Decree meant the restriction or complete abolition of the rights and freedoms entrenched in the Constitution of Lithuania. For example, Article 32 of the Constitution provides that "*a citizen may freely move and choose his place of residence in Lithuania and may leave Lithuania freely. These rights may not be restricted other than by law and if it is necessary for the protection of state security, for the protection of human health, and for the administration of justice.*" It is clear that the ban on citizens from leaving the country restricts this constitutional right (right of free movement), which was done not by a law adopted by Parliament,

---

10 See, e.g. Alberto Alemanno, 'The European Response to COVID-19: From Regulatory Emulation to Regulatory Coordination?' (2020) 11 European Journal of Risk Regulation 307, 307.

but by the Decree of the Government. Other rights and freedoms affected by the Government's Decree are: the right to liberty (Art 20), the right to respect for private life (Art 22), the right to property (Art 23), freedom of expression (Art 25) freedom of assembly (Art 36), freedom of economic activity (Art 46).

Lithuanian law recognises three special regimes of State public administration: state of emergency, extreme situation and quarantine. The problem is that these three State regimes are governed by different laws, which do not provide clearly enough the criteria for the introduction of one or another regime.

Article 144 of the Constitution provides that, when there is a threat to the constitutional system or social peace of the State, the Parliament may declare a state of emergency throughout the territory of the State, or in any part of it. The introduction of such a state may temporarily restrict the rights and freedoms referred to in Articles 22, 24, 25, 32, 35 and 36 of the Constitution. The period of the state of emergency shall not exceed six months. In cases of urgency, between sessions of the Parliament, the President of the Republic shall have the right to adopt such a decision and convene, at the same time, an extraordinary session of the Parliament for the consideration of this issue. The Parliament shall approve or overrule the decision of the President of the Republic. The state of emergency is regulated by a special law of 6 June 2002.[11] Article 3 of this Law provides that a state of emergency may be imposed when the extreme situation threatens the constitutional order of the Republic of Lithuania or the public peace and this threat cannot be eliminated without the use of the extraordinary measures entrenched in the Constitution and this Law. A state of emergency may also be introduced when the constitutional order of the Republic of Lithuania or its social peace is seriously threatened due to an extreme situation in other States.

Meanwhile, the Constitution does not regulate extreme situation and quarantine regimes. Such regimes can be introduced accordingly by the Government. The regime of extreme situation is provided by the Law on Civil Safety. This Law provides that the basis for declaring an extreme situation is an extreme event. As an extreme event the Law recognises a natural, technical, ecological or social event that endangers the life or health of the population, their social conditions, property and/or the environment. The extreme situation is understood as a situation arising from an extreme event which can cause a sudden serious risk to the life or health, property, the environment or the death, injury or other harm to the population. For example, an extreme situation in Lithuania was previously declared in 2017 due torrential rains and in 2019 due to severe drought.

In the meantime, the quarantine regime is provided by the Law on Human Communicable Diseases Prevention and Control. Under this Law, the purpose

---

[11] TAR, 2019, no 2019-10927.

of quarantine is to establish a special procedure for the work, residence, rest, travel, conditions of economic and other activities of persons, procedures for the production of products, their disposal, supply of drinking water and the provision of services, and, as a result, to limit the spread of communicable diseases. However, neither of these two Laws directly provides for the possibility for the Government to introduce such restrictions and prohibitions as were introduced in March.

With these three different special regimes of State public administration, there is still a debate in society as to which regime should have been introduced.[12] In view of the scope and nature of the restrictions imposed, a state of emergency regime should have been introduced, meaning that it should have been done by Parliament, not by the Government. However, only the Constitutional Court may answer whether the Government exceeded its competence and thus violated the Constitution by declaring an extreme situation and introducing a quarantine regime.

Since 1 September 2019, the possibility of an individual constitutional complaint has emerged in Lithuania by which a natural or legal person who has exhausted all legal remedies has the right to lodge an individual constitutional appeal. The probability that such individual complaints will arise in the future is very real since both legal and natural persons have suffered pecuniary and non-pecuniary damage as a result of the restrictions imposed by quarantine regimes. This probability has already materialised. In June 2020, a natural person applied to the Constitutional Court with an individual appeal to assess whether the Government's Decree on the introduction of quarantine violated the freedom of movement entrenched in Articles 32 and 145 of the Constitution, since persons were forbidden to leave Lithuania. However, by its decision of 2 July 2020, the Constitutional Court refused to examine this request, motivated by the fact that the petitioner did not provided evidence that he was not allowed to leave Lithuania, so his rights were not violated, and the petitioner did not use all his own possible remedies.[13] Of course, the number of such individual appeals will only increase in the future, but it can be seen from the arguments of the Constitutional Court decision that the Court so far simply fears opening floodgate for such complaints.

---

12 Egidijus Šileikis, 'Koronavirusas ir Konstitucija: karantinas ar nepaprastoji padėtis?' (Teisė.Pro, 18 March 2020) http://www.teise.pro/index.php/2020/03/18/e-sileikis-koronavirusas-ir-konstitucija-karantinas-ar-nepaprastoji-padetis/ accessed 2 April 2020; Vaidotas Vaičiatis, 'Keletas minčių apie išimtinės padėties teisinio režimo konstitucinį vertinimą Lietuvoje' (Teisė.Pro, 1 May 2020) http://www.teise.pro/index.php/2020/05/01/v-vaicaitis-keletas-minciu-apie-isimtines-padeties-teisinio-rezimo-konstitucini-vertinima-lietuvoje/ accessed 10 May 2020.

13 Decision of the Constitutional Court of 2 July 2020 in a case no 116-A-S108/20202// Internet access https://www.lrkt.lt/lt/teismo-aktai/paieska/135/ta2172/content accessed 22 September 2020.

There is, therefore, a high probability that actions for the compensation of damage will be brought against the State. This probability has also already materialised. On 8 July 2020, a private dental clinic applied to the administrative court for compensation of EUR 70,000 for damages suffered as a result of the ban on dental services during quarantine.[14] The press has also reported that about 80 other companies are promising to bring such claims against the State.[15] Should such an action be rejected by an administrative court, the plaintiff would have the opportunity to apply to the Constitutional Court and request the investigation of whether the Government's Decree to introduce quarantine was in compliance with the Constitution. If the Constitutional Court acknowledged that the Government could not establish such restrictions since Parliament had to impose a state of emergency, then the case regarding the civil liability of the State would be reopened and the question of State civil liability would be reconsidered because the illegality of the Government's actions would already be established. Even if the Government had the right to introduce a quarantine regime, the question of State civil liability can be considered in another way: were all the restrictions and prohibitions imposed by the Government proportionate to the objective pursued? Today, for example, no one can say how many people died of a heart attack, stroke or other diseases simply because hospitals were banned from carrying out scheduled operations.

Thus, the pandemic of the coronavirus revealed gaps in constitutional law, a lack of clear definition and delimitation of the competences of Parliament and the Government and the importance of the principle of proportionality. Parliament will likely review relevant laws in the near future.

2.2. TAX LAW

One of the measures taken by Parliament and the Government to reduce the effects of quarantine was to ease the tax burden. For example, declaration of personal income tax returns and payment of personal income tax was deferred to 1 July 2020. Municipalities also exempted companies from the payment of

---

14 Dalius Semėnas, 'Teismą pasiekė pirmasis verslo skundas dėl karantinio draudimų' (Verslo žinios, 8 July, 2020) https://www.vz.lt/verslo-aplinka/2020/07/08/teisma-pasieke-pirmasis-verslo-skundas-del-karantino-draudimu, https://www.delfi.lt/verslas/verslas/del-karantino-ribojimu-i-teisma-svarsto-kreiptis-dar-apie-80-imoniu-skaiciuoja-100-tukst-euru-zalas.d?id=85144169 accessed 22 September 2020.

15 Aistė Žebrauskienė, 'Dėl karantino ribojimų į teismą svarsto kreiptis dar apie 80 įmonių: skaičiuoja 100 tūkstančių eurų žalas' (DELFI.LT, 2 September 2020) https://www.delfi.lt/verslas/verslas/del-karantino-ribojimu-i-teisma-svarsto-kreiptis-dar-apie-80-imoniu-skaiciuoja-100-tukst-euru-zalas.d?id=85144169, https://www.delfi.lt/verslas/verslas/del-karantino-ribojimu-i-teisma-svarsto-kreiptis-dar-apie-80-imoniu-skaiciuoja-100-tukst-euru-zalas.d?id=85144169 accessed 22 September 2020.

real estate and land tax during the quarantine period. Parliament is also debating draft laws relating to the reduction of some taxes, e.g. personal income tax and value-added tax, the increase of the tax-free amount of personal income tax, etc. It is, therefore, likely that the tax burden will be reduced in the future. The State Tax Inspectorate also decided that new actions to recover tax debts would not be initiated against taxpayers who had suffered negative consequences as a result of quarantine and that, in the case of tax loan agreements, interest would not be applied during the entire period of the tax debt deferral.[16]

2.3. CRIMINAL AND ADMINISTRATIVE LAW

Since not everyone followed the prescribed quarantine regime and some infected patients even escaped from hospitals,[17] Parliament took measures to strengthen criminal and administrative liability for the violations of the quarantine regime. For example, Article 277 of the Lithuanian Criminal Code was amended and criminal liability for breach of the rules against epidemics or communicable diseases was strengthened. Article 277 of the Criminal Code now provides for a fine, restriction of liberty, arrest or imprisonment for up to one year, and up to five years in the event of severe consequences of the breach. The Lithuanian Code of Administrative Offences has also been amended and administrative liability has been strengthened (increased administrative fines up to EUR 1,500 or sometimes up to EUR 5,000 for various violations of quarantine regime rules).

Fourteen criminal pretrial investigations were initiated on the basis of Article 277 of the Criminal Code and several hundreds of persons were fined for infringing the quarantine rules during the quarantine period. Although, to their credit, most natural and legal persons adhered to the rules in force during quarantine, the number of infringements was still high. For example, between 50 and 100 cases of violation of quarantine rules were recorded per day.[18]

The Law on Public Procurement has been amended to address the acquisition of safeguards and other goods for public use more quickly and to simplify public procurement procedures.[19]

Quarantine has also led to changes in the area of public administration. For example, the Law on the Government has been amended. The amendments provided for the possibility of organising Government meetings remotely, as

16 TAR, 2020-04-28, no 2020-08868.

17 Ramūnas Jankauskas, 'Vilniuje po tyrimo dėl koronaviruso iš ligoninės pabėgo nepilnametė' (Diena, lt, 18 March 2020) https://www.diena.lt/naujienos/vilnius/miesto-pulsas/vilniuje-po-tyrimo-del-koronaviruso-ligonines-pabego-trylikamete-957859 accessed 12 June 2020.

18 Vytautas Budzinauskas, 'Dėl karantino pažeidimų praėjusią parą nubausti 59 asmenys' (lrt. lt, 25 March 2020) https://www.lrt.lt/naujienos/lietuvoje/2/1167440/del-karantino-pazeidimu-praejusia-para-nubausti-59-asmenys accessed 11 June 2020.

19 TAR, 2020-03-18, no 2020-05694.

well as the simplified procedure for the adoption of Government decrees and resolutions during extreme situations or quarantine regimes.[20] Other State and municipal institutions have also expanded their remote activities.

2.4. SOCIAL SECURITY LAW

The announcement of quarantine has caused a lot of social problems, such as an increase in unemployment and a reduction in the income of some workers. Parliament has therefore adopted a number of legislative amendments in the area of social security, with additional child benefits,[21] increased social allowances for pensioners and poor people,[22] and increased sickness benefits from the State Social Insurance Fund.[23] Self-employed persons who are unable to continue their business because of the quarantine regime are provided with special payments from the Guarantee Fund.[24]

Unfortunately, the consideration of social security measures often gets delayed in Parliament for political reasons. In October 2020, parliamentary elections were held in Lithuania. Therefore, the current opposition often saw the proposals of the ruling majority increasing social welfare as a tribute to the electorate or even "bribery". Political bickering often takes time to change such important laws in the area of social welfare.

3. PRIVATE LAW

3.1. PERFORMANCE OF OBLIGATIONS

Some companies reacted very drastically to the announcement of quarantine. For example, on 16 March 2020 one of the largest networks of building materials and household goods, on grounds of force majeure, stated that it would no longer pay suppliers for the goods they supplied.[25] Such statements by some entrepreneurs were responded to by the Ministry of Economy and Innovation, which circulated a letter stating that Article 6.204 of the Lithuanian Civil Code provides that when it becomes more difficult for one party to perform a

---

20 TAR, 2020-03-18, no 2020-05698.
21 TAR, 2020-05-21, no 2020-10785.
22 TAR, 2020-05-20, no 2020-10665.
23 TAR, 2020-03-18, no 2020-05705.
24 TAR, 2020-03-18, no 2020-05703.
25 '"Senukai" stabdo prekių užsakymus ir mokėjimus tiekėjams' (delfi. lt, 17 March 2020) https://www.delfi.lt/verslas/verslas/senukai-stabdo-prekiu-uzsakymus-ir-mokejimus-tieke jams.d?id=83798425 accessed 11 June 2020.

contract, that party has the right to request its contractual counterparty to alter the terms of the contract (for example, to negotiate penalties for late delivery of goods due to the logistic problems, a certain payment schedule, etc.). The Ministry called on the business community to contribute jointly and severally to mitigate the quarantine consequences and to consult business partners on their own initiative on the possibility of exempting certain penalties, interest, or other sanctions for failure to comply with part of the contractual obligations or delays in carrying out their obligations during the quarantine. The Ministry also suggested that sectoral business associations consider the possibility of adoption of a memorandum of understanding on the non-application of sanctions to each other during the quarantine period for delays in the performance of certain obligations laid down in the contracts in the event of delays due to reasonable and objective circumstances. Such a reaction from the Ministry is unusual, as the executive does not usually interfere in conflicts between business entities, and in the event of their complaints, they usually offer to settle disputes in the courts or arbitration. On the other hand, the pandemic has shown that the extraordinary situation often requires breaking the usual rules of conduct and the application of extraordinary measures. Such a reaction from the Ministry could be evaluated as a call by the State for businesses, in the event of a pandemic, to act in accordance with the principles of good faith, justice, and reasonableness, especially since the resolution of conflicts in court takes a long time. On the other hand, some may evaluate such ministerial recommendations as an order from the executive to the courts on how to resolve such disputes in the future, i.e. as a violation of the independence of the courts. However, so far, there has been no legal assessment of these ministerial reactions in the case law. The Lithuanian Banking Association responded to this invitation from the Ministry and issued a moratorium on 23 April 2020. For businesses, a moratorium (i.e. deferral of payment of loan premiums) was imposed by 1 July 2020. For natural persons, the moratorium applies to real estate loans for up to one year and, in the case of leasing contracts and consumer loans, up to six months.[26]

During the quarantine, the importance of the principles of good faith and cooperation between the parties to the obligation, as enshrined in the Articles 6.4 and 6.38 of the Lithuanian Civil Code, became clear. It should be noted that Article 6.212(1) of the Civil Code expressly provides that the fact that the debtor does not have or does not have sufficient financial resources cannot be regarded as force majeure. This is particularly important in the event of performance of monetary obligations.

It should be noted that during the quarantine period, the Civil Code was amended once and this amendment relates the execution of tourism contracts

---

[26] Association of Lithuanian Banks https://www.lba.lt/lt/moratoriumas-verslui accessed 11 June 2020.

during the quarantine regime. Although Parliament has received numerous proposals to amend the Civil Code and to regulate in detail the performance of obligations during the quarantine period, these proposals have not received support in Parliament. That fact illustrates that good faith (Art 6.158), impossibility (Art 6.62, 6.127) force majeure (Art 6.212), gross disparity (Art 6.228), changed circumstances (Art 6.204) and other doctrines enshrined in the Civil Code make it possible to ensure the stability of the Civil Code, even in such extreme circumstances. Of course, it is not yet clear how courts will apply the rules of the Civil Code when the first civil cases relating to the effects of quarantine reach them.

There were, of course, a number of obligations which the debtors could not really perform because of the quarantine introduced. In such cases, the debtor could certainly rely on force majeure. Article 6.212 (1) of the Civil Code provides that only circumstances which fulfil the following conditions are relevant to be considered when analysing the applicability of force majeure: (1) the circumstances were not present at the time of conclusion of the contract; (2) the defaulting party could not reasonably foresee them; (3) the circumstances make the contract objectively impossible to perform; (4) the defaulting party was unable to control or prevented the circumstances; and (5) the defaulting party has not assumed the risk of the circumstances or their effects. In its letter of 19 March 2020 to businesses, the Ministry of Economy and Innovation stressed that all five conditions must be met in order to find force majeure. The Ministry also invited business entities not to rush to rely on force majeure but to make wider use of Article 6.204 of the Civil Code, which provides the possibility of the modification of contract in the event of unexpected circumstances. It should be noted that some of businesses quickly reoriented their activity and continued to operate under quarantine conditions. For example, many shops started selling online; some restaurants and cafes started cooking for home delivery, etc.; and, during the first two weeks of quarantine, 80 e-shops were established in Lithuania.[27]

Article 1.129 (1)(1) of the Civil Code provides the right of the Government to declare a moratorium in which the performance of all obligations is deferred. But the Government did not declare a moratorium. However, due to the specificities of some obligations, Parliament has adopted separate legislative amendments. For example, closing the borders and barring departure to a foreign country has particularly affected tourism. In order to protect tourists, paying an advance to tourism companies for the future trip, Parliament has supplemented Article 6.751 of the Civil Code with a new rule. It provides that,

[27] 'Nuo karantino pradžios įsisteigė 80 e.parduotuvių' (Verslo žinios, 8 April 2020) https://www.vz.lt/smulkusis-verslas/2020/04/08/nuo-karantino-pradzios-isisteige-80-e-parduotuviu accessed 12 June 2020.

if the tourist and the tour operator do not agree on the reimbursement of the money paid for the failed organised future tourist trip, the tour operator shall reimburse all the money paid by the tourist no later than 90 days from the date on which the restrictions laid down in the Law on Tourism are abolished.[28] However, such an amendment to the Civil Code is contrary to Article 12(4) of EU Directive 2015/2302 (the Package Travel Directive), which provides for a period of only 14 days. The European Commission therefore in July 2020 launched a procedure of violation of EU law against Lithuania. For this reason, Parliament began to consider the draft amendment to Article 6.751 of the Civil Code in September and it is expected that this Article will be amended in the near future in line with EU law.[29]

Parliament also adopted a special law on the impact of the quarantine effects on the performance of consumer contracts for the provision of entertainment event services.[30] The Law provides that the consumer who has purchased a ticket shall not be entitled, under conditions other than those referred to in Article 4 of this Law, to unilaterally terminate the consumer contract and to demand reimbursement of the price paid for the ticket. However, the consumer has the right to terminate the consumer contract on other grounds laid down in the Civil Code and/or the rules for the provision of services approved by the service provider.

This special law also provides that, where an event does not take place as a result of quarantine bans which have made it impossible or significantly more difficult to organise events, or the date of the event is during the quarantine period, the service provider shall be entitled to set a later date of the event within 30 days of the lifting of this prohibition. The event must take place within a reasonable time from the initial date of the event, but no later than 12 months after the lifting of quarantine bans which made it impossible or significantly more difficult to organise events. In this case, the service provider does not have the right to require any additional charges from the user. The service provider must provide consumers with information about the later date of the event and other information specified in the Rules for the provision of sports, cultural and entertainment services approved by the Government. The service provider's notice of the later date of the event shall be published by the same or equivalent means and methods as information on the initial date of the event at the ticketing points. The consumer, for his/her part, has the right to notify the service provider no later than 60 days after the service provider's notification that he/she does not agree with the service provider's subsequent event date. When the consumer

---

28 TAR, 2020-05-29, no 2020-11673.

29 https://ec.europa.eu/commission/presscorner/detail/en/inf_20_1212 accessed 22 September 2020.

30 TAR, 2020-05-12, no 2020-10169.

does not agree with the later date of the event set by the service provider, the service provider shall reimburse the consumer for the event which has not taken place within 30 days of receipt of the user's notification by giving the consumer a voucher with a value of at least the amount of money paid for the ticket, without any additional charges being charged to the consumer. The voucher may cover the price of tickets for future events organised by the same service provider, or part of it. If the consumer does not use the voucher to pay the price of tickets of future events organised by the same service provider within 12 months from the date of the granting of the voucher, he/she shall be entitled to require the service provider to reimburse the consumer, no later than 14 days after the expiry of that time limit, the amount of money corresponding to the value of the voucher. If the service provider does not provide the consumer with a voucher within the 30-day time limit, the service provider must refund the price paid for the ticket to the consumer no later than 14 days after the later date of the event. Where the service provider does not set a later date for the event, the consumer shall have the right to require the reimbursement of the price paid for the ticket to the service provider, which should happen no later than 14 days after the quarantine has been withdrawn.

Other legislative changes have also been adopted to facilitate the situation of consumers. For example, the Consumer Credit Act relating to the immovable property has been amended. If the consumer debtor of credit relating to immovable property or his/her spouse becomes unemployed during the quarantine period or loses at least one-third of income, repayment premiums shall be deferred for a maximum period of three months.[31]

Of course, some transactions in the first weeks of quarantine were generally stopped. For example, the Minister of Justice stated by order of 16 March 2020 that public notaries' offices should not accept persons and notaries could not perform notarial actions. Notaries had to ensure remote consultation of individuals (by telephone and e-mail).[32] Such a decision outraged both businesses and natural persons. For example, since immovable property transactions are required in notarial form, the sale of apartments and other immovable property was halted. Natural persons also lost the opportunity to make a will in a notarial form. The Minister of Justice, therefore, changed his previous order and notaries renewed their activities on 20 March 2020. The activities of public notaries in quarantine have also encouraged notaries to make greater use of the means of modern information technology. For its part, Parliament has begun to consider legislative changes allowing some transactions, which can now be concluded only on the physical presence in a public notary's office, to be concluded remotely, such as the extension of the possibility to use an electronic power of attorney.

---

31 TAR, 2020-03-18, no 2020-05695.

32 TAR, 2020-03-18, no 2020-05472.

3.2. OTHER MEASURES TO SUPPORT BUSINESS

Special legislation has also been adopted to help businesses most affected by the introduction of the quarantine regime. For example, partial compensation for the most affected commercial lessees was introduced, provided that the lessor reduced the amount of the rent accordingly. No more than 50% of the rent may be reimbursed, up to a maximum of EUR 800,000 per company.[33] Small and medium-sized enterprises are provided for reimbursement of interest on credits of between 50 and 100%, and conditions for granting guarantees have been extended. The total value of the State's financial assistance of this kind is approximately EUR 541 million.[34] There is also a special procedure for granting loans to businesses most affected by the pandemic.[35] The Government also approved the special plan for Lithuania's future economy in July, which provides for EUR 6.3 billion to invest in the digital economy, innovation and energy over one and a half years.[36]

In order to prevent possible bankruptcy floodgate, the legislation governing bankruptcy proceedings has been amended. The amendment of the Law on the insolvency of legal persons provides that the duty of the director of a legal person to initiate insolvency proceedings does not apply during the quarantine period and for the following three months after its cancellation.[37]

3.3. LABOUR LAW

Perhaps the most adverse effects of quarantine have been experienced in labour relations. The unemployment rate in Lithuania during the quarantine period increased from 9.1% to 12%.[38] This is why Parliament and the Government found that they needed to amend the Labour Code several times. For example, amendments of the Labour Code provided for the possibility for the employer

---

33 TAR, 2020-05-03, no 2020-09261.

34 TAR, 2020-05-12, no 2020-10169.

35 TAR, 2020-04-15, no 2020-07906; INVEGA information. INVEGA is a financial entity incorporated by the State. The main objectives of the operations of the entity are as follows: provision of financial services and implementation and administration of financial and other support measures for SMEs https://invega.lt/lt/13948-2/?utm_source=newsletter&utm_medium=email&utm_campaign=news_alert_0317_aktuali_informacija_verslui_covid_19&utm_term=2020-06-09 accessed 12 June 2020.

36 https://www.lrt.lt/naujienos/verslas/4/1237362/sapoka-apie-dnr-plano-igyvendinima-viskas-priklauso-nuo-to-kaip-greitai-investuosime accessed 12 June 2020.

37 TAR, 2020-04-24, no 2020-08725.

38 'Nedarbas Lietuvoje išaugo iki 11,7 proc., tačiau besikreipiančiųjų dėl darbo skaičius mažėja' (lrt. lt, 25 May 2020) https://www.lrt.lt/naujienos/verslas/4/1181834/nedarbas-lietuvoje-paaugo-iki-11-7-proc-taciau-besikreipianciuju-del-darbo-skaicius-mazeja accessed 11 June 2020.

to declare downtime when quarantine prevents work, but, in such cases, the employee must be paid the appropriate wages. Remote working was also established.[39] In order to reduce unemployment and preserve jobs, a special wage subsidy system was provided for companies that halted their activity. EUR 56 million has been allocated for the implementation of this measure.[40]

4. PROCEDURAL LAW

No changes were made to procedural law during the quarantine period. Neither the Code of Criminal Procedure, the Code of Civil Procedure nor the Law on administrative proceedings were amended, with the exception of one amendment to the Code of Civil Procedure relating to enforcement proceedings. Article 668 of the Code of Civil Procedure now provides that the enforcement proceedings may not be diverted to cash that belongs to the debtor as State or municipal support and other benefits or compensation granted as a result of an extreme situation or quarantine.[41] Thus, all the principles of procedural law had to be valid without exception. However, the activities of the courts in the first weeks of quarantine practically stopped. The Council of Judges recommended the postponement of all oral hearings for two weeks, except in urgent cases, such as the consideration of arrest issues or child protection measures. The Council of Judges also recommended the use of remote video tools in court proceedings cases, the adoption of systems of electronic submission of procedural documents, such as by email, and to decide questions of the renewal of procedural time limits in a more liberal way.[42] Since 2013, the Lithuanian Code of Civil Procedure provides for the possibility of organising court hearings remotely by organising video or teleconferences. However, the practical implementation of these norms has been stalled due to poor material technical provision of the courts and this method of hearings has rarely been used in the past. It is therefore likely that the pandemic will encourage the State to provide adequate funding of the courts for the practical implementation of these norms.

However, oral hearings were postponed for much longer than two weeks. Even after the opening of oral hearings, some principles of procedural law were not respected. For example, when the court began to hear in oral hearing a well-known political corruption criminal case, the court did not allow

39 TAR, 2020-03-18, no 2020-05702.

40 TAR, 2020-04-07, no 2020-07196.

41 https://www.infolex.lt/ta/606815 accessed 22 September 2020.

42 'Lietuvos teismų veikla sugriežtinus COVID-19 prevencijos priemones' (Lietuvos teismai, 13 March 2020) https://www.teismai.lt/lt/naujienos/teismu-sistemos-naujienos/lietuvos-teismu-veikla-sugrieztinus-covid-19-prevencijos-priemones/7439 accessed 10 June 2020.

journalists to appear at the courtroom.[43] Thus, during quarantine, fundamental human rights such as the right to a hearing within a reasonable time, the right to be heard, the principle of publicity were violated.

Meanwhile, the introduction of quarantine measures for arbitration had no practical significance. Arbitration proceedings have not been postponed; oral arbitration hearings were held remotely. This is explained by the fact that, for example, the Rules[44] of the Vilnius Court of Commercial Arbitration already in 2018 provided for the possibility of organising hearings remotely by means of video or teleconferences. Thus, quarantine showed another advantage of arbitration compared to court proceedings.

In the early days of quarantine, there was also a problem of enforcement of court judgments. On 16 March 2020, the Minister of Justice issued an order on the activities of the bailiffs during the quarantine regime. According to the Order, bailiffs could not provide services for creditors and other persons physically, but had to serve them remotely (by phone and email). Bailiffs had to defer enforcement actions requiring the direct involvement of the bailiff, the bailiff's assistant, the parties to the enforcement proceedings and other persons.[45] However, this order was later amended and bailiffs renewed their activities.

On the other hand, it is clear that quarantine will encourage the intensive use of modern information technologies in the activities of the courts and bailiffs, and more and more cases will be electronic in the future. Already in 2019, 70% of civil and administrative cases were electronic (this means that claims and all other procedural documents may be submitted electronically by both the court and the other parties to the proceedings through a specially designed electronic court e-services portal)[46] in Lithuania.[47] There is no doubt that after quarantine this number will increase even further.

5. NEGATIVE CONSEQUENCES OF NEW LAWS AND AMENDMENTS

Parliament and the Government have adopted new legislation or changed the rules in force to protect the entire society from the threat of coronavirus.

---

43 Margiris Meilutis, Vaidotas Beniušis, 'Teismas nusprendė leisti žurnalistams stebėti E.Masiulio parodymus nuotoliniu būdu' (Klaipėda, 15 May 2020) https://klaipeda.diena.lt/naujienos/lietuva/politika/teismas-nusprende-leisti-zurnalistams-stebeti-e-masiulio-parodymus-nuotoliniu-budu-967656 accessed 10 June 2020.

44 Rules of Vilnius Court of Commercial Arbitration http://www.arbitrazas.lt/failai/2018%2001%2001%20VCCA%20Rules%20of%20Arbitration_2017-11-28.pdf accessed 10 June 2020.

45 TAR, 2020-03-16, no 2020-05472.

46 https://e.teismas.lt/lt/public/home/ accessed 10 June 2020.

47 'Kaip technologijos keičia teisėjų, prokurorų, advokatų, antstolių ir notarų darbą' (Lietuvos teismai, 9 May 2019) https://www.teismai.lt/lt/naujienos/teismu-sistemos-naujienos/kaip-technologijos-keicia-teiseju-prokuroru-advokatu-antstoliu-ir-notaru-darba/6749 accessed 10 June 2020.

However, all new legal rules have been made in haste, without forecasting or modelling the possible negative consequences of new legislation or amendments. And that such negative consequences have already arisen or will emerge in the future is already obvious. For example, the police were forced to respond to violations of quarantine regime rules, which naturally reduced the focus on other areas of public security. For example, the Police Department acknowledged that during the quarantine period there was an increase in the number of cases of domestic violence.[48] Simplification of public procurement procedures has led to an increase in the number of fraudulent public procurement contracts.[49] According to the order of the Minister of Transport, the deadline for the mandatory technical control of road vehicles during quarantine and for another 30 days after its abolition was extended.[50] This means that the number of technically unsuitable cars on the roads has increased, which could lead to an increase in the number of road accidents.

The introduction of quarantine undoubtedly adversely affected the mental and physical health of the population. During quarantine, scheduled surgery and hospitalisation were postponed in hospitals and only emergency medical services were provided. There was also no medical rehabilitation service, outpatient medical services were provided only by telephone and scheduled doctors' consultations and diagnostic procedures were postponed. It was also prohibited to provide dental services other than emergency medical assistance. A survey of oncological patients showed that 18% of patients during quarantine did not receive prescribed chemotherapy, 33% did not receive radiation therapy and 37% did not undergo prescribed surgery.[51] Thus, in the fight against one disease and focusing on one type of patient, other diseases and other patients were neglected.

6. CONCLUSIONS

The coronavirus pandemic is a kind of exam for both public institutions and society as a whole. The activities of the public authorities during the pandemic

---

48 'Karantino metu policijos taikiklyje – pranešimai apie smurtą artimoje aplinkoje' (Lietuvos policija, 10 April 2020) https://policija.lrv.lt/lt/naujienos/karantino-metu-policijos-taikiklyje-pranesimai-apie-smurta-artimoje-aplinkoje accessed 12 June 2020.

49 Margiris Meilutis, Evelina Povilaitytė, 'Pradėtas tyrimas dėl greitųjų COVID-19 testų pirkimo' (delfi. lt, 10 June 2020) https://www.delfi.lt/news/daily/lithuania/pradetas-tyrimas-del-greituju-covid-19-testu-pirkimo.d?id=84499613 accessed 12 June 2020.

50 TAR, 2020-04-03, no 2020-07076.

51 'A.Verygos botagas ir meduolis: kol gelbėjo užsikrėtusius COVID-19, kitus paliko likimo valiai' (Lrytas. lt, 12 June 2020) https://www.lrytas.lt/lietuvosdiena/aktualijos/2020/06/12/news/a-verygos-botagas-ir-meduolis-kol-gelbejo-uzsikretusius-covid-19-kitus-paliko-likimo-valiai-15230948/ accessed 12 June 2020.

revealed their weaknesses. It turned out that the State had not accumulated the necessary reserve of protective equipment, so in the first days of quarantine medical personnel lacked them. The bureaucracy of the public administration apparatus and the inability to refocus from work under normal conditions to work under extreme conditions, has also emerged. Many issues have not been resolved expeditiously for bureaucratic reasons. For example, the mere liberalisation of the authorisation procedure for the production of disinfectants for new companies was delayed by two weeks.[52] Although decisions on financial support for business have been taken expeditiously, in reality, financial support has reached the beneficiaries very late due to bureaucratic obstacles.[53]

The pandemic has also demonstrated Parliament's inability to respond promptly to threats. The political bickering in Parliament increases the importance of the Government. On the other hand, the pandemic has demonstrated the importance of the national State and the ineffectiveness of the European Union. Everything that was done was done on the initiative of national authorities, while the voice of Brussels was practically not heard.

---

52 TAR, 2020-03-05, no 2020-04998.

53 'Verslas: parama stringa dėl perteklinių reikalavimų' (15min. lt, 28 April 2020) https://www.15min.lt/verslas/naujiena/finansai/verslas-parama-stringa-del-pertekliniu-reikalavimu-662-1310176, accessed 12 June 2020.

"CORONA CONTRACT LAW" IN POLAND

When Pandemic Meets Politics

Aneta Wiewiórowska-Domagalska*

* University of Osnabrück.

This contribution presents and critically evaluates the impact of the COVID-19 pandemic on Polish contract law. Since the government refrained from introducing a state of emergency to manage the pandemic in Poland in violation of the Constitution, the constitutional dimension of the COVID-19 measures is of crucial importance for examination of the contract law, as it substantially changes the position of the parties in private law relations. The contribution therefore gives an overview of the measures introduced as a response to the COVID-19 emergency in the constitutional context and presents the classic Polish private law instruments potentially applicable to contracts in extraordinary circumstances like pandemic, as well as the extraordinary legislation introduced by the government in the area of contract law, with a view to addressing the pandemic. It ends by presenting the first cases initiated by private parties against the State Treasury.

1. INTRODUCTION

1.1. POLISH REACTION TO THE PANDEMIC

COVID-19 did not take Poland by surprise. The first case, registered on 4 March 2020, was swiftly followed by far-reaching restrictions imposed by the government, enacted as soon as 20 March 2020,[1] when the number of registered cases had reached 425 in total (70 that day).[2] As in many other countries, the change in circumstances in which contracts are performed in Poland in relation to COVID-19 was therefore (so far) not caused by the fact that a large number of people fell ill, causing market disturbances, but resulted from the restrictions imposed by the government with a view to limiting the spread of the disease. The strictness of the governmental measures did not, however, correspond with the number of registered cases.[3] The restrictions started to be lifted on 20 April,

---

1 See also Commission Staff Working Document, 2020 Rule of Law Report, Country Chapter on the rule of law situation in Poland, accompanying the document Communication from the Commission to the European Parliament, the Council, the European Economic and Social Committee and the Committee of the Regions, 2020 Rule of Law Report, the Rule of law situation in the European Union, SWD(20202) 320 final, p. 16.

2 Danuta Pawłowska, Bartosz Chyż, Dominik Uhlig, 'Koronawirus w Polsce. 314 nowych zakażonych. Łącznie ponad 35,7 tys. chorych, 1512 zmarło' (*biqdata.pl*, 29 June 2020) https://biqdata.wyborcza.pl/biqdata/7,159116,25812474,koronawirus-w-polsce-codzienna-aktualizacja.html accessed 29 June 2020.

3 The low number of the registered cases could, however, be related to the very low number of tests run at that time: see info on the increase of the test run: Arkadiusz Grochot, Monika Kamińska, 'Koronawirus w Polsce. Aktualny bilans epidemii: 35 719 zakażeń, 1 513 ofiar śmiertelnych' (*rmf24*, 4 July 2020) https://www.rmf24.pl/raporty/raport-koronawirus-z-chin/

at a time when there were 306 cases of the virus daily, and continued despite the fact that the number of cases did not seem to be decreasing – a situation that still continues as this contribution is being finalised (506 cases on 17 June 2020).[4] The rather paradoxical situation whereby the strictness of the restrictions does not seem to correspond with the number of cases of infection raises questions relating to the government's reasoning behind imposing and relaxing the measures.

1.2. PRESIDENTIAL ELECTIONS IN SIGHT

Decisions on when and whether to introduce measures in relation to situations like the pandemic are always made in a wider political context, and the effects of such measures often extend beyond the issues that the measures are supposed to address. In Poland, the response to COVID-19 had a particularly strong political background, i.e. the presidential elections that were supposed to take place on 10 May 2020. The strategy and the tactics of the Polish government's reaction to the pandemic, in relation to both the strictness of the imposed restrictions, as well as their legal basis, seem to have been directed more by the current political strategy than the epidemical necessities. This, however, has had a direct impact on the situation of parties in the context of contract law, and the recourse options that have arisen for them as a result.

Most importantly, the Polish government made a conscious decision not to announce one of the states of emergency as prescribed by the Polish Constitution. This was blatantly done to ensure that the elections would be held on the prescribed date, as introducing a state of emergency would have automatically triggered the postponement of the election date. In the end, the elections were, indeed, postponed, but not as a result of applying the Constitution,[5] and were held on 28 June 2020 and 12 July 2020 (second round). As a result, the restrictions on freedoms and the rights imposed by the government are not based on any constitutionally prescribed mechanism, which has a very significant impact on the situation in the private law area.

---

najnowsze-fakty/news-koronawirus-w-polsce-aktualny-bilans-epidemii-31-931-zakazen,nId,4377329 accessed 4 July 2020.

4 Danuta Pawłowska, Bartosz Chyż, Dominik Uhlig, 'Koronawirus w Polsce. 314 nowych zakażonych. Łącznie ponad 35,7 tys. chorych, 1512 zmarło' (*biqdata.pl*, 29 June 2020) https://biqdata.wyborcza.pl/biqdata/7,159116,25812474,koronawirus-w-polsce-codzienna-aktualizacja.html accessed 29 June 2020.

5 Without any sort of constitutionally backed procedure, as a result of an agreement concluded by two politicians of the coalition that currently holds the power in Poland: see: https://tvn24.pl/magazyn-tvn24/rozliczenie-z-gowinem-to-kwestia-czasu-kulisy-wyborczej-porazki-kaczynskiego,269,4720 accessed 15 March 2021.

1.3. PRIVATE, PUBLIC, BUT MOST OF ALL CONSTITUTIONAL

Classic private law measures, which apply when external, unusual circumstances prevent the performance of a contract as planned, focus on the impact that these circumstances have on the economic rationality or the possibility of the parties to perform under the contract. The classic instruments allow for claims to be formulated between the parties in order to restore a fair contractual balance between them, which was disturbed by the unexpected circumstances. It is, however, rather doubtful whether the rationale of introducing classic contract law measures (such as the impossibility of performance or the *rebus sic stantibus* in Poland) included such overwhelming changes to the market conditions as switching off a large part of the economy. The extent of the extraordinariness of the market conditions makes it plausible that contractual parties, acting rationally, would refrain from exercising their rights under the law. On the one hand, the classic instruments might prove to be quite ineffective (due to the general market conditions), while on the other, they might lead to contractual partners being eliminated from the market, with no viable alternatives (due to the market conditions). Instead of enforcing their rights, the parties might rather seek to renegotiate, in order to preserve the functioning of the economy in the long term.[6]

This gives even stronger rationale for the introduction of ad hoc legislative measures by the State in the case of a pandemic. These measures might take the form of public or private law intervention. The public law measures (for example: subsidies for anyone conducting business activities, tax and social security payments exceptions) provide financial support to one or both parties of a given contract, without affecting the contractual relation as such. Their immediate aim is to stimulate the economy by preventing bankruptcies and allowing the parties to perform. The measures that target private law relations, for example by freezing prices or temporarily excluding the possibility of renouncing contracts, intervene directly into the contractual relations between the parties. The rationale of the private law measures, however, focuses neither on the traditional aim of contract law, which is finding the optimal default effectiveness of contractual relations, nor on supporting a particular group of

---

6 Very symptomatic from this perspective is the guidance issued by the UK's government that urges parties to contracts that have been impacted by the COVID-19 emergency to "act responsibly" and fairly, "to protect jobs and the economy." "This includes being reasonable and proportionate in responding to performance issues and enforcing contracts (including dealing with any disputes), acting in a spirit of cooperation and aiming to achieve practical, just and equitable contractual outcomes having regard to the impact on the other party (or parties), the availability of financial resources, the protection of public health and the national interest." https://www.gov.uk/government/publications/guidance-on-responsible-contractual-behaviour-in-the-performance-and-enforcement-of-contracts-impacted-by-the-covid-19-emergency accessed 15 June 2020.

market participants who enjoy an equal position only formally (like in the case of consumer law, for example). Such legislative intervention, just like the public law measures, has a social (or market) engineering nature, where the ultimate aim is to ensure the possibility of undisturbed continuation of the market activities (preventing a market collapse by lowering the risk of large-scale bankruptcies). The crux of the problem is, therefore, correctly identifying those market areas where the legislative intervention into the private law relations will be the most efficient in terms of its impact on the entire market/supply chain. For example, a temporary freeze of rents in shopping centres may lead to the operation of delivery chains being sustained, not only the operation of the shopping centres themselves. The rationale of the "corona contract law" is therefore quite distant from the traditional paradigms of private law.

What is happening at the moment in Poland is – quite predictably – not a massive testing of private law instruments, but the imposition of a large-scale state-imposed policy, employed to maintain stability on the pandemic-stricken market. However, the real impact of the pandemic on contract law in Poland will probably manifest itself not in the effects of public law intervention, but in the fact that the measures to mitigate the economic consequences of the pandemic were introduced in violation of the constitutionally prescribed mechanisms. To understand what is happening in Poland in the area of contract law, it is therefore necessary to understand the political background of the decisions taken by the party currently governing Poland, due to the direct repercussions it has in private law relations. The strategic decision to base the functioning of the government during the pandemic on legal instruments that are used in normal circumstances (ordinances), rather than introducing a state of emergency, according to Article 232 of the Polish Constitution (with what can only be called very strong political motivation in the context of the presidential elections) has significantly changed the position of the private parties.

1.4. THE AIM OF THE CONTRIBUTION

This contribution presents and critically evaluates the impact of the COVID-19 pandemic on Polish contract law. Due to the specific Polish situation, the constitutional dimension of the Polish COVID-19 measures is of crucial importance for the examination of contract law, when attempting to take a practical, rather than a highly theoretical, approach to the analysis. Hence, the contribution explains the constitutional dimension of the Polish government's decisions and their potential consequences for the private law relations. It gives an overview of the measures introduced as a response to the COVID-19 emergency, presents the classic Polish private law instruments that are applicable in the case of impediments to the normal performance of contracts, and follows with an overview of the extraordinary legislation introduced by the government in the area of contract law with a view to addressing the pandemic. It ends by presenting the first cases initiated by private parties against the State Treasury.

2. THE RESPONSE TO COVID-19: THE CONSTITUTION SHOULD NOT STAND IN THE WAY

2.1. GENERAL

It is clear that it is not the COVID-19 pandemic itself that had a disruptive impact on the market situation, but rather the legislative measures introduced by the government with a view to limiting the spread of the virus. At the time of writing, the spread of the pandemic in Poland was at a relatively low level, when compared to other EU countries. However, the worrying factor was that, according to the European Centre for Disease Prevention and Control, the pandemic has not yet passed its peak in Poland[7] and the number of the cases remained at a relatively stable level (without a noticeable tendency to decrease).[8] This, combined with the chaotic and non-transparent information policy of the Government, the messy nature of the introduced measures, as well as their political dimension, created a situation where it was difficult to understand the true aim of the restrictions that have been imposed and subsequently lifted without a reasonable link to the epidemical situation.

2.2. THE QUESTIONABLE CONSTITUTIONALITY OF THE RESTRICTIONS

The Polish Constitution, in its Chapter XI (Extraordinary Measures), sets out rules that apply in situations of particular peril, specifying how the State is supposed to function in such circumstances. If ordinary constitutional measures are inadequate, martial law, a state of emergency or a state of natural disaster may be introduced (Art 228 of the Constitution), but only by a regulation issued on the basis of a statute. The statute must establish the principles according to which the organs of public authority function, and the degree to which the freedoms and rights of persons and citizens may be limited for the duration of the extraordinary measures. The principles, the scope and the manner of compensating for a loss of property resulting from the limitation of the freedoms

---

[7] Alice Tidey 'Poland and Sweden are the only EU countries who have not passed COVID-19 peak: ECDC' (*euronews*, 12 June 2020) https://www.euronews.com/2020/06/12/poland-and-sweden-are-the-only-eu-countries-who-have-not-passed-covid-19-peak-ecdc accessed 15 June 2020.

[8] Which might be also due to the fact that the number of tests increased substantially.

and rights of persons and citizens during such a period can also be established in a statute. All actions undertaken as a result of introducing the extraordinary measure must be proportionate to the degree of the threat and must be intended to achieve the swiftest restoration of conditions allowing for the normal functioning of the State. During the period of the extraordinary measures, the Constitution, and several other acts (including statutes on extraordinary measures) cannot be changed. Last, but not least, during such a period, and for a period of 90 days following its termination, elections for the Presidency (among others) cannot be held, and the term of office is prolonged accordingly.

Article 232 of the Constitution specifies that, in order to prevent or remove the consequences of a natural catastrophe or a technological accident exhibiting the characteristics of a natural disaster, the Council of Ministers may introduce, for a definite period no longer than 30 days, a state of natural disaster in a part of or upon the entire territory of the State. Certain freedoms and rights guaranteed by the Constitution are untouchable during the state of introduction of the extraordinary measures. Limitations on the freedoms and rights of persons and citizens only by reason of race, gender, language, faith or lack of it, social origin, ancestry or property during the introduction of any extraordinary measures are expressly excluded by Article 233 paragraph 2. In the case of a state of natural disaster, however, certain limitations may be introduced. Article 233 paragraph 3 indicates that the statute specifying the scope of limitations on the freedoms and rights of persons and citizens during a state of natural disaster may limit the freedom of economic activity, personal freedom, inviolability of the home, freedom of movement and sojourn in the Republic of Poland, the right to strike, the right of ownership, the freedom to work, the right to safe and hygienic conditions of work, as well as the right to rest (Art 233 para 3). More severe limitations are allowed in times of martial law and states of emergency (Art 233 para 1).

Article 232 is complemented by the Act on the State of Natural Disaster of 18 April 2002 (the 2002 Act),[9] which establishes the mechanism of announcing and removing a state of natural disaster, as well as the rules on how public bodies function and the scope of the limits on the rights and freedoms of humans and citizens during a state of natural disaster. According to its Article 2, a state of natural disaster can be introduced with a view to preventing the consequences of a natural disaster or to removing them. A natural disaster is understood as an event caused by the forces of nature (which includes mass cases of infectious diseases among people). The scope of the allowed limitations on rights and freedoms of humans and citizens are listed in Article 21 paragraph 1 and include (among many others) suspending activities of certain types of business, the possibility to order or prohibit certain types of business activity, the partial or

9 Official Journal 2017, item 1897.

total control over the distribution of certain types of products, the possibility of fixing prices of certain types of goods.

As the Polish Ombudsman emphasised,[10] the Polish government made a conscious decision not to introduce a state of natural disaster on the basis of Article 232, deciding instead that the instruments that the Constitution provides for managing the country in normal circumstances are sufficient to deal with the pandemic. This means, however, that the government is bound to observe all the constitutionally granted freedoms and rights and does not have the proper legal basis to limit them. Despite this, the government put forward an act, which was adopted on 2 March 2020, on specific solutions related to the prevention and eradication of COVID-19, other infectious diseases and the crisis situations caused by them (the 2020 Act),[11] which introduced changes to the Act on the Prevention and Eradication of Infections and Infectious Diseases in People of 5 December 2008 (the 2008 Act).[12] These changes provide the government with an (illegal, as it seems) authorisation to introduce restrictions to the rights and freedoms of humans. A problem that is now causing serious constitutional concerns is that the 2008 Act itself did not contain sufficient constitutional authority to introduce such restrictions. The 2020 Act allows the Council of Ministers to introduce restrictions on rights and freedom in a scope that very much reflects the potential restrictions listed in Article 21 of the 2002 Act, which, according to the Constitution, may only be introduced once a state of natural disaster has been declared. Moreover, the introduced authorisation does not contain any guidelines when it comes to the scope of the potential restrictions that it might introduce, which is required according to the Constitutional Tribunal.[13] This means that the Council of Ministers is basically unrestricted when it comes to imposing restrictions on this basis, which violates Article 92 paragraph 1 of the Constitution. However, the way the Council of Ministers used this authorisation exceeded even the flexible (and already unconstitutional) framework established by the 2008 Act.[14]

2.3. WHY NO STATE OF NATURAL DISASTER?

Introducing a state of natural disaster activates mechanisms that turned out to be unacceptable for the governing party in light of the upcoming presidential

---

10 Address of the Ombudsman to the Minister of Development of 26 June 2020, p. 2, https://www.rpo.gov.pl/sites/default/files/Wystąpienie%20RPO%20do%20MR%2C%2026.06.2020.pdf, accessed 15 March 2021.

11 Official Journal 2020, item 374 as amended.

12 Official Journal 2019, item 1239 as amended.

13 Judgment of the Constitutional Tribunal of 3 April 2012, K12/11 OTK of 2012, No 4, item 37.

14 Address of the Ombudsman to the Minister of Development of 26 June 2020, p. 9, https://www.rpo.gov.pl/sites/default/files/Wystąpienie%20RPO%20do%20MR%2C%2026.06.2020.pdf, accessed 15 March 2021.

elections, i.e. the automatic postponement of the presidential elections. In other words, the president holding the office at the moment of introducing the state of natural disaster should continue in the office until a newly elected president takes office. The aim of this solution, as confirmed by the Constitutional Tribunal,[15] is to ensure continuity of the main State organs during the period of introducing the extraordinary measures. The rational assumption is that announcing a state of natural disaster makes it impossible to organise and hold elections and the main State organs gain constitutional legitimacy to continue performing their functions, despite the fact that the nominal length of their term established in the Constitution has elapsed. The aim of the prohibition is to make sure that the State will concentrate on addressing the problems that have caused the introduction of the extraordinary measures, but also to avoid the possible manipulation of the electoral procedure and to ensure the right of citizens to make electoral decisions in a free and fully informed manner, uninfluenced by the extraordinary circumstances.

2.4. CONSEQUENCES IN THE AREA OF PRIVATE LAW

The decision not to introduce a state of natural disaster seems to be motivated solely by the fact that it would necessitate the postponement of the presidential elections.[16] This decision, however, triggered consequences when it comes to the legal situations of people who sustained damage as a result of the restrictions introduced in violation of the Constitution.[17] In a "normal situation", i.e. when the extraordinary measures are not pronounced, according to Article 417 §1 of the Polish Civil Code (CC), the State Treasury is liable for damage caused by an illegal act or omission in the exercise of the public authority. This provision enables a person who sustained damage to claim damages in full, i.e. it includes *damnum emergens* and *lucrum cessans*, within the limits of normal causality. Pronouncing a state of emergency triggers the application of the Act on Compensation for Property Losses Resulting from the Limitation of Freedom and Human and Civil Rights and Freedoms During an Emergency Situation of 22 November 2002.[18] This Act restricts the liability of the State Treasury, which

[15] Judgment of 26 May 1998, K. 17/98, OTK 1998, No 4 item 48.

[16] At certain moment the pools showed as much as 59% of support for the current president that represents the governing party, which could also be explained by the very low declared turn out: https://www.polsatnews.pl/wiadomosc/2020-04-23/prawie-60-proc-dla-andrzeja-dudy-pozostali-kandydaci-z-kilkuprocentowym-poparciem/ accessed 15 June 2020.

[17] On the subject see also: Fryderyk Zoll, Katarzyna Południak-Gierz, Wojciech Bańczyk, 'State Liability for Damage Caused by COVID-19-Related Restrictions under Polish Law' in this volume.

[18] Official Journal 2002 No 233, item 1955.

becomes liable only for damage that (a) is a consequence of restrictions on rights and freedoms established during the state of emergency; and (b) relates only to property losses (incurred expenses, lost property rights and damaged goods). The State Treasury is not, however, liable, for damage relating to the profits lost as a result of the imposed restrictions (e.g. decreased profitability of the business activity). In addition, an appropriate causal link between the event that gives rise to liability (restrictions to the rights and freedoms) and the encountered damage must be established (CC Art 361 §1). That means that the State bears liability for restrictions introduced if there is no state of natural disaster announced in full, whereas if the state of natural disaster is announced and certain restrictions are allowed, the liability only covers property losses caused by such restrictions.[19]

3. THE RESTRICTIONS ON ECONOMIC ACTIVITY IMPOSED TO COMBAT THE SPREAD OF COVID-19

3.1. THE MECHANISM OF IMPOSING THE RESTRICTIONS

The Polish government decided not to introduce a state of emergency backed by Article 232 of the Constitution, but instead introduced a long series of ordinances on the basis of Article 46(2) and (4) of the 2008 Act. The first ordinance issued by the Minister of Health on 13 March 2020 declared a state of an epidemiological threat.[20] The chaos surrounding the legislative COVID-19 strategy is best illustrated by the first ordinance. It was in force until 20 March 2020, when it was repealed by an ordinance of the Minister of Health recalling the state of an epidemiological emergency,[21] but during this time it was changed every two days.[22] On the same day (i.e. 20 March 2020), the Minister of Health

---

19 Notably, for a long time the public was fed the narrative that introduction of a state of emergency will increase the liability of the State, in particular, towards foreign companies. Łukasz Szpyrka, 'Prawie 60 proc. dla Andrzeja Dudy. Pozostali kandydaci z kilkuprocentowym poparciem' (*polsatnews.pl*, 23 April 2020) https://fakty.interia.pl/raporty/raport-wybory-prezydenckie-2020/aktualnosci/news-stan-kleski-zywiolowej-zbyt-kosztowny-dla-budzetu-panstwa,nId,4424958 accessed 15 June 2020.

20 Ordinance of the Minister of Health of 13 March 2020 declaring a state of epidemiological emergency in the Republic of Poland, Official Journal 2020, item 433.

21 Ordinance of the Minister of Health of 20 March 2020 recalling the state of epidemiological emergency in the Republic of Poland, Official Journal 2020, item 490.

22 Ordinances of the Minister of Health of 14 March 2020 (Official Journal 2020, item 441), of 16 March 2020 (Official Journal 2020, item 461), and of 18 March 2020 (Official Journal 2020, item 478), all entitled "changing the ordinance of the Minister of Health declaring a state of epidemiological emergency in the Republic of Poland."

issued an ordinance announcing a state of epidemic,[23] which was itself changed on 24 March by another ordinance of the Minister of Health.[24] The next step was an ordinance of the Council of Ministers of 31 March 2020 establishing certain restrictions, injunctions and prohibitions in connection with the occurrence of a state of epidemic.[25] It was followed by stream of ordinances issued by the Council of Ministers, either changing previous ordinances or introducing new restrictions.[26] The number of ordinances adopted, combined with the speed of the adoption and the intertwining of contents seriously questions the legitimacy of these acts, alongside their lack of constitutionality. It was simply very difficult for the addressees of the restrictions to know what the scope of the restrictions that applied at a given moment was.[27] This, combined with the informational policy of the government,[28] created severe obstacles to understanding what the restrictions truly are and how they apply.

---

23 Ordinance of the Minister of Health of 20 March 2020 declaring a state of epidemic in the Republic of Poland, Official Journal 2020, item 491.

24 Ordinance of the Minister of Health of 24 March 2020 changing the ordinance that declared a state of epidemic in the Republic of Poland, Official Journal 2020, item 522.

25 Official Journal 2020, item 566.

26 Ordinances of: 1 April 2020 (changing the ordinance of 31 March 2020, repealed by the ordinance of 10 April 2020 OJ 2020, item 568), Official Journal 2020, item 577; of 7 April 2020, Official Journal 2020, item 624; of 10 April 2020 establishing new restrictions (it repealed ordinances of 31 March, 1 April and 7 April, it was itself changed by ordinances of 15 April and 16 April, and was repealed by an ordinance of 19 April, OJ 2020, item 697), Official Journal 2020, item 658; of 15 April 2020 (changing the ordinance of 10 April 2020, repealed by the ordinance of 19 April, OJ 2020, item 697); of 19 April 2020, Official journal 2020, item 697 (it repealed ordinances of 10 April, 15 April and 16 April, was changed by the ordinance of 26 April and repealed by the ordinance of 2 May 2020, OJ 202, item 792); of 26 April 2020 Official Journal 2020, item 750 (it changed the ordinance of 19 April and was repealed by the ordinance of 2 May 2020, OJ 2020, item 792); of 2 May 2020, Official Journal 2020, item 792 (it repealed the ordinances of 19 April and 26 April, and was repealed by the ordinance of 16 May 2020, OJ 2020, item 878); of 7 May 2020, Official Journal 2020, item 820 (it changed the ordinance of 2 May and was repealed by the ordinance of 16 May 202, OJ 2020, item 878); of 16 May 2020, Official Journal 2020 item 878 (it repealed ordinances of 2 May and 7 May and was repealed by the ordinance of 29 May 2020, OJ 2020, item 964); of 29 May 2020, Official Journal 2020, item 964 (it changed ordinances of 16 and 21 May); of 30 May 2020 (it changed the ordinance of 29 May 2020); of 3 June 2020, Official Journal 2020, item 991, (it changed the ordinance of 29 May); of 5 June 2020, Official Journal 2020, item 1006 (it changed the ordinance of 29 May); of 12 June, Official Journal 2020, item 1031 (it changed the ordinance of 29 May).

27 The most drastic example would be paragraph 1(1) of the Ordinance of 1 April 2020, which entered into force as of 31 March 2020.

28 The governmental www that collects information about the restrictions http://isap.sejm.gov.pl/isap.nsf/DocDetails.xsp?id=WDU20200001031 contains description of the current measures, together with links to the ordinances. However, most of the links do not function, and it is difficult in some cases to establish the content of the ordinance using the official sources (there are instances when more than one ordinance of the Council of Ministers with a view to addressing the COVID-19 crisis was published in the course of one day) (accessed 20 and 21 June 2020).

3.2. THE IMPOSED RESTRICTIONS

The government's ordinances introduced restrictions similar to those found in other countries: a prohibition of conducting certain categories of business and restrictions regarding the ways in which businesses are to be conducted. Moreover, as of 12 March, the Government closed all care and education facilities for children; on 15 March it closed the borders; and on 25 March it restricted the possibility of travelling freely, save for necessary situations (for example grocery shopping and commuting to work; children up to the age of 16 could not even move around on the streets unattended by adults). While such restrictions did not, strictly speaking, target the freedom of economic activities, they had a very strong *de facto* impact on the market, i.e. preventing people and companies from concluding and performing contracts, as well as preventing the search for employees (especially from Ukraine).

The prohibition on conducting business activities included the organisation, promotion and management of events such as fairs and exhibitions, services relating to the improvement of physical condition, sport, entertainment, hotels, restaurants, hairdressers, beauty parlours, and certain categories of shops. For the types of business that remained open, strict rules were imposed concerning the business organisation, such as restricting the number of customers present in the business premises, strict hygiene standards (obligatory masks, gloves and disinfection), etc. Extra restrictions were imposed on shopping centres, where only certain types of businesses could remain open (pharmacies, grocery shops, financial institutions, etc.).

The restrictions began to be lifted on 20 April 2020.[29] As of 20 April, the number of people who could be in a shop at the same time increased, and persons over the age of 13 were allowed to move around the streets unsupervised, but everyone outside had to cover their nose and mouth and maintain a distance of two metres from others. On 4 May, shopping centres were re-opened,[30] as well as hotels and guesthouses (with some restrictions as to the number of people allowed), convenience stores and (as of 6 May) crèches and kindergartens. On 18 May the government allowed beauty parlours and hairdressers to reopen (following a strict sanitary regime), as well as bars and restaurants (also with sanitary restrictions). The prohibition on holding sport training sessions, as well as making movies, music recordings, etc. was also lifted at that time. As of 25 May, schools restarted providing care for children in classes 1–3, and as

---

29 https://www.biznes.gov.pl/pl/firma/sprawy-urzedowe/chce-przestrzegac-przepisow-szczegolnych/cztery-etapy-odmrazania-gospodarki accessed 15 June 2020.

30 The shopping centres were surprised and unprepared for the government's decision to reopen: Katarzyna Pachlecka, 'Otwarcie galerii handlowych to przepis pełen absurdów. Zarządcy galerii w popłochu. Wytyczne są za skomplikowane' (*dziennikzachodni.pl*, 3 May 2020) https://dziennikzachodni.pl/otwarcie-galerii-handlowych-to-przepis-pelen-absurdow-zarzadcy-galerii-w-poplochu-wytyczne-sa-za-skomplikowane/ar/c3-14943728 accessed 15 June 2020.

of 30 May there has been no obligation to cover mouths and noses in the public open spaces, subject to maintaining the two-metre distance. The limit of people in shops and restaurants was lifted, subject to certain sanitary restrictions. Hotel bars and restaurants were reopened then as well. As of 6 June, cinemas, theatres, swimming pools, fitness clubs, fairs, exhibitions, congresses were permitted to reopen, and it was again possible to organise weddings and family events for up to 150 people. At the time of writing, the prohibition still included discos, as well as travel agents and tourism organisers in shopping centres.

4. THE CLASSIC INSTRUMENTS

4.1. GENERAL APPROACH

Polish law offers several instruments that could apply in a situation like the one experienced during the pandemic, i.e. when external circumstances impact the market conditions, which in turn influence the profitability or the possibility of performing contracts; impossibility of performance, performance delay, and *rebus sic stantibus*. All these instruments rely on the traditional concepts of private law and provide for the possibility of *post factum* intervention into the contractual relationship with a view to restoring the initial rationale upon which the contractual balance was established between the parties (even if that means finding out that the contract has not been concluded or becomes extinguished).

4.2. IMPOSSIBILITY OF PERFORMANCE

4.2.1. Initial impossibility of performance

Polish law adheres to the traditional approach towards the possibility of performance, according to which the subject of performance must be possible. It distinguishes between the initial impossibility of performance, which renders the contract invalid (CC Article 387 §1), and the subsequent impossibility of performance, the consequences of which depend on the reason why the performance became impossible.

While the principle *impossibilium nulla obligatio est* has a general character that follows the very nature of obligations, the invalid nature of the contract where the performance is impossible follows from the provisions of law.[31]

---

31 Jacek Jastrzębski, 'Umowa o świadczenie niemożliwe versus umowa gwarancyjna (problem wykładni postanowień umownych)' in Józef Okolski (ed), *Księga Pamiątkowa 60-lecia Sądu Arbitrażowego przy Krajowej Izbie Gospodarczej* (Sąd Arbitrażowy przy Krajowej Izbie Gospodarczej 2010) 784–785.

The impossibility of performance must be initial, objective and permanent,[32] and may result from legal or factual circumstances. It must exist at the moment when the contract is concluded,[33] and the performance must be impossible for anyone, not only for the debtor[34] – it must be external and beyond the control of the debtor.[35] The potential settlement of performances is based on CC Article 410 that deals with undue performance (*condictio sine causa*).

4.2.2. Subsequent impossibility of performance

If the performance becomes impossible as a result of circumstances for which the debtor is not liable, the obligation expires (CC Art 475 §1). This applies if the obligation was effectively created, but subsequently became impossible to perform, not only for the debtor, but for any other entity.[36] The impossibility (factual or legal) must be permanent and objective,[37] i.e. it must be impossible to fulfil the interest of the creditor in any way, or within a timeframe that is reasonable from the point of view of the creditor, or due to the nature of the obligation. In the case of mutual performances, similarly, if one of them became impossible as a result of circumstances for which neither party is liable, the party who was to make that performance cannot demand the mutual performance, and if it received it already, it is obliged to return it in accordance with the provisions on unjustified enrichment (CC Art 495 §1) (*condictio causa finita*). If the performance is impossible only in part, then that party loses the right to the appropriate part of the mutual performance. The other party may renounce the contract if the partial performance would have no significance for it in view of the nature of the obligation, or in view of the intended purpose of the contract, which was known to the party whose performance has become partly impossible.

What is of crucial importance, according to the general contract liability principle (CC Art 471), is that the debtor is obliged to redress the damage resulting from the non-performance or improper performance of the obligation, unless the non-performance or improper performance was due to circumstances for which the debtor is not liable.

---

32 Bogusław Lackoroński in Konrad Osajda (ed), *Kodeks cywilny. Komentarz Zobowiązania część ogólna* (C.H. Beck 2017) 281 shows that this view has been presented by the legal writing since 1934.

33 Piotr Machnikowski, *System Prawa Prywatnego*, vol 5 (C.H. Beck 2013) 562.

34 Judgment of the Supreme Court of 8 May 2002, III CKN 1015/99.

35 Zbigniew Radwański in *System Prawa Cywilnego*, III part 1, (C.H. Beck 2012) 382.

36 See: judgment of the Supreme Court of 8 May 2002, III CKN 101599 and of 22 November 1973, III CRN 255/73.

37 Judgment of the Supreme Court of 5 December 200, V CKN 150/00, of 15 November 2013 VCKS 500/12.

4.3. DELAYED PERFORMANCE

Polish law distinguishes a delay in performance that results from circumstances that the debtor is not liable for (Polish: *opóźnienie*). Generally, the debtor should perform at the time established in the contract, and if the time limit for performance was not established in the contract, then immediately upon demand (CC Art 455). The consequences of such a delay are restricted to the claims established in CC Articles 481 and 482 (for pecuniary claims). Hence, the creditor may demand interest for the time of the delay, even if it suffers no damage. If the interest rate for a delay was not indicated, statutory interest for a delay is due at a rate equal to the sum of the reference rate of the National Bank of Poland and 5.5 percentage points. While the creditor may claim a higher rate of interest (if that was stipulated), the maximum amount of interest for a delay may not exceed twice the amount of the statutory interest for delay on an annual basis. If the contractual interest exceeds this threshold, the maximum interest for delay is due instead. The rules on maximum interest are mandatory and cannot be excluded or limited even by choosing a foreign law. The amount of statutory interest for a delay is announced by the Minister of Justice. Apart from the interest, the creditor is also entitled to the redress of damage on the general principles (Art 481 §3), and to claim the performance from the guarantor, if one is in place.

4.4. *REBUS SIC STANTIBUS*

Polish law also contains a *rebus sic stantibus* rule (CC Art 357^1, introduced in 1990). According to this rule, if an extraordinary change of circumstances means that the performance would be faced with excessive difficulties or would threaten one of the parties with substantial loss, the court may, after considering the interest of the parties, define the method of performing the obligations and the degree of the performance, and may even decide to terminate the contract, in accordance with the principles of community life. When terminating the contract, the court may, as far as necessary, decide upon the settlement of accounts, being guided by the principles of community life. What is important is that the change of circumstances must lead to consequences that the parties could not have foreseen when concluding the contract.[38] The circumstances must relate to a larger group of entities, or even have a general character,[39]

---

[38] Zbigniew Radwański, Adam Olejniczak, *Zobowiązania*, (C.H. Beck 2012) 301, Agnieszka Malarewicz, 'Wpływ zamiany stosunków na wykonanie zobowiązań', part 2 (2005) Monitor Prawniczy 12, 588, Maciej Mataczyński, Maksymilian Saczywko in Maciej Gutowski, *Kodeks cywilny. Komentarz*, vol I, art 357^1, (C.H. Beck 2019) 1266, Nb 5.

[39] Judgment of the Supreme Court of 19 November 2014, II CSK 191/14, http://www.sn.pl/sites/orzecznictwo/orzeczenia3/ii%20csk%20191-14-1.pdf, accessed 29 March 2021.

and do not apply to changes in individual conditions.[40] It might relate to a factual or legal situation,[41] and must exceed the normal scope of the normal contractual risks.

The Civil Code sets out further provisions applicable in the case of a change in circumstances: Article 632 §2 (contract for specific work), Article 700 (contract of tenancy), Article 907 §2 (pension). In addition, a specific rule exists (known as the "small *rebus sic stantibus*", Art 358[1] §3) that provides for the possibility of a judiciary modification of pecuniary obligations (where the object of performance from the beginning is a sum of money). In the case of an essential change in the purchasing power of money after the obligation arises, the court may, after considering the interest of the parties and in accordance with the principles of community life, change the amount or the method of making a performance in money, even if these were fixed in the decision or the contract.

5. THE COVID-19 SUPPORT MEASURES

5.1. GENERAL

To counteract the effects of the restrictions introduced by the government's ordinances, the Parliament adopted four legislative acts (at the initiative of the government), known as the "anti-crisis shields" (the fourth is in the legislative process): the Act Amending the Act on Special Arrangements for Preventing, Counteracting and Combating COVID-19 of 31 March 2020,[42] the Act on Specific Support Instruments in Relation to the Spread of the SARS-CoV-21 Virus of 16 April 2020,[43] the Act Amending Certain Acts on Protective Measures in Relation to the Spread of SARS-CoV-2 Virus of 14 May 2020,[44] and the Act on Interest Rate Subsidies on Bank Loans Granted to Provide Financial Liquidity to Businesses Affected by COVID-19 of 19 June 2020.[45]

These "Anti-Crisis Shield Acts" constitute a prime example of what properly enacted legislation should not look like. They are very chaotic (down to the numbering, which includes Articles like 15 zzzi), they introduce changes to more than a hundred legal acts, but in a very disorderly manner, sometimes just

---

40 Judgment of the Supreme Court of 7 May 1993, I CR 5/93, OSNC 1993 nr 9 item 165, of 22 April 2005, III CK 594/04, OSP 2006 nr 12 item 143 of 3 January 2016, V CSK 277/15, not published.

41 Judgment of Supreme Court of 16 May 2007, III CSK 452/06, OSP 2009 nr 2 item 19, of 17 January 2008, III CSK 202/07, LEX nr 398491, of 6 December 2006, IV CSK 290/06, LEX nr 203285.

42 Journal of Laws 2020, item 568.

43 Journal of Laws 2020, item 695.

44 Journal of Laws 2020, item 875.

45 Journal of Laws 2020, item 1068.

temporarily, creating a total lack of certainty. While the anti-crisis shields were introduced with a view to supporting Polish business, they introduce changes to a wide variety of acts, including the Act on Non-Working Days, the Code of Administrative Proceedings, the Water Law, the Telecommunications Law, or the Act on Access to Public Information. Some of the changes have a clearly political dimension and their introduction had nothing to do with the pandemic, such as the changes in the election laws (on non-working days, changing the body with the authority to establish the content of the ballot papers), or changes to the Criminal Code, which include increasing the penalty for performing an abortion, and for insulting the President of the Republic of Poland, while decreasing the penalty for administration fraud.[46] As has been commented, the changes introduced in the Shield 4.0 act violate the constitutional principle of equality before the law, the principle of proportionality, necessity and usefulness of aggravating criminal repression, as well as the principle of correct legislation and the principle of citizen's trust in the State.[47]

5.2. WHAT DO THE ANTI-CRISIS SHIELDS OFFER IN THE AREA OF CONTRACT LAW?

The Anti-Crisis Shields provide two types of instruments impacting the situations in which the parties on the market find themselves. Most of the measures take the form of public help, basically aimed at preventing mass bankruptcies and a market collapse in a longer perspective. The list includes the remission of back taxes, the postponement of tax payments and allowing payments to be made in instalments; exemption from making contributions to the Social Insurance Institution (for up to three months); "furlough" funds to compensate for lost income (EUR 250–500, to be called on up to three times, for certain category of entities), a possibility for companies on economic downtime to reduce salaries by 50%, though no lower than the minimum wage (with subsidies); subsidies for salaries; the possibility to decrease salaries and working hours to 80% for up to three months, for companies that have experienced a decrease in turnover of at least 15% in two consecutive months after 1 January 2020, as compared to the equivalent months in the previous year, or a decrease in turnover by at least 25%

46 Mikołaj Małecki, 'Zaostrzona ochrona godności Prezydenta, prymat kary więzienia – wchodzi w życie Tarcza 4.0' (*Dogmaty Karnisty*, 24 June 2020) https://www.dogmatykarnisty.pl/2020/06/wchodzi-w-zycie-tarcza-4-0/ accessed 15 June 2020, Piotr Jaźwiński, 'Wrzutki w tarczach antykryzysowych zmieniające prawo karne. Analiza' (*Konkret24*, 24 June 2020) https://konkret24.tvn24.pl/polityka,112/wrzutki-w-tarczach-antykryzysowych-zmieniajace-prawo-karne-analiza,1020839.html?fbclid=IwAR2HahnqVj1OQHwuNZ-KpHeKx8gp67Fz6V7At50XPXlUzNxyLOqN4ApKT5I accessed 15 June 2020.

47 https://kipk.pl/dokumenty/opiniakk2020.pdf?fbclid=IwAR2N-OCvmCFAN5vWHZyhaaQkzjnUDFu1F7L7YUExSaAgGu9-dkIQ6KONQhE accessed 15 June 2020.

from one month to the next after 1 January 2020. Shield 4.0 introduced rules to prevent any hostile takeovers of companies by entities from outside the EU, as well as rules facilitating the process of firing employees.

The clearly private law measures are far fewer (although it is sometimes difficult to assess, due to the effects they cause, whether a given instrument is private or public). The initial Anti-Crisis Shield set new limits on the maximum amount of non-interest bearing payments in consumer credits and introduced a possibility for tenants (meeting certain conditions) to unilaterally prolong, until 30 June 2020, lease agreements that were concluded before the act came into force (i.e. 31 March 2020) for a period that was supposed to end after that day, but before 30 June 2020. During that time, the landlords were not permitted to increase the rent. In addition, Shield 1.0 provided that companies conducting activities related to the organisation of exhibitions and congresses, or cultural, entertainment, recreational and sporting activities, or organising thematic exhibitions or outdoor events, as well as hotels, in the event that a contract with a customer is terminated as a direct result of the outbreak of the SARS-CoV-2 virus, are required to return the funds paid by the customer within 180 days of the effective termination of the contract. The termination of such contracts would not be effective if the customer agreed to receive in return a voucher from the company concerning future events in the company's scope of business, within one year from the date on which the event for which the customer paid should have been held. The value of the voucher cannot be lower than the amount paid for the performance of the existing contract by the customer. A similar regulation was introduced to change Article 47 (5)(2) of the Act on Tourist Events and Related Tourist Services of 24 November 2017, which implements Article 12 of Directive 2015/2302 of 25 November 2015 on package travel and linked travel arrangements. While that directive provides for 14 days for reimbursement in the event of the withdrawal or termination of a contract, according to Shield 1.0, the withdrawal or termination of a contract that is directly related to the outbreak of the SARS-CoV-2 virus takes effect by law 180 days after the date of making the declaration with a view to withdraw from the contract or to terminate it, which means that the tour operator effectively has 180 plus 14 days for the reimbursement. While the representatives of the Ministry of Development have stated that this is a solution ensuring compliance with Directive 2015/2302,[48] the EU Commission did not share this view and asked Poland to change the content of the provision by 2 June 2020. The Ministry has refused to issue information on the ongoing proceedings in this regard.[49]

---

48 Piotr Cybula, 'Logika ministerstwa i logika dyrektywy' (*Prawo Turystyczne*, 8 May 2020) https://prawoturystyczne.com/2020/05/08/logika-ministerstwa-i-logika-dyrektywy/ accessed 15 June 2020.

49 https://prawoturystyczne.files.wordpress.com/2020/06/odpowiedc5ba-na-pismo-pana-piotra-cybuli-1.pdf accessed 15 June 2020.

Shield 2.0 introduced changes to the regulations applicable to lease contracts for premises in shopping centres. This legislation established rules that caused the *ex lege* expiry of (all) mutual obligations from lease agreements and similar agreements concerning the use of commercial space for the duration of the epidemic. The introduced solution received very harsh reviews from the industry, which pointed out the devastating effect that it had, as well as the numerous interpretation problems arising on the basis of the introduced provisions. The allegations also referred to the lack of constitutionality, as it introduces expropriation without compensation, targeting foreign companies that own shopping centres in Poland in a discriminatory way.[50] The effects and the scope of the regulation were deemed to be so unclear that it is difficult to say even what the goal of the legislator was. To point out just one of the many problematic issues, while the act declared the expiry of the obligations, it also allowed these agreements to be renewed after the end of the epidemiological threat – an option that has thus far been unknown to contract law.

The first shields also introduced very important changes in the context of procedural law. For some time, all non-urgent terms of, among other things, civil and administrative proceedings, including enforcement, were suspended (Shield 1.0). Shield 2.0 permitted a court, or the entity conducting proceedings, to reinstate the terms of proceedings as well as to prolong the normally applicable term if a public interest or the interest of the party so required. Shield 3.0 reinstated the course of time limits. The way the issue of deadlines in proceedings was handled has caused numerous problems. It was unclear when exactly the terms were suspended,[51] as well as whether the terms were reinstated (not all professional representatives, and certainly not all parties, were aware of the effects of Shield 2.0[52]).

Shield 4.0 is more focused on private law solutions. It introduced "credit holidays" whereby borrowers who lost their main source of income after 13 March 2020 could apply to suspend the repayment of certain types of loans (consumer credits, mortgage loan contracts or credits indexed to a foreign currency) concluded in a specified period, by up to three months. During this

50 Krzysztof Woronowicz, 'Ustawa w sprawie tzw. tarczy antykryzysowej dewastuje umowy najmu powierzchni handlowych i może skutkować wywłaszczeniem bez odszkodowania' (*Gazeta Prawna.pl*, 7 April 2020) https://prawo.gazetaprawna.pl/artykuly/1467468,koronawirus-tarcza-antykryzysowa-umowa-najmu-centrum-handlowe.html accessed 15 June 2020.

51 Ewa Niesiobędzka-Krause, Paulina Chmielnicka, 'Dobre zawieszenie terminów w postępowaniu administracyjnym, ale nie wiadomo od kiedy' (*Prawo.pl*, 23 April 2020) https://www.prawo.pl/samorzad/zawieszenie-terminow-w-postepowaniu-administracyjnym-od-kiedy,499631.html accessed 15 June 2020.

52 Patrycja Rojek-Socha, 'Tarcze mieszają w terminach – nie ma pewności, czy są "zawieszone"' (*Prawo.pl*, 18 May 2020) https://www.prawo.pl/prawnicy-sady/terminy-procesowe-i-sadowe-zawieszone-czy-nie-watpliwosci,500342.html accessed 15 June 2020.

credit holiday, the lending banks may charge only payments on the basis of an insurance contract related to the loan. The suspension period does not count towards the credit period, which is prolonged accordingly. To take advantage of this credit window opportunity, an eligible borrower lodges an application with the creditor and the suspension takes place *ex lege*. The legislation offered microbusinesses low-interest rate loans of up to PLN 5,000, which are written off provided that the microenterprise is established for a period of three months from the date on which the loan is granted, and the funds from the loans are not subject to judicial or administrative enforcement. Shield 4.0 provides companies affected by the coronavirus with the possibility to take a loan with subsidised interest due to the bank (two percentage points for small and medium-sized enterprises, and one percentage point for others). The subsidy will be paid by Bank Gospodarstwa Krajowego from the funds of the Interest Rate Support Fund established for this purpose. It is meant to support entities operating in the primary production of agricultural products. A subsidised loan agreement can be signed until the end of 2020.

Shield 4.0 also introduced rules worsening the position of employees, which are applicable to commercial agents. They allow an employer who has experienced a decrease in economic turnover or a significant increase of burdens to limit the amount of severance pay to a laid-off employee, to an amount equal to ten times the minimum wage. This solution, however, applies also to the termination or dissolution of agency contracts, mandate contracts and some other contracts.[53] As an SME spokesperson stressed,[54] the Polish market is mostly composed of agents who are microenterprises, while the principals are usually large, international companies. Such a disparity makes it difficult for the agents to pursue claims against the principals. The new rules not only extend to agency contracts the rules that are to apply to employment relationships, which may cause interpretation problems, but they also make it even more difficult for agents to pursue claims against the principals. The restrictions are supposed to remain in force for the duration of the state of epidemic or an epidemiological threat, which, according to the SME Spokesperson, might be as long as two years. This would mean serious obstacles for agents conducting business activity, but also a potential inconsistency with Directive 86/653/EEC of 18 December 1986 on the coordination of the laws of the Member States relating to self-employed commercial agents (Arts 7, 8 and 17).[55]

---

53 Contracts for the provision of services, to which the provisions concerning the mandate apply, contracts for specific work or in connection with the termination of paid functions.

54 https://rzecznikmsp.gov.pl/wp-content/uploads/2020/06/WPL.341.2020.PD-.pdf, 2–3, accessed 15 June 2020.

55 https://rzecznikmsp.gov.pl/wp-content/uploads/2020/06/WPL.341.2020.PD-.pdf, 4, accessed 15 June 2020.

6. THE RATIONAL THING TO DO: THE FIRST CASES AGAINST THE STATE TREASURY

At the moment, it is still difficult to say whether the parties to private relations will make any attempt to use the classic features of contract law to address their contractual situation, and the parties will establish how effective the ad hoc measures are. What is more, it is even difficult to say with any degree of certainty, what the contents of the ad hoc measures are, and what market consequences they will bring about. The four Anti-Crisis Shields consist together of 286 pages of legislative text (just the provisions, without the grounds) and 397 articles that address not only the situation of traders, but also numerous other issues that might have (directly or indirectly) impact on the situation of traders, or which have absolutely nothing to do with that. The Polish Ombudsman has called upon the government to create a complex and coherent act that would collect the provisions addressing the situation of the traders in various sectors of the economy, but so far this request remains unanswered.[56] The Ombudsman has also pointed out that the chaotic, incoherent and unstable legal situation makes it impossible not only for traders, but also for public officials to interpret the law and to provide guidance to the traders in this respect.[57] With respect to the public law measures, while the government claims that PLN 53,694,994,304 has already been paid out,[58] there are numerous accounts relating to problems with the aid system it introduced,[59] and the unequal treatment of entities that has resulted.[60] The problem of constitutionality in relation to the COVID-19 legislation relates

---

56 https://www.rpo.gov.pl/pl/content/koronawirus-ponowna-interwencja%C2%A0-rpo-na-rzecz-przedsiebiorcow?fbclid=IwAR3yIKxQfQQYkw5zw78QPozaeAK96Jj-Q6WL9yP3kkT6dGauyVtHEbkdFLg accessed 15 June 2020.

57 https://www.rpo.gov.pl/sites/default/files/Wystąpienie%20RPO%20do%20MR%2C%20 26.06.2020.pdf, p. 2, accessed 15 June 2020.

58 https://pfrsa.pl/tarcza-finansowa-pfr.html accessed 15 June 2020.

59 Leszek Kostrzewski, '5 największych pułapek czekających na przedsiębiorców w "tarczy finansowej"' (*Wyborcza.biz*, 23 June 2020) https://wyborcza.biz/biznes/7,147584,26055559,5-najwiekszych-pulapek-czekajacych-na-przedsiebiorcow-w-tarczy.html?_ga=2.35803872.1931811601.1592209505-456000769.1587449798#S.koronawirus-K.C-B.2-L.1.male accessed 15 June 2020; Hanna Cichy, 'Kto się nie zmieści za rządową tarczą? Luki w przepisach' (*Polityka.pl*, 16 April 2020) https://www.polityka.pl/tygodnikpolityka/rynek/1952936,1,kto-sie-nie-zmiesci-za-rzadowa-tarcza-luki-w-przepisach.read, accessed 15 June 2020.

60 Ewelina Marciniak, 'Nierówne traktowanie rolników – chodzi o tarczę antykryzysową!' (*agrofakt.pl*, 2 June 2020) https://www.agrofakt.pl/nierowne-traktowanie-rolnikow-chodzi-o-tarcze-antykryzysowa/ accessed 15 June 2020, Mateusz Ratajczak, 'Tarcza antykryzysowa dla samozatrudnionych nie etatowców. Firmy-widmo będą nadużywać wsparcia' (*money.pl*, 29.04.2020) https://www.money.pl/gospodarka/tarcza-antykryzysowa-dla-samozatrudnionych-nie-etatowcow-firmy-widmo-beda-naduzywac-wsparcia-6505090705467521a.html accessed 15 June 2020, Jakub Szymczak, 'Tarcza razi niesprawiedliwością. Pracownik zwolniony z etatu na gorszej pozycji niż samozatrudniony' (*OkoPress.pl*, 1 May 2020), https://oko.press/pracownik-zwolniony-z-etatu/ accessed 15 June 2020.

therefore not only to the illegality of the restrictions imposed, but also to the chaotic, non-transparent and discriminatory nature of the ad hoc measures.

Since classic private law instruments might be ineffective, it seems that in Poland the rational choice of the aggrieved parties will be to turn against the State Treasury, on the basis of CC Article 417, claiming the illegality of government's ordinances. There are already the first cases pending in this respect. The first case was filed in May 2020, in which the owners of a fitness club chain are claiming PLN 274,000 in damages for the costs of maintaining the clubs, as well as PLN 184,000 for lost profits (the amount of profits in 2019). They argue that, despite the fact that the State has been functioning as if under a state of emergency, no such state has ever actually been introduced (argument based on the violation of the Constitution).[61] Similarly, on 19 June 2020, 84 businesses associated with the Tourism Open Organisation (Polish: *Turystyczna Organizacja Otwarta*) demanded payment of PLN 141 million in damages for losses sustained due to the illegal measures introduced by the government to combat COVID-19. It points out that the restrictions *de facto* resulted in a prohibition on conducting business activity in this industry. If the State Treasury fails to pay within two weeks, the group has threatened to proceed with a class action suit.[62]

The outcome of the cases against the State Treasury is far from certain, especially considering the emerging problems of the struggle of the Polish judiciary to remain independent from the government, representing the State Treasury. Nevertheless, that means that Polish courts will, yet again, be burdened with solving a systemic problem caused by a lack of proper legislative intervention.[63]

---

61 'Koronawirus. Jest pozew przeciwko Skarbowi Państwa za zamknięcie firmy. Opiewa na niemal pół miliona' (*Business Insider Polska*, 12 May 2020) https://businessinsider.com.pl/firmy/koronawirus-jest-pozew-przeciwko-panstwu-za-zamkniecie-firmy/q526wml accessed 15 June 2020.

62 Damian Słomski, 'Firmy turystyczne chcą odszkodowania od Skarbu Państwa. Wystawiły rachunek na 141 mln zł' (*money.pl*, 19 June 2020) https://www.money.pl/gielda/firmy-turystyczne-chca-odszkodowania-od-skarbu-panstwa-wystawily-rachunek-na-141-mln-zl-6523112586225281a.html accessed 15 June 2020.

63 Others include the problem of re-privatisation, see: Ewa Łętowska, 'Orzecznictwo sądowe jako instrument reprywatyzacji zdekoncentrowanej', Studia i Analizy Sądu Najwyższego, vol III (Biuro Studiów i Analiz Sądu Najwyższego 2016), 85–107, or the problem of consumer credits indexed or denominated in CHF: see: Aneta Wiewiórowska-Domagalska, 'Prawo z tektury. Państwo mogło zapobiec problemom frankowiczów' (*GazetaPrawna.pl*, 6 September 2019) https://serwisy.gazetaprawna.pl/finanse-osobiste/artykuly/1424985,rola-panstwa-w-kryzysie-frankowym.html accessed 15 June 2020. Łętowska points out that de-concentrated re-privatisation (i.e. re-privatisation by the courts) was more fitting for a regulation by the legislator. Legislative action would have allowed an effective approach towards the re-privatisation of property legally taken over in the past, but which is now considered a mistake of history and axiology. Re-privatisation is still carried out by the courts, but at the cost of distorting the tools that the courts use. The courts have simply been unable to notice the emerging re-privatisation business and the exorbitant nature of the re-privatisation claims.

Only when the case law decided on the basis of such claims has been established (which will take several years at least, considering the numbers involved) will it be possible to tell how deep in Poland is the curse of living during interesting times.

The re-privatisation business, under the slogan of sacred ownership, seeks to pursue dubious claims filed and enforced by specialised law firms. This has harmed the courts themselves, as they have been unable to recognise and deal with this phenomenon due to their own isolationism in judging, and because they are evaluating their own case law. It has attracted public criticism, but the problem that has inspired the criticism has its roots in the negligence of other authorities. This all leads to the social isolation of the courts, and the courts themselves are unable to prevent it because they do not sufficiently recognise the specific nature of the situations they are adjudicating.

LEGAL MEASURES AS THE RESPONSE TO AN EXTRAORDINARY SITUATION IN THE SLOVAK REPUBLIC

Martina Gajdošová*

This contribution deals with norm-making as the substantial response to an extraordinary situation caused by coronavirus, with regard to the development of law in the Slovak Republic. The contribution describes the proliferation of normative acts, such as soft law of the executive (recommendations), measures of the executive of a normative nature (prohibitions, obligations) and responses of the parliament (ad hoc COVID-19 acts). The contribution also deals with the judicial reaction. It argues that the presence of lawyers in crisis committees would ensure the respect of basic law-making principles such as human rights, adherence to procedures, constitutionality and would contribute to the sustainability of new norms.

---

* Comenius University in Bratislava, Faculty of Law, Slovak Republic. This contribution has been prepared within the project APVV-17-0056 named "The constitution of a liberal-democratic state and the radicalization of political culture".

1. INTRODUCTION

For the first time, we are faced with a special situation that affects everyone, not only in the Slovak Republic, or the European Union. All essential social relations are regulated by law, i.e. the eventuality of an extraordinary situation is known to the law and there are legal tools to manage and overcome it, or to regulate the functioning of society and the State in such a situation. All measures that "follow" this extraordinary situation have a primary goal to protect health and a secondary goal to mitigate the consequences and to renew standard relations.

It can be stated that special, new and urgent conditions mobilise legislative solutions, i.e. norm-making is activated. Of course, legislation is of fundamental importance for achieving the long-term goals. However, to solve new and acute problems, legislation is the fastest and the most operational solution with the most general impact, even though the legislative process also takes time.

The extraordinary situation of a global nature has shown that the first bodies to respond to the situation in a strictly normative way were neither global organisations, nor individuals, nor association, but the States. The experience in the Slovak Republic has shown the following course. The reality of the extraordinary situation first began to manifest itself regionally. As a result, cities, municipalities and self-governing regions, as well as various bodies were first to react. Nevertheless, the need for a nationwide resolution was quickly noticed. Normative reactions at the State level came in a form of "soft-norm-making". Various recommendations were published – mainly in the form of information leaflets for the general public against the spread of infection. This was followed by normative actions of the government. However, instead of usual legal regulations, so-called hybrid administrative acts were issued. Very quickly, in the course of a few weeks, legislative interventions at the level of acts came to reality. Ad hoc COVID-19 legislation has entered into force, fully legitimised by the new situation.

Ad hoc legislation is something undesirable, but in principle all legislation is ultimately ad hoc – for a given purpose. Ad hoc legislation is in its nature considered to be purpose-made.[1] It seems that "the time of great systematisations and law formulated as general abstract rules is coming to an end. Law becomes a tool for the regulation of relations formulated in such a way that its addressees find the most specific answer to a practical problem."[2] But ad hoc legislation is not a new topic. On the contrary, it is its permanent and substantial part of the

---

1 Karel Eliáš, 'Stabilita soukromého práva a turbulence politiky' in Kristián Csach (ed), *Ad hoc legislatíva v súkromnom práve. XIV. Dies Luby Iurisprudentiae* (Leges 2019) 38.

2 Kristián Csach, 'Predhovor' in Kristián Csach (ed), *Ad hoc legislatíva v súkromnom práve. XIV. Dies Luby Iurisprudentiae* (Leges 2019) 5.

jurisprudence, even though the ad hoc legislation is considered an anomaly.[3] We can always find a specific case or a specific situation, even a specific person for which a specific regulation was adopted as a response. Ad hoc legislation can also be dangerous for the development of the rule of law.[4]

In the spread of the disease (COVID-19), we have a legitimate source of an enormous number of normative reactions. The law has once again proved to be a tool for influencing society's homeostasis, to correct the imbalances and to grant stability to society and its development.[5] This situation has mobilised norm-making, especially in the field of public law. Regulation concerned the exercise of public power, the limits of the powers of public authorities and also their mutual relations. Since the extraordinary situation requires operational solutions, we can illustrate it by comparison to a private person who has run into difficulties – they know best what to do and how to react and look for the most effective steps. The situation is more complicated for the State since every step of a public authority must fulfil the condition *secundum et intra legem*. Therefore, many legal and sub-legal interventions were needed, as only they could regulate the acts of State bodies, i.e. the matter in question was competencies. Naturally, the private sphere has also been affected. In many fields, contractual freedom was restricted by normative acts (e.g. prohibition to terminate the lease, employer's ability to determine the conditions for the employee). Debtors were protected (temporary ban on the sale of real estate at auction, temporary suspension of execution). The conditions for obtaining aid from public sources for affected individuals were formulated. The acts had to be formulated in as much detail as possible to respond to COVID-19 and to meet the requirement of temporary measures.

Normative systems have in particular a regulating and integrating function, as well as an expressive and instrumental function.[6] Human society is "set up for normative management". This extraordinary situation showed that, in the first place – after the initial shock – norm-making started. This process was

---

3 Tomáš Gábriš, 'Leges singulares: atypické zákony z pohľadu súčasného právního realizmu' in Kristián Csach (ed), *Ad hoc legislatíva v súkromnom práve. XIV. Dies Luby Iurisprudentiae* (Leges 2019) 97.

4 "It is dangerous development, as it allows the government to use flexible structure of the private law to sanction behaviour, which it perceives dangerous for the interest of the national community. Therefore the aspect of the rule of law cannot be omitted in the domain of the private law." In connection with Polish Bill on the Institute of National Remembrance in Fryderyk Zoll, 'Does a Nation Have "Personality Rights"? On the Abuse of Civil Law by Involving it into the Political Struggle' in Kristián Csach (ed), *Ad hoc legislatíva v súkromnom práve. XIV. Dies Luby Iurisprudentiae* (Leges 2019) 123.

5 Karel Eliáš, 'Stabilita soukromého práva a turbulence politiky' in Kristián Csach (ed), *Ad hoc legislatíva v súkromnom práve. XIV. Dies Luby Iurisprudentiae* (Leges 2019) 29; the author used Viktor Knapp, *Teorie práva* (C. H. Beck 1995) 32.

6 Radoslav Procházka, Marek Káčer, *Teória práva* (C. H. Beck 2019) 92.

carried out by the State through creation of legal or sub-legal norms. Other entities operating in public or in private spheres also became involved in that process, but only in the area of alternative norms and various internal normative instructions.

2. PHASE ONE: ACKNOWLEDGING A NEW SITUATION AND PREPARING FOR ITS NORMATIVE MANAGEMENT

On 10 January 2020, the Public Health Authority of the Slovak Republic notified[7] that it had been informed by the European authorities about the occurrence of a viral pneumonia caused by a new type of coronavirus in the eastern part of China (Wuhan) and made recommendations to potential travellers in the area. The Public Health Authority continued to inform about the development of the disease and issued guidelines for regional public health authorities and the respective Ministries, to ensure that health care facilities were informed about what to do with a patient with a case suspected of this disease.

On 31 January 2020, the Public Health Authority informed[8] that the WHO's crisis committee had declared a global health emergency on 30 January 2020 in relation to the disease caused by the new coronavirus.

Subsequent measures of the State mainly concerned the preparation of medical and laboratory facilities for a possible pandemic. The information and media campaign for the public and recommendations for medical staff continued to be published. As the infectious nature of the disease is related to the movement of people, restrictions to travel were introduced, but only of a notification nature, i.e. passengers had to fill in a questionnaire for future identification.[9] As far as freedom of movement was concerned, the government continued to limit itself to recommendations not to travel.[10]

7 http://www.uvzsr.sk/index.php?option=com_content&view=article&id=3998:informacia-o-vyskyte-virusovej-pneumonie-v-ine-mesto-wuhan-sposobenej-novym-druhom-koronavirusu&catid=250:koronavirus-2019-ncov&Itemid=153 accessed 15 June 2020.

8 http://www.uvzsr.sk/index.php?option=com_content&view=article&id=4025:who-vyhlasila-pre-novy-koronavirus-2019-ncov-stav-globalnej-zdravotnej-nudze&catid=250:koronavirus-2019-ncov&Itemid=153 accessed 15 June 2020.

9 http://www.uvzsr.sk/index.php?option=com_content&view=article&id=4046:slovensko-je-na-covid-19-novy-koronavirus-pripravene&catid=250:koronavirus-2019-ncov&Itemid=153 accessed 15 June 2020.

10 http://www.uvzsr.sk/index.php?option=com_content&view=article&id=4049:odporuanie-uradu-verejneho-zdravotnictva-sr-vnsuvislosti-snvyskytom-koronavirusu-vntaliansku&catid=250:koronavirus-2019-ncov&Itemid=153 accessed 15 June 2020.

3. PHASE TWO: ACTIVATION OF SPECIAL STATE AUTHORITIES AND THE FIRST RESTRICTIONS

In the Slovak Republic, there is a legal framework for dealing with extraordinary situations of health threats provided for in a constitutional act on the security of the State in time of war, state of war, state of exception and emergency,[11] as well as the Act on the management of the state in crisis situations outside the time of war and the state of war,[12] the Act on the protection, support and development of public health[13] and the Act on civil protection of the population.[14]

On 27 February 2020,[15] the Security Council of the Slovak Republic met in order to discuss the COVID-19 response and decided to establish a Crisis Committee. On 6 March 2020, the first confirmed patient with COVID-19 disease was recorded in the Slovak Republic,[16] which triggered the first restrictions.

---

11 Article 5 sec 1 Constitutional Act No. 227/2002 Coll.: "The government may declare *emergency* only under the condition that it came or there is an imminent danger that it comes *to threat to life and health of persons, even in causal connection with the origination of a pandemic*, the environment or to threat to significant property values as a result of a natural disaster, catastrophe, industrial, traffic or other operational accident."

12 §3 of the Act No. 387/2002 Coll.: "The bodies of crisis management are a) the Government of the Slovak Republic, the Security Council of the Slovak Republic, b) ministries and other central state administration bodies, c) the National Bank of Slovakia, d) the security council of a region, e) district office, f) the security council of a county, g) municipality." §4 sec 2 of the Act No. 387/2002 Coll.: "The Government establishes a Central Crisis Committee which coordinates the activities of state administration bodies, local self-government bodies and other components intended for resolving a crisis situation in a period of a crisis situation."

13 §3 sec 1 of the Act No. 355/2007 Coll.: "The public health authorities are, to the extent provided by this Act, a) the Ministry of Health, b) the Public Health Authority, c) regional public health authorities, d) the Ministry of Defence, e) the Ministry of the Interior, f) the Ministry of Transport, Construction and Regional Development, g) Slovak Information Service."

14 §3 of the Act No. 92/1994 Coll.: "(1) For the purposes of this Act, an *extraordinary situation* means a period of threat or a period of effect of the consequences of an extraordinary event on life, health or property, ...; during it, measures are taken to save lives, health or property, to reduce the risks of threat or the necessary activities are performed to prevent spread and effects of the consequences of an extraordinary event. (2) For the purposes of this Act, an extraordinary event means a natural disaster, accident, catastrophe, threat to public health of the 2nd degree or a terrorist attack (...)." §8: "The Government declares and revokes an extraordinary situation for the endangered area or for the area, where an extraordinary event originated, if the extent of the endangered or affected area exceeds the territorial district of the region."

15 http://www.uvzsr.sk/index.php?option=com_content&view=article&id=4050:covid-19-zavery-zo-zasadnutia-bezpenostnej-rady-sr&catid=250:koronavirus-2019-ncov&Itemid=153 accessed 15 June 2020.

16 http://www.uvzsr.sk/index.php?option=com_content&view=article&id=4061:slovensko-zaznamenalo-prvy-potvrdeny-pripad-ochorenia-covid-19&catid=250:koronavirus-2019-ncov&Itemid=153 accessed 15 June 2020.

Arrivals and departures from and to Italy, visits to hospitals, prisons, nursing homes, children's homes and others were prohibited. From 10 March 2020, the Central Crisis Committee temporarily prohibited all sports, cultural and public events. It introduced a 14-day quarantine obligation for all citizens returning from affected countries (Italy, China, Iran, South Korea), i.e. a 14-day domestic quarantine together with all family members in one household.[17] The conditions were normatively regulated by the Public Health Authority in the form of a public decree.

A public decree in the Slovak Republic is an administrative act, a manifestation of the will of a public administration executive body. This normative act has a public power character in relation to persons outside the public administration and a management character in relation to persons within the public administration. The act has an authoritative character, it has a written form, it is a unilateral expression of will, it is legally binding and its adoption procedure is regulated by law.[18] At the same time, however, this act does not belong to legal regulations, i.e. it does not belong to the sources of *de iure* law, but stands on the border between legal regulations and individual administrative acts. The theory of administrative law calls them general decisions, or so-called hybrid administrative acts. It resembles an individual administrative act – its subject is largely specified, but it resembles also a normative administrative act (a legal regulation) – its addressee is defined by general features. Such acts are characterised by one-off use which is justified by an urgent public interest, e.g. for health protection, and are also temporary. Even a possible absence of a procedural mechanism for issuing hybrid administrative acts is justified by the urgency in the name of the public interest, which outweighs the private interest, and therefore there is an obligation for persons to tolerate the restriction, prohibition or obligation expressed in such an act.[19]

4. PHASE THREE: DECLARATION OF AN EXTRAORDINARY SITUATION AND EMERGENCY AND EXTENSION OF RESTRICTIONS

Following the international development (WHO Director General declared the COVID-19 pandemic on 11 March 2020) and internal development, the Slovak Government declared the extraordinary situation due to the threat to

---

17 www.uvzsr.sk/index.php?option=com_content&view=article&id=4062:informacia-zo-zasadnutia-ustredneho-krizoveho-tabu-vnsuvislosti-sncovid-19&catid=250:koronavirus-2019-ncov&Itemid=153 accessed 15 June 2020.

18 Soňa Košičiarová, *Správne právo hmotné. Všeobecná časť* (Aleš Čeněk 2015) 167.

19 Soňa Košičiarová, *Správne právo hmotné. Všeobecná časť* (Aleš Čeněk 2015) 167; Soňa Košičiarová, *Správne právo procesné. Všeobecná časť* (Heuréka 2015) 71.

public health of the second degree beginning on 12 March 2020 from 6:00 a.m. In Slovakia, similar measures were adopted as in other affected countries. The Central Crisis Committee announced[20] that kindergartens, primary and secondary schools and universities would be closed for 14 days from 16 March 2020. A mandatory 14-day quarantine was ordered for all those returning from abroad. Airports were closed, international bus and train transport stopped except for supplies. Gradually, almost all service operations (except grocery stores, pharmacies and drugstores) closed.[21]

On 15 March 2020, the government approved a proposal to declare an emergency[22] and to impose a duty to work so as to ensure the provision of health care and to prohibit the exercise of the right to strike by certain workers, namely providers of institutional health care. Mandatory quarantine was ordered in the facilities of the Ministry of the Interior.[23]

5. PHASE FOUR: FIRST LEGISLATIVE STEPS – NEW LEGAL REGULATIONS – AD HOC (COVID-19) LEGISLATION

Many acts were quickly adopted based on the government bills, which primarily responded to the spread of the disease. A large volume of legally regulated activities has moved from the personal/oral or written environment to the electronic environment. This transition to the electronic environment had to be quickly regulated in a legal way.

Numerous work activities (i.e. income making activities) have shifted to households and to the electronic environment. The whole education has been shifted to the electronic environment. In addition to the epidemiological and health aspects of the problem, the State urgently needed to address its economic and social aspects. Many activities which require personal presence and that

---

20 http://www.uvzsr.sk/index.php?option=com_content&view=article&id=4087:covid-19-ustredny-krizovy-tab-zavadza-alie-opatrenia-zatvoria-sa-koly-inletiska-karantena-plati-pre-vetkych-ktori-sa-vratia-zo-zahraniia&catid=250:koronavirus-2019-ncov&Itemid=153 accessed 15 June 2020.

21 http://www.uvzsr.sk/docs/info/covid19/Opatrenie_UVZSR_pri_ohrozeni_verejneho_zdravia_12.03.2020_prevadzky.pdf accessed 15 June 2020.

22 According to Article 5 of the Constitutional Act No. 227/2002 Coll. on the security of the state in time of war, state of war, state of exception and emergency; declared under No. 45/2020 Coll., Government Resolution No. 114 of 15 March 2020; effective from 16 March 2020. Since 19 March 2020, this emergency has been extended to the territory of the entire State; Resolution No. 115 of 18 March 2020, No. 49/2020 Coll., effective from 19 March 2020.

23 http://www.uvzsr.sk/index.php?option=com_content&view=article&id=4098:covid-19-vlada-sr-prijala-na-mimoriadnom-zasadnuti-alie-doleite-opatrenia&catid=250:koronavirus-2019-ncov&Itemid=153 accessed 15 June 2020.

serve to provide income for the population, have been interrupted. Many parents whose children needed personal care were forced to stay at home by the closure of schools and kindergartens, even if their workplace did not stop its operation. Thus, the need to deal with losses of income of employees as well as employers, entrepreneurs and to address the threat to the employment environment arose.

The first legal reactions, i.e. legislation in its true sense of the word, took place in the field of education. The Education Act, which regulates the system of school education (excluding higher education), was amended to include the competence for the Minister to decide on an extraordinary interruption of school teaching, as well as on the lock-down of school facilities, and setting other dates for the organisation of the school year provided that it was necessary due to the extraordinary circumstances.[24]

The Ministry of Justice also prepared a proposal for legal regulation of the extraordinary situation.[25] In particular, there was a general need to adjust the limitation or prescription terms in private law relations. The activity of the courts was reduced. They conducted hearings and public meetings only to the extent necessary, with the exclusion of the public for reasons of health protection.[26] In these cases, the limitation of the public presence in the court proceedings was replaced by the obligation to record each session and make it publicly available.

The way of internal acting of bodies of private persons changed. Collective bodies of legal persons established according to the regulations of civil and commercial law may use correspondence voting or allow an electronic meeting at this extraordinary time, even if this does not derive from the law or statutes. In such a way, the law interfered with the internal life of private entities, including internal norm-making. The law supplemented the way of organising and managing internal affairs. It is hard to say what will be the consequences if a person concerned by this way of organisation challenges such activities or acts. A large number of entities started to function, organise and make decisions in the electronic environment.

Legal measures in private law relations provided temporary protection for debtors. Access to the exercise of the lien was temporarily prevented, the performance of an auction was temporarily waived and the performance of an execution by sale of real estate was temporarily waived. These primary measures were shortly supplemented by an amendment[27] that protected individuals to an even greater extent by introducing a possibility of postponing the execution by

24 Act No. 56/2020 Coll. of 24 March 2020, effective from 25 March 2020.

25 Act No. 62/2020 Coll. on certain extraordinary measures in connection with the spread of dangerous infectious human disease COVID-19 and in the judiciary, of 25 March 2020, effective from 27 March 2020.

26 From 1 June 2020, the court proceedings were resumed.

27 Act No. 92/2020 Coll. of 22 April 2020, effective from 25 April 2020.

six months, until the end of 2020 at the latest. The private law area was also temporarily restricted in contractual relations since tenants received protection. The act stated that a landlord may not unilaterally terminate the lease of real estate due to the tenant's delay in paying the rent in the period from 1 April 2020 to 30 June 2020, upon proving that the delay in payment was due to circumstances related to the spread of COVID-19.

The law established the institute of temporary protection of entrepreneurs in order to create a time-limited framework for support of entrepreneurs against the negative consequences of the spread of the disease. The institute temporarily protects the entrepreneur from bankruptcy, execution and from the exercise of the lien, and such proceedings are suspended. The temporary nature is formulated directly by law until 1 October 2020, or the government may possibly extend it by a regulation until the end of 2020 at the latest.

The next act was an amendment to the Social Insurance Act and an amendment to some acts in the field of employment. The law anchored the entitlement to sickness benefits for employees and self-employed persons who were ordered to stay in quarantine or isolation, and at the same time a series of temporary measures in relation to COVID-19 disease for sickness and nursing benefits and various reliefs from compulsory social security payments were implemented.[28]

The amendment to the Labour Code affected its internal structure and further regulations on social and legal protection and safety and health at work were also amended. This is a legislative step that not only addresses this current situation, but also regulates special rules for possible similar situations in the future. The employer, who assumes a dominant position in such a situation, can order the employee to work from home, can schedule the working time and also designate taking leave for him/her. If an obstacle to work is on the side of the employer due to decision of a State body, e.g. interruption/cessation of the employer's activity, it is considered to be an obstacle to work on the part of the employer and the employee is entitled to compensation of wages to the amount of 80%, but at least to the amount of the minimum wage.[29] It is a deviation from the contractual labour law relations in favour of the decision-making competencies of the employer, while, however, at the same time the position of the employee is adequately ensured, with regard to the exceptionality of the situation.[30]

There have also been many measures introduced within the tax, customs and accounting field.[31] Electronic delivery has been favoured, many missed deadlines

---

28 Act No. 63/2020 Coll. of 25 March 2020, effective from 27 March 2020.

29 §250b of the Labour Code; Act No. 66/2020 Coll. of 2 April 2020, effective from 4 April 2020.

30 Helena Barancová, 'Domácka práca a telepráca' in Zuzana Nevolná and Milan Hlušák (eds), *Laudatio Alexander Škrinár* (Typi universitatis Tyrnaviensis 2020) 20.

31 Act No. 67/2020 Coll., on certain extraordinary measures in the financial field in connection with the spread of the dangerous contagious human disease COVID-19; of 2 April 2020, effective from 4 April 2020.

have been forgiven, deadlines have been postponed, measures have been introduced in the area of financial assistance to maintain operation in small and medium-sized enterprises and in the area of deferral of loan repayments. Later, the possibility of financial assistance to ensure the liquidity of small, medium and large enterprises was added.[32]

In the area of health care, the decision-making of collective bodies of health care subjects to electronic voting was legislatively introduced in the first place.[33] An ad hoc act was also adopted in the area of responsibility of the Ministry of the Interior.[34] Its basic tasks were to extend the deadlines for various mandatory submissions of documents, extending expiring authorisations to perform various activities (validity of identity cards, driving licenses, extension of authorised stays, etc.). An act in the area of territorial self-government enshrined the possibility of electronic deliberations of collegiate bodies (videoconferencing) and also voting on matters related to resolving a crisis situation. The Ministry of Transport and Construction was also affected by the new situation, where, in particular, the validity of various necessary documents or authorisations was extended and at the same time the number of oral hearings and local inspections in the relevant proceedings was reduced.[35] Similarly, the necessary amendments to related acts in the field of environment,[36] culture[37] and others were adopted.

A large part of the population is involved in university education and therefore in this field it was also necessary to deal with the public presence in the State examinations, postdoctoral qualification and inauguration lectures and meetings of academic bodies and to regulate these by law.[38] The meetings of collegial bodies of faculties and universities could be made in the form of videoconferences. Thus, universities were obliged to organise the State exams

---

32 Act No. 120/2020 Coll., amending and supplementing the Act No. 67/2020 Coll., on certain extraordinary measures in the financial field in connection with the spread of the dangerous contagious human disease COVID-19.

33 Act No. 69/2020 Coll. on extraordinary measures in connection with the spread of the dangerous contagious human disease COVID-19 in the area of health care, of 3 April 2020, effective from 6 April 2020.

34 Act No. 73/2020 Coll., amending and supplementing certain acts within the competence of the Ministry of the Interior of the Slovak Republic in connection with the disease COVID-19, of 7 April 2020, effective from 9 April 2020.

35 Act No. 90/2020 Coll., amending and supplementing certain acts within the competence of the Ministry of Transport and Construction of the Slovak Republic in connection with the disease COVID-19.

36 Act No. 74/2020 Coll., amending and supplementing certain acts within the competence of the Ministry of the Environment of the Slovak Republic in connection with the disease COVID-19, of 7 April 2020, effective from 9 April 2020.

37 Act No. 129/2020 Coll., amending and supplementing certain acts within the competence of the Ministry of Culture of the Slovak Republic in connection with the disease COVID-19, of 13 May 2020, effective from 21 May 2020.

38 Act No. 93/2020 Coll., amending and supplementing the Act No. 131/2002 Coll. on higher education institutions, of 22 April 2020, effective from 25 April 2020.

either with a direct audio-visual transmission or with making an audio recording available to the public during three months after the end of the crisis situation. A transition from traditional teaching to a distance form was allowed.

The norm-making competence of the government was strengthened by individual acts in the social area. It was delegated[39] that the government may introduce by a decree (implementing act) at the time of an extraordinary situation, emergency or a state of exception at this time and at the time immediately following the end of crisis the following measures: forgiveness, shortening, forgiveness of missed deadlines, preservation of claims granted before the crisis, determine the conditions of entitlements to State social benefits, change of legal procedures of competent authorities and determine the conditions for extending the performance of measures in a residence form. The government makes extensive use of this legislative power.[40] The government has also been delated to issue decrees and adjust the conditions for unemployment benefits and financial aid.[41] Thus, the government obtained the authorisation for operative norm-making in the social field in matters previously regulated by parliamentary acts.

6. INTERTEMPORAL PHASE: INTERNAL NORMATIVE ACTS OF VARIOUS BODIES

Norm-making as a response to changed conditions has manifested itself more generally, not just at the State level. Municipalities, regions, universities, professional chambers, civil society organisations and business entities began to introduce them. Their normative responses, i.e. internal normative acts, were focused mainly on two factors. The first was the adjustment of all possible processes, which until then required oral presentation, so that they could be performed online. The second factor was to respond to the passage of time, i.e. to postpone regular activities to the time "after" (various mandatory payments, internships, examinations, training, etc.). This exceptional situation did not cause changes in activities, but changed the form. A greatly enhanced use of the

---

39 Act No. 89/2020 Coll., amending and supplementing the Act No. 453/2003 Coll. on State administration bodies in the field of social affairs, family and employment services; of 22 April 2020, effective from 25 April 2020.

40 Government Regulations: No. 70/2020 Coll., No. 76/2020 Coll., No. 101/2020 Coll., No. 102/2020 Coll., No. 103/2020 Coll., No. 104/2020 Coll., No. 115/2020 Coll., No. 116/2020 Coll., No. 132/2020 Coll., No. 137/2020 Coll.

41 Act No. 66/2020 Coll., amendment to the Act No. 461/2003 Coll. on social insurance, amendment to the Act No. 448/2008 Coll. on social services; similarly also in the area of health insurance payment – to the Act No. 68/2020 Coll. – amendment to the Act No. 580/2004 Coll. on health insurance.

electronic environment for common activities will certainly be commonplace in the future. The non-standard regime of the present will very probably become a standard regime in the future.

7. DO THE COURTS ALSO INFLUENCE THE DEVELOPMENT OF LAW IN THIS TIME OF ACCELERATED LEGISLATION?

The era of hectic standardisation of human behaviour, with many restrictions of freedom in favour of the protection of the overriding interest – public health – soon found its critics. Questions as to the legality and constitutionality of individual restrictions emerged.[42]

In the overall context, it can be assessed that the measures are in principle similar in all affected countries of the world, for example also in the countries of the Council of Europe. Every interference with fundamental rights and freedoms has its constitutional limits, which are also expressed at the international law level; the European Convention on Human Rights (ECHR) is essential in this context.[43] The ECHR also assumes a legal solution for extraordinary situations, namely activation of Article 15 – derogation from the obligations of the Convention. A recent study by Jeremy McBride points out the fact that Armenia, Estonia, Georgia, Latvia, the Republic of Moldova and Romania have used this activation. The conclusion of the analysis is interesting:

> The extent to which any restrictions imposed in response to the threat posed by the pandemic will be found to be an unjustified interference with rights and freedoms under the Convention – whether with or without the invocation of a derogation – will be especially dependent upon the specific situation in a Member State, as well as their

---

[42] Slávka Henčeková Analýza právnej povahy opatrení Úradu verejného zdravotníctva SR na zamedzenie šírenia COVID-19. (30.4.2020) on-line: https://www.facebook.com/notes/sl%C3%A1vka-hen%C4%8Dekov%C3%A1/anal%C3%BDza-pr%C3%A1vnej-povahy-opatren%C3%AD-%C3%BAradu-verejn%C3%A9ho-zdravotn%C3%ADctva-sr-na-zamedzenie-%C5%A1/10222705778495168/ accessed 15 June 2020; Jozef Šátek, Vládny legislatívny chaos v prijímaní krízových opatrení. (23.4.2020, 29.4.2020), https://satek.blog.sme.sk/c/535331/vladny-legislativny-chaos-v-prijimani-krizovych-opatreni.html accessed 15 June 2020; Tlačová správa verejnej ochrankyne práv: Ombudsmanka odporúča zmeniť systém povinnej štátnej karantény. (28.4.2020), https://www.vop.gov.sk/syst-m-povinnej-t-tnej-karant-ny-je-potrebn-zmeni accessed 15 June 2020; Zuzana Gabrižová, Obnoviť kontroly podľa schengenského kódexu nie je to isté ako uzavrieť krajinu. (7.5.2020), https://euractiv.sk/section/spolocnost/news/obnovit-kontroly-podla-schengenskeho-kodexu-nie-je-to-iste-ako-uzavriet-krajinu// accessed 15 June 2020.

[43] Convention for the Protection of Human Rights and Fundamental Freedoms (No. 209/1992 Coll.).

> scope and duration. It is doubtful whether all the restrictions being imposed require a derogation to remain consistent with the requirements of the Convention but there are others which may need one, particularly if they last for a prolonged period. Although the number of Member States that have already resorted to a derogation at the same moment is unprecedented, there are many others employing the same measures as those who have done so without submitting one. It remains to be seen whether their actions will be challenged. For many, the restrictions being imposed will – even if inconvenient – seem to be a matter of common sense. However, others who are sanctioned for ignoring or who suffer serious financial losses for complying with them may take a different view.[44]

A Prague court joined the criticism of the restrictions in the Czech Republic and annulled four extraordinary measures of the Czech Ministry of Health. The judgment also attracted response in the Slovak Republic. The normative activities of the executive have raised legal issues of judicial control of such restricting acts. In the Czech Republic, the situation currently shows that measures of a general nature (e.g. issued by the Ministry of Health) are subject to review of the administrative judiciary and government decisions (e.g. measure on declaring an emergency, crisis measures on the prohibition of entry to the territory of the Czech Republic and on travel ban) are subject to the constitutional court control.[45]

In the administrative judiciary, four extraordinary measures of the Czech Ministry of Health of March and April 2020 were repealed, by which freedom of movement and freedom to conduct business was temporarily restricted.[46] This case generally depicts the substance of the dispute over the substantive jurisdiction of a State body to restrict rights and freedoms at the time of exceptional circumstances. In this case, the petitioner (individual, lawyer) did not question the principle of crisis measures of the State, but emphasised the necessity that the manner of their introduction is legal. The essence of the case is related also to the Slovak environment; there exists a similar range of sub-legal measures as well as *sui generis* acts that are close to standard legal regulations.

The general requirement is highlighted here – it is necessary to protect not only health, lives and the economy, but also a democratic State and a rule of law.[47]

---

44 Jeremy McBride, 'COVID-19 And The European Convention on Human Rights. Friday, 27 March 2020, An Analysis of Covid-19 Responses and ECHR Requirements' http://echrblog.blogspot.com/2020/03/an-analysis-of-covid-19-responses-and.html accessed 15 June 2020.

45 http://www.nssoud.cz/Nejvyssi-spravni-soud-odmitl-se-vecne-zabyvat-dvema-akty-vlady-souvisejicimi-s-nouzovym-stavem-Nasledoval-nazor-vysloveny-Ustavnim-soudem/art/32775 accessed 15 June 2020.

46 Court Judgment, Prague (Městský soud v Praze, č. j. 14 A 41/2020, 23.4.2020).

47 Czech Supreme Administrative Court Judgment (Usnesení Nejvyššího správního soudu, 1. 4. 2020, č. j. Pst 19/2019–12, p. 13).

And in this situation – the division of power in extraordinary circumstances – the court may become the guardian of power of the executive:

> the emergency regime ... temporarily suspends to some extent the effect of some "normal" constitutional and legal rules. Not only can fundamental rights and freedoms be curtailed, but also decision-making powers are concentrated in the hands of the executive, to the detriment of the legislative power. And it is a crucial task not only for the courts to ensure that after returning to the "normality" also the rule of law returns to the "normality". Historical experience shows that a real or perceived crisis can be the beginning of the destabilization of the democratic essence of the state.[48]

The court concluded that only the government (or, under certain conditions, the regional governor) may restrict fundamental rights and freedoms during emergency or a state of threat to the State. The Ministry issued a decree according to the regulations valid for the standard regime, but the legislator should have been the government according to the regulations for the extraordinary situation.[49] In this way, the material competence of the government and the individual ministries differs in standard time and in extraordinary time.

The court also added:

> if in the Czech legal environment it is not valid that in a state of exception a certain "solver of the crisis situation" assumes all the power without further legal rules, but a constitutional act on security designates a constitutional framework of the exceptional power of the government to restrict fundamental rights and freedoms, which are in more detail regulated in the Crisis Act, it cannot be allowed that any public authority replaces this clearly defined constitutional and legal framework for the restriction of fundamental rights and freedoms with its own administrative activity, to which it is otherwise entitled in the course of its "ordinary" activity. It can even be said that we recognize the degree of freedom and democracy precisely by how society can cope with exceptional situations and conditions. ... And although the court emphasizes that it has not seen any signs of abuse of the current situation in our state, considering the need to prevent this development, it has tended to adhere to the codified legislation restricting fundamental rights in times of emergency.[50]

Thus, the Czech court did not assess the abuse of power, but it stressed the need to adhere to the form. The court acknowledged that this act of the Ministry appears to be an effective tool, but effectiveness is not a measure of legality. It abolished the ministry decree.

---

48 Court Judgment, Prague (Městský soud v Praze, č. j. 14 A 41/2020, 23.4.2020, p. 131).

49 Court Judgment, Prague (Městský soud v Praze, č. j. 14 A 41/2020, 23.4.2020, p. 147).

50 Court Judgment, Prague (Městský soud v Praze, č. j. 14 A 41/2020, 23.4.2020, p. 160).

The Czech Ministry of Health filed a cassation complaint against the decision with the Supreme Administrative Court. The statements of the Ministry are essentially similar, as all the State executive bodies would use in this situation:

> We firmly support the issuance of extraordinary measures. We have done so in order to protect our citizens from the disease, which, according to experience in other countries, can have fatal consequences. It is necessary to realize that the Prague City Court dealt only with the form in which the measures were adopted, but it did not question their essence. Such a pandemic has not been here for the last hundred years, the legislative path has not yet been paved and the Government of the Czech Republic has never solved such a situation. It is therefore necessary to set up administrative practice. However, we are convinced that the Supreme Administrative Court must do so.[51]

Put simply, the Czech court contested neither the purpose, nor the effectiveness of the restrictive measures. However, it contested the legal procedure, which was not adhered to. The court proved to be the guardian of the performance of the competencies of individual executive bodies. We do not have such an example of a court judgment to repeal measures taken by executive bodies in Slovakia yet (it is not known to the author), although critical voices have been heard.

In Slovakia, however, we have an example of operative norm-making and operative intervention of the Constitutional Court – suspension of effect of certain provisions of the Electronic Communications Act – and subsequent operational intervention in trying to comply with the Constitutional Court's reservations – and again operational intervention of the Constitutional Court (repealing the suspension of effect of a part of the Act).

One of the first acts responding to COVID-19 was Act No. 62/2020 Coll. on certain extraordinary measures in connection with the spread of dangerous infectious human disease COVID-19, and which amended several acts (effective from 27 March 2020). On 14 April 2020, 34 (opposition) members of parliament filed a proposal against certain provisions of this Act with the Constitutional Court of the Slovak Republic for proceedings on the compliance of legal regulations. The proposal objected to the constitutionality of certain provisions amending the Act on the Judicial Council of the Slovak Republic, the Judges Act and the Electronic Communications Act, and also suspending their effectiveness was proposed.[52] The Constitutional Court accepted the proposal for further proceeding, and it suspended the effectiveness of certain provisions of the Electronic Communications Act. In principle, this was the strategy for using information technology regulated by law to combat the current pandemic.

---

51 http://www.mzcr.cz/dokumenty/ministerstvo-zdravotnictvi-podalo-kasacni-stiznost-proti-rozhodnuti-mestskeho-so_19183_1.html (7.5.2020) accessed 15 June 2020.

52 Act No. 185/2002 Coll., Act No. 757/2004 Coll., Act No. 351/2011 Coll.

There was a conflict with the right to privacy and the right to personal data protection. The proposers pointed to the new obligation of providers of electronic communications services (telecommunications operators) to process data of users of their electronic communication network and to provide data to the Public Health Authority of the Slovak Republic. This would have happened without the consent of the users, to the following extent: phone number, given name, surname, title, address, business name and registered office of the legal entity/place of business of the entrepreneur, geographical location data on the user's terminal device, creation of location data.

The Constitutional Court preliminarily discussed the proposal and on 13 May 2020 and it ruled[53] that it suspends the effect to some provisions of the Electronic Communications Act. The court stated that "the ongoing pandemic requires the deployment of fast and innovative solutions to protect life and health. At the same time, however, it must ensure that despite the pace of changes during this period an unintended erosion of the rule of law does not happen."[54] The court assessed the possible data collection and its subsequent use to be very broadly set and that it could be used almost without restrictions for any purpose in the pandemic context. The court pointed to the absence of sufficient guarantees, i.e. consent of the person concerned, clear definition of the purpose of the data use, supervision by a court or other independent institutions, ensuring a high level of protection and security, time limits and destruction of data and notification of persons concerned.[55]

In its reasoning, the Constitutional Court explained that it was also a part of the democratic constitutional system and society was aware of the division of power and that it perceived that the authorities adopted a legally as well as technically demanding regulation in difficult time. The court concluded that it had formulated its opinions with the aim to be helpful in a difficult situation, in order to implement the principle of constitutional cooperation of the constitutional bodies. The effect of the challenged regulation was suspended.

However, the Slovak parliament was swift and on 15 May 2020 it adopted an Act which, among other things, amended the relevant Electronic Communications Act.[56] The amended provisions take into account, *inter alia*, technical and organisational measures to protect privacy and personal data, and also data

53 Slovak Constitutional Court Judgment (ÚS SR, sp. zn. PL. ÚS 13/2020-103, 13.5.2020).

54 Slovak Constitutional Court Judgment (ÚS SR, sp. zn. PL. ÚS 13/2020-103, 13.5.2020, p. 71).

55 Slovak Constitutional Court Judgment (ÚS SR, sp. zn. PL. ÚS 13/2020-103, 13.5.2020, p. 86).

56 Act No. 119/2020 Coll. of 15.5.2020, effective from 18 May 2020, amended Act No. 351/2011 Coll. Electronic Communications Act.

processing, which is the subject of secrecy of telecommunication, exclusively to the extent necessary to identify the movements of the user concerned in order to protect life and health. The requirement to obtain the consent of the user was also introduced. The act enshrined that the authority shall destroy the data immediately after the reason for their processing has ceased to exist, it shall immediately inform the user concerned of the destruction, indicating the data which it has processed, and finally, by the end of January 2021, the authority shall submit a report on the legality of the data processing to the Constitutional Law Committee of the parliament. Since the legal regulation changed, the Constitutional Court assessed that there had been a material change in the proposal. The court also noted that the legislator adopted the given amendment after the publication of the Constitutional Court's judgment on its website and that the changes to the content of the Act may be considered "an attempt by the legislature to respond to the objections of the Constitutional Court to the shortcomings of the originally challenged legislation".[57] Therefore, on 27 May 2020, the Constitutional Court ruled that it had stopped the proceedings on compliance in this part, because it was already a different regulation in terms of content and quality. Once the court decision becomes effective, the court will continue the compliance procedure in respect of the remaining part of the proposal. On the day of the announcement of this decision in the Collection of Acts of the Slovak Republic, the validity of the judgment of the Constitutional Court concerning the suspension of the effectiveness of the affected provisions of the Electronic Communications Act expires.[58] The Electronic Communications Act was amended by Act No. 242/2020 Coll. with effect from 9 September 2020. The company providing the public network and public services is obliged to send, at the request of the State authority, information concerning the protection of persons against imminent danger and measures to prevent danger to life and health. The Public Health Authority may thus request data in the range of a telephone number during an emergency. The Public Health Authority may use this information only to prevent the emergence and spread of a pandemic or a dangerous contagious human disease and must destroy it after 60 days. The Public Health Authority is obliged to submit the report for the Constitutional Law Committee of the parliament on the lawfulness of data processing. The Public Health Authority is obliged to comply with this report until 31 March of the following year from the data proceeding.

---

57 Slovak Constitutional Court Judgment (ÚS SR, sp. zn. PL. ÚS 13/2020-185, 27.5.2020, p. 25).

58 The judgments of the Constitutional Court were published on 5 June 2020, No. 144/2020 Coll. and No. 145/2020 Coll.

8. GENERALLY ON NORMATIVE/LEGISLATIVE RESPONSES TO EXCEPTIONAL CONDITIONS: GENERALLY ON AD HOC (COVID-19) LEGISLATION

Extraordinary conditions have boosted norm-making as well as critical voices. Above all, it turned out that to solve the situation operatively means to solve it with the best possible intention and in accordance with the law, being aware of the risk of making mistakes – it concerns both the executive and the parliament. The role of the courts in this period is to be the strongest counterweight to the executive, in the sense of decision-making and a right choice of norm-making through a bill, decree or another act of normative nature, while protecting the fundamental rights and freedoms and other protected values, whether by general courts or the Constitutional Court. This judicial "control" may contribute to a clearer distinction of the norm-making competences of specific bodies in an extraordinary situation.[59] The judicial control will show who has how many competencies, whether the government as a whole, or individual ministries and authorities, who can issue which normative acts and in which way and how they have to be published. Possibly, it will also lead to a more precise distinction directly in the law. For now, the law making changed only in regard to the final stage of the process – the publication. The responsibility for publication in the Collection of Acts of the Slovak Republic was taken away from the traditional "administrator" – the Ministry of Justice, and was entrusted directly to the Office of the Government of the Slovak Republic.[60] Thus, the government gained delegated norm-making powers (previously implemented in the form of an act of the parliament) and also gained an official publication tool under "its wing".

The extraordinary situation has shown that there were no problems with publicity and, in general, with the possibility to become acquainted with the measures of the executive as well as parliament. Media of various types were bringing news and were constantly informing about the new measures. However, critical voices were heard about what was and what should have (not) been published in the Collection of Acts.

59 In the Slovak Republic, legal regulations include the constitution, constitutional acts and acts issued by the parliament (National Council of the Slovak Republic). By-laws are government regulations and decrees and measures of ministries and other State administration bodies and the National Bank of Slovakia. These are published in the Collection of Acts of the Slovak Republic. At the local level, these are generally binding regulations of municipalities and higher territorial units and decrees of local State administration. In more detail, e.g. Radoslav Procházka, Marek Káčer, *Teória práva* (C. H. Beck 2019) 157 ff. Measures as hybrid administrative acts have their various arrangements in many different specific acts.

60 The entire slov-lex portal as a public administration information system was also entrusted to the Government Office; Act No. 134/2020 Coll., amending and supplementing the Act No. 575/2001 Coll. on organisation of activity of the government and organisation of the central State administration, by which also further acts are amended, e.g. also the Act No. 400/2015 Coll. on the creation of legal regulations and on the Collection of Acts of the Slovak Republic.

In Slovakia, the Constitutional Court also acted operatively – it temporarily suspended the effect of an act that could interfere with the protection of personality and personal data (the Electronic Communications Act). The Constitutional Court's counterweight to the parliament manifested itself. However, the parliament reacted very quickly, and within a few days it corrected the provisions concerned and brought them into line with protection of the human rights guaranteed by the Constitution, international conventions, European legislation, as well as the EU Charter of Fundamental Rights.

The problem of ad hoc legislation can be looked at with regard to COVID-19, in quite the opposite way: "However, even today, are there acts not adopted more often (or especially) due to and because of specific interests rather than because of general principles? So aren't legal principles, including private law ones, just a dense compression and generalization of very specific interests? … I believe, it is not easy to answer the question, whether it is more common, that a 'system' is created from 'ad hoc' regulations, or, by supplementing missing elements in a targeted and planned way into the 'system'".[61] Also ad hoc legal norms are legal norms with general rules designated for an indefinite number of cases in the future.[62]

It is not easy to accept everything that the State has done, nor to simply reject everything that the State has done in norm-making in order to respond to the extraordinary situation. After all, with regard to the primary goal to protect health, State measures were successful.[63]

9. CONCLUSION

The accelerated development of law has shown that an extraordinary situation mobilises the State and its executive, rapidly makes the role of the executive for both the society and the State visible, and clearly strengthens it. The extraordinary situation subsequently also mobilises the parliament, and the judiciary – as a stronghold of independence in the State. The latter invokes the protection of not only health but also privacy, entrepreneurial freedom, together with all the other

---

61 Josef Bejček, 'Spontánnost soukromého právního řádu versus entropie jeho regulatorních veřejnoprávních korekcí' in Kristián Csach (ed), *Ad hoc legislatíva v súkromnom práve. XIV. Dies Luby Iurisprudentiae* (Leges 2019) 50.

62 Josef Bejček, 'Spontánnost soukromého právního řádu versus entropie jeho regulatorních veřejnoprávních korekcí' in Kristián Csach (ed), *Ad hoc legislatíva v súkromnom práve. XIV. Dies Luby Iurisprudentiae* (Leges 2019) 53.

63 Number of cases of the disease COVID-19 in the Slovak Republic at 4 June 2020: 1,525, number of deaths: 28, number of cases per 100,000 inhabitants: 28, number of deaths per 100,000 inhabitants: 0.5. http://www.uvzsr.sk/index.php?option=com_content&view=article&id=4337:prehad-potu-pripadov-ochorenia-covid-19-v-europe-k-4-6-2020&catid=250:koronavirus-2019-ncov&Itemid=153 accessed 15 June 2020.

freedoms, as well as constitutionality and observance of the principles of the rule of law. The erosion of the rule of law cannot be allowed, and in this way limits are placed and the "misconducts" of the executive or parliament are challenged by the judiciary.

Norm-making is a natural and substantial part of a human society as well as of a State. Within the development of law, an extraordinary situation results in creation of both legal regulations and sub-legal acts. Intensive norm-making begins first with "soft acts" such as recommendations, and leaflets, continues with measures of the executive of a normative nature (prohibitions, obligations and various restrictions) and finally moves to parliament and produces many ad hoc acts through an accelerated legislative procedure. Parliament authorises the government to take operational ad hoc delegated normative acts. The operational norm-making is also present at the level of self-government and internal management of organisations. What changes is the form of activities – they are transformed to electronic form, while the quality and content remain.

The lesson learnt from norm-making in an extraordinary situation, not only from Slovakia, is as follows: The State should review the legal regulations for functioning of the State in an extraordinary situation of any kind, especially with regard to the competencies of individual bodies, and their activities, including those of a normative nature. A mandatory participation of lawyers (especially constitutional lawyers) in crisis committees could be quite practical as they would pay attention to legally proper solutions to any situation. The extraordinary situation tests the abilities of various experts – in case of spreading a disease it is naturally experts in the field of public health, epidemiology, infectology and other medical disciplines, but also economists, sociologists and psychologists. However, the extraordinary situation also verifies the capability of lawyers, whether they work in public administration or elsewhere, since the law develops precisely through the deeds of lawyers.

The law has responded to new conditions, and generated conditions for transforming much human activity for livelihood online. A large number of "affected" entities have verified the viability of this form of functioning. It is likely that extraordinary measures will become new standards of work in the future even outside a crisis situation.

Ad hoc (COVID-19) legislation tries to be strictly temporary. Still, many consequences will be long lasting. However, not all legal regulations specifically deal with the situation related to the spread of COVID-19. Some legal regulations deal with the special conditions in a more general way, applicable in any crisis situation in the future. This will be another interesting part of the development of law, i.e. how it will "abandon" the ad hoc (COVID-19) legislation, and what will remain in force, because it may be useful in the future. Hopefully, it will not lead to an increase in the concentration of power of the executive.

COVID-19 AND RUSSIAN LAW

Challenge and Response

Ekaterina Dmitrikova,* Elena Sychenko,**
Anton Rudokvas*** and Andrej Novikov****

* Associate Professor, Saint-Petersburg State University, PhD in Law. Section 2 Administrative restrictions and measures of administrative coercion.

** Associate Professor, Saint-Petersburg State University, PhD in Law. Section 3 Labour and social security law in times of COVID.

*** Full Professor, Saint-Petersburg State University, Dr. Sci. in Law. Section 4 The impact of COVID-19 on the civil law in Russia.

**** Associate Professor, Saint-Petersburg State University, PhD in Law. Section 4 The impact of COVID-19 on the civil law in Russia.

The COVID-19 epidemic has become a challenge to the Russian legal system, inspiring a number of changes in it. The greatest number of novelties is noticeable in administrative law, which has to adapt to the emergence of many new restrictions on citizens' rights related to ensuring that the population of the country complies with the sanitary and epidemiological regime prescribed by the authorities. Labour law has also undergone significant mutations due to the mass transition of employees to remote mode of work. The changes also affected the right to social security, since the economic crisis triggered by the pandemic affected a large segment of the population, which required assistance from the State. The crisis situation in society and the economy has had the least impact on civil law, which is coping with new challenges using traditional legal regulation tools that have been tested for centuries. However, in the field of civil law some particular innovations took place. In general, it can be noted that in the conditions of time constraints, the share of such forms of operational modernisation of the current law has sharply increased, such as by-laws of the executive power and explanations of higher judicial instances aimed at interpreting the current legislation in relation to the new conditions.

1. INTRODUCTION

The aim of our research was to offer a review of the new Russian regulation relating to COVID 19. The authors have explored the challenges posed by COVID-19 to Russian law and the solutions adopted. The contribution does not pretend to be exhaustive because it is limited to the observation and primary analysis of the new rules of administrative law, labour law and some main issues of substantive private law and procedural law which are elaborated in connection with the topic. Certainly, the issues of data protection in the conditions of the epidemic, challenges for consumer law provoked by the restrictions imposed due to the pandemic, related problems of the law of civil and criminal procedure and some other relevant issues are still awaiting research, given that the limits of the space do not permit a complete discussion here. The research question of this contribution is the following: what are the changes that have occurred in Russian law as a reaction to the new socio-economic conditions that have developed under the influence of the COVID-19 pandemic? The latter is accompanied by a sub-research question: has the COVID-19 pandemic caused fundamental changes in any of the branches of Russian law?

2. ADMINISTRATIVE RESTRICTIONS AND MEASURES OF ADMINISTRATIVE COERCION

2.1. COVID-19: AN EXTRAORDINARY CHALLENGE FOR ADMINISTRATIVE LAW?

Changes in legislation and law enforcement practice in the field of public law in recent months in Russia are caused by an extraordinary situation that has endangered people's lives and health.[1]

This threat required State authorities to take decisions aimed at ensuring social isolation, preventing the spread of infection,[2] and improving the effectiveness of measures established to ensure the sanitary and epidemiological welfare of the public.[3] Given that the threat of spreading the disease is not limited to the territory of Russia,[4] a number of measures have been undertaken in order to "prevent the import" of the disease.[5]

On the one hand, the adoption of these measures is designed to protect the interests of an unlimited number of persons, to ensure the personal safety of each individual and society as a whole. On the other hand, it obviously involves restrictions on the rights of citizens and organisations. In this regard, questions related to the validity and proportionality of restrictions and the powers of State authorities to establish the regime under which such restrictions operate become extremely relevant.

---

1 'Coronavirus infection is included in the list of diseases that pose a danger to others.' See: On making changes to the list of diseases that pose a danger to others (Decree of the Government of the Russian Federation of 31 January 2020, no 66) http://publication.pravo.gov.ru/Document/View/0001202002030005 accessed 10 June 2020.

2 On ensuring the isolation regime to prevent the spread of COVID-2019 (Decree of the Chief State Sanitary Doctor of the Russian Federation of 18 March 2020, no 7, hereinafter, Decree no 7) http://publication.pravo.gov.ru/Document/View/0001202003190001 accessed 10 June 2020; On additional measures to prevent the spread of COVID-2019 (Decree of the Chief State Sanitary Doctor of the Russian Federation of 30 March 2020 no 9, hereinafter, Decree no 9) http://publication.pravo.gov.ru/Document/View/0001202003190001 accessed 10 June 2020.

3 On measures for ensuring the sanitary and epidemiological well-being of the public in connection with the spread of the Coronavirus infection (COVID-19) (Decree of the President of the Russian Federation of 2 April 2020, no 239, hereinafter, Presidential Decree no 239) http://publication.pravo.gov.ru/Document/View/0001202004020025 accessed 10 June 2020. See an English (non-official) version: https://drive.google.com/file/d/11SBSX4gYU7IOTEMx7OJTML057AsEc2TL/view accessed 10 June 2020.

4 The World Health Organization has recognized the spread of the disease caused by a new coronavirus as a pandemic https://ru.euronews.com/2020/03/11/pandemic-coronavirus-who accessed 10 June 2020.

5 For instance, mandatory isolation for persons arriving in Russia is established by Decree no 7.

In the Russian doctrine of administrative law, quarantine restrictions are traditionally considered as a method of administrative restriction.[6] The legal ground for restrictive measures is the provision of Part 3 of Article 55 of the Russian Constitution,[7] under which the rights and freedoms of a person and a citizen may be limited by a federal law only to the extent necessary to protect the foundations of the constitutional order, morality, health, rights and legal interests of other persons, to provide national defence and State security. The grounds for implementing restrictive measures and their legal forms are specified in federal laws.

Administrative restrictions involve establishing temporary restrictions on rights and freedoms of private individuals and organisations, establishing a total ban on the realisation of rights and freedoms, and imposing special temporary liabilities. In particular, the freedom of movement[8] and the right to conduct business may be restricted. For instance, in Saint Petersburg, all restaurants, cafes, and bars have been ordered to close.[9] Restrictive measures may be applied to persons who have not committed any illegal actions. The purpose of implementing restrictive administrative measures is to ensure the protection of public interest; their application is provided by State authorities through administrative actions, including the adoption of administrative acts.

2.2. INTRODUCTION OF A HIGH-ALERT REGIME: DISTRIBUTION OF POWERS TO ESTABLISH RULES OF CONDUCT

Prior to COVID-19, quarantine was considered as a regime that allowed the establishment of administrative, health, veterinary and other measures in order to prevent the spread of infectious diseases. The introduction of quarantine justifies a special procedure for economic and other activities, restrictions on the movement of people, vehicles, goods and animals.[10]

It should be noted that in the current situation, quarantine was not imposed on the entire territory of the Russian Federation.[11] At the federal level,

---

6 Pavel I. Kononov (ed), *Administrative law of Russia: scientific and practical course* [Unity-Dana: *Zakon i pravo* (Law and justice), 2011] 96 (in Russian).

7 The Constitution of the Russian Federation (adopted by national vote on 12 December 1993) http://www.constitution.ru/en/10003000-01.htm accessed 10 June 2020.

8 Subpara B of para 2 of Presidential Decree no 239.

9 On measures to prevent the spread of a new coronavirus disease (COVID-19) in St Petersburg (Decree of the Government of St Petersburg of 13 March 2020 no 121) https://www.gov.spb.ru/press/governor/186006/ accessed 10 June 2020.

10 Article 1 of the Federal law on sanitary and epidemiological welfare of the population (Federal Law of 30 March 1999, no 52-FZ, hereinafter, Law no 52) http://www.kremlin.ru/acts/bank/13636 accessed 10 June 2020.

11 Article 5 of Law no 52 refers this decision to the Federal level of authority.

regulatory legal acts of the President of Russia, the Government of Russia, and the Chief State Sanitary Doctor of Russia have established measures "to prevent the spread", "to counteract the spread of COVID-2019", "to ensure the sanitary and epidemiological welfare of the public", but they have not introduced the quarantine regime.

On the contrary, in the Russian regions a high-alert regime was introduced in accordance with the Federal law "On Protection of the Population and Territories in Case of Natural or Man-made Disasters".[12]

Previously, high alert was defined by the legislator as the mode of functioning of the administration and forces of the unified State system of prevention and overcoming of emergency situations, which is introduced in case of emergency.[13]

In the current circumstances, in April of 2020 Law no 68 was amended[14] to give the Russian Government and senior government officials of the constituent entities of the Russian Federation the authority to establish mandatory rules of conduct addressed to citizens and organisations when a high-alert or emergency situation is introduced.[15] The Russian Government has generally formulated prohibitions and obligations,[16] and regional authorities have been given the power to introduce their own rules and regulations in addition to those formulated by the Russian Government.

Redefining the powers and discretion of State authorities at the regional level led to imposing responsibilities and prohibitions with respect to citizens and organisations that vary in content and scope.

Refusing to satisfy the claim against the Mayor of Moscow, the court noted that under Part 3 of Article 55 of the Constitution of Russia, the right of a private individual may be restricted in order to protect the foundations of the constitutional order, health, rights and legitimate interests of other persons.[17]

---

12 As of 20 March 2020, the regulatory legal acts of State authorities of the Russian regions have introduced a high-alert regime in 45 regions. As of 29 May 2020 the regime has been introduced in 84 regions of Russia.

13 Part 6 of Article 4.1 of Federal law on protection of population and territories from natural and man-made emergency situations (Federal law of 21 December 1994, no 68, hereinafter, Law no 68) http://www.consultant.ru/document/cons_doc_LAW_5295/ accessed 10 June 2020.

14 On amendments to certain legal acts of the Russian federation on the prevention and liquidation of emergency situations (Federal law of 01.04.2020, no 98-FZ, hereinafter, Law no 98) https://rulaws.ru/laws/Federalnyy-zakon-ot-01.04.2020-N-98-FZ/ accessed 10 June 2020.

15 A vivid example is the Decree of the Mayor of Moscow on the introduction of high-alert Regime (Decree of the Mayor of Moscow of 5 March 2020, no 12-UM) https://rg.ru/2020/03/05/moscow-ukaz12-reg-dok.html accessed 10 June 2020.

16 On approval of the rules of conduct that are mandatory for citizens and organizations when a high-alert or emergency situation is introduced (Decree of the Government of the Russian Federation of 2 April 2020, no 417, hereinafter, Decree no 417) https://rulaws.ru/goverment/Postanovlenie-Pravitelstva-RF-ot-02.04.2020-N-417/ accessed 10 June 2020.

17 Decision of the Moscow City Court of 28 April 2020 in case no 3A-3877/2020 http://www.consultant.ru/cons/cgi/online.cgi?base=MARB&n=1862941&req=doc#07242890666944088 accessed 10 June 2020.

The court's decision noted that if there is a special law[18] and the justification for the purpose is provided, the right may be restricted, regardless of whether or not an emergency regime has been introduced. Considering the purpose of establishing a liability, the court noted that the legal acts imposing the public law liabilities on citizens, are aimed primarily at the protection of their health and prevention of the spread of COVID-19,[19] so citizens are obliged to exercise in good faith their rights and obligations, and not to violate the rights and freedoms of others.

While agreeing with the latter argument and recognising that the situation with the spread of the disease and the resources of the health sector in the regions differ, we believe the following: differences in the scope and content of restrictions and in the ratio of recommended and mandatory rules of conduct cannot be justified from the point of view of Part 3 of Article 55 of the Constitution of Russia if such rules are established by a regional regulatory legal act.

Restrictions and regulations for private individuals vary in content and scope in the regions. For example, in the Altai region, a Decree was issued under which all the citizens older than 65 years of age are obliged to observe the self-isolation regime; and another provision of the same document allows the operation of organisations providing notarial services.[20] The question is whether the notary violates the legislation in the field of ensuring the sanitary and epidemiological welfare of the public when they provide notarial services to the above-mentioned category of citizens in the notary office.[21]

In addition, restrictions on private individuals can be found in regional legal acts that regulate the areas which are not related to the spread of coronavirus infection. For example, in Saint Petersburg, a ban on visiting forest parks and urban forests was set as part of the fire prevention regime. Formally, the restriction is not related to the spread of the disease, but clearly contributes to the compliance with the rules of social isolation.[22]

---

18 The court recognised law no 68 as such.

19 Previously, the Constitutional Court has formulated the following position: the Constitution guarantees everyone the right to health and medical care and believes that human health is the highest inalienable good, without which many other benefits and values lose their value, and, therefore, its preservation and promotion play a fundamental role in every person's life and in the life of society and the State (Resolution of the Constitutional Court of the Russian Federation of 24 December 2013, no 30-P https://legalacts.ru/doc/postanovlenie-konstitutsionnogo-suda-rf-ot-24122013-n/ accessed 10 June 2020).

20 On individual measures to prevent the import and spread of a new coronavirus infection COVID-19 (Decree of the Governor of the Altai region of 31 March 2020, no 44 (edn of 6 April 2020) http://publication.pravo.gov.ru/Document/View/2200202003310007 accessed 26 May 2021.

21 We believe that in this situation, there are no grounds for refusing to perform a notarial action, since the provision containing the order is addressed not to a notary, but to a citizen over the age of 65.

22 On imposing a special fire prevention regime on the territory of Saint Petersburg (Decree of the Government of Saint Petersburg of 30 March 2020, no 166) http://publication.pravo.gov.ru/Document/View/7800202004010001?index=1&rangeSize=1 accessed 10 June 2020.

2.3. ESTABLISHMENT AND APPLICATION OF ADMINISTRATIVE LIABILITY MEASURES

It is no coincidence that so much attention has been paid to the validity assessment of imposed restrictions since a high-alert regime was introduced. In April of last year, administrative liability was established for violating the rules of conduct when a high-alert regime is introduced on the territory where there is an emergency threat.[23] That means that whether an act is recognised as illegal or not depends on whether or not a high-alert regime has been introduced in the relevant territory.

Under Article 20.6.1 of the Code of administrative offences of the Russian Federation, a person shall be held liable for failure to comply with the rules of conduct when a high-alert regime is introduced[24] and established at the federal level,[25] as well as with the rules established by regional regulatory legal acts in addition to Federal standards,[26] for instance, when, despite the ban, the violator provides services in a beauty salon, spa-centre or conducts training sessions inside the premises, or visits parks and squares that are forbidden to visit.

The Code was also complemented by an administrative liability for violations in the field of sanitary and epidemiological welfare committed during the state of emergency or when there is the threat of the spread of the life-threatening epidemic, or during the period of quarantine (Part 2 of Art 6.3 of the Code). The violator shall be held liable for non-compliance with the instructions issued by an official responsible for State sanitary and epidemiological supervision. Committing these violations means that, apart from being fined, organisations and individual entrepreneurs become subject to a strict penalty, such as suspension of a legal entity.

New provisions in the Code raised a number of questions referring to their application, which were clarified by the Supreme Court of the Russian Federation in order to develop a uniform practice.[27]

The liability for violations of the legislation on sanitary and epidemiological welfare is recognised as special, and a person who has committed a violation of

---

23 Article 20.6.1 of the Code of Administrative Offences of the Russian Federation (included in the Code on 1 April 2020), hereinafter, the Code www.consultant.ru/document/cons_doc_LAW_34661/ accessed 10 June 2020.

24 Article 20.6.1 of the Code of Administrative Offences of the Russian Federation provides for a written warning or a fine of 1–30 thousand rubles for citizens, 30–50 thousand rubles for individual entrepreneurs, 100–300 thousand rubles for legal entities, as a penalty.

25 Decree no 417.

26 Overview 'On Certain Issues of Judicial Practice Related to the Application of Legislation and Measures to Counter the Spread of a New Coronavirus Infection (COVID-19) on the Territory of the Russian Federation' no 1. Approved by the Presidium of the Supreme Court of the Russian Federation on 21 April 2020 (hereinafter, Overview no 1) http://www.vsrf.ru/documents/all/28857/ accessed 10 June 2020.

27 Overview no 1.

sanitary rules or hygienic standards, or who has not fulfilled the requirements or instructions of the officials responsible for sanitary and epidemiological supervision, may be held liable; for instance, when a person with an infectious disease or people who have come into contact with them do not comply with the isolation requirement if there is a suspected case.

It should be recognised that the clarifications of the Supreme Court of Russia have adjusted the law enforcement practice. Such violations as visiting squares and parks, if access to them is blocked because of the high-alert regime, non-compliance with the temporary ban on providing services, or being on playgrounds, if using them is temporarily banned, are recognised by judges not as a violation of anti-epidemic regulations and norms, but as a violation of the rules of conduct in cases where a high-alert regime has been introduced.

2.4. NEW RULES FOR CHECKING COMPLIANCE WITH MANDATORY REQUIREMENTS IN THE CONDITIONS CAUSED BY CORONAVIRUS

Speaking about the actions taken by public authorities, it would be unfair to refer only to restrictive and coercive measures. The epidemic has had a significant impact on business: entire industries have been forced to go online or suspend their operations altogether.

In the current circumstances, the decision was taken to cancel and suspend scheduled inspections.[28] For the first time, non-profit organisations, entrepreneurs, and organisations that cannot be related to small and medium-sized businesses were included in the list of entities which are subject to special rules of control and supervision. The latter are eligible for the moratorium on scheduled inspections only if the purposes of their operations are not classified as extremely high or high risk. In addition, it is planned to undertake control measures by means of remote interaction, including audio or video communication.

The new rules, aimed at reducing the administrative burden, apply to business entities, regardless of whether or not they belong to the industry most affected by coronavirus.[29]

---

28 'On the Specifics of Implementation of State Control (Supervision) and Municipal Control in 2020, and on Amending Para 7 of the Rules for the Preparation by the State Control (Supervision) Bodies and Municipal Control Bodies of Annual Plans of Scheduled Inspections of Legal Entities and Individual Entrepreneur' (Decree of the Government of the Russian Federation of 03.04.2020, no 438) http://www.consultant.ru/document/cons_doc_LAW_349478/ accessed 10 June 2020.

29 'On Approval of the List of Sectors of the Russian Economy That Are Most Affected by the Deterioration of the Situation as a Result of the Spread of a New Coronavirus Infection' (Decree of the Government of the Russian Federation of 3 April 2020 N 434 (edn from

2.5. CONCLUSION

The quarantine regime was not imposed on the entire territory of the country. Due to changes in Federal legislation, the powers of senior government officials of the constituent entities of the Russian Federation have been expanded. The analysis of judicial practice shows that private individuals do not challenge the proportionality of restrictions, but they challenge the existence of sufficient powers of regional authorities to establish a high-alert regime and restrictive measures undertaken under the high-alert regime, as well as the existence of powers of regional authorities to introduce provisions on administrative responsibility.

Temporary restrictions have been imposed under the high-alert regime. However, the consequences of such restrictions may be prolonged, primarily for organisations. This, in turn, may lead to a number of applications to the court for verification of mandatory administrative acts adopted by State authorities for the validity and proportionality of imposed restrictions.[30]

3. LABOUR AND SOCIAL SECURITY LAW IN TIMES OF COVID-19

The pandemic has been a great challenge for the authorities. It has very quickly become evident that the traditionally restricted regulation of labour is not suitable for such situations, that labour law has huge gaps in the fields of regulating the transfer of workers for remote work, and of the exchange of documents between the parties of employment contract in the electronic form. Furthermore, it is not suitable for regulating shift work during quarantine.

3.1. OVERVIEW OF CHANGES TO LABOUR REGULATIONS

The restrictions to business operations imposed to ensure public safety made the Government reflect the possible amendments to labour regulations. First, Federal law no 122-FZ adopted on 24 April 2020, provided the basis for the experiment on the use of electronic documents related to work without duplicating paper documents related to work. This experiment will run until 31 March 2021 and is aimed at establishing the conditions for further changes to the Labour Code, substituting the needed written form of all the documents related to work

26 May 2020), hereinafter, Governmental Decree N 434) http://www.consultant.ru/document/cons_doc_LAW_349344/ accessed 10 June 2020. On the contrary, the principle activity of the organisation is important for providing individual benefits.

30 See critical arguments in regard of legality of the imposed restrictions: Paul Kalinichenko, Elizaveta Moskovkina, 'Russia – With Scepter and Corona' *VerfBlog*, 2020/5/23 https://verfassungsblog.de/russia-with-scepter-and-corona/ accessed 10 June 2020.

and "live" signatures with e-documents and e-signature of both employer and employee. The participation of employers and employees in this experiment is voluntary and the employee can at any time withdraw his/her consent.

In June 2020, the amendment[31] to the Labour Code was presented to Parliament. It proposed to establish that the exchange of communications may be carried out not only in the personal presence of the parties to the employment contract but also by sending a message to a party in the form of a paper document using postal service, or electronic means. Another proposed bill[32] provides for the inclusion in the employment contract of the possibility of a temporary or partial performance by an employee of his/her work in remote form and fixes certain requirements to this agreement.

To solve the problem of regulating shift work, the Government adopted Provisional Rules of work on a rotational basis, which were valid from 29 April to 31 December 2020.[33] Under these new rules, if the shift personnel cannot arrive at the shift due to anti-epidemic measures, it is permitted to extend the period of stay on duty, taking into account the opinion of the representative body of employees for a period not exceeding three months. The extension is allowed with the employee's written consent. It is also important that these temporary provisions made it clear that the period of 14 days of observation of the workers who arrived for the shift is included in working time.

There have been several initiatives for increasing the flexibility of labour regulations. In March 2020, the Ministry of Labour proposed to amend the Labour Code providing the Government with the right to determine the notification period for upcoming layoffs or in connection with the liquidation of an organisation during an epidemic. The Government did not support the bill due to potential risks for employees.[34]

In May to June 2020, the Government and social partners considered the draft of temporary regulations of labour.[35] This draft contains mostly the norms which were expressed during the period of quarantine in the letters and the recommendations of the Labour Ministry and are very questionable in terms of

---

31 On Amendments to the Labor Code of the Russian Federation (Draft Federal law N 967986-7), http://www.consultant.ru/law/hotdocs/62788.html accessed 10 June 2020.

32 'About Modification of Article 57 of the Labour Code of the Russian Federation'. (Draft Federal Law N 966659-7), http://www.consultant.ru/cons/cgi/online.cgi?base=PRJ;n=195779;req=doc#05872584223206341 accessed 10 June 2020.

33 About the approval of provisional rules of work on a rotational basis (Decree of the Government of the Russian Federation on 28 April 2020 no 601) https://rulaws.ru/goverment/Postanovlenie-Pravitelstva-RF-ot-28.04.2020-N-601/ accessed 10 June 2020.

34 Julia Starostina, 'The Ministry of Labour Proposed a New Procedure for Changing Labour Relations in the Epidemic' (in Russian) RBC (Moscow, 24 April 2020) https://www.rbc.ru/economics/24/04/2020/5ea15cc29a7947041f6e20ed accessed 10 June 2020.

35 Olga Ignatova, 'The Ministry of Labour Proposed a Special Procedure for Remuneration and Dismissals' (in Russian) Rossiyskaya gazeta (Moscow, 29 May 2020) https://rg.ru/2020/05/29/mintrud-predlozhil-osobyj-poriadok-oplaty-truda-i-uvolnenij.html accessed 10 June 2020.

their compliance with the Labour Code. For example, it decreases the notification period for changing the conditions of labour from two months (Art 74 of the LC) to two weeks. The most spectacular norm of the present document is the acknowledgement of the priority of these temporary regulations of labour over other sources of labour law: "In the part not regulated by the present temporary regulations, labour legislation and other normative legal acts containing norms of labour law are applied."

3.2. THE INTRODUCTION OF "NON-WORKING DAYS"

The regime of non-working days is the most striking feature of the Russian approach to ensuring public safety in the pandemic.[36] The President announced a series of non-working days (in sum from 28 March to 11 May 2020) all over Russia which should be paid as working time.[37] Some measures to decrease the tax burden on employers, who were registered in the list of SME were adopted.[38]

The regime of non-working days did not cover all the organisations. As there have been several presidential decrees on this point, the trend of broadening the list of organisations which can keep working can be traced. Generally speaking, the first decree divided all organisations into four groups:[39]

1. organisations that should stop activities (all unless pointed in any other group);
2. organisations which were required to determine the number of employees to ensure their functioning (mass media, civil and municipal servants);

---

36 See also: Iuliia Ostrovskaia, 'COVID-19 and Labour Law: Russian Federation' (2020 special issue 1 vol 13) Italian Labour Law e-Journal https://illej.unibo.it/art/view/10791 accessed 10 June 2020.

37 About declaring non-working days in the Russian federation (Decree of the President of the Russian Federation of 25 March 2020 no 206) http://www.consultant.ru/document/cons_doc_LAW_348485/ accessed 10 June 2020; On the extension of measures to ensure the sanitary and epidemiological well-being of the population on the territory of the Russian federation in connection with the spread of a new coronavirus infection (COVID-19) (Decree of the President of the Russian Federation of 28 April 2020 no 294, hereinafter, Presidential Decree no 294) http://www.consultant.ru/document/cons_doc_LAW_351539/ accessed 10 June 2020.

38 For the employers included in the Unified register of SMEs, the total amount of insurance contributions in the period from 1 April to the end of 2020 is reduced from 30% to 15%. The rate of contributions to the Pension Fund will be 10%, to the mandatory medical insurance Fund-5%. Contributions to the social insurance Fund (for disability and maternity) are not paid. See Federal law no 102-FZ adopted 1 April 2020: http://www.garant.ru/news/1364993/#ixzz6SuuIzil3 accessed 10 June 2020.

39 The same pattern was followed by the following decrees: On measures to ensure the sanitary and epidemiological well-being of the population on the territory of the Russian federation in connection with the spread of a new coronavirus infection (COVID-19) (Decree of the President of the Russian Federation of 2 April 2020 no 239, hereinafter, Presidential Decree no 239) http://www.consultant.ru/document/cons_doc_LAW_349217/ accessed 10 June 2020, and the Presidential Decree no 294.

3. systemically important, as well as scientific and educational organisations for which the regime of non-working days might be spread only in coordination with the Government of the Russian Federation;
4. organisations which do not stop the activities and are not covered by the decree.

In May 2020, the President adopted a decree[40] which finished the period of non-working days and granted the power of suspension (restriction, including through defining peculiarities of the work regime, number of employees) of business activities, based on the sanitary and epidemiological situation, to the subject of the Russian Federation.

The policy of non-working days significantly influenced the labour market and the rights of workers. The number of registered unemployed for non-working days increased by almost 30%. The Chamber of Commerce and Industry commented that around three million entrepreneurs could stop operating putting more than 8.6 million people at risk of unemployment.[41]

Among the most common illegal practices used by employers are forced resignation, decreasing wages and forcing employees to take unpaid leave for the duration of "non-working" days.[42] According to the expert's calculations, about 30% of the companies which stopped working under the Presidential Decree did not pay employees, about 10% reported redundancy procedures.[43] It should be noted that the Ministry of labour[44] forbids the dismissal of workers during the period of non-working days at the discretion l of the employer.

In an organisation which remained functioning, the employer had to undertake additional measures to ensure occupational health: to organise measurement of body temperature of workers at workplaces with the mandatory removal of persons with elevated temperatures and further control of an employee calling a doctor to provide primary care at home.[45]

---

40 On determining the procedure for extending measures to ensure the sanitary and epidemiological well-being of the population in the subjects of the Russian federation in connection with the spread of a new coronavirus infection (COVID-19) (Decree of the President of the Russian Federation of 11 May 2020 no 316) http://publication.pravo.gov.ru/Document/View/0001202005110002 accessed 10 June 2020.

41 Maria Efimova, 'Either the Budget Cracks or People' (in Russian) Novaya Gazeta (Moscow, 17 April 2020) https://novayagazeta.ru/arts/2020/04/17/84949-libo-byudzhet-tresnet-libo-lyudi accessed 10 June 2020.

42 Maria Efimova, 'Either the Budget Cracks or People' (in Russian) Novaya Gazeta (Moscow, 17 April 2020) https://novayagazeta.ru/arts/2020/04/17/84949-libo-byudzhet-tresnet-libo-lyudi accessed 10 June 2020.

43 Ekaterina Sabelnikova, 'Operational Monitoring of Social Processes' *Center of macroeconomic analysis and short-term prognosis* (in Russian) www.forecast.ru/_ARCHIVE/MON_SC/2020/sm2.pdf accessed 10 June 2020.

44 Labour Ministry, *Q&A On Work Organization and Employee Rights During the Non-working Week* (in Russian) https://rosmintrud.ru/employment/54 accessed 10 June 2020.

45 Letters of federal service for supervision of consumer rights protection and human welfare (Rospotrebnadzor) about additional measures for coronavirus infection on 3 March 2020

3.3. SICK PAY IN QUARANTINE

During the pandemic, the authorities have immediately taken measures to suspend those workers who returned from the territory of countries where cases of a new coronavirus infection have been registered and adopted the temporary rules for registration of certificates of disability, appointment and payment of benefits for temporary disability in case of quarantine as well as to insured persons who live together with them.[46] These rules provided insured people returned from abroad and the people who live with them with sick leaves and sick benefits for 14 days calculated from the date of arrival.

To protect the most vulnerable elderly people, the Government introduced the opportunity of paid sick leaves for workers over 65 years.[47] Such workers are entitled to leave and the relevant benefit from the social security fund if they observe the regime of self-isolation.

Other workers in case of their contact with the COVID-positive person should be suspended from work under Article 76 of the Labour Code and will be paid sick leave under the Order of the Ministry of Healthcare and Social Development of Russia N 624n adopted on 29 June 2011.

3.4. SUPPORT OF UNEMPLOYED PEOPLE

With the growth of unemployment caused by the stoppages of business activities, the support of unemployed people has become one of the main concerns for the authorities. Already in the first speeches at the beginning of the pandemic, the President promised to raise the unemployment benefits to the sum of a living wage (about 160 US dollars). The Government adopted the temporary rules of registration of unemployed[48] which provided the mechanism of an electronic application to the employment service, regardless of the place of residence

---

no 02/3401-2020-27 http://www.consultant.ru/cons/cgi/online.cgi?base=EXP;n=618459;req =doc#07586956137747158 accessed 10 June 2020 and N 02/3633-2020-29 on 6 March 2020 https://www.glavbukh.ru/npd/edoc/97_477571 accessed 10 June 2020.

46 About the approval of temporary rules of registration of sheets of disability, appointment and payment of benefits for temporary disability in case of quarantine (Decree of the Government of the Russian Federation on 18 March 2020 no 294) http://www.garant.ru/hotlaw/federal/1332594/ accessed 10 June 2020.

47 On approval of temporary rules for registration of disability certificates, assignment and payment of temporary disability benefits in case of quarantine to insured persons aged 65 years and older (Decree of the Government of the Russian Federation of 1 April 2020. no 402) http://www.garant.ru/products/ipo/prime/doc/73730678/accessed 10 June 2020.

48 On approving temporary rules of registration of citizens in order to find a suitable job and as unemployed, as well as for the implementation of social payments to citizens recognized in the established procedure being unemployed (Decree of the Government of the Russian Federation of 8 April 2020 no 460) https://rulaws.ru/goverment/Postanovlenie-Pravitelstva-RF-ot-08.04.2020-N-460/ accessed 10 June 2020.

in Russia, as well as the mechanism of distant interviews with the potential employers. To be registered as unemployed, the person should be registered first for seeking employment and offered suitable employment opportunities.[49]

Another Government Decree has increased the maximum amount of unemployment benefits to the sum of the subsistence level, as required by the President, by the Decree no 346 adopted on 27 March 2020.[50] However, under paragraph 16 of this decree the minimum sum was still paid to first-time jobseekers (except for orphans); people who did not work more than one year; those who were dismissed for misconduct or other wrongful acts; those who worked less than 26 weeks; those who stopped individual business activities; citizens who do not have information about their average earnings. It was also fixed that the period of payment of unemployment benefits to these categories of citizens may not exceed three months in total for 12 months.

These regulations evidently could not ensure the support of a large part of the unemployed. This is why in April 2020, the President instructed the Government to ensure that the sum of unemployment benefits to be paid in April to June 2020 to persons who lost their jobs after 1 March 2020, would be equal to the subsistence level. It was immediately fixed by the Decree no 485 adopted on 12 April 2020. The mentioned paragraph 16 of the Decree no 346 was suspended until 1 July 2020.

It was also established that the unemployed will receive payments for each minor child of 3,000 roubles per month in the period April to June 2020.

However, the main problems remain: the unemployed who lost jobs before 1 March 2020 are still in many cases receiving only the minimum sum of the benefit; the period of payment of the increased sum under the most recent Decree no 485 is too short (three months); the general maximum periods of payments are too short.[51]

3.5. CONCLUSION

The acts adopted by the Government and the Labour Ministry provided certain flexibility for the regulation of employment relations in Russia. However, these

---

49 About employment of the population in the Russian federation (Law of the Russian Federation of 19 April 1991, N 1032-1) http://www.consultant.ru/document/cons_doc_LAW_60/ accessed 10 June 2020.

50 On the amounts of the minimum and maximum unemployment benefit for 2020. (Decree of the Government of the Russian Federation of 27 March 2020 no 346) http://publication.pravo.gov.ru/Document/View/0001202003300022 accessed 10 June 2020.

51 Under Article 31 of the Law of the Russian Federation of 19 April 1991 N 1032-1, the period of payment is no more than six months in the 12 months, while for certain categories of unemployed it is decreased to three months in 12 month period.

norms should correspond to the hierarchy of the sources of law, and should be complemented with the new supportive measures for the unemployed. Given that the temporary regulations, once adopted, are supposed to be valid until the end of 2020, while the increased unemployment benefit was announced only until June 2020, the huge gap in the adoption of social measures by the Government becomes evident.

We presume that the burden of the crisis under the present regulations is largely placed on business, whereas it should be distributed between the State (through providing special measures of support to business and workers/ unemployed) and the employers. Workers, as the most vulnerable party, should be protected either by means of labour law or social security law. The regime of "non-working" days, in our opinion, will have a deep and long-lasting effect on the employment market, increasing unemployment and informal work.

4. THE IMPACT OF COVID-19 ON THE CIVIL LAW IN RUSSIA

With the introduction of restrictive measures aimed at preventing the spread of a new coronavirus infection (COVID-19), actors involved in the circulation of goods and the legal community faced a number of questions about the specifics of the application of civil law during this period.

4.1. DEADLINES FOR PERFORMANCE OF OBLIGATIONS

One of the main issues of contention was the application of legal provisions on the term of performance of obligations and the limitation period in the new conditions. The fact is that in order to prevent the spread of infection, Presidential Decrees no 206 of 25 March 2020 and no 239 of 2 April 2020 declared certain periods of time as "non-working days" for the entire country. This immediately raised the question of the legal consequences of the fact that the last day of the obligation or limitation period falls on the day declared non-working according to the above-mentioned Decrees of the President of Russia.

According to the general rule laid down in Article 193 of the Civil Code of the Russian Federation (CC RF), if the last day of the term falls on a non-working day, the day of the end of the term is considered to be the next working day following it. This rule was designed to address cases when the expiration date falls on a weekend or holiday. Its formal application in the new conditions, when the non-working days according to the Presidential Decrees were extended for several weeks, would have to postpone the expiration of all the mentioned terms to the next working day following the expiration of the entire period specified in the Decrees.

The Supreme Court of the Russian Federation has proposed a restrictive interpretation of the concept of "non-working day" given in the Presidential Decrees under consideration. In determining the meaning of this concept ad hoc, the Supreme Court determined that these non-working days are among the measures established for the purpose of ensuring the sanitary and epidemiological well-being of the population, aimed at preventing the spread of a new coronavirus infection (COVID-19), and cannot be considered non-working days in the sense given to this concept in the CC RF.[52]

The opposite, i.e., a literal interpretation, would mean suspending the performance of all civil obligations without exception for a long period of time and significantly restricting civil turnover in general, which does not meet the goals of introducing non-working days aimed at creating obstacles to the spread of infection.

In addition, the establishment of non-working days in this case was not actually universal, but depended on various conditions (such as the direction of activity of the economic entity, its location, and the restrictive measures imposed in a particular subject of the Russian Federation in connection with the declaration of high alert). Above all, additional restrictive measures on movement across the territory and determining the range of economic entities whose activities are suspended may be introduced at the level of the Russian Federation's constituent entities.[53]

Similarly, in the current situation, it should be taken into account that in some cases, on days declared non-working, there may be no obstacles to the performance of the obligation, and in some cases, such performance is completely impossible. Therefore if there are no other grounds for exemption from liability for non-performance of an obligation, the establishment of non-working days in itself is not a reason for postponing the term of performance of the obligation.

If circumstances of force majeure are established in the context of the spread of a new coronavirus infection,[54] this in itself does not terminate the debtor's obligation if performance remains possible after they have lapsed.[55]

In this case, the debtor is not responsible for the delay in performance of the obligation arising as a result of force majeure, and the creditor is not deprived of the right to withdraw from the contract if, as a result of the delay arising in connection with the occurrence of force majeure, it has lost interest in performance. In this case, the debtor is not liable to the creditor for losses

---

52 Answer to question 5 of the Overview no 1.

53 Item 2 of the Presidential Decree no 239.

54 Para 3 Article 401 CC RF.

55 Para 9 of the Ruling of the Plenum of the Supreme Court of the Russian Federation dated 24 March 2016 no 7 on the application by Courts of certain provisions of the Civil Code of the Russian Federation on liability for breach of obligations (hereinafter, Ruling of the Plenum no 7) http://www.vsrf.ru/documents/own/8478/ accessed 10 June 2020.

caused by the delay in performance of obligations due to the occurrence of force majeure.[56]

Similarly, the time when the limitation of actions expires should be determined if there are no grounds for suspending it.[57]

4.2. LIMITATION OF ACTIONS

The problem of application of the rules on the limitation of actions has been resolved in the jurisprudence of courts. In connection with the restrictions and/or measures of self-isolation, the main question was: under what conditions is it possible to restore the expired limitation period or suspend it?

As a general rule, the limitation period is suspended if an extraordinary and unavoidable circumstance (force majeure) prevents the filing of a claim.

The limitation period's running shall be suspended provided that the said circumstances arose or continued to exist in the last six months of the limitation period, and if this period is equal to six months or less than six months, during the period of limitation. Accordingly, if there are more than six months left before the expiration of the limitation period, then a force majeure circumstance does not suspend its course.[58]

From the date of termination of force majeure, the limitation period continues. The remaining period of limitation, if it is less than six months, is to be extended to six months and if the limitation period is six months or less than six months, it is to be extended to the whole limitation period.[59]

The conclusion about the presence or absence of force majeure circumstances that prevented timely application to the court for protection of the violated right can be made by the court only taking into account the actual circumstances of a particular case. Thus, measures taken by State and local authorities aimed at preventing the spread of a new coronavirus infection (COVID-19), if they prevented the filing of a claim, can be recognised as grounds for suspending the limitation period in the presence of the above-mentioned conditions.

In particular, the inability of citizens to apply to the court with a claim under the restrictive measures taken (self-isolation regime, inability to apply through the Internet reception of the court or through the postal service organisation

---

56 Para 3 Article 401, para 2 ст. 405 CC RF.

57 Article 202 CC KA. Such grounds are considered by the statutory law to be: force majeure, the presence of the plaintiff or defendant in the Armed forces of the Russian Federation, transferred to martial law; the deferral of obligations established by the Government of the Russian Federation on the legal grounds (moratorium); suspension of the law or other legal act regulating the relevant relationship.

58 Para 1 Article 202 CC RF.

59 Para 4 Article 202 CC RF.

due to age, health status or other circumstances) can be considered as a valid reason for skipping the limitation period and grounds for its restoration.[60]

4.3. FORCE MAJEURE

Perhaps the main question of applying civil law in a pandemic is whether it is possible to recognise the epidemiological situation, the restrictive measures imposed by the authorities or the regime of self-isolation as force majeure or grounds for termination of an obligation due to the impossibility of its performance, including in connection with the adoption of an act of a public authority, and if this is possible, under what conditions?

Russian civil law establishes various grounds for exemption from liability for breach of obligations for citizens on the one hand, and for persons engaged in business activities on the other.[61] Citizens can be released from liability for breach of obligations in the absence of fault, that is, in a situation where the citizen, with the degree of care and prudence required by the nature of the obligation and the terms of civil turnover, took all measures for the proper performance of the obligation.[62]

On the contrary, unless otherwise provided by law or contract, a person who has failed to perform or improperly performed an obligation in the course of business activities is liable if he/she does not prove that proper performance was impossible due to force majeure (i.e. strict liability). The statutory law sets out the criteria under which a particular circumstance can be recognised as a force majeure event. For this purpose, the circumstance must be extraordinary and unavoidable in this situation, and be external to the debtor's activity under these conditions.[63]

The requirement for the circumstance to be extraordinary implies the exclusivity of the circumstance in question, the occurrence of which is not usual in specific circumstances.

Unless otherwise provided by law, a circumstance is recognised as unavoidable if any participant in civil turnover carrying out activities similar to those of the debtor could not have avoided the occurrence of this circumstance or its consequences. In other words, one of the characteristics of force majeure (along with the requirements to be extraordinary and unavoidable) is its relative nature. Circumstances, the occurrence of which depended on the will or actions of the party to the obligation, such as the debtor's lack of necessary funds, violation of obligations by its counterparties, or illegal actions of its representatives, cannot be considered force majeure.

---

60 Answer to question 5 of the Overview no 1.

61 Para 1 and 3 Article 401 CC RF.

62 Subpara 2 para 1 Article 401 CC RF.

63 Para 3 Article 401 CC RF; para 8 of the Ruling of the Plenum no 7.

Recognition of the spread of a new coronavirus infection as a force majeure event cannot be universal for all categories of debtors, regardless of the type of their activities, conditions for their implementation, including the region in which the organisation operates. For this reason, the existence of force majeure circumstances must be established taking into account the circumstances of the particular case (including the term of performance of the obligation, the nature of the unperformed obligation, the reasonableness and good faith of the debtor's actions, etc.).[64]

Circumstances caused by the threat of spreading a new coronavirus infection, as well as measures taken by State and local authorities to limit its spread, in particular, the establishment of mandatory rules of conduct when introducing a high-alert or emergency situation, a ban on the movement of vehicles, restrictions on the movement of individuals, the suspension of the activities of enterprises and institutions, the cancellation and postponement of mass events, the introduction of a regime of self-isolation of citizens, etc., may be recognised as force majeure circumstances if the court determines their compliance with the above-mentioned criteria for such circumstances. In addition, a causal link must be proved between these circumstances and the non-performance of the obligation.

As a general rule, the debtor's lack of the necessary funds is not a ground for exemption from liability for non-performance of obligations. However, if the lack of necessary funds is caused by the established restrictive measures, in particular, the prohibition of certain activities, the establishment of a regime of self-isolation, etc., it may be recognised as a ground for exemption from liability for non-performance or improper performance of obligations. An exemption from liability is permissible if a reasonable and prudent participant in civil turnover engaged in similar activities with the debtor could not have avoided the adverse financial consequences caused by restrictive measures (for example, in the case of a significant reduction in the amount of profit due to the forced closure of a public catering facility).

However, the occurrence of force majeure circumstances does not in itself terminate the debtor's obligation if performance remains possible after they have ceased. The creditor is not deprived of the right to withdraw from the contract if, as a result of a delay that objectively arose in connection with the occurrence of force majeure, it has lost interest in performance. In this case, the debtor is not liable to the creditor for losses caused by the delay in performance of obligations due to the occurrence of force majeure. If the force majeure circumstances are temporary, the party may be released from liability for a reasonable period

---

64 See more: 'Force majeure certificates' issued by the Russian Chamber of Commerce and Industry https://conflictoflaws.net/2020/force-majeure-certificates-by-the-russian-chamber-of-commerce-and-industry/?print=pdf accessed 10 June 2020.

when the force majeure circumstances prevent the performance of the party's obligations.[65]

Thus, unless otherwise provided by law, in order to be exempt from liability for non-performance of its obligations, a party must prove:[66]

(a) the presence and duration of force majeure;
(b) the presence of a causal relationship between the force majeure circumstances and the inability or delay in the performance of obligations;
(c) non-involvement of the party in the creation of force majeure circumstances;
(d) good faith acceptance by the party of reasonably expected measures to prevent (minimise) possible risks.

The highest court offers a very cautious approach to the possibility of recognising an epidemiological situation, restrictive measures or a regime of self-isolation as grounds for changing or terminating a contract due to a significant change of position (*clausula rebus sic stantibus*). Unless otherwise provided by the contract and does not arise from its essence, such circumstances that the parties could not foresee upon conclusion of the contract, can be used as a basis for change and termination of contract only in case, if in the presence of foresight of these circumstances the contract would not be concluded or would be concluded on much different terms.[67]

In connection with the discussion of the possibility of applying Article 417 CC RF "Termination of an obligation based on an act of a State authority or local self-government body" in the context of the epidemic, the question arose: did the introduction of prohibitive measures taken by State authorities make it impossible to perform civil law obligations?

The establishment of prohibitions or restrictions by an act of a State authority or local self-government body is a special case of legal impossibility to perform an obligation.[68] To apply this rule, you must have the following qualifying criteria:[69]

- inability to perform the obligation by any business entity;
- permanent impossibility of performance;
- independence of the circumstances from the actions of participants in the binding relationship.

---

65 Para 9 of the Ruling of the Plenum no 7.

66 Answer to question 7 of the Overview no 1.

67 Para 1 Article 451 CC RF; Answer to question 8 of the Overview no 1.

68 Clause 1, Article 11 The Constitution of the Russian Federation (was adopted at national voting on 12 December 1993) http://www.constitution.ru/en/10003000-01.htm accessed 10 June 2020: "State power in the Russian Federation is exercised by the President of the Russian Federation, the Federal Assembly (the Federation Council and State Duma), the Government of the Russian Federation, courts of the Russian Federation".

69 Article 416 CC RF "Termination of an obligation by impossibility of performance"; in accordance with the position of the Judicial panel on economic disputes of the Supreme

The Supreme court of the Russian Federation in relation to the coronavirus situation clarified that in order to be released from liability for non-performance of its obligations, a party must prove:

- presence and duration of force majeure circumstances;
- the presence of a cause-and-effect relationship between the force majeure circumstances and the impossibility or delay in the performance of obligations;
- non-involvement of the party in the creation of force majeure circumstances;
- bona fide acceptance by the party of reasonably expected measures to prevent (minimise) possible risks.[70]

At first glance, the prohibitive measures of State authorities made it impossible to perform obligations. For example, the Russian government has banned the export of medical masks, bandages, shoe covers, disposable overalls, chemical protection suits, etc.[71]

However, these measures are usually temporary rather than permanent, which in most cases blocks for the Russian courts the possibility of applying Articles 416 and 417 CC RF.[72]

4.4. CERTAIN TYPES OF CONTRACTS

The administrative restrictions imposed in connection with the pandemic have significantly affected certain types of civil legal relations, namely, the relations between the debtor and the creditor under a credit agreement, the lessor and the lessee of real estate, etc.

If the principle of *pacta sunt servanda* is firmly followed, ordinary citizens and small businesses operating in many sectors of the economy will be brought

---

Court of the Russian Federation, formulated in its Ruling no. 305-ES16-14210 of 30 January 2017 https://www.garant.ru/products/ipo/prime/doc/71501720/ accessed 10 June 2020, the impossibility of performing an obligation occurs only if the obligation cannot be objectively performed by any person; cf: Alexandr P. Sergeev (ed), *Commentary to the civil code of the Russian Federation. Part one (article-by-article): educational-practical comment* (2nd edn rev. and add., Prospect. 2018) 1154–1155 (in Russian); Efim A. Pavlodsky, *An accident and force majeure in civil law* (Legal literature 1978) 75–76, 85 (in Russian).

70 Answer to question 7 of Overview no 1.

71 Annex to the Government Decree 2 March 2020 no 223 'On introduction of temporary ban on the export of certain products from the Russian Federation'. "The list of products in respect of which introduced a temporary ban on the export from the Russian Federation". https://www.garant.ru/products/ipo/prime/doc/73598944/ accessed 10 June 2020.

72 At the time of writing this contribution, we have not found any cases of application by courts of Articles 416 and 417 CC RF in connection with the adoption of restrictive measures. Cf https://sudact.ru/ accessed 10 June 2020.

to the brink of ruin and bankruptcy, which in turn will inevitably lead to increased social tension. In this regard, the State authorities decided to mitigate the economic losses of business by interfering in the contractual relations of the parties in order to distribute the negative economic consequences of anti-coronavirus measures fairly.

The list of sectors of the Russian economy that are most affected by the deterioration of the economic situation as a result of the spread of a new coronavirus infection is defined by statutory law and includes:[73]

1. Air transportation, airport activities, road transport.
2. Culture, leisure and entertainment.
3. Physical culture and sports.
4. Activities of travel agencies and other organisations that provide services in the field of tourism.
5. Hotel business.
6. Public catering.
7. The activities of the organisations of additional education, private educational institutions.
8. Organisation of conferences and exhibitions.
9. Activities to provide household services to the population (repairs, laundry, dry cleaning, hairdressing and beauty salons).
10. Activities in the field of health.
11. Retail sale of non-food products.
12. Mass media and print production.

4.5. LOAN AGREEMENTS

Russian citizens often resort to borrowing money to buy housing, cars, travel services, etc. The Russian population is highly indebted.[74] Restrictive measures aimed at countering the spread of COVID-19 have led to an increase in unemployment and a significant drop in the income of citizens. In this regard, Russian legislation has established the specifics of the execution of obligations by a citizen-debtor under credit agreements and loan agreements.

First of all, the statutory law changed the terms of the loan agreement for a citizen-debtor, which consists of suspending the performance of the borrower's obligations (grace period) for the period specified in the borrower's request, but not more than six months, provided that the request is made no later than

73 Governmental Decree N 434.

74 The Central Bank expects an increase in the debt burden of Russians in 2020 https://tass.ru/ekonomika/7528485 accessed 10 June 2020.

30 September 2020.[75] This right to change the terms of the loan agreement is granted to the borrower subject to the following conditions: the amount of the loan does not exceed the maximum amount of credit established for such cases by the Government of the Russian Federation (for consumer loans of citizens – 250 thousand roubles, a loan to buy a car – 600 thousand roubles, mortgage loans not related to business activities – 1.5 million roubles); a decrease in the borrower's income (the total income of all co-borrowers) for the month preceding the borrower's request to the lender by more than 30% compared to the average income for 2019; at the time of the request, there is no grace period.[76] The meaning of the last restriction is that the citizen has already used such a benefit in the framework of consumer credit relations.

However, regardless of whether or not there are grounds for granting a grace period and whether the borrower has exercised his/her right to change the terms of the loan agreement (loan agreement) in accordance with this statutory law, the borrower may be released from liability for non-performance or improper performance of the obligation, if the violation of the obligation occurred through no fault of his/her own, including if the performance was impossible due to extraordinary and unavoidable circumstances under these conditions, including those related to the established restrictive measures (for example, if the borrower could not use the online payment system, or could not make payments in the usual way).[77]

4.6. LEASE AGREEMENT

Significant problems also arose in connection with the execution of the lease agreement for real estate by the lessee.[78] This type of lease agreement is usually concluded for a long term. The lessee assumes to pay rent at the expense of the

75 Article 6 of Federal Law on amendments to the Federal law on the Central Bank of the Russian Federation (Bank of Russia) and certain legislative acts of the Russian Federation regarding the specifics of changing the terms of a credit agreement or loan agreement (Federal Law no 106-FZ of 3 April 2020) http://www.consultant.ru/document/cons_doc_LAW_349323/ accessed 10 June 2020.

76 Article 61-1 of Federal law on Consumer Credit (Loan). (Federal law no 353-FZ of 21 December 2013) http://www.consultant.ru/document/cons_doc_LAW_155986/ accessed 10 June 2020.

77 Article 401 CC RF; Answer to question 2 of the 'Overview on certain issues of judicial practice related to the application of legislation and measures to counter the spread of a new Coronavirus infection (COVID-19) on the territory of the Russian federation no 2 approved by the Presidium of the Supreme Court of the Russian Federation on 30 April 2020' (hereinafter, Overview no 2) http://www.vsrf.ru/documents/all/28882/ accessed 10 June 2020.

78 See more on the controversial issues of the subject: Alexander Zezekalo, 'State's Regulation of Commercial Lease in Russia under COVID-19 Pandemic – Aid or Antidote?' https://www.comparativecovidlaw.it/russia/ accessed 10 June 2020.

profit received by him/her from business activities related to the lease of real estate. Usually, as tenants are the owners of cafes, restaurants, hairdressers, etc., the public-law ban on their main activities had very negative consequences for small businesses, which was compounded by the obligation to pay rent for the use of real estate in the absence of the possibility of using it.

In this regard, the legislator introduced mandatory rules which changed the terms of lease agreements in order to improve the situation of the tenant. For example, in respect of real estate lease agreements concluded before the adoption in 2020 by the organ of State power of a constituent subject of the Russian Federation of the decision on introduction of high alert or emergency regime on the territory of this constituent subject of the Federation, within 30 days from the date of application of the tenant of the relevant immovable property, the lessor is obliged to conclude an additional agreement providing for the deferred payment of the rent provided for in 2020.[79]

The postponement is granted for a period up to 1 October 2020, starting from the date of introduction of a high-alert or emergency situation on the territory of a constituent subject of the Russian Federation, subject to the following conditions:

- rent arrears are payable no earlier than 1 January 2021 and no later than 1 January 2023 in stages no more than once a month, in equal payments, the amount of which does not exceed half of the monthly rent under the lease agreement;
- deferral is available for the duration of the alert or emergency regime on the territory of the constituent subject of the Russian Federation in the amount of rent for the relevant period and in the amount of 50% of the rent for the relevant period from the date of termination of the regime of increased readiness or emergency on the territory of the constituent subject of the Russian Federation until 1 October 2020.;
- fines, interest for using other people's money or other liability measures in connection with the failure of the lessee to comply with the procedure and terms of payment of rent (including in cases where such measures are provided for in the lease agreement) in connection with the delay are not applied.[80]

The very fact that the lessee operates in the sectors of the Russian economy that have been most affected by the deterioration of the situation as a result of the

---

79 Part 1 of Article 19 of Federal Law on amendments to certain legislative acts of the Russian federation on the prevention and liquidation of emergency situations (Federal Law no 98-FZ of 1 April 2020) http://www.consultant.ru/document/cons_doc_LAW_349080/ accessed 10 June 2020.

80 Item 3 of the Requirements for the Terms and Conditions for Deferred Payment of Rent Under Real Estate Lease Agreements approved by the Government of the Russian Federation no 439 of 3 April 2020 http://www.garant.ru/hotlaw/federal/1344202/ accessed 10 June 2020.

spread of a new coronavirus infection provides sufficient grounds for granting the lessee of real estate a deferred payment of rent. In this case, it is not necessary to establish the circumstances of the impossibility of using the leased property for its intended purpose.

However, if the lessor proves that a particular tenant has not actually suffered and is not likely to suffer in a deteriorating situation as a result of the spread of a new coronavirus infection, and his/her requests are a manifestation of deliberately unfair behaviour (for example, if he/she actually uses the rental object contrary to the established restrictive measures), the court, depending on the circumstances of the case and taking into account the nature and consequences of such behaviour, may refuse to protect the right belonging to the lessee in full or in part.[81]

4.7. CONCLUSION

Reviewing the changes that took place in Russian legislation and judicial practice under the influence of the pandemic, we can conclude that they did not affect the core structure of civil law. It copes well with these challenges through the tools developed during its centuries-long development.

---

81 Answer to question 4 of the Overview no 2.

THE IMPACT OF COVID-19 IN THE PORTUGUESE LEGAL SYSTEM

A Private Law Perspective through the Principle of Good Faith

António Menezes Cordeiro and A. Barreto Menezes Cordeiro*

The COVID-19 pandemic led, in Portugal, to the publication of 250 exceptional laws. A number of principles may be extracted from these: (1) efficiency; (2) preservation of the status quo; (3) crystallisation of risk; (4) socialised damages. These principles operate in conjunction with the fundamental values of the system, notably those of good faith (bona fides) and related legal institutions: culpa in contrahendo, *abuse of rights, change of circumstances and complexity of obligations.*

* Both authors, University of Lisbon. This contribution relates to the pandemic situation and the state of legal science on 31 May 2020.

1. COVID-19 AND PORTUGAL

On 11 March 2020, the World Health Organization (WHO) declared an outbreak of acute respiratory disease, caused by the SARS-COV-2 coronavirus, to be a pandemic.[1] The disease itself has been known as COVID-19: an acronym from *coronavirus disease 2019*, the date of its identification.

In Portugal (11 million inhabitants), the first case was detected on 2 March 2020, imported from Italy. The first death occurred on the 17 March. On 31 March, there were 7,443 cases of infection and 160 deaths; on 30 April, 25,045 cases and 989 deaths; on 30 May, 32,203 cases and 1,396 deaths.[2] Compared to its most immediate neighbours, such as Spain (47 million inhabitants), where cases totalled 240,000 and deaths 30,000,[3] Portugal's situation was favourable, although the evolution of the disease in Lisbon raises cause for concern. In any case, economically, the consequences have paralleled those of other countries. Experts predicted a drop in GDP, in 2020, of between 5% and 12%: a massive reduction, with variables that change from day to day.[4]

2. SPECIAL LEGISLATION

As of early March 2020, successive pieces of legislation were published to address the COVID-19 crisis: some dealt with specific situations (e.g. credit moratoria), whilst others were more wide-ranging (e.g. the declaration of the state of emergency). We have counted: 73 in March, 122 in April and 69 in May, from orders to laws passed by Parliament, totalling 264, not counting measures adopted in the autonomous regions (Azores and Madeira) or by local authorities.[5] This legislation contains: (1) the declaration and extension of the situation of calamity; (2) the declaration and extension of the state of emergency; (3) measures relating to prevention, containment, mitigation and treatment of epidemiological infection by COVID-19; (4) measures to support the sustainability of the economy and businesses; (5) specific measures: (a) water and sanitation; (b) agriculture and fisheries; (c) tenancies; (d) banking;

---

1 https://www.who.int/dg/speeches/detail/who-director-general-s-opening-remarks-at-the-media-briefing-on-covid-19---11-march-2020 accessed 31 May 2020.

2 https://covid19.min-saude.pt/relatorio-de-situacao/ accessed 31 May 2020: information updated on a daily basis.

3 https://www.mscbs.gob.es/profesionales/saludPublica/ccayes/alertasActual/nCov-China/situacionActual.htm accessed 31 May 2020: information updated on a daily basis.

4 https://www.ecb.europa.eu/pub/economic-bulletin/focus/2020/html/ecb.ebbox202003_01~767f86ae95.en.html accessed 31 May 2020.

5 In this contribution we only intend to analyse national legislation.

(e) camping; (f) science and innovation; (g) trade and industry; (h) electronic communications; (i) culture; (j) employment; (k) civil protection; (l) transport; (m) tourism; (6) measures that place restrictions on economic activities; (7) measures relating to mobility and transport; (8) measures relating to the health and protection of families; (9) measures connected to public services; (10) exceptional publication of acts; (11) civil requisition; and (12) measures approved by the autonomous regions.

3. GENERAL LEGAL INSTITUTIONS

Portuguese law belongs to the Romano-Germanic family and has been significantly influenced by German law.[6] The Civil Code of 1966 lays down general legal institutions (instituto jurídico, instituto giuridico, Rechtsinstitut) which, with the help of legal science, can provide a just framework for some of the problems brought about by COVID-19. These legal institutions are especially required in fields not covered by exceptional rules. Their number includes *culpa in contrahendo* (Art 227), abuse of rights (Art 334), change of circumstances (Art 437), good faith in the performance of contracts (Art 762/2) and rules on supervening impossibility (Arts 790 to 797, all of the Civil Code), among others.[7] Various areas, such as employment law, also provide general legal institutions able to address the consequences of COVID-19.

4. THE PRINCIPLES PRESENT IN EXCEPTIONAL LAWS

We have isolated four principles from an analysis and identification of the common purposes of this body of legislation: (1) efficiency; (2) preservation of the status quo; (3) crystallisation of risk; (4) socialised damages.

4.1. PRINCIPLE OF EFFICIENCY

The COVID-19 pandemic made it necessary to reinforce the public services directly involved in fighting the disease. The National Health Service was

6 Marta Santos Silva, *The Draft Common Frame of Reference as a "Toolbox" for Domestic Courts: A Solution to the Pure Economic Loss Problem from a Comparative Perspective* (Springer 2017) 9 ff.

7 Catarina Monteiro Pires (ed), *Crise contratual e perturbações da prestação: Anotação ao Código Civil (Artigos 227º, 321º, 330º, 335º, 432º a 436º, 437º, 438º, 762º, 790º a 795º, 801º a 803º, 813º a 816º)* (AAFDL 2020).

provided with additional material and human resources, and more flexible procedures were introduced for the acquisition of the necessary equipment, with public funds.[8] This expansion was extended to connected areas, most notably the security forces. With all the contingencies that always occur on the ground, this was successful. Efficiency may be noted in several other areas, in particular in education. Because the epidemic prevented the continuation of classroom teaching, steps were taken to continue the academic year through telematic means: exceptionally, classes and exams were taken online. In higher education this was achieved with surprising success. The information available actually points to an increase in learning, as shown by the average scores of the exams. This is a lesson that will permit progress in future. On the high street, efficiency was pursued through take-away services and home deliveries. At an early stage, when supplies of protective materials (masks, gloves, visors and disinfectants) collapsed, it was possible to obtain them directly from abroad, through major online retailers, in particular Amazon. The law made provisions for home deliveries, and a number of companies were able to provide this essential service (e.g. prescription drugs[9]). By establishing a principle of efficiency, it becomes possible, in the interpretation and application of legal provisions, to find the most appropriate ways of addressing and solving problems. This involved giving less weight to formalism, as expressly determined in explicit rules (e.g. the continued validity of expired identity documents) and as extended, through interpretation and supplementation, to other important situations. Here, the old idea of "functional interpretation" has reclaimed significant dogmatic scope.

4.2. PRINCIPLE OF THE PRESERVATION OF THE STATUS QUO

The principle of the preservation of the status quo involves: (1) lockdown measures; (2) employment protection measures; (3) measures to protect businesses.

(1) The first good to be considered is that of human life. The lockdown seeks to protect it, in the absence of clinical solutions. This involved prohibiting movement and access to public places, closing establishments and suspending festive, social, sporting and cultural activities. Connected to the lockdown, we have the protection of housing. This explains the measures on tenancies: the admissibility of late payment, suspension of evictions and extension of contracts.

---

8 Order nº 3301-E/2020, of 15 March.

9 Order nº 4270-C/2020, of 7 April.

(2) Lockdown and social distancing gave rise to a serious socio-economic problem, through a simultaneous assault on production and on demand. Seventeen per cent of all the businesses closed, temporary or permanently.[10] The law sought to protect employment: simplified lay-off (furlough) rules, restrictions on redundancies and limited aid to companies that preserved jobs as an effective form of pressure.
(3) Employment protection was built back-to-back with protection for businesses. Requiring businesses – countless micro and small enterprises – to close meant eliminating their turnover. To prohibit redundancies was unrealistic. Instead, the State provided indirect support, through a furlough scheme, and direct support, by reducing certain outgoings, in particular with regard to taxes. This was the most difficult area of protection to provide in practice, in view of the complications involved, then and now, in granting credit.

4.3. PRINCIPLE OF RISK CRYSTALLISATION

In law, the term "risk" refers to the eventuality of losing an advantage previously secured or failure to secure an advantage when there had been a legitimate expectation of doing so. The basic rule is that risk is borne by the sphere benefiting from the advantage that is lost or fails to materialise. Every human being runs the risk of sickness and death, the owner bears that of loss or deterioration of the thing, the creditor that of his/her claim being thwarted or of his/her debtor becoming insolvent. In different contracts, there are special rules that divide risk between the parties, and there is also a margin for discretion, provided this does not entail advance waiver of rights.[11] In the context created by COVID-19, the risk of countless instances of present or potential damage would have to be borne by the beneficiaries involved. Several legal institutions, such as that of the non-imputable supervening impossibility in bilateral contracts,[12] entail sharing the risk between both parties. However, in certain cases, the exceptional laws departed from this basic parameter.

In the case of tenancy, Law 4-C/2020, of 6 April, amended by Law 17/2020, of 29 May, introduced rules that, among other things: (a) prohibit termination of residential tenancies on grounds of non-payment of rentals falling due in

---

10 Instituto nacional de Estatísticas, *Síntese INE@Covid-19* (INE, 11 May 2020) https://www.ine.pt/xportal/xmain?xpid=INE&xpgid=ine_destaques&DESTAQUESdest_boui=433015116&DESTAQUESmodo=2&xlang=pt accessed 31 May 2020.

11 Portuguese Civil Code, Article 809.

12 Portuguese Civil Code, Article 795/1.

the months when the state of emergency was in effect and in the subsequent month;[13] (b) permit deferral of rental payments, for non-residential tenants, until 1 September 2020;[14] (c) prohibit termination, in those situations, in the event of non-payment of rentals.[15]

Law 1-A/2020, of 19 March, amended most recently by Law 16/2020, of 29 May, (d) suspends eviction and similar actions, when the tenant may be left in a situation of potential homelessness;[16] (e) suspends non-renewal of tenancies by landlords, until the cessation of the protection, containment, mitigation and treatment measures relating to the pandemic.[17] The risk represented by COVID-19 crystallises in the sphere of the landlord.

In employment, Decree-Law 10G/2020, of 26 March, prohibits, in certain circumstances, collective and individual redundancies.[18] The risk is crystallised in the employer.

In banking law, Decree-Law 10-J/2020, of 26 March, imposed a legal moratorium (*lato sensu*) in relation to a series of credits.[19] Although interest remained payable on those loans, to be paid at the end of the suspension period, this measure caused the risk of customer insolvency to be shouldered by the bank.

In cases where preservation of the status quo conflicts with property rights or with rational business management, the principle of risk crystallisation requires the risk of that eventuality to be borne by landlords, employers and bankers. In this last case, provision is made for certain forms of compensation.

4.4. PRINCIPLE OF SOCIALISED DAMAGES

The COVID-19 legislation provides for various forms of direct and indirect State aid. These range from measures to boost public services and strengthen social security to bank guarantees and tax facilities. Everything that involves public funds amounts to the burden of the pandemic being borne by taxpayers. In this sense, we may speak of "socialisation of damages". The State and political and social actors must however bear in mind that only half the population pays direct taxes. The middle and upper middle class – who in Portugal enjoy very modest levels of income, in European terms – will bear the burden of the COVID-19 crisis: as happened in 2009/2014.[20]

---

13 Law 4-C/2020, of 6 April, Article 4.

14 Law 4-C/2020, of 6 April, Article 8.

15 Law 4-C/2020, of 6 April, Article 9.

16 Law 16/2020, of 29 May, Article 6-A/6, *c*).

17 Law 16/2020, of 29 May, Article 8, *a*).

18 Decree-Law 10G/2020, of 26 March, Article 13.

19 Decree-Law 10-J/2020, of 26 March, Articles 4 and 5.

20 Eurostat, *Mean and median income by household type – EU-Silc and ECHP surveys* https://appsso.eurostat.ec.europa.eu/nui/show.do?dataset=ilc_di04&lang=en accessed 25 September 2020.

5. RECOURSE TO GENERAL PRINCIPLES

5.1. BASIC CONCEPTS

The COVID-19 legislation and the broad principles that legal science is able to extract from it belong to the legal system. The situation remains highly unstable and will give rise to further legislative measures. It is not to be expected that they will depart, fundamentally, from those already adopted. We will probably see certain time limits being extended and increased employment protections. There is a likely pitfall: if not accompanied by effective support for businesses, this protection will be artificial and short-lived. The various COVID-19 measures and the principles deriving from them must now be conciliated with the fundamental values of the legal system. Good faith (*bona fides*) will play its part here: to each specific case it will bring application of the fundamental values of the system. Good faith operates through mediating principles, through which it is not exhausted. These are the principle of protection of legitimate expectations and the principle of the primacy of the underlying material content.[21]

The protection of legitimate expectations safeguards a person: (1) who is placed in a position of a reasonable belief in a given eventuality, present or future; (2) who has grounds for such expectation; (3) who, on that basis, makes an investment reflecting that expectation, i.e. expenditure or allocation of resources which cannot be restored without damage; (4) where that expectation is imputable to a person who, thereafter, must bear the consequences he/she suffers.[22,23]

The primacy of underlying material content reminds us that the law deals with real evaluations and settlements of interests: not with mere rituals or empty formalities. The primacy of material content requires us, in each specific case, to search for, locate and apply the relevant evaluations.[24] We should recall that, however simple the situations appear, it is the system as a whole that must apply in each of them. In addition to its individual application, good faith is especially embodied in four crucial legal institutions: *culpa in contrahendo*, abuse of rights, change of circumstances and complexity of contractual obligation. Let us see how these operate in the scenario of COVID-19. Through the principles enunciated below (efficiency, preservation of the status quo, crystallisation of risk and socialisation of damages), this scenario will offer scope for the protection of legitimate expectations and the primacy of the underlying material content.

---

21 António Menezes Cordeiro, *Tratado de Direito civil*, vol 1 (4th edn, Almedina 2014) 969 ff.

22 António Menezes Cordeiro, *Tratado de Direito civil*, vol 1 (4th edn, Almedina 2014) 969.

23 These four elements are generally accepted by the Portuguese Courts: STJ 19-May-2020, ECLI:PT:STJ:2020:2467.13.8TBCSC.L1.S1; STJ 9-Mar-2019, ECLI:PT:STJ:2019: 299/16.0T8VIS.C1.S1; STJ 12-Feb-2009, ECLI:PT:STJ:2009:08A4069.

24 António Menezes Cordeiro, *Tratado de Direito civil*, vol 1 (4th edn, Almedina 2014) 975.

5.2. *CULPA IN CONTRAHENDO*

Rooted in Article 227 of the Civil Code, *culpa in contrahendo* tells us that, in situations where a contract is in view, i.e. where the prospect exists of conclusion, if only potentially, of a legal transaction, the parties are subject to duties of security, loyalty and information.[25] Duties of security are intended to protect the person and financial interests of those involved, those of loyalty prohibit harmful opportunistic conduct, such as breach of secrecy or unacceptable competition, and duties of information protect the persons involved and their legitimate expectations, so that contracts are concluded on an informed and useful basis.[26]

In the field of COVID-19 law, *culpa in contrahendo* is particularly relevant in the domain of banking. Banks are required to inform their customers on their prospects for obtaining credit, responding promptly and truthfully to applications for loans. Pure silence (in some cases, of weeks or months), when contradictory to advertising, and also formal approval of operations that the banks later declare to be unfeasible, or dilatoriness in responding to applications for loans, will all be particularly inconsistent with good faith.[27]

5.3. ABUSE OF RIGHTS

As already mentioned, COVID-19 law is highly functional in inspiration. It stands not for itself, but rather for the aims it pursues. The legal positions it confers must be subject especially to the scrutiny of good faith, in order to prevent abuse of rights. We should recall that "abuse of rights" is the traditional expression referring to the inadmissible exercise of legal positions. Strictly speaking, it involves neither "abuse" nor "rights". Abuse of rights is seen in types of conduct that are inadmissible in the light of the basic values of the legal system. Foremost among these are *venire contra factum proprium*, *tu quoque* and imbalance in exercise: these are supported by abundant case law on both sides of the Atlantic.[28]

In a scenario of COVID-19, we will have abuse of rights, through *venire contra factum proprium*, for example, on the part of a subject who gives an assurance that he/she will not exercise certain exceptional rights, and later does so, causing damage, or of a banker who approves a given operation, giving written notice of this, and then goes back on his/her word, invoking credit facilities.

---

25 STJ 7-Nov.-2019, ECLI:PT:STJ:2019:153/13.8TCGMR.P1.S1.

26 António Menezes Cordeiro, *Tratado de Direito civil*, vol 2 (4th edn, Almedina 2014) 207 ff.

27 Miguel Pestana de Vasconcelos, 'Contratos de crédito bancário e COVID-19. O regime da moratória decorrente do Dec.-Lei n.º 10-J/2020' (2020) RDCom 1107.

28 António Menezes Cordeiro, *Tratado de Direito civil*, vol 5 (3rd edn, Almedina 2018) 271 ff.

The abusive exercise is deemed not to have occurred, and the "abuser" is obliged to respect his/her *factum proprium* as initially announced or, alternatively, to pay compensation for the damages corresponding to the frustrated expectations and increased expenditure.[29]

Tu quoque prohibits subjects from taking advantage of their own unlawful conduct.[30] This will be the case of someone who breaches a rule, without grounds or justification, and then, under the COVID-19 laws, invokes that same breach, in order to secure advantages. This would correspond to an extreme case of a company that intentionally defaults, in order to seek aid or subsidies.

Imbalance in exercise occurs when a subject causes great damage to another person, in order to achieve very minor advantages.[31] This will be the case, for instance, when a tenant blocks an eviction from premises for which he/she has an alternative, leaving the landlord homeless.

5.4. CHANGE OF CIRCUMSTANCES

This concept evolved over many years into that set out in Article 437 of the Civil Code, whereby a change of circumstances permits termination or modification of a contract, when: (1) the circumstances on which both parties based their intention to contract; (2) undergo an abnormal and unforeseeable change; (3) causing serious damage to one of them; (4) so that enforcement of the obligations accepted by that party is seriously inconsistent with good faith; and (5) the damage in question is not covered by the express rules on risk established in the contract.[32]

The COVID-19 crisis may be deemed to be a "major contractual basis",[33] in other words, as generating changes in a very large number of contracts, irrespective of type.[34] *A priori*, the requirements for change of circumstances are met in a great many contracts: the parties' shared basis for contracting, the anomalous and unforeseeable supervening circumstances, the serious

---

29 STJ 20-Nov.-1998, ECLI:PT:STJ:2019:97A928; Paulo Mota Pinto, 'Sobre a proibição do comportamento contaditório (venire contra factum proprium) no Direito civil' (2003) BFD, 269–322.

30 RPt 16-Jun.-2014, ECLI:PT:RPT:2004:6260/11.4TBMAI.PT.

31 STJ 28-Nov.-2002, ECLI:PT:STJ:02B3436.

32 Mariana Fontes da Costa, *Da alteração superveniente das circunstâncias: em especial à luz dos contratos bilateralmente comerciais* (2019).

33 Gerhard Kegel, 'Empfiehlt es sich, den Einfluß grundlegender Veränderungen des Wirtschaftslebens auf Verträge gesetzlich zu regeln und in welchem Sinn? (Geschäftsgrundlage, Vertragshilfe, Leistungsverweigerungsrecht)' Gutachten für den 40. Deutschen Juristentag, I (1953) 135.

34 RLx 14-Jun.-2012, ECLI:PT:STJ:876/12.9tTBBNV-A.L1.S1.

damage, the inconsistency with good faith when the contract is enforced, as if nothing had happened, and eventualities outside the specific provisions on risk. However, there is an obstacle: in many contracts, both parties are affected by the crisis. What is more, the party against whom Article 437 is invoked, may suffer extraordinary damage as a result. This matter requires careful study. What we can say is that, in the months ahead, Article 437 will be invoked on a daily basis, whenever attempts are made to enforce contracts.[35]

Intensive use of change of circumstances will foreseeably make it possible to perfect certain aspects of how it works. In particular, the need for it to be invoked extrajudicially, as already defended by the best doctrine,[36] will become clear (Arts 439 and 436/1): recourse to Article 437 on a large scale would remove the need, when it arises, for resolution through the courts.

5.5. INTRA-OBLIGATIONAL COMPLEXITY

Resulting from Article 762/2 of the Civil Code, obligational complexity explains that, in different obligations, principal renderings are complemented by accessory duties.[37] These can also be classified into duties of security, loyalty and information, and, in the obligational arena, assure the moral, physical and financial integrity of the parties, and the appropriateness of their conduct, so as not to exploit the contract for purposes for which it was not intended and to make full use of the good attributed by law: the rendering itself.

In a COVID-19 scenario, good faith in the enforcement of obligations entails respect for the function of credit positions addressed by the crisis law and special care for the fragility of some of those involved. For example, in teleworking, it will be contrary to good faith to demand excessive efforts or efforts which are rendered difficult by the failure to provide sufficient and appropriate materials. Or else, to oblige high-risk persons to make journeys which are clinically inadvisable.[38]

---

35 A. Barreto Menezes Cordeiro, 'Anotação ao artigo 437.º do CC' in Catarina Monteiro Pires (ed), *Crise contratual e perturbações da prestação: Anotação ao Código Civil (Artigos 227º, 321º, 330º, 335º, 432º a 436º, 437º, 438º, 762º, 790º a 795º, 801º a 803º, 813º a 816º)* (AAFDL 2020) 61 ff.

36 A. Barreto Menezes Cordeiro, 'Anotação ao artigo 437.º do CC' in Catarina Monteiro Pires (ed), *Crise contratual e perturbações da prestação: Anotação ao Código Civil (Artigos 227º, 321º, 330º, 335º, 432º a 436º, 437º, 438º, 762º, 790º a 795º, 801º a 803º, 813º a 816º)* (AAFDL 2020) 63.

37 António Menezes Cordeiro, *Tratado de Direito civil*, vol 6 (3rd ed, Almedina 2019) 516 ff.

38 Diogo Costa Gonçalves, 'Anotação ao artigo 762.º do CC' in Catarina Monteiro Pires (ed), *Crise contratual e perturbações da prestação: Anotação ao Código Civil (Artigos 227º, 321º, 330º, 335º, 432º a 436º, 437º, 438º, 762º, 790º a 795º, 801º a 803º, 813º a 816º)* (AAFDL 2020) 61 ff.

6. CONCLUSION

It is not foreseeable that the exceptional legislation making up COVID-19 law will be removed in the medium and long term. Everything points to it remaining in place, at least in part. Where these laws fail to keep pace with changes, or present lacunas or possible contradictions, the courts are able to intervene, drawing on the wealth of legal institutions provided by twenty-first-century law. The web of accessory duties, required by good faith in different scenarios, *in contrahendo* or in the enforcement of contracts, will give form to the increased social cohesion and solidarity that overcoming a major crisis requires. The "old" legal institutions, shaped by the crises that humankind has faced over the centuries, are fully able to offer just and predictable solutions. In relation to the COVID-19 crisis, as in other upheavals through which the Germano-Romanic system has lived, good faith, with its ability to dogmatise the system, operates as the natural law of our time: it gives a voice to legal science and its capacity, on the ground, to find harmonious and balanced solutions, even for problems beyond human control.

THE IMPACT OF THE PANDEMIC CRISIS ON THE RELATIONS BETWEEN THE STATE AND THE REGIONS IN ITALY

Giacomo Delledonne and Carlo Padula*

An analysis of the impact of the COVID-19 pandemic on the Italian constitutional order must focus on the relations between the State and the regions during the crisis. The pandemic crisis was a national one, although it affected Italian regions unequally. Furthermore, health care represents the core of regional policies: for this reason, regions almost inevitably came to the forefront during the crisis. This contribution investigates the regional response to the COVID-19 crisis against the background of the relations between the State and the regions. The contribution is divided into three parts. First, it focuses on the most important legal tool during the crisis, the Prime Minister's decrees, and their impact on the Italian regional model. Second, it focuses on how, in legal terms, the State and regional acts dealing with

* Dr Giacomo Delledonne is Postdoctoral Researcher in Comparative Public Law at Scuola Superiore Sant'Anna in Pisa. Professor Carlo Padula is Associate Professor in Constitutional Law at the University of Padua and Law Clerk at Italian Constitutional Court. This contribution is the result of joint reflections. However, sections 1, 3.2 and 4 have been written by Giacomo Delledonne, and sections 2 and 3.1 have been written by Carlo Padula. All webpages were accessed 15 June 2020. When this contribution was at proof stage, the Constitutional Court issued a major decision (judgment no 37/2021) in which it struck down some provisions of a law passed by the regional legislature of the Aosta Valley to contain the spread of COVID-19. The Court stated, among other things, that "international prophylaxis", over which the State has exclusive competence under Article 117(2) of the Constitution, covers "all measures aimed to tackle an ongoing pandemic or to prevent it".

COVID-19 can coexist. Third, it presents and discusses the measures adopted by the presidents of the regions for this purpose. In doing so, the contribution focuses on three cases: Lombardy, Veneto, and Campania.

1. INTRODUCTORY REMARKS

In many constitutional democracies, the COVID-19 crisis has triggered peculiar institutional reactions: the executives and their leaders have generally played a strong role, whereas parliaments have been called on to adapt to such a formidable challenge. The measures adopted by the Italian State institutions to face the pandemic crisis are discussed by Michele Massa in 'A General and Constitutional Outline of Italy's Efforts Against COVID-19' in this volume. In this contribution, we will focus on the interaction(s) between the State and the regions during the acute stage of the crisis.

Italian regions were among the key players in the handling of the COVID-19 crisis. This is due to several factors. First, the crisis hit the north of the country much more severely than the south. Although no region has been spared from the COVID-19 pandemic,[1] territories throughout the country have been unequally affected. Consequently, institutional reactions were marked by a dialectical relationship between the State Government and regional governments as well as between the regions themselves.[2] Second, regional competences relating to health protection have been a defining feature of the Italian model of regional State for decades. Under Article 117(3) of the Constitution, "health protection" is one of those matters in which "legislative powers are vested in the regions, except for the determination of the fundamental principles, which are laid down in state legislation".[3] As a matter of fact, health care represents the core of regional policies, and health expenditure is by far the largest item in regional budgets. Furthermore, law no 833/1978, establishing the National Healthcare Service (*Servizio sanitario nazionale*, SSN) entrusts the Minister of Health as well as regional and local governments with the power to adopt urgent bylaws (*ordinanze di carattere contingibile e urgente*) in the fields of hygiene and public health, depending on the extension of the affected area (Art 32). Third, the crisis has shown once again

---

1 As Di Cosimo and Menegus have put it, the main difference between the COVID-19 crisis and previous emergencies is that the former has not been a localised crisis: see Giovanni Di Cosimo and Giacomo Menegus, 'L'emergenza Coronavirus tra Stato e Regioni: alla ricerca della leale collaborazione' (2020) 7(Special Issue 1) BioLaw Journal – Rivista di BioDiritto 183, 185 rivista.biodiritto.org.

2 See Fulvio Cortese, 'Stato e Regioni alla prova del coronavirus' (2020) 48(1) le Regioni 3.

3 See detailed analysis by Donatella Morana, 'La tutela della salute fra competenze statali e regionali: indirizzi della giurisprudenza costituzionale e nuovi sviluppi normativi' (2018) 6(1) Osservatorio AIC 107, www.osservatorioaic.it.

that there is no strong consensus on what the Italian regional system stands for.[4] "Federalist" enthusiasm in the 2000s was followed by a strong anti-regional backlash in the wake of the economic and financial crisis. Since 2018, the debate has been marked by a strong push towards asymmetric regionalism, but the handling of the COVID-19 crisis may well prelude to another shift.

The aim of this contribution is to develop a critical analysis of the regional response to the COVID-19 crisis against the background of the relations between the State and the regions. In doing so, we will first focus on the most important legal tool in the handling of the crisis since March 2020, the Prime Minister's decrees, and its impact on the relations between the State and the regions (section 2). Second, we will look into how, in legal terms, the State and regional acts aiming to deal with COVID-19 can coexist. After that, we will present and discuss the measures adopted by the presidents of the regions for this purpose (section 3). In doing so, we will discuss and compare three cases: Lombardy, Veneto, and Campania. On the one hand, these three regions are all *ordinary regions*:[5] therefore, they have similar powers and tasks, including in the crucial area of health care. On the other hand, Lombardy and Veneto are located in the north of the country and their governments inevitably came to the forefront of public attention from the very beginning of the crisis: indeed, the first COVID-19 clusters in Italy were located in the provinces of Lodi (Lombardy) and Padua (Veneto). By 3 June 2020, more than two-thirds of the confirmed cases in Italy came from four regions in the north: Lombardy, Piedmont, Emilia-Romagna, and Veneto. Throughout the course of the pandemic crisis, institutional reactions in Lombardy and Veneto have been carefully scrutinised. Campania, in turn, is a southern region. Although the number of confirmed cases was considerably lower than in the north, there have been some small local clusters. Furthermore, the regional government of Campania has taken a very active, even creative stance: this has led to the adoption of a number of measures during the pandemic crisis.

2. THE PRIME MINISTER'S DECREES: A NEW TOOL FOR REACTING TO A HEALTH CRISIS?

As mentioned above, Article 32 of law no 833/1978 confirms that the regions have primary law-making powers regarding "public health".[6] The power to adopt urgent bylaws (*ordinanze*) in matters of public health is attributed to the

---

4 As argued by Alessandro Morelli and Annamaria Poggi, 'Le Regioni per differenziare, lo Stato per unire. A ciascuno il suo' (2020) 5(1) Diritti regionali, www.dirittiregionali.it.

5 As opposed to the five special regions provided with "special forms and conditions of autonomy" under Article 116(1) of the Constitution.

6 Article 32(2) of law no 833/1978 specifies that regional laws "lay down norms for the exercise of functions related to hygiene and public health".

Minister of Health, the presidents of the regions and the mayors, depending on the territorial scope of each *ordinanza*. This approach can also be found in Article 117 of legislative decree no 112/1998[7] as well as in Article 50(5) of legislative decree no 267/2000 (Consolidated Law on Local Government Authorities, *testo unico sugli enti locali*).

The Civil Protection Code (legislative decree no 1/2018) regulates the way to handle, among other occurrences, "emergencies of national significance".[8] According to Article 24 of the Civil Protection Code, a state of national emergency has to be agreed upon by the Council of Ministers. The legal tool for dealing with a state of national emergency are the *ordinanze di protezione civile* referred to in Article 25 of the Code: these acts are adopted by the Head of the Department for Civil Protection after seeking an agreement (*intesa*) with the affected regions, and aim to provide support to the population and to restore basic services and infrastructures. The *ordinanze* can derogate from the laws in force but must respect the general principle of the legal system (Art 25(1)).

Due to health risk related to COVID-19, on 31 January 2020, the Council of Ministers declared a state of national emergency with a duration of six months. In the framework of this state of national emergency, the Head of the Department for Civil Protection can adopt *ordinanze* "that derogate from all existing laws, with due regard for the general principles of the legal system".

However, the overall picture is somewhat more complex. When it comes to confronting major crises, the Italian Constitution provides for decrees-law, acts issued by the Government and with the same legal force as laws passed by Parliament. Under Article 77 of the Constitution (Const.), decrees-law have to be converted into law within 60 days of their publication in the Official Journal (*Gazzetta ufficiale*). However, Italian legislation also provides for these administrative *ordinanze*. If sub-State Government authorities fail to act in the event of a "grave danger for public safety and security", the State Government can act in their place (Art 120(2) Const.).

Having in mind the general framework of State, regional and local powers for tackling crises, decrees-law no 6/2020 and 19/2020, with the latter repealing the main provisions of the former, have gone a different way. The State has neither defined the measures needed to contain the infection in the decree-law itself nor resorted to *ordinanze* of the Minister of Health or the Head of the Department for Civil Protection:[9] rather, it has opted for a middle course.

---

7 Legislative decree no 112/1998 was part of a wider process of decentralisation and conferred State functions on regions and local government authorities.

8 See Article 7(1)(c) of the Code.

9 In fact, the picture is a bit more complex. The State reaction has been based on Prime Minister's decrees but also on *ordinanze* of the Minister of Health and *ordinanze* of the Head of the Department for Civil Protection. This was the case above all in the weeks before the adoption of decree-law no 6/2020 of 23 February 2020. See Andrea Cardone, 'Il baratro della necessità e la chimera della costituzionalizzazione: una lettura della crisi delle fonti

The State has resorted to decrees-law in order to define a framework for subsequent acts adopted in the form of Prime Minister's decrees (*decreti del Presidente del Consiglio dei ministri*, dPCm).[10] These decrees differ from "ordinary" *ordinanze* in that their status was regulated when the emergency had already started and, consequently, their content is "guided" by decrees-law. Moreover, *ordinanze* can derogate from legislative provisions but must respect the Constitution,[11] whereas quite different rules apply to these dPCm. The power to adopt the Prime Minister's decrees has been provided for with the specific purpose of restricting individual fundamental rights, with no derogation from legislative provisions explicitly attributed.

Articles 1(1) and 2 of decree-law no 6/2020, which have been repealed by now, were clearly unconstitutional: indeed, they contained a blanket authorisation (*delega in bianco*) that enabled unspecified "competent authorities" to adopt "all containment and management measures that are appropriate and proportionate to the evolution of the epidemiological situation". Consequently, these provisions clashed with the Constitution insofar as it states that fundamental rights have to be regulated, at least to some extent, by a law (*riserva di legge relativa*).[12]

Furthermore, the architecture of decree-law no 19/2020 gives rise to doubts: it leaves the Prime Minister a very wide choice from the point of view of both the content (30 "measures" are listed among which the Prime Minister can choose) and the territorial area.[13] It is true that the Prime Minister's decrees have a predetermined duration (maximum 30 days[14]) and must comply with the "principles of adequacy and proportionality to the risk"[15] (they can be challenged before the common judge), but these are constraints (temporariness and limits to the balancing carried out) that would also have affected decrees-law (for which the Constitutional Court is responsible for judicial review). Compared to the legislative act, free in its goal, the Prime Minister's decrees must pursue a

---

del sistema di protezione civile contro le battaglie di retroguardia' (2020) 13(Special Issue) Osservatorio sulle fonti 313.

10 As regards the relationship between decrees-law and *ordinanze di protezione civile*, see Andrea Cardone, 'Il baratro della necessità e la chimera della costituzionalizzazione: una lettura della crisi delle fonti del sistema di protezione civile contro le battaglie di retroguardia' (2020) 13(Special Issue) Osservatorio sulle fonti 313, at §2.

11 See, among others, judgments no 8/1956, 26/1961, 4/1977, 201/1987 and 127/1995 of the Italian Constitutional Court.

12 See judgment 115/2011 of the Constitutional Court; Massimo Luciani, 'Il sistema delle fonti del diritto alla prova dell'emergenza' (2020), www.rivistaaic.it, §2; Giovanni Di Cosimo, 'Tra decreti e decreti: l'importanza di usare lo strumento giusto' (2020), www.lacostituzione.info; Antonio D'Aloia, 'Poscritto. Costituzione ed emergenza: verso la fine del tunnel, con qualche speranza e (ancora) con qualche dubbio' (1/2020) BioLaw Journal §3; Chiara Tripodina, 'La Costituzione al tempo del coronavirus' (2020), www.costituzionalismo.it, §3.

13 See judgments 127/1995 and 201/1987 of the Constitutional Court.

14 Article 1(1) decree-law no 19/2020.

15 Article 1(2) decree-law no 19/2020.

purpose set by the decree-law[16] and this may suggest that they are an expression of administrative, not political, discretion.[17] The point is that the choice left to the Prime Minister is so wide that it seems to spill over into political evaluation. If a *riserva di legge relativa* is provided by the Constitution, decrees-law can hand over the enactment of implementing and detailed norms to non-legislative sources, but basic political decisions have to be made in the form of legislative norms, which have to supply the sub-legislative act with sufficient guidance. However, decrees-law no 6/2020 and 19/2020 entrust the Prime Minister with the power to decide which rights should be limited and in which parts of the national territory this should happen. For example, introducing a ban on leaving home in the north of Italy, with admitted exceptions justified by necessity and a Prime Minister's decree specifying the duration of the ban, what is meant by necessity and how it should be verified, is not the same thing as having a Prime Minister's decree deciding on whether and in which parts of the national territory to establish the ban. Basically, the inherently political power to strike a balance between fundamental rights and collective interest in public health (Art 32 Const.) has not been attributed to a constitutional organ that defines the general policy course (*indirizzo politico*) but, rather, to an organ that directs and coordinates the general policy orientations defined by the Council of Ministers in coordination with Parliament (Art 95 Const. and Arts 2 and 5 of law no 400/1988).

In Italy, an individual body has decided to limit many fundamental rights (even inviolable ones: for example, worship[18]) and the almost total lockdown, with serious social consequences and probable repercussions on the right to health itself:[19] there may be different opinions on the reasonableness of these measures[20] but it seems difficult to accept that they are posed by a single person's sub-legislative act. Moreover, Prime Minister's decrees, unlike decrees-law, are not issued by the President of the Republic, are not converted into law by Parliament, and, due to their non-legislative nature, cannot be challenged before the Constitutional Court.[21]

---

16 "To contain and contrast the health risks deriving from the spread of the COVID-19 virus, on specific parts of the national territory or, if necessary, on all of it": Article 1(1) decree-law no 19/2020.

17 See Marco Bignami, 'Chiacchiericcio sulle libertà costituzionali al tempo del coronavirus' (2020), www.questionegiustizia.it.

18 See, among others, judgment 254/2019 of the Italian Constitutional Court.

19 About risk and rights balancing see Giovanni Pitruzzella, 'La società globale del rischio e i limiti alle libertà costituzionali' (2020), www.giustiziainsieme.it, §3.

20 See, among others, Marilisa D'Amico, 'Emergenza, diritti, discriminazioni' (2020), www.gruppodipisa.it, §4.

21 Still, preventive legality control is performed by the Court of Auditors (*Corte dei conti*), which has to comply with shorter deadlines. Meanwhile, the acts under review are provisionally in force: see Article 2(4) of decree-law no 19/2020. About decree-law no 6/2020 and 19/2020 and dPCm see, among others, Ilenia Massa Pinto, 'La tremendissima lezione del Covid-19 (anche) ai giuristi' (2020), www.questionegiustizia.it, §2; Gaetano Azzariti, 'I limiti costituzionali della situazione d'emergenza provocata dal Covid-19' (2020), www.questionegiustizia.it;

The substantial fungibility between decree-law and the Prime Minister's decree is confirmed by the fact that the first Prime Minister's decree was adopted on 23 February 2020, i.e. on the same day of the enactment of decree-law no 6/2020. It seems clear, therefore, that the twisting of the decree-law (from an instrument of direct response to the emergency to a means of delegation[22]) was not necessary but it was a choice, probably depending on the innate uncertainty of the decree-law, subject to the necessary conversion by the Chambers. This factor seems to have had a greater weight in the choice, compared to the easier modifiability of the Prime Ministerial decree (in the period of greatest emergency, a decree-law was adopted every six days, therefore the need for a flexible discipline could be satisfied by the decrees-law) and to its extraneousness to the control of the President of the Republic and to the review of the Constitutional Court.

For the purposes of this contribution, which focuses on the relationship between regions and the State, the first question is: could the regions challenge decrees-law 6/2020 and 19/2020 before the Constitutional Court, although the flaws described above do not concern State-regions relations? The answer seems affirmative. As we will see, decrees-law 6/2020 and 19/2020 mainly concern regional matters (both from an objective point of view – trade, education, economic activities – and from a teleological point of view: public health) and the regions, in their own matters, can challenge State laws also for defects unrelated to the distribution of powers.[23]

Moreover, the norms in decrees-law no 6/2020 and 19/2020 give rise to some doubts regarding the nature of these dPCm. In fact, there is no strong consensus even on the nature of the *ordinanze di necessità e urgenza*: are they administrative acts in both form and substance? Do they contain norms and are administrative acts in form only?[24] Uncertainty prevails with respect to Prime Minister's decrees, which have contents equivalent to the possible (perhaps mandatory) contents of a decree-law.[25]

Antonio Ruggeri, 'Il coronavirus, la sofferta tenuta dell'assetto istituzionale e la crisi palese, ormai endemica, del sistema delle fonti' (2020), Consulta Online; Edoardo Raffiotta, 'Sulla legittimità dei provvedimenti del Governo a contrasto dell'emergenza virale da Coronavirus' (2020) BioLaw Journal.

22 See Ludovico Mazzarolli, 'Riserva di legge e principio di legalità in tempo di emergenza nazionale. Di un parlamentarismo che non regge e cede il passo a una sorta di presidenzialismo extra ordinem, con ovvio, conseguente strapotere delle pp.aa. La reiterata e prolungata violazione degli artt. 16, 70 ss., 77 Cost., per tacer d'altri' (2020), www.federalismi.it.

23 See, among others, Carlo Padula, 'Aggiornamenti in tema di ridondanza' (2019) le Regioni 738 ff.

24 See, among others, Giuseppe Morbidelli, 'Delle ordinanze libere a natura normativa' (2016) Dir. ammin. 33.; Giuseppe Manfredi, 'Potere di ordinanza (dir. amm.)' (2019), www.treccani.it; Edoardo Raffiotta, *Norme d'ordinanza* (2019) 237 ff.

25 See, among others, Giovanni Di Cosimo, 'Tra decreti e decreti: l'importanza di usare lo strumento giusto' (2020), www.lacostituzione.info; Beniamino Caravita, 'L'Italia ai tempi del coronavirus: rileggendo la Costituzione italiana' (2020), www.federalismi.it, §4; Giacomo D'Amico, *La libertà 'capovolta'. Circolazione e soggiorno nello Stato costituzionale* (2020), 169 and 176, Luca Dell'Atti – Giuseppe Naglieri, 'Le fonti della crisi. Fra esigenze unitarie e

In its case law, the Constitutional Court sticks to "substantive" criteria in order to ascertain the nature of legal acts. Even if a decree has not been adopted in the form provided for in Article 17 of law no 400/1988 with respect to regulations, it can be seen as a secondary source provided that it has the characteristics of a regulatory act (dictating general and abstract norms and innovating the legal system):

> Having in mind the distribution of this power [to adopt regulation] between the State and regions in Article 117 Const., based on objective criteria in which norms correspond to the subject matters mentioned there, it would be improper to rely on formal requisites, for instance its name or procedural non-compliance with the models of regulations provided for in general laws, to rule out that an act is a regulation. If that were the case, the constitutional distribution of competences could be eluded easily: secondary norms, surreptitiously disguised in another form, could be introduced in cases in which this is not allowed. (judgment no 278/2010, para. 16; see also judgment nos 141/2016, 274/2010, and 275/2011).

These doubts are quite relevant for the purpose of this contribution. The first question that should be answered is which legislative matters the measures contained in decrees-law no 6/2020 and 19/2020 should be ascribed to. The Italian Constitution enumerates matters in which the State has "exclusive legislative powers" (Art 117(2) Const.), matters in which there are concurring State and regional competences (Art 117(3) Const.), and specifies that "the regions have legislative powers in all subject matters that are not explicitly set aside for state legislation" (Art 117(4) Const.). However, the Constitution does not contain any criteria for "attributing" a norm to one of these subject matters. In this respect, the Constitutional Court has played a crucial role: its case law is based on a combination of the objective and teleologic criteria. In a number of cases, it is impossible to ascribe a norm to just one subject matter: for this reason, the Court has also elaborated the criteria of the prevalent subject matter and of concurring subject matters.

In material terms, the provisions of decree-law no 6/2020 show that partial or complete limitations on a number of fundamental rights were authorised: freedom of movement, freedom of assembly, right to education, religious freedom, freedom of economic initiative, and right to work, just to mention measures expressly referred to in Article 1 of decree-law no 6/2020. In spite of this, the main goals of all these measures seem to be "preventing the spread of COVID-19" (Art 1) and adopting "measures for containing and managing the emergency in order to prevent the spread of COVID-19" (Art 2): a public

garanzie costituzionali nel governo dell'emergenza da Covid-19' (2020) BioLaw Journal §2; Laura Fabiano, 'La catena della normativa emergenziale in risposta alle minacce di diffusione del Covid-19' (2020) BioLaw Journal §2.

health purpose, implementing Article 32 of the Constitution, which guarantees not only the individual right to health but also the collective interest in health. Therefore, the relevant field seems to be "health protection", in which concurring State and regional competences exist. Other matters, both concurring ("civil protection")[26] and exclusive ("international prophylaxis" and "safety",[27] referred to in Art 117(2)(q) and (h) Const.), are involved but they seem less relevant in this respect.

If the relevant subject matter falls within the concurring competences of the State and the regions, the Constitution stipulates that the State can act in two ways. First, the legislature may pass norms that determine the fundamental principles of the subject matter (Art 117(3) Const.). Second, State administrative authorities may issue administrative acts whenever administrative functions have to be exercised in a unified way: such is the peculiar meaning of the principle of subsidiarity under Article 118(1) Const.[28] In this event, the State legislature has the power to regulate the administrative functions at stake; however, the administrative act has to be adopted after seeking an agreement (*intesa*) with the affected region or the State-regions Conference.[29]

By virtue of Article 117(6) Const., in turn, State regulatory acts other than laws cannot be adopted: "Regulatory powers shall be vested in the State with respect to the subject matters of exclusive legislation, subject to any delegations of such powers to the Regions. Regulatory powers shall be vested in the Regions in all other subject matters".

According to this constitutional provision, the regional power to adopt detailed laws in the "concurring matters" is paralleled by a power to adopt regulations in the same matters. Although the Constitution said almost nothing about this before 2001, the Constitutional Court had already come to this conclusion. This had been recognised by Article 17(1) of law no 400/1988, which refers to regulations issued by the Government "in order to regulate ... the implementation and integration of laws and legislative decrees laying down fundamental principles, except for matters reserved for the regional legislatures". The prohibition for the State to adopt regulation in regional matters is well-founded: in concurring matters, the State can only lay down "fundamental

26 The state of national emergency was declared by a deliberation of the Council of Ministers on 31 January 2020, pursuant to Articles 7 and 24 of legislative decree no 1/2018 (Civil Protection Code). According to this deliberation, the necessary measures would be taken resorting to *ordinanze* of the Head of the Department of Civil Protection.

27 "Safety" should be understood not so much as crime prevention as the "protection of the public interest in the safety of people" (Constitutional Court, judgments no 21/2010 and 291/2019).

28 As mentioned above, Article 120(2) allows the State acting in place of the regions under specific circumstances (*potere sostitutivo*).

29 See, among others, judgment no 303/2003 of the Constitutional Court.

principles", which do not lend themselves to be "divided" into laws and regulations. However, Constitutional Court case law fluctuates over this.

Consequently, if the Prime Minister's decrees referred to in decrees-law no 6/2020 and 19/2020 are regulatory acts, the ensuing question is their compatibility with Article 117(6) Const. If they are administrative acts, they probably can be justified on the basis that COVID-19 has triggered a national emergency, which upholds a central intervention within the meaning of Article 118(1) Const.

However, the decrees-law should have required an agreement with the affected region or within the State-regions Conference (in case of general measures). This requirement would have been a consequence both of the constitutional principle of loyal cooperation and the case law of the Constitutional Court.[30] By contrast, the decrees-law only require advice from the Presidents of the affected regions or the President of the Regions Conference[31] (if the measure at stake affects the whole territory of Italy). By the way, the Civil Protection Code stipulates that an agreement with the regions is needed before declaring a state of national emergency (Art 24(1)) as well as before the adoption of *ordinanze di protezione civile* (Art 25(1)).[32]

Those who minimise the need for an *intesa* on the basis of the allegedly technical nature of the Prime Minister's decrees[33] are not entirely convincing. Prime Minister's decrees are grounded on advice from a Technical and Scientific Committee (see Art 2(1) of decree-law no 19/2020).[34] However, the provisions in the Prime Minister's decrees are also based on discretionary assessments and, even more importantly, on highly political judgments.

3. WHICH ROOM FOR REGIONAL *ORDINANZE*?

3.1. THE STATE LEGAL FRAMEWORK

Decrees-law no 6/2020 and 19/2020 explicitly specify room for manoeuvre of regional and local governments. Decree-law no 6/2020 stated that "pending the adoption of the Prime Minister's decrees … in case of extreme necessity and

---

30 See judgment 246/2019 of the Constitutional Court about the importance of the loyal cooperation in the field of civil protection.

31 It is clear that the President must also be the spokesman of the other presidents, especially when dPCm concerns the entire territory but "with different measures for the parts of the Republic": Fabio Cintioli, 'Sul regime del lockdown in Italia' (2020), www.federalismi.it, §6.

32 See Giovanni Di Cosimo and Giacomo Menegus, 'L'emergenza Coronavirus tra Stato e Regioni: alla ricerca della leale collaborazione' (2020) BioLaw Journal – Rivista di BioDiritto 7(Special Issue 1) 183, 185 rivista.biodiritto.org.

33 See, among others, judgments 284/2016 and 62/2013 of the Constitutional Court.

34 See, among others, Antonio Iannuzzi, 'Leggi "science driven" e Covid-19. Il rapporto tra politica e scienza nello stato di emergenza sanitaria' (2020) BioLaw Journal.

urgency the measures referred to in Articles 1 and 2 may be adopted" according to the norms illustrated above on the (regional and local) power to adopt *ordinanze* (Art 3(2)). Article 3(1) of decree-law no 19/2020 contains a similar norm, as it stipulates that, "pending the adoption of the Prime Minister's decrees referred to in Article 2(1), the regions, in case of specific situations of worsening health risk in their territories or parts thereof, can introduce measures more restrictive than those currently in force. These measures will stay in force until the adoption of the Prime Minister's decrees mentioned above. Among the measures referred to in Article 1(2), the regions can only act within the scope of their competences, with no possibility to interfere with productive activities and with activities of strategic importance for national economy". Moreover, "mayors cannot adopt urgent bylaws (*ordinanze contingibili e urgenti*) aimed to confront the emergency if they run counter to corresponding State and regional measures or regulate other objects than those referred to in section 1". Otherwise, these mayoral *ordinanze* have no legal effect (Art 3(2)).[35]

Consequently, in view of the national relevance of the health crisis, the State does not allow the adoption of regional measures, if not on an interim basis, if action is necessary and urgent in the absence of a Prime Minister's decree. In consideration of these norms, once a Prime Minister's decree has been adopted, regional *ordinanze*, regardless of whether they toughen or loosen limitations on fundamental rights, become unlawful,[36] except for new local situations, which the regions can face expecting the following Prime Minister's decree. A new structure of the relations between the State and the regions was outlined by the decree-law no 33/2020, which launched "phase 2".

Article 3 of decree-law no 19/2020 rules out all sorts of regional acts, even regional laws. Having in mind the constitutional distribution of competences, this norm can be seen as a fundamental principle in the area of health protection. According to the case law of the Constitutional Court, State norms that confer a power to adopt *ordinanze* in case of emergency on State organs are fundamental principles. Accordingly, these norms are binding on the regions, which are not allowed to enact norms, even in the form of ordinary law, inconsistent with the State *ordinanze* (see judgments no 82/2006, 284/2006, and 32/2012).

Doubts may arise in relation to specific issues not "covered" by the Prime Minister's decree. If the Prime Minister's decree has only adopted some of the measures referred to in the decree-law, can the regions take action? In all likelihood, the answer is negative: if a Prime Minister's decree has imposed only some of the limitations on fundamental rights mentioned in the decree-law, it

---

35 A similar norm was set by Article 35 of decree-law no 9/2020.

36 See Margherita Ramajoli, 'Governo, Regioni e Comuni: quale provvedimento prevale durante la ripartenza?' (2020), www.ilsole24ore.com, for whom decree-law no 19/2020 established a "hierarchy" between State dPCm and regional *ordinanze*.

has most likely *chosen* not to adopt the other measures. Accordingly, a divergent regional *ordinanza* would run counter to the decree-law,[37] except, as mentioned, in the case where a regional *ordinanza* addresses a situation that arose after the Prime Minister's decree (e.g. a cluster that broke out after the decree).

Against this background, there seems to be no room for autonomous regional measures, if not on an interim basis. In reality, as discussed in section 3.2, the regions have adopted quite many *ordinanze*, and the Government has generally avoided challenging them before administrative courts. Actually, Article 2(3) decree-law 19/2020 establishes a general safeguard clause for the acts already adopted, probably because the State-regions relations in the emergency were carried out with a collaborative method,[38] although legislative rules outline a hierarchical situation.

In fact, legal controversies concerned acts adopted either at the very beginning of the crisis or during the controversial transition to the so-called Stage Two (*fase due*) of its management. In particular, the State Government successfully challenged an *ordinanza* of the President of Marche regarding the closure of schools because of a lack of coordination with the corresponding State provisions.[39] At the beginning of May, an *ordinanza* issued by the President of Calabria tried to accelerate the re-opening of restaurants and cafés: this *ordinanza* was challenged before an administrative court and went on to be annulled.[40]

If, on the one hand, regional political autonomy has been severely limited during the fight against COVID-19, on the other hand expert and administrative decision-making have also played a significant role. In this vein, for instance, many comments have highlighted that crisis management has not been equally effective in Veneto and Lombardy. In Veneto, a much greater number of tests for SARS-CoV-2 were performed (also on asymptomatic persons, like the relatives and "acquaintances" of the sick), and a lower number of infected people have been hospitalised: this has allowed containing the spread of infection.

---

37 Differently, see Massimo Luciani, 'Il sistema delle fonti del diritto alla prova dell'emergenza' (2020), www.rivistaaic.it, 134, and Ludovico Mazzarolli, 'Sulle fonti del diritto in tempi di virus' (2020) Quaderni ammin. 22.

38 See, among others, Fulvio Cortese, 'Stato e Regioni alla prova del coronavirus' (2020) 48(1) le Regioni 3, at §2; Giovanni Di Cosimo and Giacomo Menegus, 'L'emergenza Coronavirus tra Stato e Regioni: alla ricerca della leale collaborazione' (2020) BioLaw Journal – Rivista di BioDiritto 7(Special Issue 1) 183, 185 rivista.biodiritto.org, §7; Luca Dell'Atti – Giuseppe Naglieri, 'Le fonti della crisi. Fra esigenze unitarie e garanzie costituzionali nel governo dell'emergenza da Covid-19' (2020) BioLaw Journal §2, §3.

39 See decree (*decreto*) no 56/2020 of the Regional Administrative Tribunal (TAR) of Marche. See also comments by Giovanni Di Cosimo and Giacomo Menegus, 'L'emergenza Coronavirus tra Stato e Regioni: alla ricerca della leale collaborazione' (2020) BioLaw Journal – Rivista di BioDiritto 7(Special Issue 1) 183, 185 rivista.biodiritto.org.

40 See judgment no 841/2020 of the Regional Administrative Tribunal of Calabria.

Since the very beginning of the crisis, in turn, Lombardy has ranked first in COVID-19-related infections and deaths. A number of issues have proved to be crucial for the health of regional residents: the number of protective devices supplied to doctors and citizens, the purchase of the necessary tools for performing tests, the decisions on whom to test and whom to hospitalise, the transfer of positive patients from one hospital to another, the capacity to expand intensive care units, the availability of reliable data on those infected, and the relevance of "territorial" medicine and public hygiene. To sum up, the Venetian government handled the crisis as if it were related to public health, and it tried above all to prevent infection from spreading over the regional territory. The Lombard administration, in turn, focused on hospitalisation and care of the sick.[41]

This point deserves closer scrutiny. The weakness of the regions has been highlighted for decades. On the one hand, regional governments have often been reluctant to exercise their legislative competences. On the other hand, in the exercise of their legislative powers the State Government and Parliament have overly interfered with regional competences. A long-standing claim is that the crucial component of regional autonomy is the financial regime, but Parliament has refrained from a timely and effective implementation of Article 119 Const. The COVID-19 crisis has shown that administrative decision making is of the greatest importance for citizens' lives. This applies also to technical choices that are related to the capacity of officials and experts to deliver "good administration". For regional autonomy to work and to be useful, an appropriate constitutional and legislative framework as well as efficient training and selection systems of political and administrative elites are needed.

3.2. A CLOSER LOOK AT THE REGIONAL *ORDINANZE*

In practical terms, the Italian response was based on a peculiar combination of centralisation and, to some extent, differentiation. Article 3(1) of decree-law no 6 of 23 February 2020 enabled the Prime Minister to adopt decrees (*decreti del Presidente del Consiglio dei ministri*, DPCM) to prevent the spread of COVID -19. These decrees were to be adopted upon the proposal of the Minister of Health,

---

41 See for instance the letter sent by the medical doctors of Lombardy to the regional Health Directorate (6 April 2020), at https://portale.fnomceo.it/fromceo-lombardia-nuova-lettera-indirizzata-ai-vertici-della-sanita-lombarda/; see also an interview with virologist Giorgio Palù (published 2 April 2020), at https://www.corriere.it/cronache/20_aprile_01/lombardia-non-ha-arginato-coronavirus-veneto-casi-gestiti-meglio-territorio-fbbfa2da-7448-11ea-b181-d5820c4838fa.shtml?refresh_ce-cp.; see also https://www.repubblica.it/salute/medicina-e-ricerca/2020/03/27/news/coronavirus_piu_controlli_sulla_popolazione_il_modello_veneto_per_combattere_il_virus-252479780/.

after consulting the competent ministers. Decree-law no 6/2020 also mentioned a *duty to consult* the presidents of the affected regions, in case of measures with a limited scope of application, or the President of the Conference of regional presidents, in case of measures applying to the whole national territory. As mentioned above, presidents of the regions and mayors were also enabled to act in between the adoption of the Prime Minister's decrees "in cases of extreme necessity and urgency" (Art 3(2) of decree-law no 6/2020). However, institutional practice shows that something different happened. Because of the evolving, unpredictable nature of the health crisis, some scholars argued that regional and local acts could be adopted *until the adoption of the final dPCm*.[42]

In the light of Article 3 of decree-law no 6/2020, in the three regions that are considered in this contribution the reaction to the crisis has mostly taken the form of bylaws issued by the presidents of each region (*ordinanze del Presidente della Giunta regionale*). The typical contents of these *ordinanze* can be listed as follows.[43]

1. Before the general lockdown started, some regional *ordinanze* contained significant precautionary measures. In this vein, as early as 24 February 2020 an *ordinanza* of the President of Campania recommended that the mayors of Campanian municipalities prevent mass gatherings.[44] In Campania, some economic activities, e.g. clubs, hairdresser salons and street markets, were suspended just before the beginning of the national lockdown.[45]
2. After the whole national territory was put under lockdown, regions were enabled to dictate measures stricter than those adopted by the State. The alleged goal of these regional *ordinanze* was to prevent gatherings of people: in order to meet it, the *ordinanze* strengthened restrictions on circulation within a certain distance from home, closed parks, limited bicycle circulation, and regulated the opening hours and accessibility of shops, including shopping malls.[46] In some cases, these *ordinanze*

---

42 See Giovanni Boggero, 'Le "more" dell'adozione dei DPCM sono "ghiotte" per le Regioni. Prime osservazioni sull'intreccio di poteri normativi tra Stato e Regioni in tema di Covid-19' (2020) 5(1) Diritti regionali 361, 362–363, www.dirittiregionali.it.

43 A detailed database of the regional measures in Campania, Lombardy and Veneto is available at www.osservatoriosullefonti.it (data collected by Vincenzo Casamassima, Jacopo Mazzuri, and Giacomo Menegus).

44 See O.P.G.R. Campania no 1/2020 and 2/2020.

45 See O.P.G.R. Campania no 7/2020 and 10/2020.

46 See O.P.G.R. Veneto no 33/2020. In its preamble, the *ordinanza* mentions irresponsible individual behaviour in the first weekend after the adoption of the Prime Minister's decree (DPCM) of 11 March 2020: such behaviour made it necessary to "adopt even stricter measures than those already enacted at the national and regional levels". See also O.P.G.R. Campania no 13/2020.

provided for criminal[47] or non-criminal pecuniary sanctions.[48] Special provisions applied to the public holidays of Easter, 25 April, and 1 May: these concerned, among other things, Holy Week celebrations, the opening hours of shops and the possibility to organise outdoor family gatherings.[49] These *ordinanze* generally contained a sunset clause that coincided with the sunset clause in the corresponding provisions of the Prime Minister's decrees, and were prorogued accordingly.[50]

3. After the national territory was put under lockdown, the President of Campania issued *ordinanze* establishing controls over those who came back to Campania. These *ordinanze* also imposed obligations on the companies in charge of transport services.[51] Specific measures applied to the islands in the Gulf of Naples.[52]
4. Regional *ordinanze* dictated specific norms regarding the meaning of the notion of "essential goods" defined by the Prime Minister's decree of 25 March 2020, for instance stationery and office supplies.[53]
5. In Campania, where the number of confirmed cases was relatively low, regional *ordinanze* introduced special regimes in order to prevent the emergence of local clusters. Basically, these *ordinanze* introduced prohibition to enter the territory of a specific municipality and to leave it.[54]
6. Regional *ordinanze* provided for a gradual relaxation of lockdown measures. Of course, such relaxation could only apply to those lockdown measures that had been enacted at the regional level. For instance, the obligation to circulate within a certain distance from home was eliminated.[55]

---

47 See O.P.G.R. Campania no 11/2020 (issued ahead of the general lockdown) and 15/2020. Scholars have interpreted these provisions as an example of a "cooperative model of determination of criminal offences", in which the State law-making authorities trust the regions to define some elements of a given criminal offence (Carlo Ruga Riva, 'La violazione delle ordinanze regionali e sindacali in materia di coronavirus: profili penali' (2020) 1(3) Sistema penale 231, 239).

48 See O.P.G.R. Lombardy no 514/2020; see also O.P.G.R. no 526/2020, which entrusted the regional General Directorate for Public Safety with the task of enforcing these sanctions.

49 See O.P.G.R. Veneto no 38/2020 and 40/2020, and O.P.G.R. Campania no 27/2020 and 30/2020.

50 See O.P.G.R. Lombardy no 521/2020 and 522/2020, O.P.G.R. Veneto no 37/2020, and O.P.G.R. Campania no 27/2020.

51 See O.P.G.R. Campania no 8/2020, 20/2020 and 21/2020. *Ordinanza* no 20/2020 also provided for criminal sanctions.

52 See O.P.G.R. Campania no 6/2020.

53 See Article 2 of O.P.G.R. Veneto no 38/2020.

54 See O.P.G.R. Campania no 17/2020 (Ariano Irpino), 18/2020 (Sala Consilina, Caggiano, Polla, and Atena Lucana), 22/2020 (Auletta), 26/2020 (Ariano Irpino, Sala Consilina, Polla, Caggiano, Atena Lucana, and Auletta), 28/2020 (Lauro), 29/2020 (Paolisi), 31/2020 (Lauro), 33/2020 (Ariano Irpino), 34/2020 (Paolisi), 35/2020 (Saviano), 36/2020 (Ariano Irpino), and 47/2020 (Letino). Before the beginning of the general lockdown, special measures had applied to the municipalities of Montano Antilia and Ceraso (O.P.G.R. Campania no 3/2020).

55 See O.P.G.R. Veneto no 40/2020.

The two-metre social distancing rule was replaced by one-metre social distancing.[56] Some retail activities could re-open. Many of these *ordinanze* were adopted in the second half of April 2020. A point that deserves mention is that even in this stage of the pandemic crisis the regions were sometimes slower than the State in removing restrictions: such was the case with bookshops and children's clothing stores in Veneto and Campania.[57] In turn, a Lombard *ordinanza* provided that the trade of books, stationery supplies and flowers could only take place in shopping malls.[58] Moreover, in Lombardy *ordinanze* specifically focused on street markets and fairs[59] and on sports activities.[60]

7. With an eye to the imminent launch of the dedicated app AllertaLOM, the President of Lombardy issued an *ordinanza* that allowed derogating, albeit in very broad terms, from existing norms in the field of data protection.[61]
8. Regional *ordinanze* addressed the specific needs of some regionally run services, e.g. regional public transport[62] and waste collection and treatment,[63] against the background of the COVID-19 crisis. In Lombardy and Campania, all the activities of regional administrative offices were suspended, except for fundamental services.[64] In so doing, these *ordinanze* defined basic standards of service provision that would be assured during the crisis and dictated precautionary measures. The latter included, among other things, the availability of sanitising equipment and face masks. These *ordinanze* generally contained sunset clauses and were prorogued before their effects expired.[65] Within this group, some *ordinanze* specifically addressed the circumstances and needs related to the gradual relaxation of the lockdown and the beginning of the so-called "Stage Two".[66]
9. From the second half of April, regions started adopting less restrictive measures than those contained in the Prime Minister's decrees, which was seen as problematic. In Veneto, regional residents could visit their second homes within the region.[67] Meanwhile, the Prime Minister's decree of 26 April 2020 had not eliminated such restrictions yet.

---

56 See O.P.G.R. Veneto no 42/2020.

57 See O.P.G.R. Veneto no 40/2020 and 42/2020, and O.P.G.R. Campania no 37/2020.

58 See O.P.G.R. Lombardy no 528/2020.

59 See O.P.G.R. Lombardy no 528/2020, 532/2020 and 537/2020.

60 See O.P.G.R. Lombardy no 541/2020. See also O.P.G.R. Campania no 42/2020 and 43/2020.

61 See O.P.G.R. Lombardy no 525/2020.

62 See O.P.G.R. Lombardy no 509/2020, 510/2020 and 538/2020; O.P.G.R. Veneto no 28/2020, 29/2020, 30/2020, and 39/2020; O.P.G.R. Campania no 14/2020.

63 See O.P.G.R. Lombardy no 520/2020; O.P.G.R. Veneto no 41/2020; O.P.G.R. Campania no 38/2020.

64 See O.P.G.R. Lombardy no 514/2020, 515/2020, and 517/2020; O.P.G.R. Campania no 19/2020.

65 See O.P.G.R. Veneto no 34/2020 and 36/2020; O.P.G.R. Campania no 24/2020.

66 See O.P.G.R. Veneto no 45/2020 and O.P.G.R. Campania no 40/2020.

67 See O.P.G.R. Veneto no 43/2020 and 44/2020.

10. In the run-up to the so-called "Stage Two", the President of Campania issued a new *ordinanza* with measures applying to those entering the regional territory.[68] The structure of this act was modelled after the structure of the corresponding *ordinanze* issued in March.

4. CONCLUDING REMARKS

In the preceding sections, we have summarised some peculiar aspects of the impact of the COVID-19 crisis on the relationship between the State and the regions in Italy. In doing so, we have highlighted several highly problematic issues. Pursuant to decrees-law no 6/2020 and 19/2020, a key role has been played by Prime Minister's decrees: these raise serious questions regarding the admissible limitations on fundamental rights, the involvement of the regions in State-centred decision-making processes, and respect of the distribution of legislative and administrative competencies entrenched in the Constitution. In pragmatic terms, the decision to resort to dPCm can possibly be justified bearing in mind the unprecedented nature of the crisis, which has affected the whole national territory and has impacted on the ability of the legislative to work.

From the vantage point of the relationship between the component units of the Republic (as defined in Article 114(1) Const.), the Italian approach is quite ambiguous. On the one hand, it is based on a strong centralisation of decision-making processes. As mentioned above, much of the institutional reaction was channelled through Prime Minister's decrees. These decrees were adopted after getting advice from the presidents of the affected regions or the President of the Regions Conference, depending on the extension of their scope of application. In procedural terms, this requirement is less demanding than the agreements (*intese*) between the State and the regions that are referred to in Articles 24(1) and 25(1) of the Civil Protection Code. Meanwhile, decrees-law no 6/2020 and 19/2020 not only entrusted the Prime Minister with extensive law-making power but also seemed to leave some room for autonomous regional law making. In principle, the scope for regional action seemed to be quite limited. In fact, however, the regions resorted massively to the power to adopt *ordinanze* "pending the adoption of the Prime Minister's decrees", and the State did generally refrain from challenging these *ordinanze* before the ordinary or administrative courts.[69] Consequently, the institutional reaction to the crisis was based on a peculiar mixture of centralisation and differentiation that contributed to making the Italian case quite peculiar in comparative perspective.[70]

---

68 See O.P.G.R. Campania no 41/2020 and 46/2020.

69 As noticed, among others, by Lorenzo Cuocolo, 'L'importanza delle autonomie per far fronte al Covid (e alle tendenze accentratrici' (2020) DPCE online 11(1) xv, xviii–xix.

70 See Lorenzo Cuocolo, 'L'importanza delle autonomie per far fronte al Covid (e alle tendenze accentratrici)' (2020) DPCE online 11(1) xv, xviii–xix.

For all its problematic aspects, the Italian reaction has been saluted by some scholars: in allowing for some kind of regional intervention, the legal instruments adopted by the State Government have enhanced one of the basic features of multi-level orders, namely, differentiation and limited experimentalism.[71] Such an approach should be welcomed due to the huge uncertainty on how to cope with COVID-19. As we have mentioned in section 3.1, differentiation has not been limited to the adoption of general norms in the form of *ordinanze* but has also extended to administrative decision-making.

The peculiar nature of the course of action followed by State and regional institutions during the pandemic crisis has been further emphasised by some of the arguments used by critics. One proposal for reform seems particularly telling. Some politicians relaunched the idea of having a "supremacy clause" entrenched in the Constitution to allow the State to take action in areas in which it does not possess exclusive competences in case of major crises. These proposals referred back to a provision in the draft constitutional amendment that was rejected in a referendum in December 2016.[72] However, critics have signalled that the constitutional framework currently in force provides for tools that enable the State to act in place of the regions under extraordinary circumstances. Among them, a last resort option is the *potere sostitutivo* regulated in Article 120(2) Const.[73] However, the State Government has not taken advantage of this tool designed for extraordinary circumstances during the crisis. In some respects, these proposals for reform seem to echo specific aspects of the apparently endless debate about constitutional reform in Italy. However, they also show that the appropriate role of the regions in a Republic that "recognises and promotes local autonomies" (Art 5 Const.) is far from being uncontroversial.

In sum, crisis management has been based on a number of contradictory strategies. It has relied on executive-centred law-making processes, raising significant constitutional doubts. Apparently, it has left little room for regional action. However, regions have been very active, and a kind of informal cooperation has developed, with judicial disputes between the State and the regions playing a marginal role. Still, the occasional creativity of regional presidents has not been free from the drawbacks of occasional inconsistency, with a need to reconcile local experimentalism and legal certainty.

---

71 See Enzo Balboni, 'Autonomie o centralismo contro il coronavirus' (2020) 40(2) Quaderni costituzionali 373.

72 See Stefania Parisi, 'Il sistema delle competenze e la clausola di supremazia: un "falso movimento"' (2015) 43(1) le Regioni 187; Graziella Romeo, 'The Italian Constitutional Reform of 2016: An "Exercise" of Change at the Crossroad between Constitutional Maintenance and Innovation' (2017) The Italian Law Journal, special issue, 31, 38–41.

73 See Valerio Onida, 'Perché le clausole di supremazia non servono' (Milan, 27 March 2020) Il Sole 24 Ore.

PART III

COMPENSATION FOR COVID-19 RELATED DAMAGE

TORT LAW AND THE CORONAVIRUS

Liability for Harm Caused by the COVID-19 Outbreak

Albert RUDA*

Although much attention has been paid to the impact of the COVID-19 outbreak on the existing contracts and businesses, the current crisis also poses plenty of questions from a tort law perspective. Even though the coronavirus as such may be deemed an instance of force majeure or impossibility for which no one should be held liable, it goes without saying that such a defence does not exclude liability of those persons who actually cause damage to others, in particular as regards public authorities which adopt measures to fight the crisis as such, or any person who infects another in a negligent manner, among other examples. The contribution explores some of the scenarios in which tort liability may arise as a result of the COVID-19 outbreak and subsequent measures. Unlike in other jurisdictions, where a specific statutory regimes on the protection against infections (as in Germany) or epidemics (as in Switzerland) exist, Spanish law basically faces the many challenges posed by the Corona pandemic with a general liability regime which seems rather ill-suited to that end. Therefore, the contribution analyses how those challenges can be tackled. Moreover, it analyses whether the "Principles for the COVID-19 Crisis", drafted by the European Law Institute, bring anything new in comparison.

1. INTRODUCTION

The COVID-19 outbreak has triggered an intense scholarly debate on the impact of the pandemic on existing contracts and businesses. Initially, attention was

* University of Girona. albert.ruda@udg.edu. Research Project no PID2019-104067RB-100.

paid to the protection of weak or vulnerable parties, to whether the crisis as such amounts to force majeure or impossibility, to its influence – or lack of it – on contracts which were pending performance, etc. However, the question as to whether the outbreak may lead to harms for which compensation may be sought *outside* of a contract seems to have attracted less attention. This is undoubtedly because, by definition, tort liability, as an extracontractual device or legal institute, *per definitionem* enters into play *ex post*, once damage has occurred – and, sometimes, when it is already too late to restore it. Liability issues typically come after crisis management, not before.

Since at the time of writing this contribution, the crisis is still evolving, it is probably too early to examine every single possible scenario in which tort liability may arise. Most notably, the coronavirus as such is still not fully understood from a medical or scientific perspective. Even its long-term effects are yet unknown. As infections keep occurring and the fight against the virus is prolonged, new instances of damage will appear in the near future. If anything, a defining feature of the coronavirus and the havoc it has triggered is the uncertainty it is surrounded by.[1] Therefore, liability issues may have to be examined bearing in mind that much knowledge and scientific understanding about the virus itself was – and still is – missing.

As will be shown in this contribution, such uncertainty may also have a huge impact on the claims which undoubtedly will be filed as a result of the outbreak and the measures adopted in its aftermath. Even though tort law as such may not be the best way to tackle the present situation, in Spain, in the legal system of which this contribution will mostly focus, several claims have already been filed before the courts to request liability being imposed because of damage allegedly caused by the mishandling of the crisis measures. Several judicial decisions have already been issued, and even though criminal liability has been primarily excluded, it remains to be seen if liability in tort could arise.

From a different perspective, which is the scholarly standpoint, the European Law Institute (hereafter ELI) has issued a set of "Principles for the COVID-19 Crisis" where liability is tackled on an explicit basis.[2] And although they fail to make any mention of whether liability may be based on contract or tort, it will be shown that they may be applicable to both. Therefore, the question may be asked whether such Principles bring anything new to existing solutions, in particular in contrast to Spanish law. To that regard, Section 2 below will examine the liability of private persons, in connection with whom the ELI Principles do

1 This is emphasised by José Esteve Pardo, 'Política y derecho en la incertidumbre' (*La Vanguardia*, 6 May 2020) https://www.lavanguardia.com/opinion/20200506/48992806587/politica-derecho-incertidumbre.html accessed 10 October 2020.

2 European Law Institute, 'ELI Principles for the Covid-19 Crisis' (2020) https://www.europeanlawinstitute.eu/fileadmin/user_upload/p_eli/Publications/ELI_Principles_for_the_COVID-19_Crisis.pdf accessed 1 July 2020.

indeed bring a noteworthy novelty. Nevertheless, as will be shown, the latter may be more apparent than real. Later on, Section 3 will focus on the liability of the public authorities – or, as they may also be called, Public Administrations, which is governed by its own statutory regime under Spanish law and with regard to which the ELI Principles deliberately refuse to introduce any innovation.

2. LIABILITY OF PRIVATE PERSONS

As has already been said, the kind of situations in which liability of private persons – either individuals or legal persons – may arise as a result of the COVID-19 outbreak are manifold. These include, but are not limited to, damage caused in the course of medical treatment; damage caused by negligent infection or contagion, for instance as a result of the violation of the official restrictions on mobility of the people; liability for the failure to take care of vulnerable persons, in particular the elderly; the negligent exposure of others to the risk of infection; damage caused by a defective product, whose defect precisely consists in failing to provide the safety against the risk of contagion; liability of Internet intermediaries because of the dissemination of incorrect or false information regarding the virus or the ensuing situation (so-called fake news), or even damage caused by nuisance or environmental perturbations. Even if this is a non-exhaustive list, as has been said, it is for obvious reasons not possible to go into depth in all these scenarios to analyse whether the conditions for liability to arise are met in all of them and what the consequences would be in every case. Hence, the following discussion will merely offer a general view of the tort law system, mostly from a Spanish perspective, and compare it with the ELI Principles.

Most notably, Spanish law lacks a statutory liability regime specifically tailored to tackle epidemics or pandemics. From this perspective, Spanish law departs from the model followed in other countries where a separate statutory regime exists. In particular, in Germany the legislature passed an Act on the protection against epidemics (*Infektionsschutzgesetz*) as early as 2001.[3] Among others, the Act contains provisions on "compensation in special cases" (paras 56–68). The language used is not one of liability (*Haftung*) or damage compensation (*Schadensersatz*) but merely compensation (*Entschädigung*). The general provision on the same starts from a scenario where a person has been prevented from carrying out their activity because he/she is considered a carrier, or a suspected infecting agent or ill person and must therefore be compensated for the loss of earnings (para 56.1). Such compensation may also be awarded

---

3 Gesetz zur Verhütung und Bekämpfung von Infektionskrankheiten beim Menschen (Infektionsschutzgesetz – IfSG) (20. Juli 2000) BGBl I S. 1045.

where the authority has had to adopt certain measures to fight the pandemic (para 65). As will be referred to below, such a regime has been duly updated and amended in the wake of the coronavirus outbreak.

In a similar vein, in Switzerland there has been a federal Act on the fight against transferable illnesses of the human being (or Epidemic Act) since 2012.[4] According to the same, the person who handles infectious agents or toxic products is under an obligation to adopt all necessary measures to prevent damage to persons from occurring (Art 25). As in Germany, those persons affected by measures adopted by the public authorities are also entitled to compensation (*Entschädigung*, para 63). A different provision lays down the duty to compensate the victim of damage resulting from vaccination (para 64). So-called satisfaction (*Genugtuung*) for non-pecuniary loss is capped at a maximum of CHF 70,000 (approx. EUR 65,000). However, the Swiss Epidemic Act does not provide for a liability rule applicable to the State in cases where the latter has to adopt measures to protect public health. This is further clarified in one of the official comments on the regulations passed by the Confederation to fight the COVID-19 outbreak, according to which Swiss law does not provide for a duty to compensate for damage derived from police measures towards the population. The regulations do not lay down such a duty either, for lack of statutory basis to do so.[5] As Swiss legal scholars point out, a consistent compensation system as regards the consequences of the pandemic is missing in that jurisdiction.[6] The same can be said with regard to compensation for the loss of earnings (*Erwerbausfall*) as a result of the measures adopted by the public authorities, according to the COVID-19 Act.[7]

Under Spanish law, as in many other countries, tort liability and criminal liability are decided separately. It is true that a feature of Spanish legal practice is that in many cases the criminal court also decides on the civil law issues – including compensation in tort –although both are provided for in separate sets of rules and independent from one another. This may be important because, as was mentioned in the Introduction, several criminal claims have already been

---

4 Bundesgesetz über die Bekämpfung übertragbarer Krankheiten des Menschen (Epidemiengesetz, EpG) vom 28 September 2012 (SR 818.101).

5 See Eidgenössisches Departement des Innem EDI. Bundesamt für Gesundheit BAG, 'Erläuterungen zur Verordnung vom 19. Juni 2020 über Massnah-men in der besonderen Lage zur Bekämpfung der COVID-19-Epide-mie (Covid-19-Verordnung besondere Lage; SR 818.101.26)' (2020) 10 https://www.bag.admin.ch/dam/bag/de/dokumente/mt/k-und-i/aktuelle-ausbrueche-pandemien/2019-nCoV/erlaeuterungen-besondere-lage.pdf.download.pdf/Erlaeuterungen_Covid-19-Verordnung_besondere_Lage.pdf accessed 1 July 2020.

6 See Tomas Poledna, Ralp Trümpler and Gregori Werder, 'Entschädigung von Gesundheitseinrichtungen zu Zeiten der Epidemie und Pandemie' (2020) Sondernummer ZSR 103, 111.

7 Federal Act (*Bundesgesetz*) über die gesetzlichen Grundlagen für Verordnungen des Bundesrates zur Bewältigung der Covid-19-Epidemie (Covid-19-Gesetz) vom 25 September 2020 (SR 818.102) Art 15.

filed in Spain, generally without any success and probably as part of a more general phenomenon of so-called lawfare against the Spanish government. To be more precise, an accusation of negligent homicide directed against the head of the director of the Centre of Coordination of Sanitary Alerts and Emergencies (CCAES) was dismissed by a court in Madrid.[8] In parallel, a different judge dismissed a criminal charge of administrative prevarication (*prevaricación*) for having failed to deny an authorisation to a massive demonstration in Madrid by the feminist movement on 8 March 2020.[9] Leaving these criminal accusations aside, claims in tort may be filed in the future, and some potential claimants – as will be shown below – have already expressed their readiness to do it.

In very general terms, then, it may be said that liability of private persons may arise, especially in those situations where official measures have been violated. As is well known, in the wake of the COVID-19 outbreak States have generally adopted a series of steps to curb the pandemic. In Spain, the Government decreed a state of alarm (*estado de alarma*) for the first time – affecting the whole country – on 14 March 14 2020[10] and later – affecting the region of Madrid only – on 9 October 2020.[11] Soon after, it adopted additional measures to face the economic and social impact of the virus outbreak.[12] As in other jurisdictions, the state of alarm is an exceptional situation, provided for in the Constitution (Art 116), in which the Government is allowed to impose several coercive measures, provided that they are necessary and proportionate to the situation. The fact that the World Health Organization (WHO) announced COVID-19 outbreak a pandemic and that the numbers of victims started to mount rather swiftly in the first quarter of 2020 has entailed that almost nobody has put the declaration of the state of alarm as such into question.[13]

---

8 See Rosalina Moreno, 'Inadmitida una querella contra Simón por homicidio imprudente por falta de competencia territorial' (Confilegal, 1 June 2020) https://confilegal.com/20200601-inadmitida-una-querella-contra-simon-por-homicidio-imprudente-por-falta-de-competencia-territorial/ accessed 18 June 2020.

9 See Isabel Vega et al., 'La juez del 8-M archiva la causa al no ver acreditado que el delegado del Gobierno prevaricase' (Abc.es, 15 June 2020) https://www.abc.es/espana/abci-juez-archiva-causa-no-acreditado-delegado-gobierno-prevaricase-202006121044_noticia.html/ accessed 18 June 2020.

10 Royal Decree (*Real Decreto*) 463/2020, of 14 March, por el que se declara el estado de alarma para la gestión de la situación de crisis sanitaria ocasionada por el Covid-19 (BOE no 67, 14.3.2020).

11 Royal Decree 900/2020, of 9 October, por el que se declara el estado de alarma para responder ante situaciones de especial riesgo por transmisión no controlada de infecciones causadas por el SARS-CoV-2 (BOE no 268, 9.10.2020).

12 Royal Statutory-Decree (*Real Decreto-Ley*) 8/2020, of 17 March, de medidas urgentes extraordinarias para hacer frente al impacto económico y social del Covid-19 (BOE no 73, 18.3.2020).

13 In public law scholarship see Miguel Ángel Presno Linera, 'Estado de alarma y sociedad del riesgo global' in Elena Atienza Macías and Juan F. Rodríguez Ayuso (eds), *Las respuestas del Derecho a las crisis de salud pública* (Dykinson 2020) 15, 23.

However, as time passes, it becomes clear that public authorities took probably too long to restrict travel and economic activities which made contagion more probable. Eventually, even the WHO was accused of having been too deferential to China and taken too much time to declare the pandemic.[14] A notorious case is the super-spreading event at a ski resort in Ischgl (Austria) in early March 2020,[15] but there are many other examples like international soccer matches in Bergamo (Italy) and Liverpool or other events at the national and local level. It now seems obvious that for many days in March 2020 mass gatherings were still allowed and that some governments – most notably in the UK – decided there was nothing to be done.[16] Although there seems to be still little experience on the contagion dangers of such super-spreader events, new research suggests that the health costs of one single such event may exceed several million dollars.[17] Nevertheless, claims against China, the WHO or other international organisms or entities are plagued with difficulties, because of State immunity and other doctrines which shield them.[18]

Although Spanish tort law does not as a rule require a statutory (or even a regulatory) violation as a condition for tort liability to exist, it goes without saying that in a situation like the one under comment, should someone ignore the restrictions imposed by the Government, the way towards compensation would be smoothed in a considerable way. In particular, the requirement of fault, which is the cornerstone of the general clause of liability under the Spanish Civil Code (Art 1902), would be easily met if someone left home and wandered through the streets with no apparent motive in spite of the official lockdown (popularly called *confinamiento* in Spanish), for instance. The same could be said of those patients who, after being informed they were infected, tried to escape the hospital and put others in danger – as happened in Girona, the city in which this contribution's author is based.[19] Where one knows or should reasonably have known that he/she was a carrier, a duty to prevent transmission of the virus can clearly be established.[20]

---

14 Among others see Lawrence Freedman, 'The WHO's failure on China could cost us dear' *New Statesman* (24–30 April 2020) 13.

15 See Selam Gebredikan et al., 'Ski, Party, Seed a Pandemic: The Travel Rules That Let Covid-19 Take Flight' *The New York Times* (30 September 2020) https://www.nytimes.com/2020/09/30/world/europe/ski-party-pandemic-travel-coronavirus.html accessed 10 October 2020.

16 Among many other critical voices, see Dominic Minghella, 'The 11 days that may have cost the UK' *New Statesman* (24–30 April 2020) 19.

17 See Dhaval M. Dave et al., 'The Contagion Externality Of A Superspreading Event:The Sturgis Motorcycle Rally And Covid-19' NBER Working Paper (2020) http://www.nber.org/papers/w27813 accessed 10 October 2020.

18 See Ronen Perry, 'Who Should Be Liable for the Covid-10 Outbreak', SSRN (2020) 4 et seq. https://papers.ssrn.com/sol3/papers.cfm?abstract_id=3697283, accessed 10 October 2020.

19 See La Vanguardia, 'Un paciente de coronavirus escapa del Hospital Josep Trueta con la vía aún puesta' (17 April 2020) https://www.lavanguardia.com/local/girona/20200417/48573683995/paciente-coronavirus-escapa-hospital-girona-trueta-via.html accessed 18 June 2020.

20 Similarly see Shelly Shimana, 'Coronavirus Negligence: Liability for COVID-19 Transmission' (*Petrie Flom Bill of Health* 2020) https://blog.petrieflom.law.harvard.edu/2020/04/14/coronavirus-negligence-liability-for-covid-19-transmission/ accessed 10 October 2020.

Also an employer would be liable if he/she failed to protect workers' health at work. For instance, this would be the case of a hotel which resumed its activity after lockdown but without the preventative measures required. Under Spanish law, companies are under a duty to prevent so-called "work risks" (*riesgos laborales*). In particular, employers are obliged to adopt any measures needed to protect safety and health at work, pursuant to the Act on the prevention of workplace hazards[21] (Arts 2 and 14). That entails, among others, duties of information (Art 18), supervision (Art 22), provision of adequate training to workers (Art 19), etc.[22] Also workers have a duty to abide with the preventative measures (Art 29). The employer is accountable for the infringement of their preventative obligations. Such accountability includes liabilities under public law, criminal and tort liabilities (Art 42).[23] Public authorities also have a duty to protect safety and health at work (Art 40.2 of the Spanish Constitution).

Apart from damage, which may be relatively easy to establish if there is virus contagion, it seems that the hurdles which the victim may face in these scenarios are causation and fault. As regards the first, typically the victim bears the burden of proving that the defendant caused damage[24] – for instance, through an infection due to the exposure to the virus. This is usually a rather muddy area of the law, not only because of the plethora of criteria which are used in different jurisdictions – or even a single one – as regards causation,[25] but also because it may be extremely difficult for the victim to establish the causal link. In particular, if a natural concept of causation is adopted according to the theory of equivalence of *conditio sine qua non* (*csqn*), the claimant may bear the burden of proving that his/her damage is causally attributable to the defendant's conduct because damage would not exist but for such conduct (but for test). For instance, the victim may have to prove that he/she was infected by the defendant attending a birthday party although the latter had already been diagnosed with coronavirus. However, it seems obvious that such evidence may be difficult and that there may have been alternative causes. For instance, the victim may have become infected through casual contact with an asymptomatic infected person while shopping at the supermarket, on public transport or on any other occasion

21 Act 31/1995, of 8 November, de prevención de riesgos laborales (BOE no 269, of 10.11.1995).

22 From the perspective of Austrian law, see Anton Fischer, *COVID-19 – Sorgfaltspflichten und Haftung von Leitungsorganen* (Linde Verlag 2020).

23 Also see the Royal Legislative Decree 5/2000, of 4 August, por el que se aprueba el texto refundido de la Ley sobre Infracciones y Sanciones en el Orden Social (BOE no 189, of 8.8.2000) Arts 11 and 39–47.

24 Damage is one of the constitutive elements of the claim which must be established by the claimant for the compensation claim to be accepted (pursuant to Art 217 of the Spanish Civil Procedure Act – Ley 1/2000, of 7 January, de Enjuiciamiento Civil [Official Gazette, Boletín Oficial del Estado, BOE no 7, 8.1.2000]).

25 See Pablo Salvador Coderch and Antonio Fernández Crende, 'Causalidad y responsabilidad (tercera edición)' (2006) no 1. InDret 1–27 https://indret.com/wp-content/themes/indret/pdf/329_es.pdf accessed 18 June 2020, with further references.

without any participation of the defendant at all. Even though causation may be established at a general level - exposure to an infected person may lead to contagion - it is causation at the individual level - the victim V got infected by the defendant D -that may become an insurmountable hurdle from an evidentiary perspective.

Evidentiary difficulty of this kind thus poses the question as to the applicability of any technical rules or devices in the legal system at stake to ease proof. Of course, there is the possibility to bring experts before the court to give their opinions on the scientific, epidemiological or medical aspects of evidence.[26] Nevertheless, the issue is that where causation remains uncertain there may be a need to facilitate its proof in some way. Broadly speaking, different jurisdictions have learnt to cope with causal conundrums of this sort in different settings and thus developed ways with which to alleviate the burden for the defendant. With regard to the COVID-19 outbreak, German law scholars[27] suggest that it may be possible to apply the evidentiary facilitations provided by general procedural law, in particular paragraph 287 of the Civil Procedure Ordinance.[28] In the Netherlands, one of the leading tort law scholars has submitted that one could apply proof by presumptions, the reversal of the burden of proof, the rule on alternative causation, or even proportional liability.[29] Although not all these solutions are accepted under Spanish law, it seems possible to apply at least proof by presumptions, which has been admitted - albeit in limited fashion - in cases of causal uncertainty.[30] Proportional solutions, which have been advocated by a scholarly opinion,[31] are still not widely accepted.[32]

Since, under Spanish law, accidents at work are governed by a separate statutory regime, the legal response to them departs slightly from what has been described above. The employer may be held liable for damage resulting from

---

26 See Aixa Gálvez Jiménez, 'Celebración de actos multitudinarios y crisis sanitaria del COVID-19: análisis desde una perspectiva penal' in Atienza and Rodríguez (eds), *Las respuestas del Derecho a las crisis de salud pública* (Dykinson 2020) 211, 225.

27 See Thomas Winter and Sophie Charlotte Thürk, 'Entschädigungsansprüche' in Hubert Schmidt (ed), *COVID-19. Rechtsfragen zur Corona-Krise*, (C.H. Beck, 2020) 623, 659.

28 Deutsche Zivilprozessordnung in der Fassung vom 5 Dezember 2005 (BGBl. I S. 3202; 2006 I S. 431; 2007 I S. 1781), last amended by Artikel 2 des Gesetzes vom 12 Dezember 2019 (BGBl. I S. 2633).

29 See Cees Van Dam, 'Corona en potentiële aansprakelijkheidsclaims' (*Verzekeringsrecht Aansprakelijkheid Schade en Toezicht (VAST)*, 15.5.2020) https://www.vast-online.nl/art/3753/corona-en-potentiele-aansprakelijkheidsclaims accessed 18 June 2020.

30 See Virginia Múrtula Lafuente, 'Causalidad alternativa e indeterminación del causante del daño en la responsabilidad civil', (2006) no 2 InDret 1, 15 ff. https://indret.com/wp-content/themes/indret/pdf/351_es.pdf accessed 1 July 2020.

31 See Luis Medina Alcoz, *La responsabilidad proporcional como solución a la incertidumbre causal* (Civitas 2018) 84.

32 One may find a discussion of such a rule with regard to market share liability in Albert Ruda González, 'La responsabilidad por cuota de mercado a juicio' (2003), no 3 InDret 1 https://indret.com/wp-content/uploads/2007/06/147_es.pdf accessed 1 July 2020.

a "work accident" (*accidente de trabajo*). What counts as such is very broadly defined by the General Act on Social Security (hereafter LGSS).[33] According to the same, a work accident is "any bodily injury suffered by the worker as a consequence of work carried out for another" (Art 156.1). That includes not only accidents at the workplace but also so-called *in itinere* accidents, which happen while the worker is travelling to or from work (Art 156.2.a). Accordingly, if a worker became infected by COVID-19 while on the train on the way to work, such infection would be dealt with as a work accident, and trigger liability (including in tort) by the employer.

If the worker falls ill and the illness is deemed a "professional illness" as included in an official list,[34] such illness will deserve special treatment (Art 157). For instance, the worker will not bear the burden of proving the causal link between work and damage alleged by him/her as a condition to receive social provisions such as unemployment benefits.[35] However, this is not the case with the infection with COVID-19, which lacks such a "professional" character. Therefore, the worker will have to establish that the infection happened at work or on the way to/from the same. Even though the statutory regime on the liability of the employer which is being described lays down a rebuttable presumption that any injury suffered by the worker while at work and during work time will be considered a work accident (Art 156.3), such presumption will be of little use in the case of COVID-19. The reason is that the victim may not be able to establish when or where exactly the infection took place. Unlike in other kinds of accidents at work, where it is possible to determine where the triggering event took place, the exposure to the virus may have occurred elsewhere. In spite of that, if the victim succeeds at establishing that he/she became infected while working, damage resulting therefrom will be treated according to the rules on liability of the employer.

There has actually been some controversy in this regard; since in the beginning of the COVID-19 outbreak the Spanish government was reluctant to consider infection with COVID-19 at work as a "work accident". So, a Royal Decree-Act from 10 March 2020[36] had established that the situation of workers affected by isolation measures or contagion with COVID-19 could only be "equated" or "assimilated" to a work accident with regard to the perception of

---

33 Royal Legislative Decree 8/2015, of 30 October, por el que se aprueba el texto refundido de la Ley General de la Seguridad Social (BOE no 261, of 31.10.2015).

34 The list is included in the Royal Decree 1299/2006, of 10 November, por el que se aprueba el cuadro de enfermedades profesionales en el sistema de la Seguridad Social y se establecen criterios para su notificación y registro BOE no 302, 19.12.2006).

35 However, the employer may prove that the illness at stake was caused by a cause other than work.

36 Royal Decree-Act 6/2020, of 10 March, por el que se adoptan determinadas medidas urgentes en el ámbito económico y para la protección de la salud pública (BOE no 62, 11.3.2020).

an economic benefit on the basis of temporal disability (Art 5). Such statutory provision was amended by another Royal Decree-Act on 7 April.[37] According to the latter, if the worker can prove that contagion took place while working it will be treated as a work accident (Final Disposition no 1). Such evidence may be hard to obtain unless it has been established that the employer failed to comply with existing regulations.[38] This is a major change with regard to the previous law, since under the new regime the economic benefits will not be paid by the Social Security but by the employer; moreover, the latter may be held liable for the work accident and not only be obliged to pay compensation, but may have to pay fines in the case where he/she failed to adopt measures to protect safety or health at work (pursuant to Art 164 LGSS).

Apart from causation, fault may also prove to be a hurdle for the claimant. Spanish courts have long ago abandoned their traditional stance of systematically reversing the burden of proof of fault (*culpa*).[39] Therefore, the claimant generally bears such a burden and should establish that the defendant failed to abide by the standard of conduct of a reasonable person (or a good head of the family, as the Spanish Civil Code calls him, Art 1104). Naturally, the degree of care which is required from a professional, e.g. a doctor, is higher, according to well established case law. This is also relevant in the case of professional activities, such as the organisation of groups events. In the case of sports events, for instance, organisers are under a duty to ensure the safety of participants and the public.[40] Therefore having failed to cancel an event may trigger their liability. The conduct of governments, national football associations and other organisations involved may come under scrutiny, although the focus seems to be mostly on contract law aspects.[41]

Nevertheless, the very concept of fault lies on the idea of foreseeability, since fault, under Spanish law and many other legal systems, consists in failing to foresee what the reasonable person would have foreseen under the

---

37 Royal Decree-Act 13/2020, of 7 April, por el que se adoptan determinadas medidas urgentes en materia de empleo agrario (BOE no 98, 8.4.2020).

38 See José Luis Fernández Gutiérrez, '¿Es responsable el empresario del contagio por COVID-19 de uno de sus trabajadores?' (2020) ElDerecho.com https://elderecho.com/responsable-empresario-del-contagio-covid-19-uno-trabajadores accessed 10 October 2020.

39 See Encarna Roca Trías, 'El riesgo como criterio de imputación subjetiva del daño en la jurisprudencia del Tribunal Supremo español', (2009) no 4 InDret, 1–17 https://indret.com/wp-content/themes/indret/pdf/688_es.pdf accessed 1 July 2020.

40 Pursuant to the Sports Act. See Act 10/1990, of 15 October, del Deporte BOE no 249, (17.10.1990) and the Act Ley Orgánica 3/2013, de 20 de junio, de protección de la salud del deportista y lucha contra el dopaje en la actividad deportiva (BOE no 148, 21.6.2013) Arts 2 and 3.

41 To that regard see Michele Colucci, Sean Cottrell and Rustam Sethna, 'Coronavirus and its Impact on Football' (LawInSport 2020) https://www.lawinsport.com/topics/covid19-impact/item/coronavirus-a-and-its-impact-on-football-a-sports-law-and-policy-centre-and-lawinsport-joint-survey accessed 10 October 2020.

circumstances. Although this may seem obvious, in the case of the COVID-19 it is not entirely clear what exactly was foreseeable at every single stage of the pandemic. On the one hand, the possibility of a pandemic itself was of course foreseeable. Even those who had warned us about the risks as if they were modern Cassandras were largely ignored. And, as happened in the Greek myth, havoc has ensued as a result. Among legal scholars, it seems also undisputable that disasters have received comparatively little attention.[42] However, probably no one could predict that such a disaster would actually take place.[43] Even if a pandemic was indeed foreseeable, the dimensions and seriousness of the present one were hardly foreseeable to anyone.

Bearing the latter in mind, the question may be discussed as to whether the defendant can be held liable under the present circumstances, even if fault is established. It is to this regard that the ELI Principles bring an interesting nuance to the fore. They provide that: "Given the urgent and dramatic circumstances in which doctors, health care professionals, and other providers in the medical sector have to provide services, States should ensure that these professionals are not held liable for adverse events related to the Covid -19, except in the case of at least gross negligence" (Principle no 14(1)). The ELI thus suggests that doctors and the other persons mentioned in the rule above should be exonerated from liability except in the most serious form of negligence.

At first glance, such an approach contrasts with the one adopted under Spanish law, where the tripartite classification of fault (*levissima, levis, gravis*) has long been abandoned and plays very little role in practice – if at all. At least, it is not adopted by the general statutory regime of liability based on fault (pursuant to Art 1902 CC). Nevertheless, the rule may entail less radical innovation than what appears at first sight. In some jurisdictions, a doctor who intervenes in an emergency setting may be automatically exonerated from liability – as seems to be the case under some public regional laws in Germany.[44] No one denies that the conduct of a physician who has to decide under great pressure should not be judged according to the same standards as another physician behaving in totally normal circumstances. Moreover, when assessing the doctor's conduct, one should look in retrospect bearing in mind that what is known after the event may not have been known before. The standard of care (or *lex artis ad hoc*) applicable to the doctor should thus take the changing nature of knowledge into account.[45] From this perspective, many national jurisdictions may let

---

42 A notable exception is Richard A. Posner, *Catastrophe. Risk and Response* (Oxford University Press 2014) 22.

43 See Sonia de Miguel Fernández and Juan Carlos Ruiz de la Roja, *Coronavirus. Prevención, pandemia y contención* (Catarata 2020) 121.

44 See Erwin Deutsch and Hans-Jürgen Ahrens, *Deliktsrecht* (6th edn, Vahlen 2014) 164.

45 Similarly, Manuel Ortiz Fernández, 'Algunos apuntes sobre la responsabilidad civil sanitaria ante la situación generada por el Covid-19', (2020) no 3-2 'Revista IBERC' 289–304, 296 https://revistaiberc.responsabilidadecivil.org/iberc/article/view/126 and, as regards Italian

the doctor go scot free because he/she cannot be held liable for things which could be known *ex post facto* only. It is thus at this moment that the uncertainty surrounding COVID-19 becomes most important.

At any rate, it may also be taken into account that in some cases damage may be attributed not to the defendant but to the victim him/herself. Under Swiss law, the Epidemic Act mentioned above establishes that compensation for damage may be reduced or excluded where the victim has contributed to cause the same in a substantial manner (Art 67). By contrast, contributory negligence is not even mentioned in the general tort liability regime under Spanish law, although it is well established in practice. For instance, the person who attends a crowded event where the risk of contagion is already apparent may be deemed to have contributed to his/her own harm or even to have assumed the risk of it.[46] However, the question remains unclear, at least from a Spanish perspective. It must be taken into consideration that a structured and clear theory on the assumption of risk (*asunción del riesgo*) is still missing in Spanish law.[47] The factual scenarios where use is typically made of this legal rule are sports, amusement parks or fairs, and bullfighting and related activities. Moreover, assumption of risk as such lacks any statutory recognition under Spanish law. A scholarly opinion has even suggested that there are too many doubts as to the activities to which it could be applied and one should therefore do away with this.[48] The COVID-19 outbreak does not seem to fit within the typology of situations where risk assumption is usually referred to. Nonetheless, it has been suggested that where someone creates a risky situation in a negligent manner and the victim behaves in a negligent way by assuming such a risk, the victim may be seen as having negligently contributed to damage causation, with the result that the compensation award would be reduced.[49]

3. LIABILITY OF THE PUBLIC AUTHORITIES

It seems clear that in a situation like the one created by a pandemic, the State is called upon to act swiftly to protect the population. A virus outbreak creates a risk situation which endangers not only public health but also several other

law, Luca Oliveri 'Responsabilità medica e COVID-19: prime impressioni' (Idibe 2020) https://idibe.org/tribuna/responsabilita-medica-e-covid-19-prime-impressioni/ accessed 18 June 2020.

46 As regards risk assumption in Spanish case law, see Pablo Salvador Coderch and Juan Antonio Ruiz, 'Riesgo, responsabilidad objetiva y negligencia', (2002) no 2 InDret 1–4 https://indret.com/wp-content/themes/indret/pdf/085_es.pdf accessed 1 July 2020.

47 See María Medina Alcoz, *La asunción del riesgo por parte de la víctima* (Dykinson 2004) 38.

48 See Santiago Cavanillas Múgica, 'Comentario a la Sentencia de 22 de Octubre de 1992'(1992) no 30. Cuadernos Civitas de Jurisprudencia Civil 949–958.

49 See Medina Alcoz, *La asunción del riesgo por parte de la víctima* (Dykinson 2004) 98.

legally protected interests. Therefore the State should not only provide for life[50] and health protection but also take the potentially negative consequences to the economy into consideration. So, for instance, the Spanish Constitution establishes that public authorities have a duty to protect public health through preventative measures and to provide health care and services needed to that end (Art 43.2). Consumers' right to health is also enshrined in the constitutional text (Art 51). A General Act on Health Protection[51] develops such provisions further. According to it, public administrations have to (1) inform the public about health risks (Art 10); (2) monitor or supervise the situation regarding public health (Art 12); (3) promote the provision of health care infrastructures (Art 15); (4) adopt preventative measures (Art 19); and (5) protect public health (Art 27). That everyone has a right to life and corporal integrity is also provided in many other Constitutions (e.g. Art 2.2 of the German *Grundgesetz* and Art 32 of the Italian *Costituzione*).

There is no doubt, therefore, that public authorities have a duty to act in the context of a pandemic to protect its population's health. However, it seems equally clear that public measures adopted to that end may be non-existent, ineffective, or even counter-productive or harmful. It goes without saying that the mere fact that a pandemic exists does not entail that public authorities go scot free. Quite to the contrary, there are several scenarios in which the public authorities may incur liability in a pandemic. Given the lack of a specific liability regime, it is again necessary to refer to the general liability regime.

With regard to the liability of public authorities or the State, it has already been mentioned that it is governed by a separate legal regime under Spanish law, namely, the one laid down in the Act on the Legal Regime of the Public Sector.[52] According to the same, public authorities – or public administration, as is also called – are liable irrespective of fault and whether the public service which caused damage operated in a normal or an abnormal manner (Art 32.1). Pursuant to the literal wording of the provision, liability does not require fault to be established. However, force majeure is provided for as a defence. Public authorities are also exempt from liability if the affected individual "has the duty to bear it according to legislation" (again, Art 32.1). Nevertheless, in practice liability of the public authorities is far from being strict, since courts always require that the defendant State failed to abide by a standard of care and thus

---

50 According to a study, there are signs that COVID-19 may increase suicides. See The Economist, 'Will the economic and psychological costs of covid-19 increase suicides?' (2020) The Economist https://www.economist.com/international/2020/10/05/will-the-economic-and-psychological-costs-of-covid-19-increase-suicides, accessed 10 October 2020.

51 Act 33/2011, of 4 October, General de Salud Pública (BOE no 240, 5.10.2011).

52 Act (Ley) 40/2015, of 1 October, *de Régimen Jurídico del Sector Público* (BOE no 236, de 2.10.2015).

behaved in a negligent manner. Therefore, even the law in the literature says that State liability is strict, the law in action shows it is based on fault.[53]

As has already been pointed out in Section 2, the fact that the Spanish Government has approved exceptional measures to fight or mitigate the effects of the pandemic does not prevent the liability regime mentioned above from being applied. The same can be said, with the required adaptations, as regards other jurisdictions. So, for instance, under German law, a scholarly opinion[54] has emphasised the provisions on the liability of the State (*Staatshaftung*, Art 34 of the German Constitution [*Grundgesetz*, GG]) and public officials (*Haftung bei Amtspflichtverletzung*, para 839 of the German Civil Code [BGB])[55] remain applicable.[56]

To this regard, the COVID-19 crisis poses several interesting questions. To start with, it may be discussed whether the lockdowns imposed by the Government were really necessary. Whereas in countries such as Spain, Italy or Switzerland[57] several compulsory measures have been adopted by the public authorities, other countries seem to have remained deliberately passive. As is well known, some Governments around the world have refused to decree any lockdown at all. Most notably, England[58] was reluctant to adopt so drastic a measure. However, it is also known that the circumstances forced 10 Downing Street to amend its previous stance.[59] But leaving this example aside, the fact is that other governments, in Europe, as well as in the US, have refused to order a lockdown. The cases of Sweden (with a soft lockdown)[60] and Germany (with no state of alarm at all, but other measures based on the fight of infections) may come to our mind. Leaving aside what the best strategy actually is from a medical or scientific perspective, the fact is that should lockdown be not really necessary, the Government may be accountable for having severely restricted the rights of

---

53 See Gabriel Doménech Pascual, 'Responsabilidad patrimonial de la Administración por actos jurídicos ilegales. ¿Responsabilidad objetiva o por culpa?' (2010) no 183 'Revista de Administración Pública' 179, 202 https://dialnet.unirioja.es/descarga/articulo/3359721.pdf accessed 1 July 2020.

54 See Winter and Thürk, 'Entschädigungsansprüche' in Hubert Schmidt (ed), *COVID-19. Rechtsfragen zur Corona-Krise*, (C.H. Beck 2020) 643 ff.

55 Deutsches Bürgerliches Gesetzbuch in der Fassung der Bekanntmachung vom 2 Januar 2002 (BGBl. I S. 42, 2909; 2003 I S. 738), last amended by Artikel 1 des Gesetzes vom 19 März 2020 (BGBl. I S. 541).

56 More generally, on the same, see Erwin Deutsch and Hans-Jürgen Ahrens, *Deliktsrecht* (6th edn, Vahlen 2014) 163 ff, and Steffen Detterbeck, Kay Windthorst and Hans-Peter Sproll, *Staatshaftungsrecht* (Beck 2000) 1 ff with further references.

57 Pursuant to the Verordnung über Massnahmen in der besonderen Lage zur Bekämpfung der Covid-19-Epidemie (Covid-19-Verordnung besondere Lage) vom 19 Juni 2020 (SR 818.101.26).

58 See Coronavirus Act 2020 (2020 c 7) https://www.legislation.gov.uk/ukpga/2020/7/contents accessed 18 June 2020.

59 Rather pathetically, even the Prime Minister had to fear for his life, as may be remembered.

60 The Swedish Government strategy can be found under Regeringskansliet, 'Regeringens arbete med anledning av nya coronaviruset' https://www.regeringen.se/regeringens-politik/regeringens-arbete-med-anledning-av-nya-coronaviruset/ accessed 18 June 2020.

its citizens, probably during several months, without a clear statutory basis. To this regard, banning the population from moving freely or commercial facilities from opening may have trampled fundamental rights without a clear statutory basis allowing it.[61]

Similarly, it may be open to debate whether forced testing, health data collection and supervision or tracking of the population may have violated the right to privacy and data protection. For instance, in the case of Spain, the Government entrusted a telecommunications company with the task of monitoring the geolocalisation of citizens as a measure to support the management of the COVID-19 crisis.[62] Similar measures have been adopted in other countries. For instance, the Swiss confederation put a "proximity-tracing-system" into operation, consisting in a mobile app which could be downloaded by the population on a voluntary basis.[63] To this regard, it is true that the fight against the pandemic may make it necessary to adopt several measures which imply a treatment of personal data. For instance, one may need to reduce the number of persons in a given space inside a factory or office premises. If one of the company's workers suffers from COVID-19 compatible symptoms, such a company may have to trace who that person was in contact with. The statutory ground for that is the company's duty to protect workers' health.[64] Needless to say that the duty to protect the right to health is also incumbent on the public authorities (pursuant to Art 43 of the Spanish Constitution).

However, it is one thing is to adopt protective measures regarding health and a different one to establish an indiscriminate surveillance system which may infringe on fundamental rights. Even though the Spanish Government decreed a state of alarm, as referred to above, such situation cannot imply a suspension of fundamental rights (unlike in the hypothetical case where a state of emergence or siege was decreed).[65] To that regard, Spanish legislation does indeed provide

---

61 See Presno, 'Estado de alarma y sociedad del riesgo global' in Elena Atienza Macías and Juan F. Rodríguez Ayuso (eds), *Las respuestas del Derecho a las crisis de salud pública* (Dykinson 2020) 26.

62 Order (*Orden*) SND/297/2020, of 27 March, por la que se encomienda a la Secretaría de Estado de Digitalización e Inteligencia Artificial, del Ministerio de Asuntos Económicos y Transformación Digital, el desarrollo de diversas actuaciones para la gestión de la crisis sanitaria ocasionada por el COVID-19 (BOE no 86, 28.3.2020).

63 Verordnung über das Proximity-Tracing-System für das Coronavirus Sars-CoV-2 (VPTS) vom 24. Juni 2020 (SR 818.101.25). In legal scholarship, see Ralph Trümpler and Felix Uhlmann, 'Problemstellungen und Lehren aus der Corona-Krise aus staats- und verwaltungsrechtlicher Sicht' in Martin Dumermuth et al., *COVID-19. Ein Panorama der Rechtsfragen zur Corona-Krise* (Helbing Lichtenhahn Verlag 2020) 578.

64 Pursuant to Royal Legislative Decree (Real Decreto Legislativo) 2/2015, of 23 October, por el que se aprueba el texto refundido de la Ley del Estatuto de los Trabajadores (BOE no 255, 24.10.2015) Art 19.

65 It was thus acknowledged by the Spanish Data Protection Authority. See Agencia Española de Protección de Datos. Gabinete Jurídico, 'Informe' (NREF: 17/2020) 1 https://www.aepd.es/es/documento/2020-0017.pdf, accessed 10 October 2020.

that access to clinical histories on epidemiological or public health grounds may be possible. However such access has to comply with the legislation on the autonomy of the patient.[66] According to the same, public administrations in charge of health issues may access identification data related to patients "on epidemiological grounds or to protect public health".[67] Nonetheless, it must be noted that such access is granted to health professionals and under specific circumstances provided for in statute only. Legislation on the states of alarm, exception and siege[68] does not provide any clear statutory basis for mass surveillance of data by the public authorities. According to the EU General Data Protection Regulation (hereafter GDPR),[69] processing of health data is "not prohibited" (under Art 9.1) when it "is necessary for reasons of public interest in the area of public health, such as protecting against serious cross-border threats to health or ensuring high standards of quality and safety of health care and of medicinal products or medical devices, on the basis of Union or Member State law which provides for suitable and specific measures to safeguard the rights and freedoms of the data subject, in particular professional secrecy" (Art 9.2(i)).

But from the outset, all personal data must be processed in a manner which is "adequate, relevant and limited to what is necessary in relation to the purposes for which they are processed ('data minimisation')" (Art 5.1(c) GDPR). In particular, it may be argued that there was no real need to supervise or track mobile telephone users to fight the pandemic and therefore the measures adopted by some States were neither necessary nor proportionate.[70] Nevertheless, it may also be taken into account that a data processing which seems disproportionate from the perspective of adequacy may be justified on the basis of the pre-eminence of the public interest at stake.[71] That monitoring epidemics and their spread may serve an important ground of public interest as is the protection of life is acknowledged by the GDPR itself (Recital no 46). Moreover, since

---

66 Pursuant to Act 33/2011, Art 41.

67 Pursuant to Act 41/2002, of 14 November, básica reguladora de la autonomía del paciente y de derechos y obligaciones en materia de información y documentación clínica (BOE no 274, 15.11.2002) Art 16.3.

68 Organic Act (*Ley Orgánica*) 4/1981, of 1 June, de los estados de alarma, excepción y sitio (BOE no 134, 5.6.1981).

69 Regulation (EU) 2016/679 of the European Parliament and of the Council of 27 April 2016 on the protection of natural persons with regard to the processing of personal data and on the free movement of such data, and repealing Directive 95/46/EC (General Data Protection Regulation) (Official Journal, OJ L 119, 4.5.2016, pp 1–88).

70 See Juan Francisco Rodríguez-Ayuso, 'Cumplimiento de la normativa en materia de protección de datos personales en estado de alarma por parte de las Administraciones Públicas' in Atienza and Rodríguez, *Las respuestas del Derecho a las crisis de salud pública* (Dykinson 2020) 89–106.

71 See Markus Näf and Michel Verde, 'Datenschutz und IT-Recht' in Martin Dumermuth et al., *COVID-19. Ein Panorama der Rechtsfragen zur Corona-Krise* (Helbing Lichtenhahn Verlag 2020) 398 and 420.

knowledge on the coronavirus is so incomplete the analysis on whether a measure is proportionate or not is far from being easy.[72] In conclusion, contact tracing and similar measures implying personal data processing in the context of the pandemic may be justified inasmuch as they abide with the aforementioned principles of adequacy and limitation. Therefore, public authorities would be liable provided that data was gathered which (1) was not required to put the spread of the virus on hold or (2) was kept for longer than what is strictly necessary.[73]

Apart from that, the liability of public authorities may raise other issues as well. Yet again, causation may be the crux of liability. According to the special liability regime in Spain, the causal link does not need to be direct or exclusive.[74] According to case law, proof of the causal link may become easier for the claimant whenever the public service which caused damage operated in an abnormal manner.[75] Nonetheless, it may be rather difficult to establish in a setting which is characterised by uncertainty.

Again, it is rather probable that public authorities may try to defend themselves from liability claims by resorting to the allegation of force majeure. Obviously, as a general rule the public authorities should not be liable for events which were outside of their sphere of control, unavoidable, or unforeseeable, but force majeure should not be a scapegoat either. As noted above, and even though the pandemic has put a huge pressure on public services in general and public servants in particular, the conduct of the public authorities should be subject to scrutiny, and if damage occurred such liability should not be excluded on an automatic basis.[76]

In connection with that, it may be noted that the ELI Principles, mentioned above, have refrained from introducing any novelty with regard to the liability of public authorities. It is noteworthy that even though the Principles do indeed innovate as regards liability of private persons through the exemption which has already been examined, Principle 14(3) explicitly provides that the exemption is

---

72 Similarly, with regard to Swiss law, see Andreas Zünd and Christoph Errass, 'Pandemie – Justiz – Menschenrechte', (2020) Sondernummer 'Zeitschrift für Schweizerisches Recht' (ZSR) 69, 90.

73 See José Luis Piñar Mañas, 'La protección de datos durante la crisis del coronavirus' (*Abogacía Española*, 20 March 2020) https://www.abogacia.es/actualidad/opinion-y-analisis/la-proteccion-de-datos-durante-la-crisis-del-coronavirus/ accessed 10 October 2020.

74 Instead of many, see Luis Martín Rebollo, 'Ayer y hoy de la responsabilidad patrimonial de la Administración: un balance y tres reflexiones', (1999) no 150 'Revista de Administración Pública', 317, 346, https://dialnet.unirioja.es/descarga/articulo/17461.pdf.

75 See Jesús Ernesto Peces Morate, 'La responsabilidad administrativa. El nexo causal. Últimas orientaciones jurisprudenciales' (2005) no 8 'Cuadernos de derecho local' 75 ff; also available under http://seminari.fmc.cat/ARXIUS/autors04_05/Abril_03.pdf accessed 1 July 2020.

76 Similarly Gabriel Doménech Pascual, 'Responsabilidad patrimonial del Estado por la gestión de la crisis del COVID-19', (2020) no 86-87 'El Cronista del Estado Social y Democrático de Derecho', 102, 105.

not applicable to the State. Such disparity of treatment may be open to question and create perverse incentives. For instance, it may be arguable why a private hospital may be treated more leniently than a public one in a comparable situation, e.g. negligent infection of a patient. It should also be recalled that compensation awards imposed against the State may ultimately be paid by the taxpayer, unless an internal recourse or contribution against the true author of damage is sought, which does not always happen.

In this regard, public authorities may be held liable not only for what they do (actions) but also for what they fail to do (omissions). As mentioned above, it has been suggested that the Spanish Government failed to deny an authorisation to a massive feminist demonstration which took place on 8 March 2020 in Madrid. However, it must be made clear that under Spanish law the right to demonstrate (as enshrined by Spanish Constitution, Art 21.2) is not subject to a previous public authorisation, it being sufficient for the organisers to inform the public authorities in advance.[77] According to the applicable statutory regime, the public authorities could forbid the demonstration on the condition that there was a risk of "public order disturbances" (*alteraciones del orden público*) which implied "danger to the persons or goods" (*peligro para personas o bienes*).[78] Given that the Government decreed the state of alarm several days after the demonstration (on 14 March), it may be open to debate whether such a risk actually existed on 8 March. Moreover, once again it must be borne in mind that the subsequent state of alarm did not entail the suspension of fundamental rights. To that regard, the Spanish Public Prosecutor (*Ministerio Fiscal*) issued a report according to which the mere existence of a pandemic is not ground enough to forbid demonstrations – any restrictions should be based on sufficient objective data under the particular circumstances of the case.[79] It may be conceded that this is a rather vague criterion which allows the specific question as to whether the Spanish Government should have forbidden the 8 March demonstration to remain uncertain. Seen from today's perspective, it may be submitted that having refrained from forbidding events like that was far from the wise. However, it would probably be preposterous to assume that already in early March 2020 one could have known about the pandemic what is known today.

Therefore, the State could be held liable if, for instance, it was established that it failed to provide individual emergency protection kits to its personnel. In fact,

---

77 Pursuant to Organic A.ct 9/1983, of 15 July, reguladora del derecho de reunión (BOE no 170, 18.7.1983) Art 8.

78 See Act 9/1983, Art 10.

79 See Informe del Fiscal de Sala delegado para la especialidad contencioso – administrativa de la Fiscalía del Tribunal Supremo, sobre la intervención del Ministerio Fiscal en los recursos contra la prohibición o propuesta de modificación de reuniones y manifestaciones (Art 122 LJCA), en el contexto del vigente estado de alarma (21 May 2020) https://www.fiscal.es/documents/20142/377345/DERECHO+DE+MANIFESTACIO%81N+EN+ESTADO+DE+ALARMA.pdf/cd41d243-d36b-d078-e02d-c5000190ced3 accessed 1 May 2020.

a first instance court in the Spanish city of Teruel has already decided against the Public Administration on this very ground, thereby obliging the same to provide sufficient protective kits to public servants;[80] and probably more decisions like this one will follow. Similarly, an association of victims of the pandemic has publicly announced that it will file a claim against the regional authority in Catalonia for having failed to prevent the coronavirus from spreading into nursing homes.[81] It may also be submitted that the failure to supply public hospitals with enough means to provide health care to the victims may amount to an abnormal functioning of the public authorities and thus a ground on which liability claims may be based, if it can be established that damage ensued from that shortage.[82] And even though it would be unrealistic to assume that means are unlimited in an ageing society with increasing medical needs, it may also be suggested that a shortage of resources may have added some extra difficulty to the fight against the pandemic, especially at hospitals.[83] From a tort law perspective, the analysis of such public authorities liability becomes more complicated because of the fact that causation may consist in an omission, as is the failure to adopt preventative measures. The claimants should thus establish that it was the lack of preparations, of supervision, or protection, which caused damage.[84] Moreover, the State may try to shield itself through the doctrine of discretionary powers, so the judge would not be able to review the resources allocation by the Government.[85] Against that, the victims may have to establish

80 Decision of the Labour Court (Sentencia del Juzgado de lo Social Único) from Teruel no 60/2020, (3 June 2020) https://www.ecestaticos.com/file/94084ac2e260b417deb52f736f89bd15/1591264981-4_5965289418968270572.pdf accessed 1 July 2020.

81 See Rosalina Moreno, 'Afectados Coronavirus' anuncia la primera demanda contra la Generalitat de Cataluña por su gestión en la crisis de la pandemia' (*Confilegal*, 21.5.2020) https://confilegal.com/20200521-afectados-coronavirus-anuncia-la-primera-demanda-contra-la-generalitat-de-cataluna-por-su-gestion-en-la-crisis-de-la-pandemia/ accessed 18 June 2020; According to information published in the press, the first claim to be filed against the Catalan government requests EUR 150,000 compensation for the death of an elderly person in a nursing home in Barcelona.

82 See Jose I. Ruiz de Palacios Villaverde, 'Responsabilidad patrimonial de la Administración y contagio de COVID-19' (*Lefebvre. El Derecho.com*, 30 April 2020) https://elderecho.com/responsabilidad-patrimonial-la-administracion-contagio-covid-19 accessed 18 June 2020; Similarly, Stefania Giova, 'Infezione da COVID 2019 e responsabilità della struttura sanitaria' (Idibe 2020) https://idibe.org/tribuna/infezione-da-covid-2019-e-responsabilita-della-struttura-sanitaria/ accessed 18 June 2020.

83 See Federico de Montalvo Jääskeläinen and Vicente Bellver Capella, 'La Bioética en los tiempos del coronavirus', in Atienza and Rodríguez, *Las respuestas del Derecho a las crisis de salud pública* (Dykinson 2020) 243, 247.

84 Similarly, from a Brazilian perspective, see Felipe Braga Netto, 'Coronavírus e deveres estatais:o perfil dos novos tempos' in Carlos Edison do Rêgo Monteiro Filho, Nelson Rosenvald and Roberta Densa (eds), *Coronavírus e responsabilidade civil* (IBERC, Editora Foco 2020) 235, 244.

85 See Perry, 'Who Should Be Liable for the Covid-10 Outbreak', SSRN (2020) 13 https://papers.ssrn.com/sol3/papers.cfm?abstract_id=3697283, accessed 10 October 2020.

how that discretion was badly used or incurred in a bad administration.[86] A hospital may not be liable merely on the basis that it had not enough beds, for instance.[87] However, the public authority in charge should be accountable for that fact. To that end, the emphasis may have to be put not into medical malpractice in a traditional sense but on the faulty character of health provision structure.[88]

At any rate, one should keep compensation from neighbouring concepts or legal institutes apart. Some of the measures adopted by public authorities may have expropriated particular individuals of their rights or may have restricted the possibility of their exercise. When a State – as has been the case in Spain, Italy and many other countries – decrees a lockdown and orders that hotels or restaurants should be closed, for instance, this may be done to the benefit of the public as such. Therefore, it would be unfair if the affected individuals – who may suffer economic losses as a result and even have to permanently close their business, in the worst cases – had to cope with that loss alone.

Although expropriation as different from tort law falls outside the scope of this contribution, it may be interesting to note that some jurisdictions have already provided that individuals who have had to bear a special sacrifice as a result of the COVID-19 outbreak and the subsequent measures should be "compensated" on the basis of expropriation. So, German law provides for such compensation (*Enteignungsentschädigung*) in the case where the State had to confiscate or destroy goods or adopted any other measures which diminished the value of the goods (para 65 of the Act on the protection against infections [IfSG], as amended in 2020).[89] However, it is understood by legal scholarship that such compensation may also be paid to those who were specially affected by the paralysis of the commercial activity, after their businesses were closed in the wake of the virus outbreak.[90] Even parents who may have had to take care of their children after schools were closed are not entitled to compensation for the resulting loss of earnings (new para 56.1.a IfSG), although this does not entitle entrepreneurs who may have had to keep paying salaries to their workers

---

86 Similarly, see Alexandre Pereira Bonna, 'Direito de danos, políticas públicas e a Covid-19: a pandemia que exige um novo conceito de responsabilidade civil' in Monteiro Filho, Rosenvald and Densa, *Coronavírus e responsabilidade civil* (IBERC, Editora Foco 2020) 249, 259.

87 See Ortiz, 'Algunos apuntes sobre la responsabilidad civil sanitaria ante la situación generada por el Covid-19', (2020) no 3-2 'Revista IBERC' 296 https://revistaiberc.responsabilidadecivil.org/iberc/article/view/126 accessed 1 July 2020.

88 In this vein see 'Infezione da Covid-19 e responsabilità della struttura sanitaria', 12 bis '*Actualidad Jurídica Iberoamericana*' (2020) 502, 506 ff.

89 *Gesetz zur Verhütung und Bekämpfung von Infektionskrankheiten beim Menschen* (*Infektionsschutzgesetz – IfSG*) (20. Juli 2000) BGBl I S. 1045.

90 See Winter and Thürk, 'Entschädigungsansprüche' in Hubert Schmidt (ed), *COVID-19. Rechtsfragen zur Corona-Krise*, (C.H. Beck, 2020) 639.

to receive any sum under that heading.[91] Similar rules apply under Swiss law, where private persons affected by confiscations (*Requisitionen*) and analogous measures are entitled to compensation. Again that is provided on the basis of expropriation and not tort, since when public authorities adopt those measures they are acting according to the law and not contrary to it. Therefore, the legal grounds for a compensation claim are missing.[92]

The convenience of compensating for the expropriation suffered by these categories of persons seems out of question for the reasons given above. However, it is not entirely clear to what extent jurisdictions other than Germany do actually provide for it. In the case of Spain, for instance, it seems doubtful whether current legislation allows for such compensation to be paid in all the instances mentioned above.[93]

A different issue is whether the affected persons may obtain some relief in a different way, in particular insurance. As the COVID-19 outbreak started hitting the USA, a lively debate began as to whether business closures as a result of measures decreed by the public authorities may be equated to a damage to things. Some businesses have insured against a compulsory pause of the activity but such insurance generally assumes that the pause is a result of a damage to things. In the State of New York there has been an attempt to equate both situations and thus broaden insurance protection by way of a draft bill.[94] Such discussions and initiatives seem foreign to developments in Europe. At least from a Spanish perspective, such damage would not be covered by an insurance policy which required damage to things as a condition.[95] It would be covered, however, if the policy did not require such damage but merely an interruption of business as a result of public measures to fight infections, illnesses or the like. Where the insurance policy details a list of infections or illnesses in an exhaustive manner and it does not include COVID-19, the pandemic in question would fall outside of the insurance cover.[96]

---

91 See Winter and Thürk, 'Entschädigungsansprüche' in Hubert Schmidt (ed), *COVID-19. Rechtsfragen zur Corona-Krise*, (C.H. Beck, 2020) 629–630.

92 See Poledna, Trümpler and Werder, 'Entschädigungvon Gesundheitseinrichtungen zu Zeiten der Epidemie und Pandemie' (2020) Sondernummer ZSR 109, 115.

93 In the affirmative, see Gabriel Doménech Pascual, 'Responsabilidad patrimonial del Estado por la gestión de la crisis del COVID-19', (2020) no 86-87 'El Cronista del Estado Social y Democrático de Derecho', 102, 107.

94 See State of New York, Assembly Bill A10226B (27 March 2020) https://www.nysenate.gov/legislation/bills/2019/a10226, accessed 10 October 2020.

95 Similarly, as regards Swiss law, see Ulrike Mönnich, Helmut Weiss and Oliver D. William, 'Versicherungsschutz in der Corona-Krise, hier: Deckung unter Betriebschliessungsversicherungen und Schadensaggregation in der Rückversicherung' (2020) Sondernummer ZSR 119, 123.

96 See Mönnich, Weiss and William, 'Versicherungsschutz in der Corona-Krise, hier: Deckung unter Betriebschliessungsversicherungen und Schadensaggregation in der Rückversicherung' (2020) 'Sondernummer ZSR' 135.

4. CONCLUDING REMARKS

There is little doubt that COVID-19 can give rise to a large number of legal claims of all kinds, including, of course, those for tort liability. The large number of people affected by the COVID-19 outbreak and the subsequent measures adopted by public authorities in Spain and many other countries suggests a possible avalanche of claims, with the risk of overwhelming the courts. Workers against employers, employers against public authorities, patients (or relatives of patients) against medical professionals, etc. – there is a plethora of scenarios in which the law of tort appears to be called to come into practice. In fact, the risk of avalanche seems so large that some voices have started advocating in favour of a liability law reform to shield businesses from litigation.[97]

However, the prospects for the success of such claims seems generally far from clear. On the whole, it may be rather difficult for victims to establish the causal link between the alleged harm and the defendant's conduct, for example, that the contagion took place in the workplace or at a public event, even where – as is the case of Spanish law – some legal facilitations may come to the claimant's rescue. COVID-19 is a virus which may have been caught anywhere, and even where the victim may bring prima facie evidence that he/she was in contact with an infected person such "evidence" may be deemed insufficient by courts, which are usually quite stringent as regards proof of causation. Furthermore, given that the damage may have been caused while incomplete or even contradictory information about the pandemic was available, plus the prevailing and enduring uncertainty, proof of fault may also turn out to be an insurmountable hurdle for many claimants. Although that would not definitely be the case under Spanish law, some jurisdictions are also reluctant to award compensation for purely economic losses.[98] To make things worse, tort law is a rather expensive and clumsy way to compensate damage, which makes it also ill-suited to tackle COVID-19 claims.[99] All this does not mean that tort law has no role to play at all in the aftermath of the current crisis, but it may have a more limited role than may seem at first sight.

---

97 Among others see Daniel Hemel and Daniel Todriguez, 'We can't stop the pandemic unless we change liability law' (*The Washington Post* 28 July 2020) https://www.washingtonpost.com/outlook/2020/07/28/coronavirus-tort-liability-reform/ accessed 10 October 2020.

98 As noted by Perry, 'Who Should Be Liable for the Covid-10 Outbreak', SSRN (2020) 39 https://papers.ssrn.com/sol3/papers.cfm?abstract_id=3697283, accessed 10 October 2020.

99 Similarly see Richard A. Epstein, 'Beware of Tort Liability for Covid Cases' (*Hoover Institution* 2020) https://www.hoover.org/research/beware-tort-liability-covid-cases accessed 10 October 2020.

STATE LIABILITY FOR DAMAGE CAUSED BY COVID-19 RESTRICTIONS UNDER POLISH LAW

Fryderyk ZOLL, Katarzyna POŁUDNIAK-GIERZ and Wojciech BAŃCZYK*

The COVID-19 crisis has marked nearly all spheres of our lives. To combat the spread of the virus, the Republic of Poland decided to impose severe restrictions as to the rights and freedoms of citizens and entities without applying the formal

* All authors, Jagiellonian University in Cracow and University of Osnabrück. Wojciech Bańczyk is supported by the Foundation for Polish Science (FNP). This contribution refers to the legal and factual background as of 31 August 2020.

extraordinary measures as provided by the Constitution. Businesses have been significantly affected, but it is highly disputable whether they will be compensated by the State. Two compensation regimes are potentially applicable: the one provided for in the Polish Civil Code and the other regulated in the Extraordinary Measures Compensation Law. In both cases, the conditions for the compensation are ambiguous. Therefore, the aim of this contribution is to determine the main factual and regulatory issues which might inhibit compensation of COVID-19-related damage.

1. THE POLISH STATE ON THE VERGE OF THE PANDEMIC: MANAGING IMMINENT LOSSES

On 4 March 2020, the Polish minister of health informed that the first case of coronavirus in Poland had been diagnosed.[1] Between then and 20 April 2020[2] several restrictions on conducting business activities as well as social life were imposed.

Restrictions with regard to the functioning of enterprises (e.g. shops, restaurants, hotels, gyms, hairdressers and cosmetics), as well as people's mobility (e.g. border closure affecting tourist traffic) during the epidemic, caused and are still causing various types of damage. Companies' revenues are reduced while the fixed costs (e.g. rent, employee remuneration, public law liabilities) remain unchanged. As a result, the latter tend either not to be paid, or to be paid with funds from sources atypical for the entrepreneur at hand (e.g. loan or credit). In addition, new expenditures, linked directly with the epidemic, emerge (for instance, purchase of disinfectants or costs of maintenance of unused machinery).

The government has declined to declare a state of natural disaster as provided in Article 228.1 of the Constitution.[3] It was argued that the introduction of a state of natural disaster, would have catastrophic consequences for the State Treasury,[4] because, following the Extraordinary Measures Compensation Law

---

1 https://www.gov.pl/web/zdrowie/pierwszy-przypadek-koronawirusa-w-polsce accessed 10 June 2020.

2 On 20 April, the first stage of lifting restrictions began, 4 May – the second, 18 May – the third, and 30 May – the fourth. https://www.gov.pl/web/koronawirus/nowa-normalnosc-etapy accessed 10 June 2020.

3 1997 Journal of Laws No 78 position 483 with amendments. According to the Article 228.1 of the Constitution there are three types of the states called "extraordinary measures", i.e. martial law, an extraordinary state or a state of natural disaster. The translations of the Constitution are cited after the official governmental translation. http://www.sejm.gov.pl/prawo/konst/angielski/kon1.htm accessed 12 June 2020.

4 Statement of the Vice President of the Council of Ministers Jarosław Gowin of 1 April 2020. https://tvn24.pl/polska/jaroslaw-gowin-nie-starczy-pieniedzy-na-stan-kleski-zywiolowej-4543856 accessed 10 June 2020. See also, e.g. an interview with Jarosław Kaczyński (*Gazeta Polska*, 13 May 2020); https://www.gazetapolska.pl/22348-nr-20-z-13-maja-2020 accessed 10 June 2020. Alike position is continued at a later stage, e.g. in a position of

(hereinafter EMCL),[5] the actual loss suffered as a result of limiting civil rights during this state is to be compensated. Also, the state of natural disaster forces the rescheduling of elections (Art 228.7 of the Constitution), whereas the presidential election was planned on 10 May 2020.[6] Instead, the extraconstitutional "state of epidemic"[7] was declared, and a series of special laws (so-called Anti-crisis Shields)[8] and ordinances were adopted.[9]

Not declaring[10] a state of natural disaster results in uncertainty as to the legal situation of entities whose rights were limited during the pandemic – in particular as to the basis and scope of any claims for compensation for damage caused by the restrictions in force at that time.[11] Nevertheless, the first lawsuits in this regard are already being filed.[12]

Mateusz Morawiecki (Prime Minister) from 15 September 2020 https://www.rmf24.pl/raporty/raport-koronawirus-z-chin/polska/news-firmy-domagaja-sie-odszkodowan-za-lockdown-reakcja-premiera,nId,4732695 accessed 26 September 2020.

5 2002 Journal of Laws No 233, position 1955.

6 Eventually, it was rescheduled in constitutionally dubious circumstances and took place on 28 June 2020; the second round of voting was on 12 of July 2020.

7 Rozporządzenie w sprawie ogłoszenia na obszarze Rzeczypospolitej Polskiej stanu zagrożenia epidemicznego (2020 Journal of Laws position 433).

8 E.g. ustawa z dnia 31 marca 2020 r. o zmianie ustawy o szczególnych rozwiązaniach związanych z zapobieganiem, przeciwdziałaniem i zwalczaniem COVID-19, innych chorób zakaźnych oraz wywołanych nimi sytuacji kryzysowych oraz niektórych innych ustaw (2020 Journal of Laws position 568).

9 For example: Regulation of the Council of Ministers of 10 April 2020 on establishing certain restrictions, orders and bans in connection with the outbreak of the disease (2020 Journal of Laws position 658).

10 The introduction of a state of emergency was called for by the doctrine (stanowisko Fundacji Krakowskiego Instytutu Prawa Karnego w sprawie uchwalonych w Sejmie dnia 28 marca 2020 r. ustaw o szczególnych rozwiązaniach związanych z zapobieganiem, przeciwdziałaniem i zwalczaniem COVID-19 z dnia 30 marca 2020 r., https://kipk.pl/dokumenty/stanowiskokoronawirus.pdf accessed 10 June 2020, 3–4), the judiciary (the appeal of Kraków judges from 25 March 2020: https://krakow.wyborcza.pl/krakow/7,44425,25821201,koronawirus-krakowscy-sedziowie-apeluja-do-wladz-przestrzegajcie.html accessed 10 June 2020), the Senate (https://www.senat.gov.pl/aktualnosci/art,12709,10-posiedzenie-senatu-drugi-dzien.html accessed 10 June 2020) and the Ombudsman (https://tvn24.pl/polska/koronawirus-w-polsce-rpo-adam-bodnar-powinien-byc-wprowadzony-stan-kleski-zywiolowej-4533954 accessed 10 June 2020) 9.

11 See, *inter alia*, Paweł Dudek, 'Odszkodowanie dla przedsiębiorców z powodu wprowadzenia stanu zagrożenia epidemicznego' (*Konstytucyjny.pl*, 20 March 2020) https://konstytucyjny.pl/pawel-m-dudek-odszkodowanie-dla-przedsiebiorcow-z-powodu-wprowadzenia-stanu-zagrozenia-epidemicznego/ accessed 10 June 2020; Waldemar Gontarski, 'Grożą nam miliardowe odszkodowania za stan nadzwyczajny' (*Rzeczpospolita.pl*, 5 May 2020) https://www.rp.pl/Opinie/305059940-Waldemar-Gontarski-Groza-nam-miliardowe-odszkodowania-za-stan-nadzwyczajny.html accessed 10 June 2020; Marek Isański, 'Koronawirus. Rząd nie wprowadza stanu klęski żywiołowej. To klasyczne obejście prawa' (*Money.pl*, 9 April 2020) https://www.money.pl/gospodarka/koronawirus-rzad-nie-wprowadza-stanu-kleski-zywiolowej-isanski-to-klasyczne-obejscie-prawa-opinia-6497710517995137a.html accessed 10 June 2020; Krzysztof Koźmiński, Michał Jabłoński, 'Odszkodowanie za niewprowadzenie stanu nadzwyczajnego: Czy to realna opcja?'

It should be noted that the dynamics of the phenomenon combined with its political dimension influenced the way in which the doctrinal discussion takes place – the analysis traditionally published in peer-reviewed journals is nowadays is disseminated by the press and during open online meetings. This significantly affects the research methodology – this analysis is not limited to the normative acts, court publishers and scientific analyses, but also covers the mass media releases.

The purpose of this contribution is to verify grounds, conditions and scope of liability of the State Treasury for damage caused by restrictions introduced because of the COVID-19 pandemic. Thus, after giving a brief overview of the framework for compensation claims in Polish law, two alternative compensation regimes that can apply in this respect are identified and discussed. The first issue the rules on liability for damage caused by unlawful acts and omissions of the public authority (Art 417[1] of the Polish Civil Code, (PCC)) and the second is the provisions on liability for the damage caused by legal restrictions related to the introduction of a state of natural disaster (Art 2 of EMCL). Once the grounds and premises for State's liability are defined, the analysis moves towards delineation of the scope of damage which can be compensated under the applicable provisions. Here, the scope of analysis is limited to the damage to property and does not tackle the issue of liability for personal injury. Finally, problems related to establishing a causal link between the act or omission of the State and damage are signalled, being the final impediment in case of COVID-19-related claims for damages.

(*Gazeta Prawna.pl*, 26 April 2020) https://prawo.gazetaprawna.pl/artykuly/1472218,odszkodowanie-za-niewprowadzenie-stanu-nadzwyczajnego-czy-realne.html accessed 10 June 2020; Michał Koralewski, 'Odpowiedzialność Skarbu Państwa za szkody w trakcie pandemii', LEX/el. 2020; Ewa Łętowska, 'Teza Waldemara Gontarskiego o groźbie miliardowych odszkodowań jest błędna' (*Rzeczpospolita.pl*, 6 May 2020) https://www.rp.pl/Opinie/305069966-Ewa-Letowska-teza-Waldemara-Gontarskiego-o-grozbie-miliardowych-odszkodowan-jest-bledna.html accessed 10 June 2020; Ewa Łętowska, 'To blef, że grożą gigantyczne odszkodowania za wprowadzenie stanu klęski żywiołowej', https://oko.press/prof-letowska-to-blef-ze-groza-gigantyczne-odszkodowania/ accessed 10 June 2020; Ewa Łętowska, 'Za głupstwa królów płacą ich narody (II). Reżim prawny indemnizacji w ustawie 2002 r. – przegląd' (*Monitor Konstytucyjny*, 19 April 2020) http://monitorkonstytucyjny.eu/archiwa/13518 accessed 10 June 2020; Andrzej Mikosz, 'Skutki różnicy między pandemią i epidemią' (*Rzeczpospolita.pl*, 24 April 2020) https://www.rp.pl/Opinie/304239988-Andrzej-Mikosz-Skutki-roznicy-miedzy-pandemia-i-epidemia.html accessed 10 June 2020; 'Wprowadzenie stanu klęski żywiołowej a roszczenia wobec Skarbu Państwa oraz przedłużenie kadencji Prezydenta RP' https://www.rp.pl/Bezpieczenstwo/305049974-Wprowadzenie-stanu-kleski-zywiolowej-a-roszczenia-wobec-Skarbu-Panstwa-oraz-przedluzenie-kadencji-Prezydenta-RP.html accessed 10 June 2020.

12 Marcin Łukasik, 'Pozew za koronawirusa. Zaniechanie wprowadzenia stanu nadzwyczajnego wywołało chaos' (*Money.pl*, 14 May 2020) https://msp.money.pl/wiadomosci/pozew-za-koronawirusa-zaniechanie-wprowadzenia-stanu-nadzwyczajnego-wywolalo-chaos-6510051753949313a.html accessed 10 June 2020.

2. DRAFTING THE FRAMEWORK FOR COMPENSATION CLAIMS IN CASE OF LOSS CAUSED BY THE COVID-19-RELATED RESTRICTIONS

Article 77.1 of the Polish Constitution provides that "everyone shall have the right to compensation for any harm done to him by any action of an organ of public authority contrary to the law". In this way the legislature, on the one hand, declares the strict liability of the State in this regard but, on the other, limits it only to the situations where causing damage by public authorities is unlawful.[13] This principle is reflected in Articles 417–421 PCC, which govern the conditions of such liability.

These provisions are applicable provided that the introduction of restrictions on the rights and freedoms of the individual were illegal (more precisely, contrary to the Constitution). The basis for such claims could be Article 417^1 §1 PCC. It states that "if damage is caused by a legislative act, remedy thereof may be demanded once it has been declared incompliant with the Constitution, a ratified international treaty or the law in the course of appropriate proceedings".[14] Thus, it is crucial that the provision introducing a restriction that caused the damage is declared incompliant with the above-mentioned sources of law by a competent court (with regard to the laws and the ordinances it is the Constitutional Court).[15]

Alternatively, the claim could be based on the Article 417^1 §4 PCC, according to which "if damage is caused by failure for a legislative act to be issued and the obligation to issue the same is provided for by a legal regulation, the failure to issue the act is declared incompliant with the law by the court hearing the case for remedy of damage". In this case, the unlawfulness of non-issuing the act in question is stated by the court hearing the compensation claim.[16]

It could be argued that also claims based on some other grounds might emerge (e.g. the fairness-based liability for personal harm caused by a lawful conduct of a person exercising public authority (Art 417^2 PCC)), nevertheless

---

13 Leszek Bosek, Paweł Grzegorczyk and Karol Weitz in Marek Safjan, Leszek Bosek (eds), *Konstytucja RP. Tom I. Komentarz do art. 1–86*, Art 77, I.3; Leszek Bosek, *Bezprawie legislacyjne* (Lexis Nexis 2007) point VII.2. However, this issue may be disputable due to the generalization of the concept of guilt in civil law. Maciej Kaliński, Odpowiedzialność odszkodowawcza in Adam Olejniczak (ed), *System Prawa Prywatnego*, vol 6 (3rd edn, Legalis 2018) points 161–166.

14 Translation from: Legalis.pl.

15 Robert Suwaj, Grzegorz Gudzbeler in Monika Sewastianowicz, 'Pozew za odszkodowanie za walkę z epidemią możliwy, ale sprawa potrwa dłużej' (*Prawo.pl*, 7 April 2020) https://www.prawo.pl/biznes/odszkodowania-za-ograniczenia-wprowadzane-wz-z-epidemia,499252.html accessed 10 June 2020.

16 Hubert Izdebski in Monika Sewastianowicz, 'Pozew za odszkodowanie za walkę z epidemią możliwy, ale sprawa potrwa dłużej' (*Prawo.pl*, 7 April 2020) https://www.prawo.pl/biznes/odszkodowania-za-ograniczenia-wprowadzane-wz-z-epidemia,499252.html accessed 10 June 2020.

the two aforementioned grounds seem the most common, given the nature of pandemic-related losses.

If, on the other hand, the restrictions were considered legal, compensation claims would be, in principle,[17] excluded. However, such far-reaching restrictions as introduced in the state of epidemic can hardly be considered constitutionally permissible in a State other than the extraordinary one.[18]

That being the case, the legislature is entitled to provide, by statute, a special regime of liability for damage if it was caused by restrictions during the state of extraordinary measures (Art 228.4 of the Constitution). The Polish legislature took that possibility and regulated this issue in the EMCL.

By this, two separate compensation regimes were founded, one regulated in PCC and the other in EMCL. The prerequisites for a claim to arise differ between the acts. In case of claims based on Articles 417 or 417^1 PCC, the behaviour causing the damage in question must be unlawful. In contrast, EMCL regulates the liability of the State for any conduct (its lawfulness does not need to be examined). Thus, if the conduct during the state of natural disaster is unlawful, both regimes may apply.[19]

Although the state of natural disaster was not proclaimed in a procedure required by the Constitution, some claim that due to the factual restrictions, the country has entered into such a state. This could justify granting individuals, whose interests were violated in the same way as during the state of natural disaster, protection provided for in the EMCL.

As a result, when deciding on the compensation claims related to the losses caused by the restrictions introduced because of the pandemic, the first step is to verify which compensation regime is applicable. Once the adequate regime is determined, more specific issues emerge, influencing the scope and the practical effectiveness of the protection.

3. UNLAWFUL CHARACTER OF THE NORMATIVE ACT INTRODUCING COVID-19-RELATED RESTRICTIONS

It is not clear whether the restrictions introduced in order to prevent the spread of the virus are indeed illegal (contrary to the Constitution). Most of them were

---

17 Exception provided for in Article 417^2 PCC.

18 Instead of many see the letter of the Polish Ombudsman Adam Bodnar to the Prime Minister Mateusz Morawiecki of 27 March 2020 https://www.rpo.gov.pl/sites/default/files/Rozporz%C4%85dzenia%20MZ%20COVID-19%2027.03.2020.pdf.

19 Ewa Łętowska, 'Za głupstwa królów płacą ich narody (II). Reżim prawny indemnizacji w ustawie 2002 r. – przegląd' (*Monitor Konstytucyjny*, 19 April 2020) http://monitorkonstytucyjny.eu/archiwa/13518 accessed 10 June 2020, point 4.4. claims about the state's liability for losses resulting from unlawful restrictions within extraordinary measures.

imposed based on the Article 46.4 of the Act on Preventing and Combating Infections and Infectious Human Diseases Law (PCID).[20] The PCID has already been in force for more than 10 years.[21] However, the referred provision has not never been applied before.[22] Moreover, although not formally challenged, the compliance of the PCID with the Constitution is dubious, because it establishes a state of epidemic, which, despite not being regulated in the Constitution as one of the states of emergency, entitles the State to nearly equally limit rights and freedoms of individuals.[23] Nevertheless, it does not include the guarantees, provided for by the Constitution in such cases. This issue had not been raised before 2020, probably because the provision had not yet been applied.

According to Article 417[1] §1 PCC, the law or the ordinance should be declared unconstitutional, or contrary to a ratified international agreement or to the law in the appropriate procedure. In the times before the ruling party PIS,[24] a significant part of the doctrine[25] agreed on the exclusive jurisdiction of the Constitutional Court – other courts have neither the authority to examine the conformity of the provisions with the Constitution nor to refuse to apply them.[26] This approach seems justified due to the model of constitutional control adopted in the Polish legal system.[27] However, due to the changes introduced as a result of the reform of the judiciary in Poland,[28] as well as the current functioning

---

20 Authors' translation (2019 Journal of Laws position 1239).

21 In order to combat SARS and Ebola. Druk nr 324 Sejmu VI kadencji, uzasadnienie rządowego projektu ustawy o zapobieganiu oraz zwalczaniu zakażeń i chorób zakaźnych u ludzi z dnia 10 marca 2008 r., 1.

22 In the biggest Polish judicial data bases (LEX.pl. Legalis.pl) not even one judgment referring to this provision has been registered.

23 However, the regulation of the "state of epidemic" has never before raised constitutional doubts – Marek Dobrowolski, 'Konstytucyjność stanów zagrożenia: Na przegląd rozwiązań będzie czas po epidemii' (*Gazeta Prawna.pl*, 7 April 2020) https://prawo.gazetaprawna.pl/artykuly/1467823,stany-zagrozenia-zgodnosc-z-konstytucja.html accessed 12 June 2020.

24 Fryderyk Zoll, Leah Wortham, 'Judicial independence and accountability: withstanding political stress in Poland' (2019) 42 *Fordham International Law Journal* 875, 881–882.

25 Instead of many, see Lech Garlicki, Sądownictwo konstytucyjne w Europie Zachodniej, PWN 1987, 222; Andrzej Mączyński, Agnieszka Łyszkowska, 'Bezpośrednie stosowanie Konstytucji RP przez Trybunał Konstytucyjny' in Kazimierz Działocha (ed), *Bezpośrednie stosowanie Konstytucji RP* (Wydawnictwo Sejmowe: Kancelaria Sejmu 2005) 50. In favour of the admissibility of distributed constitutional control: Ryszard Balicki 'Bezpośrednie stosowanie konstytucji' [2016] 4 *Krajowa Rada Sądownictwa*, 13, 18–19; Monika Florczak-Wątor, *Horyzontalny wymiar praw konstytucyjnych* (Wydawnictwo Uniwersytetu Jagiellońskiego 2014) 283, 339; only exceptionally, but without referring to the crisis of the Constitutional Court: Maciej Gutowski, Piotr Kardas, *Wykładnia i stosowanie prawa w procesie opartym na Konstytucji* (C.H. Beck 2017) Chapter 7, §43.

26 The court is obliged to suspend the proceeding and refer a question to the Constitutional Court.

27 Articles 188 and 193 of the Constitution.

28 Ustawa z dnia 22 grudnia 2015 r. o zmianie ustawy o Trybunale Konstytucyjnym (Journal of Laws position 2217), ustawa z dnia 22 lipca 2016 r. o Trybunale Konstytucyjnym (Journal of Laws position 1157).

of the Constitutional Court,[29] its apolitical nature becomes questionable. As a consequence, the constitutional control ceases to be reliable. In this context, the admissibility of finding a given normative act non-compliant with the Constitution by another court is considered; once again[30] the question about the admissibility of distributed constitutional control emerges.[31]

The importance of this issue becomes especially clear when taking into account that in reaction to judges' distributed constitutional control attempts, a draft amendment of the Common Courts' Proceeding Law was proposed. It was aimed at introducing disciplinary proceedings for (as a kind of obvious and glaring infringement of law as in Article 107 §1) a judge's refusal to apply a provision when its incompatibility with the Constitution or a ratified international treaty has not been declared by the Constitutional Court.[32] This draft amendment was eventually withdrawn, providing another argument in favour of admissibility of the distributed constitutional control.

Numerous arguments against the admissibility of distributed constitutional control have also been formulated in the context of the Article 417^1 §1 PCC. First, the premise (*a legislative act must be declared incompliant with the Constitution, a ratified international treaty or the law in the course of appropriate proceedings*) has purely formal character – when deciding on liability for damage, the court does not analyse the reasons for finding a legal norm unconstitutional.[33] It is argued that if during the proceedings doubts arise as to the legality of the provision on which the decision depends, the court should submit a legal

29 Fryderyk Zoll, Leah Wortham, 'Judicial independence and accountability: withstanding political stress in Poland' (2019) 42 *Fordham International Law Journal* 875, 892–894, 944, 947; Diego García-Sayán, Special Rapporteur, Presentation on the Independence of Magistrates and Lawyers at the 38th Session of the Human Rights Council (22 June 2018), https://ap.ohchr.org/documents/dpage_e.aspx?si=A/HRC/38/38 accessed 10 June 2020.

30 Previous debate took place in the 1990s, as a result the admissibility of the distributed constitutional control was rejected.

31 Ewa Łętowska, 'Aktualność sporu o zdekoncentrowaną kontrolę konstytucyjności w Polsce – uwagi na tle art. 10 Konstytucji RP' in Marek Zubik (ed), *Minikomentarz dla Maxiprofesora* (Wydawnictwo Sejmowe 2017) 799; Lech Garlicki, 'Sądy a Konstytucja Rzeczypospolitej Polskiej' [2016] 7–8 *Przegląd Sejmowy* 21–22; Tomasz T. Koncewicz, 'Emergency Constitutional Review: thinking the unthinkable? A Letter from America' (*Verfassungsblog on constitutional matters*, 29 February 2016) https://verfassungsblog.de/emergency-constitutional-review-thinking-the-unthinkable-a-letter-from-america/ accessed 10 June 2020; Mikołaj Małecki, Maciej Pach, 'Stan wyższej konieczności konstytucyjnej' [2018] 7 *Państwo i Prawo* 38; Piotr Mikuli, 'Doktryna konieczności jako uzasadnienie dla rozproszonej kontroli konstytucyjności ustaw w Polsce' [2018] *Gdańskie Studia Prawnicze*, XL, 635, 644. See also judgment of the Supreme Court [17.03.2016] case No. V CSK 377/15, judgment of the Supreme Court [23.03.2016] case No. III CZP 102/15.

32 Druk nr 69 Sejmu IX Kadencji, uzasadnienie poselskiego projektu ustawy o zmianie ustawy – Prawo o ustroju sądów powszechnych, ustawy o Sądzie Najwyższym oraz niektórych innych ustaw z dnia 12 grudnia 2019 r.

33 Przemysław Sobolewski in Konrad Osajda (ed), *Kodeks cywilny. Komentarz* (26th edn, Legalis 2020) Art 417^1, point 25.

question to the Constitutional Court in order to obtain a preliminary ruling in the relevant proceeding.[34] The examination of the lawfulness of a normative act within the compensation proceedings is excluded.[35]

Despite the prior consistency of doctrinal approach, the current crisis of the Constitutional Court means that this position may prove inadequate for the new systemic reality. Functional and teleological arguments speak for the admissibility of the verification of unconstitutionality of the act in question by the common court during the compensation proceeding.[36] Article 417^1 §1 PCC aims at safeguarding the private law entity's interests. Provided that the formal condition for a claim for damages is met only when a preliminary ruling has been issued by the Constitutional Court, in case of the inaction or political dependence of the Constitutional Court, the protection provided for in Article 417^1 §1 PCC becomes an illusion. The actual impossibility to obtain a preliminary ruling in the proper proceeding, due to the inadmissibility of distributed constitutional control, limits the right to compensation for damage caused by unlawful action of a public authority established by Article 77.1 of the Constitution. At the same time, Article 77.1 of the Constitution affects the meaning of the PCC provisions, yet itself cannot be considered a basis of claims.[37]

Another argument for the distributed constitutional control can be formed based on the results of a comparison between §1 and 4 of Article 417^1 PCC. If the damage was caused by issuing a normative act, it is necessary for the claimant to obtain a preliminary ruling of the Constitutional Court. However, if the damage was caused by the absence of a normative act, the adoption of which was required by law, the unlawfulness of the "non-adoption" of that act is determined by the court hearing the case for damages.[38] The reason for this differentiation is simple – the Polish legal system is shy of a procedure for determining whether certain inactivity of the legislature could constitute legislative omission.[39] Therefore, if declaring the unconstitutionality of an act in proper proceedings

34 Rafał Szczepaniak in Maciej Gutowski (ed), *Kodeks cywilny. Komentarz* (2nd edn, Legalis 2019) Art 417^1, point 11.

35 Zbigniew Banaszczyk, 'Odpowiedzialność za szkodę wyrządzoną przy wykonywaniu władzy publicznej' in Adam Olejniczak (ed), *System Prawa Prywatnego*, vol 6 (3rd edn, Legalis 2018) point 127.

36 Paweł Dudek, 'Odszkodowanie dla przedsiębiorców z powodu wprowadzenia stanu zagrożenia epidemicznego' (*Konstytucyjny.pl*, 20 March 2020) https://konstytucyjny.pl/pawel-m-dudek-odszkodowanie-dla-przedsiebiorcow-z-powodu-wprowadzenia-stanu-zagrozenia-epidemicznego/ accessed 10 June 2020, point IV.

37 Wyrok Trybunału Konstytucyjnego z dnia 4 grudnia 2001 r., SK 18/00, IV.3, and the sources cited there.

38 The meaning of this differentiation is underlined by Leszek Bosek, *Bezprawie legislacyjne* (Lexis Nexis 2007) point VI.1.4.

39 Zbigniew Banaszczyk 'Odpowiedzialność za szkodę wyrządzoną przy wykonywaniu władzy publicznej' in Adam Olejniczak (ed), *System Prawa Prywatnego*, vol 6 (3rd edn, Legalis 2018) point 248; Przemysław Sobolewski in Konrad Osajda (ed), *Kodeks cywilny. Komentarz* (26th edn, Legalis 2020) Art 417^1, point 72.

while maintaining appropriate guarantees becomes impossible (case of a non-functioning or politicised Constitutional Court), the court deciding on liability for damage should become competent also to declare the unconstitutionality of the act so that the conditions of Article 417^1 §1 PCC can be met.

Therefore, it is crucial to determine what criterion the common court should use when assessing whether it is possible to obtain a preliminary ruling in proceedings before the Constitutional Court. The main difficulty is to specify a criterion that would be objectively verifiable. For instance, it could be the possibility to exercise the right to a fair trial within a reasonable time limit. This criterion seems particularly justified due to the fact that there is no legal measure that would allow acceleration of the procedure before the Constitutional Court or induce the Constitutional Court to deal with a particular case within a set time frame. Thus, the unlimited freedom of the Constitutional Court in this respect may result in the practical impossibility of exercising the right to a fair trial.

The reference point when assessing whether, for example, there is a tendency not to resolve politically uncomfortable matters, could be reports of non-political or external entities, such as the Ombudsman[40] or independent non-governmental or EU organisations.[41] Currently, the analysis of the indicated sources reveals significant irregularities in this respect: cases concerning politically sensitive issues, for example abortion[42] remain undecided, while disputes in which resolution is needed due to the interests of the ruling party (see the dispute between the Sejm of the Republic of Poland and the Supreme Court and between the President of the Republic of Poland and the Supreme Court) are dealt with almost immediately.[43] This suggests that if the liability of the State Treasury for damage is caused by the restrictions introduced due to the pandemic, there are no legal means that could lead to issuing such a decision in a timely manner. Thus, in practice, the possibility of obtaining a preliminary ruling in this case might be an illusion. In such circumstances, a common court, having jurisdiction in the case for compensation, should also decide on whether the act in question is in conformity with the Constitution.

Also, most restrictions were imposed by the ordinance, not by the law. In the doctrine of constitutional law there is, in principle, no doubt that the courts

40 https://www.rpo.gov.pl/pl/raport_1/887 accessed 10 June 2020.

41 For example: Diego García-Sayán, Special Rapporteur, Presentation on the Independence of Magistrates and Lawyers at the 38th Session of the Human Rights Council (22 June 2018), https://ap.ohchr.org/documents/dpage_e.aspx?si=A/HRC/38/38 accessed 10 June 2020.

42 E.g.: the statement of the Chairman of the Polish Bishops' Conference, Stanisław Gądecki, of 12 November 2019 https://episkopat.pl/przewodniczacy-episkopatu-aborcja-ze-wzgledu-na-ryzyko-choroby-dziecka-to-dyskryminacja/ accessed 12 June 2020; Ewa Siedlecka, 'TK nie zbada legalności aborcji ze względu na wady płodu. Nie przypadkiem' (*Polityka*, 24 October 2019) https://www.polityka.pl/tygodnikpolityka/kraj/1929648,1,tk-nie-zbada-legalnosci-aborcji-ze-wzgledu-na-wady-plodu-nie-przypadkiem.read accessed 10 June 2020.

43 https://ipo.trybunal.gov.pl/ipo/view/sprawa.xhtml?&pokaz=dokumenty&sygnatura=Kpt%201/20 accessed 10 June 2020.

may control the constitutionality of the ordinances, given the judges are bound by the Constitution and the laws (Art 178.1 of the Constitution).[44] However, it is still claimed that the court, ruling in the compensation claim, may not decide on the unconstitutionality of the ordinance at hand.[45] This position should not be followed: if the court may decide on constitutionality of the ordinance in every scenario, it should also be entitled to do so if compensation is claimed. At the same time, authorities declare that the Constitutional Court should resolve a dispute on possible constitutional control of the ordinances by the courts.[46]

4. FAILURE TO INTRODUCE THE STATE OF NATURAL DISASTER IN RELATION TO THE COVID-19 EPIDEMIC AS A LEGISLATIVE OMISSION

The question of qualifying the non-imposition of the state of natural disaster as legislative omission has already been noticed in the doctrine.[47] As a rule, the above could be considered a legislative tort, if the obligation to introduce the extraordinary measures was required by law.

Meanwhile, both Articles 228 and 232 of the Constitution provide that the extraordinary measures "may be" introduced. Thus, it is claimed that these provisions do not impose any obligation in this regard.[48] This approach should be challenged. The State authorities are not free to decide on the imposition of the extraordinary measures – if they determine that the objective premises of declaring such state are fulfilled, it results in the obligation to proclaim this state.[49]

---

44 E.g. Paweł Wiliński, Piotr Karlik in Marek Safjan, Leszek Bosek (eds), *Konstytucja RP. Tom I. Komentarz do art. 1–86*, Art 178, VIII.2.

45 Przemysław Sobolewski in Konrad Osajda (ed), *Kodeks cywilny. Komentarz* (26th edn, Legalis 2020) Art 417[1], point 82.

46 Position of M. Morawiecki (Prime Minister) from 15 September 2020 https://www.rmf24.pl/raporty/raport-koronawirus-z-chin/polska/news-firmy-domagaja-sie-odszkodowan-za-lockdown-reakcja-premiera,nId,4732695 accessed 26 September 2020.

47 Michał Koralewski, 'Odpowiedzialność Skarbu Państwa za szkody w trakcie pandemii', LEX/el. 2020, point VI.

48 Marcin Miemiec, 'Stany nadzwyczajne (stan wojenny, stan wyjątkowy, stan klęski żywiołowej) w Konstytucji Rzeczypospolitej Polskiej' (2016) 106 *PPiA* 9–28 (Legalis, statement 2); Karol Dobrzeniecki, 'Stan nadzwyczajny w krzywym zwierciadle' (*Rzeczpospolita*, 31.03.2020) https://www.rp.pl/Rzecz-o-prawie/303319986-Karol-Dobrzeniecki-Stan-nadzwyczajny-w-krzywym-zwierciadle.html accessed 10 June 2020; Michał Koralewski, 'Odpowiedzialność Skarbu Państwa za szkody w trakcie pandemii', LEX/el. 2020, point 4.

49 Piotr Tuleja (4:35–7:31, 11.20–11:30) https://www.youtube.com/watch?v=3Tr3U-T08RY accessed 10 June 2020.

5. SPECIFIC LIABILITY FOR DAMAGE IN A STATE OF NATURAL DISASTER (ART 2 EMCL) IN THE LACK OF ITS INTRODUCTION

The EMCL establishes a special regime of State liability for damage caused by restrictions once the extraordinary measures are declared. Article 2.1 EMCL provides that anyone who has suffered an actual loss (*damnum emergens*) as a result of a restriction of rights and freedoms during the extraordinary measures is entitled to claim damages. However, the compensation shall be limited to the actual loss, and it does not cover the benefits which the party could have obtained if the loss had not occurred (Art 2.2 EMCL). The conditions for the State Treasury's liability are less stringent than in the case of the PCC regulation – the restrictions that contributed to the damage do not need to be unlawful. The compensation claim procedure has also been simplified. The injured party can apply for compensation to the competent voivode, indicating, *inter alia*, the value of the actual loss suffered, the time and place of its occurrence, and the limitation of rights and freedoms of the person which caused it. The decision issued by the voivode can be challenged in the court proceeding (Arts 4–6 EMCL).

This provision, therefore, functions as a guarantee. Although the State, as a result of the imposition of, for example the state of natural disaster, obtains the authority to limit the rights and freedoms of citizens significantly, their property interests remain protected as they can seek compensation under an extraordinary, simplified administrative procedure. On the other hand, the exception from the principle of full compensation provided for in the EMCL limits the financial liability of the State. It seems justified because the need to limit rights and freedoms is caused by the extraordinary circumstances and imminent threat to the State and its citizens.[50] It was noted that this mechanism does not provide for a typical compensation framework – it establishes a mechanism, which allows rather for a shared distribution of pandemic-related costs and opens up a possibility for administering aid payments.[51]

Due to the particular function of this regime, the question arises whether the aforementioned protection mechanism might apply even though the state of natural disaster has not been introduced, but nevertheless restrictions of rights and freedoms typical for the state of natural disaster were imposed. In other

50 Zbigniew Banaszczyk 'Odpowiedzialność za szkodę wyrządzoną przy wykonywaniu władzy publicznej' in Adam Olejniczak (ed), *System Prawa Prywatnego*, vol 6 (3rd edn, Legalis 2018) point 310.

51 Ewa Łętowska, 'To blef, że grożą gigantyczne odszkodowania za wprowadzenie stanu klęski żywiołowej', https://oko.press/prof-letowska-to-blef-ze-groza-gigantyczne-odszkodowania/ accessed 10 June 2020.

words, does only a formal declaration of extraordinary measures justify a claim for damages based on the Article 2 EMCL?

Some argue that the current state can be classified as a "material state of extraordinary measures".[52] Others underline that the Constitution rejects the concept of a "material state of extraordinary measures", which is clear due to the wording of Article 228.2 and 3 of the Constitution.[53] Despite this fact, the doctrine argues that compensation claims under the regime provided for in the EMCL are inadmissible because the formal condition of the EMCL application (i.e. introduction of the state of natural disaster in the appropriate procedure) is not fulfilled.[54]

At the same time, provided that a state of natural disaster has not been introduced in the way indicated in Article 228 of the Constitution, the current situation should be qualified as a hybrid state of natural disaster.[55] Reasons behind it are twofold. The state of natural disaster cannot be presumed. Also, the factual state of natural disaster cannot be legitimised simply because the restrictions typical for this state have already been introduced. At the same time, however, in the light of Article 8 of the Constitution, it is not permitted to interpret the provisions on the extraordinary measures in a manner precluding achievement of their goals.

This conclusion seems unjustified due to the guarantee function of these norms. If the legal system provides for a special protective regime in the event of a restriction of the freedoms and rights of humans and citizens during, for example a state of natural disaster, and such restrictions – in circumstances that are essentially identical to those of a state of natural disaster – are imposed, the lack of formal announcement of a state of natural disaster should not exclude the private law persons from benefiting from the aforementioned protection.[56]

52 Mikołaj Małecki, https://tvn24.pl/polska/koronawirus-w-polsce-czy-powinien-byc-wprowadzony-stan-nadzwyczajny-wyjasnia-prawnik-doktor-mikolaj-malecki-4533124 accessed 10 June 2020 M. Małecki underlines that "in the situation in which we find ourselves, in a constitutional sense, we have a state of natural disaster" (translation by the authors).

53 Piotr Tuleja (8:51–9:28) https://www.youtube.com/watch?v=3Tr3U-T08RY accessed 10 June 2020.

54 Ewa Łętowska, 'Za głupstwa królów płacą ich narody (II). Reżim prawny indemnizacji w ustawie 2002 r. – przegląd' (*Monitor Konstytucyjny*, 19 April 2020) http://monitorkonstytucyjny.eu/archiwa/13518 accessed 10 June 2020, point 1.4; Michał Koralewski, 'Odpowiedzialność Skarbu Państwa za szkody w trakcie pandemii', LEX/el. 2020, point VI; stanowisko Fundacji Krakowskiego Instytutu Prawa Karnego w sprawie uchwalonych w Sejmie dnia 28 marca 2020 r. ustaw o szczególnych rozwiązaniach związanych z zapobieganiem, przeciwdziałaniem i zwalczaniem COVID-19 z dnia 30 marca 2020 r., https://kipk.pl/dokumenty/stanowiskokoronawirus.pdf accessed 10 June 2020, point 4.

55 Piotr Tuleja, based on Art 2, 1 and 30 of the Constitution (7:30–9:52) https://www.youtube.com/watch?v=3Tr3U-T08RY accessed 10 June 2020; Marcin Krzemiński, 'Hybrydowy stan nadzwyczajny' (*Konstytucyjny.pl*, 28 March 2020) https://konstytucyjny.pl/marcin-krzeminski-hybrydowy-stan-nadzwyczajny/ accessed 14 June 2020.

56 Marcin Krzemiński, 'Hybrydowy stan nadzwyczajny' (*Konstytucyjny.pl*, 28 March 2020) https://konstytucyjny.pl/marcin-krzeminski-hybrydowy-stan-nadzwyczajny/ accessed 14 June 2020, point 5.3.2.

Otherwise, unlawful legislative omission, in principle undesirable, would deteriorate citizens' situation even further – it would impede the pursuing of compensation claims under the simplified compensation regime, hindering the use of guarantees provided for in the EMCL. Moreover, due to the difficulties in obtaining a preliminary ruling issued by the Constitutional Court, as indicated in the previous section, it may, in practice, exclude the possibility of obtaining compensation for losses suffered as a result of restrictions imposed due to the epidemic.

As a result, also in the case of the EMCL, its individual provisions should be interpreted in such a way that the guarantees provided for by the legislature in the event of introduction of extraordinary measures shall protect the individual also in case of legislative omissions. If, in accordance with the obligation arising from the Article 228 of the Constitution, the extraordinary measures were introduced, a person who suffered a loss as a result of restrictions related thereto could claim damages pursuant to Article 2 EMCL (*damnum emergens*). The person's situation must not be aggravated by legislative omission. This means that currently a person who suffered a loss as a result of restrictions related to the state of pandemic should be entitled to claim damages to the extent provided for in the EMCL pursuant to this act and, to the extent not provided for by the EMCL, pursuant to the provisions of the PCC.

6. DAMAGE RESULTING FROM THE STATE OF THE EPIDEMIC

As mentioned before, the restrictions imposed under the state of epidemic are not innocuous to the interests of the private individuals. The damage resulting from the prohibitions and obligations introduced by the State differ in type and scope. The main question is, therefore, compensation, for which damage can be claimed in court under the Polish law.

6.1. THE LIMITATIONS OF LIABILITY FOR DAMAGE OF THE STATE TREASURY (ART 2 EMCL)

As a rule, the Polish law is governed by the full compensation principle. The compensation claim, according to the Article 361 §2 PCC, can cover both actual losses, i.e. everything that was removed from the one's property (*damnum emergens*), and lost benefits, i.e. everything that did not become the property of the person but would have, provided that the damaging event had not occurred (*lucrum cessans*).[57] The damage is calculated based on comparison between

57 Judgment of the Supreme Court [10.07.2008] case No. III CZP 62/08.

the property after the damaging event and the property the person would have provided had the damaging event not taken place.[58]

However, the legislature in Article 2 EMCL decides to set aside the principle of the full compensation, limiting liability only to the actual losses. It might be challenged, whether this limitation is allowed in the light of the aforementioned principle.

The admissibility of such limitations has already been discussed in the Polish case law with regard to administrative law provisions (Art 161 §1 of the Code of Administrative Procedure). It was underlined that the limitation of full compensation is not *per se* unconstitutional and may be justified by other constitutional values which are protected by the norm in question.[59] The administrative law provision, which limits the scope of liability, is applicable if the acts of the administration causing the damage are lawful.[60] On the other hand, these norms apply in case of "an urgent administrative necessity". In this situation, due to the need to protect overriding values (mostly common interest) by immediate actions, the person might be exceptionally infringed in one's rights.[61]

In the case of the regulation of Article 2 EMCL, the framework is basically the same as in the aforementioned administrative provisions. The act causing the damage, namely the introduction of the restriction, is lawful as long as limitations are allowed in the state of natural disaster. Also, in this regard the aim of the restrictions is to protect the common interests. Due to a specific situation (e.g. the natural disaster) these interests are endangered and their protection may not be possible without limiting rights and freedoms of individual persons.[62] The decision of limiting[63] the liability of the State for the damage caused by these

58 Judgment of the Supreme Court [11.04.2014] case No. I CSK 291/13; judgment of the Supreme Court [12.02.2016] case No. II CSK 172/15. Similarly in the doctrine, e.g. Maciej Kaliński, Odpowiedzialność odszkodowawcza in Adam Olejniczak (ed), *System Prawa Prywatnego*, vol 6 (3rd edn, Legalis 2018) point 121 who underlines the factual presumptions on the hypothetical chain of events.

59 Judgment of the Constitutional Court [23.09.2003] case No. K 20/02, especially 2.3, 5.3. Also Marek Safjan, *Odpowiedzialność odszkodowawcza władzy publicznej* (Lexis Nexis 2004) 23.

60 Explicitly, e.g. Andrzej Matan in Grzegorz Łaszczyca, Czesław Martysz, Andrzej Matan, *Kodeks postępowania administracyjnego. Komentarz* (LEX 2010) Art 161, point V.1; J. Boć, *Wyrównanie strat wynikłych z legalnych działań administracji*, Wrocław 1971, 54.

61 Janusz Borkowski, Barbara Adamiak in *Kodeks postępowania administracyjnego. Komentarz* (Legalis 2019) Art 161, point 6–7; Andrzej Matan, 'Wzruszenie decyzji ostatecznej w trybie art. 161 Kodeksu postępowania administracyjnego – zagadnienia ogólne' [2009] Roczniki Administracji i Prawa: teoria i praktyka, 14–15.

62 Zbigniew Banaszczyk 'Odpowiedzialność za szkodę wyrządzoną przy wykonywaniu władzy publicznej' in Adam Olejniczak (ed), *System Prawa Prywatnego*, vol 6 (3rd edn, Legalis 2018) point 310. Similarly, on the inevitability of restrictions under the extraordinary measures: Ewa Łętowska, 'To blef, że grożą gigantyczne odszkodowania za wprowadzenie stanu klęski żywiołowej', https://oko.press/prof-letowska-to-blef-ze-groza-gigantyczne-odszkodowania/ accessed 10 June 2020.

63 Precisely about the provision limiting the State's liability – stanowisko ekspertów w zakresie konsekwencji wprowadzenia stanu klęski żywiołowej dla dochodzenia roszczeń wobec

actions can, therefore, be seen as balancing the protected interests: the right to compensation for the damage caused by imposed restriction and the common interest to impose the restrictions in question in order to diminish negative effects of the circumstances.[64]

That being the case, the need to reduce the scope of liability in case of particular infringements seems duly substantiated. Considering the above, the distinction between the *damnum emergens* and *lucrum cessans* turns out to be crucial, as only the former can be compensated within the regime of the EMCL. Although it is usually easy to classify a particular damage as *damnum emergens* or *lucrum cessans*, damage resulting from an epidemic, or more specifically, caused by the restrictions introduced in order to combat it, is difficult to categorise.

6.2. THE SCOPE OF LOSSES, WHICH CAN BE COMPENSATED: LOSING, DESTRUCTION OR DAMAGE; EXPENSES OF THE DAMAGE REMOVAL, INCREASED LIABILITIES

Under Polish law, the actual loss is usually defined as being deprived of property, its destruction or damage.[65] In case of an epidemic, it could be, for example, seizure of single-use medical equipment.[66] In principle, the compensation is calculated having in regard to the prices at the time of issuing a decision (Art 363 §2 PCC). It is assumed that the awarded damages should allow for the actual acquisition of a good or service at the time of the judicial decision. However, especially in the light of current events, it is clear that the value and the price of the property in question might be subject to intense fluctuation – they might differ substantially at the time of acquisition of the property, its loss and court decision. Thus, certain recommendations should be formulated in regard to the calculation of damages for the COVID-19-related losses.

Provided that the injured party purchased a new item or had the damaged item repaired, the incurred costs should be taken into account.[67] In particular, it would be permissible to award damages corresponding to the amount actually

Skarbu Państwa oraz przedłużenia kadencji Prezydenta RP No I.5 https://www.rp.pl/Bezpieczenstwo/305049974-Wprowadzenie-stanu-kleski-zywiolowej-a-roszczenia-wobec-Skarbu-Panstwa-oraz-przedluzenie-kadencji-Prezydenta-RP.html.

64 Tak o znaczeniu repartycyjnym – Ewa Łętowska, https://www.youtube.com/watch?v=3Tr3U-T08RY accessed 10 June 2020 (2:24:00–2:26:00).

65 Andrzej Koch in Maciej Gutowski (ed), *Kodeks cywilny. Komentarz* (2nd edn, Legalis 2019) Art 361, point 56.

66 About seizure as a typical *damnum emergens* in the state of pandemic – Ewa Łętowska, 'To blef, że grożą gigantyczne odszkodowania za wprowadzenie stanu klęski żywiołowej', https://oko.press/prof-letowska-to-blef-ze-groza-gigantyczne-odszkodowania/ accessed 10 June 2020.

67 Tadeusz Wiśniewski in Jacek Gudowski (ed), *Kodeks cywilny. Komentarz* (2nd edn, Lex 2018) Art 363, point 8; similarly Andrzej Koch in Maciej Gutowski (ed), *Kodeks cywilny. Komentarz* (2nd edn, Legalis 2019) Art 363, point 22.

spent on the purchase of such equipment at a higher price during the pandemic. Yet, the compensation should not lead to an enrichment of the injured party.[68] Thus, awarding this higher sum should not be allowed if the good or service in question had not been purchased by the injured party and their price dropped again, before the decision on the case was issued.[69]

The injured party might, instead of purchasing a good or service, incur other costs related to satisfy his/her needs in another manner, e.g. if this person's car is damaged, one can rent a vehicle for the time of repair. These costs should be included in the damage, unless the injured person in fact used the car only sporadically or has another one which can be used instead.[70] Yet, these expenses should be taken into account only, if they were actually incurred.[71] The damage in the example above is not, however, the loss of the ability to use the car during its repair (it does not diminish the victim's property), but the cost incurred to be able to travel in another way.[72] Therefore, if during the epidemic a person was temporarily deprived of the possibility to use one's own good (e.g. a car or real property) and it was economically justified and sensible to obtain a temporary replacement, actual replacement expenditures should be considered a loss.[73]

Moreover, losses can take the form of an increase of liabilities of a person.[74] Here, one of the key questions in regard to the pandemic is when the increase of liabilities during the COVID-19 crisis can be considered a loss, and, therefore, be compensated. The Polish Supreme Court ascertained that unpaid – because of reduced activity – liabilities (e.g. rent, salaries, public liabilities) as a rule cannot be compensated.[75] The same position has been upheld with regard to pandemic-related unpaid liabilities.[76] It is due to the lack of causal link between

---

68 Krzysztof Zagrobelny in Edward Gniewek (ed), *Kodeks cywilny. Komentarz* (9th edn, Legalis 2019) Art 363, point 30.

69 This may take place, in general, due to the differences in market prices – Grzegorz Karaszewski in Jerzy Ciszewski, Piotr Nazaruk (ed), *Kodeks cywilny. Komentarz* (Lex 2019) Art 363, point 6.

70 Judgment of the Supreme Court (7 judges) [17.11.2011], case No. III CZP 5/11.

71 Adam Szpunar, 'Utrata możliwości korzystania z rzeczy' 10 *Rejent* 1998, 9, 11; Andrzej Koch in Maciej Gutowski (ed), *Kodeks cywilny. Komentarz* (2nd edn, Legalis 2019) Art 361, point 58; Judgment of the Supreme Court (7 judges) [17.11.2011], case No. III CZP 5/11; Judgment of the Supreme Court [13.03.2020], case No. III CZP 63/19.

72 Judgment of the Supreme Court [13.03.2020], case No. III CZP 63/19.

73 About temporary seizure as a typical damnum *emergens* in the state of pandemic – Ewa Łętowska, 'To blef, że grożą gigantyczne odszkodowania za wprowadzenie stanu klęski żywiołowej', https://oko.press/prof-letowska-to-blef-ze-groza-gigantyczne-odszkodowania/ accessed 10 June 2020.

74 That it is a common statement – judgment of the Supreme Court [15.11.2002], case No. V CKN 1325/00.

75 Judgment of the Supreme Court [15.11.2002], case No.V CKN 1325/00.

76 Stanowisko ekspertów w zakresie konsekwencji wprowadzenia stanu klęski żywiołowej dla dochodzenia roszczeń wobec Skarbu Państwa oraz przedłużenia kadencji Prezydenta RP No I.3. https://www.rp.pl/Bezpieczenstwo/305049974-Wprowadzenie-stanu-kleski-zywiolowej-a-roszczenia-wobec-Skarbu-Panstwa-oraz-przedluzenie-kadencji-Prezydenta-RP.html. Differently, about their character as losses, see e.g. Paweł Dudek, 'Odszkodowanie dla

them and the issue of the act introducing restrictions as to the business activities of a person. The legal act causes merely a decrease in revenues. Nevertheless, if a person takes a loan or credit because of that, in order to be able to continue performing business activities, then the interests he/she would have to pay could be considered an actual loss. Similarly, if some assets require additional expenditures due to the legal impossibility of their use (case of unused machinery), or additional losses are produced (recycling expenditure with regard to unsold food after expiry date, but not the value of unsold items itself), or the person is legally obliged to buy certain goods (in the case of pandemic: disinfectants), then these costs can be regarded as an actual loss.

Finally, loss is also understood as the decrease of the value of assets.[77] In the Polish judiciary, the key example is the case of a car which, due to an accident, losses its value even if repaired afterwards.[78] A similar situation nowadays could occur in regard to real estate designated for short-term rental in tourist destinations. Their market value might drop due to the tourist travel ban, and it is uncertain whether or when it will rise again. Similar issues might appear when the value of an enterprise is examined.

6.3. COMPENSATION OF DAMAGE CLASSIFIED AS *LUCRUM CESSANS* (ART 417[1] PCC)

Provided that the claim could be based on Article 417[1] PCC (damage resulting from limitations of rights and freedoms introduced by an unconstitutional act), it could encompass both *damnum emergens* and *lucrum cessans*. Damage would cover loss of earnings, expected profit from future transactions, benefits and income from the possession of the thing, and loss of the ability to use the thing.[79] Such future losses are *per se* hypothetical, however, in order to compensate them, it must be proven that the profit was highly probable, i.e. nearly certain.[80]

przedsiębiorców z powodu wprowadzenia stanu zagrożenia epidemicznego' (*Konstytucyjny.pl*, 20 March 2020) https://konstytucyjny.pl/pawel-m-dudek-odszkodowanie-dla-przedsiebiorcow-z-powodu-wprowadzenia-stanu-zagrozenia-epidemicznego/ accessed 10 June 2020, point I.

77 Judgment of the Supreme Court [12.02.2015], case No. IV CSK 235/14; judgment of the Supreme Court [16.04.2002], case No. V CKN 960/00; Maciej Kaliński, Odpowiedzialność odszkodowawcza in Adam Olejniczak (ed), *System Prawa Prywatnego,* vol 6 (3rd edn, Legalis 2018) point 115.

78 Judgment of the Supreme Court [12.10.2001], case No. III CZP 57/01.

79 Maciej Kaliński, Odpowiedzialność odszkodowawcza in Adam Olejniczak (ed), *System Prawa Prywatnego,* vol 6 (3rd edn, Legalis 2018) point 94; similarly Adam Olejniczak in Andrzej Kidyba (ed), *Kodeks cywilny. Komentarz* (2nd edn, Lex 2014) Art 361, point 14.

80 Judgment of the Supreme Court [22 April 2015], case No. III CSK 256/14; Zbigniew Banaszczyk in Krzysztof Pietrzykowski (ed), *Kodeks cywilny. Komentarz* (9th edn, Legalis 2018) Art 361, point 49; Krzysztof Zagrobelny in Edward Gniewek (ed), *Kodeks cywilny. Komentarz* (9th edn, Legalis 2019) Art 361, point 42.

In view of the damage arising from the introduction of the state of the epidemic, it would include, in particular, lost revenue during the lockdown.

6.4. *COMPENSATIO LUCRI CUM DAMNO*: BENEFITS UNDER THE POLISH ANTI-CRISIS SHIELDS

As mentioned above, the notion of damage from Article 361 §2 PCC is defined as the difference between the actual property of the injured party and the property he/she would have, had the damaging event not happened. As a result, the court deciding on the compensation must take into account the increase in the assets of the injured person, as well as saved expenses (meaning the expenditures he/she would have incurred if the event giving rise to the damage had not occurred).[81]

However, in order to apply this principle *compensatio lucri cum damno*, the same event should be causing the damage and the benefit (or, at least, there must be a causal link between the damaging event and the profit).[82] Without the damage, the benefit would not have been gained.[83]

In the justification of the first Anti-crisis Shield, it was underlined that the restrictions introduced might cause financial difficulties of the businesses, and thus, the aim of the act was to diminish the impact of the bans.[84] However, in the government's statements, the anti-crisis shields were described rather as a mechanism to protect businesses against the pandemic crisis.[85]

In order for the liability of the State Treasury to arise, the damage should be linked with the imposed restrictions and not the epidemic itself and, to apply the *compensatio lucri cum damno* principle when calculating the compensation, there must be in a causal link between the restrictions and the State aid under Anti-crisis Shield. It must be proved that without the restrictions, the aid would not have been granted. Bearing in mind the government statements, as to the function of the anti-crisis mechanisms, this premise is not met.

---

81 Krzysztof Zagrobelny in Edward Gniewek (ed), *Kodeks cywilny. Komentarz* (9th edn, Legalis 2019) Art 361, 57; similarly Przemysław Sobolewski in Konrad Osajda (ed), *Kodeks cywilny. Komentarz* (25th edn, Legalis 2020) Art 363, point 63.

82 Przemysław Sobolewski in Konrad Osajda (ed), *Kodeks cywilny. Komentarz* (25th edn, Legalis 2020) Art 363, point 63; similarly Adam Olejniczak in Andrzej Kidyba (ed), *Kodeks cywilny. Komentarz* (2nd edn, Lex 2014) Art 361, point 15.

83 Maciej Kaliński, Odpowiedzialność odszkodowawcza in Adam Olejniczak (ed), *System Prawa Prywatnego,* vol 6 (3rd edn, Legalis 2018) point 138.

84 Druk nr 299 Sejmu IX kadencji, uzasadnienie rządowego projektu ustawy o zmianie ustawy o szczególnych rozwiązaniach związanych z zapobieganiem, przeciwdziałaniem i zwalczaniem COVID-19, innych chorób zakaźnych oraz wywołanych nimi sytuacji kryzysowych oraz niektórych innych ustaw z dnia 26 marca 2020 r., 1.

85 https://www.gov.pl/web/tarczaantykryzysowa accessed 10 June 2020.

7. CAUSAL LINK BETWEEN THE ACT OR OMISSION OF THE STATE AND DAMAGE

Regardless of the regime within which the compensation is claimed, in order to obtain it, the injured party must prove the damage, the event which caused it and the link between these two.

In Polish law, there are two elements which need to coincide so that there is an adequate causal link between the damage and the event causing it: the damage would not have occurred without the event at hand (*conditio sine qua non*) and it is its normal consequence (Art 361 §1 PCC). In case of a pandemic, therefore, one must distinguish between the consequences of the pandemic itself and the consequences of the restrictions imposed due to the pandemic. Only the latter damage can qualify for compensation.[86]

Thus, the economic damage resulting from the outbreak of the pandemic before the introduction of the restrictions shall not be compensated. The situation changes when restrictions are imposed. The damage, though, in principle, caused by the same circumstances (lack of clients at the hairdresser – people are afraid of the disease) become a result of the imposed restrictions (people do not go to the hairdresser's because it is closed due to the regulation, their fear of the virus is no longer decisive) (so-called *nova causa interveniens*).[87]

The causal link can be demonstrated by comparison of financial results of the enterprise under restrictions resulting from the state of the epidemic (e.g. lockdown), and during the epidemic, but in a period when the restrictions were already lifted. It seems of utmost importance, as the number of infected people in Poland was rather insignificant at the time when the restrictions were imposed and kept rising after the restrictions were lifted.[88]

Proving the causal link is highly improbable in cases of the damage resulting from the legislative omission. As a rule, the causality of omission is connected with a failure to perform an obligation to act.[89] The claimant should demonstrate that there was an obligation to act, the action was possible, and it would have prevented the damage.[90] Also, the damage in question must be a normal result of this legislative omission.[91]

---

86 Ewa Łętowska, 'To blef, że grożą gigantyczne odszkodowania za wprowadzenie stanu klęski żywiołowej', https://oko.press/prof-letowska-to-blef-ze-groza-gigantyczne-odszkodowania/ accessed 10 June 2020. Alike statement has been raised generally to the State's liability which is not to balance economic risks, Leszek Bosek, *Bezprawie legislacyjne* (Lexis Nexis 2007) point VII.4.2.

87 Maciej Kaliński, Odpowiedzialność odszkodowawcza in Adam Olejniczak (ed), *System Prawa Prywatnego*, vol 6 (3rd edn, Legalis 2018) point 109.

88 See: https://www.worldometers.info/coronavirus/country/poland/ accessed June 2020.

89 Franciszek Błahuta in Zbigniew Resich (ed), *Kodeks cywilny. Komentarz* (Wydawnictwo Prawnicze 1972) 870.

90 Andrzej Koch in Maciej Gutowski (ed), *Kodeks cywilny. Komentarz* (2nd edn, Legalis 2019) Art 361, point 12; similarly Zbigniew Banaszczyk in Krzysztof Pietrzykowski (ed),

However, introducing the state of natural disaster would not prevent damage but create a mechanism for its repair. A legislative omission in this respect is therefore not in any causal relationship with the occurrence of damage. The exception would be damages covering only costs related to the impediment in pursuing a civil claim within the simplified regime of the EMCL.[92] Yet, as argued in this contribution, the application of this simplified regime is not excluded.

8. CONCLUSION

In order to combat the spread of the COVID-19 virus, the Polish State decided to introduce severe restrictions as to the rights and freedoms of the private law subjects, which resulted in significant damage. Yet, despite the existence of two compensation regimes, which could theoretically be applicable in this case, it is highly disputable whether private law subjects can be compensated.

From the perspective of the general protection against unlawful State conduct, the key obstacles are related to the dubious unlawfulness of the acts imposing restrictions, factually lacking procedure of verification of the lawfulness of the act due to the reform of judiciary in Poland, and the general doubt as to admissibility of the disperse constitutional control. When examining the other grounds for compensation claims, namely the simplified EMCL framework, it turns out that the applicability of this regime also might be challenged – this time due to the fact that the state of natural disaster was not proclaimed in an appropriate manner. The analysis suggests, however, that the injured should be able to benefit from the protection granted under the EMCL as the lack of introduction of a state of natural disaster should not hinder the rights of the affected subjects. The simplified regime applies only in case of actual loss. Here the claims may encompass losing property, its destruction or damage, costs related to the repair of the goods and expenditures incurred either to be able to continue with typical activities of the person or to maintain the value and functionality of the property in the times of crises. Provided that the injured party wants to also claim the lost benefits, these could be remedied under the general PCC provisions. In both cases, however, the damage must occur as a result of the imposition of the COVID-19-related restrictions, not the pandemic itself.

Kodeks cywilny. Komentarz (9th edn, Legalis 2018) Art 361, point 23; similarly about the sine qua non test based on assessment of the hypothetical that the omitted activity had taken place – judgment of the Supreme Court [12.09.2013] case No. IV CSK 61/13.

91 Adam Olejniczak in Andrzej Kidyba (ed), *Kodeks cywilny. Komentarz* (2nd edn, Lex 2014) Art 361, point 4.

92 About the inclusion of such costs within *damnum emergens* – Maciej Kaliński, Odpowiedzialność odszkodowawcza in Adam Olejniczak (ed), *System Prawa Prywatnego*, vol 6 (3rd edn, Legalis 2018) point 93.

STATE LIABILITY FOR PERSONAL INJURIES CAUSED BY THE COVID-19 DISEASE UNDER SPANISH LAW

Sonia Ramos González*

The fundamental question about causation that arises in relation to COVID-19 infections is whether the appearance of the virus (together with its high transmission capacity among the population and its lethality) amounts in effect to force

* Universitat Pompeu Fabra. This contribution results from the research project "Coronavirus i dret privat" (2020PANDE00092), funded by the Catalan Agency for University and Research Grants (AGAUR).

majeure that breaks the causal relationship between the personal damages caused by COVID-19 and the Government's action in managing the health crisis. This contribution also addresses the issue whether, in a situation of extreme urgency, and given limited healthcare resources, a lower standard of care is expected of public health professionals than the one that would prevail under normal conditions. In addition, public administrations are likely to face claims based on tort law on the grounds that some patients were not properly attended to by medical services due to the limited health resources available, as well as the fact that some health professionals were bound to provide essential services, without being provided with the mandatory protective equipment to carry out such activity safely in accordance with the legislation.

1. INTRODUCTION

In Spain, as of 2 July 2020, the total number of deaths from the COVID-19 disease amounted to 28,368, of which 19,588 were fatalities in old people's homes and residence centres[1] (the Spanish Government has to date not made these figures public), and 52 were health professionals.[2] Based on a comparison of coronavirus deaths in 183 countries relative to their population, Spain is the country with the third highest rate of coronavirus deaths per one million population as of 1 July 2020 (606.86 deaths per million), after Belgium (853.35) and United Kingdom (657.7). Big differences show up between countries: France (444.52), Netherlands (354.77) or Germany (108.44).[3] As professor Carlo Caduff points out, the "staggering differences between countries cannot solely be explained by demography or rates of infection .... What the differences might reveal ... is that some healthcare systems are able to deal with the crisis in a better way than others".[4]

The Spanish State has adopted drastic measures aimed at containing the spread of the COVID-19 disease caused by the new SARS-CoV-2 coronavirus,

1 Rtve, 'Radiografía del coronavirus en residencias de ancianos: más de 19.500 muertos con Covid-19 o síntomas compatibles' (2 July 2020) https://www.rtve.es/noticias/20200702/radiografia-del-coronavirus-residencias-ancianos-espana/2011609.shtml accessed 2 July 2020. This data has been provided by the Departments of Health of the autonomous governments.

2 National Network for Epidemiological Surveillance (RENAVE), 'Análisis de los casos de COVID-19 en personal sanitario notificados a la RENAVE hasta el 10 de mayo en España' (29 May 2020) accessed 15 June 2020. The total number of infected health professionals amounted to 40.961.

3 Statista 'Coronavirus (COVID-19) deaths worldwide per one million population as of July 1, 2020, by country' (1 July 2020) https://www.statista.com/statistics/1104709/coronavirus-deaths-worldwide-per-million-inhabitants/ accessed 2 July 2020.

4 Carlo Caduff, 'What Went Wrong. Corona and the World after the Full Stop' Academia 8 (paper accepted for publication in Medical Anthropology Quarterly) https://www.academia.edu/42829792/What_Went_Wrong_Corona_and_the_World_after_the_Full_Stop accessed 21 June 2020.

compared to other countries, for example the Netherlands[5] or Sweden. On 14 March, the Government declared a state of alarm, based on Article 4.b of the Law 4/1981, of 1 June, governing states of emergency, for the situational management of the health crisis (Royal Decree 463/2020) – extended for the last time by Royal Decree 555/2020 until 21 June 2020 – and imposed drastic restrictions on the movement of people, suspended face-to-face educational activity at all levels of education and ordered the closure of businesses that were not of primary necessity, which among other adopted measures aimed at reinforcing the national health system throughout Spain.

It is likely that some of those who suffered personal injuries caused by the COVID-19 disease or, in case of death, their family members, will claim compensation for damages against the competent public administrations, which to date have been responsible for managing control of the COVID-19 virus epidemic. In Spain, as of 22 June 50 criminal actions have been brought against several members of the Spanish Government, as well as other members of some autonomous governments.[6] Currently, some of these criminal actions have already been closed and this has opened the door for tort law claims against public administrations (the Patient Defence Association intends to bring individual tort law claims against the Government of the Community of Madrid on behalf of 300 families who suffered the loss of family members due to the COVID-9 virus in old people's homes). In particular, a criminal action has been brought against the regional Minister of Health in Andalusia based on the failure to provide the necessary personal protective equipment to health professionals in this region.

This contribution analyses how the context of the health emergency may influence the responsibility of public administrations and, specifically, which issues of liability under Spanish law arise in this context regarding the causal link between the operation of services and the damages suffered, the concept of force majeure, as well as the general provision for "wrongful damages".

2. RELEVANT BACKGROUND

Some information from the World Health Organization (WHO) and the European Centre for Disease Prevention and Control has been selected to try to pin down the state of scientific and technical knowledge about the virus and the disease it has given rise to between January and March 2020.

---

5 Lucas Bergkamp, 'State Liability for Failure to Control the COVID-19 Epidemic: International and Dutch Law' (2020) 11(2) European Journal of Risk Regulation 343, 345 https://www.cambridge.org/core/services/aop-cambridge-core/content/view/5250CAA5A15C0D9FB9EA490404BA1AE4/S1867299X20000215a.pdf/state_liability_for_failure_to_control_the_covid19_epidemic_international_and_dutch_law.pdf accessed 14 June 2020.

6 Carlota Guindal, 'La justicia se niega a abrir una causa por la gestión de la crisis sanitaria' *La Vanguardia* (Barcelona, 22 June 2020) 14.

2.1. WHO INFORMATION AND RECOMMENDATIONS

- On 22 January, the WHO mission to China issued a statement stating that: "Data collected ... suggests that human-to-human transmission is taking place in Wuhan. *More analysis of the epidemiological data is needed to understand the full extent of human-to-human transmission*" (emphasis added).
- On 30 January 2020, the WHO issued a report indicating a total of 7,818 confirmed infections worldwide, most of them in China and 82 in 18 other countries. The WHO assessed the risk in China as very high and the global risk as also high. The recommendations made to WHO Member States included the basic principles necessary to reduce the general risk of transmitting acute infectious diseases (including measures such as avoiding contact with sick people, frequent hand washing, or within hospital facilities, reinforcing infection prevention and control practices).
- On the same date, the Emergency Committee of the International Health Regulations (IHR)[7] declared the outbreak of the new coronavirus as the 6th Public Health Emergency of International Importance.[8]
- On 3 February 2020, the WHO published the Strategic Plan for Preparedness and Response of the international community. It proposed increasing the preparedness and response measures of States, including the identification, diagnosis and treatment of cases; as well as the identification and monitoring of contacts giving priority to high-risk scenarios, such as hospitals; infection prevention and control in hospitals; implementation of security measures for travellers; and increasing awareness among the population by means of communication about the risks and commitment of the community. As regards the restriction on the mobility of citizens, the report highlights that States must carry out a risk-benefit analysis before implementing such a restriction to assess whether the benefits outweigh the disadvantages.
- The joint report from 16–24 February 2020 of the WHO/China established recommendations. For countries with imported cases and/or outbreaks of COVID-19, recommendations included: "Immediately activate the highest level of national Response Management protocols to ensure the all-of-Government and all-of-society approach needed to contain COVID-19 with non-pharmaceutical public health measures" (page 21).

---

7 The International Health Regulations (2005), approved by the World Health Assembly in 2005 and in force for 196 States since June 2007, aim "to prevent, protect against, control and provide a public health response to the international spread of disease in ways that are commensurate with and restricted to public health risks, and which avoid unnecessary interference with international traffic and trade".

8 As provided in Article 1 of the IHR, a "public health emergency of international concern" means: "an extraordinary event which is determined, as provided in these Regulations:
(i) to constitute a public health risk to other States through the international spread of disease and
(ii) to potentially require a coordinated international response".

- The report confirmed that:

  The COVID-19 virus is a new pathogen that is highly contagious, can spread quickly, and must be considered capable of causing enormous health, economic and societal impacts in any setting. It is not SARS nor influenza. Building scenarios and strategies only on the basis of well-known pathogens risks failing to exploit all possible measures to slow transmission of the COVID-19 virus, reduce disease and save lives (page 18).

  COVID-19 is spreading with astonishing speed; COVID-19 outbreaks in any setting have very serious consequences; and there is now strong evidence that non-pharmaceutical interventions can reduce and even interrupt transmission .... These measures must fully incorporate immediate case detection and isolation, rigorous close contact tracing and monitoring/quarantine, and direct population/community engagement (page 20).

- On 11 March 2020, the WHO described the situation as an international pandemic.

2.2. RISK ASSESSMENTS OF THE EUROPEAN CENTRE FOR DISEASE PREVENTION AND CONTROL (ECDC)

According to the risk assessments published since 23 February 2020,[9] the transmission risk assessment for citizens of the European Union and the United Kingdom was not moderate-high until 2 March and it was not until 12 March 2020 that a high risk level of serious disease was established for people of advanced age and with previous chronic pathologies. In the communiqué of 12 March States were urged to adopt concrete, necessary and immediate measures:

> The immediate isolation of symptomatic persons suspected or confirmed to be infected with COVID-19; the suspension of mass gatherings; social distancing measures at workplaces (for example teleworking, suspension of meetings cancellation of non-essential travel); measures in and closure of schools; ensuring the public is aware of the seriousness of COVID-19; prevention and control of COVID-19 in hospitals and long-term care facilities is an immediate priority ...; countries should identify healthcare units that can be designated to care for COVID-19 cases; countries and healthcare institutions should identify additional facilities; if resources or capacity are limited, rational approaches should be implemented: rational use of confirmatory testing, rational use of personal protective equipment, and hospitalisation and implementing rational criteria for de-isolation. Testing approaches should prioritise vulnerable populations, protection of social and healthcare institutions, including staff ....

9 ECDC, 'Risks assessments' https://www.ecdc.europa.eu/en/threats-and-outbreaks/reports-and-data/risk-assessments accessed 10 June 2020.

2.3. THE SPANISH GOVERNMENT AND MINISTRY OF HEALTH

Among the multiple statements from the Ministry of Health published since 29 January 2020 the following risk assessments are worth noting.

On 31 January 2020, two imported cases of infection of the new virus had been confirmed in Spain. Up to 1 March 73 cases of infection with the new coronavirus were confirmed in Spain, while the global risk for public health in Spain was considered moderate and the Ministry of Health maintained the containment scenario at Level 1. On 2 March with 119 confirmed infections, it was assessed as having passed Level 2, but there is no record that it became effective. On 5 March, there were three fatalities with previous pathologies. On 6 and 9 March, it was announced that specific measures had been taken in areas of significant community transmission (including Madrid, and some areas of Álava, and La Rioja); care of the elderly, avoiding unnecessary trips and encouraging people with symptoms to remain at home were recommended throughout Spain.

The Health Alerts and Emergencies Coordination Centre of the Ministry of Health had planned for three alert levels:

- Level 1: containment, because there is no uncontrolled community transmission and no massive entry of imported cases.
- Level 2: mitigation, because of community transmission to identified groups and a massive entry of imported cases.
- Level 3: generalisation. It implies that the transmission of the infection is out of control. The highest alert level.

From the declaration of the state of alarm, on 14 March, a whole series of measures were adopted including: purchase of diagnostic tests; incorporation of health professionals; increasing the capacity to produce medical equipment; and reinforcement measures in residences.

It should be remembered that when, on 17 February 2020 the Global System for Mobile Communications Association suspended the Mobile World Congress, which was due to be held in Barcelona at the end of February, for reasons of force majeure (many companies had withdrawn their participation because of their apprehension over the new virus), the WHO Director of Public Health expressed the opinion to various media outlets that there were no public health grounds preventing the holding of events of this type.[10]

---

[10] Ramon Muñoz and Ana Pantaleoni, 'El Gobierno y la OMS cuestionan el cierre del Mobile y la organización pide que las empresas asuman el coste' *El País* (Madrid, 14 February 2020) https://elpais.com/economia/2020/02/13/actualidad/1581626680_792968.html accessed 10 June 2020.

3. REQUIREMENTS FOR IMPOSING TORT LIABILITY ON PUBLIC ADMINISTRATIONS UNDER SPANISH LAW

Under Spanish law, any individual or group of people, who have suffered damage to their rights and property, is entitled to seek compensation against the competent public administration – at national, regional or municipal level – if the damage has been caused by the normal or abnormal operation of a public service and provided that there is no force majeure or that the damage caused is not one that the individual has the legal duty to bear in accordance with the law (Art 106 of the Spanish Constitution, Art 32 of the Law 40/2015, of 1 October, on the Legal Regime of the Public Sector (Public Sector Act)). In such circumstance the grounds for imposing tort liability on the administration are as follows: (1) that there be effective damage that can be financially assessed and particularised in relation to a person or a group of people; (2) that there is a causal relationship between the normal or abnormal functioning of the public service; (3) that force majeure has not intervened; and (4) that the damage is wrongful, in the sense that whoever suffers it does not have the legal duty to bear it.

The tort liability is applicable to all administrative activities, irrespective of whether the public administration has acted in the strict exercise of an administrative power, through some material activity or in omission of a legal obligation.

The administration is liable for their own acts or for the acts of their officials and agents and, in both cases, the individual who has suffered damages must bring their claim before the public administration (Art 36 of the Public Sector Act). This is without prejudice to the criminal liability of the officials and agents under the criminal law.

4. STRICT LIABILITY FOR NORMAL OR ABNORMAL OPERATION OF PUBLIC SERVICES

The liability imposed on the public administration under Spanish law is strict, so it is not required to establish the: "existence of intent, fault or negligence on the part of the Administration or its officials and agents, nor is it [required] to establish the so-called objective failure of the service, that is, a failure not attributable to any specific subject".

Once these criteria are established it: "may, with certainty, be sufficient to impose responsibility on the Administration, though their concurrence is not a prerequisite".[11]

[11] *Plaintiff v Spanish Health National Institute* [2000] ECLI: ES:TS:2000:7033 [Supreme Court].

In accordance with Spanish law, the existence of damage that the individual did not have the legal duty to bear (Art 34.1 of the Public Sector Act) is also a ground for imposing liability, even if it arises from a normal operation of the service, when the activity has been carried out within the required security standards in accordance with public policy. It must be highlighted that this ground of liability refers to the damage and not to the abnormal functioning of the public service. Among other assumptions, this ground of liability occurs, according to the jurisprudence of the Supreme Court, "when there is awareness that administrative activity gives rise to a special risk or prejudice for a person or a group of people whose harmful consequences must not be borne by the injured party"[12] or when the damages exceed "the normal consequences that we all have to face as a result of life in a society that demands better services, constituting general charges linked to the legal status of members of society".[13]

The Supreme Court has imposed liability in accordance with these terms to specific cases: it has done so to compensate injured parties for particular economic hardship they have suffered as a result of the execution of public works, provided that such damage far exceeded the inconvenience and discomfort that the performance of such activities should involve and that they had no duty to bear.[14] It has also been employed as a ground for imposing liability and awarding compensation for serious though rare side effects, even when these were known about and unavoidable, that have affected specific individuals due to the use of vaccines that were highly beneficial to public health (for example in the case of the occurrence of the *Guillain-Barre syndrome* caused by the flu vaccine):

> the obligation to accept the damage suffered cannot be imposed on the injured party when there exists no legal duty on their part to bear the risk that society must assume in terms of strict liability by virtue of the principle of solidarity, as has arisen in the particular case before the court, unlikely to be repeated owing to its exceptional nature, where a highly infrequent risk has materialised to the detriment of the claimant, though one that is foreseeable in terms of the broad scope of general vaccination campaigns, also considering … that the aims pursued were not only particular but also for general public health.[15]

Underlying these pronouncements is the view that the singular and special prejudice that an individual suffers as a result of an activity that is carried out

---

12 Ibid; *Promociones San Ciprián S.A. v Government of Galicia* [2015] ECLI:ES:TSJGAL:2015:4095 [High Court of Justice of Galicia].

13 *Hotel Miguel Ángel v Department of Public Works of Madrid* [2009] ECLI:ES:TS:2009:1749 [Supreme Court].

14 Ibid; *Gallery Center v Department of Territorial Policy and Public Works of the Generalitat of Catalonia* [2013] ECLI:ES:TSJCAT:2013:3502 [High Court of Justice of Catalonia].

15 *Plaintiff v Department of Health of the Generalitat of Catalonia* [2012] ECLI:ES:TS:2012:6645 [Supreme Court].

for in the interests and for the benefit of the wider community cannot be borne exclusively by individuals, as it constitutes a wrongful injury that is compensable.

Notwithstanding the foregoing, in the majority of cases in Spain, the grounds for imposing liability is the abnormal operation of the service or the negligent conduct of the relevant administrative officials or agents.[16]

5. UNCERTAINTY ABOUT THE RISK OF AN EPIDEMIC AS A FORCE MAJEURE EVENT

The fundamental question about causation that arises in relation to COVID-19 infections is whether the appearance of the virus (together with its high transmission capacity among the population and its lethality) amounts in effect to force majeure that breaks the causal relationship between the damages suffered and the Government's action in managing the health crisis – granted that the appearance of the virus satisfies the characteristics for establishing force majeure in the jurisprudence namely:[17] non-foreseeability, inevitability and independence from administrative action.

However, what is difficult to determine is whether these characteristics coincide in relation to the consequences that the transmission of the virus has had on public health. In view of the background described in section 2, it is true that during the months of January and February 2020 there existed a degree of uncertainty about the transmission capacity and lethality of the virus, and it does not seem apparent (without falling into hindsight bias), that the authorities could then reasonably foresee the world health crisis scenario that was to come, which would exonerate the Government from responsibility on the grounds of force majeure.

However, although the worst-case scenario was not foreseeable, it was not ruled out either,[18] and it is worth asking whether, faced with the risk of a health crisis, uncertain though not ruled out, whether the national authorities were under

---

16 Gabriel Doménech Pascual, 'Responsabilidad patrimonial del Estado y Covid-19' (2020) 86–87 El Cronista del Estado Social y Democrático de Derecho 102, 106.

17 *Plaintiff v Spanish Health National Institute* [1999] ECLI:ES:TS:1999:6050 [Supreme Court]; *Plaintiff v Department of Health of Andalusia* [2001] ECLI:ES:TS:2001:5325 [Supreme Court].

18 Regarding the lack of a Government's action to control the virus transmission from asymptomatic persons, a similar approach is argued in Jesús Alfaro, 'Carta de un jurista a un científico sobre la toma de decisiones en una epidemia' (*Derecho Mercantil España*, 8 April 2020) https://derechomercantilespana.blogspot.com/2020/04/carta-de-un-jurista-un-cientifico-sobre.html accessed 18 June 2020. Monica Gandhi, Deborah S. Yokoe and Diane V. Havlir qualifies the asymptomatic transmission as the Achilles' heel of current strategies to control COVID-19: "Ultimately, the rapid spread of Covid-19 across the United States and the globe, the clear evidence of SARS-CoV-2 transmission from asymptomatic persons, and the eventual need to relax current social distancing practices argue for broadened

an obligation to prepare their public health system and other basic capacities to respond promptly and effectively to a future health emergency and, if this is the case, whether the Spanish State reasonably complied with that obligation.

This type of obligation was already foreseen in the International Health Regulations (IHR), approved by the World Health Assembly on 23 May 2005 (in force since 15 June 2007) and signed by 196 countries, pursuant to which States were required to develop, strengthen and maintain, within the next five years following the entry into force of the IHR, their capacity to respond to public health risks.[19] In line with this goal of improving the effectiveness of nations, the Hyogo Framework for Action (HFA) 2005–2015, adopted by 168 Member States of the United Nations, also gave priority to action designed to strengthen State preparedness in the event of disasters, in order to ensure an effective response at all levels. The background described in section 2 indicates how the WHO report of 3 February 2020 also insisted on this idea of increasing and reinforcing State preparedness and response.

In any case, it is debatable whether the breach of the obligation provided in the International Health Regulations serves as the basis for filing a tort law action against the Government and for establishing a causal link between the damages and the administrative action, although some studies have already estimated the percentage of cases of infection that could have been avoided had confinement of the population been put in place a week previously.[20]

6. THE LEVEL OF DILIGENCE REQUIRED OF HEALTHCARE PROFESSIONALS IN EMERGENCY HEALTH SITUATIONS

To assess the responsibility of the health administration for the specific actions of the professionals or personnel in its service, it is necessary to assess whether in each case, with respect to each particular victim, the requirements of liability have been satisfied.

SARS-CoV-2 testing to include asymptomatic persons in prioritized settings". Monica Gandhi, Deborah S. Yokoe and Diane V. Havlir, 'Asymptomatic Transmission, the Achilles' Heel of Current Strategies to Control Covid-19' (2020) 382 New England Journal of Medicine 2158 https://www.nejm.org/doi/full/10.1056/NEJMe2009758 accessed 22 June 2020.

19 Plans adopted by the Spanish Ministry of Health are available at: https://www.mscbs.gob.es/profesionales/saludPublica/ccayes/home.htm

20 "A second counterfactual exercise shows, however, that the number of coronavirus cases would have been reduced by an additional 12.8% if the lockdown had been brought forward to March 7th, a reduction that likely would have prevented the collapse of many hospitals in Spain". Luis Orea, Inmaculada C. Álvarez, 'How effective has been the lockdown to battle COVID-19? A spatial analysis of the coronavirus propagation across provinces' (2020) 2 Efficiency Series Paper, Department of Economics, University of Oviedo https://www.unioviedo.es/oeg/ESP/esp_2020_02.pdf accessed 15 June 2020, 24.

The obligation of the administration providing health services, in accordance with established jurisprudential doctrine, is not limited to obtaining a successful outcome – namely curing the patient – but also involves employing all available means to achieve this in accordance with the *lex artis*, that is, pursuant to the existing state of medical science and technology.[21]

One of the fundamental questions in this area is whether, in a serious situation of extreme urgency, and given limited healthcare resources, a lower standard of care is expected of health professionals than would prevail under normal conditions. The traditional response in terms of tort law is that, in general, an emergency constitutes one of the circumstances that modifies the duty of care, although a specific doctrine has not been developed in this regard.[22] Spanish law does not have special provisions for physicians who provide care pursuant to emergency standards and has not promulgated new protections specifically in response to the COVID-19 pandemic.[23] However, in the specific field of health care, the required standard of care by jurisprudence is that of the *lex artis ad hoc*, pursuant to which the specific case in which medical intervention occurs and the surrounding circumstances must be considered.

Therefore, the obligation to provide compensation for damages against the health administration for the actions of its personnel should be reserved to cases involving serious negligence, that is, when the most basic or elementary duty of care standards have not been met. A similar exemption rule is included in Article 14 of the Principles for the COVID-19 Crisis, of the European Law Institute,[24] although it excludes from the rule, "the liability of the state, which remains liable pursuant to the existing specific regime of liability". Under Spanish law, the injured

---

21 Catalan Legal Advisory Commission, Opinion 182/2019, 20 June 2019 https://portaljuridic.gencat.cat/ca/pjur_ocults/pjur_resultats_fitxa/?action=fitxa&documentId=853054&language=ca_ES&mode=single *Plaintiff v Spanish Health National Institute* [2011] ECLI:ES:TS:2011:4785 [Supreme Court].

22 Richard A. Epstein, *Cases and Materials on Torts* (9th edn, Aspen Publishers 2008) 216–217; Pablo Salvador Coderch et al., *Derecho de daños* (8th edn, InDret 2019) https://indret.com/wp-content/uploads/2017/10/16.10.2019.pdf accessed 17 June 2020.

23 34 states in the United States "offer some sort of civil liability protections for physicians who provide care pursuant to emergency standards. Of those, 16 states have promulgated new protections specifically in response to the COVID-19 pandemic. Importantly, all applicable laws that provide civil immunity for providing medical care during an emergency do so conditionally. In other words, if the physician has engaged in willful or intentional misconduct or gross negligence the physician would still be subject to civil liability". Valerie Gutmann Koch, 'How States are Protecting Health Care Providers from Legal Liability in the COVID-19 Pandemic' (*Bill of Health*, 5 May 2020) https://blog.petrieflom.law.harvard.edu/2020/05/05/legal-liability-health-care-covid19-coronavirus-pandemic/ accessed 20 June 2020.

24 Principle 14 Exemption from liability for simple negligence:

"(1) Given the urgent and dramatic circumstances in which doctors, healthcare professionals, and other providers in the medical sector have to provide services, States should ensure that these professionals are not held liable for adverse events related to the COVID-19, except in the case of at least gross negligence.

party seeking to make a claim for damage arising from medical negligence, only has a basis for action seeking damages against the public administration, and not directly against the relevant personnel employed by the public administration, without prejudice to the personal responsibilities of a criminal nature that may be imposed on these parties in accordance with the corresponding legislation (Arts 36 and 37 of the Public Sector Act). These include the crimes of causing injury or homicide due to professional negligence and require a high degree of same (Arts 142.1 and 152.1 of the Spanish Penal Code of 1995).

Additionally, the Spanish Ministry of Health is likely to face claims based on the ground that some patients were not properly attended to by medical services due to the limited health resources available. However, Article 34 of the Public Sector Act provides that damages arising from facts or circumstances that could not have been prevented or avoided according to the state of scientific and technical knowledge, will not be compensable. Notwithstanding the foregoing, Article 34 of the Public Sector Act does not preclude the granting of assistance and economic benefits in applicable cases.

Another issue that will be more problematic once again is whether the State had an obligation to prepare the public health system earlier in order to minimise the impact of a health emergency, which although was not foreseeable, it was not ruled out either.

7. PRIORITISATION OF PATIENTS IN A SITUATION INVOLVING INSUFFICIENT VITAL RESOURCES

In a health emergency situation involving insufficient vital resources, professionals may be forced to apply extreme situation medical protocol, which means prioritising, in accordance with agreed medical criteria, those patients who are likely to benefit most from admission to an intensive care unit.

The Spanish Ministry of Health and 25 health, socio-health and teaching organisations have published two documents[25] in which they establish

(2) The same applies with respect to other professionals and holders of public offices who had to take quick and difficult decisions directly related to the COVID-19 crisis.

(3) These exemptions from liability do not apply to the liability of the State, which remains liable pursuant to the existing specific regime of liability".

[25] Spanish Ministry of Health, 'Informe del ministerio de sanidad sobre los aspectos éticos en situaciones de pandemia: el SARS-CoV-2' (3 April 2020) https://www.mscbs.gob.es/profesionales/saludPublica/ccayes/alertasActual/nCov-China/documentos/200403-INFORME_PANDEMIA-FINAL-MAQUETADO.pdf accessed 10 June 2020.

Spanish Society of Geriatrics and Gerontology (SEGG) et al., 'Recomendaciones sobre decisiones éticas e ingreso en UCI en situación de crisis Covid-19' (19 March 2020) https://www.segg.es/actualidad-segg/2020/03/19/consenso-segg-recomendaciones-uci-covid-19 accessed 10 June 2020.

recommendations for health professionals who are faced with a conflict of interest between the health and life of a diverse series of patients awaiting vital hospital treatment. The objective prioritisation criteria are based on the pathological situation and objective survival expectations, under the basic principle of obtaining the maximum benefit in terms of saving human lives. In both documents, it is emphasised that age should in no case be the only element to consider in the strategies employed for allocating vital resources.

Similarly, the Ministry for Health, in Order SND/265/2020, of 19 March, imposed conditions as regards the referral to health centres of elderly people from nursing homes and socio-sanitary units, if they met clinical criteria, assessed by a doctor, for referral. If they did not comply, the patient follow-up should be carried out in the residence.

Patients who died from COVID-19 and were unable to receive vital healthcare resources clearly missed out on an opportunity for treatment.[26] It should be remembered, however, that a fault liability rule applies to health professionals and in the absence of required alternative conduct, it cannot be stated that those who correctly applied the protocols acted negligently. A different matter is whether the courts can impose strict liability on the health administration to compensate for this type of damage because they consider that these patients were not obliged to accept them given that such a sacrifice exceeds the normal obligations imposed on all citizens.

On the other hand, the Spanish courts[27] have recognised that the existence of waiting lists and the consequent delay in the provision of health care as an inevitable consequence of the limited health resources available and have not sought to impose liability on the health administration unless there have been faults or unreasonable delays in the management of the waiting lists or when errors have been made in assessing patient priority:[28]

> The means available to the Administration cannot be unlimited. No one claims such a thing. Neither with respect to the health Administration, nor with respect to any other. The availability of personal and material is always limited, and this must be taken into consideration .... It is not, therefore, a matter of requiring the Administration to have unlimited means – which would be wrongful and an offence to common sense and the prevailing reality – but to prove that the material

26 In the UK context, see Clare Dyer, 'Covid-19: Woman whose father died in care home launches legal review over government's "litany of failures"' 369 (2020) https://www.bmj.com/content/369/bmj.m2405 accessed 19 June 2020.

27 *Plaintiffs v Health Department of the Generalitat of Catalonia* [2011] ECLI:ES:TS:2011:4654 [Supreme Court].

28 *Plaintiffs v Health Department of the Generalitat of Catalonia* [2011] ECLI:ES:TS:2011:4654 [Supreme Court]; *Plaintiffs v Spanish Health National Institute* [2003] ECLI: ES:AN:2003:2253.

and personnel available within the system were operative and occupied in caring for patients who had previously entered the system.[29]

8. THE LIABILITY OF THE PUBLIC ADMINISTRATION FOR INFRINGEMENT OF THE OCCUPATIONAL RISK PREVENTION REGULATIONS

In accordance with the law,[30] the Government has established that the illnesses suffered by personnel that provide service in health or social health centres, registered in the corresponding registers, as a consequence of the spread of the SARS-CoV-2 virus during the state of alarm, will be considered as a professional contingency arising from an accident at work, when being assessed by the services for the Prevention of Industrial Hazards and Health and Safety at Work.

The Social Security regulations recognise, that in the event of death due to professional illness or work-related accidents, a special lump sum compensation in the event of death due to work-related illness is awarded to the spouse, domestic partner and children.

This sort of compensation is compatible, up to the limit of the full compensation provided for the damage, with compensation resulting from any potential tort liability on the part of the administration for a possible infringement of the regulations on prevention of occupational hazards, if it were established that the victim had to engage in activities related to their employment without being provided with the necessary mandatory protective equipment to carry out such activity safely in accordance with the legislation.

Article 17.2 of Law 31/1995, of 8 November, on prevention of occupation hazards:

> An employer must provide their workers with adequate personal protective equipment for the performance of their duties and ensure that such equipment is effective when the nature of any work carried out requires their use.
>
> Personal protective equipment must be used when risks cannot be avoided or cannot be sufficiently limited by technical means involving collective protection or by measures, methods or procedures for organising work.

Any claim alleging insufficient resources cannot provide grounds for exoneration because the Administration has an obligation to provide occupational risk prevention measures and this obligation remained in force during the state of alarm, since the professionals affected were bound to provide their activity, as an

---

29 *Plaintiffs v Health Department of the Generalitat of Catalonia* [2011] ECLI:ES:TS:2011:4654 [Supreme Court].

30 Royal Decree-Law 19/2020, of 26 May.

essential service. The basis for imposing responsibility is the breach of the safe working regulations.

It is more problematic to defend the liability of the administration for the infection of professionals in centres that had sufficient personal protective equipment. But, again, the strict liability of the administration and the concept of wrongful damage, could serve as a basis for considering that the death of all health professionals as a consequence of a disease amounts to damage that exceeds the normal obligations of every citizen to live in society, which occurs as a consequence of the exercise of an activity that is carried out for the benefit and interest of the community and, therefore, cannot be borne exclusively by those entitled, constituting a wrongful injury that has to be compensated.

9. ALTERNATIVES TO THE INDIVIDUAL TORT LAW CLAIM: CLASS ACTION, COMPENSATION FUNDS AND PUBLIC AID

It should be borne in mind that any compensatory judicial remedy is a very expensive instrument to manage and compensate massive claims for damages, because it has to be resolved on a case-by-case basis, depending on the specific circumstances and, in addition, in Spain, in matters of State liability, it is necessary to initiate an administrative procedure prior to the judicial one.

From a procedural law perspective, it is not obvious whether an association legally constituted in defence of patients has the right to file a tort law claim against the public administration to defend the interests of patients who have been harmed by the operation of the public health service, even if those patients are not members of the association. That is, whether an association legally constituted can bring an administrative or a judicial class action against the Public Administration under Spanish Law.

Article 4.2 of the Spanish Law 39/2015, of 1 October, on the Common Administrative Procedure, establishes that associations and organisations representing economic and social interests own legitimate collective interests in the terms recognised by the Law and have the right to initiate an administrative procedure. Moreover, Article 19.1.b) of the Spanish Law 29/1998, of 13 July, on the Administrative Judicial Procedure, gives legal capacity to sue to associations that "are legally authorized to defend collective rights and legitimate interests."

It is debatable whether the concept of "collective interest" used by both regulations needs to be interpreted exclusively as a general interest attached to a community or group, therefore different from the sum of the private interests of each individual. In addition, the Law 29/1998 does not regulate other fundamental questions of the class actions regime (publicity of the claim and of the judicial decision, res judicata effects, enforcement of the judicial decision, etc.).[31]

However, the Supreme Court decision, of 20 September 2005,[32] has recognised that Article 11 of the Spanish Civil Procedure Law (Law 1/2000, of 7 January) is applicable as a default rule to the administrative judicial procedure according to the First Final Provision of the Law 29/1998, and Article 11 clearly recognises the right of the associations legally constituted to file a claim in defence of consumers and users who are not their members and to claim on their behalf compensation for the individual damages suffered as a result of a harmful event.

Anyway, given that the Spanish judicial system is showing signs of strain following the paralysis of judicial activity during the state of alarm, it would be advisable to take into account other less expensive compensation systems, such as compensation funds or public aid, which could establish scales to adapt the valuation of damages to the circumstances of different groups of cases.

---

31 Juan José Marín López, 'Las acciones de clase en el derecho españo' (2001) 3 InDret 4 https://indret.com/wp-content/themes/indret/pdf/057_es.pdf accessed 25 September 2020.

32 *Spanish and Catalan Organizations of Consumers and Users v Spanish Airports and Air Traffic Public Company* [2005] ECLI: ES:TS:2005:5365 [Supreme Court].

STATE LIABILITY FOR THE MANAGEMENT OF THE COVID-19 CRISIS

Gabriel DOMÉNECH-PASCUAL*

This contribution analyses whether and under which conditions the State ought to compensate for the losses caused when managing the COVID-19 crisis. It focuses, first, on instances where public authorities have accidentally caused the damage at issue either through actions or omissions. Secondly, it considers cases of State liability for lawful conduct, where public authorities deliberately have inflicted some damage on a person or a group of people for the sake of the public interest. The contribution takes Spanish law as a reference, which does not prevent the analysis from being extended to other legal systems based on similar principles.

1. INTRODUCTION

Millions of people have suffered or will suffer significant losses as a result of the COVID-19 crisis. This contribution analyses whether and under which

* University of Valencia.

conditions the State must compensate for those losses under Spanish law, whose principles on this issue are not far from those applicable in other European countries, despite appearances suggesting the contrary.[1] That obligation to compensate may arise in four types of cases.

First, there might be instances of State liability in a strict sense, where a harmful event has been accidentally caused as a consequence of actions or omissions of some public authority.

Secondly, we can think of cases where the State deliberately inflicts some damage on a person or a group of people for the sake of the public interest. Unlike instances of liability in a strict sense, where a harmful accident decreases social welfare, here the governmental measures increase – or, at least, should increase – that welfare, but at the same time they involve a special sacrifice for some people, which is to be compensated. These measures might well be deemed expropriations. However, some courts and legal scholars have considered them as instances of State liability for lawful actions.[2] Nevertheless, the big issue here is how to distinguish those measures that must be accompanied by a fair compensation (in my opinion, because they are expropriations, which are to be compensated pursuant to the Spanish Constitution[3]) from those deprivations or restrictions of rights that do not need to be compensated.

Thirdly, there might also be cases of unjust enrichment, where the Government has experienced an unjustified enrichment at the expense of a person, and it must make restitution or compensate for it.

Fourthly, the State may impose an obligation on itself to grant aid to (some of) the victims of the COVID-19 aimed at enabling them to meet their basic needs or to promote economic activity.

This contribution will focus on the first two types of cases. The analysis of these issues is arguably of great practical relevance, on the one hand, because it is foreseeable that they will generate a huge volume of litigation during the next few years, at least in Spain, and on the other hand, because the legal regime of those obligations might well influence the courses of action that both the relevant public agents and the potential victims of the COVID-19 or other similar events may take to deal with this or other analogous crisis in the future. It can be assumed that, when acting in one way or another, all of these individuals will anticipate and take into account, at least to some extent, what these obligations to compensate may be, insofar as the costs and benefits they might expect from their current decisions depend on them.

---

1 See Oliver Dör, 'Staatshaftung in Europa: Vergleichende Bestandsaufnahme' in Oliver Dörr (ed), *Staatshaftung in Europa: Nationales und Unionsrecht* (De Gruyter 2014); Ken Oliphant (ed), *The Liability of Public Authorities in Comparative Perspective* (Intersentia 2016).

2 See, e.g. Judgment of the Constitutional Court No. 28/1997, of 13 February.

3 See Article 33.3 of the Spanish Constitution. See also Article 17 of the Charter of Fundamental Rights of the European Union.

2. SPECIFIC LEGAL PROVISIONS FOR HEALTH EMERGENCIES

Several legal provisions specifically regulate State liability for damages caused by the adoption of measures in a health crisis such as the one we are now experiencing.

Article 3.2 of Organic Law 4/1981, of 1 June, on the states of alarm, exception and siege (LOEAES) establishes that "those who, as a result of the application of the acts and provisions adopted during these states, suffer ... damages or harm for acts not attributable to them, shall be entitled to compensation in accordance with the law".

Article 54.2 of Law 33/2011, of 4 October, of Public Health (LGSP), allows health authorities to take some precautionary measures in cases of emergency: the immobilisation and seizure of products and substances; the intervention of material or personal resources; the closure of facilities, establishments, services and industries; the suspension of activities; the regulation of conditions for manufacturing or marketing products and substances, as well as the operation of facilities, establishments, services and industries; and, in general, any other measure in accordance with the law if there are reasonable grounds to suspect any risk to health (para 2). And it also provides that "the costs arising from the adoption of [such measures] shall be borne by the person or undertaking responsible" (para 3 *in fine*).

These two provisions raise more questions than they resolve. They only clarify that the people who have suffered any losses as a result of those measures are not entitled to compensation if they are "responsible" for the situation which gave rise to them, i.e., if the measures are "attributable to them". Both provisions may well be interpreted as meaning that such a case occurs when the risk to public health that led to the administrative intervention was generated by those victims, either lawfully or unlawfully. For that purpose, it is irrelevant whether they created that risk by breaching the law (e.g. by not taking due care) or this risk was simply the fortuitous result of an activity they carried out in accordance with the law.

Beyond this point, several doubts arise. It should be noted, first, that neither of the two provisions refers to cases where the victims did not create the situation that prompted the administrative intervention. Neither of them considers the scenario where the risk the State tried to combat is not attributable to the victims. Article 3.2 LOEAES merely establishes that injured parties "shall be entitled to compensation in accordance with the law". In other words, it refers to the general principles applicable to this matter, which we will refer to later.

Secondly, neither of them provides anything for the cases where the measures causing the losses are unlawful, for example, because they are disproportionate. It is by no means obvious that the State should not be held liable for those infringements, not even when the illegal actions were directed against those who created the risk at issue.

Thirdly, both provisions refer to damages caused by governmental measures taken to fight a crisis like that of the COVID-19, but not for damages caused by the State having omitted the measures it should have taken to deal with this and other similar crises.

In order to answer these and other questions, there is no choice but to apply the general rules and principles established in the legislation on State liability and expropriation.

3. GENERAL PROVISIONS ON STATE LIABILITY AND EXPROPRIATION

When applying these legal norms, which are contained in Articles 32 and following of Law 40/2015, of 1 October 2015, on the Legal Regime of the Public Sector (LRJSP), and in the Expropriation Act of 16 December 1954 (LEF), to the cases we are considering, we should take into account two relevant factors.

First, such norms are extremely ambiguous and indeterminate, which entails both an advantage and a disadvantage. On the one hand, they do not provide a specific or clear answer to the questions posed by such an unusual crisis as the one we are experiencing, since they have not been designed for a situation like this. The problem is accentuated precisely by the fact that the COVID-19 crisis and the measures taken to deal with it are so extraordinary that it is extremely difficult to find in the case law of our courts criteria established in similar cases that provide a firm basis on which we can safely rely. On the other hand, that indeterminacy makes these provisions very flexible. It enables judges to adapt them to the current exceptional circumstances.

Secondly, this is, surely, one of the branches of Spanish administrative law where one can find a greater number of inconsistencies: between what our laws seem to prescribe and how they are actually applied by the courts; between the arguments that the courts use to decide and the actual content of their decisions, etc.

4. STATE LIABILITY IN A STRICT SENSE

Under Articles 32 and 34 LRJSP, the State is liable if the following conditions are met:

First, the victim needs to have suffered some damage that is: (1) actual; (2) economically assessable; (3) individualised; and (4) unlawful.

Secondly, there must be a causal link between the normal or abnormal operation of public services and that harm. This causation is excluded in cases of force majeure.

We will focus on those conditions that, in the case of the COVID-19, raise more pressing questions.

4.1. INDIVIDUALISED DAMAGES

Pursuant to Article 32.2 LRJSP, the alleged damage, to give rise to State liability, must be "individualised [*individualizado*] in relation to a person or group of people". The rationale of this condition is obvious. It would be absurd to compensate for losses suffered by the general public, since it would be the general public who, through the tax system, would have not only to pay the compensation, but also the costs of the proceedings that would have to be carried out to determine whether the State is liable or not and, eventually, the amount of money to be paid. "Compensating" the victims would paradoxically leave them worse off. The money they would cash through one pocket would be less than the money going out from the other.

It is clear that, as a result of the management of the COVID-19 crisis by the Government, most Spanish citizens have suffered or will suffer, to a greater or lesser extent, considerable losses. At the very least, the economic consequences that such management will trigger for Spanish society as a whole seem enormous. Therefore, for the above-mentioned reasons, there is little point in holding the State liable for these widespread damages. This does not preclude that the Government mitigates, in full or in part, such losses with the aim of fostering economic activity or protecting the well-being of the most needy or vulnerable people. However, tort law is not the most efficient nor the fairest legal tool for achieving that goal. State aids are surely preferable insofar as they are granted through less costly procedures and allow allocating resources to the people who need them most or who can derive the greatest social benefit from them.

Nevertheless, in my opinion, we cannot exclude the possibility of the Government having caused some individualised damages within the meaning of Article 32.2 LRJSP when managing the COVID-19 crisis. The State should eventually compensate for those special, singularly intense losses that exceed those that citizens have had to endure overall because of the management of the pandemic. It is reasonable to consider, for instance, that certain personal damages (e.g. the death of a close relative) or property damages fit into the aforementioned legal concept. Let us think that some elderly people infected with the COVID-19 died because the State illegally refused to admit them to hospital. Suppose also that some doctors and nurses became infected with the COVID-19 and died because of the negligent failure of the national health system to provide them with the necessary personal protective equipment.

4.2. UNLAWFULNESS AND NEGLIGENCE

4.2.1. *The dominant interpretation: State liability is strict*

The dominant interpretation of the provisions governing State liability in Spain has been built on two main pillars.

On the one hand, it is said that such liability is strict. This is how Article 121 of the Expropriation Act of 1954 was interpreted, whose content Article 32.1 LRJSP now reproduces in similar terms: "Individuals shall have the right to be compensated by the corresponding Public Administration for any damage they suffer to their property or rights, as long as the damage is the result of the normal or abnormal operation of public services, except in the case of force majeure or damages that the victim has no legal obligation to endure according to the law". It must be noted that this provision does not require any negligence by the injurer, unlike Article 1902 of the Spanish Civil Code, applicable in private law, which prescribes that "[t]he person who, as a result of an action or omission, causes damage to another by his fault or negligence shall be obliged to repair the damaged caused". The fact that Article 32 LRJSP omits any reference to negligence and, furthermore, provides for State liability when the damage has been caused even by the normal operation of public services indicates that such liability is strict.

On the other hand, it is established that the damage caused by the Government must be "unlawful", meaning "damage that the victim has no legal obligation to endure according to the law". The key to determining whether the State is liable or not is not whether the public service functioned normally or abnormally, it is not whether the State acted diligently or negligently, but whether the damage itself is lawful or unlawful.

This doctrine has been upheld for more than six decades by the overwhelming majority of legal scholars and practically all administrative courts. The last milestone achieved by such doctrine is the Judgments of the Constitutional Court No 112/2018, of 17 October, and No 79/2019 of 5 June, where it is stated, no less, that the referred strict-liability rule has constitutional status (as it is embedded in Article 106.2 of the Spanish Constitution[4]) and, therefore, cannot be abrogated by the legislature.[5]

4.2.2. *De facto, State liability is negligence-based*

However, there is a systematic, profound, and evident discrepancy between what Spanish courts say and what they really do, i.e. between the arguments they give to justify their decisions on this matter and their actual content. In the vast

---

4 Article 106.2 of the Spanish Constitution establishes that "[i]ndividuals shall, under the terms established by law, have the right to be compensated for any damage they suffer to their property or rights, except in the case of force majeure, as long as the damage is the result of the operation of public services".

5 See the critique by Ignacio Rodríguez Fernández, 'La responsabilidad objetiva de la Administración pública y la equidistribución del coste del bien común' (2018) 195 Revista Española de Derecho Administrativo 155.

majority of cases, despite formally reproducing the above-mentioned doctrine time and again, they apply, *de facto*, a negligence rule: the State is held liable only if the damage is the result of an abnormal operation of the corresponding public service, i.e. if public authorities omitted due care.[6] With very few exceptions, the truth is that, in practice, State liability is negligence-based, even though most legal scholars and virtually all courts maintain otherwise.

To reach this outcome, Spanish courts use several questionable arguments.[7] A neat "trick" consists in introducing the negligence rule under the guise of the causation requirement: if the public service was operated "normally", if the relevant administrative authorities took all due precautions, the courts declare that the loss at issue was not caused by such operation.[8] At other times, they just state that the strict liability regime is to be relaxed (*modulado*) in some cases, without providing a reason that convincingly justifies why an exception must be made.[9] The most frequently used strategy, however, is to resort to the "unlawfulness requirement" to apply the negligence rule without acknowledging so: if the State took due care, the victim is deemed to have a legal obligation to endure the damage suffered, which would therefore not be unlawful.[10]

This last strategy is favoured by the circularity of the concept of "damage that one does not have a legal obligation to endure in accordance with the law". To affirm that the injurer must compensate for those damages that the victim is not obliged to bear is a tautology.[11] To elude the circular reasoning that such a statement entails, another criterion is needed to determine whether that obligation exists or not. But neither legal scholars nor the courts have managed to produce a satisfactory general criterion in that regard. The most prominent authors on this issue point out that the loss must be considered unlawful "as long as there are no causes for justification that legitimise the damage in question". Initially, they also considered that such causes had to be explicitly

---

6 See, e.g. Oriol Mir, 'Responsabilidad objetiva vs. funcionamiento anormal en la responsabilidad patrimonial de la Administración sanitaria' (2008) 140 Revista Española de Derecho Administrativo 629; Oriol Mir, 'Spanien' in Oliver Dörr (ed), *Staatshaftung in Europa: Nationales und Unionsrecht* (De Gruyter 2014) 712; Miquel Martín-Casals and Jordi Ribot, 'The Liability of Public Authorities in Spain' in Ken Oliphant (ed), *The Liability of Public Authorities in Comparative Perspective* (Intersentia 2016) 470, 481, 483, 488.

7 See Letelier Wartenberg, 'La Falta de Servicio en España' (2001) 23 Revista de Derecho. Consejo de Defensa del Estado 63; Medina Alcoz, 'Mitos y ficciones en la responsabilidad patrimonial de las Administraciones públicas' (2012) 153 Revista Española de Derecho Administrativo 153.

8 See, e.g. Judgment of the Supreme Court (3rd Chamber) of 19 June 1998 (rec. 1985/1994).

9 See, e.g. Judgment of the Supreme Court (3rd Chamber) of 15 March 2018 (rec. 1016/2016).

10 See, e.g. Judgment of the Supreme Court (3rd Chamber) of 10 December 2008 (rec. 7931/2004).

11 Juan Antonio García Amado, 'Sobre algunos mitos del Derecho de daños. Causas que no causan e imputaciones objetivas bastante subjetivas' in Mariano José Herrador Guardia (ed), *Derecho de daños* (Aranzadi 2013).

established by law.[12] However, the courts have consistently refused this solution. They have considered, for example, that harm arising from public health care without negligence is not unlawful, although in this and similar cases, no legal provision explicitly imposes an obligation on the victims to endure such harm. In fact, those authors have ended up changing their opinion, and now argue that the State should be held liable if "there is no legal ground that determines or imposes as strictly inexcusable, actually intended or at least possibly accepted, the damage" at issue, which is a formula of much broader scope. The authors also give some examples of what such a ground may be (e.g. the payment of a tax or "the general burdens of social life"), but they also refrain from formulating an abstract criterion.[13]

In practice, the concept of unlawfulness works as a kind of "catch-all" concept,[14] which judges fill in depending on their intuitions.

Anyway, there is no reason to think that the negligence rule, which is *de facto* applied in Spanish public law in most of the cases of State liability, should not or will not be used in the case under consideration.

4.2.3. *Rationale of the negligence rule*

There are, indeed, good reasons to consider that, in cases where public authorities accidentally or even illegally, but not negligently, cause some damage when trying to protect public health, the victims ought to have the "obligation to endure it".

There is a vast literature on the advantages and disadvantages of negligence and strict liability rules.[15] The most relevant difference in that regard probably has to do with the volume of activity of both potential victims and injurers.

Let us suppose that due care equals the socially optimal level of care, where the marginal costs of increasing it equal its expected marginal benefits. Given this and other reasonable assumptions, we are going to skip for the sake of simplicity, one might conclude that both rules induce potential injurers to take that efficient level of care. Under both rules, the expected costs for potential injurers of taking more or less than this optimal care are greater than its benefits.

---

12 Eduardo García de Enterría and Tomás Ramón Fernández Rodríguez, *Curso de Derecho Administrativo* (Civitas 1993) vol. II, chapter XXI, IV, 2.

13 Eduardo García de Enterría and Tomás Ramón Fernández Rodríguez, *Curso de Derecho Administrativo* (Civitas 2017) vol. II, chapter XXI, IV, 3.

14 Juan Antonio García Amado, 'Sobre algunos mitos del Derecho de daños. Causas que no causan e imputaciones objetivas bastante subjetivas' in Mariano José Herrador Guardia (ed), *Derecho de daños* (Aranzadi 2013).

15 See, e.g. Hans Bernd Schäfer and Frank Müller Langer, 'Strict Liability Versus Negligence' in Michael Faure (ed), *Encyclopedia of Law and Economics. Tort Law and Economics* (Edward Elgar 2009).

By contrast, these two rules might well induce different levels of activity.[16] In a regime of negligence, potential victims bear the risk of accidents caused by injurers having acted diligently. It means that the former bear the costs of their level of activity being higher than the socially optimal one, where the marginal social costs of increasing it equal the expected additional benefits of doing so. This will induce them not to exceed that optimal level, insofar as they would pay for the excess, whose costs are, by definition, higher than its benefits.

Under this rule, potential injurers do not bear the risk of accidents when having taken due care. They will thus not bear the costs of their level of activity being higher than the socially optimal one. Consequently, this will lead them to exceed this optimal level, insofar as they would not pay for the excess.

In a regime of strict liability, potential injurers bear the risk of accidents despite having acted diligently. It means that they bear the costs of their level of activity exceeding the socially optimal one. This will induce them not to exceed that optimal level, insofar as they would pay for this excess. On the contrary, as potential victims do not bear the above-mentioned risk nor, therefore, the costs of their activity exceeding that optimal level, this rule will lead them to engage in this activity excessively, e.g. more frequently.

It must be noted that neither of these rules induces both potential injurers and victims to engage in socially optimal levels of activity. Negligence fails to do so with respect to the former, and strict liability with respect to the latter ones. Given that, strict liability seems preferable when the social costs of potential injurers engaging in an excessive volume of activity are greater than the social costs of potential victims doing the same, and vice versa.[17] In fact, in most Western legal systems, negligence is the general rule and strict liability only applies in certain cases, mainly to losses arising from "abnormally dangerous" activities carried out by tortfeasors.[18]

Consequently, it seems sensible to apply the negligence rule to the damages accidentally caused by the State when trying to protect public health against the COVID-19. This rule might create the risk that the relevant authorities excessively exercise its powers aimed at protecting public health. However, this risk seems less serious than the risk of potential victims carrying out an excessive volume of activities that could spread or worsen this pandemic. On the one hand, because the magnitude of the eventual harm seems lower in the former case. On the other hand, because several legal norms (e.g. the principles of legality and proportionality) limit the possibility of the State excessively exercising its

16 See, e.g. Steven Shavell, 'Strict Liability versus Negligence' (1980) 9 Journal of Legal Studies 1.

17 See also Keith N. Hylton, 'A positive Theory of Strict Liability' (2008) 4 Review of Law and Economics 153.

18 See, for instance, Article 5:101 of the Principles of European Tort Law, prepared by the European Group on Tort Law (hereafter, PETL).

powers, and the courts may verify whether those limits have been exceeded. By contrast, there are no clear legal rules restricting the level of activity individuals may carry out in the case of a pandemic like the COVID-19, and it would be very difficult for the courts to verify whether those rules have been violated.[19]

Moreover, strict liability might lead the Government to take excessive precautions aimed at preventing its decisions from being declared illegal by the courts, if we assume that it does not fully internalise the costs of such precautions[20] – as these costs are ultimately borne by taxpayers –, or if it overestimates the risk of making illegal decisions. In this vein, the courts of the European Union have noted that the requirement of a "sufficiently serious breach" (i.e. negligence) seeks "to avoid the situation where the risk of having to bear the losses alleged by the undertakings concerned hinders the ability of the institution concerned to fully exercise its competences in the general interest".[21] The non-existence of this requirement "would risk compromising the capacity of [EU Institutions] fully to function as regulator ... as a result of the inhibiting effect that the risk of having to bear the losses alleged by the undertakings concerned might have" on their decisions.[22]

4.2.4. Negligence in actions and omissions: standard of conduct

It must also be underlined that such negligence should be a necessary condition for State liability in both instances of losses caused by omissions or actions.

The State could only be held liable for having omitted safety measures that might have prevented the damages at issue if such omission involved a breach of the obligation to take due care, i.e. a "violation of the required standard of conduct".[23] The fact that Spanish administrative courts do not explicitly acknowledge that they apply the negligence rule to State liability has favoured that the criteria they usually apply in order to define that standard of conduct are not very transparent nor consistent. Nevertheless, it might be argued that such criteria are quite similar to those employed in the private realm.[24] In my opinion, the *de facto* rule underlying most judgments is that the administrative

---

19 For more details on the advantages of negligence over strict liability with respect to State liability, see Gabriel Doménech Pascual, 'Responsabilidad patrimonial de la Administración por actos jurídicos ilegales. ¿Responsabilidad objetiva o por culpa?' (2010) 183 Revista de Administración Pública 179.

20 See Gerrit de Geest, 'Who Should Be Immune from Tort Liability?' (2012) 41 Journal of Legal Studies 291; Jef de Mot and Michael Faure, 'The Liability of Public Authorities: An Economic Analysis', in Ken Oliphant (ed), *The Liability of Public Authorities in Comparative Perspective* (Intersentia 2016) 617. See also Giuseppe Dari-Mattiacci, Nuno Garoupa and Fernando Gómez-Pomar, 'State Liability' (2010) 4 European Review of Private Law 773.

21 Case T-429/05 *Artegodan* [2010] ECLI:EU:T:2010:60, para 55.

22 Case T-212/03 *MyTravel Group* [2008] ECLI:EU:T:2008:315, para 42.

23 In the words of Art 4:101 of PETL.

24 See, for instance, Art 4:102 of PETL.

authorities must take those precautions that are economically efficient, i.e. whose expected marginal benefits, derived from reducing the risk of accidents, exceed their marginal costs from an *ex ante* point of view.[25]

According to this criterion and in view of the information available so far, which is still limited, it might be argued that the Spanish Government omitted efficient precautionary measures that would have substantially reduced the negative impact of the pandemic. The Government disregarded for several weeks the recommendations of the World Health Organization,[26] the European Centre for Disease Prevention and Control,[27] and other public bodies and scientific organisations on how to deal with the risks associated with the COVID-19 (e.g. by purchasing protective medical equipment, testing, implementing social distancing, cancelling mass gatherings, etc.).[28] The fact that Spain is one of the countries with a highest mortality excess *per capita* during the COVID-19 outbreak suggests that our Government did not do a very good job in managing it.

Similarly, the mere fact that some of the measures adopted to tackle the present crisis that have caused losses (e.g. the closure of certain establishments) were declared unlawful would not be a sufficient condition to give rise to State liability. It is also necessary that such unlawfulness was the result of a violation of the duty to take due care. In the same vein, as said before, the European Court of Justice (ECJ) has declared that the European Union and Members States are liable for damages caused for breaches of European Union law only if the infringement at issue is "sufficiently serious".[29] In this regard, "the decisive test for finding that a breach of [EU] law is sufficiently serious is whether the Member State or the [EU] institution concerned manifestly and gravely disregarded the limits on its discretion".[30]

In order to apply this test, the courts may take into consideration several factors: "the complexity of the situations to be regulated, difficulties in the application or interpretation of the texts";[31] "the clarity and precision of the rule breached, the measure of discretion left by that rule to the national or [EU] authorities, whether the infringement and the damage caused was intentional

25 For more details, see Gabriel Doménech Pascual, 'Sobre el poder explicativo del análisis económico del Derecho. En especial, del Derecho de daños' (2019) 2 InDret.

26 See, e.g. Key planning recommendations for mass gatherings in the context of the current COVID-19 outbreak: interim guidance, 14 February 2020; Report of the WHO-China Joint Mission on Coronavirus Disease 2019 (COVID-19) 16–24 February 2020.

27 See, e.g. European Centre for Disease Prevention and Control. Outbreak of novel coronavirus disease 2019 (COVID-19): increased transmission globally – fifth update, 2 March 2020.

28 The governmental response in other countries was also questionable. See Lucas Bergkamp, 'State Liability for Failure to Control the COVID-19 Epidemic: International and Dutch Law' [2020] European Journal of Risk Regulation.

29 See, e.g. Case C-352/98 *Bergaderm and Goupil* [2000] ECLI:EU:C:2000:361, para 42.

30 Joined Cases C-46/93 and C-48/93 *Brasserie du Pêcheur and Factortame and others* [1996] ECLI:EU:C:1996:79, para 55.

31 Ibid, para 43.

or involuntary, whether any error of law was excusable or inexcusable, the fact that the position taken by a [EU] institution may have contributed towards the omission, and the adoption or retention of national measures or practices contrary to [EU] law";[32] "a breach of [EU] law will clearly be sufficiently serious if it has persisted despite a judgment finding the infringement in question to be established, or a preliminary ruling or settled case-law of the [ECJ] on the matter from which it is clear that the conduct in question constituted an infringement".[33]

The Spanish Supreme Court has established an analogous doctrine. It has declared that, even when the relevant administrative authorities have acted unlawfully, "it is necessary to leave a certain margin of appreciation" to them. If they exercised their powers in a relatively reasonable and reasoned manner, within certain margins, the eventual damage is not "unlawful", and the victims have the duty to endure it. "The contrary might seriously harm the public interest by delaying the activity of the Government in view of the permanent doubt about the legality of its decisions".[34]

4.3. FORCE MAJEURE

Article 32.1 LRJSP excludes the liability of public administrations for damages caused by the operation of public services in cases of force majeure, which Article 1105 of the Spanish Civil Code defines as those events "which cannot be foreseen or which, being foreseen, should be inevitable". Similarly, Article 34.1 LRJSP establishes that the State is not liable for "damage arising from facts or circumstances which could not have been foreseen or avoided according to the state of scientific or technical knowledge existing at the time of their production, without prejudice to any public aid that the law may establish for such cases". The Spanish Supreme Court has also added that force majeure is an event that has an origin outside the activity of the parties – here, the operation of public services – and is beyond their control.[35]

---

32 Ibid, para 56.

33 Ibid, para 57.

34 Judgment of the Supreme Court (3rd Chamber) of 5 February 1996 (rec. 2034/1993). See Miquel Martín-Casals and Jordi Ribot, 'The Liability of Public Authorities in Spain' in Ken Oliphant (ed), *The Liability of Public Authorities in Comparative Perspective* (Intersentia 2016) 483. This case law has been very controversial. In favour of it, see, e.g. Gabriel Doménech Pascual, 'Responsabilidad patrimonial de la Administración por actos jurídicos ilegales. ¿Responsabilidad objetiva o por culpa?' (2010) 183 Revista de Administración Pública 179. Against it, see, e.g. Luis Medina Alcoz, *La responsabilidad patrimonial por acto administrativo* (Civitas 2005); Tomás Ramón Fernández Rodríguez, '¿Existe un deber jurídico de soportar los perjuicios produciros por un acto administrativo declarado nulo por sentencia firme?' (2018) 205 Revista de Administración Pública 221; David Blanquer Criado, *La responsabilidad patrimonial en tiempos de pandemia* (Tirant lo Blanch 2020).

35 Judgment of the Supreme Court (3rd Chamber) of 11 July 1995 (rec. 303/1993). See also Antonio José Sánchez Sáez, 'La responsabilidad patrimonial de las Administraciones públicas

The rationale of this exclusion of liability would be that, in such scenarios, it can be considered that the damage was not actually caused by the State, i.e. the operation of public services, but by force majeure. There is no point in holding the State liable for damage that their agents could not have prevented by taking the necessary precautions.

In my opinion, the COVID-19 pandemic fits the definition of force majeure, insofar as this disease has arisen from a cause that is alien to the operation of Spanish public services and, moreover, has generated damage that could not have been avoided by adopting efficient precautions. This is also indicated by the precedent set by the National Court (*Audiencia Nacional*) in relation to the losses caused by the air traffic controllers' strike and the subsequent reaction of the Government, which decreed a state of alarm and closed the airspace in December 2010. That Court considered that the strike was a force majeure and, therefore, the losses were not attributable to the Government.[36]

However, the occurrence of force majeure does not totally exclude the possibility of the State being liable for the damages suffered by citizens as a result of the COVID-19. The damage caused by the management of this crisis was certainly unavoidable to some extent. The global nature of the pandemic and the losses suffered by citizens of almost every country of the world suggests so. Nevertheless, the public authorities of Spain and other States, through their actions and omissions, have been able to aggravate or mitigate that damage. The different impact that this pandemic has had in similar countries, depending on the different precautions taken by their respective Governments, indicates this. The exclusion of liability implied by force majeure does not extend to the damage that could have been prevented or mitigated if due precautions had been taken. The rationale is simple. To the extent that public authorities were able to prevent additional damages by adopting due care, it can be considered that the causal link – between the operation of public services and those damages – required for State liability to arise does exist.

4.4. CAUSAL UNCERTAINTY

In many cases, it will probably be difficult to prove, with the degree of certainty usually required in State liability litigation, that the damage at issue would

por incendios forestales' (2009) 179 Revista de Administración Pública 87; Concepción Barrero Rodríguez, *Fuerza mayor y responsabilidad administrativa extracontractual* (Aranzadi 2009); Jesús Conde Antequera, 'La responsabilidad de la Administración por daños derivados de fenómenos naturales: especial referencia al riesgo de inundación' (2015) 45–46 Revista Aragonesa de Administración Pública 67.

36 See Judgments of National Court (Administrative Law Chamber) of 15 April 2013 (RC rec. 108/2012); 10 July 2013 (rec. 35/2013); 18 September 2013 (rec. 55/2013); and 7 March 2014 (rec. 17/2013).

have been avoided had the Government taken due precautions. Let us take the example of deaths. Here we could find three types of uncertainties.

First, there are many cases where we cannot be certain whether people who died were infected with the SARS-CoV-2. In Spain (and other countries), the official figures of deaths from the COVID-19 only include cases where the deceased tested positive for the virus, and not all those suspected of dying from the virus were tested. In some cases, they were not tested because the relevant administrative authorities, at some point, considered that it was preferable to use the few available tests on other people. Given that and the fact that there has been a considerable "excess mortality" during the pandemic, we might well suspect that most of that excess has been caused, directly or indirectly, by the COVID-19. Nevertheless, we cannot determine with certainty which individuals who were not officially listed as having died from the virus were actually infected.

Secondly, there are instances where it is not possible to know for sure whether a person infected with the virus died from it or from another concomitant cause.

Thirdly, there will surely be many cases where we will not be able to know if the deceased, who died from the COVID-19, would have survived if the Government had taken due precautions. It might well be difficult to determine which specific deaths could have been prevented if the relevant authorities had acted diligently and which losses would have happened anyway. In some instances, it will only be possible to estimate the likelihood of the damages having occurred (avoided) if the State had taken due care.

These and other similar problems of "causal uncertainty" could be solved by applying two rules that Spanish sometimes often use in similar cases.

The first one is the "shift of the burden of proof". As a general rule, the plaintiff has to prove the causation requirement for the State to be held liable.[37] However, this burden might be "shifted" if it is easier for the defendant to produce and bring before the court evidence proving that such a requirement is not met.[38] This rule encourages evidence to be provided by the party that can provide it most efficiently, which helps to minimise litigation costs.[39] This rule might be applied, for instance, in those cases where we cannot be certain whether the people who died were infected with the SARS-CoV-2 because the Government, for whatever reason, decided not to test them. It seems obvious that the Government was the cheapest information provider in that regard.

The second rule is that of proportional liability. Spanish courts usually resolve cases of causal uncertainty through the "all-or-nothing" rule. Liability is either equal to the full losses suffered by the victim or there is no liability at

---

37 See Article 217.2 of Law 1/2000, of 7 January, on Civil Procedure (hereafter, LEC).

38 See Article 217.7 LEC. See also the Judgment of the Spanish Supreme Court (1st Chamber) of 23 December 2002 (rec. 1761/1997).

39 See Bruce L. Hay and Kathryn E. Spier, 'Burdens of Proof in Civil Litigation: An Economic Perspective' (1997) 26 Journal of Legal Studies 413.

all, and the defendant is held liable if the judge's degree of conviction about the existence of causation exceeds a certain evidentiary threshold or standard of proof, which in Spanish law is usually referred to as "reasonable certainty".[40] Nevertheless, the courts sometimes apply a "proportional liability" criterion, so that compensation equals the full losses suffered by the victim times the likelihood of (i.e. the judge's degree of conviction about) the defendant having caused the accident. The most relevant instance of proportional liability is the "loss of a chance" doctrine, which is often applied in medical malpractice cases where the abnormal operation of the public healthcare system deprived a patient of a chance of healing or survival. Here, State's liability equals the damage suffered by the victim times the probability of heal or survival if that system had functioned properly.[41]

If the probability of causation is systematically below that evidentiary threshold, the proportional rule provides the Government better incentives to take care – and eventually engage in socially optimal levels of activity – than the all-or-nothing rule.[42] Let us suppose, for instance, that such probability is always 40%, defendants actually caused damage in 40% of the cases, and such threshold is 50%. In this scenario, under the latter rule, plaintiffs would never face liability, and would surely take less than due care. Under the former rule, by contrast, their expected liability would equal the expected losses caused by their activity, which would lead them to take optimal precautions.

It seems that the management of the COVID-19 has generated many cases like those where the Spanish courts apply the proportional liability rule. It seems that some administrative authorities, by action or omission, have deprived certain individuals of a chance to heal or survive the disease, which might well be both substantial and systematically below the standard of "reasonable certainty".

5. COMPENSATION FOR EXPROPRIATION

By virtue of Royal Decree 463/2020, of 14 March, declaring the state of emergency, the Spanish Government adopted several measures aimed at

40 See Miquel Martín-Casals and Josep Solé, 'Causal Uncertainty and Proportional Liability in Spain', in Israel Gilead, Michael D. Green and Bernhard A. Koch (eds), *Proportional Liability: Analytical and Comparative Perspectives* (De Gruyter 2013) 297.

41 Miquel Martín-Casals and Josep Solé, 'Causal Uncertainty and Proportional Liability in Spain', in Israel Gilead, Michael D. Green and Bernhard A. Koch (eds), *Proportional Liability: Analytical and Comparative Perspectives* (De Gruyter 2013) 309. See also Luis Medina Alcoz, *La teoría de la pérdida de oportunidad. Estudio doctrinal y jurisprudencial de Derecho de daños público y privado* (Civitas 2007); Idem, *La responsabilidad proporcional como solución a la incertidumbre causal* (Civitas 2019).

42 See, e.g. Omri Ben-Shahar, 'Causation and Foreseeability' in Michael Faure (ed), *Encyclopedia of Law and Economics. Tort Law and Economics* (Edward Elgar 2009) 94.

managing the COVID-19 health crisis that have caused considerable losses to millions of people.

First, this Royal Decree imposed the confinement of virtually the entire population to their homes, which severely restricted their freedom of movement.[43]

Secondly, it suspended certain business and cultural activities, namely the opening of (or the public access to): retail premises, commercial establishments, hotels, restaurants, museums, archives, libraries, archives, monuments, sport facilities, parades, popular festivals, etc. Nevertheless, some exceptions were provided for: grocery stores, pharmacies, medical, optical, orthopaedic and hygiene products stores, press, gas stations, tobacconists, technological and telecommunications equipment stores, pet food stores, internet, telephone or mail order business, etc.[44]

Thirdly, it allowed the Minister of Health to "intervene in and temporarily occupy industries, factories, workshops, holdings or premises of any kind, including privately owned health centres, services and establishments, as well as those operating in the pharmaceutical sector".[45] In accordance with this provision, some firms (e.g. running private hospitals, laboratories, tourist accommodations, gas stations, etc.) were obliged to provide some "essential services" (e.g. treating COVID-19 patients, carrying out tests, providing accommodation to some workers, etc.).[46]

Fourthly, that Royal Decree also allowed the Minister of Health to "temporarily requisition all types of goods and impose compulsory personal services where this is necessary for the proper protection of public health".[47] Subsequently, in the early stages of the epidemic, some health products (e.g. protective masks) were requisitioned because of the shortages the public health system was experiencing.

Neither this Royal Decree nor any subsequent legal provision mentions the possibility of the Government providing compensation to people who have suffered losses as a result of these measures. This poses the problem of determining which of these measures are expropriations and, therefore, give rise to an obligation to compensate the victims and which ones are non-compensable regulations, which do not trigger such an obligation. Needless to say, this is a controversial and difficult issue, not only in Spanish law but also in many other legal systems.[48]

---

43 Article 7 of Royal Decree 463/2020.

44 Article 10 of Royal Decree 463/2020.

45 Article 13.b) of Royal Decree 463/2020.

46 See, for instance, Ministerial Orders TMA/277/2020, of 23 March, and SND/344/2020, of 13 April.

47 Article 13.c) of Royal Decree 463/2020.

48 In general, on how to distinguish between both types of measures, Gabriel Doménech Pascual, 'Cómo distinguir entre una expropiación y una delimitación de la propiedad no indemnizable' (2012) 2 InDret; Idem, 'Prohibido regar. ¿Expropiación o delimitación de la

Article 1 LEF gives a very broad definition of expropriation as "any form of singular deprivation of private property or of legitimate rights or economic interests".

Article 120 LEF specifies that "when, as a result of serious reasons of public order or security, epidemics, floods or other calamities, the civil authorities have to adopt measures that imply destruction, effective detriment or requisition of property or rights of individuals without the formalities required by this Law for the various types of expropriation, the injured party shall be entitled to compensation".

In view of these legal provisions, it seems obvious that requisitions made in accordance with Royal Decree 463/2020 constitute an instance of expropriation and, consequently, are to be compensated. By contrast, it is not clear whether the other abovementioned coercive measures adopted pursuant to the same Royal Decree – intervention of companies, confinement, suspension of business activities, etc. – are expropriations or, on the contrary, restrictions that do not need to be compensated.

In my opinion, the key criterion to distinguishing between both types of measures, in this and other similar cases, is whether the exercise of the right that is sacrificed by the Government is a socially undesirable activity, which is to be discouraged, or a socially desirable activity, which ought to be encouraged.[49]

In the first case, the administrative measure at issue is directed against an activity posing an excessive risk to public health. In other words, the Government causes losses to a person whose activity is disturbing public health. In such situations, it is not a good idea to compensate, since doing so would incentivise people to carry out this excessively dangerous activity, as one of the risks involved in it –that of suffering losses for reasons of public interest – would not be borne by the person performing that activity, but by taxpayers. According to this criterion, measures such as the confinement of the population and the suspension of business activities laid down in the Royal Decree 463/2020 are to be considered as non-compensable regulations, given that they ban some activities on the grounds that they are too dangerous in the current circumstances.

In the second case, the measure limits the right to engage in activities that do not pose any unacceptable risk to public health. On the contrary, the exercise of the right that is "sacrificed" in the public interest is lawful and might be considered beneficial for society. In these cases, it is therefore appropriate to

---

propiedad no indemnizable?' (2012) 39–40 Revista Aragonesa de Administración Pública 269. With respect to the measures adopted during the COVID-19 crisis, see David Blanquer Criado, *La responsabilidad patrimonial en tiempos de pandemia* (Tirant lo Blanch 2020).

49 For more details, see Gabriel Doménech Pascual, 'La responsabilidad patrimonial de la Administración derivada de la adopción de medidas cautelares' (2005) 125 Revista Española de Derecho Administrativo 65; Idem, 'Cómo distinguir entre una expropiación y una delimitación de la propiedad no indemnizable' (2012) 2 InDret.

compensate those who perform such activities, since not compensating them would discourage socially desirable behaviour. Hence, measures such as the requisitioning of medical equipment and the intervention of privately owned health facilities are to be considered as expropriations. The opposite would certainly have serious negative consequences, as it would discourage activities (e.g. the manufacture and import of such equipment) that in this and other similar situations generate huge benefits for society. It should be underlined, moreover, that this deterrent effect can also occur if the potential victims anticipate that the compensation they will get for the deprivation of their assets will be lower than the price they could obtain on the market. The Government ought to consider this potential effect when deciding whether to buy or expropriate certain assets it needs to protect public health. It must be noted that, in Spain, the requisitions of protective medical equipment in the early stages of the pandemic deterred imports and exacerbated shortages of these supplies.

This is the criterion underlying many provisions in Spanish law, and which Spanish courts usually use to resolve analogous cases.[50]

---

[50] See, for instance, Article 3.2 LOEAES and Article 54. 2 LGSP.

CORONAVIRUS AND MEDICAL LIABILITY

The Italian Perspective

Marcello Maggiolo*

Malpractice cases or public bodies' liability cases, both originated by coronavirus, are bound to be discussed in terms of liability for non-pecuniary losses and of medical liability. This contribution outlines the Italian scenario and some possible future development of the relevant law.

1. INTRODUCTION

The COVID-19 emergency currently has much more to do with contract law than with both tort in health-related issues, and medical liability. This might almost seem a paradox during a pandemic. However, there is a quite obvious reason for it. As a result of the disease and of the disruption to trade it has caused, many governments (the Italian government for sure) have been forced to adopt exceptional measures that mainly address contractual relationships.

On the other hand, malpractice cases or public body liability cases, arising out of the coronavirus, are bound to be matters for discussion in the future. Nobody yet knows how close we are to that future. There still is time in abundance for the filing of lawsuits. Nevertheless, since much has happened and continues to happen as a result of the pandemic, medical liability will become a matter of paramount relevance, whether in tort or contractually, so now is a good time to address the topic, even if how exactly the situation will develop cannot yet be known.

---

* University of Padua, School of Law, and Innsbruck University, School of Law.

This contribution will therefore examine certain principles in Italian law governing damages for non-pecuniary losses in actionable personal injury cases. First, I would like to look at the rules governing when personal injury is actionable and how the amount of any such damages are calculated. Secondly, I will focus attention on the rules on medical liability. Finally, I will say something about the current situation and future prospects.

2. NON-PECUNIARY LOSSES

On the first count, the situation in Italy was clarified by the so-called S. Martin judgments of 2008.[1] These decisions addressed the problem of non-pecuniary losses both in tort and in contract.

The problem of non-pecuniary losses in tort requires the interpretation of Article 2059 Italian Civil Code (c.c.). This rule of law states that compensation for non-pecuniary losses is awarded only in the specific cases provided for in law. Following much uncertainty, the Supreme Court (Corte di Cassazione) decided there are three groups of cases that could be said to be provided for in law according to Article 2059 c.c. The first group are those cases in which a criminal offence is involved, i.e. where the tortfeasor is liable both in criminal and in civil law.[2] The second group are those cases affected by special provisions of statutes which specifically state that compensation for non-pecuniary losses is to be awarded.[3] The third group refers to cases that involve violations of constitutional rights. It is this third group that concerns us here. Since there is a right to health according to Article 32 Italian Constitution, it follows that personal injuries give rise to a right to compensation for damages. Furthermore, according to the Corte di Cassazione, the same rule (Art 2059 c.c. as interpreted by the Court) applies in cases of non-pecuniary losses caused by breach of contractual or non-contractual obligations.[4] All cases of mental or physical harm are therefore actionable in either tort or in contract law.

As far as the assessment of this kind of damage is concerned,[5] Italian law uses a points-based system. The particular harm suffered is given a score according to

---

1 Cass., Sez. Un., 11 October 2008, Nos 26972, 26973, 26974, 26975. On the pre-existing situation, see Francesco Donato Busnelli and Salvatore Patti, *Danno e responsabilità civile* (3rd edn, Giappichelli 2013) 46 ff.

2 Art 185 c.p. (Italian Criminal Law Code).

3 E.g. Art 44 s 7, d. lgs. 286/1995 on the compensation for non-pecuniary losses caused by discrimination for gender, language, race, religious reasons; Art 2, l. 89/2001 on the compensation for non-pecuniary losses caused by an unreasonable duration of the process.

4 Matteo Maria Francisetti Brolin, *Danno non patrimoniale e inadempimento. Logiche 'patrimonialistiche' e valori della persona* (Esi 2014) 128 ff., 563 ff.; Francesco Zecchin, *Il danno non patrimoniale dal torto al contratto* (Giuffrè rancis Lefebvre 2020) 227 ff.

5 Antonina Astone, *I danni non patrimoniali alla persona: la prova* (Giuffrè 2011).

the severity of the injury, the length of the disability, the age of the victim and so on. A fixed amount of money is awarded for each number in the scoring system. The final score therefore corresponds to an amount of money to be awarded for the damage suffered.[6]

These rules form the framework for assessing medical liability.

3. MEDICAL LIABILITY: STATUTE LAW

On the question of medical liability, it should be emphasised that until the late 1970s and early 1980s, the Italian legal system afforded substantial immunity to medical professionals, hospitals and/or healthcare institutions.

The situation changed with a new sense of the doctor-patient relationship developing. Courts started to allow compensation to be awarded in cases of malpractice. The situation rapidly evolved and tilted the balance the other way, with the liability of professionals and healthcare institutions being deemed contractual in nature;[7] with causality becoming virtually presumed;[8] while the rules on the running date for the statute of limitations were adapted to the peculiarity of the offence.[9]

This sort of strict liability imposed by courts gave rise to the problem of so-called defensive medicine.[10] This very well-known issue has resulted in two laws being passed in Italy in the last few years.

The first of these was the "decreto Balduzzi" (d.l. 158/2012), which provided comprehensive public health legislation covering the organisation of hospitals, rules for the medical profession, limitations on the sale of tobacco, as well as provision on pharmaceuticals and on scientific research. Its Article 3, section 1, stated that there would be no criminal liability for simple fault on the part of a medical professional who complies with the best practice as recognised by scientific consensus. In such cases, there may only be tortious liability under Article 2043 c.c., however the court should take into account the matter of compliance with best practice in each case.[11] Article 3, section 3, stated that the damages must be awarded according to the Italian Private Insurances Code (Arts 138 and 139), i.e. applying the points system referred to above.

The new rules provided some reassurance for medical professionals who had felt threatened by the possibility of dangerous and punitive contractual

---

6 See Art 138, 139, d. lgs. 209/2005 (Private Insurances Code).

7 See Cass., 28 November 2008, no 24742 for Healthcare Institutions; Cass., 3 October 2016 for Physicians. The leading case is Cass., 22 January 1999, no 589.

8 See Cass., 26 February 2020, no 5128.

9 See Cass., 22 September 2017, no 22045.

10 See Simona Viciani, *Errore in medicina e modelli di responsabilità* (Esi, 2016) 11 ff.

11 Art 3 also provides for principles to be implemented by Presidential decrees concerning insurance duties.

liability, although they did not, and still not do, have a clear perception of how the technicalities of such rules will actually affect them in regard to tort and contract in the event of non performance or of breach.[12] The drafting itself proved, however, to be unsatisfactory, for example where Article 3 indicated the "obligation" arising from Article 2043 c.c., or where the law indicated the importance of compliance with best practice (which is relevant in terms of fault) when calculating the amount of damages to be awarded.[13]

There was therefore a need for a change to the system, with two different strands developing: one legislative, the other judicial.

From the legislative standpoint, a new Act was passed in 2017, known as "legge Gelli – Bianco" (l. 24/2017), the scope of which was narrower than that of the decreto Balduzzi. The new statute does not affect the organisational aspects of the public health system, dealing only with the medical/patient relationship. More specifically, the first part of the Act deals with the safety of medical treatments (Art 1); with the possible assignment to the regional Ombudsman of competences as relevant Public Authority (Art 2). A new Agency was put in place to draft and monitor good practices on safety in the health system (Art 3) and a duty was placed on the healthcare professionals to comply with medical treatment guidelines where such have been drawn up by registered scientific bodies (Art 5). The Act also addresses matters of privacy and transparency (Art 4). After a provision for the possibility of criminal liability for medical professionals (Art 6),[14] the law establishes both substantive and procedural rules on the civil liability of healthcare institutions and medical professionals (Art 7).

In substantive terms, the new rules respectively confirmed the nature of the liability of healthcare institutions and medical professionals, as set forth in the Decreto Balduzzi.

The situation is now perfectly clear as there is now an express provision in the law to the effect that while liability of healthcare institutions – both private and public – is contractual, i.e. it is a liability for the non-performance of an obligation (the liability of healthcare institutions is contractual even if the medical professional has been chosen by the patient and even if the medical professional is not an employee of the health institution, under sections 1 and 2), the liability of the medical professional him or herself is in tort (s 3).[15] At the same time the new law confirms the importance of good practices and

---

12 Marcello Maggiolo, *Il risarcimento della pura perdita patrimoniale* (Giufrè 2003) 100 ff.

13 Pietro A. Sirena, 'La responsabilità medica alla luce della legge Balduzzi', https://www.altalex.com/documents/news/2014/03/26/la-responsabilita-medica-alla-luce-della-legge-balduzzi#_Toc356829919 accessed 4 August 2020.

14 Article 3 of 'Decreto Balduzzi' has been repealed, and a new Article 590 *sexies* c.p. has been introduced. It deals with manslaughter or personal injuries committed by medical professionals.

15 With the obvious exception of cases where the patient and the medical doctor entered into a specific contractual agreement (s 3).

their compliance (s 3), as well as indicating how damages should be calculated in accordance with Article 138 and Article 139 of the Italian Private Insurances Code (s 4). Lastly, these rules are deemed mandatory (s 5), so they may not be waived by contractual clauses seeking to do so.

The following part of the law contains an extremely relevant procedural rule.

An action for compensation may be brought before the court only either after a pre-emptive technical assessment procedure has been carried out, pursuant to Article 696 Italian Code of Civil Procedure (c.p.c.),[16] or after an ADR procedure pursuant to d. lgs. 28/2010 (Article 8, ss 1 and 2).[17] There is also of course a right of recourse for healthcare institutions against medical professionals, but only in cases in which there has been malice or gross negligence (Art 9).[18] There also are specific rules on insurance obligations for healthcare institutions (Arts 10 and 11).[19] Most notably, again regarding the relationship with the insurance companies, the law allows the injured person to sue the insurance company directly to recover damages caused by the insured healthcare institution and/or medical professional (Art 12).

The law is quite recent and its efficiency has not yet been fully tested. It is, however, already apparent that the procedural rules have improved the chance of an injured party's being quickly and adequately compensated. This is because, as the proceeding starts with a pre-emptive technical assessment, from the outset the parties have a clear overview both of the pathology and of its causes. This is particularly true for insurance companies, for which participation in the pre-emptive technical assessment is mandatory. The result is that they are often willing to settle amicably in ways that may be favourable for the claimant, depending on the result of the technical assessment, thus avoiding wasting time and accumulating costs, as well as many of the uncertainties of the court process itself.

4. MEDICAL LIABILITY: CASE LAW

Meanwhile, case law evolved accordingly, as it was supposed to.

The whole issue of medical liability is highly sensitive and delicate, and in view of its social and economic importance, a myriad of judgments of both lower

---

16 The joinder of parties is necessary also for the insurance companies, which are moreover required to come up with a compensation proposal or to explain the reason why they do not want to present anything (s 4). A special provision relates to the appointment of specialised medical professionals in technical assessments (Art 15).

17 The eventual agreement must be reached in six months. After this deadline, it is possible to sue according to Article 702 *bis* c.p.c. (s 3).

18 The right of recourse is based on an obligation for the healthcare institution and/or the insurance company to disclose to the medical professional the legal action brought by the damaged person against them (Art 13).

19 A special Guarantee Fund for the victims of medical malpractice is formed by the Health Ministry (Art 14).

and higher courts have been made. It obviously is impossible to enter into a full examination of their contents. There was, however, one especially important day at the end of 2019 when the third section of the Court of Cassazione (which has jurisdiction on medical liability cases) decided to issue 10 judgments on medical liability, its rulings 28985 to 28994.[20] The date and the cluster of cases were by no means coincidental: it was 11 November St. Martin's day. The Court clearly linked these judgments to the ground breaking St. Martin judgments of 2008, in order to provide a general framework of rules on medical liability. The intention was for these to be a bench-mark for the years to come.[21] The purpose has an obvious implication. The judges may expect their set of rules to stand firm for the future as long as they manage to craft them convincingly. Thus, they set out to found their decisions on a sound theoretical ground. But it cannot be denied that sometimes they fell a little short.

Providing an overview of the content of the judgments is useful at this juncture.

Two judgments deal with the question of the retroactivity or the non-retroactivity of the new laws.

Decision no 28994 stated that the rule on liability in tort for healthcare professionals, i.e. Article 3 of d.l. 158/2012 (decreto Balduzzi) and Article 7 of l. 24/2017 (legge Gelli – Bianco), does not apply if the malpractice happened before those Acts had come into force. In such cases, any liability is deemed to have been contractual in nature. The second decision (no 28990), on the other and, states that the criteria for the assessment of Article 138 and Article 139 Italian Private Insurances Code apply also when the personal injury occurred before the Acts came into force. What is important from this point of view is the stage that has been reached in the proceedings, i.e. if, when the new law came into force, an assessment of the damages has already been carried out, then Articles 138 and 139 Italian Private Insurance Code apply. Lastly, again with reference to the situation existing prior to l. 24/2017 (legge Gelli – Bianco), judgment no 28987 ruled that in malpractice cases where the medical professional is guilty, the cost of the compensation must usually be equally shared through the right of recourse between the medical professional and the healthcare institution.

Another judgment (no 28985) deals with the right to self-determination.[22] In particular, on the question of the difference between personal injury and prejudice to the right to self-determination, it states that damages may be awarded

---

20 Guido Alpa, 'Orientamenti della giurisprudenza sulla nuova disciplina della responsabilità medica', 2019 C. E I., 1 ff.

21 Giovanni Comandè, 'Sulla responsabilità la Cassazione lancia il guanto di sfida' (2019) Guida al Diritto 10, 11.

22 Roberto Pucella, *Autodeterminazione e responsabilità nella relazione di cura* (Giuffrè 2010); Mariassunta Piccinni, *Il consenso al trattamento medico del minore* (Cedam 2007); Simona Cacace, *Autodeterminazione in salute* (Giappichelli 2017).

to a patient who has not expressed their informed consent to the treatment given by the medical professionals even in the absence of any malpractice on their part.

Judgment no 28989, and especially no 28986, have dealt with matters of causation, both confirming the notion of "double causation", meaning that, for there to be direct damages, the causal connection must be "material" (adequate). Indirect damages and consequent damages, on the other hand, rely on what they called "juridical" causation (substantial).

Judgment nos 28991 and 28992 deal with issues related to the burden of the proof. According to no 28991, in malpractice cases the claimant has the burden of proof to show that the medical professional has caused the aggravation of the illness or a new pathology as the case may be, whilst the defendant must prove that the aggravation or the new pathology happened due to extraordinary and unforeseeable factors that prevented the proper performance of medical duties. The burden of the proof for causation is placed on the claimant in decision no 28992,[23] while no 28994 makes it clear in this regard that medical records which are incomplete, or which have been tampered with, will assume importance in the case.[24] Other judgments deal mostly with the question of damages.

The first rule (in no 28986) concerns damage assessment where personal injury has been suffered by a person already suffering from some sort of pathology. The court moved from the distinction between cumulative physical impairment, for example where a person already blind in one eye then also loses sight in the other, and co-existing physical impairment, for example where a person has had a hip replacement and loses their sight in one eye. The difference lies in that it is self-evident that if the physical impairment is co-existing, it will not then be relevant to the damage assessment. On the other hand, in the case of cumulative physical impairment, the compensation is for the difference between the current state of invalidity and the pre-existing state of invalidity, being calculated according to the invalidity points system and corresponding scales. On the matter of damage assessment, the Court proceeds with decision no 28988 to the effect that the standards set by the law (Arts 138 and 139 Private Insurances Code), or with the courts "points" scales system for personal injury compensation, can be departed from in favour of the injured person only in exceptional and abnormal cases. Judgment no 28989 moreover emphasises the difference between loss of family relationships and any subsequent health damage, while clarifying that so-called "moral" damages (i.e. pain and suffering) can be included among the damages awarded for loss of family relationship. The judgment also addresses wrongful death, seemingly with the intention of

---

23 Roberto Pucella, *La causalità "incerta"* (Giappichelli 2007); Luca Nocco, *Il "sincretismo causale" e la politica del diritto: spunti dalla responsabilità sanitaria* (Giappichelli 2010).

24 See also Cass., 26 January 2010, no 1538 and Vittorio Occorsio, *Cartella clinica e responsabilità medica* (Giuffrè 2011) 19 ff.

clarifying the issue once and for all. The Court ruled that in a case of instant or near-instant death, no damages are claimable since such damages are not envisaged for such persons and therefore their heirs cannot inherit the claim. If, however, the death occurs after a lapse of time, the Court states that both "terminal health damage", i.e. the health damage suffered by the person during that period of time, and "terminal 'moral' damage", i.e. the pain suffered by a person who realises he/she is dying, must be awarded. Lastly, the Court of Cassazione (no 28993) examined the difference between pecuniary and non – pecuniary loss of chance, emphasising that in a pecuniary loss of chance the pre-existing situation is positive (in terms of curriculum, capabilities, experience, qualifications, etc., which offer potential earning capacity), whilst, in the non-pecuniary loss of chance the pre-existing situation is negative (a person is ill and loses the chance to get better as a result of medical malpractice).

5. MEDICAL LIABILITY AND CORONAVIRUS

So far, the Italian situation up to the end of 2019 has been considered, although further innovation had been expected. On 19 March 2019 the Prime Minister (perhaps uncoincidentally a professor in private law) proposed a bill (no 1151) of delegation to the Government for the review of the Civil Code. Article 1, point n) of the bill refers to the rules on compensation for non-pecuniary loss, which were therefore bound to change to some extent.[25] In particular, the rule of Article 1, letter n) requires the Government to rationalise the law on tortious and contractual liability for non-pecuniary loss, giving two indications for the purpose. On the one hand, it was considered that the system under Article 2059 c.c. (which stated that compensation for non-pecuniary losses could be awarded only in the specific kinds of cases provided for in law) should be made more flexible. On the other, it was deemed desirable to link the recovery of non-pecuniary losses to the constitutional importance of the interest prejudiced.

While the legal scholars were at work on the task,[26] the pandemic struck and everything changed with the issue of health developing a rather different relevance and importance. Until last year, when addressing cases of physical or mental harm, the focus had been on how much health (or lack thereof) could be converted into money.[27] Now, health is heath and its perception focuses less on

---

25 A second Article of the draft refers to civil liability: Art 1, point m) of the bill requires a rationalisation of the relationship between contractual liability, tortious liability and pre-contractual liability.

26 At the end of 2019, the Italian Society of Civil Lawyers (Associazione Civilisti Italiani), one of the prominent Italian Societies of Private Law Scholars, has drawn up a proposal for a new draft of Articles 1218, 1223, 1226, 2057, 2059 c.c.

27 Some interesting remarks along these lines in Gianfranco Palermo, 'Contributo allo studio della responsabilità per danno non patrimoniale' (2018) C. e I., 19 ff.

the economic implications or on the possibility of converting health into money. The economic relevance of health is nevertheless still there, as it is evidenced by the discussions on the desirability of creating exceptional rules.[28] Some have already been proposed.[29]

There has also been speculation on what developments the near future withholds. Giulio Ponzanelli – a renowned academic who is an expert in this field – has, for example, clearly and sharply outlined five possible case types that may arise from the current situation.[30] The first group is plain malpractice cases, the arising of which may have been caused also by the desperate conditions in which medical professionals have sometimes had to work during the coronavirus emergency. As is very well known, during the worst moments of the pandemic, medical professionals were working under unbelievable strain, in situations of great difficulty, and with great courage. There is a widespread feeling that, given such circumstances, protection against claims would be appropriate for medical professionals. To this effect, an extensive application of Article 2236 c.c. has been mooted. According to the rule, if the performance requires the physician to solve extremely difficult technical problems, possibly associated with the emergency or related structural inadequacies, there would be no liability outside of cases of malice or gross negligence.[31] The second group involves healthcare institutions and the effects of the emergency on their organisation and their performance, for example where a person has not been promptly hospitalised in an intensive care unit due to overcrowding or where a person has not been swabbed for COVID-19 quickly enough. The issue is one of the foreseeability of the risk,[32] i.e. whether the risk was foreseeable, and it seems that, at least by the end of January, it was partly foreseeable and certainly underestimated so there could be grounds for liability of the institutions, though not of the medical professionals themselves. The third group of cases, similar to the second, regards claims by the heirs of

---

28 Giovanni Comandè, 'La responsabilità sanitaria al tempo del coronavirus … e dopo' (2020) Danno e resp.

29 For instance, according to the Italian Society of Civil Lawyers (Associazione Civilisti Italiani) it is desirable that only healthcare institutions can be sued by the victims. The liability of medical professionals should, therefore, be a matter of right of recourse for the benefit of the healthcare institution.

30 Giulio Ponzanelli, 'La responsabilità sanitaria e i possibili conteziosi da Covid' (*Giustiziacivile.com*, 19 May 2020) http://giustiziacivile.com/danno-e-responsabilita/articoli/la-responsabilita-sanitaria-e-i-possibili-contenziosi-da-covid accessed 23 June 2020.

31 Luigi Mengoni, 'Obbligazioni "di risultato" e obbligazioni "di mezzi" (Studio critico)' in *Obbligazioni e negozio. Scritti II* (Giuffré 2011) 168 ff., 206 highlights that the rule contained in Art 2236 of the Italian Civil Code, rather than establishing a limitation of liability, sets a limit on the obligation itself. See also Andrea Nicolussi, 'Sezioni sempre più unite contro la distinzione fra obbligazioni di risultato e obbligazioni di mezzi. La responsabilità del medico' (2008) Danno e resp. 877 ft. 35 and Idem, 'L'interesse del creditore e il risultato dell'obbligazione' in Luigi Capogrossi Colognesi and Maria Floriana Cursi (eds), *Obligatio – obbligazione. Un confronto interdisciplinare* (Jovene 2011) 127.

32 Roberta Montinaro, *Dubbio scientifico e responsabilità civile* (Giuffrè 2012).

medical professionals who died carrying out their duties, also in this case in association with organisational and operational shortcomings. The fourth group of cases relates to residential healthcare centres for the elderly and disabled i.e. extremely vulnerable patients who are prone to catching or succumbing to the disease. Sometimes persons who were not seriously ill were unwisely admitted to residential centres where the virus spread, with dramatic consequences for the health, and sometimes survival, of other residents. The fifth and last group is made up of patients who were not treated according to the relevant therapeutic programmes due to the hospital overcrowding. Here too, the question regards the organisation of healthcare institutions and what should be expected from them.

In conclusion, it seems probable that future disputes will develop along more or less these lines and not only in Italy. It should be added that there may well be a very large number of claims, in which case it is unlikely that the matter will be left solely to the courts, so State intervention appears to be a distinct possibility.

Aside from these remarks, it can be added in a much wider perspective, and specifically in a *de iure condendo* perspective, that it might be worth considering who should benefit from compensation of non-pecuniary losses in cases of medical liability. I would like to reiterate some ideas I have already put forward elsewhere.[33]

The basic assumption is that victims of personal injury cannot really be compensated with money insofar as the non-pecuniary damage is exactly the same before and after the monetary "compensation". The harm, injury or the condition does not disappear because money is paid to the victim. There is now a widespread acceptance of the idea that providing victims with money means that they, although not truly compensated, or even not compensated at all, have a sum available to them that allows them to console themselves, whether by spending, sparing, donating, or doing whatever they please with it.[34] This *rationale* underlies all the above-mentioned judgments and statutes.

The coronavirus emergency, however, provides the opportunity to explore a somewhat different scenario. There is no reason to doubt that in malpractice and in similar cases the tortfeasor or those in breach of a contractual or legal obligations must pay, since there is no reason for granting them even partial immunity, particularly in view of usual insurance cover. It might, however, be worth reflecting on who is the most appropriate recipient of any compensation. Certainly, a part of the sum awarded should benefit the claimant. If this were not so, there would be no incentive to bringing lawsuits and no losses would be

33 Marcello Maggiolo, 'Una autentica solidarietà sociale come eredità del coronavirus: per una diversa destinazione del risarcimento del danno alla salute' (*Giustiziacivile.com*, 2 April 2020) http://giustiziacivile.com/danno-e-responsabilita/editoriali/una-autentica-solidarieta-sociale-come-eredita-del-coronavirus accessed 23 June 2020.

34 Cesare Salvi, *Il danno extracontrattuale* (Jovene 1985).

compensated, which would certainly be an undesirable result. A same time, there is no reason why the whole settlement sum should go t claimant. Provided the injured party can be afforded some consolation, a tage of the damages awarded might be used in a more sensible, efficie matic and, ultimately fairer, way, if it were granted to the healthcare syste hus benefiting the entire community.

This is, moreover, a sort of compensation in kind (and compe kind is allowed in Italy by Article 2058 c.c.). If indeed the healthca improves because of the funds raised though this proposed mechani improvement also benefits the injured person, who can potentially be with a higher level of care and expertise.

To end on a constitutional note, if Article 2 of the Italian Constitution that social solidarity is a duty for everyone, then it is a duty also for the inj person. Therefore if, as often stated,[35] the social solidarity principle is a justify factor for compensation for non-pecuniary losses, then it should also justify t allocation of a part of that sum to the wider community.

---

35 E.g. Cesare Salvi, 'La responsabilità civile' in Giovanni Iudica and Paolo Zatti (eds), *Trattato di diritto privato* (Giuffrè 1998) 32.

HARD CHOICES IN THE PANDEMIC AND GUIDELINES

Ethical and Juridical Remarks on Medical Responsibility and Liability

Antonio Da Re and Andrea Nicolussi*

This contribution proposes some legal and ethical considerations on the relationship between medical responsibility (also in the sense of medical liability) and guidelines, which over time have earned particular relevance in many legal systems. The pandemic situation has made this issue even more difficult as, on the one hand, there were no concrete guidelines and, on the other hand, several recommendations of various kinds and origins have spread, leading to confusion among healthcare professionals. In particular, the ethical-clinical recommendations developed by the Italian Society of Anaesthesia, Analgesia, Resuscitation and Intensive Care (SIAARTI) has produced an intense debate not only in Italy but also

* Antonio Da Re, University of Padua; Andrea Nicolussi, Catholic University of Milan.

abroad; indeed, SIAARTI recommendations have encouraged the publication of recommendations on the same subject in many other countries. This contribution deals with the most relevant recommendations, but mainly focuses on the Italian document since it can be considered the model for other documents. Furthermore, the restriction on access to intensive care that is based, a priori, *on age raises questions concerning not only its ethical legitimacy but also the competence of a scientific society in providing rules that may seriously infringe fundamental rights. The contribution criticises this* a priori *and extra-clinical criterion and proposes, in turn, an integrated clinical criterion, which can deal with situations of the state of emergency and the lack of resources. This integrated criterion would be more respectful of the physicians' competences and would enhance their professional role, without invading the scope and competence of the democratic institutions.*

1. THE LESSON OF THE PANDEMIC: THE IMPORTANCE OF A SYSTEMATIC APPROACH FOR HEALTHCARE ORGANISATIONS

The COVID-19 pandemic has highlighted the need to reconsider healthcare organisation in its various aspects. In particular, it has shown how important it is, on the one hand, to rebalance the relationship between the individual (not to say individualistic) dimension of health and the collective or solidarity dimension, and, on the other hand, to have a systemic vision in which to organise healthcare activities. From the perspective of the Italian Constitution, it has been an opportunity to rediscover Article 32 of the Constitution, i.e. the connection and complementarity of health both as a fundamental right of the individual and in the interest of the collectivity;[1] this is also in line with the solidarity framework of the defined Ethical and Social Relations (Rapporti etico-sociali) in which the protection of health is placed. The idea of health protection is now reconsidered both with regard to the tools useful to support it and in the context of prevention and reduction of the spread of disease. Events such as the pandemic – but also the mandatory vaccination issue – show how the concept of health safety extends beyond the, *a posteriori*, treatment of the individual patient's disease, to include far-reaching measures (for example, see Art 32, co 2, of the Italian Constitution).[2]

1 Article 32, paragraph 1, of the Constitution: "The Republic safeguards health as a fundamental right of the individual and as a collective interest, and guarantees free medical care to the indigent".

2 Article 32, paragraph 2, of the Constitution: "No one may be obliged to undergo any health treatment except under the provisions of the law. The law may not under any circumstances violate the limits imposed by respect for the human person".

Globalisation has a double face. The pandemic is a poisoned fruit of globalisation, but, at the same time, the possibility to communicate and cooperate on an international scale can facilitate the development and sharing of therapeutic responses. Furthermore, when it comes to the responsibility of healthcare professionals, it emerges once again that the individual performs his/her service within an organisational context, and thus to a certain extent, depends on the available means (in a general sense). These means include knowledge and methods (standard of skill in the sense of roman *peritia*) but also professional evaluation, and they are developed within the medical-scientific community. The former means are formalised in recommendations in those documents that we generically call "guidelines", while the ethics of professional community is properly declared in the medical code of ethics, which is now recognised by law.[3] Furthermore, the recent evolution of medical liability (responsibility in a legal sense) has been characterised by the attribution of objective standards of skill, defined by the guidelines that summarise internationally recognised experiences and studies.[4] Thus, Article 5 of Law 24/2017[5] presents a detailed set of the formal requirements of the guidelines, within which one can identify the binding recommendations for healthcare professionals; these recommendations contribute to the objective evaluation of the skill of the doctor, which, however, is valid only prima facie, without prejudice to each specific case. In other words, the law acknowledges a recent and increasingly significant phenomenon, namely the production, by the scientific and medical associations, of documents that constitute a reference point in the training and activity of individual doctors. These documents set the goal to select and reorder the guidelines, in order to eliminate or at least reduce confusion among the different sources. The pandemic has somewhat exacerbated this problem, raising the question about the role of a scientific society in such situations, and also about the purposes and the limits of its intervention. Basically, it is necessary to understand in which framework these kinds of documents can be relevant, also considering the novelty and, therefore,

---

3 See Article 1, paragraph 6, Law 22 December 2017, no 219 "Norme in materia di consenso informato e di disposizioni anticipate di trattamento", G.U. 16 January 2018, no 12 and Law 11 January 2018, no 3 on the reorganisation of the health professions "Delega al Governo in materia di sperimentazione clinica di medicinali nonché disposizioni per il riordino delle professioni sanitarie e per la dirigenza sanitaria del Ministero della salute", G.U. 31 January 2018, no 25. Concerning the legal significance of the professional code, see Italian Constitutional Court, Judgment no 259 of 2019 https://www.cortecostituzionale.it/actionSchedaPronuncia.do?anno=2019&numero=259 accessed 11 February 2021.

4 According to Carlo Castronovo, *Responsabilità civile* (Giuffrè 2018) 423 ff the guidelines are "recommendations or directions, formalized through procedure laid down by law, concerning aspects of healthcare in terms of safety".

5 Legge 8 March 2017, no 24 "Disposizioni in materia di sicurezza delle cure e della persona assistita, nonché in materia di responsabilità professionale degli esercenti le professioni sanitarie", G.U. 17 March 2017, no 64.

the *lacuna iuris* – so to speak – of extraordinary events such as the pandemic. From both a legal and ethical point of view we must take into account that such documents are drawn up in the form of recommendations, which – in the actual meaning of the term – imply a certain solicitation, if not a concrete normativity, to the recipients. Hence, a couple of corollaries can be derived. On the one hand, there is an evident responsibility, at least on the moral level, for those institutions that draw up the documents, since they give directions using a generically prescriptive language. On the other hand, there is a need to formally frame these recommendations, in order to assign them a precise and appropriate authority; indeed, they may be considered the reference point for the guidelines that will be officially recognised by the public authority.

2. THE RECENT ITALIAN DISCIPLINE OF MEDICAL RESPONSIBILITY

The problem of medical liability is urgent because, as already happened in other jurisdictions, Law no 24 of 2017 established a direct relationship between the medical responsibility of individuals and the guidelines (and the clinical practices). In particular, concerning criminal liability, Article 6 provides the exclusion of the criminal punishment of the doctor according to the compliance with the guidelines: "If the event occurred due to lack of skill, the punishment is excluded when the recommendations of the guidelines as defined and published according to the law are respected or, in the absence of these, when good clinical-assistance practices are pursued, provided that the recommendations were adequate to the specificity of the particular case".[6] Concerning civil liability, Article 7 establishes that "the judge, in determining the compensation for damage, takes into account the conduct of the healthcare practitioner according to article 5 of this law and article 590-sexies of the criminal code, introduced by article 6 of this law".[7]

---

6 In a certain sense, the law collects and updates an idea that can be derived from Article 2236 of the Civil Code ("if the service involves the solution of technical problems of special difficulty, the provider is not liable for damages, except in the case of wilful misconduct or gross negligence"), according to which, in the event of problems of special difficulty, the liability of the professionals is limited to gross technical error. See Luigi Mengoni, 'Obbligazioni "di risultato" e obbligazioni "di mezzi" (Studio critico)' in Carlo Castronovo, Antonio Albanese and Andrea Nicolussi (eds), *Obbligazioni e negozio, Scritti II* (Giuffrè 2011) 206. For more information on the technical error or *error scientiae*, see Raffaella De Matteis, *La responsabilità medica. Un sottosistema della responsabilità civile* (Cedam 1995) 123 ff.

7 This law, indeed, is questionable on a technical level both for the extra-contractual framework of liability and for the shifting of the relevance of the guidelines from the responsibility to the quantification of damages. It generates some aporias, if not antinomies, within the regulatory system, see Carlo Castronovo, *Responsabilità civile* (Giuffrè 2018) 423 ff.

Of course, the legal relevance of the guidelines concerning medical liability also finds its rationale in the need to combat or at least reduce practices of defensive medicine.[8] However, it is justified, above all, by the recognition that the standard of skill is not reduced to the mere knowledge of the individual, but the very expertise of the individual is based on the general expertise of the medical-scientific community. Similarly, medical ethics is also the result of a self-reflection of the medical community, which must also be elaborated according to certain procedures and be formalised in specific documents. Moreover, the systemic idea of a healthcare organisation was recently enriched by the concept of safety of care already expressed in paragraph 2 of Article 1 of Law 24/2017. The safety of care is no longer considered to be based exclusively on the skills and knowledge of the individual healthcare provider but on the organisation as a whole. In other words, the safety is reframed as a function of the interaction between all the components of the system; instead of being conceived as the sum of several elements – the operators, the technologies, and the organisation itself in a separate way –, safety is conceived as an overall product of the interaction of the single components. This does not mean renouncing the contribution of the professionalism and personality of the individual doctor who will always have to deal with the specificity and particularity of the different situations and different people he/she helps; rather, it means promoting the relationship between the individual and the context, organising the single components together, i.e. putting them into a relationship according to their value and efficiency. To sum

---

8 A rule of liability that avoids defensiveness and allows the doctor to act with some serenity can also be justified in Article 32 of the Italian Constitution and, once again, in a systemic idea of a health organisation. Referring to the famous Bolam Test in common law, according to which a doctor cannot be considered negligent if he/she has acted in accordance with a practice established and deemed appropriate by a certain scientific or medical community, Marc S. Stauch, 'Causation Issues in Medical Malpractice: A United Kingdom Perspective' (1996) 5 Annals Health L. 247, 248, highlights that the power of doctors resulting from the Bolam Test has an advantage in that it encourages the medical category to explore new forms of treatment and reduces the use of defensive medicine. The Bolam Test was introduced by McNair in *Bolam v Friern Hospital Management Committee* [1957] 2 ALL ER 118. As is known, the Bolam Test rule was specified in the case *Bolitho v City & Hackney Health Authority* [1998] AC 232, where Lord Browne-Wilkinson said: "In cases of diagnosis and treatment there are cases where, despite a body of professional opinion sanctioning the defendant's conduct, the defendant can properly be held liable for negligence … that is because, in some cases, it cannot be demonstrated to the judge's satisfaction that the body of opinion relied upon is reasonable or responsible. In the vast majority of cases the fact that distinguished experts in the field are of a particular opinion will demonstrate the reasonableness of that opinion. In particular, where there are questions of assessment of the relative risks and benefits of adopting a particular medical practice, a reasonable view necessarily presupposes that the relative risks and benefits have been weighed by the experts informing their opinions. But if, in a *rare case*, it can be demonstrated that the professional opinion is not capable of withstanding logical analysis, the judge is entitled to hold that the body of opinion is not reasonable or responsible". See Rachael Mulheron, 'Trumping Bolam: A Critical Legal Analysis of Bolitho's "gloss"' (2010) 69 Cambridge Law Journal 613.

up, it is necessary to reconcile the evidence-based and precision medicine with the clinical attention to the individual patient; furthermore, it is necessary to reconcile objective criteria (guidelines) with professional autonomy, which is expressed in the evaluation of and application to the specific case.[9]

Now, linking the evaluation of the medical standard of skill to an objective element such as guidelines or, as an alternative, good clinical care practice presupposes great skill by the general system of national health organisation. Hence, there is the need to regulate the guidelines, which is what the law seeks to satisfy, starting from the procedural rules necessary for their selection and legitimation.[10] The procedures provided by Article 5 of Law 24/2017 now allow distinguishing between the real and true guidelines that the healthcare professional must comply with, also considering each specific case, from those that can be conceived as pseudo-guidelines. The responsible professional has the right to know which sources he/she should refer to, without sacrificing his/her autonomy and distinguishing "good science" from "bad science". The bad science, when hasty and ill-advised, generates confusion and therefore is not immune from responsibility.[11]

---

9 As highlighted by the criminal law doctrine, the binding nature of the guidelines certainly cannot be conceived in absolute terms since it could put "at risk the therapeutic freedom of the doctor". See Matteo Caputo, 'La responsabilità penale dell'esercente la professione sanitaria dopo la L. n. 24 del 2017 … '*Quo vadit*'? Primi dubbi, prime risposte, secondi dubbi' (2017) 3 Danno e responsabilità 38 ff.; rather, they have the function of "orienting the clinical behavior". Moreover, it is the law itself that gives the opportunity to deviate from it, depending on the circumstances of the specific case. Therefore, the doctor must certainly take the guidelines into account, that is, he/she must know them and evaluate their congruence with the specific case, but he/she must not be conditioned to the point of applying them *sic et simpliciter*.

10 The guidelines are developed by the entity entrusted with a systematic and multidisciplinary evaluation of the evidence from the scientific literature; therefore, they should contain the best available evidence and provide an informative contribution, in order to help the healthcare professional in the decision-making process. The method used to draw up a recommendation must be made explicit to allow for a critical assessment of both reliability and applicability to the specific case. In the absence of guidelines, the law provides to rely on the "good clinical-care practice", which is a wider category since it refers to both concrete clinical-care practices and documents containing recommendations of good clinical-care practices. Therefore, it includes, on the one hand, the professional practices based on scientific evidence and oriented to the protection of health; on the other hand, it refers to those documents that are consistent with scientific evidence and elaborated with a declared and reconstructible methodology, not only those that bear the words "good practices". According to the Italian Supreme Court (Corte di Cassazione) – sez. IV pen.,- no 23283: judgment of 11 May 2016 in https://www.biodiritto.org/Biolaw-pedia/Giurisprudenza/Corte-di-Cassazione-sez.-IV-pen.-sent.-23283-2016-la-Cassazione-torna-sul-perimetro-applicativo-del-Decreto-Balduzzi accessed 11 February 2021 and following the definition of the US Institute of Medicine, by "guidelines" we mean the "recommendations of clinical behavior, elaborated through a process of systematic review of the literature and scientific opinions, in order to help doctors and patients to decide the most appropriate assistance modalities in specific clinical situations".

11 The distinction can be put in comparison with what is emphasised in the common law in the case *Bolitho v City & Hackney Health Authority* [1998] AC 232 in which it is required that a standard of practice must be recognised as proper by a competent, reasonable, respectable and responsible body of opinion.

3. PSEUDO-GUIDELINES AND THE NEED FOR REORGANISATION AND CONCEPTUAL CLARIFICATION

In this regulatory framework, the COVID-19 emergency has taken the medical-scientific community by surprise, raising various issues concerning which criteria to refer to in the absence of specific guidelines and true clinical assistance practices. Making a comparison with the legal dimension, we could say that the pandemic has exposed some instances of *lacuna iuris* with regard to the guidelines and also to the clinical assistance practice that should be taken into consideration in the absence of the former. Furthermore, there has been a proliferation of pseudo-guidelines that entailed the need for a careful analysis and reorganisation of those recommendations which, coming from institutional or scientific fields, concur or even interfere with the real and true guidelines, or, in the absence of any guideline, with the rationale behind the legal provision of guidelines.[12] So, they may be called "pseudo-guidelines" precisely to underline the confusion that they can create.

The first phase of the pandemic has produced problematic examples of both institutional pseudo-guidelines and scientific pseudo-guidelines. As for the former, it all began with the story of the diagnosis of so-called "patient one" that was obtained by diverging from the pseudo-guideline. Indeed, Annex 1 to the circular of the Ministry of Health of 27 January 2020, which provided checks on suspicious patients, did not allow classification of "patient 1" as a "suspected case" or "probable case", and therefore it did not authorise any diagnostic research in that direction.[13] Nonetheless, the anaesthesiologist performed the swab on the patient, immediately activating in the Codogno hospital the personal protection procedures for doctors and nurses that allowed an initial containment of the infection; this clinical intuition is remarkable and deserves

---

12 The law seems to promote legal certainty, so that the individual doctor or the evaluating judge can avoid prior examinations of the credibility and reliability of the sources. Cristiano Cupelli, '*L'eterointegrazione della legge Gelli-Bianco*: aggiornamenti in tema di linee guida "certificate" e responsabilità penale in ambito sanitario' (2017) Diritto penale contemporaneo 268 notes that this discipline, "even with all the limits of the criteria identified in secondary regulation and with the evident risk of transferring the dispute related to the scientific reliability of these sources from the criminal to the administrative office – [it] represents an appreciable effort, considering the well-known objections related to the large number of guidelines from various scientific societies, which intervene, often in opposing positions, in their areas of competence, fuelling the fear of subsequent choices, that is, of an ex post selection of the sources to justify medical conduct, above all in the court proceedings."

13 Circolare del Ministero della Salute, Direzione generale della Prevenzione Sanitaria, *Polmonite da nuovo coronavirus (2019 nCoV) in Cina*, 27 January 2020, https://www.trovanorme.salute.gov.it/norme/renderNormsanPdf?anno=2020&codLeg=72847&parte=1%20&serie=null accessed 11 February 2021.

unanimous admiration. However, despite the worthiness of this example, the question concerning the relevance of these administrative documents remains unanswered, given that they interfere with the professional autonomy of the doctor, who, in cases like these, has greater responsibility if he/she deviates from the recommendations, rather than follows them blindly.

Another example is represented by a ministerial circular that has become well known for having caused the idea of a ban on performing autopsy tests on deceased patients, precluding the possibility of a better understanding of the disease and the adequacy of certain therapies; in fact, the Ministry subsequently had to modify it. This is the Circular of the Ministry of Health entitled "Emergency indications connected to the COVID-19 epidemic concerning the funeral, cemetery and cremation sector" (8 April 2020).[14] Point C of the circular dealt the autopsy examinations and diagnostic findings and provided that: "For the entire period of the emergency phase, autopsies or diagnostic findings should not be carried out in full-blown cases of COVID-19, whether they died while being hospitalised in a hospital ward or at home." The circular did not prohibit autopsies in a Draconian way, admitting an evaluation by the judicial authority and limiting autopsies for reasons of study and in-depth analysis to the strictly necessary; however, it has actually induced misunderstandings and therefore has caused the loss of many propitious opportunities.

Unlike the two above-mentioned examples, there is a case that is worthy of more attention, namely, the pseudo-guidelines that were drawn up by a scientific association, the *Italian Society of Anaesthesia Analgesia Resuscitation and Intensive Care* (SIAARTI), entitled "Clinical ethics recommendations for the allocation of intensive care treatments, in exceptional, resource-limited circumstances".[15] Although they are not administrative guidelines, problems nevertheless arise for several reasons because they directly addressed members of an accredited association whose documents could be taken into consideration to select genuine guidelines, and because of the content of the document, which moves from the clinical to the extra-clinical dimension. The document in question was published on 6 March 2020, just as the emergency of the COVID-19 outbreaks began to spread in Lombardy and Veneto. It prescribes some criteria for dealing with the serious difficulty or even the impossibility of ensuring

14 Circolare del Ministero della Salute, Direzione generale della Prevenzione Sanitaria, *Indicazioni emergenziali connesse ad epidemia COVID-19 riguardanti il settore funebre, cimiteriale e di cremazione*, 8 April 2020, https://www.trovanorme.salute.gov.it/norme/renderNormsanPdf?anno=2020&codLeg=73832&parte=1+&serie=null accessed 11 February 2021.

15 Società Italiana di Anestesia Analgesia Rianimazione e Terapia Intensiva (SIAARTI), *Raccomandazioni di etica clinica per l'ammissione a trattamenti intensivi e per la loro sospensione, in condizioni eccezionali di squilibrio tra necessità e risorse disponibili*, 6 March 2020, https://d1c2gz5q23tkk0.cloudfront.net/assets/uploads/3017013/asset/SIAARTI_-_Covid19_-_Raccomandazioni_di_etica_clinica_%282%29.pdf?1606745834 accessed 11 February 2021.

hospitalisation in intensive care units for all patients in need and who, in normal conditions, would have found a place. These recommendations, perhaps due to their timeliness and disruptive content, have become a reference in the global bioethical debate; they have been cited and discussed in several essays, articles[16] and official documents dedicated to COVID-19, and they have been subsequently published in the world-wide (for official documents of scientific societies and bioethics committees, see the following section 5). On the formal level, these are concrete recommendations, which means that they cannot be conceived as a mere stance in the scientific debate, methodologically structured as a scientific essay and therefore open to discussion. This is a problematic aspect that is intertwined with some other perplexities concerning the purely extra-clinical criteria introduced by the document.

In this regard, they refer to the possibility of excluding the clinical criteria for the triage, as well as, occasionally, for the discharge and consequently the assistance of the sick person. As we will argue in section 4, the clinical criteria are here replaced with an *a priori* criterion, which consists in the mere setting of an age limit on admission to intensive care. The underlying logic of this recommendation – indicated in the document as no 3 – is that "it is not a question of making choices merely based upon values, but of reserving resources that could be very scarce, primarily for those who have *a greater chance of survival* and, secondly, for those who can have *more years of life saved, maximising the benefits for the greatest number of people.* In a scenario of total saturation of intensive resources, the '*first-come, first-served*' criterion would be equivalent to choosing not to cure any other patient subsequently excluded from the ICU."[17] However, the age limit criterion, which is an *a priori* criterion, i.e. without concurring with other factors for the definition of the probability of survival, is not justified by the rationale given in the document precisely because it cannot be considered *a priori*. Even lay people can see that a 65-year-old patient could have more life

---

16 See for example Robert D. Truog, Christine Mitchell, and George Q. Daley, 'The Toughest Triage – Allocating Ventilators in a Pandemic' (2020) 382(21) The New England Journal of Medicine 1973–1975; Ezekiel J. Emanuel and others, 'Fair Allocation of Scarce Medical Resources in the Time of Covid-19' (2020) 382 The New England Journal of Medicine 2049–2055.

17 SIAARTI, Raccomandazioni di etica clinica, no 3. This is our own translation of the quoted passage from the original Italian text of the Recommendations. For the English version presented by SIAARTI, see Marco Vergano, Guido Bertolini, Alberto Giannini, Giuseppe R. Gristina, Sergio Livigni, Giovanni Mistraletti, Luigi Riccioni, Flavia Petrini, 'SIAARTI recommendations for the allocation of intensive care treatments in exceptional, resource-limited circumstances' (May 2020) 86(5) Minerva Anestesiologica 469–472. The English version differs in several points from the original in Italian, as Sulmasy also pointed out: Daniel Sulmasy, 'Principled decisions and virtuous care: an ethical assessment of the SIAARTI Guidelines for allocating intensive care resources' (August 2020) 86(8) Minerva Anestesiologica 872–876. We thank Dr. Federico Zilio for his guidance and valuable support during the English translation of the text.

expectancy than a 40-year-old in a more precarious health condition, and that, therefore, the age limit criterion proves to be devoid of any medical justification and is a form of discrimination regarding a fundamental right (Art 32 Const.).

The SIAARTI document has radically gone beyond the clinical criteria (with the so-called extra-clinical criterion) and this can also lead to a possible confusion between real and true guidelines (and therefore binding) and a simple standpoint, taken – nevertheless – by accredited scientific societies. In this case – as we will discuss later – the extra-clinical criterion inevitably invades the professional autonomy concerning the need to establish priorities, but also, to some extent, it even goes beyond professional autonomy. The introduction of discriminations between "deserving" and "non-deserving" people based on the *a priori* age criterion implies the transcendence of the boundaries of medical ethics; indeed, the *a priori* exclusion of some categories of people from medical treatment should – at least – result from a democratic decision, assuming that such discrimination is constitutionally legitimate. Moreover, professional autonomy should be defined by a code of medical ethics, and not by any document made by some particular association of a medical speciality, which, if anything, may be useful as a contribution to the discussion.

4. THE *A PRIORI* AND EXTRA-CLINICAL CRITERION AND THE PREFERABILITY OF THE INTEGRATED CLINICAL JUDGMENT

The SIAARTI document is emblematic in two ways. From a formal point of view, it clearly shows the need to distinguish between binding scientific documents (real and true guidelines) and documents that are mere pseudo-guidelines; from a content point of view, it highlights the usual confusion between strictly scientific or clinical issues and the professional and legal questions. Nevertheless, these critical aspects do not obscure the merit of having clearly identified the problem of the lack of available health resources (understood in a broad sense as protective devices, ventilators, medical and paramedical staff, especially beds in intensive and sub-intensive care wards), which would have become disruptive in a few days.[18] Hence the need, as presented in the document, to establish priorities that the scarcity of resources would have made inevitable, and to do

18 In the debate, the expression "tragic choices" has also spread, echoing the title of the well-known book by Guido Calabresi and Philip Bobbitt, *Tragic choices: The conflicts society confronts in the allocation of tragically scarce resources* (W.W. Norton & Company 1978). Philip Bobbitt recently returned to the same subject, with reference to the pandemic: see 'Tragic choices, 42 anni dopo. Philip Bobbitt riflette sulla pandemia', intervista di Roberto Conti

so based on rational criteria rather than by chance. Also, the intention not to abandon doctors but to support them should be appreciated, drawing attention to the enormous pressure that threatened our health system and the onerous commitment by many doctors, health workers and social workers, at the risk of their own safety and life; gratitude to them, for what they have done during the hardest days of the pandemic will never be enough. Having said that, it is not possible to overlook the considerable limits that characterise this document. They are various and can be summarised: (1) in the presence of lexical and conceptual inaccuracies and ambiguities as well as in the assertive tone of the document itself; (2) in the lack of interdisciplinary analysis; (3) in an insufficient in-depth analysis on an ethical-normative perspective, and, finally, (4) in the adoption of a rigid and simplistic criterion such as the *a priori* age limit.[19]

4.1. LEXICAL AND CONCEPTUAL INACCURACIES

Concerning the first aspect, perhaps the most unfortunate statement is represented by the statement in point 9 of the SIAARTI Recommendations, which shows how linguistic and expressive inaccuracies can harm the contents of a scientific opinion. This point refers to the opportunity to prepare in time "a list of patients who will be deemed of deserving of ICU".[20] The wording is unpleasant because it alludes to a title of merit (the youngest age?), which some patients, unlike others, would have to access intensive care. Presumably, the drafters of the document intended to underline that, concretely, not all patients can be cured in a situation of extreme emergency. But then, what exactly makes the difference is not the merit, because all patients, without exception, deserve (even better, have the right) to be treated in various ways, including intensive ones; what makes the difference is, if anything, the potential tragic lack of sufficient resources to treat all those who would need them. In that situation, if we want to avoid grounding our decisions on subjective merit, the issue is to establish priority criteria which nevertheless are not completely detached from the medical competence in a broader sense (including professional ethics).

On this level, a decision formulated exclusively based on clinical appropriateness and proportionality may certainly be insufficient, because

(with English translation), Giustizia insieme, 17 May 2020, https://www.giustiziainsieme.it/it/diritto-dell-emergenza-covid-19/1049-tragic-choises-43-anni-dopo-philip-chase-bobbitt-riflette-sulla-pandemia?hitcount=0" \h accessed 11 February 2021.

19 For a first critical examination concerning the problematic nature of such a criterion, see Antonio Da Re, 'Il dilemma del triage. La deliberazione medica tra apriorismo e giudizio clinico' in Linda Napolitano, Carlo Chiurco (eds), *Senza Corona. A più voci sulla pandemia* (QuiEdit 2020) 69–95.

20 Again, this is our own translation of the quoted passage.

it ignores the need for a comparison between the care needs of different patients, and the necessity to establish a priority among them; in fact, the shift of attention from the individual patient to a group of patients implies that the medical decision is necessarily complemented by an evaluation of the different efficacy of the treatment for all the patients. However, asking who deserves the treatment or not because, for example, a patient falls within a certain age range is very different from asking which patients can benefit most from the proposed treatment. This second type of integrated assessment should be chosen to correctly prioritise access to intensive care. Instead, the debate seems polarised on a black-or-white alternative between the clinical criterion as such and a purely extra-clinical criterion,[21] while the tragic background (urgency and scarcity of resources) in which such decisions are made imposes that the clinical criterion (appropriateness and proportionality of the treatment referred to a single subject) is integrated (certainly not replaced) by some criteria that help to distinguish on which patients the treatment is expected to be more effective.

Point 7 then argues that "any decision to deny access to intensive care" depends on the "exceptional circumstances" and ultimately on whether "the availability of resources is overwhelmed by their need". Again, this is an imprecise and infelicitous wording. On closer inspection, this is a logical fallacy, as there is no consequentiality between the cause of the exceptional circumstances and the effect that leads to the judgment of inappropriateness of the ICU. The judgment concerning the appropriateness of care, including intensive care, must be formulated regardless of the extraordinary nature of the emergency. In other words, given the severe scarcity of resources, the concrete impossibility to ensure intensive care for all patients does not depend on a judgment of inappropriateness; indeed, the treatments can be relevant and appropriate, so much that they would be guaranteed to all in ordinary and non-emergency conditions; yet they will remain so even when, unfortunately, patients will not have access to intensive care. In such cases, if anything, we should add a priority criterion that – if one does not want to fall into the extra-clinical merit – must be based on the different efficacy of the treatment; this efficacy can also be derived from the age, but only when the age is evaluated along with other factors concerning the patient's clinical situation.

A further element of ambiguity that derives from the way the text is formulated concerns the possible extension of the *a priori* criterion to the decision of discharge of a person undergoing treatment, perhaps already successfully initiated, to make room for a new patient. This possibility is not explicitly stated in the text, but it is hard not to think that this can become the logical conclusion

---

21 See Silvia Camporesi, Maurizio Mori, 'Ethicists, doctors and triage decisions: who should decide? And on what basis?' (2020) Journal of Medical Ethics 1–3, https://jme.bmj.com/content/early/2020/07/10/medethics-2020-106499 accessed 11 February 2021: the authors, after contrasting clinical and extra-clinical judgment, opt strongly for the latter criterion.

of some assumptions that can be identified starting from the very title of the recommendations. Regarding the title, the SIAARTI recommendations concern not only the "admission to intensive treatments" but also "their suspension".[22] Furthermore, in the premises of the text, the extraordinary nature of the circumstances leads to justify not only the abstention from medical treatment but even its suspension or – as said in the text – the "discharge" of a patient already under treatment. However, point 3 of the Recommendations is silent on the possible extension of the *a priori* criterion, thus creating ambiguity concerning the title and the premises themselves; in this regard, the reason for the lack of such mention could be found in a previous SIAARTI document, once again formulated in terms of recommendations, according to which the decision not to initiate treatment and the decision to stop it would have the same ethical value.[23] This is a superficial statement, which goes beyond the acknowledgement that the suspension may be justified under certain conditions, for example when the treatment is no longer appropriate and proportionate. To peremptorily argue that "the non-initiation and the suspension of a treatment are ethically equivalent"[24] means adopting a simplifying and, once again, *a priori* approach, which does not take into account the variety of different clinical contexts. Also, the thesis of equivalence is even dangerous if applied no longer to the single patient but to the emergency circumstances and the evaluation of a multiplicity of patients in need of treatment, because it might legitimise the interruption of treatment in a patient in favour of another. Indeed, the appropriateness and proportionality for the individual patient, for whom a suspension of treatment may be justified under certain conditions, is really different from using the emergency circumstances to justify the suspension, once again employing an extra-clinical and *a priori* criterion.

Now, these limitations of how the text is formulated are worsened by the assertive and unproblematic tone used, which makes the SIAARTI document appear as not susceptible to modifications and improvements. Moreover, this is consistent with the prescriptive purpose already indicated, which generates confusion with genuine guidelines: even if the text does not mention obligations or directives, we are in any case in the presence of recommendations, which therefore are characterised by some normative intention; one should be

---

22 Again, the English version presented by SIAARTI does not respect the translation of the Italian one, even in the title; in their English version, the title is more neutral.

23 Società Italiana di Anestesia Analgesia Rianimazione e Terapia Intensiva (SIAARTI), *Le cure di fine vita e l'anestesista rianimatore: raccomandazioni SIAARTI per l'approccio alla persona morente* (update 2018) 1–50, https://www.siaarti.it/news/371329 accessed 11 February 2021. The statement is already reported and stigmatised in Andrea Nicolussi 'La legge n. 219/2017 su consenso informato e disposizioni anticipate di trattamento: il problema e le risposte della legge' (2018) Teoria e critica della regolazione sociale 2, 57–80, in particular 61, fn 7.

24 SIAARTI, *Le cure di fine vita e l'anestesista rianimatore: raccomandazioni SIAARTI per l'approccio alla persona morente* 13.

aware that they will be received by the recipients – in this specific case the anaesthetists and intensivists – not as mere indications or considerations but as rules of conduct, which are believed to be good and correct, and, therefore, to be recommended. One might point out that also the opinions of the Italian Committee for Bioethics (ICB) (Comitato Nazionale per la Bioetica – CNB) formulate Recommendations, including the one entitled *Covid-19: la decisione clinica in condizioni di carenza di risorse e il criterio del "triage in emergenza pandemica"* (Covid-19: the clinical decision in conditions of lack of resources and the criterion of "triage in a pandemic emergency"),[25] which addresses the same issue raised by the SIAARTI document. Nevertheless, this is a very different type of document and thus is not comparable with the SIAARTI recommendations. Beyond the specific content of the recommendations,[26] there is a clear difference between the recommendations made by a scientific society and those made by the CNB: the former are addressed primarily to its members, intending to guide their choices and professional behaviour; the latter come from an institutional body responsible for providing the guidelines to Parliament and the Government, and indirectly also to public opinion. Given these different purposes, it is evident that the normative force of the recommendations expressly addressed to affiliates of a scientific society can be much more binding than those presented in the opinions of the CNB.

Considering the complexity of the issue, a more prudent style that also raises some questions would certainly have benefited the document; at least it would have prevented it from being interpreted, erroneously, as genuine guidelines. In effect, the introduction presents reasonable indications on how to elaborate on the clinical decision in the context of a serious shortage of health resources: in addition to clinical appropriateness and proportionality, the document talks about the importance of guaranteeing intensive treatments to "patients with a greater chance of therapeutic success", favouring the "greatest life expectancy." Regrettably, these indications, affected by the tragic context and yet defined by a reasonable and open character, then undergo a sharp stiffening in the recommendations part, especially in the aforementioned recommendation no 3, where the age *per se* becomes the main criterion for medical deliberation.

---

25 Comitato Nazionale per la Bioetica (CNB), *Covid 19: la decisione clinica in condizioni di carenza di risorse e il criterio del "triage in emergenza pandemica"* 8 April 2020, 1–14, http://bioetica.governo.it/italiano/documenti/pareri-e-risposte/covid-19-la-decisione-clinica-in-condizioni-di-carenza-di-risorse-e-il-criterio-del-triage-in-emergenza-pandemica/ accessed 11 February 2021.

26 See the opinion of the CNB regarding the criterion of "triage in a pandemic emergency": "In such a situation as the current one characterised by a serious lack of resources, the CNB evaluates the clinical criterion as the most adequate point of reference for the allocation of the resources: any other selection criteria, for example, age, gender, social condition and role, ethnicity, disability, responsibility for behaviours that led to the disease, costs, are considered by the Committee to be ethically unacceptable", 7.

4.2. LACK OF INTERDISCIPLINARY ANALYSIS

These lexical, conceptual and argumentative limits probably depend on a fundamentally monodisciplinary approach, entirely related to intensive care and resuscitation medicine. Understandably, the strictly medical competence has had the opportunity to express its opinion here about the situation and formulate strictly clinical guidelines. However, the Recommendations are not limited to these aspects; they claim to be qualified as recommendations of "clinical ethics". However, on the basis of the remarks already formulated, it seems that any bioethics and law expertise did not significantly contribute to the drafting. The lack of interdisciplinarity constitutes a serious limitation because the bioethical enterprise is represented precisely by interdisciplinarity, and there is no doubt that similar recommendations on clinical ethics take also a bioethical value. Bioethics experts with philosophical or legal training would not have been able to provide strictly clinical guidelines, such as those prepared by the authors of the document; nevertheless, the authors should have listened to the competence from other disciplines and skills (autonomy is a value, but not when it becomes self-referential); in this way, they would have drafted a proper interdisciplinary document that would be more prudent and better argued. Probably, one might think that the time pressure imposed by the authors themselves negatively affected the final result.

4.3. INSUFFICIENT ETHICAL-NORMATIVE ANALYSIS

The document insistently returns to the exceptional nature of the pandemic context in which health facilities and doctors operate; given this, the authors hastily conclude that a single ethical-normative perspective should be assumed, namely the utilitarian one.[27] The reference to utilitarianism is explicit in the already mentioned Recommendation no 3, according to which "An age limit for the admission to the ICU may ultimately need to be set." Here, in fact, it is proposed to "to save limited resources which may become extremely scarce for those who have a much greater probability of survival and life expectancy, in order to maximise the benefits for the largest number of people". The terminology adopted (i.e. the maximisation of benefits for the greatest number) is clearly utilitarian, as is the so-called QALYs (Quality-Adjusted Life Years) methodology,[28] to which the document seems to allude, without nevertheless

27 Among the first to criticise the utilitarian approach of the SIAARTI document was Weyma Lübbe, 'Corona Triage: A Commentary on the Triage Recommendations by Italian SIAARTI Medicals Regarding the Corona Crisis', Verfassungsblog, 16 March 2020, https://verfassungsblog.de/corona-triage-2/ accessed 11 February 2021.

28 See John La Puma, Edward F. Lawlor, 'Quality-adjusted life-years: ethical implications for physicians and policy makers' (1990) Journal of the American Medical Association 263,

citing it. According to this methodology, two parameters must be taken into account: on the one hand, the years of life that can be earned thanks to a given therapy and, on the other hand, the quality of health that the patient will enjoy; based on these parameters, they make comparisons and measurements (for example, a year in very poor health conditions does not "weigh" as much as a year in good condition), finally drawing up rankings among the patients. More generally, the document attributes the adoption of certain utilitarian principles and procedures due to the extraordinary nature of the situation. This radical gap between ordinariness and extraordinariness is perplexing as if in an emergency condition we had to appeal to an extraordinary ethical code or to some principles that are valid only for that exceptional occasion. However, it is reductive to imagine that normative ethics can renounce the lexicon of the dignity of the person, of equality, of justice (not reinterpreted simplistically through the reference to the maximisation of benefits), which are principles that are valid and foundational in ordinary but also in extraordinary circumstances. It is important that we can always rely on these principles, and, even more so, in unexpected and extreme situations; based on these principles, it must be recognised that everyone, without exception and regardless of age, social status, gender, ethnicity etc., should be put in the position to be treated in the best possible way.

This recognition is not superfluous at all, first of all, because an underestimation of the principles of the dignity of the person, of equality, of justice in extraordinary circumstances could be an excuse to reduce the scope of these principles even in ordinary times, potentially triggering discriminatory kinds of logic towards the most vulnerable categories of patients. Furthermore, the fact that we base the normative ethics on these principles, which also find a solid foundation in our Constitution, does not exclude that we can discuss their concrete feasibility in conditions of extreme emergency, considering that we will have to face hard moral conflicts and dilemmas.[29] The moral question concerning the possible consequences that could be produced by adopting decisions of

---

2917–2921; Anthony John Culyer, 'Equality and Equity' in Henk ten Have (ed), *Encyclopedia of Global Bioethics* (Springer International Publishing 2016) 1150–1160.

29 For a more complete analysis of the various orientations of normative ethics, from the deontological one to the consequentialistic one, see these collections: Stephen L. Darwall, *Deontology* (Blackwell 2003); Stephen L. Darwall, *Consequentialism* (Blackwell 2003). On the difference between moral conflict and dilemma, understood in terms of a radicalisation of the conflict itself, see Carla Bagnoli, 'Moral dilemmas' in Hugh LaFollette (ed), *Wiley-Blackwell International Encyclopedia of Ethics* (Blackwell 2017): the moral dilemma is a situation where the subject is forced to violate a moral reason, whatever choice is made, in favour of one or the other horn of the dilemma. In this specific case, the violation concerns the practical impossibility (not in principle) of being able to guarantee each patient the care that would be ensured under normal conditions.

one type rather than another certainly cannot be evaded in normative ethics. However, the utilitarian approach is reductive because it undervalues the above-mentioned deontological principles, and because it fails to adequately account for the difference between people or, in other words, it tends to subordinate the good of the individual to the logic of the whole (the overall utility). A balanced and complete normative reflection will never avoid the question concerning the consequences of our choices, both personal and collective ones. Nevertheless, it would be better to adopt a non-unilateral normative approach; starting from a deontological framework, such an approach would be more complete and adequate than the utilitarian one, and it would then achieve the ethics of responsibility, which can evaluate the potential or probable consequences of our acts and the various conceivable courses of action.

From this point of view, one can only agree with the SIAARTI document when it concludes that it is necessary to set priority criteria for the admission to the ICU, foreshadowing the situation that would have soon occurred in hospitals due to the pandemic; however, what cannot be shared at all is that these criteria are conceived as *a priori* (the age limit) and following the logic of maximisation. The problem is not the questioning of the first-come-first-served criterion, which it is usually justified by ensuring equality among people and by avoiding preferences for access to care due to discretionary or even trivial reasons not founded on a clinical level. It is understandable that in triage, especially in a maxi-emergency triage, this criterion is relativised, but this should happen based on reasons that are not separate from the clinical dimension; this would allow as many patients as possible to benefit from the limited resources available, while, at the same time, it would be possible to assess which patients can realistically respond best to treatments and have a higher chance of survival in ICU. Instead, the document directly proposes not to follow the first-come-first-served criterion and it leads to the adoption of the mono-dimensional age criterion.

4.4. THE SIMPLISTIC CRITERION OF THE *A PRIORI* AGE LIMIT

The adoption of this criterion concerning its ethical-political presuppositions (are they comparing, in one way or another, human lives?) raises the basic question whether the scientific society should establish such a rigid criterion, which goes beyond the clinical dimension. This question shows how method and merit are intertwined in such a serious matter. Indeed, it is clear that the issue would have been less puzzling and perplexing if the document had simply supported the doctor on the diagnostic and therapeutic level only, providing him/her with knowledge and suggestions of good practices – still, inevitably, a knowledge in progress in the case of COVID-19. Likewise, most of the controversies would not have arisen if the document had prudently questioned which choices to adopt and, possibly, which restrictions to provide in the extreme conditions of the maxi emergency, to the attention of the medical professional community and public opinion in general. The sore point lies in the choice of recommending the doctor to rely on a rigid criterion such as the one based on the *a priori* age limit. In this regard, if this criterion is evaluated on an ethical level, i.e. as an ethical criterion, then the recommendation, on the one hand, invades the competence of the professional code and, on the other hand, it becomes paternalistic as it pretends to replace the doctor's moral conscience; otherwise, if it is evaluated as a political criterion since it grants or denies the rights to care and assistance to specific categories of patients, then it invades the competence of the authorities responsible for making decisions of this gravity in a democratic country. Moreover, it sounds paradoxical that a medical scientific society, drawing up a document of clinical ethics, eventually comes to propose a purely extra-clinical evaluation criterion. Along with the adopted modality (i.e. the recommendation style) and the issue related to the legitimacy of this document, the apriorism used is questionable, as it leads to the adoption of a decision-making automatism, which eventually removes the responsibility of the doctor. Indeed, the following point 4 of the Recommendations insists again on the age criterion including it also in the formulation of specific and general clinical criteria. Point 4 establishes that "in addition to the age, the comorbidities and the functional status of any critically ill patient presenting in these exceptional circumstances should carefully be evaluated".[30] It is important to note that the chronological age is considered first (this is not even the biological age, which would have introduced some more problematic elements), then, secondly, the evaluation of other factors are added; this priority given to the age means that the clinical criterion is once again subordinated. It would have made more sense to reverse the relationship on the clinical level, by establishing the priority of the criterion of comorbidity and functional status over the age, which nonetheless has a weight in the evaluation. The inversion of the relationship between age and comorbidities, together with the enhancement of other criteria (in the first place, the urgency), would have developed a more realistic procedure of clinical deliberation, more careful to the specific characteristic of each situation, even if it would have been more uncertain and demanding due to its open and non-*a priori* nature.

---

30 Again, our translation significantly differs from the one presented by the authors of the SIAARTI Recommendations. Our version literally translates the Italian version, where the comorbidities and the functional status of the patient are evaluated "in addition to" the chronological age; on the contrary, the English version provided by the same authors states that such criteria would be taken into consideration "together with age". This is a subtle difference, which nevertheless reveals a different hierarchy of criteria between the two versions presented by SIAARTI.

5. APRIORISM, ALGORITHM, SELECTION: A QUICK LOOK AT THE INTERNATIONAL DOCUMENTS

The question concerning the selection of the age as a criterion for admission to resuscitation soon opened an international debate in which both scientific societies and bioethics committees were involved. Compared to the SIAARTI document, the document drawn up in Germany is more thoughtful, authored by the scientific societies of German anaesthesiologists and resuscitators and also developed in collaboration with other medical categories as well as with the academy for medical ethics.[31] The German document is based on the principle according to which any criterion that makes a comparison between human lives is unacceptable, thus preventing the establishment that one life is worth more or less than another, based on age or other characteristics. The document adopts the prospect of *clinical* success as a criterion: priority must be given to patients whose treatment offers a greater probability of overcoming the *ongoing* disease. In the case of triage, all patients must be considered, not just those affected by the pandemic. Similarly, the Austrian Bioethics Commission[32] judges the age criterion, taken in isolation, is insufficient from a scientific-professional point of view and illegitimate from an ethical and legal point of view; nevertheless, for the committee, it must also be taken into account that survival in a life-threatening situation may result in permanent and irreversible dependence on intensive care. Even the *Société de Réanimation de Langue Française*, albeit in a more nuanced way, has proposed not to absolutise the age criterion, inviting instead to take into account various factors and thus to formulate a "detailed evaluation of the patient's medical characteristics".[33]

On the other hand, others were attracted by the idea of a clear criterion, easy to apply and devoid of any subjective interpretation. The *Observatori de Bioètica i Dret* (Universitat de Barcelona) identifies age as a relevant criterion for

---

31 Deutsche Interdisziplinäre Vereinigung für Intensiv- und Notfallmedizin (DIVI), *Entscheidungen über die Zuteilung von Ressourcen in der Notfall-und der Intensivmedizin im Kontext der COVID-19-Pandemie Klinisch-ethische Empfehlungen*, 26 March 2020, 1–11, https://www.divi.de/aktuelle-meldungen-intensivmedizin/covid-19-klinisch-ethische-empfehlungen-zur-entscheidung-ueber-die-zuteilung-von-ressourcen-veroeffentlicht accessed 11 February 2021.

32 Bioethikkommission – Bundeskanzleramt Österreich, Stellungnahme "Zum Umgang mit knappen Ressourcen in der Gesundheitsversorgung im Kontext der Covid-19-Pandemie", 31 March 2020, https://www.bundeskanzleramt.gv.at/themen/bioethikkommission/pressemitteilungen-bioethik/stellungnahme-zum-umgang-mit-knappen-ressourcen-in-der-gesundheitsversorgung-im-kontext-der-covid-19-pandemie.html accessed 11 February 2021.

33 Société de Réanimation de Langue Française (SRLF), *Critères d'admission et modalités de prise en charge en réanimation en contexte pandémique* (9 April 2020) point 1, https://www.srlf.org/wp-content/uploads/2020/04/20200410-Reco-Ethique-SRLF.pdf accessed 11 February 2021.

rationing the patients' admission to the hospital intensive care unit.[34] Similarly, in an internal report from the Karolinska University Hospital in Stockholm and reported in the newspaper *Aftonbladet*,[35] the criterion of biological age is used, which can be lower or higher than the personal, chronological age; in this regard, to facilitate the doctor's decision on admissibility to intensive care, some ranges are set dividing patients into those who have a biological age below 80 years, or between 70 and 80 years old, and those who have a significant impairment in more than one organ system, or are between the ages of 60 and 70 with up to two compromised organ systems.

The radicalisation of the *a priori* logic entails the development of algorithms that should facilitate a rational type of deliberation, but which end up depriving the doctor of his/her responsibility, sparing him/her any moral – certainly distressing – questions and conflicts. Actually, the renunciation by the professional of his/her own moral autonomy would be even more painful, although it would not be immediately felt. The algorithm is appealing as it constitutes a variant of the logic of *a priori* and is based on the implicit assumption that the decision resulted from the logical consequentiality of the algorithm is in itself justified, since it is devoid of any subjective interference; this, therefore, would provide a very clear directive that the professional is called to apply. However, this is a technical decision that produces a generalising automatism concerning the different, specific health conditions of patients, devaluing the clinical judgment and the correlated ethical and professional responsibility of the doctor. Moreover, the so-called technicality of the algorithm is not neutral – if it is justified to use the term "neutrality" when talking about human actions and choices. Indeed, the structure of the algorithm reflects the decision-making processes of those who built the algorithm itself; this kind of algorithm is tacitly based on several presupposed values which are not irrelevant in life-or-death circumstances. Proof of this can be found in the guidelines of the *National Institute for Health and Care Excellence* (NICE), which then lead to the preparation of an algorithm for access to intensive care:[36] once again, the ambiguous character of clinical guidelines emerges, in which, however, the reference

---

34 Observatori de Bioètica i Dret (Universitat de Barcelona), *Recomendaciones para la toma de decisiones éticas sobre el acceso de pacientes a unidades de cuidados especiales en situaciones de pandemia*, 27 March 2020, point B3, http://www.bioeticayderecho.ub.edu/sites/default/files/doc_recom-pandemia.pdf accessed 11 February 2021.

35 Olof Svensson, *Dokument visar: De prioriteras bort från intensivvård. Aftonbladet*, 9 April 2020, https://www.aftonbladet.se/nyheter/samhalle/a/lAyePy/dokument-visar-de-prioriteras-bort-fran-intensivvard accessed 11 February 2021.

36 National Institute for Health and Care Excellence (NICE), *COVID-19 Rapid Guideline: Critical Care in Adults*, 20 March 2020 (update 29 April 2020), https://www.nice.org.uk/guidance/ng159 accessed 11 February 2021; National Institute for Health and Care Excellence (NICE), *Critical Care Admission Algorithm*, 20 March 2020 (update 27 March 2020), https://www.nice.org.uk/guidance/ng159/resources/critical-care-admission-algorithm-pdf-8708948893 accessed 11 February 2021.

to extra-clinical criteria is preponderant. In fact, parameters as the age, over or under 65, and the presence or absence of persistent long-term disabilities (for example, cerebral palsy) and even learning disabilities and autism are considered; then, in all the cases the evaluation must take into account comorbidities and underlying health conditions. Two general categories of patients are therefore identified. Towards the first category, which includes adults over 65 years of age and without disabilities, doctors are invited to use the so-called Clinical Frailty Scale (CFS). This score will determine greater or lesser fragility of the patient, significantly influencing the admissibility or not to the intensive care unit, with different options that will be proposed to the doctor depending on the patient's condition (stable or worsening). The other category includes adults under 65 and patients of any age with disabilities, towards whom doctors are invited not to use the CFS, promoting instead an individualised assessment of frailty.

However, these decision-making mechanisms raise numerous issues due to their artificial, simplifying rigidity. Moreover, if they could trigger some discriminatory dynamics based on a careless language, they would become dangerous. Not surprisingly, after the protests of families and associations that take care of people with disabilities, the NICE was forced to review its guidelines (points 1.1, 2.2), providing a less rigid interpretation, enhancing the clinical assessment of each particular situation, without nevertheless renouncing the algorithm tool.

The *a priori* criterion is sometimes also extended to the suspension of treatment. The SIAARTI document implicitly presupposes this possibility, even if it shamefacedly avoids discussing the possible consequences; other documents, instead, explicitly thematise the possibility to use the *a priori* criterion in such situations, according to the questionable ethical equivalence between not starting and interrupting a treatment. Thus, the (alleged) guidelines issued by the British Medical Association (BMA)[37] explicitly stated that "Health professionals may be obliged to withdraw treatment from some patients to enable treatment of other patients with a higher survival probability. This may involve withdrawing treatment from an individual who is stable or even slowly improving but whose objective assessment indicates a significantly worse prognosis than that of another patient who requires the same resource".[38]

---

37 British Medical Association (BMA), *COVID-19 – ethical issues. A guidance note*, 1 April 2020, 1–10, here 3, https://www.bma.org.uk/media/2360/bma-covid-19-ethics-guidance-april-2020.pdf accessed 11 February 2021.

38 Even a utilitarian like John Harris, known for his very clear-cut and sometimes extreme positions, has strongly criticised the document drawn up by the British Medical Association and the National Institute for Health and Care Excellence, opportunely suggesting them to avoid any comparison of value between human lives; see John Harris, 'Why Kill the Cabin Boy?' (2019) 29 Cambridge Quarterly of Healthcare Ethics 1–6. Unlike the BMA, the Dutch corresponding association refuses the possibility of interrupting an ongoing treatment to admit a younger patient to an intensive care unit with no more available places; see Federatie Medisch Specialisten en de Koninklijke Nederlandsche Maatschappij tot bevordering der Geneeskunst (KNMG), *Draaiboek 'Triage op basis van niet-medische overwegingen*

This is a rather shocking statement, which goes far beyond the question concerning the first-come, first-served principle. In the BMA document, in order to favour a patient with a higher probability of survival, the doctor is forced to interrupt the treatment previously reserved for another patient, even if the individual is "stable or even slowly improving". This is an instrumental approach that bears serious abuses and denies any relationship between the doctor and the patient, inducing a certain automatism that would probably anaesthetise the doctor's sense of responsibility towards those who have already entrusted him/her.

Furthermore, the *Semicyuc*, the Spanish scientific society of medical intensivists, first considers the age criterion for patients over 80 years old or whose age is between 70 and 80, then suggests that "any patient with cognitive impairment, due to dementia or other degenerative diseases, would not be assisted by invasive mechanical ventilation";[39] again, this is a discriminatory statement, which has been criticised and stigmatised by the Comité de Bioética de España, as incompatible with the International Convention on the Rights of Persons with Disabilities, also signed by Spain.[40]

In the United States of America, there has been perhaps the most heated debate regarding the discriminatory nature of those measures that, in the event of an extreme emergency due to lack of resources, would have denied life-saving treatment to people with disabilities. Some associations have denounced the adoption of such measures by states such as Alabama and Washington State. Consequently, the Director of the Office for Civil Rights, Roger Severino, had to intervene with a very clear ruling, demanding that no state, even during the pandemic emergency, could discriminate patients on the basis of disability, age, race.[41]

---

voor IC-opname ten tijde van fase 3 in de COVID-19 pandemie', 16 June 2020 (update 2 September 2020), https://www.rijksoverheid.nl/documenten/publicaties/2020/06/16/draaiboek-triage-op-basis-van-niet-medische-overwegingen-voor-ic-opname-ten-tijde-van-fase-3-in-de-covid-19-pandemie accessed 11 February 2021.

39 Sociedad Española de Medicina Intensiva, Crítica y Unidades Coronarias (SEMICYUC), *Recomendaciones éticas para la toma de decisiones en la situación excepcional de crisis por pandemia COVID-19 en las unidades de cuidados intensivos*, 16 March 2020, 1–15, in particular 12, Recomendación específica no 4, https://semicyuc.org/wp-content/uploads/2020/03/%C3%89tica_SEMICYUC-COVID-19.pdf accessed 11 February 2021. The discrimination based on the cognitive level reveals the functionalist background of this approach, which defines personhood through a set of mental functions, properties or abilities. For a critical discussion, see Federico Zilio, 'Personhood and care in disorders of consciousness. An ontological, patient-centred perspective' (2020) 69 Medicina e Morale 327–346.

40 Comité de Bioética de España, *Informe del Comité de Bioética de España sobre los aspectos bioéticos de la priorización de recursos sanitarios en el contexto de la crisis del coronavirus*, 25 March 2020, 1–13, here point 9.7, http://assets.comitedebioetica.es/files/documentacion/Informe%20CBE-%20Priorizacion%20de%20recursos%20sanitarios-coronavirus%20CBE.pdf accessed 11 February 2021.

41 Office for Civil Rights (OCR) at the U.S Department of Health and Human Services (HHS), *BULLETIN: Civil Rights, HIPAA, and the Coronavirus Disease 2019 (COVID-19)*, 282020, https://www.hhs.gov/sites/default/files/ocr-bulletin-3-28-20.pdf accessed 11 February 2021.

6. CONCLUSION: PROFESSIONAL AUTONOMY WITHOUT THE *A PRIORI*

Even in times of emergency, the doctor should not stop being a doctor, but continue to orient his/her actions based on the clinical criteria that are part of his/her expertise and within which he/she forms his/her professional ethics. Undoubtedly, in circumstances characterised by urgency and a tragic scarcity of resources, the matter becomes even more complicated because the patient selection becomes inevitable; nevertheless, clinical judgment should not be abandoned for this reason, but it should be related to the circumstances of the case and integrated according to the priority imposed by the scarcity of resources. Integration, however, does not mean discarding some categories of patients according to a utilitarian and discriminatory logic and applying *a priori* rules or algorithms, which inevitably eliminates the specificity of each clinical case; rather, it is aimed at identifying patients for whom the treatment may be more effective according to clinical criteria, including urgency.

In this way, the category of effectiveness, which belongs to the dimension of profit, is combined with a principle of equity in the distribution of scarce resources, since the treatment is not precluded *sic et simpliciter* and in a utilitarian way, but is administered to those that concretely have more chance of success. It is clear that such an integration of the clinical criterion does not produce rigid solutions, nor can it provide any pre-established prescription. However, such an integrated clinical judgment, related to the circumstances of the case, is a more respectful criterion towards both the principle of equity and also the doctor's professionalism. Understandably, the *a priori* and algorithmic approach are attractive since they allow the cutting of the Gordian knot of the clinical dilemma with a clear and automatic decision; however, such a decision-making process raises perplexities for many reasons, including strictly clinical issues as well as ethical-professional ones, since the professional's conscience is relieved from all the moral questions and dilemmas, turning the doctor in a mere executor of extrinsic logics.[42]

Our examination, has aimed to summarise some basic problems of the relationship between the professional autonomy of the doctor and the criteria of expertise and ethics in the medical-scientific community, in the light of the experience of the pandemic. The abundant production, in Italy and abroad, of

---

42 The integrated clinical judgment, related to the circumstances, can never be exempt from ethical and professional responsibilities. Indeed, it is illusory to imagine that strictly clinical choices concerning aetiology, diagnosis, possible therapy, prognosis, are devoid of any ethical value as if they could be indifferent and neutral about life or death matters. In a context of severe lack of resources, those choices that imply priorities in accessing the resources cannot be morally indifferent, as these priorities establish the patients who can benefit most from medical treatment in terms of survival chances, on the basis of clinical indicators.

highly questionable documents, which are credited as clinical guidelines and then paradoxically assert extra-clinical evaluation criteria, has emphasised the need to question and discuss this event.

First of all, the dissemination of guidelines cannot deprive the doctor of the professional autonomy that takes place in the relationship with the individual patients and their particular situations. There is no doubt that autonomy is severely tested in the time of a pandemic when the health resources available are insufficient and the doctor is faced with real hard choices. But the solution to coping with such a difficult and demanding context does not consist of adopting shortcuts. In their apparently neutral technicality, these shortcuts, such as the *a priori* logic or the use of algorithms,[43] end up undermining the doctor's expertise and exempting his/her conscience from any responsibility. Indeed, even professional ethics must take into account the conscience of the individual doctor. Even admitting that the skill and conscience of the doctor are not purely individual values, as they take place in relation to the professional community, nevertheless, as Horace said, *sunt certi denique fines quos ultra citraque nequit consistere rectum* ("there are fixed limits beyond which and short of which right cannot find a resting place").

The example of the SIAARTI Recommendations shows how the dissemination of guidelines, without any conceptual reorganisation and discussion, can cause problems on various levels as also emerges from the inappropriate formulation in the premises: "The purpose of the recommendations are (*sic*) also: (A) to relieve clinicians from a part of the responsibility in the decisions making process, which can be emotionally burdensome, carried out in individual cases; (B) to make the allocation criteria for healthcare resources explicit in a condition of their own extraordinary scarcity." First, the recommendations denote an interference with the ethical-legal assessments made by the doctor, because confusion can lead him/her to have false representations on what is ethically, professionally or legally binding. As we pointed out, the SIAARTI document is neither a genuine guideline nor a source of genuine professional rules, which instead are referred to the professional code of doctors. Consequently, these recommendations cannot properly relieve clinicians of their responsibilities, which on a legal level are possibly attenuated only in relation to the compliance

43 Julian Savulescu, Marco Vergano, Lucia Craxì and Dominic Wilkinson, 'An ethical algorithm for rationing life-sustaining treatment during the COVID-19 pandemic' (2020) British Journal of Anaesthesia, 125, 25–258, support the algorithm and the utilitarian approach. However, although among these authors there is also one of the authors of the SIAARTI document (Marco Vergano), the article specifies that "age per se (without consideration of prognosis) would be ageist and arguably unlawful discrimination under the Equality Act 2010" (257). This raises at least perplexity, given the importance of age in the SIAARTI guidelines.

with genuine guidelines, provided also that the particular case does not require deviating from them. Rather, the document could even introduce some equivocal elements in the evaluation of the behaviour of doctors, who could be qualified as generally exempt from responsibility in a legal sense, within the extraordinary circumstances of the pandemic.

In fact, from the point of view of civil liability, the impossibility of ensuring all patients the assistance they needed certainly excludes liability both as contractual liability and tortious liability according to the recent Italian Law 24/2017. If the selection of patients due to the scarcity of resources is conducted on the basis of rational criteria such as the urgency or the greater efficacy of the treatment, then the exclusion of some patients for whom the treatment appears less urgent or predictably less effective is justified. These hypotheses do not properly represent a state of necessity (Tort of Necessity), because according to Article 2045 of the Italian Civil code this implies that the doctor "commits an act which causes injury (and that he) was compelled by the necessity of saving himself or others from a present danger of serious personal injury, and the danger was neither voluntarily caused by him nor otherwise avoidable".[44] Moreover, if the doctor was justified by a state of necessity, Article 2045 of the Italian Civil code provides that he/she would still have to pay an indemnity according to the fair judgment of the judge to those to whom he/she had caused damage. However, the doctor does not cause harm to any of the patients, he/she just fails/omits to administer treatment due to the scarcity of resources. The principle of patient selection adopted by each emergency department, in which triage is a good practice implemented and recognised for some time, implies that the doctor – usually the hospital – has the obligation (of skill) to follow a selection criterion that, in case of scarcity of resources, allows him/her to use those available by prioritising certain patients over others.[45] Therefore, even if the reference to the impossibility of fulfilling the obligation to treat is deemed insufficient, reference should be made to the excuse for the fulfilment of a duty, that is, the rationing of resources according to selection criteria based on medical reasons. The exclusion of civil liability implies, *a fortiori*, the exclusion of criminal liability where the provision for the

[44] The excuse of state of necessity is also provided in §904 of the BGB, but without any reference to the damage of a personal right. In fact, while §904 of the BGB states that a person acting out of necessity may damage another person's property and, in this case, will be obliged to pay an amount to the victim, it does not lay down any rule for cases where a personal right is infringed. The French Code Civil does not contain an article corresponding to Article 2045 of the Italian Civil Code or to §904 of the BGB.

[45] In the Italian legislation, the triage was foreseen by the Guidelines N. 1/1996 in the application of the decree of the President of the Republic of 27 March 1992, which states that in every emergency and acceptance unit this function must be provided as the first moment of reception and evaluation of patients related to the Emergency room. Regarding first aid, the guidelines refer to properly trained nurses, while it is clear that, regarding the anaesthesia unit, the task is referred to the doctors.

fulfilment of a duty or an obligation is specifically provided for (Article 51 of the Italian Criminal Code).[46] In this respect, during the most acute phase of the emergency and in conditions of extraordinary scarcity of resources, if criteria similar to those proposed by SIAARTI were used in certain hospitals, it should at least be admitted that the situation of special difficulty implied the application of Article 2236 of the Italian Civil Code. In fact, the Article 2236 provides that liability of professionals is limited to gross technical error and perhaps on this basis the liability of doctors who have adopted these criteria can be avoided or reduced. A similar conclusion should also apply with regard to criminal liability, although the recent law on medical liability has raised some doubts in doctrine and jurisprudence concerning the relevance of slight negligence.[47]

---

[46] See Roberto Pucella, 'Scelte tragiche e dilemmi giuridici ai tempi della pandemia' (2020) Nuova giur. civ. comm. (supplemento digitale) 29–30. According to Mirko Faccioli, 'Il ruolo dell'art 2236 c.c. nella responsabilità sanitaria per danni da Covid-19' (2020) http://www.rivistaresponsabilitamedica.it/ accessed 11 February 2021. Article 2236 of the Civil Code is applicable also in cases of emergency, because they can involve the solution of technical problems of special difficulty. Also Rocco Blaiotta, '*La colpa nella responsabilità medica*' in *Studi in onore di Mario Romano* (Jovene 2011) 775 ff highlighted the validity of the solution that makes Article 2236 of the Italian Civil Code applicable not only to situations that present a particular technical and scientific complexity, but also to cases, much more frequent, in which the doctor finds himself/herself operating in emergency situations that affect his/her cool and lucidity.

Regarding case law in the matter of emergency, see Italian Corte di Cassazione, 31 January 2008, no 13942 in *C.E.D. Italian Corte di Cassazione*, 2008, no 23925; Corte di Cassazione pen., 25 September 2007, no 44765 in *Banca dati Pluris*; Corte di Cassazione pen., 20 May 2009, no 31975 in *Banca dati Pluris*. Due regard should be given also to the judgment of Corte di Cassazione, S.U., 22 February 2018, no 8770 in *Riv. it. med. leg.*, 2018, 345 ff. For the doctrine, see Matteo Caputo, *Logiche e modi dell'esenzione da responsabilità penale per chi decide e opera in contesti di emergenza*, www.legislazionepenale.eu, 22 June 2020, 7 ff. accessed 11 February 2021.

In the UK case law "battle conditions" is the expression introduced by Mustill LJ in *Wilsher v Essex Area Health Authority* [1988] AC 1074 to describe conditions in which the medical emergency overloads the facilities, forces doctors to solve multiple problems at once and make decisions that are often improvised. See Rachael Mulheron, *Principles of Tort Law* (Cambridge 2020) 312. According to Lord Mustill in *Wilsher v Essex AHA*: "An emergency may overburden the available resources, and, if an individual is forced by circumstances to do too many things at once, the fact that he does one of them incorrectly should not lightly be taken as negligence". The particularity of the emergency situation is also underlined by Lord Donaldson, in In Re F [1990] 2 AC (HL) 17: "In an emergency, a doctor has little time to ponder the choices available. He must act in the best interests of his patient, as he sees them, but he can be more readily forgiven if he errs in his judgment of him". The judgment, in this case, concerned the duty to obtain consent to treatment in emergency situations. The case *Mulholland v Medway NHS Foundation Trust* [2015] EWCH 268 is cited by Craig Purshouse, Rob Heywood, José Miola, Emma Cave, Sarah Devaney, 'Should doctors tackling covid-19 be immune from negligence liability claims' in (2020) BMJ 370, in support of the futility of introducing specific immunities to protect doctors who are faced with the COVID-19 pandemic, as, according to the authors, the English law would already be equipped with suitable tools to take into account the particularity of emergency circumstances, as demonstrated by the case in question.

[47] See for the jurisprudence Cassazione Penale, Sezioni Unite, 22 February 2018 (ud. 21 December 2017) no 8770.

Furthermore, from this point of view, the document can be judged hasty and inappropriate; in fact, in some cases doctors may have found themselves in such a condition as to be induced to make certain tragic choices *hic et nunc*, perhaps excluding people for reasons of age and therefore applying questionable criteria. However, the adoption of these criteria could be excusable precisely because of the peculiar unforeseen conditions of extraordinary difficulties and also of stress that doctors have had to face *hic et nunc*. Instead, the document, suggesting such behaviours *a priori* and so intending to free from the responsibility, paradoxically risks achieving the opposite effect.[48]

Perhaps, rather than relieving doctors of their responsibility, the purpose of such a document should be to support them, offering indications that can accompany them in their choices and clinical deliberations, without thereby replacing their autonomy and responsibility. And, of course, the aim should also be to encourage the sharing of dilemmatic clinical choices, which are certainly "emotionally burdensome", especially on an ethical and professional level. Concerning this latter issue, the pandemic has undoubtedly raised the need for an update of the medical code of ethics about the decision-making processes in extraordinary health calamities, which can no longer be considered unpredictable. In this regard, even those who hastily drafted that document might find it useful to reflect on this matter, because the topic cannot be monopolised by a single category of doctors, although, the most exposed categories should be listened to by the general community of doctors.

Secondly, the SIAARTI document has also interfered with politics, because the *a priori* and extra-clinical criteria proposed, claiming to "make the allocation criteria for healthcare resources explicit", invades the field of the fundamental rights, presided over by the Constitution. In a democratic State, these issues are reserved to the competence of the representative bodies of the so-called "general will". The exclusion of a category of people – those over a certain age – from essential treatment cannot simply be the result of a decision by the authors of a document of a scientific association. Actually, the evident contrast between the proposed criterion – and its ideological foundation – and the fundamental principles of the Constitution suggests that even Parliament could not legitimately decide on this issue. However, no one can be satisfied with an *a priori* criterion because a democratic discussion and an open discussion on

---

48 In fact, contingencies normally reduce or exempt from liability when they are unpredictable or at least not foreseen. This also applies to the state of necessity: see Corte di Cassazione, 7 July 2016, no 13919 in *C.E.D. Corte di Cassazione*, 2016, no 640523. In the evaluation of the rationality of the selection criteria used by the doctor, it can also be assumed that the fact that the doctor induced himself/herself to follow the guideline of SIAARTI, believing it to be binding for him/her, does not count as a putative excuse, although the pseudo-guideline could be led to justify the special difficulty of the case, increased by the same confusion produced by such a document coming from an accredited scientific society.

what could be authorised in a very serious urgency and scarcity of resources cannot exclude a process of balancing between values that would be unthinkable in the normality.[49] Consider, for example, the possibility of giving precedence to medical patients because of the need not to lose professionals in dealing with a serious health crisis. Thus, even a preference in favour of people much younger than others could find a justification in a sort of "fair innings argument" of the emergency,[50] that is, the idea of preferentially granting a chance of survival to those who have still lived very little compared to what it would be a normal life and compared to someone who has already had a long and full experience of this world. But these are just some – very problematic – examples, and this is not the place to discuss them specifically. An open and in-depth discussion is needed so that it can balance the different perspectives and avoid that any priority rules can ever justify serious organisational deficiencies, as probably happened during this pandemic and could still happen if the preparation of an appropriate organisation for potential new calamities were discouraged.

Against such a background and without underestimating the importance of the general organisation, the preservation of the responsible autonomy of the individual doctor is paramount. So, it is appropriate to reverse the perspective, to avoid the risk that the emergency becomes the pretext for the establishment of a sort of "state of exception" (*Ausnahmezustand*) in health care, thus limiting autonomy and professional responsibility; the more the doctor is trained to exercise his/her professional autonomy in times of relative normality, using effective clinical guidelines but always acting through a meditated and conscious medical deliberation, the more he/she will be able to pursue this decision-making method in times of extraordinary emergency and in the presence of harrowing moral dilemmas. Likewise, the more the scientific associations have been able to offer their contribution in the advancement of medical expertise and in the updating of ethical-professional rules during ordinary times (e.g. through documents that account for the various interdisciplinary dimensions involved, but also acknowledging the limits of their competence), the more their voice will be influential and reliable, even during emergencies.

---

49 The balance between values does not mean that the framework of reference values changes, but only that the extraordinary nature of the circumstances can highlight particular needs. On a legal level, what was previously stated on the level of ethical-normative analysis applies: it is not necessary to appeal to the state of exception (*Ausnahmezustand*) and to assert exceptional principles, which would not find otherwise any justification in the ordinary condition. On the contrary, the ethical and constitutional principles remain the same, even if the extraordinary nature of the situation requires that they are applied – and balanced – in order to deal, as much as possible, with dramatic and tragic situations.

50 The "fair innings argument" is hotly debated. For a first overview, see Daniel Callahan, *Setting limits, Medical Goals in an Aging Society* (Simon and Schuster 1987); about the COVID-19 emergency, see Stefano Semplici, 'Se non ci sono ventilatori per tutti. Covid-19 e il criterio dell'età' (2020) Dialegesthai. Rivista di Filosofia https://mondodomani.org/dialegesthai/articoli/stefano-semplici-03 accessed 11 February 2021.

MOBILITY AT THE TIME OF THE CORONAVIRUS AND DAMAGE CAUSED BY VEHICLES EQUIPPED WITH ELECTRONIC SAFETY SYSTEMS

Antonio ALBANESE*

The introduction of technologies that make vehicles safer is important to address the foreseeable criticalities of road traffic due to the current needs of safe mobility and to the lower capacity of public transport as a result of social distancing measures. In this unique situation, the objective of limiting the spread of the epidemic cannot overshadow the prevention of accidents and human health must be guaranteed with respect to all possible risks. However, new safety systems are not completely failsafe. With this in mind, this contribution proposes to verify the extent to which current rules on civil liability in Italian law may offer solutions to damages caused by highly automated vehicles in terms of preventing harmful events and allocating their costs according to criteria of justice and economic efficiency. Within this logic, the analysis also looks at the rules on the distribution of compensation costs among the various parties that may be jointly and severally liable (driver, owner, custodian and manufacturer).

* Catholic University of Milan.

1. TECHNOLOGICAL INNOVATION AS A RESPONSE TO NEW NEEDS OF ROAD TRAFFIC AND THE ISSUE OF DAMAGE CAUSED BY ACCIDENTS

To permit a full return to production activities and the exercise of personal freedoms when there is still the threat of a fresh COVID-19 outbreak, safe movement of persons must be guaranteed.[1]

Unfortunately, social distancing requirements, along with fear of close physical contact, curtail public transport's capacity to meet growing consumer demand, leading to a rise in the use of privately-owned vehicles and to a switch from mass transit and carpool to single occupancy cars.[2]

The increasing traffic congestion and promotion of sustainable mobility means of transport (e.g. bicycles)[3] are only some of the factors that make it even more important to address the prevention of traffic accidents in this situation.[4]

For this purpose, though the full introduction of self-driving cars could appear currently unrealistic, the development of Advanced Driver Assistance Systems (ADAS) could offer significant short-term benefits in reducing car accidents,[5] especially where they were affordable and installable in existing vehicles.

The growing awareness of the importance of health as both a "fundamental right of the person and public interest" (Art 32 of the Italian Constitution) demands their coherent protection in a way capable of avoiding all of the potential risks of harm.

1 Julien Bert, Daniel Schellong, Markus Hagenmaier, David Hornstein, Augustin K. Wegscheider, Thomas Palme, 'How Covid-19 will shape Urban Mobility' in https://eur03.safelinks.protection.outlook.com/?url=https%3A%2F%2Fimage-src.bcg.com%2FImages%2FBCG-How-COVID-19-Will-Shape-Urban-Mobility-Jun-2020_tcm9-251727.pdf&data=02%7C01%7Cantonio.albanese%40unicatt.it%7C23fb72b5ffa44d6ef96c08d84cbdf28f%7Cb94f7d7481ff44a9b5886682acc85779%7C0%7C0%7C637343726710577024&sdata=c3RCwa8vGvo4xTmyioe7V%2FTEKqRl9WuM%2Fofz6qtSx2U%3D&reserved=0 accessed 1 July 2020.

2 In this sense the analysis of Yue Hu, Will Barbour, Samitha Samaranayake, Dan Work, 'Impacts of Covid mode shift on road traffic' in https://covid19.tabipacademy.com/2020/06/29/impacts-of-covid-19-mode-shift-on-road-traffic/ accessed 1 July 2020, shows that cities with large transit ridership are at risk for extreme traffic, unless transport systems, through new investments, can resume safe during COVID-19 conditions.

3 According to a definition of *sustainable mobility*, it is a system that will come with reasonable costs, that will operate efficiently and that will offer all populations a choice between different transport alternatives.

4 Regarding the relevance of this objective in the EU policies https://ec.europa.eu/transport/road_safety/road-safety-measures-covid-transitional-era-common-high-level-group-principles-we-exit-crisis_en accessed 1 July 2020.

5 The benefits of highly automated vehicles in making road traffic safer are analysed by Kiliaan Van Wees, Karel Brookhuis, 'Product Liability for ADAS: legal and human factors perspectives' (2005) EJTIR 357 ff.

Once more, scientific research plays a key role, in addition to fighting against the Coronavirus, in dealing with the next expected critical traffic scenario, by the design and implementation of new technologies that not only offer increased transport safety, but also promote a more efficient use of the road network.[6]

To restart economic activities, preventing at the same time the spread of the epidemic, it would help if cities, prepared to welcome autonomous vehicles and new technologies, are developed to achieve an integrated mobility system.[7]

Thus, for example, the introduction of point to point, anywhere to anywhere or last-mile automated shuttle services may be beneficial, as a more frequent service may be offered to accommodate the reduced passenger capacity of vehicles due to social distancing, without the growth in operational costs associated with the increase of human resources to be employed. Furthermore, the experience during the lockdown due to COVID-19 has taught us that in the future automated goods transport and delivery systems may have a great use to contain new infections.[8]

The needs of the present time may well be the decisive factor that forces innovation in both public and private sector transportation, by designing a safer system for the transport of people and things, in which the introduction of increasingly automated and technologically advanced vehicles plays a key role.[9]

It will require heavy investments, producing long-term social benefits that can be felt long after the pandemic is over.

Although the deployment of these technologies, which are already partially available, increases transport safety, they still cannot completely exclude the risk of harm to passengers or third parties.

---

6 On the COVID-19 epidemic as a driving force for technological innovations in the transport sector see the paper 'Automated vehicles and COVID-19 – what we can learn from it' in https://levitate-project.eu/2020/05/14/automated-vehicles-and-covid-19-what-we-can-learn-from-it/ accessed 1 July 2020, see Jack R. Nerad, 'Pandemic Will Move Autonomous Vehicle Development Forward, J.D. Power Says' in https://www.forbes.com/sites/jacknerad2/2020/08/14/pandemic-will-move-autonomous-vehicle-development-forward-jd-power-says/#4b43fea928c0 accessed 1 July 2020.

7 These considerations in James Hodgson, 'How to make cities ready for autonomous vehicles, and AVs ready for cities' in https://www.automotiveworld.com/articles/how-to-make-cities-ready-for-autonomous-vehicles-and-avs-ready-for-cities/ accessed 1 July 2020.

8 In this sense Jack R. Nerad, 'Pandemic Will Move Autonomous Vehicle Development Forward, J.D. Power Says' in https://www.forbes.com/sites/jacknerad2/2020/08/14/pandemic-will-move-autonomous-vehicle-development-forward-jd-power-says/#4b43fea928c0 accessed 1 July 2020.

9 See similar considerations in 'COVID-19's Impact on Traffic Congestion in Australia and Potential Implications for the Deployment of Autonomous Vehicles' in https://www.squirepattonboggs.com/-/media/files/insights/publications/2020/04/covid19-the-impact-on-traffic-congestion-in-australia-and-potential-implications-for-the-deployment-of-autonomous-vehicles/covid19-impact-on-traffic-congestion-in-australia.pdf accessed 1 July 2020.

To facilitate the social acceptance of these innovations, it is therefore important to check if the current legal framework, through an evolutive interpretation, may offer an adequate solution in civil liability claims in order to prevent harmful events and to allocate compensation costs pursuant to principles of justice and economic efficiency.

This includes also verifying, even by comparison with other jurisdictions, whether the Italian law system achieves both of these objectives or whether it is "preferable" that the legislator intervenes in this sector.[10]

Indeed, a regulatory adaptation is not a "logical necessity," given that in the matter of civil liability a law gap in a proper sense[11] cannot occur, because if an offence does not fall within a legal provision there will not be a liable party and the damage will remain the "responsibility" of the injured party.

From this perspective, it is therefore a question of verifying whether the current legislation on civil liability effectively guarantees the fundamental right to health against the risks of road traffic, by rules which promote, even from an economic point of view, the use of more automated and safer vehicles, charging the costs of damages caused by them on subjects who can avoid the occurrence of such harmful events.

This question will be examined following the order in which the parties may be held (jointly and severally) liable: the driver, the owner/custodian and the manufacturer of the vehicle or defective safety system.

1.1. DRIVER LIABILITY

Article 2054, paragraphs 1 and 2 Italian Civil Code (c.c.) provides for "aggravated" and "presumed" fault liability of the driver of a vehicle that is not running on rails for harm to persons or things caused by its circulation.[12] Unlike the general rule in Article 2043 c.c., it is not for the injured party to prove the wrongdoer's fault but for the driver to show he/she "did everything possible to avoid the harm".

---

10 This is the proposal of the European Parliament in its Resolution of 17 February 2017. In favour of legislative intervention see also Tatjana Evas, 'A common EU approach to liability rules and insurance for connected and autonomous vehicles. European Added Value Assessment' 2018.

11 According to Ernst Zitelmann, *Lücken im Recht* (Leipzig 1903) 27 f., there is a lack of discipline in an improper sense where the rule is not completely missing, but the case is governed by a general norm, which is inadequate with respect to the specificities of the new situation, especially considering the choices made by the legal system in other similar cases. In this regard Claus-Wilhelm Canaris, *Die Feststellung von Lückenim Gesetz* (Berlin 1964) 132 ff. uses the expression "axiological gaps" (*Wertlücken*).

12 Cass. civ. (VI) no 9646 of 13 April 2017, https://dejure.it/ (according to which the driver has the burden of proving that he/she exercised the utmost diligence, such to exclude any fault).

Although this provision does not apply to self-driving vehicles,[13] it may nevertheless be applied without any particular difficulty to cases where the driver is using advanced safety systems or the vehicle circulates autonomously but the driver can take back control of it at any time.

Moreover, the driver may also be held jointly and severally liable with the manufacturer for any damage caused by a malfunctioning of the vehicle. Indeed, to avoid liability, it is not enough to show that his/her conduct did not directly contribute to causing the injurious event or that the defective operation of the car prevented him/her from complying with the standard of due care.[14] The driver must show he/she "did everything possible" to avoid the harm which nevertheless arose.

So, this limit on liability, based on a predefined standard that considers only human conduct that is actually possible, excludes the application in Italian legislative framework of the variable criterion applied in German law pursuant to which the standard of care to which the driver is held is inversely proportional to the degree of autonomy of the vehicle.[15]

Indeed, before establishing whether the harmful event can be attributed (or not) to the driver, the reverse onus and higher evidential burden of proof are justified as they involve a risk that falls within his/her control. Consequently, it would be neither just nor efficient to require the injured party to show the harm was attributable to human error and/or a defect in the vehicle.

Differently, in the event of a collision between vehicles, to rebut the presumption of joint liability Article 2054, paragraph 2 c.c. provides that the driver must prove that he/she has not contributed to the accident.[16] If he/she shows that the accident is attributable to the malfunctioning of one or both of the vehicles involved in the collision, then he/she will not be liable for having driven the vehicle.

In any case, the insurance required by law for the circulation of the vehicle, strengthens the protection of the injured party, without denying prevention

---

13 Antonio Albanese, 'La responsabilità civile per i danni da circolazione di veicoli ad elevata automazione' (2019) Eur. dir. priv., 1000.

14 This possibility is instead admitted in legal frameworks where a corresponding Article 2054, paragraph 1, Italian Civil Code, provision is absent and, as such, the general rule on liability for negligence applies: see, e.g. Jan De Bruyne, Jochen Tanghe, 'Liability for Damage Caused by Autonomous Vehicles: A Belgian Perspective' (2017) JETL 336.

15 Julian Pehm, *Haftung für den Betrieb autonomer Fahrzeuge. Eine Komparative Sichtauf die Herausfor der ungender Automatisierung*, XXVI (Tagungsband, Karlsbader Juristentage 2018) 128. See Ernst Karner, *Liability for Robotics: Current Rules, Challenges and the Need for Innovative Concepts* in Sebastian Lohsse, Reiner Schulze, Dirk Staudenmayereds (eds), *Liability for Artificial Intelligence and the Internet of Things* (Nomos/Hart 2019) 118 (regarding to the provisions introduced in 2017 by the German reform of the *Straßenverkehrsgesetz*, that obliges the user of a potentially self-driving vehicle to retain the attention necessary to regain control at any time).

16 Recently, see Cass. civ. (VI) no 7061 of 12 March 2020, https://dejure.it/.

purposes of the driver's civil liability, given that contractual clauses result in an increase of the insurance premium in the event of accidents attributable to the insured's fault.

1.2. MANUFACTURER LIABILITY

Unlike accidents caused by traditional vehicles, where the key factor remains human error, the anticipated increase in circulation of highly automated vehicles will make the manufacturer's liability even more relevant. A greater number of on-board technologies will increase proportionally the likelihood of damage being caused by car malfunctions.

Italian law and the applicable laws in other European countries introduced by EEC Directive 374 of 1985[17] allow the vehicle to be treated as a defective product when it fails to offer the safety the public is entitled to expect.

It follows that where a malfunctioning caused an injurious event, the manufacturer will be held liable in respect of all injured parties, including road users other than the driver and passengers. This is effectively liability in tort that arises irrespective of a breach of a pre-existing obligation towards a given party.

A delimitation of the subjective spheres of damage will not arise where there is a requirement to show actual foreseeability. Indeed, Article 1225 c.c., which limits damages to what could have been foreseen when the obligation arose, does not apply, whereas the fault element, understood as the possibility to foresee and avoid the injurious event, is not required since this is a strict liability, which arises independently of any assessment of the manufacturer's conduct. The manufacturer is liable for the defect and any damage that flowed from it.[18]

Again, in terms of tortious liability, the failure to conform to a legitimate expectation of safety renders the product defective regardless of the trust between two identifiable parties. Instead, it must be assessed on a more general and abstract criterion of social expectation that appropriately considers all those who could suffer harm.

Thus vehicles, designed and socially appreciated because they provide greater safety on the road than their human driver counterparts, can be qualified as

---

17 Council Directive 85/374/EEC of 25 July 1985 on the approximation of the laws, regulations and administrative provisions of the Member States concerning liability for defective products.

18 Sometimes the foreseeability and avoidability of the damage are implicitly (and improperly) transferred from the case law to the concept of defectiveness. See Eleonora Rajneri, 'Prodotto difettoso' Dig. disc. priv. (sez. civ.), Agg. 2016 (UTET 2016), 614–615 (citing the jurisprudence which provides that liability for the defective product would not be objective since the fault of the manufacturer can be deduced from the defect). See further Trib. La Spezia no 3 of 4 January 2019, https://dejure.it/.

defective where the accident would not have occurred had it not been for the intervention of the driver-assisted system. In fact, the product would not comply with the legitimate social expectations of safety conceived before ever the product came onto the market, irrespective of any comparison across products of the same type.[19]

Likewise, the vehicle should be seen to be defective where the safety offered is greater than that offered by traditional vehicles but less than that which is socially expected,[20] as assessed by the judge with the assistance of experts and thus without the need for him/her to possess any particular technical expertise.

Therefore, while it is not enough for the vehicle to be built in conformity with applicable homologation standards,[21] it is equally unnecessary to exclude any risk of an accident. Rather, it is important to ensure a level of safety commensurate with a reasonable expectation.[22]

This way, the drawbacks of a strict liability framework, where the manufacturer bears the cost of any accident, may be avoided as it may delay the sale and marketing of its vehicles despite being safer than traditional ones.[23]

At the same time, it achieves an adequate balance, even at a procedural level, between the opposing interests of the parties involved. The injured party may satisfy the burden of proof without having to prove the malfunctioning of the specific technical features or the reasonable possibility that an alternative design would not have caused the accident. Likewise, any opportunistic conduct on the part of the manufacturer may be more easily prevented, such as an attempt to take advantage of the technological complexities of the vehicle to deny the admission of any defects.[24]

Furthermore, if the liability of the manufacturer is assessed by reference to an objective and verifiable standard of safety, it may operate as an incentive to

---

19 Jan De Bruyne, Jochen Tanghe, 'Liability for Damage Caused by Autonomous Vehicles: A Belgian Perspective' (2017) JETL 336, 360. See also Kyle Graham, 'Of frightened horses and autonomous vehicles: tort law and its assimilation of innovations' (2012) Santa Clara L. Rev. 1241, 1256 (holding instead that the social assessment of the safety of highly automated vehicles assumes widespread public awareness of them).

20 On the progressive levels of such judgment see Maurice Schellekens, 'Self-driving cars and the chilling effect of liability law' (2015) CLSR 510.

21 Cass. civ. (III) no 3692 of 15 February 2018, Resp. civ. prev., 2019 with commentary by Roberta Montinaro, *Difetto del prodotto, norme tecniche ed informazione sui rischi di danno alla salute*, 277 ff.

22 See David G. Owen, *Products Liability*[2] (West Academic Publishing 2008) 1134 ff (referencing to traditional vehicles).

23 See Maurice Schellekens, 'Self-driving cars and the chilling effect of liability law' (2015) CLSR 506–517 (assessing negative consequences of an overly rigid system of liability).

24 Therefore, the concern for a weakening in the protection afforded to injured parties manifested by Tatjana Evas, 'A common EU approach to liability rules and insurance for connected and autonomous vehicles. European Added Value Assessment' 2018, 22–23 is not shared nor does it appear necessary to introduce a specific concept of defective product that applies to self-driving vehicles.

design safer products especially if the relative cost results in less than that of foreseeable damages.

This economic assessment, however, is at the discretion of the manufacturer and does not translate into a strict rule that requires him to bear the costs of compensation only in cases where its amount exceeds the costs of investment to prevent or reduce damages. In fact, the definition of "defective product" in Article 117 Italian Consumer Code (cons. c.) would be incompatible with the introduction into Italian law (and in the Member States of the European Union) of a risky/utility test,[25] similar to the one introduced in the United States on the basis of the *Restatement (Third) on Product Liability* of 1997.

This legislation ties the appraisal of a design defect to the existence of a *reasonable alternative*, which allows assessing any decision on liability by comparison with the total costs and benefits deriving from the use of the product when compared to alternative products. This may lead to a decision that the product is safe based on a general overriding interest that prevails over the interests of the individual injured party.[26]

Conversely, the legitimate expectation of safety provided for in Article 117 cons. c. is not satisfied on the basis of a purely economic calculation that seeks to balance the collective benefits of using a particular product, including its greater safety generally, against the damages that individual parties may nonetheless suffer due to a defect that occurs in its practical use.[27]

Indeed, it is no defence to argue that a product is not defective solely on the grounds it is *ex ante* statistically safer at a collective level generally, just as the burden of the cost of damages it caused cannot fall on the injured party.

This position highlights an apparent paradox noted by those seeking to argue that the (alleged) greater safety of these new vehicles leads inexplicably to an increased manufacturer's liability since an accident is more attributable to a defect in the vehicle's functioning than to human error.[28]

It is precisely for this reason that an exclusion of the manufacturer's liability would run contrary to the principle of justice when the public utility of the product must be balanced against the collective costs associated with any damages arising from it.[29]

---

25 See Jan De Bruyne, Jochen Tanghe, 'Liability for Damage Caused by Autonomous Vehicles: A Belgian Perspective' (2017) JETL 336, 369 (reviewing the European Union framework).

26 See Eleonora Rajneri, 'Prodotto difettoso' Dig. disc. priv. (sez. civ.), Agg. 2016 (UTET 2016), 617 (noting that putting the interests of the community and those of the parties involved on the same level may at times lead to results that clash with public feeling).

27 See Aaron Twerski, James A. Henderson, 'Manufacturer's Liability for defective Product Designs: The Triumph of Risk-Utility' (2009) Brook. L. Rev. 1061 (assessing the differences between the two factors).

28 Gary E. Marchant, Rachel A. Lindor, 'The Coming Collision between Autonomous Vehicles and the Liability System' (2012) Santa Clara L. Rev. 1339.

29 Antonio Albanese, 'La responsabilità civile per i danni da circolazione di veicoli ad elevata automazione' (2019), Eur dir. priv. 1000, 1022.

This way, in fact, the damages (or the insurance premium[30]) the manufacturer has to pay can be covered by the running costs of the business, reflected in the price of the product and spread across all purchasers.[31] Furthermore, the competitive mechanisms of the market will reward those businesses that make more efficient decisions to reduce the costs required to prevent or compensate for any damages.[32]

In conclusion, the objective grounds of liability for any safety defect on the basis of legitimate expectation will certainly not discourage research and development into new technologies. Conversely, it will act as an incentive to produce even safer vehicles.

In particular, manufacturers in a position to sustain lower marginal costs to introduce new technological solutions will be encouraged to make greater investments to ensure safer vehicles.[33] This may assuage those concerned about the risks[34] of extending the manufacturer's liability since it would reduce the speed at which technologies will be introduced despite being, in principle, capable of ensuring greater transport safety.

The need for flexibility in interpreting current laws to ensure their application to new technologies does not mean that legislative intervention would be unwelcome. Uniform rules across the EU Member States would reduce the uncertainties surrounding the determination of liability in respect of highly automated vehicles. Furthermore, a re-definition and widening of the concept of product to include any services necessary for its use would allow technological development risks to be attributed to and managed by the manufacturer (e.g. network failure, hacking and cybercrime, etc.). This would improve the overall efficiency in the industry in terms of dispute resolution costs and make consumer protection more effective, thereby reflecting the objectives of European policy on defective products.[35]

---

30 However Maurice Schellekens, 'No-fault compensation schemes for self-driving vehicles' (2018) Law, Innovation and Technology 328, notes that car manufacturers, who can insure against liability for damage caused by vehicle defects, are limited and this prevents the insurer from spreading the risk on them efficiently.

31 Ronald H. Coase, 'The Problem of Social Cost' (1960) J.L. & Econ. 44 and Guido Calabresi, *The Cost of Accidents: A Legal and Economic Analysis* (Yale University Press 1970). Such distributive effect is also recognised by Gary E. Marchant, Rachel A. Lindor, 'The Coming Collision between Autonomous Vehicles and the Liability System' (2012) Santa Clara L. Rev., 1336.

32 With specific regard to the cost of damages Maurice Schellekens, 'No-fault compensation schemes for self-driving vehicles' (2018) *Law, Innovation and Technology* 329 shows that "if the compensation paid out by a manufacturer producing unsafe vehicles (casu quo his insurance premium) is substantial, this may force the manufacturer to increase the price of its vehicles, thereby making them less attractive to acquire". On the general issue see Pietro Trimarchi, *Rischio e responsabilità oggettiva* (Giuffrè 1961) 9–10.

33 Hans-Bernd Schäefer, Frank Mueller-Langer, 'Strict liability versus negligence' (2008) German Working Papers in Law and Economics issue 1.

34 Maurice Schellekens, 'Self-driving cars and the chilling effect of liability law' (2015) CLSR 511 ff.

35 On the objectives of a possible review of the matter by the EU Tatjana Evas, 'A common EU approach to liability rules and insurance for connected and autonomous vehicles. European Added Value Assessment' 2018, 5 ff. and 25 ff.

1.3. OWNER AND CUSTODIAN LIABILITY

For damages caused by autonomous or ADAS equipped vehicles, the owner, the usufructuary or purchaser with reservation of ownership are jointly and severally liable "with the driver" if they cannot show that the vehicle was being operated without their consent (Art 2054, paragraph 3 c.c.).

Assuming liability may already be attributed to the driver, and in order to guarantee compensation, the law is upheld in favour of the injured party by permitting him/her to claim damages from two distinct parties, who are jointly and severally liable albeit on separate legal grounds.[36] It follows that the owner who has paid out in damages has an action under a right of recourse against the driver for the entire amount.[37]

The owner (or alternatively the other subjects mentioned above, responsible for him/her) is also liable for damages arising from any defect in construction or vehicle maintenance irrespectively of the driver's concurrent liability pursuant to Article 2054, last paragraph c.c.

It is for the injured party to prove that there is a defect. The fact that neither it is attributable to negligence on the part of the owner is irrelevant as he/she may only exclude his/her liability by proving the damage arose from another cause.[38] It is indeed a strict liability test that does not consider the subjective conduct of the owner.[39]

Furthermore, some legal doctrine claims this provision, in respect of damages caused by a defect in construction only, was repealed by the manufacturer liability provided for in the Presidential Decree no 224 of 1988 (PC 244/1988). According to this view, the law amends the original approach taken by Article 2054 c.c., which assigned risk to the parties referred to therein although it was clearly outside their control since it was attributable to the manufacturer and not the circulation of the vehicle.[40]

This provision on manufacturer liability actually gives the rule of the civil code a new rationale.

If the strict liability of the sole owner in respect of defects in (the) building of the vehicle was previously a paradoxical outcome, now it is justified because it runs concurrently with the liability of the manufacturer.[41] This position is designed to cover definitively the cost of damages between parties jointly and

---

36 See Cesare Salvi, *Responsabilità extracontrattuale*, Enc. dir. (Giuffrè 1988) 1248. In jurisprudence, see Cass. civ. (III) no 10629 of 26 October 1998, https://dejure.it/.

37 Adriano De Cupis, *Il danno*³, II (Giuffrè 1979) 176 ff. (providing for vicarious liability).

38 Cass. civ. (III) no 1019 of 19 February 1981, https://dejure.it/.

39 Cass. civ. (III) no 4754 of 9 March 2004, https://dejure.it/.

40 Carlo Castronovo, *Responsabilità civile* (Giuffrè 2018) 759.

41 Cass. civ. (III) no 15179 of 6 August 2004.

severally liable to pay damages and who are entitled to seek recourse in respect of their costs.[42]

Before PD 224/1988 a solution of this kind was impracticable despite the case law[43] and legal doctrine[44] that recognised a concurrent liability on the manufacturer. In fact, they treated it in accordance with the general rule set out in Article 2043 c.c., with the following effect: defendants only paid out when fault was actually proven and so the owner's right of recourse was effectively nullified.[45]

The new legal framework has then strengthened the injured party's position in terms of his/her right to damages. His/her interest prevails over that of the party who, putting the defective vehicle in circulation, has to bear the risk that the damage will not, in fact, be paid out by the manufacturer.

Moreover, if there is any doubt regarding the cause of the damage, whether it is due to a human driver, a lack of maintenance or a defect in the construction, Article 2054 c.c. simplifies the procedural options available to the injured party by permitting him/her to rely on a claim against the owner[46] and his/her insurer and the onus is on the latter party to decide whether or not to bring a claim (and on what grounds) against the driver or the manufacturer.

Far from anachronistic, this approach ensures the liability of the owner continues to play a key role in the allocation of (primary and secondary) damages costs.[47]

Furthermore, on the presupposition that the damage was caused by an autonomous operation of the vehicle, there is another potential claim for damages for things that are in a person's possession pursuant to Article 2051 c.c.

In fact, this law applies when the damage arises from the innate dynamic of the thing or from some harmful agent that derives from it, and not when it simply constitutes the means to carry out an act which is itself capable of

---

42 See Antonio Albanese, 'La responsabilità civile per i danni da circolazione di veicoli ad elevata automazione' (2019) Eur dir. priv. 1042 (admitting the owner's right of recourse against the manufacturer for the entire sum of compensation) and Antonio Davola, Roberto Pardolesi, 'In viaggio col robot: verso nuovi orizzonti della r.c. auto ("driverless")?' (2017) Dann. e resp. 623 (denying any regression, thereby attributing to the owner the role of "scapegoat" in the event of a malfunctioning of the system, over which he/she has no control).

43 Cass. civ. (III) no 577 of 2 March 1973, https://dejure.it/.

44 Gianguido Scalfi, 'Responsabilità per vizi e difetti dell'autoveicolo' (1974) Resp. civ. prev. 326.

45 Carlo Castronovo, 'La legge europea sul danno da prodotti una interpretazione alternativa del D.P.R. 224/1988' (1990) Dir. comm. internaz. 13 ff.

46 With reference to Austrian and German law Ernst Karner, 'Liability for Robotics: Current Rules, Challenges and the Need for Innovative Concepts' in Sebastian Lohsse, Reiner Schulze, Dirk Staudenmayereds (eds), *Liability for Artificial Intelligence and the Internet of Things* (Nomos/Hart 2019) 121, (evidencing the issues relating to application, posed by the different frameworks in English law).

47 It is no coincidence that the German framework on damages caused by road traffic has kept the rules on owner liability unchanged. The English legislator is analogously oriented towards an introduction of the same in the project *Vehicle Technology and Aviation Bill 2016–2017*.

producing the harm.[48] In this sense, the literal interpretation of Article 2051 c.c. expressly refers to damage caused "by" the thing, as when a vehicle is the direct cause of the damage and not the instrument of human conduct.

This provision renders futile the attempts, made in other jurisdictions, to create a case of vicarious liability on the basis of a questionable anthropomorphic view that equates the autonomous operation of the vehicle to the human conduct of an auxiliary.[49]

After all, in contrast with other legal systems,[50] Article 2051 c.c. provides the injured party does not have to prove the thing is defective[51] or dangerous.[52] Instead, the custodian must show that it is defective if he/she intends to file a claim for recourse against the manufacturer.

The law thus strengthens the position of the injured party both substantially, by widening the pool of liable parties, and procedurally, by attributing the risks and costs of ascertaining some causes of the injurious event to the custodian.[53]

The requisite for liability is not the absence of any human conduct in the injurious event but the marginal role attributed to such conduct in respect of other causal factors that are directly attributable to the thing.[54]

Article 2051 c.c. may even apply to damages which arise while using the vehicle and which are causally attributable to an anomaly in its operation that has a greater incidence on causation than the human conduct.

Even though courts have held that requisite for custodian liability pursuant to Article 2051 c.c. is mere *de facto* power over the thing and not a legal title,[55]

---

48 Among the many see Cass. civ. (III) no 12300 of 28 November 1995, https://dejure.it/.

49 Ernst Karner, 'Liability for Robotics: Current Rules, Challenges and the Need for Innovative Concepts' in Sebastian Lohsse, Reiner Schulze, Dirk Staudenmayereds (eds), *Liability for Artificial Intelligence and the Internet of Things* (Nomos/Hart 2019) 120 (according to whom no one can avoid the rule on vicarious liability by utilising technical instruments in place of assistants).

50 See for example in relation to Belgium Jan De Bruyne, Jochen Tanghe, 'Liability for Damage Caused by Autonomous Vehicles: A Belgian Perspective' (2017) JETL, 336, 348–349.

51 A literal interpretation of the law, confirmed by legal comparison, does not permit the liability of the custodian to be linked in some way to profiles of non-conformity of the thing to applicable standards that are legally or socially required, as claimed by Angelo Belfiore, 'Responsabilità (Struttura del giudizio e prestazione risarcitoria)' in Antonio Albanese, Andrea Nicolussi (eds), *Le parole del diritto. Scritti in onore di Carlo Castronovo*, III (Jovene Editore 2018) 1580 fn 82.

52 Gaston Fernández Cruz, Leysser León Hilario, 'La reedificación conceptual de la responsabilidad extracontractual objetiva' (2005) Derecho PUCP 24 ff. (revealing the conceptual error inherent in considering an object "dangerous" or "risky", underlining the ambiguity in the terminology used in Art 1970 Peruvian civil code).

53 The lack of a corresponding framework in other legal systems constitutes instead a vacuum in protection: cf. Ernst Karner, 'Liability for Robotics: Current Rules, Challenges and the Need for Innovative Concepts' in Sebastian Lohsse, Reiner Schulze, Dirk Staudenmayereds (eds), *Liability for Artificial Intelligence and the Internet of Things* (Nomos/Hart 2019) 121.

54 Cesare Salvi, *Responsabilità extracontrattuale*, Enc. dir. (Giuffrè 1988), 1228.

55 Cass. civ (III) no 2284 of 2 February 2006, https://dejure.it/.

this entity cannot reasonably be seen to have the mere use and enjoyment of the thing without also the possibility of interfering in its purpose, maintenance and preservation.[56]

The party with physical possession of the vehicle is liable, irrespective of whether he/she holds the proprietary right or not, based on the fact that he/she is in a position to grant its use to other entities and, consequently, contributed to causing the risk resulting in the damage to be compensated.[57]

This *de facto* power exists regardless of the possibility to intervene to correct the automated system option since the "custodian" is liable regardless of any assessment of his actual or potential conduct.

Indeed, in many cases, the "custodian" is also the owner and as such also liable for the damage caused by the circulation of the self-driving vehicle pursuant to Article 2054, final paragraph c.c. so the injured party may seek damages on the basis of two distinct and concurrent claims of liability.

Besides, a joint and several liability is allowed when legal ownership does not coincide with the *de facto* availability of the vehicle and the custodian is not the owner of the vehicle.

The injured party may well wish to assess who is the best person to bring the claim against based on the applicable evidential burdens to be met.

In principle, this is the responsible party according to Article 2051 c.c., who places a higher evidential burden on the custodian. It is not enough for him/her to show the damage was caused by any cause other than defects in construction or maintenance.[58] Instead, he/she must show the causal link between the thing and the damage was broken by an unforeseen intervening fact.

In substance, legal scholars and courts agree that a merely subjective concept of a fortuitous event, such as any cause not attributable to the fault of the custodian, is to be excluded.[59]

It is widely recognised that the liability set out in Article 2051 c.c. is based on a *de facto* relationship with the thing and not on the custodian's act or omission which, although it is a contributory factor in causing the damage, is relevant only

---

56 According to Cass. civ. (III) no 15429 of 10 August 2004, https://dejure.it/, and Cass. civ. (III) no 26086 of 30 November 2005, https://dejure.it/, the characterising feature of the "custodian" is control over the manner of use and preservation of the object.

57 Antonio Albanese, 'La responsabilità civile per i danni da circolazione di veicoli ad elevata automazione' (2019) Eur dir. priv. 1009 and Tom Micheal Gasser, 'Legal Issues of Driver Assistance Systems and Autonomous Driving' in Azim Eskandarian (ed), *Handbook of Intelligent Vehicles* (Springer-Verlag 2012) 1529 (for the corresponding concept of "Halter" in German law).

58 This is instead the evidential burden that the defendant must satisfy in accordance with the provisions of Art 2054, final paragraph, Italian Civil Code (see Cass. civ. (III) no 1019 of 19 February 1981, https://dejure.it/).

59 *Ex ceteris* Cesare Salvi, *Responsabilità extracontrattuale*, Enc. dir. (Giuffrè 1988), 1230 and in jurisprudence Cass. civ. (III) no 295 of 13 January 2015 n. 295, https://dejure.it/, and Cass. civ. (III) no 24845 of 21 November 2014, https://dejure.it/.

from a merely factual perspective, but it is not a criterion in liability pursuant to Article 2051 c.c., not being contemplated therein.

The basis for such liability lies in the risk that the custodian created by using the thing or permitting it to be used by others.

It follows that the unforeseeability does not concern the injurious event, excluding fault, but it relates to the additional factor that breaks the existing chain of causation.[60] Its appraisal is independent of any assessment of the custodian's conduct and refers to external causes, such as natural events[61] or the conduct of the injured party itself[62] or that of a third party.[63]

However, in this case, the causal link that must be shown to be broken is tied directly to the thing being held by the custodian and not to his subjective conduct. Thus, the exclusion of liability derives from a law that is not the same as the one that applies to a negligent act, not only because of the characteristics of the intervening factor, as set out above, but also due to the type of pre-existing causal factor taken into consideration.

Neither strict liability can be equated with liability for mere causation[64] nor can the question of attributability must be confused with that of causal link.[65]

Despite the heavy burden of proof borne by the custodian, Article 2054 final paragraph c.c. may at times be in practical terms more favourable to the injured party. This is true when the fortuitous event consists in a defect of construction or maintenance, which is, according to this provision, always attributable to the owner, who may not rely on such defences to avoid liability.[66]

Other than these hypotheses, the applicability of Article 2051 c.c. to damages caused by highly automated vehicles shows a widening of the owner's liability in the event that he/she is also the *de facto* custodian of the thing.

1.4. MULTIPLE LIABLE PARTIES AND THE ALLOCATION OF DAMAGES BETWEEN THEM

Where the constitutive factors of the various types of liability examined in the preceding paragraphs are present, each liable party will be jointly and severally liable to pay damages in full.

---

60 Cass. civ. (III) no 2477 of 1 February 2018, https://dejure.it/ (for the irrelevance of such evidential burden in the area of fault).

61 Cass. civ. (VI) no 27801 of 11 December 2013, https://dejure.it/.

62 Cass. civ. (III) no 15761 of 29 July 2016, https://dejure.it/.

63 Cass. civ (III) no 18317 of 18 September 2015, https://dejure.it/.

64 Carlo Castronovo, *Responsabilità oggettiva. II) Disciplina privatistica – Dir. comp. e stran.*, Enc. giur., XXX (Treccani 1993), 9.

65 Gaston Fernández Cruz, Leysser León Hilario, 'La reedificación conceptual de la responsabilidad extracontractual objetiva' (2005) Derecho PUCP, 18 ff.

66 Cass. civ. (III) no 1019 of 19 February 1981, https://dejure.it/.

A similar provision is expressly set out in Article 121, paragraph 1, cons. c. for personal injury caused by use of a defective product. The manufacturer and the user are jointly liable for contributing to cause the harm.

This provision reflects the current interpretation of the general rule on joint and several liability set out in Article 2055 c.c. Although this provision refers specifically to "an injurious fact attributable to more than one person",[67] it is commonly held that a joint action is not necessary but rather separate harmful facts may run concurrently in respect of the same damage on grounds of negligence[68] or strict liability.[69]

Here too, each liable party must pay damages in full, in accordance with the general principles on causation and with the same consequences as joint and several liability.[70]

On this premise, Article 121, paragraph 1, cons. c. expressly sanctions joint and several obligations,[71] making Articles 1292 ff c.c. directly applicable without any need to assess the requirements for their analogous application.

Otherwise, Article 122 paragraph 3 of the cons. c. provides an exception to joint and several liability for full compensation where the negligent conduct by the user of the defective product contributed to cause damage to things belonging to a third party. In this case, the compensation due from the manufacturer is reduced in accordance with the principles set out in Article 1227, paragraph 1 c.c. which normally covers the different cases of contributory negligence by the injured party.

---

67 Analogous provision in §840 Abs. 1, German Civil Code: 'Sind fürdenaus einer unerlaubten Handlung entstehenden Schaden mehrere nebeneinander verantwortlich, so haftensie als Gesamtschuldner'.

68 See John Fleming, *The Law of Torts* (Sweet & Maxwell 1998) 175 ff (for the assessment that in American common law joint liability presupposes the indivisibility of the damage and not necessarily the participation in the conduct) and Christian von Bar, *The Common European Law of Tort*, vol I (Oxford 1998) 70 ff. (for the various solutions adopted in European legal frameworks).

69 Renato Scognamiglio, *Responsabilità civile* e danno (Giappicchelli 2010) 652 and Cass. civ. Joint Divisions no 16503 of 15 July 2009, https://dejure.it/. For an opposing position see Carlo Castronovo, *Responsabilità civile* (Giuffrè 2018) 375 ff.

70 It does not seem correct to argue that, since we are dealing with several separate obligations of compensation which all relate to the same subject matter, the right to recourse between the liable parties should be excluded, on the principle that they are all equally liable, but based on different attributable factors. See Carlo Castronovo, *Responsabilità civile* (Giuffrè 2018) 380. Indeed, in this way, the cost of the damage would fall on only one party, identified extemporaneously based on the simple fact that this party has (already) paid out compensation, while both the preventive role of civil liability and the allocative efficiency of the consequent compensation would be frustrated.

71 An analogous joint and several liability obligations are provided for in Article 2054, paragraph 3 Italian Civil Code, as against the driver and the owner of the vehicle who, in the absence of a single "harmful act" attributable to them, are liable on the basis of separate attributory factors.

Other than these hypotheses, where subjective and objective facts attributable to more than one party have to be considered – from a legal perspective – as the cause of the same injurious event, all liable parties will be obliged to compensate in full the injured party.

The remaining question is on what basis compensation can be apportioned between the jointly and severally liable parties in accordance with separate rules on liability, which are not all based on negligence.

Even though Article 122, paragraph 2 cons. c. contemplates the possibility of multiple parties being liable in various capacities, it does not provide a satisfactory solution where a liable party has paid damages in full and subsequently files a claim against the other jointly and severally liable parties. In determining the amounts due, the law requires evaluating the extent of the risk objectively attributable to each party or the seriousness of the fault and the extent of the consequences deriving from these factors. However, it fails to define the "specific relevance" of each criterion compared to the others.

These factors do not provide unequivocal directions on how to share the costs among the parties jointly liable and their heterogeneity does not allow a comparative assessment between them for the purpose of apportioning responsibility.[72]

The same rule states that if it is impossible to quantify the respective liabilities of the jointly liable parties, the damages may be apportioned equally in accordance with the provisions of the law on uncertain cases.[73] But this provision for residual cases cannot become a general rule, treating different cases in a uniform way, when the spirit of the law would require them to be treated differently.

According to some scholars, if different types of liability exist between jointly liable parties, the entire cost of the damages must fall on the negligent party.[74] This opinion does not seem to be correct given that it is based on a simplified and reductive reading of Article 2055, paragraph 2 c.c.

First, the application of this criterion in the decision-making process is not possible where the injurious event is the result of concurrent cases of strict liability only since it disregards the conduct of the parties in terms of fault.[75]

Furthermore, in cases with different types of liability, a decision to charge only those parties liable in negligence to pay damages would distort the letter and *ratio* of the law by ignoring the significant differences existing between different strict liability claims.

---

72 For criticism see Pietro Trimarchi, *Rischio e responsabilità oggettiva* (Giuffrè 1961) 304.

73 Renato Scognamiglio, *Responsabilità civile* e danno (Giappichelli 2010) 653 (proposing to extend to multiple parties with strict liability the rule in Art 2055, paragraph 3 Italia Civil Code).

74 Adriano De Cupis, *Il danno*^{3}, II (Giuffrè 1979) 181.

75 Cesare Salvi, *Responsabilità extracontrattuale*, Enc. dir. (Giuffrè 1988) 1255.

Attributing the costs of damages to the negligent party is acceptable when strict liability has essentially the aim of securing the all-assets-guarantee or facilitating the procedural position of the injured party, for example with respect to the owner of the vehicle.

Where, instead, strict liability performs a role in preventing potential harms, it would be neither fair nor opportune to charge the entire cost of the damages to the negligent party. Manufacturer of a defective vehicle cannot rebut his/her liability: since he/she is in a position that can have influence on the technical features that determine the level of safety, he/she must bear the proportional costs in damages, which the vehicle caused, together with any third-party whose negligence was contributory (e.g. the driver).

Given the impossibility of comparing fault and strict liability in terms of lesser and greater severities of facts, a possible solution would be the apportionment of damages based on the causal incidence that each fact had on the production of the harm, without assessing the seriousness of the fault.[76] It follows that the costs of damages cannot rest indefinitely with the owner when the harm derived exclusively from a defect in the construction of the vehicle.

Although this approach may appear to oppose the interests of the manufacturer, it reflects a willingness on the part of some of them to agree to extend their liability.[77]

While this position may seem inexplicable, it acknowledges a business opportunity: it is much easier to convince a consumer to purchase a vehicle equipped with electronic safety systems if the manufacturer accepts liability (and insurance costs) for any accidents. This counterbalances the extension of owner liability as compared to traditional vehicles.

Clearly, this position relies on a cost-benefit analysis that appears economically viable considering the low risk of occurrence of harmful events and so sustainable insurance costs of accidents. Ultimately, these costs may be reflected in the sale price of the good as well as spread across the total number of purchasers.

This way, a risk of market failure can be prevented by ensuring that the cost (also in terms of damages) of having a safer vehicle on the road is not borne by the individual purchaser but by all those benefiting from its increased level of safety.[78]

---

76 Marco Comporti, *Fatti illeciti: le responsabilità oggettive*, Il codice civile. Commentario (Giuffrè 2009) 292 (for the same conclusion).

77 Omri Ben-Shahar, 'Should Carmakers Be Liable When A Self Car Crashes?' *Forbes* (Chicago 22 September 2016), https://www.forbes.com/sites/omribenshahar/2016/09/22/should-carmakers-be-liable-when-a-self-driving-car-crashes/#326a855a48fb accessed 1 July 2020.

78 James M. Anderson, Nidhi Kalra, Karlyn D. Stanley, Paul Sorensen, Constantine Samaras, Tobi A. Oluwatola, *Autonomous Vehicle Technology – A Guide for Policymakers* (RAND Corporation 2016) 136 ff https://www.rand.org/pubs/research_reports/RR443-2.html accessed 1 July 2020 (for an assessment on the risks of market failure).

Any damages must be apportioned between the manufacturer of the defective vehicle and the driver who has negligently contributed to the injurious event based on the causal link with the defect and negligent conduct, respectively.

Logically, each cause must be considered equal *ex post* since the damage would not have occurred in their absence. Therefore, in apportioning the costs of damages, the assessment must take into account the extent to which the vehicle malfunction and the negligent conduct of its driver contributed *ex ante* to increase the risk of the harm that effectively occurred.

2. CONCLUSION

The civil liability of the driver provided for by the Italian Civil Code can help prevent the risk of accidents caused by vehicles that are not fully automated and in which man maintains control of driving.

Requiring the driver to prove that he/she has done everything possible to avoid the damage, this rule is consistent with the fact that the harmful event falls within his/her control. On the contrary, it would be neither just nor efficient to require the injured party to show the accident was attributable to human error and/or a defect in the vehicle.

This predefined standard of care on the one hand pushes the driver to the maximum effort due in the specific circumstance in order to avoid the damage, on the other hand makes the judicial assessment of liability easier, reducing the dispute resolution costs.

The protection of human health against road traffic risks is also strengthened by product liability regulation, leading the manufacturer to comply with objective and verifiable standards, according to social safety expectations for highly automated vehicles.

Damages the manufacturer has to pay fall within the running costs of his business and as such they are reflected in the price of the product and spread across all purchasers, in accordance with the principle of justice that the collective utility in introducing new vehicles requires the community also to bear the costs of damage resulting to individuals.

This discipline, in accordance with EU harmonised law, is substantially adequate for the issues that may arise with regard to new technologies and only needs for minor adjustments by uniform legislation.

Moreover, if there is any doubt regarding the cause of the damage, whether it is due to a human guide, a lack of maintenance or a defect in the construction, Article 2054 c.c. simplifies the procedural choices of the injured party, allowing him/her for claims against the owner and/or the custodian of the vehicle and shifting to the defendant the burden of deciding whether or not to bring a claim (and on what grounds) against the driver or the manufacturer.

This approach strengthens the position of the damaged subject both substantially, by widening the pool of liable parties, and procedurally, by attributing to the latters risks and costs of ascertaining the causes of the injurious event.

Otherwise, No-Fault Compensation schemes do not find recognition in Italian law unlike other legal systems.[79]

Given the joint responsibility of several people, the cost of compensation may be definitively and exclusively charged, through recourse, on those who, regardless of whether they are attributable to strict liability or negligence, have concretely increased the risk of the injury, while they could have played a role in preventing its occurrence.

Consistent with the aim of making road traffic safer, this conclusion can legitimately be drawn from the current law through an interpretative adjustment, without the need for a legislative amendment.

---

79 About these see Maurice Schellekens, 'No-fault compensation schemes for self-driving vehicles' (2018) *Law, Innovation and Technology* 319 ff.

PART IV

CONTRACT LAW

COVID-19 AND ENGLISH CONTRACT LAW

Hugh Beale and Christian Twigg-Flesner*

* Hugh Beale, University of Warwick, Harris Manchester College and University of Oxford; Christian Twigg-Flesner, University of Warwick.

The narrow doctrine of frustration in English contract law (under which the parties' outstanding obligations are discharged automatically) applies only when performance of a contract is impossible because of a change in circumstances. Although much-discussed, "frustration of purpose" applies only when the change has defeated the purpose for both parties and has very seldom been applied. Pre-COVID-19 law contains a few exceptions, but mostly for consumer contracts. The measures taken to relieve parties affected by COVID-19 do not involve any significant changes to contract law. Changes relevant to contracts involve delaying enforcement procedures or changes to the Financial Conduct Authority's regulatory requirements to provide for "payment holidays" for consumer credit or other financial services. Limited changes to contract law may emerge, but no significant permanent changes.

1. INTRODUCTION

In this contribution, we explore the ways in which the impact of COVID-19 on the performance of contracts would be dealt with in English law. Our aim is to provide both academic analysis and an idea of the way one common law system is (or is not) coping. We consider existing doctrine and the new legislation which has been introduced in response to the crisis and which impacts directly on contract law and the terms of existing contracts. In addition, we consider other changes which have direct impact on contracts – for example, changes to practice directions that restrict procedures that the other party may apply and changes in other forms of regulation, particularly in the requirements of the Financial Conduct Authority. Changes that have only an indirect effect on the performance of contracts, such as changes in the welfare system, are mentioned briefly.

Our analysis will concentrate on contracts between businesses and consumers (B2C) and between businesses (B2B), but we will refer briefly also to employment contracts (E2E) and to contracts between parties neither of whom is acting in the course of a business (C2C: e.g. private house sales, tenancies with "hobby landlords"). It will also look at contracts of a variety of types: for example, simple contracts for the supply of goods or services; contracts of employment; contracts for housing (both rented and on mortgage); and contracts for other financial services including loans, credit cards, insurance, etc.

First, we will set out the relevant pre-existing rules of English contract law and their potential application to the particular issues associated with COVID-19. Secondly, we will explain how the general rules are modified or replaced by particular, mainly legislative, rules in respect of particular kinds of contract. Thirdly, we examine provisions commonly found in contracts which seek to provide for unforeseen or unexpected circumstances (such as force majeure, extension of time, material adverse change and hardship clauses).

Fourthly, we highlight new legislation and other forms of regulation (such as Financial Conduct Authority requirements and Government "expectations") that impact directly on the contract rights, obligations and remedies of the parties affected by the consequences of COVID-19. We will end by considering a number of potential "pinch points" in English contract law, issues which may become problematic and on which the courts may have to develop or refine the law in the light of the effects of COVID-19, the measures taken to contain it and the way in which we think parties to contracts affected may deal with each other.

2. PRE-EXISTING CONTRACT DOCTRINE AND APPLICATION TO COVID-19 SITUATIONS

2.1. INTRODUCTION

The starting point is that English law imposes a duty on each party to perform its obligations, and to do so on time. This is normally a strict duty – we may even say an absolute one, as the common law does not (1) recognise a defence of force majeure or (2) allow for adjustment or termination of the contract on the ground of changed circumstances. In practice, very many contracts contain a force majeure clause and some have hardship or material adverse change clauses; but in the absence of such a clause, in English contract law, an unforeseen post-formation event will lead to the parties being excused or released from their future obligations only in a narrow range of circumstances.

2.2. FRUSTRATION BY SUPERVENING IMPOSSIBILITY

If performance becomes wholly impossible, either factually or legally[1] (e.g. because of a change in the law), the contract will be discharged automatically under the doctrine of "frustration", so that each party is released from any further obligation to perform, provided that

1. the impossibility occurred without the fault[2] of either party;
2. it was unforeseeable (or possibly unforeseen); and
3. the contract does not allocate the risk of inability to perform to one of the parties, either expressly or impliedly because it is one of the risks that party is expected to bear.[3]

---

1 *Fibrosa Spolka Akcyjna v Fairbairn Lawson Combe Barbour Ltd* [1943] AC 32.
2 Or the choice of either party.
3 For an instance when the claim that a contract was frustrated as a result of Coronavirus restrictions failed, see *Salam Air SAOC v Latam Airlines Group SA* [2020] EWHC 2414 (Comm).

It should be noted that factual impossibility covers only cases in which performance of the contract is literally impossible. A contract that can be performed but only at much greater cost to one party does not fall within the doctrine of frustration.[4]

Where the impossibility only relates to part of the performance (except as regards severable parts of the contract that have been performed, or should have been performed, before the event occurred[5]), the outcome will depend on whether the substance of the contract has become impossible. Thus, in *Taylor v Caldwell*,[6] the destruction of the musical hall by fire frustrated the contract even though the pleasure grounds around it were still useable. In determining whether partial impossibility constitutes frustration, the courts seem to adopt a test similar to the *Hong Kong Fir* test[7] as to when breach of an innominate term[8] will give rise to a right to terminate the contract.[9]

A temporary inability to perform is no excuse unless it lasts so long that performance of the contract becomes impossible (for example, if performance on the date set is essential or the impossibility lasts so long that it would make performance pointless), or performance in the new situation would be "radically different" to what the contract called for.[10]

If performance of the contract is neither impossible nor, in the new circumstances, would be "radically different", the party who is unable to perform will be in breach of contract and liable in damages – or at least this is the common assumption in, for example, contracts of sale and for construction.[11] The fact that performance will be far more onerous than either party could have imagined is no defence; the contract will not be frustrated and, as we have said, English law has no doctrine of changed circumstances.

An aircraft lease placed the risk of "any … occurrence of whatever kind which shall deprive [Salam Air] of the use, possession and enjoyment" of the aircraft on the lessee, which precluded the lessee's claim that the contract was frustrated by flight bans due to the pandemic imposed in Oman.

4 *Davies Contractors v Fareham UDC* [1956] AC 696.

5 See Law Reform (Frustrated Contracts) Act 1943, s 2(3).

6 (1863) 3 B & S 826 (contract to hire Surrey Gardens and Musical Hall frustrated when the music hall burned down in a fire).

7 *Hong Kong Fir Shipping Co Ltd v Kawasaki Kisen Kaisha Ltd* [1962] 2 QB 26.

8 In English law, a contract that has been broken by one party may be terminated by the other party (1) if the term broken is expressly stated to be a condition (as in *Lombard North Central plc v Butterworth* [1987] QB 527) or is so important that the court interprets it as being a condition (as in *Bunge Corp v Tradax SA* [1981] 1 WLR 711); or (2), where the term cannot be labeled as a condition (and so is an "innomimate" term), if the breach deprives the innocent party of the substance of what was contracted for (the test laid down in *Hong Kong Fir Shipping Co Ltd v Kawasaki Kisen Kaisha Ltd* [1962] 2 QB 26).

9 Treitel argues that a stricter test is needed for frustration than this: Guenter Treitel, *Frustration and Force Majeure* (3rd edn, Sweet & Maxwell 2014) 249–250, para 5-061.

10 We return to "radically different" below.

11 Later, we discuss a few exceptional cases in which the courts seem to have reached a different result, though the basis of the decisions is not clear.

Thus frustration is often an "all or nothing" outcome: either the parties are wholly released or they remain liable to perform.

It is worth noting that if an unforeseen event does cause frustration, discharge occurs automatically, not through the choice of one of the contracting parties; the parties to the contract are released from having to perform future obligations as a matter of law. Instead, in most cases,[12] the Law Reform (Frustrated Contracts) Act 1943 requires the parties to refund any payments that have been made[13] and to pay the value of any other benefits that were received before the date of discharge,[14] though in each case the court has power to reduce the amount payable to a "just sum" that reflects any costs incurred by the recipient of the money or other benefit. Costs incurred that were not covered by a pre-payment and did not result in a benefit to the other party will remain uncompensated. In other words, the regime is broadly speaking restitutionary,[15] though the Court of Appeal has pointed out that the Act must be applied according to its own terms, without "help from words which are not in the statute."[16]

2.3. IMPOSSIBILITY AS A RESULT OF COVID-19

In many instances, performance of the contract, at least within the contractual period for performance, has become impossible as a result of COVID-19 consequences. Frequently, this will be the result of travel restrictions and prohibitions of activities under government regulations. For instance, under the Health Protection (Coronavirus, Restrictions) (England) Regulations 2020,[17] many businesses were forced to close altogether for several months.[18]

---

12 The Act does not apply to certain types of contract, in particular voyage charters and contracts for the carriage of goods by sea, and contracts of sale where the goods have perished, see s 2(5). Also, the parties may agree on different provisions, s 2(3). In a commercial context such modifications would be effective and are not caught by the provisions of the Unfair Contract Terms Act 1977, see s 29(1) (exemption for a "contractual provision … authorised … by the express terms … of an enactment"). In a consumer contract, a term depriving the consumer of the entitlement to receive back any money already paid under a contract that has been frustrated, or providing for reimbursement only by other means such as a credit note or a voucher, might be unfair under Consumer Rights Act 2015, s 62.

13 s 1(2). Payments that were due but unpaid cease to be payable.

14 s 1(3). The main case where the scope of this section was considered was *BP Exploration Co (Libya) v Hunt (No 2)* [1979] 1 WLR 783 (High Court) on rather complex facts. Robert Goff J's first-instance judgment, which was upheld by the Court of Appeal ([1983] 1 WLR 232), is a detailed consideration of how the "just sum" should be calculated.

15 See Andrew Burrows (ed), *Essays on the Law of Restitution* (Clarendon Press 1991) ch 6.

16 [1983] 1 WLR 232, 243.

17 SI 2020/350 (revoked by Reg 2(1) of the Health Protection (Coronavirus, Restrictions) (No 2) (England) Regulations 2020 (SI 2020/684) with effect from 4 July 2020).

18 Many of these businesses were permitted to reopen from 4 July 2020, although others were still precluded from opening: see Schedule 2 of the Health Protection (Coronavirus, Restrictions)

A contravention of this would constitute an offence. Consequently, carrying on one of those businesses required to close would effectively be illegal during the emergency. Insofar as any contracts were entered into before the emergency arose and had to be carried out during the period of "lockdown",[19] the effect of the regulations would be to render performance illegal.

A further category of impossibility relates to physical impossibility, for example because of death or personal illness, or because of lack of transport or other essential services. These cases raise a possible difficulty in arguing frustration. Being able to obtain goods to fulfil orders taken by customers, or providing labour, material and transport, on the one hand, or on the other hand being able to accept delivery of goods or performance of services despite the closure of facilities, is normally thought to be within the party's control and therefore the risk is normally on them.[20] However, we expect the sheer scale of the lockdown during the COVID-19 pandemic, with so many industries being almost totally unable to work both in the UK and elsewhere, may lead courts to hold that extent of the difficulties encountered by suppliers and customers were outside the risks normally assumed by parties.

2.4. DELAY CAUSED BY TEMPORARY IMPOSSIBILITY

Not all of the measures taken in response to the COVID-19 pandemic will render performance of a contract permanently impossible. Many contracts can still be performed, or performance completed, at a later point in time than envisaged under the contract. Such a situation is often not such that it would constitute frustration of the contract; whether it does will depend on the extent of the disruption on the overall duration of the contract.[21] This requires asking whether the delay is such that it will deprive the other party of the substance of what they were contracting for, or make performance of the contract something "radically different". This must be "determined by an informed judgment based upon all the evidence of what has occurred and what is likely thereafter to occur."[22]

(No 2) (England) Regulations 2020 (SI 2020/684). After being allowed to re-open in the summer, many non-essential shops were required to close after Christmas 2020 and in March 2021 remain closed. Shops were permitted to reopen after 12 April 2021.

19 However, if there is a reasonable chance that performance can be completed after the closure period and before the contract duration is due to come to an end, then the temporary illegality affecting that contract will not mean that the contract has been frustrated.

20 Compare *The Sea Angel* [2007] EWCA Civ 547, in which a chartered ship was wrongly detained for a long period by port authorities. The Court held that the charter was not frustrated; delays in port were one of the risks taken by the charterer.

21 *Cricklewood Property and Investment Trust Ltd v Leightons Investment Trust Ltd* [1945] AC 221.

22 Lord Roskill in *The Nema*. See Hugh Beale (gen ed), *Chitty on Contracts* (33rd edn, Sweet & Maxwell 2018) para 23-035.

Generally, a delay has to be extensive to amount to a frustrating event, with reference to the contract and the expected impact on the contract.[23] A contract may be frustrated even though it provides for extra time for performance in certain events, if the delays are such that they are outside the clause. Asquith LJ once noted that "'delay' though literally describing what has occurred, has been read as limited to normal, moderate delay, and as not extending to an interruption so differing in degree and magnitude from anything which could have been contemplated as to differ from it in kind."[24]

2.5. ELEMENTS OF CONTRACT IMPOSSIBLE TO PERFORM

In the case of a long-term contract (such as subscription-style contracts many consumers enter into, for example, gym membership, video streaming services, etc.), or delivery of goods by instalments, performance may be interrupted or may be different from what was expected. For example, swimming pools have been temporarily closed, and streaming services have been unable to offer coverage of live sports events they would otherwise have provided. Again, this may result in frustration if the effect is sufficiently serious. In a case involving a 10-year lease of a warehouse, the contract was not frustrated when the only access road was temporarily closed for about a year.[25] This was because there was a period of three more years left after the closure had finished. Similarly, in a case involving a 99-year lease, when war broke out nine years into the lease, it was held that this did not frustrate the contract as there was expected to be a significant amount of time left after the war had ended.[26] Whilst these cases involve a commercial lease, they are indicative of how the question of frustration might be approached in the case of temporary suspension of the contract leading to partial impossibility.

We have said that English contract law does not recognise partial frustration. However, this is subject to one important qualification: if obligations under the contract are severable, then frustration can apply to severable parts without causing the entire contract to be frustrated. A simple example of a severable contract is a contract for the delivery of a quantity of goods in monthly instalments, with each instalment to be paid for on delivery. If the contract is frustrated part-way through, with some instalments already delivered, then the seller is entitled to receive payment in respect of those instalments. More importantly, severability could assist where, for some reason, some but not

23 Hugh Beale (gen ed), *Chitty on Contracts* (33rd edn, Sweet & Maxwell 2018) para 23-035.

24 *Sir Lindsay Parkinson & Co Ltd v Commissioners of Works* [1949] 2 KB 632, 665.

25 *National Carriers Ltd v Panalpina (Northern) Ltd* [1981] AC 675.

26 *Cricklewood Property and Investment Trust Ltd v Leightons Investment Trust Ltd* [1945] AC 221.

all future obligations (each of which is severable) are affected by a frustrating event.[27] In our gym example above, if the client paid for their membership on a monthly basis, payment each month and the corresponding provision of gym facilities would be treated as a severable obligations. The fact that a gym had to close for several months would therefore be treated as frustration only in respect of the severable elements affected by the (temporary) illegality.[28] However, this would only be possible if severance of the obligations under the contract was possible; had the client paid for a whole year upfront, it may be trickier to argue frustration of severable parts, and it is not clear what sort of reduction in payment a consumer would be justified in making. In the case of access to a facility which is temporarily unavailable, one might think that should be the fee for the period it is not accessible. In the case of a service where some of the service cannot be provided (such as a sports channel which cannot offer live football matches during the period), the consumer clearly has to pay something but cannot be expected to pay in full.[29] We suspect that a court would take the common sense solution of apportioning the annual fee across the weeks of the year, at least where the supplier's costs would also be incurred on a more-or-less regular basis throughout the period.

2.6. CONTRACT NO LONGER SERVES PARTY'S PURPOSE

Another common consequence of the COVID-19 pandemic will be that the reason for which one or both parties have entered into the contract has fallen away. The contract itself will still be capable of being performed but performance would be no use to one or both of the parties. For instance, many students who have vacated their student accommodation early after on-campus activities were suspended are likely to argue that they no longer have any need for their tenancy, but from the perspective of landlords, students can still live in their term-time accommodation.

It is widely said that English law recognises a doctrine of frustration of purpose. It is true that in the famous coronation case of *Krell v Henry*[30] the court held that a contract to rent a room overlooking the procession route of the King had been frustrated by the cancellation of the procession: even though the contract could still be performed in a literal sense, (as the court put it at the time), "the foundation of the contract" had been destroyed or because (or as it would now be put) performance in the new circumstances would be

---

27 See Guenter Treitel, *Frustration and Force Majeure* (3rd edn, Sweet & Maxwell 2014) 573–574, para 5-032.

28 This possibility is also envisaged in s 2(4) of the Law Reform (Frustrated Contracts) Act 1943.

29 Again, it may matter whether the contract is severable or not.

30 [1903] 2 KB 740.

"radically different." But it must be emphasised that English law will treat the contract as frustrated in such circumstances only if the *common* purpose of both parties has been frustrated.[31] It is important to appreciate that the purpose must be shared by the parties and not merely be the purpose of one of the parties, even if that purpose was known to the other party.[32] This is shown by an example given by Vaughan Williams LJ:[33] a contract to take a cab to Epsom to watch the races there would not be frustrated if the races were cancelled because of an infectious disease. Another example (already noted above) is students who no longer require accommodation near their university after face-to-face classes were suspended. The students' purpose for entering into a tenancy agreement has fallen away, but landlords let properties for the purpose of generating an income and that purpose will continue. It is clear that it does not suffice that one party's circumstances have changed unexpectedly so as to no longer need the contract. For another example, take a hotel booking for the period of the Edinburgh Festival, but the Festival is cancelled. The guest no longer needs the hotel room so the purpose for which the room was booked is no longer relevant; however, this does not affect the purpose for which the hotel entered into the contract, which is to rent out the room for payment. This contract would therefore not be frustrated.[34]

2.7. PERFORMANCE HAS BECOME MORE COSTLY

Another possibility is that the contract could still be performed, but performance would increase costs for one party. This is a situation which is covered by provisions on hardship in many other jurisdictions. English law does not have comparable provisions.

Can a contract ever be frustrated by increased expenditure? This raises the issue that the courts have said that a contract may be frustrated if performance in the changed circumstances would be "radically different". We are aware of one case that might seem to suggest this is possible. In *Metropolitan Water Board v Dick Kerr*[35] a construction contractor was prevented from working by wartime

---

31 In *Maritime National Fish Ltd. v Ocean Trawlers Ltd.* [1935] AC 524, Lord Wright noted that the authority of *Krell v Henry* "is certainly not one to be extended: it is particularly difficult to apply where … the possibility of the event relied on as constituting a frustration of the adventure … was known to both parties when the contract was made, but the contract entered into was absolute in terms so far as concerned that known possibility." (at 529).

32 Cf. *Salam Air SAOC v Latam Airlines Group SA* [2020] EWHC 2414 (Comm), involving a six-year dry-lease of an aircraft which was then grounded as a result of Coronavirus restrictions in Oman. Foxton J noted that "frustration of purpose" "has seldom been applied since it first emerged in the Coronation cases at the start of the last century." (para 49).

33 [1903] 2 KB 740, 751. See also *Herne Bay Steam Boat Co v Hutton* [1903] 2 KB 603, 689. The case was decided by the same judges as *Krell v Henry*.

34 In practice, such contracts would contain some kind of cancellation clause any event.

35 [1918] AC 119.

government restrictions and the House of Lords held (while the war was still going on) that the contractor would not be obliged to complete the work after the war because performance in the new and unknown economic circumstances would be "radically different". Even if this begins to look like a change of circumstances, we think the late Professor Sir Guenter Treitel was right to insist that it was not just the change in costs that frustrated the contract but the combination of a very long period of temporary impossibility and the change in economic conditions.[36] It is only in this way that the case can be reconciled with the many statements that frustration is not available on the basis of increased difficulty and expense in performing or financial hardship.[37]

2.8. CUSTOMER UNABLE TO PAY FOR GOODS OR SERVICES

A customer may no longer have the means to pay and therefore cannot proceed with the contract. This can arise in a number of different permutations. One instance would be an executory contract for the goods or services to be provided where the customer is not able to pay due to financial difficulties caused by the consequences of the pandemic. Another instance, affecting commercial parties as much as consumers, might arise under a loan or other credit agreement where the sum owed is to be repaid in monthly instalments. The effects of the pandemic and its consequences might affect the ability of a borrower to keep up their regular instalments. These situations would generally not amount to frustration of the contract, but be treated as a risk which the customer would have to bear.[38] However, as we will explain in the next section, there are special rules in place for certain types of credit agreements.

2.9. CONCLUSION ON THE APPLICABILITY OF THE DOCTRINE OF FRUSTRATION

It follows from what we have said that that certainly there will be cases in which contracts governed by English law are frustrated by the effects of COVID-19,

---

36 Guenter Treitel, *Frustration and Force Majeure* (3rd edn, Sweet & Maxwell 2014) para 6-031. In para 6-035 Treitel refers to another case (*William Cory & Son Ltd v Corporation of London* [1951] 1 KB 8; [1951] 2 KB 476 where the contract was frustrated by a combination of new government restrictions (a local authority by-law) and changed circumstances.

37 *Davies Contractors v Fareham UDC* [1956] AC 696. Note *Gold Group Properties Ltd v BDW Trading Ltd* [2010] EWHC 323 (TCC), where a drop of property prices by 20% did not frustrate a development agreement.

38 In a sense, this is akin to the exclusion of financial hardship situations from the scope of frustration.

because performance becomes illegal or, perhaps less frequently, physically impossible. However, the doctrine of frustration is quite narrow. It will not apply to many cases in which the impossibility is only temporary or partial; and it will not apply when the contract no longer serves one party's purpose, or has become very much more burdensome to perform. Lastly, it is an "all-or-nothing" doctrine: if it applies, the parties are automatically discharged, but if it does not apply, a party who does not perform will be liable for breach of contract unless there is a force majeure or similar clause in the contract that covers the events that have taken place.

3. RULES THAT MODIFY THE GENERAL LAW IN PARTICULAR CASES

We have found one exceptional rule of the common law that seems to "buck the trend" by, in effect, admitting a defence of force majeure. This is in contracts of employment, where it seems to be widely accepted that an employee who is temporarily prevented from working by illness is not in breach of contract.[39] We can only explain it as a customary exception.

A number of relevant statutory provisions can be invoked in instances where the common law itself would not be of assistance.

3.1. CONSUMER CREDIT

The Consumer Credit Act 1974 (CCA) governs consumer credit agreements, i.e. "an agreement between an individual ('the debtor') and another person ('the creditor') by which the creditor provides the debtor with credit of any amount."[40] An "individual" in the CCA covers not only natural persons, but also partnerships of up to three persons and unincorporated bodies.[41] This includes sole traders but not companies. A consumer credit agreement is a regulated agreement provided that it does not fall under one of the many exemptions in Part 14A of the Financial Services and Markets Act 2000 (Regulated Activities) Order 2001.[42]

---

39 Although it is widely accepted, it is not easy to find authority for the rule. The only and "early" authority cited in Hugh Beale (gen ed), *Chitty on Contracts* (33rd edn, Sweet & Maxwell 2018) para 40-178 (*Boast v Firth* (1868) LR 4 CP 1) is actually a case of permanent impossibility, as the employee had died.

40 s 8(1) CCA 1974.

41 cf s 189(1) CCA 1974.

42 See Art 60B of the Financial Services and Markets Act 2000 (Regulated Activities) Order 2001 (SI 2001/544, as amended).

Two provisions of the CCA 1974 are of particular relevance to our discussion. The first is section 129, which provides that where a borrower is unable to pay the instalments due under a regulated consumer credit agreement, and the lender seeks to enforce the agreement, the court has the power to make an order to determine payments in instalments as the court considers reasonable in the circumstances (a "time order"). In effect, the court has the power to reschedule a borrower's debt in light of the borrower's circumstances. Furthermore, in the case of goods supplied under a hire-purchase agreement, under which the contractual supplier, usually a finance company, retains ownership of the goods until the consumer has exercised the option to purchase after paying all the required instalments, section 90 of the CCA 1974 protects a defaulting borrower from repossession, provided that the borrower has already paid at least one-third of the total price of the goods to the creditor. Repossession of such "protected goods" is only permitted with a court order; and the court can of course make a time order instead.

3.2. PREPAYMENTS AND CONNECTED LENDER LIABILITY

Note that despite a Law Commission proposal for reforming the law,[43] there is insufficient consumer protection where goods were pre-paid and the business supplier becomes insolvent before the goods have been delivered or ownership has transferred to the consumer. One legislative provision of relevance is section 75 of the CCA 1974, which offers protection to consumers who used a credit card to pay for their goods, provided goods are worth more than £100/item and no more than £30,000/item. If the supplier to whom prepayment was made is unable or unwilling to give a refund, a consumer may invoke section 75 to recover the money directly from the credit card company.

3.3. PACKAGE TRAVEL

The Package Travel and Linked Travel Arrangements Regulations 2018[44] (SI 2018/634) implement the EU's Package Travel Directive (2015/2302/EU) and apply the rules from the Directive concerning due to "unavoidable and exceptional circumstances", defined as a situation beyond the control of the

---

43 Law Commission, *Consumer Prepayments on Retailer Insolvency*, (Law Commission No 368, 2016).

44 SI 2018/634, amended by the Package Travel and Linked Travel Arrangements (Amendment) (EU Exit) Regulations 2018 (SI 2018/1367) to adjust the Regulations following the UK's withdrawal from the EU.

party who seeks to rely on such a situation, the consequences of which could not have been avoided even if all reasonable measures had been taken (cf Reg 2(1)). Where such circumstances arise, termination of the contract and a full refund of the price paid by the traveller is triggered, although there is no entitlement to additional compensation.[45]

3.4. HOUSING

Space precludes a detailed treatment of housing law. Very summarily, most residential tenants who fall behind in their rent can be evicted only after a court order; and "social" landlords (local councils and housing associations, as opposed to private companies and individuals) are required to follow an elaborate protocol before evicting a tenant; among other things, landlords are required to "try to agree affordable sums for the tenant to pay towards the arrears, based upon the tenant's income and expenditure" and to assist the tenant in applying for welfare benefits.[46] Although in many cases if the tenant owes more than two months' rent, the court cannot refuse to grant possession,[47] the court has power to issue a "suspended possession order", and (particularly when the arrears have come about because of delays in the payment of Housing Benefit, or a change of circumstances such as illness of loss of job) frequently will do so if the landlord will accept the tenant's undertaking to pay the future rent and something (often a nominal amount) towards the arrears. If the tenant defaults, the landlord can immediately apply for a warrant of eviction. In the case of other tenancies, the landlord may not re-enter or regard the lease forfeited without the landlord first demanding that the default be remedied; and the tenant may apply to the court for relief against forfeiture.[48]

4. USE OF CONTRACT TERMS SUCH AS FORCE MAJEURE, MAC, HARDSHIP

The restrictive nature of the English doctrine of frustration, combined with the absence of a general principle of force majeure, puts the onus on the contracting parties to make appropriate provision for the occurrence of uncertain or unforeseeable events and their consequences through express contract terms.

45 See, e.g. Regulation 12.
46 Ministry of Justice *Pre-Action Protocol for Possession Claims by Social Landlords.*
47 See Housing Act 1988, Sch 2 Ground 8.
48 Law of Property Act 1925, s 146.

Unsurprisingly, force majeure clauses are used widely. Such clauses usually spell out in great detail which sort of events[49] will trigger the clause (often supplemented with some sort of "catch-all" wording at the end) and what the impact of this on the parties' ability to perform must be,[50] and what is to happen to the parties' obligations once the clause is engaged.

A force majeure clause must be interpreted in the way that reasonable people in the same situation, and with the same background information as the parties, would understand it.[51] In other words, each clause must be interpreted individually in the light of the circumstances known to the parties at the time, and without the help of any general doctrine that might inform the discussion, for example by providing an established meaning to the phrase "force majeure". Their application in the context of the COVID-19 pandemic will therefore depend on which events are listed as trigger events (these need to include "pandemic" or at least "epidemic"), what consequences are addressed in the clause (inability to perform, reduction in supplies), and whether what has actually happened is covered by the clause.

However, it should not be assumed that all contracts disrupted by COVID-19 will contain a force majeure clause. For instance, many contracts for the sale of private houses will have been affected by both the Government's temporary ban on[52] all but "reasonably necessary" house moves, and the British Removers Association instructions to its members to delay or cancel any house move that had not already been started. The Standard Conditions of Sale issued by the Law Society do not contain a force majeure clause and at least some solicitors

---

49 See, e.g. the detailed clause at issue in *J Lauritzen AS v Wijsmuller BV (The Super Servant Two)* [1990] 1 Lloyd's Rep 1: "Wijsmuller has the right to cancel its performance under this Contract whether the loading has been completed or not, in the event of force majeur, Acts of God, perils or danger and accidents of the sea, acts of war, warlike-operations, acts of public enemies, restraint of princes, rulers or people or seizure under legal process, quarantine restrictions, civil commotions, blockade, strikes, lockout, closure of the Suez or Panama Canal, congestion of harbours or any other circumstances whatsoever, causing extraordinary periods of delay and similar events and/or circumstances, abnormal increases in prices and wages, scarcity of fuel and similar events, which reasonably may impede, prevent or delay the performance of this contract."

50 The clause in *The Super Servant Two* required that the trigger event must "impede, prevent or delay the performance"; in contrast, the clause in *Thames Valley Power Ltd v Total Gas & Power Ltd* [2005] EWHC 2208 described the consequences as a party "unable wholly or in part to carry out any of its obligations".

51 See *Investors Compensation Scheme Ltd v West Bromwich Building Society* [1998] 1 WLR. 896 and for a general account of interpretation in English contract law, Hugh Beale (gen ed), *Chitty on Contracts* (33rd edn, Sweet & Maxwell, 2018) paras 13-041–13-107.

52 Moving house during the emergency period was permitted only "where reasonably necessary": The Health Protection (Coronavirus, Restrictions) (England) Regulations 2020, reg 6(2); it was permitted more generally from 13 May. For an account see House of Commons Library, 'Coronavirus: Advice on Home Moves' https://commonslibrary.parliament.uk/social-policy/health/diseases/coronavirus-advice-on-home-moves/ accessed 7 March 2021.

are warning that sellers who had to delay "completion" because they could not move out and therefore could not give "vacant possession" may be liable to the buyer.[53]

The absence of any doctrine of hardship or change of circumstances also leads to express provisions being included in some contracts. Not only are "Material Adverse Change" clauses common in corporate finance and mergers and acquisitions, but clauses calling for re-adjustment in the case of hardship are frequently found in longer-term contracts such as for oil and gas exploration or supply.

5. INSOLVENCY

Lastly we should point out that English law has a relatively liberal law of insolvency. We have neither the space nor the expertise to give a detailed account of English insolvency law, let alone to compare it to the law in other jurisdictions.[54] Suffice it to say that, provided that there has been no wrongdoing, businesspeople can "make a fresh start" as sole traders within a year and they may act as directors of another company unless they are disqualified for fraudulent or wrongful trading or as "unfit". Any parts of the business that remain viable can be sold off as going concerns by an administrator; this is often done within days of the administrator being appointed.[55] For consumers whose debts amount to less than £20,000 there is a simpler and much simpler and cheaper form of relief called a Debt Relief Order, which also results in most types of debts being wiped out after one year.[56]

---

53 E.g. Brachers LLP, 'What impact will coronavirus have on buying or selling a house?' https://www.brachers.co.uk/insights/what-impact-will-coronavirus-have-on-buying-or-selling-a-house accessed 10 March 2021. In many cases, however, neither party will be able to complete: if there is a "chain", the buyers may equally be unable to complete since they will only be able to pay the price once they have themselves given vacant possession to the person buying from them. Under cl 7.2.1 of the Standard conditions, "If there is default by either or both of the parties in performing their obligations under the contract and completion is delayed, the party whose total period of default is the greater is to pay compensation to the other party." In effect the liabilities will cancel each other out.

54 See Mariana Pargendler, 'The Role of the State in Contract Law: The Common-Civil Law Divide' (2018) 43 Yale J. Int'l L. 143, esp at 175–178.

55 This is done under a "pre-pack" arranged by the administrator before formal appointment: see, e.g. Julie Palmer, 'What company directors need to know about the Pre Pack Administration process' https://www.realbusinessrescue.co.uk/pre-pack-administration/process-and-procedure accessed 10 March 2021.

56 See Insolvency Service, 'Getting a Debt Relief Order' https://www.gov.uk/government/publications/getting-a-debt-relief-order/getting-a-debt-relief-order accessed 10 March 2021. The fee is £90.

6. NEW LEGISLATION OR OTHER FORMS OF REGULATION IMPACTING ON CONTRACTS

6.1. MEASURES WITH AN INDIRECT, BUT PRACTICAL EFFECT

There is not space to give a complete account of all the UK's responses to COVID-19 that will have an impact on contracts. The measures that are probably most important in practical terms are those involving income support. These have only an indirect effect on contracts, and we will briefly mention just two.[57]

First, Universal Credit, the principal benefit for those who are too ill to work, are looking for a job or have a low income,[58] has been made easier to apply for,[59] and somewhat more generous, in that the monthly amount has been increased and many of the deductions that can be made when the recipient owes money to the State or a third party were suspended unless a deduction was considered to be in the interest of the customer or the customer's family.[60]

Secondly, the Government has launched an extensive scheme for "Job Retention", under which employers may "furlough" workers on 80% of their pay up to £2,500 per month, and will be reimbursed by the Government.[61] The scheme has been extended to agency workers and in June a parallel scheme became available to the self-employed.[62] These schemes are "designed to help employers whose operations have been severely affected by coronavirus (COVID-19) to retain their employees and protect the UK's economy" rather than to protect employees, and employees have no right to be furloughed; but for very many employees the scheme has provided a lifeline – and even more so if the employer follows the Government's exhortation to pay the rest of the employee's salary. On 3 May 2020, HMRC said that 800,000 employers had

---

57 Other indirect effects will flow from Government-backed loans to businesses.

58 Universal Credit provides for living costs and the cost of renting a home (subject to local financial limits and a "bedroom tax" where the property is larger than is needed). It can also cover mortgage interest but only after a wait of 39 weeks. UC is paid in arrears, so claimants have to wait five weeks from when they apply before they will be paid. It is possible to get an "advance payment" but this must be repaid later.

59 Face-to-face interviews are no longer required and proof of identity has been simplified. In May 2020 it was reported that the relaxations have led to many fraudulent claims: see BBC News, 'Coronavirus: Benefit claims fraud could be £1.5bn' https://www.bbc.co.uk/news/business-52745983 accessed 7 March 2021.

60 See Department of Work and Pensions, 'Universal Credit: Third party payments creditor and supplier handbook' https://www.gov.uk/government/publications/how-the-deductions-from-benefit-scheme-works-a-handbook-for-creditors/universal-credit-third-party-payments-creditor-and-supplier-handbook accessed 7 March 2021.

61 HMRC, 'Check if you can claim for your employees' wages through the Coronavirus Job Retention Scheme' https://www.gov.uk/guidance/claim-for-wage-costs-through-the-coronavirus-job-retention-scheme accessed 7 March 2021.

62 HMRC, 'Check if you can claim a grant through the Self-Employment Income Support Scheme' https://www.gov.uk/guidance/claim-a-grant-through-the-coronavirus-covid-19-self-employment-income-support-scheme accessed 7 March 2021.

applied to use the scheme and 6.3m jobs were being covered.[63] The Government subsequently announced that the scheme would be extended until April 2021, and from August 2020 it was made more flexible, so that employers could bring employees back part-time and still receive support[64] – but employers would be expected to pay a percentage of the cost.

6.2. MEASURES WITH A DIRECT EFFECT ON CONTRACTS

The principal measures that have a more direct effect on contracts fall into a number of categories, namely: payment holidays, longer notice before termination of residential leases, suspension of enforcement and insolvency measures.

Three general points are worth making at the outset. First, the measures tend to be particularistic rather than relying on general provisions. This is a general characteristic of English law; as Bingham LJ said after referring to the civilian doctrine of good faith:

> English law has, characteristically, committed itself to no such overriding principle but has developed piecemeal solutions in response to demonstrated problems of unfairness.[65]

Secondly, there has been little direct interference with contract law or contract terms by means of legislation. Most of the measures involve regulation – though the practical effect may be to override the law. Thirdly, the changes tend to affect enforcement proceedings rather than the contractual obligations or rights of the parties.

We do find direct legislative interference with the terms of contracts in respect of residential tenancy agreements. For example, in the case of most privately-rented properties the landlord has been able to terminate the lease and obtain possession, without the tenant being in default or the landlord having to show a reason for the termination, after giving the tenant two months' notice.[66] This period is now extended to six months,[67] as are the notice periods required before eviction under many other types of residential tenancy.[68]

---

63 Delphine Strauss, 'Pay for more than 6m UK workers now covered by furlough scheme' https://www.ft.com/content/be2d317e-54f9-42b0-bf17-d4a9ae4d7489 accessed 7 March 2021 (noting that this total may have involved some double-counting where part-time workers are furloughed by more than one employer).

64 As with Germany's *Kurzarbeitergeld*.

65 *Interfoto Picture Library v Stilletto* [1989] QB 433, 439.

66 Housing Act 1988, s 21. The tenant is safe from termination only during the first six months.

67 Coronavirus Act 2020, Sch 29 para 7.

68 Coronavirus Act 2020, Sch 29.

The most important ground for evicting a tenant, non-payment of rent,[69] is not itself changed; instead, the courts issued a Practice Direction under which the possession proceedings that would have to be taken before the tenant can be evicted were suspended, until 20 September 2020.[70] Until then, eviction proceedings could only proceed in exceptional cases.[71] Since then the courts have been prioritising the most serious cases. These include cases with extreme alleged rent arrears accrued, that is, arrears equal to at least (i) 12 months' rent; or (ii) 9 months' rent where that amounts to more than 25% of a private landlord's total annual income from any source.[72] In addtion, until the end of March 2021 it is only in cases in which rent for six or more months is due that final "notices of evction" may be served.[73] Bailiffs were not permitted to enforce debts (including rent owed for commercial properties[74]) by seizing the debtor's assets for a similar period.[75]

Changes have also been made to insolvency, under the Corporate Insolvency and Governance Act 2020, which was introduced in Parliament on 20 May 2020[76] and received Royal Assent on 25 June 2020. Some of the changes were under discussion before COVID-19 struck: for example, to allow companies to apply for a 20-day moratorium to give them "breathing space", preventing "termination-on-insolvency" clauses operating during the moratorium or rescue proceedings and the introduction of a new restructuring procedure that can

---

69 Housing Act 1988, Sch 2, Ground 8 (e.g if rent paid monthly has not been paid for two months).

70 Initially under Practice Direction 51Z: Stay of Possession Proceedings, Coronavirus (as amended on 20 April 2020, to allow some proceedings, such as against trespassers, to continue), and now under Rule 55.29 (introduced under The Civil Procedure (Amendment No 2) (Coronavirus) Rules 2020 on 25 June 2020). The validity of Practice Direction 51Z was confirmed by the Court of Appeal in *Mehmet Arkin v Gary Ronald Marshall and others* [2020] EWCA Civ 620 (11 May 2020).

71 *Arkin v Marshall*, para 42. Eviction proceedings were not stayed in *Bernica Group v Mark Mann* (Newcastle County Court, 17 April 2020), in a case of serious anti-social behaviour where the tenant had already agreed to vacate the property (see Alice Richardson, 'Court of Appeal Holds 90-day Stay on Possession Proceedings Lawful' https://www.trinitychambers.co.uk/news/court-of-appeal-holds-90-stay-on-possession-proceedings-lawful/ accessed 29 May 2020).

72 See Ministry of Housing Comunities and Local Government, 'Guidance: Understanding the possession action process: A guide for private landlords in England and Wales', https://www.gov.uk/government/publications/understanding-the-possession-action-process-guidance-for-landlords-and-tenants/understanding-the-possession-action-process-a-guide-for-private-landlords-in-england-and-wales accessed 10 March 2021.

73 Ibid; Public Health (Coronavirus) (Protection from Eviction) (England) (No. 2) Regulations 2021, reg 2.

74 See Tribunals, Courts and Enforcement Act 2007, chapter 2.

75 Taking Control of Goods and Certification of Enforcement Agents (Amendment) (Coronavirus) Regulations 2020.

76 For a summary see Companies House, 'How the Corporate Insolvency and Governance Bill will help your business' https://www.gov.uk/government/news/how-the-corporate-insolvency-and-governance-bill-will-help-your-business accessed 10 March 2021.

involve "cram down" across certain classes of creditor. Other changes are clearly in response to the effects of the virus: for example, the temporary easements on filing requirements and Annual General Meetings, a ban on new petitions and statutory demands for three months and the suspension of directors' personal liability for wrongful trading (i.e. continuing to trade when the director knew or ought to have concluded that there was no reasonable prospect that the company would avoid going into insolvent liquidation[77]). Under section 12 of the Act,

> the court is to assume that the person is not responsible for any worsening of the financial position of the company or its creditors that occurs during the relevant period.[78]

Whilst this provision would provide some breathing space for directors, it would not affect the application of other provisions on the duties of directors under the Companies Act 2006.

For many consumers and very small businesses, it is the regulatory changes that will have the most effect on their contracts. The principal actor[79] is the Financial Conduct Authority, which now has responsibility for consumer credit – which, as we saw earlier,[80] includes credit given to sole traders and partnerships of no more than three persons. In regulating consumer credit, the FCA relies on both detailed rules, which are contained in the Consumer Credit Sourcebook referred to as "CONC", and on high level "Principles", such as Principle 6:

> A firm must pay due regard to the interests of its customers and treat them fairly.

If a regulated firm fails to comply with a rule, a private person who suffers harm as a result will have a claim for breach of statutory duty.[81] Breach of a Principle does not give rise to the same right, but the offending firm may be disciplined and the FCA may require it to pay compensation to parties who have been harmed. Equally importantly, complaints about the behaviour of firms may be referred to

---

77 Insolvency Act 1986, s 214.

78 The "relevant period" started on 1 March 2020 and ends on 30 September 2020 (s. 12(2)).

79 Other regulators are imposing parallel requirements, e.g. the energy regulator (Ofgen), see https://www.ofgem.gov.uk/system/files/docs/2020/06/open_letter_on_relaxing_network_charge_payment_terms_1.pdf accessed 10 March 2021. Contrast the role of the Competition and Markets Authority, which is concentrating on businesses that seem to be exploiting the situation to take advantage of people, for example by charging excessive prices, making misleading claims about their products or refusing to refund money after holiday, travel or other cancellations: see Competition and Markets Authority, 'CMA coronavirus (COVID-10) response' https://www.gov.uk/government/collections/cma-covid-19-response accessed 10 March 2021.

80 CCA 1974 s 8 ("an agreement between an individual ('the debtor') and any other person ('the creditor') …)".

81 Financial Services and Markets Act 2000, s 138D(2).

the Financial Ombudsman Service, which will ask whether the firm complied with the Principles, and if it did not do so may order it to pay compensation to the consumer. The result is that a firm that, for example, does not "treat its customers fairly" may be both disciplined and made to pay compensation – and the FCA or the Ombudsman may decide that it was not treating the customer even if as a matter of strict law the firm was only doing what it was entitled to. The practical effect is that the law is reformed by regulation.[82]

It is Principle 6 on which the FCA is mainly[83] relying when it is now requiring creditors to take steps to help consumers affected by COVID-19 and its effects. For example, with credit card repayments and personal loans, lenders were expected agree to a "payment holiday" of up to initially three and subsequently extended to six months (until the end of October 2020; extended later to allow applications until 31 March 2021), without affecting the consumer's credit rating,[84] and they must not call on guarantors to pay instead. The same applies to mortgages,[85] motor finance and "rent-to-own" (i.e. hire-purchase) agreements, and there must be no repossessions during the three-month period. Banks must allow customers who have a pre-arranged overdraft (a common arrangement even with customers who do not usually use the facility but want to avoid the risk of overdrawing accidentally and incurring the (often steep) charges for doing so) up to £500 interest-free for three months.[86] Under another branch of

---

82 A graphic example was provided by consumer insurance. The FSA (the relevant authority at the time) decided that a firm that sought to avoid an insurance policy on the ground of non-disclosure of a material fact by the insured – a basic rule of insurance law – was not treating the customer fairly if the insurer had not asked the consumer about the matter; and in such cases the Ombudsman would require the insurer to pay the claim. See Law Commissions, Joint Consultation Paper *Insurance Contract Law: Misrepresentation, Non-disclosure and Breach of Warranty by the Insured* (LCCP 182 /SLCDP 134, Law Commission, 2007) Part 3.

83 In relation to mortgages the FCA also relied on Principle 7 ("A firm must pay due regard to the information needs of its clients, and communicate information to them in a way which is clear, fair and not misleading") and MCOB 2.5A.1R ("A firm must act honestly, fairly and professionally in accordance with the best interests of its customer"), see FCA, 'Mortgages and coronavirus: information for consumers' https://www.fca.org.uk/consumers/mortgages-coronavirus-consumers accessed 10 March 2021. There have been some minor changes to the Rules also. For example, CONC 6.7.5. has been amended to remove the duty to set a minimum monthly repayment, if the consumer is allowed to defer payments because of the effects of the virus.

84 For a summary and links to more detailed pages see FCA, 'Coronavirus: information for consumers on personal loans, credit cards, overdrafts, motor finance and other forms of credit' https://www.fca.org.uk/consumers/coronavirus-information-personal-loans-credit-cards-overdrafts accessed 10 March 2021.

85 See FCA, 'Mortgages and coronavirus: information for consumers' https://www.fca.org.uk/consumers/mortgages-coronavirus-consumers accessed 10 March 2021 (this was amended to provide an extension for the further three months, and to allow applications to be made until 31 March 2021).

86 See FCA, 'Overdrafts and coronavirus: temporary guidance for firms' https://www.fca.org.uk/publications/finalised-guidance/overdrafts-coronavirus-temporary-guidance-firms accessed 10 March 2021.

its regulatory powers, the FCA has told insurers that the fact that the insured is now working from home, or has to leave a second home empty and unvisited, or is using a vehicle differently should not be used as a ground for rejecting claims on home or motor insurance. In some cases, a firm will not be treating a customer who is reliant on insurance fairly were the firm to refuse to renew the policy, even if the firm is not taking on new policies of the relevant kind.[87]

The concessions are limited in some respects, however. First, not all customers will benefit. The concessions apply only to those affected by the crisis – and it is easy to see cautious staff in creditor firms refusing to apply the COVID-19 concessions to people who were struggling already. Second, the concessions should not be applied "if the firm [reasonably] determines it is obviously not in the customer's interests to do so".[88]

> Where a customer was in pre-existing financial difficulty, our existing forbearance rules and guidance in CONC[89] would continue to apply. These would include for example the firm considering suspending, reducing, waiving or cancelling any further interest or charges, deferring payment of arrears or accepting token payments for a reasonable period of time.[90]

Thirdly, even when the debtor is granted a "payment holiday", interest will continue to accrue,[91] though in some cases the firm must review the rate of interest it is charging the consumer – for example with credit cards, on which the rate of interest can be very high.[92]

Fourthly, related provisions of the CCA continue to apply, such as the requirement that a creditor must give notice of sums in arrears to a debtor

---

87 See FCA, 'Insurance and coronavirus (Covid-19): our expectations of firms' https://www.fca.org.uk/firms/insurance-and-coronavirus-our-expectations accessed 10 March 2021; and, for further guidance directed to insurers, FCA, 'Coronavirus and customers in temporary financial difficulty: draft guidance for insurance and premium finance firms' https://www.fca.org.uk/publications/guidance-consultations/coronavirus-customers-temporary-financial-difficulty-draft-insurance-premium accessed 10 March 2021.

88 E.g. FCA, 'Credit cards (including retail revolving credit) and coronavirus: temporary guidance for firms' https://www.fca.org.uk/publications/finalised-guidance/credit-cards-retail-revolving-credit-coronavirus-temporary-guidance-firms accessed 10 March 2021.

89 See CONC 7.3.

90 FCA, 'Credit cards (including retail revolving credit) and coronavirus: temporary guidance for firms' https://www.fca.org.uk/publications/finalised-guidance/credit-cards-retail-revolving-credit-coronavirus-temporary-guidance-firms accessed 10 March 2021.

91 There is an exception for pay-day and similar high-cost short term credit, for which the holiday is interest-free but will last for one month only: FCA, 'Coronavirus: information for consumers on personal loans, credit cards, overdrafts, motor finance and other forms of credit' https://www.fca.org.uk/consumers/coronavirus-information-personal-loans-credit-cards-overdrafts accessed 10 March 2021.

92 See FCA, 'Credit cards (including retail revolving credit) and coronavirus: temporary guidance for firms' https://www.fca.org.uk/publications/finalised-guidance/credit-cards-retail-revolving-credit-coronavirus-temporary-guidance-firms accessed 10 March 2021.

after two missed instalments.[93] Consumer debtors who were granted a "payment holiday" have still been sent such warning notices, which are likely to confuse and worry them at the very least.[94] The introduction of the "payment holiday" through amendments to regulatory guidance is therefore not as neat as the government and FCA might have hoped – it seems that some legislative adjustments were needed to make the "payment holiday" work smoothly but this was not done.

There are of course many other measures to help consumers. Many of them have been arranged between industry, regulators and government on a voluntary basis: for example, the agreement reached with major phone and internet providers to ensure vulnerable customers or those self-isolating receive alternative methods of communication wherever possible if priority repairs to fixed broadband and landlines cannot be carried out, to treat customers who struggle with their bills fairly and appropriately as well as to remove data caps and provide more generous packages.[95]

We have said that the "concessions" required by the FCA were set initially to last three months and have been extended to six months. They may of course be extended again; but we have to hope that sooner or later things will begin to move back towards some sort of normality. Housing experts in particular fear that when the grace period is over and repossessions start again, many landlords may seek to evict tenants who have not been able to pay their rent. We are glad to see that at least some thought is being given to this. We saw earlier the protocol that "social" landlords are required to follow before evicting a tenant.[96] The Housing Minister has announced that all landlords will be required to do something similar and, interestingly, to act "in good faith" – a new departure for English housing law.[97]

However, it will not just be in housing that an end to the concessions will be a problem, especially if the end is a sudden "cliff edge" rather than a gradual "taper". We can expect many consumers to become bankrupt or use the simpler

---

93 s 86B (fixed-sum credit agreements) and s 86C (running account agreements) CCA 1974.

94 *The Guardian*, 'Borrowers on payment holidays to receive "thuggish" debt letters', 3 June 2020, https://www.theguardian.com/money/2020/jun/03/borrowers-on-payment-holidays-to-receive-thuggish-debt-letters accessed 10 March 2021.

95 See Department for Digital, Culture, Media and Sport, 'Government agrees measures with telecoms companies to support vulnerable consumers through COVID-19' https://www.gov.uk/government/news/government-agrees-measures-with-telecoms-companies-to-support-vulnerable-consumers-through-covid-19 accessed 10 March 2021.

96 Pre-Action Protocol for Possession Claims by Social Landlords (REF).

97 See Jack Simpson, 'Government's plan for rent protection after eviction ban at risk of being just "words on a page", says Shelter' https://www.insidehousing.co.uk/news/news/governments-plan-for-rent-protection-after-eviction-ban-at-risk-of-being-just-words-on-a-page-says-shelter-66386 accessed 10 March 2021. It is hoped that the Government will also follow through on its plan, announced in the Queen's Speech on 19 December 2019, to abolish the right of many private landlords under Housing Act 1988, s 21, simply to terminate a tenancy on 2 months (now three months) notice: see https://commonslibrary.parliament.uk/research-briefings/cbp-8658/ accessed 10 March 2021.

procedure of a "debt relief order" (DRO), under which their debts are written off after one year if their situation does not improve by then. But the current maximum for a DRO is £20,000. We are afraid that in order to cope with the expected numbers of insolvencies, the maximum for a DRO may need to be increased by several multiples.

6.3. CABINET OFFICE GUIDANCE ON RESPONSIBLE CONTRACTUAL BEHAVIOUR

A rather unusual document which was issued in early May 2020 is the Cabinet Office *Guidance on responsible contractual behaviour in the performance and enforcement of contracts impacted by the COVID-19 emergency.*[98] In this document, the government exhorts all individuals and businesses "to act responsibly and fairly in the national interest in performing and enforcing their contracts" (para 3) where these are affected by the COVID-19 pandemic. In particular, this means that contracting parties should be "reasonable and proportionate in responding to performance issues and enforcing contracts" (para 14), which entails "acting in a spirit of cooperation and aiming to achieve practical, just and equitable contractual outcomes having regard to the impact on the other party" (para 14). This guidance has no legal force, nor indeed any basis in law, and it is in obvious conflict with the general philosophy of English contract law. Whilst parties in a commercial relationship always have the flexibility to depart from their strict contractual obligations in the interest of their commercial relationship, such a decision needs to be weighed up against each party's wider interests and obligations to others (such as shareholders). This may explain the rather dismissive reactions to the document in blogs from law firms and barristers' chambers.[99]

---

98 Cabinet Office, 'Guidance on responsible contractual behaviour in the performance and enforcement of contracts impacted by the Covid-19 emergency' https://www.gov.uk/government/publications/guidance-on-responsible-contractual-behaviour-in-the-performance-and-enforcement-of-contracts-impacted-by-the-covid-19-emergency accessed 10 March 2021.

99 See, e.g. Charles Samek, 'Freedom of contract: Does it still exist?' https://littletonchambers.com/articles-webinars/freedom-of-contract-does-it-still-exist/; Katherine Calder and Mark Richard, 'Play fair children! – UK Cabinet Office publishes contract management guidance entreating all parties to act "reasonably" in managing Covid-19 issues' https://www.jdsupra.com/legalnews/play-fair-children-uk-cabinet-office-30763/; Fern Schofield, '"Play nicely, children": Cabinet Office guidance on responsible contractual behaviour during the pandemic' https://www.falcon-chambers.com/publications/articles/play-nicely-children-cabinet-office-guidance-on-responsible-contractual-beh; Norton Rose Fulbright, 'UK Government publishes guidance on "responsible contractual behaviour" applicable to all contracts impacted by COVID-19' https://www.nortonrosefulbright.com/de-de/wissen/publications/0a264bcc/uk-government-publishes-guidance-on-responsible-contractual-behaviour-applicable#2; all accessed 10 March 2021.

There will be situations in which each party needs some adjustment to the contract. Then we can expect the parties to negotiate voluntarily whether or not the contract, or for that matter the law, contains provisions for adjustment in changed circumstances. In this context, the *Guidance* may be relevant, as re-negotiation is more likely to leave each party reasonably satisfied if it was conducted in a co-operative way rather than in the adversarial manner that at least some Law Lords have envisaged as the norm for contractual negotiation.[100] In such a situation, mediation may help the parties to reach an acceptable compromise.[101] In other situations, however, there is less room for a mutually beneficial compromise. For example, there seem to be many disputes over whether what has happened is covered by the wording of business interruption insurance policies. This is more of a zero-sum game. If the parties each take the view that the position is unclear then of course they may readily settle for a sum representing part of the claim. If however each thinks it is likely to win if the matter goes to court, they will have little incentive to settle and indeed between them they may end up investing more in trying to win than the claim is worth.[102]

7. FUTURE "PINCH POINTS" FOR ENGLISH CONTRACT LAW

In this final section, we look ahead at those aspects of English contract law which we think might come under renewed strain because of the impact of the COVID-19 pandemic.

7.1. TEMPORARY IMPOSSIBILITY

There must be many parties who are temporarily unable to perform because of COVID-19 or the measures taken a result of it and who are not protected by a force majeure clause – not because they were deliberately taking the risk of being unable to perform but through oversight or because they are dealing on the other party's standard terms and were unable to get a force majeure clause included. We may expect some courts to be at least a little sympathetic, and it is just possible that the courts will find ways to excuse them from liability. There are a few exceptional cases, generally ignored in the books, in which courts have

100 See Lord Ackner in *Walford v Miles* [1992] 2 AC 128, 138 ("the concept of a duty to carry on negotiations in good faith is inherently repugnant to the adversarial position of the parties when involved in negotiations.")

101 See https://www.biicl.org/breathing-space accessed 10 March 2021.

102 See the analysis in George L. Priest, 'Breach and Remedy for the Tender of Non-conforming Goods' (1978) 91 Harvard LR 960.

held that a person who, for example, is too ill to work is not in breach, but that the other party may terminate the contract if the effects of the non-performance are serious.[103] The doctrinal basis of these cases is unclear; they are not cases of breach but equally they cannot be cases of frustration, as impossibility does not give the other party an option whether or not to terminate the contract. Rather, they seem to rest on interpretation of the particular contract. Perhaps an ingenious advocate in front of a sympathetic judge will be able to develop this into a more general form of relief.

7.2. SELF-INDUCED FRUSTRATION AND PRO-RATING

One of the limitations to the English doctrine of frustration is often referred to by the label "self-induced" frustration. In essence, if a party has brought about the frustrating event or its consequences for the particular contract,[104] the doctrine of frustration will not apply.[105] The cases that may need reconsideration were concerned with instances where one party had more limited resources than expected and had allocated them to other contracts. In the *Ocean Trawlers* case,[106] only three instead of five expected operating licences were issued. The licensee chose to have the three licences allocated to the licensee's own vessels rather than to two vessels that it had chartered, and claimed that the two charters were frustrated. In *The Super Servant Two*,[107] the owners had two barges and, when one was lost accidentally, they allocated the remaining barge to another contract and claimed that their contract with the plaintiffs was frustrated. In each case the court held that the contract was not frustrated as any impossibility was self-induced. The implications of this approach are that a supplier would, it seems, not be able to allocate whatever supplies or resources are available to some of its contracts and be discharged from its obligations in respect of those contracts it can no longer perform, even if the reason for its limited supplies are due to an event which would otherwise constitute frustration. Similarly, it

---

103 The best-known example is *Poussard v Spiers and Pond* (1876) 1 QBD 410, In that case, an opera singer had been engaged for a three-month run of a new opera, but was ill for the opening night and also several nights thereafter. It was held that the promoter was entitled to rescind the contract, even though the opera singer was *not* liable for breach of contract. (In contrast, in *Bettini v Gye* (1876) 1 QBD 183 it was said that at singer who did not attend rehearsals was in breach of contract (though not a sufficiently serious breach as to justify the other party in terminating the contract.) See similarly, *Minnevitch v Café de Paris (Londres) Ltd* [1936] 1 All ER 884 (employer temporarily unable to provide work). See Guenter Treitel, *Frustration and Force Majeure*, (3rd edn, Sweet & Maxwell 2014) para 5-059.

104 See the somewhat complex facts in *DGM Commodities Corp v Sea Metropolitan SA* [2012] EWHC 1984 (Comm).

105 *Maritime National Fish Ltd v Ocean Trawlers Ltd* [1935] AC 524.

106 *Maritime National Fish Ltd v Ocean Trawlers Ltd* [1935] AC 524.

107 *J Lauritzen AS v Wijsmuller BV (The Super Servant Two)* [1990] 1 Lloyd's Rep 1.

would not allow a supplier to pro-rate its available supplies among all customers and avoid liability for any shortfalls, however sensible a solution that might seem to be.

7.3. CONSIDERATION AND PERFORMANCE OF EXISTING CONTRACTUAL DUTIES

A third issue relates to contractual renegotiation. English law treats a variation to an existing contract as a new contract, so that consideration is required.[108] There is no problem over consideration if each party stands to benefit, or each gives up something, under the variation; nor if there are outstanding obligations on each side and the parties agree to rescind the original contract and replace it with a different set of obligations. However, if one party as a concession agrees to pay an additional sum if the other party simply completes performance of its original obligation, or if a creditor agrees to accept part-payment of a debt "in full satisfaction" (in other words, promises to release the debtor from any further obligation), the traditional approach was that there was no consideration and the promised concession was not binding.[109] It has long been recognised that these rules are unsatisfactory: as Lord Blackburn said in *Foakes v Beer*,

> ... all men of business, whether merchants or tradesmen, do every day recognise and act on the ground that prompt payment of a part of their demand may be more beneficial to them than it would be to insist on their rights and enforce payment of the whole.[110]

In *Williams v Roffey Bros & Nicholls (Contractors) Ltd*,[111] a contractor had promised additional payments to a struggling sub-contractor if the sub-contractor would complete the work in time for the contractor to avoid paying liquidated damages for late completion. The Court of Appeal, though purporting merely to distinguish earlier case law, effectively altered the law by holding that there was consideration if the contractor obtained a "practical benefit" from securing performance of only the sub-contractor's original obligation; and in *MWB*

---

108 There is not space to explain the doctrine of consideration here, but the essence of the doctrine is that a promise by one party is not enforceable unless the other party either does, or promises to do, something of value in exchange. For an explanation for civilian lawyers see J Cartwright, *An Introduction to the English Law of Contract for the Civil Lawyer* (3rd edn, Hart Publishing 2016) 131–143.

109 *Stilk v Myrick* (1809) 2 Camp 317 (promise to pay extra); *Foakes v Beer* (1883-84) LR 9 App Cas 605 (part payment of debt).

110 *Foakes v Beer* (1883-84) LR 9 App Cas 605, 622.

111 *Williams v Roffey Bros & Nicholls (Contractors) Ltd* [1991] 1 QB 1.

Business Exchange Centres v Rock Advertising Ltd[112] the Court of Appeal applied the same argument in a case of part-payment.[113] The *MWB* case was appealed, but the Supreme Court decided the case on the basis that the contract provided that variations were only to be effective if in writing, whereas the alleged variation was purely oral. However, Lord Sumption, speaking for the majority, contrived to cast the law on consideration for variations into doubt by saying on the one hand that the practical benefit obtained "was the very thing which the House of Lords held not to be adequate consideration in *Foakes v Beer*" and on the other that "*Foakes v Beer* ... is probably ripe for re-examination".[114] English contract lawyers were disappointed that the Supreme Court had refused to take the opportunity to sort out the law.[115] Perhaps it will get another opportunity to do so sooner than anyone thought.[116]

7.4. ECONOMIC DURESS

Lastly, as a result of the crisis, we can expect there to be cases in which party A states that it cannot or will not perform unless party B agrees to change the terms in A's favour, and B agrees because B feels that in the circumstances it has little choice. Later B may try to argue that the agreement to change the contract is voidable on the ground of "economic duress". Many of the economic duress cases have involved exactly this scenario; and it is established that if one party threatens to break the contract (an "illegitimate" threat) as a way of exacting a concession that it knows is not justified, and the other agrees only because it has no practical alternative, the variation can be avoided.[117] However, in some relevant respects the limits of the doctrine remain unclear, and in particular

112 *MWB Business Exchange Centres v Rock Advertising Ltd* [2016] EWCA Civ 553, [2017] QB 604, reversed (on other grounds) [2018] UKSC 24 [2018] 2 WLR 1603.

113 Although in *Re Selectmove Ltd* [1995] 2 All ER 531, the Court of Appeal had previously declined to apply *Williams v Roffey* to a part-payment of debt situation.

114 [2018] UKSC 24 at [18]. The doctrine of promissory estoppel, introduced into English law by Denning J in *Central London Property Trust v High Trees House Ltd* [1947] KB 130, is also relevant and indeed was applied by the CA in the *MWB* case; but it seems not to have been argued in the SC. It too is ripe for review, as it is uncertain in many respects; however, if sensible changes were made to the doctrine of consideration as applied to variations, promissory estoppel might no longer be needed.

115 In *Dan Simantob v Yacob Shavleyan t/a Yacob's Gallery* [2018] EWHC 2005 (QB), Kerr J assumed that the Supreme Court had not overruled *Williams v Roffey*, and that the part-payment of debt issue was governed by *Re Selectmove*.

116 For an interesting discussion of this case law from a Commonwealth perspective, see *Ma Hongjin v SCP Holdings Pte Ltd* [2020] SGCA 106 (Singapore Court of Appeal).

117 *North Ocean Shipping Company v Hyundai Construction, The Atlantic Baron* [1979] QB 705; *B & S Contracts and Designs Ltd v Victor Green Publications Ltd* [1984] ICR 419.

whether a threat to break a contract can ever be "legitimate" or justified.[118] If A genuinely cannot perform without an extra payment, because without the extra payment it is or will become insolvent, it is thought that the variation cannot be avoided: it can be argued that A has not made a threat but has issued a warning. But what if A wrongly but honestly believes it has legal grounds for demanding the concession? Or if A knows that it has no basis in law for its demand but honestly thinks the demand is justified commercially? Some years ago Dyson J suggested that a relevant factor is "whether the person allegedly exerting the pressure has acted in good faith or bad faith."[119] Perhaps there is a greater role for good faith in English law than is often admitted – though when Dyson J referred to good faith it is doubtful that he meant anything more demanding than the absence of fraud.

8. CONCLUSIONS

Despite the apparent inflexibility of English law when contracts are disputed by unforeseen events, the measures taken to soften the effects of COVID-19 involve little direct change to the law of contract, or indeed to their terms. Most of the measures so far taken involve temporary changes either to enforcement procedures or to the regulatory requirements that apply to consumer credit contracts of various kinds. Changes to regulatory requirements are a curious way of effectively altering the law for some categories of consumer while leaving the underlying legal principles untouched. It is not possible to explore the reasons for this approach fully here, but we suggest that it is in part due to the great reluctance on the part of English lawyers to change general contract law, which is what applies to most B2B contracts. This may be partly because law firms have invested heavily in "work arounds" (e.g. pre-drafted force majeure clauses for various types of contract) or barristers have invested in expertise at arguing around the rules, and neither wants to give up these competitive advantages. But we think that the principal reason for leaving the law somewhat inflexible is the fear that greater flexibility would mean requiring judges and lawyers to intervene more extensively in contracts and the way they are performed, and to

---

118 For a fuller discussion see Hugh Beale (gen ed), *Chitty on Contracts* (33rd edn, Sweet & Maxwell, 2018) paras 8-03–8-045.

119 *DSND Subsea Ltd v Petroleum Geo-services ASA* [2000] BLR 530 at [131]. The Court of Appeal has recently accepted that when a party threatens to do something that it is legally entitled to do (such as to refuse to renew a contract – "Legitimate Act Duress") the threat is not illegitimate, and the resulting contract will not be voidable unless the threat was made in bad faith (*Times Travel (UK) Ltd v Pakistan International Airlines Corporation* [2019] EWCA Civ 828).

apply broad standards – and that this would lead to uncertainty. Moore-Bick LJ made just this point when he said:

> There is in my view a real danger that if a general principle of good faith were established it would be invoked as often to undermine as to support the terms in which the parties have reached agreement.[120]

For this reason we do not expect the COVID-19 to have much effect, let alone a lasting effect, on general English contract law.

On the other hand, it is conceivable that the gradual development of a discrete consumer contract law[121] might be accelerated in the wake of COVID-19. It has been suggested that some of the changes made in response to COVID-19, together with the pre-existing rules for consumer credit agreements, might be indicative of an emerging principle of "social force majeure".[122] But such a principle would, much like good faith, meet the objection that it would cause more difficulties than it would solve and it seems very unlikely that the common law courts would take the initiative – so it would be a matter for Parliament rather than the courts.

---

120 *MSC Mediterranean Shipping Co SA v Cottonex Anstalt* [2016] 2 CLC 272, 291.

121 The Consumer Rights Act 2015, and the various, mostly EU-derived, statutory instruments regulating consumer contracts have already carved out a partial consumer contract law, although the separation between consumer and commercial contracts is far from complete.

122 See Iain Ramsay, 'Contract Law, social force majeure and adjusting consumer credit contracts' https://creditdebtandinsolvency.wordpress.com/2020/04/18/contract-law-social-force-majeure-and-adjusting-consumer-credit-contracts/ accessed 10 March 2021, referring to the notion of social force majeure developed by Thomas Wilhelmsson in '"Social force majeure" – A new concept in Nordic consumer law' (1990) 13 Journal of Consumer Policy 1.

"CORONAVIRUS CONTRACT LAW" IN SCOTLAND

Hector L. MacQueen*

This contribution describes the Scottish legislative response to the coronavirus pandemic, noting that the chief impact on contracts is most likely to arise from issues of the supervening illegality of particular kinds of activity normally carried out under contracts. Scottish law largely follows English law in its doctrine of frustration and its approach to force majeure clauses. This contribution accordingly suggests that the temporary interruptions to performance which the coronavirus legislation brings about may not be sufficient to discharge affected contracts. The Scottish courts may need rather to develop their very limited powers of equitable adjustment in response to changed but not necessarily frustrating circumstances. Some ways in which this might be done are suggested.

1. SOME SCENE-SETTING

A little scene-setting is necessary at the start. As a legal jurisdiction Scotland, although part of the United Kingdom for more than three centuries, has remained what it was before that union, a legal system and law wholly distinct from that of England and Wales and, indeed, what is now Northern Ireland. While much law enacted by the United Kingdom Parliament has applied throughout the united

---

* University of Edinburgh. The author is grateful for helpful comments by his colleagues, Dr D J Carr, Ms L Richardson and Professor A.J.M. Steven, and by Professor D.A.O. Edward, as well as for information provided by Scott Dickson.

territories (notably in taxation, welfare and commercial law), the situation is complicated by the variable systems of administrative and legislative devolution in Scotland, Wales and Northern Ireland. It is worth noting that there is no devolution of any kind to or within England; the United Kingdom is not a federation. The fundamental principle of Scottish devolution is that everything is devolved unless specifically reserved to the United Kingdom Government and Parliament. Amongst many other things, this means that Scottish private law and public health in Scotland are devolved matters, but not commercial law (which for present purposes includes consumer law).[1] Thus, for example, the Corporate Insolvency and Governance Act 2020, which gives some important protection from creditors and other reliefs from the requirements of company law for companies in difficulty thanks to the pandemic, is a United Kingdom Act that applies to the whole country.[2]

This background has been highlighted because it explains the sometimes-misunderstood role taken by the devolved Scottish Government in responding, first, to the threat, and then to the reality of the coronavirus pandemic in Scotland in the first half of 2020. Devolution means that the Scottish Government has the legal duty to deal with the Scottish outbreak, as do their Welsh and Northern Irish counterparts in their territories. The responsibilities of the United Kingdom Government are mainly limited to England. Entirely understandably and sensibly, the four Governments worked together from the outset of the crisis; but while the United Kingdom Government brought forward its Coronavirus Bill on 25 March 2020 elaborate provision was needed to make clear those provisions applying only to England and those applying in various different ways to the devolved territories.[3] With exceptions, the United Kingdom Act was to endure until 25 March 2022.[4] A week later the Scottish Parliament passed the Scottish Government's much shorter Coronavirus (Scotland) Bill, dealing with those matters requiring legislation that fell within devolved competence. The Scottish Act was however to expire on 30 September 2020 unless extended by Scottish Ministers to 31 March 2021 or (after 30 September 2020) to 30 September 2021.[5] Section 13 of the Act optimistically allowed Scottish Ministers to bring the Act's expiry forward in time from 30 September 2020. A further supplementary Act came into force on 26 May and was likewise to expire on 30 September unless extended or the expiry date is brought forward.[6] In both cases the expiry date was subsequently pushed back to 31 March 2021 with the continuing possibility of further extension to 30 September 2021. The secondary legislation which imposed much of the initial detail for the

1 For Scottish private law see Scotland Act 1998, s 126(4).
2 Most of this Act came into force on 26 June 2020.
3 Coronavirus Act 2020, s 100.
4 Coronavirus Act 2020, s 89.
5 Coronavirus (Scotland) Act 2020, s 12.
6 Coronavirus (Scotland) (No 2) Act 2020.

"lockdown" that began on 23 March showed the jurisdictional distinctions in their titles: the Health Protection (Coronavirus, Restrictions) (England) Regulations (SI 2020/350), the Health Protection (Coronavirus) (Restrictions) (Scotland) Regulations (SSI 2020/103), the Health Protection (Coronavirus Restrictions) (Wales) Regulations (SI 2020/353, W.80), and the Health Protection (Coronavirus Restrictions) Regulations (Northern Ireland Statutory Rules 2020/53). The Scottish Regulations have been replaced a number of times, and each of the replacements heavily amended during even brief lifespans.[7]

2. THE CONTENT OF THE EMERGENCY LEGISLATION

The separate Scottish legislation for the most part mirrors its English counterparts, however. In neither jurisdiction does the legislation have much to say of direct relevance to contract law (although the Corporate Insolvency and Governance Act 2020 does regulate termination clauses in supply contracts[8]). There is nothing to parallel the Singapore legislation giving temporary relief from the demands of performing certain types of contract where the main reason for non-performance is the COVID-19 pandemic or the operation of any rule of law made in connection with the pandemic.[9] What there is in Scotland generally limits what would otherwise be rights to enforce a contract or duties to pay contract debts. The limitations protect those who may be rendered especially vulnerable by loss of income arising from the inter-linking economic impact of job losses and business closures and suspensions following lockdown.

Both systems thus give courts and tribunals dealing with the eviction of dwelling house tenants by public and private sector landlords wide leeway during the subsistence of the Coronavirus Acts to deal with cases even where normally the landlord would have had an absolute right to evict albeit necessarily by way of court process.[10] More generally, in Scotland landlords entitled to terminate

---

7 The initial Regulations were amended 12 times before being replaced on 14 September 2020 by the Health Protection (Coronavirus) (Restrictions and Requirements) (Scotland) Regulations (SSI 2020/279) as amended from 25 September by the Amendment of the Health Protection (Coronavirus) (Restrictions and Requirements) (Scotland) Regulations 2020 (SSI 2020/300) and, from 9 October 2020, by the Health Protection (Coronavirus) (Restrictions and Requirements) (Additional Temporary Measures) (Scotland) Regulations 2020 (SSI 2020/318). These were replaced from 2 November 2020 by the Health Protection (Coronavirus) (Restrictions and Requirements) (Local Levels) (Scotland) Regulations 2020 (SI 2020/344). Their expiry date is 31 March 2021 but they had been amended 16 times up to 19 February 2021.

8 Corporate Insolvency and Governance Act 2020 ss 14–19.

9 Covid-19 (Temporary Measures) Act 2020 (No 14 of 2020), Singapore.

10 Coronavirus (Scotland) Act 2020, Sch 1; for the statutory law pre-crisis see Hector L. MacQueen and Lord Eassie (eds), *Gloag & Henderson The Law of Scotland* (14th edn, W Green 2017) paras 35.87, 35.102. Compare Coronavirus Act 2020, s 81 and Sch 9.

commercial leases for non-payment of rent must give notice to the tenant of their intention to terminate (normally, 14 days).[11] The 2020 Act extends the notice period to 14 weeks.[12] This seems less generous than the Coronavirus Act 2020, which in effect suspends the landlord's right of forfeiture or re-entry in business leases in England, Wales and Northern Ireland during the whole period of the coronavirus emergency measures.[13]

There are distinctive Scottish provisions. The six-week moratorium against further execution of judgment debts which a debtor obtains by applying for sequestration is extended to six months for the duration of the emergency period.[14] In the second Coronavirus (Scotland) Act, a new category of "student residential tenancy" was introduced to allow university students who had entered such tenancies to terminate them by reason of coronavirus if the landlord is given seven days' written notice.[15] This is a response to a situation which had apparently developed for some Scottish students after their universities' physical closure in mid-March 2020, ahead of the Government-imposed lockdown (which did not apply directly to universities).[16] Its relevance increased in autumn 2020 as students returned to their universities to find that they were "locked down" in their residences in order to control the spread of coronavirus on and from campuses when most if not all teaching was being conducted on-line rather than face-to-face.

3. PROTECTION IN PRE-EXISTING LEGISLATION

There should also be noticed at this point a number of other statutory provisions already in place pre-emergency which give the Scottish courts power to moderate the effect and enforcement of contracts, and which seem likely to be important as the impact of the coronavirus lockdown makes itself felt. The consumer protection measures referred to in the contribution on English law apply equally in Scotland, as United Kingdom measures where the Scottish Parliament has no devolved competence.[17] The Scottish legislation on residential leases has already been mentioned. The legislation on the enforcement of heritable securities (i.e. mortgages) requires the creditor to follow certain procedures in order to

---

11 See Law Reform (Miscellaneous Provisions) (Scotland) Act 1985, ss 4, 7(1).

12 Coronavirus (Scotland) Act 2020, Sch 7, paras 6–7.

13 Coronavirus Act 2020, ss 82, 83.

14 Coronavirus (Scotland) Act 2020, Sch 2.

15 Coronavirus (Scotland) (No 2) Act 2020, Sch 1, Part 1.

16 See Malcolm M. Combe, 'Scottish Landlord and Tenant Law and the Coronavirus (Scotland) (No 2) Act' (*Basedrones* 3 June 2020) https://basedrones.wordpress.com/ accessed 4 March 2021.

17 See the contribution by Hugh Beale and Christian Twigg-Flesner in this volume.

realise the security on the debtor's default or insolvency but otherwise subjects the process to no external controls. The otherwise potentially robust nature of the creditor's powers of enforcement is however tempered in relation to land used to any extent for residential purposes by the Home Owner and Debtor Protection (Scotland) Act 2010. The creditor must proceed by way of an application to a court and comply with certain pre-action requirements. The debtor may oppose the application, and certain individuals resident at the property but having no title to it, including a spouse, civil partner or cohabitant, are entitled to intervene.[18] The court must be satisfied that it is reasonable in the circumstances of the case to grant the application, and is also to have particular regard to certain factors, including the nature of and reasons for the debtor's default, the debtor's ability to fulfil its obligations within a reasonable time, any action by the creditor to assist the debtor, and the ability of the debtor and his/her household to obtain reasonable alternative accommodation.[19] If the debtor is subject to a bankruptcy process, the trustee in bankruptcy must obtain the consent of the debtor's spouse or civil partner to any sale of the family home. Should that consent not be forthcoming, the trustee may seek a judicial permission to sell. In deciding the matter, the judge takes into account the needs and financial resources of the spouse or civil partner, the debtor's children, the interest of the creditors and the length of time for which the family home was used as a residence.[20]

It is to be noted, however, that there is no similar protection available where the property is a commercial or agricultural one. Yet the crisis created by the lockdown for farming and other businesses is just as substantial for its victims as it is for the individual householder. Before the crisis the Scottish Law Commission was examining the rules on enforcement of heritable securities with a view to reform, and that review continues.[21] It is possible that the coronavirus crisis will bring the issue of judicial control and official supervision of *all* such enforcement rights to the fore in its thinking on this subject.[22] But it will be some time before the law reform process is completed, and even longer before it is translated into legislation; and by then it may be too late to ameliorate the effects of the present crisis. There is some contrast with the position where a business's debts are secured by way of a floating charge, the enforcement of which

18 Conveyancing and Feudal Reform (Scotland) Act 1970, ss 24B and 24C.

19 1970 Act, s 24(5)–(7). See Mark Higgins, *The Enforcement of Heritable Securities* (2nd edn, Sweet & Maxwell 2016) paras 7.5–7.11.

20 Bankruptcy (Scotland) Act 2016, s 113.

21 See Scottish Law Commission, *Heritable Securities: Pre-Default* (Discussion Paper No 168, 2019). A second paper, on enforcement, will follow later, and the project is expected to complete a report and recommendations by 2023: see https://www.scotlawcom.gov.uk/law-reform/law-reform-projects/heritable-securities/ accessed 4 March 2021.

22 See the comparative research paper prepared by Dr John MacLeod for the Commission and available on the Commission website cited in the previous footnote.

is normally placed in the hands of an independent "administrator". The exercise of the administrator's extensive powers is aimed at rescuing the debtor company as a going concern and achieving better results for the company's creditors as a whole and not just the holder of the floating charge.[23]

4. IMPACT OF CORONAVIRUS REGULATION ON CONTRACT PERFORMANCE

While Scottish contract law is generally not affected by the legislation introduced specifically in response to the coronavirus crisis, this is not true for many areas of activity to which contract law is highly relevant. The Health Protection (Coronavirus) (Restrictions) (Scotland) Regulations set out a number of prohibitions on various forms of business and social activity, backed up by police enforcement powers and criminal sanctions. The overall aim is to slow, control and eliminate as much as possible community transmission of the coronavirus. People were generally required to remain at home unless their work could not be carried out there or they had another reasonable excuse to move outside. Many businesses whose characteristic feature is that in their nature the ordinary conduct of business involves physical proximity with and interaction between several persons not members of the same household were compelled to close. Others were allowed to remain open, provided that they took all reasonable measures to ensure "social distancing" between customers inside and immediately outside their premises Hence the widely strung-out queues outside supermarkets, which are among the most enduring images of the reality of lockdown. Many businesses were, however, able to continue by providing for online sales with delivery by post or courier to customers' homes.

The Regulations did not entirely cut off people's capacity to enter or perform contracts. They might also continue to be formed remotely, whether or not with the permitted businesses already mentioned. The relatively newly introduced possibility of executing documents in counterpart and delivering them electronically facilitated completion of commercial contracts.[24]

---

23 See the Insolvency Act 1986, Sch B1 (added by the Enterprise Act 2002). For discussion, see Alistair D.J. MacPherson, *The Floating Charge* (Edinburgh Legal Education Trust [ELET] 2020) ch 3.

24 See the Legal Writings (Counterparts and Delivery) (Scotland) Act 2015, the background to which is in the Scottish Law Commission's *Report on Execution in Counterpart* (Scot Law Com No 231, 2013). See also Burness Paull LLP, 'Covid-19 Signing in Counterpart and Electronic Documents', 26 March 2020 https://www.burnesspaull.com/insights-and-events/news/covid-19-signing-in-counterpart-and-electronic-documents accessed 4 March 2021. I disagree with some of this article's comments about legal limitations to the possibility of counterpart execution.

5. CONTRACTS AND SUPERVENING CHANGES IN CIRCUMSTANCE

The incidence of the coronavirus by itself raises relatively few problems. One problem that may arise is the death from the illness of a party either negotiating or performing a contract. It is thought that in Scots law, unless the postal acceptance rule applies to conclude a contract before the event, the death of either offeror or offeree before acceptance means that the offer falls and ceases to be capable of acceptance.[25] Death of a party, however, does not have such a drastic effect on concluded contracts except those where the deceased's ongoing performance was highly personal in nature, as in employment, partnership, agency, a contract for services, and the grant of a guarantee. Even here, however, the contract itself may and commonly does contain provisions to govern the situation.

The supervening illegality of contracts that had already been formed before the relevant legislation came into force seems the likeliest question to be dealt with in litigation once the emergency period ends. On this subject, modern Scots law, having started from a general position that a contract was unaffected by its ceasing to be capable of performance,[26] has now very largely adopted from English law its doctrine of frustration of contract discharging the parties' obligations of performance thenceforth.[27] It has also followed the narrow approach of the English courts in the doctrine's application; the reader is referred to the contribution on English law for further discussion.[28] Likewise for the approach of Scottish courts to force majeure clauses, which is as restrictive as that of their English counterparts.[29] It seems unlikely that either frustration

---

25 Hector L. MacQueen and Joe Thomson, *Contract Law in Scotland* (5th edn, Bloomsbury 2020) para 2.51.

26 See James Dalrymple Viscount Stair, *Institutions of the Law of Scotland* (first published 1681, EUP 1981) I, x, 13; also Andrew McDouall Lord Bankton, *Institute of the Laws of Scotland* (first published 1751–3, Stair Society 1993–5) I, iv, 8; and John Erskine, *Institute of the Law of Scotland* (first published 1773, ELET 2014) III, iii, 84–6. Even before the times of the Scottish institutional writers there would have been familiarity with the impact upon contracts of measures to control the spread of infectious disease: see John Ritchie, 'Quarantine for Plague in Scotland During the Sixteenth and Seventeenth Centuries' (1948) 55 *Edinburgh Medical Journal* 691 (a reference for which I am grateful to Thomas Owen Clancy); also Andrew J.M. Steven, *Pledge and Lien* (Avizandum 2008) paras 3.43 and 3.44 on pledge and plague in sixteenth-century Edinburgh.

27 See William W. McBryde, *The Law of Contract in Scotland* (3rd edn, W Green 2007) ch 21; *Laws of Scotland: Stair Memorial Encyclopaedia*, vol 15 (Butterworths 1996, hereafter *SME*) paras 880–889; MacQueen and Thomson, *Contract Law*, paras 5.63–5.86; S.C. Styles, 'Contracts and Coronavirus' 2020 *Scots Law Times (News)* 99, 109 (2 parts).

28 See the contribution by Hugh Beale and Christian Twigg-Flesner in this volume.

29 McBryde, *Contract*, paras 21.13–18; MacQueen and Thomson, *Contract Law*, paras 4.82–4.83, 5.84–5.85.

or force majeure will apply to any contract formed before the lockdown began unless completion of its performance was due within the lockdown period.

There are some differences or uncertainties about this subject in Scots law. It is not clear how accepted if at all is the idea of "frustration of purpose" as first developed in the English "Coronation cases", especially *Krell v Henry*.[30] As settled in the great *Cantiere San Rocco* case in 1923, economic imbalances left by the discharge of a frustrated contract will be worked out as far as possible by way of the common law of unjustified enrichment;[31] the Law Reform (Frustrated Contracts) Act 1943 does not extend to Scotland and contracts governed by Scots law. Finally, it is perhaps still not entirely clear whether the Scottish courts have any more general power of "equitable adjustment" by which they could deal with the consequences of frustration or, indeed, with the problems that can be caused for a contract by post-formation changes in circumstances that do not frustrate the contract. The last, it is thought, is the problem most likely to confront Scots contract law as a result of the coronavirus pandemic and the ensuing lockdown.

6. EQUITABLE ADJUSTMENT

The argument that the Scottish courts have a power of equitable adjustment, at least in frustration cases, was first made extra-judicially in 1946 by Lord Justice-Clerk Cooper (as he then was).[32] He may have been inspired by some remarks of the Scottish House of Lords judge, Lord Macmillan, in the 1943 *Fibrosa* case in England:

> [T]he law may endeavour to effect an equitable adjustment between the parties so as to restore each as far as may be to the position which he occupied before he entered into the contract and by a process of give and take to mitigate the consequences of the contract having proved abortive. … [But] to attempt to restore matters in their entirety is to attempt the impossible. The hands of the clock cannot be turned back. Things cannot be as if they had not been. At best some sort of equitable accommodation can be achieved which must inevitably fall short of complete justice.[33]

---

30 McBryde, *Contract*, paras 21.31–21.34. Cf Laura J. Macgregor, 'The Effect of Unexpected Circumstances on Contracts in Scots and Louisiana Law' in Vernon Valentine Palmer and Elspeth Christie Reid (eds), *Mixed Jurisdictions Compared: Private Law in Louisiana and Scotland* (EUP 2009) 244–280, 266–268. *SME*, vol 15 para 886 suggests that "Perhaps, where there exists only one conceivable purpose for making a contract, such as the viewing of a very special event, then its cancellation should constitute frustration."

31 McBryde, *Contract*, paras 21.44–21.48. The leading case is *Cantiere San Rocco SA v Clyde Shipbuilding & Engineering Co* 1923 SC (HL) 105.

32 Lord Cooper, 'Frustration of Contract in Scots Law' (1948) 28(3) *Journal of Comparative Legislation* 1 (reproduced in his *Selected Papers 1922–1954* (Oliver & Boyd 1957) 124, the version referred to henceforth).

33 *Fibrosa Spolka Akcyjna v Fairbairn Lawson Combe Barbour Ltd* [1943] AC 32 (HL), 58–59.

Macmillan's comments seemed, however, to envisage only restitution as the means of making equitable adjustment between the parties to the frustrated contract. Taking a historical approach that stretched back in its examination of sources to the beginning of the seventeenth century, Cooper went further, picking out in particular the concept of risk:

> *Res perit domino* was the brocard to which appeal was often made ... the question which the courts were in use to put to themselves was – On whom should the risk of this casualty fall?[34]

The courts had established by the seventeenth century at latest a doctrine for the contract of hire whereby in some circumstances the risk of subsequent events was held to fall on neither party and the contract was thereupon discharged. *Rei interitus* applied chiefly in leases of land, whereby the destruction of the subject matter brought the contract to an end, but could also apply to hire of moveables.[35] In Cooper's own time the courts had recognised that the concept also applied to the sterilisation of the subjects such as occurred through military requisition of the land for indeterminate periods of time.[36]

But in some instances where the destruction of the hire subjects was partial rather than total the courts' approach to the matter was (and still is, insofar as the contract does not provide otherwise) to abate the amount of rent payable rather than either to discharge or leave the contract in full effect. Abatement is not a matter of setting off against the liability for rent the tenant's claim to have the subjects repaired by the landlord (a right which also exists unless the lease otherwise provides). Rather the abatement is a proportionate reduction of the rent due when unanticipated events beyond either party's control mean that the full subjects are no longer available to the tenant. Even if a tenant is contractually liable to carry out repairs to damaged subjects, that can only extend to such repairs as were within the parties' contemplation at the time of contracting.[37]

Lord Cooper thought that these rules extended beyond leases and made unnecessary the War Damage to Land (Scotland) Act 1939 under which the courts were given power to modify or suspend, not only leases, but also dispositions (sales) or heritable securities (mortgages) affecting subjects destroyed in whole

---

34 Cooper, 'Frustration of Contract' 126.

35 Cooper did not cite authority; but see Stair, *Institutions*, I, xv, 2–3; Bankton, *Institute*, I, xx, 1, 13–19; Erskine, *Institute*, III, iii, 15; *Baron David Hume's Lectures 1786–1822* (6 vols, Stair Society 1939-58), ii, 80–82, 91–93. George Joseph Bell, *Principles of the Law of Scotland* (4th edn, first published 1839, Avizandum 2010) §29, generalised the principle across all contracts. It is standard modern practice to contract out of *rei interitus* in commercial leases.

36 The major cases (in neither of which Cooper played any part) are *Tay Salmon Fisheries Ltd v Speedie* 1929 SC 593 (First Division) and *Mackeson v Boyd* 1942 SC 56 (First Division).

37 See *Gloag & Henderson* paras 11.08, 13.06, 35.08 for the modern authorities.

or in part by war damage.[38] As the Lord Advocate, the UK Government's principal Scottish law officer, at the time of the Act, Cooper's comment that "[i]t sometimes happens – *experto crede* – that an Act has to be applied to Scotland simply because a like Act has already been applied to England" may suggest that the 1939 Act was introduced against his professional advice.[39] Cooper also argued that the rules on the effect of death in contracts for the hire of work, referred to above, were an instance of the doctrine of *rei interitus*.[40] If the relevant rules developed more in the law of property and particular contracts rather than in the general law of contract, greater generalisation was possible and to be encouraged in the light of the problems thrown up by successive world wars for the law of contract.

Unfortunately, perhaps, Cooper had no opportunity to develop his ideas any further, and it is unclear how far he would have taken them; for example, in recognising the possibility of the court adjusting the outcomes of contracts in circumstances not amounting to frustration. He decided one frustration case during the Second World War in a way perhaps less flexible than his later article suggested would be appropriate. In *James B Fraser v Denny Mott & Dickson*[41] the parties in 1929 embodied in a single document a combination of what today would be called a "requirements" agreement with regard to the supply of particular types of timber, a lease of the purchasers' timber yard to the supplier, and an option for the supplier/lessee to buy the purchasers' timber yard outright should either party give notice of termination of the contract. The contract had no definite limits of time. Upon the outbreak of war in September 1939 the parties were required by emergency legislation to cease trading, although the supplier continued in occupation of the purchaser's timber yard. The Second Division of the Court of Session, headed by Lord Justice-Clerk Cooper, held that there was a single contract which had been entirely frustrated by delay of a continuing and unforeseeably long duration by at latest July 1941 (when the purchasers had sought to terminate the agreement). On the footing that the purchasers' notice of termination had been unnecessary since the trading arrangement was already frustrated so that the pre-condition for the option's exercise did not and could not arise, the court rejected a holding at first instance that while the trading part of the contract was frustrated the option remained in force. Cooper's judgment left no door ajar for the possibility of partial frustration. The actual decision was

[38] War Damage to Land (Scotland) Act 1939, s 4 (still in force). See also the War Damage to Land (Scotland) Act 1941, s 1 (also still in force) under which no rent was payable by the tenant of a dwelling house not in occupation as a result of war damage, while where the tenant remained in occupation but the accommodation in the house was substantially reduced by war damage, the rent was to be likewise reduced.

[39] Cooper, 'Frustration of Contract' 131; see the Landlord and Tenant (War Damage) Act 1939, ss 1 and 2 for England & Wales (still in force).

[40] Cooper, 'Frustration of Contract' 126.

[41] *James B Fraser v Denny Mott & Dickson* 1943 SC 293 (Second Division).

later affirmed in the House of Lords, but some of the judges there were more open to the possibility that not all provisions in a contract might necessarily fall victim to its frustration.[42]

Partial frustration might still be a usefully flexible response to some cases of unanticipated and unforeseeable changes in circumstance.[43] An old decision mentioned in the *Cantiere* case, but not referred to by Cooper, is *Ogilvy v Hume* in 1683, where an apprentice's master died three years into a five-year apprenticeship. It was held that the apprentice need not pay the two-year balance of his apprenticeship fee.[44] A similar decision is *Cutler v Littlejohn* in 1711.[45] But in *Shepherd v Innes* in 1760, where it was the apprentice who died, the master was held able to recover the full apprenticeship fee on the basis that no fault could be attributed to him in the circumstances.[46] In *Rule v Reid*, decided in 1707, Rule had before his death promised to pay Reid for arranging his funeral and educating his children. While Reid had arranged the funeral, he became too ill to see to the children's education and eventually died. His executors' claim to payment of the sum in full was upheld, on the basis that Reid had arranged the funeral and had accepted the care of the children.[47]

A further possibility not noted in Cooper's article was the potential application of the doctrine of mutuality of contract, under which if a party does not perform its side of the contract the other party need not perform its reciprocal obligations, while a party that is not performing cannot compel performance by the other party. For a long time, the doctrine has been viewed as part of the law of breach of contract.[48] But it is not so confined in its earliest statements.[49] The potential benefit of recognising its operation in frustration of contracts would be that the obligations of performance are suspended rather than discharged where the initial non-performance was attributable to relevantly changed external circumstances since the contract's conclusion.

---

42 *James B Fraser v Denny Mott & Dickson* 1944 SC (HL) 35, 39 (Viscount Simon), 48 (Lord Wright), both citing as an example *Leiston Gas Co v Leiston-cum-Sizewell Urban District Council* [1916] 2 KB 428 (CA; never overruled). Lords Macmillan and Porter appear to be against their colleagues' view at pp 41–42 and 51–52, respectively.

43 McBryde, *Contract*, para 21.45, lists contract terms which may survive frustration, such as arbitration clauses. MacQueen and Thomson, *Contract Law*, para 5.64, suggests that frustration discharges only parties' obligations of performance, not the contract itself; hence the contract can still regulate in post-frustration circumstances.

44 *Ogilvy v Hume* (1683) 2 Brown's Supplement 34 (Court of Session).

45 *Cutler v Littlejohn* (1711) Mor 583 (Court of Session).

46 *Shepherd v Innes* (1760) Mor 589 (Court of Session).

47 *Rule v Reid* (1707) Mor 6364 (Court of Session).

48 McBryde, *Contract*, paras 20.44–20.61; MacQueen and Thomson, *Contract Law*, paras 6.8–6.11.

49 See, e.g. Erskine, *Institute*, III, iii, 86: "No party in a mutual contract, where the obligations on the parties are the causes of one another, can demand performance from the other, if he himself either cannot or will not perform the counterpart; for the mutual obligations are considered as conditional." Note too Stair, *Institutions*, I, x, 16; and Bankton, *Institute*, I, xi, 13. Bell, *Principles*, §71, moves the doctrine more in the direction of breach of contract.

The arguments that Cooper did advance in his article have not yet commanded general acceptance. Today the rent abatement cases are seen typically as exceptions to a general rule that either there is frustration and discharge, or the loss lies where it falls.[50] As Saul Miller rightly pointed out in 2004, generally contractual risk rules "simply determine which one of the contracting parties bears the entire loss."[51] Thus in *Sloan's Dairies v Glasgow Corporation*,[52] for example, where fire seriously damaged the subjects of a sale of land before the buyer could take possession, it was held that risk had passed from the seller upon the contract's conclusion and that the buyer was accordingly liable for the full price. No argument for its abatement was made to the court. Miller argues accordingly that only statutory intervention can introduce a satisfactory loss apportionment scheme for the law on frustration.[53] In the third (2007) edition of his contract textbook, however, Bill McBryde wrote that the Scottish courts have "all the requisite powers" needed to effect reasonable adjustments beyond the reversal of unjustified enrichment, and cited a case in which a party to a contract frustrated for it by the acts of the other party was held entitled to an award of *quantum meruit* for work done prior to the frustration.[54] Laura Macgregor on the other hand said in 2009 that "a modern Scottish court is likely to react with surprise to the suggestion that it possesses such a power."[55]

The question was finally put to the Scottish courts in 2011, and Macgregor's scepticism borne out, in the case of *Lloyds TSB Foundation for Scotland v Lloyds Banking Group plc.*[56] This arose from the financial crash of 2008. TSB Bank had previously set up a charitable foundation (F) to which it made annual payments based upon a certain percentage of the pre-tax profits shown in its annual accounts, with a minimum payment each year of about £38,000. Bank L merged with TSB Bank in 1995 and maintained F thereafter. In 2002 a new accounting requirement came in under which L's annual accounts had to show in the profit and loss account a sum for any "negative goodwill"; that is, the amount by which the capital value of an asset acquired during the year exceeded what had been paid for it where that was the case. During the banking and financial crisis of 2008–2009 Bank L acquired another bank (HBOS) which, although of

---

50 *Gloag & Henderson*, para 11.08.

51 Saul Miller, 'Unjustified Enrichment and Failed Contracts' in Reinhard Zimmermann, Daniel Visser and Kenneth Reid (eds), *Mixed Legal Systems in Comparative Perspective: Property and Obligations in Scotland and South Africa* (OUP 2004) 437–468, 454–455.

52 *Sloan's Dairies v Glasgow Corporation* 1977 SC 223.

53 See also Angelo D.M. Forte, 'Economic Frustration of Commercial Contracts: A Comparative Analysis with Particular Reference to the United Kingdom' [1986] *Juridical Review* 1.

54 McBryde, *Contract* para 21.48. The case is *Head Wrightson Aluminium Ltd v Aberdeen Harbour Commissioners* 1958 SLT (Notes) 12 (Outer House).

55 Macgregor, 'Effect of Unexpected Circumstances' 274.

56 *Lloyds TSB Foundation for Scotland v Lloyds Banking Group plc* [2011] CSOH 105, 2012 SLT 13; [2011] CSIH 87, 2012 SC 259; [2013] UKSC 3, 2013 SC (UKSC) 169.

high capital value, was confronted with liabilities which would probably have bankrupted it but for the takeover. The price paid was therefore much less than the acquisition's capital value, by some £11.173 billion. The extreme negative goodwill of this rescue operation meant that the 2010 accounts showed Bank L in substantial profit although otherwise on its trading activities it too had suffered severe losses. F claimed the sum produced by calculating the percentage of the profit to which it was apparently entitled on the wording of the contract, some £3.5 million. Bank L, as well as arguing about the proper interpretation of the contract, made a submission that Scots law either already recognised, or should recognise, a doctrine termed "equitable adjustment" enabling the courts to address fairly such cases of changed circumstances. It was accepted that the circumstances were not such as to give rise to frustration of the contract.

At first instance in the Outer House of the Court of Session Lord Glennie rather bluntly dismissed the argument for a power of equitable adjustment: "I am not persuaded that there is such a doctrine in Scots law."[57] Part of the reasoning supporting this conclusion was that there was no equivalent doctrine in English law, an approach rightly criticised by Macgregor.[58] On appeal, the First Division of the Court of Session declared that "We are unable to find in Scots law any general doctrine of 'equitable adjustment' which would allow the court to moderate the obligation contractually owed by the respondent to the reclaimer."[59] The court added:

> While it appears that certain European jurisdictions do have some form of equitable adjustment of contracts, there is, as yet, no foundation for it, as a generality, in Scots law. It would be beyond the proper scope of judicial power to develop it in any way which would assist the respondent in this case.[60]

When the case reached the UK Supreme Court, Bank L's argument for a doctrine of equitable adjustment was scarcely needed, because it won the case as a matter of the contract's interpretation. But the Scottish judge Lord Hope of Craighead decided to address the argument in some detail. Following that analysis, his conclusion was:

> [T]he proposition that the court can equitably adjust a contract on the basis that its performance, while not frustrated, is no longer that which was originally contemplated is not part of Scots law. To hold otherwise would be to undermine

57 [2011] CSOH 105, 2012 SLT 13, [90].

58 Laura J. Macgregor, 'Long Term Contracts, Changing Circumstances and Interpretation', *Edinburgh Centre for Commercial Law Blog*, 31 July 2011 https://www.ecclblog.law.ed.ac.uk/2011/07/31/long-term-contracts-changing-circumstances-and-interpretation/ accessed 4 March 2021.

59 [2011] CSIH 87, 2012 SC 259, [28].

60 Ibid [29].

the principle enshrined in the maxim *pacta sunt servanda* which lies at the root of the whole of the law of contract. I see no need for this and, as there is no need for it, I would reject the suggestion that the court should assume that function.[61]

7. STILL ROOM FOR EQUITABLE ADJUSTMENT?

Although Lord Hope's remarks are obiter, and not part of the reasoning supporting the actual decision in the *Lloyds TSB* case, they obviously carry considerable weight. A chink of light was however left open for future argument about equitable adjustment by his acknowledgement that "[a]daptability has a part to play in any civilised system of law", and that his conclusion on the argument before him was "not the occasion to cast doubt on the ability of Scots law to find equitable solutions to unforeseen problems."[62] Lord Hope would thus seem to have a more optimistic view of judicial power to develop the law to meet new circumstances than his colleagues below in the First Division of the Court of Session.

Lord Hope also conceded that the application of enrichment principles to deal with frustrated contracts was an example of an equitable adjustment, and he noted from the law of leases the abatement of rent cases cited by Lord Cooper.[63] He additionally referred to the case of *Wilkie v Bethune*, in which a farm servant was to be paid partly in money and partly in potatoes, but the great potato blight of 1846 led the farmer to refuse to fulfil the latter part of his obligation, and the court ordered him instead to pay the servant the money equivalent to ensure the servant's "sustentation", i.e. that he could feed himself and his household. Lord Hope held that the case was an exceptional one, however, and not the source of any general principle.[64]

It may also be said that the *Lloyds TSB Foundation* case was not the best one in which to develop any notion of equitable adjustment in Scots law. This is so even if the collapse and near-collapse of many banks in 2008, and the concomitant threat to the entire global financial system, looks major enough to qualify as of a sufficiently significant nature to trigger change of circumstance rules in relation to contracts the balance of which was disturbed by these events. But as Lord Hope pointed out, the problem in the case arose from Bank L's own decision in the crisis to acquire HBOS;[65] the difficulty was, as it were, self-induced.

---

61 [2013] UKSC 3, 2013 SC (UKSC) 169, [48].

62 [2013] UKSC 3, 2013 SC (UKSC) 169, [43].

63 The cases actually cited in *Lloyds TSB* were *Muir v McIntyres* (1887) 14 R 470 (First Division) and *Sharp v Thomson* 1930 SC 1092 (Second Division).

64 *Wilkie v Bethune* (1848) 11 D 132 (First Division).

65 [2013] UKSC 3, 2013 SC (UKSC) 169, [46]. Bank L was however under immense Government pressure to save HBOS from collapse: see Ray Perman, *Hubris: How HBOS Wrecked the Best Bank in Britain* (Birlinn 2012), ch 18 ('Apocalypse Now').

Nor was there any suggestion that the sum involved would reduce Bank L finally to its knees, with all the deleterious consequences that would involve; were it otherwise, the bank would probably not have undertaken the expensive risk of litigating the matter all the way to the Supreme Court. The payment was a "one-off" brought about by circumstances which posed problems for the bank for one year only. Bank L was thus trying to escape from a bargain which would work out badly for it at a particular moment if it lost on the interpretation point. But as the same bargain might well go bad in future for F, there was no case in equity for allowing L to escape at this particular point.[66]

The *Lloyds TSB* case can thus be read more narrowly, as one where the equity of making an adjustment to the contract failed to be demonstrated, rather than as one where the possibility was decisively ruled out. Various common threads such as good faith, equity and exceptionality run through the cases of equitable adjustment apart from frustration mentioned by Lord Hope. The rent abatement cases, for example, were said by Lord Shand in 1887 to be "founded on the highest equity".[67] In *Wilkie v Bethune* the farm servant sought specific implement or damages based on the market price of potatoes. Although the various judicial opinions are not models of clarity, the case can be read as one where the court exercised its equitable discretion not to grant specific implement and awarded damages instead. This rested on the good faith interpretation of the contract of employment as one of sustenance for the servant rather than one intended to provide him with goods for resale at a profit. Certainly in the modern law it is clear that although specific implement is a matter of right in Scotland, this is tempered by the court's equitable power to refuse the remedy where performance is impossible or otherwise unenforceable, or (more significantly for present purposes) would cause undue hardship for the defender.[68] *Wilkie v Bethune* is thus indeed exceptional on its facts; but it is precisely in exceptional cases that one should expect a principle of equitable adjustment to become applicable.

Lord Cooper argued that one of the "cardinal features" of Scots law in addressing the problem of change of circumstances was that "[w]ith us law and equity have never been separated, and equity has tended to predominate."[69] The second of these observations can be fairly doubted; the late Joe Thomson once observed that in Scots law "equity has passed the age of child-bearing."[70] That extreme conclusion is implicitly challenged in general by the more recent

66 See for further comment Hector L. MacQueen, 'Change of Circumstances: CISG, CESL and a Case from Scotland' (2012) 11 *Journal of International Trade Law and Policy* 300, 302–303.

67 *Muir v McIntyres* (1887) 14 R 473 (First Division).

68 McBryde, *Contract*, paras 23.15–23.22; MacQueen and Thomson, *Contract Law* paras 7.6–7.11.

69 Cooper, 'Frustration of Contract' 124.

70 Joe M. Thomson, 'The Role of Equity in Scots Law' in Stephen Goldstein (ed), *Equity and Contemporary Legal Developments* (Hebrew University of Jerusalem 1992) 923.

and deeper analysis of the subject provided by Dr Dan Carr.[71] Nor can there be any doubt about the role equity already plays in contract law. Apart from its use to regulate specific implement, mentioned above, it also qualifies the right to withhold performance under the doctrine of mutuality and the power of a party to insist on performing despite the other party's repudiatory or anticipated breach.[72] While good faith may well be "generally an underlying principle of an explanatory and legitimating rather than an active or creative nature", "the broad principle in the field of contract law of fair dealing in good faith" has been explicitly used to require particular kinds of action by contracting parties; and many other contract rules can be recognised as manifestations of the principle.[73]

The doctrine of frustration looks unlikely to have much application in the context of the coronavirus pandemic in Scotland unless the periods of emergency lockdown extend much further than they have done down to the time of writing (7 October 2020). But a doctrine of equitable adjustment encompassing the possibility of modification of otherwise strict contract terms to prevent manifest unfairness, abatement of sums of money otherwise due, temporary suspension of performance obligations, and claims in enrichment and *quantum meruit* for work done but not completed, all short of frustration, could have a useful role to play when the parties themselves cannot agree on how to resolve the problems caused for their contracts by the legal restraints with which the pandemic has been tackled. It might be a way for the Scottish courts to put some substance behind the UK Government's guidance dated 7 May 2020 on responsible contractual behaviour in the performance and enforcement of contracts impacted by the COVID-19 emergency.[74] Similarly it could help provide the "more creative, graded, but nevertheless rigorous approach without prejudicing the underlying need for legal certainty" called for as the law's response to the effect of the pandemic on commercial contracts by the British Institute of International and Comparative Law.[75] It would likewise be consistent with the

---

71 Daniel J. Carr, *Ideas of Equity* (Edinburgh Legal Education Trust 2017); idem, 'Are Equity and Law in Scotland Fused, Separate or Inter-twined?' in John C.P. Goldberg, Henry E. Smith and P.G. Turner (eds), *Law and Equity: Fusion and Fission* (CUP 2019) ch 8.

72 Hector L. MacQueen and Shannon O'Byrne, 'The Principle of Good Faith in Contractual Performance: A Scottish-Canadian Comparison' (2019) 23 *Edinburgh Law Review* 301, 320–326.

73 See further MacQueen and Thomson, *Contract Law* para 5.26. The quotations are from Lord Hope in *R v Immigration Officer at Prague Airport ex parte European Roma Rights Centre* [2005] 2 AC 1, [60] and Lord Clyde in *Smith v Bank of Scotland* 1997 SC (HL) 111, 121.

74 See UK Cabinet Office, 'Guidance on Responsible Contractual Behaviour in the Performance and Enforcement of Contracts Impacted by the Covid-19 Emergency', 7 May 2020, updated 30 June 2020 https://www.gov.uk/government/publications/guidance-on-responsible-contractual-behaviour-in-the-performance-and-enforcement-of-contracts-impacted-by-the-covid-19-emergency accessed 4 March 2021.

75 British Institute of International and Comparative Law, 'Concept Notes on the Effect of the 2020 Pandemic on Commercial Contracts', April, May and September 2020, https://www.biicl.org/breathing-space accessed 4 March 2021.

thirteenth of the European Law Institute's legal principles for the COVID-19 crisis.[76] It would indeed be unfortunate if the *Lloyds TSB* case were held to have cut out all possibility of such an approach, especially when Lord Hope's remarks on the subject were not necessary to the actual decision of the UK Supreme Court and perhaps not based on a full review of authority and principle.

---

76 European Law Institute, 'Principles for the Covid-19 Crisis', May 2020, https://www.europeanlawinstitute.eu/fileadmin/user_upload/p_eli/Publications/ELI_Principles_for_the_COVID-19_Crisis.pdf accessed 4 March 2021.

NON-PERFORMANCE AND THE CHANGE OF CIRCUMSTANCES UNDER FRENCH LAW

Jean-Sébastien BORGHETTI*

A major issue raised by the COVID-19 crisis is whether it constitutes a lawful ground for non-performance or modification of contracts. French law traditionally took a very strict view on the binding force of contracts and acknowledged only force majeure as a cause of discharge of contract. However, the reform of contract law passed in 2016 has introduced some changes and there are now several provisions

* Université Paris II Panthéon-Assas.

in the code civil which may justify a discharge or an adaptation of contract in the case of a major change of circumstances. The COVID-19 crisis is now putting these provisions to test.

1. INTRODUCTION

The impact of the COVID-19 crisis on the national legal systems in general, and the French one in particular, is considerable. In the context of this limited contribution, however, only the impact on ongoing private law contracts[1] shall be considered. More precisely, this contribution will focus on one of the major contract law questions raised by the crisis, namely whether it constitutes a lawful ground for non-performance of contracts.

At first sight, the answer should be no. The binding force of contracts is a basic tenet of French law, which is now formulated very clearly at the beginning of the section of the Civil Code (code civil) devoted to contracts: "Contracts which are lawfully formed have the binding force of legislation for those who have made them" (Art 1103 of the new code civil). As a matter of principle, a change of circumstances, however unfavourable to one party to a contract, should not lead to a discharge of that contract. A party must therefore perform his obligations under the contract, at whatever cost to him. If he does not, the other party will be entitled to a remedy, and may, in particular, claim damages for any loss suffered as a result of non-performance.[2] There is hardly a legal rule without an exception, however, and there are cases where French law does accept a relaxation of the binding force of contracts and where a change of circumstances may lead to the contract being discharged or amended. But do these cases cover the specific circumstances of the current COVID-19 crisis?

As in other countries, emergency legislation has been adopted in France in the context of the crisis, but it deals only with specific contracts. For example, special rules have been passed which modify the rules normally applicable to the termination of tourist travel and holiday contracts[3] and in essence allow the providers of such contracts to offer a credit-note instead of a refund,

---

1 There is in French law a sharp distinction between private law and public law. While private law contracts are governed by the rules in the code civil, public law contracts (i.e. contracts concluded with a public body), such as public procurement contracts, are governed by a distinct set of rules that was initially developed by the specialised courts applying public law.

2 Throughout this contribution, "he" will be the debtor of a non-monetary obligation and "she" the creditor of that obligation (as well as the debtor of the reciprocal monetary obligation).

3 Ordonnance n° 2020-315 du 25 mars 2020 relative aux conditions financières de résolution de certains contrats de voyages touristiques et de séjours en cas de circonstances exceptionnelles et inévitables ou de force majeure, JORF no. 74, 26 March 2020, texte no. 35. In French law, an *ordonnance* is a statute adopted by the Government pursuant to an authorisation given by Parliament.

as is normally the case under French law. Likewise, penalties and other sanctions normally applicable in case of non-payment of rents of commercial and professional premises have been declared temporarily unenforceable.[4] Employment contracts, which are at any time the subject of very specific rules, have also received special attention from Parliament and the Government.[5] Most of these emergency measures were initially applicable for at least the duration of the *état d'urgence sanitaire*, or "state of public health emergency,"[6] which was in force between 24 March 2020 and 10 July 2020, and were renewed during Autumn 2020 with the arrival of the "second wave" of COVID-19, which led to reinstatement of that state of emergency until 1 June 2021.[7]

On the other hand, no rules have been adopted which purport to deal with the impact of the crisis on contracts generally. This is probably sound, as not all contracts have been affected by the crisis, and it is doubtful if a "one-size-fits-all" solution should apply to those contracts that have been affected. There is no doubt, however, that performance of countless contracts has been disturbed by the measures taken to tackle the pandemic. In particular, the strict lockdown that applied across France from 17 March to 11 May 2020, and then again from 30 October to 15 December 2020, and that led amongst other things to the closure of non-essential businesses and to severe restrictions on freedom of movement, has had a considerable impact on many contracts. Even after the end of the strict lockdown, the opening of some businesses and the performance of certain activities remained restricted for several weeks in certain parts of France more affected by the pandemic. Restaurants, bars, cinemas, theatres, museums and other such places have actually not yet reopened at the time of writing. Also, large gatherings of people remain forbidden for an indeterminate time.

To assess the impact of these measures on existing contracts, and in the absence of specific ad hoc statutory rules or contractual terms,[8] one should turn

4 Article 4 of Ordonnance n° 2020-316 du 25 mars 2020 relative au paiement des loyers, des factures d'eau, de gaz et d'électricité afférents aux locaux professionnels des entreprises dont l'activité est affectée par la propagation de l'épidémie de covid-19, JORF no. 74, 26 March 2020, texte no. 37. Prior to the adoption of this ordonnance, the Government had declared that the payment of rents relating to commercial or professional premises would be suspended during the time of the crisis. This is not what the ordonnance says, however.

5 Employment contract law, though theoretically a part of contract law, has long become a distinct and independent branch of the law, which will not be addressed here.

6 Loi n° 2020-290 du 23 mars 2020 d'urgence pour faire face à l'épidémie de covid-19, JORF no. 72, 24 March 2020, texte no. 2.

7 See especially loi n° 2020-1379 du 14 novembre 2020 autorisant la prorogation de l'état d'urgence sanitaire et portant diverses mesures de gestion de la crise sanitaire, JORF no. 277, 15 November 2020, texte no. 1.

8 Some ad hoc statutory rules have been mentioned at the beginning of this contribution. A contract can also include terms intended to deal with extraordinary situations, such as the current crisis. Subject to their precise wording, they should of course be implemented, unless they run contrary to a mandatory rule of contract law, which should rarely be the case.

to the "normal" rules of contract law. In France, as in most civil law systems, these rules are normally found in codes or statutes. There are two layers of them: (1) the general rules, which are intended to apply to all contracts and are to be found in the code civil; and (2) the rules applicable to specific types of contracts (such as contracts of sale, contracts of lease, etc.), which supplement and at times contradict the general rules, and can be found either in the code civil or in specific statutes. Given the limited size of this contribution, and since the rules applicable to specific types of contracts rarely deal with unexpected changes of circumstances,[9] only the general rules on contract law will be discussed here.

French law, however, presents an additional factor of complexity due to the reform of general contract law,[10] which was adopted in February 2016 and came into force on 1 October 2016.[11] This reform was intended first of all as a restatement of the existing law, but it did introduce some changes. Perhaps the most noted of these changes is the introduction of the possibility of a judicial revision of contracts in case of hardship, which is, of course, of special significance in the context of the COVID-19 crisis. A distinction must therefore be made based on whether the contract under scrutiny was entered as of 1 October 2016, in which case it is governed by the "new" French contract law, or before that date, in which case the rules of the "old" French contract law are applicable to it. For the sake of clarity, these two hypotheses will be considered separately.

2. CONTRACTS CONCLUDED AS OF 1 OCTOBER 2016

Not all contracts have been affected by the COVID-19 crisis, and those that have may have been impacted in very different ways. To put things simply, however, and if one takes as a starting point the most common type of contract, where one party must perform a non-monetary obligation in exchange for a price, three

---

9 However, there are provisions on the change of circumstances for example in the Tourism Code (code du tourisme) for tourist travel and holiday contracts (Art L.211-14 II) and in the Intellectual Property Code (code de la propriété intellectuelle) for publishing contracts (Art L. 131-5).

10 For a presentation and an analysis of this reform in English, see John Cartwright and Simon Whittaker (ed), *The Code Napoléon Rewritten. French Contract Law after the 2016 Reforms* (Hart Publishing 2017); Solène Rowan, 'The New French Law of Contract' (2017) 66 ICLQ 4, 805.

11 Ordonnance n° 2016-131 du 10 février 2016 portant réforme du droit des contrats, du régime général et de la preuve des obligations, JORF no. 35, 11 February 2016, texte no. 26. Parliament has confirmed the reform, and made minor changes to it, through Loi n° 2018-287 du 20 avril 2018 ratifiant l'ordonnance n° 2016-131 du 10 février 2016 portant réforme du droit des contrats, du régime général et de la preuve des obligations, JORF no. 93, 21 April 2018, texte no. 1.

main cases can be identified: (1) when the crisis has made it impossible for the debtor of the non-monetary obligation to perform; (2) when the crisis has made it impossible for the creditor of the non-monetary obligation to pay the price she had promised; and (3) when the crisis has made it impossible for the creditor of that obligation to receive performance or has rendered performance useless to her. These three cases will be considered in turn.

2.1. WHEN THE CRISIS HAS MADE IT IMPOSSIBLE FOR THE DEBTOR OF A NON-MONETARY OBLIGATION TO PERFORM

The COVID-19 crisis, and more particularly the severe lockdown measures that were in force in France for two months and then for one-and-a-half months, have made it impossible for many debtors of non-monetary obligations to perform. Here again, however, a distinction must be made. In some cases, this impossibility is definitive, while in other cases it has been only temporary.

2.1.1. Definitive impossibility to perform

In all cases where time was of the essence for the contract, the impossibility to perform due to lockdown or other restrictive measures has rendered the contract useless. Typical examples of contracts that have been affected in that way include holiday rentals, transportation and short-term accommodation contracts, as well as catering services for events that should have taken place during the lockdown period but were cancelled. In all those cases, non-performance by the debtor of the non-monetary obligation is a valid ground of termination of the contract by the creditor.[12] There can be no doubt about this, but the question is whether the debtor is liable for non-performance and should therefore pay damages for any loss caused to the creditor by non-performance.

Article 1231-1 of the new code civil provides: "A debtor is condemned, where appropriate, to the payment of damages either on the ground of the non-performance or a delay in performance of an obligation, unless he justifies this on the ground that performance was prevented by force majeure."[13] The crucial issue is therefore whether performance was prevented by force majeure. Obviously, it is for the debtor relying on force majeure to demonstrate its existence.

---

12 Art 1226 of the new code civil.

13 The English version of the code civil's new provisions is borrowed from the translation of ordonnance n° 2016-131 du 10 février 2016 by John Cartwright, Bénédicte Fauvarque-Cosson and Simon Whittaker http://www.textes.justice.gouv.fr/art_pix/Translationrevised2018final.pdf accessed 9 June 2020.

A definition of force majeure is given in Article 1218 §1 of the new code civil: "In contractual matters, there is force majeure where an event beyond the control of the debtor, which could not reasonably have been foreseen at the time of the conclusion of the contract and whose effects could not be avoided by appropriate measures, prevents performance of his obligation by the debtor." This provision thus sets out three cumulative conditions of contractual[14] force majeure. The event which prevented performance must have been: (1) beyond the control of the debtor; (2) reasonably unforeseeable at the time of the conclusion of the contract; and (3) such that its effects could not be avoided by appropriate measures.

While a pandemic as such probably does not constitute force majeure,[15] the lockdown and other restrictive measures adopted by the French Government in the context of the COVID-19 crisis certainly meet the first and third conditions set out at Article 1218 §1: they were and are beyond the control of any individual debtor, and their effects normally could not and cannot be avoided by appropriate measures. The only real issue is whether these measures were reasonably unforeseeable at the time of the conclusion of the contract. This question cannot be answered in the abstract, but only on a case-by-case basis. The closer the conclusion of the contract to the start of the first lockdown, the more foreseeable the lockdown may have been. It should be stressed, however, that Article 1218 only requires that the event should be *reasonably* unforeseeable. Given that such a lockdown was unprecedented in France, and that its eventual length was not even known at the time when it came into force, it is a fair guess that only in exceptional cases will a judge decide that the lockdown (or at least the first one) was reasonably foreseeable at the time of the conclusion of the contract and that non-performance was therefore not prevented by force majeure.

The effects of force majeure are set out by Article 1218 §2 of the new code civil. Its second sentence provides: "If the prevention [of performance caused by force majeure] is permanent, the contract is terminated by operation of law and the parties are discharged from their obligations under the conditions provided by Articles 1351 and 1351-1." When non-performance caused by force majeure is definitive, the contract is thus terminated by operation of the law. This means that the creditor does not have to give notice. Since both parties are released from their obligations, each one of them must make restitution for what he or she had received. The rules on restitution are set out at Articles 1352 to 1352-9 of the new code civil. Article 1218 does not state explicitly that the debtor relying

14 In French law, force majeure is also a relevant concept in tort law and the reform bill on civil liability that is currently under discussion sets out a different definition of force majeure in that field (Art 1253).

15 See, e.g. CA Paris, 29 juin 2006, no. 04/09052 (2003 SARS epidemic); CA Besançon, 8 January 2014, no. 12/02291 (H1N1 epidemic).

on force majeure does not have to pay damages for non-performance, but this is made clear by Article 1231-1.[16]

Except in the exceptional case where the lockdown measures were reasonably foreseeable at the time of the conclusion of the contract, these measures should therefore be regarded as amounting to force majeure and leading to the termination of those contracts whose performance they have definitively prevented, without the debtor having to pay damages.

2.1.2. Temporary impossibility to perform

The lockdown and other restrictive measures adopted in the midst of the COVID-19 crisis have made performance of many contracts only temporarily impossible, without depriving these contracts of their usefulness or their *raison d'être*. Contracts in that category include building contracts, whose performance has been delayed, or contracts for services, such as gym memberships.

If the prevention of performance of these contracts is regarded as being a consequence of force majeure, as will normally be the case, then the contract will be suspended during the time when performance was not possible. This is a consequence of the first sentence of Article 1218 §2 of the new code civil, according to which "if the prevention [of performance caused by force majeure] is temporary, performance of the obligation is suspended unless the delay which results justifies termination of the contract." Although suspension is not otherwise defined in the code, it is clear that the debtor of the non-monetary obligation does not incur any liability, penalty or other sanction for the time during which he was not able to perform, as well as for the belated completion of the contract, when a set date had been agreed upon for performance or completion (as is usually the case in building contracts, for example). This solution has been confirmed and specified by Article 4 §1 of ordonnance n° 2020-306 du 25 mars 2020 relative à la prorogation des délais échus pendant la période d'urgence sanitaire et à l'adaptation des procédures pendant cette même période,[17] which provides:

> Periodic penalty payments, penalty clauses, termination clauses and clauses providing for forfeiture, where their purpose is to penalise failure to fulfil an obligation within a specified period, shall be deemed not to have commenced or to have taken effect if that period has expired [between 12 March 2020 and the expiry of a period of one month from the date of cessation of the state of public health emergency].

---

16 The reference made to Article 1351 appears circulatory, as Article 1351, which deals with impossibility of performance, provides: "Impossibility of performing the act of performance discharges the debtor to the extent of that impossibility where it results from an event of force majeure and is definitive unless he had agreed to bear the risk of the event or had previously been given notice to perform." Article 1351-1 deals with the specific case where impossibility to perform is a result of the loss of the thing that was owed.

17 JORF no. 74, 26 March 2020, texte no. 9.

2.2. WHEN THE CRISIS HAS MADE IT IMPOSSIBLE FOR THE DEBTOR OF THE MONETARY OBLIGATION TO PAY THE PRICE

The crisis has made it impossible for many parties to pay for the goods or services they had ordered. This is not a problem when the debtor of these goods or services was himself prevented from performing, in which case the contract has been terminated either by the operation of force majeure or at the creditor's initiative. It should be noted that even before a contract is terminated, the creditor can refuse to perform his own monetary obligation by relying on the defence of non-performance (*exception d'inexécution*). Article 1219 of the new code civil provides: "A party may refuse to perform his obligation, even where it is enforceable, if the other party does not perform his own and if this non-performance is sufficiently serious." And Article 1220 even allows an anticipation of the other party's non-performance: "A party may suspend the performance of his obligation as soon as it becomes evident that his contracting partner will not perform his obligation when it becomes due and that the consequences of this non-performance are sufficiently serious for him. Notice of this suspension must be given as quickly as possible."

When the debtor has performed or has offered to perform, on the other hand, can the creditor nevertheless be discharged of her obligation to pay the price?

It is a traditional solution under French law that performance of a monetary obligation can never be prevented by force majeure.[18] The technical reason for this is that, while the debtor of such an obligation may be *de facto* incapable of paying what she owes, there can be no radical impossibility to perform as long as there is money in the economy. The fundamental reason behind this technical explanation is that insolvency cannot be regarded as a cause of discharge of contract, lest the whole economy be put at risk.[19] Admittedly, a couple of cases can be cited where the courts seemed ready to adopt the concept of "economic force majeure",[20] but it is suggested that such an evolution cannot and should not be accepted, even in the context of the COVID-19 crisis. It would constitute a major change in French contract law, with unpredictable consequences, and it is doubtful if the courts have the legitimacy to implement it, let alone four years only after Parliament reformed contract law.

---

18 See, e.g. Cass. com., 16 September 2014, no. 13-20.306, Bull. civ. IV, no. 118.

19 Insolvency proceedings under French law can have an impact on the enforceability of contracts concluded by the insolvent party. This is a complex issue, which will not be addressed here.

20 Cass. 3e civ., 19 April 1972, no. 71-10505, Bull. civ. III, no. 247; Cass. 3e civ., 10 April 1975, no. 74-10379, Bull. civ. III, no. 115.

The code civil, however, does offer some kind of relief to a party having financial difficulties. The first sentence of Article 1343-5 §1–3 of the new Code provides:

> Taking into account the situation of the debtor and the needs of the creditor, a court may defer payment of sums that are due, or allow it to be made in instalments, for a period no greater than two years.

This possibility for a court to defer payment is a matter of public policy (Art 1343-5 §5) and cannot be set aside by the parties in their contract. Of course, obtaining a delay is not as advantageous for the debtor of the monetary obligation as would be a discharge of her obligation, but the discretion granted to the court is perhaps the best way to reach a fair compromise between the interests of both parties.

2.3. WHEN THE CRISIS HAS MADE IT IMPOSSIBLE FOR THE CREDITOR TO RECEIVE PERFORMANCE OR HAS RENDERED PERFORMANCE USELESS TO HER

The lockdown and other measures connected to the COVID-19 crisis have often made it impossible for the creditor of a non-monetary obligation to receive performance or has rendered performance useless to her. For example, some people have been prevented from going to the house they had rented for their holidays, and many businesses, like restaurants, have had no use of the goods that were to be delivered to them, since they had to shut down. When the debtor was simultaneously prevented from performing, then the contract has normally been either terminated or suspended according to Article 1218 of the new code civil (see section 2.1 above). There are also cases, however, where the debtor was able to perform and insisted on performing and being paid. In such cases, can the creditor be discharged, without having to pay damages or the price he had promised?

The question is all the more crucial for the creditor of the non-monetary obligation as French law does not impose a duty to mitigate on the party suffering a loss as a consequence of the other party's fault or breach of contract. The Cour de Cassation had clearly refused to recognise such a duty before 2016[21] and the reform of contract law has remained silent about it. The debtor who cannot perform his non-monetary obligation due to the creditor not being able or willing to receive performance has therefore no duty to mitigate and he can "let his loss go", provided he falls short of being negligent.

---

[21] See Olivier Deshayes, 'L'introduction de l'obligation de modérer son dommage en matière contractuelle – Rapport français' [2010] *Revue des contrats* 3, 1139.

Article 1218 of the new code civil is of no avail to the creditor in the hypothesis contemplated here, since it addresses only the case where the debtor is prevented from performing, and not the case where the creditor is prevented from receiving performance.[22] Another provision the creditor might wish to rely on is Article 1195 of the new code civil. Before the 2016 reform, French contract law was known to have a very strict conception of the binding force of contract, whereby a change in circumstances, however important, could never result in the discharge or revision of contract (unless it constituted force majeure). Article 1195 constitutes a U-turn in that respect and is perhaps the most famous new provision in the code civil. It states that "if a change of circumstances that was unforeseeable at the time of the conclusion of the contract renders performance excessively onerous for a party who had not accepted the risk of such a change," and if the parties cannot agree on the adaptation or termination of the contract, "the court may, on the request of a party, revise the contract or put an end to it, from a date and subject to such conditions as it shall determine."

Article 1195 sets out three conditions for the remedies it provides: (1) a change in circumstances unforeseeable at the time of the conclusion of the contract; (2) the excessive "onerousness" of performance; and (3) the fact that the party bearing the price of performance did not accept the risk of such a change. This last condition can only be assessed on a case-by-case basis, but it is a fair guess that a party will rarely have accepted the risk that materialised with the measures taken in response to the COVID-19 crisis. The first condition, foreseeability, should be assessed as with force majeure. Admittedly, Article 1218 speaks of an event that was *reasonably* unforeseeable, whereas Article 1195 only refers to an unforeseeable change of circumstances, without any qualification. It is doubtful, however, if the threshold should be higher in the context of a change of circumstances than in the context of force majeure. Before the reform, the courts often said that force majeure was based on an unforeseeable event, but it was generally accepted that unforeseeability should be assessed from the standpoint of a reasonable person. If the same standard applies to Article 1195, and there is no reason why it should not, then there is no substantial difference between that provision and Article 1218 as far as unforeseeability is concerned.

It is the second condition set out by Article 1195, the excessive onerousness of performance, which is probably most problematic in the context of the current crisis. The typical case which the authors of the reform had in mind when drafting Article 1195 was the one where performance of a non-monetary obligation becomes more expensive for the debtor due to a change of circumstances, like high inflation. This is the reason why the Code speaks of performance becoming

22 As has been confirmed recently: Cass. 1re civ., 25 nov. 2020, no. 19-21.060. See however Cass. 1re civ., no. 96-13316, Bull. civ. I, no. 53, accepting that the sickness of a pupil, which prevented him from attending his school, constitutes force majeure.

excessively onerous. But what about the case where performance of the obligation becomes valueless for the creditor? Does the obligation to pay the price become excessively onerous for the debtor of that obligation when she cannot receive performance or when the thing or service received in exchange for the price has lost its value to her? If one sticks to the wording of Article 1195, the answer is no. "Onerous" (*onéreux*) is not a *terminus technicus* in French contract law, but the word normally refers in the French language to something that is high in absolute terms, and not in comparison with something else. If one adopts a rigorous approach, it cannot be said that performance of the monetary obligation is *rendered* more onerous when the good or service provided in exchange cannot be received or has lost its value, since the price itself has not changed. On the other hand, there is no doubt that the debtor of the monetary obligation gets less "value for her money" when she cannot receive performance or when the thing or service delivered to her has lost its usefulness or value. It is therefore tempting to adopt a broad conception of "onerous" at Article 1195,[23] all the more so as the Principles of European Contract Law, which were a source of inspiration for the French reform, expressly take this approach.[24]

French courts have not yet had an occasion to apply Article 1195 of the new code civil and it is therefore difficult to tell which interpretation of "onerous" they will favour. Debtors of monetary obligations can expect little relief if they adopt a narrow understanding of the term. Even if they were willing to endorse the broad approach, however, that would probably be no panacea for the debtors. First of all, the *travaux préparatoires* of the reform have made it clear that Article 1195 is not mandatory law[25] and clauses setting aside this provision have become standard terms in business contracts. Professionals are obviously wary of the courts revising the terms of their contract because of the unpredictability of the result. It is therefore likely that only a few cases will arise where a party will be able to rely on Article 1195, let alone successfully. Secondly, this provision makes it clear that the party adversely affected by the change of circumstances must continue to perform until both parties find an agreement or until the court revises or puts an end to the contract. Article 1195 thus does not offer immediate relief to the debtor of the monetary obligation. She can resist a claim for performance by the other party by invoking Article 1195, but it will take some time before the court takes a decision, and that decision may not

23 See, e.g. in favour of this approach Olivier Deshayes, Thomas Génicon and Yves-Marie Laithier, *Réforme du droit des obligations, du régime général et de la preuve des obligations* (2nd edn, LexisNexis 2018) 449.

24 Article 6:111 – Change of circumstances: "(1) A party is bound to fulfil its obligations even if performance has become more onerous, whether because the cost of performance has increased or because the value of the performance it receives has diminished."

25 Olivier Deshayes, Thomas Génicon and Yves-Marie Laithier, *Réforme du droit des obligations, du régime général et de la preuve des obligations* (2nd edn, LexisNexis 2018) 440.

be favourable to her. It might therefore be a good idea for the debtor to rely on Article 1343-5 of the new code civil alongside Article 1195.

Yet another provision which the debtor might want to rely on is Article 1186 §1 of the new code civil. It provides: "A contract which has been validly formed lapses if one of its necessary elements disappears." Article 1187 adds: "Lapse puts an end to the contract." Article 1186 §1 is actually rather mysterious, as this very general rule does not really reflect the law that applied before the reform, and no indication is given as to what the "essential elements" of the contract may be. At first glance, one might think that they are the elements necessary for the validity of a contract under French law,[26] namely: (1) the consent of the parties; (2) their capacity to contract; and (3) a content which is lawful and certain. It cannot be so, however. The "disappearance" of consent cannot result it the contract's lapsing, lest the binding force of contract be ruined. There is no reason why the fact that a party loses his capacity to enter a contract after the conclusion of an agreement should systematically lead to this agreement's coming to an end. And if the content of the contract "disappears" before performance (for example in case of destruction of the thing that has been sold), it is the rules on non-performance, and not Article 1186 §1, that should apply.

Article 1186 §2, which deals with the specific hypothesis where several contracts are necessary for the putting into effect of one and the same operation, suggests that the idea behind Article 1186 §1 is that the contract should lapse when the purpose for which it was concluded, and which was known to both parties, is frustrated. Such a rule would be too broad, however. If one takes the contract by which a fiancée orders a wedding dress, where both parties are fully aware of the final purpose of the dress, it cannot be accepted that the contract should lapse if the wedding is cancelled because the fiancée or the fiancé has decided not to marry. Unless the contract contains an express term to the contrary, this risk should be borne by the fiancée who orders the dress, and not by the dressmaker. The rule in Article 1186 §1 therefore seems workable only if there is an implied requirement that the purpose which both parties had in mind is not an activity or an event carried out or controlled by the creditor of the non-monetary obligation. This, of course, brings us quite close to the solution adopted in some of the famous coronation cases in English law.[27]

If one adopts this approach of Article 1186 §1, its scope of application overlaps partly with that of Article 1195, but the former provision is much more advantageous than the latter for the creditor of a non-monetary obligation. Article 1186 §1 provides for the automatic discharge of contract, and not just for a possible adaptation or termination at the court's discretion. It remains to be seen, however, if French courts will be willing to unleash the potential in

26 Article 1128 of the new code civil.

27 See esp *Krell v Henry* [1903] 2 K.B. 740.

this provision, which the drafters of the reform have apparently overlooked. Even if they do, Article 1186 §1 will obviously not apply in all cases where the creditor of the non-monetary obligation has lost interest in performance. For example, the owner of a restaurant could not walk out of a supply agreement on the ground that his activity has come to a halt, since it is precisely *his* activity and, unless otherwise agreed in the supply agreement, it is he who should bear the risk of its disappearance or reduction. On the other hand, one might want to apply Article 1186 §1 in the case, for instance, where someone offers a service to people purporting to attend a music festival and this festival has been cancelled due to the lockdown.

3. CONTRACTS CONCLUDED BEFORE 1 OCTOBER 2016

Contracts concluded before 1 October 2016 are governed by the provisions of the old code civil, supplemented by the massive body of case law that had developed under and around them. As has been mentioned above, French contract law before the reform was remarkable in its very strict approach to the binding force of contract. This is illustrated by the famous *Canal de Craponne* case,[28] which was decided in 1876 but remained good law until 2016. Pursuant to agreements concluded in 1560 and 1567, the successive owners of an irrigation canal had been collecting a 3-penny (*sous*) fee for the maintenance and supply of water to the peasants in the neighbouring plain. Due to the monetary depreciation over three centuries, this fee had become ridiculously low and it did not even cover the costs of maintaining the canal. In the 1870s, the current owner of the canal decided to take the matter to court in order to have the royalty revalued. The case came to the Cour de Cassation, France's highest court in civil matters, which ruled that a court had no authority to modify the terms of a contract, whatever the circumstances. In a famous dictum, the Supreme Court held that "in no case shall it be for the courts, however equitable their decision may appear, to take account of time and circumstances in order to modify the parties' agreements and to substitute new clauses for those which have been freely accepted by them."

Given this conception of contract, it should come as no surprise that French contract law before the reform offers few escape routes to parties trapped in contracts which they cannot perform, or which have lost their usefulness.[29] This is made clear by looking at the three same hypotheses which have been considered in relation to contracts concluded as of 1 October 2016.

---

28 Cass. civ., 6 March 1876 [1876] Recueil Dalloz 1, 193.

29 The special rules adopted to face the COVID-19 crisis are of course applicable to these contracts as well as to contracts concluded as of 1 October 2016.

3.1. WHEN THE CRISIS HAS MADE IT IMPOSSIBLE FOR THE DEBTOR OF A NON-MONETARY OBLIGATION TO PERFORM

As under the new contract law, the debtor of a non-monetary obligation created by a contract concluded before 1 October 2016, who has not been able to perform due to the measures taken in response to the COVID-19 crisis, can try to rely on force majeure to avoid being held liable. Article 1148 of the old code civil provides: "Damages are not due when, because of a force majeure or a fortuitous event, the debtor either was prevented from giving or doing what he was obligated to give or did what he was forbidden to do."[30]

Unlike the new Code, the old code civil did not give a definition of force majeure. However, it is generally accepted that Article 1218 §1 of the new code civil only purports to restate the traditional definition, which had been developed by the courts before 2016. The conditions of force majeure set out at Article 1218 §1 are therefore also applicable to contracts entered into before 1 October 2016.

The old Code did not explain the consequences of force majeure either, except that it relieved the defaulting debtor from having to pay damages. The courts, however, had made it clear that when force majeure makes it temporarily impossible for the debtor to perform, performance of the obligation is suspended (unless time is of the essence of the contract or the resulting delay justifies termination of the contract).[31] This is exactly the solution which has been restated at Article 1218 §2 of the new code civil. When force majeure makes performance irremediably impossible, case law was not totally clear if the contract automatically comes to an end or if the creditor needs to terminate the contract, but it was never disputed that, in such a case, force majeure leads to the discharge of contract. Here again, Article 1218 §2 of the new code civil in essence restates the old law.

There are therefore no significant differences between the old and the new law in the case where the crisis has made it impossible for the debtor of a non-monetary obligation to perform. Regardless of the date at which it was entered into, the contract is either discharged or suspended when the prevention of performance is the result of force majeure. Whether the lockdown and other measures taken to address the COVID-19 crisis meet the criteria of force majeure depends in particular on the foreseeability of such measures at the time of the conclusion of the contract. This must be assessed on a case-by-case basis,

---

30 The English version of the old code civil's articles is borrowed from the translation by David W. Gruning (with occasional amendments by the author of this contribution), accessible on the French law official website https://www.legifrance.gouv.fr/Traductions/en-English/Legifrance-translations accessed 12 June 2020.

31 See, e.g. Cass. 3e civ., 22 February 2006, no. 05-12.032, Bull. civ. III, no. 46.

but it seems likely that the question will be answered in the affirmative in most instances.

3.2. WHEN THE CRISIS HAS MADE IT IMPOSSIBLE FOR THE DEBTOR OF THE MONETARY OBLIGATION TO PAY THE PRICE

The rules which apply in this hypothesis are almost exactly the same whether the contract is governed by the new or by the old contract law. As has been explained, it is a traditional solution, which has not been altered by the 2016 reform, that force majeure does not apply for the benefit of the debtor of a monetary obligation who is unable to pay the price owed under the contract. On the other hand, the faculty for the judge to grant a delay was already recognised before 2016 and Article 1343-5 of the new code civil reproduces practically word for word the terms of Article 1244-1 of the old code civil.

Likewise, the defence of non-performance was already recognised before 2016, even though it had no explicit legislative basis. The only difference between the old and the new law in this respect is that the defence of anticipated non-performance, now codified at Article 1220 of the new code civil, was not accepted before the reform.

3.3. WHEN THE CRISIS HAS MADE IT IMPOSSIBLE FOR THE CREDITOR TO RECEIVE PERFORMANCE OR HAS RENDERED PERFORMANCE USELESS TO HER

It is in this third hypothesis that there is a significant difference between the old and the new contract law. Under the *canal de Craponne* rule that applies to contracts concluded before 1 October 2016, the courts have no power to modify or terminate a contract when a change in circumstances has made performance excessively onerous for one of the parties. A couple of cases decided in the 1990s have suggested that the party benefiting from the change in circumstances may have a duty to renegotiate the contract,[32] but this was never confirmed and, even if such a duty existed, it is difficult to see where it would lead, since a duty to renegotiate does not amount to a duty to accept a modification or termination of the contract. This is made clear by Article 1112 §1 of the new code civil, which provides: "The commencement, continuation and breaking-off of precontractual negotiations are free from control. They must mandatorily satisfy the requirements of good faith."

---

32 Cass. com., 3 November 1992, no. 90-18547, Bull. Civ. IV, no. 338; Cass. Com., 24 November 1996, no. 96-18357, Bull. civ. IV, no. 227.

In theory, the Cour de Cassation could abandon the *Canal de Craponne* rule for contracts concluded before 1 October 2016 and decide to apply a new judge-made rule to these contracts, which would mirror the rule in Article 1195 of the new code civil. In practice, however, such a reversal of the case-law rule appears extremely unlikely. Reversals of case-law are more common in France than in other jurisdictions, but it is hard to figure the Cour de Cassation turning its back to the famous *Canal de Craponne* rule, especially as this would suggest that it approves the Parliament's choice to reverse the rule it had set – something very unlikely on the part of a proud institution, which usually resents the legislator's "interfering" with its case law. Besides, applying the rule in Article 1195 to contracts concluded before the reform of French contract law would be problematic as this would mean that the contracts concerned would be governed by a rule that the parties had not anticipated and were therefore not able to set aside, even though this rule is not mandatory.

The application of the rule in Article 1186 §1 of the new code civil to contracts concluded before 1 October 2016 is perhaps less unlikely. As a general rule, it had no equivalent before the reform of contract law, but the specific instance of the lapsing of contract now codified at Article 1186 §2 was already recognised in case law. The rule in Article 1186 §1 is therefore a generalisation of a pre-existing rule and the Cour de Cassation might be willing to apply it to contracts concluded before the contract law reform. So far, however, no case can be cited which suggests that it will indeed do so and the uncertainties which have been mentioned about the limits of the rule (see section 2.3 above) do not plead in favour of its anticipated application.

4. CONCLUSION

General French contract law offers limited resources to those who would like to be discharged of their contracts in the context of the current COVID-19 crisis. When one party has been prevented from performing his non-monetary obligation due to the lockdown and other restrictive measures taken in response to the COVID-19 crisis, force majeure will normally be applicable and lead to the discharge of contract, but the parties who cannot rely on force majeure, for example because theirs was a monetary obligation or because the service or good they were to receive has become useless to them, can hardly expect a full discharge of contract. This is not surprising given the insistence on the binding force of contracts in French law, which reflects a legitimate concern for the stability of legal and economic relationships. This concern also explains the adoption of emergency rules applicable only to specific types of contracts, whose parties have been considered as deserving special attention. The question is whether this combination of general contract law and focused emergency measures will suffice to weather the major economic shock caused by the COVID-19 crisis. If this is not the case, the courts might be willing to relax the traditional rules of the code civil to grant relief to some deserving parties, as has already been done in the past, in France and elsewhere.[33]

[33] French courts are famous for having created new civil liability rules because they thought the code civil's rules made compensation too difficult. And, as is well known, it is the hyper-inflation that existed in Germany after World War One which led the German Imperial Court to grant courts the power to revise contracts in case of change of circumstances (RG, 28 November 1923, RGZ 107, 78).

THE IMPACT OF THE CORONAVIRUS CRISIS ON THE ANALYSIS AND DRAFTING OF CONTRACT CLAUSES

Force Majeure, Hardship and Deferral of Obligations

Denis PHILIPPE*

---

* Université catholique de Louvain, Visiting professor at the University of Paris; dphilippe@philippelaw.eu. The contribution is up to date as of August 2020.

This contribution analyses whether the coronavirus crisis can lead to the application of the doctrine of force majeure. The different conditions of application of force majeure are discussed (non-accountability, unforeseeability and impossibility), as its effects are not defined clearly by the literature and case law. This contribution gives some suggestions for the drafting of force majeure clauses. Of course, pandemics must be mentioned in the circumstances constituting force majeure. Then, the possibility to find alternatives in case of non-performance must be considered. Finally, a renegotiation of the contract can be incorporated into the force majeure clause. The contribution also analyses the doctrine of unforeseen circumstances and the drafting of hardship clauses. Finally, it mentions the coronavirus principles of the European Law Institute which recommends a renegotiation of the contract following the coronavirus crisis.

1. INTRODUCTION

Coronavirus has had devastating effects on our economy and the impact of the pandemic on contract law has been as virulent as the coronavirus itself. It is appropriate to introduce this contribution by recalling the milestones of the coronavirus phenomenon in view of the change in circumstances since the outbreak of the virus in Wuhan province, Hubei. On 31 December 2019, the authorities announced for the first-time clustered cases of pneumonia of unknown origin; all 41 infected people had attended the Huanan food market. The virus proceeded to spread throughout China, crippling trade with China. It then spread from China to the rest of the world, but we will not go into detail on the development of the virus itself in this contribution.

Hard-hit Europe has imposed containment measures; these have been taken at the State level. In Belgium, the containment measures were initiated on 13 March 2020. On 17 March, Luxembourg triggered a state of crisis that allowed it to take quick legislative decisions and close all construction sites. Given the scale of the pandemic, these measures have been strengthened, including the closure of many businesses and the introduction of border control. Given the temporary nature of the virus, the pandemic measures were gradually lifted in Wuhan province.

In western Europe, the pandemic was alleviated over the summer. But the crisis registered a second wave and new containment measures were decided in various countries in Europe.

The problems that can arise are manifold, but we will limit ourselves to a few examples.

You are committed to delivering goods that come from China; Chinese factories are closed because of the coronavirus. You are not able to deliver these goods. Is this a case of force majeure or hardship?

You have received an order to close your European factory; you cannot manufacture the goods and are not able to provide the goods as a result of this closure. Is it a case of force majeure?

You had to perform a service in a place abroad, but your flight is cancelled. Thus you cannot perform the service due to the coronavirus crisis.

A last example: a framework contract for the delivery of goods has been concluded; you were due to deliver by 30 March 2020 and are unable to deliver because of the coronavirus. The buyer had paid a 30% down payment – can he/she recover the deposit as a result of the force majeure?

If the contract is hit by the coronavirus crisis, the debtor can invoke force majeure if the performance of the contract is impossible, and invoke hardship if the coronavirus crisis causes a substantial imbalance. We will analyse the conditions of application of both concepts.

2. FORCE MAJEURE

After defining force majeure, we will first consider whether the coronavirus crisis meets the conditions of force majeure and then focus on drafting the clauses. We will discuss the containment measures (section 2.3) the effects of force majeure (section 2.4) and we will end with advice on the analysis and drafting of the force majeure clauses (section 2.5).[1]

---

1 See Charles Edouard Brucher, 'Force majeure and unpredictability remedies the covid-19 epidemic?' (La force majeure et l'imprévision remèdes à l'épidémie the Covid-19 ?) (2020) 4 Contracts Competition Consumption (Contrats, Concurrence, Consommation); Michaël de Potter de ten Broeck, 'A pandemic as a force majeure, A force majeure as a pandemic' (Een pandemie als overmacht, overmacht als een pandemie) (2020) 3 R.D.C.-TBH 246–278. See Michel Storck, 'Synthesis, Failure to perform the contract' (Synthèse, Le défaut d'exécution du contrat)in Jurisclasseur civil, update 1 June 2020, no 10, Articles 1224–1230. Martine Behar Touchais, 'The impact of a health crisis on contracts in commercial law. On the occasion of the Covid-19 pandemic' (L'impact d'une crise sanitaire sur les contrats en droit commercial; À l'occasion de la pandémie de Covid-19) (2020) 15–16 The Enterprise and Business Legal

2.1. DEFINITION

Article 1147 of the Civil Code exempts the debtor in case of "foreign cause" (cause étrangère) or force majeure.[2]

Force majeure is not defined in the Civil Code. It is generally admitted in law that force majeure exempts the debtor from an obligation when circumstances arise with the following characteristics:

- unaccountability to the party who invokes it;
- unforeseeability and unavoidability;
- irresistibly resulting in an impossibility to carry out the contractual obligation.

It has the effect of dissolving the contract if the obstacle is final, and suspending it if the obstacle is temporary.[3] The force majeure can also affect only a part of the contract.

Table 1. Force majeure

HYPOTHESIS			**REGIME**	
Circumstances		Effects	Notification	Suspension
Unaccountable	Unpredictable	Impossibility of execution		Dissolution

Source: Compiled by the author.

Week (La Semaine Juridique Entreprise et Affaires) 1162; Julia Heinich, 'The Impact of the Coronavirus Epidemic on Business Contracts: From Force Majeure to Unforeseen Events' (L'incidence de l'épidémie de coronavirus sur les contrats d'affaires: de la force majeure à l'imprévision), (2020) D. 616; Patrick Wéry, *Notary Directory, Bonds Obligations (Répertoire Notarial), Volume IV, Book 1/1, The general theory of the contract* (Théorie générale du contrat) (Larcier 2010) 1017; Aloïs Van Oevelen and Annick De Boeck, *Overmacht* (Intersentia 2015); Sophie Goldman and Stéphanie Lagasse, 'Contractual imbalance arising during performance due to external circumstances' (Comment appréhender le déséquilibre contractuel en droit commun ?) in *News in general contract law* (Droit commun des contrats: questions choisies) (Brussels 2016) 112–127; Britt Weyts, 'The classic doctrine of force majeure in the law of obligations, more topical than ever' (Het klassieke leerstuk van overmacht in het verbintenissenrecht, actueler dan ooit) (2020) R.G.D.C. 442; Paul-Alain Foriers and Charlotte de Leval, 'Force majeure and contract' (Force majeure et contrat) in Patrick Wéry (ed) *The law of contractual obligations and the bicentenary of the Civil Code* (Le droit des obligations contractuelles et le bicentenaire du code civil) (La Charte 2004), 241.

2 These two terms have the same meaning, Patrick Wéry, *Notary Directory, Bonds Obligations (Répertoire Notarial), Volume IV, Book 1/1, The general theory of the contract* (Théorie Générale du contrat) (Larcier 2010) 562.

3 Ludo Cornelis, *General Theory of Commitment* (Algemene theorie van de verbintenis) (Intersentia 2000) 649, no 518; Pascale Guiomard, 'Influenza, epidemics and force majeure in ten stops' (La grippe, les épidémies et la force majeure en dix arrêts) (2020) Dalloz actualité.

The Supreme Court can exert control on the conditions of application and effects of the force majeure but the factual assessment is done by the judge of the merits.[4]

2.2. CONDITIONS OF APPLICATION

2.2.1. Unaccountability to the party that invokes it

Force majeure must be, at least in French law, external to the party that invokes it. It is often felt in Belgian law, that an external cause is not necessarily required and that the disruptive event must simply not be attributable to the party who invokes it.[5] This applies, for example, to the case of a disease (in this case, coronavirus), as its cause is directly external to the party that invokes it, since it is a virus that comes from abroad and spreads at an impressive rate. But the debtor is liable for the non-performance of his/her subcontractor.[6]

What if several faulty and unaccountable causes contribute to non-execution? For example, the seller was scheduled to deliver on 30 November 2019; delivery is more than two months behind schedule and the seller then invokes force majeure due to the coronavirus crisis. In this case, the seller will remain responsible.[7] Let us take another example: under a framework long-term supply contract, the seller had to contractually keep a stock of 1,000 cases from China; he/she had not kept such a stock and claimed a shortage of parts because he/she could no longer buy from China due to the coronavirus. The buyer may rightly refuse the application of force majeure; indeed, his/her contractual fault, the failure to maintain sufficient stock, contributed to the non-performance of the sales contract.[8]

2.2.2. Unforeseeability

In its decision of 15 February 1951,[9] the Supreme Court rejected the application of force majeure considering that the debtor could have foreseen the occurrence of the event and taken adequate measures to avoid the damage caused by this event.

---

4 Patrick Wéry, *Notary Directory, Bonds Obligations (Répertoire Notarial), Volume IV, Book 1/1, The general theory of the contract* (Thoérie Générale du contrat) (Larcier 2010) 565.

5 Stéphanie Michaux and Denis Philippe, *Obligations, Theoretical and practical treatise* (Obligations, Traité théorique et pratique) (Kluwer 2002) 4.23.

6 Patrick Wéry, *Notary Directory, Bonds Obligations, Volume IV, Book 1/1* (Répertoire notarial, Les obligations, Volume IV, Livre 1/1), *The general theory of the contract* (Théorie Générale du contrat) (Larcier 2010) 565.

7 See on this issue, Denis Philippe, *Changing circumstances and upheaval of the contractual economy* (Changement de circonstances et bouleversement de l'économie contractuelle) (Bruylant 1986) 621.

8 See Cass. 6 December 1985, case F-19851206-2.

9 Pas., 1951, I, 389.

Unforeseeability must be assessed reasonably, taking into account the circumstances of the case. It must be assessed at the conclusion of the contract.[10]

Unforeseeability is assessed *in abstracto* i.e. a prudent person acting under the same circumstances. In France, some authors emphasise that unforeseeability is not an essential condition of application of force majeure.[11]

The notion of unforeseeability is relative: the pandemic was envisaged in 2013 in a report of the German[12] parliament, and Bill Gates explained at a conference in 2015 that we were not prepared for the next pandemic. Does this mean that the current coronavirus pandemic was predictable? We must refer to the prudent and diligent person placed under the same circumstances and here we will all agree that this pandemic and its effects were not foreseeable.[13]

Based on the evidence mentioned above, the existence of the virus had to be relied upon as early as 15 January 2020. In other words, this event had to be taken into account by the parties in their contractual negotiations as of that date. The buyer will not be able to avail him/herself of the unpredictability of the coronavirus at this time.

It is important to distinguish the *unforeseeability of the event* on the one hand, and the *unforeseeability of its effects on the contract* on the other hand.[14] If the event is foreseeable but its effects on the contract are not, the debtor will still be able to avail him/herself of the unpredictability. Let us return to the development of the coronavirus. Who could have foreseen on 15 January, when the coronavirus could be taken into account by the contracting parties, that it would result in such a spread on other continents and especially in Europe?

Let us take the following example. On 5 February 2020, you commit to make a product delivery for 1 April 2020; you know of the coronavirus and its effects in China at this time, but you do not know that your factory will have to be closed on 18 March 2020 under the Belgian ministerial decree; therefore, you can always avail yourself of the unpredictability of the measures decreed by the Belgian government, as they were unpredictable on 5 February 2020.

---

10 Stéphanie Michaux and Denis Philippe, *Obligations, Theoretical and practical treatise* (Obligations, Traité théorique et pratique) (Kluwer 2002) 4.19.

11 Paul-Henry Antonmattéi, 'Contribution to the study of force majeure' (Contribution à l'étude de la force majeure), *Library de droit privé,* Volume 220, (L.G.D.J. 1993) 64 ff.

12 Report on risk analysis in civil protection, 3.1.2013, German Bundestag 17th parliamentary term, printed matter 77/1205, no 2.3., 5. 'How to apprehend pandemics having regard to SARS' (comment appréhender une pandémie en se référant au SARS).

13 Stéphanie Michaux and Denis Philippe, *Obligations, Theoretical and practical treatise* (Obligations, Traité théorique et pratique) (Kluwer 2002) 4.16.

14 Charles Edouard Brucher, 'Force majeure and unpredictability remedies the covid-19 epidemic?' (La force majeure et l'imprévision remèdes à la pandémie de Covid-19) (2020) 4 Contracts Competition Consumption, made no difference between the event and its effects; we think however that the distinction between both is not only easy to draw, but gives a more precise view on the issue.

What if a contract was entered into after the first wave? We find that the second wave was foreseeable but the debtor could argue that the scope of the effects of the second wave could not have been foreseen.

What was not foreseeable is the global effect of the coronavirus crisis; we can argue that in March 2020, for instance, parties could not have foreseen the length and the fluctuating effects of the pandemic and thus the effects were not foreseeable, but what can be reproached is the non-insertion of a force majeure clause: when the future is uncertain and can cast doubt on the performance of your obligations, it is wise to insert a change of circumstances clause.

2.2.3. Impossibility to perform

If alternative solutions exist, the condition of impossibility to perform is not met. The fact that the performance of the obligation becomes excessively burdensome is not sufficient.[15] Let us take the following example.

You, an intermediate Belgian supplier, are committed to selling goods; the only supplier is from China and the Chinese company is closed. You are clearly in a force majeure situation. But if *alternative* supply opportunities are present, the debtor must resort to them. Let us take the previous example; if an Argentinian supplier can supply the same goods, you, an intermediate Belgian supplier, have to turn to this other supplier. If the price is substantially higher, you will have to see if you can invoke hardship in such a situation, which we will analyse later.

The impossibility must be reasonably assessed.[16] The Belgian Court of Cassation has had the opportunity on several occasions to state this.[17] The Paris

15 Patrick Wéry, *Notary Directory, Bonds Obligations (Répertoire Notarial), Volume IV, Book 1/1, The general theory of the contract* (Théorie Générale du contrat) (Larcier 2010) 564.

16 Alois Van Oevelen, 'Force majeure and imprecision in Belgian contract law' (2008) TPR 608, no 5; Patrick Wéry, *Notary Directory, Bonds Obligations (Répertoire Notarial), Volume IV, Book 1/1, The general theory of the contract* (Théorie Générale du contrat) (Larcier 2010); Rémy Cabrillac, *Law of Obligations in Private Law Series* (Droit des obligations, série de droit privé) (Dalloz 2002) 110, no 154; Marcel Fontaine, 'Scope and limits of the principle of convention-law' (Portée et limites du principe de la convention-loi) in X. Gods (ed), *Contractual Obligations* (Editions of the Young Bar Association 1984) 188; Jacques Heenen, 'The responsibility of the maritime carrier and the notion of force majeure' (La responsabilité du transporteur maritime et la notion de force majeure) (notes Cass. April 13, 1956) (1957) RCJB 94; Michaël de Potter de ten Broeck, *Changed circumstances in contract law* (Gewijzigde omstandigheden in het contractenrecht) (Intersentia 2017) 46; Jean François Germain, Yannick Ninane, Jean van Zuylen, 'La force majeure dans le droit commun des obligations contractuelles' (La force majeure dans le droit commun des obligations contractuelles) in *The Force Majeure* (La force majeure) (Anthemis 2013); François Glansdorff, 'La force majeure' (2019) J.T. 355. Stéphanie Michaux and Denis Philippe, *Obligations, Theoretical and practical treatise* (Obligations, Traité théorique et pratique) (Kluwer 2002); Paul-Henri Antonmattéi, 'Contribution to the study of force majeure' (Contribution à l'étude de la force majeure), *Library de droit privé*, Volume 220 (L.G.D.J. 1993).

17 Cass. 13 May 1996 Pas. 455, and Cass. 21 September 1991, R.W. 1991-91, 682.

Commercial Court was also of this opinion.[18] In a case dated 20 May 2020, the definition of force majeure was adjusted so as to consider execution impossible when it was carried out under unreasonable economic conditions. By accepting this clause, the Court ruled in favour of the existence of an event of force majeure represented by the coronavirus.

Alternatively, what if the impossibility is the result of another standard to be met? Let us take a simple example. You have to deliver goods that come from Russia; Russia is under embargo following the events in Ukraine; you are unable to deliver as a result of the embargo and it is a *fait du prince* constituting force majeure; therefore the standard to be met takes precedence over the contractual commitment. The impossibility is assessed *in abstracto*.[19]

What if there is a conflict of standards? What if the standard to be respected is the protection of life and health covered by Article 2 of the European Convention on Human Rights which urges you not to work, while the containment measures allow you to continue working? The protection of life and health should in principle take precedence, and this hypothesis will be returned to in the study of containment measures later.

The *mere fact of running out of liquidity* is not a case of force majeure and it is written that the debts of sums of money do not fall under the scope of force majeure by referring to the adage *genera non pereunt.*

In a judgment of 28 June 2018,[20] the Court of Cassation confirmed that financial incapacity cannot constitute a case of force majeure, even if this incapacity is due to external circumstances which constitute a case of force majeure for the debtor. We will nuance the effects of this judgment in the following paragraph with respect to the impossibility of use.[21] It is not our ambition to here take up all the measures that have been taken by the banks and by the public authorities to help businesses.

Let us remember, however, that under Article 1244 of the Belgian Civil Code, the judge may grant terms and time to the unfortunate and, in good faith, the debtor. It seems pretty obvious to me that this article will be able to find application in the wake of the coronavirus crisis.

---

18 Trib. Com. Paris, 20 May 2020, R.G. 20200 16407.

19 Stéphanie Michaux and Denis Philippe, *Obligations, Theoretical and practical treatise* (Obligations, Traité théorique et pratique) (Kluwer 2002) 4.15.

20 Cass. 28 June 2018, C.17.0701.N/1.

21 See also in French law, Martine Behar Touchais, 'L'impact d'une crise sanitaire sur les contrats en droit commercial. À l'occasion de la pandémie de Covid-19' (2020) 15–16; La Semaine Juridique Entreprise et Affaires, n°15 and Cass., 16 September 2014, no 13-20.306: ECLI:FR:CCASS:2014:CO00708 -2.

2.2.4. *Various questions: evidence, lease and case law*

2.2.4.1. Burden of proof

In case of obligation to procure (obligation de résultat), for instance the supplier cannot deliver the good in the due time, the burden of proof rests with the debtor who invokes force majeure and the debtor will be well advised to retain all the evidence of force majeure. In case of obligation of means (obligation de moyen), it is up to the creditor to proof the wrongdoing of the debtor; if the creditor succeeds, the debtor must then prove the force majeure to be exempted of liability.[22]

2.2.4.2. Lease agreement

What if a store has to close? The tenant refuses to pay on the grounds of force majeure; the owner counters by saying that the lack of liquidity is not a case of force majeure as stated above. It will then be necessary to refer to Article 1722 of the Belgian Civil Code, which states that the lease is void in the event of a loss of the rented premises; the impossibility of use may give rise to the application of this Article because it can be equated with the loss of the rented premises. Alternatively, it can be considered that if the tenant is deprived of enjoyment, the landlord does not fulfil his/her obligations to make available the rented property as contractually agreed, the tenant then being entitled to suspend the payment of rents.[23]

The case law is divided on this matter. Some decisions follow the reasoning exposed in the foregoing paragraph.[24] Others consider that the lessee cannot invoke the force majeure because the performance obligation to pay a sum of money is never impossible; it is an application of the adage *genera non pereunt*.[25]

Reading the lease agreement may prove valuable in the search for the solution to this question; in fact, the use of the property rented for a particular purpose (e.g. clothing store) is often expressly provided for. Force majeure will then be

---

22 Patrick Wéry, *Notary Directory, Bonds Obligations (Répertoire Notarial), Volume IV, Book 1/1, The general theory of the contract* (Théorie Générale du contrat) (Larcier 2010) 562.

23 See Mathieu Higny, 'The payment of rent and charges to the lessor in the lease of an immovable property facing the coronavirus' (Le paiement du loyer et des charges au bailleur dans le bail d'un bien immeuble face au coronavirus) (2020) J.T. 265–272.

24 See J.P. Etterbeek, 30 October 2020, 20A870; Jean Van Zuylen, 'Coronavirus et force majeure: questions choisies', (2020) Revue générale de droit civil 382 ff.

25 See J. Paix Woluwe Saint Pierre, 2 July 2020, Leuven 10 November 2020, nr 20A957/2.

more easily applied since the property can no longer be available as stipulated in the contract.[26]

2.2.4.3. Jurisprudence

Of course, the case law remains scarce. One example is a judgment of the Colmar Court of Appeal of 12 March 2020.[27] A foreigner appeals a first-degree order. He cannot appear at the hearing; the court recognises a case of force majeure in these terms:

> The appellant, Mr. A X, could not be brought to the hearing at the Court of Appeal, because of the exceptional and insurmountable circumstances, of the character of force majeure, related to the ongoing epidemic of Covid-19; in effect, we were informed in the morning that a foreigner detained at the Geispolsheim CRA with symptoms of the virus was being screened and had been in contact with the staff of the Order of Malta during an hour-long interview. The staff of this association is therefore subject to a 14-day confinement. However, the concomitant presence in this centre of this person and Mr. To X, who himself was also assisted by the staff of the Order of Malta in drafting his act of appeal; therefore, the person concerned is also likely to have been in close contact with the foreign person who may be affected by this virus. Therefore, these exceptional circumstances, resulting in the absence of Mr. A X at today's hearing, are of the character of force majeure, being external, unpredictable and irresistible, given the time required to rule and the fact that, within that time, it will not be possible to ascertain the absence of a risk of contagion and to have an escort authorized to take Mr. X to the hearing. In addition, the Geispolheim CRA indicated that it did not have any equipment to hear Mr. A X in the context of a video conference, which it follows that such a solution is also not possible for this audience. Accordingly, the hearing takes place in the absence of Mr. To X, that Master F G-H, a lawyer at the Colmar bar, who was committed to the law, agreed to represent.

I have referred to this judgment because it is recent and it illustrates the exceptional situation in which we find ourselves, although the facts do not concern contract law.

---

26 See also in French law, Martine Behar Touchais, 'The impact of a health crisis on commercial law contracts. On the occasion of the Covid-19 pandemic' (L'impact d'une crise sanitaire sur les contrats en droit commercial; À l'occasion de la pandémie de Covid-19) (2020) 15–16 The Enterprise and Business Legal Week 9, 12, 14, 15, 16, 18; Bail commercial – Le sort des loyers dans les baux commerciaux à l'épreuve de la crise du covid-19: quid de l'exception d'inexécution ? – Libres propos par Louis Perreau-Saussine, 01/05/2020 La Semaine Juridique – Notariale et immobilière. The *exceptio non adimpleti contractus* can also be invoked by the lessee if the usage of the lease contract is mentioned in the contract and that the lessor is not able to give this usage due to the coronavirus crisis and its effects.

27 6th (6ème), foreigners (étrangers), judgment 20/01098 (jugement 20/01098), published at *Dalloz (publié chez Dalloz)*, doctrine.

2.3. THE *FAIT DU PRINCE*

We can highlight that the *fait du prince* represents the intervention of the public authorities in the contract and can therefore constitute a force majeure case.[28]

As noted in the introduction, the pandemic required State intervention in different parts of the world. States have taken various measures to prevent the spread of the virus, which have had a substantial impact on the economy and on contracts.

Under Belgian law, we have, to date, different successive ministerial orders, on 13, 18, 23 and 27 March, 17 April and 8, 13, 15 May 2020, relating to the containment following the coronavirus. Other orders have been successively adopted.

Let us take, for example, Articles 2 and 3 of the 18 March 2020 orders:

> Art. 2. Telework at home is mandatory in all non-essential enterprises, regardless of size, for all staff members whose duties are appropriate. For functions to which telework at home cannot apply, companies must take the necessary measures to ensure compliance with the rules of social distance, the maintenance of a distance of 1.5 meters between each person. This rule is also applicable for employer-organized transportation. Non-essential companies unable to comply with the above measures must close.
>
> Art. 3. The provisions of Article 2 do not apply to businesses in the crucial sectors and to essential services covered by the annex to this order. However, these companies and services are required to implement, as far as possible, the telework system at home and the rules of social distance.

Ministerial order dated 3 April broadened the services listed in Article 3 and now include "producers, suppliers, service providers and subcontractors of goods, works and services essential to the activities of these enterprises and services".[29] By Ministerial order dated 17 April, the containment was prolonged until 3 May; garden centres and do-it-yourself retailers could be reopened.

In Luxembourg, a regulation was issued on 18 March and modified on 8 April. Article 3 of the regulation prohibits commercial and artisanal activities except essential services. Measures to alleviate these prohibitions were decided on 17 April.[30] In many countries, a distinction was made between essential and other services.

---

[28] See Stéphanie Michaux and Denis Philippe, *Obligations, Theoretical and practical treatise* (Obligations, Traité théorique et pratique) (Kluwer 2002) 4.32.

[29] Various decrees have been issued in specific areas.

[30] Numerous news orders have been issued since then; an inventory of these measures can be found on the website of the State of Luxembourg (https://covid19.public.lu/dam-assets/covid-19/toolbox/nouvelles-mesures/affiche/11-01-2021/10206-DISA-Cov19-Mesures-Jan21-A4-v4.pdf accessed 31 March 2021).

Essential services can therefore be provided during periods of confinement. However, the rules of telework and social distancing must be respected, but unlike non-essential services, only where possible. Given the importance of health and the dangers of contamination, the concept "as far as possible" must be interpreted in the sense that the best efforts must be made to respect the rules of telework and social distancing.

This ministerial order has since then been modified several times, to alleviate or to strengthen the containment measures.[31]

2.4. EFFECTS: THEORETICAL ASPECTS[32]

The first step is to *inform* the co-contractor of the force majeure event and its effects on the contract. This is not expressly provided for by law but may be based on Article 1134, paragraph 3, of the Civil Code, which provides for the good faith implementation of the conventions.

Notification can be preventive; for example, coronavirus occurs but may pose risks to the performance of the contract; the contractor is directly notified even if the execution of the contract is still possible. It can be circumstantial; it comes at a time when the contract is impossible to perform. If it is circumstantial, it must also be detailed: the debtor must explain why he/she invokes force majeure. Since communication between contractors is essential, we can only advise preventive notification.

As the law is silent on notification and its forms, its necessity and content will be left to the judge's discretion.

Force majeure results in the dissolution of the contract if the effect is final, and the suspension of the contract if it is temporary. It will result in the dissolution of the contract if, although the effect of the event is only temporary, the duration of the suspension causes the performance of the obligation to lose its purpose.[33]

---

[31] See more recently, Ministerial Order of 28 October modified by the Ministerial Order of 1 November 2020, M.B. 1/11/2020, éd. 1. Ministerial Order of November 28 November 2020 M.B. 29 November 2020.

[32] Patrick Wéry, *Notary Directory, Bonds Obligations (Répertoire Notarial), Volume IV, Book 1/1, The general theory of the contract* (Théorie générale du contrat) (Larcier 2010) 568; Stéphanie Michaux and Denis Philippe, *Obligations, Theoretical and practical treatise* (Obligations, Traité théorique et pratique) (Kluwer 2002) 4.43 ff.

[33] Patrick Wéry, *Notary Directory, Bonds Obligations (Répertoire Notarial), Volume IV, Book 1/1, The general theory of the contract* (Théorie générale du contrat) (Larcier 2010) 568; Denis Philippe, 'La force majeure temporaire et la suspension des obligations contractuelles', *Le droit des obligations dans la vie de l'entreprise* (La Charte 2017) 219–243.

The force majeure operates for the future, and therefore *ex nunc*, unlike the termination by fault or annulment of the contract which operate in principle *ex tunc*. Force majeure therefore has no retroactive effect.[34] This effect *ex tunc* is considered an application of the broader figure of the caducité of the convention because of the disappearance of its object.[35]

The solution is, however, disputed as some consider that there is no reason to submit dissolution by application of risk doctrine and termination for wrongful non-performance to two different legal regimes.[36] I believe that it makes sense for force majeure to operate *ex tunc*; indeed, it is by the impossibility of performance that the contract ceases its effects; there is no justification for nullifying the past that has been properly executed; in the event of annulment, for example, the contract was flawed at its conclusion; the resolution aims at sanctioning the gross negligence of a contracting party which undermines the trust, past, present and future, that could have been placed in this contracting party. But this sanction is not needed in case of force majeure.

Is it possible to estimate that the contract could be dissolved before its performance has been made impossible (anticipatory breach)? The case law does not rule on this issue, but the possibility of terminating the contract even before the breach is verified is recognised in the draft reform of Belgian contract law, in the Vienna Convention on International Sale in Articles 71 ff. What can be done when the debtor is at fault in the above hypothesis, must also apply in case of force majeure. A solution that guarantees the effectiveness of the contractual relationship must be found and it is not useful to enclose one of the parties in a meaningless contractual relationship.

What are the effects of force majeure on the parties' performance in a unilateral contract?

The debtor is relieved of his/her obligation.[37] In case of unilateral contract, the contract is terminated.[38]

---

34 Patrick Wéry, *Notary Directory, Bonds Obligations (Répertoire Notarial), Volume IV, Book 1/1, The general theory of the contract* (Théorie Générale du contrat) (Larcier 2010) 576; Stéphanie Michaux and Denis Philippe, *Obligations, Theoretical and practical treatise* (Obligations, Traité théorique et pratique) (Kluwer 2002) 4.48.

35 Oliver Vanden Berghe, Chapter 4 – 'Force majeure' in Oliver Vanden Berghe (ed), *Manage the duration and end of commercial contracts – Managing the duration and termination of commercial contracts* (Gérer la durée et la fin des contrats commerciaux – Gérer la durée et la fin des contrats commerciaux) (Larcier 2009) 61–63.

36 François Glansdorff, 'Force Majeure' (2019) J.T. 6772, 355–358, esp 19.

37 Patrick Wéry, *Notary Directory, Bonds Obligations (Répertoire Notarial), Volume IV, Book 1/1, The general theory of the contract* (Théorie générale du contrat) (Larcier 2010) 572; Henri De Page, *Treaty of civil law*, Volume II, 1964, 811.

38 Stéphanie Michaux and Denis Philippe, *Obligations, Theoretical and practical treatise* (Obligations, Traité théorique et pratique) (Kluwer 2002) 4.46.

What in the case of synallagmatic contracts?

The doctrine of risk (théorie des risques[39]) is applied. Authors have the habit of quoting the adage *res perit creditori:* the thing perishes at the creditor's risk. In other words, the creditor cannot claim anything from his/her co-contractor.[40]

However, there are three exceptions to this principle:

- When the debtor was already put in default;
- When the parties have, by a contrary clause, extended the debtor's liability to the case of force majeure;
- Where the debtor is bound, as a result of a particular legal provision, to act in case of force majeure.[41]

Thus, the debtor, for instance the supplier of goods which cannot be delivered due to the coronavirus crisis, is discharged from its obligation and also, in principle, from all obligations of the contract.[42]

If the co-contractor remains required, it will be said that the loss of the contract is for him/her: the burden of risk falls on him/her.

If, on the other hand, this co-contractor is also relieved of its commitments, it will be said that the loss of the contract is extinguished for the debtor of the obligation because of the external cause: the burden of risk then falls on that debtor (*res perit debitori*).[43] In practice, if the seller is unable to deliver for force majeure, he/she is released while the buyer is also exempt from paying the price.

What happens in the event of a sale with a down payment? The seller cannot deliver given the force majeure finding its cause in the coronavirus. The buyer has made a 30% down payment – is he/she entitled to a refund of this down payment?

Based on the principles set out above, we have seen that the supplier is released from its obligation to deliver, and based on risk doctrine, the customer

39 See for a criticism of this doctrine in case of force majeure, Michaël de Potter de ten Broeck, *Changed circumstances in contract law* (Gewijzigde omstandigheden in het contractenrecht) (Intersentia 2017) 308.

40 Cass., 27 June 1946, *Pas.*, 1946, I, p 270, obs. Raoul.Hayoit de Termicourt.; *R.C.J.B.*, 1947, p 268, obs. André de Bersaques. See also on the lease, *supra*, section 2.2.4.3.

41 See for more nuances, Stéphanie Michaux and Denis Philippe, *Obligations, Theoretical and practical treatise* (Obligations, Traité théorique et pratique) (Kluwer 2002) 4.45 and 4.46; Patrick Wéry, *Notary Directory, Bonds Obligations (Répertoire Notarial), Volume IV, Book 1/1, The general theory of the contract* (Théorie Générale du contrat) (Larcier 2010) 572.

42 Ibid, 569.

43 Patrick Wéry, 'Subsection 3 – The liberating foreign cause, risk theory and unpredictability' (La cause étrangère libératoire, la théorie des risques et l'impérvision) in *Law of Obligations* (Droit des obligations), Volume 1 (Larcier 2011) 538–562; Pierre Harmel, *The sale (La vente), Effects of extinguishing obligations* (Effets de l'extinction des obligations), *Notary Directory, Book 1, Sale General Theory* (Répertoire Notarial, Livre I, Vente: Théorie générale) (Larcier 1985) 592.

should not pay the price. Thus, there will be a restitution of the down payment.[44] However, if expenses have already been advanced by the seller, the seller will be able to keep them.[45]

The force majeure is partial when it has an effect on certain obligations of the contract only; for instance, the contract foresees three deliveries; only one of these is hit by force majeure;[46] the contract can be performed for the other deliveries. But, for the delivery affected by the force majeure, the seller is exempt from delivery and the buyer is discharged from payment of the price.[47] Also the obligations which are accessory to the obligations hit by the force majeure are extinguished.[48]

We have already underlined that force majeure leads to the suspension when it has only temporary effects.[49] This is the case for the effects of coronavirus. What makes this crisis peculiar is that the coronavirus has had at least two waves and thus the effects vary in the time and the moment of recovery is uncertain. The suspension will lead to termination when the contract loses its utility.[50] For instance, it could be after the first or the second wave.

We can point out that in certain circumstances, obligations can survive the end of the contract, like the non-compete clause or the confidentiality clause.

2.5. RECOMMENDATIONS FOR THE DRAFTING OF A FORCE MAJEURE CLAUSE IN A CONTRACT

Excellent studies have been devoted to these clauses[51] and it is not the subject of this brief contribution to carry out a new analysis of the clauses, but simply to show how to cope with the coronavirus crisis through these clauses. We recommend that you carefully plan the renegotiation of the contract. After this pandemic, the force majeure clause will no longer be drafted as before.

---

44 Jean Van Zuylen, 'Coronavirus and force majeure: questions choisies' (2020) R.G.D.C. 382; Civ. Brussels (4th ch), 26 April 1991 (1991) J.T. 603.

45 See for the application of similar principles in terms of conditions precedent Benoït Kohl, Chapter I 'Elements constituting the sale' in *Real estate sales* (Larcier 2012) 7–27.

46 Patrick Wéry, *Notary Directory, Bonds Obligations (Répertoire Notarial), Volume IV, Book 1/1, The general theory of the contract* (Théorie Générale du contrat) (Larcier 2010) 576; Stéphanie Michaux and Denis Philippe, *Obligations, Theoretical and practical treatise* (Obligations, Traité théorique et pratique) (Kluwer 2002) 4.57.

47 Patrick Wéry, *Notary Directory, Bonds Obligations (Répertoire Notarial), Volume IV, Book 1/1, The general theory of the contract* (Théorie Générale du contrat) (Larcier 2010) 575.

48 Stéphanie Michaux and Denis Philippe, *Obligations, Theoretical and practical treatise* (Obligations, Traité théorique et pratique) (Kluwer 2002) 4.57.

49 Cass. 13 January 1956, *Pas.*, 1956, I, 460.

50 See Stéphanie Michaux and Denis Philippe, *Obligations, Theoretical and practical treatise* (Obligations, Traité théorique et pratique) (Kluwer 2002) 4.51.

51 See Marc Gouden, 'Contractual liability arrangements' (Clauses aménageant la responsabilité contractuelle) in Denis Philippe (ed), *The drafting of international contracts (La rédaction des contrats internationaux: conseils aux praticiens & approche de droit comparé)* (Bruylant 2012) 56.

Let us recall the structure of the force majeure clause which corresponds to that of the concept of force majeure that we have shown in the table above, but let us now put the renegotiation in the spotlight.

Figure 1. Force majeure clause timeline

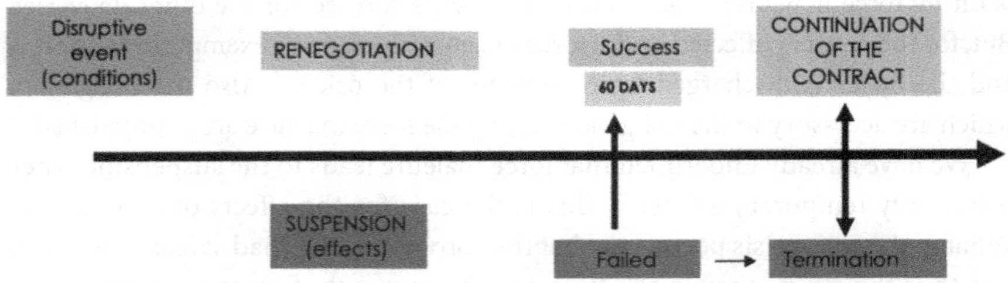

Source: Produced by the author.

It is known that in addition to defining the concept and its conditions of application (externality, unforeseeability and impossibility of performance) the clause often sets out the circumstances that may give rise to the invocation of force majeure and it is certain that the term pandemic will now be included.

Let us take the following clause:

> No Party shall be liable for any failure to perform its obligations where such failure is as a result of Acts of God (including fire, flood, earthquake, storm, hurricane or other natural disaster), war, invasion, act of foreign enemies, hostilities (whether war is declared or not), civil war, rebellion, revolution, insurrection, military or usurped power or confiscation, terrorist activities, nationalisation, government sanction, blockage, embargo, labour dispute, strike, lockout *pandemic* or interruption or failure of electricity [or telephone service], and no other Party will have a right to terminate this Agreement under Clause 19 (Termination) in such circumstances.

We added the pandemic to the earlier clause. The advantage of inserting the circumstance will be to avoid discussion on whether the coronavirus constitutes a hypothesis of force majeure; some believe that previous causes of death (e.g. H1N1) are not a case of force majeure, so the current pandemic is not in itself a case of force majeure.

We will now proceed with the analysis of components of the clause that have caught our attention in the context of this pandemic.

2.5.1. *Notification*

The following clause can be taken:

> The party invoking the force majeure case should, immediately after the occurrence, send an express and recommended notification to the other party.

A notification is important, as we have seen, for the fluidity of communication between contractors; this notification, may take place in a preventive manner, which is not expressly provided for in this clause. This preventive notification is important in the case of COVID-19, given the evolutionary nature of this pandemic on the contract. Looking at the various ministerial orders that have been issued in Belgium. We no longer believe it is appropriate in the digital age to require a recommended mail notification.

Another more comprehensive clause is:

> The Contractor shall forthwith notify the Buyer as soon as the said Special and Excepted Risks have ended.
>
> The termination of the force majeure shall similarly be notified.
>
> The affected Party shall also provide notice to the other Party of
>
> 1. with respect to an ongoing Force Majeure Event, the cessation of the Force Majeure Event, and
> 2. the affected Party's ability to recommence performance of its obligations under this Agreement
>
> as soon as possible, but in any event, not later than seven (7) days after the occurrence of each of (1) and (2) above or, where the affected Party has (acting reasonably) vacated the Site, or its relevant property, as the case may be, as a result of such Force Majeure Event, not later than seven (7) days after the date it becomes or should have become aware of such occurrence.

2.5.2. *Effects and renegotiation*

> The contracting parties are momentarily untied, totally or partially, from their obligations in the case of force majeure having the unpredictability and being beyond the will of the parties, which is responsible for the party availing itself of the written proof of the force majeure nature of such a case within thirty days.
>
> If, due to force majeure, one of the parties is prevented from fulfilling its contractual obligations for a period of more than three months, the contracting parties meet to determine the conditions for the continuation of the contract or the termination of the contract.

We can only stress the importance of renegotiating the contract. If the contract is concluded now, a specific provision for COVID-19 may also be provided, if its influence on the contract can be coped with now.

As we know, COVID-19 is working like waves with a permanent movement; thus it is possible that more than one renegotiation will be required.

Thus we advise incorporation of a renegotiation clause with less strict deadlines due to the uncertainty of the effects of the pandemic. We can assume that the contract will be renegotiated and that, if the contract loses its purpose, it will be terminated, for instance:

> If, due to force majeure as previously defined, one of the parties is prevented from fulfilling its contractual obligations, the performance of the contract is suspended. Parties shall during this period of suspension, renegotiate the contract. If the force majeure event disappears, the contract will be performed as contractually foreseen or with the adequate adaptation due to the effect of the force majeure event during the period of suspension.
>
> If the force majeure event continues later to prevent the fulfilment of contractual obligations, and the performance of the contract becomes useless, parties are entitled to terminate the contract.

Among the elements of the renegotiation is the deferral of payment obligations. Thus, the return of the deposit in the event of force majeure can be foreseen if, as a result of COVID-19, the performance cannot take place.

2.5.3. Booking clause

A contract may provide that machines are reserved for the contractor to carry out work. It is feared that the co-contractor will not provide the raw materials, plans and other instructions intended to carry out this work. These must be supplied by a subcontractor who is in a containment situation and cannot deliver the raw materials

Some elements in the drafting of the clause:

- First, as soon as the first forebodings of difficulty of execution appear, the contractor must be notified;
- A time limit for cancellation of reservations to reallocate the machines must be stipulated;
- If force majeure is not proven, a penalty may be provided for the booking fee;
- If force majeure is proven, a renegotiation can be planned with indications of the risks to be borne on both sides.

2.5.4. Delivery of masks or respirators

A renegotiation can be planned if the number of masks ordered does not arrive due to a force majeure caused by the coronavirus. Clauses about respirators can also be inserted. For the buyer, it will be the clause providing penalties in case of delay that will be preferred, but from the perspective of a Belgian seller who is intermediate, it will be the force majeure clause that is needed to exempt him/her from liability if the masks do not arrive from a foreign supplier. The two clauses can be combined: no liability for the first fortnight and then a penalty clause beyond that period.

2.5.5. *Obligation to limit one's own damage*

> In the event of force majeure, the contracting parties are required to make every effort to remove and/or lessen the difficulties and damage caused, in which case the other party will be constantly kept informed of the situation. Otherwise, the defaulting party may be claimed damages by the other party.

We can only insist on the appropriateness of providing a renegotiation clause in the contract in case of force majeure; this will allow the parties to better develop alternative solutions. For example, if the goods cannot come from China, a supply from Argentina may be considered and a price renegotiated; the survival of the contract is at stake.

2.5.6. *During the suspension*

> Buyers shall be at liberty to procure from other suppliers any deficiency of deliveries caused by the operation of this clause.

If the suspension causes the contract to lose its usefulness, it can be foreseen that the contract will be dissolved. Thus, let us take the example where you order goods on 1 February in China. You had to insert these goods into a product to be delivered by the 1 March. You cannot make the delivery on 1 March, as the products did not arrive from China. Therefore, the force majeure will have a final effect since the delivery of the product has lost all utility for the final buyer.[52]

In addition, the post-suspension or post-confinement period may also be provided; the suspension may have changed the supply conditions leading, for instance, to a price increase.

2.5.7. *Damage and costs*

> For delays and non-performance of obligations due to force majeure, neither party can claim penalties, interest or any other compensation or participation in the injury suffered by the party because of force majeure.

This clause is quite obvious, but it avoids any discussion. Sometimes during the suspension period, costs are incurred; for example, the seller carries out

---

52 See Denis Philippe, 'Temporary force majeure and the suspension of contractual obligations' (La force majeure temporaire et la suspension des obligations contractuelles) in *The law of obligations in the business* (Le droit des obligations dans la vie de l'entreprise) (La Charte 2017) 219–243.

transport or stores goods. It will be useful to predict who will bear the costs of transportation or storage.

3. HARDSHIP OR *IMPRÉVISION*

3.1. DEFINITION

The doctrine of unforeseen circumstances is intended for having the adjustment of the contract admitted when circumstances with the following characteristics arise:

- unaccountability to the party that invokes it;
- unpredictability and unavoidability;
- inevitably leading to an upheaval in the contractual economy.[53]

Hardship leads to renegotiation of the contract.

Table 2. Structure of the hardship clause

HYPOTHESIS			**REGIME**	
Circumstances		Effects	Notification	Renegotiation
Unaccountable	Unpredictable	Frustration of purpose Excessively expensive Disruption of the contractual economy		Dissolution in case failure of the Negotiations

Source: Compiled by the author

3.2. CONDITIONS OF APPLICATION

Hardship or impracticability will also be very common during the coronavirus crisis; indeed, the difficult circumstances that the virus imposes on us will often make it much more difficult to perform the contract. For example, as a

53 See for a comparative analysis, Denis Philippe, *Changement de circonstances et bouleversement de l'économie contractuelle* (Bruylant 1986), 'Unexpected circumstances in European contract law' in Ewoud Hondius and Hans Christoph Grigoleit (eds), *Common Core of European Private Law* (Cambridge University Press 2011), and 'France and related jurisdictions', ibid, 144 ff.

result of containment measures (telework) the execution of your services has become excessively difficult. The doctrine of unforeseen circumstances it is not expressly recognised in Belgian[54] law and it is therefore highly recommended to arrange it contractually as will be explained in section 3.4.

Let us take the example outlined above. You cannot source from China and you invoke force majeure. There is an alternative source of supply in Argentina but the cost is twice as high, and choosing that source of supply would lead to an important loss for you; you can invoke hardship to renegotiate the contract.

For the application of this doctrine, we can refer to what we have outlined on the unaccountability and unpredictability in terms of force majeure. The upheaval of the contractual economy is different from the impossibility that finds application in force majeure. Indeed, execution should not be impossible but excessively onerous. This is the case in the aforementioned example of supply in Argentina.

Upheaval of the contractual economy can cover three different effects:

- the performance of the obligation becomes excessively burdensome;
- the original equilibrium between the obligations is disrupted;
- the purpose of the contract is frustrated.[55]

The effect of the unforeseen circumstances doctrine is the adjustment of the contract and not the suspension or dissolution. Thus, in the example mentioned above, the price difference between the Argentine product and the Chinese product can be shared between parties, for example, halved.

3.3. RECOGNITION OF THE DOCTRINE OF UNFORESEEN CIRCUMSTANCES IN BELGIAN LAW

This doctrine has long been rejected as in France.[56] But recent decisions of the Supreme Court are more favourable to the recognition of this doctrine.

---

[54] We are not going to repeat what we have already written and we refer to the most recent article by Denis Philippe, 'La théorie de l'imprévision' in Pascal Ancel and André Prum (eds) *Reforming contract law: Comparative analysis around Luxembourg law* (Réformer le droit des contrats ? Analyse comparée autour du droit luxembourgeois) (Larcier 2020) 467; Denis Philippe, 'Les clauses relatives au changement de circonstances dans les contrats à long terme' in Denis Philippe (ed), *La rédaction des contrats internationaux* (Bruylant 2012) 143.

[55] See Denis Philippe, *Changing circumstances and upheaval of the contractual economy* (Changement de circonstances et bouleversement de l'économie contractuelle) (Bruylant 1986), Chapter II, no 1.3.3.1.

[56] See Denis Philippe, *Changing circumstances and upheaval of the contractual economy* (Changement de circonstances et bouleversement de l'économie contractuelle) (Bruylant 1986) Chapter II, no 1.1., p. 155; Cass., 30 October 1924, *Pas.*, 1924, I, 565; Denis Philippe, 'The point about ... unforeseen circumstances' (Le point sur ... l'imprévision) (2007) J.T. 728 ff.

In an important decision of 19 June 2009, the Supreme Court applied the hardship in a case of long- term international steel sales contract. During the performance of the contract, the price registered an unforeseeable increase of 70%. The Supreme Court applied the Vienna Convention on the Sale of Good (CISG) and considered that the matter of unforeseen circumstances was governed but not settled by the Vienna Convention and made an application of Article 7.2. CISG which allows the judge, in case of a gap, to complete the law with the general principles underlying the Convention. The Supreme Court decided that the Unidroit Principles are such general principles and made an application of Article 6.2.2. of the Unidroit Principles on unforeseen circumstances.

Another important case is the decision of the Supreme Court of 14 October 2010.[57] In this case, in the contract organising the divorce, the husband agreed to pay to his previous wife alimony of the equivalent of €250 in 1979. More than 20 years later, the income of the husband decreased whereas the income of the wife increased. The husband claimed relief; the wife refused; the judge of the merits as the Supreme Court considered that this refusal amounted, in the circumstances of the case, to an abuse of rights.

We know that in France, *imprévision* has been rejected since the Canal de Craponne case of 31 March 1876, but has been expressly recognised in the reform of the Civil Code, Article 1195.[58]

> Art. 1195. – If a change of circumstances that was unforeseeable at the time of the conclusion of the contract renders performance excessively onerous for a party who had not accepted the risk of such a change, that party may ask the other contracting party to renegotiate the contract. The first party must continue to perform his obligations during renegotiation.
>
> In the case of refusal or the failure of renegotiations, the parties may agree to terminate the contract from the date and on the conditions which they determine, or by a common agreement ask the court to set about its adaptation. In the absence of an agreement within a reasonable time, the court may, on the request of a party, revise the contract or put an end to it, from a date and subject to such conditions as it shall determine.

---

57 See Jean Van Zuylen, 'Some thoughts on the economic usefulness of the contract at the beginning of the decision of the Cour de cassation of 14 October 2010' (Quelques réflexions sur l'utilité économique du contrat au départ de l'arrêt de la Cour de cassation du 14 octobre 2010), (2012) DAOR 6 ff.; Denis Philippe, 'The judge and the revision of the contract: The upheaval of the contractual economy', (Le juge et la révision du contrat: le bouleversement de l'économie contractuelle) 'The judge and the contract' (Le juge et le contrat), The Charter, (La Charte) 2014, pp 377–407; Denis Philippe, 'The upheaval of the contractual economy in Belgian law' (Le bouleversement de l'économie contractuelle en droit belge) (2015) Revue de Droit International et de Droit Comparé 159–164.

58 See 'Contract Law Reform: The Debate', (2014) Law and Heritage, no 240; Patrick Dupichot, 'The new judicial termination for unforeseen circumstances' (La nouvelle résiliation judiciaire pour imprévision) in Philippe Stoffel Munck (ed), *Reform of Contract Law and Business Practic* (Réforme du droit des contrats et pratique des affaires) (Dalloz 2015) 75 ff.

In Belgium, a draft of reform of the Civil Code on the law of contractual obligations has been approved by the previous government. Article 5.77 of this draft has inserted a provision similar to Article 1195.[59]

The Belgian draft, not yet officially translated, is largely inspired by the French law.[60]

We can discuss briefly the main conditions of application. Unfortunately, due to the non-recognition of this doctrine over the decades, the implementation of it was very scarce.[61]

- Unforeseeable circumstances. We have seen that the Supreme Court considered that the 70% increase in the price of steel at the beginning of this millennium was unforeseeable; the coronavirus crisis would also be considered as unforeseeable.[62]
- The performance must be excessively onerous. The 70% increase in the price of steel (the raw material to manufacture steel pipes) makes the contract excessively onerous;
- The risk must not be assumed by the debtor; for instance, if you enter into a contract for sale of land where it is uncertain that you can build on it (speculative piece of land), you cannot invoke the doctrine of unforeseen circumstances if, after the conclusion of the contract, you do not receive the building permit.

We can regret that French and Belgian law do not accept frustration of purpose. The Belgian drafters mention in the preparatory works that excessively onerous includes the substantial alteration of the economic balance between the obligations of the parties, and this precision is welcome. For instance, you enter into a long-term patent licence contract. After one year, a new patent has been

---

59 The text has been approved on first reading by the former government; now, the same draft has been deposited at the Parliament under the number 55K0174001 and we hope that this text will be adopted shortly.

60 Denis Philippe, 'The introduction of unforeseen circumstances in Belgian law' (L'introduction de l'imprévision en droit belge), *Business Law in evolution* (Le droit des affaires en évolution) (Larcier 2018) 55–68.

61 However, the doctrine of unforeseen circumstances has been recognised through other concepts, like force majeure or caducité but it does not seem opportune to discuss these applications in this contribution. See Denis Philippe, *Changing circumstances and upheaval of the contractual economy* (Changement de circonstances et bouleversement de l'économie contractuelle) (Bruylant 1986), Chapter II, no 3, p. 169; Patrick Wéry, L'imprévision et ses succédanés, observations sub Liège, 27 June 1995, (1996) J.L.M.B. 108); see also for an application of the force majeure in case of unforeseen circumstances, Michaël de Potter de ten Broeck, *Changed circumstances in contract law* (Gewijzigde omstandigheden in het contractenrecht) (Intersentia 2017).

62 See on this condition, Denis Philippe, *Changing circumstances and upheaval of the contractual economy* (Changement de circonstances et bouleversement de l'économie contractuelle) (Bruylant 1986) no 1.3.2.3., esp p 631.

discovered that deprives the licence contract of the old patent of utility. This is an application of the frustration of purpose; the above-mentioned French and Belgian provisions cannot apply in this case.

These provisions introduced the renegotiation of the contract by the parties which is to be welcomed; the negotiations must be done within a reasonable time which is also opportune although too vague.

The French provision foresees the intervention of the judge without any specific provision; the Belgian provision designates a specific judge (the "as referee" judge) who can take a decision in an urgent proceeding. This must also be approved because the life of the contract must be safeguarded.

It is to be welcomed that these provisions favoured the renegotiation of the contract by the parties. The intervention of the judge can be considered as the ultimate recourse.

3.4. RECOMMENDATIONS FOR CONTRACT REDACTION

A short clause can be put forward:

> In the event of a fundamental change in circumstances that place an unfair burden on one of the parties arising from this Protocol, the parties will consult with each other to jointly find fair adjustments to that agreement.

The clause does not mention circumstances, and therefore the pandemic is excluded. If you write a clause with exemplative circumstances, you will naturally have to include the pandemic from now on. Thus, one can take the following clause:

> If owing to changed circumstances *such as* changes in monetary values or discriminatory Governmental action or regulations, *pandemics* or differential customs duties unduly discriminating against the origin from which A is then supplying to B, the continued operation of which is causing undue hardship to either party, that party shall have the right to require the other party to participate in a joint examination of the position with a view to determining whether revision or modification of the provisions hereof is required and if so what revision or modification would be appropriate and equitable in the circumstances.

If the contract is concluded now, a specific provision for COVID-19 may also be provided, if its influence on the contract can be foreseen now. Thus, it can be expected that if the contractually planned source of supply dries up, the parties will renegotiate in order to find another source of supply and share the costs.

The post-containment situation can also be more accurately organised through hardship clauses. It is possible that the performance of the contract will be much more difficult and that a renegotiation will have to be undertaken between contracting parties.

Once more, the drafting of the clause is more complex due to the volatility of the effects of the coronavirus; the performance of the obligations can be first suspended, then become excessively burdensome; thereafter, the effects of the coronavirus crisis become definitive or the situation reverts to normal.

We can propose the next clause:

> In case of hardship, a party can require a renegotiation of the contract. If the definitive adaptation of the contract cannot be found rapidly, parties will in a period of one week, proceed to a temporary adaptation of the obligations until a definitive adaptation is agreed upon.

3.5. EUROPEAN LAW INSTITUTE CORONAVIRUS PRINCIPLES

The European Law Institute (ELI) has adopted legal principles to be respected during the coronavirus crisis.

A specific principle (principle 13), concerns the effects on the contractual obligations. It would be opportune to quote this principle:

1. Where performance of a contract is temporarily or definitively prevented directly or indirectly due to the COVID-19 outbreak or the European States' decisions taken in relation to the COVID-19 outbreak, States should ensure that existing law on impossibility or force majeure apply in an effective way and provide reasonable solutions. In particular, the contractual allocation of risk in these instances should be evaluated in the light of existing contracts, background legal regime and the principle of good faith.
2. Where, as a consequence of the COVID-19 crisis and the measures taken during the pandemic, performance has become excessively difficult (hardship principle), including when cost of performance has risen significantly, European States should ensure that, in accordance with the principle of good faith, parties enter into re-negotiations even if this has not been provided for in a contract or in existing legislation.
3. In conformity with the principle of solidarity, States should ensure that the consequences of the disruption of contractual relationships, such as the cancellation of travel arrangements, should not be at the sole risk of one party, in particular of a consumer or SME.

ELI underlines good faith and renegotiation in these difficult circumstances.[63]

[63] See the article on the website of the Institute ELI Publishes Principles for the COVID-19 Crisis www.europeanlawinstitute.eu accessed 19 March 2021.

4. CONCLUSIONS

There is no doubt that the coronavirus is, and will be, invoked by the debtor to be exempt from the performance of its obligations or to adapt the contract in a wide range of situations. Most of the conditions of application of force majeure and hardship are frequently fulfilled as unforeseeability and non-accountability but each case must be analysed carefully.

In case of force majeure, to assess the impossibility of performance, it must be considered whether alternative performance solutions are feasible and due to the successive waves of the coronavirus crisis, a renegotiation will be the most appropriate remedy.

In case of hardship, the assessment of substantial imbalance requires a careful analysis of the effects of the coronavirus on the overall economics of the contract.

We will witness a firework display of interrogations. One can only advise insertion of a clause in the contract organising force majeure and hardship and a judicious drafting of the clause would allow control, at least in part, of uncertainty. Due to the uncertainties linked to the covid crisis, we think that proactivity, flexibility and possibilities of initiative must be present in the clause.

Renegotiation and mediation are key to solving the problems having arisen due to the coronavirus crisis.

REMARKS ON THE EFFECTS OF THE PANDEMIC ON LONG-TERM CONTRACTS

Guido ALPA*

The coronavirus epidemic is shaping a situation that can be considered an event of force majeure, characterised by unpredictability, exceptionality and uncertainty in its duration and then impossibility of performing and termination of contract. It is necessary to take into account also the provisions adopted by national legislators concerning limitation of economic activities, working, travelling, moving, etc. These limitations result in orders and prohibitions, modifying the performance of contracts, sometimes causing impossibility. In Italian law, these events are considered "factum principis," *whose legal effects are similar to force majeure. Factum principis and force majeure affect long-term contracts, and may cause temporary supervening impossibility or supervening excessively onerous nature of the performance. In the first case, the performance may be postponed, in the second the contract shall be terminated. The Italian Civil Code's provisions suggest how the risk may be allocated between the parties in different situations submitted to the judge.*

* University of Rome – La Sapienza.

1. THE CORONAVIRUS AS AN EVENT OF FORCE MAJEURE AND AS A *FACTUM PRINCIPIS*

The coronavirus epidemic was defined as an *emergency* by decree-law no 6 of 23 February 2020[1] and a *pandemic* by the World Health Organization on 20 March 2020. The Organization stated that "The COVID-19 emergency committee has agreed unanimously that the epidemic still constitutes an international public health emergency",[2] and on 4 May it added that it is still a global public health emergency.[3] These declarations, formulated internationally, shape a situation that can certainly be considered an event of force majeure: it is unforeseeable, exceptional and uncertain in its duration.

In Italy, the first provisions were adopted by the Government, in the form of Prime Minister's decrees and then in the form of Council of Ministers' decrees, as well as by individual Ministers in the form of ministerial decrees; the Parliament was involved in the conversion of those decrees into statutes. Support was given to the sanitary system, to businesses in the form of tax credits, to big firms in the form of guarantees, pursuant to the Law-decree no 34/2020.

Many limitations were introduced to individual freedoms, commercial businesses and professional activities.

To react to the effects of the pandemic, we wondered whether it was preferable to introduce one or more statutes concerning long-term contracts, or to leave the solution of all questions to the Civil Code.

We additionally wondered whether, in the past, there have been events similar to the situation caused by the coronavirus and how the legal system reacted.

If we look at the provisions enacted during the Second World War, we find limitations on matters of property that have left traces in the civil code, such as confiscation and rationing. If we go back in time, during the First World War we note that detailed legislation regarding contracts was introduced,[4] and that, for

---

1 Containing "Urgent measures for the containment and management of the COVID-19 epidemic emergency", converted, with amendments, by law no 13 of 5 March 2020, subsequently abrogated by decree-law no 19 of 2020 with the exception of Article 3, paragraph 6-bis, and Article 4.

2 Source: WHO Website (2020) https://www.who.int/news-room/detail/01-05-2020-statement-on-the-third-meeting-of-the-international-health-regulations-(2005)-emergency-committee-regarding-the-outbreak-of-coronavirus-disease-(covid-19) accessed 10 June 2020.

3 According to the data distributed by the WHO, on 20 May 2020, there were 4,761,559 infections and 317,529 deaths (Health Emergency Dashboard).

4 For some references, see Pietro Cogliolo, *La legislazione di guerra nel diritto civile e commerciale* (UTET 1917); Vittorio Scialoja, *I problemi dello Stato italiano dopo la guerra* (Zanichelli 1918); of interest is Pietro Perlingieri and Antonella Tartaglia Polcini (eds), *Le prolusioni dei civilisti* (Edizioni Scientifiche Italiane 2012), where you can find Filippo Vassalli, *Della legislazione di guerra e dei nuovi confini del diritto privato* 1697, Francesco

example, rental contracts were amended, establishing the extension of contracts and the fixing of rental fees.

In other terms, for reasons of public benefit it was considered necessary to interfere in the contractual freedom of the parties, limiting it, with specific, extremely detailed provisions.

Today, the Italian legislator has not followed this model. Also, the specific provisions, being rather limited in their subject, exclude the possibility that they can be applied to all contracts and all circumstances without any generalisation.[5] The first doctrinal contributions pointed in this direction.[6]

The only general provision which could be considered of general relevance is Article 3 of Law-decree no 6/2020, which states that the observance of epidemic measures shall be taken in consideration in evaluating cases of late or partial payments.

According to the first commentators, this provision should exonerate the debtor from negligence for delays in performance. However, if the rules of supervening impossibility are applied, the solution is identical to the one already provided for by the code.[7] Therefore, this rule does not add much to the result that can be reached without it.

For matters concerning contracts, the solution has therefore remained entrusted to the civil code[8] without prejudice to the caveats which will be referred to below.

Ferrara sr., *Diritto di guerra e diritto di pace* 1727 and Alfredo Ascoli, *I Trattati di Versailles e di St. Germain e i principi di diritto civile* 1795; for an accurate reconstruction of this emergency law, see Laura Moscati, 'La legislazione di guerra e il contributo della civilistica romana' (2016) RISG 349.

5 But cf Giuseppe Sparano, 'Effetti della pandemia sui contratti. Tesi dell'unitarietà' (2020), Giust civ com http://giustiziacivile.com/obbligazioni-e-contratti/editoriali/effetti-della-pandemia-sui-contratti-tesi-dellunitarieta accessed 10 June 2020.

6 See, among the first ones, the essays published on Giust Civ com (2020), including, of a general nature, Aurelio Gentili, 'Un proposta sui contratti d'impresa al tempo del coronavirus' http://giustiziacivile.com/obbligazioni-e-contratti/approfondimenti/una-proposta-sui-contratti-dimpresa-al-tempo-del accessed 10 June 2020; Claudio Scognamiglio, 'L'emergenza Covid 19: quale ruolo per il civilista?' http://giustiziacivile.com/obbligazioni-e-contratti/editoriali/lemergenza-covid-19-quale-ruolo-il-civilista accessed 10 June 2020; Alberto Maria Benedetti, 'Il "rapporto" obbligatorio al tempo dell'isolamento: una causa (transitoria) di giustificazione?' http://giustiziacivile.com/obbligazioni-e-contratti/editoriali/il-rapporto-obbligatorio-al-tempo-dellisolamento-una-causa accessed 10 June 2020; Stefano Verzoni, 'Gli effetti, sui contratti in corso, dell'emergenza sanitaria legata al COVID-19' http://giustiziacivile.com/obbligazioni-e-contratti/approfondimenti/gli-effetti-sui-contratti-corso-dellemergenza-sanitaria accessed 10 June 2020; Raffaele Di Raimo, 'Le discontinuità che seguono i grandi traumi: pensando al credito (e al debito), mentre la notte è ancora fonda', http://giustiziacivile.com/obbligazioni-e-contratti/editoriali/le-discontinuita-che-seguono-i-grandi-traumi-pensando-al-credito accessed 10 June 2020.

7 For the first comments, see Vincenzo Cuffaro, 'Le locazioni commerciali e gli effetti giuridici dell'epidemia' (2020) Giust civ com http://giustiziacivile.com/obbligazioni-e-contratti/editoriali/le-locazioni-commerciali-e-gli-effetti-giuridici-dellepidemia accessed 10 June 2020.

8 See decree-law no 18 of 2020 containing measures to support employment, on contracts of legal patronage (Chapter V, further measures – Art 83 ff, suspension of hearings/proceedings),

According to the general principles of private law, limitations to contractual autonomy provided for by a public body constitute a *factum principis*, exonerating the debtor from fulfilling his/her obligations and excluding any fault. Here, there is no order of an authority, but a natural event and breach is due to an external cause; but the natural event should be unforeseeable.

A natural predictable event, such as hail or frost, is not in itself a reason exempting the debtor from liability. Roman jurists already considered this problem and had resolved it by taking into account the extent of the fortuitous event and its unpredictability.[9]

Parties may negotiate risk allocation: in the event in which the parties have divided the risks deriving from unforeseeable events, the *factum principis*, even if intervening, does not exonerate the debtor. On this matter, in a decision issued 60 years ago, which remains unamended up to this day, the Court of Cassation stated that "to be exempt from liability due to breach, the debtor cannot invoke the impossibility of the performance, even if due to *factum principis*, when the contract includes the possibility of the occurrence of an event that prevents performance and the debtor has willingly assumed the risk for himself or when the debtor has willingly placed himself in the condition of being subject to a possible mandatory measure".[10]

2. PERSONAL PERFORMANCE AND PROTECTION OF FUNDAMENTAL RIGHTS

The "Coronavirus decrees" have made reference to modes of rendering an employment contract and the largest number of scholarly contributions have been published on this matter.[11]

It is, however, clear that in long-term contracts in which the rendering of a physical performance was provided for, performance cannot be demanded by the creditor where it imposes on the debtor the risk of exposure to the virus.

---

on contracts for holidays and purchase of tickets to access shows of any kind (Art 88) and on some public tender contracts (Art 91 that added paragraph 6-bis to Art 3 decree law no. 6 of 2020, converted with amendments to law no 13 of 2020).

9 Ulpiano L. 15, §2, ff loc. cond.
The French Civil Code provides that 'Si le bail est fait pour plusieurs années, et que, pendant la durée du bail, la totalité ou la moitié d'une récolte au moins soit enlevée par des cas fortuits, le fermier peut demander une remise du prix de sa location, à moins qu'il ne soit indemnisé par les récoltes précédentes' (Art 1769).
This rule derives from Roman Law. Roman jurists pondered the matter in reference to the leasing of agricultural holdings. In particular, if the owner had to reduce the rental fee when the harvest was destroyed by a force majeure event, such as frost, hail, flooding. The response was positive, but only when the destruction depended on an extraordinary natural event.

10 Cass. Civ. 9 November 1960 no. 2979, Foro It 1960, no 373.

11 See the special dossier 'Emergenza Covid-19' (2020), Giust civ com http://giustiziacivile.com/editoriali/speciale-emergenza-covid-19 accessed 10 June 2020.

Such performance is for instance one that requires contact with other persons or travelling by public transport, or one that exposes the debtor to an unsafe workplace. Its execution would put the performer's life or health in danger, and the protection of the fundamental rights of life and health exempt the debtor from his/her obligation: the performance cannot be demanded according to the principle of good faith (Arts 1175 and 1375 Civil Code[12]). This will be the case for the entire period of time in which the epidemic continues, or until the moment in which provisions authorising the return of activities in safe conditions supervene.[13] The contract providing a performance that places the worker's life or health at risk is against mandatory rules and public order, and must therefore be considered null and void due to the illegality of the content of the contract. However, in this case it is also necessary to take into consideration the given circumstances.[14]

3. TEMPORARY SUPERVENING IMPOSSIBILITY: SUSPENSION OF CONTRACTS AND WITHDRAWAL

In order to ascertain that the debtor's breach does not imply any liability, the civil code requires that (1) the performance has become objectively impossible and that (2) the debtor is not at fault. This result is reached by coordinating Articles 1218 and 1256, which provide the following:

> Article 1218. *Liability of debtor.* The debtor who does not exactly render due performance is liable for damages unless he proves that the non-performance or delay was due to impossibility of performance for a cause not imputable to him.
>
> Article 1256. *Definitive impossibility and temporary impossibility.* An obligation is extinguished when its performance becomes impossible for a cause not imputable to the debtor.
>
> If the impossibility is only temporary, the debtor is not liable for delay in performance as long as it continues to exist. However, the obligation is extinguished if the impossibility continues until, depending on the source of the obligation or the nature of its subject matter, the debtor can no longer be held bound to perform the obligation or the creditor is no longer interested in the performance.

---

12 Article 1175 Italian Civil Code: '*Fair behaviour.* The debtor and the creditor shall behave according to rules of fairness'. Article 1375: '*Performance according to good faith.* The contract shall be performed according to good faith'.

13 A contract for services that are infringing fundamental rights – also with the consent of the interested party – would be null and void due to violation of dignity and public order: Maria Rosaria Marella, 'Il fondamento della dignità umana. Un modello costituzionale per il diritto dei contratti' (2007) Riv. crit. dir. priv. 67.

14 As occurs in the case of work performed on a public holiday: Court of Cassation 15 July 2019 no 18887.

On this matter, the Court of Cassation has stated that:

> The debtor's liberation due to supervening impossibility of performance may only occur, according to the provisions of Articles 1218 and 1256 Italian Civil Code, if and when the objective element of the impossibility to render the performance itself, considered alone, and the subjective element of absence of malice by the debtor in causing the event that has made the performance impossible both exist.[15]

Having ascertained the impossibility and the imputability, it is necessary to verify whether the impossibility is permanent or only temporary.

As stated in the beginning of this contribution, there is no clear understanding of how long a pandemic emergency will last. Hence, issuing legislative provisions – by which the restrictions to personal liberties due to reasons of public safety have been partly superseded – must be evaluated on a case-by-case basis, with reference to the specific circumstances.

In the event that the debtor does not fulfil his obligations – legitimately – for the stated reasons, the creditor can in turn refuse to fulfil his/her obligations. In fact, it has been stated that:

> exercising the exception of breach according to Article 1460 Civil Code,[16] that can also be applied in reference to contracts of continuous or periodic execution, and also for associated contracts, is separate from the responsibility of the counterparty, as the interest of the party in not carrying out his performance without a counter-performance merits protection, and this in order to prevent a situation of inequality for the counterparty; thus, said exception can be granted also in the event in which the breach depends on the supervening relative impossibility of performance due to reasons that are not imputable to the debtor.[17]

In long-term contracts, in which performances may be divided, split, or be subject to separate deliveries, the performances already carried out should be remunerated and the creditor must pay the price:

> The provision of Article 1458, paragraph one Italian civil code, for which, in long term contracts, the effect of the termination does not extend to the performances already carried out, does not mean that the breaching party has the right to a counter-performance, considering the fact that the non-retroactive mode of the

15 Cass civ (III) 8 June 2018 no 14915, https://pluris-cedam.utetgiuridica.it accessed 10 June 2020.

16 It is "*exceptio inadimpleti contractus*" provided by Article 1458 Italian Civil Code: "*Defence based upon non-performance.* In contracts providing for mutual counter-performances, each party can refuse to perform his obligation if the other party does not perform or offer to perform his own at the same time, unless different times for performance have been established by the parties or appear from the nature of the contract".

17 Cass civ. (III) 19 October 2007 no 21973, https://pluris-cedam.utetgiuridica.it accessed 10 June 2020.

termination concerns performances "carried out", not those "not carried out", not nullifying the need to observe the bilateral nature or the regulations of the termination.[18]

In the event of temporary impossibility, it is the creditor who must prove that he/she has no interest in maintaining the contract, the effects of which are suspended, and in this case the creditor can legitimately withdraw, according to Articles 1256 para 2 and 1464 Italian Civil Code. The code balances the parties' interests, again from an objective point of view, pursuing the certainty of private engagements and their functionality for market needs.

This implies that the contractual relationship must be preserved,[19] as the relationship itself is of value and the parties have not only incurred costs and taken time to be able to establish it, but have also made plans to enjoy the effects arising from it. Additionally, the debtor could still perform the service in the future, and this delay may be worthwhile for the creditor.

Calculating the advantage is not left to the creditor's arbitration: his/her interest in not continuing with the contract is subject to evaluation by the judge, who takes into account the nature of the performance and the circumstances of the case to examine the choice of the party that has withdrawn from the contract.

While the suspension of the contract must not benefit the debtor to the creditor's detriment, likewise the withdrawal must not benefit the creditor to debtor's detriment.

4. THE SUPERVENING EXCESSIVELY ONEROUS NATURE OF THE PERFORMANCE

From a general perspective, the pandemic could raise costs and prices that could damage one party, or preclude its opportunity to make profits. In long-term contracts, this implies a supervening imbalance between the performances: the performance due by one party becomes excessively onerous.

Concerning excessive onerousness, the Italian Civil Code provides:

> Article 1467. *Contract for mutual counter-performances.* In contracts for continuous or periodic performance or for deferred performance, if extraordinary or unforeseeable events make the performance of one of the parties excessively onerous, the party who owes such performance can demand dissolution of the contract, with the effects set forth in article 1458.

---

18 Cass. civ. (II) 7 December 2012 no 22202, https://pluris-cedam.utetgiuridica.it accessed 10 June 2020.

19 In the interpretation of contracts, Article 1367 Italian Civil Code provides that the contract or its clauses shall be interpreted in a way in which it could have some effects instead another one according to which it could have none.

> Dissolution cannot be demanded if the supervening onerousness is part of the normal risk of the contract.
>
> A party against whom dissolution is demanded can avoid it by offering to modify equitably the conditions of the contract.

First of all, it must be ascertained whether the contract stipulated between the parties is for periodic performance, or whether it is a long-term contract for continuous performance. The relevant issue is not whether the event has caused a considerable increase or decrease in the value of each performance considered per se, but rather whether there is an imbalance of performances, i.e. a variation in value considered in reference to the bilateral relationship.

However, there is doubt that the debtor could invoke the rules of excessive onerousness in cases connected with the effects of the pandemic. The sum due has not reduced or increased in value but has rather remained the same. What has changed for the debtor is the value of the counter-performance of the creditor, but this does not entail that the debtor's possible incapability to pay should be a burden on the creditor.[20]

Onerousness does not automatically imply difficulty in payment for the debtor; it merely implies an abnormal bilateral relationship, or rather a non-normal risk. The debtor cannot impose on the counterparty the assumption of the risk (or part thereof) for the sole reason that it has become more difficult for him/her to carry out the performance. In our case, on a general level, there has not even been a monetary devaluation[21] and listings on the stock exchange quotations, which initially decreased considerably due to the impact of the pandemic, began to rise again after a few days.

In order to apply the rules of excessive onerousness, the impact must be of a considerable extent; the simple oscillation of prices is a normal contractual risk, which the debtor cannot benefit from:

> The normal risk of a contract that, according to paragraph two of Article 1467 Italian Civil Code, does not validate the dissolution due to supervening excessive

---

20 Aurelio Gentili, 'Una proposta sui contratti d'impresa al tempo del coronavirus' (2020), Giust civ com http://giustiziacivile.com/obbligazioni-e-contratti/approfondimenti/una-proposta-sui-contratti-dimpresa-al-tempo-del accessed 10 June 2020; Ugo Salanitro, 'La gestione del rischio nella locazione commerciale al tempo del coronavirus' (2020) Giust civ com http://giustiziacivile.com/obbligazioni-e-contratti/editoriali/la-gestione-del-rischio-nella-locazione-commerciale-al-tempo-del accessed 10 June 2020; Raffaello Morello, 'Gli effetti sui contratti dell'emergenza sanitaria determinata dalla diffusione del coronavirus e l'applicazione dei rimedi previsti dal Codice civile' (2020) Giust civ com http://giustiziacivile.com/obbligazioni-e-contratti/approfondimenti/gli-effetti-sui-contratti-dellemergenza-sanitaria accessed 10 June 2020.

21 Cass Civ (II) 13 January 1995 no 369, https://pluris-cedam.utetgiuridica.it accessed 10 June 2020.

> onerousness, also includes fluctuations in value of the performances that originated from the regular and normal market fluctuations.[22]

It is therefore a complex evaluation, as the Court of Cassation underlines:

> The matter of applicability, to a given contract, of Article 1467 Civil Code on supervened onerousness must be resolved by the judge, with specific reference to the actual case and the action actually brought, being obliged, for this purpose, to not only consider the nature and structure (from a pure classificatory point of view) of the contract on which termination is requested, but also the modes and times of fulfilling the reciprocal performances connected with the contract itself.

Therefore, besides the nature and structure of the contract, also the modes and times of fulfilling the reciprocal performances connected with the contract itself seem to be relevant.[23]

In order to avoid termination of the contract, which is the effect of applying Article 1467, the creditor may offer to the counterparty a fair reduction of their performance:

> Article 1467 Italian Civil Code does not force the respondent, who wishes to avoid the termination of the contract, to offer an amendment to the conditions of the contract such as to precisely re-establish the balance between the respective positions that existed at the time of conclusion, considering the fact that by logically combining the three paragraphs of the article in question, one can deduce that the supervening onerousness of the considered performance gives the right to termination solely if it is excessive (paragraph 1) and does not come under normal risk of the contract (paragraph 2), with the consequence that the offer to amend the contract is to be considered fair if it returns the contract to a bilateral dimension that, if it had existed at the time of the conclusion, the burdened party would not have the right to request termination.[24]

The amendment to the economic terms can only be requested by the respondent party in the proceeding.[25] In contracts where both parties are creditors and debtors, it lies with the respondent, i.e. the party that holds the role of respondent, to offer the reduction to fairness, while the burdened party cannot request it, and can only request termination of the contract, should the prerequisites exist.

---

22 Cass Civ (III) 17 July 2003 no 11200, https://pluris-cedam.utetgiuridica.it accessed 10 June 2020.

23 Cass civ (II) 8 August 2003 no 11947, https://pluris-cedam.utetgiuridica.it accessed 10 June 2020.

24 Cass civ (II) 11 January 1992 no 247, https://pluris-cedam.utetgiuridica.it accessed 10 June 2020.

25 Cass civ (II) 5 January 2000 no 46, https://pluris-cedam.utetgiuridica.it accessed 10 June 2020.

5. CONTRACTS FOR PECUNIARY OBLIGATIONS

As previously stated, no all-encompassing rules can be dictated for all types of contracts and for all circumstances. Some demonstrative examples are provided below.

It is certainly correct to maintain that the fulfilment of the obligation to pay a sum of money or transfer a fungible item should always be considered possible, and that it therefore cannot imply excessive onerousness (*genus numquam perit*). Furthermore, paying the amount in legal currency is never excessively onerous.

Likewise, it is correct to maintain that the application of the principle of social solidarity[26] and the principle of good faith cannot constitute the grounds for a reduction of the payment or for the suspension of payments. If the performance is possible and there are no fluctuations in price that are considered to be excessive, demanding fulfilment is legitimate and the debtor cannot ask for the contract to be terminated.[27]

Evaluations must therefore be made on a case-by-case basis, depending on the type of contract and bearing in mind the circumstances of any case. For specific long-term contracts, the civil code has considered the advantages and disadvantages suffered by the parties, such as profits and losses, and has introduced corrective measures that serve to preserve the contract under fair conditions. However, these are corrective measures regarding specific contracts, and cannot be extended jointly and automatically to all.

6. FORCE MAJEURE, *FACTUM PRINCIPIS* AND SPECIAL CONTRACTS

6.1. LEASES AND RENTALS

Leases have received particular attention. For residential leases, it has been asked – with regard to the prohibitive measures aimed at containing the pandemic – whether the ban on travelling from one region to another, and, for the first two months of lockdown, the ban on all travel, influenced current leases of houses

---

26 Provided by Italian Constitution by Article 2, concerning the principle of social solidarity, which may be applied by the judge, as ruled by Const Court 21 October 2013 no 248, www.cortecostituzionale.it, and Const Court 26 March 2014 no 77, www.cortecostituzionale.it accessed 10 June 2020.

27 Aurelio Gentili, 'Un proposta sui contratti d'impresa al tempo del coronavirus' (2020) Giust civ http://giustiziacivile.com/obbligazioni-e-contratti/approfondimenti/una-proposta-sui-contratti-dimpresa-al-tempo-del accessed 10 June 2020, §§3 following. On risk, see Mario Bessone, *Adempimento e rischio contrattuale* (Giuffrè 1969); Guido Alpa, Mario Bessone, Vincenzo Roppo, *Rischio contrattuale e autonomia privata* (Jovene 1982); Guido Alpa, 'Rischio contrattuale (Diritto vigente)', *Enciclopedia del diritto XI* (1999) 1144.

used by the tenant for their holidays. The fact that the tenant is not able to travel to a holiday home is completely separate to the underlying contractual relationship, as the asset is still available to the lessee and the owner cannot use it freely in the lessee's absence. *A fortiori*, when the house is full of furniture and items belonging to the tenant, it is unavailable to the owner and therefore the contract cannot be terminated. Likewise, Article 1583 Italian Civil Code, which provides for the reduction of payment for repairs to the item that cannot be enjoyed by the lessor, is not applicable. In this case, the item has no flaws or need for repairs.

In addition, in this case *factum principis* implies the ban of moving from one place to another, but it does not concern the use of holiday homes and is not a good reason to escape one's obligations.

The situation is undoubtedly different if the mayor's orders have prohibited many residents living in a dwelling in the municipality during the period of the pandemic. This would certainly constitute a *factum principis* that affects non-residents, making it impossible for them to live in the area. This in turn results in it being impossible to use the house, which is a good reason to avoid payment of lease fees for the duration of the ban.

The case of a property leased for commercial use is more complicated. When the lease implies access to the public, yet the public cannot access the property due to limits of movement established by the authorities, or if there has been a ban on opening, the lessee cannot use the premises that he/she has leased nor carry out activities requiring contact with the public. This is the situation hotels are now facing, as specific restrictions to use have been imposed. Closing down a business relates to the activity, which entails that the risk falls on the hotelier, whereas closing the building concerns the property, and accordingly the risk is borne by the owner.

In both cases, the remedies offered by the civil code are not sufficient to divide the risk equally. Additionally, one cannot say that it is preferable for the risk to fall on the owner rather than on the entrepreneur, as both of their interests are worthy of protection; moreover, the owner could be an entrepreneur in turn, and rely on the payment of the rental from his/her tenant to, in turn, pay for other rentals or instalments of a mortgage or loan that must be paid back.

A distinction has been proposed with regards to whether the *factum principis* falls on the business activity or on the property. Where it relates to the business activity, the risk should be borne by the business owner, be it an entrepreneur or a professional. Where it falls on the property due to having been ordered to close, the risk should be borne by the landlord.[28] The ideal result would be for the risk to be borne by whomever the limitation happens to impact more closely.

---

[28] Ugo Salanitro, 'La gestione del rischio nella locazione commerciale al tempo del corona virus' (2020) Giust civ com http://giustiziacivile.com/obbligazioni-e-contratti/editoriali/la-gestione-del-rischio-nella-locazione-commerciale-al-tempo-del accessed 10 June 2020.

However, this solution is not totally satisfactory: if business cannot be conducted, the ban affects the entrepreneur. However, it also affects the owner, as he/she must guarantee enjoyment of commercial use, which is something he/she is not capable of as commercial activities are not permitted for his/her tenants. It is true that in this case, it is not a matter of faults in the property (as would be the case if the property did not have a certificate of suitability for use) and therefore the prohibition is not connected with the property itself. Likewise, it is also true that the tenants are prohibited from doing business due to an external reason that is not imputable to them.

Ordinarily, the lessee has the right to indemnity when the contract is terminated – this indemnity doubles if the lease for the carrying out the new business is similar to the one already carried out. In other words, the carrying out of commercial activity is a value that favours the owner when he/she re-leases the property. Contact with the public, knowledge of the business premises by the public, the conducting of the business activity in that location, the use of the hallmark of the firm, are all elements that contribute to consolidating goodwill. This means that contact with the public is a circumstance which is relevant for the law.[29]

However, it seems fair for the risk to fall on the professional or entrepreneur lessee, if regardless of the restrictions, they can carry out their business, even if in worse conditions than normally. For instance, they can resort to remote working organised in the leased premises, or carry it out, as is the case of restaurants, pizza parlours, and bars that make food and drink to take away, serving clients on demand and at home.

Professionals who can carry out their business remotely find themselves in this situation. The case is different for those professionals, such as doctors, dentists and private clinics, who need contact with the patients to be able to carry out their work.

These cases indicate that the risk must be administered jointly, and that having the risk fall on one or the other party based on chance does not correspond to reasons of fairness. This is why authors suggest applying the principle of good faith or the principle of solidarity (provided by Art 3 of the Constitution) in order to share the risk between the parties caused by exceptional circumstances.[30]

A special rule is provided by the civil code in cases of renting out something productive, for instance a field, a workshop or something that gives products per se. In this case, if an order from the authorities affects productivity (where it is clearly a case of *factum principis*), and the parties respectively suffer a loss

---

29 One of the first cases decided by the Tribunal of Rome on 29 May 2020 reduced the due rates of 70% per 2 months.

30 Francesco Macario, 'Per un diritto dei contratti più solidale in epoca di "coronavirus"' (2020) Giust civ com http://giustiziacivile.com/obbligazioni-e-contratti/editoriali/un-diritto-dei-contratti-piu-solidale-epoca-di-coronavirus, accessed 10 June 2020.

or gain an advantage, it is possible to request an increase or a reduction in the rental fee (Art 1623 Italian Civil Code). Here, it suffices that the imbalance is notable: in this case, it is not the favoured party that must offer the reduction to fairness, but the disadvantaged party that, resorting to an action similar to the action *quanti minoris* of a sale, can ask the judge to rebalance the performances.

6.2. PROCUREMENT CONTRACT

With regard to procurement contracts, the civil code contains rules that are less rigid than the ones examined, as they take into consideration variations that may supervene, not due to external circumstances, but due to decisions by each contracting party. For instance, variations in the project and the extent of the work (Art 1660 Italian Civil Code) allow the party that sees a reduction in profit to withdraw, with the right to a fair compensation.

If the variations depend on external circumstances, such as a geological occurrence, the party to the contract that believes the onerousness of his/her performance to have increased can request fair payment (Art 1664 Italian Civil Code).

The case of the pandemic and its possible effects on rising prices may be solved with the application of the cited rule, which provides the party encumbered by the increase or decrease of costs of materials or labour, on the condition it is higher or lower than one tenth of the agreed price, the possibility for to ask for the prices to be reviewed.

However, if the parties have established a fixed price and not a unit price, the variations caused by unforeseeable external agents are not relevant.[31]

In case of excessive onerousness of the execution of the work due to supervened extraordinary and unforeseeable events, it is permitted to take into consideration the needs of the damaged party.[32] This is also the case with increases in the costs of materials and labour.[33]

7. THE LACK OF A PROVISION ON RENEGOTIATION IN THE ITALIAN CIVIL CODE

The coronavirus has highlighted the insufficiency of the rules provided by the civil code that foresees the hypothesis of suspension of the effects of a contract

31 Cass civ (I) 9 September 2011 no 18559, https://pluris-cedam.utetgiuridica.it accessed 10 June 2020.

32 Cass civ (I) 21 December 1996 no 11469, https://pluris-cedam.utetgiuridica.it accessed 10 June 2020.

33 Cass civ (II) 29 August 1990 no 8949, https://pluris-cedam.utetgiuridica.it accessed 10 June 2020.

due to unforeseeable and exceptional external circumstances but allows the creditor to invoke withdrawal.

In the event of supervening unforeseen circumstances that make performance impossible, or more onerous, even if temporarily, parties are not compelled to renegotiate.

The obligation of renegotiation was provided for by the Government in a bill of law filed a year ago, which revises the civil code (Bill of law 19 March 2019, Senate Records, no 1151), and it would be advisable that the approval of the provision on renegotiation be brought forward.[34] There may also be a solution entrusted to mandatory mediation and negotiation via professionals, including long-term contracts in the realm of areas entrusted to these terms of extrajudicial settlement of disputes.

---

[34] In this sense, see the proposals drawn up by the Association of Italian Civil Law Specialists, to which the cited doctrinal contributions refer.

GOVERNMENT EMERGENCY INTERVENTION IN PRIVATE CONTRACTS IN TIMES OF COVID-19

A User's Guide

Juan José GANUZA and Fernando GÓMEZ POMAR*

---

* Both authors, Universitat Pompeu Fabra. This contribution results from the research project "Coronavirus i dret privat" (2020PANDE00092), funded by the Catalan Agency for University and Research Grants (AGAUR). We are grateful to Pablo Salvador, Cándido Paz-Ares, José Massaguer, María Paz García Rubio, Gabriel Doménech, Carles Vendrell, Carlos Gómez Ligüerre, and participants at the Law and Macro Conference 2020 for comments and suggestions on an earlier draft of this contribution. All remaining errors are our own.

This contribution provides a preliminary analysis of the legal instruments that governments use to provide emergency regulation of contracts in the wake of the turmoil resulting from the COVID-19 pandemic. We identify the acute liquidity concern afflicting virtually all agents along the contractual chain in a large number of sectors as the most pressing problem. We then introduce some of the main criteria to understand and design response measures in the area of private contracts in times of emergency: (1) the systemic and urgent character of response measures; (2) keeping things simple, minimising ex ante controls and transaction costs; (3) the urgency of preventing a chain reaction of defaults along contractual networks and the economy at large; (4) the relational value of existing contracts and the ways to preserve it; (5) how tailor-made agreements in M&A and finance have developed over time means to cope with the impact of extraordinary contingencies.

1. INTRODUCTION

The health emergency associated with COVID-19 has put enormous pressure on the foundations of family, social and economic lives across Europe and the world at large. It has also challenged the resilience of contracts and economic relationships, as well as the consistency and wisdom of the law that governs them.

Understandably, the harsh economic impact that has resulted from the various measures adopted to combat the spread of the contagion and provide health systems with the means and time to cope with the pandemic, coupled with the prospects of an ensuing economic recession have forced many economic agents to figure out how to absorb the losses already suffered or anticipated or, alternatively, to explore ways of shifting – or sharing, if one prefers a more "polite" term – current or expected losses to other parties in existing contractual relationships.

Several means of intervening in ongoing contracts have been proposed, discussed, and implemented in the midst of the dramatic disruption of the normal functioning of society and in the wake of the uncertain future ahead in terms of economic and social well-being. In this contribution, we try to offer some guidance on how to think and implement a number of legal tools that can be deployed to minimise the negative impact of the recent and current disruption following the public health emergency on the functioning of contracts.

These ideas on what to do with contracts in situations of macro-economic alarm are based on criteria that we believe to be legally and economically sound and also pass the test of reality in light of the experience of measures adopted in Spain and other European countries to cope with the consequences of COVID-19 in the realm of contracts. For obvious reasons, we will refer to several policies implemented in Spain, but we also use illustrations from several other European jurisdictions (France, Germany, Italy and Portugal).

Our preferred approaches are fit for a crisis that, in the short term, represents an acute and serious liquidity problem for economic agents, both consumers and firms of all types at every level of the contract chain. In 2020 and perhaps even in early 2021, many agents in the economy will be short of liquid assets to pay their liabilities (liquidity or cash flow shock). Later, it may happen that liabilities of individuals and firms exceed their assets, making their situation (their business in the case of firms) unsustainable in the mid- and long-term.

Clearly, the severity and duration of the short-term and longer-term shocks will depend on how long the measures to contain the pandemic will last, and how intensely they will impact the income prospects of households and the demand and supply for firms.

In this contribution we focus on the liquidity or cash flow shock in the short term and how legal rules affecting contracts should be designed and deployed to improve matters quickly and effectively to resist the blow. Not that we think the mid- and long-term are less relevant, or do not pose interesting questions for legal policy affecting existing contracts. Quite the contrary. The unknowns, however, clearly grow with the length of the perspective. First, how the experience of the pandemic may affect consumer decisions in the future and thus, whether demand patterns pre-COVID-19 will be restored any time soon. For instance, will people continue to cut travelling and restaurant-going even when the peak of the health emergency is past? Second, whether the economic recovery in Europe and other parts of the world is quick or slow are still highly uncertain. All these factors, to a large extent, will shape how best to deal with longer-term effects of the pandemic.

With the cash flow shock in mind, we posit a relatively narrow set of criteria to address the issues: (1) the systemic and urgent nature of the measures that need to be implemented; (2) a preference for simple interventions, which minimise *ex-ante* requirements and transaction costs; (3) the crucial importance of preventing a spiral of defaults that may spread throughout the economy; (4) the recognition that contracts are valuable assets that deserve protection and the importance of considering the most appropriate measures overall to do so; (5) the existence of "tailor-made" contracts, which have their own adjustment mechanisms that can be used and trusted. Finally, we conclude with an optimistic plea to reflect upon how contracts can contribute to the recovery that all countries, to a greater or lesser extent, will need.

Even when focusing on the short term, as we do, we acknowledge that there are interesting areas that we do not address here. A number of the issues we consider here would also be applicable to employment contracts. Given their legal and regulatory characteristics, that moreover differ significantly from country to country – more so, we would say, than commercial contracts – we prefer to leave them entirely out of the contribution.

The same is true for bankruptcy issues. Bankruptcy law and insolvency institutions not only pose interesting questions about long-term survival of firms once the liquidity shock has been absorbed, but also affect immediate financing decisions of firms attempting to overcome the short-term impact of the pandemic, since agents will anticipate that there are chances, perhaps even large ones, that the cash flow problems coupled with protracted decrease in demand or supply capacity means that they may end up in bankruptcy.

Finally, we do not deal with issues of financial regulation or economic regulation more generally, even if we concede that regulatory instruments are often intertwined with those explicitly belonging to the governance over private contracts. We do not even address regulation in regard to the macro-economic shock that COVID-19 has produced in many economies, in Europe and elsewhere. In recent times, interest on the macro-economic effects of legal regulation of the financial sector and the economy at large, and whether regulation may be used by governments with similar counter-cyclical goals and properties of other more traditional macro-economic tools (fiscal policy and monetary policy) has expanded very significantly. We simply refer to the numerous contributions in this expanding area of research.[1]

2. LARGE-SCALE AND URGENT RESPONSES ARE NEEDED FOR A SYSTEMIC AND PRESSING PROBLEM

The first idea concerns the adequateness of means and ends. For a systemic and pressing problem, we must apply systemic and urgent measures, not measures with a delayed effect nor those focusing merely on individual characteristics of the contractual relationship. It is time for the law with an eye on macro-economics,[2] not on micro-economics.

There seems to be no doubt that the pandemic, the measures to combat it and its economic consequences are of a general, systemic and immediate nature. To put it in economic terms, they represent a macro shock with effects already in the very short term. It is a sudden impact on the contractual and economic

1 Jonathan S. Masur and Eric A. Posner, 'Should Regulation Be Countercyclical?', (2017) 34 Yale Journal on Regulation 743; Daniel Tarullo, 'Time-varying Measures in Financial Regulation' (2020) 83(1) Law and Contemporary Problems 1; Erik Gerding, 'Against Regulatory Stimulus' (2020) 83(1) Law and Contemporary Problems 49; Iris H-Y Chiu, Andreas Kokkinis and Andrea Miglionico, 'Regulatory Suspensions in Times of Crisis: The Challenges of Covid – 19 and Thoughts for the Future', Law Working Paper No. 517/2020, European Corporate Governance Institute 1–36; Yair Listokin, 'Law and Macroeconomics: The Law and Economics of Recessions' (2017) 34 Yale Journal on Regulation 791; Yair Listokin, *Law and Macroeconomics* (Harvard University Press 2019).

2 Yair Listokin, *Law and Macroeconomics* (Harvard University Press 2019); Yair Listokin, and 'Law & Macroeconomics: What Took So Long?' (2020) 83 (1) Law and Contemporary Problems 145.

framework of the countries most affected by the emergency. It is true that some sectors, activities and households are going to incur, at least in the near future, only a slight adverse impact, but the seismic waves resulting from the fall in supply and demand for goods and services of many different kinds are already being strongly felt in almost every corner of the economy. As has been argued,[3] "[a]mong the critical questions policy makers are facing are how best to support small businesses and how to reduce the number of otherwise viable businesses that will be forced into bankruptcy as a result of COVID-19 and efforts to slow its spread."

To confront an urgent and systemic problem we cannot resort to instruments whose effects, despite how beneficial they may be, will not be felt for months or even years. We do not have time for that. The effects of the measures adopted, although imperfect, must be immediate. Otherwise, they will be practically worthless to prevent the destruction of valuable contractual relations and supply networks that may follow soon as an outcome from a liquidity earthquake that is not properly mitigated.

In order to mitigate the negative effects of the impact, it is essential that protections be made available immediately, not in the future and even less so in the distant future, which is even more uncertain and involves decisions that cannot be even remotely foreseen. As Yair Listokin says, "[u]sing case by case adjudication to remedy recessions would be a heroic task – far better to rely on more systematic responses to macro-economic problems".[4]

When millions of contracts are at stake at the same time, we cannot afford to resort to instruments that require high administrative and decision-making costs to produce results. This is why, in order to deal with the emergency associated with the coronavirus, the court systems should not be the preferred institution to intervene in contracts, not even as an adjudicator to settle disputes resulting from a contracting party's unilateral decision to deviate from an agreement. This view is not just the result of courts being unable to resolve the matters quickly – they are unable to do so, and even less so in times of lockdown and their aftermath-but also because the cost of each resolution for the parties and for society as a whole would be too high. The swift intervention in contractual arrangements that the situation calls for cannot depend on the resolving millions of lawsuits between contracting parties. Even with a well-equipped and uncongested justice system, the above remains true, since the delay and cost of relying on judicial intervention is necessarily high. It is not an appealing option in pressing times.

We believe, therefore, that those who, undoubtedly with good intentions, wish to entrust the immediate response in the contractual sphere to general

---

3 Todd Baker and Kathryn Judge, 'How to Help Small Businesses Survive COVID-19' in Katharina Pistor (ed), *Law in the Time of COVID-19* (Columbia Law School 2020) 109.

4 Yair Listokin, 'Law & Macroeconomics: What Took So Long?' (2020) 83(1) Law and Contemporary Problems 146.

doctrines in contract law requiring ad hoc interpretation and adjudication, taking into account all relevant circumstances, have not considered the full picture. Doctrines such as hardship[5] (and similar ones in other legal systems, as in France (*imprévision*), Spain (*rebus sic stantibus*), Germany (*Wegfall der Geschäftgrundlage*), and Italy (*eccessiva onerosità sopravvenuta*) are unlikely to produce the needed results with the needed expediency and immediacy.

Those doctrines are ill-suited mechanisms for the current emergency, not only because they lack immediacy[6] but because of the unpredictability and overall cost to the judicial system and society as a whole that would follow from subjecting hundreds of thousands, perhaps millions, of contracts to an uncertain and distant judicial decision on whether the conditions for contract modification or termination were satisfied. In most legal systems (certainly so in Spain, but their general nature allows us to conjecture that other legal systems are perhaps not too dissimilar in this respect[7]) those doctrines do not even set a sufficiently clear negotiating framework for the parties to be able to reach a mutually acceptable agreement to modify the contract, and even less so in an entirely novel scenario such as the one triggered by COVID-19. In other words, relying on general clauses in need of court interpretation and decision in view of all circumstances of the case at hand is neither feasible nor desirable to address systemic events and macro shocks that suddenly impact an economy. Even less

---

5 Although its scope seems to be limited in Common Law jurisdictions: Klaus Peter Berger and Daniel Behn, 'Force Majeure and Hardship in the age of Corona: A Historical and Comparative Study' (2020) 6(4) McGill Journal of Dispute Resolution 115–117. For economic justifications of the narrow scope of performance excuses in Common Law systems, see Victor Goldberg, *Rethinking Contract Law and Contract Design* (Edward Elgar 2015) chs 11 and 12.

6 In some legal systems the statutory rules expressing doctrines such as *rebus sic stantibus*, hardship, *imprévision*, and the like, clarify that the use of rebus does not justify the suspension of performance while the terms of the contract are being renegotiated or the court is being asked to make an adjustment for the change in circumstances. Thus, Article 1195 of the French Code Civil states that a defaulting party who has not assumed the risk of an unforeseeable change of circumstances "… may demand a renegotiation of the contract with his counterpart. It will continue to enforce its obligations during the renegotiation". Article 6.2.3 (2) of the Unidroit Principles on International Commercial Contracts 2016, similarly provides that a claim does not allow for suspension of performance. In other legal systems, although the issue is not specifically addressed, it is clear that if a contracting party, when invoking rebus, unilaterally decides to suspend its performance, or to reduce it to a certain extent, it does so at its own peril and at the risk of the outcome of the renegotiation and, if it comes to it, the court decision, which may not be infrequent not uncommon in these cases where a contracting party acts unilaterally.

7 Thomas Rüfner, 'Change of Circumstances', Nils Janssen and Reinhard Zimmermann (eds), *Commentaries on European Contract Laws* (Oxford University Press 2018) 909, writes: "Even in Germany, after almost a hundred years of scholarly debate, it is far from clear, what the *Geschäftsgrundlage* is, which circumstances belong to it, and which ones do not. When is a change of circumstances fundamental enough to warrant the granting of relief? When does performance become excessively onerous? None of these questions, can be answered with a satisfactory degree of certainty."

so when societies are confronted by a problem that affects many (if not all) contracts in an asymmetric manner and has highly uncertain medium-term impact.

Countries who have experienced comparable dramatic macro shocks, such as Germany, know this well. In fact, Germany, the birthplace of the modern version of the ancient *rebus sic stantibus* doctrine, with a reasonably well-established case law on the doctrine and a court system fuelled by one of the highest per capita expenditures on the administration of justice, has not substantially relied on the doctrine – codified since 2002 in §313 of the BGB – of the disappearance of the basis of the agreement (*Wegfall der Geschäftsgrundlage*) in the current situation, at least for the short term. They have preferred to set special and urgent – yet temporary – measures of intervention in a wide but not universal scope of contract. The German Law of 27 March 2020 has established various general measures aimed at adapting existing contracts to the emergency. These include a moratorium on payments in favour of consumers and small and medium-sized enterprises (SMEs) that are particularly affected by the situation, a suspension of judgments and evictions on both residential and commercial property leases for default due to COVID-19 and on the payment of rent until the end of June 2020, as well as deferments and suspensions of early acceleration on consumer credit.[8] Currently, §313 BGB has not been seen – rightly so, and without much ado – as an effective means of providing relief under a systemic and pressing shock.[9]

---

8 On some of the German measures, see Martin Schmidt-Kessel and Christina Möllnitz, 'Coronavertragsrecht – Sonderregeln für Verbraucher und Kleinstunternehmen' (2020) Neue Juristische Wochenshrift 1103.

9 The argument in the text does not imply that there is a lack of proposals in academic and legal circles advocating the application of §313 BGB in "Corona and post-Corona times" to allow courts to modify existing contracts with the purpose of sharing the risks of the negative economic consequences of the pandemic, albeit not as the main tool to provide immediate relief to contract parties: Gerhard Wagner, 'Corona Law' (2020), 3/2020 Zeitschrift für europäisches Privatrecht 536–539; Marc-Philippe Weller, Markus Lieberknecht and Victor Habrich, 'Virulente Leistungsstörungen – Auswirkungen der Corona-Krise auf die Vertragsdurchführung' (2020) 2020(15) Neue Juristische Wochenschrift 1021; Martin Häublein and Maximilian Müller, 'Wer trägt das Pandemierisiko in der Geschäftsraummiete?' (2020) Neue Zeitschrift für Miet- und Wohnungsrecht 486–492 (for commercial leases). Before the pandemic, however, several German scholars argued in favour of a very narrow scope for §313 BGB in situations of economic turmoil, such as the ones brought about by COVID-19 and the associated public health measures: Hannes Unberath, 'Long-Term Contracts and the DCFR – Interpretation and Adjustment', Gerhard Wagner (ed), *The Common Frame of Reference: A View from Law & Economics* (Sellier 2009) 152–153; Thomas Rüfner, 'Change of Circumstances' in Nils Janssen and Reinhard Zimmermann (eds), *Commentaries on European Contract Laws* (Oxford University Press 2018) 910. Undoubtedly, risk sharing when the contract party who has been hit by the consequences of the pandemic is risk averse is a relevant dimension of how to treat contracts in the post-COVID world, but probably it is even more important to achieve *ex post* efficiency and mobilisation of the assets under contract to their most valuable uses. In terms of encouraging efficient renegotiation of existing contracts to adapt to the circumstances after the pandemic, there are more sophisticated instruments than the application of hardship or similar doctrines.

3. SIMPLICITY AND EASE OF IMPLEMENTATION

The second idea is easy to express but hard to accomplish: keep things simple. Interventions in contracts to provide redress against liquidity shocks to one contract party must be designed to be as simple as possible, easy and quick to implement, and accompanied by specific measures that minimise transaction costs necessary for the intervention to have a positive impact.

Given the urgency, in the short run, it seems preferable to "over-assist" with a given measure (have it reach some people who do not truly require it), than to leave out a significant number of those who really do need support to cope with the emergency. Clearly, the number and complexity of requirements and procedures to qualify for the benefits of the emergency measures over existing contracts is at odds with the simplification mandate. This also calls for *ex post* controls rather than *ex ante* checks and verification requirements.

In reality, European Governments seem to have been aware of the need for simplicity. Often, they have skipped *ex ante* certifications and proofs before having individuals and firms eligible for many of the adopted measures. In part, this flexibility is linked to the immediate constraints imposed by the lockdown prevailing during the public health emergency. Still, the rationale for *ex post* verification – and eventually, sanctions in case of misuse of the entitlements – should not be limited to the special circumstances in which the population of various European countries have been placed for several months. The advantage of *ex post* mechanisms relates to the reduction in transaction costs and the ensuing gains in access and speed in implementation compared to relying more on *ex ante* screening devices. Deterrence of misconduct, however, should be part of the necessary toolbox to ensure that those who actually depend on receiving the benefits from the protective impact of the emergency measures, and without interference from the ones who pretend they are in need but are not. Achieving deterrence in this area is likely to require the use of sanctions that go beyond mere restitution of benefits unfairly and undeservedly enjoyed.

It is however difficult for the legislator, even in the midst of an emergency, to transcend common features or requirements linked to formalisation, documentation and registration that are seen as standard in ordinary times. In extraordinary times, the concern about the delays associated with such sources of transaction costs should be given extra weight compared to periods of business as usual, so it is highly unlikely that the benefits from such formalities would outweigh their costs in an emergency.

It is thus hard to understand that the Spanish lawmaker when adopting an emergency moratorium in mortgage loans in favour of debtors in a specially vulnerable situation due to the pandemic and its economic effects,[10] has been

---

10 The Spanish RDL 8/2020, as modified shortly thereafter by RDL 11/2020 and RDL 15/2020. The measure initially provided for in the first Spanish RDL was limited to mortgage loans for

unable to leave aside the involvement of registries and notaries. Worse, when the Spanish RDL 11/2020 has tried to expand the scope of protection for families and the most vulnerable groups as a result of the COVID-19 health crisis, and extended the mortgage moratorium also to credit agreements without a mortgage security,[11] it has still kept formalisation requirements that are not generally necessary – no notarial document is legally required for the binding nature of the agreement – and are exceedingly costly and hard to satisfy, especially during times of lockdown and when mobility is still restricted.

4. STOP THE SPREAD NOT ONLY OF THE VIRUS BUT ALSO OF DEFAULTS DUE TO LACK OF LIQUIDITY

The third organising idea that we consider highly relevant has to do with the importance of preventing a possible uncontrolled spiral of defaults. In situations of severe and sudden decline in income and earnings for families and firms, there is a significant risk of generating a pattern of defaults that spreads throughout the entire contractual chain: end customers do not pay their counterparties, the latter do the same with their own suppliers and so on. This process has an enormous destructive capacity for contracts that provide value for the contracting parties and can put at risk a significant portion of the productive economy of a country. Emergency measures affecting existing contracts must seek to provide means of ensuring that this undesirable dynamic does not begin or, once underway, is halted as soon as possible. Erecting reasonably effective backstops against the spread of contract defaults appears as a realistic and appealing goal for emergency measures dealing with existing contracts.

In the abstract, the sooner we are able to stop the possible chain of defaults, the better. The closer the first link – the one through which the final payment is made – is to successfully halting the risk of escalating defaults, the easier it will be to prevent liquidity-related panics and to avoid initial losses from spreading to "healthy" sectors of the entire economic and contractual systems.

Intervention at or close to the first level to avert the spread of defaults requires the injection of external funds – ultimately, in most realistic scenarios, with some public support – which can come in various forms. One such form

---

the acquisition of a primary residence, but the second RDL extends the intended scope of the moratorium to include loans or credits secured by mortgages for the acquisition of property used for economic activity by entrepreneurs and professionals who suffer a substantial loss of income or a substantial decrease in revenue of at least 40%, as well as to residences other than those in a the standard rental situation where the mortgage debtor, individual, owner and lessor of such properties, has stopped receiving rental income from tenants.

11 The Spanish regulation on emergency relief for unsecured credit debtors, with some slight variation, is substantially similar to that of the moratorium on mortgage loans and follows the same logic (definition of vulnerability, application, effects, duration, etc.).

is the direct provision of public funds or assistance.[12] Another is the use of tax deferrals, which means that the taxpayer can receive credit from the tax authority for the amount of tax due in order to meet other payment obligations.[13] Finally, it is possible that the funds come from the private financial sector with public guarantees that, to a greater or lesser extent,[14] facilitate not only their allocation to those who otherwise would be considered as too high a risk to receive financing but also to make the terms of the contract more advantageous than what would be obtained under normal market conditions, especially in the current situation.[15]

Some countries, such as Italy, have determined for financial contracts with credit institutions that any funds committed by the creditors, but not yet received by or made available to firms (in general or certain categories of firms, such as SMEs, or firms in sectors particularly hard hit by the public health emergency) cannot be suspended or revoked within a given period of time – some months, ideally, sufficient time for the firms to recover – even if the contracts contain clauses that would allow creditors not to provide additional funds.[16] In a similar vein, Portugal has also banned the revocation of lines of credit or approved loans.[17]

It is true that in some cases acting upon the first link in the contract chain may not be feasible for a number of reasons. For example, due to informational or logistical barriers, or for other related reasons, it may be difficult for liquidity

---

12 Some States, such as Denmark, have opted for quasi-universal household income maintenance policies, allowing households to continue to pay all their obligations while also easing the liquidity situation of those companies who should normally make the payments by having them covered by the State during the emergency. In addition, Denmark approved a compensation scheme to help companies meet fixed expenses due between 9 March and 9 June 2020 (including rental payments). Companies in any sector of activity which anticipate a drop in revenue of more than 40% as a result of COVID-19 and whose total fixed costs between 9 March and 9 June exceed a certain limit could benefit from this plan. A maximum amount of aid was set, and the proportion of costs that could be covered by the aid may not exceed the estimated reduction in revenue caused by COVID-19, except for businesses that have been forced to shut down.

13 In Spain (and in other countries, such as Italy) tax moratoriums have been introduced for self-employed individuals and SMEs, so that what would otherwise be used to pay taxes can be immediately used to meet other payment obligations.

14 This is the scheme adopted in Spain, as provided for in the Spanish RDL 8/2020, and later developed by several decisions by the Council of Ministers and resolutions emanating from the Ministry of Economic Affairs. Comparable schemes have also been implemented by other European countries, such as France, Germany and Italy.

15 On rationales for Government lending in general and in emergencies, Nadav Orian Peer, 'Public Purpose Finance: The Government's Role as Lender' (2020) 83 (1) Law and Contemporary Problems 101.

16 Article 56.2 of the Italian Law on validation and implementation of the d-l of 17 March 2020, n. 18. The measure was adopted for the benefit of SMEs (within the meaning of European Commission Recommendation 2003/361 of 6.5.2003).

17 Portuguese Decreto-Lei No. 10-J/2020, of 13 March 2020.

support measures that could actually avert a chain of defaults to reach the first level (where the first default may take place). Additionally, the State's budget may not be able to take on the excessive costs associated with sustaining the initial step to preserve existing payment dynamics.[18] When this is the case, perhaps another link in the chain can reasonably be accessed relatively early on to provide the funds to short-circuit the expansion of defaults.

Moratoriums on payments can also be established, allowing the debtor to finance him/herself temporarily by saving the amount of the payment that would otherwise have been due at the expense of his/her contractual counterpart.

4.1. MORATORIUMS AS A MEANS OF PROVIDING LIQUIDITY TO DEBTORS

Many countries have adopted moratoriums of different nature and scope together with the legal and economic measures that have accompanied public health measures in response to the epidemiological emergency and its distorting effects on supply, demand and income. In addition to tax moratoriums, which effectively function as a substitute for direct injections of public funds, we find moratoriums in the financial sector for families and also eventually for micro-enterprises and SMEs in a number of European countries (Germany, Italy, Portugal, Spain), as well in the residential and commercial leasing sector in a few countries (Spain, Portugal). Moratoriums of a more general nature for households and small businesses experiencing difficulties in meeting their current obligations have also been adopted in Germany and Italy.

A moratorium as a means of providing liquidity to a debtor who is temporarily deprived of liquid assets should be designed and implemented carefully to avoid

---

18 There are intelligent mechanisms to address the challenge of maintaining the payment system through the direct injection of liquidity to households, which has low administration costs and potential for recuperation by the Government: N. Gregory Mankiw, A Proposal for Social Insurance during the Pandemic http://gregmankiw.blogspot.com/, accessed 1 July 2020.
Mankiw's idea is that the State will send each family with an income below a certain level I (those with higher incomes are expected to have a certain amount of savings), an amount of money X during the N months that the negative impact on their income is expected to last. At the same time, an additional tax is introduced, payable in June 2021, or deferred over a number of years, equivalent to N*X*(I2020/I2019), where I2020 is the income for 2020 and I2019 is the income for the previous year. You would never pay more than N*X. Thus, those who have no income in 2020 would pay nothing, those who earned half as much as in the previous year would pay back only half in instalments, and only those who maintained their income in 2020 would pay back the entire amount they received from the State, returning an interest-free loan that they would have received from the Government.
There have been criticisms of such broad measures, as being insufficiently targeted and lacking the intensity and depth to avert the problems of those more in need: Pamela Foohey, Dalié Jimenez and Christopher K. Odinet, 'CARES Act Gimmicks: How Not to Give People Money During a Pandemic and What to Do Instead' (2020) University of Illinois Law Review 81.

triggering or aggravating a "spillover effect" that would generate an undesirable chain reaction of defaults. Let us have a look at different layers or types of moratoriums.

4.2. MORATORIUMS ON DEBTS *VIS-À-VIS* THE GOVERNMENT

The "safest" moratoriums from the point of view of avoiding a run on payments would undoubtedly be those where the State is the counterpart. The State can operate in an emergency situation – and in others – especially with the support of a central bank, as a sort of "creditor of last resort". This makes it possible to predict that a spiral of defaults would not be generated as a result of the deferment of payments that results from such moratoriums. In most cases, monetary obligations with the Government are not of a contractual nature (tax liabilities as the paramount example), although it is true that some firms have liabilities of a contractual nature with the Government, as in public procurement. The case of moratoriums in Government debts is important to consider, since it makes particularly clear the rationale for the moratorium as a means of providing liquidity to the debtor at the expense of the creditor and what factors should bear on advocating or rejecting its use as an emergency measure, depending on the creditor's ability to act as a backstop to the expansion of a spiral of successive defaults.

4.3. MORATORIUMS IN FINANCING AGREEMENTS WITH CREDIT INSTITUTIONS

The next step in decreasing order of confidence as to the risk of triggering a chain reaction of defaults (that is, still fairly secure) refers to moratoriums in financial contracts where the creditor is a financial institution.[19] Here, at least if moratoriums for debtors with an immediate liquidity problem do not last long – or, when extending for more time, they are at least partially guaranteed by the Government – we can still be reasonably confident that such moratoriums would not be risky in terms of successive defaults. It seems that the position adopted and announced by the European Central Bank in the face of the emergency makes it possible to anticipate that European financial institutions will be in a reasonably good position to provide liquidity to large groups of the population who need it, at least in the short term and perhaps even longer.

Among the measures introduced in various European countries, we observe stays and moratoriums on debt contracts with financial institutions addressed

---

[19] When the counterpart in the financing contract is not a financial institution the issue is more problematic, as will be argued when we consider other moratoriums, such as with leases.

at groups that have been more seriously affected or threatened by the health emergency and its economic effects. Indeed, in Spain, the Spanish RDL 8/2020 establishes a moratorium of three months[20] on the payment of mortgage loans intended for the purchase of the main place of residence[21] for debtors who are vulnerable as a result of the emergency situation (families with reduced income, self-employed persons with a significant decrease in revenue, and in both groups, those who are highly unlikely to be able to make short-term credit payments given the ratio between credit payments and income).

The mortgage moratorium under the Spanish RDL 8/2020 also covers non-debtor guarantors, co-signers and mortgagors in a state of economic vulnerability, who now may claim the benefit of subsidiary liability (*excusión* is the technical term in Spanish law) i.e. to require the entity to exhaust the main debtor's assets before attempting to enforce the guarantee or the mortgage, even when such benefit had been waived in the contract.

The legal moratorium has also been extended to loans secured by real estate mortgages whose purpose was the acquisition of property for an economic activity by entrepreneurs and professionals who are suffering a substantial loss of income or a substantial drop in revenue (at least 40%) as a result of the pandemic. The same applies to homes other than the principal residence that are rented out and for which the mortgagor, the owner and lessor of the home, has not received rent from the tenant due to the circumstances relating to COVID-19.[22]

A similar moratorium has also been granted to debtors in credit agreements without mortgage guarantees, whatever the purpose of the credit,[23] again also for the benefit of individuals – including the self-employed and professionals – in a vulnerable situation. This moratorium also applies to the guarantors of such loans who are in a state of economic vulnerability (Art 9.2 RDL 11/2020).[24]

In Italy, moratoriums have been approved on mortgage loans for the purchase of principal residences. The Italian d-l of 2 March 2020 no. 9, established the possibility of a moratorium of up to nine months on the payment of mortgage credit instalments (for amounts less than EUR 250,000) for employees who have had their employment contracts suspended or their working hours reduced by

20 Initially, the Spanish RDL 8/2020 did not specify a precise duration. The later RDL 11/2020 clarified that the duration is three months.

21 For their part, the professional associations (AEB and CECA) in the finance sector have encouraged their members to offer voluntary moratoriums beyond what is legally required.

22 This extension is made available in the Spanish RDL 11/2020.

23 This expansion is also the result of the amendments made to the financial moratorium by the Spanish RDL 11/2020.

24 Despite the fact that this issue is not expressly regulated in the provisions governing the moratorium, from the wording of Article 13.4 of the Spanish RDL 8/2020 (as amended by RDL 11/2020), and from the regulation of the moratorium applicable to consumer financing, it seems clear that the moratorium results in the extension of the term of the loan or credit for as long as the legally granted moratorium lasts.

at least 30 days. Pursuant to the Italian d-l 17 March 2020 no. 18, this moratorium was extended to self-employed persons who had suffered a decrease in their quarterly revenue of at least one-third.

Italy has also established a moratorium on payments (recurring and non-recurring payments) of financing contracts for small and medium-sized businesses which did not have a deteriorated credit situation (that is, close to an event of default) before the health emergency erupted. The moratorium was initially determined to last until 30 September 2020.[25] It is accompanied by significant Government guarantees, which cover the additional use of credit lines and loan proceeds to a certain extent, as well as the principal and interest payments subject to the deferment.

In Portugal, measures have also been taken[26] in favour of financial debtors (both firms and consumers) who are not in arrears in the payments due and have been affected by the impact of COVID-19. Payment of interest and capital was suspended until 30 September 2020, and the contract automatically extended for a time equivalent to the time of suspension, and the guarantees, bonds and other payment securities are similarly extended.

In Germany, Article 240 §3 EGBGB has established, in the absence of a contrary agreement of the parties, an automatic (*ope legis*) deferment of all payments by consumers for principal, interest and other recurring charges in credit contracts, both with a real estate security and without it, for a period of three months if the consumer has suffered a loss of income as a result of the emergency associated with COVID-19 that makes it impossible for him/her to afford such payments. Additionally, it is provided that if the debtor and creditor do not reach an agreement regarding the number of months of extension after the moratorium, the contract will be extended by three months beyond the projected duration and the benefits payable by the debtor will be temporarily deferred until the end of the extension period. These measures are supplemented by a suspension of the creditor's right to acceleration or early termination in the event of a default, a worsening of the debtor's financial situation, or a decrease in the value of collateral, in all cases until the end of the moratorium period.

The German legal provision establishes, however, an escape valve in order to prevent the moratorium – which is broad since it covers all financing contract commitments of consumers who are vulnerable due to the emergency – from having unmanageable consequences for the financing party, by making it clear that the measures described above cannot be imposed on a financing party if, in light of all relevant circumstances, including those associated with the pandemic,

---

25 Article 56.2 of the Italian Law on the validation and conversion of the d-l of 17 March 2020, no. 18.

26 Portuguese Decreto-Lei No. 10-J/2020 of 13 March 2020. See, Nuno Manuel Pinto Oliveira, 'COVID-19, contratos de crédito, contratos de arrendamiento y contratos de viajes del sector turístico en Portugal' (2020) VII(2) Revista de Derecho civil 89.

they are too costly for the financing party. Such refinements to the availability of debt moratoriums in contracts serve a valuable goal (avoid imposing the provision of liquidity to a contract party who is ill-placed to face it) but they probably come at the cost of increasing the complexity, the length and the cost of the emergency liquidity provision.

4.4. MORATORIUMS ON RENTAL LEASES

Another area in which a moratorium on payments could be considered are leases. There is no doubt that many economic agents (both consumers and firms) have to make lease payments at critical times when their income is impaired, at least in the short term.

The truth is, however, that most European countries have not adopted moratoriums in this area. In the majority of cases, instead, Governments have limited their intervention on leases, as will be discussed in the next section, to suspending the ability of landlords to terminate the contract due to default by the tenant and the ensuing eviction of the latter from the leased premises.

Some European jurisdictions have added to this a prohibition on enforcing penalties and guarantees for non-payment by the tenant for as long as the emergency situation lasts. The explanation for this attitude seems to be tied to the main theme of this section: a moratorium implies obtaining liquidity at the expense of the contractual counterparty, and there is no way to be certain that the contractual counterparty in a lease contract is well equipped – in general and under the current unique circumstances in particular – to provide such liquidity without triggering successive and subsequent defaults and, ultimately, the dreaded spiral of defaults.

The exception to this trend is to be found in the Iberian Peninsula.[27] Spain has adopted a complex regime of intervention – essentially implying moratoriums, but also other effects – in both residential and commercial leases.

In relation to residential leases, tenants of a main place of residence who are in a vulnerable position and whose landlord is a large holder of residential property[28] are entitled to the following, depending on the choice by the landlord (unless a deferment or a total or partial waiver of rent had already been agreed

27 A measure with similar effects has also been adopted in Scotland where the landlord's right to terminate the contract for non-payment of rent generally requires prior notice to the tenant, who in turn has a time to pay the amount due. In the context of COVID-19, the period during which the tenant has the right to pay has been extended in commercial leases from the current 14 days to 14 weeks.

28 "Large holders" are defined by the Spanish emergency lease legislation as individuals or legal entities who are holders of (1) more than 10 urban properties (excluding garages and storage rooms) or (2) built-up area of more than 1,500 square meters.

by the parties): (1) a moratorium on rent payments or (2) a 50% waiver of rent. The moratorium or debt cancellation will be in effect for the duration of the state of alarm or for as long as the situation of vulnerability continues, up to a maximum of four months.

In the event of a moratorium, the rent shall be deferred by dividing the payments into instalments over a period of at least three years, which shall be calculated from the time the moratorium ends or the situation of vulnerability has passed, but always within the term of the rental contract. The tenant is not penalised in any way and does not have to pay interest on the liquidity advance that results from the deferment and the subsequent instalment payments.

If the landlord is not a large holder, the moratorium is not mandatory. Instead, there is an obligation to negotiate and explore alternatives, but if, in the end, the landlord does not accept a deferral or a waiver, the moratorium is not compulsory. For such cases (although there are others), the Spanish RDL 11/2020 approved a financial line of credit with complete guarantee coverage by the State of bank financing for tenants in a situation of vulnerability, as a result of the expansion of COVID-19, in order to fund housing rent payments for up to a maximum of six monthly payments.

With a similar purpose, a new aid programme has also been created to alleviate the economic burden of tenants of principal residences who find themselves in situations of vulnerability due to their obligations to pay rent or to repay the transitional financing aid for rent payments. It is specified that the amount of this aid may be up to 900 euros per month and 100% of the rent payments or, if applicable, 100% of the principal and interest of the loan that may be taken out to meet the rent payments for the principal residence.[29]

In Spain, a moratorium on commercial leases and leases of an ongoing industry or business has been adopted under RDL 15/2020. The measure is intended to benefit self-employed persons and SMEs[30] that lease property and are experiencing financial difficulties that affect their ability to pay rent. The difficulty of making payments is dependent on whether their business activity has been officially suspended or whether, even if it has not been suspended, they have experienced a decrease in revenue of 75% or more. In these cases, if the lessor is a large property holder,[31] the lessees are entitled to apply for a moratorium on the payment of rent (assuming that a moratorium or reduction of rent had not already been agreed to), for the period that the state of alarm

---

29 In a similar vein, in Portugal, the Lei No. 4-C/2020, of 6 April 2020, provides for public interest-free loans to tenants in vulnerable situations and in severe difficulties to pay rent.

30 The concept of SME that has been adopted in the Spanish emergency legislation is narrower than that in general EU Law (essentially, the notion in the 2003 European Commission Recommendation 2003/361 of 6 May 2003).

31 With the same meaning of this term as that provided for residential leases by the Spanish RDL 11/2020.

lasts and, if the difficulty continues, for the following months up to a maximum of four months. The deferred rent must be paid at the end of the moratorium by means of instalments over at least the following two years of the contract (always within the term of the contract) and without any penalties or interest being charged to the tenants for the deferral.

For other landlords ("small holders"), a mechanism for renegotiation of rent is provided, similar to what has been established for residential leases, in order to obtain a temporary and extraordinary deferral of the payment of rent, but it seems to be evident from the legal text that this is not mandatory for the landlord. In order to "grease" the voluntary deferral agreement, the rental deposit is allowed to be used to cover one of the periods of rent deferral, with the deposit being returned within one year after the end of the moratorium.

In Portugal, protective measures have been adopted for lessees[32] affecting the payment of rent for both residential and non-residential leases. For residential leases, payment default by the tenant during the period of the health emergency will not be taken into account to allow termination for non-payment.

For commercial rentals, the Portuguese intervention is even more ambitious, since businesses open to the public for retail activities or performance of services that are now closed, or whose activities have been suspended, have been allowed to defer the payment of rent due during the months in which the health emergency is in effect and for an additional month on top. The deferred amount will be paid in instalments over the 12 months following the end of the moratorium. In Portugal, however, no distinction has been made between large and small holders.

The Spanish and Portuguese moratoriums on rent (and perhaps even more so the latter, since it applies to all kinds of lessors in terms of size) present a certain risk of forcing lessors who may not be well placed to provide liquidity to their tenants to do so, and thus initiating in some cases a chain of defaults with undesirable consequences. If the lessor is an entity with sufficient financial muscle (direct or indirect), it is likely that it would be able to provide its tenants with the emergency liquidity they require. However, we cannot assume that all lessors are in such a position. That may be the case even if the imposition is restricted to the so-called "large holders", especially if we consider that the number of properties that make a lessor a large holder is rather low and does not guarantee an increased ability to finance tenants in the short term. For example, a small real estate company with seven apartments and five commercial premises qualifies under the Spanish emergency regulations as a large holder. It is not obvious that such a lessor is in a position to provide liquidity to its tenants, much less to all of them at the same time. This could lead to a chain of defaults – the

32 Portuguese Lei No. 4-C/2020 of 6 April.

real estate company defaults on its suppliers of goods and services and stops paying its employees – which is what is so crucially important to contain.

4.5. OTHER MORATORIUMS

In Europe, other moratoriums have been approved in various other sectors.[33] For example, in Germany, §240 §1 EGBGB has provided for a general moratorium for consumers and SMEs[34] in respect of their payment obligations arising from ordinary contracts such as those for communications, energy, electricity and mandatory insurance. This moratorium ran temporarily until 30 June 2020, but was not automatic. It was based on the request of the consumer whose personal or family's well-being or the SME whose business' viability may be at risk if forced to continue making payments under such contracts. In response, the supplier of the goods or services could challenge the moratorium if he/she could demonstrate that failure to collect payment would threaten the viability of his/her own business.

The moratorium, despite providing for the aforementioned escape valve for the creditor, goes to the trouble of expressly excluding leases and employment contracts from its scope of application. There are obvious reasons to exclude employment contracts since workers are not generally in a good position to provide liquidity to their employers through a moratorium on wages and salaries.[35] In fact, a similar exclusion could have been introduced for non-employment service contracts since we cannot assume that the service provider in those contracts is well equipped to provide liquidity to the client, except for services such as those mentioned above, including energy, communications, and possibly others that are typically provided by very large companies. The same also applies to leases, as previously argued. One cannot generally assume – as the measures at stake

---

33 In Spain, although there are no moratoriums in the strict sense of the kind adopted in Germany and Italy that we will summarise, some measures have been taken with a similar goal in mind. The Spanish RDL 11/2020 (Art 28) extends the group of potential recipients of electricity vouchers to the self-employed who have seen their revenue reduced by at least 75% in the month prior to which the voucher is sought to apply in relation to the average revenue of the previous six-month period. Similarly, Article 29 of the Spanish RDL 11/2020 establishes measures aimed at guaranteeing the ongoing supply of energy and water to homes during the state of alarm, such that while the state of alarm is in effect, the supply to domestic consumers in their principal residence may not be suspended for reasons other than the need to ensure the security of supply, people and facilities, even if such a suspension option is provided for in the supply or access contracts signed by the consumers.

34 In this case, the concept (broader than that used in Spain for the non-residential rental moratorium) is based on the notion in the European Commission Recommendation 2003/361 of 6 May 2003.

35 In fact, in the case of temporary suspensions of employment contracts (ERTEs, in the Spanish legal jargon) this liquidity is mostly provided by the State, which assumes a large proportion of the wages that are earned during this period.

are of a general nature, not considering the circumstances of a given individual contract – that landlords, across the board, are able to provide liquidity to their tenants in the current circumstances. It seems that, in general, there may be other agents (starting with the Government) who could offer such financing to tenants experiencing difficulties without the risk of sparking a string of successive defaults.

In Italy, Article 4 of Decree No. 9 of 2 March 2020 provided for the suspension of payments for electricity, water, gas and urban waste management for residents of the municipalities most affected by the pandemic until 30 April 2020.[36]

Once again, there is a risk of forcing economic agents to provide liquidity even if they are not necessarily well equipped to do so in the short term. Certainly, it is more common, that the providers of communications and energy services are large companies with sufficient financial margins to take on the mandatory short-term financing of their customers. This may not be necessarily the case, and therefore, and thus it may seem reasonable to establish (as Germany has done) safety valves to cover those scenarios. On the other hand, safety valves add uncertainty to the provision of liquidity support through contract moratoriums and increase transaction costs in the implementation of the emergency measures.

5. CAUTION AND MINIMUM INTERVENTION: KEEPING CONTRACTS ALIVE (WHEN POSSIBLE)

The various options for intervening in ongoing contracts can have very distinct contractual effects and their costs prove to be equally diverse. We examine these options and conclude with an unsurprising recommendation: better to opt, in principle, for the least costly and intrusive ones.

5.1. TERMINATION OF THE CONTRACT AND ITS COSTS

The most drastic – and probably costly – general mechanism to intervene in an existing contract is to terminate it. A contractual relationship that was alive and well before the outbreak of the pandemic was presumably in place because it created value for the parties, and thus (absent negative effects that are hard to establish at such level of analysis) for society. An ongoing contract is in general a valuable asset. If the law terminates the contract, the value associated with that contract is destroyed. We can label such value the "relational value" of an existing contract.

[36] Article 72 of the Italian Law on validation and conversion of d-l no. 18 contains this provision, developing a system for the payment of suspended invoices in instalments.

This value exists not only because there are very often specific, unamortised investments that lose all their capacity to generate value once the contractual relationship expires, especially if the expiration is abrupt. This is not only the case because a contract is a source of value in relation to other contracts with the clients or counterparts of one of the contracting parties (the "goodwill" as often referred to in agency and distribution contracts). What is most decisive is that the network of reciprocities[37] that takes place within a living contractual relationship and which operates as an incentive mechanism for behaviours that produce social value – and which depends crucially on the plausible continuity of the relationship – lapses when the contract ends. This is of enormous relevance in a multitude of contractual environments: supply and distribution chains – relationships between input producers and final producers, between manufacturers, wholesalers, retailers and final customers; leases, professional and other service contracts, recurrent financing contracts and many more.

The costs for the parties and society in general associated with the termination of a contractual relationship are potentially very high. Even when the relational element can be seen as typically less relevant (think of a mortgage loan contract relating to the purchase of a private home or other asset), the termination of the contract coupled with enforcement of the guarantee also generates relevant costs for the parties. The debtor who sees his/her property foreclosed loses wealth, the usage of the asset and also the idiosyncratic value that most owners place upon their property. Moreover, foreclosure produces significant negative external effects, such as costs for the justice system, as well as a reduction in property prices in areas where there are numerous foreclosures.

Resorting to a broad measure of termination of contracts as a means to intervene in emergency situations does not seem in principle an attractive option. On the contrary, the above arguments point to the general desirability of preventing the costs associated with contract termination. The more so when the defaults and disruptions in the contract that may underlie termination are linked to a public health emergency, which presumably will be only transitory – although the current one is proving not to be so short-lived. Incurring the social losses that result from the termination of existing contracts, due to a temporary disruption, does not seem an appealing strategy for both legal systems and societies.

5.1.1. Restricting termination to preserve the relational value of contracts

It is therefore unsurprising that during the present emergency situation various legal systems have adopted multiple measures with the aim of restricting the

---

37 See, on the relational dimension of contracts, Juanjo Ganuza and Fernando Gómez, 'Contracts without Courts' (2021 forthcoming) Journal of Economics and Management Strategy, and the extensive economic and law and economics literature referenced there.

termination of existing contracts, with its associated costs, and have decidedly opted to promote the continued conservation of ongoing relationships.

France has adopted perhaps the broadest and most general measure aimed at preserving the continuity of contracts despite instances of non-performance linked to or aggravated by the pandemic. The French emergency laws determine that contractual penalties and liquidated damages provisions, penalty clauses, acceleration terms and clauses stipulating the termination of contractual obligations for a certain term will not take effect if the date on which performance was due falls within the period between 12 March 2020 and one month after the end of the state of emergency. Following one month after this period (that is, two months from the expiration of the state of emergency) the clauses in question will regain effect if compliance has not yet taken place before that date. If the date of non-performance is prior to 12 March, the clauses in question take effect, but are suspended until one month after the end of the state of emergency.[38]

Other countries and jurisdictions have adopted measures restricting contractual termination in the field of lease contracts, being aware of the significant costs, for the parties and for society, that the termination of these relationships may entail.

Germany[39] initially suspended, until 30 June 2020, the landlord's right to terminate the lease (for housing, commercial and office premises) on the grounds of non-payment of rent and similar amounts accruing between 1 April and 30 June 2020, where the non-payment is credibly linked to the effects of COVID-19. The obligation to pay the rent – and the lessor's right to claim it – is not suspended, rather simply the lessor's right to terminate the lease for non-payment of rent for that particular time period. The German emergency law does not prevent – unlike the French rule – the enforcement of guarantees for non-payment, or the accrual of interest for late payment.

In Portugal, payment defaults occurring while under the state of emergency were not be taken into account to reach the number of failed payments that are necessary for terminating a residential lease.

In England and Wales, where the legal tradition is usually very reluctant to intervene in tenancy relationships, especially in commercial ones, it was established that landlords may not evict tenants of commercial premises or offices for non-payment of rent or similar amounts until 30 June – this date being subject to extension. However, the tenant's obligation to pay the rent remains (including default interest for late payment) and the lessor may take any legal action other than eviction, such as the enforcement of any type of guarantee existing in relation to the obligation to pay the rent – guarantees, among others.

---

38 French Ordonnance n° 2020-306 of 25 March 2020 on the extension of time limits during the period of public health emergencies and the adaptation of procedures during that period.

39 Article 240 §3 EGBGB.

In Spain, no general provisions have been adopted to suspend the termination of the contract and eviction in the field of leases. However, the moratorium passed by RDL 11/2020 and 15/2020 for residential and commercial areas, respectively, legally imposes a postponement of the payment of rental income for certain groups of tenants – namely the vulnerable, in the residential sector, and commercial tenants seriously affected by the economic downturn linked to the health emergency, in the non-residential. In this way, termination and eviction of tenants will be excluded for the tenants covered by the moratorium while it remains in force, simply because the rent will not be due during its duration.

It is true that in Spain certain additional measures were introduced to preserve rental relationships. Thus, it has been generally provided[40] that housing tenants may extend, for up to six months, contracts that expire between the entry into force of RDL 11/2020 and two months after the end of the state of alarm. With less general scope, in relation to tenants in vulnerable situations, Spanish law has introduced[41] the possibility to suspend evictions when these vulnerable tenants do not have housing alternatives. Suspension will last until the appropriate measures are adopted by the social services, with a maximum period of six months.

It is likely that a more general measure suspending the termination of rental contracts, for a period sufficient to cover the disruption caused by the health emergency and thus to prevent that leases that are viable and produce value for the parties are wiped out by short-term defaults would have been welcome. It is possible, though, that the Spanish legislator is implicitly relying on the suspension of the procedural terms and deadlines that was introduced early in Spain during the state of emergency. An express rule, however, such as the German or French ones, would have provided greater clarity.

The above does not mean that termination would always be inefficient after the change in circumstances following the pandemic, especially if their consequences are not merely transitory. Let us consider the following example concerning a commercial lease. One year before COVID-19, premises in a prime location owned by L were rented to T, who runs a very successful fine restaurant in the premises. Assume that the rent is 100, and the value for T of the use of the property is 110. Presumably, the lease contract holds value for the parties over alternative contracts (with other landlords or tenants). Now, when the pandemic erupts, the restaurant has to be closed to the public for two months. During this time, the value of the lease for T is just 50 (it is only used as the basis for catering services, not to serve food in the premises), and moreover T has liquidity problems and can only pay up to 50 as rent. It makes sense not

40 Article 2 Spanish RDL 11/2020.

41 Article 1 Spanish RDL 11/2020.

to terminate the lease if the disruption in the business of the restaurant is only temporary, and restricting the ability of the landlord to terminate the contract due to the non-payment of rent by the tenant while the restaurant is closed by public order is probably wise.[42] But if the pandemic will have a lasting effect on the demand for fine dining due to health fears in the population, and the value of the lease for T (after the forced closure) goes down to 80, while a retailer R would value the use of the property at 90, it is efficient that the lease contract between L and T is terminated, and a new lease with R is signed.[43]

5.1.2. Restricting termination to avoid liquidity and solvency risks

The wariness of contractual termination in an emergency situation may be due to reasons largely unconnected with the objective of preserving the relational value of the contract or avoiding the costs of enforcement on valuable assets following termination. It can also be explained by reasons related to problems of liquidity – and possibly even solvency – that may affect a contract party, and the consequent spiral of defaults that can occur as a result of restitution obligations accompanying the termination of the contract that that party may be unable to comply with.

This problem is likely to be particularly important in the transport and tourism sectors. There, massive cancellation and termination of contracts by clients undoubtedly may reach significant proportions, precisely at a time where companies in the transport, travel and tourism sector are being hit very hard and experience very serious cash flow problems. When,. following cancellation by the clients, firms were forced to give back promptly all advance payments and deposits made in regard of the services that have been cancelled, the current liquidity shock would be exacerbated and probably lead to a number of insolvencies in those sectors.

42 If only to avoid extreme cases of a landlord trying to get advantage of the vulnerability of the tenant due to the liquidity constraint and the value of the goodwill attached by T to the rented premises, trying to force a renegotiation raising the rent to, say, 105.

43 If T could use legal doctrines such as hardship, *rebus sic stantibus* or *Wegfall der Geschäftsgrundlage* (as argued, for instance, by Gerhard Wagner, 'Corona Law' (2020) 2020(3) Zeitschrift für europäisches Privatrecht, 536–539, and Martin Häublein and Maximilian Müller, 'Wer trägt das Pandemierisiko in der Geschäftsraummiete?' (2020) Neue Zeitschrift für Miet- und Wohnungsrecht 486–492) to reduce rent to, say, 75, the efficient outcome (termination and new lease to R) would be impeded or at least discouraged. It may make sense to encourage renegotiation between L and T, but there are more subtle – and at the same time, less reliant on court's ability to rewrite contracts– ways to do it. For instance, having payments between the parties contingent on the observation ex post as to whether the rent in the contract with R is higher than the renegotiation offer made by T. The sharing of risk of adverse events that may fall upon T (and other contract parties similarly situated) cannot be, in the dire economic environment following the pandemic, the main, let alone the only goal of legal intervention on existing lease agreements.

It is clear that the closure of hotels of all kinds, as well as the widespread, almost complete in many cases, disruption of passenger transport lines, especially in the medium and long distance, has frustrated the travel plans of many consumers. Moreover, the situation for this sector, in terms of its disruption of normal operations and its ability to meet the requirements of the contracts, is expected to perhaps last longer than for most other industries.

It may seem natural to think that if the provision of the service is not possible, given the closure of the establishment or the suspension of means of transportation, there is no other solution than the cancellation of the contract due to supervening impossibility and, with it, the return of payment already made, that is, the amounts advanced by the traveller for the transport or hotel reservation, sometimes reaching the full contract price. In the case of package travel contracts, EU law expressly provides for this effect in cases of cancellation due to extraordinary circumstances. Article 12.2 of the package travel Directive[44] provides that "… the traveller shall have the right to terminate the package travel contract before the start of the package without paying any termination fee in the event of unavoidable and extraordinary circumstances occurring at the place of destination or its immediate vicinity and significantly affecting the performance of the package, or which significantly affect the carriage of passengers to the destination. In the event of termination of the package travel contract under this paragraph, the traveler shall be entitled to a full refund of any payments made for the package but shall not be entitled to additional compensation".

The risk in an emergency situation such as the current is that the accumulation of these cancellations and requests for reimbursement, although foreseeably small on average, in aggregate terms may represent a serious problem of liquidity and perhaps even solvency for the tour operator or transport company.

Presumably with this problem in mind, Article 36 of the Spanish RDL 11/2020[45] has introduced some provisions to try to mitigate such consequences. In general, it contemplates that as a consequence of the measures adopted during the state of alarm, contracts – typically for the purchase of consumer goods or the provision of services, although transport or accommodation contracts are not specifically mentioned – will be impossible to enforce. The consumer maintains its right to terminate the contract, but subject to certain conditions. First, its exercise is significantly limited in time (period of 14 days from the impossibility

---

44 Directive (EU) 2015/2302 of the European Parliament and of the Council of 25 November 2015 on package travel and linked travel arrangements, amending Regulation (EC) No 2006/2004 and Directive 2011/83/EU of the European Parliament and of the Council and repealing Council Directive 90/314/EEC.

45 The wording of the provision was so confusing that it has been amended twice in less than three months, first by the Spanish RDL 15/2020, and later, with effect on 10 June 2020, by the RDL 21/2020. On this complex interpretive task, see Ángel Carrasco Perera, 'Este bucle es intrincado. El art 36.1 RDL 11/2020 (COVID) pasa por tercera vez por la peluquería del BOE' (2020) Centro de Estudios de Consumo 1–7.

of performance). Second, the restitutionary effects from cancellation are subordinated to a negotiated process of review of the terms of the contract, including the offer by the company of substitute vouchers for the reimbursement. Only if 60 days pass without an agreement on an alternative, the obligation to return deposits or advance payments will become effective. For reimbursement, unless otherwise agreed, a maximum period of 14 days is provided.

For package travel contracts that had to be cancelled due to COVID-19 the Spanish Government also tried to impose a novel way out. The Spanish RDL 11/2020 provided in its original version of 31 March 2020 that the consumer could be given a voucher to be used within one year from the end of the validity of the state of alarm and its extensions, for an amount equal to the refund that would have corresponded in accordance with the Spanish General Law on Consumer Protection. If the organiser of the trip, on the other hand, had been reimbursed by the suppliers of services included in the contract for the anticipated quantities for the trip, it would proceed, depending on whether that reimbursement had been total or partial, with the total or partial cancellation of the voucher and with the restitution to the consumer of the corresponding quantities. The refund to the consumer had to take place within a period not exceeding 60 days.

Now, the Spanish RDL 21/2020 has returned to a more orthodox (in view of the provisions of the package travel Directive) regime, by which the one-year voucher has to be accepted by the consumer in lieu of the full reimbursement of deposits or advancements, and the firm has to provide the restitution requested by the consumer within a 14-day period. Vouchers, so it is added, need to contain a sufficient financial security (in ways, however, that remain unspecified).

Similar, in fact more far-reaching, measures can be found in Italy. For contracts for shows and cultural events of all kinds, vouchers[46] with a one-year duration have been provided for, which consumers must request within 30 days and the company responsible for the event must send the consumer within the same period.[47] In relation to contracts for all means of transport, accommodation and travel packages,[48] it has been provided that the company, after receiving

---

46 A very similar solution has been introduced in Germany for contracts related to services and events in the cultural field, including sport events, conferences, swimming pools, gyms, and music and language courses. Instead of a price refund, consumers would receive an equivalent in-kind voucher (Gutschein). The Law was sponsored by the CDU/CSU and SPD parliamentary fractions and entered into force on 20 May 2020.

47 Article 88 of the Italian Law on the validation and conversion of d-l no. 18.

48 For package travel, Germany has also passed a law that entered into force on 31 July 2020, providing also for vouchers in favour of consumers who had booked their travel prior to 8 March 2020. The vouchers are not mandatory for customers, who can claim restitution of advance payments and deposits. To enhance the appeal of the vouchers, and thus, the rate of acceptance by consumers, the Government provides guarantees up to the full value of the voucher. If the voucher is not redeemed by the end of 2021, firms have to immediately refund all deposits and payments made by the consumer.

the request from the consumer, should proceed (within 30 days or 60 days in some cases of travel packages) to reimburse the price or amounts advanced or to deliver a voucher for the same amount valid for one year.[49]

In Portugal,[50] for travel and accommodation arranged through travel agencies, and also for direct reservations of accommodation, when the required services were foreseen for the period between 13 March and 30 September 2020, customers have the right to a voucher for the full amount anticipated, or a rescheduling of the travel or stay before the end of 2021. Only when the voucher is not used or the services have not been rescheduled within that period of time, the customer is entitled to reimbursement of deposits and advance payments, to be made by the firm within a 14-day period. The same applies in favour of unemployed consumers.

Many of these measures generated a negative uproar in the Spanish legal literature[51] on the basis that they imply reduction in the level of consumer protection enshrined in consumer legislation (and, in the case of package travel contracts, specifically in the package travel Directive, EU Directive 2015/2302).

In Europe more generally, the situation of the travel and hotel industries stirred a vibrant debate on the matter, particularly in regard to consumer rights in Directive 2015/2302 on package travel, and passenger rights in Regulations 261/2004,[52] 1371/2007,[53] 1177/2010[54] and 181/2011.[55]

The European Commission advocated the preservation of the status quo in the consumer *acquis*, albeit in a Recommendation of 13 May 2020,[56] it suggests the use of vouchers to be offered to passengers or travellers, as an alternative to reimbursement in money, but subject to voluntary acceptance by the customer. The Commission also recommended that vouchers should be valid for a minimum of one year, be covered by protection against insolvency of the

49 Article 88 bis of the Italian Law on the validation and conversion of d-l no. 18.

50 Portuguese Decreto-Lei No. 17/2020, of 23 April 2020.

51 Manuel Jesús Marín López, 'Efectos del COVID-19 sobre contratos de consumo: el artículo 36 del RD-L 11/2020' (2020) Centro de Estudios de Consumo 1–24; Pascual Martínez Espín, 'El fin de los bonos de viaje o no: depende' (2020) Centro de Estudios de Consumo 1–4.

52 Regulation (EC) No 261/2004 of the European Parliament and of the Council of 11 February 2004 establishing common rules on compensation and assistance to passengers in the event of denied boarding and of cancellation or long delay of flights, and repealing Regulation (EEC) No 295/91.

53 Regulation (EC) No 1371/2007 of the European Parliament and of the Council of 23 October 2007 on rail passengers' rights and obligations.

54 Regulation (EU) No 1177/2010 of the European Parliament and of the Council of 24 November 2010 concerning the rights of passengers when travelling by sea and inland waterway and amending Regulation (EC) No 2006/2004.

55 Regulation (EU) No 181/2011 of the European Parliament and of the Council of 16 February 2011 concerning the rights of passengers in bus and coach transport and amending Regulation (EC) No 2006/2004.

56 Commission Recommendation (EU) 2020/648 of 13 May 2020 on vouchers offered to passengers and travellers as an alternative to reimbursement for cancelled package travel and transport services in the context of the COVID-19 pandemic.

carrier or the organiser of the travel, refundable even before the expiration of the one-year period, and transferrable to other passengers or consumers. The Commission also encourages Member States to actively consider setting up guarantee schemes for vouchers to ensure reimbursement in case of insolvency of the issuer of the voucher.

Numerous Member States,[57] however, prefer a more intense use of vouchers, and issued a joint statement underscoring the need of additional flexibility in the European rules. The underlying principle is that that vouchers should be more heavily relied upon, even without the consumer's consent, provided that certain features accompany the temporary issuance of the vouchers: transparent information, non-discrimination, a common length of voucher validity, maximum flexibility of use and a clear right of reimbursement immediately at the end of validity in the event of non-use of vouchers.

The idea underlying measures as the ones referred to above, in our view, does not seem totally objectionable in terms of substance, even acknowledging the existence of implementation problems. The concern behind the rules is well-founded and the voucher mechanism appears to be an interesting instrument for keeping the contract alive and avoiding a flood of claims for reimbursement in a very short time against the same firm.[58] In the present emergency situation, consumer protection understood as the full and exact observance of each and every consumer right in an ordinary period should allow for some exceptions in order to achieve larger macro-economic goals. Given the extraordinary, urgent and temporary nature of the intervention, the preservation of the productive framework in the tourism and transport sector, among others, and the reduction of the risk of insolvency and a spiral of defaults and bankruptcies seems a powerful reason.[59]

In fact, probably the most significant criticism that may be raised against solutions such as the ones in Article 36 of the RDL 11/2020 is that they impose upon consumers whose contracts in the travel and tourism field have been frustrated in their execution due to the effect of the pandemic a across the board to provide liquidity to firms in those industries. In the Spanish case, that liquidity provision lasts at least for two and a half months.

---

57 BE, BG, CY, CZ, EL, FR, IE, LV, MT, NL, PL and PT.

58 As indicated in the text, in other countries with a major tourism industry and seriously affected by the emergency, such as Italy or Portugal, similar measures have been adopted, also aimed at mitigating this risk.

59 Needless to say, not every sacrifice in the altar of short-term avoidance of a liquidity crisis and a wave of bankruptcies is justified. But the insistence on exact and complete preservation of consumers' right of reimbursement at all costs is perhaps also an extreme position. A middle ground is feasible, especially if vouchers are transferable and can be redeemed against the Government. In general, on the tension between macroeconomic goals and legal constraints, Yair Listokin, *Law and Macroeconomics. Legal Remedies to Recessions* (Harvard University Press 2019) 139.

This measure, given its general nature, does not weigh the ability of consumers to actually provide this liquidity to tourism and transport companies. For many consumers, it is true that, given that the amounts at stake are likely to be not very large (price of a hotel reservation, a planned holiday or a plane or train ticket)[60] such financing at their expense will be bearable on an individual basis. But there is no certainty that this will be the case. There might be consumers with a liquidity problem of their own. Even for amounts that are not seemingly too high, it does not make sense to impose the financing of companies for two and a half months on consumers when the companies' ability to perform has become impossible during the health emergency.

However, the idea of the voucher should be maintained as an instrument for preserving the contract by rendering performance of the specific hotel or transport service to a later date, without necessarily forcing the consumer to finance the contractual counterpart if he/she cannot or does not want to. One possibility to combine both objectives in some way would be to make the voucher immediately redeemable at the expense of the Government, so that the consumer could receive the amount directly from the tax authorities, and the latter could obtain a credit against the issuer of the voucher payable through taxation once the situation in those sectors has normalised or, even, if it becomes necessary in the future to give public aid to the companies in those sectors, deductible from any aid that might correspond to the issuer. In a similar vein, it has been suggested that the bond should be made into a security that would allow the consumer holding the bond to transfer it in exchange for money or to finance it by guaranteeing its amount.[61] Another possibility is to allow the credits represented by the voucher (and also others deriving from different COVID-19-related moratoriums) to become the assets of investment vehicles that may attract attention from investors who are in a better position to provide liquidity to both sides of the contract.[62]

5.2. MODIFYING THE CONTENT OF THE OBLIGATION: DEBT REDUCTION AND SUSPENSION

An attenuated intervention (compared to cancellation or termination) may be found in a modification of the content of the contract, at least in some forms of

---

60 The aggregate amount may be important for a given firm, possibly determining liquidity or even solvency problems, as all reimbursements accumulate suddenly in a short period of time.

61 See the Commission Recommendation of 13 May 2020. In Spain, Ángel Carrasco Perera, 'The "COVID-bonus" issued by travel agencies in favour of consumers' (2020) (in https://www.ga-p.com/publicaciones/el-bono-covid-emitido-por-las-agencias-de-viajes-en-favor-de-losconsumidores/ accessed 1 July 2020).

62 We are grateful to José Massaguer for this suggestion.

it. By the content of the contract we do not refer here to terms or clauses ancillary to those of the parties' main obligations, such as penalty clauses, liquidated damages terms or guarantees relating to the performance by the obligor.[63] We are thinking here of direct intervention affecting, to a greater or lesser extent, the main performance due under the contract. In particular, when referring to monetary obligations, the amount due. For other types of performance (for instance, the provision of services), it would be hard to imagine that a general law in times of emergency would be in the position to determine a modification in the nature and quality of the services to be rendered, although it is imaginable that a suspension in the provision could be decreed across the board in an emergency situation.

In short, it is feasible to consider, in times of a pressing macro-economic shock, a waiver of the monetary obligations for individuals and firms most directly affected by the pandemic and its consequences. As a measure of broad and general application, it does not appear advisable, either for the majority of contracts containing monetary obligations, or even for the majority of contracts of a given kind (loans, payments of certain goods). This is true, we believe, both if the policy is implemented through ad hoc legislative measures for the emergency situation or through a general and non-case dependent reading of some rules and doctrines in contract law (both the ones applicable to all contracts or those that govern a particular type of contract).

An indiscriminate elimination or reduction, whether general or by sector, of a party's payment obligations means that a fraction (greater or lesser depending on the amount) of the losses initially suffered by those contract parties directly affected by COVID-19 is transferred to the other party or parties. Such a transfer of the losses from the pandemic to someone else, merely because he/she is the counterparty in a contractual relationship, does not seem appealing, absent concrete and compelling justifications for the transfer of the losses. Broad appeals to risk sharing do not appear sufficient to this effect.

To make the argument clearer and more concrete, let us think of a one-year commercial lease in 2020 between A (landlord) and B (tenant). The monthly rent is equal to 50. In January and February 2020, B receives a monthly income from the commercial activity in the leased premises equal to 100. Due to the state of emergency and the lockdown measures, B is forced to suspend retail activity for three months and stops receiving the 100 per month that he/she

[63] We have already pointed out that some countries (France) have temporarily suspended the effects of such clauses insofar as it has been considered that they may contribute to or amplify the breach and threaten the continuation of the contract. Moreover, tinkering with liquidated damages and penalty provisions may be, under certain circumstances, a valuable tool to encourage renegotiation of the contract by the parties leading to more efficient outcomes or to speedier reutilisation of assets under contract rendered idle by the consequences of the pandemic. This is left, however, for later work.

normally would (let us leave aside, for simplicity, the possibility that he/she can make some online sales, as well as other costs from the retail activity). The forced suspension of sales has therefore resulted in a loss of 100 per month for B.

This loss, moreover, is irreversible. It can be transferred on to others, in whole or in part, but it does not disappear, in the same way that insurance coverage does not make losses caused by accident go away, it simply transfers them from the insured's pocket to the insurer's pocket.[64] The income from the period of forced closure is gone forever. Passing it on to the counterparty does not eliminate it, and extending the rental contract at its end for a period of time equivalent to that of suspension does not erase the losses. As a Spanish classical author wrote in 1562: "If you spent your money wrong, you may earn more; but the time spent cannot be recovered. Days go by and never come back".[65]

In principle, it is B, the party who receives the loss immediately and directly, who should bear it, unless we believe that there is some good reason to shift it onto others. If, for the entirety of the emergency period, a 100% deduction is imposed on the payment of the rental income from the business premises (or, equivalently, the lease is suspended for the duration of the closure), of the loss initially suffered (100), B could transfer half (50, the amount of the rental income) to the lessor, so that A would be absorbing 50% of B's losses. If the rent is reduced by 50%, A would be assuming 25% of B's losses and similarly with other percentages of rent reduction.

If instead of a rent reduction, a general suspension of commercial leases is implemented during the validity of the health emergency (say, three months), the effect is exactly the same as a 100% rent reduction. Of the 100 per month loss that B experiences directly, when rent payment is suspended, half shifts to A. Nothing changes the fact that at the end of 2020 the lease will be extended for the three months of suspension. It is true that B will pay 50 each month to A during that additional time, but it is in exchange for enjoying the premises during the extension, not because of what happened during the suspension period. Moreover, it inevitably implies a real use of resources, since no other tenant could use the property and thus, A will not be able to obtain rent from another tenant other than B during the three months of the extension of the lease.

Therefore, although suspension and moratorium are often spoken of as if they were identical in their substance and effects, this is incorrect. The truth is that a suspension of the contract is equivalent to a 100% payment reduction for the time of suspension, and cannot be identified with a moratorium. In a moratorium, what happens is that the counterpart (the lessor, in our example)

---

64 Although this coverage, without a doubt, if the one who can suffer the loss is risk averse, means an improvement in welfare because he/she would be free from risks that reduce his/her welfare.

65 The original Spanish reads: "*Si gastaste mal tu dinero, puedes tornar a ganar otro tanto; pero el tiempo gastado no se puede cobrar. Pasan los días y nunca vuelven*". The author, Fray Diego de Estella, was a sixteenth-century religious writer and a master of Spanish classical prose.

finances the amount subject to the moratorium to the debtor for the duration of the moratorium. However, the lessor bears nothing of the underlying loss generated by the debtor's liquidity difficulty. The effect of the moratorium is purely financial, and the cost of financing, if the moratorium results in the accrual of interest to be paid by the debtor, is borne by the debtor and not by the counterparty.

Clearly, if the moratorium is accompanied, as it has been in Spain in the area of financing and lease contracts, by a provision that determines that the financing is to be provided to the debtor at zero interest (without surcharges or interest on arrears), the cost of providing the financing during the moratorium period falls on the creditor and, from this point of view, is a "reduction" of payments, but a reduction corresponding only to the financial cost of the deferral, not to the underlying loss that leads to the state of illiquidity of the monetary debtor.

It is only when the contract is purely financial that a contract suspension and a pure moratorium are similar (although not identical). But this is because the very nature of the contract makes the effect of both purely financial. Let us think of a financing contract with a duration of one year (until 31 December 2020), in which the debtor has to pay 100 to the creditor monthly. If there is a pure three-month moratorium (April, May, June) on that contract, the creditor is financing the 300 of the income of the affected months for six months (those remaining until the end of 2020). If a suspension of the contract occurs that entails the extension of its duration for a time equivalent to that of suspension, what happens is that the creditor is financing the 300 of the income corresponding to the length of suspension for nine months (until the end of the contractual period now extended).

Ultimately, a waiver (or suspension, which is equivalent) imposed generally[66] on payment obligations accrued in the emergency period entails transferring a portion of the losses initially suffered by the debtor of the payment over its counterpart in that contract. There is no general reason why such a general shift of losses is necessarily desirable through contracts in general or any particular type of contract (beyond insurance). Even less so when both parties to the

66 The Spanish RDL 11/2020 does call for a rent reduction of large homeowners in favour of tenants of principal residence in a situation of vulnerability, as it requires the landlord to choose between (1) a 50% reduction in rental income for the duration of the state of emergency and the following monthly payments if that period is insufficient in relation to the situation of vulnerability caused by the COVID19, with a maximum of four months in any case and (2) a moratorium on the payment of rental income for a maximum period of four months, to be returned in three years without surcharge or interest. In short, at the landlord's discretion, a 50% reduction of the rent is imposed for four months or a reduction of the financial cost of financing the amount of the four months' rent for a period of three years. However, despite the fact that the notion of large holder in RDL 11/2020 is probably over-inclusive, it seems that a difference is likely to exist in the capacity to absorb losses between the lessor and a lessee who is specifically in a very vulnerable situation. This kind of measure, however, has not been common in other European countries.

contract are firms. It is worth noting that, for good reason, in most countries there have been no widespread measures of this kind implemented in the midst of the emergency situation.

A generalised shifting of losses of the type described above requires solid grounds to justify it and reasonable criteria for determining its extent. In order to verify the presence of both conditions, we believe that a wide variety of factors and circumstances should be considered, which require a detailed analysis of the contract and the situation of the contracting parties. We believe that this is not possible in an emergency situation in which intervention of contracts must be immediate and general, which is incompatible with a precise analysis to this effect. This will only be possible, if at all, "when the dust settles", and requires a complex analysis, not merely intuitive risk sharing.

5.3. PURELY FINANCIAL DISRUPTION: THE MORATORIUM

As mentioned above, a moratorium on payment in favour of a contract party means that the counterparty to the contract is granted financing for the amount of the payment due and for the period of the moratorium. The moratorium may (or may not) be accompanied by a reduction equivalent to the cost of such financing if the moratorium is set as "free of interest or surcharges".

In section 4 we have already extensively analysed the use of moratoriums in different contractual fields by legislators in various countries during the course of the COVID-19 health emergency. We will now mention only two general ideas. The first, that a moratorium is a less aggressive instrument of intervention into a valid contract than termination and a reduction in the amount of the debt. Moreover, by focusing on the issues of liquidity and short-term financing, evaluation of its benefits and costs, as well as its design, is simpler than that of other more intrusive intervention alternatives.

Furthermore, moratoriums appear to be an effective tool for dealing with pressing liquidity concerns afflicting debtors, especially when the number of people involved is or may be high. The experience of the major recession that followed the financial crisis that started in the United States in 2007 reveals that for debtors in difficulty, measures with an immediate impact on their short-term payments are more effective than measures that could add to their total debt, but which materialise in later periods. Ganong and Noel's[67] empirical analysis shows that mortgage debt reductions that do not diminish short-term payments but

---

67 Peter Ganong and Pascal Noel, 'Liquidity vs. Wealth in Household Debt Obligations: Evidence from Housing Policy in the Great Recession' 2018 NBER Working Paper No. 24964 1–52; Peter Ganong and Pascal Noel, 'The Effect of Debt on Default and Consumption: Evidence from Housing Policy in the Great Recession' 2017 Working Paper Harvard Joint Center on Housing Studies 1–77.

concentrate on the long-term amount of debt, do not have a significant impact on defaults and the levels of spending of households who are in difficulty with their mortgage debts. When a default produces immediate costs, it is the outcome from short-term shocks in income and is not sensitive to future projections or anticipations of the debt burden that will be felt in later periods, let alone those even further away in time.

6. PERSONALISED SOLUTIONS FOR TAILORED CONTRACTS

Tailored contracts are also facing the consequences of the public health emergency and its economic impact. There are contracts that are intensely negotiated and adapted in every detail to the characteristics of the transaction and the interests of the contracting parties. M&A or large corporate finance contracts are paramount examples of these. Clearly, disputes over events arising from COVID-19 will also be important in such contracts. The large investor or company that had agreed to buy a company in the luxury goods sector at a fixed price and has not yet received it, as the transaction is in the interim period, will no doubt be very alarmed that the turnover expectations of the company that has just been bought will be much lower than expected. The bank that has just granted substantial financing to a large company in the tourism sector will be very concerned at how the financial covenants that had been included in the contract to allow new provisions of financing to be granted are now bound to be breached.

We do not believe that there is ample room in these areas for general intervention on contracts in the midst of the emergency. The effects of the emergency may constitute a serious obstacle to the implementation of the contract as the parties had foreseen. This is for two reasons. The first is that liquidity problems that may arise in this area probably can better be handled through other tools than general emergency legislation in the contract realm. Secondly, these contracts typically possess negotiated mechanisms to deal with this kind of problem. Parties and/or their advisors accumulate experience of previous large macro-economic disruptions, perhaps not of a pandemic, but of other equally, or almost equally, economic turmoil.

Those instruments and the contractual terms inserting them into the text of the contract were, almost certainly, not thinking of the COVID-19 pandemic and its consequences. But it is hard to imagine that the general legal measures regarding contracts that we can design and apply in this state of emergency will be better suited to maximising the value of the contract than those that have been refined and calibrated over a long period of time to assess contractual solutions to unexpected events in M&A and financial contracts. In M&A, one should mention MAC and MAE clauses (Material Adverse Change and Material

Adverse Event)[68] with their complex scheme of "carve-outs" and "carve-ins", together with other more general mechanisms such as representations and warranties and their reaffirmation or modification at different points in the contractual process. In financing contracts, we also find MAC and MAE clauses, typically projected towards the future solvency of the debtor – unlike in M&A contracts in which they have a partly retrospective function in relation to the valuation of the company purchased when the contract was concluded. But there are also other agreements which attempt to gauge how the debtor's financial situation will influence the provisions of the contract and, where appropriate, the maintenance of the financing. It seems more prudent to let the specific instruments take precedence over the general ones that we may devise in times of emergency, however controversial the application of the former may be in such difficult times as the one we are living in.

7. EPILOGUE: THE RECOVERY AND CONTRACTS

When the storm – the health emergency with its toll of disease and death – has passed, or at least has subsided, many countries will face a severe economic recession, with the consequences of job losses and the closure of businesses. We will then have to think about recovery and the instruments we will need to make it swift and robust.

Unlike other historical episodes (the Civil War in Spain; Second World War in most of Europe), there will not be a need to rebuild physical infrastructures following the catastrophe. What we will have lost – human lives and then jobs and businesses – is not susceptible to reconstruction. But societies can regain their economic and social footing and restore, in time, the lost levels of human welfare for those who have remained and those who will follow.

To that end, we do not believe that the contributions of law and economics are secondary. They must be called upon to contribute to creating the conditions for a solid and accelerated recovery. The channels for communicating impulse in an economy are the contracts that economic agents enter into. These agents will continue to need strong contract law to keep the channels clear of interference and capable of circulating the goods and services that pass through them. Many of these contracts, including those that already exist, will be partly burdened by

68 Matthew Jennejohn, Julian Nyarko and Eric L. Talley, 'COVID-19 as a Force Majeure in Corporate Transactions' Working Paper, Columbia Law School (2020) (in https://papers.ssrn.com/sol3/papers.cfm?abstract_id=3577701, accessed 1 July 2020); Robert Miller, 'Material Adverse Effect Clauses and the COVID-19 Pandemi' University of Iowa Legal Studies Research Paper (2020) (in http://ssrn.com/abstract=3603055 accessed 7 October 2020); Albert Choi and George Triantis, 'Strategic Vagueness in Contract Design: The Case of Corporate Acquisitions' (2010)119(5) Yale Law Journal 848.

the unfortunate legacy of the health crisis and the subsequent economic crisis. In order to resolve the problems and disputes that arise, we must use the best contract law that we can conceive of and apply. This also includes hardship and similar doctrines, although not the ones of a state of emergency, but of a time of recovery. Doctrines that respond to the spirit of reviving contracts and lead to the efficient use of resources, not looking back to the ashes of what was destroyed by COVID-19 and will never come back.

FORCE MAJEURE AND HARDSHIP IN THE CORONA CRISIS

Some Contract Law Reflections on ELI Principle no 13

Carmen Jerez, María Kubica and Albert Ruda*

The Principles for the COVID-19 crisis, drafted by the European Law Institute in May 2020, provide a set of criteria that deserve analysis within the framework of contract law. In particular, its Principle no 13 lays down a rule on force majeure and hardship in light of which national contract laws may be re-examined. Consequently, an event considered to amount to force majeure will usually entail in the contract that the debtor at stake will be relieved of the duty to compensate for non-performance. Therefore, force majeure does not necessarily lead to the termination of the contract. The present contribution, thus, analyses the new Principle no 13 from the perspective of (mostly) Spanish contract law, the CISG and several soft law instruments.

* Carmen Jerez, Autonomous University of Madrid, carmen.jerez@uam.es; María Kubica, Universidad Loyola Andalucía, mlkubica@uloyola.es; Albert Ruda, University of Girona, albert.ruda@udg.edu.

1. INTRODUCTION

The worldwide crisis caused by the emergence of the COVID-19 reveals that the system of remedies against a contractual breach, laid down by uniform sales law and soft law instruments, is designed for crisis situations between contracting parties, but it is unsatisfactory both in scenarios of generalised misfortunes that affect the planet, and, simply, when impediments occur that are beyond the control of the parties.[1] This justifies that institutions dedicated to the study of law (as is the case of the European Law Institute) immediately publishes principles applicable to contracts affected by the COVID-19 crisis. The text of the European Law Institute (ELI) Principles for the COVID-19 crisis contains a proposal of 15 basic measures (principles) adapted to these circumstances, both of public and private law.[2] The purpose of this contribution is to briefly analyse its Principle no 13, dedicated to force majeure and hardship, and to compare it with Spanish law. At the same time, the authors intend to explain its content and suggest some reflections. To do that, a previous delimitation of concepts is necessary.

The principle of freedom of contract, present in all market economies, means not only that the parties to a contract can freely choose whether to celebrate it or not, but also that the agreement reached should be honoured (*pacta sunt servanda* or sanctity of contracts).[3] In other words, it is the main principle of contract law[4] that the parties are bound by their promises, the latter being the very reason of the contract conclusion.[5]

On the other hand, an agreement constitutes a consensual risk allocation mechanism. Generally, fixing the terms of the contract at the time of its conclusion allows allocation of future risks although the circumstances surrounding the contract conclusion may suffer drastic alteration. "The risk of change is on the party on whom it falls."[6] Nevertheless, in some exceptional cases

---

1 Proof of this are the controversies generated by Article 79 CISG, which required the uniform reinterpretation of a United Nations Committee of experts in 2007 (coincidentally, held in Wuhan): Alejandro M. Garro, 'CISG-AC Opinion No 7, Exemption of Liability for Damages under Article 79 of the CISG', Columbia University School of Law. Adopted by the CISG-AC at its 11th meeting in Wuhan (2007).

2 The Principles are available under the ELI website. https://www.europeanlawinstitute.eu/fileadmin/user_upload/p_eli/Publications/ELI_Principles_for_the_COVID-19_Crisis.pdf accessed 1 July 2020.

3 For Spanish law see, among others, Díez Picazo, *Fundamentos del Derecho Civil Patrimonial*, vol 2. *Las relaciones obligatorias* (6th edn, Civitas 2008) 133 ff. For Comparative Law, cf Willem H. Van Boom, 'Impossibility, Impracticability and Unforeseen Circumstances' (2020) SSRN Electronic Journal 1.

4 Marc-Philippe Weller, *Die Vertragstreue* (Mohr Siebeck 2009).

5 See Gottfried Schiemann, 'Das Rechtsgeschäft' in Julius von Staudinger, *Kommentar zum BGB, Eckpfeiler des Zivilrechts* (Sellier De Gruyter 2013) 131 ff.

6 See Van Boom, 'Impossibility' 1.

enforcing the obligations imposed by contract can lead to inequitable results.[7] In those circumstances, when some extrinsic factors have a negative impact on the contract equilibrium, risk allocation, by some considered a basic function of contracts and contract law,[8] become a crucial point again.[9]

Amongst the aforementioned exceptions, one can point out two: namely, force majeure or impossibility and hardship or unforeseen circumstances. Broadly speaking, in case of the former we deal with impossibility to perform due to circumstances beyond the control of the promisor/debtor[10] while the latter concerns situations where the promisor's performance, though not impossible, has become excessively onerous (hardship), so different that the economic basis on which the contract was made has disappeared due to subsequent change in circumstances (German *Wegfall der Geschaftsgrundlage)* or impracticable by the occurrence of a contingency the non-occurrence of which was a basic assumption on which the contract was made (United States' *Commercial Impracticability).*[11]

In Spain and all those legal systems that respect the rule "impossibilium nulla obligatio" of Roman origin two clearly distinguished concepts of impossibility exist: subsequent (supervening) and initial objective. The former arises after contract formation; meanwhile the latter already exists at the time the parties enter into the contract. Only supervening impossibility leads to non-performance and can be dealt with under the force majeure excuse. Initial impossibility is a matter of validity of the contract, which renders the agreement null and void.[12] The Spanish Civil Code (CC) encompasses the supervening impossibility in Article 1182 regulating the concept of "due thing loss". According to the later, "the obligation consisting of deliver a certain thing, when it is lost or destroyed without fault of the debtor and before he enters into arrears, will be extinguished".

---

7 Philip Ridder and Marc-Philippe Weller, 'Unforeseen Circumstances, Hardship, Impossibility and Force Majeure under German Contract Law' 22 ERPL 371, 372.

8 See Pablo Salvador Coderch, 'Alteración de circunstancias en el art. 1.213 de la Propuesta de Modernización del Código Civil en materia de Obligaciones y Contratos' (October 2009) InDret 41.

9 In that vein as to rebus sic stantibus clause Isabel González Pacanowska, 'Alteración sobrevenida de circunstancias en los contratos sinalagmáticos: de la rebus sic stantibus a la alteración extraordinaria de circunstancias', *Estudios sobre incumplimiento y resolución* (Aranzadi Tomson Reuters 2015) (ebook, available online https://proview.thomsonreuters.com/ accessed 1 July 2020) and Ángel Carrasco Pereira, *Derecho de contratos* (Aranzadi 2010) 1044.

10 See Van Boom, 'Impossibility' 1.

11 Dionysios P. Flambouras, 'The Doctrines of Impossibility of Performance and Clausula Rebus Sic Stantibus in the 1980 Convention on Contracts for the International Sale of Goods and the Principles of European Contract Law – A Comparative Analysis' (2001) 13 Pace Int'l L. Rev. 261, 277–278.

12 See Christoph Brunner, *Force Majeure and Hardship under General Contract Principles: Exemption for Non-Performance in International Arbitration* (Kluwer Law International 2009) 77.

Accordingly, Article 1184 CC amplifies the scope of application of the Article 1182 to services that result legally or are physically impossible.[13]

As to the *rebus sic stantibus* doctrine that in Spain lacks substantive regulation, its development having come from the judiciary, case law has established the following requirements for its application:

(1) The party/ies obligation/s must be one of continual performance (*obligación de tracto sucesivo*); the obligation of instantaneous execution falls within the scope of its application only if their fulfilment has been deferred until a certain time in the future;
(2) Presence of a supervening alteration of the business base due to the fact that (a) the equivalence between the parties' benefits is destroyed, or (b) the common business purpose is unattainable;
(3) The business base disappearance should be extraordinary and unforeseeable at the time of the conclusion of the contract;
(4) Risk cannot be an element of the contract (e.g. aleatory contract) nor can the supervening alteration form part of the risk assumed by one of the parties in a contract in question;
(5) Foreseeability must be assessed in relation to the type of contract entered into and the amount of information to which the contracting parties have access.

The latter item is related to the assumption of the risks in the contract itself, so that one could speak of a tacit assumption of risk in all those cases in which the risk has been foreseeable and not foreseen by the parties.[14] "Radical unforeseeability" of not only changed circumstances, but also of its consequences, required initially by the Spanish case law, has led consequently to almost practical impossibility of the clause application. Nevertheless, the last global financial crisis of 2008–2014 brought about a change in the Spanish Supreme Court's approximation to this element.[15] From this moment on, the "unforeseeability" requirement is satisfied

---

13 See Luis Díez Picazo, *Fundamentos del Derecho Civil Patrimonial*, vol 2. *Las relaciones obligatorias* (6th edn, Civitas 2008) 690. For more details see also Manuel Albaladejo García, XV-1 *Comentarios al Código Civil y Compilaciones Forales* (Madrid (1989) 353; Ricardo de Ángel Yagüez, *Comentario del Código Civil del Ministerio de Justicia* (Edersa 1991); Ángel Carrasco Perera, *Comentarios al Código* Civil *y Compilaciones Forales*, vol XV-1 (Edersa 1989) 374; Ángel Cristóbal Montes, *El incumplimiento de las obligaciones* (Tecnos 1989) 149; Antonio Morales Moreno, *La modernización del derecho de obligacione*s (Civitas 2006); Fernando Pantaleón Prieto, 'Las nuevas bases de la responsabilidad contractual', (1993) *Anuario de Derecho civil* 1719–1746, among others.

14 See Luz M. Martínez Velencoso, 'Riesgo Negocial v. Cláusula "Rebus Sic Stantibus"' (2011) 1 InDret 5–6 and Javier Lete, 'Le changement de circonstances en droit espagnol' in Javier Lete et al. (eds), *La recodification du Droit espagnol des obligations en France et en Espagne* (Université de Poitiers 2016) 237, 238.

15 See SSTS 30 June 2014 (RJ 2014, 3526), 15 October 2014 (RJ 2014, 6129), confirmed later on by SSTS 18 July 2019 (RJ 2019, 3010) and 6 March 2020 (RJ 2020, 879).

in all those instances in which to maintain the contract unchanged could not be reasonably required from the disadvantaged party. Thus, foreseeability should not "be appreciated with respect to an abstract possibility of the production of the alteration or circumstance determining the change, considered in itself, but in the economic and business context it influences".[16] Therefore, if the elements necessary for the foreseeability judgment were materially inaccessible, or even if they were accessible, forming a judgment is not possible at exceptional cost, changing circumstances could be classified as unforeseeable.[17]

1.1. SOLUTIONS TO THE UNPREDICTABLE AND INSUPERABLE EVENT

The factual assumption from which we depart is an unpredictable and insuperable event, which occurs after the conclusion of the contract but before its performance.

We understand by an unpredictable and insuperable event one that is totally outside the sphere of control of the contracting parties and that prevents, directly or indirectly, the performance of the contract, in whole or in part, provisionally or definitively.[18] The COVID-19 pandemic and the subsequent sanitary measures adopted by the governments of the States constitute a perfect example. A particularity in this sense is presented by German law, which embraces a very broad concept of impossibility (*Unmöglichkeit*) that also includes economic impossibility.[19] As regards force majeure, §275 BGB, which regulates, *inter alia*,

---

16 See again STS 30 June 2014 (RJ 2014, 3526).

17 Luz M. Martínez Velencoso, 'La Ruptura de la Economía Negocial tras el Covid-19 (un análisis desde el moderno Derecho Europeo de Contratos)' 12 bis *Actualidad Jurídica Iberoamericana* (2020) 326, 331. See also Fernando M. Alejandre García-Cerezo, Álvaro Luna Yerga and María Xiol Bardají, 'Crisis Económica y Cláusula Rebus Sic Stantibus: ¿Cambio de Vía en la Jurisprudencia Reciente del Tribunal Supremo?' (2013) 3 *Revista Aranzadi* Doctrinal; Cristina De Amuntágui Rodríguez, *La Cláusula Rebus Sic Stantibus* (Tirant lo Blanch 1993); Joaquín Ataz López, 'Art 1.452', in Rodrigo Bercovitz Rodríguez-Cano (ed), *Comentarios al Código Civil*, t. VII, (Tirant lo Blanch 2013) 10.235–10.249; Carrasco, *Derecho de Contratos* (Aranzadi 2010) 1044; Morales, *La Modernización del derecho de obligaciones* (Civitas 2006); Francisco Javier Orduña Moreno and Luz M. Martínez Velencoso, *La Moderna Configuración de la Cláusula 'Rebus Sic Stantibus'* (Civitas 2013); Sixto Sánchez Lorenzo, 'La Frustración del Contrato' in Sixto Sánchez Lorenzo (ed), *Derecho Contractual Comparado. Una Perspectiva Europea y Transnacional* (2nd edn, Civitas 2013) 1377–1437; Lis Paula San Miguel Pradera, 'La Excesiva Onerosidad Sobrevenida: una Propuesta de Regulación Europea', (2002) *Anuario de Derecho civil* 1115–1132.

18 The ELI Principle no 13.1 refers to the temporary or definitive nature of the impediment and the direct or indirect incidence of the event on the result, but not expressly to the total or partial nature of the breach it causes. However, this last variable is implicit in the solutions provided (in particular, in point 2, when dealing with renegotiation).

19 Divergences exist as to whether the economic impossibility is also regulated by §275 II BGB or is an assumption that only fits in §313 BGB. In favour of the latter solution, among others,

the supervening impossibility not attributable to the debtor, does not explicitly require that the situation that originates the non-performance is unpredictable. However, scholars, either by the influence of international instruments or soft law,[20] or by deduction from the initial impossibility doctrine, promotes unpredictability[21] (and the other requirements of force majeure, namely, insuperability and inevitability) to essential standards of this institution in German law.

The solutions adopted by the internal regulations for the unforeseeable and unavoidable event that causes a breach of contract are diverse, but there are also points in common:

(1) First, the commonly shared solution in Latin systems is the so-called force majeure, by virtue of which the debtor is exempted from liability for the non-performance. In common law systems it is considered an

Wilhelm Canaris, *Schuldrechtsreform 2002* (CH Beck 2002) XII; Reinhard Zimmermann, *The New German Law of Obligations* (OUP 2006) 46; Reiner Schulze, '§275 BGB' in Reiner Schulze and others (ed), *Bürgerliches Gesetzbuch Handkommentar* (Nomos 2011) para 20. This strand of the legal scholarship distinguishes between practical impossibility (§275 II BGB) and economic impossibility (§313 BGB). However, scholars also indicate that the term "economic impossibility" can create confusion, pointing out that both precepts regulate cases of hardship. The difference between one and the other lies in that §275 II BGB focuses on the great disproportion that the creditor's interest in performance supposes (the debtor's interest in obtaining the corresponding benefit does not play any role here) and it consists of comparing this interest with the expenses in which the debtor has to incur to fulfil his/her obligation. On the other hand, §313 deals with the cases in which the circumstances that form the foundation of the contract must have been seriously altered since its formation. The classic example of the case subject to the first provision is the one in which two parties sign a contract for the sale of a ring and before the seller transfers possession of the ring to the buyer the ring accidentally falls to the bottom of a lake. Technically, the ring could be located and removed from the lake, but the expenses associated with this operation would suppose a very high cost for the debtor. The second provision regulates, for example, the cases in which the global market price has increased excessively and unexpectedly. See Basil S. Markesinis, Hannes Unberath and Angus C. Johnston, *The German Law of Contract: A Comparative Treatise* (Hart Publishing 2006) 413–414 and Ridder and Weller, 'Unforeseen Circumstances, Hardship, Impossibility and Force Majeure under German Contract Law' 22 ERPL' 374–385. For a comparison between Spanish and German laws on the issue now see Albert Ruda-González, 'El impacto del Covid-19 en el Derecho europeo de contratos. En especial, el caso de Alemania' (2020) *Instituto de Derecho Iberoamericano* https://idibe.org/tribuna/impacto-del-covid-19-derecho-europeo-contratos-especial-caso-alemania accessed 1 July 2020.

20 See Brunner, *Force Majeure and Hardship under General Contract Principles: Exemption for Non-Performance in International Arbitration* (Kluwer Law International 2009) 86–87 and Ridder and Weller, 'Unforeseen Circumstances' 371, 373.

21 Since the debtor is obliged to verify if he/she is indeed capable of fulfilling the contract before signing it. Ilya Kokorin and Jeroen Van der Weide, 'Force Majeure and Unforeseen Change of Circumstances. The Case of Embargoes and Currency Fluctuations (Russian, German and French Approaches)' (2015) III Russian Law Journal 46, 62.

implicit term.[22] This solution is expressly included in the United Nations Convention on Contracts for the International Sale of Goods, signed in Vienna on 11 April 1980 (hereinafter, CISG) (Art 79) and the UNIDROIT Principles (Art 7.1.7). This does not mean that the contract is terminated or extinct, but simply prevents the creditor from exercising the following remedies:

(a) the action to perform the contract, as long as the impediment lasts; and,
(b) the action for damages, definitely, as regards the specific non-performance.

Force majeure, however, will play a less important role in these legal systems in which contractual liability is based upon fault. In this regard, an unpredictable and insuperable event beyond the control of the contracting party that prevents contractual performance will never allow the negligence of said party to be established. It is at this point that the concept of force majeure becomes less necessary to avoid unfair results.[23] Traditionally, the Latin and Germanic systems departed from the fault principle (although the objective tendency imposed by the CISG is not without an influence on them). Thus, §§276 and 280 BGB and Articles 1101 and 1104 of the

22 John Cartwright, *Contract Law* (Hart Publishing 2007) 237. International contracts contain, more frequently than national ones, force majeure clauses, which contemplate the consequences that situations such as war, epidemic, fire, strikes and other unforeseeable and unavoidable events would have on the contract. They provide that when non-performance is justified as a result of force majeure, there will be no liability of the debtor for the delay in performance, provided that he/she notifies the creditor presenting evidence of the facts. They also set forth the obligation of the debtor to adopt the necessary measures to limit the effects of the damage in the interest of the creditor. The best doctrine explains that these clauses are not really necessary, "since all legal systems provide for the same legal consequence (exemption from the obligation to indemnify for damages if the breach of contract is due to *force majeure*)", and even common law considers it an implicit clause (see Sixto Sánchez Lorenzo, *Cláusulas en los contratos internacionales. Redacción y análisis* (Atelier 2012) 405 ff, 411). The clauses also often specify that if the duration essentially deprives the parties (or one of them) of their legitimate expectations, they will have the right to terminate the contract by notifying the other party within a reasonable time. The benefits obtained during the previous phase of the contract deserve a compensation in form of the payment of the equivalent (that is, the bargain basis of the contract is rebalanced, with a view to its liquidation). Although the concept of force majeure is foreign to common law, it is often used in contractual clauses, and the doctrine of frustration or other technical means lead to results similar to those of civil law. See William Swadling, 'Force majeure and Frustration: Introduction and Relationship' in Ewan McKendrick (ed), *Force majeure and Frustration of Contract* (2nd edn, Routledge 1995) 5 and Günther H. Treitel, *Frustration and Force Majeure* (Sweet & Maxwell 1994) 3. Also Ole Lando, 'Non-performance (Breach) of Contracts' in Arthur Hartkamp and others (eds) *Towards a European Civil Code* (4th edn, Wolters Kluwer 2011) 695 ff.

23 See Ridder and Weller, 'Unforeseen Circumstances Hardship, Impossibility and Force Majeure under German Contract Law' 22 ERPL 373.

Spanish Civil Code,[24] require (as a general rule) the fault of the debtor for compensation to proceed. However, very soon for most scholars of both countries it became clear that this fault was to be presumed. Consequently, the debtor has to prove that the non-performance was not due to his/her negligence.[25]

(2) A second solution, more typical of Anglo-Saxon law, but which civil law systems received through the harmonisation of contract law,[26] is the consideration of the excessive onerousness arising from the contract for one of the parties (hardship), due to a change of circumstances beyond the control and will of the contracting parties.[27] This situation differs from force majeure in as much as there is an alteration of the bargain base, to the extent that it is very burdensome for one of the parties to perform; however, the unavoidable and insuperable event is at the origin of both situations.

There are three solutions normally associated with hardship: termination of contract, judicial modification of the contract, or the obligation of the parties to renegotiate it, again seeking a balance between the reciprocal obligations of the parties to perform. According to systematisation by Hondius and Grigoleit,[28] a distinction is made between open and closed legal systems. The first has developed (either by case law or in legislation) a general doctrine of hardship that applies exceptionally and provides for the adjustment of the contract in

---

[24] Royal Decree (*Real Decreto*) 24 July 1889 *por el que se publica el Código Civil* (Gaceta de Madrid no 206, 25.7.1889).

[25] Bruno Rodríguez-Rosado, 'Los sistemas de responsabilidad contractual: entre la responsabilidad por culpa y la strict liability' (2014) 4 Revista de Derecho civil 155, 165–166.

[26] In this regard, see the study by González Pacanowska, 'Alteración sobrevenida de circunstancias en los contratos sinalagmáticos: de la rebus sic stantibus a la alteración extraordinaria de circunstancias', *Estudios sobre incumplimiento y resolución* (Aranzadi Tomson Reuters 2015) 141–213. The author advocates, as an intermediate solution, the re-adaptation of the contract, in order to avoid its termination ("the all-or-nothing solution hardly satisfies", p 209) and provides criteria that contribute to this solution that may arise in the different situations.

[27] Cartwright, *Contract Law* (Hart Publishing 2007) 235 justifies the exemption of liability of the one who contracted based on circumstances that allowed foreseeing a certain balance of benefits, and which later suffered profound alteration for reasons beyond the control of contracting parties. The risks assumed by the contractor are those that were foreseeably based on the existing circumstances at the time of contracting. If the circumstances were different, other than what the parties thought, at the time of the contract, we would be facing a vitiating factor. If the circumstances change after the performance, there is no problem for the parties. But if the contract was concluded under determined circumstances, certain and correctly understood by the parties, and, unexpectedly, before performance, an essential alteration of these circumstances occurs, any of the parties may allege the imbalance of performances ("the changed circumstances affect the contractual balance") and invoke a remedy under the new circumstances, "such as a release from the contract, or an adjustment of the terms of the contract".

[28] Ewoud Hondius and Hans Christoph Grigoleit, 'Introduction: An approach to the issues and doctrines relating to unexpected circumstances' in Ewoud Hondius and Hans Christoph Grigoleit (eds), *Unexpected Circumstances in European Contract Law* (CUP 2011) 3 ff.

case of unexpected circumstances. Within this category fall Austria, Germany, Greece, Italy, Lithuania, the Netherlands, Portugal, Spain, Sweden, and after the 2016 Contract Law Reform also France and finally the Draft Common Frame of Reference (DCFR). This reform departs from the French legal tradition, allowing the judge to review the contract in cases of imbalance in accordance with Article 1195 and gives the victim of such an imbalance the right to request the renegotiation of the contract.[29] The jurisdictions in the second group either lack a general doctrine on hardship, or have established this doctrine (most countries), but this doctrine does not allow them to adjust the contract as a general rule. Amongst the countries included in this category, one may find Belgium, the Czech Republic, Denmark, England, Ireland, Scotland and Slovenia. Since internal systems do not normally provide for the renegotiation of the contract (this is rather typical of uniform law),[30] in order to safeguard this remedy, the contracting parties should rather introduce it as a contractual clause[31] (renegotiation is not expressly foreseen under the CISG, whereas exemption from liability is).[32]

---

29 More details on the *imprévision* doctrine can be found in Bénédicte Fauvarque-Cosson, 'Does Review on the Ground of *Imprévision* Breach the Principle of the Binding Force of Contracts' in *The Code Napoléon Rewritten: French Contract Law after the 2016 Reforms* (Hart Publishing 2017) 187–207.

30 Articles 6.2.1–6.2.3 (in particular, the latter), of the UNIDROIT Principles on International Commercial Contracts (2016).

31 See Sánchez Lorenzo, *Cláusulas en los contratos internacionales. Redacción y análisis* (Atelier 2012) 421–432, especially 424. The author explains that, in the drafting of hardship clauses, it is usually provided that "if any of the parties had obtained a benefit prior to the termination of the contract, due to any act of the other party carried out in performance of the contract, he must compensate the other part by paying a sum equivalent to the value of the benefit obtained". It is the responsibility of the party alleging the difficulty, to notify the other party, with proof of the facts, and to use all means to mitigate the damage where possible.

32 We can consider that, in terms of excessive onerousness, the Convention can be abided by, as regards the available remedies, by resort to international uniform law on commercial contracts (specifically, the UNIDROIT Principles), as has already been done by the case law. For example, the Belgian Court of Cassation ruled in this regard [Belgium 19 June 2009 Court of Cassation (Scafom International BV v Lorraine Tubes SAS), available at http://cisgw3.law.pace.edu/cases/090619b1.html accessed 1 July 2020]. The parties had concluded a contract for the sale of steel pipes. After the conclusion of the contract and before delivery, the steel price unexpectedly increased by approximately 70%. The seller tried to renegotiate a higher contract price, but the buyer flatly refused and insisted on delivering the products at the agreed price. The contract did not include any price adaptation clause. The decision of the court of first instance was reversed by the Antwerp Court of Appeal. That court decided that the CISG did not regulate the issue of excessive onerousness (*rebus sic stantibus* clause) and applied French national law by allowing the seller's counterclaim for an amount based on a higher price. However, the *Cour de Cassation* rejected the application of French internal law and declared that the change of circumstances that was not reasonably foreseeable at the time of the conclusion of the contract and that was of such a nature that it increased the burden of performance of the contract in an extraordinary and disproportionate manner, may constitute an impediment within the meaning of Article 79 of the treaty, even if performance

Most legal systems tend to associate hardship with force majeure, placing it within the concept of exoneration from or mitigation of liability caused by supervening events rather than as a case of invalidity of the contract due to its weaknesses or defects present *ab initio* of the agreement,[33] which is reasonable.

Common Law systems present some peculiarity within the models exposed, with their doctrine of irremediable frustration of contract as a consequence of an unpredictable and inevitable event.[34] John Cartwright explains that, for the doctrine to be applicable, certain requirements must be met (test for frustration).[35] The remedies applicable in this case are drastic: "the contract is automatically discharged and neither party is held to perform. There is no room

was not literally impossible. Nevertheless, the decision ends by integrating the provisions of Article 79 CISG with the UNIDROIT Principles, considering that this norm is insufficient to regulate the consequences of excessive onerousness, and declaring that the party affected by the changed circumstances is entitled to a renegotiation of the contract. The CISG Advisory Council Opinion No. 20 Hardship has nevertheless rejected this gap-filling function of UNIDROIT Principles and together with it, the availability under the CISG of such remedies as the renegotiation, adjustment and termination of the contract.

Among the voices in favour of admitting excessive onerousness in the scope of Article 79 CISG, we may distinguish that of the Director of the UN International Law Branch who presided over the works on drafting and adopting the CISG (John O. Honnold, *Uniform Law for International Sales under the 1980 United Nations convention* (3rd edn, Kluwer 1999) 543–544); in the same sense, Ugo Draetta, 'Force Majeure clauses in international trade practice' (1996) 5 Int'l Bus LJ 547, 555; and Peter Schlechtriem, *Uniform Sales Law. Convention on contracts for the international sale of goods* (Manz 1986) 102. The latter, although in the final version of the Convention the proposal of the Norwegian delegations and of the old FRG regarding excessive onerousness was not included in Article 79 (John O. Honnold, *Documentary history of the uniform law for international sales: the studies, deliberations, and decisions that led to the 1980 United Nations Convention with introductions and explanations* (Kluwer 1989) 350). Among the judicial decisions that have applied the rule in this regard, together with the aforementioned one, we may mention, for example, *Schiedsgericht der Handelskammer* Hamburg of 21 March and 21 June 1996, available at http://cisgw3.law.pace.edu/cases/960321g1.html accessed 1 July 2020, which compared the exemption standard established in Article 79 with the causes that give rise to exemption in accordance with national legal doctrines of force majeure, economic impossibility and excessive onerousness; and the ruling of the Polish Supreme Court on a drastic rise in coke fuel prices, where the case was returned to the Court of Appeal on the basis that said court had not taken into account the possible application to the facts of the case of the doctrine of excessive onerousness encompassed within Article. 79 CISG. The Polish Supreme Court declared that under the "impediment" of Article 79 we must also understand the economic impossibility of fulfilling the obligation, and it emphasise that this impossibility is related to the predictability of the damage referred to in Article 74.2 CISG. Poland 8 February 2012 Supreme Court, available at http://cisgw3.law.pace.edu/cases/120208p1.html accessed 1 July 2020. On the contrary, the judgment of the *Tribunale Civile di Monza* of January 14, 1993 affirmed that Article 79 was of a different nature than the *hardship* or Italian doctrine of *eccessiva onerosità sopravvenuta*, http://cisgw3.law.pace.edu/cases/930114i3.html accessed 1 July 2020.

33 Com. 36 in Garro, 'CISG-AC Opinion No 7, Exemption of Liability for Damages under Article 79 of the CISG' Columbia University School of Law. Adopted by the CISG-AC at its 11th meeting in Wuhan (2007) 1.

34 As shown by Rodrigo Momberg Uribe, *The effect of a change of circumstances on the binding force of contracts* (Intersentia 2011).

35 See Cartwright, *Contract Law* (Hart Publishing 2007) 241.

for judicial variation of the contract".[36] Unlike *civil law* systems, the termination "is not retroactive", "those obligations which have already accrued due are left undisturbed".[37] The snapshots of this assumption are the well-known coronation cases, in which the rental of balconies in London to contemplate the parade after the coronation ceremony of Edward VII in 1902 was rendered meaningless due to an unpredictable and unavoidable event that prevented the parade from taking place.[38] Finally, it is necessary to consider the concrete cases to determine the scope of application of the doctrine, including within it the events that in other civil law countries could be classified under the concept of force majeure or impracticability. Thus, frustration applies: to cases of supervening destruction of the object of the contract; to the performance that, while assumed by the parties to be possible, due to a supervening event became impossible; to the impracticability in the sense given to it by German doctrine combined with the temporary impossibility or looming illegality (but not impracticability in general); when the object of the contract or the debtor become unavailable (e.g. by requisition, conscription, detention in war, etc.).[39]

1.2. ELI PRINCIPLE NO 13: STRUCTURE AND CONTENTS

Principle no 13 is entitled "*Force majeure*[40] and Hardship", and is divided into three paragraphs, listed in a very logical and rational manner:

(1) The first refers to force majeure (Principle no 13.1). It starts from the assumption that force majeure or impossibility is already regulated by States' legal frameworks and – without alluding to the applicable remedy on an explicit basis – that these regulations should apply in an effective way. In doing so, it introduces the criterion of "reasonable solutions", which will be examined below, and which refers to the guidelines of "contractual allocation of risk".

---

36 See Van Boom, 'Impossibility Impracticability and Unforeseen Circumstances' (2020) SSRN Electronic Journal 1, 7.

37 See Cartwright, *Contract Law* (Hart Publishing 2007) 241.

38 Despite having estimated a first claim for rent payment, in a second case brought before the courts, the latter adopted an intermediate solution, according to which neither the amount advanced as a reservation should be returned, nor the amount not yet paid in price concept could be required. The courts maintained this doctrine for 40 years. After this period, the English case law took a turn and admitted that the termination of the contract, with the reciprocal restitution of benefits, is an adequate solution for cases of frustration of the contractual end due to a supervening alteration of the circumstances, with the right to claim the restitution of the benefit made. See Manuel García Caracuel, *La alteración sobrevenida de las circunstancias contractuales* (Dykinson 2014) 71–73.

39 See Van Boom, 'Impossibility Impracticability and Unforeseen Circumstances' (2020) SSRN Electronic Journal 1, 7.

40 Our italics.

(2) The second paragraph focuses on the cases of hardship (Principle no 13.2). In these cases, the Principles' text refers directly to the applicable remedy, namely the renegotiation of the contract, irrespective of whether it is expressly provided for in domestic legislation or in the contract, or even if it is not provided for at all in any of them.

(3) The last paragraph refers to cases where a "disruption of contractual relationships" take place (Principle no 13.3). In these cases, the principle of solidarity is introduced as a guideline for action, to avoid that one of the parties in the contract must assume all the risks generated by the force majeure.

1.3. THE PRINCIPLE OF GOOD FAITH AS THE AXIS OF THE PROPOSAL

Contractual good faith seems to be the key to the solutions provided to the three scenarios regulated in the Principles: force majeure (Principle no 13.1), hardship (Principle no 13.2) and disruption of the contractual relationship (Principle no 3.3). In the first two cases, good faith is mentioned on an explicit basis, while in the last one the principle of solidarity – which may be derived from the principle of good faith– is referred to, which is why the latter principle may be deemed to be contained implicitly in this third rule as well.

Contractual good faith operates thus, in the cases in which an unavoidable and insuperable event occurs as a hindrance within the stage where the contract should be performed, as a limit to the principle of the binding force of contracts (or *pacta sunt servanda).* In these circumstances, it can be said that good faith acts as a limit to the normal application of the remedies provided for breach of contract.[41] However, the role of good faith does not end there: good faith acts as an ordering criterion of the consequences for the parties of the event amounting to force majeure or hardship. And it does so by providing solutions adapted to the three situations that may arise:

First of all, and as a general rule for all cases, good faith entails the non-performing debtor's exemption from liability, insofar as there is no causal link between his/her conduct – action or omission – and the harmful result connected to the violation of the creditor's right. It would be contrary to good faith to request that the debtor assume the risk of such circumstance, i.e. the

41 As suggested by Beatriz Fernández Gregoraci, *Comparative Corona Law* webinar, 22 May 2020, (organised by Professors Karin Sein and Hugh Beale) contractual good faith is a limit for the recourse to certain remedies when the appropriate circumstances are not met (she specifically refers to the termination of the contract).

pandemic, which hinders the contract performance and that is as alien to the debtor as much as to the creditor (force majeure). The performance claim remains unaffected, but the creditor must wait for normality to return to exercise it. The debtor must collaborate by mitigating the damage (that is, by performing the contract as soon as possible).

Secondly, and taking a further step, good faith prevents the situation that, if the performance becomes excessively burdensome for one of the contracting parties, the creditor's claim for performance can be kept intact. Under such circumstances, good faith imposes on the parties a duty to renegotiate the terms of the contract, since as a consequence of the unforeseeable and insuperable event an alteration of the circumstances that were taken into account at the time of contracting and that therefore constituted the basis of the contract has taken place.

Lastly, and in the event that the contract becomes void of content or no it longer makes sense to one or both contractors to keep the contract with its binding effects, good faith imposes the sharing of the risk between them (solidarity principle) as a solution. Again, it would be contrary to the good faith to impose only on one of the contracting party the risk-taking of an event that is as foreign to him/her as to the other contracting party.

2. FORCE MAJEURE (PRINCIPLE NO 13.1)

Principle no 13.1 provides as follows:

> Where performance of a contract is temporarily or definitively prevented directly or indirectly due to the COVID-19 outbreak or States' decisions taken in relation to the COVID-19 outbreak, States should ensure that existing law on impossibility or force majeure applies in an effective way, and provides reasonable solutions. In particular, the contractual allocation of risk in these instances should be evaluated in the light of existing contracts, background legal regimes and the principle of good faith.

As its literal wording provides, the Principle's first paragraph refers to force majeure and, with good reason, rests on the assumption that in most countries force majeure is provided for as a defence. Principle no 13.1 thus limits itself to asking States to guarantee the correct application of the rules and that the solutions provided are reasonable. The criteria to be taken into account for the allocation of the risk posed by an unforeseeable and unavoidable event (COVID-19) that affects the execution of the contract are the following:

(1) the contractual content;
(2) the rules of the legal system applicable to the specific case; and,
(3) good faith.

The Principle is thus interesting for the following reasons:

(1) To start with, it is noteworthy that the ELI Principles assume that the pandemic amounts to a force majeure. This is actually far from obvious, even though some address the issue to the contrary – as is the case of insurers in Spain.[42] Under Spanish law, for instance, the general rule is that the debtor is not held liable for those events which were unforeseeable or being foreseeable, were unavoidable (Art 1105 CC). Therefore, in those jurisdictions which deal jointly with fortuitous event and force majeure, as is the case under Spanish law, the distinction between both becomes mostly irrelevant,[43] even if there is some scholarly debate about that.[44] As a leading legal scholar put it, force majeure and *casus* are equivalent from an Spanish perspective, in that they set a limit to the debtor's liability, which is that breach occurs as a result of an event falling outside of the debtor's sphere of control.[45] The Principle's starting point is different, since there is no mention of *unforeseeable* events and the emphasis is put on *impossibility* or force majeure. This makes the discussion on whether a pandemic was foreseeable or not redundant.

(2) As has just been noted, force majeure or impossibility seem to be used as synonymous or equivalent expressions by the Principle under comment. Therefore, emphasis seems to be put on the fact that the pandemic could not be avoided and as a result of it the contract performance ceases to depend on the will of the parties. At any rate, the term force majeure is used, in contrast to some proposals in Spain that tend to replace it with the synonym "impediment" (*impedimento*).[46] Along with the temporary

---

42 A report written by a law firm on the request of the insurer sector concludes that the COVID-19 outbreak does not actually amount to force majeure. See Carlos Berbell, 'La pandemia de coronavirus no ha sido imprevisible y no cumple el requisito de fuerza mayor' (*Confilegal*, 26 May 2020) https://confilegal.com/20200526-la-pandemia-de-coronavirus-no-ha-sido-imprevisible-y-no-cumple-el-requisito-de-fuerza-mayor accessed 1 July 2020.

43 Among others, see José Luis Lacruz et al., *Elementos de Derecho civil*, II-1, *Derecho de obligaciones* (Dykinson 2011) 175.

44 See summarily Eugenio Llamas Pombo, 'Artículo 1105' in Andrés Domínguez Luelmo (ed), *Comentarios al Código Civil* (Lex Nova 2010) 1216; Jacinto Gil Rodríguez, 'Responsabilidad por incumplimiento' in Lluís Puig Ferrio et al., *Manual de Derecho* civil, vol 2 (3rd edn, Marcial Pons 2000) 307–308.

45 See Luis Díez Picazo, *Fundamentos del Derecho Civil Patrimonial. Introducción,* vol 1. *Teoría del Contrato* (6th edn, Civitas 2007) 727 and 733. According to the same, with regard to natural phenomena and events one should focus on the debtor's ability to foresee them, having the statistical recurrence or frequency of the same into account. Also see Ferran Badosa Coll, *Dret d'obligacions* (Barcanova 1990) 383–384.

46 See Article 1209 of the official Proposal drafted by Comisión General de Codificación, *Propuesta de Modernización del Código Civil en materia de Obligaciones y Contratos* (BOE 2009) www.mjusticia.gob.es/cs/Satellite/1292338957019 accessed 1 July 2020. Similarly, Arts 518–24 of Asociación de profesores de Derecho civil, *Propuesta de Código Civil* (Tecnos 2018)

or definitive nature of the impediment which lies at the very core of the impossibility idea, and which is directly or indirectly caused by COVID-19, it may be interpreted that the rule includes, even in an implicit manner, that force majeure will be applied irrespective of whether the breach is of a total or partial nature. This seems to be in line with what is provided by Spanish law, where liability exemption because of force majeure could be possible even if the impossibility affected performance merely in part. At any rate, the Principle under comment assumes that some force majeure rule exists ("existing law"), which is not always true. Common law, for instance, developed only the doctrine of frustration of contract, although the results may be equivalent in practice.[47]

(3) It is also worth mentioning that for the Principle under comment it is enough for the rules on force majeure to operate in this context that the contract performance is prevented in either a direct or an indirect way (Principle no 13.1). Therefore, it is not required that one of the parties is affected on an individual level and in an immediate way, but the impossibility may result from the general situation which derives from the pandemic. In adopting such a broad scope, the Principle refuses to adopt a restrictive definition of force majeure under which only those consequences strictly linked to the virus outbreak as such fall within the force majeure concept. Moreover, the Principle does not require that the impossibility be attributable to the virus outbreak or the States' decisions in an exclusive way. Therefore, it may be interpreted that force majeure may be deemed to exist even if the contractual party affected by it behaved in a negligent way and thus the breach was partly attributable to the latter. It may be assumed that in such a setting the exemption of liability may be partial only. This is in line with Spanish law, where force majeure may operate as a total or partial defence.

(4) Principle no 13.1 is a call addressed to States to ensure that the rules on force majeure lead to reasonable results in the present context of the pandemic. It is thus assumed that there is an "existing law", whatever its contents are, which provides some solution to the force majeure setting. In most jurisdictions, such a rule does indeed provide for the exemption of the debtor's liability for the specific breach derived from the impediment or impossibility at stake (as in the case of Art 1105 Spanish CC). In the current setting, the impediment is caused by the COVID-19 itself or by the sanitary and security measures adopted by the States on this occasion.

---

www.derechocivil.net/images/libros/obra_completa.pdf accessed 1 July 2020. The latter is an official proposal drafted by a private organization as is the Society of private law professors.

47 See Swadling, 'Force majeure and Frustration: Introduction and Relationship' in Ewan McKendrick (ed), *Force majeure and Frustration of Contract* (2nd edn, Routledge 1995) 5 and Treitel, *Frustration and Force Majeure* (Sweet & Maxwell 1994) 3. Also see Lando, 'Non-performance (Breach) of Contracts' in Arthur Hartkamp and others (eds), *Towards a European Civil Code* (4th edn, Wolters Kluwer 2011) 695 ff.

Such a solution is the one generally adopted and is in accordance with the criterion of good faith. It may be suggested that requesting performance in the pandemic's scenario may even amount to an abuse of right, which is against the good faith. Again, this is the approach adopted by Spanish law (Art 7.2 CC).

(5) As has been partly said above, Principle no 13.1 is not addressed to the parties in a contract or even to a judicial authority but to the State as such. The Principle is understood as an admonition to the State itself, which should ensure that its "existing law" on force majeure operates in a proper or admissible manner in the pandemic's scenario. It goes without saying that the COVID-19 outbreak is indeed a force majeure instance and that force majeure rules should provide a solution to it. The possibility that a given legal system does not simply provide for such a rule or either categorises the current pandemic as a different event or concept, other than force majeure, is not provided for by Principle no 13.1. However, a functional approach would suggest that such Principle is also applicable to those other rules or principles which in a given jurisdiction fulfil the same role as force majeure does where it exists.

At any rate, the addressee of Principle no 13.1 seems to be primarily the legislature (in civil law systems) or the judge (in common law systems), which should review the existing law on force majeure to assess whether it leads to reasonable results. As is well known, several jurisdictions have passed emergency measures by means of which specific solutions have been provided, in particular as regards those contracts which were still pending performance.[48] The classical institute of force majeure provided for in some civil codes, such as the Spanish one (Art 1105), may thus be displaced on an exceptional basis by public law measures adopted by the Government during the pandemic's crisis. Seen from this angle, Principle no 13.1 may appear as a call to the legislature to reform existing rules or to supplement or complete them through new ones related to the COVID-19 outbreak.

(6) Principle no 13.1 does, however, provide for the possibility that the contract already included some clauses or articles on force majeure, in which case the contract should be "evaluated". Notably, the Principle does not state who should evaluate the contract at stake, although in most jurisdictions it may be assumed that such a task will fall on the judges' shoulders. The standard against which the evaluation should be done is threefold: (i) the "existing contracts";

[48] See Carlos Gómez Ligüerre, 'Fuerza mayor' (2020) 2 *InDret* https://indret.com/fuerza-mayor accessed 1 July 2020.

(ii) background legal regimes; and (iii) the good faith principle. It is not entirely clear how a contract may be evaluated against other "existing contracts", what these contracts are, or how the judge should get access to the contracts which the parties had concluded in previous occasions. It may be suggested that having previous contracts entered into by the same parties may not be entirely useful, since they may have been signed before the COVID-19 outbreak and thus irrelevant. If, in the absence of a contractual clause, domestic law contains a rule other than the debtor's exemption, but the solution can still be deemed reasonable, the latter should be applied, provided that it is in accordance with good faith. At any rate, the Principle under comment partly departs from the law of some jurisdictions, such as Spain. Under the Spanish Civil Code, the contracting parties may establish that one of them may bear the risk of force majeure. However, no other rule entitles the judge to review the contract on the basis of other "existing contracts". Even though good faith operates as a principle governing contract law (Art 1258 CC), the judge may take the very contract in which such a clause is included as a whole, to see how the risks and benefits are allocated between the parties.

(7) It may be observed that Principle no 13.1 does not provide a substantive rule on force majeure, in the sense that the Principle does not provide *what* should be the consequences of force majeure as such, but merely *how* they ought to be, namely, that they ought to be reasonable. Since force majeure operates at the stage of the execution or performance of the contract and not at the one of the contract formation, it may be assumed that force majeure does not affect the existence of the contract as such. In that regard, the Principle provides for the possibility that the contract itself allocates the risk in some way. Therefore, one may assume that the contract is preserved, which is in accordance with the principles of *pacta sunt servanda* or the sanctity of contracts. Typically, force majeure operates at a different level, namely, by affecting the debtor's liability. This is also in line with Spanish law, according to which the contract binds the parties (Arts 1088 and 1255 CC) but force majeure exempts the debtor from liability for breach (Art 1105 CC). The creditor retains the claim for performance, which may be subsequently exercised when normality is recovered. Among the remedies for non-performance, the creditor may under these circumstances exercise his/her right to suspend his/her own performance or *exceptio non adimpleti contractus* – in the unlikely event that the debtor requests it.

(8) Although the Principle under comment does not explicitly so provide, it may be considered that debtor and creditor should collaborate to mitigate the damage, so that performance takes place as soon as possible. This is in line with the principle of good faith, which is mentioned by the Principle.

3. HARDSHIP (PRINCIPLE NO 13.2)

Principle no 13.2 provides that:

> Where, as a consequence of the COVID-19 crisis and the measures taken during the pandemic, performance has become excessively difficult (hardship principle), including where the cost of performance has risen significantly, States should ensure that, in accordance with the principle of good faith, parties enter into renegotiations even if this has not been provided for in a contract or in existing legislation.

Pursuant to its literal wording, Principle 13 paragraph 2 refers to the hardship or excessive burden which is laid on the debtor's shoulders as a result of a drastic alteration of the circumstances which formed the basis on which the contract was agreed upon, or as a consequence of the measures adopted by the public authorities on the occasion of the COVID-19 outbreak.

Rightfully, the ELI starts on the grounds that the domestic jurisdictions generally fail to provide a statutory solution to the hardship which takes place. Accordingly, the rule lays down that, in good faith, the solution consists in the renegotiation of the contract by the parties themselves. And this, regardless of whether such possibility was not provided for:

(a) either in the contract itself;
(b) or in the legal system which is applicable to the particular contractual relationship at stake.

The Principle is remarkable for several reasons:

(1) The renegotiation of the contract seems to be considered a duty or obligation derived from the principle of good faith, which is therefore imposed on the parties. The Principle under comment tells States that they should ensure that parties go into that renegotiation. Therefore, if one of the parties fails to perform, it will be possible for the other to go to court – i.e. a State authority or organ – to request the same to adapt the contract accordingly. This is in contrast with those legal systems which lack a general provision on hardship. For instance, under Italian law (Codice civile, Art 1467) it is statutorily provided that extraordinary and unforeseeable events may lead to contract termination, but this is not the only way out, inasmuch as conservation of the contract may also be possible.[49]

[49] See Enrico Gabrielli, *El contrato. Incumplimiento y tutelas* (Lex 2020) 53–101. According to the same, if the unforeseeable and extraordinary nature of an event after the conclusion of the contract determines the excessive onerousness of the service assumed by one of the

(2) The adaptation of the contract to the new circumstances should be governed by the search for a new balance of the contractual obligations. If the circumstances that formed the basis on which one party was contracted have changed, the new basis of the contract should be in accordance with the new circumstances. Otherwise the result would be contrary to good faith and could constitute an abuse of right by the other contracting party. In principle, it may be assumed that renegotiation should be aimed at removing the excessive difficulty which hinders performance. A mere appearance of negotiation in which parties do not really go into detail or lack the will to find a new balance within the contract would be against the principle of good faith.

(3) In any case, the solution of Principle no 13.2 (renegotiation), is compatible with the application of the rule on force majeure to which reference is made in the preceding paragraph (Principle no 13.1), that is, the exoneration of liability of the debtor for non-performance (in accordance with the legal regime provided for in most jurisdictions). It may be assumed that such liability may be excluded in the course of the renegotiation.

(4) Principle no 13.2 must also be read in connection with the rule to be found in the following paragraph (Principle no 13.3), so that, when the parties fail to reach an agreement on the adaptation of the contract to the new circumstances, the termination of the contract can take place, if:
    (a) the Judge admits the discharge of the contract as a solution to the conflict, on the request of one of them; or,
    (b) both contracting parties, without the need to retort to the judge, agree to terminate the contract.

4. DISRUPTION OF CONTRACTUAL RELATIONSHIPS: SOLIDARITY (PRINCIPLE NO 13.3)

Principle no 13.3 provides that:

> In conformity with the principle of solidarity, States should ensure that the consequences of the disruption of contractual relationships, such as the cancellation of travel arrangements, should not be at the sole risk of one party, in particular of a consumer or SME.

---

contracting parties, it is possible to terminate the contract and render it without effect, provided that the risk was not assumed by that contracting party (and it is also not the usual rule that such a party does so) and whenever it is not possible to avoid the termination of the contract by offering new conditions that balance the contractual obligations again fairly. For a Spanish law perspective, see Lete, 'Le changement ...' 238, with further references.

According to its literal wording, this third and last paragraph refers to those cases in which, according to the principle of solidarity (derived from good faith or fairness), the extinction of the contractual relationship is imposed as a solution. Unlike the previous paragraphs of Principle no 13, the third one provides an example, namely, the cancellation of trips, which is very well chosen and on which legal scholarship has obviously expressed its concerns given the seriousness of the issue. There is no doubt about the opportunity to deal in this rule with contractual relationships with consumers and SMEs. Principle no 13.3 refers to them on an explicit basis to avoid being forced to assume the risk of damages generated in relation to the contract by COVID-19.

There are several aspects of the Principle under comment that can be emphasised:

(1) The change in the language in Principle no. 13.3 in contrast to the previous paragraphs of the same Principle is noteworthy. The paragraph under comment does not use the expressions force majeure, "impossibility" (cf. Principle no 13.1), "hardship", or "excessive difficulty" (Principle no 13.2) but speaks of a "disruption of contractual relationships". It may be understood that the latter is a broad category which may embrace both force majeure and hardship. An alternative interpretation of the Principle is the one according to which should hardship occur, the parties have the duty to renegotiate (pursuant to Principle no 13.2), and if renegotiation fails, then there is a "disruption" of the contractual relationship. According to the principle under comment, then, what should be avoided is that the disruption results in one sole party bearing the whole risk. If this is so, it may be understood that revision by a judge in the case of disruption is subsidiary, should renegotiation fail. The Principle is not entirely clear to that regard.

(2) The question thus may arise as to what is the relationship between this third paragraph and the previous two. One possible interpretation consists of understanding that the solution provided in Principle 13.3 for cases of force majeure and hardship is subsidiary to the ones contained in the two previous paragraphs. According to that, paragraph 3 should be applied as an alternative to the adaptation of the contract when it has become void of content or the contractual purpose has been frustrated, either by the judge's ruling, or by mutual agreement of the parties. However, it may also be understood as a limit to what the judge or the parties can do. Even where the judge steps in or the parties renegotiate, the result should not consist of laying all the consequences of the contractual disruption on one party alone. Since the Principle expressly mentions consumers, it may be submitted that the same result would probably be achieved in most jurisdictions through the application of consumer law provisions. Making the consumer bear an excessive burden would be against the desirable contractual balance, at

least from a Spanish law perspective – at least if the result derives from a contract clause which was not negotiated by the parties.[50]

(3) Principle no 13.3 does not explicitly provide how the disruption of the contractual relationship should take place in particular. "Disruption" is a broad and neutral term as to include termination or extinction of the contract, but also modification of the contact by a judge. The ELI Principles do not adopt any criteria as to whether termination should take place through the notification to the other party or not.[51] Neither provide whether modification has any priority. Under Spanish law, for instance, there is much debate as to whether the court should modify the contract or merely terminate it.[52] It may be assumed that under the conditions created by the pandemic, the termination of the contract will require the agreement of the contracting parties or a judicial decision to that regard, since termination is not due to the breach of the contract by one of the contracting parties, but to the frustration of the end of the contract.

(4) In case of termination of contract based on Principle no 13.3, the parties must put an end to the contractual relationship in such a way that, if one of them had received a benefit as a result of the contract, the balance of the contractual obligations between the two contracting parties should be guaranteed, through the subsequent distribution of the benefits (either in kind or through an equivalent) if necessary to achieve this purpose. This rule implicitly includes a possible restitution or distribution, if needed, of what was received in exchange for the thing which was the object of the contract, when the debtor could not deliver it but received some compensation in lieu instead.[53]

5. CONCLUSIONS

Principle no 13 on "force majeure and hardship" deals jointly with two legal institutions, which may seriously affect contracts. The Principle as such does

---

50 Article 80.1.c) and 82 of the Royal Legislative Decree (*Real Decreto Legislativo*) 1/2007, of 16 November, *por el que se aprueba el texto refundido de la Ley General para la Defensa de los Consumidores y Usuarios y otras leyes complementarias* (Spanish Official Gazette, Boletín Oficial del Estado [BOE] no 287, 30.11.2007).

51 Following the CISG model of resolution for non-performance by notification to the other party, some civil law systems that traditionally required the judicial discharge of the contract have evolved in that direction (recently, the French Civil Code as a result of the 2016 reform).

52 See Isabel Espín Alba, *Cláusula rebus sic stantibus* (Reus 2020) 140.

53 Once again, it is a matter of avoiding that only one of the parties bears the heavy burden of the contract risks, but also of ensuring that none of them takes advantage of the situation. That could result in an enrichment, which it would be contrary to the good faith to keep to oneself.

not provide a full or complete regulation on how these situations should have an impact on the contract, if at all. Therefore, the Principle does not say anything as to whether a party may terminate the contract or whether it should be kept as it was. Instead, Principle no 13 is focused on preventing some situations or results, which are deemed to be unfair or undesirable, from occurring. This is why the principle of good faith is mentioned in the first two paragraphs, and the principle of solidarity, in the third one.

Whereas good faith may be deemed one of those common ideas which are universally accepted, this is not necessarily so with the idea of solidarity. Due to its brevity, the Principle does not explain to what regard solidarity is different from good faith. It may be deduced that renegotiation which becomes desirable as a result of the COVID-19 outbreak should take place in good faith; thus the parties should truly strive at finding a solution in common (Principle no 13.2). And if there is force majeure, the consequence attached to it by the legal system should be assessed by the States against the background of good faith (Principle no 13.1). This may be read as a call to the legislatures to review their positive rules on force majeure – or impossibility – or to judges to review the way in which the institution is applied. However, when the negative results from the contract being disrupted have to be allocated between the parties, the issue is one of solidarity (Principle no 13.3). Solidarity calls for a fair distribution of the risk between both parties, thus preventing that one of them takes advantage of the situation.

Seen from this perspective, Principle no 13 sets some minimum standards to be observed by the States in the aftermath of the COVID-19 outbreak. No new law is automatically needed, but in the face of a huge crisis like the present one, the existing legal regimes should be reviewed to avoid unfair results.

The key to this provision rests on the fact that the principle of contractual good faith is the axis of the solutions sought for situations that, in stages, may arise, and which may be enumerated as follows (even if the list is not comprehensive):

(1) Maintenance of the contract;
(2) Adaptation ("renegotiation") of the contract; and
(3) Termination ("disruption") of the contract.

Rightly, the Principle seems to assume that, while force majeure is provided for as a legal institution in most jurisdictions (it is "existing law", as the provision reads), the same does not happen with the regard to the adaptation of the contract due to hardship (no reference to "existing law" is thus made). At any rate, disruption of the contract, should it occur, should be in line with solidarity and not be too cumbersome for one of the parties.

Notably, then, the Principle fails to provide what the particular legal effect or consequence of force majeure should be. This may be the reason why a scholarly opinion seems to suggest that the Principle under comment does not bring anything new, at least as regards hardship.[54] However, even if as regards force majeure this is left open to the "existing law" of States, a minimum is set: that the solution should not violate good faith. By contrast, in the case of hardship the Principle does indeed provide a legal effect, which is that a duty to renegotiate applies. It could be argued that the ELI Principles may have missed the opportunity to state that force majeure merely exempt the debtor from liability. However, the ELI may have been reluctant to interfere with the law of particular jurisdictions at that level of precision.

Apart from that, the Principles do not provide how the renegotiation of contract should take place, apart from the fact that it should be "in accordance with the principle of good faith" (Principle no 13.2). In particular, it fails to provide what happens if one of the parties refuses to renegotiate or adopts a merely passive stance, or even worse, if it boycotts any renegotiation attempts.

Finally, it may be submitted that the way in which Principle no 13 uses terminology may create some doubt. Interestingly enough, the Principle rests on the idea of contractual solidarity, which is alien to many jurisdictions. However, the relationship to the principle of good faith unfortunately remains in the dark. Therefore, even if the ELI makes clear that in no way should one party be forced to bear the whole risk of "disruption", Principle no 13 fails to provide specific guidelines with which to allocate such a risk in a "solidary" manner between the parties.

54 See Ángel Carrasco Perera, 'Al fin la madre de todas las batallas del COVID 19: *rebus sic stantibus*. Con ocasión de una reciente propuesta institucional' (CESCO Publicaciones Jurídicas 2020) 2 http://centrodeestudiosdeconsumo.com/images/Al_fin_la_madre_de_todas_las_batallas_del_covid_19-_rebus_sic_stantibus.pdf accessed 1 July 2020.

CORONAVIRUS' IMPACT ON BROADCASTING RIGHTS FOR THE SPANISH PROFESSIONAL FOOTBALL LEAGUE

Antoni Rubí-Puig*

The spread of SARS-CoV-2 and the measures adopted by public authorities to prevent health risks posed by COVID-19 led organisers of sport events worldwide to cancel all ongoing competitions. The Spanish Professional Football League or

* Universitat Pompeu Fabra. This contribution results from the research project "Coronavirus i dret privat" (2020PANDE00092), funded by the Catalan Agency for University and Research Grants (AGAUR).

"LaLiga" was suspended for almost three months, and pending matches for the 2019–2020 season resumed with a new and tight calendar. Such unexpected changes in the championship undoubtedly diminished the value of LaLiga broadcasting rights and generated losses to their national and international holders. This contribution discusses the application of Spanish contract law to identify any possible claims that broadcasters could have to seek some relief. On close inspection, it is unlikely that broadcasters could enjoy any remedies to claim damages, to terminate their payment obligations or to adjust their contracts with LaLiga's organiser. However, due to the particularities of the football broadcasting market, voluntary renegotiation of contracts is expected to occur.

1. A LONG FOOTBALL BLACKOUT

The coronavirus has profoundly affected professional and amateur sports.[1] As authorities around the world began to react to prevent the spread of COVID-19, sports went into an almost complete blackout. Competitions that were still in progress were abruptly interrupted and their organisers were left unsure whether and under what conditions they could be resumed. At the time of writing some, such as the Tokyo 2020 Olympics, have been postponed to 2021, whereas others have been cancelled. In many countries, all sports facilities and venues were forced to temporarily close. Professional athletes in several jurisdictions could only train from their homes, and some of them decided to withdraw from tournaments. As all major sport competitions and events were suspended, no live sports were available on TV or on the internet for months.

Many of this blackout's economic and legal repercussions are yet to emerge. The impossibility to hold the competitions or other sports events as initially planned has had a tremendous impact on the long- term agreements in force, the economic investments their parties made, and other contractual networks involved in one of the most lucrative markets in the entertainment industry: sport broadcasting rights.

In this contribution, I focus on Spanish professional football and more specifically on the broadcasting rights for the Spanish Professional Football League or "LaLiga". This league competition is the most important one in Spain and it also has many followers worldwide. The main football governing body in Spain is the *Real Federación Española de Fútbol* (RFEF), which is responsible for organising the "Copa del Rey" and "Supercopa de España" competitions and for

[1] This chapter was completed on 20 September 2020. Any developments in sport competitions that have taken place after this date – in particular, the Spanish Professional Football League 2020-2021 season – have not been considered.

managing the Spanish national football team. The *Liga de Fútbol Professional* (LFP or LaLiga), which forms part of RFEF and comprises 42 football clubs, is responsible for organising state football leagues, among others, the first division of the Spanish football league. Just behind the English Premier League and the German Bundesliga, LaLiga is one of the most popular professional sports leagues in the world.

As of the date of writing, LaLiga has been suspended for almost three months. During this period, broadcasting rights agreements in place have presumably remained valid and enforceable and all their obligations binding for their parties. The governmental measures and the general situation have nevertheless prevented LFP from performing its main obligations under those agreements: arranging and developing the fixtures. As broadcasters had been unable to exploit the entitlements they bid for, they had already suffered some economic losses, mainly a reduction in the number for subscribers of premium-TV services and of advertisers and sponsors. Their obligations to pay LaLiga have not necessarily been affected: a right to recoup a part of the payments they made or a right to avoid some instalments is not necessarily granted by Spanish Contract Law under current circumstances. As cancelled fixtures have already been rescheduled, the broadcasters' main interest when agreements were concluded is safeguarded. However, the commercial value of their entitlements may have eroded: concentration of fixtures in a shorter period of time and change of timetables would probably attract fewer audiences and fewer advertisers.

2. CANCELLATION OF MAJOR FOOTBALL EVENTS IN SPAIN: A CHRONOLOGY

Organisers of the major football competitions in Spain had already adopted some measures to face the risks posed by the COVID-19 pandemic before the Spanish Government's main reaction. On 11 March 2020, RFEF issued Circular no 62, by which all non-professional football and futsal competitions at the national level were suspended for a two-week period.[2] The day after, LaLiga followed track and suspended all competitions for the same period and grounded its decision on Royal Decree 664/1997 on the protection of workers against risks related to exposure to biological agents in the workplace.[3]

2 https://www.rfef.es/normativas-sanciones/circulares/circular-62-20192020 accessed 12 June 2020.

3 LaLiga had already informed all teams on 9 March that the scheduled fixtures for the following two weeks had to be played behind closed doors pursuant to instructions by the *Consejo Superior de Deportes*.

On 14 March 2020, the Spanish Government declared the state of alarm for the management of the health crisis caused by COVID-19.[4] Based on Article 116.2 of the Spanish Constitution and the Organic Act 4/1981, the Government passed Royal Decree 463/2020, which, *inter alia*, ordered the closing of all football stadiums and other sports premises and establishments.[5] As the Royal Decree was not sufficiently clear as to whether teams of players could train, the *Consejo Superior de Deportes* intervened and informed some clubs that they had to refrain from calling their players into training.

On 23 March RFEF and LaLiga officially announced the suspension of all professional football championships until the Spanish Government considered that competitions could be resumed without any health risks for players, referees or any other concerned individuals.[6]

On 28 April the Spanish Government presented the *Plan para la transición a una nueva normalidad*, a de-escalation plan to progressively end all mobility restrictions and other limitations ordered because of the pandemic.[7] The plan is structured in four different phases and has been applied in an asymmetric way as to territories and industries or fields of activity depending on various health and technical indicators. In regions that transitioned to Phase 1, professional leagues were allowed to resume training. A health protocol was officially passed on 30 April.[8] After some individual training onsite, team training in groups of 10 players were approved, and during the second half of May, most professional football players in the first divisions were called by clubs to restart team training.

On 23 May, the President of the Spanish Government announced that professional competitions and namely LaLiga could resume from 8 June 2020 onwards. LaLiga subsequently informed that pending fixtures for the 2019–2020 season would resume on 11 June. The announcement established a new calendar in which all pending matches were rescheduled. Because of the proximity of

---

4 Royal Decree 463/2020, declaring the state of alarm for the management of the health crisis posed by COVID-19 (*Real Decreto 463/2020, de 14 de marzo, por el que se declara el estado de alarma para la gestión de la situación de crisis sanitaria ocasionada por el COVID-19* (BOE no 67, 14.3.2020)). The state of the alarm established under this norm has been subsequently extended for additional two-week periods by other Royal Decrees (RD 476/2020 of 27 March; RD 487/2020 of 10 April; RD 492/2020, of 24 April; RD 514/2020, of 8 May; RD 537/2020 of 22 May and RD 555/2020 of 5 June).

5 Article 10.3 and Annex.

6 https://www.rfef.es/noticias/acuerdo-comision-seguimiento-del-convenio-coordinacion-rfef-laliga accessed 12 June 2020.

7 https://www.mscbs.gob.es/profesionales/saludPublica/ccayes/alertasActual/nCov/planDesescalada.htm accessed 12 June 2020.

8 *Orden SND/388/2020, de 3 de mayo, por la que se establecen las condiciones para la apertura al público de determinados comercios y servicios, y la apertura de archivos, así como para la práctica del deporte profesional y federado.*

summer with very high temperatures in most of Spain, the number of fixtures per week increased and new hours planned. Coordination with some international competitions such as the Champions League were also considered in devising the new calendar. Furthermore, the beginning of the new 2020–2021 season was adjourned and is expected to take place one month later than usual.

3. BROADCASTING RIGHTS IN SPANISH LAW

The main regulation governing broadcasting rights in Spanish professional football is Royal Law-Decree 5/2015 (RLD 5/2015).[9] Although insufficient in several aspects, this regulation contributed to many doubts that had been raised for decades about the legal nature of broadcasting rights, their ownership allocation or their marketability options.

3.1. LEGAL NATURE

Prior to RLD 5/2015, sports broadcasting rights were not specifically regulated and were only indirectly mentioned in Spanish Law.[10] However, broadcasting rights had already been conceived as subjective rights with an economic dimension which entitled their holders to broadcast, rebroadcast or otherwise exploit the audiovisual footage of football matches.[11] Courts assumed the legal status of these exclusive rights in cases in which RFEF and LFP were claiming that clubs had a right to exclude journalists from the stadiums. Although such claims were dismissed as freedom of information was ruled to prevail, courts qualified broadcasting rights as economic exclusive entitlements when balancing them with professional journalists' fundamental rights.[12]

---

9 Royal Law-Decree 5/2015, of 30 April, on urgent measures in relation to the marketing of the rights to exploit audiovisual content of professional football competitions (*Real Decreto-ley 5/2015, de 30 de abril, de medidas urgentes en relación con la comercialización de los derechos de explotación de contenidos audiovisuales de las competiciones de fútbol profesional* (BOE no 104, 1.5.2015)).

10 Act 21/1997, of 3 July, on Broadcastings and Rebroadcastings of Sports Competitions and Events (*Ley 21/1997, de 3 de julio, reguladora de las Emisiones y Retransmisiones de Competiciones y Acontecimientos Deportivos* (BOE no 159, 4.7.1997)) (repealed by General Act 7/2010, of 31 March, on Audiovisual Communication (*Ley 7/2010, de 31 de marzo, General de la Comunicación Audiovisual*)).

11 See José Massaguer, 'Naturaleza, protección y titularidad de los derechos audiovisuales sobre acontecimientos deportivos' (1997) ADI 18, 287–289.

12 See Court of Appeals of Madrid, Judgment of 30 March 1996 (Roj: SAP M 12/1996). The legal disputes between media outlets and sports organisers have been recurrent in Spain.

3.2. PROTECTION

Sports events as such, and particularly football matches, are not protected under Spanish copyright law.[13] Football matches are not considered authorial works and neither are professional players considered to be authors who contribute to a collective work. This exclusion does not, however, prevent protectability of other elements under copyright law. In this regard, the Court of Justice of the European Union (CJEU) has ruled that the audiovisual production, recording and broadcasting footage of sporting events, as well as some particular elements such as anthems, may be protected by copyright or some related rights.[14]

As sports events which are the necessary subject matter of broadcasting rights are not protectable as such under intellectual property law, organisers have to resort to the general protection tools for subjective rights, including unfair competition actions, and indirectly through rights of entrance and admission into the football stadiums ("house right").[15]

3.3. OWNERSHIP

Article 2.1 of RLD 5/2015 now makes clear that initial ownership of broadcasting rights in professional football belongs to the clubs or entities participating in the competition at stake.

Before RLD 5/2015 was passed, even though it was generally assumed that broadcasting rights for a sports event could be initially vested upon its organiser,

---

13 See Supreme Court, 1st Chamber, Judgment no 439/2013 of 25 June 2013 (Roj: STS 3872/2013).

14 See joined cases C-403/08 and C-429/08 *FAPL v QC Leisure* and *Karen Murphy* [2011] ECR I-09083. Some EU Member States, such as France and Italy, have established some special neighbouring rights for sports event organisers in their national sports laws. See in this regard Asser Institute, *Study on sports organisers' rights in the European Union* (Publication Office of the European Union 2014).

15 Rights of entrance are grounded on the right of property or other possessory rights. The arena right or house right has been particularly discussed in German scholarship. See Götz Schulze, 'Das private Hausrecht. Schutzrecht für die Gebrauchsnutzung von Räumen' (2015) JZ 8, 381–391. In Spain, a right of admission is expressly regulated under Article 59.1 e) of *Real Decreto 2816/1982, de 27 de agosto, por el que se aprueba el Reglamento General de Policía de Espectáculos Públicos y Actividades recreativas*, which prohibits the public from "entrar en el recinto o local sin cumplir los requisitos a los que la Empresa tuviese condicionado el derecho de admisión, a través de su publicidad o mediante carteles, bien visibles, colocados en los lugares de acceso, haciendo constar claramente tales requisitos".
The house right is not absolute and has to be balanced with the fundamental right of the public to receive information. This general limit, which has generated several disputes and controversial legal intervention, is now regulated in Article 19 of General Act 7/2010, of March 31, on Audiovisual Communication, which besides rights of entrance, regulates the availability of short news reporting. See also case C-283/11, *Sky Österreich* [2013] ECR I-nyr.

deciding who the organiser should be was not straightforward in the case of professional football.[16] First, by definition, two different teams participate in a match; and second, the match would be played within a competition or league organised by another person. Leagues and cups might be institutionally arranged or organised in distinct ways.[17] Furthermore, all potential rightsholders operate within a complex network of contracts in which other stakeholders, such as players, stadium owners, broadcasters or television rights agencies would participate. In other terms, broadcasting rights may belong to the organiser of the competition or to the organisers of particular matches and, in the latter case, rights may be allocated to both teams, or to just one of them.

When deciding on ownership, courts generally understood that broadcasting rights for competitions belonged to clubs, with the exception of some particular events such as a cup final.[18] The Spanish Competition Authority has suggested that because of the reciprocity of matches, broadcasting rights should be owned by the host club and not shared with the visitor team.[19]

3.4. COLLECTIVE MANAGEMENT

Article 2 of RLD 5/2015 establishes that participation in an official professional football competition will necessarily entail the transfer of the powers to commercialise broadcasting rights held by the participating clubs to the organising entity.[20] So it is LaLiga which jointly manages and markets the

---

16 See for a general discussion of this problem in association football and other sports, Jesús Alfaro, 'Derechos de propiedad en la retransmisión televisada del fútbol' in Juan Carlos Sáenz, Fernando Oleo and Aurora Martínez (eds), *Estudios de derecho mercantil: En memoria del Profesor Aníbal Sánchez Andrés* (Thomson-Civitas 2010) 139–169.

17 See Patricia Galán, 'Derechos de explotación audiovisual de las competiciones del fútbol profesional en España (II): Titularidad', http://www.sennferrero.com/es/opinion/436-derechos-de-explotacion-audiovisual-de-las-competiciones-del-futbol-profesional-en-espana-ii-titularidad accessed 12 June 2020.

18 See Audiencia Nacional, Judgment of 1 March 2013 (Roj: SAN 843/2013): "Currently, the original holders of the audiovisual rights for La Liga and Copa del Rey are the football clubs themselves, with one exception: the audiovisual rights to the Copa del Rey's final, which belong to the Royal Spanish Football Federation (RFEF)".

19 See Comisión Nacional de la Competencia, *Informe sobre la competencia en los mercados de adquisición y explotación de derechos audiovisuales de fútbol en España*, 2008, 32–34 https://www.cnmc.es/sites/default/files/1185836_7.pdf accessed 12 June 2020. This solution was clearly influenced by the 1997 German Supreme Court Judgment in the *Europapokalheimspiele* case (BGH Urt. v. 11.12.1997 – NJW 1998, 756).

20 Also individual football players would have transferred or otherwise licensed to their clubs all image rights that are necessary for the general exploitation of broadcasting rights. See in this regard Organic Act 1/1982 on the civil protection of the rights to honour, individual and family privacy and own image; and Article 7.3 of Royal Decree 1006/1985, which regulates the special employment relationship of professional athletes.

broadcasting rights for the Spanish Professional Football League (LaLiga and "Segunda División").[21]

LaLiga periodically organises public tenders, in which different rights packages are independently offered. Packages are devised according to different limitations, such as temporal or geographical ones. Also, exclusivity is generally granted for the exploitation of broadcasting rights. Packages are usually contracted for a period of three seasons.[22]

Before making the tender public, LaLiga has to request a report on the established conditions from the Spanish Competition Authority (CNMC).

Packages may include bundles of rights which entitle the bidder to exploit matches through live broadcasting, webcasting or streaming or delayed broadcasting. Also, packages will include other content, such as highlights or clips of matches. Pursuant to Article 4 of RLD 5/2015, tenders must specify the date and time of each of the fixtures which are included in a package and their conditions.

Broadcasting rights are allocated by means of a public, transparent, competitive and non-discriminatory procedure, which should be based on objective criteria, including, *inter alia*, the economic viability of bidders' offers, the interest of the competition in the market at stake, and the bidder's expected contribution to the growth and future value of broadcasting rights.

Pursuant to RLD 5/2015, the same bidder may not be directly or indirectly granted exclusive broadcasting rights in two or more packages aimed at the same national market. Exceptionally, a bidder may be granted more than one package for the same market, if no other bidders have presented any offers for the packages at stake.

Rents obtained by LFP are then distributed among all clubs participating in the competition at stake. Distribution is made according to different factors established under Article 5 of RLD 5/2015, most notably the final position each team has had in the league in previous years. In 2019, LaLiga distributed EUR 1,578 million among the different clubs in the first and second division of the Spanish professional football league.[23] FC Barcelona and Real Madrid were

---

21 LaLiga may directly market broadcasting rights or may appoint an entity to carry out any tasks dealing with the promotion and commercialisation of the competition's audiovisual rights. In this regard, concerning the international tender of broadcasting rights for the seasons 2021–2022, 2022–2023 and 2023–2024, LaLiga has appointed Mediaproducción, S.L.U. This company will thus be unable to participate as an interested audiovisual operator and to submit any bids for the offered packages. See the text of the tender at https://assets.laliga.com/assets/2020/02/20/originals/da392bb8f58de537e3d72c51df17c774.pdf accessed 12 June 2020.

22 Following the criteria established by the Competition Authority and the Supreme Court, agreements to exploit broadcasting rights for a period longer than three years were deemed to be anti-competitive *per se*. RLD 5/2015 established this maximum term as mandatory. However, this maximum term has now been eliminated from RLD 5/2015. See below section 3.6.

23 See https://www.laliga.com/transparencia/gestion-economica/derechos-audiovisuales accessed 12 June 2020.

the clubs that received more rents. The first clubs in the rank receive an average of 3.5 times the amount that the last club in the division earns from broadcasting rights. Before RLD 5/2015 was passed, earnings from broadcasting rights grossly diverged among clubs: the first team in LaLiga could receive ten times more rents from broadcasting rights than the last ranked one.

Clubs have an obligation to allocate some of the received amounts to different types of funds.[24] The purposes of these funds are diverse and include, among others, promotion of the Spanish Professional Football Leagues in the Spanish and international markets, stimulation of amateur football and local federations, contributions to social security benefits for professional players or compensations to teams that are relegated to lower leagues.

3.5. COMPETITION LAW

One of the major issues with collective management of broadcasting rights is the risk of engaging in anti-competitive practices against Articles 101 and 102 TFEU and Spanish Competition Law. RLD 5/2015 requires tenders to be examined by the Spanish Competition Authority with the aim of guaranteeing market competition, transparency and non-discrimination.[25]

In an array of reports, CNMC has examined LaLiga's broadcasting rights tenders and analysed potential anti-competitive effects.[26] CNMC has suggested, *inter alia*, that the tenders go beyond the scope of rights that LFP may jointly commercialise based on RLD 5/2015 and that they include rights that should be marketed by the clubs themselves. It has also advised that reserving some advertising and sponsorships rights runs afoul of being anti-competitive and that the content of different packages and awarding criteria are not sufficiently transparent.

3.6. AMENDMENTS TO RLD 5/2015 DURING THE PANDEMIC

RLD 5/2015 was amended on 21 April 2020.[27] One of the most significant changes concerns the suppression of the three-year maximum term for broadcasting

24 See Article 6 of RLD 5/2015.

25 Sports have generally enjoyed an idiosyncratic autonomy but they are not excluded from EU Law and namely from competition law. The CJEU has made clear in various landmark cases that EU Law will cover sports in different areas. See case 36/74, *B.N.O. Walrave* [1974] ECR -01405; Case C-415/93, *URBSF v Bosman* [1995] ECR I-4921; and Case C-519/04 P, *Meca-Medina v Commission* [2006] ECR I-6991. See generally Stephen Weatherill, *Principles and Practices in EU Sports Law* (OUP 2017) 288 and ff.

26 See CNMC, Reports of 4 September 2017 (INF/CNMC/174/17); 18 April 2018 (INF/DC/055/18); 18 April 2019 (INF/DC/085/19) and 6 February 2020 (INF/DC/03/20).

27 DF 5ª of *Real Decreto-ley 15/2020, de 21 de abril, de medidas urgentes complementarias para apoyar la economía y el empleo* (BOE no 112 of 22.4.2020) ("RLD 15/2020").

rights agreements.[28] LFP's President has already announced the intention to offer packages for a five-year term in future tenders.[29]

Some mandatory contributions of clubs have been modified. A new fund has been established for the international promotion of Spanish sports. For this purpose, a new foundation has been created: *"Fundación España Deporte Global"*.[30]

4. THE NEW NORMAL? SOLUTIONS UNDER SPANISH CONTRACT LAW

4.1. PROBLEM AT STAKE

At of time of writing, all professional football championships in Spain have been suspended for three months. During this time, the companies that were granted the rights to broadcast LaLiga have been unable to use and exploit these entitlements in their respective territories. Depending on audiences' preferences in each territory, it is likely that, as a consequence, broadcasters have already lost subscribers, as well as advertising and sponsoring revenues.

On 11 June 2020, the First Division of the Spanish Professional Football League resumed the pending matches for the 2019–2020 season. Although the risk of a definite cancellation of some matches cannot be disregarded, the current scenario, at the time of writing, may be described in terms of a delay in performance rather than a total or partial non-performance. In any case, even if some of the fixtures were definitively cancelled, as broadcasting agreements are usually concluded for a three-year term, most of LaLiga's obligations in connection thereto would have been already performed, or its performance during next seasons would still be in the interest of broadcasters.

A delayed performance of matches may, however, be the source of other types of losses. As more fixtures will be held per week at different time slots, audiences' attention and interest are likely to decline. The fact that matches would be played behind closed doors and with no spectators allowed into the stadiums is a further matter of concern which is said to reduce viewers' appeal for the live broadcasts. A reduction in the number of viewers will affect the willingness to pay advertisers and sponsors to have their brands connected to the matches.

In light of the erosion of value that broadcasting rights packages have experienced, a question arises as regards the allocation of such losses: should the

---

28 Article 4.4.f) RLD 5/2015.

29 https://www.expansion.com/directivos/deporte-negocio/2020/04/24/5ea31696e5fdeaba198b4574.html accessed 12 June 2020.

30 Article 6.1.f) RLD 5/2015.

broadcasters assume all financial losses, or should they have some mechanism to shift them in whole or in part to the LFP?

4.2. ALLOCATION OF RISKS BY THE PARTIES

Spanish Contract Law does not actually provide straightforward solutions to all disputes that may arise because of the temporal impossibility of holding matches and broadcasting them to fans around the world. Most of the rules on contracts are set forth in the Spanish Civil Code 1889 (SCC), which contains an outdated fragmentary legal regime to deal with breach of contract cases. Due to the insufficient guidance that this array of provisions supplies, the Supreme Court's case law has to be considered as well.

The starting point to deal with the allocation of losses or risks in broadcasting agreements is the text of each contract. Broadcasting agreements may include provisions that would allocate risks posed by the occurrence of a pandemic or, more generally, a force majeure provision. Although they are not frequent in Spanish contractual usage, parties may have also established MAC (material adverse change) or MAE (material adverse effect) provisions in their agreements. With grounds on private autonomy or freedom of contract, parties may thus have regulated specific solutions to deal with the economic consequences of cancellations or adjournments of matches, such as, for instance, setting some penalties for the LFP or granting broadcasters a right to a price reduction.

As the final broadcasting agreements between LFP and broadcasters are confidential, the texts of the initial tenders for broadcasting rights issued by LFP may be examined with the aim of identifying intended possible solutions. In this regard, for instance, section 5.10. of the tender for LaLiga broadcasting rights in the Spanish territory establishes that "LaLiga shall not be held liable towards the Candidates or the Successful Bidders for any loss, damage or harm (including indirect damage and loss of profit) in relation to the content of [this tender] or the content of the future broadcasting agreement to be concluded with the Successful Bidder."[31] Force majeure is referred only as an event that would unilaterally prevent broadcasters from exploiting their rights.[32]

---

31 LaLiga, *Bases para la solicitud de ofertas para la comercialización de los derechos de explotación de contenidos audiovisuales del Campeonato Nacional de Liga de Primera y Segunda División para las temporadas 2019/2020 a 2021/2022* https://files.laliga.es/201805/28172653laliga---bases-solicitud-de-ofertas-espana.pdf accessed 12 June 2020. The international tender of broadcasting rights for the seasons 2021–2022, 2022–2023 and 2023–2024 contains similar provisions.

32 See *Bases para la solicitud de ofertas para la comercialización de los derechos de explotación de contenidos audiovisuales del Campeonato Nacional de Liga de Primera y Segunda División para las temporadas 2019/2020 a 2021/2022* https://files.laliga.es/201805/28172653laliga---bases-solicitud-de-ofertas-espana.pdf accessed 12 June 2020, section 5.3. Also one such force majeure event would enable LFP to terminate their contracts with broadcasters (section 4.3.7).

As it is likely that parties in the broadcasting agreements did not attach particular effects to the COVID-19 pandemic, general solutions under Spanish Contract Law may be discussed.

4.3. DELAYED PERFORMANCE AS BREACH OF CONTRACT

Delays in performance may be deemed a breach of contract, since performance by one of the parties does not strictly conform to the promises made to the other party. For this reason, LaLiga may fear some actions by the bidders for a potential breach of contract. However, in spite of a non-conforming performance, broadcasters do not necessarily have a right to claim any compensation, release or adjustment of their agreements.

Spanish Contract Law contains a traditional legal regime for delay in performing an obligation which is grounded on the notion of *mora* (Art 1100 SCC). Unless otherwise established by the parties, legal effects of delay will require a notice of default dispatched by the creditor to the debtor. If the time of performance was not legally relevant and the delay does not render performance out of interest for the creditor, the debtor will still be able to perform its obligations under the contract and will have to compensate any damages caused by the delay (Arts 1101 and 1108 SCC). Debtors will be able to exonerate themselves from liability for damages if the delay was caused by events outside of their sphere of control, namely in cases of force majeure (Art 1105 SCC). Because LFP can still perform its main obligations under the broadcasting agreement and the schedule of specific matches was not essential, LFP would not be deemed in breach of the contracts pursuant to this traditional regime.

However, aside from pecuniary obligations, this traditional regime has been mostly castoff by courts and scholars. In the last decades, the Supreme Court's case law has advanced a more modern approach, in line with international contract law developments, which shifts the focus from non-performance of unilateral obligations to breach of bilateral contracts. Breach of contract is thus conceived as any departure from the agreement, which is not necessarily limited to its wording but also to other duties that may be customary or be based on good faith.[33] From this standpoint, any non-conformity may qualify as a breach of contract. However, this would not necessarily entail the aggrieved party to use all remedies in place. Some of them, such as a claim for damages, would generally require a finding of negligence or of intentional breach. Other remedies, such as termination, would be available only for fundamental breaches.

---

33 See Fernando Gómez, 'El incumplimiento contractual en Derecho español' (2007) InDret 3; and Antonio Manuel Morales, 'La noción unitaria de incumplimiento en la propuesta de modernización del Código Civil' in Isabel González and Carmen Leonor García (eds), *Estudios sobre incumplimiento y resolución* (Thomson-Aranzadi 2014) 23–46.

5. REMEDIES AND DEFENCES UNDER SPANISH CONTRACT LAW

5.1. GENERAL REMEDIES FOR BREACH OF CONTRACT

Specific performance, damages and termination are the three main remedies for breach of contract under Spanish Law.[34] A brief discussion of their main elements reveals their inadequacy to address the coronavirus' impact on broadcasting right agreements. Given the prospects of considering the pandemic and the adopted government measures an external unforeseeable event, and given the difficulties of qualifying the breach as fundamental, this general toolset of contractual remedies would hardly be of utility to broadcasters.

Specific performance does not appear as a helpful remedy in the current circumstances. As it is unfeasible to arrange the matches pursuant to the initially agreed calendar, specific performance becomes impossible. Rescheduling the matches involves an alternative performance, which would not satisfy creditors' initial expectations under the contracts. When specific performance is unworkable, the aggrieved party may claim damages amounting to the value of performance ("*reparación por equivalente*").

Damages may be used as the sole remedy or may be coupled with other remedies such as specific performance and termination. Generally, damages would require a finding of negligence or of intentional breach. An aggrieved party would be entitled to expectation damages, that is, the amount that would put him/her in the utility situation he/she would have, had the contract been performed as agreed (Art 1106 SCC). As a general rule, the award of damages covers only those losses that were foreseen or foreseeable at the time of concluding the contract (Art 1107 SCC); that is, causation may become a relevant question. For this reason, doubts may arise as to which particular broadcasters' losses are causally linked to changes in the championship calendar. Damages for moral prejudice caused by a breach of contract can also be awarded. Parties may agree to provisions excluding or limiting the compensation of damages. Damages would not be available when the breach that is said to cause the losses stems from an external event beyond the party's sphere of control.

Whereas the reduction of price is not established as a general remedy for breach of contract, it may be conceived as equivalent to damages from a practical perspective. In this vein, the reduction of the price may be regarded as the diminishment of value in the entitlement that was granted to an aggrieved party. Once again, damages will not be available if harm was caused by a force majeure event.

---

34 For a comprehensive study of remedies for breach of contract in Spanish Law, see Ángel Carrasco, *Derecho de Contratos* (2nd edn, Thomson-Aranzadi 2018) ch 21–24.

Termination of contract is restricted to fundamental breaches (Art 1124 SCC). Considering that broadcasting agreements are concluded for a three-year period, a change of calendar during a fraction of the term would hardly qualify as a fundamental breach. Payment obligations by broadcasters are not specifically linked to individual matches, and therefore reciprocity can only be assessed in relation to the contract as a whole. Besides, claims for termination would not be available when the breach at stake is excusable, for instance, when it was originated by an external event beyond the party's sphere of control.

5.2. IMPRACTICABILITY AND FORCE MAJEURE

As has been advanced, the application of particular remedies depends on specific requirements and is also modulated by external causes. If the event that produced the breach was beyond the parties' control, and the contract did not specifically allocate the consequences of its occurrence, general provisions in the Civil Code may apply.

The main force majeure provision in the Spanish Civil Code is Article 1105, which establishes that "[a]side from the cases expressly mentioned in the law or when an obligation so establishes, no one will be responsible for those events that could not have been foreseen or, if foreseen, were inevitable." This provision must be put in connection with Article 1184 SCC, which excuses performance in cases of legal or physical impossibility.[35] As the preamble of RLD 15/2020 has advised, this legal regime is outdated and unfit to address the social and economic repercussions of the COVID-19 pandemic.[36]

In any case, if a particular event which was unforeseeable, or a particular legal restriction renders performance of a contract impossible, the debtor may be exonerated from liability towards the creditor. Besides, the debtor may be released from performing its obligations under the contract.

If performance by the other party is still feasible – which would be the general case for pecuniary obligations – he/she would not be able to avoid payment or to seek reimbursement of any amounts that were already paid. In other terms, risk of the event that renders performance impracticable is in general wholly allocated to the payer.

---

35 Article 1184 SCC: "The debtor will also be released if the obligations to make when performance becomes legally or physically impossible". See also Article 1183 SCC which sets forth that: "The obligation to deliver a certain thing will be extinguished if the thing is lost or destroyed, provided that the debtor was not negligent or late in performing".

36 See *Real Decreto-ley 15/2020 de medidas urgentes complementarias para apoyar la economía y el empleo*: "Asimismo, si se acude a la regulación del Código Civil referida a la fuerza mayor, tampoco ofrece una solución idónea porque no ajusta la distribución del riesgo entre las partes, aunque puede justificar la resolución contractual en los casos más graves".

Application of this legal regime to broadcasting rights agreements reveals that even in cases in which matches were cancelled, broadcasters would not have a right to avoid paying the different instalments they agreed to or to recoup any already paid instalments. Whereas LFP would initially have a right to release itself from its duties to arrange the fixtures that were to be broadcasted during the lockdown and avoid financial liabilities for breach, broadcasters cannot resort to force majeure to seek relief.

In this regard, two distinct events should be analysed: the pandemic itself and the governmental restrictions established under the alarm decrees. Although some measures were initially adopted by LFP and RFEF, the restrictions that have made the initially scheduled calendar of matches impracticable have been ordered by public authorities in various regulations. Such restrictions would easily meet the requirements of legal impossibility under Article 1184 SCC and would enable LFP to be released from its obligations. These restrictions have not made payment obligations by broadcasters impracticable though.

As for the pandemic, courts or other adjudicators would have to analyse particular circumstances that may make the effects of SARS-CoV-2 and COVID-19 unpredictable and unavoidable. In the past, some Spanish courts have qualified Influenza A virus subtype H1N1 as sufficiently unforeseeable and thus as a force majeure event that would release breaching parties from liability.[37] Therefore, the COVID-19 pandemic is likely to be categorised as force majeure that would excuse LFP from performance and liability, but not as an event that would affect payment obligations by broadcasters.

Notwithstanding the previous considerations, reliance on force majeure requires that the impediment at stake could not reasonably be expected to be accounted for at the time of concluding the contract. As has been mentioned, it is likely that the parties considered possible cancellations or adjournments of matches and allocated all risks of such events to the broadcasters exclusively.

5.3. WITHHOLDING PERFORMANCE DURING SUSPENSION OF EVENTS

The cancellation of matches in other competitions, such as the French league, prompted some pay-TV broadcasters to announce that they were suspending their due instalments. Similar announcements have not occurred regarding LaLiga rights.

Spanish contract law does not provide a general right to withhold performance or a general regime for anticipatory breach.[38] Some defences may

37 See Court of Appeals of Madrid, Judgment of 10 December 2013 (Roj: SAP M 21843/2013).

38 Withholding performance is established as a remedy for some contracts such as sales. See Article 1502 SCC.

be available to justify withholding performance as reactions to allegations of breach of contract: a party may justify the suspension of performance if he/she shows that his/her counterparty was in breach (*non adimpleti contractus* and *non rite adimpleti contractus* defences).

In any case, withholding performance would demand the counterparty's breach to be fundamental. As already discussed, because broadcasters' payment obligations are not linked to specific matches, fundamentality of breach would hardly concur to justify any withholding of performance.

5.4. HARDSHIP AND *REBUS SIC STANTIBUS*

LaLiga's temporal suspension and the subsequent rescheduling of matches are likely to result in a diminishment of the value of performance that broadcasting rightsholders receive. As has been described, the rearrangement of fixtures, with more than one round per week, may lead to saturation and loss of appeal for viewers and advertisers. Whereas some viewers may have cancelled their subscriptions, others might be reluctant to sign up or to pay a fee to watch a particular match. A reduction in viewers will cause a decrease in the demand of advertising and other promotional practices.

The diminishment of the value of performance that a party receives due to an unexpected change of circumstances may qualify as hardship if some conditions are met.[39] The Spanish Civil Code does not contain a specific regulation on hardship and its contours have been defined by the Supreme Court under the doctrine of *rebus sic stantibus*.[40] In an array of cases decided during the last decade and motivated by the Great Recession, the Supreme Court has established under which conditions a party may resort to this doctrine to terminate a contract or to adjust its own obligations.

Before describing the required conditions to apply the doctrine, some caveats are necessary. First, the Supreme Court's case law has, to some extent, been pendulant and has not always provided sufficient guidance. Second, the application of the doctrine is highly exceptional and, despite some highly criticised judgments, the majority of decisions have rejected applying the doctrine to the facts at dispute.[41] Third, most of the cases have dealt with real estate contracts.

---

39 See Article 6.2.2. UNIDROIT Principles of International Commercial Contracts.

40 This is in sharp contrast with other close jurisdictions which have rules dealing with unexpected changes in the cost or value of performance. See Article 1467 of the Italian Codice Civile, Article 1195 of the French Code Civil or §313 of the German Bürgerliches Gesetzbuch. See also Articles 6.1.1–6.2.3 of the UNIDROIT Principles, Article 6:111 of the Principles of European Contract Law, Article III.-1:110 Draft Common Frame of Reference; or Article 89 CESL.

41 See Supreme Court Judgments no 591/2014 of 15 October 2014 (Roj: 5090/2014) and no 333/2014, of 30 June 2014 (Roj: 2823/2014).

The Supreme Court has traditionally identified four different requirements: (1) an extraordinary change of circumstances after the agreement was concluded; which (2) was unforeseeable; (3) alters the agreement's basis in a way that destroys the balance of rights and obligations between the parties; and (4) produces an excessive disproportion between the parties' obligations.[42]

The most recent Supreme Court judgment dealing with *rebus sic stantibus* may shed some light into its potential implications for broadcasting agreements.[43] In the Judgment of 6 March 2020, the Court had to examine, *inter alia*, whether a media company that was responsible for commercialising advertising and sponsoring slots in the Galician public TV and radio systems could rely on the doctrine to excuse some obligations that it had agreed to. In particular, the party alleged that because of an unexpected audience decrease, it could not meet the minimum annual threshold of revenues it had guaranteed under the contract.

The Supreme Court identifies three factors that rule out applying the doctrine to the case. First, *rebus sic stantibus* would mostly be applicable to long-term contracts, a condition that is not met in the case at stake, where parties had agreed to a two-year term and an automatic one-year extension, during which the alleged imbalance occurred. Second, the economic impact should be substantial. The Court considers a decrease in advertising investment from EUR 25.9 million in 2007 to EUR 24.1 million in 2008 not to be drastic. And third, the doctrine would not apply to events that fall within the normal risks of the contract – such as in the case, variations in advertising investment – and that the parties may have expressly or implicitly allocated. When examined in connection with broadcasting agreements, these factors are likely to preclude applying the doctrine.

5.5. RENEGOTIATION OF CONTRACTS

A key aspect of broadcasting rights agreements is the limited pool of potential parties to them. On the one hand, it is evident that LFP or any other competition organiser holds a monopoly position in all contracts concerning the championship at stake. On the other hand, the number of potential bidders in each geographical market who might be interested in exploiting broadcasting rights would be small and include just a few media companies. Besides, some of these companies would operate globally and bid for broadcasting rights in different territories.

---

42 See Pablo Salvador, 'Alteración de circunstancias en el art. 1213 de la Propuesta de Modernización del Código Civil en materia de Obligaciones y Contratos' (2009) InDret 4.

43 Supreme Court, Judgment no 156/2020 of 6 March 2020 (Roj: STS 791/2020).

This market structure has two immediate consequences: first, contracts will in many cases be concluded by repeated players, a condition which reduces opportunism; and second, reputational effects can be rapidly observed and spread across different players.[44]

Due to these conditions, LFP might have sufficient incentives to renegotiate their contracts on a voluntary basis with the aim of sharing the negative consequences of the league's suspension.[45] LFP may particularly have a strategic incentive in renegotiating broadcasting agreements because of the expected effects that this may have in the value of future tenders.[46] Refusals to reallocate some risks are likely to decrease future bidders' willingness to pay.

Spanish contract law sets forth an obligation to renegotiate in good faith (Art 7 SCC). Duties to disclose relevant information and to mitigate harmful consequences are in place. Also, as regards to broadcasting rights, the dominant position of LFP should be considered to prevent anti-competitive behaviour.

Finally, broadcasting rights agreements are embedded into a broader contractual network, in which an array of different bilateral contracts can be found.[47] Because of interdependence, renegotiation of one type of contract may lead to renegotiation in other network edges. For instance, one of the most affected vertices, clubs, may also expect a decrease of revenues if broadcasters might finally avoid their payment obligations or reduce their amounts. Any intended renegotiation of contracts in the most relevant node or vertex should consider how parties are likely to pass on readjustments of losses and risks to other stakeholders in the network.

6. CONCLUSIONS

The suspension of LaLiga championship for three months and the rescheduling of matches have undoubtedly diminished the value of broadcasting rights and generated losses to their holders. An examination of Spanish contract law rules on performance reveals that broadcasters would hardly have any option to claim damages, to be released from payment obligations or to readjust their agreements with LFP.

---

44 Louis Kaplow and Steven Shavell, 'Economic Analysis of Law', in Alan Auerbach and Martin Feldstein (eds), *Handbook of Public Economics* (Elsevier 2002) 1707.

45 The law and economics literature on renegotiation is vast. For a brief summary of expected readjustments see Robert E. Scott, 'The Law and Economics of Incomplete Contracts' (2006) Annu. Rev. Law. Soc. Sci 2.

46 The institutional setting in which broadcasting rights agreements are concluded and performed, which combines informal and formal mechanisms to induce cooperation, may be conceived as a form of relational contract.

47 See Fabrizio Cafaggi (ed), *Contractual Networks, Inter-Firm Cooperation and Economic Growth* (Edward Elgar 2011).

However, voluntary renegotiation of broadcasting agreements is likely to happen in the shadow of formal legal enforcement with the aim of shifting some of the losses to the LFP, clubs and other interested stakeholders. A market structure with a limited group of parties who engage in some form of repeated interaction may provide sufficient incentives to LFP to move away from the allocation of risks established both under the contract and the default provisions in the SCC.

PRESCRIPTION AND LAPSE OF RIGHTS UNDER THE SPANISH STATE OF EMERGENCY

Antoni VAQUER*

This contribution discusses the regulation contained in the Royal Decree establishing the state of emergency in Spain on suspension of the running of the periods of prescription in a private law system that does not have a general rule on suspension. Since the Spanish legislator has suspended the running of the periods for all citizens and claims as long as the emergency state has been in force, it is questionable whether this solution is efficient in terms of protection of people who, because of illness caused by COVID, are unable to pursue a claim once the emergency state has come to an end. Moreover, the Spanish Civil Code still distinguishes usucapio inter presentes *and* usucapio inter absentes, *the latter requiring a longer period, but the Royal Decree does not contain any rule on acquisitive prescription.*

* University of Lleida.

1. THE LEGAL FRAMEWORK

The Royal Decree 463/2020, of 14 March,[1] that declared the state of emergency in Spain because of the pandemic caused by COVID-19, contains three (additional) dispositions concerning prescription and lapse of rights.

The first (Second Additional Disposition) deals with procedural periods and establishes (in Spanish) in its first paragraph that "se suspenden términos y se suspenden e interrumpen los plazos previstos en las leyes procesales para todos los órdenes jurisdiccionales. El cómputo de los plazos se reanudará en el momento en que pierda vigencia el presente real decreto o, en su caso, las prórrogas del mismo" (dates are suspended, and periods established in procedural laws are suspended and interrupted, own translation).

The second (Third Additional Disposition) tackles administrative periods and lays down along the same lines that "se suspenden términos y se interrumpen los plazos para la tramitación de los procedimientos de las entidades del sector público. El cómputo de los plazos se reanudará en el momento en que pierda vigencia el presente real decreto o, en su caso, las prórrogas del mismo" (dates are suspended and periods for complying with public sector procedures are interrupted. The running of the period will start to run again right at the moment when this Royal Decree or its extensions cease to be in force, own translation).

The third (Fourth Additional Disposition) is devoted to private law periods: "Los plazos de prescripción y caducidad de cualesquiera acciones y derechos quedarán suspendidos durante el plazo de vigencia del estado de alarma y, en su caso, de las prórrogas que se adoptaren" (periods of prescription and lapse of any actions and rights are suspended as long as the state of emergency or its extensions are in force, own translation).

The regulation has precedents in other jurisdictions on the occasion of disasters,[2] although it is a bit incoherent. The Second Additional Disposition combines suspension and interruption linked to the same legal effect: "computation will start to run again" (*"reanudará"*), meaning that the period is extended without resetting the chronograph; this matches with suspension but not with interruption. Furthermore, the Spanish Civil Code does not regulate suspension of prescription periods; prescription periods may only be interrupted. Only the Civil Code of Catalonia regulates these (Arts 121-15–121-19; moreover, Art 122-3 regulates suspension of the running of lapse periods). Hence, it is not surprising that these exceptional rules have raised a number of questions.

---

1 See its text here: https://www.boe.es/boe/dias/2020/03/14/pdfs/BOE-A-2020-3692.pdf accessed 4 March 2021.

2 For example, on the occasion of hurricanes Katrina and Rita in Louisiana. See Benjamin West Janke, 'Revisiting *Contra Non Valentem* in Light of Hurricanes Katrina and Rita' (2008) 68 Tulane Law Review 497.

2. "TÉRMINOS" AND "PLAZOS", SUSPENSION OR INTERRUPTION

Because of the obscurity of the rules, the State Attorney issued a report[3] intended at clarifying the legal text. This is a sort of authentic interpretation of the legal text. First, the report makes a distinction between the terms "*término*" and "*plazo*". For the State Attorney, "*término*" means "fixing a certain date", whilst "*plazo*" refers to "a period of time between an initial and a final day". Therefore, the second Additional Disposition may be translated as "dates are suspended, and periods set out in procedural laws are suspended and interrupted in respect to all jurisdictional orders. Computation of periods will start to run again once this royal decree is no longer applicable". Since suspension and interruption are not synonyms, the report admits that the legal text contains a contradiction: the running of the period may be suspended or interrupted, but not both at the same time. Moreover, the legal consequences of suspension and interruption are not the same. The State Attorney resolves the contradiction by arguing that the wording of the Royal Decree should be interpreted as "start to run again" and not as "renew". A purposive interpretation leads to the same outcome: a period implies a burden for the citizens, because periods are established in their interest. Hence, the report argues that "citizens had the chance to fulfil the formality before the state of emergency was declared, time passed by cannot be regained, yet once the state of emergency ends, they have a new chance to fulfil the formality during the time before expiry of the period". The same interpretation applies to the Third Additional Disposition on administrative periods.

Of course, this interpretation is possible when taking into account the wording of the rule, but it is very disadvantageous for citizens. Interruption and renewal imply that periods run afresh, and it is irrelevant how much time has already passed and what the current situation of the concerned person is when the state of emergency comes to an end, as the chronograph has been reset.

Additionally, the report was silent on "suspension of *términos*": what is meant with the suspension of a certain date? The running of a period can be suspended, while a fixed date cannot. If a certain formality has to be fulfilled on a certain date and the law declares this to have become impossible, suspension in its literal meaning could only mean that the date dictating the deadline for the fulfilment of the formality would be moved to the day after the state of emergency has ended once the state of emergency has ended, the date is the day after of ending. This would undoubtedly collapse courts and administrations due to the accumulation of all suspended "*términos*" onto one day.

---

3 See its text here: http://www.icpm.es/downNews/3262_Informe%20AE.pdf accessed 4 March 2021.

It is by no means surprising that the State proceeded to amend itself shortly after. The Royal Decree-Law 16/2020, of 28 April, on procedural and organisational measures facing COVID-19 in the field of the administration of justice, contains a specific provision dealing with the problem created by the Royal Decree 463/2020. Article 2 states that procedural "*términos y plazos*" suspended by the latter will start to run afresh, being the first day of the new period the day after that suspension stops. Even with the amending clarification, the meaning of the provision remains incoherent: the running of the period is interrupted immediately after the period should start to run again after suspension. Furthermore, a "*término*" cannot be interrupted.

Literally, this interruption affects procedural periods covered by the Second Additional Disposition. Therefore, the Fourth Additional Disposition dealing with private law periods remains untouched.

3. PRESCRIPTION AND LAPSE OF RIGHTS

Because the Spanish Civil Code has no rule on suspension of prescription periods, the legislator has decided to introduce a provision linked to the state of emergency establishing the suspension of the running of the periods (literally, in the legal provision suspension refers to the periods, but it has to be assumed that what is suspended is the running of the period and not the period itself). According to the Fourth Additional Disposition, periods of prescription and of lapse of rights are suspended between the date in which the Royal Decree entered into force and the date in which the state of emergency ends.

This is not the first time that the Spanish legislator rules suspension of the running of periods outside the Civil Code. The Act of 1 April 1939[4] suspended retrospectively[5] all periods of prescription concerning persons and assets affected by the Spanish civil war. Two points must be outlined: first, the suspension covered expressly both acquisitive and extinctive prescription. Second, it had no general effect but is limited to "cases in which because of the situation of persons, of assets, or of necessary means, the exercise of such rights and actions has not been possible". As Pedro del Olmo[6] has highlighted, the intervention of the legislator in cases of pandemic or civil war is evidence that the current law does not allow inferring the feasibility of suspension based on cases of impediments beyond creditor's control. Only the Commercial Code enshrines an ancient rule (Art 955) on suspension of prescription of commercial claims, yet it has been seldom applied.

---

4 See its text here: https://www.boe.es/datos/pdfs/BOE/1939/097/A01989-01990.pdf accessed 4 March 2021.

5 From the day before the civil war broke out (17 July 1939).

6 Pedro del Olmo, 'Silencio, la prescripción duerme', Almacén de Derecho https://almacendederecho.org/silencio-la-prescripcion-duerme accessed 4 March 2021.

3.1. POSTPONEMENT OF EXPIRY

It has already been stressed that the Spanish Civil Code does not regulate suspension of prescription. Catalan law does, but without ruling on the postponement of expiry. Postponement of expiry would have been a very useful tool in relation to fixed dates occurring during the state of emergency. The legislator could have said that "*términos*" are postponed, so that formalities could be fulfilled, for instance two months after the end of the state of emergency. This has not been the case and it is still unknown what will happen in the future with all the formalities that should have been fulfilled on a certain date within the period of the state of emergency. Along the same lines, expiry of the prescription period could have been postponed for, for instance, six months after the end of the state of emergency. Nevertheless, this option is excluded by the law in force.

3.2. SUSPENSION IN CASES OF IMPEDIMENT BEYOND CREDITOR'S CONTROL

As the pandemic is the immediate cause of the general suspension, the legislative mandate is in force in all Spain, irrespective of the impact of infection in each territory and of the existence of a particular civil law ruling the issue. Catalonia has its own civil law with a modern regulation of limitation of actions mainly based on the Principles of European Contract Law (PECL). Therefore, suspension of prescription is ruled, with one of the grounds being an impediment beyond creditor's control, as no one should be reproached for not pursuing a claim they cannot pursue.[7] It must be supposed that the Spanish legislator considers the pandemic as an impediment and resorts to the old motto *agere non valenti non currit prescription*. However, even if the rule is well-intentioned it deserves some criticism.

The rule incorporated in the Royal Decree suspends the running of the period irrespective of the remaining time of the period. Every period is suspended regardless of, to provide an example, a general five-year period of prescription (Art 1964 Spanish Civil Code) had only begun to run. This is unnecessary taking into account that the state of emergency should only last for short periods of time in western democracies. The PECL and other civil codes establish suspension only when the impediment becomes evident close to the end of the prescription period. Thus, Article 14:303(2) PECL and Article III.-7:303(2) Draft Common Frame of Reference (DCFR) suspend the running of the period when the impediment arises or subsists within the last six months of the prescription period; the same is laid down in §206 German Civil Code (BGB).

---

7 Reinhard Zimmermann, *The New German Law of Obligations* (OUP 2005) 145.

Article 121-15 of the Civil Code of Catalonia mirrors PECL and the BGB as it sets out that the impediment must exist within the last six months of the period; additionally, it stresses that the effects of suspension never take place before these last six months, even if the impediment raised previously. Since the Royal Decree is in force in all Spain without any distinction, Article 121-15 has temporarily been *de facto* abrogated, because all periods of prescription are suspended.

One could be tempted to conclude that the rule passed by the Spanish legislator provides Catalan citizens with a more effective protection against the negative consequences of the pandemic in the exercise of claims and rights than the Catalan Civil Code does. However, this is not true. The rule drafted by the State is general and does not take into consideration the concrete personal situations of citizens. Suspension is general because of the pandemic, but it does not soften the law of prescription in view of personal situations. If interruption and suspension serve to temper the blind and objective periods of prescription,[8] a general suspension solves only partially the problems that a pandemic and similar disasters may cause. The following example illustrates the situation.[9] Dolores, from Madrid, could claim damages from Juan because of a car accident on 29 May 2019. The limitation period of claims for damages is one year according to Article 1968.2 Spanish Civil Code.[10] I will explain later that suspension of periods has come to an end on 4 June 2020. The period begins to run again on that date after a 70-day suspension. But Dolores is infected with coronavirus just after the ending of the state of emergency, resulting in acute respiratory distress,

---

8 Benjamin West Janke, François-Xavier Licari, 'The French Revision of Prescription: A Model for Louisiana?' (2010) 85 Tulane Law Review 43.

9 It has to be taken into account that Spanish scholars consider that a conflict such as the one used as an illustration in the text is deemed to be linked to the law of delicts; a procedural character is expressly denied. Therefore, the law applicable to the prescription of the claim is decided in accordance with Regulation 864/2007, Rome II (RRII). However, unlike Great Britain, where the criteria settled in the Regulation have been expressly extended to solve internal conflicts of law (see *The Law Applicable to Non-Contractual Obligations (England and Wales and Northern Ireland) Regulations 2008, Regulation 6* (https://www.legislation.gov.uk/uksi/2008/2986/contents/made accessed 4 March 2021)), Spain did not rule the issue. The prevailing view is that since Article 25.2 RRII allows – but does not impose – its application to purely internal situations, conflicts on torts resulting from the plurality of legislations must be solved applying State legislation. Hence, Article 10.9.1 of the Spanish Civil Code has to be applied. According to this provision, "Non-contractual obligations shall be governed by the law of the place where the event from which they result took place" (translation by the Spanish Ministry of Justice, https://www.mjusticia.gob.es/es/AreaTematica/DocumentacionPublicaciones/Documents/Spanish%20Civil%20Code.pdf, accessed 4 March 2021). In case of a traffic accident, regional laws of the place where the accident took place ruling the issue – including prescription of claims– must be applied.

10 Courts consider that the three-year period of Article 121-21.d) Catalan Civil Code does not apply to car accidents because this is a special statute.

for which she requires hospitalisation for two months. Despite suspension ruled by the State, her claim will probably be negatively affected by the prescription period. If the principle underlying suspension of the running of periods is that the creditor must have a fair chance of asserting the claim,[11] suspension laid down under the Spanish state of emergency is useless. By contrast, if Dolores were from Barcelona, after having benefitted from the general suspension, as force majeure within the last six months of the period is a ground for suspending the running of the period in Catalan law, she would not have to fear that the claim is affected while she stays in the hospital. It has to be concluded that once the exceptional suspension comes to an end, the ordinary legislation, including the regular grounds of suspension, are applicable.

Hence, a general rule suspending the running of the prescription period where it lacks a regulation of suspension is not as efficient as it may seem at first glance. Suspension of prescription is based on personal circumstances of the claimants. Even the most objective ground for suspension, an impediment beyond creditor's control, takes into account the impact of the circumstances on a specific claimant, as suspension must be rejected if a minimum degree of negligence in pursuing the claim can be attributed to the claimant.[12] General Franco, who enacted the statute of 1939, did not suspend the running of the periods for everyone, but solely for those who could not exercise their claims because of the civil war. The more recent example of New York after the terrorist attack of 11 September goes along the same lines, for Executive Order 113.7 issued by Governor Pataki temporarily suspended the statutes of limitation on civil actions "so far as it bars actions whose limitation period concludes during the period commencing from the date that the disaster emergency was declared", but later after cutting off the general suspension of the statutes of limitation the Governor extended the suspension for those persons directly affected by the disaster until 8 November 2001, under Executive Order 113.28.122.[13]

The previous arguments are also useful for the regulation contained in the project of a Common European Sales Law (CESL). In contrast to PECL and the DCFR, CESL did not incorporate impediments beyond creditor's control as a ground for suspension of the running of prescription periods.[14] This missing ground becomes more evident in times of coronavirus.

---

11 Reinhard Zimmermann, 'Article 14:303', in Nils Jansen, Reinhard Zimmermann (eds), *Commentaries in European Contract Laws* (OUP 2018) [1].

12 Palandt, Ellenberger, *Bürgerliches Gesetzbuch* (Beck 2020) §206, [4]; Staudinger, Peters, Jacoby, *BGB*, §206, (Otto Schmidt/De Gruyter 2019) [26].

13 Benjamin West Janke, 'Revisiting *Contra Non Valentem* in Light of Hurricanes Katrina and Rita' (2008) 68 Tulane Law Review 497, 521–522.

14 See Esther Arroyo i Amayuelas, Antoni Vaquer, 'Prescription in the Proposal for a Common European Sales Law' (2013) 9 European Review of Contract Law 38, 50–51.

3.3. LAPSE OF RIGHTS

The Spanish Civil Code does not systematically regulate the lapse of rights. This is a scholarly creation. There is a series of cases that case law has qualified as lapse in contrast to prescription, but any substantive rule is missing. According to case law, lapse of rights periods are fixed periods of time in which a right or an action has to be exercised; once the period has expired, the exercise of the right is not allowed. Lapse of rights affect mainly powers of legal configuration or potestative rights and actions. One of its main features is that the running of the lapse period can neither be interrupted nor suspended.[15] Therefore, suspension of the running of lapse periods entails an innovation in Spanish law. As with prescription, likewise suspension affects generally any lapse period irrespective of the personal situation of the claimant in relation to the ability to pursue the right.

Conversely, Catalan civil law regulates the lapse of rights and admits suspension of the running of the period where the parties may dispose of the legal relationship. The grounds for suspension are the same that are applicable to prescription. Consequently, the critical observations made in relation to suspension of prescription periods in the Royal Decree apply to lapse of rights.

One last question tackles conventional periods of lapse of rights, this is to say, the pact establishing that a certain power can only be exercised within a fixed period of time. Spanish scholars have accepted the feasibility of such periods and the Civil Code of Catalonia contains a specific rule in Article 122-4. In view of the broad terms of the Royal Decree, one may think that suspension affects these periods too. However, it has been argued that a general suspension must be restrictively construed because it implies an unjustified interference with freedom of contract and only force majeure can become a ground for suspension,[16] although there is no legal provision in State law. In Catalan law, an impediment beyond creditor's control suspends the running of the conventional periods of lapse of rights.[17]

---

15 Albert Lamarca Marquès, 'Limitation of Actions' in Sjef van Erp, Antoni Vaquer (eds), *Introduction to Spanish Patrimonial Law* (Comares 2006) 352. However, occasionally the Supreme Court in some peculiar cases had accepted suspension of the period of lapse of rights; see Luis Díez-Picazo, Antonio Gullón, *Sistema de derecho civil,* vol I (13th edn, Tecnos 2016) 381, footnote 3, and Ángel Carrasco Perera, *Derecho civil* (1st edn, Tecnos 1996) 380, who quote a few decisions considering that a conciliation hearing hat a suspensive effect that were handed down before the new Act on civil procedure was enacted in 2000. The latest editions of Carrasco do not mention these decisions.

16 José Manuel Busto Lago, '¿Se suspenden también los plazos de caducidad convencionales?' (2020) Revista CESCO http://centrodeestudiosdeconsumo.com/images/7._JOSE_MANUEL_BUSTO_LAGO_-_Se_suspenden_tambien_los_plazos_de_caducidad_convencionales.pdf accessed 4 March 2021.

17 Esteve Bosch Capdevila, 'Article 122-4' in Albert Lamarca, Antoni Vaquer (eds), *Comentari al llibre primer de Codi civil de Catalunya. Disposicions preliminars. Prescripció i caducitat* (Atelier 2012) 672.

4. ACQUISITIVE PRESCRIPTION

The Fourth Additional Disposition of the Royal Decree 463/2020 speaks of "periods of prescription and rights". Prescription may refer to extinctive and to acquisitive prescription, that is to say, the method of acquiring property by meeting statutory requirements of continuous possession *(usucapio)*. There are two solid arguments to conclude that the Royal Decree is referring only to extinctive prescription:

(1) The wording of the disposition tackles both prescription and lapse of rights. The common denominator between both institutions is that they focus on the exercise of claims, rights and actions, not on the acquisition of property rights.
(2) The precedent in the Act of 1939 mentions expressly extinctive and acquisitive prescription, whilst the Royal Decree 463/2020 does not.

Therefore, even if the rationale is the same for extinctive and acquisitive prescription, there is no legal provision that prevents possessors from completing acquisitive prescription under the state of emergency. It has to be recalled that the Spanish Civil Code still distinguishes between *usucapio inter presentes* and *inter absentes.* According to Article 1957, "Ownership and other real rights in respect to real property shall be prescribed by possession for ten years as to persons present, and by twenty years in respect to those absent, when held in good faith and under a just title".[18] Presence and absence are not legal concepts, but mere factual situations.[19] It is hard to understand that if the length of the period required to acquire ownership by possession depends on the ancient distinction between staying and not staying physically in the place where the asset is located, the lockdown in Spain and the consequent restriction of movement has not been taken into account as a ground for suspension of the running of the period.

By contrast, the Catalan Civil Code contains a rule on suspension of the running of the acquisitive prescription period[20] (one only period of three years for movable and 20 for immovable assets irrespective of presence or absence). Suspension benefits persons not able to act for themselves or by means of an agent. Since the wording is close to Article 121-15 on suspension of prescription

18 Translation by Clifford Stevens Walton, *The Civil Law in Spain and Spanish-America, including Cuba, Puerto Rico and the Philippine Islands* (W.H. Lowdermilk & Co 1900).

19 Agustín Luna Serrano, 'Article 1957' in *Comentario del Código civil*, t. II (Spanish Ministry of Justice 1991), 2141.

20 Article 531-26 CCCat: Possession required for acquisitive prescription is suspended in the cases in which acquisitive prescription takes place: a) against persons who cannot act by themselves or by means of an agent, as long as this situation persists (own translation).

because of an impediment beyond creditor's control, it can be concluded that physical impossibility resulting from lockdown becomes a ground for suspension of the running of acquisitive prescription, although probably the provision was not intended for such a situation.[21] Hence, in Catalonia periods of extinctive and acquisitive prescription are suspended because of the pandemic.

5. THE END OF THE SUSPENSION

The Royal Decree 537/2020, of 22 May, extended for the fifth time the state of emergency in Spain. Despite the fact that the state of emergency was still in force,[22] the Royal Decree contained three rules cutting off suspension. According to Article 8, from 4 June 2020 the suspension of procedural periods ended; according to Article 9, from 1 June the computation of administrative periods started to run again or started afresh depending on what the law had established; and according to Article 10, suspension of prescription and lapse of rights periods ended on 4 June 2020. Additionally, the three discussed Additional Dispositions of Royal Decree 463/2020 were expressly repealed. It was surprising that the state of emergency suspension of periods came to an end, although freedom of movement was still restricted. Even more surprising was that suspension of periods ended on different dates depending on the character of the periods. It has to be borne in mind that Royal Decree 463/2020 aligned the end of suspension of the running of periods with the end of the state of emergency. No legal provision referred to the "*términos*" supposed to be suspended. Interruption seems to have been restricted to some administrative periods, although the wording of Article 2 of the Royal Decree-law 16/2020 ruled that all procedural periods had been interrupted and not suspended. The same has happened under the new state of emergency declared in October 2020: despite restrictions to freedom of movement, no suspension has been established. All in all, one could refer to the situation as a complete chaos.

6. CONCLUDING REMARKS

The legal consequences of the coronavirus show the huge importance of modernised rules on prescription. The Spanish regulation of prescription in the Civil Code has been modified only once since it entered into force in 1889, an

---

21 Pedro del Pozo, Antoni Vaquer, Esteve Bosch, *Derecho civil de Cataluña. Derechos reales* (6th edn, Marcial Pons 2018) 98–99.

22 The state of emergency was in force until June 21, 2020, according to Royal Decree 555/2020, of 5 June. Later on by means of the Royal Decree 926/2020, of 25 October, Spain was again under a state of emergency (in force at the time of delivering this contribution).

amendment restricted to reduce the general period of prescription from 15 to 5 years. Suspension is not ruled. Therefore, the State legislator has intervened in order to try to avoid the adverse consequences of lockdown on the exercise of claims and rights. Nevertheless, the intervention is far from satisfactory. On the one hand, it is restricted to extinctive prescription. On the other hand, the confusing intervention is overbroad since it has introduced a general suspension that does not take into consideration the personal situations and the real chance to pursue the claims. Additionally, as in many other aspects, the State legislator has disregarded regional laws and, in particular, has overlapped a general suspension with the specific grounds for suspension in the civil law of Catalonia that provide a much more efficient regulation.

PARAMETERS FOR APPLYING THE RULES ON FORCE MAJEURE TO COVID-19 IN SPAIN

Angel CARRASCO*

* University of Castilla-La Mancha, Toledo.

The aim of the contribution is to analyse how the spread of COVID-19 affects contractual relationships under Spanish law. A case-by-case approach is adopted – the key difficulties and paradoxes associated with the application of the current legal framework are determined by analysing the most typical difficulties encountered by the contractors due to the pandemic. The legal context is comprehensively presented: the core practical issues related to the functioning of the institution of force majeure are examined. The common problematic scenarios caused by the COVID-19 crisis are addressed, i.e.: the practical impact of the all-risk clauses on the risk distribution, the disappearance of causa of the contract, the tension between labour law mechanisms and force majeure. Finally, the possibility of classifying COVID-19 contingency as a force majeure contingency is examined (both the undisputed and the debatable force majeure contingencies are discussed).

1. INTRODUCTION

Everyone is acutely aware of how COVID-19 has impacted our lives since February 2020. In this context, the temporal border marked by RD 463/2020,[1] establishing a "state of alarm" in the country, has severely limited the freedom of movement and imposed the closure of a great number of commercial activities alongside other public regulatory packages in the areas of employment, transport, health, tourism, etc. A series of Royal Decrees followed, which have affected very solid sectors of the Spanish legal system, including private law. "COVID-19 as a force majeure event" was already being discussed when the virus seemed to be located exclusively in China, because the paralysis of that country was bringing about dysfunctions in the global supply of goods and services, and, therefore, in the possibility of fulfilling supply or manufacturing contracts even in Spain.[2] However, after RD 463, the rise of the term "force majeure" has been extraordinary in Spain.[3] One could argue it has gone "viral".

---

1 Real Decreto 463/2020, de 14 de marzo, por el que se declara el estado de alarma para la gestión de la situación de crisis sanitaria ocasionada por el COVID-19, "BOE" núm. 67, de 14/03/2020.

2 And elsewhere, obviously. See, Shannon Rose Selden and others, 'Roundtable: Contract Enforceability in the Age of Covid-19' (2020) 21 Business Law International, available at https://www.ibanet.org/Publications/business-law-international-september-2020.aspx, accessed 12 November 2020. Also, Sergio García Long (ed), *Derecho de los Desastres: Covid-19* (Pontificia Universidad Católica del Perú 2020).

3 Alonso Arana, 'Nuevas medidas (económicas y sociales) contra el COVID-19. Análisis normativo RDL 8/2020' (2020) Aranzadi digital num. 1, BIB 2020\9598; Buades Feliu, 'Algunas reflexiones sobre la pandemia del COVID-19, la declaración de Estado de Alarma, los supuestos de fuerza mayor y los contratos entre empresarios con obligaciones de

In the recent scenario of pandemia, the cognitive limits between Force Majeure and Rebus sic Stantibus rule have been almost blurred.[4] "Experts" and "pagans" relentlessly muddle around this aspect of COVID-19, giving social notoriety to a classic academic device. And, naturally, it has begun to be strategically managed in the dynamics of contractual performance and renegotiation.[5]

2. PARAMETERS FOR APPLYING FORCE MAJEURE

2.1. THE TWO EXONERATING EFFECTS OF FORCE MAJEURE

If an obligation arising from a contract or a law is affected by force majeure, making performance impossible, there are two exonerating effects for the debtor.[6] First, his/her obligation is extinguished or suspended (Arts 1182–1184 of the Civil Code (CC)).

Second, the debtor is not liable for the harm caused to the creditor by the material breach (Art 1105 CC). Additionally, there is a third effect, which no longer derives from force majeure, but from the bilateral structure of the contract in which is embedded a mutual consideration (the "synallagma"), a contract in which each obligation becomes *cause* of the opposite one: the counterparty is also released from performing what is due from him/her, as a quid pro quo outcome of the inhibited performance of the debtor (Art 1124 CC).

---

tracto sucesivo' (2020) Diario LA LEY, nº 9610, 8; Ángel Carrasco Perera, 'Permítame que le cuenta la verdad sobre COVID y Fuerza Mayor' (2020) CESCO www.centrodeestudiosde consumo.com accessed 12 November 2020; De Miguel Asensio, 'Medidas de emergencia y contratos internacionales' (2020) LA LEY UNIÓN EUROPEA, nº 81; Gomez Ligüerre, 'Fuerza mayor' (2020) InDret, www.indret.com accessed 12 November 2020.

4 Álvarez Segismundo, 'Pandemia, fuerza mayor y cláusula rebus sic stantibus a la luz de la Jurisprudencia' (La Ley 2020), avaliable at https://diariolaley.laleynext.es/dll/2020/04/23/pandemia-fuerza-mayor-y-clausula-rebus-sic-stantibus-a-la-luz-de-la-jurisprudencia, accessed 12 November 2020.; Pasquau Liaño, 'Covid-19: los contratos también se contagian. Hay fórmulas para mitigar el colapso judicial' (La Ley 2020), avaliable at https://diariolaley.laleynext.es/dll/2020/06/25/covid-19-los-contratos-tambien-se-contagian-hay-formulas-para-mitigar-el-colapso-judicial, accessed 12 November 2020. Chantal Moll, '¿Es la cláusula "rebus sic stantibus" la solución a todos los problemas jurídicos del Covid-19?' (La Ley 2020), avaliable at https://diariolaley.laleynext.es/dll/2020/07/07/es-la-clausula-rebus-sic-stantibus-la-solucion-a-todos-los-problemas-juridicos-del-covid-19, accessed 12 November 2020.

5 As to the case law in the second half of 2020, Ángel Carrasco Perera, 'Debtor's Release by COVID-Hardship (rebus sic stantibus) in Financial Debts. Spanish Trends' (December 2020), Journal of International Banking Law and Regulation.

6 As to Spanish law, Ángel Carrasco Perera, *Derecho de contratos* (2nd edn, Aranzadi 2017), Chapter 20. In international settings, Christoph Brunner, *Force Majeure and Hardship under General Contract Principles* (Wolters Kluwer 2008).

2.2. AN "ALL RISK" CLAUSE IS INDEED AN ALL RISK CLAUSE

The contract is the first source for the solution of problems or confrontations generated by the COVID-19 risk. If the contract merely provides for a typical force majeure clause, it is likely to be of no use to us, because the starting question is whether our case (COVID-19) is in fact contained in that clause. However, the contract may share, or more specifically assign, risks, or it may introduce a clause with a specific remedy for risks. It is possible that a clause assigns or shares *all risks in general*, in which case COVID-19 is one of them. For example, a clause stating that whenever one party informs the other that it cannot perform for a reason beyond its control and which was not foreseeable, the parties will negotiate for 10 days and, should the negotiations fail, the non-defaulting party may leave by paying an exit amount of 15% of the contract budget. This clause cannot be eliminated by COVID-19 as force majeure, but applies to COVID-19, whether force majeure or not.

Contractual practice affords other examples. When the contract warrants the creditor a "minimal guaranteed amount" of rent or payment, the debtor's assumption of risk becomes unavoidable under this cap. When the lessor enjoys an exoneration clause that releases him/her from bearing any inconvenience for the use that encumbers the premises, the lessee cannot escape this burden by proving that such or such use inconveniency is to be deemed force majeure.

Take now an example of a wedding, which is very illustrative. In the contract with the hotelier, the bride and groom have agreed that, if the banquet is suspended by decision of the bride and groom within the 20 days prior to the appointed date, the bride and groom (or whoever agreed to pay) must pay 25% of the contract price. It is clear that this is an *all risk* clause, even if it is the case that the wedding is suspended because the bride and groom have been hospitalised because of COVID-19. One may counter that this is not fair, because before COVID-19 there were an X number of risks that could lead the bride and groom not to hold the event (including a sentimental break-up), but after COVID-19 the risk is much higher, with a resulting X+COVID-19; in other words, today there is a greater probability that the bride and groom will have to pay the penalty, and this increased risk has no bearing in a reduction in the price penalty charged for the banquet. This is true, but the bride and groom have to bear that higher risk, because an 'all risk' clause is indeed an all risk clause.

As a rule, a force majeure risk sharing or assignment clause cannot be deactivated because the promisor claims that force majeure (i.e. COVID-19) has made such a clause unenforceable. A risk clause cannot be deactivated by the occurrence of a risk that is covered by the clause. The risk, then, is part of the clause, and does not destroy it.

2.3. CONTRACTUAL FORCE MAJEURE FOCUSES ON CONSIDERATION OWED UNDER A CONTRACT (OR LAW)

Another wedding example seems appropriate. Taken ill by COVID-19, the star musician who had been hired for the wedding event cannot perform. The illness is force majeure, the obligation is thus extinguished (or suspended) (but he/she does not get paid either). The additional staff hired by the employer to serve the banquet are taken ill by COVID-19. This does not affect the mutual consideration of the service contract between the bride and groom and the company, it is a concurrent circumstance, and it is an issue that falls on the employer if he/she does not reach an agreement with the bride and groom. Let us suppose the sad contingency of the bride's death due to COVID-19. This event does not affect the bilateral structure, nor has it made it impossible to fulfil either of the two reciprocal obligations. Naturally, neither the wedding nor the banquet will take place; most likely an agreement will be reached. However, if this is not the case, the relatives or the groom can terminate the hospitality contract due to the *unexpected disappearance of the "causa" (total failure of the consideration).* We can call these surrounding contingencies "improper force majeure", with the meaning that I will further explain and with the consequences that I will detail below.

Article 160(2) of the Consumers Act (Holidays Packages) reads as follows: "Notwithstanding the provisions of the previous paragraph, when there are unavoidable and extraordinary circumstances in the place of destination or in the vicinity that significantly affect the performance of the combined trip or the transport of passengers to the place of destination, the passenger shall have the right to terminate the contract before the start of the trip without paying any penalty. In this case the passenger shall be entitled to a full refund of any payment made, but not to additional compensation". The rule is correct: the contingency affects the synallagma, the holiday trip that the company will not be able to provide as it should. So does Article 160(3)(b). In Article 297(a) of the Maritime Navigation Act, if the passenger does not show up for boarding, he/she must pay the ticket, unless the cause of failure to board is the death or illness of the passenger or family members who accompanied him/her and the carrier has been notified without delay. These contingencies are not force majeure , because the passenger (or his/her heirs) are not unable to pay. It would be an unexpected disappearance of the 'causa', to which the law assigns the exonerating effects of force majeure.

2.4. FORCE MAJEURE IS NOT THE SAME AS THE FACTUAL REQUIREMENTS OF AN EXCEPTIONAL RULE

We move on to a different scenario. Let us imagine that the COVID-19 law confers a unique right or eliminates an ordinary charge in favour of the self-employed employer who has lost 50% of the average turnover of the previous three months during the state of alarm. The employer receives a subsidy, the payment of his/her taxes is deferred, he/she is entitled to an ICO (State-owned bank) loan, etc. Fifty per cent of the decrease in average turnover is the factual requirement of the law or laws that confer such advantages to the self-employed, but such does not become a force majeure contingency in contractual relations with third parties. The law insulates an issue (turnover decrease up to 50%) and endorses to that issue a specific "liberating" effect for a class of debtors (tax duties of self-employed employers). But the law does not need to frame such issue as "force majeure". No other debtors are entitled to become totally or partially free from their *commercial* duties by mere pointing to the fact that they are self-employed employers who have lost 50% of the average turnover of the previous three months during the state of alarm.

2.5. IN WHOSE INTEREST IS IT TO CLAIM FORCE MAJEURE?

Resorting to force majeure as exonerating ground is mainly only in the interest of (1) the promisor who has received or expects to receive consideration that is immune to the impossibility of giving, and (2) the promisor who seeks to avoid the effects (payment of interest, etc.) of likely delay on his/her part. Normally the former will not occur in bilateral contracts, because the promisor who is released by force majeure also loses the right to consideration and must return it if it has already been collected. If the transaction was good for both parties, both parties lose the respective utility that the exchange produced. If the contract was beneficial for both parties, any legal rule is likely to be superfluous, because the parties will come to an agreement as long as COVID-19 does not prevent them from finding the formula in which the contract will again be beneficial.

There is only one case of a bilateral contract where this does not happen. It is precisely in the most classic of all types of contract, the sale and purchase of a specific good (Art 1452 CC). If the good is lost or destroyed due to no fault of the seller before delivery, the buyer is left without the good and has to pay. But it is not enough that the delivery is "impossible", the good must have been *lost* or *destroyed*. Such a scenario does not seem to be possible in a COVID-19 risk contingency.

2.6. THE FORCE MAJEURE TO CARRY OUT A TEMPORARY COLLECTIVE REDUNDANCY PROCEDURE ("ERTE") IS NOT THE FORCE MAJEURE UNDER CONTRACT LAW

According to Article 22 RDL 8/2020, collective redundancies and the reduction in working hours stemming from the loss of business caused by COVID-19, including the suspension or closure of commercial premises, temporal lockouts of public sites, contract suspensions, limitations in transport facilities, ban or restriction of freedom of movement with regards to persons and assets, shortage of industrial inputs, etc., will be deemed force majeure contingencies within the meaning of Article 47 of the Workers' Statute Act, thus vesting in the employer the right to terminate or suspend employment contracts, with the statutory compensation. Although this COVID-19 rule is semantic, it does not pretend any kind of ultra-activity beyond the limits of the Labour Law. The contingency, which the employer may use to carry out collective redundancy procedure, is not per se a contingency which may be asserted in order to excuse a material breach of a commercial contract.

2.7. THERE ARE TIMES WHEN FORCE MAJEURE "HAPPENS" ONCE, AND OTHER TIMES WHEN IT "HAPPENS" TWICE

When force majeure first happens, the risk and harm rests with the person on whom it occurs. Let us imagine that a rule dictates that people with asthma can no longer go to gyms, and Peter is an asthmatic who has paid a quarterly fee. Force majeure has happened on him and him alone. Since Peter is not required to train or attend the gym, the risk does not impact the contractual expectations of the gym. But let us imagine that the government forbids gyms to be opened to the public, which was the case after the proclamation of the state of alarm by Royal Decree 463. The first time the force majeure happens, it is on Peter (he will no longer be able to cycle in the gym). But this risk is bound to strike a second time, which is the definitive one. The definitive force majeure is borne by those who can no longer offer what they are paid for. The risk of not cycling in the gym is suffered by Peter, the risk of the contract as a whole is suffered by the gym: Peter rescinds by frustration and the gym does not get paid.

As we will see later in the text with regard to the lease of business premises closed to the public by RD 463/2020, there are times when people are absent-minded about the person by whom the risk must be borne on the second time. In other words, whether Peter has to bear the burden of not cycling but still has to pay, or whether the gym lost the right to remuneration as a consequence of Peter not been able to use the gym. As a matter of curiosity: a lot of people (not only the owners of gyms) thought during the state of alarm that Peter and only

Peter was the person to bear the disaster. We imagine further that because of COVID-19, the government prohibits commercial establishments from selling products manufactured in China. The risk is borne by the Chinese and by the companies that own the establishments. Will it be borne the second time by the lessor, who will have to lower the rent according to the loss of earnings? Will it be borne by the shopping mall's commonhold association that passes the condominium charges on to the establishment? The risk will not be borne by them, because what the establishment sells and how much it sells is not internal to the structure of the bilateral lease contract.

Where the legislator has clearly made the risk fall *irreversibly*, it is not possible to react in the contract by an exit or similar contractual device which makes it reversible against the other party. Force majeure is not borne a second time and is not spread through the veins of the contract. Consider the following example:

During the month following the entry into force of this royal decree-law, suppliers of electricity, natural gas and water may not suspend supply to those consumers who are vulnerable consumers.

Another fitting example would be:

Debtors falling within the scope of this royal decree-law may request from the creditor, up to 15 days after the end of the validity of this royal decree-law, a moratorium on the payment of the loan secured by a mortgage for the purchase of their habitual residence.

We know that the legislator has wanted the risk to fall irreversibly on the banks because the application of moratorium *interest will not be allowed for the period of validity of the moratorium.*

Another example:

Companies providing electronic communications services shall maintain the provision of publicly available electronic communications services contracted by their clients on the date of the start of the application of the state of alarm, so that they cannot suspend or interrupt them.

Finally, a clear example in the field of employment:

Force majeure and the economic, technical, organisational and production causes underpinning the measures to suspend contracts and reduce working hours provided for in Articles 22 and 23 of Royal Decree-law 8/2020 of 17 March may not be understood *as justifying the termination of employment contracts or redundancies.*

2.8. IS THE "COVID-19 CONTINGENCY" A FORCE MAJEURE CONTINGENCY?

"Is COVID-19 a force majeure event?" In current times, one always hears this question as soon as one enters a legal forum. And, what is worse, it is usually answered by the questioner, without any hesitation.[7] But the question is a trap and the answer to the trap is sophistry. It is a poorly framed question and therefore it has no answer.

What is a "COVID-19 contingency"? Amongst other possibilities, it is the following:

1. COVID-19 as a virus harmful to health or life: It is a force majeure event if the debtor of consideration in the form of work is affected by it. Not only artists, but also many other freelancers can be found in this case. But the question remains open in corporate cases. Here it *depends.* In any case, force majeure does not encompass COVID-19, but merely illness or death.

   If a freelancer cannot paint your house because of the virus, it is force majeure. If a paint company claims to have all its employees on leave because of the virus, it is not "proper" force majeure.

2. COVID-19 *as prohibitive or imperative government measures*: contained in RD 463/2020, RRDL 8/2020, 9/2020, 10/2020, 11/2020, 15/2020, and implementing regulations, are a case of force majeure preventing contractual performance, but not because it is "COVID-19", but because it is a regulatory prohibition (*factum principis*). For example, see Article 36 RDL 11/2020: the impossibility of performance stems from the 'measures' (which impose closure), not from the "COVID-19 risk". This is a very important distinction when considering sub-Article 4 thereof.
3. COVID-19 *as a general economic disaster*: disruption of production chains, disappearance of customers, impracticality of factory work, etc. This, in principle, says nothing. It is like asking whether a general strike or a flu epidemic or torrential rains are force majeure. *It depends.* It can be "improper" force majeure.

---

7 Further to the previous references, Ángel Serrano de Nicolas, 'Fuerza mayor y cláusula rebus sic stantibus entre la imposibilidad sobrevenida y la excesiva onerosidad por el confinamiento derivado del Covid-19' (La Ley 2020), available at https://diariolaley.laleynext.es/dll/2020/04/24/fuerza-mayor-y-clausula-rebus-sic-stantibus-entre-la-imposibilidad-sobrevenida-y-la-excesiva-onerosidad-por-el-confinamiento-derivado-del-covid-19, accessed 12 November 2020; Blanco González and Durán Vargas, 'Las relaciones contractuales en los tiempos del COVID-19. Incidencia de la cláusula rebus sic stantibus en los contratos tras el impacto de la pandemia y el Real Decreto 463/2020', (2020) 4 Actualidad Civil.

4. COVID-19 as a *precautionary principle*: Put into practice by companies or individuals fleeing from the risk of contagion. The precautionary principle is not in itself force majeure. *It depends.* It can be "improper" force majeure.

2.9. COVID-19 CONTINGENCIES: "PROPER" AND "IMPROPER" FORCE MAJEURE CONTINGENCIES

The following are undisputed force majeure contingencies, which we shall refer to as "proper contingencies": (1) Legislative prohibition (due to COVID-19) in respect of an agreed consideration being given on its own terms. (2) Legislative prohibition (due to COVID-19) in respect of an activity being carried out that is necessarily *instrumental* to giving the promised consideration. (3) Absolute individual impossibility of performance through no fault of said individual, e.g., consideration in the form of personal provision of a service, the promisor thereof having been infected by the virus. (4) Absolute generic impossibility of performance by whichever promisor who had "stepped into the shoes" of the affected obligor, e.g. because the input for the manufacture of the product comes exclusively and necessarily from China and from nowhere else, and the Chinese market is closed.

These others are debatable force majeure contingencies, which we shall refer to as "improper contingencies": (1) Unenforceability of performance conduct, because it would compromise personal resources of the promisor with reasonably likely *exposure to COVID-19 infection*. (2) Unenforceability of performance conduct, because it would compromise personal resources of the *counterparty*, due to reasonably likely exposure to the infection. (3) Unenforceability of performance conduct that would entail an extraordinary cost overrun not offset by the contract price. (4) Non-absolute, but unique impossibility of the promisor to perform in the prescribed manner and within the prescribed time limit. (5) Unexpected disappearance of the "causa" (recall the death of the bride).

When does "improper" force majeure become exonerating force majeure? This should be the case when:

1. When the costs of procuring performance by the promisor are grossly disproportionate to the requirement of good faith, and in addition the promisor offers to cover the cost of trust suffered by the promisee, as explained below.
2. When the cost overrun for the promisor is supplementary to additional incidental and unexpected remuneration for the promisee, who has benefited from the pandemic, a so-called COVID *windfall*. For instance, the importer of facemasks is experiencing difficulty in procuring the goods in time to fulfil its orders with retail sellers because there is a shortage or a disruption in its source (China). In its turn, retail sellers are making huge profits in a business that until de COVID-19 was yielding a poor turnover.

3. When the failure to give the consideration also incorporates *a precautionary principle to protect the interests of the counterparty*. There is a type of contract where the COVID-19 contingency (1) jeopardises the promisor's people or organisation, or (2) compromises the promisor or promisee's own organisation's safety. When the promisor (e.g. *Mobile World Congress*) paralyses the performance because (matter of fact, not verbally) it has considered (also) the health interests of the counterparty's organisation or of both parties, then force majeure becomes "proper".

   In other words, if, by suspending his/her performance, the promisor is also managing, for the promisee, third party interests within the meaning of Article 1888 CC,[8] *he/she does not need other conditions to raise his/her contingency to the rank of "proper" force majeure.*

4. When the contingency is temporary and suspensive, and the interests of the other party are not severely compromised by the suspension – one has to be less demanding in declaring that a debtor is inexcusably in delay than in declaring that a debtor is released from his/her obligation.
5. The requirements for force majeure must be relaxed when the stranded costs, which the promisor will have to bear in order to get out of the "impossible" contract, are greater than the stranded costs which the promisee will have to bear for the same reason. The less of an incentive the promisor has for declaring force majeure, the more should be deemed the debtor's declaration made in good faith: the debtor is paying for the force majeure more than what the creditor is losing.
6. "Improper" force majeure becomes irrelevant if the interested party (promisee) proves that the promisor had made a bad contract regardless of the COVID-19 contingency. If the counterparty proves that, due to COVID-19, the other party aims to procure a motive to get rid of a (irrespective of COVID-19) bad deal, the force majeure is not to be considered.

2.10. THE "ACID TEST" FOR JUMPING INTO A PROPER FORCE MAJEURE CONTINGENCY

Let us suppose that people regarding the pandemic (not the "government COVID-19 measures") as force majeure are right. It is clear, as was said, that in most cases this is not the case. Nevertheless, the situation of inactivity, closure and panic that deeply affects economic activity is understandable. Let us hypothetically accept

[8] Christian von Bar, Eric Clive and Hans Schulte-Nölke, 'Book V. Benevolent intervention in another's affairs' in Christian von Bar, Eric Clive and Hans Schulte-Nölke (eds) *Principles, Definitions and Model Rules of European Private Law* (Verlag Dr. Otto Schmidt 2009) 395 ff.

that the COVID-19 pandemic is a "quasi force majeure", seeking a name for it with exonerating purposes. In this case, the subsequent rule follows:

However impure ("improper") the force majeure of the hindering contingency, an *interpretative effort* can be made in favour of the promisor, who is personally unable to perform on the terms contracted, but in that case said promisor, who is extraordinarily released, *must pay the other party the proven costs that this party has faced as a result of the failure of the contract.* In other words, the promisor does not compensate for the interest in the performance not obtained by the promisee, but for the costs of reliance invested in the contract.

I am certain that with this prophylactic measure there will be fewer promisors who, taking advantage of COVID-19, will be ready to declare at the drop of a hat impeding force majeure contingencies.

2.11. CLOSED LEASED COMMERCIAL PREMISES: WHO BEARS THE RISK?[9]

In news made public on 14 April in various media, the following controversial, perhaps even absurd, statement could be read: "Commercial businesses launched an SOS yesterday after being closed for a month. In a statement signed by seven employers' organisations (CEC, Anceco, Amicca, Comertia, Acotex, Eurelia and Fece), representing 510,000 establishments and 1.7 million jobs, they warned that the situation is critical. Given the seriousness of the situation generated by the current health crisis, several of the main business associations informed the government that businesses are unable to meet current costs, especially the rent of commercial premises".

These words embody a by no means isolated opinion. Given the enormous increase in written legal opinions on COVID-19 and force majeure, it is not unusual to read that tenants of commercial premises closed down by government COVID-19 measures still have to pay rent. Rental assets lobbies even claim to have won the match pointing to the infamous Article 1 of Royal Decree-law 15/2020.

---

9 See Rius Fuentes-Lojo, 'Cláusula rebus sic stantibus y arrendamiento de local de negocio. La posible suspensión del contrato', (2020) 4 Actualidad Civil; Carlos Cabrera Padrón, 'El arrendamiento de los locales de negocios en la crisis del coronavirus: la cláusula rebus sic stantibus un invitado que ha llegado para quedarse', (La Ley, 2020), available at https://diariolaley.laleynext.es/dll/2020/05/13/el-arrendamiento-de-los-locales-de-negocio-en-la-crisis-del-coronavirus-la-clausula-rebus-sic-stantibus-un-invitado-que-ha-llegado-para-quedarse accessed 12 November 2020; Ángel Carrasco Perera, 'Locales de negocio cerrados por COVID: la barbarie o el lobby hacen su agosto (segunda versión, reforzada para los incrédulos)' (Centro de Estudios de Consumo 2020); José Ramón García Vicente, 'Arrendamiento y pandemia (i) y Arrendamiento de local de negocio y pandemia' (Blog Asociación de Profesores Derecho Civil, 2020); Antonio Orti Vallejo, 'Apunte sobre la suspensión de la obligación de pago de la renta de los locales de negocio a los que les ha sido prohibida la apertura' (Centro de Estudios de Consumo 2020).

This apprehension can only arise from defective legal training. RD 463/2020 prohibits certain commercial businesses from remaining open to the public. The measure affected many existing establishments on rented premises, which had to close to the public. Undoubtedly, this is a force majeure measure, not because the COVID-19 is a case of force majeure as is commonly repeated, but because there is a *factum principis* that makes it impossible to perform. The confusion lies in not clearly knowing what element exactly it is impossible to perform. The performance that is made impossible is not the carrying out of business as such, because the *performance of commerce is not a performance owed by the lessee to the lessor as part of its owed consideration.* The obligation that is extinguished or suspended is the obligation of the lessor to *provide continuously the useful enjoyment of the rented property.* Force majeure first strikes the lessee, but in the end the lessor bears the cost. And since *in the lease agreement, because it is a continuing contract, the risk of impeding contingencies is never shifted to the lessee* (unlike in a sale and purchase under Art 1452 CC), the lessee may suspend payment and/or terminate the agreement due to the impossibility the opposing party is facing. Therefore, the lessee *does not have to pay rent.* Obviously, the lessor cannot evict for non-payment of rent.

Twenty centuries of Roman and Civil Law have tirelessly taught that there is an essential difference between those who sell something and those who rent it. Those who sell, shift the risk of the property to the buyers from the moment the contract is made, and furthermore, are only liable to the buyers in that these will not be deprived of the property by the action of a third party (*peaceful possession*). The person leasing out *never shifts the risk of future non-use to the lessee.* This is because the lessor is obliged, among other things, to provide the lessee continuously with the *useful use of the property*, which, unlike the buyer's peaceful possession, our Civil Code very appropriately calls *peaceful enjoyment* (Art 1544(3)). I give you an example that goes back to the time of the Digest. I rented a room to a lens polisher whose work needed a lot of natural light; the neighbour, making use of his/her right, and without overstepping, erected a wall in his/her property, and the polisher no longer had the light he/she required. The lessor, even if through no fault of his/her own, has ceased to provide useful enjoyment in accordance with the intended use, so he/she will not be able to collect the rent, and being a non-temporary contingency, the polisher can terminate. I take the example from Pothier, *Traité du contract du louage*, no. 113, based in turn on the case of Gayo in Digest 19, 2, 25, 2.

The principle of law that rested on various Roman sources was brilliantly expressed by Domat in his *Lois Civiles*, IV, III. It will not be translated here as it is better left in French: "la cessation de cet usage, quelle qu'en soit la cause, doit tomber sur le bailleur" [*The deprivation of this use, whatever its cause, is to be borne by the lessor*] The outstanding Roman texts are Dig. 19, 2 15,1 (*"if I'm not able to the fruitful use of the lease*, no matter what the cause"); according to Servio, whom Ulpiano quotes in 19, 2, 15, 2, the landlord has to answer to the settler "for every force that cannot be resisted", and he gives several examples of force majeure, and always for the reason that *It is just to hand down the land in a way that the lessee may lucratively use it.* The passage in 19, 2, 25, 2 is the one already referred to, that "the lights in a cenacle are darkened" by the neighbour's lawful exercise of the right to build. Since the risk is never shifted to the settler, if the estate you have rented to me is confiscated, you are bound by the act, even if you are not the cause of the confiscation. "So I think," says Africano in 19, 2, 33, "that the same must be observed, so that you will return to me the rent which I would have paid, of course, for that time which I would not have enjoyed; and you will not be obliged to answer for more … (For) if the use of it is prevented by *a person or people to whom you cannot impede to act*, you will be obliged to do nothing more than giving up the collection of the rent or return the payment already made".

Antonio Gómez, famous author of the *Variae Resolutiones Iuris Civilis*, devotes Chapter III of Book II of the same to the lease agreement. It begins with a basic distinction between sale and purchase, according to which in the lease the risk of the property is never fully shifted to the lessee, because the lessor must not procure either ownership or "possession", but a continuous *fruitful use*, because in this contract the rent *is paid as consideration for a use able to yield profits*, so that if the property perishes, the payment of rent necessarily ceases. But let us go beyond the loss of the property.

Let us suppose that the land was handed down to the tenant, but the tenant cannot profit from its use, for instance due to an impediment raised by a third party; the lessor is not bound to pay damages, but it is also deprived of the right to the rent.

The question is completely different if the drop in sales of the establishment do not stem from the imperative closure, but from the depression of the market as a result of the collective risk of COVID-19. Here there is no impeding force majeure. What suffers is the commercial operation, but this does not belong to the *causa* of the lease. The only relevant measure for the lessee, and a very relevant one at that, is the analogical application of Article 1575 CC, as the only course to give rise to the *rebus sic stantibus* (unforeseeability and excessive hardship) clause.

2.12. WHO BEARS THE SUNKEN, UNPROFITABLE COSTS OF CONTRACT FAILURE?

The analogy with public contracts cannot be applied (cf Art 34 RDL 8/2020) because, as these involve public services, the public authority is subject to the principle of maintaining the contractor's economic equilibrium. Therefore, when government COVID-19 measures adversely affect public contractors, the government has to bear to some extent the contractor's unamortised costs.

Article 36(2) RDL 11/2020 requires that the establishment that cannot perform its service with the consumer due to the government COVID-19 measures, has to return the sum it was charged (which is logical), but can deduct the expenses that have become useless due to the failure of the contract. This measure is exceptional and can only be explained by the fact that the government has understood that it is reasonable for consumers to have to pay part of the cost of the business risk, for a kind of social solidarity.

In the absence of any special provision,[10] sunk costs are internalised by the sufferer and cannot be passed on. In an force majeure contingency, this happens on both sides: everyone loses what they invested in the business. In debatable contingencies, as explained above, the promisor can only raise his/her contingency to force majeure if he/she decides to bear the counterparty's trust costs.

There are other incidental costs, which are apportioned according to the nature of the case and the law that governs it. Typical cases are the unexpected incidental costs of maintaining travellers unable to reach their destination. According to the law, the service provider bears these costs (Arts 161(7) of the Consumers Act and 292 of the Maritime Navigation Act).

2.13. IN FINANCIAL CONTRACTS WITH NON-CONSUMER COUNTERPARTIES, ANY NON-PERFORMANCE BY THE PROMISOR IS ATTACHED TO THEM

There is no "COVID-19 risk" that enables the debtor not to comply with his/her financial obligation.[11] In RDLs 8 and 11/2020, the legislator has taken care to clarify that during the financial moratoriums provided for the benefit of specially considered individuals (consumers, particularly vulnerable natural or legal persons or companies), no late payment interest will be accrued, but that this rule will not apply to any case not covered by the special rule. There is no COVID-19 risk here that could be asserted by the non-privileged borrower. And the rule is not unfounded. Loan contracts are not synallagmatic. If the promisor were able to assert COVID-19 risk in order to suspend payments, the counterparty (lender) would have no instruments to pass on force majeure through the mutual consideration. It would be an unfair *win-win* contingency for the promisor.

10 Which is the case, for instance, of English Law (*Frustrated Contracts Act* 1943), Cfr. Günter H. Treitel, *Frustration and Force Majeure* (3rd edn, Sweet & Maxwell 2014) Ch. 15.

11 Simon Rayney, 'Using Force Majeure Clauses in Relation to Inability to Pay: A Forlorn Hope', (2020) 17 International Corporate Rescue, 276; Ángel Carrasco Perera, 'Debtor's Release by COVID-Hardship (rebus sic stantibus) in Financial Debts. Spanish Trends' (December 2020), Journal of International Banking Law and Regulation.

2.14. WATERFALL THEORY

The "waterfall theory" is one of the most widespread hypotheses where the force majeure card is being shuffled. The direct promisor claims force majeure to not perform (or not perform in time); whether he/she accepts it or not (he/she will fight to justify that COVID-19 is not force majeure), his/her promisee has to somehow enforce this non-performance with COVID-19 against his/her own promisee, and delay or suspend his/her own performance. Of course, he/she can assert the same COVID-19 force majeure that he/she was not accepting from the upstream promisor. And with danger, because he/she could find him/herself bound to consider that there is force majeure vis-à-vis its debtor, without being sure that he/she will be able to assert the same in a dispute vis-à-vis its own creditor.

If the first promisor fails to perform with regard to an essential *input*, and things are such that (e.g. an EPC contract) the promisee cannot seek alternative performance to meet its own performance, the said promisee is *not in* force majeure as against its own creditor *unless the first promisor could present a* force majeure case, which the first promisee could oppose. In other words, the first promisee has a force majeure case when the first promisor could then defend him/herself with force majeure against the final promisee, if the latter acted by subrogation or had the first claim assigned. Otherwise, the first promisee (and second promissor) are not in force majeure, even if he/she cannot do anything about it.

Putting myself in the difficult position of the intermediate contracting party, for purely strategic purposes, I would limit myself to a softer defence: the "contractor" is in default and claims force majeure, which the promisee does not accept. However, that excuse to comply makes it impossible for the first promisee to perform with its own promisee. It is, however, a waterfall that the final promisee knew about because he/she knew that the intervention of the contractor was necessary, and it is not something that the first promisee put in later on its own and whose risk he/she has to bear. The risk of the contractor was a risk that affected both of promisees, and especially the final creditor knows that its immediate debtor cannot do a hedge deal now and find another one. And the first promisee just stands there, in the twilight of "sharing a common risk", without using force majeure. Because it is substantially different, to claim that this risk that happens to the first promisee is its force majeure, that the final promisee has to tolerate it rather than to state that this risk that happens is "our common risk" and both promisees have to share its cost because both bear the happening of the fatal contingency.

2.15. WHAT IS REINSURED IS INSURED

Insurance companies have COVID-19 as an enemy on several fronts. But it seems appropriate to highlight the one that is actually less specific to the sector, and more specific to insurance as an ordinary payment obligation. It is not that COVID-19 is insured, which it is not, but rather that *sometimes* losses are insured that do not arise from a *material* contingency and it turns out that the *pandemic* has not been registered as a cover exclusion clause. Health insurance, life insurance, death insurance, income protection insurance, credit insurance, and surety insurance are the outstanding cases.

It is time to ask, always anxiously, if the insurance company can release itself by claiming the force majeure exception. Suppose that the premium was not adjusted upwards for the increased risk generally caused by COVID-19; or that the law prevented (as in personal insurance) this adjustment for increased risk. The answer is obvious: if the premium was adjusted upwards, the entire risk belongs to the insurer; if the premium was not adjusted and this imbalance is not attributable to the malice of the insured, the entire risk remains with the insurer. The only exception is in the case where the insurer has recourse to Article 11 of the Insurance Contract Act, under which he/she is allowed to adjust the premium.

RD-law 15/2020 has attributed to the "Consorcio de Compensación de Seguros" (CCS) a function of extraordinary and last resort reinsurer against these losses. Article 7 RDL 15/2020 authorises it to accept in reinsurance the risks assumed by private insurance companies authorised to operate in the credit and surety lines of insurance, who so request. There is a certain retroactive effect of the rule.

Let us note that this change also has a meaning in ordinary force majeure terms. *From the moment an insurer can reinsure a risk, that risk ceases to be force majeure (if it ever was) for the insurer.*

2.16. EVENT TICKETING PLATFORMS

There are various ticket platforms, though the most popular in Spain is perhaps *Ticketea*. Most of them were caught by the COVID-19 storm.

Many music concerts and public performances of a recreational nature were contracted before COVID-19, and the ticket fees had been paid. It is certain that the concerts will not be held. A problem arises as the tickets were obtained through a platform manager or independent entrepreneur, different from the sponsor of the event. Now a refund is requested. The price of the tickets was charged by the platform, which is a mere carrier, but in the price of the ticket a carrier's fee was included. The sponsor of the event does not intend to return to the customer the premium that was kept by the platform manager. Should the manager return the part of the price that represented the remuneration of his/her ticket agency services to the customer?

The answer is *no*. Obviously, this manager already performed, performance which is, moreover, irreversible. The singer on duty will not sing and the promoter will not pay him/her, although he/she will certainly have to suffer, at the very least, the loss of the expected profits. But the tickets were sold, the manager's duty was performed and concluded. Therefore, the COVID-19 risk has impacted both parties (customer and platform) after the risk was definitely located with the customer, who can no longer distribute it by contract. Now the sales commission for the ticket is for the customer a wholly frustrated investment. However, it is his/her risk. Additionally, unless otherwise agreed, it is not a good solution that the promoter also bears the risk of the sales commission.

Strictly speaking, this scenario can be generalised to many structures of social life. Let us imagine that I had purchased a fabulous trip to the Far East, for which the Spanish authorities, or the authorities of the destination, prescribe special vaccinations that must be administered one month before the trip. I pay for the vaccinations, which might not be cheap, and finally COVID-19 puts an end to my dreams of travelling. It is clear that the consumer definitely suffers the "frustration" of the cost of the vaccine, although there was neither failure in the administration of the vaccine nor did such a vaccine fail to bring about its proper effect, regardless that in the end the travel failed to materialise. One could imagine countless similar scenarios: there is an endless number of contracts that could have been concluded one month before a trip, which are now useless following the cancellation of the travel plans. The customer must know that with COVID-19 he/she has irretrievably lost two things – the pleasure of the trip and the equipment bought for it. We have yet to see whether the customer will get back what he/she advanced to the travel company.[12]

12 This peril has not been offset by Commission Recommendation (EU) 2020/648 of 13 May 2020 on vouchers offered to passengers and travellers as an alternative to reimbursement for cancelled package travel and transport services in the context of the COVID-19 pandemic.

PORTUGAL'S COVID-19 LEGISLATION AND THE CHALLENGES RAISED FOR THE CHANGE OF CIRCUMSTANCES REGIME

Henrique Sousa ANTUNES*

During the recent period of Portugal's financial bailout, following the severe effects of the global financial crisis of 2008, the courts demonstrated a clear reluctance to accept claims for contract termination or modification due to change of circumstances. Within this framework, the Portuguese legislator's responses to the pandemic raises challenges for the change of circumstances regime. The legislative activity to which COVID-19 has given rise tests the traditional understanding regarding the foundations of the institute, certainly with regard to cases related to the pandemic, but also regarding situations of unenforceability with different grounds.

* Catholic University of Portugal.

1. INTRODUCTION: DISRUPTION TO CONTRACT OBLIGATIONS CAUSED BY COVID-19

As has been the case in many legal orders, the appearance of COVID-19 and the measures taken by the State as a result of the pandemic present a challenge for Portuguese contract law. COVID-19 has emerged in the different countries as a direct or indirect cause of non-fulfilment of obligations or, at least, as a reason for adjusting the contractual position of the parties, due to the great sacrifice connected with fulfilment of the duties to be performed.

Disruption to contract relations may be seen in situations where performance becomes impossible, either temporarily or definitively, and in cases where, although performance is still possible, fulfilment by the debtor appears to be unenforceable since the performances are clearly disproportionate or because fulfilment of the obligations would be excessively onerous. A distinction should be made between these two situations.

Identifying performance as being temporarily or permanently impossible presupposes that COVID-19 prevents its fulfilment. A number of examples may be found, including, in particular, certain effects of the state of emergency measures decreed by the public authorities: a trip has been cancelled, a school has closed, a show has been postponed, the debtor failed to carry out a building contract or to supply goods. The impossibility may also be due to the debtor being infected with the new coronavirus: the debtor was unable to enter into a promised contract, or to be represented in that act, or was physically unable to fulfil a personal provision to which he/she had committed (e.g. painting artwork, composing music, directing a film, producing a text). There are many examples, of course.

These are situations in which the obligation is extinguished due to the appearance of a "logical imperative".[1] Identifying a situation as impossible implies, then, determining which party should assume the loss resulting from that extinguishment. Is the creditor still required to perform the counter-obligation or is he/she, instead, exonerated from such counter-performance? The following questions will serve as illustrations: Are passengers of a cancelled flight entitled to demand a refund of any sums paid? Can parents legitimately refuse to pay monthly school fees or, at least, demand a reduction in the price? Are music festival-goers entitled to have the price they paid for the ticket refunded? Can a sponsor of a sporting competition be exonerated from paying the sponsorship sum because the event has been suspended?

In general terms, Article 795(1) of the Portuguese Civil Code places the burden of the loss of the counter-performance on the debtor: "When in a

---

1 Nuno Pinto Oliveira, *Princípios de Direito dos Contratos* (Coimbra Editora 2011) 564.

bilateral contract one of the performances becomes impossible, the creditor is not bound to counter perform and is entitled, if he has already done so, to demand its restoration in the terms laid down for unjust enrichment". As a result of the community impact of COVID-19, the legislator adapted the application of this general principle in several areas.

The situation of unenforceability is different. Performance is possible but involves considerable sacrifice for the debtor. Extinguishment of the obligation is not an imposition by the nature of things. Modification or extinguishment of the obligation occurs "as a result of a practical (normative) imperative, whereby the obligation is modified or extinguished as a result of good faith, embodied in the (sub)principle of proportionality".[2]

The pandemic has had a significant economic impact on many business sectors, leading to imbalance in the performance agreed or, to those who are disadvantaged, lacking the financial capacity to satisfy the commitments they have agreed with third parties. This latter situation is evident in the culture, sport and tourism sectors, and in many commercial activities, namely gyms, hairdressers and restaurants, and affects both business owners and employees.

The topic we have chosen for this brief contribution relates, precisely, to the relevance of unenforceability caused by COVID-19. The aim, in particular, is to consider the institutes which, classically, the law provides the debtor with to protect his/her interests, and to assess, in the light of this, the reach of the legal instruments created by the legislator in the current times. The main challenges we wish to address are definition of the scope of application of the general rules and of the special regimes on unenforceability, and the difficulties in making the new rules compatible with the theoretical and practical framework of the general law.

2. UNENFORCEABILITY IN PORTUGUESE LAW

Unenforceability in the field of contracts includes two situations: where the performances are clearly disproportionate, i.e. economic impossibility, and where fulfilling the obligations is excessively onerous, i.e. practical or moral impossibility.[3]

Performance is said to be disproportionate when the cost of compliance has increased or the value of the counter-performance has decreased to an extent that changes the equilibrium of the contract. Fulfilling obligations is considered to be excessively onerous when, for material or personal reasons, demanding performance would clearly affect the principle of good faith.

---

2 Ibid.

3 For all, see Nuno Pinto Oliveira, ibid 566 ff.

The spread of SARS-CoV2 has brought about global implications of both these kinds. In general, examples of economic impossibility are a dramatic increase in the costs of the raw materials needed to perform services or to provide goods, or frustration of the intended benefits of entering into the contract.[4] On the other hand, practical impossibility might be the supervening shortage of raw materials or labour or, in our opinion, the repercussions of a serious deterioration in the debtor's patrimonial situation in the contracts to which he/she is a party. The concept of moral impossibility covers personal constraints that prevent fulfilment of the provision (for example the death of a close relative, provision of family support, accompanying of other dependent persons).

The stability of the contract may be affected by a situation where the performances are clearly disproportionate. This is a lesson in comparative law that the Portuguese law has welcomed.[5] In some soft law solutions that serve as a reference for international trade and legal orders in general, changes of circumstances that give rise to situations of fundamental imbalance in the provisions exonerate the debtor.

According to the UNIDROIT Principles of International Commercial Contracts (PICC), the disadvantaged party may request renegotiation of the contract in the case of hardship (Art 6.2.3.) "where the occurrence of events fundamentally alters the equilibrium of the contract either because the cost of a party's performance has increased or because the value of the performance a party receives has diminished" (Art 6.2.2.). Likewise, Article 6.111 of the Principles of European Contract Law (PECL) on "Change of Circumstances" reads: "(1) A party is bound to fulfil its obligations even if performance has become more onerous, whether because the cost of performance has increased or because the value of the performance it receives has diminished. (2) If, however, performance of the contract becomes excessively onerous because of a change of circumstances, the parties are bound to enter into negotiations with a view to adapting the contract or terminating it ...".

And in the case of situations of economic or personal sacrifice of the debtor that exceed the limits of reasonableness? Although some legal orders admit *difficultas praestandi* as a reason for impossibility of performance, this solution seems to be reserved for very limited situations of practical impossibility (a ring falling to the bottom of the ocean serves as a paradigm) or situations of moral impossibility (the debtor's personal impediments). This is the case in German law (§275(2) and (3) of the Civil Code – BGB).[6]

---

4 See, in particular, *Unidroit Principles 2016*, Article 6.2.2., comments, 218 ff.

5 For a comparative law perspective, see Ewoud Hondius, Hans Christoph Grigoleit (eds), *Unexpected Circumstances in European Contract Law* (Cambridge University Press 2011).

6 In a dialogue between the German law and the Portuguese law on the subject, see Catarina Monteiro Pires, *Impossibilidade da Prestação* (Almedina 2017) 438 ff, and *Contratos. I. Perturbações na Execução* (Almedina 2019) 22 ff.

From a traditional perspective, Portuguese law seems to reject any general relevance of excessive onerousness in the fulfilment of obligations.[7] *Difficultas praestandi* does not constitute a cause of impossibility of performance or late performance not attributable to the debtor, and the obligation is not therefore extinguished.[8] In the preparatory work for the Portuguese Civil Code, Vaz Serra proposed that extraordinary difficulty (limit of sacrifice) should be admitted as a reason for exonerating the debtor. The solution was rejected, however, due to the fears that the uncertainty and discretion would bring to the certainty of the regime. Today, there are those who advocate a return to Vaz Serra's option, in the following terms (inclusion of an Art 790-A in the Civil Code): "If the performance is excessively difficult, in such manner that it would be grossly contrary to good faith to require fulfilment, the debtor may be exonerated from the obligation or may obtain modification of it".[9]

Without prejudice to the above, Portuguese law lays down some specific situations in which excessive onerousness for the debtor is considered, for example:

1. on monetary compensation – "Compensation shall be fixed in money, whenever natural restoration is not possible, does not fully repair the harm or is excessively onerous for the debtor" (Art 566(1) of the Civil Code);
2. on the impossibility of restitution – "If a loan is of a thing other than money and restitution becomes impossible or extremely difficult due to a reason not attributable to the borrower, the latter shall pay the value that the thing has when the obligation is due" (Art1149 of the Civil Code).

Some legal theory, however, recognises that cases of excessive onerousness may prove to be so severe that the absence of a response in the law is untenable. It therefore proposes providing the debtor with the benefit of applying the principle of good faith in fulfilment of obligations, abuse of rights, collision of duties or the criterion of excusability.[10]

In our view, situations of excessive onerousness should be assessed in the light of the requirements for termination or modification of the contract due to change of circumstances (Arts 437–439 of the Civil Code).

With regard to this legal institute, there must be a change of the circumstances on which the parties based the decision to contract, that change must be

7 Thus, João de Matos Antunes Varela, *Das Obrigações em Geral*, vol II, (7th edn, Almedina 1997) 68 ff.

8 See Maria de Lurdes Pereira, *Conceito de Prestação e Destino da Contraprestação* (Almedina 2001) 75 ff.

9 Nuno Pinto Oliveira, *Princípios de Direito dos Contratos* (Coimbra Editora 2011) 571.

10 See José Carlos Brandão Proença, *Lições de Cumprimento e Não Cumprimento das Obrigações* (3rd edn, Universidade Católica Editora 2019) 224 ff.

unexpected, one of the parties must have suffered harm, the principle of good faith must be seriously affected, the harm must not fall within the risks inherent in the contract, and the injured party must not be in default at the time of the change of circumstances.

By subjecting situations of excessive onerousness to an appreciation of these conditions, the law could be sensitive to the debtor's situation, while still respecting the primacy of the principle of *pacta sunt servanda*. And the different situations of unenforceability would be dealt with homogeneously, with the strictness that contract stability requires. The suggested distinction between clear disproportionality of performances and fulfilment of obligations that is excessively onerous is rejected.

The scope of our reflection goes further, however. Should the debtor's lack of economic resources be included within excessive onerousness? Can the debtor benefit from modification or extinguishment of the obligation if, by reason of the supervening occurrence of a situation of unemployment, suspension of an employment contract, or closure of his/her own commercial or industrial establishment, he/she is deprived of the financial conditions that allow him/her to pay service charges (e.g. water, electricity, communications, etc.), rent, credit repayments, or the amount due if a promised contract is entered into?

In general, Portuguese legal theory does not afford relevance to the debtor's lack of economic resources in terms of fulfilment of his/her obligation, this only being relevant to the application of the legal institutes of bankruptcy or insolvency.[11] We have argued a different approach.[12] And, as will shall see, this may be restated in times of COVID-19.

It might be noted that, although the economic imbalance of the performances serves as a reference for the issue of change of circumstances in codifications of soft law, these codifications embrace the formula of excessive onerousness. And, in this context, the rules of the Draft Common Frame of Reference of European Private Law (DCFR) appear to add legitimacy to the debate on the pertinence of the debtor's lack of economic resources, by appealing to a criterion of justice. In Article III.1:110 – Variation or termination by court on a change of circumstances, we may read:

> (1) An obligation must be performed even if performance has become more onerous, whether the cost of performance has increased or because the value of what is to be received in return has diminished. (2) If, however, performance of a contractual obligation or of an obligation arising from a unilateral juridical act becomes so onerous because of an exceptional change of circumstances that it would be manifestly unjust to hold the debtor to the obligation a court may (vary or terminate the obligation …).

---

11 In this sense, see, for all, Inocêncio Galvão Telles, *Direito das Obrigações* (7th edn, Coimbra Editora 1997) 365, note 1.

12 Henrique Sousa Antunes, 'A alteração das circunstâncias no direito europeu dos contratos' (2014) 47 Cadernos de Direito Privado 3 ff.

It appears that determining whether there is injustice associated with maintaining the obligation includes an assessment of the debtor's economic situations: "... the assessment of justice may lead the court to examine, for the application of the provision, factors which are external to the contract itself, e.g. the economic situation of the promisor, its relative position on the market and even its related contracts with third parties".[13] A case-by-case analysis of situations submitted for the court's appreciation is a requirement for the fulfilment of the general clauses:

> In any case, the assessment of the onerousness of the performance as being excessive or severe is difficult and a case-by-case analysis cannot be avoided. Furthermore, such an assessment cannot be made by means of arithmetical parameters, but is a task for the court that has to consider the circumstances of the particular case in order to establish the seriousness of the consequences for the debtor in maintaining performance as agreed.[14]

A different approach only seems to be admissible if there is a concrete intervention by the legislator.

3. THE CHALLENGES RAISED BY THE LEGISLATOR'S RESPONSES TO THE PANDEMIC

The legislative activity to which COVID-19 has given rise has tested the traditional understanding regarding the foundations of the institute of contract termination or modification due to change of circumstances, and it has brought with it several challenges to the legal application of the regime, certainly with regard to cases related to the pandemic, but also regarding situations of unenforceability with different origins.

First, in passing different laws that interfere with the fulfilment of obligations with the aim of freeing the debtor from the excessive onerousness that would result from performance, the legislator chose not to limit the relevance of change of circumstances to situations where performances are clearly disproportionate. And, unequivocally, a debtor's lack of the economic means to fulfil the obligations by which he/she is bound serves as a basis for several of those measures.

Then, the legislator departed from the requirement to demonstrate the existence of harm and a causal link between the change of circumstances and the harm, when it protected situations affected by the economic implications of

---

13 Rodrigo Momberg Uribe, *The effect of a change of circumstances on the binding force of contracts – Comparative perspectives* (Intersentia/Metro 2011) 202.

14 Ibid.

the pandemic. What effects will this approach have regarding the injured party's burden of proof in situations not covered by the law?

Thirdly, the application of the requirement that the principle of good faith must be seriously affected is, by the nature of things, silenced in the legislation passed within the scope of COVID-19. Will this silencing constitute a reason for softening the strictness of the requirement in a judicial context of assessment of the pandemic's impact in situations not covered in the law?

Moreover, the legislator's reaction to the social and economic emergency caused by COVID-19 disregarded any risk sharing executed by law or by agreement of the parties. It did so in recognition of the prevalence of unenforceability over risk sharing. This prioritising seems to favour a restrictive interpretation of the criterion of risk assumption and, also, of acceptance of exceptional circumstances in which, although the injured party bears the burden of the risk, good faith dictates modification of the contract due to change of circumstances.

In fifth place, the COVID-19 legislation allowed debtors with payments in default to benefit from moratoria if the debt relates to an asset with an existential dimension. In our opinion, the civil judge could not take a different approach, given the protection afforded to human dignity.

Lastly, although our list does not profess to be exhaustive, the passing of wide-ranging legislation to cover the contractual implications of the measures taken as a result of the pandemic enhances the importance of the legislator in terms of taking a position on how to exercise contract termination due to change of circumstances and on the timeframe of the effects of this. The aim is to provide certainty to all economic agents affected by the consequences of COVID-19.

3.1. RELEVANT CIRCUMSTANCES

According to most of the legal theory and case law, it is the concept of basis of the transaction (*Geschäftsgrundlage*) that allows the impact of the change of circumstances on the binding force of the transaction to be recognised (interpretation of the first requirement of Art 437 of the Portuguese Civil Code). Accordingly, only those facts which, with respect to one or both parties, essentially determined the will to negotiate, and therefore condition the binding effect of the representations made, will be taken into account. Now, the economic capacity to honour the commitments made is certainly not an implicit condition for concluding the contract which the counterparty would have accepted or good faith would have required.

If we take this approach, the debtor's economic situation at the time of fulfilment tends to be irrelevant. Knowing, however, that the requirements of Article 437 of the Civil Code, listed above, are cumulative, we believe that taking the requirement of good faith separately requires reinterpretation of the circumstances to be taken into account, in the light of the theory on the *rebus sic stantibus* clause. Circumstances which, existing at the time the contract was concluded, were irrelevant, gain relevance in the light of good faith: "… provided that demanding the obligations … assumed (by the injured party) seriously affects the principles of good faith" (Art 437(1) of the Civil Code).

It must be said that this debate is less relevant in the context of COVID-19, since the classical approach has always accepted the institute of contract termination or modification due to a change of the circumstances forming the "broad basis of the transaction" (Kegel): this concept includes situations that affect the social existence of the parties, examples of which are economic crises, revolutions, unforeseeable changes to the law or natural disasters. The consequences of the pandemic therefore fall within the "broad basis of the transaction".

There are, however, several concerns. During the recent period of the country's financial bailout, following the severe effects of the global financial crisis of 2008, the Portuguese courts demonstrated a clear reluctance to accept claims for contract termination or modification due to change of circumstances. We may consider, for example, the Supreme Court of Justice Ruling of 23 January 2014, on a claim based on supervening economic insufficiency. The ruling stated:

> unlike mistake, where the basis of the transaction is unilateral, relating exclusively to the mistaken party, in change of circumstances it is bilateral, relating simultaneously to both parties …. It follows, *tout court*, that a change of the parties' personal circumstances is not capable of falling within the institute. Namely the invoked 'significant decrease in the claimants' purchasing power and the situation of unemployment that the claimant has found herself in since October 2009'. An extension, indeed, of the prohibition on it being invoked as grounds for demanding any reduction, discount or abatement of the debt, or postponement of its due date, such as results from *beneficium competentiae* or *ne egeant* in Roman law.[15]

The contrast with the current situation may be seen with an example. Decree-Law No. 10-J/2020, of 26 March, set out exceptional measures to protect the credits of families, businesses, private charitable institutions and other social economy entities, as well as a special regime of personal guarantees of the State, within the scope of COVID-19. The preamble highlights the debtor's lack of economic means as a reason for the measures:

> The consequences for the economy (of COVID-19 and the state of emergency) require the adoption of urgent measures in order to protect Portuguese families, with regard to mortgages on permanent privately-owned residences, and national companies to

15 Case 1117/10.9TVLSB.P1.S1 (reporting judge: Granja da Fonseca).

> ensure that their treasury and liquidity are strengthened, to mitigate the effects of the fall in economic activity. Sole traders, private charitable institutions, non-profit organisations and other social economy entities are also covered by this protection regime.

Accordingly, any influence of the COVID-19 legislative approach on a court's appreciation of situations of economic impact from the pandemic that are not covered by the legal regimes approved may give rise to a contradiction of decisions being invoked, considering the case law of the 2008 crisis.

Let us now consider the existence of other cases of unenforceability, not caused by the pandemic. In our opinion, the main utility of the concept of "broad basis of the transaction" can be found in the justification of a competence of the legislator, motivated by risk sharing: "In the case of risks resulting from the social situation, disturbance to the broad basis of the transaction should, in strict terms of justice, be borne by all those who share that same situation".[16] While, from a distributive justice perspective, a change of the "broad basis of the transaction" argues in favour of broad legislative intervention that softens the debtor's responsibility, the judicial tendency to regard the debtor's economic situation as irrelevant in the absence of a change of the "broad basis of the transaction" appears to offend the constitutional principle of equality: the performance is unenforceable, and that should be sufficient.

In the area of judicial review of contracts, the concept of excessive onerousness must be immune to the individual or collective impact of the change of circumstances. The concept of "broad basis of the transaction" is, insofar as commutative justice is applied, useless. Let us repeat: the performance is unenforceable, and that should be sufficient.

3.2. THE CAUSE OF THE HARM

Contract termination or modification due to change of circumstances is dependent on proof of a causal link between that change and the harm suffered by the counterparty. The binding force of contracts can only be adjusted if the patrimonial loss suffered or the personal sacrifice endured are due to unexpected subsequent facts.

The COVID-19 legislation at times waives proof of harm and at other times dispenses with proof of the causal link between the pandemic and the harm (fulfilment of the *conditio sine qua non*). We will illustrate each of these situations.

As we know, Decree-Law No. 10-J/2020 set out exceptional measures to protect the credits of families, businesses, private charitable institutions and

---

[16] Mariana Fontes da Costa, *Da Alteração Superveniente das Circunstâncias (Em especial à luz dos contratos bilateralmente comerciais)* (Almedina 2017) 403.

other social economy entities. The entities in question benefited from moratoria on the payment of capital, rents, interest, commission or other charges on the credit transactions they had contracted, and from a prohibition on the revoking, in whole or in part, of credit facilities in their favour and loans granted (Art 4). What conditions must be met to modify those contractual credit relations? Companies and social economy entities are required, in short, to have their registered office and economic activity in Portugal, and must not be in default with the burdened financial institutions and with the Tax and Social Security Authorities (whereas in the case of mortgage credit for the permanent privately-owned residence of a natural person, there is an additional requirement of proof of personal or professional effects caused by COVID-19 – Art 2).

Law No. 4-C/2020, of 6 April, established exceptional rules for situations of late payment of rent owed pursuant to urban housing and non-housing rental contracts, within the scope of the pandemic. Support is granted to tenants and to landlords. A distinction was made between housing and non-housing rentals. In the case of the former, it is necessary to demonstrate a fall of at least 20% in the income of the tenant's or of the landlord's household and, in addition, a debt-to-income ratio of the tenant greater than 35% or, in relation to the landlord, evidence of the causal link between the fall in income and the non-payment of rents by tenants under the provision set out in the same law (Art 3(1)). For non-housing rentals, the support measures are, to put it succinctly, justified by the legal or administrative suspension of the tenants' business (Art 7).

In the aforementioned Decree-Law, the legislator waived any proof of the existence of harm to the companies being benefited. In Law No. 4-C/2020 it is required that a loss of income be demonstrated, but without requiring the tenant to prove that such loss was a result of the pandemic. While, pursuant to Article 4(1) of Ministerial Implementing Order No. 91/2020, of 14 April, intended to execute Article 3 of Law No. 4-C/2020, "the fall in income … corresponds to a decrease in income of over 20% resulting from a fact related to the epidemiological situation caused by COVID-19", the reality is that the only requirement is a comparison of income between the periods considered (sub-paragraph a)).

The contrast with the judicial decisions in the context of the 2008 global financial crisis is great. One example is the Supreme Court of Justice Ruling of 10 January 2013, on a claim to modify a credit facility agreement, on the grounds of economic insufficiency.[17] It was claimed that the international financial crisis had affected the wine production financed with the credit obtained.

The ruling reads: "It is a fact that the 'subprime' crisis originating in the United States of America triggered an international financial crisis that spread to the economic sphere and deepened in 2008, 2009 and 2010 and gave rise to

[17] Case 187/10.4TVLSB.L2.S1 (reporting judge: Orlando Afonso).

the current crisis in Portugal, but that economic crisis (which is not denied) does not lead, *per se*, and in general terms, to the application of Article 437 of the CC. There must be a direct correlation that is factually demonstrated in the proceedings between the general economic crisis and the specific economic activity of a given agent in order for us to speak of an unexpected change of circumstances".

And, yet, the following was deemed to have been proven in the proceedings:

> 14 – In the summer of 2007, the excess of mortgages granted in the United States of America, which became known as the 'subprime crisis', triggered an international financial crisis that spread to the economic sphere and deepened in 2008, 2009 and 2010, creating a situation of generalised recession among economies, which is felt in Portugal, namely through an increase in unemployment, an increase in the number of families resorting to social assistance, a decrease in consumption and company closures, a decrease in GDP and an increase in external debt; 36 – Sales of the company 'DD, Ld[a]' fell, when compared to 2006, 5.24% in 2007, 38.25% in 2008 and 55.66% in 2009; 37 – Which was due to the crisis described in 14; 38 – For the same reason, purchasers of wine from that company either do not pay or delay payment.

The legislator's COVID-19 options compel the COVID-19 judge to rethink his approach to the economic impacts of a change of the "broad basis of the transaction". The legal waiver of a causal link between the change of circumstances and the harm is based on a criterion of the high probability of the sacrifice being attributable to the change of circumstances, and this likelihood, in a judicial context, leads to a presumption of fact.

Accordingly, the COVID-19 judge must set aside the approach used during the recent global financial crisis. When judging cases that are not governed by the pandemic legislation, the use of a presumption of fact on causality appears to be an imperative of equality, when the conditions being assessed are identical or materially equivalent and when the facts correspond to the timeframe of the laws passed. It seems clear to us, therefore, that when the judge considers a claim for termination of a contract covered by a moratorium established by the legislator, he/she must presume causality between the harm that the interested party is called upon to demonstrate and the implications of COVID-19.

Meanwhile, the judge does not appear to be allowed to exclude the application of a COVID-19 law on the grounds of demonstration of absence of harm or of a causal link between the change of circumstances and the harm, considering the hierarchical parity of the laws (Civil Code and the COVID-19 legislation) and the relation of speciality between them.

In our opinion, the judge is therefore prevented, in the context of COVID-19 legislation, from ascertaining whether the causal link has been established, namely confirmation of the *conditio sine qua non*, or affording negative relevance to a virtual cause (in other words, the possibility of limiting or excluding the application of the effects set out in the law on the grounds of a demonstration that, in the absence of the pandemic and the measures taken by the public authorities in relation to it, another fact would have caused the same harm).

Another question concerns assessment of the continuation of COVID-19 impacts beyond the timeframe of the protections established by the legislator. As the application of the special law is excluded, the competent rules are Articles 437–439 of the Civil Code. Considering the extent of the benefits afforded by the COVID-19 legislation, the end of the measures will indicate cessation of a relationship of probability between the pandemic and the harm. The use of a presumption of fact in this case appears, then, to be ruled out. Moreover, the judge can call on instruments that help to dilute the causal connection between COVID-19 and the economic effects due to it as a consequence of the passage of time. In this regard, we may mention abuse of rights (Art 334 of the Civil Code) and contributory fault (Art 570 of the Civil Code).

3.3. SERIOUS EFFECT ON THE PRINCIPLES OF GOOD FAITH

In the Civil Code, good faith is designed as a requirement that is dependent on the cumulative confirmation of the other conditions for contract termination or modification due to change of circumstances. The law seems to be unaware of the polarising nature of that principle, thus allowing for interpretations that would bind the debtor to fulfil the obligation, even though such a requirement would seriously affect the principle of good faith. If the change were to circumstances other than the basis of the transaction or if it were covered by the risks inherent in the contract, good faith would be of no use as grounds for contract termination or modification due to change of circumstances. As we have stated, we have a different interpretation. We acknowledge, however, that several authors have called on good faith to play a key role in contract review, in particular with regard to the allocation of risk.[18] And some have gone even further, as in the words of Menezes Cordeiro:

> the person who, by operation of fact or of law, revolutionary or otherwise, since both are subject to the investigation of the Science of Law …, finds himself with abnormal difficulty in complying with certain obligations cannot, *a priori*, be deprived of correction, imposed by material justice, contained in good faith, and deposited in the Civil Code by the legislator of 1966. This reasoning applies to general difficulties of an economic nature.[19]

---

18 Thus, Mário Júlio de Almeida Costa, *Direito das Obrigações* (12th edn, Almedina 2009) 347. For all, see Mariana Fontes da Costa, *Da Alteração Superveniente das Circunstâncias (Em especial à luz dos contratos bilateralmente comerciais)* (Almedina 2017) 384 ff.

19 *Da Boa Fé no Direito Civil* (Coimbra 1997) 936.

The predominance of good faith was, in fact, Vaz Serra's understanding, in the preparatory work for the Portuguese Civil Code:

> from what is said in the text we may conclude that the contract may be terminated or revised even if the requirements of the basis of the transaction theory are not met ..., if good faith so justifies. In fact, it may happen that, although good faith would not oblige the other party to accept the presumption in question, the situation has become such that it is objectively inadmissible for that other party to impose on the presuming party that the contract will be performed without any modification. It is then termination or modification based on justice or objective good faith, as a means of ensuring respect for these in a situation that appears profoundly different from that which existed when the contract was made.[20]

The COVID-19 legislation is based on a presumption of material justice, constructing situations of unenforceability due to excessive onerousness without a concrete assessment of the economic impact of the pandemic on the beneficiary's circumstances. The legislator waives any assessment of the impossibility in practice of fulfilling the obligation, sufficing itself, basically, with objective criteria of loss of income.

The choice of the Portuguese legislator is understandable, considering the general and abstract nature of the law and the need for efficacy of the measures taken. Criticism of the vague nature of some of the formulas used, particularly by the German COVID-19 legislator, such as the effect on the reasonable standard of living of the consumer or on the economic basis of the activity of a micro-enterprise (*Gesetz zur Abmilderung der Folgen der COVID-19-Pandemie im Zivil-, Insolvenz-, und Strafverfahrensrecht – Vom 27 März 2020*) is thus avoided.

The contrast between these approaches is all the more striking if we note that, unlike the German legislator, the Portuguese legislator did not carry out the weighing up exercise which, by reason of the existence of two parties, the principle of good faith would determine. The conditions for the unenforceability of fulfilment of the obligation are, clearly, dependent on an assessment of the debtor's situation, but also, simultaneously, on an appreciation of the creditor's needs: "Therefore, even when the supervening events have made the performance of the affected party excessively onerous, if the counter-performance is also severely burdened by the new circumstances, the relevant provisions are not applicable".[21]

Knowing the relevance of good faith in change of circumstances in line with the civil law, has the legislator made it legitimate for the judge to use presumptions

---

20 'Resolução ou Modificação do Contrato por Alteração das Circunstâncias' (1957) 68 Boletim do Ministério da Justiça 319 ff.

21 Rodrigo Momberg Uribe, *The effect of a change of circumstances on the binding force of contracts – Comparative perspectives* (Intersentia/Metro 2011) 203.

of fact in situations that are not covered by the COVID-19 legislation passed? It cannot be denied that identical cases will justify converging approaches, relieving the injured party of the burden of proof. Only the irrelevance of the creditor's situation appears to be excluded, by virtue of the different nature of the legislative and judicial activities.

In these terms, it seems acceptable to soften the severity with which the requirement was interpreted in relation to the impacts of the financial and economic crisis in Portugal's recent past.

3.4. CHANGE NOT COVERED BY THE RISKS INHERENT IN THE CONTRACT

Contract termination or modification due to change of circumstances is not admitted if the injured party has assumed the risk of that change. However, it is often accepted that there is a basis for risk sharing when the "broad basis of the transaction" is affected. Overlooking the risk assumed in a contract or established by law is justified, since "in cases where coexistence in society is affected ... the State is often unable to (or refuses to) provide a response to claims for compensation for its citizens, or only does so in an insufficient and often belated manner".[22]

The pragmatism of risk sharing determined by the legislator demonstrates the prevalence of unenforceability over risk. It should be noted, however, that other situations of community reach fall through the cracks of the law. And, in any case, even if it is a case of collective unenforceability, it cannot be accepted that, due to the specific nature of the excessive onerousness, the answer may differ between distributive justice and commutative justice. The topic prompts some thoughts.

The COVID-19 measures taken within the cultural or artistic fields or relating to the tourism sector (Decree-Law No. 10-I/2020, of 26 March, and Decree-Law No. 17/2020, of 23 April, respectively) serve as an example. In any case, and generally speaking, restitution is excluded by a new opportunity for performance, ruling out an immediate refund of the amount of payment, established in Article 795 of the Civil Code.

Risk sharing is asserted. The following is written regarding tourism:

> This regime seeks to strike a balance between the financial sustainability of the economic operators and the rights of consumers, which, notwithstanding the current context, may not be suppressed or eliminated. To this extent, although some consumer rights may undergo temporary and localised changes, the regime established offers

22 Mariana Fontes da Costa, *Da Alteração Superveniente das Circunstâncias (Em especial à luz dos contratos bilateralmente comerciais)* (Almedina 2017) 403, note 1028.

> distinct protection for consumers who are in a situation of unemployment and, as such, in a particularly vulnerable state (preamble of Decree-Law No. 17/2020).

The solution was to replace the immediate reimbursement of the payment with a refund conditional on the absence of a rescheduling of the trip or the use of a voucher issued by December 31, 2021 (Art 3(1)–(3) of Decree-Law No. 17/2020). However, risk sharing is limited to the unenforceability for the counterparty: "Up until 30 September 2020, travellers who are in a situation of unemployment may claim a refund of the total amount spent, to be made within 14 days" (Art 3(6) of Decree-Law No. 17/2020).

Risk sharing is also suggested by the European Law Institute (ELI), in Principle 13(3) of the ELI Principles for the COVID-19 Crisis: "In conformity with the principle of solidarity, States should ensure that the consequences of the disruption of contractual relationships, such as the cancellation of travel arrangements, should not be at the sole risk of one party, in particular of a consumer or SME".

In Portuguese case law, risk is often treated as consideration for the advantage expected from entering into the contract. In this sense, it is up to the debtor to assume the loss corresponding to the non-use of the benefit, without the law or the parties having pronounced specifically on the aforementioned burden. A criterion of implicit risk distribution prevails, attributing the loss of the benefit pursued to the party who was bound by the performance.

It appears that maintaining the indicated guidance is out of line with the relevance given to situations of unenforceability by the COVID-19 legislation. If we take as a reference the implications of the current economic situation on compliance with promissory contracts previously entered into, the Supreme Court of Justice Ruling of 10 April 2014[23] will serve as an example. The court had to consider the modification or termination of a promissory contract for sale and purchase due to the frustration of the forecast resale value of the property the purchase of which had been promised, as a result of the financial and real estate crisis of 2007 and the subsequent insolvency of the injured party. The ruling reads:

> In the tumultuous world of our modern business society, the pursuit of gain is the ambition that is patently evident in its most visible form, and this situation determines the type of relationship that will direct the conduct of the various commercial agents and also command the domestic behaviour of each of the citizens who will conduct business in this commercial context. Good business ethics, understood as a value linked to the organisation aimed at ensuring the company's good results in the market, is associated with obtaining profit, that is, return on the result of the services provided to clients. This specific commercial activity also involves the

---

23 Case 1167/10.5TBACB-E.C1.S1. (reporting judge: Silva Gonçalves)

> contingency of the risk of losing the monetary value that the entrepreneur provided for financial investment, an event that may materialise as a result of, in the meantime and negatively, changes in the particularities of the market in which the proposed plan is included. This characteristic risk, more precisely the conscious acceptance of the degree of uncertainty in obtaining the expected return on a given financial application or investment made, will have to be singularly calculated and taken into consideration by the investor in the position he takes before each planned deal.

In my opinion, applying the change of circumstances regime is incompatible with the use of a *ubi commoda, ibi incommoda* principle, thereby seeking to preserve the contract's binding force. Another formula that also appears unsatisfactory is the economic balance of the contract, which considers, together, the law, the contract clauses, the type of business, the commercial practices and the effects of the parties' motivations when establishing the contract's content.[24] I believe that the injured party should only be prohibited from invoking change of circumstances if the law allocates the risk to him, if the parties expressly stipulate this, and in aleatory contracts. Any other approach would overturn the primacy of good faith, subordinating it to the simple teleology of risk.

A stricter understanding of the concept of risk can be read from the unenforceability that gives rise to the COVID-19 legislation. We may note, for example, that, in the wording of the German law, risk is not formulated as a requirement of exclusion, but rather as a criterion for consideration (§313 of the German Civil Code – BGB, entitled "Interference with the basis of the transaction":

> (1) If circumstances which became the basis of a contract have significantly changed since the contract was entered into and if the parties would not have entered into the contract or would have entered into it with different contents if they had foreseen this change, adaptation of the contract may be demanded to the extent that, taking account of all the circumstances of the specific case, in particular the contractual or statutory distribution of risk, one of the parties cannot reasonably be expected to uphold the contract without alteration; … (translation provided by *Bundesministerium der Justiz und für Verbraucherschutz*).

In addition, in the context of the pandemic, the need to restrict the scope that the courts give to risk-taking appears to be reinforced, given the overwhelming manner in which the law modified the content of contracts. Knowing that the legislator acted without conducting the weighing up exercise required by the separate application of the principle of good faith and silencing the different response which, by virtue of the law or the contract, the risk would determine, the role of the courts should fall in line.

---

24 Mariana Fontes da Costa, *Da Alteração Superveniente das Circunstâncias (Em especial à luz dos contratos bilateralmente comerciais)* (Almedina 2017) 383 ff.

Thus, if maintaining a contract seriously affects good faith, equality will even determine paralysis of the risk sharing exercised by the parties or by the law (allowing, at least, modification of the contract). Inspiration is derived from Principle 13(1) of the ELI Principles for the COVID-19 Crisis, on the impossibility of performance:

> Where performance of a contract is temporarily or definitively prevented directly or indirectly due to the COVID-19 outbreak or States' decisions taken in relation to the COVID-19 outbreak, States should ensure that existing law on impossibility or *force majeure* applies in an effective way, and provide reasonable solutions. In particular, the contractual allocation of risk in these instances should be evaluated in the light of existing contracts, background legal regimes and the principle of good faith.

3.5. ABSENCE OF DEFAULT OF THE INJURED PARTY AT THE TIME OF THE CHANGE OF CIRCUMSTANCES

It will be recalled that, according to Article 438 of the Civil Code, the existence of default of the injured party at the time when the change of circumstances occurred prevents contract termination or modification. Although this rule is present in some of the measures taken by the COVID-19 legislator, we discover acknowledgement of the prevalence of existential values when this condition is not a requirement.

Article 4 of Law No. 7/2020, of 10 April, in the wording given to it by Law No. 18/2020, of 29 May, determined a prohibition on the suspension of water, electricity, natural gas and electronic communications supply services until 30 September 2020. In doing so, the legislator included users of those services who had payments overdue, in the following terms (Art 4(4) and (5)):

> 4 – In the event that there are amounts overdue relating to the supply of the services referred to in paragraph 1, a payment plan shall be drawn up; 5 – The payment plan referred to in the previous paragraph is defined by agreement between the supplier and the client, and shall commence from the second month following the end of period set out in paragraph 3 (30 September 2020).

This option of the legislator highlights the humanist framework to which the Law should, by definition, be subject, suggesting that, also in the context of the application of Article 438 of the Civil Code, good faith justifies the application of exceptions to the rule that an injured party in default may not benefit from contract termination or modification due to change of circumstances. Ultimately, the dignity of the human person, on which the legal order is founded, acts as a criterion (Art 1 of the Constitution of the Portuguese Republic).

Meanwhile, the application of this default requirement needs to be expanded on, and a standard solution provided by the legislator will certainly produce benefits: which point in time serves as a reference for the default? The declaration of the pandemic by the World Health Organization? The appearance of the first cases in Portugal? The first declaration of a state of emergency?

4. THE EXERCISE OF RIGHTS

The dimension of the change of circumstances in times of COVID-19 has justified the law overriding the affected party and the judge, bringing greater legal certainty to the management of contractual relations. From the same perspective, it would be important for the Portuguese legislator to make an explicit statement on how to exercise the right to terminate the contract and when termination would produce effects.

In the absence of an agreement of the parties on modification of the contract, this can be enforced judicially.[25] There is, however, a difference of opinion in the legal theory on the judicial or extra-judicial nature of contract termination due to change of circumstances. Among others, the following arguments are presented in favour of the extra-judicial exercise of termination: the principle of freedom of form (Art 219 of the Civil Code); the general rules on termination (Art 436(1) of the Civil Code); the competence of the court to assess the legitimacy of an extra-judicial exercise; the contribution made to preventing backlogs in the courts; the delay in judicial decisions; the production of immediate effects.[26]

In my opinion, judicial exercise of termination is required, considering the wording of the law (namely Articles 437(2) and 439 of the Civil Code), due to the complexity of the analysis of the requirements regarding change of circumstances, the benefits of legal certainty, the potential for litigation that, foreseeably, extra-judicial termination would give rise to, the possibility of preventing the duration of the judicial proceedings from harming the injured party with judicial acceptance of retroactive termination.

I acknowledge, however, that it would be beneficial a legislative intervention on this issue, particularly in the context of the pandemic's effect on the social existence of the parties.

---

25 Catarina Monteiro Pires, 'Efeitos da alteração das circunstâncias' (2013) 145 O Direito 187 ff.

26 See Mariana Fontes da Costa, *Da Alteração Superveniente das Circunstâncias (Em especial à luz dos contratos bilateralmente comerciais)* (Almedina 2017) 507 ff.

5. CONCLUSIONS

Following the above analysis, we may now summarise the main conclusions reached:

1. As has been the case in many legal orders, the appearance of COVID-19 and the measures taken by the State as a result of the pandemic present a challenge for Portuguese contract law. COVID-19 has emerged in the different countries as a direct or indirect cause of non-fulfilment of obligations or, at least, as a reason for adjusting the contractual position of the parties, due to the great sacrifice connected with fulfilment of the duties to be performed.
2. Disruption to contract relations may be seen in situations where performance becomes impossible, either temporarily or definitively, and in cases where, although performance is still possible, fulfilment by the debtor appears to be unenforceable since the performances are clearly disproportionate or because fulfilment of the obligations would be excessively onerous.
3. Performance is said to be disproportionate when the cost of compliance has increased or the value of the counter-performance has decreased to an extent that changes the equilibrium of the contract. Fulfilling obligations is considered to be excessively onerous when, for material or personal reasons, demanding performance would clearly affect the principle of good faith.
4. In my view, situations of excessive onerousness should be assessed in the light of the requirements for termination or modification of the contract due to change of circumstances (Arts 437–439 of the Civil Code).
5. With regard to this legal institute, there must be a change of the circumstances on which the parties based the decision to contract, that change must be unexpected, one of the parties must have suffered harm, the principle of good faith must be seriously affected, the harm must not fall within the risks inherent in the contract, and the injured party must not be in default at the time of the change of circumstances.
6. The legislative activity to which COVID-19 has given rise has tested the traditional understanding regarding the foundations of the institute of contract termination or modification due to change of circumstances, and it has brought with it several challenges to the legal application of the regime, certainly with regard to cases related to the pandemic, but also regarding situations of unenforceability with different origins.
7. During the recent period of Portugal's financial bailout, following the severe effects of the global financial crisis of 2008, the courts demonstrated a clear reluctance to accept claims for contract termination or modification due to change of circumstances.
8. Any influence of the COVID-19 legislative approach on a court's appreciation of situations of economic impact from the pandemic that are

not covered by the legal regimes approved may give rise to a contradiction of decisions being invoked, considering the case law of the 2008 crisis.

9. While, from a distributive justice perspective, a change of the "broad basis of the transaction" argues in favour of broad legislative intervention that softens the debtor's responsibility, the judicial tendency to regard the debtor's economic situation as irrelevant in the absence of a change of the "broad basis of the transaction" appears to offend the constitutional principle of equality: the performance is unenforceable, and that should be sufficient.
10. The COVID-19 legislation at times waives proof of harm and at other times dispenses with proof of the causal link between the pandemic and the harm (fulfilment of the *conditio sine qua non*). The legal waiver of a causal link between the change of circumstances and the harm is based on a criterion of the high probability of the sacrifice being attributable to the change of circumstances, and this likelihood, in a judicial context, leads to a presumption of fact.
11. The judge is prevented, in the context of COVID-19 legislation, from ascertaining whether the causal link has been established, namely confirmation of the *conditio sine qua non*, or affording negative relevance to a virtual cause (in other words, the possibility of limiting or excluding the application of the effects set out in the law on the grounds of a demonstration that, in the absence of the pandemic and the measures taken by the public authorities in relation to it, another fact would have caused the same harm).
12. The COVID-19 legislation is based on a presumption of material justice, constructing situations of unenforceability due to excessive onerousness without a concrete assessment of the economic impact of the pandemic on the beneficiary's circumstances. The legislator waives any assessment of the impossibility in practice of fulfilling the obligation, sufficing itself, basically, with objective criteria of loss of income.
13. Knowing the relevance of good faith in change of circumstances in line with the civil law, has the legislator made it legitimate for the judge to use presumptions of fact in situations that are not covered by the COVID-19 legislation passed? It cannot be denied that identical cases will justify converging approaches, relieving the injured party of the burden of proof.
14. In the context of the pandemic, the need to restrict the scope that the courts give to risk-taking appears to be reinforced, given the overwhelming manner in which the law modified the content of contracts.
15. The waiver of absence of default of the injured party by the COVID-19 legislator with regard to essential goods highlights the humanist framework to which the Law should, by definition, be subject, suggesting that, also in the context of the application of Article 438 of the Civil Code, good faith justifies the application of exceptions to the rule that an injured party in default may not benefit from contract termination.

16. The passing of wide-ranging legislation to cover the contractual implications of the measures taken as a result of the pandemic enhances the importance of the legislator in determining how to exercise, judicially or extra-judicially, contract termination due to change of circumstances and on the timeframe of the effects of this. The aim is to provide certainty to all economic agents affected by the consequences of COVID-19.

PARTICULAR CORONA CONTRACT LAW IN GERMANY

Why Does General Contract Law not Suffice?

Martin SCHMIDT-KESSEL and Christina MÖLLNITZ*

* Both authors, University of Bayreuth.

In order to handle the economic consequences of the COVID-19-pandemic, the German legislator has issued a number of specific rules for certain contracts for a limited period of time. The fact that legislation saw the need for such measures raises the question whether established German contract law is not sufficient to deal with the consequences of a large-scale crisis. This contribution therefore outlines in a first step how the rules of general contract law in Germany apply to contracts affected by the COVID-19-crisis. The second step is dedicated to an analysis of the interaction between the particular rules within the emergency regulation and the general contract law and will conclude with some first tentative answers to the general question concerning the reasons to amend German law by the Corona Contract Law legislation.

1. INTRODUCTION

The COVID-19-pandemic has so far caused unprecedented, far-reaching State intervention into the economy in many, if not all, States around the world.[1] However, a complete public law takeover of the whole economy has not taken place. This results in the fact that COVID-19 has become a stress test also to established contract law: the consequences of the pandemic and of State interventions to contractual relationships have to be dealt with by contract law. However, many national legislators seem not to sufficiently trust the established contract law rules and their application by courts. They have been and still are enacting specific emergency legislation for (all or certain) contracts. Sometimes supervisory authorities are also stepping in to clarify the regulatory framework.

The German legislator has also become active and established some special rules of Corona Contract Law for a limited period of time and only for some particular situations: with the Act of 27 March 2020 a new Article 240 of the *Einführungsgesetz zum Bürgerlichen Gesetzbuch* (Introductory Act to the

---

1 For a first comparative view see Katherina Pistor (ed), *Law in the Time of COVID-19* (Columbia Law School 2020).

German Civil Code (Introductory Act)) was enacted. This Article 240 contains a moratorium for payments on so-called *wesentliche Dauerschuldverhältnisse* (essential long-term contracts) in favour of severely affected consumers and micro-entrepreneurs (Art 240 §1 Introductory Act), a ban on termination for delayed payments under real estate rental and lease contracts (Art 240 §2 Introductory Act), as well as statutory deferrals, termination bans and other changes for interest and redemption payments for consumer credit agreements including mortgages (Art 240 §3 Introductory Act).[2] With the Act of 15 May 2020 a further provision (Art 240 §5 Introductory Act) was established, which enables the organisers of leisure events cancelled for COVID-19 reasons and leisure facilities closed to replace obligations to refund payments to their clients by issuing vouchers.[3]

At least on first sight these interventions seem to be astonishing from a broader perspective: German contract law in general provides for a series of instruments to master consequences of large-scale crises to contracts.[4] In particular the doctrines of impossibility (§§275, 326 BGB), the doctrine of fundamental change of the contract basis (§313 BGB) and the rights to end long-term contracts for serious reason (generally §314 BGB, moreover for instance §§490, 543, 626, 648a BGB) seem to be well established and broadly tested as well as flexible enough to produce sufficient solutions to cope with the COVID-19 crisis in the contract law. We therefore asked ourselves the question for what reasons the German legislator issued the above-mentioned additional provisions and whether it was a right decision to do so. And we started to prepare a comparative research project on exactly this question: Why did or do many legislators and governments react by specific rule-making notwithstanding that their legal orders are well-experienced in dealing with (other) large-scale crises also affecting many contracts and contract parties and in providing for many general rules on risk distribution? In short: What does Corona contract law reveal about the classical instruments? Are there gaps or deficiencies in the well-established law, which could be interpreted as lack of preparedness of the respective legal orders? Did (and do) the specific enactments and decisions reach the political goals attached to them? Is there a kind of general pandemic contract law emerging?

---

2 On this Act see our broad analysis: Christina Möllnitz and Martin Schmidt-Kessel, 'Commentary to article 240 EGBGB', *Uhlenbruck Insolvenzordnung* (15th edn, Vahlen 2020) 355–388 (para 1–186). Moreover, see Martin Schmidt-Kessel, Christina Möllnitz, 'Coronavertragsrecht – Sonderregeln für Verbraucher und Kleinstunternehmen' [2020] Neue Juristische Wochenschrift 1103; Thomas Rüfner, 'Das Corona-Moratorium nach Art. 240 EGBGB' [2020] Juristenzeitung 443.

3 This provision is not meant to apply to refunding of payments for package travel under Directive (EU) 2015/2302 and the several passengers rights Regulations.

4 Many authors have started to analyse these general rules as their application to contracts in the current crisis, *inter alia*, Marc-Philippe Weller, Markus Lieberknecht, Victor Habrich, 'Virulente Leistungsstörungen – Auswirkungen der Corona-Krise auf die Vertragsdurchführung' [2020] Neue Juristische Wochenschrift 1017.

We would like to present here the results of a first preparatory step: How do German general contract law and the new German rules from the emergency legislation interact? For this purpose, we will first roughly outline how the rules of general contract law apply to contracts affected by the crisis. Then we will analyse step by step the particular rules within the emergency regulation and their interaction with general contract law. Finally, we will conclude with some first tentative answers to our general question concerning the reasons to amend German law by the Corona Contract Law legislation.

2. COVID-19 UNDER GENERAL CONTRACT LAW

The German emergency legislation on Corona contract law is confronted with well-established institutions of contract law and rules for breach of contract. Most of them were applied to the consequences of two World Wars, the revolution(s) of 1918, the hyperinflation from 1923/24, the world economic crisis from 1929, the transformations of the economic system following 1948 and 1989 and to several serious international crises. Surprisingly enough, no cases concerning the consequences of the so-called Spanish influenza seem to have been reported.[5] The range of legal institutions, principles, rules and remedies of general contract law to be possibly applied to Corona cases lasts from the classical rules of impossibility and impracticability in §§275, 326 BGB to the various rules on non-conformity (in particular §§535, 536 BGB for lease contracts), the fundamental change of circumstances in §313 BGB and the various rights to end the contract for serious reason. In contrast, leaving aside some particular transpositions of EU Directives (§§651n(1) no 3, 676c no 1 BGB on package travel and payment services) and international conventions (§701(3) BGB on innkeeper's liability and Article 79 CISG) German contract law legislation does not use the topic of force majeure, whereas the concept is widely used in contract clauses in Germany.[6]

2.1. §275 BGB AND THE DOCTRINE OF IMPOSSIBILITY

The *locus classicus* of external disturbances of the performance of a binding contract under German law is the doctrine of impossibility. This doctrine first covers cases of factual impediments to performance, §275(1) BGB, which in

5 But see the criminal decision by the Reichsgericht concerning an earlier epidemic situation of cholera in 27 RGSt 280.

6 For the interpretation of such clauses in COVID-19 cases see Klaus Bacher, 'Die Corona-Pandemie und allgemeinen Regeln über Leistungsstörungen' [2020] MDR 514, paras 18–21. Cf Amtsgericht Augsburg, ReiseRecht aktuell 2005, 84 (for Sars-CoV 1).

a COVID-19 scenario might, e.g. (have) happen(ed) in cases of illness of the debtor itself. However, in such a case the debtor would usually be held to be obliged to organise (and pay for) another (sub)supplier and thereby to overcome the impediment, unless the debt is exclusively linked to the person of the debtor. Economic distress would not help the debtor in such a case because of the dogma of unlimited liability with one's own assets. For exactly the same reason, monetary obligations will usually not be affected by §275 BGB.

Similarly, §275(1) BGB also covers cases of legal impediments. Quarantine and containment measures by the public administration are typical cases for this kind of impossibility.[7] However, also in those cases the obligee of a debt other than highly personal is again held to "buy" a substitute performance if this would be legally possible.

In both cases of impediments the duty to organise a substitute is limited by the defences for economic or personal impracticability in §275(2) and (3) BGB if the economic costs or the personal efforts to render performance become unacceptable compared to the interest of the creditor.[8] In a COVID-19 scenario extra costs for rendering performance due to illness of persons or quarantine or containment measures could trigger this defence. Moreover, risk of infection may raise issues of personal impracticability of performance. However, this economic threshold only limits claims for specific performance, whereas the debtor may remain liable for damages for fault.

Two additional points have to be emphasised in relation to the doctrine of impossibility: First, §275 BGB does not cover temporary impediments as far as performance can be made up for later as well. For these cases, an application of §275 BGB (not of §326 BGB) by way of analogy is usually accepted.[9] Second, the provision (with its restrictions as to the legal consequences) also applies to impediments, which only render parts or certain elements of performance impossible or impracticable. For example, if the place of delivery is impossible or impracticable due to a Corona-related impediment, the claim for performance would not be enforced as to this element of performance. However, it has not been decided so far, how such an elementary impossibility or impracticability could be dealt with in terms of changing the modus or kind of performance. For the classical partial impossibility §326(1) 1st sentence BGB refers to the rules on price reduction in §441(3) BGB; for the cases under consideration, this might not always suffice.

---

7 Klaus Bacher, 'Die Corona-Pandemie und allgemeinen Regeln über Leistungsstörungen' [2020] MDR 514, para 24.

8 It is not entirely clear from legal writing whether this interest of the creditor only refers to its interest in specific performance by the debtor (or its servants or agents) or by its general performance interest (which would considerably weaken the defence based on §275(2) BGB). Cf Peter Schlechtriem, Martin Schmidt-Kessel, *Schuldrecht Allgemeiner Teil* (6th edn, Mohr Siebeck 2005) para 483.

9 Bundesgerichtshof, 3 March 2013, BGHZ 197, 21, para 26.

2.2. REMEDIES FOR NON-CONFORMITY

Rules on conformity, which are only regulated in the provisions for particular types of contract, may also apply to certain situations of disturbances caused by Corona. This is rather obvious for cases of a non-conforming package travel due to Corona restrictions, where the particular broad notion of conformity under the Directive (EU) 2015/2302 and its transposition in §651i BGB applies.

Less self-evident is the application of rules for non-conformity when Corona related restrictions lead to dysfunctional consequences for a performance by the debtor. This is intensively discussed for business premises, which can or may not be used by the business due to Corona restrictions.[10] This idea might surprise as far as such restrictions are completely lacking a connection to the substance of the premises. However, the argument to a certain extent is in line with the general tendency of conformity being understood as a function of the performance. The question has not been decided yet, but will probably go to the courts.

2.3. *GESCHÄFTSGRUNDLAGE* AND CHANGE OF CIRCUMSTANCES

In a crisis of such a dimension every German lawyer would, *inter alia*, think in terms of *Geschäftsgrundlage* to solve the upcoming cases. There had been little discussion on such a change of circumstances by an epidemic or pandemic event before the COVID-19 pandemic started. Since 2002 the doctrine established by the *Reichsgericht* in 1923[11] is codified in §313 BGB. The doctrine, at first hand, aims for continuity of the contract, which may be modified for this purpose (§313(1) BGB), whereas the contract may only be terminated if one party may not reasonably be expected to uphold the modified contract (§313(3) BGB).

With the notions of *große Geschäftsgrundlage* (large contractual basis) and *kleine Geschäftsgrundlage* (small contractual basis) German academics are attempting to systematise the cases covered and use the category of *große Geschäftsgrundlage* to deal with situations, in which the entire social existence of both contracting parties is shaken (mass calamities).[12] Usually, non-performances of contracts due to wars and natural disasters are classified

---

10 Marc-Philippe Weller, Chris Thomale, 'Gewerbemietrecht – Mietminderung in der Corona-Krise' [2020] Betriebsberater 962; Silvio Sittner, 'Mietrechtspraxis unter Covid-19' [2020] Neue Juristische Wochenschrift, 1169, 1170/71; Martin Häublein, Maximilian Müller, 'Wer trägt das Pandemierisiko in der Geschäftsraummiete?' [2020] Neue Zeitschrift für Miet- und Wohnungsrecht 481, 483–485; Hans-Michael Krepold, 'Gewerbemietverträge in Zeiten der Corona-Pandemie' [2020] Wertpapiermitteilungen 726, 729–731.

11 Usually 103 RGZ 328 is seen as the decisive judgment: see Konrad Zweigert, Hans Georg Rupp, Gerhard Kegel, *Die Einwirkung des Krieges auf Verträge* (de Gruyter 1941) 100.

12 Werner Flume, *Allgemeiner Teil des Bürgerlichen Rechts: Das Rechtsgeschäft*, vol II (Springer-Verlag 1965) 523.

as disturbances of the *große Geschäftsgrundlage*. For the COVID-19 pandemic the classification is discussed intensively.[13] On the other hand, the classification does not imply significant differences in the treatment of the situations covered by §313 BGB: it may be easier to plead §313 BGB but its application is neither self-evident nor is it presumed. In current academic writing, however, there is an agreement that the COVID-19-pandemic is at least in principle suitable to affect the *kleine Geschäftsgrundlage*, i.e. to meet the requirements of §313 BGB.[14]

The first criterion for §313 BGB is the fundamental change of the circumstances. This criterion is concretised by several groups of cases. For the coronavirus crisis the groups of aggravation of the necessary performance efforts (beyond §275(2) and (3) BGB), frustration or disruption of the purpose of the contract and legal changes are probably the most important ones. Economic distress and lack of liquidity are only rarely accepted as relevant circumstances in this context.[15]

Second, the fundamental change of circumstances must happen outside of the risk allocation organised by the contract and the applicable law. Particular contract clauses on pandemics or – more generally – on force majeure, might exclude the application of §313 BGB. Moreover, the risk allocation by particular legislation has to be considered and may prevent the doctrine of fundamental change of circumstances to be applied. The dogma of unlimited liability with one's own assets counts as a core element of the legal risk allocation, which is usually the decisive counter-argument against the application of §313 BGB in cases of economic distress and lack of liquidity of the debtor.

Article 240 Introductory Act in this context does not generally exclude the application of §313 BGB to contracts suffering from the COVID-19-pandemic. However, Article 240 Introductory Act certainly does override §313 BGB, where the provision provides for a sufficient answer to a change of circumstances. The termination bans enacted by the emergency legislation could conflict with the relevant legal consequences of §313(3) BGB. On the other hand, Article 240 Introductory Act should not be interpreted as a general valuation by the legislator that the dogma of unlimited liability with one's own assets should be restricted under §313 BGB to cope with the Corona crisis.

---

13 In favour of große Geschäftsgrundlage, *inter alia*, Christina Möllnitz, Martin Schmidt-Kessel, 'Commentary to article 240 EGBGB' *Uhlenbruck Insolvenzordnung* (15th edn, Vahlen 2020) para 85; Alexander Schall, 'Corona-Krise: Unmöglichkeit und Wegfall der Geschäftsgrundlage bei gewerblichen Miet- und Pachtverträgen' [2020] Juristenzeitung 388, 392. Against such a classification, *inter alia*, Marc-Philippe Weller, Markus Lieberknecht, Victor Habrich, 'Virulente Leistungsstörungen – Auswirkungen der Corona-Krise auf die Vertragsdurchführung' [2020] Neue Juristische Wochenschrift 1017, 1021; Thomas Pfeiffer, *juris Praxiskommentar*, §313 para 13.4 (R 3 April 2020).

14 Thomas Pfeiffer, *juris Praxiskommentar*, §313 para 13.4 (R 3 April 2020).

15 Thomas Finckenauer, *Münchener Kommentar zum BGB* (8th edn, 2019) §313 para 306.

2.4. ENDING THE CONTRACT FOR SERIOUS REASON

German law finds itself in the rather unique position that every long-term contract may be brought to an end for good reason and that this right to unilaterally end the contract by notice may be modified or restricted for certain cases but not generally be excluded. The respective provisions – generally §314 BGB, for specific contracts, *inter alia*, §§543, 626, 648a BGB – do cover termination for breach and also ending for other *wichtige Gründe* (serious reasons). These provisions have to be given some thought, albeit depending on the individual case. This is particularly the case where the crisis causes a fundamental breach of the contract (e.g. by delays of payment). However, also the lack of prospects for the future of a contract may trigger §314 BGB in some cases, in which the provision interacts also with §313 BGB.

However, looking at Article 240 Introductory Act reveals a completely different direction of the legal development: the termination bans and the restriction to restitutionary remedies show that the legislator tended to favour continuity of contracts rather than ending them – even in cases of a (hypothetical) breach of contract. As the legislator apparently classifies the Corona crisis as a temporary phenomenon, it is obvious to prevent breakdowns of supply chains and other contractual relationships. In this sense, the various termination rights will – according to the legislator's plan – probably not play a major role in the reaction of the legal order as a whole. However, this is likely to change if the temporary crisis turns into a longer-lasting state.

3. THE MORATORIUM FOR CONSUMERS AND MICRO-ENTREPRENEURS (ART 240 §1 INTRODUCTORY ACT)

The core element of the German Corona contract law is a moratorium on claims against consumers and micro-entrepreneurs who are faced with serious financial difficulties as a result of the COVID-19-pandemic. Article 240 §1 Introductory Act applies to "essential long-term contracts" concluded before 8 March 2020 and is designed as a right of the debtor to refuse performance. This right could be exercised until 30 June 2020 at the latest; contracts that do not contain a continuing obligation are not covered from the outset. The obligation of the other party to the contract is not affected by the debtors' refusal; this obligation is to be performed as laid down in the contract. Nevertheless, the other party is entitled to object to the refusal by the debtor if the non-performance is unacceptable (in the sense of Article 240 §1(3) Introductory Act) for him/her as well.

The moratorium is laid down separately in Article 240 §1 Introductory Act for consumers (in particular §1(1), (3) 1st sentence) and micro-entrepreneurs (in particular §1(2), (3) 2nd sentence), but in each case structured in the same way. It does not apply to certain rental and lease agreements that are covered by Article 240 §2 Introductory Act and not at all to loan agreements and labour contracts, Article 240 §1(4) Introductory Act. Article 240 §1(4) Introductory Act forbids deviations at the expense of the consumer or the micro-entrepreneur.

3.1. CONTRACT PARTIES PROTECTED

The personal scope of application of Article 240 §1(1) Introductory Act is limited to contracts between consumers and traders following the definitions given by §§13, 14 BGB. The corresponding right in §1(2) protects – irrespective of the contractual partner – micro-entrepreneurs as defined in Recommendation 2003/361/EC of the European Commission of 6 May 2003. According to this recommendation, a micro-enterprise is an enterprise which employs fewer than 10 persons and whose annual turnover does not exceed EUR 2 million. There is no right to refuse for small and medium-sized enterprises.

3.2. MATERIAL SCOPE OF APPLICATION

The moratorium is limited to *wesentliche Dauerschuldverhältnisse* (essential long-term contracts). The provision itself and the legislative materials provide for some hints as to which contracts are covered by this requirement. Simple sales contracts are obviously excluded from the scope of application. For consumers such essential contracts cover services of general interest to the consumer (Art 240 §1(1) 3rd sentence). For micro-entrepreneurs, Article 240 §1(2) 3rd sentence, an essential long-term contract is defined as a contract that is essential to cover the services necessary for the "reasonable continuation of the business". According to the legislative materials[16] of this Act, the provision, *inter alia*, covers contracts for compulsory insurance, electricity, gas and telecommunications.

What is necessary in the meaning of the provision is that it is not to be decided according to the individual preferences of the consumer but using objective standards. The provision also covers non-monetary contributions

16 The Draft for the Act was prepared to a large extent within the Federal Ministry of Justice and for Consumer Affairs but introduced to the Parliament not by the Federal Government but by the Members of Parliament of the three parties supporting the Federal Government. This official Draft to Article 240 §§1-4 Introductory Act takes the number BT-Drs. 19/18110.

by the debtor.[17] In these cases, the long-term contract must be existential for the micro-entrepreneur, for example through his/her dependence on a single customer (e.g. service providers on the verge of bogus self-employment).

3.3. CONDITIONS OF THE RIGHT TO REFUSE

Consumers may refuse to perform their obligation if the performance is not possible due to the COVID-19-pandemic without endangering their reasonable maintenance or the reasonable maintenance of their relatives. For micro-entrepreneurs, the moratorium applies if performance is not possible without jeopardising the economic basis of his/her business or if the micro-entrepreneur is not capable to perform. An indirect connection with the pandemic is sufficient, as the provision only refers to "circumstances attributable to the pandemic".

Due to the proximity of Article 240 Introductory Act to insolvency law, a recourse to the standards of the Insolvency Act is reasonable to determine the economic situation. For the micro-entrepreneur, relevant risks will exist in the event of insolvency (§17 Insolvency Act) and over-indebtedness (§19 Insolvency Act). The imminent insolvency (§18(2) Insolvency Act) is also sufficient with regard to the debtor's burden to actively refuse performance. The debtor must therefore use liquid assets and reserves.

In principle, these standards also apply to consumers, although practical indications may arise in the event of unsuccessful enforcement attempts or due to the use of services relating to basic needs within the meaning of Book 2 of the German Social Security Code. In addition, after job loss, unpaid leave or short-time work, it is sufficient for the monthly household income to fall below the basic requirements if no significant liquid assets are available for the consumer.

Moreover, §1(1) 1st sentence no 1 mentions the case that "the entrepreneur cannot provide the service". The provision therefore suspends the debtor of the need to "buy" his/her ability to perform on the market or to compensate for the loss of personnel or the inability to procure materials and infrastructure.

3.4. DUPLIC OF THE CREDITOR

The refusal of performance by the consumer or the micro-entrepreneur might also endanger the economic basis of the creditor's business or the maintenance

---

17 This point is disputed in academic writing, pro Martin Schmidt-Kessel, Christina Möllnitz, 'Coronavertragsrecht – Sonderregeln für Verbraucher und Kleinstunternehmen' [2020] Neue Juristische Wochenschrift 1104; contra Thomas Rüfner, 'Das Corona-Moratorium nach Art. 240 EGBGB' [2020] Juristenzeitung 443, 446.

of the creditor or his/her relatives. Therefore, if the debtor and creditor are thus in comparable financial difficulties, Article 240 §1(3) Introductory Act decides in favour of the creditor. In this case, the debtor only has the right to terminate the contract.

3.5. LEGAL CONSEQUENCES

The right to refuse performance is a defence; it must be expressly exercised. Mere non-performance as such is not sufficient. If the debtor refuses the performance, the claim in question is not enforceable until 30 June 2020 even if it has been enforceable before the debtor exercised the right to refuse performance. Default and termination due to delay are excluded.

The claim to the respective counter-performance is not affected by the refusal – despite the absence of an explicit regulation within Article 240 §1 Introductory Act. This results from the purpose of the regulation to protect the maintenance of the consumer and the necessary foundation of the respective business. If the contractual partner of the consumer or micro-entrepreneur that are in the existential need of the performance was not still obligated to perform the purpose of the provision would not be met.

3.6. RELATION TO GENERAL CONTRACT LAW

The (limited) general moratorium established by Article 240 §1 Introductory Act is in several respects not congruent with the rules of German general contract law. However, since §275 BGB applies to temporary impossibility only by analogy, the overlap with Article 240 §1 Introductory Act is limited. Both provisions can also be applied in parallel. On the other hand, §275 BGB only in very rare circumstances protects a debtor of monetary obligations, which form at least the overwhelming part of obligations, to which Article 240 §1 Introductory Act applies. Moreover, §275 BGB is connected to §326 BGB: If the debtor is not obliged to perform due to an impossibility, there is also no entitlement to counter-performance according to §326 BGB. However, the application of §326(1) BGB would prevent an essential objective of Article 240 §1 Introductory Act to leave the counter-performance unaffected by the moratorium. Accordingly, the analogy with §326(1) BGB is excluded, where the *Coronanotbedarfseinrede* (Corona distress defence) applies. If, on the other hand, there is a final impossibility or unreasonableness within the meaning of §275 BGB, the application of §326(1) remains unaffected.

The doctrine of change of circumstances in §313 BGB does not usually help a debtor of payment obligations either. The doctrine follows the law in particular in so far as economic distress of such a debtor is concerned and only in rare constellations provides for a way out of the distress.[18] In particular, the simple lack of liquidity for reasons, which lie outside of the contractual relationship, does not form a case of change of circumstances.[19] Following the Second World War, Germany even had established a separate *Vertragshilfegesetz* (Contract Help Act)[20] to cope, *inter alia*, with situations of economic distress of the debtor. Therefore, the overlap between both instruments is considerably limited. As far as both rules are applicable, Article 240 §1 Introductory Act will form part of the legal risk distribution under the contract.[21] Therefore, if the moratorium by the defence under the emergency legislation sufficiently solves the situation of distress, §313 BGB may not be applied. For the same reasons, Article 240 §1 Introductory Act also cannot be circumvented by cancellation of the contract pursuant to §314 BGB due to its regulatory purpose.

Moreover, even where §1 does not apply, the provision shows that the legislator intended to solve the temporary disturbances of contracts by the COVID-19-pandemic by temporary measures only. Even where the provision does not apply, ending the contract on the basis of §313 BGB purely because of economic distress and lack of liquidity will be excluded by the legal risk distribution enacted by §1 as long as the disturbances do not last longer than the period(s) referred to by the Act.

4. BAN OF TERMINATION FOR LATE PAYMENT IN CASE OF REAL ESTATE RENT AND LEASE (ART 240 §2 INTRODUCTORY ACT)

Tenants and leaseholders of real estate cannot refuse to perform their payment obligations under Article 240 §1(1) or (2) Introductory Act. This exposes them to the risk of termination of their contracts (mainly under §§543, 573 BGB). Article 240 §2 Introductory Act, therefore, orders an exclusion of the termination of the default of payment, as far as it concerns missing payments in the months April, May and June 2020.[22] Tenants may now be able to conduct claims about possible exclusions of the obligation to pay rent (e.g. according to §§326(1), 536, 313 BGB) with less risk. §2 applies to both professional premises and housing. According to §2(3), the ban on termination is mandatory in favour of the tenant.

---

18 Thomas Finckenauer, *Münchener Kommentar zum BGB* (8th edn, 2019) §313 para 306.

19 Thomas Finckenauer, *Münchener Kommentar zum BGB* (8th edn, 2019) §313 para 224–226.

20 See Bundesgesetzblatt (Federal Official Journal) Part I (1952) 198. The Act, which was finally abolished in 2000, see Bundesgesetzblatt (Federal Official Journal) Part I (2000) 908, had equipped the judge with a discretionary power to order "contract help" thereby changing the contract.

21 Cf section 2 for the relevance of this argument.

22 The Federal Constitutional Court, however, has rejected a first constitutional complaint as inadmissible for purely procedural reasons, see Bundesverfassungsgericht, COVID-19 und Recht 2020, 87.

4.1. LIMITED TERMINATION BAN

The ban on termination precludes the effects of a nevertheless declared termination. In cases where the claim to rent or lease does not exist anyway the termination ban remains ineffective. The termination ban also prevents landlords to rely on effectively agreed cancellation clauses for payment delays.

The provision requires that the non-payment by the tenant is "based on the effects of the COVID-19-pandemic". The explanation to the Draft only mentions unwillingness to pay and inability to pay for reasons other than the COVID-19-pandemic as examples where the exclusion of termination should not be relevant. Therefore, §2 does not provide the tenant with the possibility of freely setting priorities in the disbursement of his/her funds. An existential threat to the tenant is not necessary to ban the termination. However, a considerable loss of income or a considerable increase in costs is necessary. These disadvantages must not be compensated by other consequences of the crisis – such as State compensation for loss of earnings or additional expenses that threaten the tenant's existence. In addition, existing liquid reserves must be used and spent; a simple operating loss of a company, for example, will not suffice. In the case of group companies, liquid reserves of the parent company may also have to be taken into account.

4.2. LEGAL CONSEQUENCES

Based on Article 240 §2 Introductory Act, the landlord cannot terminate the contract because of the delay in payment. The provision only covers terminations solely due to late payment. In cases with a variety of reasons for the termination the termination ban is therefore not applicable. The termination ban applies to the non-payment of payments in the period from 1 April 2020 to 30 June 2020. Termination rights already created before 1 April 2020 are not affected by §2. Moreover, evictions from legally binding executory titles are not prevented by §2.

The regulation does not provide for further legal consequences. In particular, §2 – unlike §§1, 3 – does not establish rights to refuse performance or statutory deferral. *A fortiori*, the claim itself as well as the default with it remains unaffected. Damages caused by delay or interest on arrears are also not excluded by the new regulation.

Remedies which functionally include the termination or counteract the effects of the prohibition of termination are banned by Article 240 §2 Introductory Act to prevent its circumvention. This includes damages including termination according to §§280(1), (3), 281 BGB. The same shall apply, *mutatis mutandis*, if §§320, 321, 273 BGB would counteract the ban on termination.

4.3. INTERPLAY WITH GENERAL CONTRACT LAW

The ban of rights to terminate the contract is a very limited instrument for the rental and lease relationships covered. As opposed to Article 240 §1 Introductory Act the provision is directed against general contract law and its results in case of economic distress and lack of liquidity. This does not only restrict the typical remedies of termination for late payment in §§543, 573 BGB but also does not leave §313 BGB unaffected. Article 240 §2 Introductory Act allocates the risk of remaining bound by the lease contract to the landlord despite lack of payment. This risk allocation excludes termination for change of circumstances also, where the situation of economic distress of the tenant would allow the landlord to terminate without any lack of payment. Other consequences under §313 BGB and the right to have the contract modified under §313(1) BGB, in particular, remain unaffected. The German legislator clarified this effect later on by introducing an additional Article 240 §7 Introductory Act.

5. DEFERRAL AND TERMINATION OF CONSUMER CREDIT AND MORTGAGE AGREEMENTS (ART 240 §3 INTRODUCTORY ACT)

For consumer loan agreements, the new provisions provide for an *ipso iure* deferral. The deferral is accompanied by measures for the protection against termination and options for adjusting the contract. Article 240 §3 Introductory Act is characterised by the basic idea that creditor and debtor should find joint solutions for dealing with the consumer's (temporary) liquidity shortage as amicably as possible. The regulations are therefore partly dispositive, §3(2), and provide for a discussion between the entrepreneur and the consumer about an amicable settlement and other support measures.

5.1. SCOPE OF APPLICATION

Article 240 §3 Introductory Act is only applicable to consumer loan agreements as defined in §491 BGB which were concluded before 15 March 2020. The provision therefore covers both classical consumer credits (§491(2) BGB) and mortgage agreements (§491(3) BGB). The deferral applies exclusively to claims for repayment, interest or redemption payments. Other claims in connection with the loan agreement (e.g. fees or claims for damages caused by delay) are not covered.

5.2. DEFERRAL ARRANGEMENT

Any claims of the creditor for repayment, interest or redemption payments due between 1 April 2020 and 30 June 2020 are automatically deferred for a period of three months from the former due date. As a prerequisite, the consumer needs to have lost income due to the exceptional circumstances caused by the COVID-19-pandemic, which makes it unreasonable to expect him/her to provide the owed payment. The deferment is to be calculated separately for each claim and is effective for three months in all cases.

The proven loss of income must reach a level that makes the owed payments covered by §3 unacceptable for the consumer. Performance is unacceptable in particular if the debtor's or his/her relatives' reasonable maintenance is endangered. The explicit recourse to the loss of income does not exclude the consideration of the debtor's liquid assets. Rather, the determination of unacceptability requires a comprehensive consideration of all circumstances of the individual case and thus also the existence of liquid assets at the debtor.[23]

Under §3(6), the deferral does not apply if it is unacceptable for the creditor as well. Here, all circumstances of the individual case have to be taken into account, including the change in the general living conditions caused by the COVID-19-pandemic. §3 (as opposed to §1) provides for a comprehensive weighing of interests in which the pandemic is only one possible consideration. This also includes, for example, cases of previous breaches of contract or other notorious unreliability on the part of the consumer.

5.3. TERMINATION BAN

In addition to the deferral, the termination of the loan by the creditor due to default of payment, significant deterioration in the financial circumstances of the consumer or the value of one of the securities provided for the loan is excluded until the expiry of the deferral, Article 240 §3(3) Introductory Act. The provision is mandatory in favour of the consumer. However, the ban of termination does not apply if this ban is unacceptable for the creditor.

5.4. RENEGOTIATION AND EXTENSION OF THE CONTRACT PERIOD

Article 240 §3(4) Introductory Act requires the creditor to offer the consumer an opportunity to discuss the possibility of an amicable arrangement and

[23] For a first case see Amtsgericht Frankfurt Zeitschrift für Bank- und Kapitalmarktrecht 2020, 260.

available support options. The regulation establishes a legal obligation. The primary consequence of a breach of this obligation – as well as the failure to reach an agreement – is the extension of the contract duration by three months and the postponement of the due date of all claims by the same period. In addition, claims for damages by the consumer may also be considered if the consumer has suffered verifiable causal damage as a result of the omitted negotiations.

5.5. INTERPLAY WITH GENERAL CONTRACT LAW

The particular rules for consumer loan contracts provide for a complete structure of risk allocation and by Article 240 §3(3) Introductory Act particularly emphasise the continuity of the contractual relationship. The provision thereby completely overrides the instrumentarium of general contract law exactly for the situation of economic distress of the consumer. In particular, §3 leaves no room for an application of §313 BGB. However, due to the general reluctance of courts and academics to apply the doctrine to cases of lack of liquidity, the overlap between the two provisions is likely to be very limited.

6. VOUCHERS FOR FAILED LEISURE ACTIVITIES (ART 240 §5 INTRODUCTORY ACT)

The somewhat "younger" Article 240 §5 Introductory Act takes a different approach to overcoming the difficulties of the pandemic. It will support the (mainly entrepreneurial) organisers of failed leisure activities as well as operators of leisure facilities that had to be closed. The general rules of German contract law require the organisers and operators to pay back entrance fees or other fees and charges that have been paid for the access. In order to prevent a large outflow of liquidity and thus a possible insolvency of the organisers of leisure activities §5 authorises the organisers to issue vouchers instead of refunding their clients. Only if the client does not redeem the voucher by 31 December 2021, he/she can demand payment of the voucher amount. In practice, the provision therefore leads to a compulsory loan without the duty to pay interest of the clients for the organisers.[24] If the conditions of §5 are not met, the substitution of the original reimbursement claim by the voucher fails if the client does not accept the voucher on the basis of a separate agreement.

---

24 Cf also Wolfgang Voit, *Beck Online Commentary BGB* (45th edn, 2020) Art 240 EGBGB para 2, 3, who questions the constitutionality due to the transfer of the risk of insolvency.

6.1. SCOPE OF APPLICATION

The scope of application only grants this right to organisers of leisure events as well as to operators of leisure facilities. The provision itself names music, culture and sport events and facilities as examples but also contains the very broad term of "other leisure activities" and "other leisure facilities". It is here necessary to take the reasoning behind the provision into consideration. Article 240 §5 Introductory Act is justified by the idea that the clients have already regarded the money invested as "not necessary" for their living expenses as they dedicated it to leisure activities (which corresponds to the limited scope of Article 240 §1 Introductory Act to essential long-term contracts). The provision is only applicable to tickets and other authorisations that were purchased before 8 March 2020. After this date, the legislator saw the organisers of the event in a position to recognise possible obstacles, so from then on they sold the tickets at their own risk. There is no time limit for the application of §5. The right to issue vouchers can be exercised as long as there still are impediments caused by the COVID-19-pandemic.

6.2. CONDITIONS FOR ISSUING A VOUCHER

The right to issue a voucher is restricted to impediments for the realisation of an event or the opening of a leisure facility caused by the COVID-19-pandemic. The provision especially aims for prohibitions of large events or the legally forced closure of certain facilities – be it a general one for all these kinds of facilities or a specific one due to a quarantine measure.

The purpose of the provision requires a broad understanding of the causal link of the impediment and the pandemic. Therefore, reasonable precautionary decisions by the organiser are sufficient for the right to issue a voucher. If facilities remain closed even after the shutdown due to the burdensome precautionary measures, the purpose of Article 240 §5 Introductory Act – insolvency prevention – would not be met if these facilities were not allowed to issue vouchers.

The provision also requires the existence of any kind of reimbursement claim. The provision is not limited to reimbursement due to impossibility (§§346, 326(4) BGB) but also to restitutionary claims following avoidance, withdrawal or termination for anticipatory breach.

6.3. CONSEQUENCES OF THE RIGHT TO ISSUE A VOUCHER

The right to issue vouchers instead of reimbursing is not automatic but the organisers and operators have to actively choose to issue vouchers. Dogmatically, the provision grants an *Ersetzungsbefugnis* (right to substitute) so that the original reimbursement claim is substituted by the claim from the voucher. In practice, the provision leads to a replacement of the reimbursement claim by a claim with a later due date creating the effects of a deferral. Nevertheless, there are some differences to a deferral as the original claim does no longer exist as well as the clients have the possibility to attend other events using their vouchers and are not limited to a monetary claim.

The right to substitute requires the organisers and operators to issue vouchers that value-wise must include the full admission price or all other charges including any advance booking fees. It is therefore forbidden to bind the voucher to any upcoming event or a special replacement event only. According to the purpose of the provision, the value of the voucher must correspond to the value of the reimbursement claim. If a gym membership for a year grants some reduction compared to the price for a single month the value of the voucher has to be based on the percentage of the annual price and not be calculated according to the monthly price.[25] The voucher must also contain the information that it was issued because of the COVID-19-pandemic and under which conditions the holder may request payment of the value of the voucher.

The provision does not grant any preferential rights for the holders of Corona-vouchers in regard to the purchase of new tickets for future events. Moreover, §5 accepts the fact that holders of the voucher might have to make an additional payment for the replacement event if the tickets for this event are issued at a higher price.

6.4. UNACCEPTABILITY DUE TO PERSONAL CIRCUMSTANCES

To balance the interests of the organisers and operators with the ones of the clients Article 240 §5(5) no 1 Introductory Act grants the holder of the voucher the right to claim immediate payment of the value of the voucher, if being referred to the voucher is unacceptable for the client in view of its personal circumstances. The application of this exception is limited to vouchers that are issued in accordance with §5.

The reference to unacceptability due to personal circumstances gives judges the possibility to take into account the specificities of each individual case. Nevertheless, the exception is only applicable to exceptional cases. The mere loss of interest in a future event does not lead to the unacceptability of a voucher as this is not an exceptional circumstance but dealt with by §5(5) no 2 granting the payment of the voucher after 31 December 2021. The explanation to the Draft

[25] Cf also Wolfgang Voit, *Beck Online Commentary BGB* (45th edn, 2020) Art 240 EGBGB para 2, 3, with additional examples.

assumes that the conditions of the exception are likely to be fulfilled, if the holder of a ticket planned to attend the event as part of a holiday trip and could only make up for the missed date by incurring high travel costs or if the holder of the voucher is not able to pay existentially important costs of living such as rent or energy bills without the reimbursement (cf §1).[26] Unreasonableness might also arise when a long-term contract like a gym membership is terminated before the voucher has been redeemed. In this case, the client cannot be forced into a longer contractual relationship just to get the possibility to redeem the voucher.

6.5. SERIES OF EVENTS

§5(1) 2nd sentence contains a special provision for a series of events. If the purchased ticket or other entitlement includes participation in several leisure events and only part of these events could or can take place, the organiser is entitled to give the holder a voucher for the value of the unused part. The provision disables the clients to rely on an exception according to §5(5) no 1 if they are not interested in the remaining events of that series as well as disabling the provisions of the German contract law that are prohibiting a partial performance.[27]

6.6. RELATIONSHIP TO GENERAL CONTRACT LAW

The rule on vouchers as a substitute to restitution of the price is of a rather particular character because it presupposes the remedies of general contract law (including §313 BGB) and moderates their restitutionary consequences. In this respect §5 is of an accessory character. Moreover, on the restitutionary level the provision falls outside of the typical scope of the instruments dealing with large-scale disasters: §275 BGB provides no effective defence against the claims for restitution of the price. §314 BGB and its siblings do not apply to restitution. Finally, §313 BGB could perhaps come to similar results as §5, if the provision would allow for termination of contract on particular conditions deviating from the usual restitutionary consequences – theoretically conceivable but not really likely. Therefore, Article 240 §5 Introductory Act lays down an additional exception to the dogma of unlimited liability with one's own assets and thereby deviates again from general contract law.

26 This official Draft to Article 240 §5 Introductory Act takes the number BT-Drs. 19/18697.

27 The interplay of the provision with the rules on partial non-performance treated as complete non-performance because of an overall lack of interest of the creditor in a partial performance (in particular in the context of §323 (5) 1st sentence) still needs to be discussed.

7. CONCLUSIONS

The particular rules of German Corona contract law established by Article 240 Introductory Act have more in common than a first view into the pure text of the rules reveals. All four of them revolve around the same two basic structural decisions: first, they are of a provisional nature usually emphasised by sunset clauses. Second, they are focussing on lack of liquidity of a contract party, which is protected for a short period of time. These structural decisions are taken by the legislator in view of protecting consumers and avoiding formal insolvency proceedings to keep business structures intact and to prevent a large Corona transformation to the detriment of the national economy.

For this purpose, the German legislator (carefully, with no real discretion for the judges) modifies, restricts and overrides the classical German instruments of contractual crisis management (impossibility, change of circumstances and termination for serious reason), which represent the market economy core dogma of unlimited liability with one's own assets. Therefore, the interventions should be understood as being a (time-limited) reaction to the finding that large-scale crises cannot be managed only by market-compliant instruments – a finding which exactly corresponds to other historical experiences with distortions to the *große Geschäftsgrundlage* in contract law.[28]

Finally, these results show that the interventions of the German legislator by emergency legislation were not so much a reaction to weaknesses of the classical market oriented institutions of contract law. It was rather a sign of a significant deficit in preparation of contract law to large-scale crises affecting the *große Geschäftsgrundlage*, where the dogma of unlimited liability with one's own assets is not (entirely) suitable to sufficiently address the situation. Therefore, in 2020 the German legislator was forced to reinvent the wheel of a crisis-proof pandemic contract law without being able to resort to well-prepared emergency measures and model rules in the sense of a *vorsorgliches Vertragsrecht* (precautionary contract law). It is for academia now, to develop such models to prepare for the next large-scale crises.

[28] Thomas Finckenauer, *Münchener Kommentar zum BGB* (8th edn, 2019) §313 para 18.

IMPOSSIBILITY, FORCE MAJEURE AND COVID-19 UNDER SWISS AND AUSTRIAN CONTRACT LAWS

Andreas FURRER, Angelika LAYR and Jeremias WARTMANN*

The COVID-19 pandemic and the enactment of legislation to slow the spread of the virus are affecting large parts of the economy, including contractual relationships. This contribution examines the legal situation and possible remedies, according to Swiss and Austrian general contract law while taking account of the developments in European contract law. Both jurisdictions allow for contractual force majeure clauses to allocate risks in connection with unforeseeable or changing circumstances. As there is no statutory definition of force majeure, the individual contracts need to be examined, and COVID-19-specific clauses for newly concluded contracts should be introduced. In the absence of a contractual agreement, the concepts of delay of performance or impossibility might be applicable for adaptation or termination of the contract. If the contractual equilibrium is severely disrupted by the changing circumstances, the doctrine of clausula rebus sic stantibus *could apply.*

* All authors, University of Lucerne.

1. INTRODUCTION

The COVID-19 pandemic led to the enactment of strict and far-reaching measures (COVID-19 Measures) to slow the spread of the virus. Switzerland,[1] as well as Austria,[2] passed laws that comprise, *inter alia*, limitations on cross-border travel, the closure of educational institutions and non-essential businesses, the prohibition of events and new rules in export controls. These legal acts will expire at a given date unless they are extended or revoked earlier.[3] Contract law is not directly governed within these measures but is affected directly or indirectly nevertheless: the performance of existing contracts may be delayed, impossible or unduly burdensome for one of the parties. This contribution examines the remedies for such situations under Swiss and Austrian general contract law,[4] while also situating these approaches within the broader context of European contract law.

2. CONTRACTUAL FORCE MAJEURE CLAUSES

Swiss and Austrian general contract law are based on the principles of freedom of contract and *pacta sunt servanda*. Under these principles, if the parties agree

---

1 Primarily the Ordinance on Measures to Combat the Coronavirus (COVID-19) of 13 March 2020 of the Swiss Federal Council (Classified Compilation of Swiss Law (CCSL) no 818.101.24). This ordinance covers measures directly aiming to prevent the spread of the virus, for which the Federal Council derives its powers primarily from Article 7 Act on Epidemics of 28 September 2012 (AE, CSSL 818.101). Additionally, the Federal Council has enacted ordinances to address the broader ramifications (e.g. economic and social), which are based upon the Federal Council's emergency powers of Article 185(3) Federal Constitution of the Swiss Confederation (SFC, CCSL 101); see also Andreas Stöckli, 'Regierung und Parlament in Pandemiezeiten' (2020) 139 Zeitschrift für Schweizerisches Recht, Sondernummer 'Pandemie und Recht' 9, 21.

2 Federal Act on provisional measures to prevent the spread of COVID-19 (Bundesgesetz betreffend vorläufige Maßnahmen zur Verhinderung der Verbreitung von COVID-19; COVID-19-Maßnahmengesetz), BGBl I 12/2020, 15 March 2020 and corresponding ordinances and further acts. A list of COVID-19-legislation can be found https://www.sozialministerium.at/Informationen-zum-Coronavirus/Coronavirus---Rechtliches.html accessed 5 March 2021.

3 In Switzerland, emergency ordinances based upon Article 185(3) SFC expire after six months unless submitted to the Federal Assembly for approval or transformation (Art 7d Government and Administration Organisation Act (GAOA), CCSL 172.010). Whether the limitations of Article 7d GAOA also apply to measures based upon Article 7 AE is subject to debate, while the text explicitly refers only to Article 185(3) SFC, scholars want to apply Article 7d GAOA to Article 7 AE based upon considerations of separation of power and legislative history (Frédéric Bernard, 'La loi sur les épidémies à l'épreuve du nouveau coronavirus' [2020] Jusletter 30 March 2020, no 21; Stöckli 'Regierung und Parlament in Pandemiezeiten' (2020) 139 Zeitschrift für Schweizerisches Recht, Sondernummer 'Pandemie und Recht' 9, 21 ff).

4 Accordingly, the legal rules only concerning specific contracts (e.g. sale, lease, employment) are not included.

on a later fulfilment of their respective obligations, each party bears a certain risk for future events and the behaviour of the counterparty. To a certain extent, every contract is based on a risk assessment and risk decision.

To deal with this risk, the parties often define the term of force majeure, which allows for adjustments in case of changing or unforeseeable circumstances. Such clauses enable the parties to define not only the notion of force majeure but also its consequences.

If a contract does not define force majeure, case law can provide definitions: Swiss jurisprudence defines force majeure as an unforeseeable, extraordinary event that occurs with unavoidable external force.[5] Similarly, according to the Austrian Supreme Court (*Oberster Gerichtshof*; OGH), force majeure is an elementary external event, which does not occur and cannot be expected to occur with a certain frequency and regularity and cannot be prevented even by exercising the utmost reasonable care.[6] The OGH has, for instance, classified the SARS epidemic of 2002–2004 as a case of force majeure in connection with a travel contract.[7]

In view of the intensity and the global impact of the virus on the economy, the measures taken suggest that COVID-19 constitutes an exceptional elementary external event. This is also underlined by the World Health Organization (WHO) classifying the COVID-19 outbreak as a pandemic[8] and numerous countries applying emergency law. Ultimately, the wide range of possible circumstances necessitates that the specific circumstances of a contract are used to assess whether COVID-19 constitutes force majeure. For instance, one might think of the different situation of a factory closure by official orders in contrast to a voluntary precautionary shutdown.

As force majeure clauses regularly require that the event was not foreseeable at the time of the conclusion of the contract, the parties should introduce specific clauses to allocate the risks associated with COVID-19 Measures in newly closed contracts.

---

5 '[U]nvorhersehbares, aussergewöhnliches Geschehnis, das mit unabwendbarer Gewalt von aussen hereinbricht'; BGE 102 Ib 257 consid 5, p 262; Corinne Widmer Lüchinger and Wolfgang Wiegand in Corinne Widmer Lüchinger and David Oser (eds), *Basler Kommentar: Obligationenrecht I: Art. 1-529 OR* (7th edn, Helbing Lichtenhahn Verlag 2019) no 12 Article 103 SCO; Andreas Furrer and Rainer Wey in Anton K. Schnyder (ed), *Handkommentar zum Schweizer Privatrecht: Obligationenrecht – Allgemeine Bestimmungen: Art. 1–183 OR* (3rd edn, Schulthess Verlag 2016) no 12 Article 103 SCO.

6 'Höhere Gewalt ist ein von außen her auf den Betrieb einwirkendes außergewöhnliches Ereignis, das nicht in einer gewissen Häufigkeit und Regelmäßigkeit vorkommt und zu erwarten ist und durch äußerst zumutbare Sorgfalt weder abgewendet noch in seinen Folgen unschädlich gemacht werden kann.'; RIS-Justiz RS0029808.

7 OGH 14 June 2005, 4 Ob 103/05h.

8 World Health Organization, 'WHO announces COVID-19 outbreak a pandemic' (12 March 2020) http://www.euro.who.int/en/health-topics/health-emergencies/coronavirus-covid-19/news/news/2020/3/who-announces-covid-19-outbreak-a-pandemic accessed 9 June 2020.

In this context, reference can be made to the model force majeure clause of the International Chamber of Commerce (ICC), which was updated in 2020.[9] The update primarily pertained to the wording of the clause. However, one of the substantive amendments introduces an explicit duration of 120 days from the start of the impediment, after which either party may terminate the contract. Yet, it remains doubtful whether such a predetermined duration suits a clause intended to regulate unpredictable events, especially considering the wide variety of contracts affected by widespread disruption such as the COVID-19 pandemic.

By allowing parties to regulate cases of force majeure proactively, Swiss and Austrian contract law are consistent with the notion of freedom of contract, which also underlies the contract law of all European countries and also the fragments of a European Union contract law and the projects on a European Private Law.[10] This openness allows parties to tailor the definition and effects of force majeure to their specific needs, which reduces the potential for conflicts and, if they arise, fosters their amicable and expedient resolution. Additionally, in the context of an ongoing pandemic or other prolonged significant events, specific clauses are an instrument to provide relative certainty to the parties even in the absence of executive or legislative action or before a judicial consensus on the issue has emerged.

3. IMPOSSIBILITY AND DELAY

If there is no contractual force majeure clause, the concepts of (subsequent) impossibility and delay of performance might apply to adjust or terminate contracts. These concepts are regulated individually in both the Swiss and Austrian codification. This differentiated approach stems from Roman contract law, which has influenced both Switzerland and Austria.[11] This approach contrasts with the unified approach to the breach of contract introduced in

---

9 https://iccwbo.org/publication/icc-force-majeure-and-hardship-clauses/ accessed 1 May 2021.

10 The notion of party autonomy features prominently, e.g. in: art 1:102 Principles of European Contract Law (PECL), II.-1:102 Draft Common Frame of Reference (DCFR) or art 1 of the (withdrawn) Proposal for a Common European Sales Law (CESL). Party autonomy is also contained in: art 6 United Nations Convention on Contracts for the International Sale of Goods (CISG) or art 1.1 UNIDROIT Principles of International Commercial Contracts (PICC).

11 Filippo Ranieri, *Europäisches Obligationenrecht: Ein Handbuch mit Texten und Materialien* (3rd edn, Springer Verlag 2009) 555 and 855; Jens Kleinschmidt in Nils Jansen and Reinhard Zimmermann (eds), *Commentaries on European Contract Laws* (OUP 2018) no 8 Introduction before Article 8:101 PECL; The SCO was in part also influenced by the ABGB (as well as by other neighbouring codifications and codifications of the cantons): Claire Huguenin and Barbara Meise, 'OR 2020: Braucht die Schweiz ein neues Vertragsrecht? – Eine Einführung' [2015] Schweizerische Zeitschrift für Wirtschafts- und Finanzmarktrecht (SZW) 280, 282 ff.

modern private law and private codices. These instruments contain a unified notion of breach of contract, originating in common law and Scandinavian law.[12] Besides Switzerland and Austria, other European countries following a civil law approach use a differentiated system.[13] In Switzerland, numerous scholars presented a draft for an updated general part for the code of obligations (OR 2020) to fundamentally modernise the more than 100-year old general part, which would have followed the unified approach.[14] However, the Federal Council rejected the proposal, citing a lack of necessity and too much risk.[15]

3.1. SUBSEQUENT IMPOSSIBILITY

COVID-19 Measures may render an obligation impossible by preventing a party from performing it. Under Swiss,[16] as well as Austrian[17] law, impossibility

---

[12] Article 8:101 PECL, III.-1:102(3) DCFR, Article 87 CESL (Proposal), Article 30 and 53 CISG, Article 7.1.1 PICC; Jens Kleinschmidt in Nils Jansen and Reinhard Zimmermann (eds), Commentaries on European Contract Laws (OUP 2018) no 10 and 15 Introduction before Article 8:101 PECL; Filippo Ranieri, *Europäisches Obligationenrecht: Ein Handbuch mit Texten und Materialien* (3rd edn, Springer Verlag 2009) 855; cf Harriet Schelhaas in Stefan Vogenauer (ed), *Commentary on the UNIDROIT Principles of International Commercial Contracts (PICC)* (OUP 2015) no 1 Article 7.1.1 PICC.

[13] However, Germany has recently adopted a unified approach (§280 BGB); with further references: Ulrich Magnus, 'Chapter 17: Performance and Breach of Contract' in Larry A. DiMatteo and others (eds), *International Sales Law: Contract, Principles & Practice* (Nomos 2016) no 98.

[14] Article 118 SCO 2020; with explicit reference to CISG, DCFR, PECL and PICC: Markus Müller-Chen in Claire Huguenin and Reto M. Hilty (eds), *Schweizer Obligationenrecht 2020: Entwurf für einen neuen allgemeinen Teil* (Schulthess Verlag 2013) no 4 ff Vorbemerkungen zu Articles 118–134 SCO 2020; similar: Nadja Erk, 'Vorschlag eines neuen Leistungsstörungsrechts im OR 2020' [2015] SZW 329, 332.

[15] Modernisierung des Allgemeinen Teils des Schweizerischen Obligationenrechts: Bericht des Bundesrates in Erfüllung der Postulate 13.3217 Bischof und 13.3226 Caroni vom 31 January 2018 https://www.ejpd.admin.ch/dam/bj/de/data/aktuell/news/2018/2018-01-310/ber-br-d.pdf.download.pdf/ber-br-d.pdf accessed 25 September 2020.

[16] Viktor Aepli, *Zürcher Kommentar: Art. 114-126 OR: Erlöschen der Obligation* (3rd edn, Schulthess Verlag 1991) no 44 Article 119 SCO; Rolf H. Weber, *Berner Kommentar: Schweizerisches Zivilgesetzbuch: Das Obligationenrecht: Allgemeine Bestimmungen: Die Folgen der Nichterfüllung: Art. 97-109 OR* (Stämpfli Verlag 2000) no 131 and 139 Article 97 SCO; Oliver Kälin, 'Unmöglichkeit der Leistung nach art. 119 OR und clausula rebus sic stantibus' [2004] recht 246, 248; Hans Giger in Willi Fischer and Thierry Luterbacher (eds), *Haftpflichtkommentar: Kommentar zu den schweizerischen Haftpflichtbestimmungen* (Dike Verlag 2015) no 11 Article 97 SCO; Andreas Furrer and Rainer Wey in Anton K. Schnyder (ed), *Handkommentar zum Schweizer Privatrecht: Obligationenrecht – Allgemeine Bestimmungen: Art. 1–183 OR* (3rd edn, Schulthess Verlag 2016) no 43 Article 97 SCO; Wolfgang Wiegand in Corinne Widmer Lüchinger and David Oser (eds), *Basler Kommentar: Obligationenrecht I: Art. 1-529 OR* (7th edn, Helbing Lichtenhahn Verlag 2019) no 16 Article 97 SCO; permanence is also present in cases where there is a chance that the performance might be possible in the future, but the end of the impossibility is either not in sight or not before a contractually defined end date or period of time; see Viktor Aepli, *Zürcher Kommentar: Art. 114-126 OR:*

requires a permanent obstacle to performance. In case of a merely temporary impossibility, the rules for delay by the debtor apply (see below section 3.2).[18] Subsequent impossibility means that the obstacle arises after the conclusion of the contract.

Whether the requirements of impossibility are fulfilled must be carefully analysed by considering the specific obligations undertaken by the parties. In Switzerland, the threshold of impossibility is generally not met if the creditor cannot use the debtor's performance for the envisaged purpose (e.g. if a property is rented without specifying a use and, subsequently, the lessee cannot get a permit for the intended use).[19] However, an obligation is considered impossible in the exceptional case that the intended use of the performance forms an integral part of the contract (e.g. a property is rented specifically as a dentist's office, and an unforeseen change to the law prevents the dentist from further practising dentistry).[20] On the debtor's side, the performance is not impossible if it has only become more onerous for the debtor.[21] However, in exceptional

---

Erlöschen der Obligation (3rd edn, Schulthess Verlag 1991) no 123 Article 119 SCO; Andreas Thier in Heinrich Honsell (ed), *Kurzkommentar Obligationenrecht: Art. 1-1186 OR* (Helbing Lichtenhahn Verlag 2014) no 7 Article 97 SCO.

17 In Austrian law, the possibility that the contract cannot be fulfilled in the future needs to be close to certain; among others OGH 10 December 2002, 10 Ob 326/02t; OGH 28 September 2007, 5 Ob 107/07g; Rudolf Reischauer in Peter Rummel and Meinhard Lukas (eds), *ABGB* (4th edn, rdb.at 2018) §920, no 4; Andrea Holly in Andreas Kletečka and Martin Schauer (eds), *ABGB-ON* (1.05 edn, rdb.at 2019) §1447, no 12.

18 Article 102 ff SCO; §§918 ff ABGB.

19 Example decided in: BGE 62 II 42, consid 1 pp 43 ff; Viktor Aepli, *Zürcher Kommentar: Art. 114-126 OR: Erlöschen der Obligation* (3rd edn, Schulthess Verlag 1991) no 31 ff Article 119 SCO Andreas Thier in Heinrich Honsell (ed), *Kurzkommentar Obligationenrecht: Art. 1-1186 OR* (Helbing Lichtenhahn Verlag 2014) no 12 Article 97 SCO; Andreas Furrer and Rainer Wey in Anton K. Schnyder (ed), *Handkommentar zum Schweizer Privatrecht: Obligationenrecht – Allgemeine Bestimmungen: Art. 1–183 OR* (3rd edn, Schulthess Verlag 2016) no 38 Article 97 SCO.

20 Example decided in: BGE 57 II 532, consid 1 p 534; Andreas Thier in Heinrich Honsell (ed), *Kurzkommentar Obligationenrecht: Art. 1-1186 OR* (Helbing Lichtenhahn Verlag 2014) no 12 Article 97 SCO; Hans Giger in Willi Fischer and Thierry Luterbacher (eds), *Haftpflichtkommentar: Kommentar zu den schweizerischen Haftpflichtbestimmungen* (Dike Verlag 2015) no 16 Article 97 SCO; Andreas Furrer and Rainer Wey in Anton K. Schnyder (ed), *Handkommentar zum Schweizer Privatrecht: Obligationenrecht – Allgemeine Bestimmungen: Art. 1–183 OR* (3rd edn, Schulthess Verlag 2016) no 37 Article 97 SCO.

21 BGE 135 III 212, consid 3.1 p 218; 4A_189/2012, consid 5.2; Rolf H. Weber, *Berner Kommentar: Schweizerisches Zivilgesetzbuch: Das Obligationenrecht: Allgemeine Bestimmungen: Die Folgen der Nichterfüllung: Art. 97-109 OR* (Stämpfli Verlag 2000) no 134 Article 97 SCO; Oliver Kälin, 'Unmöglichkeit der Leistung nach art. 119 OR und clausula rebus sic stantibus' [2004] recht 256, 250; Andreas Thier in Heinrich Honsell (ed), *Kurzkommentar Obligationenrecht: Art. 1-1186 OR* (Helbing Lichtenhahn Verlag 2014) no 9 Article 97 SCO; Hans Giger in Willi Fischer and Thierry Luterbacher (eds), *Haftpflichtkommentar: Kommentar zu den schweizerischen Haftpflichtbestimmungen* (Dike Verlag 2015) no 13 Article 97 SCO; Michaela Eichenberger in Jolanta Kren Kostkiewicz and others (eds), *OR Kommentar: Schweizerisches Obligationenrecht* (Orell Füssli 2016) no 3 Article 119 SCO; Andreas Furrer and Rainer Wey in Anton K. Schnyder (ed), *Handkommentar zum Schweizer Privatrecht: Obligationenrecht – Allgemeine Bestimmungen: Art. 1–183 OR* (3rd edn, Schulthess Verlag 2016) no 33 Article 97 SCO.

circumstances, the Swiss Federal Supreme Court (*Bundesgericht*; BGer) has held that a performance is impossible where the onerousness has amounted to such an extent that demanding performance would be contrary to good faith.[22] Furthermore, the performance is impossible if it would pose an unacceptable risk to the debtor's life or health.[23]

COVID-19 creates difficulties in determining whether impossibility applies. This question cannot be answered in the abstract. The following points can guide the determination: (1) COVID-19 (Measures) – from today's point of view – are temporary phenomena, which is why in many cases the measures will constitute a delay rather than an impossibility. However, a permanent obstacle for contract performance (and, therefore, impossibility) is present if the obligation was to be fulfilled at a specific date (*Fixgeschäft;* e.g. delivery of goods for Easter sales, funeral speech or delivery of a wedding cake). (2) The COVID-19 Measures have an impact on the creditor's use of property (e.g. a restaurant must remain closed). It must be examined whether such obstacles cause impossibility. (3) COVID-19 and the Measures may render an obligation more onerous and may pose a risk to the debtor's health (e.g. contact with clients). It must be determined if these added difficulties amount to impossibility.

Once impossibility has been established, the consequences can be determined according to the following considerations.

The Swiss Code of Obligations (SCO) regulates cases of subsequent impossibility in Articles 97 and 119. Since Article 97 SCO only deals with the impossibility for which the debtor is responsible, Article 119 SCO is the primary legal basis in the present context. Article 119 SCO applies if the debtor is not responsible for the impossibility,[24] for which the debtor bears the burden

22 BGE 135 III 212, consid 3.1 p 218; see also Thomas Coendet, 'Subjektive Unmöglichkeit als regulatives Prinzip: Über die Funktion der subjektiven Leistungsunmöglichkeit als notwendiges systematisches Regulativ gegenüber dem Schuldnerverzug' [2009] recht 128, 128; see criticism in Andreas Furrer and Rainer Wey in Anton K. Schnyder (ed), *Handkommentar zum Schweizer Privatrecht: Obligationenrecht – Allgemeine Bestimmungen: Art. 1–183 OR* (3rd edn, Schulthess Verlag 2016) no 33 Article 97 SCO.

23 Rolf H. Weber, *Berner Kommentar: Schweizerisches Zivilgesetzbuch: Das Obligationenrecht: Allgemeine Bestimmungen: Die Folgen der Nichterfüllung: Art. 97-109 OR* (Stämpfli Verlag 2000) no 128 Article 97 SCO; Hans Giger in Willi Fischer and Thierry Luterbacher (eds), *Haftpflichtkommentar: Kommentar zu den schweizerischen Haftpflichtbestimmungen* (Dike Verlag 2015) no 14 Article 97 SCO; Andreas Furrer and Rainer Wey in Anton K. Schnyder (ed), *Handkommentar zum Schweizer Privatrecht: Obligationenrecht – Allgemeine Bestimmungen: Art. 1–183 OR* (3rd edn, Schulthess Verlag 2016) no 36 Article 97 SCO.

24 Viktor Aepli, *Zürcher Kommentar: Art. 114-126 OR: Erlöschen der Obligation* (3rd edn, Schulthess Verlag 1991) no 58 Article 119 SCO; Andreas Thier in Heinrich Honsell (ed), *Kurzkommentar Obligationenrecht: Art. 1-1186 OR* (Helbing Lichtenhahn Verlag 2014) no 3 Article 119 SCO; Laurent Killias and Matthias Wiget in Anton K. Schnyder (ed), *Handkommentar zum Schweizer Privatrecht: Obligationenrecht – Allgemeine Bestimmungen: Art. 1–183 OR* (3rd edn, Schulthess Verlag 2016) no 12 Article 119 SCO.

of proof.[25] The BGer and numerous scholars apply Article 119 SCO to both objective (i.e. no-one can fulfil the obligation) and subjective (i.e. the debtor cannot fulfil the obligation, while others could) impossibility,[26] whereas others wish to treat subjective impossibility as a delay.[27]

The courts have developed criteria on the basis of which it is determined whether the debtor is responsible for the impossibility of performance. For example, if the performance would require the debtor to act illegally, he/she is not responsible for the impossibility if this prohibition was not foreseeable.[28] When assessing the foreseeability, the debtor's expertise must be taken into consideration.[29] When comparing the required lack of responsibility to the standard of force majeure, the BGer has held that force majeure is not the applicable test under Article 119 SCO. While force majeure excludes responsibility within the meaning of Article 119 SCO, Article 119 SCO does not require that the lack of responsibility be caused by force majeure.[30]

---

[25] Oliver Kälin, 'Unmöglichkeit der Leistung nach art. 119 OR und clausula rebus sic stantibus' [2004] recht 246 251.

[26] See for the terminology: BGer 2C_390/2016 consid 5.3.1; Obergericht Zürich PP180004 consid IV.2; Michaela Eichenberger in Jolanta Kren Kostkiewicz and others (eds), *OR Kommentar: Schweizerisches Obligationenrecht* (Orell Füssli 2016) no 3 Article 119 SCO; Andreas Furrer and Rainer Wey in Anton K. Schnyder (ed), *Handkommentar zum Schweizer Privatrecht: Obligationenrecht – Allgemeine Bestimmungen: Art. 1–183 OR* (3rd edn, Schulthess Verlag 2016) no 31 Article 97 SCO.

[27] BGE 57 II 532 consid 1 pp 534 ff; BGer 4C.344/2002 consid 4.2; BGer 4A_189/2012 consid 5.2; Handelsgericht Zürich HG140166 of 16 February 2017, consid 5.2.1; Thomas Coendet, 'Subjektive Unmöglichkeit als regulatives Prinzip: Über die Funktion der subjektiven Leistungsunmöglichkeit als notwendiges systematisches Regulativ gegenüber dem Schuldnerverzug' [2009] recht 128, 129; Wolfgang Wiegand in Corinne Widmer Lüchinger and David Oser (eds), *Basler Kommentar: Obligationenrecht I: Art. 1-529 OR* (7th edn, Helbing Lichtenhahn Verlag 2019) no 1+4 Article 119 SCO; contradictory: BGer 2C_390/2016 consid 5.3.1; differently: Viktor Aepli, *Zürcher Kommentar: Art. 114-126 OR: Erlöschen der Obligation* (3rd edn, Schulthess Verlag 1991) no 49 Article 119 SCO; see also Laurent Killias and Matthias Wiget in Anton K. Schnyder (ed), *Handkommentar zum Schweizer Privatrecht: Obligationenrecht – Allgemeine Bestimmungen: Art. 1–183 OR* (3rd edn, Schulthess Verlag 2016) no 6 Article 119 SCO.

[28] BGE 42 II 367 consid 1 p 372; BGE 57 II 532 consid 2 p 535; BGer 4A_562/2011 consid 4.3; see also Viktor Aepli, *Zürcher Kommentar: Art. 114-126 OR: Erlöschen der Obligation* (3rd edn, Schulthess Verlag 1991) no 56 Article 119 SCO; Oliver Kälin, 'Unmöglichkeit der Leistung nach art. 119 OR und clausula rebus sic stantibus' [2004] recht 246, 248; Jolanta Kren Kostkiewicz in Jolanta Kren Kostkiewicz and others (eds), *OR Kommentar: Schweizerisches Obligationenrecht* (Orell Füssli 2016) no 7 Article 97 SCO; Corinne Widmer Lüchinger and Wolfgang Wiegand in Corinne Widmer Lüchinger and David Oser (eds), Basler Kommentar: Obligationenrecht I: Art. 1-529 OR (7th edn, Helbing Lichtenhahn Verlag 2019) no 3 Article 103 SCO; see on foreseeability of COVID-19 Measures: Benjamin V. Enz, 'Risikozuordnung in Verträgen und die COVID-19 Situation: Teil 1: Anwendungsbereich der clausula rebus sic stantibus, der Unmöglichkeit nach Art. 119 OR und der Kündigung aus wichtigem Grund' [2020] Jusletter 18 May 2020, no 15.

[29] BGE 54 II 333 consid 4 pp 337 ff; BGE 111 II 352 consid 2a p 355.

[30] BGE 57 II 508 consid 3 p 511; see also Rolf H. Weber, *Berner Kommentar: Schweizerisches Zivilgesetzbuch: Das Obligationenrecht: Allgemeine Bestimmungen: Die Folgen der Nichterfüllung:*

In case the requirements of Article 119 SCO are met, the impossible obligation ceases to exist.[31] If this obligation was part of a bilateral contract, then the party released is liable for consideration already received, and any consideration not yet received ceases to be owed (Art 119(2) SCO).[32] If the debtor exempted from performance under Article 119 SCO receives compensation for the obligation that has become impossible, and if this compensation is closely related in economic terms (representative commodity, e.g. insured sum), the creditor can decide whether to receive this compensation. If the creditor chooses this substitute, he/she again remains liable for the obligation.[33]

The legal situation in Austrian law is comparable. In the event of a subsequent impossibility for which the debtor is neither responsible (*zufällige nachträgliche Unmöglichkeit*[34]) nor was the event foreseeable – especially cases of force majeure[35] – the contract will terminate automatically. The debtor will be released

---

Art. 97-109 OR (Stämpfli Verlag 2000) no 242 Article 97 SCO; see also the exculpation under Article 97 SCO: Eugen Bucher, *Schweizerisches Obligationenrecht: Allgemeiner Teil ohne Deliktsrecht* (2nd edn, Schulthess Verlag 1988) 347; Hans Giger in Willi Fischer and Thierry Luterbacher (eds), *Haftpflichtkommentar: Kommentar zu den schweizerischen Haftpflichtbestimmungen* (Dike Verlag 2015) no 34 Article 97 SCO; Andreas Furrer and Rainer Wey in Anton K. Schnyder (ed), *Handkommentar zum Schweizer Privatrecht: Obligationenrecht – Allgemeine Bestimmungen: Art. 1–183 OR* (3rd edn, Schulthess Verlag 2016) no 119 Article 97 SCO; Wolfgang Wiegand in Corinne Widmer Lüchinger and David Oser (eds), *Basler Kommentar: Obligationenrecht I: Art. 1-529 OR* (7th edn, Helbing Lichtenhahn Verlag 2019) no 42 Article 97 SCO.

31 Wolfgang Wiegand in Corinne Widmer Lüchinger and David Oser (eds), *Basler Kommentar: Obligationenrecht I: Art. 1-529 OR* (7th edn, Helbing Lichtenhahn Verlag 2019) no 11 Article 119 SCO.

32 The legal nature of the obligation to restore the consideration, which affects the period of prescription, is subject to debate. On contractual basis: Laurent Killias and Matthias Wiget in Anton K. Schnyder (ed), *Handkommentar zum Schweizer Privatrecht: Obligationenrecht – Allgemeine Bestimmungen: Art. 1–183 OR* (3rd edn, Schulthess Verlag 2016) no 19 Article 119 SCO; Wolfgang Wiegand in Corinne Widmer Lüchinger and David Oser (eds), *Basler Kommentar: Obligationenrecht I: Art. 1-529 OR* (7th edn, Helbing Lichtenhahn Verlag 2019) no 18 Article 119 SCO; BGer: suggests openness for contractual basis: BGE 137 III 243 consid 4.4.7 pp 251 ff; left open: BGE 114 II 152 consid 2d) pp 158 ff; earlier explicitly based upon unjust enrichment: BGE 63 II 252 consid 3 p 258.

33 Eugen Bucher, *Schweizerisches Obligationenrecht: Allgemeiner Teil ohne Deliktsrecht* (2nd edn, Schulthess Verlag 1988) pp 424 ff; Viktor Aepli, *Zürcher Kommentar: Art. 114-126 OR: Erlöschen der Obligation* (3rd edn, Schulthess Verlag 1991) no 125 ff Article 119 SCO; Michaela Eichenberger in Jolanta Kren Kostkiewicz and others (eds), *OR Kommentar: Schweizerisches Obligationenrecht* (Orell Füssli 2016) no 7 Article 119 SCO; Laurent Killias and Matthias Wiget in Anton K. Schnyder (ed), *Handkommentar zum Schweizer Privatrecht: Obligationenrecht – Allgemeine Bestimmungen: Art. 1–183 OR* (3rd edn, Schulthess Verlag 2016) no 27 Article 119 SCO; Wolfgang Wiegand in Corinne Widmer Lüchinger and David Oser (eds), *Basler Kommentar: Obligationenrecht I: Art. 1-529 OR* (7th edn, Helbing Lichtenhahn Verlag 2019) no 15 Article 119 SCO.

34 §1447 ABGB.

35 Andrea Holly in Andreas Kletečka and Martin Schauer (eds), *ABGB-ON* (1.05 edn, rdb.at 2019) §1447, no 16.

from the obligation to perform, and the creditor's obligation ceases.[36] The creditor can neither demand performance nor claim damages; however, the creditor can demand the return of the sum already paid in fulfilment of his/her obligation (e.g. deposit or price of already paid concert tickets). Alternatively, the creditor may demand a substitute the debtor has received (*stellvertretendes Commodum*).[37] §880 Austrian General Civil Code (ABGB) covers a special case of subsequent impossibility specifically intended for legal prohibitions.[38] The case law on §880 ABGB is sparse, but the OGH applied §880 in cases where the contractual performance becomes unlawful due to an official order after the conclusion of the contract.[39] The legal consequence is the *ex lege* termination of the contract.

It is difficult to assess to what extent COVID-19 Measures can be considered foreseeable for contracts that have been concluded before these Measures were enacted. The fact that the BGer considered a party's expertise to influence foreseeability suggests that there is not one specific date at which the COVID-19 Measures could be considered foreseeable for all parties. Accordingly, the foreseeability will likely be assessed differently for large, globally active corporations compared to small local stores. Since the debtor is only exempted from liability if the change to the law was not foreseeable, parties need to be particularly careful if a contract is concluded during the validity of the COVID-19 Measures but is only to be performed after these measures have expired. If the measures are extended, and the performance of the contract becomes impossible, the debtor runs the risk of being held responsible because such an extension might be considered foreseeable. In such cases where both parties are aware that there might be a risk of impossibility, but neither party caused the impossibility, the debtor remains solely responsible.[40]

3.2. DELAY BY THE DEBTOR

According to Swiss and Austrian law, the rules for delay apply if the impossibility of performance is merely temporary.[41]

36 §1447 ABGB; Andrea Holly in Andreas Kletečka and Martin Schauer (eds), *ABGB-ON* (1.05 edn, rdb.at 2019) §1447, no 43.

37 §§1447, 1435 ABGB; Rudolf Reischauer in Peter Rummel, *ABGB* (3rd edn, rdb.at 2002) §1447, no 4; Andrea Holly in Andreas Kletečka and Martin Schauer (eds), *ABGB-ON* (1.05 edn, rdb.at 2019) §1447, no 43.

38 Silvia Dullinger in Peter Rummel and Meinhard Lukas (eds), *ABGB* (4th edn, rdb.at 2018) §880, no 1; Georg Graf in Andreas Kletečka and Martin Schauer (eds), *ABGB-ON* (1.05 edn, rdb.at 2019) §880, no 1.

39 OGH 1 Ob 302/97 m = SZ 71/30; OGH 1 Ob 164/01 a = SZ 74/160; OGH 6 Ob 77/01 v = MietSlg 53.221; OGH 5 Ob 205/73 = JBl 1975, 206; OGH 17 November 1983, 7 Ob 716/83; OGH 6 Ob 503/94 = RdW 1995, 177; Georg Graf in Andreas Kletečka and Martin Schauer (eds), *ABGB-ON* (1.05 edn, rdb.at 2019) §880, no 3.

40 BGE 88 II 195 consid 5 p 203.

41 Article 102 ff SCO (Switzerland); §918 ff ABGB (Austria).

Under Swiss law, if the contract stipulates a deadline for the performance, exceeding this deadline immediately constitutes a delay (Art 102(2) SCO); otherwise, a formal reminder is necessary (Art 102(1) SCO). Delay applies regardless of fault; however, many of the creditor's remedies (e.g. claims for damages) during delay are only available if the debtor is at fault.[42] The effects of delay are twofold: on the one hand, the debtor is subject to additional liability. On the other hand, the creditor has different options to determine the future of the contract.

Article 103(1), which lays down the additional liability, stipulates that the debtor is liable for damages caused by late performance (special provisions for monetary obligations in Arts 104ff SCO). However, the debtor is only liable for such damages if the debtor is at fault, which is presumed.[43] Furthermore, Article 103(1) SCO provides that in case of delay, the debtor is responsible for accidental damage, including force majeure.[44] However, the debtor can avoid the responsibility for accidental damage if the debtor either proves that the delay is not his/her fault or that the damage would have occurred even if the performance had been timely.[45]

If the delay is caused by COVID-19 Measures, then the considerations under Article 119 SCO apply *mutatis mutandis* to the exculpation for damages for delay, i.e. the debtor might not be responsible for damages if COVID-19 Measures caused the delay. However, if the debtor's performance was delayed independent of COVID-19 Measures, the debtor may be responsible for damage caused by these measures because, as mentioned above, the debtor is liable for accidental damage.

---

42 Eugen Bucher, *Schweizerisches Obligationenrecht: Allgemeiner Teil ohne Deliktsrecht* (2nd edn, Schulthess Verlag 1988) 359 ff.

43 Rolf H. Weber, Berner Kommentar: *Schweizerisches Zivilgesetzbuch: Das Obligationenrecht: Allgemeine Bestimmungen: Die Folgen der Nichterfüllung: Art. 97-109 OR* (Stämpfli Verlag 2000) no 41 Article 103 SCO; Hans Giger in Willi Fischer and Thierry Luterbacher (eds), *Haftpflichtkommentar: Kommentar zu den schweizerischen Haftpflichtbestimmungen* (Dike Verlag 2015) no 2 Article 103 SCO; Andreas Furrer and Rainer Wey in Anton K. Schnyder (ed), *Handkommentar zum Schweizer Privatrecht: Obligationenrecht – Allgemeine Bestimmungen: Art. 1–183 OR* (3rd edn, Schulthess Verlag 2016) no 20 Articlel 03 SCO.

44 Rolf H. Weber, Berner Kommentar: *Schweizerisches Zivilgesetzbuch: Das Obligationenrecht: Allgemeine Bestimmungen: Die Folgen der Nichterfüllung: Art. 97-109 OR* (Stämpfli Verlag 2000) no 48 Article 103 SCO; Andreas Furrer and Rainer Wey in Anton K. Schnyder (ed), *Handkommentar zum Schweizer Privatrecht: Obligationenrecht – Allgemeine Bestimmungen: Art. 1–183 OR* (3rd edn, Schulthess Verlag 2016) no 26 Article 103 SCO; Corinne Widmer Lüchinger and Wolfgang Wiegand in Corinne Widmer Lüchinger and David Oser (eds), *Basler Kommentar: Obligationenrecht I: Art. 1-529 OR* (7th edn, Helbing Lichtenhahn Verlag 2019) no 12 Article 103 SCO.

45 Andreas Thier in Heinrich Honsell (ed), *Kurzkommentar Obligationenrecht: Art. 1-1186 OR* (Helbing Lichtenhahn Verlag 2014) no 7 Article 97 SCO no 4 Article 103 SCO.

The responsibility to pay damages under these provisions does not affect the original obligation.[46] But under a bilateral contract, the creditor, after providing appropriate additional time for performance,[47] has the option to forego subsequent performance and claim damages for non-performance or withdraw from the contract (Art 107 SCO). Such a claim for damages must meet the requirements of Article 97 SCO, which include the debtor's fault.[48] In certain cases (e.g. when it is clear that timely performance will not be possible), no additional time limit is required (Art 108 SCO).

Similarly to Swiss law, the concept of delay according to the Austrian ABGB does not require fault; delay according to §918 ABGB applies if the performance is still possible but is not performed or accepted at the proper time, in the agreed manner or at the proper place. In these cases, the creditor has a right to choose: the creditor can (1) insist on performance; or (2) withdraw from the contract by setting an adequate extension.[49] Such extension is not necessary if a fixed date was agreed upon for the performance of the contract (*Fixgeschäft*), or if it is obvious that the debtor is not in the position to perform within a reasonable time.[50] In case the extension period expires, the contract will be dissolved by withdrawal.[51] In connection with COVID-19 Measures, the length of the extension period will be of particular interest. It will strongly depend on the individual case what duration is appropriate. In case of delay, the debtor bears the risk of accidental loss from the time of the agreed delivery (*Gefahrtragung*). If the debtor is at fault, he/she will also be liable for damages.

---

46 Andreas Furrer and Rainer Wey in Anton K. Schnyder (ed), *Handkommentar zum Schweizer Privatrecht: Obligationenrecht – Allgemeine Bestimmungen: Art. 1–183 OR* (3rd edn, Schulthess Verlag 2016) no 6 Article 103 SCO; Corinne Widmer Lüchinger and Wolfgang Wiegand in Corinne Widmer Lüchinger and David Oser (eds), *Basler Kommentar: Obligationenrecht I: Art. 1-529 OR* (7th edn, Helbing Lichtenhahn Verlag 2019) no 7 Article 103 SCO.

47 The duration of the additional time depends on the specific circumstances. Cf the extensive discussion and references to jurisprudence in Rolf H. Weber, *Berner Kommentar: Schweizerisches Zivilgesetzbuch: Das Obligationenrecht: Allgemeine Bestimmungen: Die Folgen der Nichterfüllung: Art. 97-109 OR* (Stämpfli Verlag 2000) no 54 ff Article 107 SCO.

48 Eugen Bucher, *Schweizerisches Obligationenrecht: Allgemeiner Teil ohne Deliktsrecht* (2nd edn, Schulthess Verlag 1988) 379 ff; Andreas Furrer and Rainer Wey in Anton K. Schnyder (ed), *Handkommentar zum Schweizer Privatrecht: Obligationenrecht – Allgemeine Bestimmungen: Art. 1–183 OR* (3rd edn, Schulthess Verlag 2016) no 43 Article 107 SCO; Wolfgang Wiegand in Corinne Widmer Lüchinger and David Oser (eds), *Basler Kommentar: Obligationenrecht I: Art. 1-529 OR* (7th edn, Helbing Lichtenhahn Verlag 2019) no 16 Article 107 SCO.

49 Rudolf Reischauer in Peter Rummel and Meinhard Lukas (eds), *ABGB* (4th edn, rdb.at 2018) §918, no 9.

50 The legal consequences of subsequent impossibility (see above) apply in these cases.

51 §918 ABGB; Stefan Perner, Martin Spitzer and Georg Kodek, *Bürgerliches Recht* (5th edn, Manz 2016) 172; Rudolf Reischauer in Peter Rummel and Meinhard Lukas (eds), *ABGB* (4th edn, rdb.at 2018) §918, no 11; Michael Gruber in Andreas Kletečka and Martin Schauer (eds), *ABGB-ON* (1.06 edn, rdb.at 2019) §918, no 33.

Attention should be paid to the provisions in the 2. COVID-19-Justiz-Begleitgesetz.[52] The Austrian legislator has introduced special provisions for liquidity problems caused by COVID-19.[53] For contracts concluded before 1 April 2020 with payments due between 1 April and 30 June 2020, §3 2. COVID-19-JuBG the default interest is limited to the statutory default interest rate of 4% per year, irrespective of the contractual agreement. Further, the creditor does not have to reimburse the costs of extrajudicial debt enforcement measures. These provisions only apply if the delay in payment is due to a considerable impairment of the economic performance caused by COVID-19. Moreover, the COVID-19-JuBG, *inter alia*, exempts the debtor from contractual penalties in case of delay because of a considerable impairment of the debtor's economic capacity or restrictions on economic activities due to COVID-19.[54] This mandatory legal provision applies to contractual relationships entered into before 1 April 2020 even if the parties agreed on a no-fault contractual penalty. This is particularly surprising and questionable as §1336(2) ABGB already allows courts to balance the parties' interests by reducing excessive penalties.

It remains to be seen if this provision will stand up to constitutional scrutiny, as it is hard to explain why cases of delay because of COVID-19 should be treated differently from cases where the delay was caused by other events, like terrorist attacks or earthquakes.

3.3. DELAY BY THE CREDITOR

Not only the debtor may be in delay but also the creditor. According to Swiss law, this is the case when the creditor, without good cause, refuses the performance properly offered or to carry out preparations he/she is obliged to make and without which the debtor cannot perform (Art 91 SCO). For the creditor to be in delay the requirements are the following: (1) the debtor must be able and willing to perform the obligation properly;[55] (2) the debtor must,

---

52 2. Federal Act on Complementary Measures regarding COVID-19 in Judiciary (2. Bundesgesetz betreffend Begleitmaßnahmen zu COVID-19 in der Justiz; 2. COVID-19-JuBG), BGBl I 24/2020, 4 April 2020.

53 Further, there are specific provisions for rental contracts or loan agreements, which cannot be addressed within the scope of this contribution.

54 §4 2. COVID-19-JuBG.

55 BGE 79 II 280 consid 2 p 282; BGE 111 II 463 consid 5a p 469; Marius Schraner, *Zürcher Kommentar: Die Erfüllung der Obligationen: Art. 68-96 OR* (3rd edn, Schulthess Verlag 2000) no 60 ff Article 91 SCO; Rolf H. Weber, *Berner Kommentar: Schweizerisches Zivilgesetzbuch: Das Obligationenrecht: Allgemeine Bestimmungen: Die Folgen der Nichterfüllung: Art. 97-109 OR* (Stämpfli Verlag 2000) no 79 ff Article 91 SCO; Gregor Mercier in Anton K. Schnyder (ed), *Handkommentar zum Schweizer Privatrecht: Obligationenrecht – Allgemeine Bestimmungen: Art. 1–183 OR* (3rd edn, Schulthess Verlag 2016) no 15 ff Article 91 SCO; Stefan Leimgruber in Corinne Widmer Lüchinger and David Oser (eds), *Basler Kommentar: Obligationenrecht I: Art. 1-529 OR* (7th edn, Helbing Lichtenhahn Verlag 2019) no 3 ff+6 Article 91 SCO.

in general, properly offer the performance to the creditor;[56] (3) the creditor must refuse to accept the offered performance, which can be realised by not performing necessary preparations (e.g. a client not providing necessary documents to his/her attorney), not co-operating during performance (e.g. not allowing builders on the building site) or not performing accompanying actions (e.g. refusing to provide a receipt);[57] and, finally, (4) such refusal must be without good cause. A "good cause" must be an objective reason outside the creditor's sphere, it is irrelevant whether the creditor is at fault (i.e. delay also applies if the creditor cannot accept due to illness, accident, personal emergency, etc.).[58]

COVID-19 may create situations in which the creditor causes a delay, e.g. by not being able to accept a delivery because of full warehouses due to a decrease in sales. Whether delays occur in these cases depends on whether the refusal is made without good reason. Determining what constitutes a good cause can only be done in light of the specific contract. Besides the following cases there is little guidance on how major events impact this assessment: (1) during the First World War a Swiss seller sold oranges to a German buyer to be handed

56 BGE 79 II 280 consid 2 p 282; BGE 111 II 463 consid 5a p 469; BGE 119 II 439 consid 2b) p 439; Marius Schraner, Zürcher Kommentar: Die Erfüllung der Obligationen: Art. 68-96 OR (3rd edn, Schulthess Verlag 2000) no 74 ff Article 91 SCO; Rolf H. Weber, *Berner Kommentar: Schweizerisches Zivilgesetzbuch: Das Obligationenrecht: Allgemeine Bestimmungen: Die Folgen der Nichterfüllung: Art. 97-109 OR* (Stämpfli Verlag 2000) no 96 ff Article 91 SCO; Gregor Mercier in Anton K. Schnyder (ed), *Handkommentar zum Schweizer Privatrecht: Obligationenrecht – Allgemeine Bestimmungen: Art. 1–183 OR* (3rd edn, Schulthess Verlag 2016) no 7 ff Article 91 SCO; Stefan Leimgruber in Corinne Widmer Lüchinger and David Oser (eds), *Basler Kommentar: Obligationenrecht I: Art. 1-529 OR* (7th edn, Helbing Lichtenhahn Verlag 2019) no 4 ff Article 91 SCO. The offer may not be conditional upon an unjustified requirement: BGE 88 II 111 consid 7 p 115; BGer 4C.277/2005 consid 5. For the exception to offer performance: BGE 59 II 305 consid 5 pp 307 ff; BGE 109 II 26 consid 4b) p 32.

57 BGE 42 II 219 consid 3 p 224; BGE 59 II 305 consid 5 pp 306 ff; BGE 109 II 26 consid 4 pp 31 ff; BGer 4A_446/2015 consid 3.3.2; Marius Schraner, *Zürcher Kommentar: Die Erfüllung der Obligationen: Art. 68-96 OR* (3rd edn, Schulthess Verlag 2000) no 113 ff Article 91 SCO; Rolf H. Weber, *Berner Kommentar: Schweizerisches Zivilgesetzbuch: Das Obligationenrecht: Allgemeine Bestimmungen: Die Folgen der Nichterfüllung: Art. 97-109 OR* (Stämpfli Verlag 2000) no 141 ff Article 91 SCO; Gregor Mercier in Anton K. Schnyder (ed), *Handkommentar zum Schweizer Privatrecht: Obligationenrecht – Allgemeine Bestimmungen: Art. 1–183 OR* (3rd edn, Schulthess Verlag 2016) no 17 ff Article 91 SCO; Stefan Leimgruber in Corinne Widmer Lüchinger and David Oser (eds), *Basler Kommentar: Obligationenrecht I: Art. 1-529 OR* (7th edn, Helbing Lichtenhahn Verlag 2019) no 7 ff Article 91 SCO.

58 Marius Schraner, *Zürcher Kommentar: Die Erfüllung der Obligationen: Art. 68-96 OR* (3rd edn, Schulthess Verlag 2000) no 125 ff Article 91 SCO; Rolf H. Weber, *Berner Kommentar: Schweizerisches Zivilgesetzbuch: Das Obligationenrecht: Allgemeine Bestimmungen: Die Folgen der Nichterfüllung: Art. 97-109 OR* (Stämpfli Verlag 2000) no 155 ff Article 91 SCO; Gregor Mercier in Anton K. Schnyder (ed), *Handkommentar zum Schweizer Privatrecht: Obligationenrecht – Allgemeine Bestimmungen: Art. 1–183 OR* (3rd edn, Schulthess Verlag 2016) no 21 ff Article 91 SCO; Stefan Leimgruber in Corinne Widmer Lüchinger and David Oser (eds), *Basler Kommentar: Obligationenrecht I: Art. 1-529 OR* (7th edn, Helbing Lichtenhahn Verlag 2019) no 13 ff Article 91 SCO.

over in Switzerland. Before the delivery, Germany banned the import of oranges, and the buyer argued that this import ban constituted a good cause not to accept the goods. The BGer rejected this argument by holding that the delivery in Switzerland was still possible.[59] However, doctrine concludes that there would be a good cause if the ban covered the place of delivery.[60] (2) In a decision of 1943, the Supreme Cantonal Court of Zurich held that war measures that prevent the acceptance constitute a good reason for refusing acceptance because they are objective measures that affect the economy as such and, therefore, do not come from the sphere of the creditor.[61] The doctrine argues further from an economic perspective that the fact that a good is no longer needed due to changes in the creditor's economic situation is not sufficient to establish a good reason.[62] It is unclear whether this statement also holds if large parts of the economy are severely disrupted, and, thus, the impediment affects more than the sphere of one creditor.

Unlike a delay by the debtor, a delay by the creditor generally[63] does not provide a claim for damages and does not allow the enforcement of the creditor's acceptance or preparatory actions.[64] This shows that the acceptance or preparatory actions are generally not full obligations but lesser duties (*Obliegenheiten*). While they are not directly enforceable, the law provides the debtor with other remedies.[65]

---

59 BGE 44 II 407 consid 1 pp 409 ff.

60 Marius Schraner, *Zürcher Kommentar: Die Erfüllung der Obligationen: Art. 68-96 OR* (3rd edn, Schulthess Verlag 2000) no 128 Article 91 SCO; Rolf H. Weber, *Berner Kommentar: Schweizerisches Zivilgesetzbuch: Das Obligationenrecht: Allgemeine Bestimmungen: Die Folgen der Nichterfüllung: Art. 97-109 OR* (Stämpfli Verlag 2000) no 160 Article 91 SCO.

61 Supreme Cantonal Court of Zurich, consid II in [1943] Schweizerische Juristen-Zeitung (SJZ) 362, 363.

62 Marius Schraner, *Zürcher Kommentar: Die Erfüllung der Obligationen: Art. 68-96 OR* (3rd edn, Schulthess Verlag 2000) no 127 Article 91 SCO; Rolf H. Weber, *Berner Kommentar: Schweizerisches Zivilgesetzbuch: Das Obligationenrecht: Allgemeine Bestimmungen: Die Folgen der Nichterfüllung: Art. 97-109 OR* (Stämpfli Verlag 2000) no 158 Article 91 SCO; Stefan Leimgruber in Corinne Widmer Lüchinger and David Oser (eds), *Basler Kommentar: Obligationenrecht I: Art. 1-529 OR* (7th edn, Helbing Lichtenhahn Verlag 2019) no 1 Article 92 SCO.

63 In exceptional circumstances or if agreed by the parties, the acceptance or preparatory actions can be elevated to a fully enforceable obligation, which may provide a claim for damages in case of delay (Rolf H. Weber, *Berner Kommentar: Schweizerisches Zivilgesetzbuch: Das Obligationenrecht: Allgemeine Bestimmungen: Die Folgen der Nichterfüllung: Art. 97-109 OR* (Stämpfli Verlag 2000) no 54 ff Article 91 SCO).

64 BGer 4A_446/2015 consid 3.3.2; Marius Schraner, *Zürcher Kommentar: Die Erfüllung der Obligationen: Art. 68-96 OR* (3rd edn, Schulthess Verlag 2000) no 22 ff Article 91 SCO; Rolf H. Weber, *Berner Kommentar: Schweizerisches Zivilgesetzbuch: Das Obligationenrecht: Allgemeine Bestimmungen: Die Folgen der Nichterfüllung: Art. 97-109 OR* (Stämpfli Verlag 2000) no 50 ff Article 91 SCO.

65 Peter Gauch and others, *Schweizerisches Obligationenrecht: Allgemeiner Teil: ohne ausservertragliches Haftpflichtrecht* (10th edn, Schulthess Verlag 2014) no 101 ff.

First, the delay by a creditor precludes the delay by the debtor and the accompanying consequences.[66] Secondly, depending on the nature of the obligation, the debtor has rights to free him/herself unilaterally but is not obligated to exercise them.[67] These rights include the deposition or sale of the goods to be delivered or withdrawal from the contract if the obligation does not pertain to goods (Art 92 ff SCO).

The applicable provision for delay by the creditor in Austrian law is §1419 ABGB (*Annahmeverzug*). As under Swiss law, delay by the creditor only exists if the debtor is willing and able to perform.[68] The creditor is in delay if he/she refuses to accept the performance duly offered – which means the agreed goods, in the agreed quantity and quality at the right time and place[69] – by the debtor. A creditor who is not able to store the delivered goods because of full warehouses will be in delay irrespective of the reasons which led to this situation.[70] Unlike under Swiss law, the creditor is in delay irrespective of whether there was a good cause for the delay. Furthermore, fault is no prerequisite, but if the creditor is at fault, he/she might also be liable for damages on the grounds of tort law.[71]

Delay by the creditor does not release the debtor from obligation, nor does it constitute a right to withdraw from the contract.[72] In principle, the creditor must stay willing to perform but can free him/herself from the obligation by depositing.[73] According to the ABGB[74] the sale of goods by the debtor to discharge his/her duty (*Befreiungsverkauf*) is only permissible in exceptional

---

66 BGE 82 II 460 consid 2 p 466; BGer 4C.277/2005 consid 5; Rolf H. Weber, *Berner Kommentar: Schweizerisches Zivilgesetzbuch: Das Obligationenrecht: Allgemeine Bestimmungen: Die Folgen der Nichterfüllung: Art. 97-109 OR* (Stämpfli Verlag 2000) no 25 ff Article 92 SCO; Stefan Leimgruber in Corinne Widmer Lüchinger and David Oser (eds), *Basler Kommentar: Obligationenrecht I: Art. 1-529 OR* (7th edn, Helbing Lichtenhahn Verlag 2019) no 1 Article 92 SCO.

67 Stefan Leimgruber in Corinne Widmer Lüchinger and David Oser (eds), *Basler Kommentar: Obligationenrecht I: Art. 1-529 OR* (7th edn, Helbing Lichtenhahn Verlag 2019) no 1 Article 92 SCO.

68 Johannes Stabentheiner in Andreas Kletečka and Martin Schauer (eds), *ABGB-ON* (1.04 edn, rdb.at 2018) §1419, no 2.

69 See criteria according to §1413 ABGB; RS0103510; OGH 12 March 1996, 10 Ob 2035/96d; Johannes Stabentheiner in Andreas Kletečka and Martin Schauer (eds), *ABGB-ON* (1.04 edn, rdb.at 2018) §1419 no 2.

70 RIS-Justiz RS0131860; OGH 15 December 2017, 1 Ob 218/17s.

71 Rudolf Reischauer in Peter Rummel, ABGB (3rd edn, rdb.at 2002) §1419, no 2; Johannes Stabentheiner in Andreas Kletečka and Martin Schauer (eds), ABGB-ON (1.04 edn, rdb.at 2018) §1419 no 3.

72 Johannes Stabentheiner in Andreas Kletečka and Martin Schauer (eds), *ABGB-ON* (1.04 edn, rdb.at 2018) §1419 no 2 ff; RIS-Justiz RS0033457; OGH 23 October 1986, 7 Ob 690/86.

73 OGH 23 October 1986, 7 Ob 690/86.

74 In contrast to the provisions in the Commercial Code (Unternehmensgesetzbuch; UGB), dRGBl 219/1897; according to §373(2) UGB the debtor is authorised to sell the goods after notification. No prior notification is necessary in case of perishable goods, imminent danger or when the notification is otherwise unfeasible.

cases; such as for perishable goods or in the event of disproportionate costs of deposit.[75]

Under Austrian law, too, acceptance is a lesser duty (*Obliegenheit*). The primary legal consequence is that the creditor bears the risk of accidental loss.[76] In the above example of delay by the creditor because of full warehouses, the buyer would be obliged to pay the purchase price even if the goods were destroyed by a storm[77] but may demand a substitute, like insurance payments (*stellvertretendes Commodum*).

For synallagmatic contracts – as a natural consequence – the creditor is also a debtor liable for his/her obligation; e.g. the buyer must perform the payment. If he/she refuses to do so, the legal consequences of delay by the debtor apply.

3.4. FORCE MAJEURE IN SWISS AND AUSTRIAN CONTRACT LAW EMBEDDED IN THE INTERNATIONAL CONTEXT

As shown in the previous sections, the differentiated approach to breach of contract in Swiss and Austrian general contract law provides different remedies depending on the type of breach of contract. However, the commonality is that damages generally require fault (or another form of responsibility, e.g. responsibility for a third party). In the contractual context, fault is presumed, and, accordingly, the burden of proof for the exculpation lies with the person in breach of contract. As shown above, force majeure is a possible reason for exculpation.

Conversely, international instruments generally hold the person in breach of contract liable for damages regardless of fault.[78] However, these systems then allow for exceptions for certain impediments, which are sometimes explicitly referred to as force majeure or, in the other cases, perform a similar function.[79]

---

75 Rudolf Reischauer in Peter Rummel, *ABGB* (3rd edn, rdb.at 2002) §1419, no 11; Johannes Stabentheiner in Andreas Kletečka and Martin Schauer (eds), *ABGB-ON* (1.04 edn, rdb.at 2018) §1419 no 11.

76 RIS-Justiz RS0033438; OGH 11 June 1981, 7 Ob 639/80; Rudolf Reischauer in Peter Rummel, ABGB (3rd edn, rdb.at 2002) §1419, no 13; Johannes Stabentheiner in Andreas Kletečka and Martin Schauer (eds), *ABGB-ON* (1.04 edn, rdb.at 2018) §1419 no 7.

77 Accidental loss was also assumed for cases of currency devaluation caused by legislation: OGH 1 March 1950, 1 Ob 97/50.

78 Thomas Rüfner in Nils Jansen and Reinhard Zimmermann (eds), *Commentaries on European Contract Laws* (OUP 2018) no 18 Article 8:108 PECL; cf Harriet Schelhaas in Stefan Vogenauer (ed), *Commentary on the UNIDROIT Principles of International Commercial Contracts (PICC)* (OUP 2015) no 4 Article 7.1.1 PICC; Ulrich Magnus, 'Chapter 17: Performance and Breach of Contract' in Larry A. DiMatteo and others (eds), *International Sales Law: Contract, Principles & Practice* (Nomos 2016) no 7, 21 and 32.

79 Article 88 CESL (proposal); Article 7.1.7 PICC; Article 8:108 PECL; III.-3:104 DCFR; Article 79 CISG; Thomas Rüfner in Nils Jansen and Reinhard Zimmermann (eds), *Commentaries on European Contract Laws* (OUP 2018) no 17 Article 8:108 PECL; Ingeborg Schwenzer, 'Die *clausula* und das CISG' in Wolfgang Wiegand, Thomas Koller and Hans Peter Walter (eds), *Tradition mit Weitsicht: Festschrift für Eugen Bucher zum 80. Geburtstag* (Stämpfli Verlag 2009) 723 ff.

Although the Swiss and Austrian fault-based system differs from the international instruments, the unifying factor is that force majeure or similar impediments serve to limit the parties' responsibility for factors outside their control. Ultimately, and despite their different approaches, both systems support the idea that there are factors for which the debtor is not liable. This similarity was also pointed out in the rejected proposal for a new Swiss general contract law. This proposal would have abandoned the fault-based system in favour of the system followed by some modern national contract laws and international instruments.[80] However, this change would have probably been of little practical significance because, on the one hand, fault is presumed and must be disproven, and, on the other hand, the test for fault applies a partly objective standard. These two factors narrow the gap to the international standards in practice.[81]

4. CONTRACT ADAPTATION IN CASE OF CHANGED CIRCUMSTANCES (*CLAUSULA REBUS SIC STANTIBUS*)

The subsequent impossibility of performance must be distinguished from those cases in which performance is still possible but the balance between performance and consideration presupposed by the contracting parties is disturbed by external circumstances. This leads to the following question: Is it from a legal point of view relevant if the governmental measures or restrictions make the performance of a contract by one contracting party useless or unprofitable (e.g. minimum quantities under framework contracts, massive price increases due to COVID-19)?

The change of circumstances and their implications on contracts are an inherent and long-standing problem in private law that was already discussed under Roman law.[82] The underlying problem is the conflict between the principle of *pacta sunt servanda* on the one hand and the unacceptable situations that may

80 The proposal would have introduced a similar provision for exceptions (Art 121 SCO 2020). The accompanying commentary makes particular reference to the rules in the CISG and PICC: Markus Müller-Chen in Claire Huguenin and Reto M. Hilty (eds), *Schweizer Obligationenrecht 2020: Entwurf für einen neuen allgemeinen Teil* (Schulthess Verlag 2013) no 1 ff Article 19 SCO 2020 no 1 Article 121 SCO 2020.

81 Nadja Erk, 'Vorschlag eines neuen Leistungsstörungsrechts im OR 2020' [2015] SZW 329, 332 ff; Markus Müller-Chen in Claire Huguenin and Reto M. Hilty (eds), *Schweizer Obligationenrecht 2020: Entwurf für einen neuen allgemeinen Teil* (Schulthess Verlag 2013) no 2 Article 121 SCO 2020; cf similar conclusions regarding the BGB: Thomas Rüfner in Nils Jansen and Reinhard Zimmermann (eds), Commentaries on European Contract Laws (OUP 2018) no 18 Article 8:108 PECL.

82 Franz Bydlinsky, 'Zum Wegfall der Geschäftsgrundlage im österreichischen Recht' [1996] Österreichisches Bankarchiv (ÖBA) 499, 499; Heinrich Honsell, *Römisches Recht* (8th edn, Springer 2015) 142.

arise out of changed circumstances which the parties did not foresee and which render the performance unduly burdensome for one party on the other hand.[83]

As with force majeure, both Swiss and Austrian law allow the parties to introduce their own clauses for (or the exclusion of) contract adaptation in case of changed circumstances. They can define both the requirements for and consequences of changed circumstances.[84] Such clauses for contract adaptation generally supersede judicial contract adaptation.[85] These clauses may range from specific (e.g. a predetermined price increase if inflation rises above a certain threshold) to general in their wording.

To the latter category belongs the ICC hardship clause, which was, along with the previously mentioned ICC force majeure clause, updated in 2020. With this update, the ICC hardship clause now contains versions permitting contract adaptation instead of being limited to contract termination if negotiations fail.[86] This change can prove beneficial, especially in the context of COVID-19, when adaptation allows contractual relationships to continue and sustain at least some economic activity to the extent the situation permits.

When drafting contracts, standard clauses (such as the ICC hardship clause) may guide the parties. Yet, major events, such as COVID-19, underline that the parties should each pay particular attention to these clauses, taking into account both the duration of the contract and the specific contractual risks (such as loss or increase of sales; logistics; price developments) and adapt standard clauses where necessary. Beyond hardship clauses themselves, COVID-19 impressively demonstrates how important it is for the parties to be aware of the nature and the impact of these risks on their specific contractual relationship.

In the absence of a party agreement, Swiss case law recognises that in exceptional cases contracts may be adapted by the court under *clausula rebus sic stantibus*. Such an adaptation requires that: (1) the circumstances have changed since the contract conclusion; (2) that these changes were neither avoidable nor foreseeable; (3) that they have caused a grave inequality in the contractual

83 Franz Bydlinsky, 'Zum Wegfall der Geschäftsgrundlage im österreichischen Recht' [1996] Österreichisches Bankarchiv (ÖBA) 499, 499.

84 Peter Jäggi, Peter Gauch and Stephan Hartmann, *Zürcher Kommentar: Art. 18 OR – Auslegung, Ergänzung und Anpassung der Verträge: Simulation* (4th edn, Schulthess Verlag 2015) no 656 ff; Christoph Müller, *Berner Kommentar: Schweizerisches Zivilgesetzbuch: Das Obligationenrecht: Allgemeine Bestimmungen: Art. 1-18 OR mit allgemeiner Einleitung in das Schweizerische Obligationenrecht* (Stämpfli Verlag 2018) no 575 ff Article 18 SCO.

85 There are limited exceptions to this rule, e.g. in case the clause is not permissible or it contains a gap (Peter Jäggi, Peter Gauch and Stephan Hartmann, *Zürcher Kommentar: Art. 18 OR – Auslegung, Ergänzung und Anpassung der Verträge: Simulation* (4th edn, Schulthess Verlag 2015) no 726).

86 Fabio Bortolotti, 'ICC Force Majeure and Hardship Clauses 2020: Introductory Note and Commentary' https://iccwbo.org/content/uploads/sites/3/2020/07/icc-forcemajeure-introductory-note.pdf, June 2020 accessed 1 October 2020 7 ff.

quid pro quo; and that (4) the party does not act contradictorily (e.g. fulfilling the contract without any reservations).[87]

Furthermore, some scholars and the BGer argue that a party may withdraw from a contract (under the provisions concerning error (*Irrtum*), Arts 23 ff SCO) if it mistakenly assumed that a circumstance would materialise in the future and there was no question in the party's mind that this assumption would prove correct (*Irrtum über zukünftige Sachverhalte*).[88] This error must pertain to a circumstance that is essential for the type of contract concluded and has been considered essential by the party which made the wrong assumption.[89] Whether an error can even pertain to a future circumstance and the precise requirements for such an error are subject to debate. Furthermore, even if an error may pertain to the future, the precise relation to *clausula rebus sic stantibus* and, in some cases, impossibility remains unclear.[90]

In Austrian law, the *clausula* problem is known as the doctrine of *Wegfall der Geschäftsgrundlage*. This doctrine concerns the typical circumstances which the contracting parties presume when concluding the contract and raises the question of whether a misconception about these circumstances entitles to challenge or adjustment of the contract if the performance becomes unduly burdensome for one of the parties.[91] The dogmatic classification of the doctrine is still not clear.[92]

---

87 BGE 127 III 300 consid 5b) p 305; see also Oliver Kälin, 'Unmöglichkeit der Leistung nach art. 119 OR und clausula rebus sic stantibus' [2004] recht 246, 251 ff; Giovanni Molo and Flavio Amadò, 'Covid-19: implicazioni giuridiche per le imprese' [2020] Novità fiscali 3, 14; Benjamin V. Enz, 'Risikozuordnung in Verträgen und die COVID-19 Situation: Teil 1: Anwendungsbereich der clausula rebus sic stantibus, der Unmöglichkeit nach Art. 119 OR und der Kündigung aus wichtigem Grund' [2020] Jusletter 18 May 2020, no 3 ff.

88 Fundamentally: BGE 109 II 105 consid. 4b) p 109 ff, see also BGE 118 II 297 consid. 2b) p. 300; with extensive references on the differing opinions: Peter Jäggi, Peter Gauch and Stephan Hartmann, *Zürcher Kommentar: Art. 18 OR – Auslegung, Ergänzung und Anpassung der Verträge: Simulation* (4th edn, Schulthess Verlag 2015) no 699.

89 Bruno Schmidlin, *Berner Kommentar: Mängel des Vertragsabschlusses: Art. 23-31 OR* (2nd edn, Stämpfli Verlag 2013) no 90 Article 24 SCO.

90 Regarding the application to COVID-19 Measures: Benjamin V. Enz, 'Risikozuordnung in Verträgen und die COVID-19 Situation: Teil 1: Anwendungsbereich der clausula rebus sic stantibus, der Unmöglichkeit nach Art. 119 OR und der Kündigung aus wichtigem Grund' [2020] Jusletter 18 May 2020, no 16 ff; see also Ernst Kramer, 'Neues zur clausula rebus sic stantibus' [2014] SJZ 273, 282; Peter Jäggi, Peter Gauch and Stephan Hartmann, *Zürcher Kommentar: Art. 18 OR – Auslegung, Ergänzung und Anpassung der Verträge: Simulation* (4th edn, Schulthess Verlag 2015) no 701.

91 Franz Bydlinsky, 'Zum Wegfall der Geschäftsgrundlage im österreichischen Recht' [1996] Österreichisches Bankarchiv (ÖBA) 499 499.

92 See for example Leopold Pfaff, 'Die clausel: rebus sic stantibus in der Doctrin und der österreichischen Gesetzgebung' in *Festschrift zum siebzigsten Geburtstage Sr. Excellenz Dr. Joseph Unger* (Cotta 1898) 221; Karl Larenz, *Geschäftsgrundlage und Vertragserfüllung* (2nd edn, Beck 1957); Peter Rummel, 'Anmerkungen zum gemeinsamen Irrtum und zur Geschäftsgrundlage' [1981] Juristische Blätter (JBl), 1; Ferdinand Kerschner, 'Wegfall der Geschäftsgrundlage bei unwiderruflichen Sozialleistungen' [1988] Wirtschaftsrechtliche Blätter (WBl) 211; Franz Bydlinsky, 'Zum Wegfall der Geschäftsgrundlage im österreichischen

Starting points were sought in the law of error (*Irrtum*[93]) or judicial contract adaptation.[94] Jurisprudence applies this doctrine in rare cases as *ultima ratio* and when changes are fundamental so that insisting on performance would violate the principle of good faith.[95] The possible consequences are primarily an amendment of the contract or if an amendment is impossible, the termination of the contract.[96]

Contract adaptation under *clausula rebus sic stantibus* allows for substantial judicial discretion and can only be considered under the specific circumstances of the contract. Due to the significance of the principle of *pacta sunt servanda*, the courts are reluctant to apply *clausula rebus sic stantibus*. Nevertheless, the exceptional circumstances caused by the COVID-19 pandemic may in individual cases prove sufficient to justify contract adaptation. In an early Swiss domestic arbitral award, the tribunal stated in an *obiter dictum* that *clausula rebus sic stantibus* would apply to the lease of a restaurant that could no longer operate due to the COVID-19 Measures if there were not already specific provisions for the reduction of rent.[97]

Unlike the different approaches to liability addressed above, the Swiss and Austrian approach to contract adaptation in case of changed circumstances more closely aligns with international instruments, which contain similar provisions.[98]

Recht' [1996] Österreichisches Bankarchiv (ÖBA) 499 499; Günther H. Roth, 'Vom Wegfall der Geschäftsgrundlage zur richterlichen Vertragsanpassung' in Erwin Bernat (ed), *Festschrift Heinz Krejci zum 60. Geburtstag Bd. 2* (Verlag Österreich 2001) 1251; Ernst Kramer, 'Wegfall der Geschäftsgrundlage – ein Binnenvergleich im Rahmen des deutschen Rechtskreises' [2015] JBl 273.

93 A wrong assumption about future developments is merely an irrelevant error of motive (*Motivirrtum*), According to §901 ABGB, an error in motive is only considerable if the motive was made a contractual condition. Typical circumstances, which all parties assume, are not covered.

94 Kramer, 'Wegfall der Geschäftsgrundlage – ein Binnenvergleich im Rahmen des deutschen Rechtskreises' [2015] JBl 284; according to Kramer the legal basis for judicial contract adaptation can be found in §914 ABGB, according to which the contract is to be understood in such a way that it is in line with the practice of good faith *'Übung des redlichen Verkehrs'* (with reference to OGH 2 October 2013, 7 Ob 91/13b).

95 RIS-Justiz RS0017524; OGH 10 March 1988, 8 Ob 527/88; *ultima ratio* RIS-Justiz RS0017454; OGH 29 May 2013, 2 Ob 173/12y.

96 OGH 14 June 2005, 4 Ob 103/05h.

97 Schenkel & Serrago Rechtsanwälte AG, *Schiedsgerichtsentscheid betreffend Mietzinsherabsetzung infolge Betriebsschliessung Covid-19 Coronavirus* (2020) https://www.rechtsanwalt-luzern.ch/fileadmin/files/schenkelrechtsanwaelte.ch/Engagement/Entscheid_Mietzinsherabsetzung_infolge_Covid-19.pdf accessed 11 May 2020, consid 6.

98 Articles 6.2.1 ff PICC; Article 89 CESL (proposal); Article 6:111 PECL; III.-1:110 DCFR; Larry A. DiMatteo, 'Chapter 22: Excuse: Impossibility and Hardship' in Larry A. DiMatteo and others (eds), *International Sales Law: Contract, Principles & Practice* (Nomos 2016) no 47, 50 and 51; As a general trend: Filippo Ranieri, *Europäisches Obligationenrecht: Ein Handbuch mit Texten und Materialien* (3rd edn, Springer Verlag 2009) 851; Notably, the CISG does not explicitly provide for contract adaptation in case of changed circumstances. Yet, it remains unclear whether such adaptation is possible; see: CISG Advisory Council, 'Opinion No. 20: Hardship under the CISG'

As under Swiss and Austrian law, these instruments require that contract adaptation be reserved for the most egregious disruptions to the contractual equilibrium.[99] Such systems equally grant substantial judicial discretion by allowing courts to adapt contracts instead of limiting them to termination.[100] These instruments differ from Swiss and Austrian law insofar as they contain explicit provisions for contract adaptation. Other countries, such as Germany and France, have introduced explicit provisions as well.[101] Recently, the German LG Heidelberg ruled that §313 BGB (the provision for contract adaptation) is not applicable and the tenant is obliged to lease payments during COVID-19 related closure, in case of a commercial lease agreement for business premises.[102] However, the decision emphasises the necessity for a case-by-case assessment in light of the specific circumstances and contractual provisions. In the particular case, the agreement of a sales-dependent lease rate with a fixed minimum amount indicated the reasonableness of the continuing lease payments. In Switzerland, the proposed updated general contract law would have included an explicit provision for changed circumstances.[103] Furthermore, and in contrast

---

http://cisgac.com/file/repository/Opinion_No_20_CISG_and_Hardship_Official_.pdf, 2–5 February 2020, accessed 1 October 2020; see for further reference the list of court decisions and arbitral awards in footnote 16 on p 7; Thomas Rüfner in Nils Jansen and Reinhard Zimmermann (eds), *Commentaries on European Contract Laws* (OUP 2018) no 17 Article 6:111 PECL; Ewan McKendrick in Stefan Vogenauer (ed), *Commentary on the UNIDROIT Principles of International Commercial Contracts (PICC)* (OUP 2015) no 4 Introduction to Section 6.2 of the PICC; Larry A. DiMatteo, 'Chapter 22: Excuse: Impossibility and Hardship' in Larry A. DiMatteo and others (eds), *International Sales Law: Contract, Principles & Practice* (Nomos 2016) no 26 ff; see also the comments on the issue in CISG Advisory Council, 'Opinion No. 7: Exemption of Liability for Damages Under Article 79 of the CISG' http://www.cisgac.com/file/repository/CISG_Advisory_Council_Opinion_No_7.pdf, 12 October 2007, accessed 1 October 2020, in particular para 23 ff.

99 Ewan McKendrick in Stefan Vogenauer (ed), *Commentary on the UNIDROIT Principles of International Commercial Contracts (PICC)* (OUP 2015) no 4 Article 6.2.1 PICC. Introducing the clause regarding changed circumstances by reiterating that *pacta sunt servanda* is the central principle even if circumstance render the performance more onerous: Article 6.2.1 PICC; Article 89(1) CESL (proposal); Article 6:111(1) PECL; III.-1:110(1) DCFR. For a restrictive interpretation of Article 6.2.2 PICC: ICC Arbitration 9479, February 1999 in Michael Joachim Bonell (ed), *The UNIDROIT Principles in Practice: Caselaw and Bibliography on the UNIDROIT Principles of International Commercial Contracts* (2nd edn, Transnational Publishers 2006) 786, 791.

100 Article 6.2.3(4)(b) PICC; Article 89(2) CESL (proposal); Article 6:111(3)(b) PECL; III.-1:110(2)(a) DCFR.

101 Germany: §313 Bürgerliches Gesetzbuch (BGB); France: Article 1195 Code civil, which was only added in 2016 and introduced the general possibility of contract adaptation in case of changed circumstances into French civil law (Thomas Rüfner in Nils Jansen and Reinhard Zimmermann (eds), *Commentaries on European Contract Laws* (OUP 2018) no 14 Article 6:111 PECL).

102 LG Heidelberg, 30.7.2020, 5 O 66/20, BeckRS, 19165.

103 Article 19 SCO 2020; Hans-Ueli Vogt in Claire Huguenin and Reto M. Hilty (eds), *Schweizer Obligationenrecht 2020: Entwurf für einen neuen allgemeinen Teil* (Schulthess Verlag 2013) no 1 ff Article 19 SCO 2020.

to the international instruments,[104] most scholars argue that Swiss law does not require renegotiations before a contract adaptation is possible.[105]

In a broader context, parties should be aware that different legal systems vary substantially regarding the permissibility and requirements of judicial contract adaptation.[106] Accordingly, the parties should consider whether they want to introduce a contractual hardship clause in light of the law applicable to their contract.

5. CONCLUSION

The COVID-19 pandemic triggered the widespread use of emergency legislation affecting large parts of the economy and the contractual relationships underlying them. This contribution has examined how Swiss and Austrian general contract law deal with such an upheaval.

We have shown that both countries pursue a similar system of addressing obstacles to the performance of contracts. Both countries offer considerable latitude for parties to introduce their own force majeure clauses to regulate such occurrences. In the absence of such a clause, the primary consideration is whether COVID-19 and COVID-19. Measures rendered the original obligation impossible, and it, therefore, ceases to exist.

In some cases, however, the obstacle will not be permanent, and the rules concerning delay apply instead. Finally, both systems allow for contract adaptation if changing circumstances have severely disrupted the original contractual equilibrium as *ultima ratio*.

In the broader European context, the Swiss and Austrian openness to parties introducing their own force majeure clauses and the possibility of adapting contracts in case of changed circumstances aligns well with international instruments. On the contrary, the differentiated system for breach of contract and the fault-based system of damages operates differently from these instruments. Nevertheless, both systems allow exceptions to the liability in cases of, or similar to, force majeure.

---

104 Article 6.2.3(1)+(3) PICC; Article 89(1) CESL (proposal); Article 6:111(2) PECL; III.-1:110(3)(d) DCFR.

105 With further references: Peter Jäggi, Peter Gauch and Stephan Hartmann, *Zürcher Kommentar: Art. 18 OR – Auslegung, Ergänzung und Anpassung der Verträge: Simulation* (4th edn, Schulthess Verlag 2015) no 744; Christoph Müller, *Berner Kommentar: Schweizerisches Zivilgesetzbuch: Das Obligationenrecht: Allgemeine Bestimmungen: Art. 1-18 OR mit allgemeiner Einleitung in das Schweizerische Obligationenrecht* (Stämpfli Verlag 2018) no 644 Article 18 SCO.

106 Fabio Bortolotti, 'ICC Force Majeure and Hardship Clauses 2020: Introductory Note and Commentary' https://iccwbo.org/content/uploads/sites/3/2020/07/icc-forcemajeure-introductory-note.pdf, June 2020 accessed 1 October 2020, 7; CISG Advisory Council, 'Opinion No. 20: Hardship under the CISG' http://cisgac.com/file/repository/Opinion_No_20_CISG_and_Hardship_Official_.pdf, 2-5 February 2020 (accessed 1 October 2020) para 0.3.

CORONAVIRUS AND ITS IMPACT ON CONTRACTS IN GREECE

Eugenia DACORONIA*

To face COVID-19, this current, exceptional, and unforeseeable pandemic, the extraordinary procedure of enacting Acts of Legislative Content was followed in Greece, a procedure provided by the Greek Constitution in exceptional circumstances. Accordingly, as of the 25 February 2020 to 1 May 2020, nine Acts of Legislative Content were issued. They have been ratified by law and have been followed by a considerable number of ministerial decisions, necessary for their implementation. These acts contain provisions imposing measures for the prevention and limitation of the spread of COVID-19, including the lockdown of enterprises for a certain period as well as provisions for the regulation of such lockdowns to specific contracts. The purpose of the present contribution is to briefly present these provisions as well as the provisions of the Greek Civil Code which apply when events of force majeure, such as the pandemic of the COVID-19, occur.

* National and Kapodistrian University of Athens (EKPA), Law School.

1. INTRODUCTION

A pandemic[1] is an epidemic of an infectious disease that has spread across a large region, for instance, across multiple continents or worldwide, affecting a substantial number of people. A widespread endemic disease with a stable number of infected people is not a pandemic. Widespread endemic diseases with a stable number of infected people, such as recurrences of seasonal influenza, are generally excluded from the definition of "pandemic", as they occur simultaneously in large regions of the globe, rather than being spread worldwide. After the 1918 influenza pandemic (Spanish flu), COVID-19 was added on the list of the current pandemics.

The 2019–2020 COVID-19 pandemic is expected to have a profound negative effect on the global economy, potentially for years to come, with substantial drops in Gross Domestic Product (GDP), accompanied by increases in unemployment noted around the world. Apart from its impact on health, the coronavirus has induced a lockdown of economic life in the majority of countries around the world, having a serious impact on everyday life with adverse effects on all aspects of it.

To face COVID-19, this current, exceptional and unforeseeable pandemic, the extraordinary procedure of enacting Acts of Legislative Content was followed in Greece, a procedure provided by the Greek Constitution in exceptional circumstances. More precisely, according to the Greek Constitution, under extraordinary circumstances of an urgent and unforeseeable need, the President of the Republic may, upon the proposal of the Cabinet, issue acts of legislative content.[2] Such acts must be submitted to Parliament for ratification, as specified in the provisions of Article 72 §1 of the Constitution (debate and vote in Plenum are required), within 40 days of their issuance or within 40 days from the convening of a parliamentary session. Should such acts not be submitted to Parliament within the above-mentioned time limits or should they not be ratified by Parliament within three months of their submission, they will cease to be in force.

Accordingly, as of 25 February 2020 to 1 May 2020, nine Acts of Legislative Content were issued which have been ratified by law and have been followed by a considerable number of ministerial decisions, necessary for their implementation. These acts contained provisions imposing measures for the prevention and limitation of the spread of COVID-19. These measures include, amongst others: the compulsory submission to clinical and medical examination, vaccination medical treatment, etc. of those who are reasonably suspected of directly or indirectly transmitting the disease, precautionary hospitalisation,

---

[1] From Greek πᾶν, *pan*, "all" and δῆμος, *demos*, "people", https://www.lexico.com/en/definition/pandemic accessed 16 June 2020.

[2] 1975 Constitution of Greece, as revised by the Parliamentary Resolution of 27 May 2008 of the VIIIth Revisionary Parliament, Article 44 §1.

vaccination, medical treatment, etc. of travellers coming from areas where the spread of the virus is prevalent, temporary travel restrictions to countries where the virus is prevalent and the temporary prohibition of the operation of school units and of educational structures of all degrees, public or private, of places of religious worship, as well as of theatres, cinemas, museums.[3] Almost a general lockdown has been imposed in the whole country, with several serious economic consequences. Notably, all seasonal hotels had to close down as from 14 March 2020 and all shops as from 18 March 2020 (for the necessary period of two or three months), with very minor exceptions for some shops (e.g. bakeries or shops for take-away food), which were allowed to operate.

The issues of whether, to what extent and for how long these restrictions, reducing all kinds of human rights (right to movement, to education, to the exercise of religious beliefs etc.), are justified in view of the extraordinary condition under which they were imposed and the need to protect public health, is left to public law academics to answer. What a private law academic is called to answer is the impact of COVID-19 and the above measures on contracts. Whether parties to contracts are still obliged or excused from their obligations under the contract; how Greek law tackles these matters; and what means are provided by Greek law to face these difficulties.

2. IMPACT OF CORONAVIRUS ON CONTRACTS: FORCE MAJEURE

Non-performance of an obligation can be due either to fault or to chance (fortuitous) events (in a broad sense). These (fortuitous) events are subdivided into chance (fortuitous) events (in a strict sense) and events of force majeure.[4] The courts in Greece accept, in principle, a wide notion of the term force majeure, considering as force majeure all events that could not be foreseen and averted even by means of extreme care and prudence,[5] thus, adopting, from the two theories on the subject, the subjective (or relative) theory and not the objective one.[6] Irrespective of which theory is to be adopted, however,

---

3 Act of Legislative Content of 25 February 2020, published in the Government Gazette (*Fyllo Efimeridas tis Kyvernissis*, FEK) A' 42/25.02.2020, ratified by L 4682/2020, FEK A' 76/03.04.2020.

4 Michael Stathopoulos, Antonios G. Karampatzos, *Contract Law In Hellas* (3rd edn, Kluwer Law International 2014) p 171, no 258.

5 Greek Court of Cassation (*Areios Pagos*, AP) 266/1995, Greek Justice (*Elliniki Dikaiossini*, EllDni) 1996, 671; 16/1995, Legal Tribune (*Nomiko Vima*, NoV) 44, 192; 1592/1988, Journal of Greek Jurists (*Efimeris Ellinon Nomikon*, EEN) 1989, 754; 1850/1987, NoV 36, 1646; 267/1976, NoV 24, 790; 698/1973, NoV 22, 186; 462/1970, NoV 18, 1305.

6 For a short presentation of these two theories (in English) see Stathopoulos, Karampatzos, *Contract Law In Hellas*, p 172, no 259 and (in Greek) Apostolos Georgiades, *Law of*

war, earthquakes,[7] and other similar occurrences always constitute force majeure, and apart from the consequences on the fulfilment of the performance, they constitute the ground for the suspension of all kinds of obligations for the period of their existence. The COVID-19 pandemic, which entailed unforeseen and non-imaginable governmental prohibitions, also belongs to these events. The provisions on force majeure may not only lead to a suspension of the obligation, but also to the partial or total dismissal of the obligation without any claims from the counterparty.

3. SUSPENSION OF THE PRESCRIPTION PERIOD

The Greek Civil Code (GCC) devotes a whole chapter (chapter 10, Articles 247–280) to prescription and term of extinction of a right.[8] The provisions on prescription apply to all kinds of claims unless otherwise provided. More particularly, Articles 247–278 GCC refer to the prescription of claims, and Articles 279, 280 GCC to term of extinction of a right, to which, as Article 279 GCC provides, the provisions on prescription also apply by analogy. In contrast to Roman Law, where prescription was an institution of a more general nature, which had as a consequence the acquisition, loss and deactivation of rights due to their exercise or omission to exercise (*praescriptio acquisitiva* or *praescriptio extinctiva*),[9] the GCC adopts a narrow notion of prescription and, according to it, only the claim, i.e. the right to seek performance from another, consisting of an act or omission, is prescribed (Art 247 GCC).[10]

Prescription period is the statutory period of time after which the claim for remedy is prescribed. According to the general rule of Article 249 GCC, unless stipulated otherwise, claims are prescribed after 20 years have passed since the claim was initiated.[11] It is otherwise stipulated, e.g.:

- in Article 250 GCC, which enumerates various categories of claims (such as claims of merchants, manufacturers and craftsmen for the supply of goods

Obligations. General Part (2nd edn, P. N. Sakkoulas Publications 2015) §23, pp 262–263, nos 31–32; Michael Stathopoulos, *Law of Obligations. General Part* (5th edn, Sakkoulas Editions, 2018) §6, p 371–373, nos 101, 102; Dimitra Papadopoulou-Klamari in Georgiades, Stathopoulos, *Civil Code. General Principles* (2nd edn, P. N. Sakkoulas 2016) vol I^{B}, Article 255, nos 14, 15.

7 Papadopoulou-Klamari in Georgiades, Stathopoulos, *Civil Code*, Article 255 no 17.

8 For a list of relevant bibliography see Apostolos Georgiades in Georgiades, Stathopoulos, *Civil Code, General Principles*, vol I^{B}, Introd. Remarks on Articles 247–280.

9 See Panagiotis Ladas, *General Principles of Civil Law*, (2009) vol II, §29 no 9; Pavlos Stymfaliades, *General Principles of Civil Law* (1953) §77, p 238.

10 Georgiades in Georgiades, Stathopoulos, *Civil Code*, Introd. Remarks on arts 247–280 nos. 4, 5.

11 Apostolos Georgiades, *General Principles of Civil Law* (4th edn, 2012) pp 334–336; Pinelopi Agallopoulou, *Basic Concepts of Greek Civil Law* (in English) (2005) p. 98; AP 343/2007, published in Isokratis, the Legal Data Bank of the Athens Bar.

and for expenses incurred, of hotel-owners, innkeepers and those whose profession is to provide food, for lodging and supply of food as well as for any other catering for their customers and for expenses incurred, of doctors and midwives, lawyers, notaries public and bailiffs for their remuneration and for expenses incurred, etc.), that are prescribed after five years have passed since the claim was initiated, or

- in Article 937 §1 GCC, which provides that torts are time-barred five years after the victim has had knowledge of the damage and of the person bound to pay damages, and without regard to such knowledge, in 20 years from the commission of the act.[12]

The GCC also contains rules of prolongation of the prescription period by either interrupting it (Arts 260–270 GCC)[13] or suspending it (Arts 255–259 GCC)[14] for certain reasons. When the prescription is interrupted, the time of prescription that has already passed is cancelled, and the period of prescription starts counting from the beginning.[15] For instance, the rules on interruption apply when the debtor recognises his/her obligation in any way (Art 260 GCC), or when the creditor files an action for the claim (Art 261 GCC).[16] When the prescription is suspended, the period of suspension does not count for the completion of the prescription (Art 257 §1 GCC). The prescription continues after the cessation of the suspension but may not be completed before the lapse of six months thereafter (Art 257 §2 GCC).

Force majeure is explicitly mentioned in the GCC as one of the reasons for the suspension of the prescription. To be more precise, it is stipulated (Art 255 sentence 1 GCC)[17] that the prescription period is suspended for as long as the

---

12 For more about prescription in tort law in the Greek legal system (in English) see Eugenia Dacoronia, *Prescription in Tort Law: Greece* in Israel Gilead and Bjarte Askeland (eds), *Prescription in Tort Law* (Intersentia 2020) pp 379–411.

13 For an analysis of said arts see, among others, Papadopoulou-Klamari in Georgiades, Stathopoulos, *Civil Code*, arts 260–270; Agallopoulou, *Basic Concepts of Greek Civil Law*, pp 101, 102.

14 For an analysis of said arts see, among others, Papadopoulou-Klamari in Georgiades, Stathopooulos, *Civil Code*, arts 255–256. See also (in English) Symeon Symeonides in Konstantinos Kerameus and Phaedon Kozyris, *Introduction to Greek Law* (3rd edn, 2008) pp 98, 99.

15 For an analysis of said arts see, from the most recent bibliography, Papadopoulou-Klamari in Georgiades and Stathopoulos, *Civil Code*, arts 260–270; Agallopoulou, *Basic Concepts of Greek Civil Law*, pp 101, 102; AP 343/2007, published in Isokratis, the Legal Data Bank of the Athens Bar.

16 Georgiades, *General Principles of Civil Law*, pp 343–351.

17 See, among others, Chrysoula Michailidou in Apostolos Georgiades, *Brief Interpretation of the Civil Code (= Syntomi Ermineia tou Astikou Kodika/SEAK)* (2010) vol I, Article 255 nos 1–6; Papadopoulou–Klamari in Georgiades, Stathopoulos, *Civil Code*, Article 255, nos 14–18; AP 738/2016, published in Isokratis; 1657/2008, NoV 57, 1084; 1285/2005, published in Isokratis.

obligee is prevented by force majeure from pursuing his/her claim within the last six months of the period of prescription. A definition of force majeure is not given in the GCC, but it is generally accepted[18] that force majeure is defined as any unforeseeable event, which renders the pursuing of the claim impossible, even though the utmost care and diligence has been demonstrated. The coronavirus pandemic, like natural disasters and wars, is an event of force majeure, so the prescription of a claim is suspended for as long as the obligee is prevented from pursuing his/her claim within the last six months of the period of prescription.

4. IMPOSSIBILITY OF PERFORMANCE: EXEMPTION FROM OBLIGATION

Articles 370 ff GCC contain principles regarding bilateral contracts and regulate the consequences of the impossibility of performance, which differ depending on whether the impossibility is due to the fault of the other party (Art 381 GCC), to the fault of the party who has the obligation to render the performance (Art 382) or is not due to fault (Art 380 GCC). In particular, Article 380 GCC on impossibility of performance by one party not due to fault provides that if the impossibility of performance of one of the contracting parties is not due to his/her fault, the other contracting party is also absolved from the obligation to counter-perform. If the counter-performance has already been fulfilled, it may be recovered, according to the provisions of unjust enrichment (Arts 904 ff GCC). However, the other party is not released from his/her obligation to counter-perform if he/she sought from the debtor whatever the latter acquired because of the impossible performance.

As cases of impossibility of performance due to the pandemic are, as a rule, cases where impossibility is due to an unexpected and unforeseeable event (force majeure) and not to the fault of the debtor, Article 380 GCC applies. The other party to the contract is also dismissed from his/her counter-performance, which can be sought back on the basis of the provisions of unjust enrichment if already fulfilled.

5. DELAY OF THE PERFORMANCE: RIGHT TO RESCISSION

According to the Greek Civil Code, in case of delay in rendering the performance, the right of rescission from the contract is, in principle, given to the creditor, if the debtor, who is responsible for the delay, is at fault (see Arts 382, 383 GCC).

---

18 Konstantinos Simantiras, *General Principles of Civil Law* (4th edn, 1988) no 1058; Maria-Christina Kalogera in Georgiades, Stathopoulos, *Greek Civil Code* (1978) vol 1, Article 255 no 2; Papadopoulou-Klamari in Georgiades, Stathopoulos, *Civil Code*, Article 255, no 14.

As a rule, when the delay is not due to the debtor, no right of rescission is provided by law.

As proposed in Greek doctrine,[19] however, a right of rescission can be given, even if the debtor is not at fault, in the following cases:

1. If it has been agreed that the performance was to be made exclusively at an appointed time or exclusively within an appointed deadline, where the creditor shall be entitled to rescind by the mere reason of delay, irrespective of whether the debtor is at fault. If the creditor, however, prefers to seek performance, he/she has the obligation to announce that immediately to the debtor, otherwise he/she loses such right (Art 401 GCC).[20] The ratio behind this provision is that the time of performance is of such importance to the creditor in these contracts, that he/she can be freed, even if the debtor is not at fault.
2. When the creditor has no more interest in the fulfilment of the performance. This lack of interest, however, must be accepted only in extraordinary cases, after balancing the particular circumstances, so as not to overturn the above-mentioned basic position of the law, which is to grant the right of rescission only when the debtor is at fault. The application by analogy of Articles 343 §2 and 380 GCC can be the ground for granting the right of rescission even if the debtor is not at fault.[21] A direct application of Article 343 §2 GCC is not possible, as it is explicitly stipulated in the said paragraph that in order for the creditor to decline acceptance of the delayed performance within a reasonable time from when the offer or the invitation by the debtor is made, and seek compensation for non-performance, the debtor should be in default. The debtor, though, *is not* in default, and, according to Article 342 GCC, if the delay in performance is due to an event for which he/she has no liability.[22]
3. Especially for the contracts for work, where the master of the work is granted by Article 686 sentence 1 GCC the right of rescission, irrespective

---

19 See in detail Michael Stathopoulos, *Probleme der Vertragsverbindung in rechtsvergleichender Betrachtung*, AcP 1994, 566 f; Stathopoulos, *Law of Obligations*, §21, pp 1421–1424, nos 67–75, where he also notes (p 1422, fn. 91) that the requirement of fault for the rescission is not correct *de lege ferenda* and justifies that (p 1424–1427, nos 75, 76) by reference to other legal systems which recognize the rescission for contractual violations, irrespective of fault.

20 For an analysis of Article 401 GCC see Stathopoulos, *Law of Obligations*, §21, p 1443–1446, nos 103–107; Stamatis Koumanis in Georgiades *SEAK* I, Article 401 GCC; Ioannis Karakostas, *Civil Code* (2006) Article 401, p 591–596; Panagiotis Papanikolaou in Georgiades, Stathopoulos, *Civil Code* (1979) vol II, Article 401, p 396–400.

21 It is to be noted here that the new §323 of the BGB, after the 2002 amendment, does not require fault for the rescission, but only a deadline to be set for fulfilling the performance.

22 For a detailed justification of this approach see Stathopoulos, *Law of Obligations*, pp 1422, 1423 nos 68–71.

of the contractor's fault. In particular, Article 686 GCC stipulates that if the contractor delays the beginning of the work, or if, without it being the fault of the master, he/she delays its execution in whole or in part in such a way that is contrary to the contract and renders the timely completion of the work impossible, the master of work can rescind the contract and does not have to wait for the expiration of the period set for delivery. In case the contractor is in default, all rights of the master of work, because of the default, are kept.

4. Under certain circumstances to be judged in each particular case, a delay in performance after a certain time can be considered, according to the requirements of good faith (Art 288 GCC), as an impossibility of performance and can entail the consequences thereof.
5. In contracts of long duration, which can be terminated for good reason, the long delay in fulfilling the contract can also be considered, according to the requirements of good faith (Art 288 GCC), as a good reason for terminating the contract.

Adopting the above position, we are of the view that, in the case of the pandemic and due to it, if the creditor has no more interest in the fulfilment of the performance, then the right of rescission should be recognised for him/her. This could be the case, for example if merchandise ordered cannot be delivered to the creditor by the debtor in time because of various prohibitions and lockdown of shops in another country due to the pandemic, and this bears as a consequence the justified, under the particular circumstances, lack of interest in the fulfilment on the part of the creditor.

6. UNFORESEEN CHANGE OF CIRCUMSTANCES: JUDICIAL REVIEW

A typical example of the national legal tradition is the introduction into the GCC, and on a wide scale, of general clauses which are based on the principle of equity. Such general rules had long been a feature of Greek custom.[23] Thus, explicit provisions are found in the GCC regarding the civil protection of personality (Art 57 GCC), the prohibition of the abuse of a right (Art 281 GCC), the possibility of dissolution or adjustment of a contract by reason of an unforeseen change in circumstances (Art 388 GCC), etc.

---

23 For a short presentation of the evolution of Greek Civil Law (in English) see Eugenia Dacoronia, 'The evolution of the Greek Civil Law. From its byzantine – roman origins to its contemporary European orientation' in Hector L. MacQueen, Antoni Vaquer and Santiago Espiau, *Regional Private Laws And Codification In Europe* (Cambridge University Press 2003) pp 288–305.

Focusing on this last possibility, it has to be first underlined that a contract, from the moment that it is concluded, is binding upon the contracting parties. The binding nature of contracts (*pacta sunt servanda*) is a basic principle of the GCC. Nevertheless, in certain cases, this commitment may prove onerous and harsh for one of the parties, particularly if the circumstances which existed at the time of the conclusion of the contract have changed in such a way as to destroy the balance of the contract to the detriment of one of the parties. The GCC deals with this problem by an express provision – that of Article 388 GCC, which is one of the most basic and most forward-looking of those contained in the GCC. Starting out from the principle of the inviolability of contracts, the provision provides, on strict conditions, for the concession of this principle in recognising the possibility of a judicial dissolution or of revision of a reciprocal contract in the event of an unforeseen change in circumstances and of upsetting of the balance between performance and counter-performance. The provision of Article 388 GCC is none other than a special expression of the principle of good faith which is formulated generally as to the law of obligations in Article 288 GCC, which lays down that: "The debtor is obliged to effect the performance as good faith requires, after consideration also of common usage." Article 288 GCC could basically lead to similar solutions in the absence of Article 388 GCC. Nevertheless, in practical terms, the adoption of the special provision in the GCC is useful because it gives clearer and more particular expression to the will of the legislator in this connection. However, it is accepted that when the conditions of Article 388 GCC are not met, the possibility of resorting to Article 288 remains as an "*ultimum refugium*".[24]

As stated,[25] a combination of views and criteria are found in Article 388 GCC, drawn both from classic theories on the need for an equilibrium between performance and counter-performance (here of course in order to deal with the *ex post facto* upsetting of any initial balance) or on the *clausula rebus sic stantibus* (but on strict terms today), and more modern doctrines which have been developed internationally in the 20th century. Those are particularly the cases of the German doctrine of the collapse of the underlying basis of the transaction (*Wegfall der Geschäftsgrundlage*) and the French theory of the unforeseen (*théorie de l' imprévision*). The basic idea, however, which permeates the institution is that of *bona fides*.[26]

Crucial circumstances of the time of the contract, which are taken into consideration by the parties when entering a contract usually are, for example, the price index, tax legislation and in general, any other economic conditions,

---

24 Stathopoulos, Karampatzos, *Contract Law In Hellas*, p 192, no 292.

25 Stathopoulos, Karampatzos, *Contract Law In Hellas*, p 192, no 292.

26 For a detailed analysis of Article 388 GCC see Stathopoulos in Georgiades, Stathopoulos, *Civil Code*, Article 388, p 365–374; Apostolos Chelidonis in Georgiades *SEAK* I, Article 388.

the security of the country, peace and other political or social parameters, the usual weather conditions of the place of performance, etc.[27] It is mentioned in Greek jurisprudence that all particular cases cannot be foreseen in detail, as each time the particular judgment depends on the particular circumstances of the case[28] and how these have changed.

Accordingly, Greek courts have applied Article 388 GCC when there was:

- an abrupt increase on the value of the property due to the depreciation of the Greek drachma in 1953, which was the Greek currency till the introduction of the Euro;[29]
- a considerable depreciation of the currency, in such a manner which adversely affected the parties' calculations (in such case, the debtor of the monetary performance was obliged to perform not in the deflated currency, but "in the equivalent of healthy currencies");[30]
- a change of statutory provisions;[31]
- a general economic crisis, as the one Greece experienced after 2010, with the imposition of strict measures of austerity which had chain effects to all aspects of the Greek society;[32]
- extreme natural phenomena, floods, earthquakes, etc. or
- revolutions, wars, etc.

On the contrary, the courts did not apply Article 388 GCC in cases of:

- a non-considerable depreciation, even if it exceeded small fluctuations and was unforeseen, when it did not exceed the usual measure, according to common experience and logic;[33]
- increase in the value of the performance by 35%;[34]
- small fluctuation of the buying power of the Greek drachma due to depreciation of foreign currencies;[35]

---

27 Michael Stathopoulos, *Law of Obligations*, §22, p 1483, no 18.

28 See, among others, AP 1487/2005, NoV 54, 394; Piraeus Court of Appeal 48/2010, published in Isokratis, the Athens Bar data bank.

29 AP 34/1965, NoV 13, 736.

30 AP 672/1963, NoV 12, 398; AP 62/1957, NoV 5, 534; AP 766/1954, NoV 3, 361.

31 Thessaloniki Court of Appeal 534/1955, EEN 23, 192.

32 See AP 841/2017; 1088/2017; 207/2017; 998/2014, all of them published in NOMOS data bank.

33 AP 1171/2004, published in NOMOS; AP 1138/1990, EllDni 1991, 808; AP 672/1963, NoV 11, 159; AP 509/1962, NoV 11, 159; Court of Appeal of the Aegean 68/1975, NoV 24, 810; Athens Single-member Court of First Instance 5036/1976, EEN 44, 88.

34 AP 399/1961, NoV 10, 83; see also Greek Council of the State (Symvoulio tis Epikrateias, StE) 530/1953, EEN 20, 530.

35 Samos Multi-member Court of First Instance 6/1974, Justice (Dikaiossini, Dni) 1974, 329.

- non-renewal of a hotel license;[36]
- rainfall in the month of October.[37,38]

The COVID-19 situation falls no doubt among the cases of an unforeseen change in the circumstances which upsets the balance between performance and counter-performance. Thus, there is a field for judicial termination or of revision of a reciprocal contract if the parties do not find an amicable solution.

7. IMPACT OF CORONAVIRUS ON SPECIFIC CONTRACTS

The above-mentioned urgently enacted Acts of Legislative Contents also tried to give equitable solutions to the problems the lockdown generated in various sectors of the Greek economy. As an example, reference is made hereinafter to certain measures enacted in relation to specific contracts. It remains to be seen whether these measures were sufficient and – even more importantly – efficient, as it is still too early to judge.

7.1. CONTRACTS REGARDING TOURIST ENTERPRISES

In an effort to give solutions to and to balance the conflicting interests of the parties to contracts related to the tourist sector, exceptional measures have been enacted with the Act of Legislative Content of 13 April 2020. More precisely, Articles 70 and 71 of the Act of Legislative Content of 13 April 2020,[39] ratified by L 4690/2020,[40] adopt measures addressing the termination of contracts between tourist enterprises or between tourist enterprises and customers and introduce the possibility of granting a credit note of equal value, valid for 18 months as of the date of issuance, instead of a refund. If the credit note has not been used at its maturity, the enterprise is obliged to pay the customer or the other enterprise an amount of money equal to the value of the credit note.

It must be noted that, apart from the above-mentioned legislative intervention in contracts, the Greek legislator, in an effort to also protect tourist enterprises from eventual tort actions against them if a client contracts the

36 Patras Court of First Instance 812/1964, EEN 31, 745.

37 Patras Court of First Instance 971/1964, EEN 31, 868.

38 For an enumeration of all above cases, see also Stathopoulos, *Law of Obligations*, §22, pp 1501–1503, nos 42, 43.

39 FEK A' 84.

40 FEK A' 104.

coronavirus when in their establishments, exempts tourist enterprises from any civil liability against any person, directly or indirectly related to COVID-19, if said enterprises apply the conditions set in the special health protocols which the law provides. The injured party bears the burden of proving the damage suffered and the causal link between the improper application of the conditions set in the special medical protocols and the damage (Art 60 §5 of L 4688/2020[41]). The special health protocols for the period for which they are necessary and on the basis of which tourist enterprises[42] should operate, in derogation of their usual operating conditions, are specified in a Joint Ministerial Decision, issued after an opinion of the National Committee on the Protection of Public Health against COVID-19.

7.2. LEASE CONTRACTS

Concerning lease contracts, Article 2 §1 of the Act of Legislative Content of 20 March 2020,[43] ratified by L 4683/2020,[44] provides that the tenant of a professional lease for the establishment of a business, for which special and extraordinary measures have been taken regarding the suspension or provisional prohibition of the operation for preventive or repressive reasons that are related to COVID-19, is exempted from the obligation to pay 40% of the total rent for the months April and May 2020, by way of derogation from the applicable lease provisions. The partial non-payment of the rent does not give birth to a right of termination of the contract against the lessee or to any other civil claim. Article 2 §2 of the Act provides that §1 thereof also applies to contracts of lease for housing, when the lessee is working at a business of the type mentioned in §1 and whose employment contract has been temporarily suspended because of the measures for the prevention of the spread of the coronavirus.

It should be mentioned, however, that it is doubtful whether the existence of this regulation of the law means that the application of Article 388 GCC is excluded and that a judicial revision of the contract cannot take place. A judicial revision of the contract would not be allowed only if the special legislation regulating, in a certain way, the consequences of the change of circumstances, explicitly mentioned, at the same time, that the application of Article 388 GCC was excluded.

---

41 FEK A'101.

42 Article 1 §1 of L 4276/2014 (FEK A' 155) determines the categories of enterprises which belong to the tourist sector.

43 FEK A' 68.

44 FEK A' 83/10.04.2020.

7.3. EMPLOYMENT CONTRACTS

Regarding employment contracts, a number of Acts of Legislative Content were enacted, providing, *inter alia*, the following:

- *The Act of Legislative Content of 11 March 2020*,[45] ratified by above mentioned L 4682/2020, provides that until 10 April 2020, a period that can be extended by a joint Ministerial Decree, the employer can decide that the employee will offer his/her services through teleworking (Art 4 §2). The Act also provides for a special purpose paid leave to employees for as long as educational institutions in Greece are closed because of the COVID-19, on the condition that they use one day of their annual leave for every three days of the special leave. Two-thirds of the employees' remuneration during this leave is paid by the employer, and one-third by the Greek State (Art 4 §3).

Teleworking was established in Greece by Article 5 of L 3846/2010,[46] in which the conditions were set as follows:

1. The employer must give in writing to the employee, within eight days, all relevant information about the work that needs to be carried out. If the employee must be "tele-on duty" then the limits must be set as well as time periods for responding.
2. If the normal employment is converted to teleworking, a three month period is set in which both parties could revert back by giving a 15-day notice period.
3. In any case, the employer shall bear the expenses of teleworking and shall provide the employee with all technical support, as well as replacement in case of need.
4. The employer, within two months of signing the contract, notifies in writing the teleworking employee the contact information of the personnel representatives in the company.

- *The Act of Legislative Content of 20 March 2020*,[47] ratified by the above mentioned L 4683/2020, provides that the employer whose enterprise is severely impacted because of the compulsory, extraordinary and provisional measures in the market imposed for combating the spread of COVID-19 or who has been on a temporary lockdown on the basis of the extraordinary provisions, may provisionally transfer personnel to another enterprise of the

---

45 FEK A' 55/11.03.2020.

46 FEK A' 66/11.05.2020.

47 FEK A' 68/20.03.2020.

same group, after a relevant agreement between themselves. The enterprises of the group that are going to make use of this possibility must maintain the same number of employees (Art 10 §§1 and 2).

Enterprises who have been on a temporary lockdown by order of the public authority and for all the period during which the measures to combat the spread of COVID-19, are obliged not to reduce the number of their personnel and terminate their contracts as of 18 March 2020. Termination of the employment contract is prohibited and, if effected, it is void (Art 11 §1). Enterprises severely impacted because of the compulsory measures may suspend the employment contracts of all or part of their personnel, in order to adjust their operational needs to the unfavourable conditions created for up to one month from the publication of the Act in the Official Gazette, a period that can be extended by a Joint Ministerial Decision of the Minister of Finance and of the Minister of Labour and Social Affairs, depending on the way the phenomenon develops. In a case where enterprises make use of the aforementioned measure, they are prohibited from dismissing any of their employees and shall be obliged to keep the same employees under the same terms and conditions of employment as of the 21 March 2020, for an equal period of time to the suspension period; if any dismissal is effected, it shall be null and void (Art 11 §2 A).

Employees whose employment contracts have been suspended, either following a lockdown by order of the authorities or a decision of their employer according to Article 11 §2 A, are entitled to a special State benefit. The same State benefit is due also to employees who have been terminated or resigned during the period from 1–20 March 2020. During the suspension period, the employees are entitled to full social security coverage, borne by the State (Art 11 §2 B).

- *The Joint Ministerial Decision (CMD) 12998/23 March 2020*[48] of the Minister of Finance and of the Minister of Labour and Social Affairs, implementing the Act of Legislative Content of 14 March 2020,[49] ratified by L 4682/2020, as well as the Act of Legislative Content of 20 March 2020, ratified by L 4683/2020, and after the relevant legislative authorisation, provides that the lockdown imposed by the authorities is regarded as force majeure and absolves employees of enterprises who have been on a temporary lockdown by order of the public authority from the obligation to render services and their employers from the obligation of salary payment (Chapter A, A.1., Article 1§1). In this case and, for as long as the obligatory lockdown is in force, the employment contracts are suspended (Chapter A, A.1., Article 1§2). The Ministerial Decision also stipulates that fixed-term employment contracts that are due to expire during the lockdown shall also

48 FEK B' 1078/28.03.2020.

49 FEK A' 64/14.03.2020.

be suspended and that the employment contract shall continue after the lockdown is lifted for the rest of its term (Chapter A, A.1., Article 1§3). All unpaid leave which was agreed between such employers and employees were *ipso jure* revoked as from 28 March 2020, date of publication of the CMD (Chapter A, A.1., Article 1 §4).

Employees of enterprises whose activity has been suspended receive, as an emergency financial aid, an amount of EUR 800, called special purpose compensation, which covers a period of 45 calendar days, provided that they do not have an employment contract with another employer (Chapter A, A.1., Article 3 §1).

Employees of enterprises whose activity has been suspended following the lockdown, or of enterprises that have been severely impacted and who have resigned or their employment contract was terminated during the period starting 1 March 2020 and ending 20 March 2020 are entitled to a state benefit, called special aim compensation, of EUR 800 (Chapter A, A.3., Article 1§1). Teleworking employees are not entitled to such compensation (Chapter A, A.2., Article 4§1). Also, as a matter of exception, employers may agree with some of their suspended employees (not exceeding 10%[50]) to provide telework in order to cover temporary needs of the business (Chapter A, A.2., Article 4§3).

- By the *Act of Legislative Content of 1 May 2020*,[51] ratified by L 4690/2020,[52] enterprises severely impacted may extend the suspension up to 60% of the contracts already suspended for a maximum period of 30 days, but not later than 31 May 2020 (Art 10 §1). For enterprises, whose compulsory lockdown continues by order of the public authority during the month of May 2020, the suspension of their employees' employment contracts is extended for as long as the lockdown continues.

8. EPILOGUE

The COVID-19 pandemic has not only upset contracts creating a lot of financial problems, not easily tackled, but also signals the beginning of a new era, an era where teleworking will be established where possible, e-commerce will flourish, and other upheavals will take place. As with everything, there are two sides to this: the rapid and useful changes, dictated by this unexpected, to non-specialists, pandemic, that lead to an e-world, constitute the good side. The other side is the alienation, the lack of real, human contact. Much effort is needed to ensure this situation does not persist for too long.

---

50 Circular of the Ministry of Labour and Social Affairs of 31.03.2020 (Prot. no: οικ. 13738/413).

51 FEK A' 90/01.05.2020.

52 FEK A' 104/30.05.2020.

THE IMPACTS OF COVID-19 IN HUNGARIAN CONTRACT LAW

Attila MENYHÁRD*

The legal and social consequences of the COVID-19 epidemic raise challenges in legal systems. Incompleteness of contracts requires statutory or judicial intervention in order to reach the most efficient risk allocation in contractual relationships. In Hungarian contract law implied terms, impossibility and judicial amendment of contracts on the grounds of clausula rebus sic stantibus provide the doctrinal framework for such an assessment. These doctrines provide the legal framework for balancing the conflicting interests of the binding force of contracts and the demand for adjusting social and legal relationships to changing circumstances. Contracts are to be assessed on a case-by-case basis, but it is argued here that commercial and non-commercial transactions require different approaches and that direct legal and indirect social consequences should be considered differently.

Contracts create trust in the promise of the other party. This trust complies with the moral duty to keep promises. Contracts are social relationships and it seems to be evident that, if social and economic circumstances change, the contract has to be adapted to such changes. This requirement seems to be incompatible with the principle of binding force of contracts. Contracts are never complete due to high transaction costs. For this reason, they are not able to allocate the

---

* Eötvös Loránd University.

risks of unforeseen changes in the future. Thus, social and economic changes call for legislative or judicial adaptation of contracts to these new circumstances, although such intervention is normally unwelcomed and seen as an intrusion into the parties' private autonomy. The problems emerging with statutory restrictions and changes of social behaviour due to the COVID-19 crisis is the same in Hungary as elsewhere and the toolkit of Hungarian private law to be used in such situations seems to be similar to those of other European jurisdictions, with certain peculiarities.

1. CHANGES OF CIRCUMSTANCES AND BINDING FORCE OF CONTRACTS

Contracts create rights and obligations in the system of private law. They are, however, not simply legal phenomena but they channel market mechanisms and they also establish social relationships.[1] Contracts create trust and reliance upon the promise of the other party and the main function of contract law is protecting this reliance. The binding force of a contract creates incentives for the promisor to perform and makes it reasonable for the promisee to prepare its own performance and to invest in it. This trust is the key for planning and is the basis of the modern society and economy. As contracts are social relationships, they are to be adjusted to unpredictable changes of social and economic circumstances because the promisor made the promise assuming those circumstances including predictable changes of them. The requirement of keeping promises is one of the fundamental values of our societies. However, this shall not mean that promises are to be kept even if it becomes unexpectedly and unpredictably hard for the promisor to do so. In other words, promises can be understood as being conditional upon the circumstances of making the promise.

The possibility of changes of circumstances involves risks and contracts are risk-allocation mechanisms. In a perfect world, contracts would be perfect, that is, the parties considered all the possible risks of future changes, addressed them and allocated such risks while negotiating the terms and conditions of the contract. Such a contract is a complete contract. Even if concluding a complete contract could theoretically be possible, the transaction costs of predicting, negotiating and allocating risks of rather low probability would be too high. From the point of view of social welfare, transaction costs of allocating low probability risks should be avoided at the contracting stage and left to *ex post* risk allocation mechanisms provided by the law: courts and by the legislator. The judgment of the English court in *Paradine v Jane*[2] awarding the rental fee

---

1 Ian R. Macneil, 'The Many Futures of Contract' (1974) 47 Southern California Law Review 691, 715, Josef Kohler, *Philosophy of Law* (The Macmillan Company 1921) 51.

2 [1647] EWHC KB J5.

to the landlord in spite of the fact that the tenant was not able to use the land due to war, simply on the ground that the contract did not contain an exception for such a case, was based on clear-cut arguments but sounds unacceptable and somewhat cynical for us today.

Contracts are necessarily incomplete, and it is the task of private law to provide solutions for re-allocating the risks if unforeseen and unpredictable circumstances made performance much more difficult for the promisor than what was expected at the time of concluding the contract. This is also supported by the idea of promoting social justice in contractual relationships. The gaps of incomplete contracts can be filled by implied terms or by concretising general clauses like good faith and fair dealing and deriving rights and obligations therefrom as to the contractual relationship of the parties via the construction of the contract (*ergänzende Vertragsauslegung*). Both general private law rules and doctrines such as hardship, impossibility, frustration of purpose or, *clausula rebus sic stantibus*, and specific rules applicable to contracts may address such cases. The legislator also may intervene with ad hoc legislation if changes of circumstances affect a wide range of contracts and appear as a social problem.

Such doctrines pointing in the same direction, however, are just elements of the reasoning provided by courts. The judgment is the result of weighing values that are relevant and interplay in such scenarios. As to the binding force of contracts, party autonomy, self-reliance, objective value of the exchange and reliance on the promise of the other party are the relevant values that may have different strengths according to the facts of the case.[3] In the flexible system of private law,[4] the judgment of the court upon the binding force of a contract is the outcome of counter-weighing these relevant values according to their strengths under the given circumstances. That is, the more informed and voluntary the consent was, the less relevant the objective value of the exchange is. Lack of information concerning unforeseen circumstances may undermine the original value of the exchange. In the flexible system of private law, such changes would be more drastic, were the courts to be more inclined to re-allocate the risks between the parties or deprive the contract of its binding force entirely.

2. THE IMPACTS OF COVID-19 ON THE BINDING FORCE OF CONTRACTS

There is no generic answer or approach that could be identified as a leading policy in the course of assessing the consequences of legislative steps and

3 Franz Bydlinski, 'A "Flexible System" Approach to Contract Law' in Herbert Hausmanninger et al. (eds), *Developments in Austrian and Israeli Private Law* (Springer 1999) 9.

4 Walter Wilburg, 'Zusammenspiel der Kräfte im Aufbau des Schuldrechts' 163 AcP, 1964, 364.

social reactions triggered by COVID-19 in contractual relationships. Thus, the doctrinal and regulatory framework is provided here but no ultimate answers are given. Such answers and statements can be formulated only as of the result of analysing the actual contractual relationship, having regard to all the circumstances of the specific case. Today, it is rather difficult to predict how courts would react and approach the relevant issues: rules and doctrines rooted in the historical development of contract law are not designed for allocating the consequences of wide-ranging social events in a massive number of contracts. If the supervening event which destroyed the value of performance or made performance significantly harder for the obligor affected the society as a whole, courts may be reluctant to re-allocate risks and incline to establish that the consequences of such events shall be borne by each member of the society and no exceptions should be provided from this. That is, the greater the number of potential plaintiffs, the less willing courts are to intervene by reshaping the contract.[5]

In the course of assessing the impacts of COVID-19 in contractual relationships, a distinction must be made between the impacts of the epidemic in society as a matter of fact on the one hand and the impact of the specific legislation including administrative measures on the other hand. Change of behaviour of the members of the society is a legally relevant fact of a very different nature from statutory or administrative restrictions. Thus, the consequences of them are to be assessed separately, although they quite often overlap in legal relationships. If there was any kind of risk allocation stipulated by the parties for such circumstances in the contract; if there was a relevant provision in the contract, it is still a question if it is valid and enforceable considering its compliance with public policy, good morals and unenforceability of unfair contract terms in consumer contracts and in standard form contracts. If there is no valid and enforceable risk allocation stipulated by the parties, risk allocation is the task of the State either via the judiciary or by the legislative power.

The impact of COVID-19 affected society as a whole in a way that has never been experienced before. It influenced the preferences and the behaviour of all members of society: the impacts of the coronavirus in the welfare society were unprecedently wide. That is why the case law in the periods between the First and the Second World War as well as after the transition in 1989/1990 in Hungary is not necessarily authoritative in this respect. These judgments, however, may still bring important insights and may outline arguments, doctrines and approaches that provide the legal framework for assessing the impact of COVID-19 in contractual relationships. They are inevitably the proper starting

---

5 Helmut Koziol, 'Compensation for Pure Economic Loss from a Continental Lawyer's Perspective' in Willem H. van Boom et al. (eds), *Pure Economic Loss* (Springer 2004) 149. The arguments are valid in contract law as well.

point for assessing these cases, but the courts may revise their case law entirely, having regard to the specific features of COVID-19, namely, that the epidemic is international, it affects society as a whole and the consequences of it stem from the mixture of administrative measures and social behaviour.

The administrative and statutory measures in Hungary were similar to the package adopted in other European jurisdictions: moratorium for debtors of bank-financed loans and credits including financial leasing, freezing bankruptcy procedures and enforcement of judgments or decrees of tax authorities and other administrative bodies, prohibitions of unilateral termination of certain lease contracts, introducing caps for fees for lease and interests of consumer credits and moratorium for payment of certain types of taxes and other public duties. These were only temporary ad hoc interventions addressing legal relationships in the short run. That is, the gaps these statutory interventions inevitably left are to be filled with general doctrines and such doctrines are to apply for establishing the impacts of changes of circumstances in the long run as well. As the first step of the protection against the COVID-19 epidemic, the Hungarian Government declared a state of emergency on 11 March 2020, consequently, the Government became empowered to suspend and deviate from the provisions of certain acts, as well as to take other extraordinary measures. In the course of the state of emergency, among others:[6]

1. stricter control rules were introduced at the borders and the Hungarian healthcare and police workers, soldiers and government officials were allowed to leave the country only with permission;
2. digital working schedule was introduced in Hungarian schools and exceptional judicial pause was ordered at the Hungarian courts;
3. the Government established 10 action groups to handle certain types of duties;
4. general curfew restrictions came into effect, according to people were allowed to leave their residence for defined reasons;
5. the Hungarian debtors were granted with an extension to repay their actual instalments (debt moratorium);

6 Those measures were adopted in 25 legislative measures, in particular with Government Decree 40/2020. (III. 11.) on declaring state of emergency; Government Decree 47/2020. (III. 18.) on immediate measures necessary in order to reduce the coronavirus pandemic's effect on the national economy; Government Decree 186/2020. (V. 6.) on different rules applicable in the course of the state of emergency to State and municipal lease agreement and on amending the rules of Government Decree 47/2020. (III. 18.) on immediate measures necessary in order to reduce the coronavirus pandemic's effect on the national economy with respect to lease agreements; Government Decree 249/2020. (V. 28.) on the different application of the provisions of Act XLIX of 1991 on bankruptcy and liquidation proceeding and Act V of 2006 on public company information, company registration and winding-up proceedings, the Act LVII of 2020 on terminating the state of emergency; Act LVIII of 2020 on the temporary rules connected to the state of emergency's termination and on the epidemiological preparedness.

6. leases in certain sectors – such as tourism and catering industry – must not be terminated unilaterally;
7. the Government established the so-called national defence management groups in order to secure the continuous operation of companies that are essential from the aspect of the Hungarian economy;
8. certain deadlines of social insurance and family aid rules were prolonged;
9. tax advantages were granted especially for micro and small businesses;
10. military forces were allowed to be seconded to Hungarian hospitals in order to control the use of medical supplies;
11. the Hungarian Parliament adopted Act XII of 2020 on the defence against the coronavirus, which also empowered the Government to take extraordinary measures in the course of the state of emergency, and also amended the Hungarian Criminal Code;
12. new types of student loans and rules of decreased time employment were introduced, furthermore, special taxes were imposed to banks and retailers;
13. some conditions of obtaining a degree in the Hungarian higher education were simplified;
14. the rules of legal entities' operation – with special regards to adopting resolutions by the decision-making body – were modified in order to decrease the direct contact among people;
15. the deadline of leases concluded in relation to State – or municipality-owned apartments were prolonged;
16. some deadlines in Hungarian insolvency proceedings were also prolonged; and
17. the rules of requesting permission from the authorities and the operation of the public education were modified.

In addition to this, the Government launched a special supporting system and proceeding in order to enhance the competitiveness of certain industrial sectors' incumbents. Furthermore, some types of corporate transactions (such as transferring or acquiring shares, increasing capital, transforming, merging or demerging, etc.) intended to execute by foreign investors, became subject to the permission of the Minister for Innovation and Technology. The Parliament terminated the state of emergency, therefore, the Government's regulations passed under the extraordinary legislation have been repealed. At the same time, the Parliament adopted a Temporary Act which declared general preparedness with respect to the pandemic and includes temporary rules which still apply to a certain scope of questions and circumstances, such as: (1) employment law relationships; (2) leases; (3) legal entities' and business associations' everyday operation; (4) financial reporting obligations. The rules of corporate transactions intended to execute by foreign investors and some of the travelling restrictions also remain in effect in accordance with the Temporary Act.

Beyond the specific ad hoc legislation and in context of the applicable general doctrines of private law, the most predictable approach of courts could be that the COVID-19 epidemic and the administrative or statutory measures implemented to deal with it have an overall impact on the society and each member of society has to bear its consequences. Intervention in contractual relationships would mean that some the members of society would be exempted from consequences that others would have to bear. From the point of view of social justice, this would not seem to be legitimate. Structural interventions, such as protecting consumers, debtors or other weaker players of the market economy can be justified but such interventions require specific legislation. This may mean further restrictions upon the conduct of market actors (creditors, landlords, etc.) in stronger positions. It cannot be excluded that the temporary statutory measures applied to re-allocate the risks may be partially postponed. This also means that courts would not play a decisive role in re-allocation of risks where this is justified. The legislator will be cast with the central role in this scenario.

All in all, at the end of the day, contracts are always open for renegotiation by the parties. Courts or the legislator will allocate the risk of failure of such renegotiation. The binding force of a contract plays only a secondary role compared to trust in the performance of contracts.[7] In other words, the question is whether contractual parties are interested in maintaining their contractual relationship or not. If they are, they will renegotiate it. The party interested in keeping the trust of the other party has a stronger incentive to renegotiate the contract.

3. THE RELEVANT DOCTRINAL AND REGULATORY FRAMEWORK OF PRIVATE LAW

Hungarian private law, like other European jurisdictions, presents a wide range of doctrines and rules addressing the impact of changes of circumstances that were unforeseeable for the parties at the time of conclusion of the contract. The complexity of doctrines is the result of two peculiarities. First, these impacts are covered with different rules and doctrines, either specific or general, that have different preconditions and different consequences. Such consequences can be termination of the contract (impossibility, exercising the right to terminate the contract), judicial amendment (hardship) or exoneration from liability for breach of contract. Secondly, rules and doctrines not specifically addressing the issue of changes of circumstances may also play an important role in managing these cases. Such doctrines of fundamental importance are assuming "implied terms" or applying "*ergänzende Vertagsauslagung*" in the course of construing the contract.

---

7 Hugh Collins, *Regulating Contracts* (OUP 1999) 97.

3.1. IMPLIED TERMS AND *ERGÄNZENDE VERTRAGSAUSLEGUNG*

There are cases where the law implies a term to a contract which the parties did not negotiate and did not insert themselves. *Ergänzende Vertragsauslegung* does the same but anchors this to the general clause of the requirement of good faith and fair dealing, which is an inherent part of Hungarian private law with the same meaning and function as *Treu und Glauben* in German law.[8] The traditional Hungarian legal thought accepted that the gaps in the contract can and are to be filled with rights and obligations derived from the requirement of good faith and fair dealing. Implied terms or *ergänzende Vertragsauslegung* have the same function.[9] They are to establish contractual rights and obligations that were not stipulated by the parties and they do so in order to have the contract complying with the general values and requirements of the society. Terms implied by any of the relevant doctrines belong to the fundamentals of the contracts and they mostly relate to the existence or non-existence of facts, assumed to be so obvious and the failure of them has such a low probability that the parties did not consider it necessary to stipulate them explicitly. Some of the most typical of such assumptions are that the object of the contract exists, the party is capable of providing personal services, it is possible to attain the purpose of the contract which was obvious for the other party too (that is why it can be implied), etc.[10]

As to *ergänzende Vertragsauslegung* via application of the general clause of good faith and fair dealing, before the Second World War, legal doctrines of traditional Hungarian private law followed the German pattern. The requirement of good faith and fair dealing is a part of the Hungarian private law and, since it is explicitly provided in §1:3 of the Hungarian Civil Code amongst the introductory provisions as a general clause, it is an inherent content of all of the private law relationships including contracts. Contracting parties are imposed with this obligation even if they never stipulated or negotiated for it. General clauses are to be concretised by the courts in order to implement relevant social values on a case-by-case basis, having regard to the specific facts of the case. That is, courts may derive concrete rights and obligations from the requirement of good faith and fair dealing as between the contracting parties even if they never negotiated and stipulated such rights and obligations. This holds for the current Hungarian private law as well, although it is not reflected in contemporary Hungarian court practice. This abstinence fits into the general tendency that – contrasted with other jurisdictions in Europe – Hungarian courts are relatively

8 Földi András, *A jóhiszeműség és tisztesség elve* (ELTE ÁJK Budapest 2001) 105.

9 Kelemen László, *A jóhiszeműség és tisztesség a magánjogban* (Ablaka György Nyomdája Szeged 1937) 88.

10 E.g. *Taylor v Caldwell* [1863] 3 B&S 826; *Krell v Henry* [1903] 2 KB 740.

reluctant to apply general clauses. The reason for this attitude is not very clear. They may feel the content of general clauses is too vague, there also might have been bad experiences from socialist area of using these clauses for direct political purposes and the parties also rely on general clauses quite often as an ultimate argument, so courts accept these arguments with certain caution. A further reason may be that a great number of judges are accustomed to the attitude that they are the "servant of the law," where "law" is understood as the legislator's order. They may become uncertain while applying norms having vague content. Anyway, the regime of Hungarian private law is open for establishing implied terms via the construction of the contract (*ergänzende Vertragsauslegung*). This is an opportunity that courts can take if they think it just and reasonable under the circumstances of the case if the application of ordinary rules does not lead to a socially satisfactory result.

3.2. IMPOSSIBILITY

The circumstances of conclusion of the contract may change and such changes may result in unenforceability. Initial impossibility makes the contract null and void. If the performance becomes impossible after the conclusion of the contract as a result of changes in circumstances, such impossibility results in termination of the contract and converts the obligation of performance in kind into a liability for damages. Hungarian contract law addresses impossibility as a form of breach of contract. From this, it follows that if the obligor was responsible for impossibility, he/she shall be liable according to the liability for breach of contract. Performance of a contract may become impossible due to physical circumstances (e.g. the object of the contract was destroyed) or because the contract has lost its purpose. This was the case, for example, where the shareholder's agreement had been terminated *ex lege* due to impossibility because the registration was rejected by the court.[11] The court also established that the purpose of lease contract was frustrated and terminated due to impossibility if the tenant concluded it in order to establish an industrial area but finally the industrial area did not come into existence on grounds for which none of the parties was responsible.[12] The contract terminates due to impossibility also if the performance of the contract would impose such a hardship on the obligor that the performance of it should not be expected.[13] This is the case, for example, when the parties exchanged their flat but one of them became ill after concluding

[11] Supreme Court, Legf. Bír. Gfv. IX. 30.279/2005. sz. EBH 2006 no 1428.
[12] Supreme Court, Legf. Bír. Pfv. VIII. 20.056/2007 sz. BH 2007 no 370.
[13] Supreme Court, Legf. Bír. Gf. III. 30 496/1985. sz. BH 1986 no 489.

the contract and the treatment is only available for her in the original place of living.[14] Impossibility may occur as a result of changes of the legal environment. This is the case when the performance of the contract qualifies as an unlawful conduct.[15]

Implied terms or *ergänzende Vertragsauslegung* play a fundamental role in the context of impossibility: the doctrine of frustration of purpose assumes that rights and obligations established in the contract are conditional upon certain presumptions (purpose) even if they are not stipulated by the parties. If this ground of the contract disappeared, the contract shall not be enforceable (*Wegfall der Geschäftsgrundlage*). This conclusion is also valid in Hungarian private law.[16]

Thus, impossibility seems to provide a complete toolkit for addressing the impacts of COVID-19 in contractual relationships in Hungarian contract law. As to direct consequences of statutory restrictions the legal impossibility, while as to the consequences of changes of social behaviour the impossibility due to frustration of purpose may provide an answer.[17] This is, however, not so much the case. If the contract is not very clear as to allocating the risk of such a phenomenon as the COVID-19 pandemic, the question is, whether a term is to be implied that the rights and obligations stipulated by the parties should be conditional upon the absence of such restrictions or hardship or not. The answer does not come from the inherent logic of private law. It is a policy issue to be decided by the court and different approaches should be followed in commercial and non-commercial contracts. In *Krell v Henry*,[18] the landmark case for implied terms and frustration of purpose in English contract law, the court rejected the plaintiff's claim for the rental fee of a flat rented by the defendant in the plaintiff's building in order to view the march of the participants, including the King, as part of the celebration process of coronating King Edward VII. The contract obviously did not contain any clause for the case of cancellation of the celebration. The celebration, however, was postponed due to the illness of the Crown Prince. The court established that celebration including the march was an implied term of the contract because it was clear for the parties that the

---

14 Supreme Court, P. törv. III. 20 346/1984. sz. BH 1985 no 101.

15 Supreme Court, Legf. Bír. Gfv. X. 31.639/2001. sz. BH 2002 no 235.

16 E.g. Supreme Court, P. törv. III. 20 346/1984. BH 1985. no 101. (the contract shell be deemed as terminated due to impossibility if performance was hardened as a result of illness of the party); Supreme Court, Legf. Bír. Gf. III. 30 496/1985., BH 1986. no 469. (if the contract can be performed only with unforeseeable difficulties while to overcome such difficulties shall not be expected from the party, the contract terminates due to impossibility); Supreme Court, Legf. Bír. Pfv. VIII. 20.056/2007., BH 2007. no 370. (the contract for lease of land shall be deemed as terminated due to economic impossibility if the exploiting land according to the contractual purpose becomes impossible).

17 Whether temporary impossibility shall or may result in termination of the contract or only postponing the time of performance as an excuse for breach of contract, depends on the nature and on the content of contract.

18 [1903] 2 KB 740.

defendant would pay the agreed price in order to view the march. If there was no such a celebration, the defendant never hired the flat and the contract was never concluded. That is, as a result of frustration of purpose, the contract lost its binding force and was not to be enforced. In the case of *Herne Bay Steam Company v Hutton*,[19] however, the court came to a different conclusion even though the facts of the case were rather similar. In this case, the defendant hired a boat from the plaintiff with the intent that he would take passengers to the Royal naval fleet, obviously for a certain price, while the King visited it as part of the celebration. As the celebration was postponed, this attempt failed, and the defendant repudiated the contract arguing that it lost its purpose due to cancellation of the event he intended to take passengers to. The plaintiff argued that the purpose of the contract was to hire the boat which was not frustrated at all and claimed the agreed rental fee. The court decided in favour of the plaintiff. The court established that the purpose of the contract was not frustrated because the Royal naval fleet was still there, and it was still possible to show it to passengers of the hired ship from the water. Thus, the purpose of the contract was not frustrated, and the defendant did not have the right to repudiate it. The facts of the two cases were very similar but for one exception: while in *Krell v Henry* it was the defendant's private purpose to view the coronation, in *Herne Bay Steam Company v Hutton* it was a profit-making opportunity for the defendant; it was his venture. The difference of the underlying policy resulting in different risk-allocation in the two cases was the same as the policy of the dividing line between private law and commercial law.

This policy has nothing to do with any kind of speciality of the English legal system but reflects the needs and demands of the market economy and welfare state to apply different rules, standards and values to "business to business" than "business to consumer" transactions. This does not depend on the existence of a commercial or enterprise code in codified legal systems. This may hold for Hungarian contract law too. Thus, according to the firm view of the author of this contribution, establishing impossibility due to frustration of purpose in commercial relationships should fall under much stricter requirements and should be less probable than in non-commercial ones. This view is supported by the approach followed by courts in international commercial legal disputes.[20] If the performance interfered with statutory or administrative restrictions and became impossible due to unlawfulness, the differences in the outcome in commercial and non-commercial transactions are much less justified.

An important peculiarity of impossibility is that it gives a "black or white" answer as to the binding force of contract: the contract either remains binding or not. It does not provide a playing field to the State to intervene in transactions

---

19 [1903] 2 KB 683.

20 *Tsakiroglou & Co Ltd v Noblee Thorl GmbH* [1962] AC 93.

with reshaping the rights and obligations of the parties. This fits very well to the market paradigm in the sense that it does not give a new contract to the parties without the consent of all of them, but it leaves them to decide if they want to renegotiate the contractual relationship or not. This, however, can be a social disadvantage if termination of the contract affects the position of third parties,[21] or if renegotiation brings excessively high transaction costs, which is not the optimal solution. This is the case, in particular, with long-term contracts, because the parties invest in performance with calculating pay-off on a longer run. That is why terminating a long-term relationship would result in high transaction costs. It is not only less efficient but can be unjust as well.

3.3. *CLAUSULA REBUS SIC STANTIBUS*

In long-term contractual relationships, parties are particularly exposed to the consequences of changing circumstances which increases the risks of incomplete contracts. The transaction costs can be reduced by adapting contracts to the changed circumstances while keeping the original balance of rights and obligations and complying with social values rather than terminating the relationship via the doctrine of impossibility. The doctrine of adapting contract to changing circumstances with a judicial amendment is, in general, called *clausula rebus sic stantibus*, which may be established on general clauses, especially the requirement of good faith and fair dealing, or on specific rules on different levels of abstraction in private law. Such amendment of the contract is reasonable in long-term relationships. In such contracts, there is a high probability of incompleteness, i.e. that risks occur which are not allocated by the parties due to high transaction costs. Doctrines of frustration of purpose or impossibility of performance make the contract unenforceable. Thus, parties should renegotiate their contract and reach a new consent if they want to uphold their legal relationship. Contrary to this, doctrines of hardship pave the way for revising the contract with the consequence that one of the parties finds itself in a contract which it might have never concluded and without having the opportunity to quit or to renegotiate.

As far as long-term contracts are concerned, there is a specific rule provided for hardships in the Hungarian Civil Code. According to this rule, the court may amend the contract at the request of the parties in a long-term contractual relationship, if, due to a circumstance that occurred after the conclusion of the contract, the performance of the contract according to the original conditions would interfere with the legally protected interests and the possibility of a change in the circumstances was not foreseeable at the time of conclusion

21 E.g. the Gaz de Bordeaux case, Conseil d'État 30 March 1916, DP 1916 3.25.

of the contract, provided that the change was not caused by the party and the change in circumstances fell outside the normal business risk.[22] There are strong arguments for the court not being entirely free in designing the amendment of the contract but may amend it only using the non-mandatory rules provided in the Civil Code. Contracts may be amended by the legislator as well, although such interventions in a private law relationship are exceptional; changes in social and economic circumstances may make such an intervention legitimate. The legislative intervention of amending the contract is a circumstance that occurred after the conclusion of the contract, opening the opportunity for amending a long-term contract, if, as the result of the statutory amendment, the contract would violate the legally protected interest of the party.[23] In such cases, the amendment of the contract by the court shall not overwrite the content provided by the legislator.

Both courts and the legislator have appropriate tools for restoring social justice in private law relationships. The task of the legislator and the judiciary is the same. It does not make a difference if private law relationships are shaped by the legislator or courts, insofar as legislative measures are flexible enough for opening the opportunity of judicial interpretation. If following the legislative measure courts cannot assess individual cases on their merits, the premise that the same cases should be assessed the same way while different cases should be assessed different ways may not prevail. As a result, corrective justice may not be implemented properly. From this point of view, judicial measures are far more preferable than statutory intervention.

In order to give an impression of the different attitudes of the legislator and the courts in Hungary, I shall mention two cases. The first is a judgment of the Constitutional Court from the beginning of the 1990s. According to the preliminaries of the case, during socialism, the State provided cheap long-term loans on a low level of fixed rate of interests in order to subsidise certain groups of the population, including victims of floods of the Tisza river. The legal technique for providing such loans was that the payment of the loan was made by the State-owned OTP Bank, actually the only bank providing services to consumers. After the change of the economic system into a market economy, interest rates increased dramatically, and these long-term cheap loans paid on a fixed-rate caused big losses to the OTP. The solution for the problem was to compensate the loss of the OTP with funds from the central budget of the State. Subsidising these loans became a huge burden on the central budget because the interest rates available on the market were about six to eight times higher. In order to consolidate this burden, the interests of these loans were increased with a statutory amendment of these contracts to half of the market rates. The statute also provided an option for the debtors, according to which if debtors

22 §6:192 Hungarian Civil Code.

23 §6:60 (2) Hungarian Civil Code.

paid the 60% of the debt, the remaining 40% was cancelled.[24] The debtors turned to the Constitutional Court in order to have the statutory increase of the interest revised in the light of the constitutional order. The Constitutional Court established that the State has the right to intervene in contractual relationships if such intervention complies with the test of *clausula rebus sic stantibus* provided in the Civil Code. This provision allowed judicial intervention in long-term contracts if, as the result of changing the circumstances, the contract violates the protected interests of the party.[25] The Constitutional Court held[26] that the consequences of the transition into market economy established hardship and raising the interest rates was compatible with the Constitution. It is remarkable, that in the other case, in a very similar situation, when the State Insurance Company claimed for relief of too burdensome insurance policies provided to agricultural entrepreneurs, on the very same ground at the ordinary court, the ordinary court rejected the claim arguing that the consequences of economic and social changes affecting the society as a whole, are to be borne by everyone equally and no one shall be relieved of the consequences of such impacts.[27]

These two judgments provide a good example of how important the moral baseline is when it comes to assessing justice. If the change of circumstances was the consequence of events affecting the society as a whole or, at least, a wide range of market players or consumers, there are two possible contradicting answers: on the one hand, such changes obviously provide a ground for intervening in the contractual relationship; on the other hand, the consequence of such changes is to be borne by everyone equally, that is, this is not the proper ground for State intervention. This makes the problem a policy issue and the State is to decide if such consequences are to be re-allocated or not.

I believe that a key factor in the emerging direct State intervention is the changing role of the State in society. Private law is modelled after the liberal market where the role of the State is enforcing transactions insofar as they were concluded voluntarily and on an informed basis. Thus, limits of freedom of contract address market failures and protection of public policy: they are not designed to protect parties from the impacts of economic changes. They can be capable only in a limited way to protect vulnerable parties or weaker groups of society. Consumer protection became an important policy of private law, but considering the rules covering consumer contracts, they follow such a regulatory approach that it is hardly compatible with the internal logic of private law. Ad hoc legislation, often used as statutory amendments of contractual relationships

---

24 Act no CIV upon the central budget of the Hungarian Republic §§64–68.

25 According to the relevant rule of §241 of the Civil Code (1959) the court might have amended a contract when it violated any substantial rightful interest of one of the parties in consequence of a circumstance arising in the long-term relationship of the parties following the conclusion of the contract.

26 Constitutional Court, 32/1991 (VI.6.) AB hat.

27 Supreme Court, Legf. Bír. Gf. I. 30 197/1991. sz., BH 1992. no 123.

does have a strong regulatory nature, which is much more inherent to public administrative law than to private law. The regulatory approach is reflected in detailed rules with less flexibility to adjust their application to the specific circumstances of the cases and also in the mandatory nature of such norms which is typical for such legislation. This is to be seen, however, as a reflection to the demand of the society vis-à-vis the State.

In the model of market economy, the demand of the society vis-à-vis the State was to provide a legal framework for enforcing transactions, to abstain from intervention and to allow a great playing field to the market players. In the modern welfare state, the demand of society is to provide social security, the highest possible standard of living and protection against evil things that may occur to us. The reaction of the State to such demands is a growing paternalism with an intervention into the life of the citizen, including his or her private law relationships. Under such social demands, the values of the market economy and democracy are less important for the society. The members of the society focus on the quality of the services provided by the State much more than on freedom involving responsibility.

As far as COVID-19 measures are concerned, the legislative intervention in contractual relationships implemented so far is only temporary and its scope is also limited to specific relationships, especially rent and lease. There is no relevant permanent legislation adopted so far. The consequences of COVID-19 show a certain similarity to the consequences of the transition into a market economy in 1989/1990 insofar as they affect society as a whole because of the influence on life and position of almost all members of society. The biggest part of the transactions involved are not discrete ones but are elements of contractual chains or relate to other contractual relationships in a complex system of legal relationships. In the modern society and economy, contracts are to be assessed as social relationships and also are to be seen as elements of a more complex system of interrelations. Judicial intervention is designed for discrete transactions and the scope of the judgment is limited accordingly. That is why, as a general attitude, it is likely that courts will be reluctant to intervene in contractual relationships and re-allocate the risks of COVID-19 by amending the contracts. Such interventions would, however, be inevitably necessary to fill the gaps left by statutory intervention or to correct the legal relationship in order to keep the coherence of the relationship broken by the statutory intervention. An example of such a need for intervention is correcting the duration of financial lease if the parties could not agree upon it. The moratorium provided for financial credits and extending the deadline of payment for the debtors till the end of the year 2020 covers financial lease as well but does not extend the duration of the lease.[28]

---

[28] 1.§ of Government Decree 47/2020. (III. 18.) on immediate measures necessary in order to reduce the coronavirus pandemic's effect on the national economy.

The problem is that financial lease is a legal relationship designed for a definite period of time where the lessee has a call option as the defined period expires. If the lessee comes into the position to exercise the option before the fee, i.e. the credit, was paid, the creditor of the financial lease would lose its ownership and the credit becomes unsecured. Such a situation would disrupt the structure of the financial lease. In order to avoid this, the duration must be adjusted to the extended deadline of payment. If the parties were not able to renegotiate their contract, there is a need for statutory or judicial amendment of the contract. If the legislator fails to fix it, courts would certainly do that with the application of *clausula rebus sic stantibus*.

4. LIABILITY FOR BREACH OF CONTRACT

§6:142 of the Hungarian Civil Code provides that the party causing damage to the other party by breach of contract shall be required to compensate for it. He/she shall be exempted from liability if he/she proves that the breach of contract was caused by a circumstance that was outside of his/her control and was not foreseeable at the time of concluding the contract, and he/she could not be expected to have avoided that circumstance or averted the damage. Practically, the obligor can be exonerated only by proving that *force majeure* caused the breach. The key factor of exoneration from liability is the concept of "beyond control". If the cause of the breach of contract fell within the control of the party, he/she could hardly argue successfully that it was not foreseeable at the time of concluding the contract, and that he/she could not be expected to have avoided that circumstance or averted the damage. The phrase "beyond control" has no precedent in Hungarian contract law, neither in theory nor in practice. It is a legal transplant taken from products of harmonisation of private law, especially from the CISG (Art 79), the PECL (Art 8:108), the DCFR (3:104) and from the UPICC (Art 6.2.2., Art 7.1.7). The main goal of the legislator was to express that compliance with the required standard of conduct or duty of care shall not be a ground for exoneration. The rule establishes strict liability in the sense that the absence of fault shall not be enough ground for exoneration. In the context of a contractual relationship, this rule is not about responsibility or about establishing the consequences of a wrongful behaviour but it is about pure risk allocation: the obligor undertook an obligation voluntarily for the agreed price. Thus, the cost of performance shall be borne by the obligor in order to shift the costs where the benefits are. The protection of the reliance on the promise of the obligor also requires such strict liability. The fact that the party breaching the contract was not able to influence the circumstance resulting in a breach of contract does not qualify the ground as falling "beyond control". Beyond control shall be understood in the context of Hungarian contract law as expressing *force majeure*. Circumstances that the obligor was not able to influence and could not be avoided even with the utmost duty of care, may still be qualified as falling under the scope of the party's control.[29]

The global pandemic caused by COVID-19 certainly could not have been foreseeable at the time of contracting provided that the contract was concluded before the pandemic. In most of the cases, most probably the statutory restrictions and their consequences would fell beyond the obligor's control and would result in exoneration from liability for breach of contract. The influence of expanding COVID-19 on the behaviour of the members of society would be less likely qualified as a circumstance falling beyond the obligor's control.

5. CONTRACTUAL SIDE-OBLIGATIONS AND SPECIFIC CONTRACTS

The legal impacts of COVID-19 in contractual relationships shall be assessed in the context of the contract as a whole. Contractual rights and obligations may be directly or indirectly relevant in the course of assessing the legal consequences of the epidemic. In Hungarian law of obligations, the parties are imposed with the duty to cooperate,[30] which does not imply an obligation to accept an offer for the amendment of the contract but it may imply obligations to tolerate non-compliance with the contract to a certain extent[31] and may require positive steps in order to help the obligor to perform. The duty to cooperate is a general clause open for concretisation according to the facts of the case and shall be concretised in the light of other rights and obligations stipulated in the contract.

In Hungarian contract law, there are specific contracts that are covered by specific rules as far as changes of circumstances are concerned. Such contracts are the contract for alimony and maintenance, gifts, contract for work on goods (including building contracts) and lease. From the point of view of impacts of the COVID-19 epidemic, the rules covering impossibility of contract for work on goods and building contracts and the rules covering cases where the tenant was not able to use the rental could be relevant.

---

29 Opinion of the New Civil Code Advisory Board to the Supreme Court, https://kuria-birosag.hu/hu/ptk?tid%5B%5D=498&body_value= accessed 11 March 2021 [the opinions of the Advisory Board do not have identification numbers and date but are published at the homepage of the Supreme Court].

30 §6:62. Hungarian Civil Code.

31 The nature of the general clause of this rule does not exclude such conclusion but it is not yet confirmed in court practice. Implied, however, with other rules of non-performance. E.g. the obligee has the right to rescind the contract on the grounds of delay of the obligor if he/she provided a reasonable additional deadline for performing the contract. If, however, the deadline was strict or the obligor is able to prove that the purpose of performance was frustrated due to the delay, he/she does not have such an obligation as a precondition of exercising the right to rescind the contract (§6:154. Hungarian Civil Code).

If performance of a contract for work on goods or building contract becomes impossible for a reason for which neither of the parties is liable, and the cause making performance impossible occurred within the contractor's scope of interests, the contractor shall not claim remuneration. If the cause making performance impossible occurred within the customer's scope of interests, the contractor shall be entitled to the contractor's fee. However, the customer may deduct the amount of the costs saved by the contractor due to the performance becoming impossible, as well as the amount the contractor earned or could have earned elsewhere without difficulty in the time freed up. If the cause of impossibility occurred within or outside of both parties' spheres of interest, the contractor shall be entitled to the pro-rata fee of the work performed and costs. The customer may require the contractor to hand over the commenced but unfinished work; in such a case, the rules of unjustified enrichment shall apply.[32]

Lease contracts play a central role in satisfying social and economic needs. That is why how risks are allocated in this type of contractual relationships is a critical issue. The starting point in Hungarian contract law is that the landlord is imposed with the duty to provide the use. From this follows that if the object of the lease cannot be used by the tenant, it is basically the risk of the landlord. The Hungarian Civil Code (1959) was very clear that if the tenant was not able to use the leased property for reasons not attributable to him/her, he/she had the right to claim for a reduction of the rental fee. This rule changed with the Civil Code (2013) stating that the tenant shall have the right to such reduction if the ground preventing him/her from using the property fell outside the scope of his interests.[33] It is not clear why the legislator changed this formula but it is obvious that risk allocation does not turn on simply on the tenant's actual position but has to be assessed on the ground if the cause of impossibility to use the object of the lease does fall in the scope of the landlord's or the tenant's interests. "Scope of interests" does not have a clear meaning in Hungarian contract law and no guidelines have been developed so far for assessing it. This may result in a need for a complex approach of leases. In so far as statutory restrictions are concerned (e.g. limitation for opening hours of shops), these risks can be allocated to the landlord on the ground that it is the landlord's fundamental obligation to provide the use to the tenant. In so far as social behaviour is concerned, the conclusion shall be the opposite: if the lessee hires a certain object in order to use it for business purposes, the decreasing demand for the services shall be deemed as the risk of the lessee.

---

32 §6:248 Hungarian Civil Code.

33 §6:336 (2) Hungarian Civil Code.

6. CONCLUSIONS

Contracts create social relationships. In the modern economy and society, contracts are to be seen not simply as discrete transactions but as interrelated with other legal relationships, often in great complexity. In the past century, the courts of European jurisdictions, including the Hungarian one, developed and elaborated doctrines like implied terms, frustration of purpose, impossibility, *clausula rebus sic stantibus* for re-allocating the risks of unforeseen contingencies. Binding force of contracts and the need for adapting social and legal relationships to changing circumstances create contradictory demands in society and the economy. Balancing these conflicting social interests requires a complex and differentiated approach. Thus, there is no clear-cut answer as to the allocation of the risks of the COVID-19 epidemic in contractual relationships. Risk allocation shall be different in commercial and non-commercial relationships and shall be different according to the nature of the consequences of the epidemic. That is, the direct impacts of the statutory restrictions, the indirect consequences of statutory restrictions and the consequences of changes in social behaviour are different in their nature and require different assessment with different conclusions. In the course of judicial revision of contracts, there is a need for a case-by-case analysis, having regard to the circumstances of the specific case as well as assessing rights and obligations in their complexity. Consumer contracts require structural interventions which would be the task of the legislator instead of courts. Due to the complexity of legal relationships, the most probable baseline of courts is that they are reluctant to intervene in individual relationships mainly because the consequences of COVID-19 epidemic affect the society as a whole. Correction of individual relationships may be unjust for social justice if risks that affect each member of the society are re-allocated in certain relationships while remaining untouched in others. When it comes to filling the gaps of specific ad hoc legislation, courts would certainly play an important role. Specific contracts of high social importance, like lease, rent, contract for work on goods and building contracts are addressed with specific relevant rules while remedies for breach of contract and side-obligations like the duty to cooperate are also parts of the puzzle when presenting the legal landscape. The COVID-19 epidemic is so wide-ranging and affects so deeply the society as a whole that, given the complexity of legal relationships, the doctrines and case law developed so far are not necessarily applicable anymore. Most probably, parties that have maintained the legal relationship, preserving trust and reliance as a priority will manage the problem with practice in transactions. The unpredictable outcome of judicial revision also calls for solutions based on renegotiation and mutual consent.

DEFERRAL OF PAYMENTS UNDER A CREDIT AGREEMENT AS AN EXTRAORDINARY MEASURE DUE TO THE EPIDEMIC

A Slovenian Approach

Miha Juhart*

The SARS-CoV-2 epidemic (COVID-19) poses a particular challenge to many disciplines and requires the State to take action at various levels of engagement. One example of this is a credit agreement. To mitigate the effects of the epidemic on the solvency of borrowers, the Slovenian legislator adopted the Intervention Measure Act on Deferred Payments of Borrowers' Obligations. The essential measure is the deferral of payment as stipulated, meaning the suspension of the maturity date of all obligations under the credit agreement until the end of the deferral period for 12 months. During this period, the interest shall be charged on the deferred part of the principal at the regular interest rate. The borrower may apply for the deferral of payment if the epidemic affects his/her ability to repay the loan. The bank must offer the borrower the conclusion of an annex to the credit contract if he/she fulfils

* University of Ljubljana, Faculty of Law.

all conditions for the application. In the deferral period, the borrower is bound by a special reporting obligation concerning his/her solvency and ability to make a repayment.

1. INTRODUCTION

The SARS-CoV-2 epidemic (COVID-19) poses a particular challenge to many disciplines and requires the State to take action at various levels of engagement. Contract law is probably not the only area where measures would be necessary or even vital. However, the epidemic and, above all, the enforcement of related measures is a cause that significantly affects the content of contractual obligations. Therefore, States adopt various regulations to resolve the situations that have arisen and enact special rules introducing specific interim solutions that interfere with existing contractual relationships. Of course, no universal approach exists for such actions, and each State should take into account the specific features and circumstances and, above all, consider whom and in what way to help in these unpredictable situations. Therefore, legislative solutions that interfere with contract law cannot be easily copied but must be viewed comprehensively and in conjunction with measures taken in other areas that may take into account interests that contract law solutions ignore or regulate in favour of counterparties.

In doing so, a distinction must be made between contracts where the principal obligation of the parties is a one-off performance and contracts involving a more permanent contractual relationship. The latter is characterised by the fact that an essential element of the contract is the period during which the mutual obligation between the parties lasts. A typical example of such contracts are lease and credit agreements.[1] From the perspective of the epidemic, of particular interest are those contracts that arose before the epidemic and which can be expected to continue after it has ended. The content of most often concluded credit agreements meets these requirements. If we start from the assumption that these credit agreements were concluded before the epidemic and the lender has already provided the cash principal of the loan to the borrower, the question arises as to how the epidemic affects the borrower's obligation to repay the loan.

2. THE BORROWER'S OBLIGATIONS AND THE EPIDEMIC

The borrower's obligation to pay the loan back is an obligation to pay a certain amount of money, and the application of general rules of contract law for

1 In Slovenian law, a credit agreement is a loan agreement concluded by a bank or other financial organisation as a lender and the subject of which is money.

pecuniary obligations is minimal. Slovenian legal doctrine and case law have made it abundantly clear that the debtor of a pecuniary obligation cannot invoke either the subsequent impossibility of performance or the changed circumstances.[2] The Supreme Court of the Republic of Slovenia ruled that money is the most generic thing, so the subsequent inability of performance is out of the question.[3] The debtor's pecuniary obligation may change his/her financial position, and thus the latter becomes insolvent after the conclusion of the contract, but such a change does not mean that impossibility of performance has occurred. A pecuniary obligation can always be fulfilled, and the debtor's weaker financial position does not create an impossibility of performance. Slovenian law in Article 112 of the Code of Obligations[4] regulates the impact of changed circumstances on a contractual obligation as a special legal institution. A party whose fulfilment of an obligation becomes significantly more challenging may request that the court annul the contract. The condition for this is that the performance of the party's obligation has become difficult after the conclusion of the contract for reasons for which the party is not responsible, to such an extent that the contract no longer meets the expectations of the parties. It would be unfair to maintain such a contract as it is.[5] Again, the position is unequivocal that the changed circumstances cannot be invoked by the debtor of the pecuniary obligation. Due to the difficulty of fulfilling the pecuniary obligation, the termination of the contract cannot be requested due to changed circumstances.[6] The debtor of a pecuniary obligation must always count on the possibility that his/her financial situation will change and, therefore, payment will become more difficult for. This is especially true for the borrowers, who cannot count on the fact that the loan will not have to be repaid, even though their profitability will deteriorate for reasons beyond their control.

Therefore, we can conclude that the epidemic in principle has no specific impact on credit agreements. This means that borrowers must fulfil all their obligations under credit agreements even during the epidemic and the validity of emergency measures that may significantly affect their profitability. Due to non-payment of the pecuniary obligation, all general legal consequences of non-fulfilment occur, which are determined by law or specially agreed by the contract between the parties.

---

2 Stojan Cigoj, *Teorija obligacij, Splošni del obligacijskega prava* (A Theory of Obligations, General Part of Obligation Law) (Uradni list, Ljubljana 1981) 330 ff.

3 Supreme Court of the Republic of Slovenia Judgment and Decision III Ips 93/2003 of 18 May 2004.

4 Official Journal of the Republic of Slovenia, no 97/07, 64/16 and 20/18.

5 See in more detail Cigoj, Teorija 334; Peter Grilc, *Gospodarska/finančna kriza kot spremenjena okoliščina* (The Economic/Financial Crisis as a Changed Circumstances) (Pravni letopis 2011) 1; Mile Dolenc in Miha Juhart and Nina Plavšak (eds), *Obligacijski zakonik s komentarjem* (Code of Obligations with Commentary) (GV Založba, Ljubljana 2004) 599.

6 Supreme Court of the Republic of Slovenia Judgment and Decision III Ips 17/1993 of 7 April 1993.

3. THE PITFALLS OF A SPECIAL LAW ON MEASURES AFFECTING EXISTING CONTRACTS

As borrowers are unable to rely on the general rules of contract law (in the event of a deterioration of their solvency because of the epidemic) to adjust or facilitate their obligations, the legislator can come to their aid. The legislator may adopt a special law to facilitate the borrower's obligations due during the epidemic or even later if the borrower's solvency is significantly impaired due to the effect of measures taken due to the epidemic. However, the adoption and entry into force of such a law raises several general legal issues. The legislator must count, above all, on the possibility that creditors will request a review of the constitutionality of any law that interferes with existing contracts and changes the contractually agreed obligations of the contracting parties. The case law of the Constitutional Court of the Republic of Slovenia has been abundantly clear regarding the constitutional protection of contractual freedom, not only referring to Article 33 of the Constitution and the guarantee of private property and inheritance but also linking legal protection to certain other rights and freedoms such as the inviolability of personal rights and the resulting freedom of action under Article 35 of the Constitution and free economic initiative under Article 74 of the Constitution. The following position is the leading one:

> One of the basic principles of the law of obligations is the freedom of regulation of bonded relations. Such general autonomy of contractual parties in concluding contracts on the basis of the law of obligations is also founded in the general freedom of conduct emanating from the integrity of personal rights as provided for by Article 35 of the Constitution, and in the free economic initiative guaranteed in Article 74 of the Constitution.[7]

This position has been reconfirmed several times and has been taken up in some other decisions of the Constitutional Court.[8] Therefore, today there is no doubt that the freedom to regulate obligations or contractual freedom enjoys constitutional protection as a fundamental right or freedom of the individual. The Constitutional Court case-law is also undoubtedly clear on this issue:

> That is why individual legal restrictions of free contractual intent will only be in conformity with the Constitution if they satisfy the constitutional requirements with regard to admissibility of imposing restrictions on constitutional rights, in the

7 Decision of the Constitutional Court No. U-I-202/93 of 6 October 1994.

8 See, e.g. the decisions of the Constitutional Court of the Republic of Slovenia Nos. U-I-123/95 of 5 March 1998, U-I-340/96 of 12 March 1998 and U-I-165/08 of 1 October 2009.

> disputed case especially the conditions of Article 15 (3) of the Constitution, and in the case of carrying out an economic activity also the conditions of Article 74 (2) of the Constitution.[9]

The significance of this view is, of course, twofold and has positive and negative elements. From a positive perspective, it means that the legislator does not pose unlimited power to interfere with and restrict contractual freedoms. However, any legislative interference with contractual freedom can be assessed with instruments developed based on Article 15 of the Constitution and taking into account the proportionality test.

> In the event that a statutory regulation interferes with an individual human right, the Constitutional Court assesses the admissibility of such interference from the perspective of the existence of a constitutionally permissible aim (Article 15 (3) of the Constitution) and the perspective of the principle of proportionality (Article 2 of the Constitution) ... Besides the requirement that the interference with human rights is based only on a constitutionally permissible goal (Article 15 (3) of the Constitution) the established constitutional case-law requires the assessment whether this is in line with principles of the rule of law (Article 2 of the Constitution), namely that principle, which prohibits undue state interference even in cases where they pursue a constitutionally permissible goal (the general principle of proportionality). The Constitutional Court shall determine the existence of undue interference with the application of a proportionality test. This test involves assessing three aspects of the interference: 1) whether the interference is necessary at all; 2) whether the assessed interference is suitable for achieving the pursued goal; 3) whether the severity of the consequences of the assessed interference with the affected human right is proportional to the value of the pursued goal or the benefits that will result from the interference (principle of proportionality *stricto sensu*). Only if the interference passes all three aspects of the test is it constitutionally permissible.[10]

From a negative perspective, it means that contractual freedom is not unlimited, but can be limited by law in a constitutionally justified manner. Restriction of contractual freedom is, after all, part of civil law itself, which began to set the limits of contractual freedom long before the affirmation of contractual freedom as a constitutional category. From the constitutional perspective, a law that interferes with existing treaties can also be reproached for having a retroactive effect. It could be false retroactivity, which in Slovene constitutional theory is presented as the effect of law, the prescribed consequence of which occurs after the publication of the regulation, but the operative part of this consequence

9 Decision of the Constitutional Court No. U-I-202/93 of 6 October 1994.

10 Decision of the Constitutional Court No. U-I-219/03 of 14 November 2003.

in the law relates to circumstances (facts) from the time before the law was published.[11] Again, this is a category of constitutional law that is not absolutely prohibited but is admissible if an individual statutory provision or measure passes the proportionality test mentioned above.[12] The purpose of this contribution is not to discuss the constitutional problems of a special law that interferes with existing contracts, but to analyse the potential content of such a regulation.

In addition to the dilemma of constitutional acceptability of interfering with the existing credit agreements, the legislator must take into account some other starting points before adopting such a law, which can be an essential element in applying the proportionality test, especially in assessing the severity of consequences. The legislator must decide whether the special regime should apply to all credit agreements or only to credit agreements where the creditors are persons exhibiting certain features. Thus, the validity of special measures may be limited to consumer credits only, but may also cover the credits of economic operators. Furthermore, an essential element is the demonstration of reduced solvency because of the epidemic itself or other measures taken in this regard. Even during the epidemic, some borrowers were more or less uninterrupted in their economic activity, generating income on this basis and thus maintaining their ability to pay. For other borrowers, however, the situation may have deteriorated sharply. Some have lost their jobs, which usually also means a significant deterioration in solvency. Others have been prevented, restricted, or entirely banned from engaging in economic activities due to the introduction of other measures related to the epidemic. This, in turn, is associated with lower revenues and poorer solvency. Since the epidemic itself or the measures taken because of the outbreak affect both borrowers-consumers and borrowers-economic operators, it is reasonable that special measures interfering with existing credit agreements apply to all credit agreements.

4. SLOVENIAN DEFERRED PAYMENTS ACT

4.1. THE MEASURE OF DEFERRAL OF PAYMENTS UNDER A CREDIT AGREEMENT

To mitigate the effects of the epidemic on the solvency of borrowers, the Slovenian legislator has decided to determine special measures that may affect credit agreements concluded before the outbreak. As one of the first regulations

11 Lovro Šturm in Lovro Šturm (ed), *Komentar Ustave Republike Slovenije* (A Commentary of the Constitution of the Republic of Slovenia) (Fakulteta za podiplomske državne in evropske študije, Ljubljana 2002) 57 and 1040.

12 Decision of the Constitutional Court No. U-I-158/11 of 28 November 2013.

after the beginning of the epidemic, the Intervention Measure Act on Deferred Payments of Borrowers' Obligations (the Deferred Payments Act) was adopted.[13] The Act entered into force on 29 March 2020, while the epidemic in the Republic of Slovenia was declared on 12 March 2020.[14] The Act applies to borrowers who are economic operators, other persons engaged in business activity and consumers (Art 2(2) of the Deferred Payments Act). The essential measure by which the legislator wishes to help the borrower is the deferral of payment as stipulated in Article 5(1) of the Act. Deferred payment under this provision means the suspension of the maturity date of all obligations under the credit agreement until the end of the deferral period. In the wording, the legislator is not precise enough, as he talks about the institution of deferral of payments, and, in the definition of the institution, about the deferral of obligations, which is a broader concept since the obligation of payment is only one type of obligation. According to the purpose of the provision, this provision should be interpreted narrowly and, even though a broader term is used in the definition, the deferral should be limited in substance to obligations of payment. No reason exists for the deferral to cover other obligations of the borrower, especially the obligations assumed by the borrower in commercial credit agreements as commitments. The epidemic has no impact on the borrower's reporting obligation, but the problem of financial and non-financial commitments is significantly different and cannot be solved by deferral, which is a mechanism that takes into account primarily the borrower's solvency.

The final maturity date of the credit agreement shall be extended for the duration of the deferral, which means that they shall not mature during the deferral. After the suspension, the fulfilment of obligations shall continue as agreed, and the repayment period shall be extended for the duration of the deferral. By amending the Deferred Payments Act in Article 2 of the Act Determining the Intervention Measures to Contain the COVID-19 Epidemic and Mitigate its Consequences for Citizens and the Economy,[15] it is specifically stipulated that during the deferral period, interest shall be charged on the deferred part of the principal at the regular interest rate agreed upon at the time of concluding the credit agreement. This is an amendment to the credit agreement if the borrower requests a payment deferral, which occurs directly stemming from law and the parties do not have to agree on it.

However, the legal nature of the amendment to the credit agreement is not entirely clear. We may ask whether this is an amendment based on the unilateral

---

13 Official Journal of the Republic of Slovenia, Nos 36/20 and 49/20.

14 The method of adopting legal regulations in the Republic of Slovenia was not adapted to the emergency situation and the law went through a relatively long adoption process, although the Government adopted it and sent it to the Parliament on 17 March.

15 Official Journal of the Republic of Slovenia, Nos 49/20 and 61/20.

exercise of the constitutive right or an agreement to amend the contract. I find the argument for the first position mainly in the fact that by its content it is a borrower's right, which the bank may not waive if all the conditions for deferral of payment set by law are met. A further argument is also the statutory amendment to the contract, which changes the time of loan repayment and the total amount of payments of the borrower, which is a consequence of interest on the principal at the time of payments deferral. Another possible interpretation is that the credit agreement is amended only by concluding an annex, to which Article 5(2) of the Deferred Payments Act refers. The annex, however, must contain an agreement on the consequences provided by law. Therefore, this is not regarded as a modification of the contract, the content of which is the result of the will of the parties, but the content of the modification is determined by law, which seems unusual and superfluous. In this respect, a better solution would be to amend the credit agreement with a statement, and the bank would have a duty to prepare a new statement of liabilities complying with the legally prescribed rules. Such a method would be more practical and more considerate to the borrower, who would save time by concluding an annex.[16] However, the position that the amendment of the contract requires the conclusion of an annex has a certain advantage, as in this case the bank's obligations regarding the contents that fall within the scope of pre-contractual explanatory duty can be incorporated into the contract amendment procedure. For an informed decision of the borrower regarding the amendment of the credit agreement, it is essential that the borrower is acquainted with the changed content of the obligation, and above all, with the new amount of payments he/she owes due to interest during the deferral period. For the above-mentioned reasons, the view that a modification of the credit agreement only occurs with the conclusion of an annex seems more appropriate. Of course, upon such an interpretation, the bank is bound by a contractual obligation (Art 17(1) of the Code of Obligations) and is obliged to conclude an annex to the contract at the request of any borrower who meets the conditions of the Deferred Payments Act.

4.2. THE DURATION OF THE DEFERRAL

In the Deferred Payments Act, the time dimension of the effect and enforcement of a deferred payment measure is unusual. It is even less common that deferred payment covers liabilities that have not yet matured (until the declaration of a

[16] The borrower, of course, has the option to object to the statement if it is not drawn up in accordance with the law.

virus epidemic) (Art 2(1) of the Deferred Payments Act). The deferral of payment is set for 12 months, which is a relatively long period, especially since the agreed duration of the loan is not taken into account. In the case of short-term loans, this can create a very unusual situation where the borrower has to repay regular instalments of the loan after the end of the epidemic. However, when he/she repays the last instalment, there may be a time gap for the 12-month deferred instalment to mature based on the Deferred Payments Act.

The question also arises as to whether the borrower can request a shorter deferral period. Article 2(6) of the Deferred Payments Act stipulates that the parties may agree on a different deadline for deferred payment if it is more favourable for the borrower. What is more favourable for the borrower is a unique question that is challenging to answer unambiguously, primarily because for the period of deferral there is a legal change in the loan agreement and additional interest on the principal. Sometimes a deferral period of fewer than 12 months will be more favourable for the borrower, especially if he/she does not want to bear the credit burden or wants to release it as soon as possible. However, it may happen that the borrower's ability to repay the loan will be weakened by a more extended period, and he/she will strive for a longer deferral of payment.

There is no doubt that any terms and conditions for a loan extension can be concluded based on a special agreement between the bank and the lender. It is a general possibility for the contracting parties to regulate their mutual relationship within the framework of their autonomy. There is also no doubt that the borrower cannot request from the bank to extend the deferral of payments for a period exceeding 12 months. However, various interpretations are possible regarding the shorter deferral period. With a plain grammatical interpretation of Article 2 of the Deferred Payments Act, the shortening of the deferral period is also possible only based on an agreement between the bank and the borrower. However, if we consider the purpose of the law, the answer may be different. Deferred payment is a special measure, the exercise of which is the borrower's optional right. If the borrower does not decide to exercise the right, the credit agreement shall not be amended. However, if the borrower chooses to exercise this right, the law provides a 12-month deferral of payment obligations. Therefore, the provision should be interpreted in such a way that the period of validity of the deferral depends on the will of the borrower and the bank is obliged to accept any request for a shorter period, if so requested by the borrower. We can start from the assumption that the borrower's request for a shorter period reflects his/her interest. The purpose of the law is to help a borrower whose ability to repay a loan is limited or hampered by the effects of measures due to the epidemic. Therefore, the payment deferral should last as long as necessary for the borrower to establish economic activity and generate income. The 12-month deadline is set only as the deadline for deferral that the bank is obliged to accept.

4.3. APPLICATION OF DEFERRAL TO CREDIT AGREEMENTS CONCLUDED AFTER THE DECLARATION OF AN EPIDEMIC

However, the provision of Article 2(7) of the Deferred Payments Act that the provisions of the Act shall also apply to credit agreements concluded after its entry into force is very unusual. These contracts are concluded at a time when the effect of measures to control the epidemic is not an unexpected event affecting the economic life of the borrower. Therefore, no particular reason exists for these contracts to be subject to a measure designed to eliminate the effects of measures that are unexpected for borrowers and significantly affect their ability to repay the loan. Such a provision can negatively affect the willingness of banks to enter into new credit agreements, as the expiry of the grace period will allow the eligible borrower to exercise this option.

However, it is not clear what effect the special agreement between the parties has, if the borrower waives the exercise of his/her right or assures the bank that he/she does not meet the conditions for exercising the right to deferment under Article 2 of the Deferred Payments Act. In principle, there is no doubt about the validity of such contractual arrangements, if certain general assumptions are met. In particular, the bank must not take advantage of its stronger position and impose such provisions. The status of the borrower can also be an important circumstance. Restrictions on the borrower's legal situation are easier to be accepted in commercial contracts. In the case of consumer contracts, exclusionary agreements can very quickly have the nature of inadmissible contractual terms, which of course means that these agreements are null and void.

To conclude, the answer to the question of the validity of such clauses is challenging to formulate. Given the general legal principles that the contracting parties must exercise due diligence in concluding a contract, I do not see an appropriate basis for such an effect, unless the escalation of measures would further change the circumstances. It is entirely unclear to me why special arrangements should apply to contracts concluded with knowledge of the existence of the epidemic and the possible consequences thereof.

4.4. APPLICATION FOR APPROVAL OF DEFERRED PAYMENTS

The Deferred Payments Act also stipulates a special method of enforcing a special measure of deferred payment. The measure is enforced at the request of a borrower who meets the prescribed conditions. Both economic entities and natural persons who are borrowers of Slovenian banks and are connected to Slovenia (registered office, citizenship and permanent residence) are entitled to deferral.

A special condition for entitlement to deferred payment is the impact of the epidemic on the ability to repay the loan (Art 2(4) of the Deferred Payments Act).

The strictest condition is prescribed for large companies as defined by Article 55 of the Companies Act.[17] A large company is entitled to deferred payment if the repayment of the loan could cause liquidity problems to the extent that the solvency of the company would be jeopardised. For other companies (micro, small and medium-sized) and other economic operators, it is sufficient that for business reasons related to the consequences of the virus epidemic, they cannot guarantee the repayment of obligations under the credit agreement with the bank. The same applies to individuals or consumers. The consumer qualifies for deferred payment if, due to circumstances related to the consequences of the virus epidemic, he/she is temporarily unable to secure repayment of obligations under the credit agreement with the bank. This can be proven by lower benefits due to loss of employment or reduced hours or a similar measure of the employer, such as furloughing its workers. The burden of proof for the existence of this condition lies with the borrower.

Providing evidence is facilitated by the presumption under Article 2(5) of the Deferred Payments Act, which stipulates that eligibility does not have to be specifically substantiated by an economic operator if it performs an activity for which a government or municipal decree stipulates a temporary ban on goods due to the virus epidemic. An additional condition for entitlement to deferment with economic operators is that the entity has settled due liabilities from mandatory contributions, taxes, and other duties as of 31 December 2019, or that on the day of submitting the application for deferral the entity is in a situation where the payment of liabilities arising from mandatory contributions, taxes, and other duties is deferred or their repayment in instalments is allowed under the legal provisions.

The borrower must state in the application (request) addressed to the bank all the circumstances that demonstrate the right to payment deferral, and economic operators must additionally state the management plan on measures to establish liquidity. The law specifically sanctions the borrower's false statements in the request for approval of the loan deferral. If the borrower provides false information, the bank may, by Article 4 of the Deferred Payments Act, suspend or shorten the period of deferred payments.

The period in which the borrower can request a payment deferral is also very peculiar. This deadline is set by Article 2(3) of the Deferred Payments Act and stipulates that the application must be submitted no later than six months after the declaration of the end of the virus epidemic.[18] From the purpose of the statutory provision, one can deduce that the borrower can submit an application immediately after the entry into force of the law, i.e. during the period of validity

---

17 The legal definition complies with Commission Recommendation of 6 May 2003 concerning the definition of micro, small and medium-sized enterprises (C (2003) 1422).

18 The end of the epidemic in the Republic of Slovenia was declared on 1 June 2020.

of measures due to the epidemic. The period of six months after the declaration of the end of the epidemic is relatively long and unfavourable, especially for banks, which will be uncertain about the borrower's decision to apply for a deferral. However, it is not entirely clear from the Deferred Payments Act when the effect of the deferral occurs or whether the deferral applies to already due and unpaid liabilities from the credit agreement or only to liabilities that will mature after the submission of the application. It is only clear from Article 2(1) of the Deferred Payments Act that the deferral does not apply to obligations that mature after the declaration of the epidemic.

In this lacuna, the most reasonable interpretation is that the deferral period commences on the due date of the borrower's oldest outstanding liability due after the declaration of the epidemic. With such an interpretation, the borrower has the opportunity to influence the beginning and the end of the deferral by paying all due obligations up to the moment for which he/she wants the deferral to take effect. Of course, the ability to pay overdue liabilities can be a circumstance that affects the assessment of entitlement to the deferment, so borrowers are generally expected to rush through deferred payment applications. However, there is no reason to explain that the payment deferral would not be applied retroactively for liabilities that mature after the declaration of the epidemic, but even before the entry into force of the Deferred Payments Act.

4.5. MODIFICATION OF THE CREDIT AGREEMENT

By submitting the application, the borrower expresses his/her will to request a modification of the credit agreement. No specific provisions exist on the legal nature and consequences of such a statement, so the general rules of contract law and some specific rules governing the credit agreement must be applied. If we accept the position that the contract is amended by concluding an annex to the contract, the borrower's request has the legal nature of a request to conclude a contract against the one bound by the contractual obligation. The question, however, arises whether such a request can be considered an offer to enter into a contract, especially if the borrower has no information on how his/her contractual obligation will change. In the case of consumer loans, in particular, an additional question arises as to how to take into account certain special rules of consumer protection set out in the Consumer Credit Act in the context of such an amendment to the credit agreement.[19] One of the fundamental forms of consumer protection is the pre-contractual informed consent.[20] The purpose

---

19 Official Journal of the Republic of Slovenia, No 77/16.

20 See Andreja Fakin, *Splošne predpogodbene dolžnosti informiranja: pravna podlaga vzpostavitve in možne sankcije za njihovo kršitev* (General Pre-Contractual Information Duties: Legal Basis of Establishment and Possible Sanctions for Infringement) (Podjetje in delo 2015) 1.

of the informed consent is to provide the consumer with comprehensive and comprehensible information on the content of the obligation and the potential risks he/she assumes by concluding the contract. Prima facie, the 12-month deferral option is a desirable option for consumers. This is especially true for those whose incomes have decreased or will decrease due to the epidemic. However, the deferral of payment under Article 5 of the Deferred Payments Act is not without consequences for the content of the obligation, so the amounts of instalments will change after the deferral termination. This change also largely depends on the amortisation schedule of an individual loan, and above all on what part of the principal has already been repaid.

Therefore, I believe, it is vital that the consumer who wishes to exercise his/her right to defer payments and thus modify the credit agreement be provided in advance with information on changes in the content of the obligations that will arise resulting from exercising the right. The consumer can make an informed decision regarding the exercise of the right to deferment only if he/she has a clear understanding of what his/her obligation will be after the modification with all relevant data and including the new calculation of the APR. I believe such comprehensive information must be provided to the consumer by the bank, and if it is not provided, the legal consequences of waiving the obligation to conclude a consumer credit agreement under Article 17 of the Consumer Credit Act occur. This provision stipulates the right of the borrower to withdraw from the contract by a unilateral statement. In this case, the right of withdrawal understandably applies only to the modification. If the consumer avails him/herself of the option of withdrawal, the contract shall apply as originally agreed. The consumer must exercise his/her right of withdrawal within one month of the conclusion, unless there is a legal consequence that, despite the shortcomings in the conclusion, the modification remains in force.

4.6. BORROWER REPORTING

Article 4 of the Deferred Payments Act stipulates a special reporting obligation for specific borrowers who have been granted deferred payments by concluding an annex to the credit agreement. The reporting obligation applies to borrowers who are economic operators. They must report to the bank once a month on the implementation of the liquidity recovery plan and other changes in the business situation. If the reporting entity omits monthly reporting or provides untrue information in the report, the bank may suspend or shorten the period of deferral of payments. The law does not specify how the bank shall exercise this right. Therefore, we can conclude that the bank shall exercise this right by a unilateral statement, which acts as an amendment to the credit agreement. The effect of the amendment to the contract occurs when the borrower receives a statement from the bank that the bank has enforced the suspension or shortening of the payment deferral due to a breach of the reporting obligation. The bank may do the same if it assesses from the content of the report that the interruption or shortening of the payment deferral period is justified. The bank may do so in particular if it considers that the borrower's economic situation has improved since the end of the epidemic, so that the delay is no longer economically justified.

Banks are likely to take into account, in particular, the volume of operations, financial flow and other financial indicators after the end of the epidemic. In this respect, the law provides banks with an extensive power. However, it is not entirely clear what the legal protection of the borrower is if a dispute arises between him/her and the bank as to whether the bank is entitled to suspend or shorten the deferral of the loan. Since the borrower must eventually repay the entire loan, it is primarily a dispute over the payment of contractual and default interest, which will have to be decided by the court.

5. CONCLUSION

The regulation of the Slovenian Deferred Payments Act is very special. Nevertheless, it was quickly established in business practice. Although there are quite a few ambiguities in the law that have been highlighted, the law has been applied without any particular difficulties so far. It is obvious that it has been accepted by both banks and borrowers. So far, it does not appear that a request for a review of constitutionality has been initiated. Therefore, such a review is unlikely, as the end of the epidemic was declared in the Republic of Slovenia.[21] Supervision over the application of the law is performed by the Bank of Slovenia, which has also published the first data. In the first month of the Deferred Payments Act, banks received 22,230 applications from borrowers for deferred payment in the amount of EUR 267 million, which represents 3.3% of all loans.[22] The Bank of Slovenia estimates that the movement of applications in the coming months will depend mainly on the time and intensity of the restart of the economy, as allowed by the situation with coronavirus.

---

21 Ordinance on the revocation of epidemic of contagious disease SARS-CoV-2 (COVID-19), Official Journal of the Republic of Slovenia, No 68/20.

22 https://www.bsi.si/mediji/1496/v-prvem-mesecu-22230-vlog-za-odlog-placil-obveznosti-kreditojemalcev accessed 16 March 2021.

THE PANDEMIC AND CHANGE OF CIRCUMSTANCES IN ITALY

Andrea Nicolussi*

*The contribution is divided into two parts. The first describes the essential lines of the discipline of contingencies (change of circumstances in a broad sense) in Italian law with some comparisons with English common law. In particular, two subdivisions of the subject are presented. The former is the distinction between contingencies that disrupt the exchange covered by the contract in a qualitative sense and contingencies that disrupt the exchange covered by the contract in a quantitative sense. The latter is the distinction between typical contingencies, that is, legally foreseen and disciplined, and atypical contingencies, that is, not governed by the contract or by the law and which can make the fairness (*equità, aequitas*) criterion intervene. After this premise, the author analyses two hypotheses of lease contracts, those for commercial use and those for the residence of university off-site students, which can be considered examples of typical contingencies and atypical contingencies, respectively. The author concludes with a reference to quantitative contingencies with regard to which he takes into consideration the remedies of termination, equitable adjustment and renegotiation.*

* Catholic University of Milan.

1. CHANGE OF CIRCUMSTANCES IN GENERAL

Of the events that have happened to man in our time, the COVID-19 pandemic is probably the most extraordinary of the last decades, not only because of the tragic effects it has had on the lives of many people, especially the most vulnerable, but also for the suspension of normal social life for, already, more than a year across much of the world. The restrictions on personal freedom imposed by the State on citizens to protect the community's interest in health, one of the highest constitutional values (Art 32 Italian Constitution), were introduced for the first time since the birth of the Republic in 1948. It is obvious that the question of their effects on that dense web of innumerable legal relationships that had arisen in pre-pandemic daily life has emerged. For civil law, these relationships are related mainly to contracts and in particular to long-term contracts, which were affected by this extraordinary and – at least for the majority of people – unpredictable event. Events like this once again show how each contract is historically conditioned. The change in the circumstances in which it was conceived shows that it depended on those circumstances present at the time of its adoption or at least on the developments that could have been foreseen. However, this consideration must be understood in conjunction with the principle of self-responsibility (the burden of predicting and regulating subsequent occurrences) which is connected to the principle of freedom of contract (freedom to enter into the contract as the regulatory centre of gravity of the obligations arising from the contract).[1] The issue of lacunae that emerge after the contract has been concluded must be resolved coherently and in accordance with the terms of the contract, but there are also rules that the legal tradition has long developed to fill such lacunae. The pertinent issue is that of the measure of self-responsibility: to what extent do the parties have the burden of predicting and contracting the risks of any contingencies and to what extent instead does an integrative and heteronomous rule of allocation of unregulated risks make sense.

A subsequent occurrence that in civil law legal systems traditionally is dealt with by the law without the need for a contractual provision is the impossibility of performance for reasons not attributable to the debtor. In civil law systems, in fact, the contract is seen mainly as a source of obligations, and in turn the obligation, a concept derived from Roman law, is conceived as a duty that reaches a limit in the subsequent impossibility of performance. Hence, the rule that the impossibility of an obligation leads to the automatic termination of the contract and thus also to the extinction of the counter-obligation. It follows that if neither the parties nor the law impose a guarantee, the obligations following

---

[1] Angelo Belfiore, *La presupposizione* (Giappichelli 2003) 31 ff (where the criterion of self-responsibility is based on Art 1374 Italian Civil Code).

from a contract in their essence find their limit in the (possible) subsequent impossibility of performance.

In other words, there is no burden on the parties to foresee the subsequent impossibility of performance as a cause for exemption from the liability of the debtor even when the obligation derives from a contract.

On the other hand, in common law systems the principle of the primacy of the contract has been affirmed with more force (sanctity of contract) and obligations arising from contracts have a certain particular discipline different from that of other types of obligations. Moreover, there is always the memory and still some, even if limited, relevance of *Paradine v Jane*[2] in which the Court required the tenant to pay the rent despite the fund being requisitioned by the German prince and therefore the tenant was unable to enjoy the fund. *Paradine v Jane* radicalises the principle of self-responsibility: whatever happens, if you are contractually bound, you cannot be released from your contractual obligations except by a cause foreseen by the contract as a legitimate excuse. In a very broad sense, contractual duties are absolute, and absence of fault is no defence.[3] As we know, in English law the principle of absoluteness of the obligation has been questioned and the law of contract has admitted the relevance of subsequent impossibility,[4] but it is understood as a frustration of the contract, rather than as a reflection on contracts of a rule generally valid for obligations.

In civil law, and in particular in Italian law, impossibility is an objective concept. It indicates that with the means provided by the contract it is not objectively possible to fulfil the obligation, i.e. to achieve the result due, in terms of entitlement, to the creditor. Therefore, "impossibility" is quite distinct from greater difficulty of performance.[5] The distinction is also well known in English law where it is stated that mere hardship cannot frustrate the contract.[6]

However, unlike English law, there is contractual protection in Italian law for the case of serious difficulty in fulfilling the obligations deriving from a contract. This special discipline operates in a sense that is completely different from common law. Indeed, the Italian Civil Code provides, among the first codes in Europe, for termination (*risoluzione*) for excessive onerousness.[7]

---

2 [1647] EWHC KB J5.

3 Patrick Selim Atiyah, *An introduction to the law of contract* (Clarendon Press 1995) 214.

4 *Taylor v Caldwell* [1863] 3 B & S 826. In general, see Patrick Selim Atiyah, *An introduction to the law of contract* (Clarendon Press 1995) 231 ff.

5 The impossibility of performance is objective, but relative because the principle of good faith requires an interpretation of the title from which the obligation derives and a determination of which means were required to achieve the due result. Only in relation to these means can the subsequent impossibility be judged. See Luigi Mengoni, 'Responsabilità contrattuale' in Carlo Castronovo, Antonio Albanese and Andrea Nicolussi (eds), *Obbligazioni e negozio, Scritti II* (Giuffrè 2011) 328 ff.

6 Patrick Selim Atiyah, *An introduction to the law of contract* (Clarendon Press 1995) 240 ff.

7 Article 1467 Italian Civil Code: "*Contract for mutual counter-performances.* In contracts for continuous or periodic performance or for deferred performance, if extraordinary or

Comparing termination for subsequent impossibility and that for subsequent excessive onerousness, the two fundamental models of contingency on which the Italian legal system is based emerge. The former can be seen as a *qualitative* contingency and the latter as a *quantitative* contingency. If it is not possible for Titius to perform the service promised to Gaius due to a circumstance that has occurred, the exchange will not be possible because there is no possibility of remedying such a situation. Possibly a guarantee with indemnity may be provided,[8] but we are no longer on the level of the original contractual exchange in a qualitative sense: *aliud pro alio.*

With regard to quantitative contingencies, the excessive burden that arose highlights another model of contingency which affects the contractual exchange: a contingency that disrupts the relationship of economic equivalence between services agreed with the contract, but does not change the quality of the exchange, and therefore allows remedy in the sense of adjustment (adaptation). This is a "remediable" contingency because the contract can continue as the qualitative result is still possible. Hence, it can also be said that in the case of impossibility the contract cannot be continued, while in that of excessive onerousness the contract can be continued. This perspective is perhaps the essential distinction between contractual contingencies, i.e. between those that qualitatively alter the balance of the exchange and those that alter it quantitatively compared to what was originally set in its object.[9] In other words, the possibility of a *reductio ad equitatem* (equitable adjustment) is the consequence that specifically differentiates quantitative contingencies from qualitative ones.

In reference to impossibility, Article 91 of Decree-Law of 17 March 2020, no 18 in which Article 3 paragraph 6-bis of Decree-Law of 23 February 2020, no 6 is inserted provides that "compliance with the containment measures referred to in this decree is always assessed for the purposes of exclusion, pursuant to and for the purposes of Articles 1218 and 1223 Italian Civil Code, of the liability of the debtor, also in relation to the application of any forfeiture or penalties related to delays or omissions". However, the norm has been given an interpretation that reduces it to the obvious, on the basis of which compliance with containment

---

unforeseeable events make the performance of one of the parties excessively onerous, the party who owes such performance can demand dissolution of the contract, with the effects set forth in Article 1458. Dissolution cannot be demanded if the supervening onerousness is part of the normal risk of the contract. A party against whom dissolution is demanded can avoid it by offering to modify equitably the conditions of the contract".

8 Cass Civ 9 November 1960 no 2979, Foro It 1960, no 373 stated that "to be exempt from liability due to breach, the debtor cannot invoke the impossibility of the performance, even if due to *factum principis*, when the contract includes the possibility of the occurrence of an event that prevents performance and the debtor has willingly assumed the risk for himself or when the debtor has willingly placed himself in the condition of being subject to a possible mandatory measure".

9 This distinction is the result of the most advanced survey on subsequent occurrences carried out by Angelo Belfiore, *La presupposizione* (Giappicchelli 2003) 16 fn 28.

measures should constitute an impossibility due to non-attributable reasons.[10] To be precise, the measures do not necessarily constitute definitive impossibility but mostly configure temporary impossibility from which consequences not necessarily identical to those of definitive impossibility could derive.

Moreover, in the midst of the two general categories of typical contingencies – impossibility and excessive onerousness – contingencies are expected that affect the quality of the exchange but in a relative way and therefore can also admit a quantitative remedy. These are temporary impossibility and partial impossibility, which can lead to qualitative or quantitative reflections on the contract.[11]

In particular, the model of Article 1464 Italian Civil Code identifies a sort of middle ground where qualitative contingency does not operate automatically by terminating the contract, but allows space for deliberation between the alternative of maintaining the contract with a reduction in the consideration and that of withdrawal where the creditor has no appreciable interest in the fulfilment of the obligation. The rule therefore leaves room for manoeuvre also in the sense of maintenance of the relationship, and from this point of view it lends itself to be assessed as a reference point of qualitative contingencies that only affect the contract to a certain degree without implying an automatic dissolution as in the case of subsequent impossibility.

2. ATYPICAL CONTINGENCIES AND EQUITABLE REMEDY: COLLISION BETWEEN THE RIGHTS OF CREDITORS AND A CONSTITUTIONAL VALUE

It should be noted that the matter of contractual lacunae is regulated by the Civil Code in Article 1374 on the basis of which the contract obliges the parties not only to what is expressed in it but also to all the consequences that derive from it according to the law, or, failing that, according to customs and fairness in the civil

---

10 See Aldo Angelo Dolmetta, 'Rispetto delle misure di contenimento della pandemia e disciplina dell'obbligazione' (2020), IlCaso.it https://blog.ilcaso.it/news_892/11-04-20/«Rispetto_delle_misure_di_contenimento»_della_pandemia_e_disciplina_dell'obbligazione accessed 15 June 2020.

11 Article 1256 Italian Civil Code provides that: "*Definitive impossibility and temporary impossibility*. An obligation is extinguished when its performance becomes impossible for a cause not imputable to the debtor. If the impossibility is only temporary the debtor is not liable for delay in performance as long as it continues to exist. However, the obligation is extinguished if the impossibility continues until, depending on the source of the obligation or the nature of its subject matter, the debtor can no longer be held bound to perform the obligation or the creditor is no longer interested in the performance". Article 1464 Italian Civil Code provides that: "*Partial impossibility*. When the performance of a party has become only partially impossible, the other party is entitled to a corresponding reduction in the performance due by it, and may also terminate the contract if it has no appreciable interest in partial performance".

law sense (*equità, aequitas*). As has been said perspicuously, "fairness (Art 1374) and good faith (Art 1375) constitute the two different figures through which the covenant system is self-integrated, just as the legal system is self-integrated through analogy".[12] Naturally, the term self-integration must be understood in the sense of judicial integration of contractual lacunae, but respectful of the logic of the contract in question. More precisely, the rules generated by fairness (*equità, aequitas*) will be "a function, on the one hand, of the logic of the contractual agreement which they will integrate and, on the other hand, of the need for balancing on both parties the cost of the contingency the lack of foresight of which was attributable equally to both parties".[13] According to an American author, the foundation of a possible equitable adjustment can be found in the principle of autonomy itself. In fact, it is argued that autonomy requires identifying whether the parties reasonably expected their counterpart to be flexible if things went awry, in which case the advantaged party should have agreed to an adjustment without litigation. The court's adjustment under these circumstances is framed merely as a form of specific performance.[14] When an event occurs that prompts an imbalance in the contract and is attributable to an event unexpected by both parties, the problem of an equitable intervention on the contract arises. The extent of the lacuna depends on the interpretation of Article 1467 Italian Civil Code. If it is considered that the requirement of extraordinary and unforeseeable events applies only to the remedy of termination, and that therefore Article 1467 Italian Civil Code does not exhaust all the hypotheses (cases) of relevance of significant imbalances generated by contingencies, then it cannot be excluded that when serious contingencies occur an equitable remedy can intervene. On the other hand, in the disciplines of contractual types (specific contracts), it is the Italian Civil Code itself that provides for revisions of the contract such as for service contracts (Art 1664 Italian Civil Code) or for rent (Art 1623 Italian Civil Code).

A particular case of atypical contingency is the undue hardship (*inesigibilità*) that derives from a mixture between good faith and fairness and corresponds to the *Unzumutbarkeit* of German law where it was founded on the principle of *Treu und Glauben*: the performance cannot be claimed due to circumstances that occurred because fulfilment implies the sacrifice of a value higher than the credit (the right of the creditor): there is a collision between two values which in the legal system have respectively higher rank and lower rank.[15] In Italian civil law,

12 Angelo Belfiore, *La presupposizione* (Giappichelli 2003) 30.

13 Angelo Belfiore, *La presupposizione* (Giappichelli 2003) 23.

14 Robert A. Hillman, 'Maybe Dick Speidel Was Right about Court Adjustment' (2009) 46 San Diego L. Rev. 3 595, 604.

15 On undue hardship (*inesigibilità*), see Luigi Mengoni, 'Responsabilità contrattuale' in Carlo Castronovo, Antonio Albanese and Andrea Nicolussi (eds), *Obbligazioni e negozio, Scritti II* (Giuffrè 2011) 333 (who also directly relate the issue to fair dealing pursuant to Article 1175 Italian Civil Code, but considering it to gravitate to the general orbit of objective good faith.

reference is made to the principle of good faith and fair dealing (*correttezza*). The concept of undue hardship is not derived so much from the principle of good faith as a criterion for assessing behaviour for the purposes of liability, but corresponds more precisely to the obligation of fair dealing both for the debtor and the creditor (Art 1175 Italian Civil Code). In this case it translates into a criterion of exemption from the liability of the debtor and correlatively into the complaint (for abuse of right) of the possible behaviour of the creditor claiming fulfilment. Scholars tend to exhaust the issue with reference to fair dealing, but in this hypothesis, it is not only protection of reliance that comes into play, but also a real comparison of values that are balanced to reach what could be considered an equitable solution according to good faith. A classic example is that of the singer who does not go to the theatre because she has to care for her son who is in hospital suffering from serious illness. Performance is still possible.[16] However, the creditor, undoubtedly, can be considered incorrect if they demand fulfilment by imposing a similar sacrifice on the debtor, but at the same time the claim could be considered unfair due to the disproportionality between credit and value to be sacrificed.[17] It is clear that the conditions determined by the pandemic have affected all those obligatory relationships in which the debtor is physically exposed to contagion and therefore in general the performance is not due. Moreover, in the case of an employed worker there is also the obligation of the employer to take the necessary measures to protect the physical integrity of the workers (Art 2087 Italian Civil Code). Obviously, the question presents itself differently in cases where it is the debtor's duty to face the danger of contagion or it must be assumed that the contracting party has foreseen this contingency and the debtor has accepted the ensuing risk. Therefore, doctors cannot excuse their obligation to treat a patient under the pretext of a risk of contagion, at least as long as equipment to protect their duty, e.g. masks or disinfectants and if ready, vaccination, is made available to them.

A more problematic example can be seen in cases where the fulfilment of the obligation does not jeopardise health. One could, for instance, think of bank loan contracts in which the debtor of the instalments is at some point in serious

---

Article 1175 Italian Civil Code provides that: "*Fair behaviour ('Comportamento secondo correttezza')*. The debtor and the creditor shall behave according to rules of fair dealing", while Article 1375 provides that: "*Performance according to good faith*. The contract shall be performed according to good faith").

16 Luigi Mengoni, 'Responsabilità contrattuale' in Carlo Castronovo, Antonio Albanese and Andrea Nicolussi (eds), *Obbligazioni e negozio, Scritti II* (Giuffrè 2011) 333–334 (for more examples).

17 In Italian legal culture, good faith (*buona fede*) and fairness (*equità, aequitas*) are clearly distinct categories. The first protects reliance between parties who enter into a legal relationship and therefore is a source of rules of conduct and of responsibility. The second is, instead, a criterion of attribution to the judge of the power to balance the interests of the parties and therefore to fill a lacuna or sometimes even to derogate from a general rule.

difficulty due to losing their job through no fault of their own. Good faith could justify the idea that the claim of the sum in question is a case of undue hardship (*Unzumutbarkeit*), in the sense of a suspension of the power to claim the credit when its payment could be said to be less important than another value of higher constitutional rank, such as the payment of health expenses for oneself or for children.[18]

The core element of this idea was taken up, to some extent, by German law which introduced the category of "essential long-term obligations" (*wesentliche Dauerschuldverhältnisse*). Article 240 §1(1) 3rd sentence of the *Einführungsgesetz zum Bürgerlichen Gesetzbuch* (Introductory Act to the German Civil Code), enacted with the Act of 27 March 2020, includes a definition of this type of obligation that describes them as those that require services of appropriate general interest (*Wesentliche Dauerschuldverhältnisse sind solche, die zur Eindeckung mit Leistungen der angemessenen Daseinsvorsorge erforderlich sind*).[19] Irrespective of what one may think of this category of obligations, this represents further proof that contracts cannot be reduced to their text and to the freedom of contract, nor can we assume that for the parties the terms were valid irrespective of what may supervene. Especially when it comes to long-term contracts, where essential interests are at stake, an opportunity for a rebalancing intervention by the law arises, whenever extraordinary circumstances supervene.

3. TYPICAL AND ATYPICAL CONTINGENCIES IN THE LEASE

The pandemic and the containment measures adopted have posed some dilemmas with regard to lease contracts. In particular, two types of these contracts are considered, those for commercial use and those of a transitory nature for off-site university students. Before discussing them, a premise on some fundamental questions is useful.

A first point is that the Italian legislator has not specifically addressed the problem, with the notable exception of leases involving sport facilities,[20] unlike

18 Andrea Nicolussi, 'Etica del contratto e contratti di durata per l'esistenza della persona' in Luca Nogler and Udo Reifner, *Life time contracts* (Eleven International Publishing 2014) 153.

19 The "essential long-term contracts" recall the category proposed and discussed in Luca Nogler and Udo Reifner, *Life time contracts* (Eleven International Publishing 2014).

20 Article 216 co. 3 of Decree-Law 19 May 2020 no 34, converted with modification by law 17 July 2020, no 77, states that: "The suspension of sporting activities … is always assessed, pursuant to articles 1256, 1464, 1467 and 1468 Italian civil code … as a factor of supervening imbalance in the structure of interests agreed with the lease of gyms, swimming pools and sports facilities owned by private individuals. Due to this imbalance, the tenant has the right, limited to five months from March 2020 to July 2020, to a corresponding reduction in the rent which, subject to proof of a different amount by the interested party, is assumed to be equal

the German legislator, who adopted the new Article 240 §2 of the Introductory Act to the German Civil Code, applicable to both commercial and residential premises and provides the exclusion of termination in case of late payment, as long as it concerns non-payment in the months of April, May and June 2020.[21] As there is no such act in Italy, the solution to the problems raised by the pandemic needs to be further researched within the Italian legal system. In Italian law, the discipline of leasing seems to observe a distinction between circumstances that arise which affect the use in a material (physical) sense of the rented property and circumstances extrinsic to use in the proper sense. It is one thing that a supervening circumstance compromises the material possibility of using the asset such as the collapse of a wall or an authority's ban on using a certain apartment; it is another thing where a circumstance arises which nullifies the ulterior purpose of the use of the apartment such as the fact that during the holiday in the mountains the ski slopes were closed or with regard to university students living in an apartment off-campus when the university was closed or, finally, to quote a famous British Coronation case, the fact that the parade for Edward VII was cancelled and the tenant of the apartment unable to attend. This distinction between circumstances affecting the material possibility of using the asset and extrinsic circumstances is also derived from the obligations provided for by the Italian Civil Code in relation to leased property. Article 1575 Italian Civil Code provides that the lessor must keep the matter in place to be utilised for the agreed use and Article 1587 Italian Civil Code provides that the tenant must take delivery[22] of the thing and observe the diligence of the good family man in using it for the use determined in the contract or for the use that could otherwise be presumed under the circumstances.[23] As can be seen, there is no room for the tenant's use to be included in the performance or due result of the lessor, which involves circumstances extrinsic to the material consistency of the asset. Thus, also Article 1581 Italian Civil Code maintains this criterion linked to the material profile with regard to subsequent defects of the thing.

---

to 50% of the contractually established fee". It seems possible to argue that, given the express reference to Articles 1256, 1464, 1467 and 1468 Italian Civil Code, here the Italian legislator did not introduce a new legal principle but rather restated a pre-existing one, inferred from the aforementioned articles. If this were the case, the novel aspect of the law would be only the exact quantification of the reduction in the rent.

21 See, in this book, the contribution by Martin Schmidt-Kessel and Christina Möllnitz, 'Particular Corona Contract Law in Germany – Why Does General Contract Law Not Suffice?'.

22 The expression "take delivery" literally translates the formula of the Italian legal text ("*prendere in consegna*"). It refers to taking charge of the thing which implies an obligation of protection and responsibility for any material damage to the thing itself.

23 However, such a rule gives rise to possible uncertainties as one might imagine, for example, referring to cases such as the English leading case in the matter of necessity *Liverpool City Council v Irwin* [1977] AC 239. See Patrick Selim Atiyah, *An introduction to the law of contract* (Clarendon Press 1995) 206.

From a comparative perspective, this is confirmed in English law in which subsequent impossibility is such if it affects the object of the lease contract making the property unusable by the tenant. It is precisely for this reason that *Krell v Henry*[24] (the case of the apartment rented to attend the parade in honour of Edward VII, then cancelled) is not considered a case of impossibility. In fact, the cancellation of the parade did not affect the objective use of the asset but an extrinsic circumstance on which the landlord had no power. In other words, this circumstance cannot be considered as part of the performance or result due by the debtor. Thus, in English law if, despite the contingency, the leased thing retains some function for the tenant, in general the risk of not being able to use the thing for what could have been the main purpose is borne by the tenant. The person who rented a boat to see the naval review by the King and take a ride with friends on the Thames cannot claim frustration of contract because of the cancellation of the event owing to the King's illness.[25] Nor can Mr. Schlesinger, who had rented an apartment in London, but was unable to travel to London due to the subsequent closure of the borders at the time of the First World War.[26] Again in this case, English jurisprudence considered that the apartment could still be used, for example by subleasing it.

Although opinion has not been lacking among Italian scholars that in cases similar to *Krell v Henry* we can refer to impossibility also under Italian law,[27] it does not seem that the specific interest in attending the parade from the apartment is a result of the debtor's performance and therefore the possible cancellation of the parade may constitute an impossibility. If anything, it is a question of establishing from what other point of view this interest may be contractually relevant, and of course even before this, whether the interest is relevant at all.

As is known, in English law the answer to this question is as follows. *Krell v Henry* is considered a hypothesis of frustration of the common venture because the parade takes on the value of an extrinsic circumstance necessary for the contract in question. The tenant's interest in using the apartment to attend the parade assumes the *conditio sine qua non* (indispensable condition) of the contract which allows the landlord to obtain extraordinary and otherwise unachievable gains from his apartment and explains the willingness, on the other hand, of the tenant to pay a high rent to be able to live in the apartment for a few days. Where the owner is aware of the purpose for which a person hires something, and when he well knows that what has been hired would in fact be useless for any other purpose, and where the price is grossly inflated

24 [1903] 2 KB 740.
25 *Herne Bay Steamboat Co v Hutton* [1903] 1 KB 20.
26 *London Northern Estates v Schlesinger* [1916] 1 KB 20.
27 Angelo Belfiore, *La presupposizione* (Giappichelli 2003) 101 fn 125.

because of the special use contemplated, then it is reasonable to say that this use is the common object of both parties, and not merely the individual motive of the hirer.[28]

In Italian law, a relevance of atypical contingencies implies an equitable intervention on the contract which must be related to the regulatory indices contained in the contractual type (specific contracts) regulation. In this regard, Article 1623 Italian Civil Code can be taken into consideration. It pertains to the regulation for the *affitto*, which is a subtype of lease characterised by the enjoyment of a productive, movable or immovable thing, such as agricultural land, animals, machines, etc. If, as a consequence of a legal provision or by order of the competent authority, the contractual relationship is significantly modified so that the parties suffer a loss and an advantage respectively, an increase or decrease in the rent can be requested or, according to the circumstances, the termination of the contract. It is therefore possible to ask whether Article 1623 Italian Civil Code expresses a general rule that can also be extended to rentals. The fact that rentals concern productive things to be managed by the tenant is not a sufficient reason to believe that the changes indirectly produced by legal provisions that affect the mutual relationship of a contract cannot be treated similarly where they concern the lease. The sense of Article 1623 Italian Civil Code seems to obviate that risks deriving from measures that increase or decrease the productivity of the thing are interactions borne on one side only. The logic seems to be that of a sort of prohibition of enrichment of one or the other party connected to these measures, a logic that legitimises an equitable intervention on the contract. It should be noted that if the authority's provision reduces the productivity of the property, a sort of partial impossibility occurs, while the hypothetical increase would be more properly an enrichment of the tenant. Unlike termination for excessive onerousness pursuant to Article 1467 Italian Civil Code, the disadvantaged party can directly request rent increase or reduction, unless, based on the circumstances, he prefers the dissolution of the contract.

4. LEASES FOR COMMERCIAL USE AND TYPICAL CONTINGENCIES

The distinction between use in the proper sense of the thing (object of the contract) and extrinsic circumstances can be used to examine two types of cases that pandemic has brought to light in Italy.

The first relates to leases for commercial uses and the second to leases of apartments by off-site university students (away from home).

---

28 Patrick Selim Atiyah, *An introduction to the law of contract* (Clarendon Press 1995) 234.

As far as leases for commercial uses are concerned, it is a question of establishing how and if the property can be used following the introduction of measures linked to the pandemic. The scholars who have already dealt with these cases in Italy have made distinctions according to whether the room (site) where the commercial activity takes place can possibly still be used, for instance for the storage of the goods that are sold remotely or if the place is used for direct sale to the public and therefore the prohibition of public access or perhaps of the activity itself makes it impossible for it to be carried out. In many cases, bars, restaurants, hotels and shops have been closed and therefore there is no doubt that the circumstance that has arisen has affected the use of the property in its physical form.

Therefore, according to one scholar, the risk should be borne by the lessor.[29] This would result from the peculiar risk allocation of subsequent occurrences in the leasing discipline (regulation), which derives from the set of rules for which the lessor is not obliged to guarantee any enjoyment of the property, but more precisely the suitability of the thing for the agreed use (Art 1575 Italian Civil Code), or to the use determined in the contract or that may otherwise be assumed under the circumstances *(arg. ex* Article 1587 Italian Civil Code). According to a different scholar, since the emergency measures limit the tenant's activity, the risk is pertinent to their sphere, therefore they cannot transfer it to the lessor, who still guarantees the enjoyment of the property anyway.[30] Otherwise, if one followed a different solution, this would make the lessor participate in the risk of "activity of the tenant", without the lessor participating in the benefits and sharing the choices. Nor can this distribution of risk be considered in any way foreseen and accepted by the parties, in the absence of indices to that effect obtainable from the contract.[31]

---

29 Ugo Salanitro, 'Una soluzione strutturale nell'emergenza: locazioni commerciali e impossibilità temporanea' (2020) NGCG (forthcoming); Ugo Salanitro, 'La gestione del rischio nella locazione commerciale al tempo del corona virus' (2020) Giust civ com http://giustiziacivile.com/obbligazioni-e-contratti/editoriali/la-gestione-del-rischio-nella-locazione-commerciale-al-tempo-del accessed 15 June 2020.

30 See Aurelio Gentili, 'Un proposta sui contratti d'impresa al tempo del coronavirus' (2020) Giust civ com http://giustiziacivile.com/obbligazioni-e-contratti/approfondimenti/una-proposta-sui-contratti-dimpresa-al-tempo-del accessed 15 June 2020, §3; Raffaello Morello, 'Gli effetti sui contratti dell'emergenza sanitaria determinata dalla diffusione del coronavirus e l'applicazione dei rimedi previsti dal Codice civile' (2020), Giust civ com http://giustiziacivile.com/obbligazioni-e-contratti/approfondimenti/gli-effetti-sui-contratti-dellemergenza-sanitaria accessed 10 June 2020, §3.3; Massimo Zaccheo, 'Brevi riflessioni sulle sopravvenienze contrattuali alla luce della normativa sull'emergenza epidemiologica da Covid-19', (2020) Giust civ com http://giustiziacivile.com/obbligazioni-e-contratti/editoriali/brevi-riflessioni-sulle-sopravvenienze-contrattuali-alla-luce accessed 15 June 2020, §§3 ff.; Luca Guerrini, 'Coronavirus, legislazione emergenziale e contratto: una fotografia', (2020) Giust civ com http://giustiziacivile.com/obbligazioni-e-contratti/articoli/coronavirus-legislazione-emergenziale-e-contratto-una-fotografia accessed 15 June 2020, §4.

31 Aurelio Gentili, 'Un proposta sui contratti d'impresa al tempo del coronavirus' (2020) Giust civ com http://giustiziacivile.com/obbligazioni-e-contratti/approfondimenti/una-proposta-sui-contratti-dimpresa-al-tempo-del accessed 15 June 2020, §3, and fns 10 and 11.

According to other authors, the solution should not consist in an either/or decision making one party or the other bear the entire risk, but the Solomonic solution that they promote is argued in a less rigorous way with a generic reference to the principle of good faith or to a heterodox *Drittwirkung* (third party effect) of the principle of solidarity (provided for by Article 2 Italian Constitution). However, neither good faith nor solidarity are technically equitable criteria in Italian law. Therefore neither of them can justify a compromise solution.

As for leases for commercial use, the tenant who carries out a commercial activity (business) on his/her premises, such as a pizzeria without the sale of takeaway products, is affected by subsequent occurrence (by COVID-19 lockdown measures) precisely in the materiality of the use of the property, given that the public (and the employees themselves during the lockdown) cannot access the premises.[32]

It follows that this case can be traced back to temporary impossibility and to a certain extent also to partial impossibility, since mostly things belonging to the tenant (furniture, equipment, etc.) will remain in the pizzeria. Based on Article 1256 Italian Civil Code the lessor is not responsible as long as the impossibility persists. The tenant's position is less clear, because in general it cannot be argued that he/she cannot use the leased property at least to a certain extent, for example as a warehouse for the goods and the things and furnishings of the premises. Therefore, instead of completely excluding the payment of the fee as should be the case by applying the rule of temporary impossibility, one could imagine a reduction of the fee on the basis of Article 1464 Italian Civil Code.[33] On the other hand, in terms of taking on risks in leasing for commercial uses, if it is true that the item is not considered a productive one as in the contract of *affitto*, and therefore the tenant has no management obligations, the law nevertheless recognises the contribution of the tenant at the start-up of the premises, granting him/her an indemnity in the event of termination (Arts 34 and 35 of Law 27 July 1978, no 392). It follows that the prohibition of public access to the premises affects not only the use agreed in the contract that the lessor must grant to the tenant but also other interests of the tenant that are protected by law.[34]

32 This is the case also for private clinics and those professionals, such as doctors, dentists, who need contact with patients in order to do their job.

33 To this line of reasoning adheres Trib. Rome (V) *ordinanza* 29 May 2020, r.g. no 18779/2020.

34 Termination of the contract as the only remedy in this case would consist of an overly rigid solution. On the one hand, it would displease the tenant, because it would prevent them from continuing their commercial activity as soon as the restrictive measures were lifted; on the other hand, it would displease the lessor because they would have to look for another trader who might also want changes in the premises. In Germany, as for micro-entrepreneurs, Article 240 §1(2) 3rd sentence defines an essential long-term contract as a contract that is essential to cover the services necessary for the "reasonable continuation of the business".

5. TEMPORARY RENTAL FOR UNIVERSITY ATTENDANCE AND ATYPICAL CONTINGENCIES

The pandemic has affected the rental relationships entered into by university students. Many students left their rented apartments and returned to their home towns from which, due to coronavirus lockdown measures, they were not able to return. On the other hand, if they had stayed, they would not have been able to attend the lessons that had been suspended.

In Italy, rental regulation (Art 5 of Law 9 December 1998, no. 431) contemplates the subtype of temporary rental for university needs which derogates from the general regulation of rentals for housing needs regarding the duration and allows the lessor to make the most of the apartment from an economic point of view. These contracts, pursuant to Article 4 of Ministerial Decree 30 December 2002 (Ministry of Infrastructure and Transport), must expressly refer to the fact that the off-site tenant is enrolled on a university course at the local university, duly indicated.[35] It follows that the purpose of the use of the apartment, i.e. to enable a student to attend university, finds legal and contractual recognition, but the risk of events that occur that affect this purpose is not specifically regulated by law.

The subsequent occurrence of containment measures and the closure of universities, unlike in commercial leases, does not affect the use of the apartment. The containment measures have affected the purpose of the rental of the apartment which is linked to the housing needs of the off-site student. It is therefore an atypical contingency which constitutes neither a supervening impossibility nor a case of excessive supervening onerousness. Those who advocate for a vision of the contract focused on self-responsibility will consider the subsequent occurrence as a risk that the tenant must bear, given that this risk is not a case of impossibility. In other words, if you analyse it as a mere individual motive, the only way to make it legally relevant would be to make it a condition in the sense of Article 1353 Italian Civil Code (the parties may make the effectiveness or termination of the contract or a single agreement subject to a future and uncertain event), or otherwise provide for a specific contractual clause with a different solution. But it may seem insufficient to treat it as an individual motive if you consider that the requirement is a legally necessary element for the framing of the contract as temporary lease for university needs.

If the purpose of attending university courses is a requirement foreseen by the law for this contractual subtype, it cannot be denied that this requirement is an indication of the legal relevance of this tenant students' interest. Therefore, it cannot be qualified as a mere motive of a contractual party. Consequently,

---

35 See Mario Trimarchi, 'Le locazioni abitative transitorie' in Vincenzo Cuffaro (ed), *Le locazioni urbane. Vent'anni di disciplina speciale* (Giappicchelli 1999) 129–130 (where reference to Cass civ (III) 20 August 1997, no 7750, and Cass civ (III) 4 April 1997 no 10797 occurrence of containment measures and the closure of universities).

it could be considered that in the absence of a precise legal rule for the case of containment measures and closure of universities, fairness (*equità, aequitas,*) may take over (Art 1374 Italian Civil Code). The result could be that the subsequent occurrence does not legitimise a suspension of the fee payment obligation, but a reduction of the same such as to make both parties bear the contingency. In essence, although this is not a partial impossibility, a similar rule could apply. Moreover, an equitable intervention to fill the lacuna in the contract does not seem to contradict the law of rental contracts, especially since the link between rental contract and university attendance is in a certain sense a common venture in these types of contract: on the one hand, it justifies exceptions to the regulation of leases for residential use in the interest of the lessor, on the other hand, it can justify the importance of the tenant's interest in using the apartment for those needs. It may also be relevant that these types of contracts allow the landlord to obtain a higher price than what he/she would normally obtain by renting the apartment for normal and non-transitory housing needs. Furthermore, without prejudice to the distinction between circumstances affecting the material use of the property and circumstances extrinsic to material use, the principle that the use of the property can also be obtained presumptively based on the circumstances shows that the lease is not closed on the relevance of interests not expressly regulated by the contract. Of course, Article 1587 Italian Civil Code provides this criterion with regard to material use. However, the relevance of interests that do not concern the performance proper (the result due to the creditor) is confirmed also in the principle deriving from Article 1623 Italian Civil Code, which shows that in these contracts the risk-allocation procedure is not exclusively referred to the fortuitous criterion (force majeure). Room for an equitable adjustment, in other words, does not seem precluded. It goes without saying that the question remains to determine more precisely the criteria for a judicial reduction of the rent that could tend to cover the costs of the lessor and a percentage of the fee related to the maintenance of the contract and the residual use of the apartment, for example for the storage of their belongings, during the time when students are forced to stay in their home town. Finally, if the lessor is a professional, Article 2, paragraph 2, c) Consumer Code gives consumers and users the so-called fundamental right "to fair dealing, transparency and *fairness* (equità, aequitas) in contractual relations" (emphasis added).

6. SUBSEQUENT OCCURRENCES THAT CAUSE IMPRACTICABILITY: REVISION AND RENEGOTIATION OBLIGATION

As for the Italian legal system and with regard to the cases in which a subsequent occurrence alters the contractual balance from an economic point of view –

due to which the exchange in a qualitative sense remains possible – a problem arises concerning the insufficiency of termination for subsequent excessive onerousness which is confined in the exceptionality by the requirements of the unpredictability and extraordinary nature of the event.[36] Furthermore, Article 1467 Italian Civil Code provides termination as the main remedy and only secondarily that of equitable adjustment (*reductio ad aequitatem*).

However, the regulation of specific contracts provides some examples of equitable intervention (equitable adjustment) on the contract that ignore the rigorous criterion of the extraordinary and unpredictable nature of the event and above all the primacy of the remedy of termination. For instance, in the case of the contract of *affitto*, where there are supervening events that are simply not foreseen, Article 1664, paragraph 2 Italian Civil Code prescribes an equitable compensation in favour of the contractor as a consequence of the considerably higher onerous burden of their performance. In the final analysis, the idea that the failure to regulate any contingency implies in any case the conclusion that, the person on whom fate has fallen has taken the risk, can be simplistic and, above all, unfair. In reference to the case of Article 1664, paragraph 2 Italian Civil Code a different distribution of risks can also be explained in relation to the fact that the contract is characterised by being "foreordained to meet the creditor's needs (preferences)" and is "organized through a system of rules that give the latter a higher-level position".[37] Similarly, Article 1623 Italian Civil Code shows that a subsequent occurrence that disrupts the economic equilibrium can justify an equitable intervention. Basically, it is not obvious that the issue of excessive onerousness is monopolised, except for exceptions such as the last one considered, by a rule that limits its relevance to extraordinary and unpredictable facts and requires termination. Hence, the serious question of whether fairness can work to resolve problems of excessive onerousness arising from unforeseen rather than unforeseeable facts, either in the sense of termination or in that of

---

36 A reference to the fairness (*equità, aequitas*) integration criterion, pursuant to Article 1374 c.c., can be found in Rodolfo Sacco, 'I rimedi per le sopravvenienze' in Rodolfo Sacco and Giorgio De Nova, *Il contratto* (4th edn, UTET 2016) 1708 ff., who, however, seems to reserve to fairness (*equità, aequitas*) only the task of presiding over the renegotiation, because "termination kills the contractual relationship", while "renegotiation should serve to cure it". In reality, the survival of the contract is not an absolute value and sometimes the adjustment may prove unfair to the party on whom it discharged risks in a way that makes it exit the market. Think of a manufacturer who, having to pay a higher price for the supply of a component, instead of terminating the contract and looking for a cheaper alternative solution, was forced to buy the goods at that price, ending up off the market compared to the competition. Fairness (*equità, aequitas*), if it is intended as a supplementary criterion of the lacuna that emerged with the occurrence, should not therefore exclude the remedy of termination. See Tommaso Mauceri, 'Sopravvenienze perturbative e rinegoziazione del contratto' (2007) 4 Europa e dir. priv. 1095, 1111.

37 See Tommaso Mauceri, 'Sopravvenienze perturbative e rinegoziazione del contratto' (2007) 4 Europa e dir. priv. 1095, 1111.

revision without allowing the creditor the possibility to choose between keeping the revised contract or accept termination (*recesso*) on the model of Article 1664, paragraph 1 or 2, Italian Civil Code.[38] Fairness (*equità, aequitas*), however, would certainly not have the serious defect of a rule such as that recently proposed by Art 1, *i)*, of the "Delegation to the government for the revision of the Civil Code" bill (of 19 March 2019, no. 1151) which establishes as a guiding principle or criterion "to provide for the right of the parties to contracts that have become excessively burdensome for exceptional and unforeseeable reasons to demand their renegotiation according to good faith or, in case of failure to agree, to request the adjustment of the contractual conditions in order to restore the proportion between the performances originally agreed by the parties".[39] It would be an

38 With regard to Article 1664 Italian Civil Code according to several authors, the exceptionality of this provision derives from its relationship with the derogation from the provisions of Article 1467 Italian Civil Code: see, for example, Oreste Cagnasso, *La concessione in vendita. Problemi di qualificazione* (Giuffrè 1983) 65 ff. However, a different conclusion can be drawn after an in-depth analysis of Article 1664 of the Italian Civil Code in relation to its practical scope, and the general consideration according to which the exceptionality of a norm does not derive simply from a relationship of *species ad genus* of a purely logical type, but depends on specific reasons for a value judgment on the basis of which it is justified to sterilise its regulatory potential: Tommaso Mauceri, 'Sopravvenienze perturbative e rinegoziazione del contratto' (2007) 4 *Europa e dir. priv.* 1095, 1116 (with reference to Luigi Caiani, 'Analogia', *Enciclopedia del diritto II* (Giuffrè 1958), 367–370 and Angelo Belfiore, 'Interpretazione della legge e analogia', *Annali Seminario giur. Catania VI* (Giuffrè 2006) 15 ff.).

39 It would be a rule similar to that contained in Article 6:111 Principles of European Contract Law: "If, however, performance of the contract becomes excessively onerous because of a change of circumstances, the parties are bound to enter into negotiations with a view to adapting the contract or terminating it, provided that: (a) the change of circumstances occurred after the time of conclusion of the contract, (b) the possibility of a change of circumstances was not one which could reasonably have been taken into account at the time of conclusion of the contract, and (c) the risk of the change of circumstances is not one which, according to the contract, the party affected should be required to bear. (3) If the parties fail to reach agreement within a reasonable period, the court may: (a) terminate the contract at a date and on terms to be determined by the court; or (b) adapt the contract in order to distribute between the parties in a just and equitable manner the losses and gains resulting from the change of circumstances. In either case, the court may award damages for the loss suffered through a party refusing to negotiate or breaking off negotiations contrary to good faith and fair dealing". In favour of renegotiation according to the principle of good faith are Francesco Macario, *'Per un diritto dei contratti più solidale in epoca di "coronavirus"'* (2020) Giust civ com http://giustiziacivile.com/obbligazioni-e-contratti/editoriali/un-diritto-dei-contratti-piu-solidale-epoca-di-coronavirus, accessed 15 June 2020, and Antonio De Mauro, 'Pandemia e contratto: spunti di riflessione in tema di impossibilità sopravvenuta della prestazione' (2020) Giust civ com http://giustiziacivile.com/obbligazioni-e-contratti/editoriali/pandemia-e-contratto-spunti-di-riflessione-tema-di-impossibilita accessed 15 June 2020. The Italian Court of Cassation, the court of last resort in private matters, in its report on the "emergency" contractual law, echoing Vincenzo Roppo, *Il contratto* (Giuffrè 2011), 972–973, opined that the principle of good faith postulates the renegotiation as "a path needed to adapt the contract to the circumstances and needs that have arisen": therefore "the renegotiation, in the face of contingencies that alter the exchange relationship becomes an obligatory step, which preserves the originally agreed cost and revenue plan, with the consequence that anyone who avoids the obligation to restore it commits a serious violation of the contractual regulation".

innovation that could be criticised for both defect and excess: defect because it would maintain the serious limit of exceptionalism and unpredictability; excess because it would impose in these cases the rigid obligation of renegotiation which, in spite of what was foreseen, could be revealed to be against good faith itself in all those cases in which imposing the adaptation of a contract would discharge costs on the party not affected by the risk that could put it out of business.[40] An example that could imply the obligation of renegotiation could be that of a contract for the supply of a certain health product whose production costs have increased enormously due to the excess demand for the raw material following the coronavirus COVID-19 pandemic and the consequent requests for this product. However, a different case can also be imagined. The increases in the production costs of the healthcare product covered by the contract are due to the increase in the cost of a component that is located abroad, but there are companies that produce a similar product with more readily available materials and therefore at a price closer to that agreed between the parties. In the second case, it is difficult to find a reason according to the good faith principle for imposing on the buyer the maintenance of a contract that has become excessively burdensome for the counterparty when the buyer no longer has an interest in maintaining the contract, being able to satisfy his/her interest by returning to the market.

An equitable solution would instead have the advantage of avoiding rigidity both in excess and in defect, furthermore explaining what seems to be the criterion substantially adopted also by §313 German Civil Code which formally

---

The Court goes so far as to propose the remedy of the specific performance (Art 2932 c.c.) transforming the obligation to renegotiate into an obligation to agree on an adjustment of the contract. (see the text here: http://www.cortedicassazione.it/cassazione-resources/resources/cms/documents/Relazione_Tematica_Civile_056-2020.pdf accessed 2 October 2020). An opening toward the rule of mandatory renegotiation and the judicial power to intervene in the contract in case of non-fulfilment of this obligation is found in Trib. Rome (VI) *ordinanza* 27 August 2020 (for a comment, see Giuseppe Portonera, 'Rinegoziazione contrattuale e COVID-19: a proposito di una recente ordinanza del Tribunale di Roma' (2020) Filodiritto https://www.filodiritto.com/rinegoziazione-contrattuale-e-covid-19-proposito-di-una-recente-ordinanza-del-tribunale-di-roma accessed 2 October 2020).

40 A criticism of the reference to good faith as the basis for the renegotiation obligation can be found in Emanuele Tuccari, *Sopravvenienze e rimedi nei contratti di durata* (CEDAM 2018) 121 ff who focuses mainly on the uncertainty that this rule ends up determining on contracts, also exposing the system that adopts it to the risk of discouraging investments, especially foreign ones. The criticism is acceptable even if some concern on the topic of competition between legal systems cannot be kept silent. On this subject, let me refer to Andrea Nicolussi, 'Europa e cosiddetta competizione tra ordinamenti giuridici' (2006) 1 Europa e dir. priv. 83. For a recent recovery of the theme, cf Anne Peters, 'The Competition between Legal Orders' (2014) 3 International Law Research 45 (for a series of considerations also regarding the advantages of a competition which, however, should not be casual, but orderly, complementary to the legislation of a State matrix and in any case such that fundamental principles are not renounced).

brings into play undue hardship (*Unzumutbarkeit*) and hypothetical will (which seems to simply perform the function of keeping the operation in the logic of the contract as provided for in Article 1419 Italian Civil Code for a different hypothesis) to legitimise the equitable adjustment of the contract.

Of course, the possibility of renegotiation is not to be excluded and can be considered as one of the alternatives between the direct intervention of the judge and that mediated by the attempt to renegotiate by the parties. Indeed, fairness (*equitá, aequitas*) should allow a preventive assessment of the peculiarities of the relationship which could reveal reasons for excluding the maintenance of the contract where its revision would result in an excessive cost compared to the return of the parties to the market.

The equitable bridging of the contract lacuna caused by subsequent occurrences will need a rational explanation with regard to the particularities of the case in question, to the specific problems it highlights and to the intrinsic logic of the contract in question, necessary for opening the narrow door of fairness (*equitá, aequitas*).[41]

41 As is well known, even this narrow door of fairness (*equità, aequitas*) is strongly opposed by many common law jurists, but it would be an oversimplification to say that everyone opposes it. Certainly, after the famous ALCOA court's adjustment, John Dawson wrote that the ALCOA court's adjustment remedy was thoroughly "bizarre": the two main Dawson's reasons were that courts lack the knowledge and resources to write a better contract than the parties, and that courts do not have the power or authority to do so. See John P. Dawson, 'Judicial Revision of Frustrated Contracts: The United States' (1984), 64 B.U. L. Rev. 1, 28, 30–38. However, important defences of the Alcoa's approach were written, for instance, by Richard E. Speidel ('The New Spirit of Contract' (1982), 2 J.L. & COM. 193, 206–208; 'Court-Imposed Price Adjustments Under Long-Term Supply Contracts' (1981), 76 Nw. U. L. Rev. 369, 395–400, 421; 'Excusable Nonperformance in Sales Contracts: Some Thoughts About Risk Management' (1980), 32 S.C. L. Rrv. 241, 276–79). More recently see Robert A. Hillman, 'Maybe Dick Speidel Was Right about Court Adjustment' (2009), 46 San Diego L. Rev. 3 595, where the Author reviews his point made in Robert A. Hillman, 'Court Adjustment of Long-Term Contracts: An Analysis Under Modern Contract Law' (1987) Duke L.J. 1. Both Dawson's reasons are criticised. The court's lack of knowledge argument does not take into consideration both the fact that courts are not without guidance and that judges take on hard cases all of the time (for instance, the substantive and remedial complexities of securities, patent, and antitrust cases). As for the court's lack of power argument, objections can be raised both from the point of view of fairness and from that of autonomy on which this argument is based. In fact, "assuming that the parties had agreed at the outset to be flexible in the face of onerous unanticipated circumstances and that a court can approximate the modification the parties should have made, the court's adjustment is either a form of specific performance or a legitimate method of filling a gap in the contract" (606–607).

CORONAVIRUS, THE MILLENNIUM AND THE FINANCIAL CRISIS

Ewoud HONDIUS*

Coronavirus may be a new issue, but epidemics are not. Legal issues related to epidemics are of all times. Two disasters which struck in recent times were the millennium bug and the financial crisis. This contribution deals with the question how Dutch law has coped with the Corona crisis. More in particular it addresses how the 1992 Civil Code's new provision on unforeseen circumstances has been (non) applied in practice. The contribution then turns to two international developments: the work of the International Chamber of Commerce – see also the contribution by Denis Philippe in this volume – and the work of the Common Core of European Private Law (Trento) project.

* Utrecht University. e.h.hondius@uu.nl. The author is grateful to the anonymous peer or peers for their useful comments.

1. INTRODUCTION

The coronavirus has all of us in its grips. Apart from medical and ethical questions, it raises legal and economic issues. Is the train passenger entitled to repayment of the fare when travel is suspended? Is there recourse for the air passenger who has been left stranded at a Moroccan airport? May the small retailer call in force majeure or a hardship clause when he/she can no longer pay the rent? Is the Government empowered to commandeer medicine from unwilling pharmaceutical companies?

Coronavirus may be a new issue, but epidemics are not. Legal issues related to epidemics are also of all times. It therefore seems a good idea when trying to answer the questions to look back to the past. I do not have in mind a full-fledged historical survey of the pest or Spanish influenza or the Mexican flu. No doubt a systematic study of these disasters will be undertaken. What springs to one's mind is a comparison with two more or less recent occurrences of a comparable nature.

The first occurrence is a problem which during the last millennium change raised wide-spread anxiety, and was known as the millennium-bug or Y2K. It refers to events related to the formatting and storage of calendar data for dates beginning in the year 2000. Problems were anticipated, and did arise, because many programmes represented four-digit years with only the final two digits – making the year 2000 indistinguishable from 1900. The assumption of a twentieth-century date in such programmes could cause various errors, such as the incorrect display of dates and the inaccurate ordering of automated dated records or real-time events. In 1979 an IBM-employee warned of the problems anticipated at the time of the millennium change. The effects of the millennium bug have, in reality, been much smaller than was anticipated and not at all comparable to the coronavirus, but the solutions offered at the time may still be helpful in the present coronavirus era. It was suggested that traders and consumers prepare checklists, that the burden of proof be discussed, and codes of practice written. Mediation and arbitration were to prevent the judiciary being flooded with claims.

A second disaster which struck the world was that of the 2007 financial (Lehman) crisis. Like the millennium bug, this crisis raised legal issues, which often could best be solved by way of arbitration and mediation. In 1974, the Organisation for Economic Cooperation and Development adopted the Trade Pledge. This involves agreement of Member States to avoid taking trade restrictive or other actions designed to stimulate exports or to artificially defend their current account positions. The financial crisis has raised a number of legal questions, one of which is whether or not contracts may be modified or abrogated[1] in case of a

---

1 A similar question is whether parties may be obliged to renegotiate the contract. This question is taken up by Rodrigo Momberg in his PhD 'The effect of a change of circumstances on the binding force of contracts' (Intersentia 2011).

change of circumstances.[2] The issue is not wholly novel. It has been the subject of debate ever since medieval times.[3] Do all contracts contain an implicit clause that they are only valid when the circumstances remain unchanged: the *clausula rebus sic stantibus*? European jurisdictions provide different solutions to this question. But do they in fact diverge where practical issues are concerned?

This contribution will deal with the question how Dutch law has coped with disasters such as the two mentioned above. It will then move on to international developments. Several international groups of scholars have studied this phenomenon. More in particular, the work of the International Chamber of Commerce and that of the Trento Group will briefly be dealt with.

This approach is an old-fashioned method. It will not focus on the more fashionable topic of disaster law, which in the Netherlands has chiefly been dealt with by Daniel Farber and Michael Faure.[4]

2. DUTCH LAW: A BRIEF GLIMPSE

In December 1915, a Haarlem-based cotton company sold a quantity of "sarongs" to Stork, to be delivered in Rangoon (Myanmar). Due to the First World War, shipping was hampered. For a long time, it was impossible to deliver the sarongs at all, let alone on time. After the war, it was disputed that the Cotton Company[5] was still obliged to deliver. There are more landmark cases in the Netherlands, as well as elsewhere: such as the English coronation – not corona! – cases, the French *Canal de craponne* and the German hyperinflation cases, but the sarongs case surely has remained the landmark case.

But the main development of interest in the Netherlands has been the adoption of a legislative provision in the 1992 Civil Code on unforeseen circumstances. The provision, paragraph 258 BW, reads as follows:

1. Upon the demand of one of the parties, the court may modify the effects of a contract or it may set aside, in whole or in part, on the basis of unforeseen circumstances of such a nature that the other party according to standards of reasonableness and fairness, may not expect the contract to

---

2 This contribution will use the words "change of circumstances" interchangeably with "unexpected circumstances".

3 Famous cases include the French *Canal de Craponne* case (*DP* 76.1.195, *Grand arrêts* no 94) and the English coronation cases *Krell v Henry* [1903] 2 KB 740 and *Herne Bay Steam Boat v Hutton* [1903] 2 KB 683.

4 Daniel Farber, Michael Faure (eds), *Disaster Law* (Elgar 2010) 673 p. Likewise the French 2016 Contract Law Reform has introduced the possibility of contract revision by the parties in case of "imprévision".

5 Hoge Raad 8 January 1926, *Nederlandse Jurisprudentie* 1926, 203.

be maintained in unmodified form. The modification of setting aside may be given retroactive effect.
2. The modification or the setting aside shall not be pronounced to the extent that it is common ground that the person invoking the circumstances should be accountable for them if this follows from the nature of the contract.
3. For the application of this Article, a party to whom a contractual right or obligation has been transmitted, is treated as a contracting party.

The reader may find of interest the idea that the initiative has hereby been shifted from the legislature to the court. However, it is fair to observe that the judiciary does not partake of this option often.[6] It has therefore been held that the Dutch system nonetheless may be qualified as a closed system.

3. INTERNATIONAL CHAMBER OF COMMERCE

One of the international organisations which have put "Hardship and force majeure in international commercial contracts" on the agenda is the International Chamber of Commerce.[7] From 1974–1991, Marcel Fontaine (Louvain-la-Neuve) chaired its *Working Group on International Contracts*. In April 1975, the Working Group opted for "*hardship clauses*" as its first theme. The outcome of this was the ICC *Clause on hardship*. Although preference was given by the Group to Article 97 of the former Estonian Civil Code:

Alteration of balance of contractual obligations

4. If the circumstances under which a contract is entered into change after the entry into the contract and this results in a material change in the balance of the obligations of the parties due to which the costs of one party for the performance of an obligation increase significantly or the value of that which is to be received from the other party under the contract decreases significantly, the injured party may demand amendment of the contract from the other party in order to restore the original balance of the obligations.
5. Amendment of a contract under the circumstances in subsection (1) of this section may be demanded if:
   a. at the time of entry into the contract, the injured party could not have reasonably expected that the circumstances might change, and
   b. the injured party could not influence the change in the circumstances, and

6 Translated by Hans Warendorf, Richard Thomas and Ian Curry Sumber (eds), *The Civil Code of the Netherlands* (2nd edn, Wolters Kluwer 2013) 1301 p.

7 Fabio Bortolotti, Dorothy Ufot (eds), *Hardship and force majeure in international commercial contracts/Dealing with unforeseen events in a changing World* (International Chamber of Commerce 2018) 232 p.

   c. the risk of a change in the circumstances is not borne by the injured party pursuant to the law of the contract, and
   d. the injured party would not have entered into the contract under significant different terms if the party had known of the change in the circumstances.
6. Amendment of a contract may also be demanded if the circumstances under which the contract was entered into had already changed before the contract was entered into but became known to the injured party after the contract was entered into.
7. The injured party may also demand amendment to the contract retroactively, but not as of a time earlier than the time when the balance of the obligations changed.
8. If the bases for amendment of a contract exist but, due to the circumstances, amendment of the contract pursuant to subsection (1) of this section is not possible or would not be reasonable with respect to the other party, the party aggrieved by alteration of the balance of the obligations may withdraw from the contract or, in the case of a long-term contract, cancel the contract pursuant to the procedure provided for in Par. 196 of this Act.

Pascale Accaoui Lorfing (Paris) argues for a contract clause with the following content: "In the context of contractual provision on change in circumstances that impacts the contract equilibrium, arbitrators may intervene when parties try to renegotiate and fail to agree on contract adaptation". Christoph Brunner (Berne) argues that force majeure is nearly always determined by looking into a contract clause and not into the law. Filip De Ly (Rotterdam) pleads for modernisation of the *ICC Force Majeure Clause 2003* – "The revision work of the task force is to be encouraged to take a fresh look at the Clause and, based on its analyses, to come forward with a new clause which may serve the interests of the international business community". H. Ercüment Erdem (Istanbul) sketches the changes in the *ICC Clause* since 2003. Klaus Peter Berger (Cologne) sees the force majeure clause as "the most prominent example of a transnational legal principle of the new Lex Mercatoria". Mercédeh Azeredo da Silveira finally focuses on economic sanctions as half-way between diplomatic action and military action.

4. EUROPE: THE TRENTO PROJECT

The Common Core of European Private Law project is based on the combined ideas of Rodolfo Sacco and Rudi Schlesinger ("the two Rudi's"). Sacco (1923–) is the godfather of Italian comparative law[8] and the author who coined the idea

---

[8] Witness his *Introduzione al diritto comparato* (Giuffré 1979) and his *I Grandi sistemi giuridici* (Cedam 1996).

of "legal formants".[9] Having held a chair in Trieste and Pavia, since 1971 he has been associated with the University of Torino. Schlesinger (1909–1996) was an American of German extraction who taught in Cornell, where he came up with the theory of the common core of legal systems. According to this theory, jurisdictions may have widely diverging points of departure, but in fact the outcome of litigation is often the same. Thus, even if specific performance is the prevailing remedy in continental law, in fact courts will often award damages, just like in common law jurisdictions. Schlesinger set out to test his ideas in a celebrated research project on formation of contract.[10] It was in Italy that the project was to be continued on a much larger scale. In 1993, Mauro Bussani and Ugo Mattei founded the Common Core of European Private Law project.[11] Three sub-groups were established, on Contract, Property and Tort. All three are taken in a wide sense, including, for instance, environmental liability and ecological damage[12] and the enforcement of competition law in Europe.[13] The three groups have come together annually, first in Trento, and then – when the two convenors continued their careers elsewhere – in Torino. Apart from the meetings of the three working groups there are also plenary sessions, where not only general issues are discussed but outsiders are also invited to critically evaluate the group's methodology.[14] There is open access to the three groups, which provides a rare chance for young graduates to mingle with old diehards of comparative law.

It was the Contract group chaired by James Gordley which in 2000 put unexpected circumstances on the agenda. Chaired by Hans Christoph Grigoleit and Ewoud Hondius, a group of scholars edited a volume of national reports and case studies.[15] The subject matter also had to be demarcated. Notions such as *abus de droit*, *force majeure*, good faith, impossibility, interpretation, mistake, unfair contract terms and unjust enrichment may indeed be of relevance.

A mistake of one party or a mutual mistake of both parties with regard to factors that were already present before or at the time the contract was concluded differs significantly from the occurrence of unexpected events arising

---

9 Rodolfo Sacco, 'Legal formants: a dynamic approach to comparative law' (1991) 39 American Journal of Comparative Law 1–34 and 343–401.

10 Rudi Schlesinger (ed), *Formation of Contracts/A Study of the Common Core of Legal Systems* (Oceana 1968) 2 vols, 1 727 p.

11 See among their various publications Mauro Bussani and Ugo Mattei (eds), *Opening up European law* (Stämpfli 2007) 283 p.

12 Monika Hinteregger (ed), *Environmental liability and ecological damage* (Cambridge University Press 2008) 697 p.

13 Thomas Möllers and Andreas Heinemann (eds), *The Enforcement of Competition Law in Europe* (Cambridge University Press 2008) 713 p.

14 See for instance Günter Frankenberg, 'How to do projects with comparative law – notes of an expedition to the common core' 6 Global Jurist 2006.

15 Ewoud Hondius, Hans Christoph Grigoleit (eds), *Unexpected circumstances in European contract law* (Cambridge University Press 2011) 692 p.

after the conclusion of the contract. A clear distinction between pre-existing and supervening factors is meaningful for the doctrinal treatment of unexpected circumstances, because it is generally easier for the parties to recognise and control pre-existing factors than future developments. Furthermore, by submitting themselves to a contractual agreement, the parties are aware that they generally assume the risk of future changes and they may only be relieved from this risk under exceptional circumstances. A lack of information about pre-existing factors, on the other hand, will in most jurisdictions allow parties to terminate a contract even if they are not heavily burdened by the contract. The absence of a relevant mistake is a precondition for the binding effect of the contract and the assumption of risks provided therein. Hence, if a party is mistaken about certain factors that were present at the time of contracting, the case should only be treated according to the respective rules on mistake.

5. UNCERTAINTY, THE LACK OF PRECEDENTS AND HARMONISATION BY ADVANCING THE LEGAL DISCOURSE

As mentioned above, the uncertainty of judgments on unexpected circumstances is an unavoidable characteristic of the conflict between legal security and the binding force of contract on the one hand and the requirements of equity on the other. There are possibilities for strengthening certainty on the comparative level by further harmonisation with regard to the doctrinal background in general and the mechanism of adjustment in particular. Yet, there is another structural source of uncertainty that is particularly important in cases of unexpected circumstances. That is the lack of reliable precedents in many jurisdictions.

Many cases in which relief on the basis of unexpected circumstances is discussed are quite eccentric and rare. Some national reporters have had difficulties identifying precedents similar to our cases at hand and some may have had to go back several decades. Especially in continental countries, the question may be raised whether "old" precedents still have - persuasive - value as they reflect an antiquated legal and social background and could arguably be overruled if they were submitted to the respective Supreme Court today.[16]

Further harmonisation of the law in Europe may enlarge the basis of precedents. It would mean that instead of a meagre trickle of cases, every Member State would fully profit from the case law of the other Member States of the European Union. However, harmonisation on the basis of precedents does not necessarily depend on a common Civil Code.[17] The American example

16 Ewoud Hondius (ed), *Precedent and the law/Les précédents et le droit* (Bruylant 2007) 19 p.

17 See Ilka Klöckner, *Grenzüberschreitende Bindung an zivilgerichtliche Präjudizien*, PhD thesis Freiburg 2005, (Mohr 2006) 254 p.

shows that the various states of the Union refer to the case law of other states. The process of harmonisation by precedents may be enhanced by a restatement of European contract law without binding effect. In fact, in Europe several such restatements are available such as the DCFR (Draft Common Frame of Reference), the PECL (Principles of European Contract Law), the Principles of the *Association Henri Capitant des Amis de la Culture Juridique Française* and the *Société de Législation Comparée*, the *Acquis*-Principles, the *Gandolfi* Code, the Feasibility Study of the European Group of Experts (Art 92),[18] as well as other international instruments, such as the UNIDROIT Principles for International Commercial Contracts.

There is a considerable amount of similarity between the different European legal systems both in terms of the results achieved as well as in terms of their doctrinal approach. Hence, even without a uniform mandatory European rule on unexpected circumstances, courts and practitioners may profit from an analysis of cases from other European legal systems. Such an exchange is particularly important in cases of unexpected circumstances as, due to the variety of the potentially relevant factors, the legal doctrines applied and their requirements are necessarily vague and as it may always be argued that the solution will greatly depend on the facts of the individual case. Furthermore, it should be stressed again that, as far as precise doctrinal guidelines are concerned, no legal systems seem to have presented a comprehensively convincing approach to the problem of unexpected circumstances so far.

6. "OPEN" VERSUS "CLOSED" LEGAL SYSTEMS

The outcome of the Trento research team has been a distinction between "open" and "closed" legal systems. The distinction is based on the criterion whether or not a jurisdiction recognises a general rule under which the contract can be adjusted to unexpected circumstances by the courts. The distinction led to the following groups: as "open" legal systems we qualified those of Austria, Germany, Greece, Italy, Lithuania, the Netherlands, Portugal and Sweden. We characterised as "closed" jurisdictions those of Belgium, Denmark, England, France, Ireland, Scotland and Slovenia. To a certain extent this distinction goes along with the classic division into legal families. Not very surprisingly, the common law tradition and the French influence ("closed" jurisdictions) led to similarities in the doctrinal approach to cases

18 A European contract law for consumers and businesses: publication of the results of the feasibility study carried out by the Expert Group on European contract law for stakeholders' and legal practitioners' feedback, May 2011. See Reiner Schulze and Jules Stuyck (eds), *Towards a European Contract Law – An Introduction* (Sellier 2011).

on the one hand, as did the German tradition ("open" jurisdictions) on the other hand.[19]

However, the distinction between "open" and "closed" jurisdictions did not survive the test wholly unscathed as far as the outcome of our cases is concerned. Thus, the distinction between "open" and "closed" jurisdictions is a rough doctrinal approach rather than a clear indication of differences with regard to the result of a certain case. It is fair to say that the recognition of a general and flexible rule providing for relief in cases of unexpected circumstances may make it easier for the courts to set aside a contract. Yet, the strict requirements for relief and the variety of other legal concepts dilute the effects of any particular doctrine. In a jurisdiction such as the Netherlands, for example, where a provision in the Civil Code allows adjustment of the contract in case of a change of circumstances, this provision is used so rarely that one may occasionally ask whether this is not rather a "closed" system. Likewise, Slovenia, which we qualified as a "closed" jurisdiction, seems to be on the borderline with the "open" systems. The distinction was drawn based on doctrinal aspects and the differences between the two groups remain on a doctrinal level.

7. CONVERGENCE AS TO THE GENERAL ISSUE OF THE BINDING CHARACTER OF THE CONTRACT TERMS

Before turning to a more systematic analysis of the doctrinal concepts, it is remarkable to observe that in most cases there is a clear tendency as far as the results are concerned, i.e. whether or not a certain unexpected event justifies suspending the binding character of the terms of contract and limiting the principle of *pacta sunt servanda*. It should be noted, however, that these tendencies only relate to the suspensory effect as such while the legal consequences (adjustment or termination) may vary in detail. I shall examine these tendencies in the four different groups.

7.1. EQUIVALENCE OF EXCHANGE IS SUBSTANTIALLY AFFECTED

(1) With regard to the first group of cases in which the "equivalence of the exchange has been affected" we can conclude that under the law of all jurisdictions long-term agreements can lose their binding effect if, in the

19 Rodrigo Momberg in his PhD thesis *The Effect of a Change of Circumstances on the Binding Force of Contracts* (Utrecht University/Intersentia 2011) arrives at a similar distinction between "receptive" and "non-receptive" systems.

course of time, the initially fixed price grows out of proportion to the value of the object.[20] In many jurisdictions, the right to terminate long-term contracts is an essential element of their contract law. Such a right is, in effect, based on the rationale that in the course of long-term agreements unexpected effects can occur that cannot be provided for by the parties in advance. This correspondence becomes evident under the German rules on unexpected circumstances which contain a separate section dealing with the effects of unexpected events on long-term contracts (§314 BGB) besides the general provision on *Störung der Geschäftsgrundlage* (§313 BGB).

(2) There is generally much reservation as to the question whether extraordinary inflation can affect credit agreements. Only some of the "open" jurisdictions mitigate the consequences for the burdened party while applying very strict standards.[21] This reservation can be referred to the nominal value principle under which the amount of a monetary debt is based on its nominal and not on its "real" value. Inflation is a ubiquitous phenomenon of the economy and distinctions between regular and excessive conditions are hard to draw. Unsurprisingly, due to its speculative nature, the jurisdictions are even more reluctant to grant relief in the case of a foreign currency agreement.[22]

(3) We can observe a tendency towards relief in cases in which government intervention has strongly affected the contractual equilibrium, even though the "closed" jurisdictions are more reluctant to grant relief. This trend can be attributed to the consideration that government action is often elementary to the parties' interests and evidently beyond their control.

(4) Under a majority of jurisdictions, unexpected benefits do not trigger any form of relief, even if the benefits are out of proportion with the

---

[20] "Canal de Craponne": *Long-term agreement – devaluation of the price agreement.*
Early in the twentieth century, farmers A and B entered into a contract under which A promised to build and maintain an irrigation channel; B was entitled to extract water at a fixed price. The contract was concluded for an unlimited period of time. Almost 100 years later, A's successors ask for an increase in the price arguing that, due to inflation and a rise in the cost of maintenance as well as labour, the agreed price has become completely inadequate.
Is the claim by A's successors justified? Are they, alternatively, entitled to terminate the contract?

[21] Extraordinary inflation: *Hardship due to extraordinary inflation; hardship resulting from a foreign currency agreement (Extraordinary inflation).*
A receives a loan from the B-Bank. Under the agreement, the interest rate is fixed at 10% for five years. In the last 20 years before the agreement, the rate of inflation had been relatively stable within a range of 1 to 6%. In the third year after the conclusion of the agreement, the economic situation begins to destabilise and inflation rises quickly to 50%.

[22] *B-Bank asks for an adjustment or for a termination of the contract (Variation: foreign currency agreement).*
The loan agreement between A and the B-Bank provides for repayment and interest in a foreign currency. In the last 10 years before the agreement, the relevant exchange rate had been relatively stable within a range of 20%. Subsequently, the national currency is 80% compared to the foreign currency.
A asks for an adjustment or for a termination of the contract.

consideration.[23] It appears that one-sided windfall profits arising from the contract do not elicit the same inclination for equitable compensation as excessive losses.

7.2. RECIPIENT'S USE OF GOODS OR SERVICES IS SUBSTANTIALLY AFFECTED

(1) In the cases from the second group where the "recipient's use of goods or services is substantially affected", government intervention seems to be, again, a clear example for judicial intervention: relief is predominantly granted if the lease of a petrol station becomes worthless to the lessee as petrol is no longer available due to confiscation in wartime.[24] However, in the majority of the jurisdictions an export ban that is already present at the time of contracting does not justify relief for the burdened party even if both parties expected that the ban would be suspended.[25] The reason for upholding the contract in this case is that the parties knew about the risk of the ban and the misjudgement of an identified risk is held not to justify a relief.

(2) When a promised work of construction (in our case: a cellar) becomes useless to the client due to a natural disaster (destruction of the rest of the building), all legal systems give him the right to cancel the completion

---

23 Unexpected benefit: *Long-term lease – extraordinary increase of the rental value*
B leases business premises from A for a fixed period of 15 years. Shortly after concluding the contract, the character of the area changes strongly and unexpectedly: A military airport located nearby is shut down and an enormous amount of public funds is invested in the area (infrastructure, etc.). As a consequence, B's business soars and his profits are 500% of what he could reasonably have expected. By the same token, the rental value of comparable business premises in the same area rises to 500% of the amount A and B have agreed upon. A claims that the leasing price is to be adjusted accordingly or, alternatively, that the agreement is to be terminated.
Is A's claim justified?

24 Confiscation of petrol: *government intervention makes the use of a rented petrol station impossible*
A leases a petrol station from B. Due to the outbreak of war, the Government confiscates all petrol in that area and it is impossible for A to obtain petrol from any source. As a result, A can make no use of the petrol station. He stops the payment on the lease.
Is A's refusal to pay the rent justified?

25 Export ban: *Purchaser of technical equipment is affected by export ban*
Firm A purchases technical equipment which is to be produced by firm B. The parties know that firm A plans to resell the equipment to Iraq. At the time of contracting, exports to Iraq are illegal but the parties expect that the status quo will change before the time of delivery. The parties are aware that the equipment can only be sold to Iraq at a reasonable price. When firm B has completed production and offers delivery, exports to Iraq are still illegal and no change is in sight. Firm A refuses acceptance and payment.
Is A's refusal to accept and pay justified?

of the work because it has become useless. With regard to the question of compensation, the jurisdictions are basically divided into two groups: according to one approach, the contractor remains entitled to the full contract price less the expenses he saves by not having to carry out the work, e.g. wages, material, etc. (Belgium, Czech Republic, Denmark, France and Slovenia). Thereby the contractor is awarded his contractual profits and the risk that the contract has become useless is allocated to the client. The argument for this is that the house is in his sphere of risk and control. In other jurisdictions, the contractor's claim for his contractual profits is reduced by some form of equitable adjustment and therefore the risk is distributed between both parties (the Netherlands, Portugal, England and Ireland). This solution is based upon the notion that the risk in question is not rooted in the house itself but in the natural disaster which is beyond either party's control.[26]

(3) In the hotel reservation case the four events presented[27] display different tendencies: there is broad correspondence with regard to the conclusion that the frustration of individual purposes (exhibition cancelled) and disturbances in transport (strike) do not relieve the customer from his contractual obligations as these risks fall in the sphere of the customer. There is a certain tendency towards relief in the case involving terrorist threats; however, much seems to depend on the facts (e.g. the probability and the foreseeability of the attacks). A clear tendency for relief can be stated in the coronation case: the fact that the price reflects the procession leads most reports to conclude that the hotel owner has to bear the risk.

---

26 Destruction of cellar: *Renovation of cellar becomes useless due to the destruction of the building by a natural disaster*
A agrees to refurbish B's cellar into a wine cellar. The work is scheduled to start one month after the agreement. Before the work has started, B's house is completely destroyed during a violent summer storm. However, the cellar of the house remains fully intact. B immediately informs A and asks him not to perform. A insists on the agreement. He argues that B's cellar is still intact, that he has reserved two weeks to carry out the work and that he has already purchased the necessary materials.
Is B obliged to pay the contract price or, alternatively, to compensate A for his losses?

27 Hotel reservation: *Individual purpose of the visit frustrated; strike by airport personnel; general safety endangered; coronation case*
A booked a room at B's hotel, but:

a) The exhibition he wants to visit is cancelled at the very last moment.
b) A terrorist movement declares that it is to launch a campaign against tourists in that town.
c) An unforeseeable strike by airport personnel prevents A from travelling to the city where the hotel is located at the specified time.
d) The coronation procession scheduled on the respective date is cancelled. The room has a view of the street where the procession was supposed to take place. Due to the extraordinary event, the agreed price is ten times higher than the regular price.

Is A entitled to cancel the reservation?

(4) With regard to the shop rental case, a clear majority of the jurisdictions denies relief to the shop owner who claims that the business environment has developed unfavourably. This risk is considered not to be unusual and therefore the shop owner could and should have provided for it by implementing a protective term.[28]

7.3. FAILURE OF A SPECIFIED PURPOSE (OTHER THAN A) AND B))

Both of the cases that were dealt with in the third group "specified purposes" show a tendency in favour of relief:

(1) The assumption that the sold property will be used for cultural purposes will suffice for setting aside the agreement if it is used for other purposes because this assumption is – similarly to the coronation case – reflected in the price.[29] Here, the requirements of equity can quite easily be reconciled with the principle of *pacta sunt servanda* on the basis of "conventional" doctrines (especially constructive interpretation).

(2) In the case of divorce, the investment of one spouse in the property of the other one can give rise to a claim for compensation in most jurisdictions if divorce law does not provide for just results.[30] This solution can be based on the consideration that the reliance on the durability of the marriage should be legally protected.

---

28 Shop rental: *Renting a retail outlet; unexpected business environment at a shopping centre*
A is the owner of a bookshop. He contracts with B to rent business accommodation in B's shopping centre. The fixed period of the lease is five years. The shopping centre has just been built and a large part of the accommodation is still unoccupied. Both parties expect at the time of contracting that a variety of shops (the hotel and catering trade, retail sales) will be located there. One year later almost all the accommodation is rented, but three-quarters of the shopping centre consists of restaurants and cafes. For that reason most potential customers visit the shopping centre after A closes the doors of his bookshop.
Is A entitled to an adjustment or to a termination of the contract?

29 Sale of real estate involving expectation of cultural use: *Use of real estate by transferee does not comply with expectations of the transferor*
A sells his family home to B at a price far below its market value. Both parties assume that B would dedicate the house to cultural purposes only. However, this assumption was not inserted in the contract as an explicit condition. B changes his mind and gives it to one of his daughters instead.
Is A entitled to ask for the difference between the agreed price and the market value or, alternatively, to reclaim the house?

30 Investment in spouse's house is frustrated by divorce: *Equitable compensation if divorce laws lack a basis for compensation*
Before A and B marry, they enter into a prenuptial agreement in which they agree on the separation of property. During the marriage A buys a house and A and B use the house as their family home. The price of the house is EUR 500,000. A is the sole proprietor of the house, but B has contributed EUR 100,000 to the purchase price. In addition, B carries out extensive

7.4. MUTUAL MISTAKE AND MISCELLANEOUS ISSUES

(1) In the fourth group, a clear tendency can be stated in the case in which the parties of a share deal were mutually mistaken concerning the market value of shares.[31] Here, the burdened party is generally entitled to set aside the agreement on the fixed price, as both parties share the responsibility for the mistake. Another tendency is that the party burdened by the false price fixing is not entitled to enforce a price agreement that reflects the "true value" because the other party's reliance on the written price agreement must equally be taken into account. Notable exceptions are the common law jurisdictions of England and Ireland where no remedy is granted and thereby the risk of the mutual mistake is allocated only to the party burdened by the "false" price calculation in the written contract.

(2) In the impediments of production beyond the seller's control case,[32] the effect of unexpected circumstances on the respective rules on breach of contract was analysed. The question here is whether the seller would be excused from his liability in damages due to the unexpected nature of the impediment. Even though many jurisdictions tend to solve this case on the basis of their ("conventional") doctrines on breach of contract, a clear distinction between the "open" and "closed" jurisdictions can be observed. The main reason for this is that the distinction between the "open" and the "closed" jurisdictions is in line with the division between systems that apply a fault liability regime with regard to contractual damages and those jurisdictions that provide for strict liability. On the basis of their strict liability regime, there is a clear tendency to holding A liable for damages

---

renovation work before they move in. The renovation would have cost EUR 50,000 if professional services had been employed. After A and B have lived together in the house for one year, they separate and then divorce. Divorce law does not provide a basis for compensation.
Is B entitled to compensation for his contributions to the family home?

31 Share deal – mutual mistake: *False determination of the market value in a share deal*
A holds shares of X corporation. He agrees to sell the shares to B at the current price as listed by the stock exchange on the day of contracting. In the written contract, the parties set a price of EUR 10 per share. However, the actual price per share on the day of contracting is EUR 12. The Internet service from which the parties derived the price had displayed an incorrect number. When A discovers the correct price, he demands that the purchase price be increased to EUR 12.
Can A ask for a price of EUR 12 per share? Can he, alternatively, terminate the contract?

32 Impediments of production beyond seller's control: *Production of contractual goods is inhibited by a strike/ restriction of electricity supplies*
A agrees to deliver some goods to B on a certain date, but:

a) The workers of a subcontractor go on strike.
b) Due to problems with the State energy production and distribution system the Government decides to cut the electricity supply at night thereby making it impossible to work at night.

As a result, A cannot deliver the goods for an uncertain period of time.
Is B entitled to terminate the contract and to ask for damages?

among the "closed" jurisdictions. The findings of the "open" jurisdictions remain somewhat vague due to the limited factual basis of the given case. However, it becomes quite clear that, subject to the factual details of the case, A has strong arguments to challenge his liability in many of the "open" jurisdictions. The lack of a clear tendency reflects the division as to the liability regime, but also the ambivalence of the risks in question. While neither strikes nor the energy supply are under the complete control of the seller, one may argue that he is closer to these sources of risk than the purchaser.

(3) With regard to the disclaimer case,[33] it may be observed that a general disclaimer will predominantly be regarded as invalid in both the "open" and in the "closed" jurisdictions. There are, however, some exceptions (Belgium and France from the group of the "closed" and Germany, Portugal and Spain from the group of the "open" jurisdictions). The rationale for the majority perspective is that unexpected events are beyond the parties' imagination and thus beyond their dispositions. One may also draw the conclusion that the equity principles from which the doctrines governing unexpected circumstances are derived are qualified as *ius cogens*.

8. THE PREFERENCE FOR OPENLY ADDRESSING THE ISSUE

Let us now turn to the doctrinal distinction between "conventional" and "exceptional" concepts. The doctrines that specifically address the issue of unexpected circumstances and identify the unexpected event as the source for relief (e.g. *Wegfall der Geschäftsgrundlage*, doctrine of assumptions, *clausula rebus sic stantibus*) have been referred to as "exceptional" doctrines. "Conventional" doctrines, on the other hand, are the traditional doctrines of contract law, which are based on the parties' (hypothetical) intentions or on flaws in the mechanism of contracting. Such doctrines can address unexpected events with reference to the contractual agreement (e.g. interpretation, mistake, impossibility of performance and *laesio enormis*).

---

[33] Disclaimer: *Disclaimer concerning the rights arising from unexpected circumstances; other clauses related to unexpected circumstances*
The construction company A agrees to build a double-floor building on B's land for the price of EUR 2,000,000. In the contract the parties stipulate a disclaimer which excludes "all the rights of both parties arising from unexpected circumstances". Two weeks after the construction work has begun a granite rock, which could not have been detected by the parties before the conclusion of the contract, is revealed on B's land. As a result the costs of the construction increase by 300%. Can A ask for an adjustment of the contract or can he terminate the contract in spite of the disclaimer?

In favour of the "conventional" concepts one may argue that they are in harmony with the principle of *pacta sunt servanda*: if the parties' (hypothetical) intentions can be referred to as the basis of relief or if flaws can be identified in the contracting process, there is no conflict between the contract and an equitable allocation of risks. The harmonising character of the "conventional" concepts may make it easier for the courts to set the contract aside.

However, quite often the "conventional" concepts provide no precise and persuasive rationale for relief in cases of unexpected circumstances – even if they are referred to by the courts. If the contract does not address the unexpected event explicitly or by clear implication, relief cannot be based on the parties' actual intentions. Hence, "conventional" concepts are always dealing with hypothetical assumptions as to what the parties would have agreed upon if they had foreseen the event. This reconstruction of the parties' hypothetical intentions will often be fictional. If the parties have not foreseen the risk in question, it is equally fictional to qualify their non-perception as a mistake. Therefore, in many cases of unexpected circumstances the application of a "conventional" doctrine amounts to concealing the essential equitable conflict between the (flawless but silent) contract and the extrinsic effect caused by the unexpected event in question.

The "exceptional" doctrines, on the other hand, openly address the conflict between the contract and the requirements of equity in the light of the unexpected event in question. These doctrines and their application reveal that in most cases the problem of unexpected circumstances cannot be solved with reference to the intention of the parties and that an external standard of law is to be applied in the assessment of the event and its consequences for the contract. This becomes evident in the "open" jurisdictions, where on the basis of a general "exceptional" doctrine the contractual agreement itself can be adjusted to match the requirements of equity.

The European model rules on contract law presented so far all propose to recognise such a general "exceptional" doctrine. The conflict between the principle of *pacta sunt servanda* and the requirements of equity is particularly evident in the rules of the DCFR, which are based on the PECL. In Article III.-1:110 DCFR and Article 6.111 PECL the principle of sanctity of the contract is confirmed as the general rule. However, at the same time, it is confronted with the relevant exceptions in the case of a change of circumstances.

9. MINIMUM REQUIREMENTS FOR SETTING ASIDE THE CONTRACT

As I have already mentioned and as the national reports illustrate, there are various "exceptional" doctrines, specifically addressing the issue of unexpected circumstances both in the "open" and in the "closed" jurisdictions. In the "open" jurisdictions, these doctrines will allow for termination as well as adjustment of the contract, while in the "closed" jurisdictions termination is generally the only remedy available.

Even though the different concepts vary strongly in detail, we can identify three basic prerequisites for the application of such "exceptional" doctrines, as far as their doctrinal justification is concerned: (1) The transaction must have been affected *fundamentally* by a certain event. (2) The event affecting the transaction *must not have been provided for in the contract or foreseen by both parties* at the time of the conclusion of the contract. (3) The burden resulting from the event may *not be attributed to one party by any particular legal rule.* This postulate accounts for the principle of *lex specialis derogat legi generali.*

These requirements can be characterised as "minimum conditions": even though further restrictions may (and often do) apply under the law of the individual jurisdictions, these requirements must be met in any case if the contract is to be challenged successfully.

10. DISTINCTION BETWEEN ISSUES OF INITIAL MISTAKE AND OF UNEXPECTED EVENTS ARISING AFTER THE CONCLUSION OF THE CONTRACT

The process of harmonisation on the basis of precedents involves the problem of languages. An Estonian case on change of circumstances will have little impact in Portugal if it is not available in a language which is accessible to Portuguese lawyers. A database in the present European *lingua franca* – and ideally in more than just one language – would therefore be necessary. This need not necessarily be a database in the formal sense, such as the former CLAB.[34] A more user-friendly option is ECTIL's Yearbook of Tort Law, which is discussed at annual meetings in Vienna. It is clear from the preceding paragraphs that contract revision in case of changed circumstances is now widely accepted in European jurisdictions, but whether it is up to the parties concerned to arrive at such revision remains an open issue.

34 DG SANCO's one time database on unfair contract terms (*clauses abusives*) – see Thomas Wilhelmsson in Torbjörn Andersson, Bengt Lindell (eds), *Festskrift till Per Henrik Lindblom* (Iustus 2004) 781–800.

PART V

CONSUMER LAW

SPANISH CONSUMER LAW IN THE COVID-19 EMERGENCY

Álvaro Luna and Pablo Salvador Coderch*

---

* Álvaro Luna, Cuatrecasas; Pablo Salvador Coderch, Universitat Pompeu Fabra and Cuatrecasas. This contribution results from the research project "Coronavirus i dret privat" (2020PANDE00092), funded by the Catalan Agency for University and Research Grants (AGAUR) and was written within a contractual research framework between the Universitat Pompeu Fabra and the Barcelona office of the law firm Cuatrecasas.

As a consequence of the COVID-19 emergency, Spanish consumer contract law was amended through Section 36 of Royal Decree-Law 11/2020, of 31 March. Paragraphs 1, 2 and 3 of Section 36 provide the possibility of adjusting consumer sales and services contracts, and if the parties do not reach an agreement within 60 days, the consumer can terminate the contract. We defend in this contribution that Section 36 must never be understood as an alibi for opportunistic termination and, therefore, both the adjustment and termination requests must meet standards of good faith and fair dealing.

The legal issue analysed and answered in this contribution is the scope of Section 36, paragraphs 1–3, of Royal Decree-Law 11/2020 in relation to the principle of conservation of contracts. This contribution analyses Section 36 in the light of the good faith principle. Renegotiation, adjustment and even termination are possible but only in good faith.

Section 36, paragraphs 1–3, of Royal Decree-Law 11/2020 allows for the termination of consumer sales and services agreements due to the impossibility of compliance caused by the measures adopted to deal with the COVID-19 pandemic under the state of alarm and their extension by the Spanish Government, validated by the Congress of Deputies (the Spanish lower chamber of representatives), and even later, during the de-escalation and the so called "new normal" phases, until the health crisis is over. This regulation is based on the principles of contract preservation and good faith and seeks to guide contract adaptation within the framework of reasonable negotiation between traders and consumers. In our opinion, the objective of reconciling the broad power of termination established by law with the preservation and adaptation of contracts is manifested in the explanation of this regulation discussed in this contribution.

1. STATE OF ALARM

On 14 March 2020, the Spanish Government declared a state of alarm to handle the health crisis caused by COVID-19 (Royal Decree 463/2020, of 14 March).

Section 116.2 of the Spanish Constitution of 1978 (SC) regulates the state of alarm, which the Government may decree for 15 days, with any extension subject to approval by the Congress of Deputies.

Born as a reaction to the Spanish Civil War (1936–1939) and to the dictatorship of General Franco that followed it (1936–1975), Article 116 of the SC established a staggered regulation: state of alarm, state of emergency and state of siege.

Organic Law 4/1981, of 1 June, developed the constitutional provisions. The declaration of the state of alarm is possible if extraordinary circumstances make it impossible to maintain normality through the ordinary powers of the competent authorities (Sec 1.1), and the alteration of normality is due, as is the case of the pandemic of COVID-19, to "health crises, such as epidemics and serious contamination situations" (Sec 4.b). The Government can appoint the competent authorities during the state of alarm (Sec 9) and limit the movement of people at specific times and places (Sec 11.a).

Section 116 allowing the confinement of the entire Spanish population for an extended period such as the first wave of the pandemic from March to June 2020 is not without constitutional controversy. In any case, similar lockdown measures, although generally less stringent, have been established in almost all comparable legal systems.

Royal Decree 463/2020, of 14 March, declaring the state of alarm throughout Spain (Sec 1), established that the competent authority was the Government, with the functions referred to in the Royal Decree delegated to four ministries (Defence; State; Transportation, Mobility and Urban Agenda; and Health) in their respective areas of responsibility (Sec 4.2). It also limited the movement of people on roads and public spaces to essential activities (Sec 7).

However, by 16 September 2020, Spain was the fifth country in the world by number of estimated diagnosed deaths caused by COVID-19 per million inhabitants: 642.16 (Peru is first with 966.79; Belgium is second with 869.37; Bolivia is third with 655.94 ... UK, eighth: 626.63; USA, nineth: 597.07; Italy, tenth: 589.64; Sweden, eleventh: 574.58).[1] The legal provisions for extending the state of alarm every fortnight ended up channelling progressively broader deconfinement measures (Royal Decrees 476/2020, 487/2020, 492/2020, 514/2020, 537/2020, Resolution of 3 June 2020).[2] Although an early assessment would be premature, if more and better precautionary measures had been taken in January and February 2020, stricter ones could have probably been avoided later on.[3]

---

1 Statista, https://es.statista.com/ accessed 16 September 2020. Data must be analysed with extreme caution: different countries use different methods to calculate the number of deaths from COVID-19, and some of them change their methods with some frequency. As of 16 September 2020, one of the most reputable sources is www.coronavirus.jhu.edu accessed 16 September 2020, from Johns Hopkins University & Medicine. In the text, the authors have opted for death per million inhabitants instead of absolute figures.

2 State of alarm expired at 00:00 on 21 June 2020.

3 On 12 February 2020, GSMA (Global System for Mobile Communications Association), an industry organisation that represents the interests of mobile networks operations, cancelled the 2020 edition of Mobile World Congress in Barcelona, "because the global concern regarding the coronavirus outbreak ... make it impossible for the GSMA to hold the event" (Statement of Mr. John Hoffman CEO of GSMA). Other economic agents took similar decisions before March (e.g. Giorgio Armani cancelled the AW20 Show due to coronavirus fears on 23 February). In Spain, the coincidence of political public meetings, demonstrations, and football matches at the end of February and beginning of March objectively increased contagion risks. The role of the World Health Organization before and during the pandemics has also been an object of controversy, but this issue is not analysed in this contribution. WHO announced COVID-19 outbreak as a Public Health Emergency of International Concern on 11 February 2020, and as a pandemic on 11 March 2020.

2. SPANISH CONSUMER LAW IN COVID-19 TIMES

The Spanish Government has adopted several measures that directly affect consumer contracts and relations.[4] The main ones are described below.

2.1. STAY OF PROCEDURAL AND CIVIL DEADLINES

RD 463/2020 ordered the interruption of the terms and deadlines provided in procedural laws for all jurisdictional orders, with some exceptions (second additional provision), during the entire state of alarm. This provision is understood to reach the legal obligations with procedural projection.[5]

RDL 11/2020 ordered the suspension, for a maximum of six months, of eviction and foreclosure procedures for rent arrears subject to the 1994 Spanish Urban Leases Act affecting vulnerable households with no alternative housing options (Sec 1).

RD 463/2020 suspended prescription and limitation deadlines ("*plazos de prescripción y plazos de caducidad*") on any claims and rights during the state of alarm (fourth additional disposition).[6]

2.2. MORATORIUM ON PAYMENTS

Under RDLs 8/2020 and 11/2020, debtors undergoing "circumstances of economic vulnerability", as defined by the law, can request a three-month moratorium (which may be extended by resolution of the Council of Ministers) from their creditors to pay the principal and interest of mortgage loans (taken out to purchase a main residence, a property to carry out the activity of individual entrepreneurs or professionals, or rented residences where the owner and mortgage debtor has not been paid rent during the state of emergency and up to a month after it is lifted) and credits not secured by a mortgage.

---

4 During the state of alarm, the Government adopts measures through a Royal Decree-law (RDL), which must be subsequently validated by the Congress of Deputies (Sec 86 of the SC). To date, all the measures have been validated, although it has voted in favour of processing the Royal Decree-laws as bills.

5 The suspension of the procedural terms and deadlines was lifted with effect from 4 June 2020, coinciding with the resumption of judicial activity (Sec 8 RD 537/2020). Despite the initial indication that terms were merely suspended, the lawmaker has agreed to restart calculating them completely (Sec 2.1 RDL 16/2020) and has even agreed that the period for the announcement, preparation, formalisation and filing of appeals against judgments and other resolutions that end the procedure and that are notified during the suspension of deadlines established in RD 463/2020, of 14 March, and those that are notified within the following 20 business days (Sec 2.2 RDL 16/2020) will be doubled.

6 This suspension was lifted with effect from 4 June 2020 (Sec 10 RD 537/2020).

RDL 19/2020 further provided a new moratorium on financial debt for agreements reached between the debtor and the financial institution that are subject to the provisions of sectoral framework agreements between financial institutions through their associations. This moratorium supplements the legal moratorium applicable in circumstances of special vulnerability, established under RDL 8/2020 and 11/2020.

2.3. CONTRACT EXTENSIONS AND MORATORIUM

The lawmaker has provided the following:

- The interruption, during the state of alarm and its extensions, of the periods to return products bought at stores and online (Sec 21 RDL 8/2020).[7]
- An extraordinary six-month extension of main residence lease agreements subject to the 1994 Spanish Urban Leases Act (Sec 2 RDL 11/2020).
- An automatic moratorium up to a maximum of four months on paying rent to lease a main residence under an agreement subject to the 1994 Spanish Urban Leases Act, which is granted to those in a situation of vulnerability when the lessor is a company or public entity providing housing or a large housing asset holder (an individual or legal entity owning over 10 urban properties, excluding parking lots and storage units, or a built surface over 1,500 m^2). This also applies to Social Housing Fund leases (Sec 3 and ff. RDL 11/2020).
- Measures to help users and consumers pay their bills, offering them the option to postpone any unpaid bills or pay them in instalments. This applies to bills submitted from the date the state of alarm entered into force until 30 June 2020 if they meet certain conditions (RDL 19/2020).

Although there are doubts on interpretation of the previous measures because of the urgency with which they had to be adopted (many of them having to be subsequently clarified by the lawmaker), perhaps the most controversial, for its contents and form, has been Sec 36 RDL 11/2020, which provides for the termination of purchase of goods and services agreements and package tours without penalty for consumers and users.

We will focus on Section 36, paragraphs 1, 2 and 3 of RDL 11/2020, on purchase and services agreements, excluding number 4, on package tours.

7 Although the subjective scope is not clear from the wording of the Section, from the explanatory statements of the law, it seems that this measure aims at protecting consumers deprived of their freedom of move during the state of alarm.

3. RIGHT TO TERMINATE CONSUMER CONTRACTS: THE TEXTUAL EDGES OF SECTION 36 OF THE RDL 11/2020

Section 36 of RDL 11/2020, of 31 March, sets out urgent supplementary social and economic measures to deal with COVID-19:

> **Section 36, paragraphs 1, 2 and 3. Right to terminate certain consumer and user contracts without penalty**
>
> Sec 36.1. If, as a consequence of the measures adopted by the competent authorities during the state of alarm, the de-escalation or the new normal phases, the contracts signed by consumers and users, be they for the sale of goods or the provision of services, including those of successive tract, cannot be performed, the consumer and user will be entitled to terminate the contract during 14 days from the date of impossible performance, provided that the measures that made it impossible to perform such contract remain in force. The option to terminate the contract can only be admitted when it is not possible to obtain, from the proposal or review proposals offered in good faith by each of the parties, a solution to restore the reciprocity of interests of the contract. Adaptation proposals may include, among others, the offer of vouchers for reimbursement, which in any case will be subject to acceptance by the consumer or user. For these purposes, it will be understood that it is not possible to obtain a proposal for adjustment that restores the reciprocity of interests of the contract after 60 days from the request for contractual termination by the consumer or user without agreement between the parties on the review proposal.[8]
>
> Sec 36.2. When the performance of the contract is impossible according to the previous section, the trader[9] must return the sums paid by the consumer or user, except for expenses incurred, duly itemized and provided to the consumer in the same way as payment was made within a maximum of 14 days, unless the consumer and user expressly accept different terms.
>
> Sec 36.3. Regarding contracts for the provision of services of successive tract, the trader may offer options for the recovery of the service afterwards. Only if the consumer could not or did not accept this recovery, must the amounts already paid for the period of the service not provided for that cause be returned or, with the consumer's agreement, future fees for the provision of the service can be reduced. Likewise, the trader will refrain from submitting new monthly bills until the service can be provided normally, without this resulting in the termination of the contract, except in case of the parties' mutual agreement.

---

8 This is the current wording of Section 36.1, which has been modified by RDL 15/2020 and RDL 21/2020, of June 9.

9 For the purposes of this note, and following European Union directives, "trader" means any natural person or any legal person, irrespective of whether privately or publicly owned, who is acting, including through any other person acting in its name or on its behalf, for purposes relating to its trade, business, craft or profession.

3.1. "IF, AS A CONSEQUENCE OF"

Conditional and modal, the sentence announces a series of circumstances that will trigger the legal effects provided by Section 36. Note that the text uses the term "consequence", which according to its first meaning in the Royal Spanish Academy Dictionary[10] is a "fact or event that follows or results from another," and it has a broader scope than "effect," defined as what follows by virtue of a cause. Thus, it is not required that there be a single cause; there may be several (and, in turn, each of them potentially originating the result by itself or in conjunction with all or some of the others). Direct or immediate causation is not required either, as it can be more or less approximate. Therefore, courts have wide latitude when assessing the factual assumption of the Section. Compare this to the "necessary consequence" in Section 1107.1 of the Spanish Civil Code (SCC).

3.2. "MEASURES ADOPTED"

The term "measures" corresponds to its sixth meaning in the Royal Spanish Academy Dictionary: "provision, prevention," and "adopted" is synonymous with "taken." Measures are, therefore, decisions of individuals or organisations, not natural events or occurrences, and for the purposes of Section 36, they must come from the competent authorities.[11] The degree or intensity of the measures is relevant only insofar as it must generate the consequences that the precept will establish next.

3.3. "DURING THE VALIDITY OF THE STATE OF ALARM, THE DE-ESCALATION OR THE NEW NORMAL PHASES"

Section 36.1 establishes a clear time frame: the measures must have been adopted during the state of alarm, the de-escalation or the new normal phases, neither before nor after.[12] However, when the new normal phase is over, and if, as a result of a pandemic outbreak or another similar circumstance, a new state of alarm is

---

10 Founded in 1713, the Royal Spanish Academy is Spain's official institution with a mission to ensure the stability of the Spanish Language (see: https://dle.rae.es/ accessed 17 June 2020).

11 According to the general understanding, the lawmaker clarified this circumstance in RDL 21/2020.

12 The original wording of Section 36.1 exclusively refers to the measures adopted during the state of alarm and its extensions, which raises the question of what should happen in relation to the consequences of the measures after the end of the state of alarm, or the consequences of any measures that may be adopted after the state of alarm has been lifted. In line with the Plan for the Transition to a New Normality, of 28 April 2020, which is the

declared, Section 36.1 would not apply, unless another provision so established. Naturally, the question is what happens if, shortly after the end of the new normal phase – one, two or three months – i.e. when the health crisis is over, a new health crisis arises. The reasonable answer would be that the closer in time, the easier it is to accept the continuity of cases and circumstances and apply Section 36.1.

3.4. "CONTRACTS SIGNED BY CONSUMERS AND USERS"

The subjective scope of Section 36 is clear. It is an issue of the law of contracts, not of any other legal acts (e.g. notices, payments or withdrawals) or business transactions that are also legal (e.g. waivers or debt acknowledgements). But the law reads "signed", a term whose first meaning in the Dictionary of the Royal Spanish Academy is "to sign at the bottom or the end of a writing", a requirement that would exclude, beyond all reason, express but verbal or tacit contracts. But this is not the meaning derived from the general regulation of contracts with consumers and users (Section 59 ff of the Spanish Consumer Protection Act, "SCPA"), and "to sign" has a second meaning, "to agree" and a third one, "to oblige oneself to contribute", which help prevent interpretation nonsense. The reference admits a plausible meaning, according to which the existence of the contract is not to be presumed since, even in the case of tacit contracts (e.g. self-service in a restaurant), a conclusive behaviour on the part of the consumer is, by definition, required.

Therefore, Section 36 will apply to consumer contracts in the strictest sense, i.e. "entered into between a consumer or user and a trader" (Sec 59.1 of the SCPA) rather than to contracts between traders or between individuals, subject to the general rules of contract law, which, however, takes into account extraordinary situations (e.g. *rebus sic stantibus clause*, force majeure, impossibility of compliance and obstacle to compliance). The concepts of consumer, trader, producer and supplier are those included in consumer legislation (Secs 3, 4, 5 and 7 of the SCPA, respectively).

3.5. "BE THEY FOR THE SALE OF GOODS OR THE PROVISION OF SERVICES, INCLUDING THOSE OF SUCCESSIVE TRACT"

"Sales contract" has a clear legal meaning in Spanish law (Sec 1445 of the SCC), and it is obvious which sales are excluded (Secs 2 and 3 of the United Nations

---

plan for the country's gradual de-escalation of the confinement (https://www.lamoncloa.gob.es/consejodeministros/resumenes/Documents/2020/PlanTransicionNuevaNormalidad.pdf accessed on 17 June 2020). RDL 21/2020 modified the wording of the Section and also included the measures that can be adopted during the de-escalation and new normality phases, which will last until the health crisis is totally overcome.

Convention on Contracts for the International Sale of Goods, of 11 April 1980 (CISG); share purchase agreements: cf Sec 325 of the Spanish Commercial Code). It is, however, easily extensible to contracts that include the (possibility of) transfer of property (or legal and peaceful possession) of goods in exchange for a price (call option, leasing or renting) and to any final distribution contracts with similar results.

Timed and onerous assignments of the use of goods and lease of assets do not fall within the scope of Section 36. For real estate leases, emergency regulation as a result of the pandemic included in Section 2 ff of the same RDL 11/2020 covers the most relevant adverse situations involving rent arrears for vulnerable households.

It would not be unreasonable to defend that long-term contracts should be included in the different scenarios foreseen in Section 36 by which the use and possession of the goods are transferred throughout their useful life or which place the holder in a legal and economic position similar to that of the holder of a surface right.

For movable assets, the solution, *mutatis mutandis*, is the same. A short-term lease should not be understood as included in the scenarios of Section 36, but if its duration and conditions bring the lessee closer to the position of a quasi-owner, the issue will, once again, be debatable. Then, the application of the discussed rule can be argued.

Section 36 discusses buying and selling of goods without distinguishing between movable and unmovable, and tangible and intangible things (rights), though it could have done so. Doubts can arise if Section 36 is compared to Section 59 bis 2. of the SCPA, where "goods" are "tangible movable things," but there is a circumstance that suggests a broad understanding: COVID-19 is a pandemic that substantially and materially affects the entire world. It is not as the 2008 recession, a crisis caused by real estate and financial upheaval. Its generality and universality point to the broad construction of the rules issued to mitigate its consequences.

Sales contracts border lease of works contracts in the latter's obligation to carry out the works, not only to deliver them, but their overlap is almost universal if the contractor assumes the obligation to provide a substantial part of the materials necessary to manufacture or produce the works (cf Sec 1588 SCC: there is a lease of works contract whether the contractor provides only the work or also supplies the material. However, compare this with Section 3.2 of the CISG). Any doubts are cleared if "service provision contracts" are also included in the factual assumption: the distinction between works and services lease contracts does not depend on the material nature of the provision (preparing a legal opinion: lease of works; legal advice and defence: lease of services), but the legal intensity of the obligation assumed, as means (services) or results (work). If the trader in the contract with the consumer assumes an obligation of results, then it will be necessary to analyse, under the general rules, whether the impossibility as an effect of the measures adopted during the state of alarm justifies the suspension of contract compliance or, rather, its termination. But, in principle, in the works contract, there is an obligation of result, and the consumer does not assume *ab initio* the risk of performing the service that is not finally delivered, so it does not need a specific power of suspension or termination, *ex* Section 36.1, hence, the limitation of the rule to lease of services contracts. Expressly included are contracts of successive ("that happens or follows from one thing to another") tract ("time lapse") i.e. those whose legal fulfilment is not instantaneous but takes place over time through a series of actions the obliged party must perform.

3.6. "RESULT OF IMPOSSIBLE PERFORMANCE"

Compliance, in principle, is payment, fulfilment of the obligation and the counter obligation of each of the parties (Sec 1157 SCC), and it must become ("result") "impossible", i.e., literally "not possible" (Dictionary of the Spanish Royal Academy, first meaning) or "extremely difficult" (second meaning). A restriction of the literal meaning to the legal or physical impossibility of Section 1184 SCC or the loss of the due thing of Section 1182 SCC would be contrary to the nature of things in the context of the COVID-19 pandemic, one that it simultaneously affects the entire world, again, in its literal and complete sense, in all circumstances. In practice, the literal interpretation of the Section would affirm that "*genus nunquam perit*" should not prevent the debtor affected by the subjective impossibility (and supervening as a consequence of the measures adopted during the state of alarm) to obtain financial resources to fulfil a payment obligation to resort to Section 36.[13]

3.7. "THE CONSUMER … WILL BE ENTITLED TO TERMINATE THE CONTRACT DURING 14 DAYS …"

Section 36 enables the consumer and user to terminate the contract during 14 days from its impossible performance. This is a power of termination, but not of termination for breach of the other party; the 14-day period for impossibilities

[13] It is not a peaceful matter. Against it, see Ángel Francisco Carrasco Perera, of 10 April 2020 "*Imposibilidad de cumplimiento por Covid. ¿pero imposibilidad para quién*? (Impossibility of compliance due to COVID. But, ¿whose impossibility?) (https://www.linkedin.com/pulse/imposibilidad-de-cumplimiento-por-covid-pero-para-carrasco-perera, accessed 17 June 2020).

that occurred before 4 June 2020, will be counted from that date[14] and not, as the Section suggests, from the date of impossible performance. This is predicated on the obligations of the parties, regardless of which one has been affected by the measures adopted as a result of the state of alarm. The contractual failure does not have to be symmetrical: it is enough that one of the two main obligations of the sale or service contract has been affected for the contractual balance to be considered broken.[15] But the break of the contractual balance must be true, as Section 36 does not grant a power of denunciation or withdrawal *ad nutum*, arbitrary or opportunistic and contrary to good faith.[16] This comment allows for subjective impossibility but not for strategic behaviour.

3.8. GOOD FAITH AND RECIPROCITY OF INTERESTS

"The claim for termination of the contract can only be admitted when it is not possible to obtain, from the proposal or review proposals offered by each of the parties in good faith, a solution that restores the reciprocity of interests of the contract."

Indeed, the nucleus of this provision is the principle of good faith: the "*Nemo auditur suam turpitudinem allegans*" standard is fully applicable to the factual

14 RD 463/2020 ordered the suspension of prescription and limitation deadlines (*plazos de prescripción y plazos de caducidad*) on any claims and rights, thus including the right to terminate contracts later regulated in Section 36. The suspension of the procedural terms and deadlines was lifted with effect from 4 June 2020.

15 A literal interpretation of the Section would affirm that payment obligations fall under the scope of Section 36, but this is unclear in the doctrine.

16 For some, the right to terminate a contract granted by Section 36 is not an *ex novo* right, since the consumer will only have the right to terminate the contract when termination was already possible under the rules of the Spanish Civil Code (basically, Art 1124 SCC) and the SCPA. The only thing Section 36 does is modify the way of exercising that right of termination (mainly shortening the period to exercise the right and including a forced negotiation for 60 days). See Manuel Marín López, '*Efectos del COVID-19 en los contratos con consumidores: el art. 36 del RD-Ley 11/2020*' ('Effects of COVID-19 on consumer contracts: art. 36 of RD-Law 11/2020') in http://centrodeestudiosdeconsumo.com/images/Efectos_del_COVID-19_en_los_contracts_with_consumers-_el_art_36_del_RD-ley_112020.pdf: "Outside the cases in which the law establishes specific rules on the termination of the contract (e.g. Arts 66.bis.2 and 121 of the SCPA), the case law of the Spanish Supreme Court on Section 1124 SCC sets out that the termination is applicable when the contract is bilateral or synallagmatic; the creditor (i.e., the consumer) has not breached its own obligation, and the obligation breached by the debtor (the seller or provider) is essential, in the sense that the breach is serious and definitively frustrates the purpose of the contract, since the subsequent debtor's performance, even if possible, no longer meets the expectations of the creditor. In conclusion, the right to terminate the contract applies, under Section 36, when the consumer has the right to terminate it under the Spanish Civil Code or the applicable consumer protection regulations." Accessed 17 June 2020.

assumption of Section 36. The claim for termination is subsidiary[17] to a serious offer to renegotiate the contract by each of the parties, not only by the trader. The wording suggests that the parties must negotiate a solution that restores contractual economy and makes it possible, if it still is possible (it cannot always be), to survive after rebalancing the contract in good faith. Again, neither traders nor consumers and users can act in bad faith, and bad faith is the manifest or proven absence of impossibility. It develops a very broad notion of impossibility, fitting the universal and sudden nature of the COVID-19 pandemic. At the same time, its broadness is counterbalanced by the required observance of good faith.

3.9. "THE ADJUSTMENT PROPOSALS MAY INCLUDE … THE OFFER OF SUBSTITUTE VOUCHERS FOR REIMBURSEMENT"

The text uses "may," but the reference is not idle: it draws a line of preference for preservation of the contract over termination. "*Pacta sunt servanda*," the contract preservation principle includes its reasonable modificative novation ("among others"). In some contracts, compliance time is essential, but in most cases, the offer of reasonable alternatives for future or staggered times makes sense under the principle of good faith. Remember that the rule's factual assumption is that the contract is impossible to perform as a consequence of the measures adopted by the public authorities during the state of alarm or during the de-escalation or new normality phases: "as a consequence" is not the same as "on occasion." Proposals, reads the precept, may include offering vouchers instead of a refund, but there is no requirement that the object of the vouchers be identical to the unfulfilled benefits. It is enough for them to be reasonably similar (a different trip, accommodation, or menu) but functionally comparable, and there is no limitation in this regard (e.g. a trip with the same price to another destination, accommodation in a different establishment, or a different performance in the same opera house).

3.10. LACK OF AGREEMENT AFTER 60 DAYS

"For these purposes, it will be understood that it is not possible to obtain a proposal for a review that restores the reciprocity of interests of the contract after 60 days from the request for contractual termination by the consumer or user without agreement between the parties on the review proposal."

---

17 For the purposes of clarification, Section 36 uses the term *"resolución"* in Spanish, which is commonly used in situations where one of the parties has incurred a breach of contract. The correct term, in line with the majority doctrine, should have been *"terminación."*

The sentence is time-focused ("it will be understood that it is not possible to obtain a proposal … after"), but its meaning is clearly conditional. It will be understood that it is not possible to obtain a proposal for review if 60 days have elapsed since the request for cancellation without agreement of the parties. But the conditioning is not only procedural. There must be a request by any means, although it is not subject to form, and it is time-based (60 days must have lapsed without agreement). In addition, good faith will normally require a negotiation under the parameters of correction consistent with what is agreed by the parties, sectorial uses and, of course, what is determined by law. Note that the power to terminate the contract granted by Section 36 is superimposed on the general power of withdrawal, itself expressly unconditional, established by Section 68 of the SCPA,[18] whose minimum and non-derogable period of performance is 14 days from receipt of the goods (Sec 71 of the SCPA). However, Section 36 does not refer to it or repeat it, but it has its own regulatory autonomy, basically a self-contained rule that focuses on contractual good faith. Therefore, a manifestly unfounded termination request, i.e. an arbitrary request, can be disregarded, and the trader may prove the clear bad faith of the consumer. Timing has another meaning here. It is to show that, normally, the request for termination will not be in bad faith, that proof of it and the time elapsed without agreement will suffice for the contract to be terminated. But a consumer's bad-faith is not unimaginable. As we will see in the next section, the obligation of the trader to return to the consumer the sum paid presupposes that the acquired goods have not suffered any deterioration other than the expected, reasonable, tear and wear, so a partial depreciation should probably be discounted. The purchaser of a household appliance that has been used for years, but which it has not paid for, cannot claim in good faith the full refund of the price paid. This brings us to the second part of the precept, which we will discuss below.

3.11. REIMBURSEMENT OF SUMS PAID BY THE CONSUMER

"In cases in which the performance of the contract is impossible under the previous section, the trader must return the sums paid by the consumer or user, except for expenses incurred, duly itemized and provided to the consumer in the same way as payment was made, within a maximum of 14 days, unless the consumer or user expressly accepts different terms."

When performance is impossible, and the 60-day period following the request for resolution lapses without the parties' agreement, the restitution of the contractual benefits will apply in a new 14-day period. The trader will have

[18] The SCPA does not grant the right of withdrawal for all consumer contracts but mainly for contracts agreed at a distance (e.g. online, by phone or mail), and those agreed outside commercial premises (e.g. door-to-door sales). See Sections 92 and ff of the SCPA.

to return the sums paid by the consumer, but Section 36 does not displace the rules of mutual restitution of benefits. Even if it does not refer to the consumer returning the goods, it must be understood as bound by application of the general rules (cf Sec 1303 of the SCC). It does not make the regulations on unjust enrichment inapplicable either (Sec 1901 of the SCC), since Section 36 does not substantiate any kind of unfounded enrichment by either party. COVID-19 is a general pandemic, and the emergency legislation tries to cushion its effects for everyone's benefit. But it does not allow the purchaser of a practically depreciated but not yet fully paid car to resort to Section 36 for self-enrichment and then purchase of a new vehicle. Section 36 naturally allows the previous reading: not only because it does not exclude applicability of the general rules beyond what is expressly provided, but also because the reference to the expenses incurred arises from the same principle, and thus explicitly considers it as being into force. It protects the consumer, but it does not justify the consumer's expectations of unjustified enrichment. The trader can discount the expenses incurred, which are not only return, transfer or renaming, but also repair and, where appropriate, fine-tuning of the returned property.[19] Hence the requirement that expenses be properly itemised – by concepts, units and amount – and provided to the consumer, who can discuss their origin and amount. The consumer may not, however, return a used item and claim its price as new. In any case, the trader cannot deduct expenses that were not actually incurred, and this raises the question of what can be deducted when the consumer returns a used and perhaps poorly maintained item. Again, the principle that vetoes unjust enrichment will prevent the consumer from making unfounded profit from a widespread alarm situation. The same results from a systematic interpretation of Section 36, paragraph 3, which expressly assumes that the consumer has no right to ask for the part of the price for the services historically provided.

In the same vein is the last point of that paragraph, which allows for an express agreement on different conditions for settlement of the contract. The parties can change the meaning of the precept but by agreement. The pandemic justifies the oversight of the rights of consumers and users but not the destruction of contractual law. It would be, again, contrary to the nature of things and to the literal wording of the precept.

---

19 The legitimacy of the trader's right to deduct expenses has been questioned to the extent that it could contradict the European Union regulations (see Manuel Marín López: Training capsules. Civil capsule: "Art. 36. Right to terminate consumer contracts" available at https://vimeo.com/404964804 accessed 17 June 2020). Regarding the scope of these expenses, others have advocated for a restrictive interpretation of the rule. First, the Ministry of Consumption (whose interpretation is not binding), which has issued a note on the rights of consumers and users facing the situation caused by the coronavirus, where it refers to "the expenses originated for the reimbursement, which must be suitably itemized and which, in no case, may entail a penalty for the user." (https://www.mscbs.gob.es/profesionales/saludPublica/ccayes/alertasActual/nCov-China/documentos/COVID19_Nota_derechos_consumidores.pdf accessed 17 June 2020).

3.12. CONTRACTS FOR SERVICES

"Regarding contracts for the provision of services of successive tract, the trader may offer options for the recovery of the service afterwards. Only if the consumer could not or did not accept this recovery, must the amounts already paid for the period of the service not provided for that cause be returned or, with the consumer's agreement, future fees for the provision of the service can be reduced."

The trader affected by the alarm situation who has not been able to provide the service may offer to the consumer options for recovery afterwards, i.e. after the measures that, in fact or in law, have prevented it from rendering its services are lifted. Such options and their specific content are left to free negotiation and, where appropriate, agreement by the parties. But if the consumer cannot accept the option, – e.g. because it is physically impossible to continue to receive the service – or does not want to accept it, then it will be entitled to a refund for the amounts for the services not provided or to reduce the amount of future fees. The extent or rate of reduction depends on the agreement between the parties, although the law seems to assume that compensation will normally be partial. A conservative idea underlies the contract, tending to the distribution over time of the consequences of the disruption caused by the interruption of the service. But, in any case, the private arrangement that the trader and consumer can reach prevails, whether it be a price reduction or a total allocation of the fees paid for services not provided to future fees. It only happens that the underlying legal principle advocates the preservation of the contract and the cushioning of the effects of the impossibility to perform it.

4. SUSPENSION OF MONTHLY BILLS

"Likewise, the trader will refrain from submitting new monthly bills until the service can be provided normally, without this resulting in the termination of the contract, except in case of mutual agreement by the parties."

The final paragraph of Section 36.3 establishes a default rule which seeks a balance between preservation and termination of the contract, giving the parties the possibility of reaching different balance. The rule is very favourable to the recipient of the services that cannot be provided normally, but in many cases, it is not necessarily the most appropriate for the economy of the contract. Consider the case of unavailable services, whose provision is periodic and cannot be postponed, that cannot be carried out for a time, the loss for its frustrated recipient is total, and in such cases, the default rule of Section 36.3 makes sense. But there are many cases in which the provision of the service will only be postponed. In those cases, the legal solution is doubtful. Think of a gym, a social club, a teaching or rehab centre that temporarily stops its services to its registered members, but the day after the state of alarm is lifted or relaxed, the premises open their doors, and services return to their users. In this environment, adapting the contract to charge a part of the fee that covers fixed costs while it temporarily ceases to provide its services makes sense. Note that a pandemic is not an earthquake, a fire, a bombing, so the facilities must be maintained, and shortly after reopening is authorised, they go back to providing their services. A contractual and social rebalancing that separates fixed costs from variables could have been considered as the default solution, probably the most appropriate for business contractors, but this was not adopted by the lawmaker. In the field of consumer contracts, it simply remains a reflection on reasonable solutions to safeguard contracts and, ultimately, the general interest with the best possible functioning of the economic and social system.

5. CONCLUSION

Section 36 of Spanish Royal Decree-Law 11/2020 allows termination of sales contracts and contracts for services entered into between a consumer or user and a trader, if as a consequence of measures adopted by the authorities during the COVID-19 emergency, performance becomes impossible. Impossibility is to be widely construed but always under the principles of good faith and contract preservation. Section 36 must never be understood as an alibi for opportunistic termination.

CONSUMER LAW AND COVID-19 IN PORTUGAL

Jorge Morais Carvalho and Sandra Passinhas*

Periods of crisis have a negative impact on the level of consumer protection, with the emphasis on other objectives, in particular those linked to the functioning of the market. This contribution aims at demonstrating that, in Portugal, measures adopted to face the economic and social effects of COVID-19 can be characterised as twofold: those that reduce the level of consumer protection and those that aim to protect particularly vulnerable consumers. Evidence will be given in the following fields: tourism (package travel, hotel or short-term accommodation bookings), services of general interest (in particular, water, electricity, gas and telecommunications provision), credit agreements (both mortgage credit and consumer credit), electronic payments, sale of goods, and the price-reduction commercial practice of sales.

---

* Jorge Morais Carvalho, NOVA School of Law, Lisbon; Sandra Passinhas, Universidade de Coimbra.

1. INTRODUCTION

Although the first signs of an imbalance in the consumer/trader relationship pre-existed,[1] the issue of consumer protection, understood as such, has its historical landmark in the famous speech of John F. Kennedy, delivered in Congress on 15 March 1962. In that speech, the American President Kennedy stressed that "consumers, by definition, include us all", adding that, although they are not organised and are not heard, they constitute the largest economic group acting in the market, being influenced by (and influencing) all the decisions taken at this level.

Consumer law was born and developed in the following decades in unique conditions of peace, economic growth and democracy.[2] It developed, in particular, in places and at times of greatest economic growth. In recent human history, conditions had never been more favourable for the State and its citizens, its representatives, including producers, distributors and traders, to be concerned with the adoption of greater protection of the consumer.

The economic crisis erupted in 2008, with particular vigour in those States where consumer protection had triumphed, and shook the perfect conditions for peace, economic growth and democracy necessary for the development of consumer law.[3] The crisis fundamentally called into question the assumption of economic growth, although its effects on peace and democracy should not be overlooked.

The pandemic crisis that we are currently experiencing – and which still seems to be at its beginning – once again calls into question the ideal conditions for the development of consumer law, first because it affects economic growth, but also peace and democracy may be weakened in many geographical contexts.

The legislative and regulatory measures adopted over the last few months reflect precisely this trend in times of crisis, with consumers being deprived of protection in order to relieve traders of some costs, while at the same time accentuating the protection of groups of consumers who are particularly unprotected by the economic difficulties they face. The focus is no longer on consumer law, which is fundamentally centred on granting rights to the middle class, but rather on the rights of the poorest.[4]

After a general explanation of the basis of consumer law, an analysis of some rules approved in recent months is carried out, as an example of the proposition that we argue in this contribution that the level of consumer protection decreases in times of crisis.

---

1 António Menezes Cordeiro, 'Da Natureza Civil do Direito do Consumo' (2004) 136-IV O Direito 605, 608; Jorge Morais Carvalho, *Manual de Direito do Consumo* (7th edn, Almedina 2020) 25 ff.

2 Carlos Ferreira de Almeida, *Direito do Consumo* (Almedina 2005) 211.

3 Carlos Ferreira de Almeida, 'A Crise do Direito do Consumo' in Nuno Piçarra and Jorge Bacelar Gouveia (eds), *A Crise e o Direito* (Almedina 2013) 215.

4 Jorge Morais Carvalho, 'COVID-19 e Direito do Consumo' (2020) Número Especial COVID-19 Revista do Ministério Público 277, 279.

2. BASIS OF CONSUMER LAW

The traditional basis for the approval and identification of laws concerning consumer law do not differ significantly, basing themselves essentially on the need for consumer protection, due to the existence of an unbalanced relationship between the consumer and the trader,[5] since it is assumed that the latter has, on the one hand, more and better information, not only technical but also legal, regarding the business in question, and, on the other hand, a superior financial capacity. It should be noted that this imbalance is not a prerequisite for the specific qualification of someone as a consumer.

The protection of the markets should also be included among the basis of consumer law.

One of the main objectives of consumer law is to stimulate consumer confidence so that they purchase more goods and services,[6] with consumption being identified as an important factor in economic growth. The costs associated with consumer protection laws, which generally increase in proportion to the increase in protection,[7] tend to favour large companies over smaller ones, since they have greater capacity to adapt and resist any reductions in profit margins. Consumer protection can be a factor in competition between companies.[8]

3. CRISIS OF 2008 AND POST-CRISIS OF 2008

Even before we look at the measures taken in the context of the pandemic between March and June 2020, let us look at some examples of the consequences of the 2008 economic crisis.

This crisis hit those countries where the success of consumer law had been most intense over the previous decades. As Carlos Ferreira de Almeida states, "consumption has been at the core of the hurricane",[9] first due to the uncontrolled increase in credit and consumption, followed by its abrupt reduction.

---

[5] Jorge Pegado Liz, *Introdução ao Direito e à Política do Consumo* (Editorial Notícias 1999) 294; Jean Calais-Auloy and Frank Steinmetz, *Droit de la Consommation* (7th edn, Dalloz 2006) 1; Gilles Paisant, *Défense et Illustration du Droit de la Consommation* (LexisNexis 2015) 39.

[6] Carlos Ferreira de Almeida, 'A Crise do Direito do Consumo' in Nuno Piçarra and Jorge Bacelar Gouveia (eds), *A Crise e o Direito* (Almedina 2013) 217; António Pinto Monteiro, 'O Direito do Consumidor em Debate: Evolução e Desafios' in Jorge Morais Carvalho (ed), *I Congresso de Direito do Consumo* (Almedina 2016) 11, 25.

[7] António Menezes Cordeiro, 'A Tutela do Consumidor de Produtos Financeiros' in *Liber Amicorum Mário Frota – A Causa dos Direitos dos Consumidores* (Almedina 2012) 51, 53.

[8] Cristina Torres, 'MEO – O Direito do Consumo e as Empresas: A Proteção dos Consumidores como Fator Competitivo' in Jorge Morais Carvalho (ed), *I Congresso de Direito do Consumo* (Almedina 2016) 131, 137.

[9] Carlos Ferreira de Almeida, 'A Crise do Direito do Consumo' in Nuno Piçarra and Jorge Bacelar Gouveia (eds), *A Crise e o Direito* (Almedina 2013) 216.

In addition to a clear "deficit in the practical application"[10] of consumer law provisions, a phenomenon of stagnation, or even a decrease, in the level of consumer protection could be observed in the years following the onset of the crisis.

At the European level, the trend towards maximum harmonisation directives is a good example that market protection currently prevails over consumer protection. For example, in transposing the Consumer Rights Directive, Austria had to repeal a rule stipulating that the time limit for exercising the right of withdrawal did not start to run until the consumer received the first invoice. In Portugal, when transposing the Directive on the sale of goods, a hierarchy of consumer rights in the event of non-conformity with the contract will have to be established.

In Portugal, some legal regimes have also pointed in the direction of a step backwards, such as Law no 58/2012, which created an extraordinary regime of protection for mortgage debtors in a very difficult economic situation, with requirements so demanding that it seems to have been adopted with the aim of reducing consumer protection. Also, Law no 10/2013, Law no 47/2014 and Decree-Law no 205/2015 can be given as examples of this trend.

Between 2016/2017 and 2019, with the recovery of the economy, both globally and particularly in Portugal, the trend seems to have reversed, with new consumer protection rules having been approved in some areas, particularly around the digital economy. At least, looking back today, we have not found in the last two or three years any examples of that trend of stagnation or decrease in the level of consumer protection and, on the contrary, legislative production has been intense both at national and European level.

Since 2020, we have been once again faced with a crisis, still with unknown extent and reach, but this has already prompted legislative interventions to restrict some consumer rights, essentially with the aim, currently, of ensuring the subsistence of some professionals in sectors most affected or other public interests.

4. PACKAGE TRAVEL AND BOOKINGS IN HOTELS OR LOCAL ACCOMMODATION ESTABLISHMENTS

In the tourism sector, the first measure adopted focused on trips made by final year students of the various levels (high school, college, university), which are quite common in Portugal and usually take place during the Easter holidays.

Article 11 of Decree-Law no 10-A/2020 of 13 March 2020 (amended more than a dozen times), ratified by Law no 1-A/2020 of 19 March 2020 (also with

---

10 Gilles Paisant, *Défense et Illustration du Droit de la Consommation* (LexisNexis 2015) 257.

several amendments) prohibited those trips and determined that the travel agencies or other entities are obliged to reschedule them, unless otherwise agreed between the parties.

In the meantime, a legal regime applicable to package travels and to reservations in hotels or local accommodation (*alojamento local*) establishments[11] has been approved. The Decree-Law no 17/2020 of 23 April 2020 establishes exceptional and temporary measures relating to the tourism sector, within the scope of the COVID-19 disease pandemic.

In essence, the cancellation of package trips or reservations in hotels or local accommodation establishments (scheduled for the period between 13 March 2020 and 30 September 2020) does not allow the traveller to immediately terminate the contract and the consequent right to reimbursement, which can only be made at the beginning of 2022.

Travellers who are unemployed may request reimbursement of the entire amount spent until 30 September 2020 (Arts 3-6 and 4-8).

Apart from this situation, travellers (only) have the right to opt for (1) the issuance of a voucher, transferable, of equal value to the payment made and valid until 31 December 2021; or (2) the rescheduling of the trip or booking until 31 December 2021.

If the voucher is not used or the rescheduling is not made by 31 December 2021, the traveller will then be entitled to a refund, which must be made within 14 days.

Unlike what would result from the application of the general provisions (see Art 795-1 of the Civil Code) and other special provisions applicable to the sector, the traveller will have to wait until 2022 to obtain the refund.

Regarding the cancellation of reservations in hotels and local accommodation establishments, Article 4 contains some additional provisions.

Thus, this regime does not apply to refundable bookings, in which case the cancellation rules agreed by the parties should apply. Although there is no similar provision for package trips, the *ratio* of this provision also extends to them, so if special rules for cancellation have been stipulated, they should apply. Thus, for instance, if the traveller can cancel the trip up to day X, incurring a penalty of 10%, the cancellation up to day X gives the traveller the right to immediate reimbursement of everything he/she has already paid above that 10%, even if the trip has already been cancelled in the meantime.

Article 4-5 states, in turn, that "rescheduling can only be carried out directly with the hotel or local accommodation establishment". It cannot, therefore,

---

11 In English, on this topic, see Jorge Morais Carvalho and Pedro Policarpo, 'Regulating Airbnb in Portugal' (2018) 6 EuCML 256; Sandra Passinhas, 'Collaborative Economy in Portugal: the case for passenger transport and short-term accommodation' in José Manuel Carril Vázquez, Rafael Garcia Pérez and Marcos López Suárez, *Economía Colaborativa y Derecho: Aspectos Civiles, Mercantiles e Laborales* (Thomas Reuters Aranzadi 2019) 355 ff.

be carried out via the online platform. What happens with the right to issue a voucher? In an *a contrario sensu* interpretation, it seems that this right can be exercised via the online platform. However, this possibility will depend on the contractual relationship between the traveller and the platform.

As the preamble to the law states, "this scheme seeks to strike a balance between the financial sustainability of traders and the rights of consumers which, despite the current context, cannot be removed or eliminated". The rights cannot be removed, but they are reduced, in order to ensure the sustainability of the economic sectors concerned.

Only the most vulnerable consumers – in this case those who are unemployed – are particularly protected.

5. SERVICES OF GENERAL INTEREST

The legal regime of services of general interest is provided, in Portugal, by Law no 23/96 of 26 July 1996, encompassing the following utilities: water, electricity, gas, electronic communications, postal services, wastewater collection, urban solid waste management, and transport services. Since all these services are at the core of human needs and social relations, the legislator dismissed the concept of consumer (defined in Art 2-1 of the Portuguese Consumer Act[12] as "every person that acquires goods or services for purposes which are outside his/her trade, business, craft or profession from someone that is acting for purposes relating to his/her trade, business, craft or profession")[13] and adopted the operative concept of "user", wider in its spectrum, since it allows the inclusion both of legal persons and of natural persons that are acting for purposes related to their trade, business, craft or profession. The stricter concept of consumer plays a residual role in this field, namely in the very contingent aspect of dispute resolution, that is mandatory to professionals only when the acquirers of the service are consumers, and upon their unilateral decision (Art 15).[14]

---

12 Law No. 24/96 of 31 July 1996.

13 Jorge Morais Carvalho, 'O conceito de consumidor no direito português' (2018) 15 Estudos de Direito do Consumidor 185–232; Paulo Duarte, 'O conceito jurídico de consumidor, segundo o artigo 2.º, n.º 1, da Lei de Defesa do Consumidor' (1999) 75 *Boletim da Faculdade de Direito da Universidade de Coimbra*, 649–703; Carlos Ferreira de Almeida, *Direito do Consumo* (Almedina 2005) 29; Teresa Estévez Abeleira, 'Análises de la noción de consumidor en el derecho português desde la perspectiva del derecho español' (2016) 10 Estudos de Direito do Consumidor, 31.

14 See also Article 14 of Law no 24/96. About the unilateral arbitration, see Jorge Morais Carvalho and João Pedro Pinto-Ferreira, 'Reflexão sobre a Arbitragem e a Mediação de Consumo na Lei de Defesa do Consumidor – A Lei n.º 63/2019, de 16 de Agosto' (2020) 13 RIAC 9 ff; Paulo Duarte, 'A Chamada 'Arbitragem Necessária de Litígios de Consumo' no Domínio dos Serviços Públicos Essenciais' in *Estudos de Direito do Consumo – Homenagem a Manuel Cabeçadas Ataíde Ferreira* (DECO 2016) 452 ff. About consumer ADR in Portugal, see

The legal regime of services of general interest is designed as utmost protective to users and quite stringent to professionals. As a general principle, the professional must comply with the diligence required by the provision of these services, and according to a good faith principle. The interests of users must always be taken into consideration. Therefore, Law no 23/96 requires, first, a high level of quality on the provision of those services, according to patterns further consolidated in the many sectoral regulations applicable. During the lockdown period the provision of several services was severely jeopardised. For example, post services had to face an increased number of deliveries, since online transactions were the preferred (and sometimes only) means of contract conclusion, and with respect to water, electricity, gas and communications, traders struggled with urgent repair works.[15] Secondly, traders are in charge of giving clear and adequate information about the provision of the service and the terms of the contract. The right of the users to information was particularly important during the pandemic. The several legislative acts successively enacted and the different responses according to the service at stake, – created a strong need of information and assistance to users. Thirdly, Law no 23/96 impinges upon the execution of the contract. On one hand, Article 5 states that the provision of the service cannot be suspended, except when a qualified delay occurred, and a specific written notice is given to consumers. This notice should specify the reason for the suspension and inform the user about the means available to avoid the suspension of the service (Art 5-2 and 3). The proceeding is thus more stringent to professionals than the one imposed by the general principle *exceptio non adimpleti contractus* set out in Article 428 of the Portuguese Civil Code. On the other hand, Article 10 sets a short prescription period for claims arising from debts related to essential services contracts. As a general rule, the time limit is six months after the provision of the service.

As a consequence of the pandemic crisis, it was foreseeable that many consumers would have difficulties in paying for these services, especially more vulnerable consumers.[16] Law no 7/2020 of 10 April 2020 would, therefore, prohibit

---

Jorge Morais Carvalho, 'Consumer ADR in the European Union and in Portugal as a means of ensuring consumer protection' in Christine Riefa and Séverine Saintier (eds), *Vulnerable Consumers and the Law: Consumer Protection and Access to Justice* (Routledge 2021) 193 ff; João Pedro Pinto-Ferreira and Joana Campos Carvalho, 'Consumer ADR in Portugal' (2018) 2 EuCML 89; Jorge Morais Carvalho, João Pedro Pinto-Ferreira and Joana Campos Carvalho, *Manual de Resolução Alternativa de Litígios de Consumo* (Almedina 2017); Sandra Passinhas, 'Alterações recentes no âmbito da resolução alternativa de litígios de consumo' in Instituto Jurídico da Faculdade de Direito de Coimbra (ed), *O contrato: na gestão do risco e na garantia da equidade* (2015) 357 ff.

15 These factors gave rise to several complaints before the regulatory entity, ANACOM. Further information can be found here: https://bit.ly/2WNThh0 accessed 11 March 2021.

16 Concerning the concept of vulnerability in Portuguese Consumer Law, see Sandra Passinhas, 'O lugar da vulnerabilidade no direito do consumidor português' (2019) 15 Estudos de Direito do Consumidor 257.

the suspension of the provision of water, electricity, gas and communications (Art 4), regardless of the cause thereof. The prohibition was in force during the emergency state (that lasted until 2 May) and for the following month (June 2020). More recently, Law no 18/2020 of 29 May 2020 extended the prohibition until 30 September 2020. According to Article 4-4 and 5, an agreement for payment between the provider and the consumer should be concluded meanwhile, and the payment will be due from November on. However, this agreement for payment was suggested without further explanations or enforcement.[17]

Since Law 18/2020 entered into force, the suspension of a service became subject to stringent requirements. It is not available for all consumers; rather, it requires a situation of unemployment, a diminution of the family income over 20%, or a situation of infection with coronavirus in the family.[18] The rationale of this limitation is not clear. Services of general interest fulfil essential needs of the users; they presuppose a situation of vulnerability that flows from the nature of the service itself. To demand an individual consideration of consumers, and an assessment of their personal situation, might turn into a strong limitation in the number of beneficiaries.[19] Further, the measure seems to be exclusive for individuals, refusing protection to other subjects (users, in the definition of Law 23/96) that might be facing difficulties, as is the case of small businesses.

As regards the prescription period, Law 1-A/2020 of March 19 temporarily suspended the running of the prescriptive period from the 9 March. The suspension lasted until 3 June, a period of 87 days. It must be considered that the temporary suspension of the prescription period encompassed the time limitation period within any legal proceeding that might have initiated or commenced, so professionals have their collecting period of six-month period extended accordingly to Law 1-A/2020 for 87 days. A different solution would lead to an unjust and unacceptable enrichment of users in default.[20]

---

17 The lack of regulation raised problems of coordination with and within sectorial provisions. For example, in the energy sector, the regulatory entity (ERSE) issued, first, Regulation 356-A/2020, of 7 April, on exceptional measures on energy sector. Later, ERSE issued a necessary interpretative note on the coordination of Regulation 356-A/2020 with Law no. 7/2020.

18 Ministerial Ordenance 149/2020, 22 June 2020.

19 The original version of Law no. 7/2020 limited this requirement to consumers of communications services. The distinction of this service from the general regime set for water, electricity and gas provision could also be criticised.

20 Paulo Pimenta, 'Prazos, diligências, processos e procedimentos em época de emergência de saúde pública (DL nº 10-A/2020, de 13 de Março, Lei nº 1-A/2020, de 19 de Março, e Lei nº 4-A/2020, de 6 Abril)' at https://www.direitoemdia.pt/magazine/show/683 accessed 11 March 2021; Teixeira de Sousa/Delgado de Carvalho, 'As medidas excepcionais e temporárias estabelecidas pela L 1-A/2020, de 19/3 (repercussões na jurisdição civil)' at https://blogippc.blogspot.com/2020/03/as-medidas-excepcionais-e-temporarias.html accessed 11 March 2021; José Oliveira Martins, '(Ainda a) Lei n.º 1-A/2020, de 19 de março – uma segunda leitura' Revista Julgar Online, available at http://julgar.pt/ainda-a-lei-n-o-1-a2020-de-19-de-marco-uma-segunda-leitura/ accessed 11 March 2021.

One of the consequences of the pandemic was the temporary suspension of employment (lay off) and unemployment. Many businesses quickly shifted to remote work, where possible, and abandoned operations in an office setting when COVID-19 became a pandemic and the Government required or encouraged people to stay at home. Those circumstances resulted both in difficulties of debtors to comply with their contracts (as discussed above), but also, in several situations, loss of interest in a concluded contract (for example, if the employee was working in a distant city and returning home became possible). In the field of essential services, 24-month binding contracts are common in Portugal so many consumers would have to comply with a service contract that was no longer useful.

Law no 7/2000 would allow a departure from the *pacta sunt servandae* principle to consumers in a situation of unemployment or diminution of family income of over 20% as regards their telecommunications contract. According to Article 4-3, consumers were entitled to unilaterally terminate their communications contract, without payment of any compensation to the provider. Again, it is difficult to understand the limited scope of this provision. Permanence clauses are normally agreed upon between providers and clients, also in the field of electricity and gas. These services might not be necessary in a situation where someone has moved out of their current residence in order to live at the family home instead, whether temporarily or permanently.

Law no 18/2020, of 29 May 2020, introduced slight modifications to this scheme. In general, consumers were entitled to choose between termination or temporary suspension of the telecommunications contract. No penalties or additional charges could result from this temporary suspension, and the contract would be revived from 1 October 2020 on. The legislator refused to broaden the protection's scope to other contracts, which, it must be underlined, results in a shortfall of consumer protection.

As regards the provision of telecommunications service, it should also be emphasised that during the lockdown, the digital platform has evolved into the primary workplace for many, if not most, companies and organisations, e-learning has become regular, and video chatting adopted as the normal means for social interaction. It resulted in increased demand for electronic communications, that was foreseen by Decree-Law no 10-D/2020 of 23 March 2020. It provided that companies that offered public communications networks or publicly available electronic communications should give priority to the continued provision of critical services, namely Voice and Short Message Services (SMS) supported on fixed and mobile networks; uninterrupted access to emergency services; data services supported on fixed and mobile networks; and distribution services of television signals (linear and digital terrestrial). To ensure the continuity of critical services, enterprises offering public communications networks or publicly available electronic communications services were also entitled to take exceptional measures, for example, to establish priorities in the resolution of network failures and disturbances. They were also in charge of network and traffic management, including capacity reservation on the mobile network. The aim of this provision was to ensure the continuity of electronic communication services to priority customers, such as hospitals and security forces, as well as to determine the critical electronic communication services that should be continuously provided to consumers.

6. CREDIT AGREEMENTS

Since the beginning of the pandemic period, credit agreements relating to residential immovable property have been subject to political intervention. The crisis introduced potentially severe social and economic consequences, and, for several families, loans would become increasingly unaffordable, resulting in defaults (and, ultimately, increasing forced sales).

One may say that after implementation of Directive no 2014/17/EU of the European Parliament and of the Council of 4 February 2014 on credit agreements for consumers relating to residential immovable property[21] by Decree-Law no 74-A/2017, of June 23,[22] consumers entering into credit agreements relating to immovable property benefit from a high level of protection as regards the execution of the contract. First, consumers who are in debt of more than one credit to the same financial institution are entitled to choose the debt they want to comply with. This is the so-called *designatio*,[23] where the debtor elects a credit, among several, to be paid, when full compliance is not possible.[24] The *designatio* is foreseen in Article 783 of the Portuguese Civil Code, and Article 26 of Decree-Law 74-A/2017 imposes on creditors a specific duty of information about the consequences of default and a duty of notice to the consumer to declare which debt is to be designated. This is a particularly important instrument, since it allows the consumer, for example, to comply with the credit agreement relating to his/her residential immovable property instead of complying with the obligations deriving from a consumer credit agreement. In the short term, a family home might be more protected from executive proceedings.

Other provisions must also be referred to. First, non-compliance by the consumer does not lead automatically to maturity of all instalments or to

---

21 Implementing European Parliament and Council Directive 2014/17/EU of the 4 February 2014 on credit agreements for consumers relating to residential immovable property – OJ L 60, 28 February 2014, 34–85.

22 For a general overview, Sandra Passinhas, 'O regime jurídico do crédito aos consumidores para imóveis de habitação' (2018) 14 Estudos de Direito do Consumidor 415.

23 In Roman Law: "*Quotiens qui debetur ex pluribus causis unum debitum solvit, est in arbitrio dicere quod potius debitum voluerit solutum; et quod dixerit id erit solutum*" (D.43.6.1).

24 Pires de Lima and Antunes Varela, *Código Civil Anotado*, vol II, (3rd edn, Coimbra Editora 1986) 34–35; Almeida Costa, *Direito das Obrigações* (12th edn, Almedina 2009) 998.

termination of the contract. The minimum requisite is the default of three successive payments. The creditor must allow the payment in an additional period of 30 days and is in charge of a qualified duty of information concerning the effects of non-payment. Only after the three-month default and the additional period of 30 days occur, does maturity of all instalments and termination of the contract become effective. Secondly, the consumer has the right to the revival of the credit agreement relating to residential immovable property until the forced sale of the property. Nevertheless, full compliance of all credits in arrears and existence of no other claims is required.

The first measure adopted to mitigate the adverse systemic impact of COVID-19 was the suspension of executive proceedings over residential immovable property, by Law No 1-A/2020 of 19 March 2020. This provision included credits already in arrears, namely non-performed loans. Although these credits are often transmitted to non-financial entities, Law No 1-A made no distinction according to the qualification of the creditor. The scope of protection was the family residential property, regardless of the type of credit at stake.

Soon after, Decree-Law no 10-J/2020 of 26 March 2020 established further measures aiming at protecting vulnerable families that entered into a credit agreement relating to immovable property.[25] The protection granted by Decree-Law no 10-J/2020 consisted of the deferral of payment of capital and/or interests, without charges for consumers. Consequently, the credit agreement, along with collaterals and other ancillary contracts (e.g. insurance contracts), were automatically extended. To be eligible for this protection, the debtor has to demonstrate the family's vulnerability. In particular, a situation of unemployment, lay off, leave of absence for disease or family care, should exist. For professionals, a substantial reduction of their income should be proven. As of 18 March 2020, debtors should not be in a situation of arrears for more than 90 days or in a situation of foreclosure or insolvency. Compliance by the debtor with responsibilities before the Tax Office and Social Security Office is also required. The requirements are, thus, very strict and the measure showed very limited scope. On one hand, it only protects debtors that faced difficulties after (and due to) the pandemic crisis. Debtors who were already in a situation of non-compliance were excluded from this protection; it should be pointed out, however, that these debtors would then face even more difficulties in the execution and regularisation of the credit agreement. On the other hand, the protection set by Decree-Law 10-J/2020 does not encompass consumer credit agreements. This limited scope of the protective measure was not uncontroversial. It is understandable that the Government was

---

25 Miguel Pestana de Vasconcelos, 'Contratos de crédito bancário e COVID-19. O regime da moratória decorrente do Dec.-Lei 10-J/2020' (2020) Revista de Direito Comercial, available at https://www.revistadedireitocomercial.com/contratos-de-credito-bancario-e-covid-19-o-regime-da-moratoria accessed 11 March 2021.

imposing on financial institutions a *moratoria* in their credit agreements, and that would justify the *de minimis* protection. However, from the point of view of the consumer, the nature of the credit might not be relevant; the difficulties of payment arising from unemployment, lay off or diminution of income would affect the capacity to comply with all credit contracts.

The European Bank Association (EBA) on 12 March 2020 had supported the measures taken and proposed by national governments and EU bodies to address the adverse systemic economic impact of the coronavirus in the form of general *moratoria*. A second statement issued on 25 March 2020 clarified the implications of *moratoria* on the prudential and accounting treatment of the exposures, in particular that generalised payment delays due to legislative initiatives and addressed to all borrowers do not lead to any automatic classification in default, forborne or unlikeliness to pay. The EBA emphasised there should be no flexibility in relation to consumer protection; therefore, it called on all lenders to act in the interest of consumers. It reminded financial institutions to grant such measures in compliance with EU law, such as the Mortgage Credit Directive and the Consumer Credit Directive, in particular concerning the importance of full information disclosure, especially of any potential charges and costs, and the transparency and clarity of terms and conditions. It also noted the importance of careful consideration from a legal and reputational perspective of any new and additional charges specifically introduced in relation to contingency measures, which are ostensibly designed to alleviate the pressure on consumers and businesses, and any cross selling of products to consumers. From a prudential perspective, the acceptance of temporary measures should not automatically lead to negative implications for the consumer's credit rating based on loan reclassification.

Following the EBA Statement, the Portuguese Association of Specialised Credit Institutions (ASFAC) created a private *moratorium*, that all of its members are actually granting to their clients. Not only is the private moratoria set by ASFAC available for the large field of consumer credit it also appears to be more flexible and less stringent to debtors. The Portuguese Association of Banks issued a Protocol, subscribed by eight financial entities, granting a private *moratorium* to debtors of consumer credit. It is also less strict in the provision of evidence concerning the financial situation of debtors and their family. The Portuguese Association of Leasing, Factoring and Renting (ALF) also provided moratoriums to its customers, credit lines, advance payments to suppliers, offers of insurance to volunteers, among other financial measures to support the economy.

Decree-Law no 10-J/2020 was later amended by Decree-Law no 26/2000, of 16 June, which extended both the duration of the moratorium and the protective scope of the measure. As regards the moratorium, it was extended until 31 March 2021. Therefore, until that date, consumers might benefit from the deferral of payment of capital and/or interests, without charges. Further, the credit agreement, collaterals and other ancillary contracts will be automatically extended. As regards the protective scope, the measure now encompasses both mortgage credit and consumer credit agreements for educational or professional training purposes (Art 3-2-b), in order to protect consumers affected by the crisis who face liquidity shortages and difficulties in timely payment of their financial and other commitments.

7. ELECTRONIC PAYMENTS

The Statement on Consumer and Payment Issues in light of COVID-19, issued by EBA on 25 March, encouraged consumers and merchants to take necessary sanitary precautions when providing, or making use of, point-of-sales terminals to pay for goods in-store that required a PIN, including by considering all payment methods available, such as contactless or remote payments. It also called on payment service providers to contribute to measures that limit the spread of COVID-19 and, to that end, to facilitate consumers' ability to make payments without the need for physical contact.

In Portugal, Decree-Law 10-H of 26 March 2020 provided temporary measures concerning electronic payments, that were in force until 30 June 2020: charges with payments by card were suspended and the use of electronic cards could not be refused or limited for payments beyond a certain threshold. The Portuguese banking system, coordinated by the Bank of Portugal, also decided to increase the exemption for strong consumer authentication limit for contactless payments at the point of sale up to the maximum thresholds of EUR 50 per transaction. With regard to contactless payments, it was noticed that after the regulation of March, 20% of consumers adopted this payment method. Taking this into consideration the Bank of Portugal and SIBS (the leading payment services provider in Portugal) agreed to keep the maximum threshold of EUR 50.

One might conclude, in the field of electronic payments, that the pandemic drove innovation in the setting of product intervention. In the electronic payments sector, the crisis offered an opportunity for change, and it received a positive answer from the regulator.[26] The quest for more substantial reforms, namely increasing safety, is, nevertheless, ongoing. Directive (EU) 2015/2366 of the European Parliament and of the Council of 25 November 2015 on payment services in the internal market, implemented in Portugal by Decree-Law 91/2018 of 12 November 2020, set out rules concerning strict security requirements for electronic payments and the protection of consumers' financial

26 Concerning the consideration of consumer interests in financial regulation, see Lisa Kastner, *Civil Society and Financial Regulation* (Routledge 2018) 23 ff.

data, guaranteeing safe authentication and reducing the risk of fraud, as well as the transparency of conditions and information requirements for payment services. However, as empirical evidence reported several cases of fraud in this area[27] the safety issue remains on the policy agenda.

8. SALE OF GOODS

The legislator has also adopted some exceptional provisions on the sale of consumer goods.

Article 18-A of Decree-Law no 10-A/2020 of 13 March 2020 added by Decree-Law no 24-A/2020 of 29 May 2020 has as its heading "extension of the deadlines for the exercise of consumer rights" and establishes that "the deadlines for the exercise of rights [remedies] provided for in Article 5-A of Decree-Law no 67/2003, of 8 April 2020, in its current wording [the Consumer Sales Act, which transposed Directive 1999/44/EC], whose expiration took place between 18 March 2020 and 31 May 2020 are extended until 30 June 2020".

This measure clearly reinforces consumer' rights, aiming to respond to the impossibility or difficulty of contact with the trader during the pandemic period, either by the possible closure of premises or the need for consumer enclosure.

Article 5-A-1 of Decree-Law no 67/2003 establishes time limits (1) to notify the trader of a lack of conformity (two months or one year from the date on which the consumer detected the lack of conformity, depending on whether the goods are movable or immovable, respectively); and (2) for the expiration of the action (two or three years from the date of notification, depending on whether the goods are movable or immovable, respectively).

The extension provided for in Article 18-A of Decree-Law no 10-A/2020 implies that, if the time limit for notification, for instance, expired on 19 April (because the lack of conformity in the movable property was detected on 19 February), the notification can still be made until 30 June. Similarly, if the deadline for filing the suit expires on 19 April (because the complaint was made on the same day in 2018), it is extended until 30 June.

What if the period of the legal guarantee of conformity (or of liability of the seller) – which is not extended by this new legal regime – ends between 18 March and 31 May without the consumer having informed the trader of the lack of conformity? Under Article 5-A-1 of Decree-Law no 67/2003, the remedies

---

27 For risk allocation in this sector, see Mafalda Miranda Barbosa, 'Serviços de pagamento, gestão do risco e responsabilidade civil – algumas reflexões a propósito da nova diretiva dos serviços de pagamento (DSP2)' (2017) Revista de Direito Comercial, available at https://static1.squarespace.com/static/58596f8a29687fe710cf45cd/t/5b03e1191ae6cf47920d32c2/1526980891565/2017-18.pdf 11 March 2021.

would expire on that date, and notification of the lack of conformity would not be possible at a later time. However, an interpretation of Article 18-A of Decree-Law no 10-A/2020 should be made taking into account its teleology, allowing the notification of the lack of conformity to be made after the end of the time limit of the legal guarantee of conformity up to 30 June.

A problem raised by Article 18-A is highlighted here. By providing for the extension of the time limits that ended between 18 March and 31 May until 30 June, the time limits that ended later (between 1 June and 29 June) will actually end on the scheduled date, i.e. earlier than these.

Using an example, let us imagine that consumer A detected the lack of conformity on 20 January, consumer B on 31 March and consumer C on 1 April. Consumers A and B will be able to notify the trader by 30 June, while consumer C, despite having detected the lack of conformity later, can only do so by 1 June.

As it is possible to verify from our earlier discussion, only a few amendments were made in the legislation regarding the sale of goods during the pandemic crisis. An interpretation of the legislation according to the circumstances would probably have been sufficient, but a legislative correction was the chosen solution. This legal regime may raise some problematic issues, which can however be resolved through an interpretation taking into account its objective.

9. SALES

Decree-Law no 20-E/2020 of 12 May 2020 establishes an exceptional and temporary regime motivated by the ongoing pandemic with regard to price-cutting sales.

The problem of price reductions is on the threshold between consumer law and competition law: on the one hand, the objective is to ensure that consumers are aware of prices, guaranteeing that there is an effective difference between the price set before and after the promotion; on the other hand, it intends to defend the regular functioning of the markets.

The matter is regulated in Portugal by Decree-Law no 70/2007 of 26 March 2007.

Article 3 contains an exhaustive list of price-reduction commercial practices: sales (*saldos*), promotions (*promoções*) and liquidation (*liquidação*). Traders may only advertise a price reduction if it consists of one of these practices (Art 3-3) and may not use an expression that does not correspond to the practice used (Art 3-4).

It should be noted that since the price of goods or services can be freely fixed, the trader may at any time make a discount. Contrary to what might be assumed from the wording of the law ("only commercial practices with a price reduction are permitted in the manner referred to in the preceding paragraph"), it is not a question of allowing the practice, but of announcing it to the public.

Thus, if a good costs EUR 20 in a particular shop and, in the following week, the trader puts it on sale for EUR 10, without advertising the discount, it is a price reduction, which is valid and does not have to respect the legal regime in question (with the exception of the few rules that do not depend on the existence of a price reduction, such as Arts 7-2 and 9). What is not allowed is to announce that a discount is granted and not to comply with Decree-Law no 70/2007.

If the concept of promotion (*promoção*) is quite broad, covering any price reduction, regardless of the duration and period of the year, the concept of sales (*saldos*) is more limited.

Decree-Law no 10/2015 of 16 January 2015 has significantly altered the teleology underlying the concept of sales (*saldos*), which are no longer characterised by the fact that they take place at the end of the season, on dates predefined by the law (between 28 December and 28 February and between 15 July and 15 September) and may take place in any period of the year, provided that they do not exceed, in total, four months per year. Decree-Law no 109/2019 of 14 August 2019 went even further, slightly extending the maximum duration of sales (*saldos*), which now corresponds to 124 days per year (Art 10-1). The sales (*saldos*) are currently characterised solely by their objective: accelerated disposal of goods or services (Art 3-1-a).

It is precisely with the aim of helping traders to sell their products that Article 3 of Decree-Law no 20-E/2020 stipulates that "sales [*saldos*] that take place during the months of May and June 2020 are not subject to the maximum limit for sales [*saldos*] of 124 days per year, provided for in Article 10-1 of Decree-Law no 70/2007".

The preamble of the Decree-Law states that it is "imperative to note that commercial premises that have remained closed or whose activity has been suspended have been deprived of the possibility of disposing of their respective products, either directly or through the services provided, now accumulating stocks in the respective inventories, which it is essential to dispose of, not only to allow for the emptying and renovation of products, but also to boost the respective economic activity". The preamble also adds that it is important "to introduce solutions that will allow traders to dispose of their stocks, which will involve, in particular, the provisional modification of the system of price-reduction commercial practices, creating sales or service opportunities for economic operators and new opportunities for consumers to purchase goods and services".

The legal regime recognises that the advertising of sales (*saldos*) is particularly effective (probably in the consumer's subconscious) for the marketing of goods and services, having a more significant effect on the consumer's decision to contract than the advertising of promotions (*promoções*), which would always be accessible to traders under Decree-Law no 70/2007 without the need for any amendment to the legal regime.

It is much more doubtful that simply allowing the commercialisation of goods and services on sale creates "new opportunities" for consumers. The opportunities are already there, and the legal regime only allows the price-reduction to be advertised in a more efficient way for the trader.

Article 4 of Decree-Law no 20-E/2020 also states that "the economic operator that intends to sale during the months of May and June 2020 is exempt from issuing, for this period, the declaration, foreseen in Article 10-5 of Decree-Law no 70/2007 addressed to the Food and Economic Security Authority". The advertising of sales during this period is therefore made a little more flexible.

It is interesting to note that in Spain, the message intended to be conveyed is different regarding promotions made on premises. The second additional provision of Orden SND/399/2020 of 9 May 2020 for the easing of certain national restrictions, established after the declaration of the state of alarm in application of phase 1 of the Plan for the transition to a new normality states that "the traders may not advertise or adopt commercial practices that may have, as an effect, the agglomeration of people on premises or in its neighbourhood. This restriction does not affect sales or promotions in e-commerce".

It is therefore prohibited in Spain, during this period, to advertise promotions or sales on premises. The objective of avoiding agglomeration therefore overlaps with the objective of ensuring the disposal of stocks by traders.

10. CONCLUSION

Policymakers, as demonstrated, have introduced a number of reforms against the expressed preferences of consumers and financial services providers. As regards consumers, their rights were watered down by commitment, mainly, of touristic professionals. As for credit providers new regulations were set and new costs were imposed. Consideration of the pandemic crisis as catalyst for positive change in the market dynamics is, thus, very limited, and, actually, can be concentrated only in electronic payments field.

Periods of crisis have a negative impact on the level of consumer protection, with the emphasis on other objectives, in particular those linked to the functioning of the market and ensuring business safeguards. This aspect reveals the fact that consumer protection rules are a cost for companies, being seen as more positive in times of prosperity, especially by large companies, which have a greater margin for compliance, and as less positive in times of crisis such as the one we are experiencing today. Also, at this time the effect is particularly harmful for large companies. Take the example of air transport and passengers' rights in the event of flight cancellations.

Measures adopted in times of crisis are usually divided in those that reduce the level of consumer protection in general and those that aim to protect particularly vulnerable groups of consumers, who are usually most affected by the crisis.

In recent months we have witnessed precisely the adoption of measures that fall within these two groups. In the first group, we highlight the exceptional schemes concerning the rescheduling of bookings in hotels. In the second group, we can include measures concerning the protection of the user of services of general interest or the borrower of home loans.

DIGITAL PLATFORMS AND COVID-19

Gerhard DANNEMANN, Christoph BUSCH and
Hans SCHULTE-NÖLKE*

The present contribution discusses the impact of the COVID-19 pandemic on the platform economy and in particular on the triangular contractual relationships between online platforms, suppliers and customers. It places this discussion in the

* Gerhard Dannemann, Humboldt University of Berlin and University of Oxford; Christoph Busch, University of Osnabrück; Hans Schulte-Nölke, University of Osnabrück.

context of the ongoing debate about the future of platform regulation, including the Model Rules for Online Platforms which were recently adopted by the European Law Institute. Particular attention is given to "price gauging" for products such as face masks or sanitisers, policies to prioritise essential products on platforms selling goods, and measures undertaken by accommodation platforms to regulate pandemic-related frustration and non-performance of supplier-customer contracts. The contribution explores the legality of adopted measures. It furthermore argues that imposing a general duty of transparency and fairness on platform operators as market-shapers could help platform operators, platform users and courts as guidelines when they have to adapt to unforeseen future developments.

The COVID-19 pandemic is not only a public health emergency, but also a source of unprecedented economic disruption. Digital platforms have been affected by the pandemic in different ways. Some platforms have seen their operations disrupted, as is the case for accommodation platforms such as Airbnb, Homeaway or Booking which suffered from COVID-19 related prohibitions of travel and of providing accommodation. Others have seen a sharp upturn in business, in particular retail platforms such as Amazon and eBay which took over some of the business of high street vendors who ran out of supplies or whose shops were closed due to the pandemic.

Against this background, this contribution explores how platforms have reacted to the current crisis and what this means for the ongoing debate about the future of platform regulation. This also provides an opportunity to test the Model Rules for Online Platforms which were recently adopted by the European Law Institute.[1] The pandemic has triggered a wide range of reactions and policy changes among platforms from measures against price gouging and misleading health claims to the prioritisation of "essential products" and adjustments to cancellation policies for travellers.

This contribution has six sections. In section 1 we will look at how online marketplaces address the widespread problem of price gouging regarding products such as face masks or hand sanitisers. Section 2 takes a closer look at how Amazon changed its shipping policy and decided to prioritise "essential products". Section 3 deals with issues of COVID-19 related frustration and non-performance of contract and compares how different accommodation platforms have reacted to the changed circumstances in which accommodation providers had to operate. Sections 4 and 5 examine whether the presented

[1] ELI Model Rules on Online Platforms https://www.europeanlawinstitute.eu/projects-publications/completed-projects-old/online-platforms/ accessed 23 June 2020. The present authors were co-reporters of this project together with Aneta Wiewiórowska-Domagalska and Fryderyk Zoll; on the project see further Christoph Busch, Gerhard Dannemann, Hans Schulte-Nölke, Aneta Wiewiórowska-Domagalska and Fryderyk Zoll, 'The ELI Model Rules on Online Platforms' (2020) Journal of European Consumer and Market Law 61.

COVID-19 measures taken by platforms are lawful and discuss a general duty of fairness and transparency on platforms, attempting a broader look at what lessons can be learned from how platforms have operated during the pandemic for the future of platform regulation. Section 6 offers "Tentative conclusions".

1. POLICING OF EXCESSIVE PRICES

During the first weeks of the pandemic, there were numerous reports of price gouging on digital platforms, in particular for products such as face masks and hand sanitiser. In some cases, such products were offered with a mark-up of up to 1,000%.[2] In view of such reports, not only sellers, but also online marketplaces came into focus. In March 2020, the Italian Competition Authority launched investigations against Amazon and eBay regarding the marketing of hand sanitiser, face masks and other medical products sold via these two platforms.[3] These two proceedings concern not only cases of price gouging, but also problematic health claims for certain products, an issue which will not be dealt with further in the present contribution.

While marketplace operators do not themselves sell products at extortionate prices, they may profit indirectly from cases of price gouging through the commissions which they charge. In order to avoid the impression that they are profiteers of the pandemic, several digital platforms have taken action to combat price gouging. For example, eBay stated on its website:

> We have a zero-tolerance policy on price gouging on our marketplace to ensure buyers are able to find essential items at reasonable prices. As of May 27, 2020, we have removed or blocked more than 20 million listings that are in violation of our policy related to COVID-19.[4]

However, the platforms' approach to price gouging has attracted criticism from various sides. While consumer organisations criticise that platform operators do not do enough against excessive prices, traders who sell their products on Amazon complain that the platform's fight against price gouging has resulted in excessive action, taking down legitimate and reasonably priced offers. According

---

2 Hannah Walsh, 'eBay and Amazon failing to prevent sellers profiteering during coronavirus crisis' (25 March 2020) https://www.which.co.uk/news/2020/03/online-marketplaces-coronavirus-update-ebay-and-amazon accessed 20 June 2020.

3 Autorità garante della concorrenza e del mercato, 'The Authority begins investigating Amazon and eBay for misleading claims and excessive price increases' (Press release, 12 March 2020) https://en.agcm.it/en/media/press-releases/2020/3/PS11716-PS11717 accessed 20 June 2020.

4 EBay, 'We are Actively Removing Price Gouging, Prohibited Items from eBay's Marketplace', https://www.ebayinc.com/stories/news/we-are-actively-removing-price-gouging-prohibited-items-from-ebays-marketplace accessed 20 June 2020.

to press reports, Amazon mistakenly suspended many seller accounts because a rather banal error was made in the algorithmic verification of the sales prices.[5] Apparently, the system treated an e.g. French or German comma, which separates the full euro amount from the cent figures, as an English comma, which would help the reader to identify groups of three noughts (as in 1,000,000 for 1 million). Therefore, the system misread a price of "10,00 EUR" as 1000 EUR and triggered an automatic "maximum price error" which may lead to an account suspension.

Sellers who offer products at excessive prices risk violating national bans on price gouging. In addition, offering goods at extortionate prices could also violate the Unfair Commercial Practices Directive (2005/29/EC). This directive does not contain any specific regulation on excessive pricing. However, such conduct could possibly fall under the general clause stipulated in Article 5(2) of Directive 2005/29/EC, if one assumes that price gouging is contrary to the requirements of professional diligence and likely to materially distort the economic behaviour of the average consumer.[6]

Platform operators will be shielded in most cases by the liability exemption for host providers under Article 14 of the E-Commerce Directive (2000/31/EC) as long as they do not have actual knowledge of the illegal activity. In addition, Article 15(1) of Directive 2000/31/EC specifies that "Member States shall not impose a general obligation on providers [...] to monitor the information which they transmit". Thus, as a general rule, platform operators will only be obliged to take action if they have been notified about individual cases of price gouging.

From a policy perspective, it is questionable whether such a platform-friendly solution is appropriate. While policing trademark infringements or fighting hate speech on digital platforms involves intricate legal and factual evaluations, identifying usurious prices for hand sanitisers is relatively simple and easy to automate. One of the lessons which could be learned from the COVID-19 pandemic would be to include in the prospective EU Digital Services Act a provision which establishes a duty of care of digital platforms to take action against obvious cases of price gouging.

The automated enforcement of anti-price-gouging rules will inevitably lead to algorithmic errors (both false negatives and false positives). Therefore, it must be ensured that platform users whose accounts are wrongly blocked have an effective right of appeal against the platform operators. The mandatory rules for complaint handling mechanisms stipulated by the P2B Regulation (EU) 2019/1150, which will be applicable from 12 July 2020, are a first step in this direction.

---

5 Michael Gassmann, 'Amazons Komma-Problem bringt deutsche Händler in Bedrängnis' (15 May 2020) https://www.welt.de/wirtschaft/article208012899/E-Commerce-Amazons-folgenschwerer-Kommafehler.html accessed 20 June 2020.

6 Christine Riefa, 'Coronavirus as a Catalyst to Transform Consumer Policy and Enforcement' (2020) Journal of Consumer Policy https://doi.org/10.1007/s10603-020-09462-0 accessed 20 June 2020.

2. PRIORITISATION OF ESSENTIAL PRODUCTS

2.1. AMAZON'S NEW SHIPPING POLICY

During the early weeks of the COVID-19 crisis, online retailers and digital marketplaces were overwhelmed by a surge in demand, in particular for household staples and medical supplies such as face masks, because of product shortages at physical stores.[7] The situation was aggravated when bricks-and-mortar shops had to close during the lockdown. Fulfilment centres had difficulties coping with the sudden surge in demand. At the same time, enhanced cleaning and social distancing measures had to be implemented at warehouses, which further complicated matters. Some online retailers reacted by making next-day delivery unavailable in some regions or by imposing quantity limits on specific items.[8] In March 2020, Amazon announced plans to hire an additional 100,000 employees in the United States as a reaction to the surge in demand and the new logistics challenges.[9]

In a further bid to ease the pressure on its fulfilment centres, Amazon took the decision to change its shipping policy and announced that it would "temporarily prioritise" essential items as of 17 March 2020.[10] In practical terms, this meant that Amazon would stop the intake of "non-essential" items at its fulfilment centres. As a result of this policy change, only products considered "essential" were eligible for shipping via Amazon's fulfilment service. According to Amazon, the category of "essential products" included items such as medical supplies, household staples, beauty products, groceries and pet supplies.[11]

Under the new shipping policy, third-party sellers were still able to sell products falling outside these categories. But they were no longer able to use "Fulfilled by Amazon" (FBA), a service that allows sellers to ship their products

---

7 Greg Bensinger, 'We Need Amazon During the Coronavirus. That's a Problem' *New York Times* (New York, 31 March 2020) https://www.nytimes.com/2020/03/31/opinion/covid-delivery-amazon.html accessed 20 June 2020.

8 James F. Peltz and Emmanuel Morgan, 'Amazon taught us to rely on fast delivery. In the coronavirus era, it can't keep up' *Los Angeles Times* (Los Angeles, 18 March 2020) https://www.latimes.com/business/story/2020-03-18/amazon-delivery-coronavirus accessed 20 June 2020.

9 Dana Mattioli, 'Amazon to Hire 100,000 Warehouse and Delivery Workers Amid Coronavirus Shutdowns' *Wall Street Journal* (New York, 17 March 2020) https://www.wsj.com/articles/amazon-to-hire-100-000-warehouse-and-delivery-workers-amid-coronavirus-shutdowns-11584387833 accessed 16 June 2020.

10 Karen Weise, 'To Focus on Necessities, Amazon Stops Accepting Some Items in Warehouses' *New York Times* (New York, 17 March 2020) https://www.nytimes.com/2020/03/17/technology/amazon-coronavirus.html accessed 20 June 2020.

11 Krystal Hu and Jeffrey Dastin, 'Amazon warehouses receive only vital supplies in U.S., Europe amid coronavirus' *Reuters* (London, 17 March 2020) https://www.reuters.com/article/us-health-coronavirus-amazon-com-exclusi/exclusive-amazon-warehouses-receive-only-vital-supplies-in-u-s-europe-amid-coronavirus-idUSKBN2142IM accessed 20 June 2020.

to their customers via an Amazon warehouse. For non-essential products, third-party sellers on Amazon were thus limited to the "Fulfilled by Merchant" (FBM) scheme, which requires sellers to manage their inventory themselves and to ship their own orders. However, for many third-party sellers this was not a viable option. In particular, for one-person businesses or "solopreneurs" whose business model relies on Amazon's shipment service, switching from FBA to FBM was not possible, as they were lacking the necessary logistics capacity. For the same reason, switching to selling their products through other platforms that do not offer fulfilment services was also not an option.

In mid-April, Amazon again changed its shipping policy and announced that it would resume accepting shipments of non-essential products to their fulfilment centres.[12] However, in order to allow Amazon to continue prioritising certain product categories, the intake of products would still be limited by quantity on an item-by-item basis.

From a legal perspective, the question arises as to whether the prioritisation of "essential products" is permissible. In particular, the differentiated treatment of different platform users could be problematic from a competition law perspective (see section 2.2). Furthermore, Amazon's approach may also conflict with the fairness rules of the new P2B Regulation (see section 2.3).

2.2. DIFFERENTIATED TREATMENT UNDER ARTICLE 102(C) TFEU

According to Article 102(c) TFEU, the application of "dissimilar conditions to equivalent transactions with other trading parties" can amount to an abuse of dominance, if it places the other parties at a competitive disadvantage. The application of this provision presupposes that Amazon is found to be dominant on the relevant market in geographic and product terms. This will depend, in particular, on the extent to which other platform operators such as eBay, AliExpress or other online marketplaces compete with Amazon. The answer to this question is likely to be different for different EU Member States.

In those Member States where Amazon is found to be dominant, the key question will be whether its conduct can be considered an abuse of dominance. First of all, it should be emphasised that not every unequal treatment of platform users is objectionable from a competition law perspective. Second, Amazon's prioritisation policy, is not an "outright" form for self-preferencing unlike other types of behaviour by online platforms that have been under investigation

12 Dana Mattioli, 'Amazon to Expand Shipments of Nonessential Items, Continue Adding Staff' *Wall Street Journal* (New York, 13 April 2020) https://www.wsj.com/articles/amazon-seeks-to-hire-another-75-000-workers-11586789365 accessed 20 June 2020.

by the European Commission[13] and by national competition authorities.[14] Defining the legal boundaries for a differentiated treatment of the type that is here at issue is difficult.[15] Several interrelated questions arise in this context. Does Amazon's conduct qualify as differentiation of "equivalent transactions"? Which categories of products can be considered "equivalent"? Are scarves and neck tubes equivalent to face masks? These are tricky questions which have to be assessed on an item-by-item basis.

What is problematic in this context, is that Amazon decides whether an item falls into the "essential product" category and is not willing to argue about its decision: "We determine if a product is a household staple, a medical supply or both based upon the listing. At this time, we are not accepting requests to re-classify listings."[16] Amazon locuta, causa finita?

Finally, it has to be determined whether there is an objective justification for the differentiated treatment of different product categories. Here, too, one can have very different views. On the one hand, one could argue that Amazon's change of shipping policy is justified as it helps to ensure vital supplies in times of crisis.[17] On the other hand, one could explain Amazon's decision as an attempt to keep its customers satisfied in times of limited shipping capacity. While the first reading of Amazon's behaviour is more benevolent, the latter would indicate a less altruistic motive.

2.3. FAIRNESS AND TRANSPARENCY RULES UNDER THE P2B REGULATION (EU) 2019/1150

Legal limits for a prioritisation of "essential products" could in future also result from the P2B Regulation (EU) 2019/1150 which aims at promoting fairness and

---

13 See, e.g. Case AT.39740 Google Search (Shopping), 27 June 2017; see also European Commission, 'Antitrust: Commission opens investigation into possible anti- competitive conduct of Amazon' (Press release, 17 July 2019) http://europa.eu/rapid/press-re lease_IP-19-4291_en.htm accessed 20 June 2020.

14 See, e.g. Italian Competition Authority, 'A528 – Amazon: investigation launched on possible abuse of a dominant position in online marketplaces and logistic services' (Press release, 16 April 2019) https://en.agcm.it/en/media/press-releases/2019/4/Amazon-investigation-launched-on-possible-abuse-of-a-dominant-position-in-online-marketplaces-and-logistic-services accessed 20 June 2020.

15 For a more detailed analysis see Inge Graef, 'Differentiated Treatment in Platform-to-Business Relations: EU Competition Law and Economic Dependence' (2019) 38 Yearbook of European Law 448.

16 Amazon Sellercentral Europe, 'Temporarily prioritizing products coming into our fulfillment centers' https://sellercentral.amazon.de/gp/help/external/help.html?itemID=F37V7QBB8WSVF43&language=en_ES&ref=efph_F37V7QBB8WSVF43_relt_200917490 accessed 19 June 2020.

17 This is the view expressed in a message by Amazon CEO and founder Jeff Bezos from 21 March 2020: "We're providing a vital service to people everywhere, especially to those,

transparency for business users of online intermediary platforms. The regulation, which is applicable from 12 July 2020, is essentially limited to setting transparency requirements for online platforms.[18] While Article 8 P2B Regulation emphasises that the contractual relationships between platform operators and platform users should be "conducted in good faith and based on fair dealing", the P2B Regulation falls short of providing for a general fairness test against which a decision to prioritise essential products could be measured.[19] Nor does the P2B Regulation contain a general prohibition of differentiated treatment by platform operators. Article 7 P2B Regulation only contains a transparency rule for self-preferencing by vertically integrated platforms, which most probably would not cover the type of shipping policy change made by Amazon in March 2020.

However, Amazon's decision to prioritise essential products could run into conflict with Article 4 P2B Regulation. The provision formulates requirements for the case that a platform operator decides to restrict or suspend the provision of its online intermediation services to a given business user in relation to individual goods or services offered by that business user. Article 4(1) P2B Regulation requires the platform operator to provide the business user concerned, prior to or at the time of the restriction or suspension taking effect, with a statement of reasons for that decision on a durable medium. More importantly, under Article 4(3) P2B Regulation, the platform operator must give the business user the opportunity to clarify the facts and circumstances in the framework of an internal complaint-handling process as required under Article 11 P2B Regulation. Amazon's statement that they "are not accepting requests to re-classify listings", would in all likelihood run afoul of this provision.

3. PLATFORM MEASURES TO REGULATE PANDEMIC-RELATED FRUSTRATION AND NON-PERFORMANCE OF CONTRACT

The COVID-19 pandemic has given rise to very different legal questions for those platforms whose business was severely disrupted by the pandemic. This disruption of platform activities will frequently have been felt most severely in supplier-customer contracts. The performance of these contracts may

like the elderly, who are most vulnerable." https://blog.aboutamazon.com/company-news/a-message-from-our-ceo-and-founder accessed 20 June 2020.

18 For an overview see Christoph Busch, 'Towards Fairness and Transparency in the Platform Economy? A First Look at the P2B Regulation' in Alberto De Franceschi and Reiner Schulze (eds) *Digital Revolution – New Challenges for Law* (Beck and Nomos 2019), 57.

19 Christoph Busch, 'Towards Fairness and Transparency in the Platform Economy? A First Look at the P2B Regulation' in Alberto De Franceschi and Reiner Schulze (eds) *Digital Revolution – New Challenges for Law* (Beck and Nomos 2019) 61–63.

have become impossible or the purpose of the contract frustrated due to the COVID-19 pandemic.

Contract laws can deal with situations such as these under the doctrines of impossibility, frustration, basis of transaction (*Wegfall der Geschäftsgrundlage*), *force majeure* or *clausula rebus sic stantibus*.[20] Contracts may contain provisions on extenuating circumstances which may apply to the COVID-19 pandemic. National legislators may furthermore have enacted rules which deal specifically with the allocation of contractual risks and liabilities due to the COVID-19 outbreak.

Online platforms where customers can book accommodation are particularly affected by COVID-19 cancellations and can provide an interesting case study for pandemic-related frustration and non-performance of contract. The accommodation contract itself may be affected by illegality if COVID-19 legislation prohibits the renting of hotel rooms, holiday flats or other accommodation as part of legislative containment and distancing measures. Similarly, travellers may be prohibited from leaving their country of residence, or from entering the country or region of their chosen destination. Or they may be unable to travel long-distance because all flights have been cancelled. There may also be cases of frustration of purpose, for example if the accommodation was booked for guests at a wedding ceremony which was subsequently prohibited or cancelled by the person who was to officiate. The legal consequences may differ between different legal systems, and also depend on further circumstances.

As a general trend, though, illegality of the performance will render the contract unenforceable or void, and payments made under such a contract can be claimed back, so that the loss falls mainly on the accommodation provider. On the other hand, the risk whether a traveller will be able to use accommodation for the intended purpose is likely to lie with the traveller, as would frequently be the risk of being able to obtain immigration clearance and travel.

We have compared the cancellation policies of three major accommodation platforms, namely Airbnb, Booking and Homeaway.[21] It is interesting to note how differences between how these platforms operate shape their COVID-19 cancellation policies. Airbnb goes furthest in determining the contractual relationship between the supplier and the customer by submitting these contracts to Airbnb's own standard terms. These contain detailed provisions on extenuating circumstances which in some situations allow an accommodation

---

20 See, e.g. Hein Kötz, *European Contract Law* (Gill Mertens and Tony Weir tr, 2nd edn, OUP 2017) ch 15. The DCFR contains a provision on impediments which are beyond the debtor's control (Art III.-3:104) which relieves the debtor of liability. Article III.-1:110 on "Variation or termination by court on a change of circumstances" deals with the situation where performance has become more onerous due to the changed circumstances.

21 Booking.com has published guidance which apparently applies worldwide. Policies for Airbnb and Homeaway may vary from country to country; as examples, we have chosen the policies published on these companies' UK websites.

provider or a traveller to cancel the contract even after a contractually stipulated cancellation period, or the period for a consumer withdrawal right has expired. Such extenuating circumstances under Airbnb's general standard terms include:[22]

> **Unexpected serious illness or injury** affecting a host or member of the travelling party. …
>
> **Transportation disruptions** that make it impossible to travel to your destination, including road closures and flight cancellations where there are no alternative methods of travel. …
>
> **Train, bus, or ferry cancellations** where no alternate trips were available on the same day. …
>
> **Epidemic disease or illness** that suddenly affects a region or an entire group of people. … Any updates to our policy regarding the outbreak of a disease, and the scope of policy application, will be determined based on announcements by the World Health Organization and local authorities.
>
> **Travel restrictions** imposed by a government, law enforcement agency, or military that restrict travel to or from the listing or experience location. …
>
> **Changes to visa or passport requirements** that make it impossible to travel to the destination. This doesn't include lost or expired travel documents.

Furthermore, Airbnb has issued specific COVID-19 policies.[23] These establish a cut-off point: only bookings made on or before 14 March 2020 for stays between 14 March and 15 July 2020 could be cancelled freely due to the pandemic. And while Airbnb leaves the extenuating circumstances rules otherwise unaffected for hosts, restrictions are imposed on guests. The 15 March version of Airbnb's COVID-19 policy stated that bookings made on or after 15 March "will not be covered under our extenuating circumstances policy except where the guest or host has contracted COVID-19".

From 30 March onwards, Airbnb imposed further, and apparently retroactive restrictions.[24] Such bookings:

> will not be covered under our extenuating circumstances policy, except where the guest or host is currently sick with COVID-19. COVID-19-related circumstances

---

22 https://www.airbnb.co.uk/help/article/1320/what-if-i-need-to-cancel-because-of-an-emergency-or-unavoidable-circumstance accessed 19 June 2020.

23 https://www.airbnb.co.uk/help/article/2701/extenuating-circumstances-policy-and-the-coronavirus-covid19 accessed 9 June 2020. These could be understood as "updated to our policies" on epidemic illnesses, but also seek to cover travel restrictions.

24 http://web.archive.org/web/20200323180243/https://www.airbnb.co.uk/help/article/2701/extenuating-circumstances-policy-and-the-coronavirus-covid19; https://www.airbnb.co.uk/help/article/2701/extenuating-circumstances-policy-and-the-coronavirus-covid19 accessed 9 June 2020.

> not covered include: transport disruptions and cancellations; travel advisories and restrictions; health advisories and quarantines; changes to applicable law; and other government mandates such as evacuation orders, border closures, prohibitions on short-term rentals, and lockdown requirements.

For these restrictions, Airbnb gives the following reasons:

> Our extenuating circumstances policy is intended to protect guests and hosts from unforeseen circumstances that arise after booking. After the declaration of COVID-19 as a global pandemic by the World Health Organization, the extenuating circumstances policy no longer applies because COVID-19 and its consequences are no longer unforeseen or unexpected.

It is interesting to note in contrast that Airbnb's standard terms on extenuating circumstances use "unforeseeable" or "unexpected" only in connection with "property damage, maintenance, and amenity issues" and "serious illness or injury", but not with epidemic illnesses or travel restrictions.

Several questions arise in this context. The first, perhaps minor question relates to the retroactive restrictions imposed on 30 March for bookings made between on or after 15 March, namely that a guest or host need to be "currently sick" with COVID-19 rather than having "contracted" COVID-19, and possibly also through adding a list of reasons which do not entitle to cancel.

The second, more important question is whether national law rules on extenuating circumstances can be restricted through Airbnb's standard terms in this way, thus placing the risk on the traveller (who often will be a consumer) that performance becomes impossible in particular because temporary bans on providing accommodation have been extended or reinstalled. Hosts, who would often have to return payments under the various doctrines dealing with extenuating circumstances, are thus allowed to shift the risk that their performance has become illegal onto the guests.

As Airbnb has taken on the role of regulator for the effect of COVID-19 on supplier-customer contracts, parties may also place reliance on these policies being legally effective. Will such reliance on Airbnb's policy statements protect a platform user even if a court finds later that Airbnb's representations do not conform with the law? Will compromises concluded between suppliers and customers in the assumption that Airbnb's statements were correct be affected by error of law? Either situation could lead to Airbnb becoming liable under its contracts with platform users for having provided rules which are subsequently rejected by the courts. (Airbnb might seek to defend such claims by asserting that their "cancellation policies" were intended to take effect only in Airbnb's own contractual relationships with hosts and guests but not in the supplier-customer contract, but that is not the impression which a typical user would obtain from reading these policies.) Courts may also uphold Airbnb's COVID-19 policies (and be it as "authentic interpretation" of its extenuating policy rules), which would reinforce the platform's role as regulator of supplier-customer contracts.

At any rate, Airbnb's COVID-19 policies show how intensively the platform-supplier contract and the platform-customer contract can interact with the supplier-customer contract, with the platform taking on the role of a regulator.

The risk of becoming liable for questionable legal statements or for any other interference in the supplier-customer contract is something which the accommodation platform Booking is apparently keen to avoid. This platform issues no guidance but limits itself essentially to the advice that its platform users should check themselves for applicable domestic laws on whether booked accommodation may still be provided, and to check their supplier-customer contracts for the legal consequences.[25]

Yet another approach is taken by Homeaway. Like Booking, Homeaway does not attempt to regulate the supplier-customer contract through its own standard terms. For dealing with COVID-19 related cancellations, Homeaway has instead adopted a nudging policy for facilitating cancellations by travellers, but also by accommodation providers irrespective of whether either party has a right to cancel the contract. Guests wishing to cancel the contract are advised to contact their host. Hosts are allowed to cancel a contract with "COVID-19" as a reason without negative effects on their ranking in search results, which would otherwise dip by any cancellation effectuated by a host. Hosts are also advised to offer guests wishing to cancel the contract due to COVID-19 at least a reimbursement of 50%, better of 100% of the contract price, or to move the dates of the booking, or to offer a voucher type solution whereby payments made under the cancelled booking will be counted towards a new booking made within the next year.

The nudging effect on hosts is reinforced by using the host's response as a criterion for ranking the host's accommodation on the Homeaway website. Hosts who move the booking or who allow cancellation and a full refund, or a full voucher, receive the equivalent of a five-star review for the purpose of ranking. Hosts who do not comply with Homeaways's recommendations will receive the equivalent of a one-star review for the purpose of ranking.

While this is fairly ingenious, questions arise as to the transparency of this procedure, which apparently is disclosed neither to guests nor to potential travellers browsing through Homeaway's website. That would be a violation of the transparency requirement under Article 4 para (1) ELI Model Rules. Homeaway's policies may also give the impression to hosts that they have the

25 "Cancellation due to Coronavirus is dependent on several factors, including where you're travelling to, your country of origin, your arrival date, and your reason for travelling. Individual reservation policies are set by the property you've booked. As such, it would not be appropriate to make a universal change to our policy." https://www.booking.com/covid-19.en-gb.html accessed 5 June 2020.

right to insist on payment even where performance of the contract has become legally impossible. Similarly, cut-off dates set in Homeaways's COVID-19 policies (bookings made by 13 March for stays between 13 March and 30 June 2020) may generate the impression in hosts and guests alike that these are legally relevant.[26]

We can also note that neither Airbnb's regulation model nor Homeaway's nudging model take into account whether any particular risk which has materialised due to the COVID-19 pandemic would normally, as a matter of law (background law or mandatory provisions), fall on the guest or on the host.

All three models adopted by these three major accommodation platforms – regulation, nudging, non-interference – are per se compatible with the ELI Model Rules. These do not encourage, prohibit, or regulate the platform's interference with the supplier-customer contract, except that the platform may become liable under Article 20 for non-performance of the supplier-customer contract in cases where the customer can reasonably rely on the platform's predominant influence. Our present view is that this is still the preferable solution.

4. ARE THE COVID-19 MEASURES TAKEN BY PLATFORMS LAWFUL?

The following presents some preliminary considerations on the general obligations of platforms and the legality of COVID-19 measures based on the examples which were explained above. Perhaps the most difficult questions concern the extent to which platforms are within their entrepreneurial rights when interfering with the supplier-customer relationship through COVID-19 measures, and which criteria could be applied to assess the legality of such measures. A basis for these considerations could be the working hypothesis that the law of platforms evolves towards a general duty of fairness and transparency towards platform users, which the courts can develop by carefully extending individual provisions of the existing law and by crystallising these into certain specific obligations.

4.1. PLATFORMS INTERFERING WITH THE SUPPLIER-CUSTOMER RELATIONSHIP

It is a common feature of the above examples that COVID-19 related measures taken by platforms interfere, to different degrees, with the supplier-customer relationship. Platforms can be observed as remotely controlling the

26 https://www.homeaway.co.uk/discoveryhub/tips-and-resources/improve-performance/covid-19-emergency-policy accessed 5 June 2020.

supplier-customer relationship from the pre-contractual phase onwards.[27] This can occur via the platform's own standard terms, which may more or less force the supplier and the customer to adopt specific terms which regulate their relationship. Platforms have many ways of providing incentives to either party to a supplier-customer contract to behave in a certain way. Platforms which process payments have what may be the most powerful instrument, namely, to allocate a payment, either by allowing a supplier to keep the customer's payment, or by refunding the payment to the customer even against the will of the supplier.[28]

In some cases, platform policies on cancellation of, for example accommodation contracts may deprive suppliers or customers of rights that they are actually entitled to under the contract between those two parties. When platforms prioritise certain products or services, this disadvantages products or services offered by other suppliers and may also disadvantage customers who would like to order the non-prioritised products or services. And platform policies against price gouging may inadvertently prevent suppliers from charging what in fact is a reasonable price.

Can affected suppliers or customers demand the platform to refrain from such measures or claim compensation? That depends, *inter alia*, on whether the platform has, by taking the measure in question, violated its duties towards these users.

4.2. POSSIBLE LEGAL OBLIGATIONS INFRINGED BY COVID-19 MEASURES OF PLATFORMS

Several of the provisions against which the COVID-19 measures of platforms have to be measured have already been addressed in connection with the above examples. If one summarises those that may be of particular importance for the establishment of obligations of platforms towards their users, the result is a rather short list. The most important source of obligations of platforms are the contracts which the platform operator concluded with its users when they created their account. Each of these contracts is primarily governed by one applicable national law. In practice, the most important question will frequently be whether the general terms and conditions of the platform are valid and effective. Within the EU, if the user is a consumer, the Consumer Rights Directive 2011/83

27 See also Christoph Busch, 'Self-regulation and regulatory intermediation in the platform economy' in Marta Cantero Gamito and Hans-W. Micklitz (eds), *The Role of the EU in Transnational Legal Ordering: Standards, Contracts and Codes* (Elgar 2020) 115 at 117–118 (with further examples of remote controlling of contracts by digital platforms).

28 Cf BGH (German Federal Supreme Court) 1 April 2020, Case VIII ZR 18/19 (regarding Amazon's A-to-Z Guarantee) and 22 November 2017, Case VIII ZR 83/16 (regarding PayPal's Buyer Protection).

and the Directive on Unfair Terms in Consumer Contracts Directive 93/13 will apply.

Further obligations of platform operators may arise from unfair commercial practices law, which is also – at least partially – shaped by EU-law, in particular Directive 2005/29 on unfair business-to-consumer commercial practices. Moreover, the P2B-Regulation 2019/1150 on promoting fairness and transparency for business users of online intermediation services lays out several obligations of platforms. Further legal obligations of platforms result from competition law and public law, including data protection law, which will not be dealt with here.

It is clear that the existing EU law displays a rather patchy image. As we have seen, there is presently no express rule in EU law that places platforms under a general obligation to act fairly towards its users or which would have imposed a general principle of good faith and fair dealing.[29] At the current state of EU law, the Member States might close the gaps in this fragmentary field of EU law and implement more general duties of platforms.[30] Some have already done so. Readers may know that French law provides for a general obligation de loyauté, which, on a closer look, primarily results in an obligation to provide information.[31] Under German law, general duties of platforms could possibly be developed by the courts through interpretation of general principles such as good faith, in particular by setting aside unfair terms in the standard terms of platforms.[32]

Looking more closely at a platform's legal obligations towards its users, the list becomes more multifaceted. The above-mentioned ELI Model Rules on Online Platforms can give an impression of the duties which platforms may have. These ELI Model rules, of course, do not represent the existing law, but they combine elements that can actually be found within EU law and certain national legal systems and can thus give an indication for a fuller set of duties which platforms may have towards their users.

According to the ELI Model Rules, platforms have many information duties as well as a duty to comply with the requirements of professional diligence regarding reputation systems.[33] Moreover, platforms may have, to a limited

---

29 See, e.g. Paolo Siciliani, Christine Riefa and Harriet Gamper, *Consumer theories of harm – An economic approach to consumer law enforcement and policy making* (Hart 2019) 9, who argue that "a general duty to trade fairly" still needs to be developed.

30 See Friso Bostoen, 'Neutrality, fairness or freedom? Principles for platform regulation' (2018) 7(1) Internet Policy Review.

31 Cf Article L. 111-7 II *Code de la consommation* as amended by *Loi* no 2016-1321, Article 49; Judith Rochfeld and Zolynski, 'La "loyauté" des "platefomes". Quelles plateformes? Quelle loyauté?' (2016) Dalloz IP/IT, 520.

32 §242 BGB contains the general principle of good faith and fair dealing, whereas §307 BGB subjects standard terms to a general good faith based control.

33 See in particular Articles 3–6, 13–15 ELI Model Rules on Online Platforms for information duties and Articles 5(2) and 6 for standards of professional diligence in reputation systems.

extent, a duty to protect their users, in particular against other users.[34] Platforms also have to react if they obtain knowledge that misleading information has been placed on the platform by one of its users.[35] To the extent that platforms have such duties, part of the sanctions can be a liability for damages.[36]

4.3. POLICIES OF PLATFORMS IN THE COVID-19 CRISIS

When examining the legality of the COVID-19 measures taken by platforms, one must take into account the purposes of these measures. As the examples show, platforms have their own, often rather individual policies with their own purposes. Platforms are certainly concerned with protection against infections, be it that of their own employees or delivery services, their customers or the general public. The prioritisation of certain goods and services can serve, among other things, to ensure that the population is supplied with goods that are particularly important during the pandemic given that the bricks-and-mortar shops are closed. However, COVID-19 related measures can also have multiple purposes, including predominantly self-serving purposes of platforms such as increasing customer satisfaction, winning new customers and maximising sales and profits in times of limited shipping capacity.

If a platform takes measures to regulate potential disputes between its users, such measures can also serve rather different purposes.[37] The platform may have the goal of acting as an honest broker who helps users to find a fair and uncomplicated solution. However, the platform may also be driven by its desire to bind one of its user groups, for example the tenants of short-term accommodation, and may thus implement biased solutions in favour of this user group which are to the disadvantage of the landlords. Alternatively, they may shift the risk of future disruptions caused by the pandemic onto the customer. It goes without saying that the choices and values that underlie the platforms' policies are, at least, not necessarily committed to the common good, but they may also serve the – often legitimate – goals of the platform operator.[38]

It is important to note that these policies are usually not enforced by way of individual human decisions. Normally, the platform operator will just use an algorithm which imposes decisions in individual cases. Quite generally, platforms operate in such a way that the imposition and enforcement of

---

34 See in particular Article 8 ELI Model Rules on Online Platforms.

35 Article 9 ELI Model Rules on Online Platforms.

36 Article 24 ELI Model Rules on Online Platforms.

37 For a detailed analysis see Rory Van Loo, 'Federal Rules of Platform Procedure' (2020 forthcoming), The University of Chicago Law Review.

38 José van Dijck, Thomas Poell and Martijn de Waal, *The Platform Society: Public Values in a Connective World* (OUP 2018) 4.

legal obligations only makes sense if they are formulated in a way that can be translated into algorithms.

This leads to the more general question of what legal systems can and should do to shape and control the policies and measures which platforms have adopted in response to the pandemic. Regulating contractual relationships and enforcing rules and values in the electronic environment of, often globally operating, platforms is not a new task for the law. However, in a crisis, the nature of this task may change, and the situation may call for a new appreciation as to how principles and rules are to be applied, and how these may be enforced.

4.4. FUNCTIONS OF PLATFORMS IN THE COVID-19 CRISIS

When evaluating how the law regulates the operations of platforms during and subsequent to the pandemic one needs to consider the specific functions which platforms have assumed in the COVID-19 crisis. It became apparent that platforms, at least many of them, have advanced to being critical infrastructure and have provided a fairly pandemic-resistant market infrastructure at times when local shops had to close.[39] Platforms may also help to fight the pandemic and its consequences by supplying necessary goods and taking specific COVID-19 measures for avoiding infections. One could even assume that the long closure of almost all bricks-and-mortar shops except for those who were selling food, toiletries or pharmaceutical products was only possible because the platform economy was prepared to close the emerging supply gaps without a significant risk of infection.

In order to be able to perform their infrastructural function in the pandemic, platforms must have a certain range of action, which may in some cases even extend to intervening in the legal relationship between suppliers and customers. This may be supported by a proportionality test. The greater the crisis and the more necessary the proposed measures to maintain supply or to combat infections, the more platforms may be allowed to take measures that interfere with the contractual rights of their users. This could in particular apply to the measures adopted to prioritise the delivery of essential goods. On the other hand, it is rather doubtful whether the extraordinary circumstances of the COVID-19 pandemic justify a platform's interference with the contract between an accommodation provider and a traveller which seeks to regulate the rights and obligations without regard to the law which applies to this relationship.

---

39 On Amazon see for example: Wendy Liu, 'Coronavirus has made Amazon a public utility – so we should treat it like one' *The Guardian* (London, 17 April 2020) https://www.theguardian.com/commentisfree/2020/apr/17/amazon-coronavirus-public-utility-workers accessed 20 June 2020.

Where platforms are entitled to intervene in a supplier-customer relationship, this should be subject to a two-stage test. The first step is to determine the normal rights and obligations of the platform and of the user independent of any crisis. These rights and obligations may already be shaped by rules for an unforeseen change of circumstances which can apply in the given situation. Otherwise, in a second step, one could then ask whether, due to the exceptional circumstances surrounding the COVID-19 crisis, the platform is entitled to take measures which would not be permitted under normal circumstances.

Legal systems must then police these measures and, in order to enforce the law, ensure that platforms become liable if they resort to unlawful measures in the course of the COVID-19 pandemic. When monitoring and regulating platforms to this effect, legislators, courts and other public authorities should have to take into account the special importance of platforms in the pandemic.

5. A GENERAL DUTY OF FAIRNESS AND TRANSPARENCY OF PLATFORMS AND ITS EMANATIONS

5.1. "NET NEUTRALITY" AS A MODEL FOR A GENERAL PRINCIPLE OF PLATFORM NEUTRALITY?

The above examples raise the question of whether digital platform operators should be subject to a general principle of neutrality which prohibits unequal treatment of platform users. A model for such a principle of "platform neutrality" could be the principle of "net neutrality", as it is, for example, laid down in Article 3(3) Telecom Single Market Regulation (EU) 2015/2120.[40] According to this provision, "providers of internet access services shall treat all traffic equally when providing internet access services, without discrimination, restriction or interference". This regulation takes into account the essential role of internet access providers as providers of infrastructural services in the digital world. By analogy, the providers of large online marketplaces could also be regarded as infrastructure service providers, which could justify regulation along the lines of infrastructure regulation.[41] However, the examples show that a mere principle of neutrality may be too narrow to address the legal issues that arise. Above all,

---

40 On this idea see Friso Bostoen, 'Neutrality, fairness or freedom? Principles for platform regulation' (2018) 7(1) Internet Policy Review.

41 See K. Sabeel Rahman, 'The New Utilities: Private Power, Social Infrastructure, and the Revival of the Public Utility Concept' (2018) 39 Cardozo L. Rev. 1621; see also José van Dijck, David Nieborg and Thomas Poell, 'Reframing platform power'(2019) 8(2) Internet Policy Review (underlining the infrastructural power of digital platforms).

neutrality would enforce equal treatment, not necessarily fair treatment.[42] At least when it comes to the extent to which platforms can intervene in the legal relationship of suppliers and customers for solving pandemic-related disputes, a mere principle of equal treatment would not help much.

5.2. GENERAL DUTY OF FAIRNESS AND TRANSPARENCY OF PLATFORMS TOWARDS THEIR USERS

A more fundamental way of dealing with increased rights of platforms to interfere with supplier-customer contracts in a crisis such as the present one could be to limit the powers of platforms by a general duty of fairness and transparency towards their users. The principles of fairness and transparency can be seen as underpinning the French legislation on platforms in particular,[43] but also the ELI Model Rules, which state in Article 1 that their aim is to "contribute to fairness and transparency".

Such a general duty of fairness and transparency[44] can also be derived from unfair commercial practices law and be part of the general duty to comply with the requirements of professional diligence. Article 8 of the P2B Regulation expressly seeks to ensure that "contractual relations between providers of online intermediation services and business users are conducted in good faith and based on fair dealing". Against this background, the individual obligations of platforms provided for in the P2B Regulation could be construed as still incomplete emanations of a larger principle whereby platforms have a general duty of fairness and transparency.

Such a general duty would have the advantage that it becomes easier for the courts to develop specific aspects of this duty for certain situations. This is particularly evident when an unexpected situation, such as the current COVID-19 pandemic, occurs, for which the legislature could not be prepared, and where certainty of contracts becomes less of an issue. A general duty would also have the further advantage that it could be used not only to substantiate the "hard" legal obligations of platforms, but also as a yardstick for seemingly "soft" actions by platforms, against which, for example, the observed "nudging" could be measured.

---

[42] The French *Conseil d'État*, for example, was also sceptical about transferring the principle of neutrality from telecommunication to platforms, cf rapport 'Le numérique et les droits fondamentaux' (2014) 21.

[43] Particularly clearly, e.g. in the report of the French *Conseil d'État*, 'Le numérique et les droits fondamentaux' (2014), 21.: "les plateformes devraient être soumises à une obligation de loyauté envers leurs utilisateurs, tant les utilisateurs non professionnels dans le cadre du droit de la consommation que les utilisateurs professionnels dans le cadre du droit de la concurrence."

[44] *Yam Seng Pte Ltd v International Trade Corp Ltd* [2013] EWHC 111 (QB); *Al Nehayan v Kent* [2018] EWCH 33 (Comm); *Bates & Ors v Post Office Ltd (No 3)* [2019] EWHC 606 (QB).

Some of the possible specific obligations that may follow from a general duty of platforms based on their role as creators and shapers of markets have already been formulated in the ELI Model Rules, namely information and transparency duties and the duty to protect users of the platform. It appears highly likely that the COVID-19 pandemic will require the courts to further develop specific obligations of platforms which can be based on such a general principle.

5.3. PROCEDURAL DIMENSION OF FAIRNESS

The envisaged general duty of fairness and transparency for digital platforms would have both a substantive and a procedural dimension. While the determination of substantive fairness standards requires a very difficult balancing of different interests, the minimum requirements for procedural fairness appear relatively clear. For decisions that have far-reaching consequences for platform users, such as account suspensions and terminations, a platform must grant its users a procedural recourse. Amongst the examples presented above, such a recourse was lacking regarding the takedown of listings for alleged price gouging and the prioritisation of 'essential' products.

The P2B regulation will bring some improvements. Article 11(1) P2B Regulation requires platform operators to set up an internal complaint management system that is easily accessible and free of charge for commercial platform users and ensures that complaints are dealt with "within a reasonable time frame". The regulation does not specify the maximum duration or the structure of the complaint procedure. Article 11(2) P2B Regulation limits itself to some rather general phrases requiring, for example, that platform operators shall "duly consider" complaints and process them "swiftly and effectively". In a future revision of the P2B Regulation these requirements should be further specified. A possible source of inspiration could be the draft report of the European Parliament's Committee for Legal Affairs, which contains a detailed proposal regarding fair procedural rules for content moderation systems in social networks.[45]

5.4. SUBSTANTIVE DIMENSION OF FAIRNESS

One example of a substantive obligation which can be derived from a general duty of fairness and transparency could be an obligation of platforms to be neutral and fair towards their different users when they intervene in the relationship between suppliers and customers in order to address problems resulting from

45 European Parliament, 'Committee on Legal Affairs, Draft Report with recommendations to the Commission on a Digital Services Act: adapting commercial and civil law rules for commercial entities operating online', 2020/2019(INL), 22 April 2020.

the crisis. A particular difficult question in this context is the extent to which the platform must respect the existing rights and obligations in the relationship between the supplier and the customer, i.e. whether the platform, before adopting measures, must establish whether, for example, the customer is entitled to terminate the supplier-customer contract and to recover any advance payment as a consequence of the COVID-19 pandemic. Obviously, platforms are generally neither judges nor arbiters, and they also have generally some discretion as to whether they want to intervene at all. It should also be obvious that they are not entitled to completely ignore or attempt to override the law which applies to the contractual relations with which they might interfere, as this could lead to very rough "justice" being administered by platforms in such cases. Where platforms cross this line and instruct users to adopt a solution which clearly contradicts the applicable law, they may become liable for giving questionable advice or for interfering unduly with the supplier-customer contract.

5.5. ROLE OF PLATFORMS IN ENFORCING CUSTOMER RIGHTS

During the current crisis, some platforms have also become more involved in the enforcement of rights and obligations. Customer rights, in particular consumer rights, can be enforced in a number of different ways, be it in advance through administrative bodies such as, for example, the UK Competition and Markets Authority (CMA), be it subsequently through ADR, arbitration, court proceedings (including collective actions), or again by administrative action. In the current crisis, there is an increased risk that subsequent enforcement will benefit only a small proportion of those affected or even come too late because, for example, the businesses which are obliged to provide a refund will be unreachable or insolvent.

One interesting aspect of platforms in this context is that they may take on the function of intermediary preventative enforcers. It has been reported that enforcement agencies such as the CMA for the United Kingdom and the European Commission instructed platforms to act against COVID-19 related unfair commercial practices on their sites. In a similar vein, the Italian competition authority (AGCM) sent a request for information to the main online sales platforms about the distribution of hand disinfectants and disposable respirators.[46] Since then, the AGCM has initiated several additional investigations into excessive price increases.[47] As a result of this official activity,

46 https://en.agcm.it/en/media/press-releases/2020/3/ICA-Coronavirus-the-Authority-intervenes-in-the-sale-of-sanitizing-products-and-masks accessed 20 June 2020.

47 https://en.agcm.it/en/media/press-releases/2020/3/ICA-Coronavirus-the-Authority-begins-investigating-Amazon-and-eBay-for-misleading-claims-and-excessive-price-increases accessed 20 June 2020.

eBay, Amazon and other platforms have reportedly introduced price gouging policies and committed to reporting COVID-19 related unfair commercial practices to the authorities.[48] Such rather informal measures seem to have a measurable impact. On the initiative of the German Ministry of Justice and for Consumer Protection, the network of European Consumer Protection Cooperation (CPC Network) conducted a Europe-wide survey on offers relevant to the coronavirus crisis on online trading platforms. The results of the survey show that some online trading platforms still have a significant number of misleading offers. There were also positive examples: several platforms took efficient action against consumer deception in connection with corona-relevant products.[49]

Where platforms have been mandated or requested by the authorities to take action against certain COVID-19 related malpractice by their users, they have some leeway as to which approach they will adopt to tackle the problem, and should not be held liable for any slight negligence if they, for example, misjudge the legal situation under the contract between suppliers and customers.

6. TENTATIVE CONCLUSIONS

We only had the time and space to touch upon these questions and to offer some tentative thoughts. The above nevertheless shows that some fundamental legal questions might need to be rethought for two overlapping reasons. The first reason is the general rise of the platform economy, and the second is the current COVID-19 pandemic, which focuses attention on the role of many platforms as critical infrastructure and which serves as a catalyst which accelerates ongoing long-term developments towards further digitalisation of society, economy and law.

The examples given here show that platforms are by far not just matchmakers, but also very active shapers of the market. This is not a new phenomenon, but the pandemic has accelerated and intensified this ongoing development. Platform interventions in the market are reaching a new quantitative and qualitative dimension. Legal systems must scrutinise these developments and respond where this is required in order to ensure that its values and rules are respected. In doing so, due regard must be given to the special function of platforms as an integral part of the general infrastructure for supplying the population with goods and services. The COVID-19 pandemic has underlined how important this

---

48 Christine Riefa, 'Coronavirus as a Catalyst to Transform Consumer Policy and Enforcement', (2020) Journal of Consumer Policy https://doi.org/10.1007/s10603-020-09462-0 accessed 20 June 2020.

49 https://www.bmjv.de/SharedDocs/Pressemitteilungen/DE/2020/052620_Sweep.html accessed 26 June 2020.

function has meanwhile become: many platforms have proven to be essential for combating the pandemic and its many adverse consequences. The COVID-19 pandemic has also revealed a nascent general duty of fairness and transparency towards their users, some aspects of which had already manifested themselves in EU law and the laws of Member States. This general duty has a procedural and a substantive dimension, both of which need to be further developed. The present work on a Digital Services Act provides a good opportunity for this. The ELI Model Rules on Online Platforms are a possible source of inspiration. Although they were developed before the pandemic, they also point in the direction of a general duty of platforms to act fairly and transparently towards their users.

TOWARDS A RENAISSANCE OF PRICE CONTROL IN CONTRACT LAW?

Preliminary Observations on COVID-19 and Price Regulation on the Consumer Market

Mateusz Grochowski*

This contribution addresses the dilemma of retail price regulation on the consumer market in the economic realities triggered by the COVID-19 pandemic. It discusses the reinvigoration of discussion over price control that ensued in numerous countries as a result of the rapid increase of prices of certain goods (such as medical products and everyday-use utensils). It attempts to preliminarily frame the underlying policy premises of price regulation triggered by the pandemic. It also seeks a more in-depth understanding of the rationale of price review in the extraordinary market conditions, as well as the general rules for allocation of tasks in this regard between public and private law. In so doing, the text focuses primarily on the EU consumer law and attempts to understand what concept of price control it rests on and to what extent it may provide a response to the price concerns in the outcome of COVID-19.

* Ph.D., LL.M. (Yale), Senior Research Fellow in the Max Planck Institute for Comparative and Interntional Private Law in Hamburg, Germany, Assistant Professor in the Institute of Law Studies of the Polish Academy of Sciences, Warsaw, Poland, Affiliated Fellow in the Information Society Project (Yale Law School) (grochowski@mpipriv.de). The text benefited from the discussion at the seminar "Excessive v. unfair prices during coronavirus crisis" at the Robert Schuman Centre for Advanced Studies at the European University Institute in Florence.

1. COVID-19 AND PRICE SURGES: MAPPING THE PHENOMENON

The immense and rapid consequences of the coronavirus pandemic triggered for the global economy elicited profound market fluctuations and drew rather gloomy prospects for the post-pandemic realities. One of the most immediate spheres which experienced almost immediate and conspicuous change after the pandemic outbreak were retail prices on the consumer market.[1] Even before the strict health measures were introduced, the spreading awareness of the incoming pandemic resulted in a prompt surge of prices for several everyday-need products, which proliferated even further in the course of the lockdown. The rise of prices in the era of the pandemic was elicited by a rapidly growing demand for particular types of goods and services[2] and an increase of manufacture and supply costs. In this way, the COVID-19 pandemic led to a new incarnation of the age-old concept of "economy of shortage".[3] In the circumstances of the pandemic, the economy developed several insular shortages of supply, which led to a noticeable surge of prices for particular products.[4] This pertained especially to medical supplies (especially of an everyday use, such as face masks, gloves and disinfectants), as well as for some food products and other basic goods.[5]

The rising prices triggered profound social and economic concerns and created an instant plea for rethinking the market policy agenda. Indeed, several countries[6] introduced measures intended to limit the uncontrolled growth of

---

1 For an in-depth analysis of this dynamic see Nick Paumgarten, 'The Price Of The Coronavirus Pandemic' [2020] *The New Yorker*.

2 Andreas Mundt, 'The Bundeskartellamt in times of COVID-19: adaption of workflows and implications for our enforcement practice' (2020) 8 Journal of Antitrust Enforcement 254; 'COVID-19 Could Lead To The Return Of Inflation – Eventually' [2020] *The Economist*. This conclusion is not, however, all-embracing; for instance, on particularities on the food market see a FAO report: http://www.fao.org/giews/food-prices/food-policies/detail/en/c/1270543/ accessed 27 July 2020.

3 The concept initially coined by János Kornai, *The Socialist System: The Political Economy Of Communism* (Princeton University Press 1992).

4 Ramsi A. Woodcock, 'The Hidden Shortages Of The Market Economy' https://lpeblog.org/2020/06/03/the-hidden-shortages-of-the-market-economy/#more-3580 accessed 27 July 2020.

5 See generally Ramsi A. Woodcock, 'The Efficient Queue And The Case Against Dynamic Pricing' (2020) 105 Iowa Law Review 1791; John Noble, 'Competition law in times of crisis – tackling the COVID-19 challenge: a producer perspective' (2020) 8 Journal of Antitrust Enforcement 294 ff; Rik Chakraborti, Gavin Roberts, 'Anti-price gouging laws, shortages, and COVID-19: big data insights from consumer searches' [2020] https://papers.ssrn.com/sol3/papers.cfm?abstract_id=3613726, 4-5, accessed 3 March 2021.

6 Not in all countries have the consumer protection measures been initiated and created by the State agencies. For instance, in Germany, they were instigated by consumer associations (who opposed overpricing in retail sale of face masks); cf Will Hayter, 'Tackling the COVID-19 challenge – a perspective from the CMA' (2020) 8 Journal of Antitrust Enforcement 251.

prices on the consumer market, usually by imposing statutory ceilings on retail prices of particular goods[7] and by initiating antitrust investigations.[8] Although the actual life-span and efficacy of these actions have been uneven,[9] they undoubtedly created a visible trend in global market policy, which – to a degree unprecedented in recent years – endorsed the possibility of direct intervention into prices on the consumer market. Most of these measures were intended to entail redistributive effects on the market, and rested on public law instruments. They were framed both in an overall fashion (especially in a form of mandatory price thresholds), or with a stronger focus on individual market conduct (e.g. through checks on price practices of particular firms, usually with use of antitrust and antidiscrimination tools).[10] All these interventions shared the common basic rationale, i.e. the general concern that the negative externalities of price increase (especially when it amounts to price gouging) are so high in the context of the pandemic that they legitimise temporary deviation from the general hands-off approach towards price control which is commonplace in the present-day liberal market economy.[11]

Even in these instances, however, the eventual framing at the policy level and enforcement of such measures has been undertaken by a State.

7 That was, amongst others, the case for Italy, France, the United Kingdom and Poland, where prices of certain products – considered as particularly vulnerable at the time of the pandemic – were legislatively limited with pre-set thresholds – see, e.g. Kate Beioley, Jim Pickard, 'UK Watchdog Seeks Powers To Tackle Coronavirus Profiteering' [2020] *Financial Times* https://www.ft.com/content/6af426bc-bfa3-4acb-86e0-c72eb0333e7e accessed 27 July 2020; Mikolaj Piaskowski and Michal Derdak, 'Poland: COVID-19 Special Legislation: Maximum Prices And Costs Of Loans' [2020] *Global Compliance News* https://globalcompliancenews.com/poland-COVID19-special-legislation-maximum-prices-and-costs-of-loans-06042020/ accessed 27 July 2020; Alberto Mingardi, 'Italy's COVID Price-Control Fiasco' [2020] *The Wall Street Journal* https://www.wsj.com/articles/italys-COVID-price-control-fiasco-11589842827 accessed 27 July 2020; Penelope Giosa, 'Exploitative Pricing in the Time of Coronavirus – The Response of EU Competition Law and the Prospect of Price Regulation' [2020] Journal of European Competition Law & Practice 499, 506.

8 Such checks were carried out e.g. in Ireland, Germany, Greece and in several non-EU countries, such as e.g. US states, Canada and Australia; see Isolde Goggin, 'How the Irish Competition and Consumer Protection Commission is responding to the COVID-19 challenge' (2020) 8 Journal of Antitrust Enforcement 249; Andreas Mundt, 'The Bundeskartellamt in times of COVID-19: adaption of workflows and implications for our enforcement practice' (2020) 8 Journal of Antitrust Enforcement 254; Rod Sims, 'Competition law in times of crisis – tackling the COVID-19 challenge: Australian Competition and Consumer Commission' (2020) 8 Journal of Antitrust Enforcement *passim*; Will Hayter, 'Tackling the COVID-19 challenge – a perspective from the CMA' (2020) 8 Journal of Antitrust Enforcement 251.

9 See e.g. Alberto Mingardi, 'Italy's COVID Price-Control Fiasco' [2020] *The Wall Street Journal* https://www.wsj.com/articles/italys-COVID-price-control-fiasco-11589842827 accessed 27 July 2020.

10 See also a review of food pricing policies introduced worldwide at: National policy responses to limit the impact of COVID-19 on food markets, The Food and Agriculture Organization of the United Nations (FAO), http://www.fao.org/giews/food-prices/food-policies/detail/en/c/1270543/ accessed 14 June 2020.

11 The essence of this premise has been convincingly encapsulated by David S. Evans, 'Planning for catastrophes' (2020) 8 Journal of Antitrust Enforcement 275: "[w]e can generally count

The choice of public law instruments in price control cannot be, however, overrated for its impact on both the legal order and the market dynamics. All price regulatory mechanisms by nature interfere directly with the sphere of contract law. At the most obvious level, they restrict private autonomy and curb the array of agreements that may be effectively concluded in the selected parts of the economy. At the same time, every price control instrument also directly affects a more profound concept of contract law, namely free bargaining. The measures taken to counteract price gouging in the COVID-19 era were naturally interfering with this essential feature of contract law (at least in its version endorsed in EU law), constraining free determination of value and price.

This leads to a foundational concern that will be further explored throughout this contribution: whether and to what extent price control instruments adopted (or: adoptable) for the consumer market in the outcome of the COVID-19 require specific public law measures and to what extent the same effect can be achieved at the level of the existing toolbox of contract law. The principal questions addressed in this contribution tackle regulatory policy in the consumer market. The analysis attempts to understand better what should be the optimal division of labour between private (contract) and public law in regulating price surges in the case of extraordinary change of economic and social circumstances (such as those in the COVID-era economy). In so doing, the contribution addresses the existing price control instruments at two levels: (a) their general fitness for the underlying values and policy agenda of contract law to serve as a price control tool and (b) their applicability of the already existing institutions and instruments of contract law in order to moderate retail prices on the consumer market. In discussing these issues, the following remarks will focus primarily on EU private law and the contract law jurisdictions of the Member States. In its more profound dimension, the argument presented below encompasses also the general legal and economic premises of price control and the general theoretical framework of contracts in the free market economy.

---

on the price mechanism to allocate resources to their highest valued uses and to provide signals to firms on where to invest. In times of catastrophe traditional markets may not work well. Some catastrophes could cripple the ability to make transactions based on pecuniary prices, resulting in the need for some forms of barter. For others, society may decide that it is not desirable to allocate certain scarce resources based on the willingness, and ability, to pay." On a partial critique of this attitude see however Tommy Thompson, 'Price Controls On COVID-19 Treatments Would Be Misguided' [2020] *The Press Enterprise* https://www.pe.com/2020/06/04/price-controls-on-COVID-19-treatments-would-be-misguided/ accessed 14 June 2020; J.D. Tuccille, 'Price-Gouging Laws Will Do More Harm Than Good During The Coronavirus Pandemic' [2020] *Reason* https://reason.com/2020/03/16/price-gouging-laws-will-do-more-harm-than-good-during-the-coronavirus-pandemic/ accessed 27 July 2020.

2. CONTRACT LAW AND PRICE CONTROL

The debate about the COVID-19-triggered surge of prices builds on a more foundational question: to what extent irregular – even if temporary – market circumstances may justify regulatory intervention in value/price relation by means of contract law. Classically, the attitudes vis-à-vis price scrutiny oscillate between procedural and substantive fairness.[12] The first approach, being in principle more autonomy-oriented, builds on the assumption that direct price control cannot be reconciled with individual freedom to make market valuations. From this vantage point, contracts provide a platform for setting prices through bargaining – and the price in itself should be kept beyond the ambit of any arbitrary steering. The regulatory focus is shifted here solely upon the procedural dimension of price-setting. It accentuates the need to guarantee the lack of substantial imbalances between parties and hence endorses necessity of equal opportunities for all contractors involved in price-setting.

The procedural approach towards price determination is the foundational premise in all contract law systems that build on the liberal paradigm. Price, considered under this view as a product of free market dynamics, is in principle exempted from any in-depth framing, both by legislation and courts.[13] What follows from this basic assumption is that legal bearing on price-setting is mostly concerned with the proper process of making and expressing a choice by each party. In this way, the procedural approach is construed by the classic instruments such as defects of consent and formal requirements.[14] All of them focus on the process of reaching the decision about setting value/price relation, and set aside both the amount of price and its relationship to any actual market value.

At the same time, contract law jurisdictions usually depart from this general approach in a few regards, by replacing the procedural price control with a substantive approach (conceptually rooted in the Roman concepts of *iustum pretium* and *laesio enormis*). They focus not on controlling the process

---

12 Cf. e.g. Horst Eidenmüller, 'Justifying Fair Price Rules in Contract Law' (2015) 11 European Review of Contract Law, 220; Daniel Kahneman et al., 'Fairness as a Constraint on Profit Seeking: Entitlements in the Market' (1986) 76 The American Economic Review 728; Martijn W. Hesselink, 'Could a Fair Price Rule (or its Absence) be Unjust? On the Relationship between Contract Law, Justice and Democracy' (2015) 11 European Review of Contract Law 185.

13 On the theoretic framing of price control in the free-market economy cf Niamh Dunne, 'Price Regulation in the Social Market Economy' (2017) LSE Law, Society and Economy Working Papers 3/2017; Steven N.S. Cheung, 'A theory of price control' (1974) 17 Journal of Law & Economics 54–67.

14 The latter instrument is also commonly used by EU contract law to enhance decision-making schemes – see for instance Peter Mankowski, 'Formvorschriften und Europäisches Privatrecht' in Hans Schulte-Nölke, Reiner Schulze (eds), *Europäisches Privatrecht im Gemeinschaftsrecht*, (Bundesanzeiger 2002) 186–189.

of establishing the price, but on its final outcome.[15] They rest on the premise that particularly conspicuous imbalances in parties' consideration justify the intervention of contract law in the substance of an agreement (by its cancellation or alteration).[16] At a deeper layer, the bulk of these instruments assume that substantial price fairness should be evaluated with reference to the particular bargaining situation between parties. In other words, price fairness is almost never[17] established with sole reference to an objectified (average) price[18] in the relevant market sector.[19]

The range of these tools differs substantially across jurisdictions. Most of the instruments at stake focus though on the same factual pattern – i.e. taking advantage by one party of its superior bargaining position, in order to stipulate grossly disproportionate profits or minimise risks. The concepts typically used in this domain usually rest on the Roman-rooted concept of *laesio enormis*,[20] which centres around disproportionality between the value of parties' counter-performances.[21] Some contract law systems adopt this formula almost straightforwardly, putting disproportion in value in the foreground.

---

15 See Alphonse M. Squillante, 'The Doctrine of Just Price – Its Origin and Development' (1969) 74 Comparative Law Journal 334f; Arthur T. von Mehren, 'The Comparative Study of Law' (1991–1992) 6/7 Tulane Civil Law Forum 43, 49–51.

16 On comparative remarks see, e.g. Aleksander Grebieniow, 'Remedies for Inequality in Exchange. Comparative Perspectives for the Evolution of the Law in the 21st Century' (2019) 23 European Review of Private Law 9–24 with further references.

17 See, however, §943 of the Austrian Civil Code (ABGB), discussed further in this section.

18 The same outcome, yet in a slightly different way, is achieved also in US law, on grounds of the unconscionability doctrine; cf e.g. Jane P. Mallor, 'Unconscionability in Contracts between Merchants' (1986) 40 Southwestern Law Journal 1073. As the author observes further, "[i]n almost all cases in which courts have found unconscionability, elements of both procedural and substantive unfairness have existed. Courts require no set ratio of procedural to substantive unconscionability; they usually use a loose sliding scale." The opposite attitude, confined to objectified economic indicators, is proper rather for competition law – see Hardin Ratshisusu, Liberty Mncube, 'Addressing excessive pricing concerns in time of the COVID-19 pandemic – a view from South Africa' (2020) 8 Journal of Antitrust Enforcement 256.

19 Contract law tends to adopt this point of reference rather exceptionally, when it is needed to establish a price that has not been determined unambiguously by the parties; see, e.g. Article 73 of the Common European Sales Law, which sets forth that in such a case the price could be ascertained by reference to "the price normally charged in comparable circumstances at the time of the conclusion of the contract or, if no such price is available, a reasonable price" (on the content and hierarchy of these criteria cf Dirk Looschelders, Mark Makowsky, in Martin Schmidt-Kessel (ed), *Der Entwurf für ein Gemeinsames Europäisches Kaufrecht. Kommentar* (Sellier 2014) 417 ff.).

20 Cf. e.g. John A. Jolowicz, 'The Origin of Laesio Enormis' (1937) 49 Juridical Review 50; James Gordley, 'Equality in Exchange' (1981) 69 California Law Review 1587, 1638–1645; Raymond de Roover, 'The Concept of the Just Price: Theory and Economic Policy' (1958) 18 Journal of Economic History 418.

21 See e.g. Cf. Jacolien Barnard, 'Unfairness of price and the doctrine of laesio enormis in consumer sales' (2013) 76 Tydskrif vir Hedendaagse Romeins-Hollandse Reg (Journal for Contemporary Roman-Dutch Law) 524ff.

In this way, §943 of the Austrian Civil Code (ABGB) allows to claim dissolution[22] of an agreement that provides substantive disproportion in parties' positions (defined as a 50% difference in value at the moment when the agreement was concluded).[23] In other systems, objective imbalance of performances is supplemented with subjective exploitation of particular need or weakness of one contractor by the counterparty. This attitude is adopted in German law (§138 (2) BGB), which renders exploitive contracts null and void. The exploitation in question is defined as using weakness of a counterparty (defined as "predicament, inexperience, lack of sound judgement or considerable weakness of will"), which leads to disproportion of performances stipulated in the agreement. By introducing this provision, German law purposefully departed from the classic *laesio enormis* model – based on pure inequality of parties' considerations – and replaced it with a more complex and situation-specific scheme.[24] This model is followed also in Article 388 of the Polish Civil Code, which vests courts not only with an *ex officio* power to rescind an agreement, but also to modify it in a way that would restore adequacy of parties' considerations.[25] Other jurisdictions – with French[26] contract law as one of the most prominent representations[27] – depart from this attitude, following an assumption that price determination is the domain of unconstrained parties' valuation.[28] At the

---

22 Under Polish law the mechanism in question is more strongly oriented towards judicial enforcement – since it vests courts with an *ex officio* power to rescind or modify an agreement to restore adequacy of parties' considerations; see also Aleksander Grebieniow, 'Remedies for Inequality' at 20.

23 Cf. Lukas Klever, *Laesio enormis. Von der Natur der Schadloshaltung wegen Verkürzung über die Hälfte* (Manz 2019) 77ff. The Polish provision, in turn, in its current shape provides an open-ended standard of "excessive disproportion between considerations stipulated for both parties." At the same time, the rule in question does not rest merely on disproportion in considerations, but also requires a specific type of disproportion in bargaining power, where one of the contractors "exploits a forced situation or the inefficiency or inexperience of the other party".

24 Cf. e.g. Manfred Wolf, Jörg Neuner, *Allgemeiner Teil des Bürgerlichen Rechts* (C.H. Beck 2016) at 564; Hans-Peter Haferkamp, in Mathias Schmoeckel, Joachim Rückert, Reinhard Zimmermann (eds), *Historisch-kritischer Kommentar zum BGB, vol I, Allgemeiner Teil. §§1–240* (Mohr Siebeck 2003) 713ff.

25 See also Aleksander Grebieniow, 'Remedies for Inequality' at 20.

26 This assumption was substantiated explicitly in Article 1168 of the Code Civil (in the meaning introuced by the 2016 reform of the French law of obligations). It prescribes that in mutual agreements (*contrats synallagmatiques*) lack of equivalence in parties' performances is not solely a basis for nullity, unless the law provides otherwise. Correspondingly, under Article 1591 of the Code Civil the price in a sale agreement is to be determined solely by the parties.

27 On the earlier representations of this approach in French contract law doctrine see also James Gordley, 'Myths of the French Civil Code' (1994) 42 American Journal of Comparative Law 459, 474, 478.

28 As Arthur T. von Mehren explains this averse towards price scrrutiny, "The laesio enormis theory did not become obsolete because of an emergent view that the principle of equivalence was not basic to contractual justice. Rather value was increasingly seen not as intrinsic but

same time however, these systems also adopt various instruments that prevent glaring exploitation. Such measures may be introduced by both specific legal constructions,[29] as well as by reference to general corrective measures in contract law (such as defects of consent[30]).

The common denominator for all these concepts is their situation-specific focus. They are concerned about incidental and situational grounds for the abuse of bargaining power, regardless of whether they result from systemic characteristics of the market or merely from incidental superiority of one contractor over the other. Building on such a functional paradigm provides these instruments with flexibility and creates a potential for a response to changing market or social realities. In this way, they are able to address the consequences for retail prices instigated by the pandemic, which were predominantly of an incidental and somewhat fleeting nature. The picture of price control in consumer market has, however, one more substantial component which also needs to be considered in the COVID-19 context: EU consumer protection.[31]

3. AN ELEPHANT IN THE ROOM: PRICE CONTROL AND EU PRIVATE LAW

The general reluctance towards price interventions in contract law was plainly reflected in the policy agenda and institutional structure of EU private law, in particular consumer protection rules. It further distilled and conceptually refined the foundational distinction between the procedural and substantive attitude towards price fairness, choosing the former as the principal and preferred solution.

In the most prominent form, this approach was encapsulated in Article 4(2) UCTD,[32] which excludes from the ambit of fairness control the terms that

---

as based upon individual decisions and prefeiences. To the extent that these decisions are generalized and cooidinated by the market, the contract price and the market or just price are identical unless the contracting process was defective because of error, fraud, or the like; ... where individual preferences anif decisions are too particularized or too diverse to be generalized and coordinated by the market, the proposition that value is not intrinsic but rests on individual preferences and decisions again leaves no place for the just price theory. In all these situations, the satisfaction of an appropriate standard of procedural justice was – and continues to be – taken to warrant the justness of the transaction." (Arthur T. von Mehren, 'The Comparative Study' at 50).

29 See e.g. Articles 1674–1685 of the French Code Civil, which allow to subvert contracts for sale of real property which stipulate the price below 1/12 of the property's value.

30 James Gordley, 'Equality in Exchange', at 1601.

31 Hans-Peter Haferkamp, in Mathias Schmoeckel, Joachim Rückert, Reinhard Zimmermann (eds), *Historisch-kritischer Kommentar zum BGB*, vol I, Allgemeiner Teil. §§1–240 (Mohr Siebeck 2003) 708ff.

32 Council Directive 93/13/EEC of 5 April 1993 on unfair terms in consumer contracts (OJ L 95, 21.4.1993, 29–34).

determine "the main subject matter of the contract" and "the adequacy of the price and remuneration, on the one hand, as against the services or goods supplies in exchange, on the other". This attitude builds on a clearly minimalistic stance towards market valuations, adopted by parties in the form of a bargained-for price. UCTD ascribes hence itself into a liberal concept of contract law, based on the strong endorsement of individual autonomy, understood as a right to self-determine the valuation of goods and services on the market.[33] What is nonetheless particularly notable is that EU consumer law adopts this premise as an exceptional void in the system of review of consumer agreements. The CJEU case law further entrenches this attitude by clearly opting for a strict reading of Article 4(2),[34] which favours a much stronger consumer protection policy than a liberal market agenda.[35] In other words, Article 4(2) indicates that the distributive effect is rather a general rule on the grounds of consumer law, which only in the case of direct price intervention gives way before the idea of commutative justice.[36] This general attitude is supplemented in the further part of Article 4(2), which allows for carrying out a fairness test on price terms when they are non-transparent and were not drafted in "plain intelligible language"). It implies that at least one of the parties could be plausibly unable to fully comprehend these terms and hence it would be impossible to reach meaningful bargaining over the price (which in turn eradicates the market-liberty rationale of the "main subject matter" exemption). In this way, UCTD highlights the procedural dimension of fairness, allowing for substance-based review only if parties were unable to take part in price-setting on an equal footing.[37]

---

33 See e.g. Thomas Wilhelmsson, 'Varieties of Welfarism in European Contract Law' (2004) 10 European Law Journal, 728f; Glenn Heirman, 'Core terms: interpretation and possibilities of assessment' (2017) 6 Journal of European Consumer and Market Law, 30; Yesim M. Atamer, 'Why Judicial Control of Price Terms in Consumer Contracts Might Not Always Be the Right Answer – Insights from Behavioural Law and Economics' (2017) 80 Modern Law Review 627–629.

34 See e.g. CJEU decisions: of 30 April 2014, *Árpád Kásler and Hajnalka Káslerné Rábai v OTP Jelzálogbank Zrt.*, C-26/13 (ECLI:EU:C:2014:282) p. 42; of 26 February 2015, *Bogdan Matei and Ioana Ofelia Matei v SC Volksbank România SA*, C-143/13 (ECLI:EU:C:2015:127) p. 49; of 23 April 2015, *Jean-Claude Van Hove v CNP Assurances SA*, C-96/14 (ECLI:EU:C:2015:262) p. 31; of 20 September 2017, *Ruxandra Paula Andriciuc and Others v Banca Românească SA*, C-186/16 (ECLI:EU:C:2017:703) p. 34–36.

35 Cf. also Sergio Cámara Lapuente, 'Control of Price Related Terms in Standard Form Contracts in the European Union: The Innovative Role of the CJEU's Case- Law' in Yesim M. Atamer, Pascal Pichonnaz (eds), *Control of Price related Terms in Standard Form Contrats* (Springer 2019) 76–78.

36 As the *travaux preparatoires* over Article 4(2) may suggest, the idea of excluding price control beyond the unfairness check in Article 4(2) UCTD was not considered initially as an essential part of the directive. The provision was introduced at the final stages of the legislative process over UCTD, through the Council's amendment. It did not constitute hence a part of the original design of unfair terms control and was introduced only at the final stages of UCTD drafting – cf Hans-Wolfgang Micklitz, in Norbert Reich, Hans-Wolfgang Micklitz, Peter Rott, Klaus Tonner, *European Consumer Law* (Intersentia 2014) 138.

37 See also Yesim M. Atamer, Pascal Pichonnaz, 'Control of Price Related Terms in Standard Form Contracts: General Report' in Yesim M. Atamer, Pascal Pichonnaz (eds), *Control of*

The same preference for procedural attitude is also followed in the EU rules on unfair market practices in UCPD.[38] It refers to retail prices on the consumer market in its several provisions, though at the same time perceives this issue principally through a prism of procedural guarantees for making free and unconstrained consumer decision-making. The UCPD is concerned mostly with the way the price is presented to a consumer and what impact it may exert on the consumer's cognition and market choices. In Article 6(1)(d), which may serve as a clear example of this bearing, UCPD prohibits practices that would deceive consumers about "the price or the manner in which the price is calculated, or the existence of a specific price advantage", by providing untrue information in this regard or by presenting it in a misleading way. This formula clearly departs from any kind of substantial considerations, being concerned exclusively with the way a consumer may understand the price and its relation to the value of a good.[39] It does not tackle upon any objective value/price relation, along with other substantive criteria.[40] This attitude fits directly into the general concept of unfair commercial practice, which under Article 5(2)(b) UCPD "materially distorts or is likely to materially distort the economic behaviour with regard to the product" of the average non-professional on the relevant market. The UCPD approach reiterates the general assumption of contract law neutrality towards price calculation and fits well into the framework established previously by UCTD.

On closer inspection, however, the hands-off attitude of EU private law towards price calculation turns out to be rather ostensible. Although both the UCTD and UCPD attempt to steer clear of direct distributive effects of price control,[41] strong trends towards price control are apparent in the intersection between consumer and competition protection. Like its US counterpart, EU competition law recognises price unfairness as a self-standing ground for

---

Price related Terms in Standard Form Contrats (Springer 2019) 28–32; Michael Schillig, 'Directive 93/13 and the Price Term Exemption: A Comparative Analysis in the Light of the Market for Lemons Rationale' (2011) 60 International and Comparative Law Quarterly 933, 940–945.

38 Directive 2005/29/EC of the European Parliament and of the Council of 11 May 2005 concerning unfair business-to-consumer commercial practices in the internal market and amending Council Directive 84/450/EEC, Directives 97/7/EC, 98/27/EC and 2002/65/EC of the European Parliament and of the Council and Regulation (EC) No 2006/2004 of the European Parliament and of the Council, OJ L 149, 11.6.2005, 22–39.

39 In line with this general assumption, Article 7(4)(c) counts information about components of the final price (such as fiscal burdens and shipping costs), and (alternatively) the way how the bare price and the additional costs were calculated (if one of them was not pre-determined by the supplier).

40 This attitude is further confirmed by the CJEU case law, which interprets price checks under UCPD through the prism of procedural guarantees – see judgment of 12 May 2011, *Konsumentombudsmannen v Ving Sverige AB*, C-122/10 (ECLI:EU:C:2011:299) p. 35–41.

41 Cf. Thomas Wilhelmsson, 'Varieties of Welfarism in European Contract Law' (2004) 10 European Law Journal 728f.

antitrust intervention. Under Article 102(a) TFEU, the abuse of a dominant market position may be constituted, amongst others, by "directly or indirectly imposing unfair purchase or selling prices" on the retail consumer market. The robust body of CJEU case law which interprets this concept (founded mostly on the milestone *United Brands* decision[42]) provides a generally clear set of criteria for the assessment of whether a particular price can be considered abusive.[43] It should be noted that the sole magnitude of price increase may be an independent reason for finding this practice as an abuse of a dominant position.[44] The price control schemes in question are enforced primarily by the market regulatory authorities, through injunctions and financial penalties – namely, by the protection of collective consumer interests. They may be coupled with interim measures, which amount to temporary suspension of a particular pricing practice.[45] In the realities of the pandemic, the latter solution may seem particularly efficient in counteracting excessive price surges. In this way, Article 102(a) TFEU lays the foundation for an "internally redistributive welfarism",[46] which supplements a more neutral attitude of EU private law.

The price control mechanisms in EU private law also have, however, their more individualised dimension. First of all, the protection against abusive price fixing, provided for in Article 102(a) TFEU, may also allow for the direct protection of individual rights, through private claims for damages.[47] The actual effectiveness of this instrument is, nonetheless, limited. Private enforcement of competition law is usually not time-efficient in terms of its market impact and, by nature, is effective only *ex post*, when a market abuse already took place

---

42 ECJ judgment of 14 February 1978, *United Brands Company and United Brands Continentaal BV v Commission of the European Communities*, C-22/76 (ECLI:EU:C:1978:22).

43 See e.g. Pinar Akman, Luke Garrod, 'When are Excessive Prices Unfair?' (2011) 7 Journal of Competition Law & Economics 408ff; Thomas Ackermann, 'Vodafone: Price Regulation as a Substitute for Intervention under Article 102 TFEU' (2010) 1 Journal of European Competition Law & Practice 426f.

44 CJEU in the judgment of 5 October 1988, *Société alsacienne et lorraine de télécommunications et d'électronique (Alsatel) v SA Novasam*, C-247/86 (ECLI:EU:C:1988:469). On the relevance of this decision for the price gouging phenomena related to COVID-19 cf Francisco Costa-Cabral, Leigh Hancher, Giorgio Monti, Alexandre Ruiz Feases, 'EU Competition Law and COVID-19' (2020) TILEC Discussion Paper, DP 2020-007, 9.

45 On the particular relevance of interim measures for counteracting excessive pricing in the COVID-19 era, Francisco Costa-Cabral, Leigh Hancher, Giorgio Monti, Alexandre Ruiz Feases, 'EU Competition Law and COVID-19' (2020) TILEC Discussion Paper, DP 2020-007, 11–13.

46 Thomas Wilhelmsson, 'Varieties of Welfarism in European Contract Law' (2004) 10 European Law Journal 729.

47 Under the Directive 2014/104/EU of the European Parliament and of the Council of 26 November 2014 on certain rules governing actions for damages under national law for infringements of the competition law provisions of the Member States and of the European Union (OJ L 349, 5.12.2014, 1–19). Generally on consumer injuries caused by excessive pricing see Daniel A. Crane, 'Optimizing Private Antitrust Enforcement' (2010) 63 Vanderbilt Law Review 679–687.

and inflicted harm. Apart from the administrative enforcement, which (at least within one jurisdiction) may build on a pre-conceptualised and coherent policy agenda, private schemes are by nature much more heterogeneous and random, depending on individual proactivity and profit/cost evaluation.[48]

Secondly, despite its apparent neutrality towards substantive price control, the EU private law *sensu stricto* also creates several entry points for scrutinising the price/value relation in particular consumer agreements. The bulk of them, somewhat surprisingly, turned out to be Article 4(2) UCTD itself. The "core terms" exception constitutes an extraordinary concession for market liberty, which constraints effective consumer protection. For these reasons, both at the EU[49] and the domestic level, this concept is understood rather narrowly – with dubious cases resolved typically in favour of the application of the unfairness test. In this way, although the most typical and clear forms of price remain beyond the scope of control, Member States' case law tends to allow for verification of other types of payments imposed by professionals (e.g. various bank fees,[50] as well as the sums charged in the case of earlier withdrawal of the invested capital[51]). Apart from this, the chain of reforms of EU law throughout the past years further strengthened the focus on price fairness. The playground for this change has been principally the calculation of prices by algorithms,[52] where the EU introduced several fairness-oriented instruments, including transparency of price personalisation and a general right to object to being subjected to personalised decision-making.[53] The problem over algorithmic pricing makes the problem of price regulation even broader, asking fundamental

48 On theoretical and practical frictions and concerns in private enforcement of competition law with regard to excessive pricing see Michal Gal, 'The Case for Limiting Private Litigation of Excessive Pricing' (2020) 16 Journal of Competition Law and Economics; Frank Maier-Rigaud, Ulrich Schwalbe, 'Private Enforcement Under EU Law: Abuse of Dominance and the Quantification of Lucrum Cessans' (2013) 2 CPI Antitrust Chronicle November 3ff; Roger van den Bergh, Sonja Keske, 'Private Enforcement of European Competition Law: Quo Vadis?' (2008) 3 European Review of Contract Law.

49 Hans-Wolfgang Micklitz, in Norbert Reich, Hans-Wolfgang Micklitz, Peter Rott, Klaus Tonner, *European Consumer Law* (Intersentia 2014) 138.

50 See e.g. the instances discussed by Yesim M. Atamer, 'Why Judicial Control of Price Terms in Consumer Contracts Might Not Always Be the Right Answer – Insights from Behavioural Law and Economics' (2017) 80 Modern Law Review 624–627, 644–657 and Yesim M. Atamer, Pascal Pichonnaz, 'Control of Price Related Terms' 34.

51 See e.g. Polish Supreme Court in resolution of 24 January 2020, III CZP 51/19.

52 More generally on this issue also Oren Bar-Gill, 'Algorithmic Price Discrimination. When Demand Is a Function of Both Preferences and (Mis)perceptions' (2019) 86 The University of Chicago Law Review; Frederik Zuiderveen Borgesius, Joost Poort, 'Online Price Discrimination and EU Data Privacy Law' (2017) 40 Journal of Consumer Policy.

53 See e.g. Tycho de Graaf, 'Consequences of Nullifying and Agreement on Account of Personalized Pricing' (2019) EuCML No. 5/2019, 185. On the other dimension of data protection and price control – namely, on the price-related outcome of legal limits on commodification of personal data and privacy – see also Caleb S. Fuller, 'Privacy law as price control' (2018) 45 European Journal of Law and Economics 225, 229–233.

questions about price fairness[54] and the substantive/procedural divide in price review. From this perspective, the question of post-COVID-19 price regulation is only a part of a more profound renaissance of debate over the concept and regulatory toolbox of price scrutiny. Even if the measures introduced to combat price gouging turned out to be only temporary, they would bring an undoubted contribution to the discussion about rationale and means of price control at the EU and domestic level.

4. PRICE CONTROL AND DISTRIBUTIVE CONCERNS IN CONSUMER LAW

The pandemic reestablished a consumer expectation, well-recognised throughout the 20th century economic history – "to be protected against scarcity and profiteers".[55] An era of economic turmoil and social anxiety creates a natural plea for a higher level of market paternalism, including more restrictive price scrutiny. This creates not only a higher pressure on governments to behave more proactively in market dealings, but also overthrows in part the usual resilience towards market intervention, shared to various degrees by all liberal market economies.

The exceptional market circumstances triggered by the COVID-19 pandemic may potentially fit well into this picture. An ever growing demand for particular products and services – many of which were vital for health and life or personal/family problems of individuals – put many consumers in a conspicuous market necessity. This triggered, in turn, an increased risk of situational exploitation by imposing excessive prices for essential products. Clearly not every increase of price should be considered as a wrongful price gouging. Apart from increasing demand, a surge in price typically also reflects a growth in production and supply costs, which in many instances could be also a direct spillover of the pandemic. This creates a clear *caveat* for more differentiated and situation-specific responses to price control on the consumer market (and may partly support a case for combining public and contract law instruments, as will be discussed below).

---

54 Cf. especially Akiva Miller, 'What Do We Worry about When We Worry about Price Discrimination – The Law and Ethics of Using Personal Information for Pricing' (2014) 19 Journal of Technology Law & Policy.

55 So, in the context of post-World War I economic realities, Frank Trentmann, *Empire of Things. How we Became a World of Consumers, from the Fifteenth Century to the Twenty-First* (Allen Lane 2016) p. 278; see also Guido Calabresi, *The Future of Law and Economics. Essays in Reform and Recollection* (Yale University Press 2016) 53f, who commences his argument on price control rationale using as an example the system of rationing of goods in the US during the Second World War.

What is also important (especially for the early stages of the COVID-19 pandemic), some parts of the consumer market turned out to be *de facto* low-competitive. Due to the lockdown and substantial disruption in postal and delivery services, many consumers could refer to a limited number of suppliers – mostly those that operated locally and were available mostly in a direct way, in brick-and-mortar stores (e.g. stores and pharmacies available in a consumer's neighbourhood). This had a twofold outcome for pricing on the consumer market. First, it created an even stronger opportunity for instant increase of retail prices for the goods in the highest demand, by building upon the emergence of local *de facto* monopolies or oligopolies of suppliers. This process was particularly clear for smaller or more isolated markets (especially small towns and the countryside), where, in the pre-COVID-19 era local brick-and-mortar trade supplied only the essential products (such as alimentary, basic tools and fuel), while the other products were supplied mostly by more remotely-located firms or, to an increasing extent, through online purchases. Secondly, a more intense geographic clustering of markets mostly disabled competition-based mechanisms of establishing prices offered to consumers. Temporarily increased locality of markets decreased a drive towards the balanced price/value allocation and could have pushed firms towards harvesting profits by the exploitation of consumers' decision-making constraint.

On a more profound level, the increased trends towards price control rest on the particular type of mistrust towards the free market. The necessity to regulate prices is strongly underpinned by a conviction that in unusual circumstances, where the normal production/demand relation is substantially distorted, the regular price-setting through market bargaining and competition cannot function properly.[56] This, in turn, would easily skew the allocation of goods between market actors that would take place under regular circumstances. For obvious reasons, this situation may cause several materially negative outcomes in various economic and social domains. In particular, it deprives some individuals (unable or unwilling to pay an exceptionally high price) of goods that may be essential to them in the era of the pandemic. This individual hardship may entail further consequences in the scale of the entire society. Again, one of the most conspicuous instances of this problem is retail prices of medical products on the consumer market. An immense surge of prices for face masks or disinfectants not only hinders individual security (in the medical or emotional sense), but also puts under threat the safety of the entire population. In this way, the distributive effect of price control may also have a direct impact on other collective goods and values, beyond distributive justice understood in simple terms.

---

56 As has been already observed, "At a fundamental level, the coronavirus is testing the assumption that market forces will always yield the right mix and quantity of products at the right price." – Maurice Stucke, Ariel Ezrachi, 'COVID-19 and competition – aspiring for more than our old normality?' (2020) 8 Journal of Antitrust Enforcement 314.

5. PRICE CONTROL WITHIN AND BEYOND CONTRACT LAW: PREMISES OF CHOICE

The current framework of the EU consumer law provides complex and somewhat blurred prospects for reviewing price surging in the outcome of the COVID-19 pandemic. Seemingly, the division of labour within EU law allocates price control schemes almost exclusively in the hands of public enforcers of competition law. The basis provided in this regard by Article 102(a) TFEU allows for the horizontal review of prices and application of injunctions and penalties in a coherent way, centralised at the state level. This architecture strongly enhances the creation of a consolidated political agenda for price control, which may occur particularly important in the face of social and economic challenges posed by the pandemic. Maintaining coherent political premises of price review is particularly important in the spheres where too far-reaching price control may produce adverse negative externalities or where it should be framed in order to achieve particular regulatory aims.

Regarding the former, if the price increase results from a disruption in a supply chain of the product, intervention into spontaneous price-setting may further this disruption, making the distribution process less profitable for some participants or for the entire chain – which, in turn, may trigger a decrease in supply or deterioration in quality.[57] The centralised price control would be more efficient in the instances where the possibility to accrue higher profit due to unexpected circumstances can also provide an incentive for more innovation on the consumer market. It may pertain both to broadening the market offer (e.g. by devising new techniques of antivirus personal protection) and to enhancing availability of the existing offer to consumers (for instance, by improving brick-and-mortar distribution network or developing online channels of supplying goods and services).[58] This may prove particularly meaningful in

---

57 On price control as a way of allocating costs along a supply chain also Tsjalle van der Burg, 'How price controls can cut the number of COVID-19 bankruptcies' [2020] *LSE Blog*, https://blogs.lse.ac.uk/COVID19/2020/05/14/how-price-controls-can-cut-the-number-of-COVID-19-bankruptcies/ accessed 27 July 2020. In the further perspective, excessive price control may also increase inflation, see, e.g. 'COVID-19 Could Lead To The Return Of Inflation – Eventually' [2020] *The Economist*; on the reverse price increase dynamics in some supply chains see also Martijn Snoep, 'Competition enforcement in times of crisis – a perspective from the ACM' (2020) 8 Journal of Antitrust Enforcement 268.

58 Separtely, the pandemic-related price increase opens a question whether swift price increase amounts to inpracticability of an agreement or to a Force Majeure excuse – cf Andrew A. Schwartz, 'Contracts and COVID-19' (2020) 73 Stanford Law Review Online 48, 49f; Sarman Shetty, Pranav Budihal, 'Force Majeure, Frustration and Impossibility. A Qualitative Empirical Analysis', https://www.lawctopus.com/wp-content/uploads/2020/08/Force-Majeure-Frustration-Impossibility-A-Qualitative-Empirical-Analysis-.pdf, accessed 1 October 2020.

the situations when particular innovations (e.g. advances in medical techniques) are required expediently. In this situation, a substantial price increase may serve as a way of distributing the cost of innovation in the society, working hence as an indirect fiscal instrument.

In both instances contract law measures turn out less favourable and, potentially, counter-productive. Due to their decentralised character and randomness (based on an individual decision to protect one's rights), they hardly allow for construing any thorough and consistent policy premise. Civil courts are also, self-evidently, not equipped to construe such programs of economic and social steering, as well as to provide an assessment of price adequacy and fairness in a general perspective that would reach beyond a particular consumer agreement.[59]

At the same time, however, the centralisation of administrative response comes at the cost of its granularity. In a natural way, it is capable of addressing general classes of problems and overall market patterns losing a grip on more idiosyncratic or harder noticeable problems triggered by price gouging. For instance, although a public law price threshold may address well excessive pricing of sanitising gels – and penalise particular professionals for exploitive conduct vis-à-vis consumers as a class – it can hardly encompass a situation where price, though not excessive globally, becomes abusive towards a particular consumer. This may happen both due to introduction of individualised price increases (e.g. when a professional can realise that a consumer is in a particular need of a purchase), as well as when the general raise of price affects various consumers unevenly and is excessive only for a minor fraction of them. In this way the pandemic revealed a substantial hidden potential of contract law (and consumer law in particular) as price control devices. Although the response provided by contract law is much more random and decentralised, by virtue of these features it is usually much more sensitive towards details and capable of grasping more divergent or atypical circumstances of particular cases.

It also cannot be overlooked that the unquestioned advantage of price control solutions is that they are already available and pretty well-established at the conceptual level. Developing a more thorough set of administratively-enforced "emergency laws",[60] that could allow for centralised market steering, comes by nature with a higher social cost and at a slower pace. Although the initial stages of the pandemic witnessed lots of "ad interim" regulatory solutions imposed by

[59] Cf. e.g. Michal Gal, 'The Case for Limiting Private Litigation of Excessive Pricing' (2020) 16 Journal of Competition Law and Economics; Yesim M. Atamer, 'Why Judicial Control of Price Terms in Consumer Contracts Might Not Always Be the Right Answer – Insights from Behavioural Law and Economics' (2017) 80 Modern Law Review.

[60] See Tsjalle van der Burg, 'How price controls can cut the number of COVID-19 bankruptcies' [2020] *LSE Blog*, https://blogs.lse.ac.uk/COVID19/2020/05/14/how-price-controls-can-cut-the-number-of-COVID-19-bankruptcies/ accessed 27 July 2020.

the executive power, the more stable and thorough regulatory response (that could encompass longer-lasting economic consequences of the pandemic or respond to its further waves) requires – at least in principle – stronger democratic legitimation, preceded with a discourse about the social allocation of costs and benefits of such market intervention.

On top of these observations, price control through contract law also provides a broader array of instruments to address the problem of excessive prices than publicly-enforced competition law. This pertains not only to the measures based on the concept of procedural fairness, but also to more substance-oriented instruments, especially to various constructions based on the *laesio enormis* concept. The former, being a cornerstone idea of price regulation in the EU private law, is clearly justifiable in the ordinary economic realities, where the value/price dynamic remains roughly stable and regular.[61]

The circumstances of the pandemic, along with the high risk of opportunistic price gouging, clearly draw attention to instruments of the second genre and advocate for deeper insight into the substantive premises of pricing consumer goods on the retail market. In this regard, domestic contract law is traditionally stronger confined to the substantive rather than the procedural dimension. In this way, domestic contract law revealed its new, and somewhat unexpected, face. In the reality of the pandemic, it may clearly turn out to supplement EU private law in the spheres where consumer protection policy may advocate for extraordinary measures, focused on the substance of market dealings, not only on equality of arms in bargaining. In this way, general contract law instruments may supplement not only public law measures, but also the EU private law framework – in both regards amending them with more specific and context-sensitive solutions.

6. CONCLUSIONS: COVID-19 AND THE NEW OPENING FOR PRICE FAIRNESS IN EU CONTRACT LAW?

The COVID-19 pandemic forced substantive reconsideration of many prevailing ideas and well-established convictions. The rapid and profound economic change brought about by the lockdown and the accompanying market disruption reopened a long-forgotten debate about the legitimacy of price control in a free-market economy. As was observed only a few years before the pandemic outbreak, "[i]t is distinctly unfashionable to talk of just prices. The very term

61 Pragmatically, this outcome rests strongly on the actual effectiveness of enforcement of consumer law, which requires detailed insights into the cost- and time-effectiveness of consumer disputes in particular Member States, as well as into the existing system of state- and non-state institutional support for consumers.

seems to betray a lack of sophistication, an appeal to a fruitless query abandoned ages ago."[62] The pandemic prominently reversed these tides, replacing the "if" question with a "how" problem. For the reasons discussed above, a certain degree of price regulation seems inevitable to provide both a necessary degree of market steering in the extraordinary circumstances, as well as to guarantee the fairness of pricing individual consumers for goods and services (especially in the areas with a particularly high risk of exploitation or deprivation of every-day essentials).

Even if this change turns out eventually to be only temporary, it is likely to entail more long-lasting consequences for understanding the role of social justice and protective measures in contract law.[63]

The reinvigoration of the price control conundrum, triggered by distortions on the consumer retail market, plays one of the key roles in this regard. On the one hand, it created a plea for better understanding of the already existing concepts of price fairness and their institutional representations in the contract law agenda.[64] On the other hand, it posed a more profound question about optimal allocation of tasks in price review between contract and competition law – and consequently, about the possible role of the former.

From this perspective, regulatory concerns introduced by the COVID-19 pandemic provide a convincing argument that withdrawal – to a limited extent – from a general "no substantive price control" paradigm might be conceptually sound or convincing as a policy prospect in the irregular market circumstances, where the typical ways of establishing value/price relation are getting skewed.[65] The market disruption that ensued in the outcome of the pandemic allowed a more profound question to be asked about the actual role of contract law as an economic and social steering enterprise. The extraordinary circumstances caused by the health hazard and massive lockdown created a strong plea for higher social sensitivity of private law, both at the domestic and at the EU level.[66] The economic turmoil substantially

---

62 Robert C. Hockett, Roy Kreitner, 'Just Prices' (2018) 27 Cornell Journal of Law and Public Policy 771.

63 Cf. Hans-Wolfgang Micklitz, 'The COVID-19 Threat: An Opportunity to Rethink the European Economic Constitution and European Private Law' (2020) 11 European Journal of Risk Regulation, 250 and *passim*; Safieddine Bouali, 'COVID-19 Pandemic and Abuse of Economic Dependence. Short-run Market Vulnerability and Exploitative conduct' (2020), https://hal.archives-ouvertes.fr/hal-02564678 accessed 14 June 2020.

64 Reinvigoration of price control discourse has been typical for deep economic crises, usually associated with major social and political distress – for historical evidence of such discussion in the post-World War I US see, e.g. Nathan Isaacs, 'Revival of the Justum Pretium' (1920–1921) 6 Cornell Law Quarterly 381ff.

65 Will Hayter, 'Tackling the COVID-19 challenge – a perspective from the CMA' (2020) 8 Journal of Antitrust Enforcement 251.

66 See also generally Hans-Wolfgang Micklitz, 'The COVID-19 Threat: An Opportunity to Rethink the European Economic Constitution and European Private Law' (2020) 11 European Journal of Risk Regulation 249.

reinforced those actors on the consumer market who already enjoyed bargaining prevalence, and created areas of particularly prominent consumer weakness.[67] Obviously, any intervention into the substance of prices means constraining private autonomy and making an arbitrary decision in the field that normally should depend solely on parties' own assessment of the relative value of the particular good. In the consequence, although none of the measures discussed above formally excludes bargaining (but rather attempts to channel and restrict it),[68] they incessantly depart from a classically liberal paradigm of contract law.

In some instances, however, this departure may seem justifiable. As has been said above, contract law does not seem to be the optimal domain for pursuing price regulation policies. The more natural and better-suited platform for such interventions is undoubtedly public law, which may better accommodate public policy agenda and develop tools for legitimised intervention into free market dynamics (especially on the grounds of competition law). Contract law, based on a different set of paradigms, perceives price control as a tightly-framed exception and is much more open towards procedural than substantive fairness. This is also the case for the EU private law, much more regulatory in nature than the classic contract law frameworks. Notwithstanding this classic thread of discussion about price checks, the extraordinary and profound consequences of the pandemic bring about a pressing need to rethink this attitude and to conceptualise a new approach towards price regulation by means of contract law. It may undoubtedly supplement the administrative instruments and intervene in the spheres that require more flexible and sensitive criteria of assessment and sanctions.

The future of the post-COVID society and market is highly unclear and far from conclusive prospects. Nonetheless, some legal developments instigated by the pandemic might plausibly become persistent and permanently shape the legal order. The stronger awareness of contract law towards conspicuous price abuses, accompanied by a more critical attitude towards the classic liberal paradigm, may undoubtedly count among them. The final outcome of this change, which will form between the legislation, the case law and the market practice, is yet still to come.

---

67 On the particular type of consumer vulnerability caused by the pandemic-caused market conditions, Monique Goyens, Agustin Reyna, 'Public interest in EU policymaking after COVID-19: five short-term lessons from a consumer perspective' (2020) 8 Journal of Antitrust Enforcement 280.

68 Cf Guido Calabresi, *The Future of Law and Economics. Essays in Reform and Recollection*, (Yale University Press 2016) 54, who discusses this feature by reference to the rationing system in the US retail market of the World War II era.

RESIDENTIAL AND COMMERCIAL LEASES AMIDST THE CORONAVIRUS CRISIS

The Spanish Case in Context

Carlos Gómez-Ligüerre and Rosa Milà-Rafel*

* Both authors, Universitat Pompeu Fabra. This contribution results from the research project "Coronavirus i dret privat" (2020PANDE00092), funded by the Catalan Agency for University and Research Grants (AGAUR). The authors thank the comments made by an anonymous reviewer to a previous draft of the contribution. Errors remain the sole responsibility of the authors.

The Spanish emergency lawmaker has been prompted to take protective measures for tenants during the COVID-19 crisis. Such measures distinguish between residential and commercial leases. All of them are presented in the present contribution from a critical perspective. Commercial leases deserve special attention due to their economic relevance, and because of the intense debate among Spanish scholars on the applicability of the rebus sic stantibus *doctrine, or any of its equivalents, to adapt the contract if commercial tenants are affected by the exceptional measures imposed by the Government to deal with the COVID-19 health crisis.*

1. THE TENANT'S PROTECTIVE MEASURES IN CONTEXT

Tenancy market is a case study in each and every micro-economics course.[1] Legislation is prompted to grant quick and effective solutions to the demand of residential and commercial spaces, while supply is rigid. While demand reacts in the short term on several economic and social grounds, such as the mobility rate of the population, supply is subject to the availability of buildings and premises. In the case of residential leases, the obvious connection between affordable housing and the effective deployment of fundamental rights[2] makes the issue very sensitive from both the social and legal perspective. Lawmakers all over the world face the difficulties of promoting a fair and affordable rental market. Subsidies for promoting more rentals seek equilibrium with the liberalisation of the market, the protection of property rights and securing tenure.[3]

---

1 See, among others, Hal R. Varian, *Intermediate Microeconomics. A Modern Approach* (8th edn, W. W. Norton & Company 2010) 1 ff.

2 The European Court of Human Rights (ECtHR) has stressed the relationship between the right to respect for family life and for the home (Article 8 of the European Convention of Human Rights) and person's housing rights. See, among other decisions, *McCann v The United Kingdom* (Application 19009/04).

3 It is worthy referring to the scientific reports by country published by the experts of the TENLAW group: Tenancy Law and Housing Policy in Multi-Level Europa, hosted by the Zentrum für Europäische Rechtspolitik (Zerp)- Universität Bremen, https://www.uni-bremen.de/jura/tenlaw-tenancy-law-and-housing-policy-in-multi-level-europe accessed 13 June 2020.

The situation sounds familiar to every specialist in the field, and the situation in Spain is no different. Tenancy regulations face similar problems all over Europe, where housing problems prompt legislative measures everywhere in order to amend negative side effects produced by the market. The crisis caused by COVID-19, common to all European jurisdictions, has enhanced the necessity to protect tenants. This contribution presents the legislative measures taken by the Spanish emergency lawmaker, forced to deal with a tenancy market that presents some specific features, which make the issue much more complicated in Spain than in other European countries.

The current situation of the tenancy law in Spain can be summarised by three different structural problems: legislative, geographical and economical.[4]

From the legislative perspective, Spanish tenancy law is governed by a clear distinction between residential and commercial leases. The former are subject to mandatory rules in favour of tenants, in particular on rent updates and securing tenure, while the latter are widely based on the freedom of contract. Such a distinction has been blurred by the spread of the short-term leases agreed through internet platforms, mostly devoted to tourist rentals, excluded from the scope of the mandatory rules on residential leases. Rents have skyrocketed in some areas and many local and regional governments argue for rent controls.

Geography, in its turn, explains the existing tensions in the access to residential leases. Spain has a population of roughly 47 million habitants (47,100,396 million according to the estimated census of 2018),[5] and almost 26 million houses (25,712,744, according to the last estimation).[6] Such data suggest that Spain should not suffer from a housing problem. However, reality challenges this data. In Madrid and Barcelona, the two biggest Spanish cities, demand for housing overwhelms supply. The same mismatch exists in other populated urban areas. The problem most probably resembles the situation in other European countries, where the liveliest and most economically active cities attract large cohorts of population. What is different in Spain is the unbalanced proportion between home ownership and rental rates.

For several legal, economic and social reasons, the Spanish population has historically preferred home ownership rather than renting a property. In fact, home ownership has benefitted in the last decades from generous public

---

4 For a more detailed explanation, see Elga Molina Roig, National Report for Spain, TENLAW: Tenancy Law and Housing Policy in Multi-Level Europa, https://www.uni-bremen.de/fileadmin/user_upload/fachbereiche/fb6/fb6/Forschung/ZERP/TENLAW/Reports/SpainReport_16092014.pdf accessed 13 June 2020.

5 Spanish Statistical Office, 'General statistics on population' https://www.ine.es/dyngs/INEbase/es/operacion.htm?c=Estadistica_C&cid=1254736176951&menu=ultiDatos&idp=1254735572981 accessed 13 June 2020.

6 Spanish Ministry of Transport, Mobility and Urban Agenda, 'Housing stock estimation', https://apps.fomento.gob.es/BoletinOnline2/?nivel=2&orden=33000000 accessed 13 June 2020.

policies, mostly in the form of tax incentives. According to the last available data, 76.3% of the Spanish population live in their own properties.[7] This percentage narrows the market for residential leases, easily overwhelmed by demand, and the interplay between supply and demand pushes up rentals.

Finally, economics shows a close connection between residential leases and economic vulnerability. In the aftermath of the past financial crisis, many Spanish debtors were unable to pay their loans and thousands of mortgages were foreclosed.[8] Many Spanish families lost their properties, and subsidised rentals were adopted as the sole solution for citizens in a situation of economic vulnerability, since financial institutions tightened the economic requirements to grant mortgages. On 14 March 2020, the Royal Decree 463/2020[9] declared the national emergency due to COVID-19. Since then, the Spanish Government has enacted several protective provisions for tenants. All of them refer to a combination of the following: (1) the moratorium on the payment of the rent; (2) the extension of the lease term; (3) the suspension of the eviction proceedings.

These measures are similar to the ones taken by other European lawmakers.[10] All of them try to avoid the detrimental effects that the general lockdown of most economic activities might have in both residential and commercial leases. They all aim at softening the impact of the crisis for households and business alike.

In the Spanish case, though, the regulatory frame differs to some extent from the situation in other European jurisdictions also prompted to protect tenants. Spanish private law does not contain a general rule on hardship or any other equivalent legal doctrine. The contractual provisions in the Spanish Civil Code are clearly outdated, and one of their flaws is that they still maintain factual impossibility as the only ground for discharging contracts. The specific regulation

7 See Eurostats, Distribution of population by tenure status, type of household and income group (Last update, 5 June 2020) https://appsso.eurostat.ec.europa.eu/nui/show.do?dataset=ilc_lvho02&lang=en accessed 13 June 2020. The Spanish percentage is close to the European Union average (70% of its citizens live in their own dwellings). However, data are subject to great variance between EU countries. The percentage of ownership varies from the 51.5% in Germany to the 96.4% in Romania. Spain is, indeed, in the higher part of the table per countries, only below Eastern countries, and in a similar level to Belgium (72.3%), Greece (73.5%), Italy (72.4%), and Luxembourg (71.2%). See, also, Alice Pittini (ed), *The State of Housing in the EU 2019* (available at https://www.housingeurope.eu/resource-1323/the-state-of-housing-in-the-eu-2019 accessed 2 October 2020).

8 For a general overview of the impact of the past financial crisis in the Spanish real-estate market, see Sergio Nasarre Aznar, *Los años de la crisis de la vivienda* (Tirant lo Blanch 2020).

9 Official Journal no 67, of 14 March 2020.

10 See the comparative charts on Konstantin Kholodilin, *Housing Policies Worldwide during Coronavirus Crisis: Challenges and Solutions*, DIW focus, No 2, April 2020 (available at https://www.diw.de/de/diw_01.c.758176.de/publikationen/diw_focus/2020_0002/housing_policies_worldwide_during_coronavirus_crisis__challenges_and_solutions.html accessed 2 October 2020).

on tenancy is also lacking a rule on the effects of supervening circumstances in the rental agreement. Therefore, tenants, landlords, their lawyers, as well as the courts do not have a regulatory framework able to solve the disputes that the COVID-19 outbreak is causing. The problem is much more acute when dealing with commercial leases, where, as has been said, specific regulations have been traditionally deferent to freedom of contract and where, consequently, contractual diversity is higher than in residential leases.

2. RESIDENTIAL LEASES

2.1. GENERAL PROVISIONS

As comparative studies on the topic have shown, national regulations on residential leases present a high level of diversity.[11] Several factors explain this, from the rate of social mobility to the financial incentives attached to residential leases, as well as the existence of tax benefits and the financial structure of each jurisdiction. In Spain, diversity also exists within the same market, again making the situation idiosyncratic in comparison to other European jurisdictions. A brief introduction to the current legislative situation will help to better understand the impact of the protective measures for tenants of residential leases adopted during the COVID-19 crisis.

The Spanish regulation on residential leases is formed by a variety of mandatory rules underpinned set off by different statutes, all of them in force and applicable to the leases agreed during the respective periods of validity. The successive reforms on the issue have always been adopted respecting the existing status quo of the residential leases already in force, being applicable only to contracts agreed after the enactment of each new piece of legislation. Reforms have included "grandfather clauses" excluding existing contracts from their scope of application.

Such a legislative policy has turned into a great normative complexity. Different legal regimes based on different legislative purposes co-exist. It is, in fact, not unusual that different tenants in the same building are subject to different rules depending on the time in which their contracts were concluded.

For the majority of the past century, Decree 4104/1964[12] was in force. The statute strengthened the position of tenants. Residential leases were open-ended contracts, securing life-long tenure, and landlords were only allowed to increase the rent according to the official retail price index. Such regulation had a

---

11 See the comparative study carried out by Christoph U. Schmid (ed), *Tenancy Law and Housing Policy in Europe. Towards Regulatory Equilibrium* (Edward Elgar 2018).

12 Official Journal no 312, of 29 December 1964.

devastating effect on the Spanish housing market. Few owners were interested in renting their properties and the offer of dwellings for rent decreased dramatically.

In 1994, the enactment of the current Urban Leases Statute (Ley 29/1994, de 24 Novembre de Arrendamientos Urbanos, (LAU))[13] intended to change the situation by making residential leases more attractive to potential landlords. The new rules provided by Articles 6–28 LAU introduced measures aimed at promoting an increase in the offer of residential leases. The main incentives were sought by shortening the mandatory lease's minimum length and by allowing the updating of the rent at the end of each mandatory term.

Since its enactment, the LAU has been amended several times. The most relevant modifications were enacted in 2013 and 2019.[14] For the purpose of the present contribution, it is enough to summarise the provisions regarding length and mandatory extensions of the contract and the provisions dealing with the rent updates.

As for the length of contracts, Article 9 LAU sets forth that the tenant can extend the contract up to five years or less if the landlord is an individual, or up to seven years or less if the landlord is a legal entity. During these periods, extensions are mandatory for the landlord who cannot terminate the contract. Once such periods expire without notice of termination from the landlord or the tenant to the other contractual party, the agreement is automatically renewed for an additional term of three years.[15] Therefore, under Spanish tenancy law, the time schedule for residential leases is five or seven years plus a subsequent term of three years.

As for the rent, and putting aside some legal provisions regarding the increase or substitution of the rent due to improvements or upgrades in the quality of the property, updating is only allowed upon termination of the contract or its legal extensions.[16] Non-payment of the rent allows the landlord to terminate the contract.[17] Spanish Civil Procedural Act (Ley 1/2000, de 7 January, de Enjuiciamiento Civil) provides the landlords with specific eviction proceedings.

The legal provisions referred to are mandatory. It implies a high degree of standardisation of the contracts for residential leases in Spain, at least in the core issues regarding the length of the tenure, the way of securing it and rent updates.

---

13 For a general comment to the statutory regulation and its application by the Spanish courts, see Fernando Pantaleón Prieto (dir), *Comentario a la Ley de Arrendamientos Urbanos* (Civitas 1995); Rodrigo Bercovitz Rodríguez-Cano (coord), *Comentarios a la Ley de Arrendamientos Urbanos* (6th edn, Aranzadi 2013); Xavier O'Callaghan Muñoz (dir), *Comentarios a la Ley de Arrendamientos Urbanos* (Edersa 1995); Alejandro Fuentes Lojo, *Novísima suma de arrendamientos urbanos* (Bosch 2007).

14 Royal Decree-Law 7/2019, of 1 March, on urgent measures concerning housing and leases (Official Journal no 55, of 5 March 2019).

15 Article 10 LAU.

16 Article 18 LAU.

17 Article 27 LAU.

2.2. SPECIAL MEASURES INTRODUCED TO PROTECT TENANTS OF RESIDENTIAL LEASES DURING THE COVID-19 EMERGENCY PERIOD

The LAU does not contain provisions dealing with force majeure or hardship.[18] On the one hand, it could seem odd that the LAU, whose provisions refer to a long-term contract, fails to provide a legal solution for the adjustment of contractual obligations in the case of unforeseen circumstances that affect either the landlord's or the tenant's ability to perform. On the other hand, it is debatable to what extent such a change of unforeseen circumstances may affect the performance of a contract, which only forces the landlord to maintain the peaceful use and enjoyment of the property, and the tenant to pay for the rent.

The landlord will breach the contract if he/she is no longer able to provide the use of the property as agreed. Such a case will discharge the tenant from his/her obligation to pay the rent. From the landlord's duties' perspective, impossibility turns into the breach of the contract and it has to be solved according to the rules governing termination in such scenarios. In its turn, the tenant will breach the contract if he/she fails to pay the rent. Since paying money is the paradigmatic example of generic obligation and *genus nunquam perit*, it is harder to envision another solution than the termination of the contract in the case of the tenant's financial impossibility to pay the rent.[19]

The above-mentioned reason might explain the lack of general provisions in the LAU regarding the impact of unforeseen circumstances. They do not deserve a specific legal solution other than the general one provided for by the breach of contract.

The Spanish legislator was aware that such an argument could work rather well in individual cases, but did not provide a fair answer to a pandemic situation affecting dramatically huge parts of the population. For that reason, the Royal

[18] Outside the supervening necessity by the landlord of the property for familiar reasons and the legal subrogation of the tenant in case of death or divorce.

[19] In the aftermath of the former financial crisis, the possibility to apply impossibility doctrines to tenants struggling with financial setbacks was discussed in depth under Spanish law. Courts dismissed the application of such doctrines. Financial debtors are obliged to pay and difficulties to get the funds cannot amount to factual impossibility. See, among others, the decisions rendered by the Spanish Supreme Court, Civil Chamber, on 17 January 2013 (ECLI:ES:TS:2013:1013) and on 18 January 2013 (ECLI:ES:TS:2013:679). In fact, financial inability is not considered as an excuse to discharge the performance of money debts. See, Rona Serozan, 'General Report on the Effects of Financial Crises on the Binding Force of Contracts: Renegotiation, Rescission or Revision' in Martin Schauer and Bea Verschraegen (eds), *General Reports of the XIXth Congress of the International Academy of Comparative Law* (Springer 2017) 99–114. And the comments on US law at Allan Farnsworth, *Contracts* (4th edn, Wolters Kluwer 2004) 633, and from a comparative perspective, Hanes Rösler, 'Hardship in German Codified Private Law: In Comparative Perspective to English, French, and International Private Law' (2007) 15 Eur. Riv. Priv. 483.

Decree 11/2020, of 31 March,[20] which is one of several provisions enacted as a response to the crisis caused by the COVID-19, set forth measures to address the impact of the crisis on residential leases. The measures are designed to protect tenants unable to pay the rent and qualify as individuals in a "special situation of economic vulnerability" for the purposes of this regulation. These measures can be summarised as follows.

First, the suspension of all eviction proceedings against tenants without alternative housing has been ordered. The suspension will last until for six months after the end of the state of emergency, unless before that time social services are able to find alternative housing for the tenant.

Second, tenants are allowed to extend for six months contract leases which otherwise would expire before the end of the state of alarm. Landlords are forced to accept such an extension.

Third, tenants are allowed to ask for a moratorium on the payment of the rent, although the legal regime differs depending on the qualification of the landlord:

1. If the landlord is qualified as "large scale landlord" or "large owner", they are obliged to attend to the request of the tenant. Once the moratorium terminates, the tenant must pay the deferred rent, in monthly instalments over the following three years or for the duration of the lease agreement if that expires earlier.[21] Alternatively, such "large owners" might agree on a reduction of 50% of the rent during the whole national emergency period and four months after its end.
2. If the landlord does not qualify as "large owner", they are not forced to accept the postponement of the rent asked for by the tenant. The tenant is then entitled to seek financing from the public fund the Spanish Government has created for that purpose.

Such protective measures will surely provide relief to some tenants in dire straits. Nonetheless, it is debatable to what extent they offer a proper response to the crisis and its impact on residential leases from the legal and economic perspectives.

Tenants qualified as beneficiaries are those included in the legal condition of "special economic vulnerability". The requirements to be included in such a category, listed by the Royal Decree 11/2020, are quite strict: potential

---

20 Official Journal no 91, of 1 March 2020. The Royal Decree 11/2020 has been amended by the Royal Decree 2/2021, of 26 January (Official Journal no 91, of 1 April 2021). The preventive measures referred to in the text correspond to those in force after the amendment.

21 Such an extension may have a negative effect on sureties and other kind of warrants to the contract since Article 1851 Spanish Civil Code sets forth the termination of the surety if the contract is extended without the consent of the guarantor. Such consent is not requested by the emergency legislation and its absence may provoke the termination of the surety.

beneficiaries must prove that they are unemployed as a result of the COVID-19 crisis or that their income has been reduced dramatically, and that the rent amounts to more than the 35% of the whole income of the family unit (not only the income of the tenant). Thus, protective measures do not apply to all tenants. In addition, since protective measures only apply to residential leases subject to the LAU, those subject to other regulations on the matter, mostly those subject to the Decree 4104/1964, are excluded.

Although landlords are a necessary party in each residential lease, they are left out. Protective measures focus on tenants, probably to too high an extent. The Spanish lawmaker shifted the costs of the crisis from tenants to landlords.[22] This is clear when taking into account the concept of "large owner" referred to in the emergency rules. The landlord is qualified as a "large owner" if they are a legal person or an individual renting more than 10 properties or, in total, an area greater than 1,500 m^2. The concept is unknown by the LAU, which solely made a distinction between legal persons and individuals when regulating the mandatory minimum length of the lease. As already seen, legal entities renting out residential properties are forced to grant a minimum length of seven years, instead of the regular five-year term provided by the LAU. In the emergency regulation, those entities are also forced to admit the postponement of the payment of the rents by the tenant, unless they agree on a reduction of the rent. It could make sense if it is assumed that such businesses enjoy a stronger financial situation than individuals. However, in the emergency legislation, some individuals, considered as "large owners", are subject to the same obligation to agree either on the postponement of the rent or on its reduction.

The combination of the two former ideas explains the critiques made by legal scholars and professionals in the sector. The protective measures tend to be insufficient for many tenants, while those benefitted by the emergency regulation transfer the risks and costs of the crisis to landlords. Landlords, in turn, are unable to recover the property due to the general suspension of eviction proceedings.

The solution, despite its flaws, can be justified from a social perspective since it avoids the situation where many families lose their homes in the short term. Nevertheless, these measures lack a sound economic appeal since they do not avoid in the mid and long term the domino-effect in the whole economy that may be caused by the non-payment of the rents to landlords. Instead of general rules on rent reduction or a moratorium on the payment of the rent,

22 The economic effect of the legislative solution may be especially detrimental in Spain. As the Consideration of the Royal Decree 11/2020 acknowledges, 85% of the Spanish landlords are individuals, that is to say, they offer properties in the market without a proper business structure and, therefore, without a strong financial endowment and without access to the specific regulation for the business insolvency.

it would probably be more appropriate to provide a general prohibition on the termination of residential leases due to the non-payment of the rent and to the extent that such non-payments are caused by the COVID-19 crisis. Such approach would assure housing to vulnerable tenants without detriment to contractual relationships beyond the duration of the crisis. This is the German solution set forth by the Section 2 of the new §240 EBGB[23] to be applied to leases and usufructuary leases.[24]

A solution solely based on the temporary suspension of the termination and the subsequent eviction in cases in which the non-payment is attached to the crisis is much more respectful towards the contract, avoids unfair and opportunistic practices, and limits the financial effects of the non-payment on the landlord's side. Spanish emergency rules on residential leases can be risky for the economy and for many families as well. They can benefit some tenants whose financial difficulties are unrelated to the COVID-19 crisis, but they exclude some tenants who are facing financial difficulties due to the crisis, and they transfer to the landlords the general costs of the impact of the crisis in residential leases. The Spanish solution seems to be too targeted.

3. COMMERCIAL LEASES

3.1. GENERAL PROVISIONS

The LAU includes several provisions referring to commercial leases in Articles 29–35. Unlike rules on residential leases, such legal provisions are default rules. A greater extent for freedom of contract is legally permitted. Commercial leases are much more diverse than residential ones and parties entering into these kinds of contracts are more sophisticated on average than those entering into residential leases.

The impact of the COVID-19 crisis has also been different on commercial leases than on residential leases. The lockdown has caused the temporary closing

23 The new version of the Article was drafted by Article 5 of the *Gesetz zur Abmilderung der Folgen der Covid-19 Pandemie im Zivil-, Insolvenz- und Strafverfahrenrecht* enacted on 27 March of 2020.

24 According to which: "(1) Landlords are not permitted to terminate leases for land or premises merely on the ground that the tenant does not make a rental payment in the period from 1 April 2020 to 30 June 2020 despite its being due, insofar as non-payment is due to the effects of the Covid-19 pandemic. The link between the Covid-19 pandemic and non-payment must be satisfactorily demonstrated. Other rights of termination remain unaffected …." For a comment on the provision, see Silvio Sittner, 'Mietrechtspraxis unter Covid-19' (2020) NJW 1169.

of many commercial facilities. For the sake of public health, many businesses were forced to close for several weeks, and the shutdown has prevented tenants from obtaining income from their economic activity. Hence, in addition to the general liquidity problem affecting any tenant, in the case of the commercial leases the problematic issue has been to decide if commercial tenants are forced to pay the rent during the period in which they are not allowed to carry out their businesses.

The question has provoked an intense debate among Spanish legal scholars,[25] and it is not duly addressed by the emergency legislation enacted in response to the COVID-19 crisis. Some contracts will surely include a provision for force majeure or similar cases. The problem arises when there is no contractual provision, and it is more acute under Spanish law than under other European legal systems. As has been said, the LAU does not provide a solution for this case, deferring the problem to general remedies for breach of contract. Such a solution appears unfair in this situation since commercial tenants – unlike residential ones – are not allowed to take advantage of the leased property.

The general regulation on contracts contained in the Spanish Civil Code does not give a proper legal answer. The Spanish Civil Code lacks a regulation on the effect of supervening circumstances in long-term contracts. Following closely the Roman tradition, the Spanish Civil Code only contemplates impossibility as a way of discharging contractual obligations. Such impossibility has been understood as a factual one.[26] It is something adverse and beyond the scope of control of the affected contractual party that makes performance objectively impossible. Although the shutdown of commercial premises prevents tenants from carrying on with their economic activities, it is far from clear that this situation makes the tenant unable to pay the rent, since payment of monetary debts is, due to the generic condition of money, always possible.

---

25 Some legal scholars claim that commercial tenants are not obliged to pay the rent during the period in which they are not allowed to carry out their businesses on the grounds of Article 1554.3 of the Spanish Civil Code or the analogic application of Article 26 LAU. In this vein, see Ángel Carrasco Perera, 'Locales de negocio cerrados por COVID: la barbarie o el lobby hacen su agosto (segunda versión, reforzada para los incrédulos)' (2020), *Centro de Estudios de Consumo*, http://centrodeestudiosdeconsumo.com/images/Locales_de_negocio_cerrados_por_COVID-_la_barbarie_o_el_lobby_hacen_su_agosto.pdf accessed 13 June 2020. In contrast, others claim that commercial tenants are obliged to pay the rent during the shutdown of the commercial premises. See Fernando Pantaleón Prieto, 'Arrendamiento de local de negocio y suspensión de actividades empresariales' (2020) Almacén de Derecho, https://almacendederecho.org/arrendamiento-de-local-de-negocio-y-suspension-legal-de-actividades-empresariales accessed 13 June 2020.

26 Articles 1182–1186 Spanish Civil Code.

Spanish legal scholars struggle with the issue, and it will certainly be the object of judicial decisions in the near future. The lack of legal regulation on frustration, commercial impracticability or *rebus sic stantibus* poisons the debate, since there is no general legal frame for examining under which circumstances some degree of discharge, if any, is acceptable.[27] This situation may change in the near future since the Spanish Government is committed to the necessary modifications of the legislative framework in order to introduce in the Spanish Civil Code a provision on the *rebus sic stantibus*.[28] So far, the Spanish emergency lawmaker has made provisions to help commercial tenants, but as will be seen in the next section, rules enacted on the topic fail to give a clear solution.

3.2. SPECIAL MEASURES INTRODUCED TO PROTECT TENANTS OF COMMERCIAL LEASES DURING THE COVID-19 EMERGENCY PERIOD

In Spain, the Royal Decree-Law 15/2020, of 21 April[29] (RDL 15/2020) introduced specific measures to protect tenants of commercial property during the COVID-19 crisis. The decree can be summarised as follows.

3.2.1. Mandatory moratorium on commercial leases if the landlord is a large-scale landlord

The main measure introduced by the RDL 15/2020 is the mandatory moratorium on the payment of rent. However, this measure is not applicable to all commercial leasing contracts. Only self-employed tenants and SMEs that face financial hardship and inability to comply with their rental obligations can benefit under this provision. The economic activity carried out by these tenants is required to meet either of two requirements. Namely, that either their business activity has been suspended as a consequence of the measures adopted by the Government, or that they have suffered at least a 75% reduction in their economic turnover,

---

27 Following the example of the countless legal provisions on the topic already in force in many European jurisdictions (see §313 German Civil Code, Article 1195 French Civil Code or Article 1467 Italian Civil Code) as well as the proposals made by soft law (Art 6:111 PECL, Art 6.1.1 PICC, Art III.-1:110 DCFR or Art 89 CESL), the Spanish Codification Commission made in the year 2009 a proposal for including in the Spanish Civil Code a provision on the issue. Unfortunately, Spanish lawmakers have procrastinated over the debate for introducing such modification in the Spanish Civil Code.

28 See Additional Provision 6 of the Act 3/2020, of 18 September (Official Journal no 250, of 19 September 2020).

29 Official Journal no 112, of 22 April 2020.

although their commercial activity has not been directly suspended. In addition, the landlord must be a public housing company or a large-scale landlord – that is, as explained earlier, a natural or legal person who owns more than 10 urban properties or with an area of more than 1,500 m^2.

In these cases, the tenant has the right to demand from the landlord, within one month from the entry into force of the RDL 15/2020, a moratorium on the payment of rent, provided that the parties have not previously reached an agreement. This rental moratorium must cover the same period as the state of emergency and, if the tenant's inability to comply with their rental obligations remains, during the subsequent months, up to a maximum of four months. Once the moratorium terminates, the tenant must pay the deferred rent, in monthly instalments over the following two years or for the duration of the lease agreement if that expires earlier. Finally, the tenant does not have to pay interest or penalties for the deferment of the said rent.

3.2.2. *The mechanism of renegotiation for other commercial leasing contracts*

For tenants of commercial lease agreements who cannot benefit from the mandatory moratorium, the RDL 15/2020 provides for a rent renegotiation mechanism. In particular, it allows the tenant to request a moratorium on the payment of the rent from the landlord, provided that the parties had not previously reached an agreement. The granting of this moratorium depends on the intention of the landlord, so in effect, in such cases, granting a moratorium is dependent on a voluntary decision of the landlord. However, if the landlord accepts the moratorium, then they reserve the right to use the deposit – paid by the tenant at the beginning of the contract to cover the tenant's default or misuse – to recover either part of or the total amount of the deferred rent. In such cases, the tenant must repay the deposit within one year or during the term of the lease if it expires beforehand.

4. HARDSHIP DOCTRINES AND THEIR POTENTIAL APPLICATION TO COMMERCIAL LEASES

4.1. HARDSHIP DOCTRINES AS THE TENANTS' ULTIMATE REMEDY AGAINST THE COVID-19 CONTINGENCY

The economic consequences caused by the COVID-19 pandemic have given rise to serious liquidity problems for both consumers and companies, which in the case of commercial leases has resulted in a situation where many commercial tenants are unable to comply with their rental obligations. In such circumstances, the parties will often have agreed to renegotiate the leasing agreement – rent reduction or moratorium – especially if they have invested a significant amount of time and money in complying with its terms.[30] In some cases, as explained above, the Government has intervened, approving emergency legislation to adapt lease agreements to the current circumstances. However, the emergency protective measures do not resolve the situation faced by all tenants. In consequence and as a last resort, the party negatively affected by the change of circumstances will have sought court assistance seeking adaptation or termination of the contract based on an exceptional doctrine addressing unexpected circumstances. Although Spain has not integrated such doctrines into legislation, the Spanish Supreme Court recognises the *rebus sic stantibus* doctrine.

From the point of view of legislative policy, it is not advisable to rely solely on this doctrine to remedy an urgent, general, and systemic problem, such as the one that has arisen with the COVID-19 pandemic and the legal consequences it has given rise to. The *rebus* doctrine requires that the courts address the legal fallout on a case-by-case basis, inevitably involving a process which could implicate a substantial time commitment. In addition, relying on the courts to handle a large volume of leasehold contracts affected by the COVID-19 contingency will impose substantial pressure and costs on the Spanish judicial system.[31] It is revealing that the European legal systems that have general rules based on the hardship doctrine – such as Germany and France – have not relied on its general application to remedy contractual problems caused by the health crisis and have instead adopted ad hoc legislation to provide the solution. Although in Spain, equivalent legislation has been passed to deal with the effects of the COVID-19 crisis on commercial leases, these measures have benefited only a small number of tenants.

This section provides an analysis of under which conditions the COVID-19 crisis and the measures taken during the pandemic can be considered as amounting to such an unforeseeable and extraordinary change of circumstances that the obligation of the tenant to pay the rent under the lease becomes an excessively onerous one. And, consequently, in which cases adaptation and, as a last resort, termination of the lease, is justified to make the contract reasonable

---

30 Marta Ceniani, Barbara Luppi and Francesco Parisi, 'Chapter 3. Law and economics: the comparative law and economics of frustration in contracts' in Ewoud Hondius and Cristoph Grigoleit (eds), *Unexpected Circumstances in European Contract Law* (Cambridge University Press 2011) 37.

31 Juan-José Ganuza and Fernando Gómez, 'Los instrumentos para intervenir en los contratos en tiempos de COVID-19: guía de uso' (2020) 2 InDret, 560–561. In the same vein, Ángel Carrasco Perera, 'Al fin la madre de todas las batallas del Covid 19: *rebus sic stantibus*. Con ocasión de una reciente propuesta institucional' (2020) *Centro de Estudios de Consumo*, http://centrodeestudiosdeconsumo.com/images/Al_fin_la_madre_de_todas_las_batallas_del_covid_19-_rebus_sic_stantibus.pdf accessed 13 June 2020 and Matilde Cuena Casas, 'Moratoria en los arrendamientos de locales de negocio y suspensión de actividad económica a causa de la pandemia por COVID-19. Legislando para la foto' (2020) *Hay Derecho* (www.hayderecho.com) accessed 13 June 2020.

and equitable in the new circumstances, in the light of the good faith principle as well as the *rebus sic stantibus* doctrine.

4.2. REQUIREMENTS OF THE *REBUS SIC STANTIBUS* DOCTRINE ACCORDING TO THE SPANISH SUPREME COURT

In Spanish law, the adaptation or termination of a contract due to the unexpected change of circumstances is not provided for in the Civil Code of 1889, although the notion has been admitted by the Civil Chamber of the Spanish Supreme Court since the mid-20th century, based on the doctrine of the *rebus sic stantibus*. The basis for its application is to be found in the principle of contractual good faith in accordance with Article 1258 of the Civil Code. Less frequently, Spanish jurisprudence has resolved the problems arising from the unexpected changes of circumstances based on alternative doctrines, such as interference with the basis of the contract doctrine.

The Spanish courts apply the *rebus* doctrine as a remedy to restore the equilibrium of the contract under contracts involving reciprocal obligations. Its application may lead, in the first place, to adaptation of the contract and, only exceptionally, to the termination of the contract if alteration of the contractual terms fails to rebalance the equilibrium of the contract.

The requirements set forth by the Civil Chamber of the Spanish Supreme Court as to the application of the *rebus sic stantibus* doctrine are as follows: (1) a complete and fundamental alteration of the circumstances at the time of performance of the contract from those prevailing when the contract was entered into; (2) the existence of an unprecedented or exorbitant disproportion between the performances of the contracting parties, which breaks the balance between these performances; (3) that all this arises due to supervening and radically unforeseeable circumstances;[32] (4) that there are no other remedies available to avoid or prevent damage;[33] and (5) that it refers fundamentally to contracts involving continuing relations, although no judgment rules out the possibility to apply the doctrine to non-continuing contracts with a time lag between the formation of the contract and its performance.[34]

---

32 Supreme Court Judgments of 17 May 1957 (RJ 1940/2164); 129/2001 of 20 February 2001 (ECLI:ES:TS:2001:1176); 197/2007 of 1 March 2007 (ECLI:ES:TS:2007:1964); and 781/2009 of 20 November 2009 (ECLI:ES:TS:2009:7112).

33 Supreme Court Judgments, First Chamber, of 6 June 1959 (RJ 1959/3026); of 24 June 1993 (RJ 1993/5382); 1234/2001 of 28 December 2001 (ECLI:ES:TS:2001:10409); 274/2003 of 21 March 2003 (ECLI:ES:TS:2003:1967); 197/2007 of 1 March 2007 (ECLI:ES:TS:2007:1964); and 781/2009 of 20 November 2009 (ECLI:ES:TS:2009:7112).

34 Supreme Court Judgment, First Chamber, 197/2007 of 1 March 2007 (ECLI:ES:TS:2007:1964).

4.3. THE *REBUS SIC STANTIBUS* DOCTRINE DOES NOT APPLY TO THE RISKS ASSIGNED TO ONE OF THE PARTIES BY THE CONTRACT OR THE LAW

One of the basic functions of contract law is the allocation of the risk among the parties due to change of circumstances.[35] However, the parties might not have considered some unexpected circumstances at the time of the conclusion of the contract. The *rebus sic stantibus* doctrine aims to address the problem of assigning contractual risks in cases involving unexpected alteration of circumstances.[36] Contractual risks amount to the possible failure of the interests that the contracting parties wished to achieve under the contract, due to the occurrence of events that arose after the contract being entered into and which were not attributable to the parties.[37]

In the case of commercial leases affected by the COVID-19 crisis and the measures taken during the pandemic, the contractual risk to be assigned is the risk of the diminishing profitability of the tenants' business due to the change of circumstances. Such risk may be classified as a supervening modification of the circumstances and is not attributable to any of the contractual parties. However, it would be more challenging for the tenant to prove that in such cases the requirements of unforeseeability of the risk and excessive onerousness concur.

Regarding the unforeseeability requirement, the Spanish Supreme Court has taken the view that the risk is not unforeseeable if it has been anticipated and provided for by the contracting parties. In other words, the *rebus sic stantibus* doctrine is not applicable if one of the parties has expressly accepted the risk of changing circumstances arising in the contract. In addition, if this risk has been implicitly accepted by one of the parties, by virtue of the circumstances or the nature of the contract, then it cannot be deemed unforeseeable.[38] Once these elements of risk have been duly accepted by the contracting parties, it is not for the courts to reassign them in a different fashion.[39]

In long-term leases between professionals, the parties are likely to agree to a price revision clause, if they are fully aware of the risk at the time of contracting and that the subsequent renegotiation of the contract will be costly. The existence of this type of clause excludes the application of the *rebus* doctrine, since once the contingency has arisen, it cannot be described as unforeseeable.[40]

---

35 Alan Mitchell Polinsky, 'Risk Sharing Through Breach of Contract Remedies' (1983) 12 Oxf. J. Leg. Stud. 427.

36 Cristina de Amunátegui Rodríguez, *La cláusula rebus sic stantibus* (Tirant Lo Blanch 2003) 176.

37 Ángel Carrasco Perera, *Derecho de contratos* (2nd edn, Aranzadi Thomson Reuters 2017) 976.

38 Judgment of the Supreme Court, Civil Chamber, 5/2019 of 9 January 2019 (ECLI:ES:TS:2019:13).

39 Günter H. Treitel, *Frustration and force majeure* (2nd edn, Thomson Sweet & Maxwell 2014) 1.

40 Judgment of the Supreme Court, Civil Chamber, 333/2014 of 30 June 2014 (ECLI:ES:TS:2014:2823).

Consequently, the question of the predictability of the COVID-19 risk in leasing contracts cannot be answered conclusively in the abstract, and the contractual allocation of risk must be analysed on a case-by-case basis.

Secondly, if the contract does not attribute the risk explicitly or implicitly to one of the parties, the risk must be assigned by applying the risk imputation criteria as established in the relevant legislation. The legal rules governing the interpretation of certain unforeseen events take priority in terms of application with respect to the doctrine of *rebus sic stantibus* (*lex specialis derogat legi generali*). Consequently, the *rebus* doctrine is a subsidiary remedy, applicable only to leasing contracts in the absence of an express provision in the general or special legislation adopted to deal with the COVID-19 crisis.

In the case of commercial leases affected by COVID-19, it is necessary to take into consideration the special regulation approved by Royal Decree-Law 15/2020 that only provides for a mandatory moratorium on leases for business or industrial premises entered into between self-employed tenants or SME and large-scale landlords. However, this special regulation has not been considered an obstacle to apply the *rebus* rule in cases falling inside its parameters.[41]

4.4. THE DEVELOPMENT OF THE SPANISH SUPREME COURT'S CASE LAW ON THE *REBUS SIC STANTIBUS* DOCTRINE, MARKET RISKS AND LEASEHOLD INTERESTS

4.4.1. *The traditional doctrine of the Spanish Supreme Court*

The application of the *rebus sic stantibus* doctrine by the Spanish Supreme Court up to 2014 has been very restrictive and has been followed only in exceptional cases. This reluctance can be explained given that, as a general principle, an obligation must be performed even if performance has become more onerous for the debtor.[42] The Supreme Court has applied a strict interpretation of the *rebus* rule, thereby avoiding transferring the risk to the other contractual party.[43]

---

41 In favour of the application of the rebus in all cases, see the judgment of the Court of First Instance number 20 of Barcelona, of 18 January 2021. See also Fernando Pantaleón Prieto, 'Arrendamiento de local de negocio y suspensión de actividades empresariales' (2020) *Almacén de Derecho* https://almacendederecho.org/arrendamiento-de-local-de-negocio-y-suspension-legal-de-actividades-empresariales accessed 13 June 2020.

42 Ewoud Hondius and Hans Christoph Grigoleit, 'Overview: Concepts dealing with unexpected circumstances' in Ewoud Hondius and Hans Christoph Grigoleit (eds), *Unexpected Circumstances in European Contract Law* (Cambridge University Press 2011) 127–129.

43 Ángel Carrasco Perera, 'Reivindicación y defensa de la vieja doctrina *rebus sic santibus*. Sentencia de 15 de octubre de 2014 (RJ 2014, 6129)' (2015) 98 Cuadernos Civitas de Jurisprudencia Civil 184.

In addition, market fluctuations and changes in the financial position of the parties were considered as a foreseeable risk for those involved when entering into a contract, as evidenced by economic history.[44] Based on these arguments, the First Chamber of the Spanish Supreme Court rejected, in its judgment 243/2012 of 27 April 2012,[45] an application to increase the rent based on a *rebus* clause by the landlord of a long-term parking lot located inside a shopping centre. The Supreme Court was of the view that the passage of time in long-term contracts and the economic transformation of a country cannot serve as a basis for modifying the contract based on the *rebus* doctrine, since such circumstances are foreseeable.

4.4.2. *The Spanish Supreme Court's flexible approach to the* rebus *doctrine during the 2008 economic and financial crisis*

After the economic and financial crisis of 2008, the First Chamber of the Spanish Supreme Court announced – in its judgments 333/2014 of 30 June[46] and 591/2014 of 15 October 2014[47] – a revision of its interpretation of the *rebus* doctrine. The Court abandoned the view that the *rebus* doctrine is a "dangerous practice", applicable only in very exceptional circumstances, in favour of making its application requirements more flexible. The most relevant aspect of these two judgments is that they recognise that an economic recession can be considered as amounting to an extraordinary and unforeseeable market change, capable of altering the basis of contractual obligations. However, in the court's view the application of the *rebus* clause did not arise automatically, but only after taking into consideration the circumstances of each individual case.[48]

An example of the Spanish Supreme Court's flexible approach to the *rebus* doctrine during the 2008 economic and financial crisis, can be found in its judgment 591/2014 of 15 October 2014,[49] concerning a commercial lease agreement. The court upheld the modification of the rent that arose under the hotels' long-term lease, despite the fact that the contract contained a clause permitting the tenant to withdraw from the lease after a certain date, paying the amount determined in a liquidated damages clause. During the 2008 economic crisis, the tenant had suffered losses of three million euros due to the reduction in the number of clients. The Supreme Court upheld reduction of the rent as this had been excessively onerous and that the risk involved had been

---

44 Judgment of the Supreme Court, Civil Chamber, 597/2012 of 8 October 2012 (ECLI:ES:TS:2012:6202).

45 ECLI:ES:TS:2012:2868.

46 ECLI:ES:TS:2014:2823.

47 ECLI:ES:TS:2014:5090.

48 Judgments of the Supreme Court, Civil Chamber, 333/2014 of 30 June 2014 (ECLI:ES:TS:2014:2823) and 591/2014 of 15 October 2014 (ECLI:ES:TS:2014:5090).

49 ECLI:ES:TS:2014:5090.

unforeseeable. The court was of the view that the 42.3% fall in the hotel sector was not foreseeable at the time the contract was entered into.

This judgment has been subject to criticism, since it seems unreasonable to uphold the view that the tenant, an international company involved in operating in the hotel sector, could not have taken into account the potential risk of being affected by an economic crisis when entering into a long-term contract.

4.4.3. Return to the traditional doctrine of the Supreme Court

Although in the judgments of the Spanish Supreme Court cited in the previous section, the First Chamber applied a broad interpretation of *rebus* doctrine, in subsequent judgments the First Chamber has returned to its traditional view of the doctrine and has rejected the revision of contracts affected by the economic crisis that commenced in 2008, because: "the problem caused by the financial crisis is an event that occurs in the context of the debtor's business activities, which cannot be considered, unforeseeable or inevitable".[50]

In relation to a commercial lease agreement, the judgment of the Supreme Court, First Chamber, 57/2019 of 15 January 2019,[51] effectively reversed its previous judgment 591/2014 of 15 October 2014, as both judgments had produced contrary decisions on similar facts. In the judgment 57/2019 of 15 January 2019 the Supreme Court has taken the view that the *rebus sic stantibus* clause cannot be applied as the basis for reducing the rent due under a long-term hotel lease. The judgment concludes that the risk arising from the decrease in the operating income of the hotel due to the deteriorating economic situation and market instability, must be considered as being typical of the tenant's business activity, a company dedicated to hotel management. In addition, in the contract the parties had attributed such risk to the tenant by agreeing a guaranteed minimum rent, as well as a clause that allowed the tenant to withdraw from the contract early after paying the amount determined in a liquidated damages clause.

4.5. ADAPTATION OR TERMINATION OF COMMERCIAL LEASES AFFECTED BY THE COVID-19 CRISIS IN THE LIGHT OF THE *REBUS SIC STANTIBUS* DOCTRINE

To address the issue of adaptation or termination of commercial leases affected by the COVID in the light of the *rebus sic stantibus doctrine* it is necessary to

---

50 Judgment of the Supreme Court, Civil Chamber, 742/2014 of 11 December 2014 (ECLI:ES:TS:2014:5210).

51 ECLI:ES:TS:2019:57.

distinguish two situations that we consider should be treated differently by the Spanish courts.

First, the commercial lease may have been affected by the exceptional measures imposed by the Government to deal with the COVID-19 health crisis. At the outset of the health crisis, this may have resulted in the suspension of all economic activity carried out in the business premises by the tenant[52] and, after the most severe phase of the pandemic had subsided, by measures that continued to have consequences for its economic activity, such as capacity restrictions.[53] Such measures put in place by the Government will have entailed that tenants do not obtain income from their economic activity or that their turnover has been drastically reduced.

It is in such circumstances that the Spanish courts can be willing to accept adaptation of the leasing agreement based on the *rebus* doctrine, provided that the tenant has not assumed the risk contractually and is in a position to prove that the obligation to pay the rent has become excessively onerous, since business cannot be developed as usual as the consequence of an unforeseeable scenario.[54] This argument implies that landlords assume those risks that prevent tenants from using the leasehold interest for the purpose agreed by both parties. If, on the contrary, Spanish courts understand that landlords only guarantee the premises availability and they do not assume the risks of the business, the *rebus* doctrine will not play a role.[55]

Secondly, once the measures imposed by the Government to address the health crisis are lifted, tenants may be affected by another consequence arising

---

52 See Article 10 of the Royal Decree 463/2020, of 14 March 2020, which declared the state of alarm.

53 On 28 April 2020, the Spanish Council of Ministers approved the Plan for the Transition towards a New Normality which establishes the main parameters and instruments for the adaptation of the whole of society after the crisis caused by COVID-19. The plan allows, provided certain conditions exist, the opening of premises and establishments to the public, but maintaining certain restrictions.

54 In favour of the application of the *rebus* doctrine in such cases, see the judgment of the Court of First Instance number 20 of Barcelona, of 18 January 2021. In this vein, see Ángel Carrasco Perera, 'Reivindicación y defensa de la vieja doctrina *rebus sic santibus*. Sentencia de 15 de Octubre de 2014 (RJ 2014, 6129)' (2015) 98 Cuadernos Civitas de Jurisprudencia Civil 191–193.

55 It seems again much more cautious the German solution, based on the exclusion of eviction claims due to the non-payment of the rent during the emergency period (see §240 EBGB). It is also revealing that German scholars agree on the inability of the Geschäftsgrundlage doctrine (§313 German Civil Code) to address the issue. See, Alexander Schall, 'Corona-Krise: Unmöglichkeit und Wegfall der Geschäftsgrundlage bei gewerblichen Miet- und Pachtverträgen' (2020) 8 Juristen Zeitung 388–396; Jürgen Hübner, 'Das Gesetz zur Abmilderung der Folgen der COVID-19-Pandemie im Geschäftsraummietrecht – nicht mehr als ein erster Schritt' (2020) Zeitschrift für Immobilienrech 273.

from the COVID-19 crisis, namely the economic fallout.[56] In this context, there can be little doubt that a substantial number of tenants are experiencing a noticeable decrease in their economic turnover arising from the activity carried out in the business premises where they hold a leasehold interest.

In such circumstances, based on the most recent Spanish Supreme Court judgments on the matter, analysed above, the courts will find it difficult to uphold demands seeking the adaptation of lease agreements based on the *rebus sic stantibus* doctrine. Owners of leasehold property cannot be taken to assume market risks to the same extent as the risk of an economic crisis. According to the judgment of the Supreme Court, First Chamber, 57/2019 of 15 January 2019,[57] the deterioration of the economic situation and market instability risks must be considered as being typical of the tenant's business activity.

---

56 See the macroeconomic projections for the Spanish economy for the period 2020-2023, published by Bank of Spain, 'Macroeconomic projections for the Spanish economy (2020-2023)', December 2020, https://www.bde.es/bde/en/areas/analisis-economi/analisis-economi/proyecciones-mac/Proyecciones_macroeconomicas.html accessed 13 March 2021.

57 ECLI:ES:TS:2019:57.

THE JURIDICAL IMPACT OF COVID-19 IN PORTUGUESE TENANCY CONTRACT LAW

Ana Isabel da Costa Afonso*

In response to the public health emergency derived from the COVID-19 disease, Portugal opted for a relatively strict lockdown. Most business activities were suspended and citizens were put under an obligation of confinement. This has created serious disruptions in people's lives and professional activities. In this contribution I will address the specific measures the Portuguese legislator brought into force to solve problems that arouse in tenancy contracts, namely, the adjournment of the obligation to pay rent and the suspension of eviction's effects. Since the legislative measures do not have a general scope that could comprehend all of the tenancy contracts and provide for only a limited and very specific set of solutions, I believe that it is necessary to turn to other legal provisions of a more general approach in order to give an adequate response to the problems encountered in tenancy contracts as a consequence of the pandemic.

The COVID-19 public health crisis urged national legislators to take immediate and exceptional measures on contract law to mitigate the anticipated economic and financial calamity. In Portugal, right after the state of emergency had been declared varied legislative provisions brought into force. The Portuguese legislator's approach was not to create a general set of provisions on contracts

* Faculty of Law of the Catholic University of Portugal.

but to define some specific solutions for some specific types of contracts, mainly credit, employment and tenancy contracts. The aim of this contribution is to address the specific legislative intervention on tenancy contract law, analysing its extent and – given its limited scope – questioning whether a classical and more generic instrument such as the "unexpected change in circumstances", enshrined in Article 437.º of the Portuguese Civil Code, may provide a necessary and adequate solution to the disruption of the tenancy contracts, caused by the pandemic.

1. SPECIFIC LEGISLATIVE MEASURES

As a result of the declaration of the state of emergency,[1] Law num. 1-A/2020 came to force on 19 March 2020. This law contained two extraordinary and transitory measures aimed at protecting tenants: one determining the suspension of the effects of contract termination by landlords (see Art 8.º) and the other, suspending eviction procedures when the residential tenant is put in a fragile situation due to the lack of premises to inhabit (see Art 7.º, n.º 10). Shortly after its publication, the Law's extent was clarified and broadened by Law num. 4-A/2020, of 6 April: on the one hand, it laid down the suspension of the effects of all forms of termination of the contract not grounded on breach of contractual obligations by the tenant, including lawful termination by the landlord, mutual consent revocation and automatic expiry based on the corresponding contractual or legal provisions (Art 8.º);[2] on the other hand, it added to the suspension of the effects of eviction procedures grounds "a ponderous social reason" (see Art 7.º, num. 11).

1 By Decree of the President of the Republic n.º 14-A/2020, on 18 March.

2 According to the Portuguese regime of tenancy contract law, the contract may be terminated by the landlord through a declaration of will both when the duration of the contract is indeterminate and when it lasts for a fixed period. If nothing else is agreed upon, when the fixed period is reached, the contract will be automatically renewed for the same amount of time of its initial duration or (after the change introduced by Law n.º 13/2019 of 12 February) for at least three years in residential contracts and five years in non-residential contracts, when the initial fixed duration is shorter than this time (see Arts 1096.º and 1110.º, n.º 3 and n.º 4 of the Civil Code). The Law n.º 1-A, 19 March, referred to "denúncias" wording that, apart from not being the most correct, corresponds only (within the legal framework of tenancy contract law) to the extinction of a contract with an indefinite duration (see Arts 1101.º and 1110.º-A of the Civil Code). The appropriate legal term referring to the extinction of a fixed time duration (when the automatic extinction is not agreed upon) is opposition to renewal, in Portuguese, "oposição à renovação". This clarification, made by the Law n.º 4-A, was therefore necessary. The Law's scope was extended to include also the suspension of the effects of an automatic extinction of the contract (in Portuguese "caducidade", cf Art 1051.º CC), of termination by mutual consent (see Art 1082.º CC), as well as the six-month moratorium for property restitution provided by Article 1053.º CC, when the contract is automatically extinguished for reasons other than the contractual term ending (expiration of the six-month term will be postponed to after legislative measures to protect the tenant due to the pandemic are revoked). About the modifications recently made to tenancy contract termination

The suspension of the effects of contractual termination and also of the eviction procedures is thus applicable to both residential and non-residential tenancies: the first provision expressly provides for both types; as for the latter, the Law's extension – referring not only to absence of a place to inhabit but also to ponderous social reasons – makes way to apply the second provision not only to residential but also to non-residential tenancy contracts. The legislative's purpose is crystal clear: evictions would either put tenants in a very fragile situation or create an undesired movement of people on the streets looking for new premises to inhabit or to establish their professional activities or enterprises in. The legal provision of the contractual termination suspended effects remained in force until 31 December 2020, according to the Law num. 58-A/2020 of 30 September. The date has been extended to 30 June 2021 by Law num. 75-A/2020 of 30 December 2020. Suspension of the eviction's procedures has meanwhile been revoked by Law num. 16/2020 of 29 May 2020, but later on implemented again by Law num. 4-B/2021 of 1 February 2021.

With respect to the tenancy contract law another provision was brought into force, among the legislative measures to implement the declaration of a state of emergency: first numbered Article 10.º of the Government Decree num. 2-A/2020 of 20 March, later renumbered Article 12.º of the Decree num. 2-B/2020 of 2 April, maintained in Decree num. 2.º-C/2020 of 17 April, it stated that the closing of premises and the suspension of businesses activities could not be invoked either as a ground to terminate a contract or to enforce eviction from the premises.[3] Being coerced by law to suspend their activities, termination of the contract would most unlikely be grounded, yet the legislator was cautious enough to declare its prohibition.[4] I understand that this provision forms the protection of the tenant, being therefore applicable only to the landlord. Averting possible quarrelling around the qualification of the contract, the legislator states the application of the norm not only to pure non-residential tenancy contracts but also to other contractual manners of exploiting the

---

norms, cf Ana Isabel Afonso 'Sobre as mais recentes alterações legislativas ao regime do arrendamento urbano', in Ana Isabel Afonso (coord) *Estudos de Arrendamento Urbano, vol. I* (Porto Universidade Católica Editora 2020), pp. 26–32. About the modalities of contractual extinction in general, see Romano Martinez, *Da cessação do contrato* (Almedina 2017) and on the extinction of tenancy contracts in particular, Menezes Leitão, *Arrendamento Urbano* (Almedina 2019) pp. 135–178.

3 Except for first need or considered essential goods and services, the businesses activities that require public contact were suspended (Arts 7.º, 8.º, 9.º and Annexes I and II of Decree n.º 2-A/2020).The same measure was contained in Decree n.º 2-B/2020 (Arts 9.º, 10.º, 11.º, Annexes I and II), which implemented the renewal of the state of emergency declared by the Decree of the Republic President n.º 17-A/2020, of 2 April, and later maintained in Decree n.º 2-C/2020 of 17 April (Arts 9.º, 10.º, 11.º, Annexes I and II), which renewed for the second time the state of emergency.

4 The right to terminate the contract is only recognised to the landlord when the tenant does not use the premises for more than a year (Art 1072.º, CC). It is possible, however, that the parties to a non-residential tenancy contract may have agreed on something diverse.

premises.[5] After the termination of the declaration of state of emergency,[6] this provision (that impedes termination of the contract or eviction from the premises on the grounds of business activity suspension) is now included in Article 8.º-A of Law num. 14/2020, of 9 May.

The third set of exceptional rulings on tenancy contract law, which was specifically devoted to it, is Law num. 4-C/2020 of 6 April. This Law aims to deal with the tenants' difficulty to comply with the obligation to pay the rent in the due time, when they are suffering from a substantial reduction of income, in the case of residential tenants, or prevented from earning any profit, in the case of the non-residential tenants, since many premises and enterprises were put on hold on account of the public health emergency. The original legal solution allowed adjournment of the rental payment, due during the state of emergency period and the following month, for the next 12 months after that period is finished. Each instalment, of not less than one-twelfth of the total amount in debt, should be paid together with the monthly corresponding rent (see Arts 4.º and 8.º). Since the order of suspension was maintained for some business activities after the state of emergency was terminated, minor modifications have been introduced to Law num.4-C by Law num. 17/2020 of 29 May to adjust the law's extent to those situations: the adjournment of the rental payment was delayed to one month after the business activity was reinitiated. Law num. 45/2020 of 20 August introduced further modifications on non-residential tenancy contracts and extended the debt settlement period from 12 to 24 months, starting on 1 January of 2021 until 31 December 2022. The answer provided by the Portuguese legislator to face the liquidity crisis of the tenant was therefore to preserve the contracts settling a moratorium that temporarily transfers the burden of liquidity to the landlord.

Alongside the moratorium solution, the Law states (see Arts 4.º and 9.º) that a contract cannot be terminated on grounds of material breach by failure to fulfil the obligation to pay the rent in the due time and also that the landlord cannot ask for legal indemnification for damages resulting from late payment (20% of the due amount, see Art 1041.º, num. 1 of the Civil Code) or other contractual penalties (liquidated damages or others).[7]

---

5 It is therefore undoubtedly applicable to "shopping centre" contracts, which are qualified in Portuguese juridical practice as atypical contracts or atypical non-residential tenancies. For further considerations on the qualification of "shopping centre" contracts, consult Ana Isabel Afonso, *Os contratos de instalação de lojistas em centros comerciais – Qualificação e regime jurídico* (Publicações Universidade Católica 2003).

6 Which happened on 3 May, by Governmental Declaration (cf Council of Ministers' Resolution num. 33- A/2020, of 30 April).

7 The legislative technique is not the most accurate since the landlord's prohibition to demand legal or contractual indemnification is only stated in the third chapter of the Law (see Art 9.º, n.º 2), pertaining only to non-residential tenancy. Nonetheless the same prohibition is applicable to residential tenancy given that delaying the rent payment is not attributable to the tenant, that is to say is legally grounded.

As previously mentioned, both residential and non-residential tenants may be entitled to postpone payment of rent, although based on different grounds. The Law considers the situation of the residential tenant who has suffered a reduction of household income of more than 20% (when compared with the previous month or the corresponding period of the previous year) or is put in a situation where the payment of the rent surpasses 35% of household income (Art 3.º, n.º 1, a) and b)). The tenant willing to benefit from the legal solution shall inform the landlord of its intention (by a written notification, five days before the due date) and show proof of the income's reduction (Art 6.º e 3.º, num. 2). This proof shall be made according to the terms stated in Ministerial Ordinance num. 91/2020 of 14 April, Articles 6.º and 7.º, either by presentation of a document issued by the entity responsible for the payment of the revenues (for example, in the case of employment income, payment receipt issued by the employer) or, when exhibit of a document is not possible, by an honour-bound declaration of the tenant himself/herself. Residential tenants were also conceded the right to benefit from financial aid, as stated on Article 5.º, num. 1, which consists of a no interest allowance from the IHRU, I.P.[8] As for the non-residential tenant, he/she may benefit from the rent payment postponement legal solution when the functioning of his/her enterprise has been suspended, by governmental Decree or administrative authority decision, because of the pandemic, for as long as the suspension of the activity persists and during the following three months (see Art 7.º and 8.º of Law num. 4-C, as revised by Law num. 17 and Law num. 45). Although in the original version of the Law the tenant was not legally bound by the obligation to inform the landlord of his/her intention to postpone the payment of the rent – unlike the residential tenant –, we considered that the duty to perform the contract in good faith obliges him/her to do so (Art 762.º, num. 2 of the Civil Code). In its second revision of Law n.º 4-C, the legislator has explicitly filled the gap, obliging the tenant to inform the landlord of the intention to access the law's protective solution (Art 8.º-A of Law num. 4-C, added by Law num. 45).

Having temporarily moved the burden of the liquidity deficit from the tenants to the landlords, the legislator created a new problem (since the risk transference may be unsustainable for the landlord) that has been accounted for only to a limited extent. In the first version of Law num. 4-C it was exclusively for residential tenancy that the landlord was granted a no interest allowance (from the IHRU, I.P.) and only when there is a significant reduction of his/her income as a consequence of the lack of payment by the tenants (Art 5.º, num. 3 of Law num. 4-C). The landlord must prove a reduction of more than 20% of family revenue (in comparison to the previous month or of the same period of the

8 Instituto Público da Habitação e Reabilitação Urbana (Public Institute of Urban Housing).

previous year), such that it comes under the level of the social support index,[9] and also that the revenue decrease was caused by the failure of the tenants' rent payments (Art 3.º, c) and d) of Law n.º 4-C plus Ministerial Ordinance num. 91/2020). Law num. 45 also entitles a non-residential landlord to an allowance but with costs, albeit reduced, and only for the difference between the amount of the monthly rent due and a percentage of maximum effort permitted of the landlord's income (Art 8.º, num. 5). Thus, the State's financial aid intervenes only when the landlord is him/herself put in an unsustainable liquidity deficit.

The provisions of Law num. 4-C are applicable not only to non-residential tenancy contracts but also to other contractual forms of commercial exploitation of the immovables, not purely qualified as tenancies (see Arts 1.º, num. 2 e 10.º), which is the case with "shopping centre" contracts. Articles 8.º, 9.º and 10.º of Law num. 4-C/2020 (as well as currently Art 8.º-A of Law num. 14/2020) provided the first legal steps to address the problems encountered in this specific type of contract. Shopping centre business owners could therefore defer payment of the rents (according to what was above referred), and would not be accountable for this delay; the shopping centre management was not allowed to terminate the contracts, either on the grounds of failure to perform payment of the rent in due time, or based on the suspension of business activities. Article 168.º-A, num. 5 of Law num. 27-A/2020 of 24 July, has, however, settled a specific provision for "shopping centre" contracts: until 31 December 2020, shopping centre tenants are exempted from payment of the fixed amount parcel of the rent due, having only to pay the variable portion (calculated upon a percentage of the revenues) apart from the contribution to the shopping centre costs.

2. OTHER APPLICABLE LEGAL SOLUTIONS

It may well be concluded that there are only very specific and limited provisions to address the problems aroused in tenancy relationships as a result of the pandemic consequences. In the absence of a complete or more consistent extraordinary regime, we have to look for other legal solutions, specifically those of the tenancy contract, and also the more general legal responses to contractual performance under risk occurrence.

2.1. THE URBAN TENANCY CONTRACT LEGAL REGIME

Within the tenancy legal framework, there are two provisions related to the consequences of a definite or temporary impossibility to use and profit from

[9] In Portuguese, IAS (Indexante dos Apoios Sociais, that is, Social Support Index): presently equals EUR 438,81, according to the Ministerial Ordinance n.º 27/2020 of 31 January.

the rented immovable property. Both are contained in the Portuguese Civil Code, one in Article 1040.º, admitting a proportional reduction of the rent due when the tenant is totally or partially prevented (for reasons not attributable to him/her) from enjoying the premises, and the other one in Article 1050.º, recognising the tenant's right to terminate the contract when, for reasons he/she cannot be responsible for, he/she is prevented from enjoyment of the premises, therefore placing the contractual risk in the landlord's sphere.[10] These norms are not, however, adequate to solve problems that arise in tenancy contractual relationships as a consequence of the pandemic and the legal duty to confinement at home. To start with they cannot be applicable to residential tenancies, since the tenant is not being impeded from enjoying the premises (on the contrary, tenants are, generally, forced to stay at home, probably using the premises more than ever). With respect to non-residential tenancy contracts, I find the provision stated in Article 1050.º Civil Code may be interpreted in a way to allow the commercial tenant to terminate the contract, since he/she is prevented from exploiting the property for reasons not attributed to him/her, when coerced to suspend business activity, but it is doubtfull, since there is no physical impossibility to use the premises. Nonetheless, we see no obstacle to this interpretation of Article 1050.º in the legislative exceptional and transitory measure to prohibit termination of the contract on the grounds of the suspension of activity in the premises, stated in the successive Decrees that contained the regulation of the state of emergency above referred (and now on Art 8.º-A of Law num. 14/2020), because we consider it respects only the landlord and not the tenant. In what concerns the other norm, contained in Article 1040.º of the Civil Code, providing for a reduction of the rent proportional to the duration and to the extent of impossibility to enjoy the immovable, we have to stress that it will seldom be applicable to non-residential tenancies with suspended activities. In fact, when the impossibility to exploit the premises is attributable neither to the tenant nor to the landlord, the former is only allowed to ask for a reduction of the rent when the impossibility lasts for more than one-sixth of the duration of the contract (see num. 2 of Art 1040.º of the Civil Code), which would hardly be the case since the suspension of activities did not exceed two or three months, which corresponds to much less than one-sixth of the non-residential contract's typical duration (up to more than three years). However, this may be a possibility for those tenants whose businesses have not been allowed to reopen for more than a year.

---

[10] The risk of deprivation or decreasing of the premises usage falls on the tenant sphere when it does not exceed a sixth of the contract duration; from then on the burden is attributed to the landlord. Article 1050.º places the contractual risk in the landlord's sphere. Cf António Menezes Cordeiro, in António Menezes Cordeiro (coord), *Leis do arrendamento urbano anotadas* (Almedina 2014) pp. 69–72 and 99.

2.2. GENERAL CONTRACT LAW SOLUTIONS

Although it has been maintained that the existence of a specific legal regime is an impediment to apply the "*rebus sic stantibus*" solution contained in Article 437.º of the Portuguese Civil Code – the legislator would have restored the contractual equilibrium disrupted by the pandemic and its corresponding legislative restrictions[11] – we understand that the limited and very specific range of the legal measurements, as stated above, leaves room for the necessary search of other legal solutions, including general provisions such as Article 437.º of the Civil Code. In this norm, the Portuguese legislator has addressed the problem of a fundamental change in circumstances, which, although not being regulated in the contract's clauses, constitutes the basis to the contract's content and even the decision to contractually bind in itself. The aggrieved party is entitled to terminate the contract or to ask for a modification of the contract's clauses when obligation to perform, as originally agreed, violates the good faith principle and is not included in the contractual risks.[12] The pandemic is, undoubtedly, a non-foreseeable fundamental change in circumstances that is not included in the contractual risks. Although the tenancy contract is not definitely frustrated – the situation is merely temporary – and the use or occupation of the premises is not physically impossible, there is a supervening event that may frustrate the purpose of the contract rendering the obligation to perform as initially agreed so burdensome as to violate the good faith commands.

There are, in fact, some situations where Article 437.º of the Civil Code may provide an appropriate legal answer. I am thinking about the case of short-term tenancy contracts made with students or for specific, temporary, professional reasons. Since on-campus lectures have been suspended, students do not need to

---

11 Maria Raquel Rei, 'Arrendamento', in *Novo coronavírus e gestão da crise contratual – Contratos em especial e responsabilidade*, https://www.cidp.pt/evento/2-videocast-novo-coronavirus-e-gestao-da-crise-contratual-contratos-em-especial-e-responsabilidade/80 accessed 15 June 2020.

12 The supervening change in circumstances must be anomalous or exceptional (though not necessarily unforeseeable, as is being stated by a relevant part of the Portuguese legal literature and is also my understanding), must not be included in the contractual risks and shall damage the aggrieved party at a level that asking for performance as initially agreed upon would be a violation of good faith. For further and more profound considerations on the legal requirements of Art 437.º, see, within Portuguese literature on the theme, António Menezes Cordeiro, *Da boa fé no Direito Civil*, vol II (Almedina 1984) 903 ff, esp 1106 ff, 'A crise e a alteração das circunstâncias' RDC, I (2016) 1, 7–63; Luís Carvalho Fernandes, *A teoria da imprevisão no Direito Civil português* (Quid Iuris 2001) 281–294; Pedro Pais de Vasconcelos, *Teoria Geral do Direito Civil* (Almedina 2005) 744–753; Almeida Costa, *Direito das Obrigações* (Almedina 2006) 330–348; Mariana Fontes Costa, *Da alteração superveniente das circunstâncias – em especial à luz dos contratos bilateralmente comerciais* (Almedina 2017) 329–470; Henrique Sousa Antunes, 'Anotação ao art. 437.º', in AAVV. *Comentário ao Código Civil – Direito das Obrigações – Das Obrigações em geral* (Universidade Católica Editora 2018) 154–159.

stay away from home, spending unnecessary money on rent and they wish to terminate the contract, based on the frustration of its purpose, or to modify the contract period, postponing it until face-to-face teaching is reinitiated. The same may happen to a tenancy contract for a professional purpose: the suspension of certain activity can definitely erase its aim or opportunity and the interest of the tenant in the contract can be definitely compromised. These cases cannot be solved under the provision of Article 1050.º of the Civil Code because there is no impossibility to use and benefit from the space itself, but, for reasons not ascribable either to landlord or to tenant and, furthermore, not included within the contractual risks, utilisation of the premises no longer serves the interest of the tenant. In these situations, I believe that the tenant should be able to terminate the contract under the provision of Article 437.º of the Portuguese Civil Code.

Nonetheless, contractual termination under Article 437.º will not, in general, correspond to a desirable solution for either landlord or tenant. The tenant will be aiming to a proportional reduction of the rent or the possibility to postpone payment until profits are more balanced. The extraordinary reduction of consumption, since so many people have been forced to stay at home, not only impacts those whose activities are suspended by law, but also the enterprises that, although remaining with open doors, have no or almost no clients. Take for example the case of a hotel being exploited as a rented immovable. There was no legal command to suspend the activities of hotels but needless to say that the number of occupants may well have been reduced to zero or to just a few clients. Since the hotel activity was not suspended, the solution of the rent payment adjournment stated in Law num. 4-C/2020 is not applicable and the hotel owner is not entitled to postpone payment, but surely the payment of rent in the due time will be an excessively onerous duty for the tenant. The owner of the hotel will not be interested in its termination but preferably in an agreed temporary adjustment of the contract. As for the landlord, it is unlikely that he/she would rather have an empty non-profitable premise than agreeing to an adjustment to contractual conditions.

In my opinion the most adequate legal solution, in these cases, is to apply the principle of good faith and bind the contractual parties to renegotiate the contract (see Art 762.º, num. 2 of the Civil Code). As I see it, in these situations, the preferable solution is not the resources contained in Article 437.º of the Civil Code, but rather the good faith principle solution of binding the contractual parties to renegotiate it.[13] Prioritising this solution to a possible immediate

---

13 Recognising this possibility in Portuguese doctrine, António Pinto Monteiro, Júlio Gomes, 'A "hardship clause" e o problema da alteração das circunstâncias (breve apontamento)', in *AAVV. Juris et de Iure – nos vinte anos da Faculdade de Direito da Universidade Católica Portuguesa – Porto* (Universidade Católica Portuguesa 1998) 39. Considering that a fundamental change in contractual circumstances entitles the aggrieved party to require the other one to cooperate

application of Article 437.º of the Civil Code seems to be more adequate, flexible and efficient (no one else as the parties to the contract will be more aware of their own interests) than a heteronomous more costly and protracted intervention of the court.[14]

If the parties fail to reach an agreement, intervention of the court will then be necessary to find an equitable solution. Asserting the obligation to renegotiate the contract (or to adjust the contractual terms during the crisis period) is, nonetheless, of the utmost relevance because it is not limited to giving the parties a possibility or an opportunity to solve their contractual matters, it goes further, imposing them the duty (whose non-fulfilment they could be liable for) to actively negotiate a solution in good faith.[15]

From my perspective, adjustment or termination of the contract under Article 437.º and obligation to renegotiate the contract according to principles of

---

in a modification of the contract, see Nuno Pinto de Oliveira, 'Em tema de alteração das circunstâncias: a prioridade da adaptação/modificação sobre a resolução do contrato' in Elsa Vaz de Sequeira, Fernando Oliveira e Sá (eds) *AAVV. Edição comemorativa do cinquentenário do Código Civil* (Universidade Católica Editora 2017) 265. Refusing a general recognition of a legal duty to renegotiate the contract, exceptionally admitting to it as a concrete densification of the duty to perform under good faith, cf Mariana Fontes Costa, *Da alteração superveniente das circunstâncias – em especial à luz dos contratos bilateralmente comerciais* (Almedina 2017) 473–486. Henrique Sousa Antunes, 'Anotação ao art. 437.º', in *AAVV. Comentário ao Código Civil – Direito das Obrigações – Das Obrigações em geral* (Universidade Católica Editora 2018) 159, maintains that Article 762.º, n.º 2, gives (only) rise to an encumbrance to renegotiate. Catarina Monteiro Pires, 'Efeitos da alteração das circunstâncias' (2013) 145 O Direito 204, upholds the duty to negotiate under good faith, sustained in Art 762.º, n.º 2. On the same path, see also Diogo Costa Gonçalves, 'Anotação ao art. 762.º of the Portuguese Civil Code', in Catarina Monteiro Pires (ed), *Novo coronavírus e crise contratual – Anotação ao Código Civil* (AAFDL 2020) 74–78. Consult also António Menezes Cordeiro, 'O princípio da boa fé e o dever de renegociação em situação económica difícil' RDS V (2013) 3, 487–535.

14 Although I think that an obligation to renegotiate the contract may be grounded in duty to perform the contract under good faith, I do not think that renegotiating the contract needs to be considered a requirement for a judicial remedy, such as adjustment or termination, under Article 437.º. The aggrieved party will naturally turn to the contractual partner to solve matters before deciding to take it to court or will have a legitimate reason for not doing so. In case it corresponds to an opportunistic behaviour it should be sanctioned for that and that only. Accordingly, Mariana Fontes Costa, *Da alteração superveniente das circunstâncias – em especial à luz dos contratos bilateralmente comerciais* (Almedina 2017) 484. Stating that before asking for adjustment or termination, renegotiation of the contract must be complied with, see Horst Eidenmüller, 'Neuverhandlungspflichten bei Wegfall der Geschäftsgrundlage' (1995) 13 ZIP (Zeitschrift für Wirtschaftsrecht) 1071. Being aware of all the difficulties imposing a duty to renegotiate a contract may bring along (such as specifically stressed by Ewoud Hondius and Hans Christoph Grigoleit, *Unexpected circumstances in European Contract Law* (Cambridge University Press 2011) 9–10) we, nonetheless, are prone to consider that the PECL solution (Art. 6:111 (2)) was, on this particular matter, better than the one contained in DCFR (Book III, Art. 1:110 (3) (d)), since the latter converts renegotiation into a requirement for a remedy.

15 I am certainly aware of all the limits and difficulties of a renegotiation to face a contractual crisis and have no intention to embark on a "Neuverhandlungseuphorie", as referred by Horst Eidenmüller, ibid.

good faith (sustained in Art 762.º, n.º 2) are two autonomous solutions, the latter not being a requirement to use the first resource. Nonetheless, they both pertain to the same juridical axiological question (correct the contract disruption caused by an anomalous event) and are grounded in the same good faith principle (not only to identify the disruption but also to mend it).

2.3. THE SPECIAL CASE OF SHOPPING CENTRE CONTRACTS

As stated above, on 24 July 2020, the Portuguese legislator created a specific solution for shopping centre contracts, which stayed in force until 31 December 2020: the shop owner is exempt from paying the fixed part of the retribution and need only pay its variable parcel (a percentage of the transactions), apart from contributing to the costs of the shopping centre's functioning (see Art 168.º-A, 5, added to Law num. 2/2020 by Law num. 27-A/2020). Considering the specificities of this atypical contract – they include a "joint-venture", cooperative element, that is absent from typical commercial tenancies[16] – and being aware of the difficulties shoppers could have had in settling a fair solution as a result of a contractual renegotiation, the Portuguese legislator conceived a singular response for the shopping centre contracts' disruption that, in my opinion, is not as adequate, equitable and efficient as one would wish for. Torn between the usual controversial demands of certainty and material adequacy, we can well understand and subscribe to a legislative option for a specific and certain solution, especially in a moment of a global crisis like the present. However, when aiming for certainty and a fair protection of one of the contractual parties, the legislator has to be careful to avoid interpretative doubts and creating new inequalities. One of the questions initially raised was the intended date that the provision's enforcement would begin: 25 July 2020 (set in Law num. 27-A (see Art 26.º)) or 1 April 2020 (date of enforcement of Law num. 4-C, applicable in general to all non-residential tenancies rents). This question has subsequently been answered by the legislator through an authentic interpretation of Art 168.º-A, n.º 5.[17] But other interpretative difficulties remained. How is the variable parcel calculated: as contained in the contract – typically it is only due when it surpasses the fixed parcel and only for the exceeded amount – or by applying the agreed percentage to the monthly revenues? Has the legislator taken into consideration that some shop owners only pay a fixed parcel? Do the specificities of the "shopping centre contracts" justify conceding to the business owners the privilege of not paying

16 See Ana Isabel Afonso, *Os contratos de instalação de lojistasem centros comerciais – Qualificação e regime jurídico* (Publicações Universidade Católica 2003) esp 148–161 and 228–233. On cooperation as a structural class of contracts, consult Ferreira de Almeida, *Texto e enunciado na teoria do negócio jurídico* (Almedina 1992) 533–536.

17 See Law num. 4-A/2021, of 2 February 2021, that stipulated 13 March 2020.

a fixed retribution, in comparison to other non-residential tenants operating outside a shopping centre?

Before the innovative provision for the shopping centre tenants was created, they were subject to the same solutions of all tenants in general, contained in the above-referred Law num. 4-C and Law num. 14 (Art 8.º-A).This means that the rents due from April to July could be delayed if the premises had been closed or the business activities suspended. There has been no general order to close shopping centres so those businesses that were allowed to remain functioning could keep selling goods and rendering services to the public. Since the legal moratorium appeared to us as a limited solution – exclusively applicable to those whose business activities had been suspended and allowing only a deferment of the rent and not a proportional reduction or some other solution – we considered it would be an adequate solution to oblige the contractual parties to renegotiate the agreement terms under good faith, bearing in mind that these contracts include an atypical "joint-venture" element that should not be left out when dealing with the problem of excessive burden caused by a supervening non-foreseeable event. An individual commercial business owner (in Portuguese "lojista") should not sustain the entire risk of the business activity's suspension. In the absence of specific contractual provisions – "hardship clauses" either do not exist or do not usually address suspension of activities due to public authority decisions or public health emergencies – and given the limited scope of the legal solution we understood parties in a shopping centre contract should, when necessary, renegotiate the contract adjusting it to the economic downturn. As far as I am concerned, the actual legal solution is too invasive of private autonomy, creates some uncertainties and inequalities and does not reach every case. How to address, for example, the case of shop owners who remained with open doors and are contractually bound to pay only a fixed amount of money: they do not benefit either from rent payment adjournment since their business activities have not been suspended, or from the new solution of Article 168.º-A, n.º 5, as their payment is not calculated upon a variable parcel. Failing to reach every individual case, the specific legal solution still needs to be combined with other more general instruments of contract law. With respect to shopping centres, in my opinion, it would have been better to leave things as they were, combining rent payment adjournment with the obligation to renegotiate the contract to adjust it to a crisis period, equitably distributing the risk between the two parties, considering the specificities of the individual case.

3. FINAL REMARKS

In order to face the consumer's and entrepreneur's liquidity difficulties caused by the public health emergency crisis, European Union Member State provided an immediate and exceptional response of varied content and range, but mainly consisting in direct financial State aid or in allowing deferment of payments, without penalties, of taxes, credit instalments or even rents. When the creditor is not the State (or a public entity) but a private person the payment adjournments may introduce a new problem, translating the liquidity deficit to the other party to the contract.

Allowing deferment of rent payment in urban tenancy contracts has only been enforced in Portugal and Spain[18] and with some significant differences between them. The Portuguese solution appears to us too wide, since all landlords without exception or variance shall endure the rent adjournment consequences (being only able to ask for an allowance when their financial position goes below acceptable), and too limited, in another way, as commercial tenants whose profits have fallen down considerably (more than 50%) may not benefit from the legal solution (applicable only to those whose business activities have been put on hold). Up to a certain point, these differences were considered by Spanish legislator.[19]

A different solution that may be envisaged to solve the tenant's liquidity difficulties would be to equally distribute the risk of the rent payment during the crisis between the two parties, tenant and landlord, and the State, each being accountable for payment of one-third of the rent. With this solution the tenant would not have to worry about paying the monthly rent plus the deferred parcel when the economic upturn is still very uncertain, the landlord would not be deprived (even if temporarily) from the rent income and there would be a partial socialisation of the risk. For non-residential tenancies and after business activities are reinitiated the same equal partition of the risk could be applicable during a period of three to four months proportionally to the profit decrease of the establishment. Being in my opinion equitable, this solution has two set-backs: landlord does not receive full payment; together with other measures implemented, it could exceed State's financial capacities.[20]

---

18 In German, for example, the specific legal solution is to impede termination of contract based on failure to pay the rent during the period between 1 April and 30 June, but only when breach is a consequence of the pandemic (see Art 240 §2 of EGBGB). On the German specific rules to mitigate the effects of coronavirus in contracts, see Martin Schmidt-Kessel and Christina Möllnitz, 'Coronavertragsrecht – Sonderregeln für Verbraucher und Kleinstunternehmen' (2020) 16 NJW (Neue Juristische Woche) 1103–1107.

19 The *Real Decreto Ley* 11/2020, of 31 March, BOE, num. 91 of 1 April (see Arts 3–9) distinguishes the position of the landlord between being an enterprise or not, a public entity or a "gran tenedor de vivienda", only these having to endure the consequences of one of two options: adjournment of the rent and a 50% reduction of its amount. When the landlord is a "pequeño tenedor", adjournment of the rent is not imposed, but the parties are obliged to renegotiate the contracts and, in case it fails, State support may be available. The *Real Decreto Ley* 15/2020 of 21 April, BOE, num. 112 of 22 of April, concedes the legal benefit to autonomous and SME not only when their activities have been suspended but also when revenues have fallen behind 75%, and also defines a variant solution when the landlord is a "pequeño tenedor" (see Arts 1–5).

20 Meanwhile, on 30 December 2020, financial State aid has been introduced to support payment of rent. See Article 8.º-C of Law num. 75-A/2020.

Although I agree that in a time of systemic crisis, such as this, contractual disruptions may not be completely left to general legal instruments such as "unexpected change in circumstances", immediate and exceptional legal responses being indispensable,[21] it is also true that when specific solutions do not provide an equitable and adequate answer, parties will need to turn to general instruments based on the principle of good faith.[22] There is no reason for a general, anticipated, mistrust of contractual power: obligation to renegotiate the contract in good faith can be an adequate and efficient tool in a crisis period.

---

21 Such as stressed by Juan José Ganuza and Fernando Gómez Pomar, 'Los instrumentos para intervenir en los contratos en tiempos de COVID-19: guia de uso' (2020) 2 InDret 560–561, to face an urgent, systemic problem, urgent and systemic measures are required instead of solutions focused on the individual characteristics of the contract. According to these authors, its lack of immediacy, its unpredictability and its high costs that make the "rebus sic stantibus" instrument an inadequate solution for an event with such a high impact on the economy.

22 Applying general civil law instruments to contractual corona crisis, see, in Germany, Constantin Willems, 'Das Allgemeine Vertragsrecht in den Zeiten der Corona-Pandemie' (2020) 3 Zeitschrift für das Juristische Studium in www.zjs-online.com, and Marc-Philippe Weller, 'Virulente Leistungsstörungen – Auswirkungen der Corona-Krise auf die Vertragsdurchführung' (2020) 15 NJW 1015–1022. In Portugal, see the above quoted *Novo coronavírus e crise contratual* (coord Catarina Monteiro Pires) (AAFDL 2020).

NUDGING CONSUMERS TOWARDS SUSTAINABLE PRACTICES REGARDING PLASTICS IN A POST-COVID-19 EUROPE

Marta Santos Silva and Luísa Cortat Simonetti Gonçalves*

Producers and consumers play an important role in the fight against plastic pollution, particularly as far as single-use plastics (SUPs) are concerned, that depend on product eco-design and change in consumption patterns. The EU acknowledges the role of producers and consumers, and established goals for Member States, often in the form of rules addressed to the industry. The challenges caused by SUPs were, however, increased by the COVID-19 pandemic that led to an exponential production of protective equipment, such as masks and gloves, food packaging and take-away containers. This contribution thus purports to address the question of how nudging can foster sustainable practices regarding plastics in Europe during and after the coronavirus crisis. Based on the understanding that behavioural insights are useful to both policy and lawmakers and on statistical information available on the impact on consumer choice and the environment, this contribution demonstrates the utility of nudges in the particular COVID-19 scenario and concludes that consumers shall be given a prominent role in the

* Marta Santos Silva, Maastricht University and KU Leuven – the author for correspondence or queries. Luísa Cortat Simonetti Gonçalves, Academy of European Law (ERA) and Graduate Institute Geneva. The authors would like to thank the anonymous peer-reviewer for their comments.

orchestration of the transition to a sustainable plastics economy. In order to do so, the contribution: (1) describes the omnipresence of plastics in the products offered to consumers; (2) contextualises the European approach to SUPs in the pursuit for a circular economy; (3) summarises the impacts of the coronavirus crisis on the environment and on the law in Europe; (4) describes the role of stakeholders in a sustainable plastics economy; and (5) sets the importance of addressing consumer behaviour through nudging in the fight against SUPs.

1. THE OMNIPRESENCE OF PLASTICS IN THE WORLD OF CONSUMERS

Since their first appearance in 1907, several kinds of polymers have been developed, and we know all of them as "plastic". Plastics are used for applications as diverse as packaging, electric and electronic equipment, construction, agriculture, healthcare, automotive,[1] clothing, cosmetics, furniture, and toys.

Plastic products and materials are a popular product in modern daily life. They are durable, water resistant, highly functional, and versatile, and may be purchased for a relatively low cost.[2] They have been rapidly and deeply ingrained in people's day-to-day lives[3] in such a way that we can speak today of an "addiction to plastics".[4]

The appealing advantages of this material and its convenient use led to the growth of "single-use" or disposable plastics (SUPs), which can be defined as "products and packaging made wholly or partly from plastic that is not conceived, designed, or placed on the market to accomplish – within its life

1 John N. Hahladakis, Eleni Iacovidou, Spyridoula Gerassimidou, 'Plastic waste in a circular economy' in Trevor M. Letcher (ed), *Plastic Waste and Recycling: Environmental Impact, Societal Issues, Prevention, and Solutions* (Academic Press 2020) 481.

2 Directive (EU) 2019/904 of the European Parliament and of the Council of 5 June 2019 on the reduction of the impact of certain plastic products on the environment [2019] OJ L 155, Preamble 1; WWF UK, 'Ten tips to reduce your plastic footprint' https://www.wwf.org.uk/updates/ten-tips-reduce-your-plastic-footprint, accessed 9 August 2020.

3 Directive (EU) 2019/904 of the European Parliament and of the Council of 5 June 2019 on the reduction of the impact of certain plastic products on the environment [2019] OJ L 155, Preamble 1; Communication from the Commission to the European Parliament, the Council, the European Economic and Social Committee and the Committee of the Regions. A European Strategy for Plastics in a Circular Economy [SWD(2018) 16 final] COM(2018) 28 final https://ec.europa.eu/environment/circular-economy/pdf/plastics-strategy.pdf accessed 9 August 2020; Jerneja Penca, 'European Plastics Strategy: What promise for global marine litter?' (2018) 97 Marine Policy 197, 197.

4 Sharon George, 'Plastics we cannot live without' in Trevor M. Letcher (ed), *Plastic Waste and Recycling: Environmental Impact, Societal Issues, Prevention, and Solutions* (Academic Press 2020) 449, 449.

span – multiple trips or rotations by being returned to a producer for refill or reused for the same purpose for which it was originally conceived".[5]

SUPs consist of straws, cotton buds, plastic cutlery, plastic plates and rubber gloves, and represent about half of the plastic produced worldwide.[6] This plastic ends up in landfills or in the oceans, giving rise to the largest environmental disaster caused by humankind,[7] together with climate change.

Data are alarming: estimations show that, every year, at least eight million tons of plastic end in the oceans, and that, if this pace continues, by 2050 the oceans will have more plastics than fish.[8] However, beyond the visible objects "microplastics" are also part of the problem. Natural interactions make plastic pieces slowly break up into 0.1 to 5 mm large floating plastic particles that are eaten by fish, other marine species and also humans.

Larger and smaller plastic pieces of plastic together form what is called the "plastic soup",[9] that endanger ecosystems[10] and human health[11] and are thus an existential threat to Europe and the world.

---

5 Directive (EU) 2019/904 of the European Parliament and of the Council of 5 June 2019 on the reduction of the impact of certain plastic products on the environment [2019] OJ L 155, Preamble 1.

6 Jefferson Hopewell, Robert Dvorak and Edward Kosior, 'Plastics recycling: challenges and opportunities' (2009) 364 Philosophical Transactions of the Royal Society. Series B. Biological Sciences 1526, 2115.

7 Laura Parker, 'Planet or Plastic? A whopping 91% of plastic isn't recycled' (*National Geographic*, 20 December 2018) https://www.nationalgeographic.com/news/2017/07/plastic-produced-recycling-waste-ocean-trash-debris-environment/ accessed 18 November 2019.

8 Athanasios Valavandinis and Thomais Vlachogianni, 'Microplastics in the Marine Environment: Ubiquitous and Persistent Pollution Problem in the World's Oceans Threatening Marine Biota' (*Researchgate*, 30 June 2014) www.researchgate.net/publication/263477975 accessed 9 August 2020.

9 The "plastic soup" was first described in 1997 by the sailor Charles Moore, when taking a shortcut on the way between Hawaii and California. He reported to major news and interview programs the Great Pacific Garbage Patch, describing it as a *plastic soup* twice the size of Texas. Patricia Bauer, 'Great Pacific Garbage Patch' (*Encyclopaedia Britannica*) https://www.britannica.com/topic/Great-Pacific-Garbage-Patch accessed 12 August 2020.

10 *Litterbase*. 2017, https://litterbase.awi.de/interaction_graph accessed 29 August 2017; Cees Van De Guchte, 'Marine Litter' (*Sixth Meeting of the UN Open-Ended Informal Consultative Processes on Oceans & the Law of the Sea* 6–10 June 2005) https://www.un.org/Depts/los/consultative_process/documents/6_guchte.pdf accessed 12 August 2020.

11 Research shows that we are already drinking, eating and even breathing plastics. Alvise Vianello, 'Simulating human exposure to indoor airborne microplastics using a Breathing Thermal Manikin' (2019) Nature, Scientific Reports 9, Article number 8670; Damian Carrington, 'We are living on a plastic planet. What does it mean to our health?' (*The Guardian*, 6 September 2017), https://www.theguardian.com/environment/2017/sep/06/we-are-living-on-a-plastic-planet-what-does-it-mean-for-our-health/ accessed 8 September 2017; Peter Haffner, 'An Intimation of the Apocalypse' (*NZZ Folio* 07/2009), https://www.plasticgarbageproject.org/en/plastic-garbage/problems/plastic-garbage-gyre/peter-haffner-an-intimation-of-the-apokalypse/ accessed 19 August 2020.

2. THE REGULATORY CONTEXT OF THE SINGLE-USE PLASTIC DIRECTIVE (SUPD)

The environmental disruption caused by plastic waste has been known for decades. However, traditional regulatory solutions have not yet effectively dealt with this problem. Internationally, there is almost no mention of plastic pollution, with only scattered and unstructured provisions in instruments such as the London Protocol (2006), Annex V of the International Convention for the Prevention of Pollution from Ships, or MARPOL (2011), the Basel Convention (through an amendment that entered in force in December 2019), the Agreement on Government Procurement, or GPA[12] (from 2014 onwards), and the Sustainable Development Goals[13] (2030 Agenda for Sustainable Development). The regulations that refer to plastic pollution are very recent and have not yet sufficiently reduced plastic pollution or its impacts.[14]

Plastic pollution has been mainly addressed by national or local governments, through legal bans or use of restrictions.

By August 2017, 40 countries around the world already had bans or restrictions in place, and these mainly concerned plastic bags and straws.[15] As for Europe, to mention a few examples, in 2015, France banned oxo-fragmentable bags;[16] in 2016, 2017 and 2018, Italy, France and Belgium (Brussels) respectively, banned ultra-lightweight plastic bags; in 2018, Denmark banned plastic bags and in 2019, Italy banned non-biodegradable plastic cotton buds. Iceland has initiatives

---

12 United Nations Environmental Program – UNEP. *Global Programme of Action for the Protection of the Marine Environment from Land-Based Activity* (1995) https://www.unenvironment.org/resources/toolkits-manuals-and-guides/global-programme-action-protection-marine-environment-land accessed 14 August 2020.

13 United Nations Sustainable Development Knowledge Platform, *Sustainable Development Goals* (2015) https://sustainabledevelopment.un.org/?menu=1300 accessed 12 August 2020.

14 Luísa Cortat Simonetti Gonçalves and Michael Gerbert Faure, 'International Law Instruments to Address the Plastic Soup' (2019) 43 William & Mary Environmental Law and Policy Review 3, 870; Luísa Cortat Simonetti Gonçalves, *Legal Remedies against the Plastic Pollution of the Oceans: An Analysis of the Attempts from Public International Law and Private Initiatives to face the Plastic Soup* (Proefschriftmaken 2020).

15 G. Cabrera, 'Countries with plastic bag bans. August 28, 2017' (*ABC*, 28 August 2017) https://www.abc.net.au/news/2017-08-28/countries-with-plastic-bag-bans/8850284?nw=0 accessed 14 August 2020.

16 "Bioplastics" is a misleading term in the sense that it refers to a broad range of materials, most of which are not good for the environment. See, e.g. Geert Bergsma, Lonneke de Graaff, Sanne Nusselder and Ingrid Odegard, 'Biobased Plastics in a Circular Economy: Policy suggestions for biobased and biobased biodegradable plastics' (*CE Delft*, 2017) 4 https://www.cedelft.eu/en/publications/2022/biobased-plastics-in-a-circular-economy accessed 14 August 2020. In this context, oxo-fragmentable refers to the kind of plastic that does not degrade when exposed in the environment, but merely breaks faster into smaller pieces.

for plastic waste management in ports[17] and, since 2014, the Netherlands has had, for the same purpose, a Green Deal under implementation at the ports of Rotterdam and Amsterdam.[18]

In 2020, several countries established measures fighting plastics. France banned plastic eating ware and cotton buds. In continental Spain and the Balearic Islands, all single-use consumer plastics will need to be "easily recyclable" or otherwise replaced by biodegradable alternatives, and wet wipes must now be clearly labelled to prevent them from being flushed.[19] In Portugal, eating and drinking ware, cotton buds and oxo-degradable plastics are forbidden, and resistant plastic bags became more expensive.

The EU soon recognised the advantages of a coordinated action[20] to prevent the fragmentation of the single market and its adverse effects.[21] In a scenario of increasing supply chain complexity and with the high number of bordering markets, harmonisation could benefit businesses and consumers.[22]

---

17 European Commission [2018] Commission Staff Working Document Impact Assessment Reducing Marine Litter: action on single use plastics and fishing gear. Part 1/3 https://ec.europa.eu/environment/circular-economy/pdf/single-use_plastics_impact_assessment.pdf accessed 9 August 2020, 30.

18 Green Deal. GD166 – Scheepsafvalketen (16 July 2018) https://www.greendeals.nl/sites/default/files/downloads/GD166-samenvatting-Scheepsafvalketen.pdf accessed 26 July 2018.

19 European Commission [2018] Commission Staff Working Document Impact Assessment Reducing Marine Litter: action on single use plastics and fishing gear. Part 1/3 https://ec.europa.eu/environment/circular-economy/pdf/single-use_plastics_impact_assessment.pdf accessed 9 August 2020, 33–34.

20 For an economic analysis of up and downsides of tort law harmonisation, see e.g. Michael Faure, 'How law and economics may contribute to the harmonisation of tort law in Europe' (*Researchgate*, 2003) https://www.researchgate.net/publication/241873105_How_law_and_economics_may_contribute_to_the_harmonisation_of_tort_law_in_Europe#read accessed 14 August 2020. On the harmonisation of tort law in Europe from a legal perspective see Marta Santos Silva, *The Draft Common Frame of Reference as a 'toolbox' for domestic courts* (Springer 2017) 66 ff.

21 European Commission [2018] Commission Staff Working Document Impact Assessment Reducing Marine Litter: action on single use plastics and fishing gear. Part 1/3 https://ec.europa.eu/environment/circular-economy/pdf/single-use_plastics_impact_assessment.pdf accessed 9 August 2020, 33. It is worth noticing that the European Commission recommended that in respect of "the application deadlines in Article 17(1), second sub-paragraph, of the SUP Directive" EU Members States would not "apply measures such as bans on single use plastic products and marking of sanitary items before the 3rd of July 2021". They considered that a "harmonised application of these rules across the EU is necessary to ensure the proper functioning of the internal market and give sufficient time to economic operators to adapt their production and business models" https://ceoe-tenerife.com/wp-content/uploads/2019/11/Administrative-letter-to-MS.SUP-implementation.pdf accessed 12 August 2020.

22 European Commission [2018] Commission Staff Working Document Impact Assessment Reducing Marine Litter: action on single use plastics and fishing gear. Part 1/3 https://ec.europa.eu/environment/circular-economy/pdf/single-use_plastics_impact_assessment.pdf accessed 9 August 2020, 5.

The EU started legislating on plastic pollution in 1994, when the Directive 94/62/EC on Packaging and Packaging Waste[23] set targets for packaging recycling and for the reduction of the per capita consumption of lightweight plastic carrier bags. In 2006, Regulation (EC) No 1013/2006 of 14 June 2006 on shipments and waste[24] set procedures for transboundary waste transport, including to third countries, and the REACH (Registration, Evaluation, Authorisation and Restriction of Chemicals) Regulation[25] established a general framework on chemicals intended to facilitate the placing on the market of recycled materials. In 2008, the CLP (Classification, Labelling and Packaging) Regulation aimed at ensuring that the hazards posed by chemical substances were clearly identified and communicated. In the same year, an amendment to the Directive 2008/98/EC on waste (Waste Framework Directive)[26] required Member States to identify products that are the main sources of littering and to take measures to halt the generation of marine litter. However, none of them was considered properly implemented.[27]

By 2018, around 26 million tons of plastic were being generated in Europe every year,[28]and this meant the entire system was in urgent need of an overhaul. So that year the EU Plastics Strategy[29] was introduced.[30] The European Commission set up four concrete pillars to help achieve a more sustainable use of plastics throughout the value chain, namely: improving the economics and quality of plastics recycling; curbing plastic waste and littering; driving innovation and investment towards circular solutions; and harnessing global action.

---

23 European Parliament and Council Directive 94/62/EC of 20 December 1994 on packaging and packaging waste [1994] OJ L 365.

24 Regulation (EC) No 1013/2006 of the European Parliament and of the Council of 14 June 2006 on shipments of waste, OJ L 190.

25 Regulation (EC) No 1907/2006 of the European Parliament and of the Council of 18 December 2006 concerning the Registration, Evaluation, Authorisation and Restriction of Chemicals (REACH), OJ L 396.

26 Directive 2008/98/EC of the European Parliament and of the Council of 19 November 2008 on waste and repealing certain Directives, OJ L 312.

27 Edward Kosier and Irene Crescenzi, 'Solution to the plastic waste problem on land and in the oceans' in Trevor M. Letcher (ed), *Plastic Waste and Recycling: Environmental Impact, Societal Issues, Prevention, and Solutions* (Academic Press 2020) 415, 429.

28 European Commission [2015] Closing the Loop – An EU Action Plan for Circular Economy https://eur-lex.europa.eu/resource.html?uri=cellar:8a8ef5e8-99a0-11e5-b3b7-01aa75ed71a1.0012.02/DOC_1&format=PDF accessed 12 August 2020, 2.

29 Communication from the Commission to the European Parliament, the Council, the European Economic and Social Committee and the Committee of the Regions. A European Strategy for Plastics in a Circular Economy [SWD(2018) 16 final] COM(2018) 28 final https://ec.europa.eu/environment/circular-economy/pdf/plastics-strategy.pdf accessed 9 August 2020.

30 For a detailed chronological overview, see Tim Elliott, Hannah Gillie and Alice Thomson, 'European Union's plastic strategy and an impact assessment of the proposed directive on tackling single-use plastics items' in Trevor M. Letcher (ed), *Plastic Waste and Recycling: Environmental Impact, Societal Issues, Prevention, and Solutions* (Academic Press 2020) 605–610.

The EU Plastic Strategy is embedded in a broader context, namely that of the EU Action Plan for the Circular Economy,[31] already considered as having a leading role on the plastic-related agenda if compared with other global major economies such as the United States.[32]

This instrument aims to introduce a transition from a linear into a circular economy[33] in Europe, "closing the loop" of each product's life cycle, rather than endorsing single-use and the waste of material after any kind of use. The intention is that the value of products and resources is maintained for a longer time and waste is minimised;[34] thereby, the EU becomes a lower carbon, resource efficient and ultimately more competitive economy.[35]

The plastics industry is viewed as a priority area[36] for the transition of the EU into a circular economy,[37] given the concerning numbers of plastics that are not recycled and, therefore, end up in landfills or oceans every year.[38] In their "Action Plan for the Circular Economy", the Commission reaffirmed the need to establish a more sustainable plastics industry by preparing a strategy which would address "the challenges posed by plastics throughout the value chain".[39]

In the EU Plastics Strategy, the European Commission described its goal of achieving a "smart, innovative and sustainable" plastics industry, where product design and the production process respect the needs of reuse,

---

31 European Commission [2015] Closing the Loop – An EU Action Plan for Circular Economy, https://eur-lex.europa.eu/resource.html?uri=cellar:8a8ef5e8-99a0-11e5-b3b7-01aa75ed71a1.0012.02/DOC_1&format=PDF accessed 12 August 2020.

32 Madeline June Kass, 'Fishing for Plastic: EU Targets Marine Pollution', (2019) 58 Natural Resources & Environment.

33 The term was popularised by Ellen MacArthur. See Ellen MacArthur Foundation, 'What is a circular economy?' (*Ellen MacArthur Foundation*, 2017) https://www.ellenmacarthurfoundation.org/circular-economy/concept accessed 12 August 2020.

34 European Commission [2015] Closing the Loop – An EU Action Plan for Circular Economy https://eur-lex.europa.eu/resource.html?uri=cellar:8a8ef5e8-99a0-11e5-b3b7-01aa75ed71a1.0012.02/DOC_1&format=PDF accessed 12 August 2020, 2.

35 European Commission [2015] Closing the Loop – An EU Action Plan for Circular Economy https://eur-lex.europa.eu/resource.html?uri=cellar:8a8ef5e8-99a0-11e5-b3b7-01aa75ed71a1.0012.02/DOC_1&format=PDF accessed 12 August 2020.

36 European Commission [2015] Closing the Loop – An EU Action Plan for Circular Economy https://eur-lex.europa.eu/resource.html?uri=cellar:8a8ef5e8-99a0-11e5-b3b7-01aa75ed71a1.0012.02/DOC_1&format=PDF accessed 12 August 2020.

37 European Commission [2015] Closing the Loop – An EU Action Plan for Circular Economy https://eur-lex.europa.eu/resource.html?uri=cellar:8a8ef5e8-99a0-11e5-b3b7-01aa75ed71a1.0012.02/DOC_1&format=PDF accessed 12 August 2020, 13.

38 This concerns 1.5% to 4% of global plastic, around 5 to 13 million tons of plastic. European Commission [2015] Closing the Loop – An EU Action Plan for Circular Economy https://eur-lex.europa.eu/resource.html?uri=cellar:8a8ef5e8-99a0-11e5-b3b7-01aa75ed71a1.0012.02/DOC_1&format=PDF accessed 12 August 2020, 3.

39 European Commission [2015] Closing the Loop – An EU Action Plan for Circular Economy https://eur-lex.europa.eu/resource.html?uri=cellar:8a8ef5e8-99a0-11e5-b3b7-01aa75ed71a1.0012.02/DOC_1&format=PDF accessed 12 August 2020, 14. Séverine Herbots, *The role of European Trade Actors in the Plastics Strategy* (Hasselt University 2020), unpublished.

repair and recycling[40] through a cooperative effort of citizens, governments and industries.[41] By 2030, the EU wishes that: all plastics are reusable or recyclable; more than half of plastics waste generated in Europe is recycled; new companies embrace circular solutions to the plastics production chain and that the secondary plastic market increases fourfold as compared to 2015.[42]

It was within the EU Plastics Strategy context that, in May 2019, shortly after its proposal,[43] the EU formally approved[44] pioneer legislation to prevent and tackle marine litter by, among other things, phasing out unnecessary single-use plastics, introducing economic incentives to reduce consumption and transition to reusable systems, and establishing high collection rates and extended producer responsibility schemes (EPR).[45]

The Single-Use Plastics Directive (SUP Directive or SUPD) aims at coordinating marine litter prevention policies and measures.[46] The measures set forth apply to all EU Member States, who will have to transpose and implement the SUP Directive into their national legislation by mid-2021.[47] Even though some consider it under-ambitious as far as target setting,[48] its entry into force on

---

40 European Commission [2018] A European Strategy for Plastics in a Circular Economy. SWD (2018)16 def, 5.

41 Communication from the Commission to the European Parliament, the Council, the European Economic and Social Committee and the Committee of the Regions. A European Strategy for Plastics in a Circular Economy [SWD(2018) 16 final] COM(2018) 28 final https://ec.europa.eu/environment/circular-economy/pdf/plastics-strategy.pdf accessed 9 August 2020. See also Joseph Sarkis, Maurie J. Cohen, Paul Dewick and Patrick Schroeder, 'A brave new world. Lessons from the COVID-19 pandemic for transitioning to sustainable supply and production' (2020) 159 *Resources, Conservation and Recycling* 1, 1–4.

42 Communication from the Commission to the European Parliament, the Council, the European Economic and Social Committee and the Committee of the Regions. A European Strategy for Plastics in a Circular Economy [SWD(2018) 16 final] COM(2018) 28 final https://ec.europa.eu/environment/circular-economy/pdf/plastics-strategy.pdf, 5, accessed 9 August 2020.

43 European Commission, 'Single-use plastics: New EU rules to reduce marine litter' (*European Commission. Press Release Database*, 28 May 2018) http://europa.eu/rapid/press-release_IP-18-3927_en.html accessed 12 August 2020.

44 Rethink Plastic Alliance, 'Press release: EU agrees unprecedented cuts to single-use plastics' (*Rethink Plastic Alliance*, 19 December 2018) https://rethinkplasticalliance.eu/news/eu-agrees-unprecedented-cuts-to-single-use-plastics/ accessed 12 August 2020.

45 Zero Waste Europe, 'Unfolding the Single-Use Plastics Directive: Policy Briefing' (*Rethink Plastic Alliance*, May 2019) https://rethinkplasticalliance.eu/wp-content/uploads/2019/05/ZWE_Unfolding-the-SUP-directive.pdf accessed 9 August 2020.

46 European Commission [2018] Commission Staff Working Document: Implementation Plan accompanying the document proposal for a Directive of the European Parliament and of the Council on the Reduction of the Impact of certain plastic products on the environment https://eur-lex.europa.eu/legal-content/EN/TXT/PDF/?uri=CELEX:52018SC0256&from=EN accessed 11 August 2020, 3.

47 Zero Waste Europe, 'Unfolding the Single-Use Plastics Directive: Policy Briefing' (*Rethink Plastic Alliance*, May 2019) https://rethinkplasticalliance.eu/wp-content/uploads/2019/05/ZWE_Unfolding-the-SUP-directive.pdf accessed 9 August 2020.

48 Noreen O'Meara, 'Tackling the plastics pollution crisis through the EU Single-Use Plastics Directive: context, scope and implementation challenges' (2020) 25(6) Environmental Liability 235.

3 July 2017 cements "a key piece of European legislation into the history of the human response to tackling the major challenge of marine plastic pollution".[49]

3. CORONAVIRUS AND ITS IMPACT ON THE ENVIRONMENT AND THE LAW IN EUROPE

All seemed set for a successful implementation in 2021 of the SUP Directive, if it was not for the fact that Europe was swept by COVID-19 in 2020.

From the moment it was declared officially as a pandemic on 11 March 2020[50] COVID-19 had devastating consequences, also for the environment. It allegedly brought about a decrease in CO2 emissions by 17% in comparison with 2019[51] due to the sharp decrease in commuting,[52] but plastics had a comeback with a massive surge of plastic products such as face masks, water and hand sanitiser bottles, visors, cotton buds, packaging[53] and take-away food containers.[54] This represented several steps backward in a well-settled European journey towards elimination of single-use plastics by 2030.

---

49 Tim Elliott, Hannah Gillie and Alice Thomson, 'European Union's plastic strategy and an impact assessment of the proposed directive on tackling single-use plastics items' in Trevor M. Letcher (ed), *Plastic Waste and Recycling: Environmental Impact, Societal Issues, Prevention, and Solutions* (Academic Press 2020) 605, 622.

50 World Health Organization, 'WHO Timeline – COVID-19' (*World Health Organization*, 27 April 2020) https://www.who.int/news-room/detail/27-04-2020-who-timeline---covid-19 accessed 9 August 2020.

51 Corinne Le Quéré, Robert B. Jackson, Matthew W. Jones, Adam J. P. Smith, Sam Abernethy, Robbie M. Andrew, Anthony J. De-Gol, David R. Willis, Yuli Shan, Josep G. Canadell, Pierre Friedlingstein, Felix Creutzig, and Glen P. Peter, 'Temporary reduction in daily global CO2 emissions during the COVID-19 forced confinement' in Nature Climate Change (2020) 10 https://www.nature.com/articles/s41558-020-0797-x.pdf accessed 4 August 2020.

52 COVID-19 Consumer Law Research Group, 'Consumer Law and Policy Relating to Change of Circumstances Due to the COVID-19 Pandemic' (2020) 43 Journal of Consumer Policy 437, 441 https://link.springer.com/article/10.1007/s10603-020-09463-z accessed 12 August 2020 and Frank Boons, Martin Burgess, Steffan Hirth, Helen Holmes, Sherilyn MacGregor, Josephine Mylan, Matthew Paterson, Maria Sharmina, Daniel Welch, Luke Yates, Alison L. Browne, Ulrike Ehgartner, Mike Hodson, Claire Hoolohan, Andrew Mcweekin, Filippo Oncini, Malte B. Roedl, Alan Warde, Harald Wieser and Chunhua Ye 'Covid-19, Changing social practices and the transition to sustainable production and consumption. Version 1.0' (*ResearchGate*, May 2020) https://www.researchgate.net/publication/341214697_Covid-19_Changing_Social_Practices_and_the_Transition_to_Sustainable_Consumption_and_Production accessed 15 August 2020.

53 COVID-19 Consumer Law Research Group, 'Consumer Law and Policy Relating to Change of Circumstances Due to the COVID-19 Pandemic' (2020) 43 Journal of Consumer Policy 437, 441 https://link.springer.com/article/10.1007/s10603-020-09463-z accessed 12 August 2020.

54 Angeli Mehta, 'The war on plastics runs into a perfect storm with Covid-19' (*Ethical Corp*, 2 June 2020) https://www.ethicalcorp.com/war-plastics-runs-perfect-storm-covid-19 accessed 11 August 2020; Gillian Flaccus, 'Coronavirus fears spur cities to reverse hard-fought bans on single-use plastic' (*Fortune*, 8 April 2020) https://fortune.com/2020/04/08/coronavirus-reverse-bans-single-use-plastic/ accessed 11 August 2020.

In earlier recommendations, the World Health Organization (WHO) discouraged the generalised use of protective equipment by the population. It stated that medical masks should be reserved for health care workers, due to the concern that the use of masks in the community would create a misleading sense of security, leading people to neglect other essential measures.[55] However, considering the risks of pre- and asymptomatic transmission, updated information, and the difficulties of social distancing in many contexts, the WHO "updated its guidance to advise that to prevent COVID-19 transmission effectively in areas of community transmission, governments should encourage the general public to wear masks in specific situations and settings as part of a comprehensive approach to suppress SARS-CoV-2 transmission".[56] Following such recommendation, States started demanding that citizens use disposable[57] masks[58] and gloves and, with people staying longer at home, an increase in the amount of food and take-away packages was also observed.[59] Being a global pandemic, COVID-19 thus risks to cause billions[60] of SUP products to end up in landfills or floating in the seas.[61]

---

55 See World Health Organization, 'Advice on the use of masks in the context of COVID-19' (*World Health Organization*, 6 April 2020) https://apps.who.int/iris/bitstream/handle/10665/331693/WHO-2019-nCov-IPC_Masks-2020.3-eng.pdf?sequence=1&isAllowed=y accessed 5 August 2020.

56 See World Health Organization, 'Advice on the use of masks in the context of COVID-19' (*World Health Organization*, 6 April 2020) https://apps.who.int/iris/bitstream/handle/10665/331693/WHO-2019-nCov-IPC_Masks-2020.3-eng.pdf?sequence=1&isAllowed=y accessed 5 August 2020.

57 Although the use of fabric (reusable) masks is generally considered less detrimental for the environment, it also contributes to the growth of plastic pollution, namely through the release of microplastics to the environment during washing. See Plastic Soup Foundation, 'Ocean Clean Wash. 2017' (*Plastic Soup Foundation*, 2017) https://www.plasticsoupfoundation.org/en/what-we-do/microplastics/ocean-clean-wash/ accessed 15 August 2020.

58 Face masks typically contain polypropylene (PP) that acts as a protective layer against fluid droplets.

59 United Nations Conference on Trade and Development, 'Growing plastic pollution in wake of COVID-19: how trade policy can help' (*UNCTAD*, 27 July 2020) https://unctad.org/en/pages/newsdetails.aspx?OriginalVersionID=2440 accessed 5 August 2020.

60 Globally, the sales of disposable face masks are estimated to raise from $800 million in 2019 to $166 billion in 2020. See United Nations Conference on Trade and Development, 'Growing plastic pollution in wake of COVID-19: how trade policy can help' (*UNCTAD*, 27 July 2020) https://unctad.org/en/pages/newsdetails.aspx?OriginalVersionID=2440 accessed 5 August 2020.

61 Although world-wide consolidated numbers are not yet available, the specific statistics already known are a clear indication of the seriousness of the issue. For instance, as early as February 2020 – so, even before the WHO declared COVID-19 a pandemic situation – Gary Stokes documented 70 surgical facemasks on a 100-metre length of beach in Hong Kong. See *The Economist*, 'Sea of trouble: COVID-19 has led to a pandemic of plastic pollution' (*The Economist*, 22 June 2020) https://www.economist.com/international/2020/06/22/covid-19-has-led-to-a-pandemic-of-plastic-pollution accessed 5 August 2020. Similarly, since the coronavirus broke out in the United Kingdom, the Thames river is filled with latex gloves. See *The Economist*, 'Sea of trouble: COVID-19 has led to a pandemic of plastic pollution'

In this scenario, one could think regulation should be strengthened, but in fact there has been some leniency in the application of certain regulations – or at least some aspects of them – or they have been suspended.

This has been certainly so at the national level. In the UK, where ban on plastics have been postponed for six months, bag charges have been waived, and so have in Scotland deposit-return for bottles.[62] In Italy, the "plastic tax" that meant to charge 0.45 euro per kilogram of single-use plastic produced from virgin feedstock (i.e. not recycled)[63] was supposed to come into effect on 1 July 2020, but in April the Government decided to postpone it to 1 January 2021 because of the pandemic.[64]

The EU regulations themselves provide for a *cum grano salis* reading for reasons of public health. That is, for example, the case of Directive 2008/98/EC on waste, Article 13 of which states that waste collection practices can be adapted in the context of the COVID-19 crisis with the objective of protecting public health.[65]

(*The Economist*, 22 June 2020) https://www.economist.com/international/2020/06/22/covid-19-has-led-to-a-pandemic-of-plastic-pollution accessed 5 August 2020. During an eight-week lockdown in Singapore, the residents discarded extra 1,470 tons of plastic waste from takeout packaging and food delivery alone. See Shashank Begali, 'The COVID-19 pandemic is unleashing a tidal wave of plastic waste' (*LA Times*, 13 June 2020) https://www.latimes.com/world-nation/story/2020-06-13/coronavirus-pandemic-plastic-waste-recycling accessed 5 August 2020. If historical data is a reliable indicator, it can be expected that around 75% of the used masks, as well as other pandemic-related waste, will end up in landfills, or floating in the seas. UN News, 'Five things you should know about disposable masks and plastic pollution' (*UN News*, 30 July 2020) https://news.un.org/en/story/2020/07/1069151 accessed 5 August 2020.

62 Angeli Mehta, 'The war on plastics runs into a perfect storm with Covid-19' (*Ethical Corp*, 2 June 2020) https://www.ethicalcorp.com/war-plastics-runs-perfect-storm-covid-19 accessed 11 August 2020. Wales, however, is allegedly committed to the bans and restrictions of the use of single-use plastics. See BBC News, 'Coronavirus: Calls to delay single-use plastic ban until 2022' (*BBC*, 1 June 2020) https://www.bbc.com/news/uk-wales-52864403 accessed 12 August 2020.

63 Italian Government, 'Bilancio di previsione dello Stato per l'anno finanziario 2020 e bilancio pluriennale per il triennio 2020-2022' (*Gazzetta Ufficiale*, 27 December 2019) https://www.gazzettaufficiale.it/atto/stampa/serie_generale/originario accessed 12 August 2020, arts 634 and 640.

64 Parlamento Italiano, 'Misure fiscali e finanziarie per l'emergenza Coronavirus' (*Camera dei deputati*, 26 July 2020) https://temi.camera.it/leg18/temi/misure-fiscali-e-finanziarie-per-l-emergenza-coronavirus.html accessed 11 August 2020. For an overview in the US, see Jessica Heiges, Kate O'Neill, 'COVID-19 has resurrected single-use plastics – are they back to stay?' (*The Conversation*, 14 July 2020) https://theconversation.com/covid-19-has-resurrected-single-use-plastics-are-they-back-to-stay-140328 accessed 12 August 2020 and Victoria Zuber, 'How nudge theory can help empty our plastic-filled "drawers of shame"' (*World Economic Forum*, 24 June 2020) https://www.weforum.org/agenda/2020/06/how-we-can-nudge-theory-can-help-us-empty-our-drawers-of-shame/ accessed 2 August 2020.

65 Practical Law EU, 'COVID-19: European Commission publishes guidance document on waste management during COVID-19 pandemic' (*UK Practical Law*, 2020) https://uk.practicallaw.thomsonreuters.com/w-025-0445?originationContext=document&transitionType=DocumentItem&contextData=%28sc.Default%29&comp=pluk accessed 8 August 2020.

The European Commission held firm in the face of lobbying by the plastics converters' trade body, which wanted it to delay its implementation of a SUPs ban by at least a year.[66] The Commission justified its stand because of the pressure on waste-management systems owing to the pandemic.[67] This point of view may have gained momentum with the publication, by a large group of international scientists, of a policy paper proving that reusable safety ware is not less safe than single-use plastic safety ware.[68] Moreover, the European Council announced on 21 July 2020, that "a new own resource based on non-recycled plastic waste will be introduced and applied as of 1 January 2021".[69] The amount owed will be calculated based on the national contribution on the weight of non-recycled plastic packaging waste, at a rate of 0.80 euro per kilogram.[70]

The Guidance on the SUPD that the European Commission had initially planned to adopt in July 2020[71] – and that is now targeted for Spring 2021– will be decisive in clarifying how stakeholders are due to implement the Directive in these times of coronavirus crisis.

A draft version leaked to the press on 11 August 2020, and it raises concerns as to whether the ultimate objective of eliminating SUPs will be effectively achieved.

The Plastic Soup Foundation argues that the current draft offers companies many escape routes from the SUP Directive, mainly because of the approach to multipacks, the frequent replacement of bans by extended producer liability and the concept of "single-use".[72]

---

66 Frédéric Simon, 'EU dismisses industry calls to lift ban on single-use plastics' (*EURACTIV*, 15 April 2020) https://www.euractiv.com/section/circular-economy/news/eu-dismisses-industry-calls-to-lift-ban-on-single-use-plastics/ accessed 12 August 2020.

67 Frédéric Simon, 'EU dismisses industry calls to lift ban on single-use plastics' (*EURACTIV*, 15 April 2020) https://www.euractiv.com/section/circular-economy/news/eu-dismisses-industry-calls-to-lift-ban-on-single-use-plastics/ accessed 7 August 2020.

68 'Health Expert Statement Addressing Safety of Reusables and COVID-19' (4 June 2020) https://storage.googleapis.com/planet4-international-stateless/2020/07/0c3a6a32-health-expert-statement_updated.pdf accessed 15 August 2020.

69 See A29, European Council, 'Special Meeting of the European Council (17, 18, 19, 20 and 21 July 2020) – Conclusions' (*European Council*, 21 July 2020) https://www.consilium.europa.eu/media/45109/210720-euco-final-conclusions-en.pdf accessed 11 August 2020.

70 European Council, 'Special Meeting of the European Council (17, 18, 19, 20 and 21 July 2020) – Conclusions' (*European Council*, 21 July 2020) https://www.consilium.europa.eu/media/45109/210720-euco-final-conclusions-en.pdf accessed 11 August 2020, para 146.

71 A group of consultants led by Ramboll, supported by Deloitte, Prognos, IEEP and Wood, has assisted the Commission in these tasks and has carried out stakeholder consultations and workshops during the course of 2020 and 2021. European Commission, Transposition and implementation of the Directive on the reduction of the impact of certain plastic products on the environment (2019) https://ceoe-tenerife.com/wp-content/uploads/2019/11/Administrative-letter-to-MS.SUP-implementation.pdf accessed 9 August 2020.

72 Plastic Soup Foundation, 'EU offers companies many escape routes from SUP directive' (11 August 2020) https://www.plasticsoupfoundation.org/en/2020/08/eu-biedt-bedrijven-veel-ontsnappingsroutes-uit-sup-richtlijn/ accessed 12 August 2020.

As for the latter, the draft Guidance clarifies the concept of "multiple trips or rotations", used in the definition of single-use product. It defines them as the "expected number of times the product can be used; expected number of washing or dishwasher cycles; ease of use features, etc."[73] Regrettably, the definition remains vague and may be potentially used to justify actions that harm the environment. For instance, a company may increase the amount of plastics used in cutlery, plates or glasses in order to make them thicker, and thus resistant to multiple washings, but the consumer's perception that such products are intended for single-use only might remain.

An upside of the draft relates to the clarification of the "refillable" characteristic. The Draft Guidance states that, in order to be considered a refill, there must be a set-up and operational re-use system.[74] This clarification is pertinent because the possibility, in theory, of re-entering the cycle is irrelevant if the practical circumstances do not make it feasible. However, the draft excludes such set-up and operational re-use system as a requirement to establish "re-usability" – the mere fact that the plastic product may be re-used by the consumer is considered enough not to be considered a single-use product. This could possibly mean that the fact that an ice-cream container may be used by consumers to freeze leftovers could stop it from being classified as "single-use product", even if consumers most often dispose of ice-cream containers and do not re-use them.

The clarification of which products are subject to the SUP Directive on the one hand and the Packaging Waste Directive on the other[75] must be praised, as it is useful to prevent possible conflict of laws in the future.

However, another downside of the draft, and one of the biggest ones, relates multipacks, that are excluded from the scope of SUP Directive.[76]

---

73 European Commission, 'First Draft for Discussion with Member States: Commission guidance in accordance with Directive (EU) 2019/904 of the European Parliament and of the Council of 5 June 2019 on the reduction of the impact of certain plastic products on the environment' (August 2020) https://drive.google.com/drive/u/0/folders/1A5CIkXnFTt3ynlXQ5y0mUTFEDr_i_Pmk accessed 12 August 2020, 9.

74 European Commission, 'First Draft for Discussion with Member States: Commission guidance in accordance with Directive (EU) 2019/904 of the European Parliament and of the Council of 5 June 2019 on the reduction of the impact of certain plastic products on the environment' (August 2020) https://drive.google.com/drive/u/0/folders/1A5CIkXnFTt3ynlXQ5y0mUTFEDr_i_Pmk accessed 12 August 2020, 11.

75 European Commission, 'First Draft for Discussion with Member States: Commission guidance in accordance with Directive (EU) 2019/904 of the European Parliament and of the Council of 5 June 2019 on the reduction of the impact of certain plastic products on the environment' (August 2020) https://drive.google.com/drive/u/0/folders/1A5CIkXnFTt3ynlXQ5y0mUTFEDr_i_Pmk> accessed 12 August 2020, 11–12.

76 European Commission, 'Annex to the First Draft for Discussion with Member States: Commission guidance in accordance with Directive (EU) 2019/904 of the European Parliament and of the Council of 5 June 2019 on the reduction of the impact of certain plastic products on the environment' (August 2020) https://drive.google.com/drive/u/0/folders/1A5CIkXnFTt3ynlXQ5y0mUTFEDr_i_Pmk accessed 12 August 2020, topic 3.

"Multipacks" are packages that contain more than one portion packed separately inside, such as cookies, sandwiches, or yogurts. Similarly to the definition of "multiple trips or rotations", this definition is also vague. Beyond that, such a definition may have the collateral damage of encouraging the industry of producing even more plastic in order to separate goods and thus avoid the SUPs prohibition.

In a nutshell, the draft Guidance, which is supposed to clarify the legal terms in the SUP Directive, may still be too vague and leave room for misinterpretation or misused application by stakeholders. These preliminary concerns regarding the Commission's guidance should, however, be re-analysed in the future, in the light of the Guidance version which is actually to be adopted.

4. THE ROLE OF STAKEHOLDERS IN A SUSTAINABLE PLASTICS ECONOMY

The complexity and broadness of the plastic pollution problem, especially regarding SUPs, which are widely distributed for consumers' use, makes it imperative that solutions involve all players in the plastic chain.[77] So, it comes as no surprise that, upon the deadline for implementation of the SUPD, Members States must ensure that manufacturers, producers, retailers, importers, sellers (regardless of the selling technique used, including distance contracts), and anyone placing on the EU market any of the items addressed under the SUP Directive comply with the measures established therein. Companies will have to pay for the costs of waste management, clean-up and awareness-raising measures for the SUPs they produce and sell, as prescribed by the Extended Producer Responsibility (EPR) schemes, as well as to comply with other requirements established under the SUP Directive.[78]

In that sense, measures established in the SUPD and addressed to the industry include – aligning with the polluter-pays principle – extended producer responsibility schemes.[79] This applies for food containers, flexible packets and

---

77 For a more detailed discussion on the involvement of governments, companies, and civil society, see Luísa Cortat Simonetti Gonçalves, *Legal Remedies against the Plastic Pollution of the Oceans: An Analysis of the Attempts from Public International Law and Private Initiatives to face the Plastic Soup* (Proefschriftmaken, 2020). See also Séverine Herbots, *The Role of European Trade Actors in the Plastics Strategy* (Hasselt University 2020), unpublished.

78 Zero Waste Europe, 'Unfolding the Single-Use Plastics Directive: Policy Briefing' (*Rethink Plastic Alliance*, May 2019) https://rethinkplasticalliance.eu/wp-content/uploads/2019/05/ZWE_Unfolding-the-SUP-directive.pdf Z-accessed 9 August 2020.

79 See point 21 of Article 3 and Article 8(2) of Directive (EU) 2019/904 of the European Parliament and of the Council of 5 June 2019 on the reduction of the impact of certain plastic products on the environment [2019] L 155/1 https://eur-lex.europa.eu/legal-content/EN/TXT/PDF/?uri=CELEX:32019L0904 accessed 12 August 2020.

wrappers containing food, beverage containers with up to three litres capacity, cups for beverages, lightweight plastic carrier bags, wet wipes, balloons, tobacco products with filter,[80] and fishing gear and components.[81]

Still addressing the industry, the EU Plastic Strategy[82] launched a pledging campaign for the use of recycled plastics in new products, indicating the possibility of applying economic tools to reward such use.[83] The initiative seemed to create the appropriate momentum, since, by the end of 2018, 70 companies and business associations submitted their voluntary pledges, including big corporations already known by their negative contributions to plastic pollution because of the amount they produce,[84] such as Coca-Cola, Nestlé, P&G, and Unilever.[85] Also, a collective of 147 stakeholder organisations representing the entire plastic value chain have formed the "circular alliance" and signed a declaration listing numerous specific measures aimed at increasing the uptake of recycled plastics and developing and revising the design of their products to meet the recycling guidelines.[86]

In such a scenario, the role of consumers naturally also had to be included. "Economic and other incentives to support sustainable consumer choices and promote responsible consumer behaviour can be an effective tool for achieving the objectives of this Directive".[87] Sustainable growth should

---

80 Annex Part E of Directive (EU) 2019/904 of the European Parliament and of the Council of 5 June 2019 on the reduction of the impact of certain plastic products on the environment [2019] L 155/1 https://eur-lex.europa.eu/legal-content/EN/TXT/PDF/?uri=CELEX:32019L0904 accessed 12 August 2020.

81 Para 23 of Directive (EU) 2019/904 of the European Parliament and of the Council of 5 June 2019 on the reduction of the impact of certain plastic products on the environment [2019] L 155/1 https://eur-lex.europa.eu/legal-content/EN/TXT/PDF/?uri=CELEX:32019L0904 accessed 12 August 2020.

82 Communication from the Commission to the European Parliament, the Council, the European Economic and Social Committee and the Committee of the Regions, 'A European Strategy for Plastics in a Circular Economy' [2018] [SWD(2018) 16 final] COM(2018) 28 final https://ec.europa.eu/environment/circular-economy/pdf/plastics-strategy.pdf, accessed 9 August 2020, annex III.

83 European Commission, 'A European Strategy for Plastics in a Circular Economy (brochure)' (*European Commission*, 2019) https://ec.europa.eu/environment/circular-economy/pdf/plastics-strategy-brochure.pdf accessed 15 August 2020, 12.

84 Luísa Cortat Simonetti Gonçalves, *Legal Remedies against the Plastic Pollution of the Oceans: An Analysis of the Attempts from Public International Law and Private Initiatives to face the Plastic Soup* (Proefschriftmaken, 2020) 103–105.

85 European Commission, 'European strategy for plastics – voluntary pledges' (*European Commission*, 4 March 2019) https://ec.europa.eu/growth/content/european-strategy-plastics-voluntary-pledges_en accessed 12 August 2020.

86 Eleonora Foschi and Alessandra Bonoli, 'The Commitment of Packaging Industry in the Framework of the European Strategy for Plastics in a Circular Economy' (2019) 9 Adm. Sci. 1, 8.

87 Communication from the Commission to the European Parliament, the Council, the European Economic and Social Committee and the Committee of the Regions. A European Strategy for Plastics in a Circular Economy [SWD(2018) 16 final] COM(2018) 28 final https://ec.europa.eu/environment/circular-economy/pdf/plastics-strategy.pdf accessed 9 August 2020, para 26.

involve a dematerialisation of the economy by transition to an access-based consumption model or *servitisation* in a broad sense.[88] The old Theodore Levitt quote "customers don't want quarter inch drills, they want quarter inch holes" illustrates this business model:[89] rather than focusing on the traditional unsustainable "make, use, dispose" approach, it focuses on selling functionalities of products rather than products themselves.

An important means for incentive – also referred to by the EU Plastics Strategy – consists of green public procurement. Considering that public procurements account for "an average of 12 percent of gross domestic product (GDP) in OECD countries, and up to 30 percent of GDP in many developing countries",[90] Green Public Procurement (GPP) is already being used as a means to foster sustainability and environmental protection. It uses environmental criteria for contracts and biddings.[91]

However, stimuli such as green subsidies are very costly to society (capital needs, to mention an example, to be collected via distortive taxes on labour) and in the current COVID-19-caused scenario of pre-economic recession[92] it is unlikely that governments will invest capital in such economic incentives. It comes, then, as one more reason why the importance of consumers' engagement has increased during the pandemic.

Moreover, despite the mentioned initial progress in the actions involving the industry, the European Plastics Converters (EuPC) industry association

---

88 "Servitisation" in a broad sense is used as a synonym for what the European Economic and Social Committee called "functional economy", both being based on consuming services rather than buying products. For details, see Fryderyk Zoll, 'From a Product-Based Economy to Services? Legal Aspects of an Economy in Transition' in Bert Keirsbilck and Evelyne Terryn (eds), *Consumer Protection in a Circular Economy* (Intersentia 2019) 149 and, in the same volume, Petra Weingerl and Janja Hojnik, 'Servitization' and Movables. Legal Initiatives and Challenges in Slovenia' Bert Keirsbilck and Evelyne Terryn (eds), *Consumer Protection in a Circular Economy* (Intersentia 2019) 225.

89 Elsie T. Freeman 'Buying quarter inch holes: public support through results' (2000) 25 Archival Issues 91.

90 UN Environment, 'Global Review of Sustainable Public Procurement' (*UN Environment*, 2017) https://www.unenvironment.org/resources/report/2017-global-review-sustainable-public-procurement#:~:text=The%202017%20Global%20Review%20of,in%20the%20past%20three%20years accessed 3 March 2020.

91 This use of environmental criteria is made with the effects on the market as a whole and the potential distortions within the EU trade market in mind. Thus, "public procurement should be performed in a non-discriminatory and transparent manner that gives rise to undistorted competition, thus allowing administration to obtain best value for money". Stefan E. Weishaar, 'Cartels, Competition and Public Procurement: Law and Economics Approaches to Bid Rigging' (Edward Elgar 2013) 2.

92 Even in the best-case scenario – which already did not happen –, a global economic crisis of unknown proportions is expected for at least 1.5 years following the pandemic. See, e.g. ING, 'Four scenarios for the global economy after Covid-19' (*ING*, 2 April 2020) https://think.ing.com/articles/four-scenarios-for-the-global-economy-after-covid-19/ accessed 12 August 2020.

requested, in April 2020, the postponement of the implementation of the SUPD due to the COVID-19 pandemic.[93] Although denied by the European Commission, the request indicates a movement of the European industry against advances in banning SUPs. The structured spread of the news, initiated by the plastic industry world-wide, that reusable plastics could play on the contamination from the new virus, added up to such a movement.[94] Therefore, the pandemic "reset the clock" and increased the importance of addressing "psychological and behavioral barriers, including a perception that reused or recycled products may not be hygienic. Fear-driven habits and mistrust developed under extreme stress often stick long after the source of stress disappears".[95] The steps taken now may influence years of action to the ban of SUPs.

5. THE IMPORTANCE OF ADDRESSING CONSUMER BEHAVIOUR THROUGH NUDGING IN THE FIGHT AGAINST PLASTICS

Addressing plastic pollution through legislation alone is often ineffective because it may fail to overcome the resistance of consumers and producers to laws that imply behavioural changes. In Brazil, for instance, where plastic pollution has been addressed at the regional level, either the Government went back on laws because of non-compliance[96] or laws proved inefficient.[97] Consumer demands have a great potential of being the core orchestrator of the transition to a sustainable plastics economy.

This directly relates to two of the roles that civil society should play within a comprehensive approach to fight plastic pollution, namely, the prevention

---

93 European Plastics Converters, 'Open Letter' (*European Plastic Converters*, 8 April 2020) https://fd0ea2e2-fecf-4f82-8b1b-9e5e1ebec6a0.filesusr.com/ugd/2eb778_9d8ec284e39b4c7d84e774f0da14f2e8.pdf accessed 12 August 2020.

94 Plastics Industry Association, 'Letter to the US Department of Health and Human Services' (*Politico*, 18 March 2020) https://www.politico.com/states/f/?id=00000171-0d87-d270-a773-6fdfcc4d0000 accessed 12 August 2020.

95 Grzegorz Peszko, 'Plastics: The coronavirus could reset the clock' (*World Bankblogs*, 7 April 2020) https://blogs.worldbank.org/voices/plastics-coronavirus-could-reset-clock accessed 12 August 2020.

96 That was the case of the Metropolitan region of Vitória and São Paulo. In the latter, over 40 municipal legislations regarding bans on plastic bags were object to judicial actions from the plastic industry. See Luísa Cortat Simonetti Gonçalves and Paula Castello Miguel, 'Dever Fundamental de Proteção ao Meio Ambiente e Políticas Públicas no Estado de São Paulo para Banimento de Sacolas Plásticas', forthcoming.

97 That was the case of Rio de Janeiro. Daiane Costa, 'Lei Contra Sacolas Plástica não Pega no Rio' (*O Globo*, 15 April 2015) https://oglobo.globo.com/economia/defesa-do-consumidor/lei-contra-sacolas-plasticas-nao-pega-no-rio-15876913 accessed 15 August 2020.

of *green*[98] and *bluewashing* (or corporate social responsibility) by increasing social awareness and to sensitise the industry towards the adoption of sustainable production patterns.[99]

Focusing on consumers as main agents for change fits the New Circular Economy Action Plan published in March 2020,[100] that aims to "empower consumers to make sustainable choices for their own benefit and that of the environment".[101] It is also in line with the concerns raised in the context of the European Strategy for Plastics regarding the complex and diffuse nature of individual behaviour.[102]

The question is thus begged whether consumers are ready and willing to engage in such transition to minimal material-based consumption patterns, letting go of the relationship developed with plastic products and some of the conveniences of contemporary life. This is particularly so as alternative materials are often pricier and less readily accessible, such as recycled plastics, which are not always available nor affordable, and have a shorter life cycle.[103]

So how to incentivise consumers to increase demand for sustainable plastic economies?

Nudging, a growing trend in the US and recently in Europe as well,[104] offers a yet relatively unexplored but high potential for fostering sustainable practices,

---

98 Greenwashing may be defined as the "act of misleading consumers regarding the environmental practices of a company or the environmental benefits of a product or service". See Terrachoice, 'Sins of Greenwashing' (*UL*, 2007) https://www.ul.com/insights/sins-greenwashing accessed 15 August 2020.

99 Luísa Cortat Simonetti Gonçalves, *Legal Remedies against the Plastic Pollution of the Oceans: An Analysis of the Attempts from Public International Law and Private Initiatives to face the Plastic Soup* (Proefschriftmaken 2020) 108.

100 European Commission, 'Circular Economy Action Plan: For a cleaner and more competitive Europe' (*European Commission*, March 2020) https://ec.europa.eu/environment/circular-economy/pdf/new_circular_economy_action_plan.pdf accessed 5 August 2020.

101 European Commission, 'Changing how we produce and consume: New Circular Economy Action Plan shows the way to a climate-neutral, competitive economy of empowered consumers' (*European Commission*, 11 March 2020) https://ec.europa.eu/commission/presscorner/detail/en/ip_20_420 accessed 5 August 2020.

102 European Commission, 'A European Strategy for Plastics in a Circular Economy (brochure)' (*European Commission*, 2019) https://ec.europa.eu/environment/circular-economy/pdf/plastics-strategy-brochure.pdf accessed 15 August 2020, 13.

103 Cheryl Katz, 'Piling Up: How China's Ban on Importing Waste Has Stalled Global Recycling'. (*Yale Environment 360*, 7 March 2019) https://e360.yale.edu/features/piling-up-how-chinas-ban-on-importing-waste-has-stalled-global-ecycling#:~:text=AFP%2FGetty%20Images-,Piling%20Up%3A%20How%20China%27s%20Ban%20on%20Importing%20Waste%20Has%20Stalled,the%20U.S.%20scrambling%20for%20alternatives.&text=Recycled%20aluminum%20and%20glass%20are%20less%20affected%20by%20the%20ban accessed 24 August 2019. Yen Nee Lee, 'The world is scrambling now that China is refusing to be a trash dumping ground' (*CNBC*, 16 April 2018) https://www.cnbc.com/2018/04/16/climate-change-china-bans-import-offoreign-waste-to-stop-pollution.html accessed 20 March 2020.

104 Robert Baldwin, 'From regulation to behaviour change: giving nudge the third degree' (2014) 77 *The Modern Law Review* 6, 831, 831 and Alberto Alemanno and Anne-Lise Sibony (eds),

particularly as far as plastics are concerned. In their seminal work on nudging, Richard Thaler and Cass Sunstein defined "nudge" as "any aspect of the choice architecture", meaning the context in which people make decisions,[105] "that alters people's behaviour in a predictable way without forbidding any options or significantly changing their economic incentives".[106]

As is well described in the best-selling book by Nobel in Economics laureate Daniel Kahneman,[107] people use two cognitive systems for collecting information and for making decisions: system 1, a quicker, more impulsive system; and system 2, a slower, "lazier" system, which demands more reflection and is therefore less relied upon in daily life for collecting information and making decisions. The impact of the existence of these two systems in decision making is that people are, quite commonly, irrational agents who take decisions while being influenced by several cognitive and psychological biases.[108] Individuals are thus seen as constrained by limitations of information, cognitive capacity, and self-control and as tending to rely on a series of heuristics and shorthand methods of using information. As a result, they tend to take decisions which do not serve their welfare.[109]

Nudges may be seen as a transition from "fast" to "slow" thinking.[110] They are policy design choices or actions that apply insights from behavioural science and aim to improve the typical biased and in that measure irrational consumers' choices.[111] In order for an aspect of a choice architecture to classify as nudge

---

Nudge and the Law: A European perspective (Hart Publishing 2015), Christoph Busch, 'The future of pre-contractual information duties: from behavioural insights to big data' in Christian Twigg-Flesner (ed), Research Handbook on EU Consumer and Contract Law (Edward Elgar 2016) 221, 229.

105 Avishalom Tor, 'The Critical and Problematic Role of Bounded Rationality in Nudging' in Klaus Mathis and Avishalom Tor (eds), *Nudging – Possibilities, Limitations and Applications in European Law and Economics*. Richard Thaler and Cass Sunstein, *Nudge: Improving Decisions About Health, Wealth, and Happiness* (Penguin 2009) 3.

106 Richard Thaler and Cass Sunstein, *Nudge: Improving Decisions About Health, Wealth, and Happiness* (Penguin 2009) 6.

107 Daniel Kahnemann, *Thinking Fast and Slow* (Farrar, Straus and Giroux 2011).

108 Christoph Busch, 'The future of pre-contractual information duties: from behavioural insights to big data' in Christian Twigg-Flesner (ed), *Research Handbook on EU Consumer and Contract Law* (Edward Elgar 2016) 4.

109 Robert Baldwin, 'From Regulation to Behaviour Change: Giving Nudge the Third Degree' 77 The Modern Law Review 6, 831–857.

110 Ollie Boesen, 'Is Nudge Theory the Answer to our Single-Use Plastic problem?' (*Huffington Post*, 15 June 2018) https://www.huffingtonpost.co.uk/entry/can-nudge-theory-be-the-answer-to-our-single-use-plastics_uk_5b1a5624e4b01fbe42a7d48b?guccounter=1&guce_referrer=aHR0cHM6Ly93d3cuZ29vZ2xlLmNvbS8&guce_referrer_sig=AQAAAJI6p_x8Xm5DkvYCjQddkZMy0Ntwkb8ZwXRHjGwmDIta3Qh_Cyxn927wyOUaqaRTY4Hs8QAYz_acKRRwVF0ag8FHYMUhMweuKMaRct09QP1nyc_SwZN_yjf0qw6v8tF1EkNRuj0IQClS1wA96qEhBVbnwqbVKL1dHrSPUG8Bz9yy accessed 12 August 2020.

111 UN Environmental program, 'Nudge to action: Behavioural Science for Sustainability' (*UN Environment*, 3 March 2017) https://www.unenvironment.org/news-and-stories/story/nudge-action-behavioural-science-sustainability accessed 12 August 2020.

it must thus produce a "predictable behavioural effect" and use only rationally neutral behavioural tools.[112]

At the heart of nudging is a philosophy entitled "libertarian paternalism".[113] On the one hand, the nudge is paternalistic, as it stimulates choices that are seen as welfare enhancing for the individual; on the other hand, the nudge is libertarian, because it does not constrain the freedom of the agent, who is the one deciding on the course of action he/she ultimately will take.[114]

According to the definition of "nudge" by Thaler and Sunstein, legitimate nudges are only those which make deciding agents better-off as judged by themselves. This could seem to exclude situations where behavioural tools are used to pursue social welfare goals, such as a more sustainable society,[115] but in the paper which coined the term "libertarian paternalism", Thaler and Sunstein had defined it as a policy "selected with the goal of influencing the choices of affected parties in a way that will make those parties better off".[116] According to this broader definition, nudges seem to encompass the possibility of advancing social welfare goals or other socially oriented goals, even though these goals do not – or at least not perceived as such – promote individuals self-reported well-being.[117]

Nudges are subject to criticism. There are doubts as to their efficacy when the behaviour that is to be changed is the result of collective processes and policies. It is argued that the way individuals answer to nudges depends on the cultural, economic, social, institutional context of the agent and that they can easily "counter-nudge".[118]

---

112 Avishalom Tor, 'The Critical and Problematic Role of Bounded Rationality in Nudging' in Klaus Mathis and Avishalom Tor (eds), *Nudging – Possibilities, Limitations and Applications in European Law and Economics* (Springer 2016); Richard Thaler and Cass Sunstein, 'Nudge: Improving Decisions About Health, Wealth, and Happiness' (Penguin 2009) 3.

113 Richard Thaler and Cass Sunstein, *Nudge: Improving Decisions About Health, Wealth, and Happiness* (Penguin 2009).

114 See, however, Robert Baldwin, 'From Regulation to Behaviour Change: Giving Nudge the Third Degree' 77 The Modern Law Review 831, 835 who classifies nudges in three degrees, of which in only the first the decision-making autonomy of the individual is truly respected.

115 Avishalom Tor, 'The Critical and Problematic Role of Bounded Rationality in Nudging' in Klaus Mathis and Avishalom Tor (eds), *Nudging – Possibilities, Limitations and Applications in European Law and Economics*, 3–4 and 6; Robert Baldwin, 'From Regulation to Behaviour Change: Giving Nudge the Third Degree' 77 The Modern Law Review 6, 831.

116 Richard Thaler and Cass Sunstein, *Nudge: Improving Decisions About Health, Wealth, and Happiness* (Penguin 2009) 3, 175.

117 Avishalom Tor, 'The Critical and Problematic Role of Bounded Rationality in Nudging' in Klaus Mathis and Avishalom Tor (eds), *Nudging – Possibilities, Limitations and Applications in European Law and Economics*, 4.

118 Robert Baldwin, 'From Regulation to Behaviour Change: Giving Nudge the Third Degree' 77 The Modern Law Review 6, 838–841. See also the case study on the Toronto's plastic bag legislation, which disclosed different impacts across behavioural and demographic groups: Nicholas Rivers et al., 'Using nudges to reduce waste? The case of Toronto's plastic bag levy' (2017) 188 Journal of Environmental Management 153–162.

The disclosure of the practice of nudging, as transparency towards agents would require, is also said to affect their effectiveness as they "typically work better in the dark".[119] The main criticism of nudging is indeed its potential for manipulation,[120] i.e. the intentional, hidden steering of people's choices by promoting and shaping decision-making processes that people would not usually appeal to in order to make rational decisions.[121] Yeung calls it "liberal manipulation critique".[122]

However, the potential of nudge theory in fighting SUPs is undeniable, and there is a large array of measures that can be taken to persuade consumers to take more sustainable behaviours.

Industry as well as food delivery and food pick-up platform and apps[123] can, due to the inertia bias, send plasticware with take-away orders only upon express request of the customer, for example. This is particularly so, as during lockdowns, quarantines and home-office takeaway is by nature ordered for consumption at home, where it can be expected that there is durable cutlery available.[124] By changing the default option from "adding plasticware with orders", to "adding plasticware with orders only upon request", plasticware would likely rarely be added to orders, as previous experiences – take the famous organ donation default option experiment[125] – show. In addition to reducing plastic waste and contributing to more sustainable and sustained consumption habits, this option would also allow restaurants to save costs and help them grow their goodwill.[126]

There are several other nudges that could be used to help minimising or even eliminating consumption or SUPs during the COVID-19 pandemic.

---

119 Luc Bovens, 'Nudges and Cultural Variance: a Note on Selinger and Whyte' (2010) 23 Knowledge, Technology & Policy 3–4, 483.

120 T. M. Wilkinson, 'Nudging and Manipulation' (2012) 61 Political Studies 2, 341, 347, Daniel M. Hausman and Brynn Welch, 'Debate: to nudge or not to nudge' (2010) 18 The Journal of Political Philosophy 1, 123 128.

121 T. M. Wilkinson, 'Nudging and Manipulation' (2012) 61 Political Studies 2, 341, 347.

122 Karen Yeung, '"Hypernudge": Big Data as a mode of regulation by design' (2017) 20 Information, Communication and Society 1, 118, 123 ff.

123 That is the case, for example, of Too Good to Go, a platform operating in Central Europe that has recently helped restaurants that closed due to the COVID-19 lockdown. See Helen Hammett, 'How one startup is leading the fight against food waste' (*Marketing Week*, 7 July 2020) https://www.marketingweek.com/too-good-to-go-food-waste/ accessed 12 August 2020.

124 Victoria Zuber, 'How nudge theory can help empty our plastic-filled 'drawers of shame'' (*World Economic Forum*, 24 June 2020) https://www.weforum.org/agenda/2020/06/how-we-can-nudge-theory-can-help-us-empty-our-drawers-of-shame/.

125 Countries where people are automatically enrolled as organ donors have a much bigger pool of donors. In these opt-out countries, an average of 90% of people donate their organs. See Francesca Schaibe 'Stanford University. "Opt Out" Policies Increase Organ Donation' (*Stanford Sparq*) https://sparq.stanford.edu/solutions/opt-out-policies-increase-organ-donation accessed 12 August 2020.

126 Victoria Zuber, 'How nudge theory can help empty our plastic-filled 'drawers of shame'' (*World Economic Forum*, 24 June 2020) https://www.weforum.org/agenda/2020/06/how-we-can-nudge-theory-can-help-us-empty-our-drawers-of-shame/.

Consequently, consumers would opt for washable masks, refillable drinks and food containers and fabric shopping bags. Consumers would opt for drinking and eating in (with the necessary observance of social distancing and other sanitary precautions) whenever regulations would not prohibit it. Whenever takeaway is the only option, they would reject plastic cutlery with takeaway and buy local instead of online, preferring businesses that minimise packaging.[127]

A nudge may not in itself be the answer to the fight of single-use plastics. However, it can help fight the current plastics emergency, help consolidate sustainable habits and push society forward in the journey towards a more sustainable plastics economy.[128]

6. CONCLUDING REMARKS: THE WAY AHEAD

The severity of plastic pollution and its consequences to nature and human health are already well established. Yet, legal research about the fight against plastic pollution[129] has been demonstrating that traditional (hard and soft) law alone does not yet provide convincing solutions for the plastic soup problem.[130] Moreover, changes in production and consumer patterns are key to the issue and thus it is essential to analyse private initiatives and paths to influence private action.

The role for transitioning from the linear to the circular economy model has been placed particularly in the industry, and, particularly, on product design,

127 Amazon has a "Frustration-Free Packaging (FFP)" program in place that encourages manufacturers to package their products in easy-to-open packaging that is 100% recyclable and ready to ship to customers without additional Amazon boxes. They claim to, have reduced the weight of outbound packaging by 33% in the past five years, and have eliminated more than 1.5 billion shipping boxes. See Sustainability Question Bank from Amazon https://sustainability.aboutamazon.com/question-bank#?category=packaging; see also Amazon, Sustainable Packaging Initiatives, https://sustainability.aboutamazon.com/environment/packaging-and-products/packaging and Packaging Gateway https://www.packaging-gateway.com/features/amazon-packaging-waste/ (11 July 2019); Deborah William, 'Amazon packaging waste: Current operations and future plans' (*Packaging Gateway*, 11 July 2019) https://www.packaging-gateway.com/features/amazon-packaging-waste/.

128 Victoria Zuber, 'How nudge theory can help empty our plastic-filled 'drawers of shame'' (*World Economic Forum*, 24 June 2020) https://www.weforum.org/agenda/2020/06/how-we-can-nudge-theory-can-help-us-empty-our-drawers-of-shame/ accessed 12 August 2020.

129 Luísa Cortat Simonetti Gonçalves and Michael Gerbert Faure, 'International Law Instruments to Address the Plastic Soup' [2019] William & Mary Environmental Law and Policy Review 43(3), 870; Luísa Cortat Simonetti Gonçalves, *Legal Remedies against the Plastic Pollution of the Oceans: An Analysis of the Attempts from Public International Law and Private Initiatives to face the Plastic Soup* (Proefschriftmaken 2020).

130 COVID-19 Consumer Law Research Group, 'Consumer Law and Policy Relating to Change of Circumstances Due to the COVID-19 Pandemic' (2020) 43 Journal of Consumer Policy 437, 441 https://link.springer.com/article/10.1007/s10603-020-09463-z accessed 12 August 2020, 439.

operations, and infrastructure optimisation,[131] and so is the case regarding transitioning to a circular economy for plastics.

The European Strategy for Plastics in a Circular Economy places design and production, and thus the industry, at the core of the transition to a circular economy for plastics,[132] but it stresses that "civil society, the scientific community, businesses and local authorities will have a decisive role to play".[133]

Some movements were observed in Europe that were aimed at implementing the European Single Use Plastics Directive (SUPD), but they were interrupted or slowed due to COVID-19 pandemic. This interference happened through postponements or delays in regulations from Member States – as with the cases of UK, Scotland, and Italy – and from the EU, with the delay in the official publication of the Guidance on the SUPD. The interference also happened through an increase in the consumption of single-use plastics in protection equipment such as masks and gloves, and in food packaging and takeaway containers.

Such a scenario was aggravated by the industry's stand of pushing for further postponements in the implementation of regulations and spreading news about the fear that reusable items would be unsafe by not protecting against SARS-CoV-2 infection. Therefore, if consumer behaviour was already an essential aspect in the agenda against plastic pollution, now it is even more so.

Coping with the challenges ahead in terms of plastic waste management will require a cooperative approach from local to national governments as well as businesses and consumers.

Even though the COVID-19 pandemic is regarded, and rightly so, as a tremendous global crisis, the EU, governments, businesses, and consumers have a choice. Either they choose to deepen the sustainability gap, or they choose to transform this crisis into an *opportunity* of reassessing and reorganising aspects we have been struggling with, and to integrate behavioural insights into Consumer and Environmental Law and policy.

---

131 Ellen MacArthur Foundation, 'What is a circular economy?' (*Ellen MacArthur Foundation*, 2017) https://www.ellenmacarthurfoundation.org/circular-economy/concept.

132 Communication from the Commission to the European Parliament, the Council, the European Economic and Social Committee and the Committee of the Regions. A European Strategy for Plastics in a Circular Economy [SWD(2018) 16 final] COM(2018) 28 final https://ec.europa.eu/environment/circular-economy/pdf/plastics-strategy.pdf accessed 9 August 2020, 5.

133 Communication from the Commission to the European Parliament, the Council, the European Economic and Social Committee and the Committee of the Regions. A European Strategy for Plastics in a Circular Economy [SWD(2018) 16 final] COM(2018) 28 final https://ec.europa.eu/environment/circular-economy/pdf/plastics-strategy.pdf accessed 9 August 2020, 8.

PART VI

LABOUR AND SOCIAL LAW

FUNCTIONAL AND SYSTEMIC IMPACTS OF COVID-19 ON EUROPEAN SOCIAL LAW AND SOCIAL POLICY

Luka Mišič and Grega Strban*

In this contribution, the authors address functional or short-term and systemic or long-term effects of the COVID-19 epidemic on European social law and social policy. They focus on the legal and factual status of mobile workers and self-employed persons, the coordination of sickness benefits in kind and cross-border provision of healthcare services in times of a health crisis, and, most notably, on the potential resurrection of the national welfare state that is challenging the further development of the European social model and the European Union's deeper social integration. Since the epidemic appears to still be in full swing and since Member States' anti-corona measures seem to be complemented on a day-to-day basis, the authors' deliberations are based on general assumptions regarding free movement of workers and self-employed persons, social security coordination, and the nature of the European social model, coupled with what they perceive to be key challenges posed by the COVID-19 epidemic in the field of European social law and social policy, also affecting, at least indirectly, national rules and policies.

* Both authors, University of Ljubljana.

1. INTRODUCTION

As with other branches of law, social security law was placed in a two-fold position during the current COVID-19 epidemic. On the one hand, a number of social rights were *de iure* or *de facto* suspended either at the national level or at the level of the European Union (EU). On the other hand, new social rights or other rights with a social aim were introduced throughout Europe in order to tackle present and future negative effects of the epidemic, such as increased health needs of the population, changed family obligations, higher levels of unemployment, poverty and social exclusion, especially among vulnerable groups, self-employed persons, persons employed on grounds of civil law contracts, etc. Member States (MS) introduced, for example, care time for employees with children and other special family benefits, telemedical consultations, e-medical prescriptions, short-time work, facilitated telework, temporary or partial unemployment benefits, suspension of social security contribution payment obligations, simplified procedures for claiming social rights, special social assistance measures, etc.[1] Proposals on universal access to social and health services and proposals for an universal[2] basic income quickly re-entered the public debate as governments tried to fight increased levels of poverty and social exclusion on the one hand and keep market-demand high on the other.

The epidemic displayed once again, in the field of social security, the vivid interplay between the law and life's reality, in which the former commonly struggles to keep up with the latter, relying on generality and high levels of abstraction as a means of covering equally all potential future cases. However, this time it seems that (national) legislators were caught completely off guard, trying hard to instantly adapt to previously unknown challenges posed by the unprecedented epidemic in different areas of public and private life. Unsurprisingly, the European values of transnational solidarity and integration were, at least in the first few weeks of the epidemic, placed in the back seat, whilst national legislators and/or governments struggled to keep their communities, economies and/or themselves afloat. As Zielonka pointed out at the very beginning of the epidemic, "[v]irtually overnight, national capitals have effectively reclaimed sovereignty from the European Union without asking either their own people or Brussels for permission … Gone is globalisation and

---

1 A list of measures for several MS is available with the European Social Insurance Platform (*ESIP*) https://esip.eu/covid-19-pandemic accessed 5 June 2020.

2 In times of crisis, general measures come before individual assessment, since the latter, due to the number of pending cases, commonly can no longer be carried out on time. See Ulrich Becker 'Sozialpolitik und Sozialrecht in Krisenzeiten' in Ulrich Becker et al., *Existenzsicherung in der Coronakrise: Sozialpolitische Maßnahmen zun Erhalt von Arbeit, Wirtschaft und sozialem Schutz im Rechtsvergleich* (2020) Working papers law (MPI) 11.

European integration. Back is the heroic struggle of states for national survival".[3] These were the words of a chilling prediction of things to come. The ease with which the common European identity and sense of solidarity were forgotten in a significant number of MS, even if only briefly, questions the fragile future of European social integration. The latter is, as follows, traditionally limited by politically acceptable narrow EU competences in the field, with additional barriers posed by the diversity of national social security systems, fear from social dumping and social tourism, and the ongoing rise of Euroscepticism, xenophobia and nationalism, feeding itself on the great centre-periphery divide.[4]

Beginning with (1) an outline of the European Social Model (ESM) and its characterisation, the authors examine the recent COVID-19 epidemic that struck Europe and what seems to be a short-term *functional* impact it had on (2) social security coordination and/or free movement of workers, self-employed persons and jobseekers within the EU and (3) cross-border access to sickness benefits in kind (i.e. health care). The authors also address the long-term *systemic* impact it could have on (4) the rise of the national welfare state, challenging the common development of European social law and social policy.

The aim of this contribution is to discuss, in the first place, the potential role that the recent epidemic might have had or still might have on the future development of the ESM or, in other terms, the future of European social integration, whilst addressing social security rights in the EU, directly affected by and during the epidemic. In the widest sense, the authors define European social integration as an ongoing process of Europeanisation of national social law and social policy. In a narrower context, which is the context of this contribution, European social integration relates to a shift of powers in the field of social protection from MSs to the EU, with the aim of guaranteeing a higher level of social welfare and social protection for all EU citizens as an end in itself, whilst developing the ESM independently, not as a mere facilitator of the common market.

2. SOCIAL INTEGRATION AND THE ESM

According to Schoukens, a social model in social science literature refers to "developed labour law systems and redistributive social security systems,

---

3 Jan Zielonka 'Has the coronavirus brought back the nation-state?' (*Social Europe*, 26 March 2020) https://www.socialeurope.eu/has-the-coronavirus-brought-back-the-nation-state accessed 4 June 2020.

4 On the centre-periphery dichotomy in the EU see, fore and foremost, Damjan Kukovec, 'Law and the Periphery' (2015) ELJ 406–428. For a more recent discussion that also encompasses centre-periphery dynamics see Damjan Kukovec 'Subject-object dialectics and social change' in Samo Bardutzky, Elaine Fahey (eds), *Framing the Subjects and Objects of Contemporary EU Law* (Edward Elgar Publishing 2017) 45–63.

providing income protection and cost compensation for recognized contingencies such as old age survivorship, work incapacity, unemployment, health care and family burden."[5] It is based on horizontal and vertical solidarity and, according to the author, in its most complete form consists of a subsidiary social assistance scheme, providing the individual with minimum subsistence.[6] Horizontal solidarity describes the relationship between good and bad risks, for example between the old and the young, whilst vertical solidarity describes the relationship between high- and low-earners within a redistributive social model. Traditionally, social models were grounded in the notion of intranational solidarity and formed part of the bounded nation-state. Redistributive social security systems in Europe were developed in the wake of the Second World War. They were, however, adjusted to the industrial society of the time and rested on the now long passed assumption of stable full-time employment, exercised with a single permanent employer.[7] The latter was a rule resident in the same nation-state, possibly same municipality or region, as the (male) worker. Today, social security is clearly no longer a purely local, regional or even national affair, even if it is, as observed by Pieters, first and foremost regulated by national law, also in its cross-border aspects.[8] Family structures, forms of work organisation and patterns of mobility have changed, which, especially in the now enlarged EU, begs the question whether the right to social security can still be guaranteed by MSs alone, based on the principle of territoriality, or does it call for (a greater) involvement of the EU,[9] and if so, should EU involvement (re)enforce the notion of MS to MS solidarity or should it have the sole utilitarian aim of enabling efficient functioning of the common market. If the ESM is understood solely as a common market accelerator, then the COVID-19 epidemic should not have a long-term, *systemic* effect on it, since markets are supposed to recover one way or the other and even come back stronger. If the ESM is understood as a solidarity-promoting mechanism, then the possible return to the nation-state that might have been triggered by the epidemic could put a final hold on future EU social integration. However, before any further investigation, the current ESM has to be analysed.

---

5 Paul Schoukens, *EU Social Security Law: The Hidden 'Social' Model* (Tilburg University 2016) 5–6.

6 Paul Schoukens, *EU Social Security Law: The Hidden 'Social' Model* (Tilburg University 2016) 5–6.

7 See Grega Strban, 'Family Benefits in the EU. Is it Still Possible to Coordinate Them?' (2016) MJ 776.

8 See Danny Pieters, *Social Security: An Introduction to the Basic Principles* (Kluwer Law International 2006) 125.

9 Grega Strban, 'The Right to Social Security: From State to EU Responsibility?' in Carlo Amatucci (ed), *Legal Science: Functions, Significance and Future in Legal Systems II* (University of Latvia Press 2020) 186.

In 2002, following the path of selective Europeanisation of policy functions, Scharpf described social Europe as "a road not taken".[10] Almost two decades later, it seems that the historical asymmetry between social and economic or market Europe remains deeply embedded, meaning also that the ESM is, as above-mentioned, in the first place a common market accelerator. Even if competences in the field of social security are shared between the MS and the EU, the latter holds only very limited competences in harmonising the substance of social security systems. They concern equal treatment of men and women – a commodifying basic principle, established in order to prevent unfair competition in the common market – legally non-binding cooperation between MSs in the form of the Open Method of Coordination (OMC) and the recent European Pillar of Social Rights.[11] At the same time, no common EU social security scheme exists. A European unemployment benefit scheme,[12] even if a fiscal stabilisation mechanism and not a social (insurance) scheme, has to this day not yet seen the day of light, whilst a European social assistance scheme, a common pot from which economically inactive EU citizens taking advantage of their free movement rights could profit, seems far-fetched to say the least.

The EU, however, holds wider competences in the field of social security coordination as to ensure that mobile EU citizens, especially workers and self-employed persons, do not suffer from a reduction or loss of benefits due to the presence of a cross-border element. If national social security systems in the EU were not coordinated, free movement (of workers), thus also functioning of the common market, would suffer severely. Principles such as equal treatment, single applicable legislation, aggregation of periods, or export of benefits allow EU citizens to reside, work or look for work, under special conditions, in any MS without being treated less favourably than nationals of the host MS or nationals of their MSs of origin that did not take advantage of their free movement rights. However, EU law does not unify national social security systems, even if, paradoxically, their coordination is achieved by means of a Regulation[13] as a unifying measure.[14] Unification is limited to formal social security law which

---

10 Fritz Scharpf, 'The European Social Model: Coping with the Challenges of Diversity' (2002), JCMS 645, 647.

11 See Grega Strban, 'The Right to Social Security: From State to EU Responsibility?' in Carlo Amatucci (ed), *Legal Science: Functions, Significance and Future in Legal Systems II* (University of Latvia Press 2020) 190.

12 See, for example, Michael Coucheir, Grega Strban and Harald Hauben (eds), '*The Legal and Operational Feasibility of a European Unemployment Benefits Scheme at the National Level*' (2016) Ceps Special Report No. 145.

13 Consolidated Version of Regulation (EC) 883/2004 of the European Parliament and of the Council of 29 April 2004 on the coordination of social security systems [2004] OJ L166/1.

14 Grega Strban, 'The Right to Social Security: From State to EU Responsibility?' in Carlo Amatucci (ed), *Legal Science: Functions, Significance and Future in Legal Systems II* (University of Latvia Press 2020) 191.

governs the application of substantive social security law in cross-border situations, with the aim of eliminating positive and negative conflicts of national social security law that could result in double coverage and double (or more) contribution payment obligations, full or partial lack of coverage, additional administrative burdens, etc. At the same time, the EU holds no competences in the field of social assistance, such as social care services, minimum income protection. Social assistance is guaranteed within a residence-based scheme, traditionally limited to competences of the national legislator due to tax financing and the aim of preventing poverty and social exclusion, not active income replacement due to the occurrence of a particular contingency. Unlike social security (insurance), social assistance remains uncoordinated[15] and in the full domain of national welfare states. Special non-contributory benefits, that meet special needs of social security benefit recipients and thus have a mixed nature, remain coordinated but are not exportable. Even if social security coordination rules extended, through the 50 years of its development, to third country nationals and economically non-active EU citizens, with the just mentioned special non-contributory cash benefits added to the system of coordination,[16] the links with the labour market would only become loosened,[17] not cut. According to Van Raepenbusch, national social security rules have been, by means of case law of the Court of Justice, further de-territorialised in favour of the accomplishments of the internal market.[18]

3. SOCIAL INTEGRATION AND THE ESM AFTER COVID-19

According to the above-mentioned characteristics, can the ESM even be described as a fully-fledged supranational social model, or is it merely a set of

---

[15] It also falls outside the scope of EU rules on equal treatment of men and women, remains limited under general secondary free movement rules, but is considered a social advantage under Article 7 of Regulation (EU) No 492/2011 of the European Parliament and of the Council of 5 April 2011 on freedom of movement for workers within the Union, thus being subject to equal treatment of national and mobile workers. See Consolidated Version of the Regulation [2011] OJ L141/1.

[16] See Simon Roberts, 'A Short History of Social Security Integration' in Yves Jorens (ed), *50 Years of Social Security Coordination. Past – Present – Future* (European Commission 2009) 26.

[17] See Simon Roberts, 'A Short History of Social Security Integration' in Yves Jorens (ed), *50 Years of Social Security Coordination. Past – Present – Future* (European Commission 2009) 26.

[18] See Sean Van Raepenbusch, 'The Role of the Court of Justice in the Development of Social Security Law of Persons Moving Within the European Union' in Yves Jorens (ed), *50 Years of Social Security Coordination. Past – Present – Future*, (European Commission 2009) 52.

rules, preventing the clash of national social models for the sake of the common market and market citizenship? Either way, a lack of EU competences in the field of social protection, effectively limited to social security coordination, reveals what is general knowledge. First, the EU is still first and foremost a market-driven project. Second, long-term financial sustainability of the European national welfare states, together with its main characteristics, which, according to Scharpf,[19] may be regarded as forming part of MS' constitutional identities,[20] is considered to be almost off the table when it comes to supranational rulemaking procedures.[21] If MSs were politically less protective of their national social models, the EU may have gained transparent[22] additional competences in harmonising national social security systems, whilst social security coordination might have included pure social assistance benefits as well.[23] However, the belief that additional competences, especially in the wake of an economic crisis caused by the COVID-19 epidemic, would lead to increased levels of welfare and social protection, might be considered wishful thinking. According to Bologna, who is referring to Fuchs, Eurozone MSs were forced, due to a rigid monetarist policy followed by EU institutions, to recover their post-crisis competitiveness by means of decreasing the level of their welfare systems (e.g. benefits for unemployed persons, retired persons), labour law protection and prerogatives of company agreements.[24] Additionally, as observed by Schoukens,

> social security systems in the EU are not so much assessed on their merits with regard to redistribution or equity; nor with regard to their adequacy of protection. They are assessed in terms of their efficiency and efficacy, their sustainability and transparency, in relation to their economic soundness, the budget and underlying

---

19 See Fritz Scharpf, 'The Asymmetry of European Integration, or Why the EU Cannot Be a "Social Market Economy"' (2010) Socio-Economic Review 233.

20 In a functional sense, according to Marjan Kos, 'The Relevance of National Identity in European Union Law and Its Potential for Instrumentalisation' [2019] ZZR 46, "constitutional identity is understood by the Member States courts as a limitation on the substance of EU law, which is not allowed to interfere with their core constitutional values." Basic principles of national social security systems, such as the presence of a social state principle, means of financing, scope of coverage, existence of a safety net, etc., can be considered MS' constitutional identities.

21 Luka Mišič, 'The National Welfare State, Four Categories of EU Citizens, and the Pursuit of Liberal Equality' in Moriz Kopetzki et al. (eds), *Autoritäres vs Liberales Europa* (Jan Sramek Verlag 2019) 13.

22 For the "hidden social model", that in-part seems very much hidden but much less social, see Paul Schoukens, *EU Social Security Law: The Hidden 'Social' Model* (Tilburg University 2016).

23 On the (non) coordination of minimum subsistence benefits see Gijsbert Vonk, 'The EU (non) co-ordination of minimum subsistence benefits: What went wrong and what ways forward' (2020) EJSS https://journals.sagepub.com/doi/full/10.1177/1388262720928772 accessed 21 June 2020.

24 Silvio Bologna 'The European Unemployment Benefit Scheme: Legal Basis for Resocialising Europe' (2017) Economia & lavoro 11–12.

> fiscal policies … Social security policy in the EU is mainly approached from the perspective of activation ….[25]

If the EU did possess additional competences in harmonising national social security systems, any post-COVID-19 economic crisis could lead to a direct decrease of social protection for the sake of market competitiveness. Since its competences remain limited, changed fiscal soundness conditions, following a great increase in MS' public debts, and monitoring procedures will most likely indirectly and in the long run affect national social security systems and levels of labour law protection in a negative way. Unless, of course, the EU, shaken by the epidemic, steers away from the predominant "growth at all cost" paradigm. A "social" change of heart could allow MSs to spend more on social protection (e.g. longer provision of unemployment benefits, higher family benefits, enabled access to social assistance benefits), social services (e.g. strengthening of public health insurance schemes and public healthcare providers, additional financing of homes for the elderly), or general welfare of the population (e.g. shorter working hours or working days, facilitated telework), without risking scrutiny by EU bodies and institutions. If, however, additional social protection measures are enabled for business and market salvation only and are thus of a temporary, crisis-prevention nature, they might become obsolete and burdensome after the economy is restored. Conversely, crisis-prevention legislation that lowers the level of social welfare and social protection of the population has a tendency to linger.[26]

So far, the biggest "breakthrough" in the last years in the field of social policy was when EU institutions jointly proclaimed the European Pillar of Social Rights, a soft-law document,[27] lacking the tools needed to bring the European market-driven project truly closer to a socially-driven project. A project that would offer equal opportunities to all EU citizens and not merely those who participate in the common market and thus contribute to the European centres' common good, as a rule within a *quid pro quo* relationship between the centres' and the socially and economically underdeveloped periphery.[28] As it stands, the fight against poverty and social exclusion, apart from the indirect impacts of EU social funds, remains firmly within the competences of MSs. Meanwhile, EU

---

25 Paul Schoukens, *EU Social Security Law: The Hidden 'Social' Model* (Tilburg University 2016) 40.

26 In Slovenia, for example, some savings measures introduced in 2012 with the Fiscal Balance Act remain in force today, after years of experiencing high yearly growth.

27 So far, the European Pillar of Social Rights has led, for example, to the passing of the Council Recommendation of 8 November 2018 on access to social protection for workers and the self-employed [2019] OJ L387/1.

28 See Luka Mišič, 'Equality of Opportunity in the EU: Rethinking the European Pillar of Social Rights in Light of Free Movement as a Supranational Principle of Justice' (2020) ZZR 58 ff.

competences in the field of social security coordination protect the functioning of the common market and enable the free movement of economically active EU citizens, the short-term mobility of all EU citizens and the long-term mobility or residency in a host MS of economically inactive EU citizens. The latter, however, ought to possess sufficient resources for themselves and their family members in order to fulfil the conditions of the Citizens' Directive[29] and its associated case law of the Court of Justice of the EU.[30]

If the ESM is (also in its transparent part) only a tool of the common market, then the question of further social integration and the impact of the COVID-19 epidemic seems irrelevant. One the one hand, social integration does not exist separately from market integration; on the other hand, markets are, as above-mentioned, bound to recover. From this perspective, all impact of the COVID-19 epidemic is first and foremost short term and *functional*, unless, as above-mentioned, the EU uses the epidemic for a major change of course in its fiscal and social policy, rethinking the way in which national social security systems are perceived in light of fiscal soundness criteria. Then, the EU, even if not deepening the ESM, could deepen its social dimension indirectly, through increased long-term levels of public spending within MSs and their social security systems.

4. FREE MOVEMENT AND WORK

After general opposition against closures as an *ultima ratio* public health measure, followed by occasional tip-toing and then a swift shutdown of national borders within the EU, the free movement of workers, services and persons was the first victim of the COVID-19 epidemic. As put bluntly by Pochet, "the closing once more of national borders has been a highly symbolic trend, demonstrating that 'other' Europeans are still considered as potentially dangerous, disease-carrying foreigners."[31] The closures of national borders meant that, at least until exceptions for special categories of persons were provided, migrant, frontier and posted workers and self-employed persons were unable to perform their economic activities in the common market. The same applies to wholly or partially unemployed persons seeking employment in a different MS.

---

[29] Consolidated Version of Directive 2004/38/EC of the European Parliament and of the Council of 29 April 2004 on the right of citizens of the Union and their family members to move and reside freely within the territory of the Member States [2004] OJ L158/77.

[30] See Luka Mišič, 'Equality of Opportunity in the EU: Rethinking the European Pillar of Social Rights in Light of Free Movement as a Supranational Principle of Justice' (2020) ZZR 59–63.

[31] Philippe Pochet, 'Four scenarios for Europe's future after the crisis?' (*Social Europe*, 30 April 2020) https://www.socialeurope.eu/four-scenarios-for-europes-future-after-the-crisis accessed 4 June 2020.

The closures, however, might have proved to be a significant issue in cases where production or provision of services in a particular MS was not suspended, whilst foreign workers or self-employed persons were unable to (effectively) perform their economic activities due to the fact they reside outside the MS of employment. The latter especially applies to frontier workers, migrating from the MS of residency to the MS of employment on a weekly or even daily basis, meaning that any prescribed quarantine, either in the host MS or MS of origin, meant that they were *de facto* unable to work. The need to showcase a recent proof of good health from the MS of origin also may have contributed negatively to their free movement, as it is safe to say that health documents were not always easy to come by on time, especially in times when mass testing was still unavailable. Other factors, such as changed family obligations (due to closure of schools and kindergartens and additional assistance needed by the elderly), also have to be considered, since workers that reside in close proximity to their workplaces possess better chances of balancing professional and private or family life. Another potential condition for entry into the territory of another MS is the so-called vaccination passport. It is foreseen as a document, in either paper or electronic form, indicating that a mobile EU citizen is vaccinated against COVID-19. It is, however, unclear whether the legislative action concerning the vaccination passport will remain with the MSs or whether the EU will try to overcome its complementing and supporting competences in the field of public health (protection) by introducing uniform conditions concerning the said document.[32] In doing so, it would prevent different national approaches and situations in which individual MSs could introduce or unnecessarily prolong disproportionate measures limiting free movement (entry and residence rights) of persons and/or workers, which might, if neglecting the fundamental goals of the EU, represent a breach of EU law. Either way, any introduction of such conditions could have a serious negative effect on free movement of economically active persons if they too would have to possess a proof of vaccination upon entry. Even more so, voluntary vaccination would become *de facto* compulsory.

During the epidemic, the inability of employers to rely on foreign workers possibly led to a downfall in production and consequent imposition of measures such as part-time work, shorter working hours, wage or in-work benefit

---

32 Compare Article 168 of the Treaty on the Functioning of the European Union [2012] OJ C326/47 and Articles 27 and 29 of the Directive 2004/38/EC of the European Parliament and of the Council of 29 April 2004 on the right of citizens of the Union and their family members to move and reside freely within the territory of the Member States amending Regulation (EEC) No 1612/68 and repealing Directives 64/221/EEC, 68/360/EEC, 72/194/EEC, 68/360/EEC, 72/194/EEC, 73(148/EEC, 75/35/EEC, 7/35/EEC, 90/364/EEC, 90/365/EEC and 93/96/EEC, OJ L158/77.

reductions or even suspension or termination of employment contracts. In the latter case, it will be interesting to see whether principles of equal treatment and prohibition of discrimination on grounds of (national) citizenship, as embedded in primary and secondary EU law, were fully followed when it came to the possible selection of domestic and/or foreign workers who lost their employment as an indirect effect of public health constraints on free movement. The same applies to all types of reduction or suspension of rights or employee benefits, no matter the cause, such as downfall in production due to lack of available labour, lack of supply or demand, or due to the imposition of a limited number of workers allowed in the workplace. The potential issue of non-nationals, who possibly became unemployed or subject to loss, deduction or suspension of rights or in-work benefits before host MS' nationals on arbitrary grounds, coincides with the communitarian sense of shared identity and belonging, limited to citizens or permanent residents of the nation-state. In MSs that border the European periphery, such as Austria or Germany, potential discrimination treatment of foreign workers can also attribute to the above-mentioned centre-periphery divide, especially in cases of manual labourers unable to perform work from home. From this perspective, the closure of borders due to the COVID-19 epidemic might have had a more profound, *systemic* affect, contributing to (covert) unequal treatment of migrant, posted or frontier workers, especially when moving from low-income MSs. They are deemed necessary in regular times for the sake of steady economic growth, but considered an inconvenience in times of crisis.[33]

Another functional impact of the epidemic concerning (potentially) mobile EU citizens relates to different deadlines and their potential prolongations set out in secondary EU law, such as time limitations concerning lawful posting of workers (24 months), export of unemployment benefits to another MS (three to six months), timely registration with the employment services of the host MS (seven days), timely return of unemployed persons to the MS of residency (e.g. frontier workers, seasonal workers), etc. It is safe to say that a number of services provided across borders (posting) were not concluded on time, and that a number of job-seekers that exported their unemployment benefits were unable to effectively seek employment, meaning all lost periods should be prolonged without facing disproportionate administrative obstacles by competent social security institutions. The same applies to delays or other issues resulting from (timely) unavailability of employment services' officers.

---

33 It will be interesting to see how the United Kingdom deals with a shortage of skilled labourers from low-income MS in light of (a no deal) Brexit, coupled with post-COVID-19 recession or crisis.

5. FREE MOVEMENT AND HEALTH CARE

Concerning EU rules on the export of sickness benefits outside the MS of insurance (competent MS), three situations have to be distinguished.[34] First, where the person receiving treatment resides outside the competent MS. He/she is entitled to receive sickness benefits in kind in the MS of residence, according to its national legislation, on account of the health insurance carrier in the competent MS. Second, where the person (e.g. student, tourist) receiving treatment temporarily resides in another MS for non-medical reasons (unplanned medical treatment). He/she is entitled to receive sickness benefits in kind in the MS of temporary residence, according to its national legislation, on account of the health insurance carrier in the competent MS, but only insofar medical treatment is *necessary*, meaning that a lack of treatment would lead to an unforeseen early return to the competent MS. Third, where the person receiving treatment temporarily resides in another MS for medical reasons (planned medical treatment). After obtaining prior authorisation for particular treatment that is included among sickness benefits in kind in the competent MS but cannot be provided within a medically justifiable time he/she is entitled to receive timely treatment in another MS, according to its national legislation and on account of the health insurance carrier in the competent MS. Independently from EU law provisions, national social security rules might provide additional situations in which cross-border provision of medical services is guaranteed and reimbursed by the health insurance carrier in the competent MS, for example when all means of available medical treatment have been exhausted in the competent MS, whilst medically recognised and potentially effective treatment is available in another MS or third-country.

The authors presuppose that the COVID-19 epidemic affected the export of sickness benefits in kind within the EU in two main ways. First, the changed and increased medical needs of the population, coupled with a common lack of protective and logistical capacities, and possibly also with high levels of health care privatisation, may have prorogued a number of medical services that would have been provided under regular circumstances. This means that the suspension of particular services (or even all non-necessary or non-urgent treatment) may have led to patients' early unforeseen departures to MSs of competence in cases of unplanned medical treatment, or to a deterioration of their health in cases of planned medical treatment. However, it is important that in cases where an EU citizen was legally temporarily residing in another MS and got infected, unplanned treatment was provided regardless of his/her (national) citizenship, taking into account only the planned duration of the stay. It is also possible that in some MSs which have experienced a severe overflow

[34] See Grega Strban, 'The Right to Health in the EU' in Elisabeth Brameshuber et al. (eds), *Festschrift Franz Marhold* (Manz 2020) 842 ff.

of their medical capacities, treatment had not been provided within a medically justifiable time due to the COVID-19 epidemic, and that patients have thus become eligible to obtain planned treatment in another MS whose medical capacities are less affected by the epidemic. If put in practice even in times of limited free movement and great public health concerns, this would be a truly European solution. As long as the epidemic lasts, patients from MSs with severe epidemiological situations could become entitled to receive timely medical treatment in MSs whose epidemiological situation is better and whose medical capacities are coping with the number of receiving patients. Needless to say, growing numbers of patients seeking treatment from other MSs could trigger not only the aforementioned public health concerns, even if treatment is not related to COVID-19, but also communitarian sentiments of national citizens (voters) who, after experiencing the epidemic, might feel over-protective of their public healthcare systems.

The second way in which the COVID-19 epidemic affected the export of medical benefits relates to the closure of borders. As long as no exceptions for special categories of persons, such as persons planning to obtain timely medical treatment in another MS, were introduced, their right to health was denied on grounds of public health protection. In both cases, it is key that – from a standpoint of equal treatment and prohibition of discrimination on grounds of (national) citizenship – medical services were or were not provided on grounds of objective, appropriate and proportionate criteria, and not on the sole criteria of citizenship or due to the presence of a cross-border element. Unequal treatment concerning EU citizens from different MSs may have occurred in situations in which MSs reopened some, but not all national borders, especially in cases in which the reasons behind such decisions were of political, economic, historical or cultural nature (possibly arbitrary reasons), not stemming from objective epidemiological differences between two or more MSs. The same applies to the prior discussion on migrant, posted and frontier workers and self-employed persons. From this perspective, what again seems a purely *functional* and short-term effect of the COVID-19 epidemic on European social security law and social policy, may reveal a deeper, value-based system of mutual cooperation and trust or exclusionism and distrust among different MSs.

Additionally, the epidemic also affected the cross-border provision of healthcare services on grounds of the Cross-Border Healthcare Directive,[35]

---

35 Directive 2011/24/EU of the European Parliament and of the Council of 9 March 2011 on the application of patients' rights in cross-border healthcare [2011] OJ L84/54. It should be noted that the Directive does not apply to public vaccination programmes against infectious diseases which are exclusively aimed at protecting the health of the population on the territory of a MS and which are subject to specific planning and implementation measures (see Article 1). Vaccination against infectious diseases might also not be included in the "basket of services" from compulsory health insurance but provided by the state on behalf of the state budget, thus excluding non-residents.

reflecting the parallel (dual or complementary) route for exporting the right to medical benefits that began with the now famous cases of *Kohll* and *Decker*, after which prior authorisation conditions, enshrined in the Regulation, were deemed an obstacle to free movement, even if in line with the provisions of the Regulation.[36] A patient, wishing to obtain medical treatment in another MS and commonly asking for reimbursement only after having returned to the competent MS, was most likely unable to do so either due to the suspension of particular medical benefits' provision, both with private and public providers, either due to the shutdown of borders, as long as no exceptions were provided for cross-border healthcare consumers. If the patient planned his/her treatment well in advance, deciding not to obtain treatment in the public healthcare system in the competent MS but in another MS, the deferral might have led to a deterioration of his or her health. The cross-border case, however, is no different from purely national cases in which the provision of some or even the majority of medical benefits in kind were suspended.

6. THE RISE OF THE NATIONAL WELFARE STATE

The seemingly outdated idea of a national welfare state as a bounded community that is based on the principle of solidarity and wealth redistribution, which is not only tolerated by its members out of rational fear from contingencies or social exclusion and poverty but also due to a shared sense of belonging and common identity, could gain and/or maintain momentum even after the COVID-19 epidemic settles. A true communitarian understanding of the nation-state and its social and economic institutions excludes, as a rule, all non-members or outsiders from participation,[37] and the recent crisis once again revealed the lack of transnational solidarity within the EU, put under additional pressure due to the slow common European vaccine supply. Frontiers of solidarity, especially in regard to social assistance schemes, aimed at fighting poverty and social exclusion are commonly determined by their financial capacities. According to Lenaerts,

> [f]inancially, public authorities must strike the right balance between the number of persons who contribute to the functioning of the welfare system and the number of persons who benefit from it ... Understood as a criterion limiting the personal scope of social solidarity, the concept of membership guarantees the financial stability of national welfare systems.[38]

---

36 See Grega Strban, 'The Right to Health in the EU (2020) ERA Forum 395, 396.

37 For an in-depth discussion on communitarianism in social security see Luka Mišič 'Theories of Political Philosophy as Guiding Principles in Social Security' (2018) Studies on Labour Law and Social Policy 274 ff.

38 Koen Lenaerts, 'European Union Citizenship, National Welfare Systems and Social Solidarity' (2011), Jurisprudence 398.

From the point of view of long-term financial sustainability, the potential economic crisis coming as an aftermath of the epidemic could once again reinforce the idea of – at least particular categories of –[39] mobile EU citizens as non-contributing individuals, even if economically active, and reinforce fear of social tourism. At the same time, a major drop in domestic levels of employment could lead to the witch-hunt for morally ineligible mobile, frontier and posted workers and self-employed persons, even if they contribute to the common good by means of contribution and tax payment and even if their jobs are commonly unwanted by nationals of the host MS in times of economic growth and full employment. A lack of (at least initial) common action in the fight against COVID-19 could additionally portray the EU as redundant, thus powering Eurosceptic and nationalistic sentiments, whilst reinforcing the divide between European centres and the periphery, also growing wider with the above-mentioned fear from social dumping. Needless to say, the current situation constitutes a bad environment for the debate on furthering European social integration, especially in long-term periods of reducing MS' public debt that as a rule increased during the fight against short- and long-term negative effects of the epidemic.

7. CONCLUSION

The COVID-19 epidemic has had a major impact on free movement of workers and self-employed persons. Especially in case of frontier workers, what at first glance seems to be a *functional* and short-term effect of the epidemic, may prove to have revealed once again the rooted divide between the European centres and the periphery. The economic crisis as an aftermath of the epidemic could, from this perspective, raise associated questions of social tourism and social dumping, reinforcing the idea of a bounded national welfare state. In such conditions, where long-term financial sustainability of national welfare systems and the stability of MS' labour markets will possibly be put under severe pressure, every discussion of further European social integration and the creation or development of an inclusive ESM is especially difficult.

The same applies to the question of granting more competences in the field of social protection to the EU, even if the latter could, by means of the hidden ESM, use the crisis as an opportunity to indirectly set trajectories for national social models. Another *functional* and short-term effect of the epidemic is the suspension of (particular) medical services both in internal as

[39] On (non-)deserving EU citizens, see Luka Mišič, 'The National Welfare State, Four Categories of EU Citizens, and the Pursuit of Liberal Equality' in Moriz Kopetzki et al. (eds), *Autoritäres vs Liberales Europa* (Jan Sramek Verlag 2019) 3 ff.

well as cross-border situations. However, potential unequal treatment of other MS' citizens, their categorisation as a public health threat, *de facto* mandatory early, unforeseen returns to MSs of competences, etc., could reveal a deeper, communitarian-based belief of the supremacy of the nation-state. Where else, if not in social security law, grounded in the principle of solidarity and wealth redistribution, can such tendencies be observed best?

European-wide, transnational solutions are needed if we want the EU to function in the long run. Being part of a common union is great in stable times of growth and in cases when rights and benefits come before obligations. However, in a time of clear, unavoidable and recurring crisis stonger connections at both the national and supranational level are needed.

LABOUR LAW MEASURES ADOPTED IN RESPONSE TO COVID-19 IN GREECE

Ioannis Skandalis*

Several urgent labour law measures have been adopted in Greece as a response to COVID-19 through consecutive Legislative Acts, which were further clarified through numerous Ministerial Decisions. For this purpose, the Greek government resorted to an extraordinary fast-track legislative procedure provided by the Greek constitution, which enables the executive power to legislate in cases of emergency. The said measures are subsequently ratified by law. The adopted labour law-related measures aimed to inject some flexibility in the labour market and to guarantee a basic level of income by the State for those employees whose employment contracts were suspended, by also safeguarding the maintenance of as many working positions as possible. The purpose of this contribution is to present these measures by emphasising the interpretative issues that they set. The crucial question that the present contribution attempts to answer is: How do the adopted measures fit in the wider context of Greek labour law?

---

* Law School of the National and Kapodistrian University of Athens (EKPA), Greece. I would like to warmly thank my colleagues, Nicola Countouris, Professor of Labour and European Law at UCL and Ioannis Katsaroumpas, Lecturer in Employment Law at the University of Sussex for their comments on previous drafts of the present contribution. Any remaining errors or omissions are entirely attributed to the author.

1. INTRODUCTION

Greece was one of the first countries to adopt restrictive measures at an early stage of the COVID-19 pandemic.[1] In the field of labour law, a large number of measures have been adopted through consecutive Legislative Acts (LA(s)), as well as through Ministerial Decisions (οικ.),[2] some of which were clarified further through administrative guidelines.

The adopted measures aimed at safeguarding the following objectives: First of all, the reduction of labour cost for enterprises that did not operate during the coronavirus crisis through the automatic suspension of individual employment contracts of their employees. In this way, the main contractual obligations of the parties were temporarily suspended and, thus, the employees did not provide their services and the employers did not pay salaries. Secondly, for those enterprises that were affected by COVID-19, the legislative measures introduced the option to suspend the entirety or a specific number of their employment contracts so as to reduce their employment costs. In parallel, the adopted measures also attempted to safeguard the survival of employment positions through certain rules that introduced prohibition on dismissals; whilst, at the same time, a certain level of basic income was guaranteed for employees, whose employment contracts were suspended by the State. Finally, the measures aimed at providing a certain level of flexibility in order for the enterprises, whose activities were not paused, to continue to operate to a certain extent (e.g. through telework, transfer of employees within a group of undertakings, operation through security personnel).

At the time of writing, and in the light of a relatively small number of coronavirus-related deaths and contagions in Greece, the majority of enterprises are currently still operating; however, most of them are doing so by adopting a variety of particular safety measures. Currently, the most challenging issue for Greece relates to the detailed prescriptions under which enterprises in the

---

1 The outbreak of COVID-19 was declared a Public Health Emergency of International Concern by the World Health Organization on 30 January 2020 (see: WHO website https://www.who.int/emergencies/diseases/novel-coronavirus-2019/events-as-they-happen accessed 19 June 2020).

2 For the adoption of the analysed measures, the Greek government made use of an extraordinary procedure of a fast-track legislative process enabling the executive power to legislate in cases of emergency, see Effrosyni Bakirtzi, 'COVID-19 and Labour Law: Greece' (2020) 13 Italian Labour Law e-Journal Special Issue 1 https://doi.org/10.6092/issn.1561-8048/10785 accessed 19 June 2020. In general, the process that was followed was the adoption of Legislative Acts (LAs) on the basis of Article 44 paragraph 1 of the Greek Constitution, which were then clarified as to their exact details of application by relevant Ministerial Decisions. The possibility for such clarifications through Ministerial Decisions was provided in the text of the LAs.

tourist industry might be allowed to operate again.[3] In parallel, due to the long-term implications of COVID-19 for businesses, some of the labour law measures were prolonged for a certain period of time and this will be emphasised in the relevant sections.

In light of the above, it is necessary to deal with the following crucial question: How do the adopted measures fit within the wider context of Greek labour law? In this regard, the present contribution will emphasise on the appropriate interpretation of the new measures within the framework of Greek labour law.

The present contribution is structured as follows: After the present brief introductory section, the following two sections refer to the measures that are, or have been, in force for a considerable period of time. The section "other measures" analyses the rest of the measures, which were in effect mainly until 31 May 2020, in order to offer the complete view and a better understanding of the function of the measures. This is followed by a concluding section. It should be noted that emphasis is placed on the wider interpretative issues set by the measures, rather than on the technical details characterising their implementation.

2. THE "CO-OPERATION" MECHANISM

Article 31 of the recently enacted Law 4690/2020[4] introduces a mechanism under the name "Co-operation", which aims at the maintenance of full-time employment contracts, and constitutes the most recent COVID-19-related measure within the Greek labour market. The duration of such mechanism was initially set from 15 June 2020 to 15 October 2020 (exceptionally – for particular undertakings – until 31 December 2020), and subsequently extended until 30 June 2021 (through Art 105 of Law 4790/2021). The mechanism is applicable to full-time employees for all enterprises with a specified minimum reduction of their level of income (i.e. at least 20%, in comparison to the reference month and depending upon the month of participation of the mechanism).

In particular, if an enterprise is eligible, on the basis of relevant financial data, to participate in this mechanism, the employer has the option to reduce up to 50% of the weekly working hours of all or part of the employees, however without relevant employment contracts being converted to part-time ones.[5]

---

3 Just to underline the importance of tourism in the Greek economy, it is estimated that, during 2018, tourism contributed 30.9% to GPD and 25.9% to total employment (see analytically at SETE – Greek Tourism Confederation website https://sete.gr/en/strategy-for-tourism/basic-figures-repository/2018/greek-tourism-basic-figures-2018/ accessed 19 June 2020).

4 See also Ministerial Decisions 22804/Δ1.7772/12.6.2020 and οικ. 23103/478/13.6.2020.

5 This system resembles the "short-time work" arrangement adopted in Germany in the context of COVID-19 measures, see: Arthur Sullivan, 'Short-time work: A vital tool in Germany's

Employees included in the mechanism are entitled to receive on top of their wage for reduced working hours, an additional support from the Greek State amounting to 60% of their net salary corresponding to the time where they do not perform any work (i.e. 60% of their lost income). It is also provided that if the net earnings of the employees, after the above adjustment, are less than the minimum statutory salary or wage, the difference is covered by the Greek State. It is not explicitly determined whether the reduction of the working time might take place through the reduction of working hours per day or through the reduction of working days (i.e. job rotation system). In this regard, it appears that the employer has both options available and might choose the option covering better its business needs on the basis of the managerial prerogative.[6] Employers shall also maintain the same nominal salaries of the employees for as long as the employees participate in the mechanism.

It is further provided that employers are not allowed to terminate the employment contracts of employees participating in this mechanism and, if they do, such terminations shall be considered null and void. This provision clearly aims at safeguarding the employment positions of the concerned employees. An interpretative issue that the prohibition of dismissals sets is whether dismissals may take place for exceptional reasons, not related to COVID-19. Thus, in light of the research question of the present contribution, it is crucial to situate the above exceptional provisions on termination within the wider framework of the Greek labour law on dismissals. In this regard, it is clarified that, in principle, under Greek law, the termination of employment contracts of indefinite duration does not need to be justified by a specific reason.[7] However, in extreme cases,

---

economic armoury against coronavirus' *DW* (30 March 2020) https://www.dw.com/en/short-time-work-a-vital-tool-in-germanys-economic-armory-against-coronavirus/a-52952657 accessed 19 June 2020.

6 For a similar approach, see Labour Law Bulletin (DEN) http://www.den.gr/Post/396/782/el/Nomos-4690-2020-%E2%80%93-Oi-kurioteres-kata-ti-gnomi-mas-diataxeis/ accessed 19 June 2020.

7 See analytically Dimitris Zerdelis, *Labour Law: Individual Labour Relations* (Sakkoulas 2019) 1208 ff (in Greek). However, a dismissal under Greek law might also be evaluated for abusiveness under Article 281 of Greek Civil Code (if said dismissal is against the principles of good faith and/or bona fides). Within such an evaluation, the court will eventually judge, even indirectly, the reason for the dismissal. Finally, there is an ongoing academic debate in Greece as to whether the ratification of the revised European Social Charter ((Rev)ESC) through law 4359/2016 has rendered the justification of dismissal necessary on the basis of relevant Article 24. On this issue, contradicting decisions of lower courts have been issued (indicatively in favour of the approach that the dismissal should be based on a valid reason after the ratification of (Rev)ESC is case 2245/2019 of the Court of First Instance of Athens; whilst case 237/2019 of the Court of First Instance of Athens adopted the opposite view). The Greek Supreme Court through its decision 1512/2018 has ruled that the above ratification has not affected the status of Greek law on dismissals, given that on the basis of Greek legislation compensation is, in principle, due in every case of dismissal, even if this is duly justified. Thus, the requirement for employees' adequate compensation, if their employment contract

as for instance when an employee might commit a criminal offence against the enterprise, the employer might bring proceedings against the employee and, afterwards, proceed to dismissal without the payment of the dismissal compensation (Art 5 of Law 2112/1920).[8] Hence, the interpretative issue being set is whether the employer utilising the co-operation mechanism is captured by the prohibition on dismissals, even in cases where the employee might commit offences or does not fulfil its contractual obligations on purpose. We consider that the provision interpreted in light of its purpose should be approached so as to prohibit dismissals relating to technical, organisational and economic reasons. Meanwhile, the prohibition should not extend to dismissals justified by an important reason related to the person of the employee (e.g. commitment of criminal offence), provided that the relevant reason is indeed genuine.[9] However, the explicit wording of the provision that refers to the prohibition of any dismissal could possibly lead the courts to the contrary interpretation of the prohibition of any dismissal, irrespective of the reason justifying it. This approach might also be supported by the fact that, as already mentioned, the termination of employment contracts of indefinite duration does not need to be justified. In this sense, and given also that the invalidity of dismissals has

---

is terminated without any valid reason is satisfied by existing Greek law. Conversely, the opposite theoretical view supports that the compensation provided by Greek law in every case of dismissal does not satisfy the requirement of (Rev)ESC for adequate compensation. On the legislative side, Article 48 of Law 4611/2019, which was enacted during May 2019, provided for the need for dismissal justification by stipulating that the termination of an employment contract of indefinite duration is valid only if it is based on a valid reason, within the meaning of Article 24 (Rev)ESC, but the above article has been abolished retroactively from its voting a few months later by the new Greek government elected on the 7 July 2019 through Article 117 para 2 of law 4623/2019 (on August 2019). For an extensive analysis of the current status of dismissals under Greek law, see Dimitris Zerdelis, *Labour Law: Individual Labour Relations* (Sakkoulas 2019) 1241 ff (in Greek). Dimitris Zerdelis, 'The protection against dismissal following law 4611/2019', (2019) Labour Law Review 369 ff (in Greek). Konstantinos Rizos, *Termination of employment contract* (Nomiki Vivliothiki 2020) 116 ff (in Greek).

8 For analysis of the relevant conditions applying to this case, see Georgios Leventis and Costas Papadimitriou, *Individual Labour Law* (DEN 2011) 868–875 (in Greek).

9 By way of analogy, we could refer here to the case of protection against dismissal offered by Greek labour law for employees being members of the board of trade unions. In particular, although said employees might only be dismissed on the basis of particular reasons provided by law and after a permission granted by a special Committee (Arts 14 and 15 of Law 1264/1982, as in force); in cases where the protection is claimed by employees, who committed serious offences, which were not included within the specific reasons justifying their dismissal, Greek courts by resorting to Article 281 GCC ruled that the concerned employees abused the relevant protection for reasons being irrelevant to the safeguarding of trade union freedom and, thus, the dismissal was considered lawful, see Ioannis Skandalis, 'The application of Article 281 GCC to employees' rights' in Costas Papadimitriou and Gianna Karimbali-Tsiptsiou (eds), *The Labour and Civil Law in open discussion: 17th Panhellenic conference of EDEKA* (Sakkoulas 2019) 208–211 (in Greek).

serious implications for the enterprise under Greek law,[10] we consider that businesses will be very hesitant to proceed with dismissals during the period of the prohibition for any reason whatsoever.

Further to the above, the situation of the mechanism of "co-operation" within Greek labour law regime renders it essential to interpret the mechanism vis-à-vis part-time work legislation in order to evaluate its compatibility with such legislation. In this regard, the following initial observations should be made.

First, in Greek labour law, the standard type of labour contract, which is deemed to offer the wider protection for employees, is the full-time labour contract of indefinite duration.[11] In this context, the co-operation mechanism attempts to safeguard such relationships by also accommodating a certain degree of flexibility for enterprises through the possibility of unilateral reduction of working hours. However, such reduction is temporary and does not lead to the transformation of full-time employment contracts into other types of contracts (e.g. part-time, job rotation). Additionally, the State covers part of employees' lost income, due to the participation in the mechanism. Secondly, in general, under Greek law, the transformation of full-time employment contracts to part-time ones requires the employee's agreement. Even more forcefully, it is provided that any dismissal that might take place, due to the employee's refusal to accept an employer's proposal to transform a full-time employment relationship into a part-time one is null and void (Art 38 para 8 of Law 1892/90, as in force).[12]

Moreover, specific provisions exist regarding the job rotation system, which is a category of part-time work being based on the provision of work on a full-time basis per day, but for fewer days per week or fewer weeks per month, or fewer months per year. This working arrangement could be based, under Greek law, on the prior agreement between employer and employees. However, under certain conditions, it might also be imposed unilaterally by the employer on the basis of Article 38 para 3 of Law 1892/1990, as in force.[13] In particular, for the lawful unilateral imposition of job rotation by the employer, it is required, in the first place, to have a downsizing of the enterprises level of activities and, secondly,

---

10 Given that the invalid dismissal is deemed as never having existed, the most common legal consequence is the payment of salaries in arrears from the moment of the dismissal until the discussion of the employee's claim before the competent court. For an analysis of the consequences of invalid dismissal under Greek law, see Dimitris Zerdelis, *Labour Law: Individual Labour Relations* (Sakkoulas 2019) 1335 ff. (in Greek).

11 See Georgios Leventis and Costas Papadimitriou, *Individual Labour Law* (DEN 2011) 130 (in Greek).

12 Ioannis Skandalis, 'Part-time work: A critical approach of changes adopted through law 4635/2019' (2020) Labor Law Bulletin (DEN) 26 ff. (in Greek).

13 See analytically Georgios Leventis and Costas Papadimitriou, *Individual Labour Law* (DEN 2011) 200–202 (in Greek). Costas Papadimitriou, 'The Greek labour law face to the crisis: a dangerous passage towards a new juridical nature' (2013) ELLN Working Paper Series, December 2013. Dimitris Zerdelis, *Labour Law: Individual Labour Relations* (Sakkoulas 2019) 692–693 (in Greek).

the employer shall proceed with prior information and consultation with the workers' representatives or the entirety of the employees (if no representatives exist). Additionally, it is explicitly provided that such measures shall be imposed for the safeguarding of the employment positions and for a maximum duration of nine months per calendar year. In this regard, although the unilateral imposition of the job rotation structure requires the satisfaction of the above conditions, there is no guarantee of a minimum level of employment and income, given that in theory such a system might lead to a minimum of employment of even one day per week. The only limit to such a possibility is the option of employees to claim that the imposed system of unilateral job rotation has been abusively imposed by the employer, in contradiction with Article 281 of the Greek Civil Code (GCC),[14] which will render the imposition of such measure null and void. In order to be acknowledged that a right has been exercised abusively under Greek law, it is required that such exercise profoundly exceeds the limits of the principles of good faith, bona fide or the economic or social purpose of the right, according to Article 281 of GCC. Thus, it is quite dubious whether the courts will accept a relevant employee's claim, given that the mere excess of the above principles, at the stage of the unilateral imposition of the job rotation system, is not adequate, but the excess on behalf of the employer should be profound.

The interpretation of the newly introduced co-operation mechanism within the context of part-time legislation of Greek law, leads to the following points:

- The imposition of the co-operation mechanism does not require the prior consent of the employees, as it is the case for the conversion of a full-time working arrangement to a part-time one, but it might be imposed unilaterally by the employer on the basis of relevant business needs. This could be justified by the temporary character of the measure and by the fact that the full-time employment relationship, in cases where the co-operation mechanism is utilised, is not converted to part-time.
- The imposition of the co-operation mechanism does not require prior information and consultation with employees for its imposition, as is the case with the unilateral imposition of job rotation system, but it guarantees that the employees will, at the very least, receive half of their salaries by the employer, as well as that 60% of their lost income will be covered by the State, which does not apply to the job rotation system. However, this is an indication of the limited participation of the Greek social partners within the implementation of COVID-19 labour law measures in Greece.
- The choice for the imposition of unilateral job on rotation remains available for enterprises as a generally applicable option, provided that the relevant

14 For an analysis of Article 281 GCC, see Apostolos Georgiadis, *General Principles of Civil Law* (P.N. Sakkoulas 2018) 267 ff.

conditions are being satisfied. However, in each particular case, it should be evaluated whether the access to the co-operation mechanism might serve business needs and whether the conditions for the use of the mechanism are being satisfied as well. If this is the case, it appears that the co-operation mechanism should be preferred as offering a better level of employees' protection, since 60% of their lost income will be covered by the State. In this sense, the unilateral imposition of job rotation by the employer outside the context of the co-operation mechanism, despite the fact that relevant conditions for access to the co-operation mechanism are satisfied, may be deemed abusive. However, the imposition of unilateral job rotation by the employer may not be considered abusive, if, on the basis of objective criteria and factors, it can be proven that the enterprise requires less than 50% of employee's work, which is the maximum amount of working time reduction allowed by the co-operation mechanism.

3. MEASURES FOR SEASONAL EMPLOYMENT

Articles 32 ff of Law 4690/20[15] includes specific rules for seasonal employment (e.g. employees in touristic enterprises), which has also been affected by COVID-19. In order for the rules below to be understood, it should be borne in mind that under Greek law specific rules apply to certain categories of employees working in enterprises operating seasonally. The most characteristic case is employees working in seasonal hotels, who shall make an application for being re-employed for the next season, and if the hotel attains particular levels of occupancy, there is an obligation to hire a particular percentage or even the entirety of the said employees for the next season (Art 8 of law 1346/1983).[16] This is the reason why the employment contracts of employees in seasonal hotels are characterised by Greek legal theory as fixed-term employment contracts of a peculiar type.

According to Article 32 para 3 of law 4690/20, the employment contracts of seasonal enterprises which did not operate were suspended. Additionally, Article 32 paras 1 and 2 provide that main and ancillary tourist seasonal accommodations and hotels, which re-hired seasonal employees, as well enterprises, which re-hired drivers of tourist buses who were employed in 2019, could suspend the employment contracts of part or the entirety of these employees for the period from 1 June 2020 until 30 September 2020. However, if the above enterprises reached certain rates of occupancy, they were obliged

15 See also Ministerial Decision οικ. 23102/477/12.6.2020.

16 For the employment status of seasonal employees, see analytically Georgios Leventis and Costas Papadimitriou, *Individual Labour Law* (DEN 2011) 138–142 (in Greek).

to revoke permanently the suspension of their employee's contracts, who may then participate in the co-operation mechanism. In both cases, there was a prohibition of dismissals for the whole period of suspension and if a dismissal took place, it would be deemed null and void.

Article 37 of law 4690/20 offered the choice to enterprises of the tourist, transport, cultural and athletic sectors, which were considered affected by COVID-19 on the basis of relevant lists issued by the competent ministries, to extend the suspension of employment contracts until 30 June 2020 or 31 July 2020, depending on their code of activity. In such a case, the prohibition of dismissals covered the whole suspension period and it is further extended for 30 days following the end of the suspension, during which the employers shall also retain the same terms and conditions of employment of the concerned employees (Art 37 para 5 of law 4690/20 and Ministerial Decision οικ. 23102/477/12.6.2020). In every case of suspension, the employees were entitled to receive the exceptional state benefit of EUR 534 per month.

It is further provided by Article 33 of Law 4690/2020, that seasonal employees who were not re-hired in 2020 (and who were employed during 2019 – under full or part-time employment – and have received regular unemployment benefit) were entitled, under particular conditions, to receive financial remuneration equal to their last monthly unemployment benefit for June, July and August 2020 on the condition of being still registered with the Manpower Employment Organisation (OAED).

In light of the above, the measures adopted for seasonal employment were supplementary and exceptional to the generally applicable regime on seasonal employment and they aimed at injecting some flexibility into the enterprises of the tourist sector in order to reduce the negative effects of COVID-19. In parallel, the said measures aimed at safeguarding the employment positions in these enterprises by also providing for a certain level of income replacement for employees by the Greek State. Thus, from a mere legal perspective, no particular interpretative issues arise from the situation of these measures within the wider context of the existing labour law regime. However, in a wider context, given that for the enterprises in the tourist sector the next stage of their operation appears to be at least marred with uncertainty, some additional supporting measures will be required.

4. OTHER MEASURES

For the measures that will be analysed in the present section, the following distinction of enterprises is crucial: The first category of measures refers to enterprises whose operation has been temporarily ceased through decision of public authority, e.g. restaurants and hairdressers. The second category of measures applies to enterprises being severely affected by the coronavirus crisis, such as real estate entities, entities offering cleaning services, etc., and the third category applies to the rest of the enterprises (also including the affected ones). It is also emphasised that enterprises which are back to operation, after pausing their activities, are considered for labour law purposes as affected by COVID-19. The following analysis is structured according to the above distinction.

4.1. ENTITIES WHOSE OPERATION CEASED THROUGH ADMINISTRATIVE DECISIONS

For enterprises whose operation ceased through administrative decisions, it is provided that every labour contract is automatically suspended for the period that these enterprises do not operate, which means that the parties are free from their main contractual obligations, i.e. the employees do not offer their services and the employers do not pay salaries. This measure was mainly valid until 31 May 2020, but may also apply to a limited number of enterprises which still do not operate, according to relevant administrative decisions.

In a wider context, according to Article 656 of GCC, the employer is not required to pay employees' salary in case that the employer is prevented from accepting employees' services, due to force majeure.[17] A definition of force majeure is not given in the above article, but it is generally accepted that force majeure constitutes any unforeseeable event that could have not been prevented, even if the utmost care and diligence has been demonstrated.[18] In this regard, Article 656 of GCC could also apply in the context of COVID-19 for the non-payment of employees' salaries, since the non-operation of the enterprise due to COVID-19 could undoubtedly be considered as a force majeure event preventing employers from accepting employees' services.[19] However, for the purposes of legal certainty, the legislator opted for the *ex lege* suspension of the employment relationships in enterprises that ceased their operation through a decision issued by the public authorities.

In particular, the automatic suspension of labour contracts was extended until 31 May 2020[20] on the basis of the continued suspension of operation

17 For an analysis of the concept of force majeure under Article 656 GCC, see Dimitris Zerdelis, *Labour Law: Individual Labour Relations* (Sakkoulas 2019) 914 ff. (in Greek).

18 Konstantinos Simantiras, *General Principles of Civil Law* (4th edn, Ant. Sakkoulas 1988) no 1058 (in Greek).

19 See also Dimitrios Vasileiou, 'Reduction of activity and prohibition of enterprises functioning due to coronavirus pandemic covid-19 and employment relations after Ministerial Decision 12998/232/2020' (2020), Employment Law Review Working Paper 1/2020, 3 (in Greek) https://eergd.gr/eergd-wp-1-2020 accessed 19 June 2020.

20 LA 14.03.2020, Article 10 of LA 01.05.2020 and Ministerial Decisions οικ.17788/346/8.5.2020 and οικ. 19221/379/19.5.2020.

of enterprises through administrative decisions, by also providing for the possibility of further suspension in cases where suspension of operation might be prolonged for specific enterprises. It was also provided that fixed-term employment contracts were also suspended and would continue when the enterprise would be back in operation (i.e. the duration of the fixed-term employment contract extends for a period corresponding to the duration of the suspension). However, Ministerial Decision 19221/379/19.5.2020 clarified that the suspension of fixed-term employment contracts would not apply in cases where, by the nature of the fixed-term contract, the prolongation of its duration might not be possible, for example where the fixed-term employment contract was used for the substitution of another employee during illness, and the ill employee is back at the workplace, after the end of suspension.

On the side of the employees' protection, the relevant measures also provided that the dismissals of employees are prohibited for the period of the suspension of the employment contracts, and if a dismissal takes place, the dismissal shall be deemed null and void. Additionally, the employees of the above undertakings were entitled to a special purpose compensation of EUR 800 paid by the State, which corresponded to 45 days (i.e. monthly amount of EUR 534 or EUR 17.8 for each day of suspension). It is clear that Greece did not adopt the legislative approach of other countries, such as the UK, where governments undertook the coverage of part of employees' salary (i.e. 80%).[21] On the contrary, the Greek Government made an evaluation of a particular amount that could cover the basic needs of the employees[22] and awarded that amount, irrespective of the actual salary received by each employee, prior to the suspension of the employment contract. However, this choice also resulted in odd cases, where part-time employees who received less salary than the financial support found themselves in a better financial position during the suspension of their employment contracts due to COVID-19. At the same time, employees working in enterprises whose operation was suspended through a relevant decision of public authority continued to have social security insurance calculated on their full salary and the corresponding social security contributions were covered by the Greek State.

---

21 In particular, in the UK workers on temporary leave (furloughed workers), during coronavirus, are entitled to 80% of their wages, up to a monthly cap of £2,500 by the state, see Chartered Institute of Personnel and Development official website https://www.cipd.co.uk/knowledge/fundamentals/emp-law/employees/furlough accessed 19 June 2020.

22 However, the rationale behind the granting of a particular amount as state benefit for employees whose employment contracts were suspended might only be inferred implicitly, since there is no formal reference to the measures as to the way, through which the level of the state benefit has been determined, e.g. the needs that were taken into consideration, etc. It is also worth mentioning that the amount of the benefit is less than minimum salary, which from 1 February 2019 is set at EUR 650 for full time employees (Ministerial Decision 4241/127/30.01.2019 and Article 103 of law 4172/2013), see Dimitris Zerdelis, *Labour Law: Individual Labour Relations* (Sakkoulas 2019) 796–797 ff (in Greek).

The crucial issue being considered in light of the research question of the present contribution, is the implications of COVID-19 on the employment relationships, in the absence of specific legislative intervention. In this regard, it is considered that, even if the analysed measure on the suspension of employment relationships – under particular conditions – has not been adopted, the coronavirus pandemic would be considered a force majeure event, which entails that the employer would not be obliged to pay salaries, if prevented to accept employees' services due to COVID-19. However, it is dubious whether a potential second wave of the coronavirus pandemic would be equally considered as a force majeure event under Article 656 GCC, given that in such a case the lack of foreseeability might not be taken for granted. Thus, a potential new cessation of operation of particular enterprises due to the recurrence of the coronavirus pandemic would render the ad hoc legal intervention necessary in order to avoid legal uncertainty regarding its implications on employment relationships. The intervention was also necessary for the social support of employees, whose employment contracts were suspended.

4.2. ENTERPRISES AFFECTED SEVERELY BY COVID-19

In the case of affected enterprises, employment contracts were not automatically suspended, but employers had the choice to suspend the employment contracts of their employees. The enterprises affected by the COVID-19 were determined on the basis of their code of activity that was declared to the tax authority. The list of said entities was dynamic and has been occasionally renewed, following the evolution of the coronavirus.

By virtue of a mutual decision issued by the Ministries of Finance and Labour, dated 28 March 2020 (12998/232/2020), it was provided that the suspension could initiate at any point from 21 March 2020 until 20 April 2020 at the latest, whilst once initiated, the duration of the suspension should be 45 days and could not be interrupted or revoked. However, through more recent measures (Art 10 LA 01.05.2020, Ministerial Decision οικ. 17788/346/8.5.2020 and Circular οικ. 19221/379/19.5.2020), it has been provided that the employer might revoke the suspension, even prior to the completion of 45 days, if required by relevant business needs. Additionally, the measure of suspension could have been implemented gradually to different employees.

The potential choice of the employer, whose entity is deemed affected by COVID-19 as per the above, to suspend the employment contracts of all or some of its employees had the following implications: First, employees whose employment contracts were suspended were entitled to a special purpose compensation of EUR 800, paid by the State corresponding to a period of 45 days. In parallel, these employees enjoyed full social security insurance calculated on their full salary and the relevant social security contributions were covered by the State. Secondly, employers were not allowed to terminate the employment contracts of their employees, and such terminations, starting from 18 March 2020, would be considered null and void. In this regard, it was provided that these entities were obliged to retain the same employees with the same terms and conditions of employment (as applicable on 21 March 2020) for the whole period of suspension, as well as for 45 days after the conclusion of the measure of suspension. This measure did not cover employees who resigned from their position, retired or had fixed-term employment contacts that expired after the end of the suspension. In this sense, the ratio of this measure was to extend the prohibition of dismissals for an additional period of 45 days following the end of suspension;[23] whilst, as mentioned above, for businesses that ceased their operation due to an administrative decision, the prohibition of dismissals covered only the period of the suspension. The prohibition of dismissals covers not only employees whose employment contracts were suspended, but the entirety of the personnel.

On a final note, particular provisions provided the possibility of the revocation of suspension of employment contracts for urgent, non-deferred operational needs (Circular no.14676/253/2020 and Ministerial Decision 17239/Δ1.5936/2020), as well as for the extension of suspension and its permanent revocation for particular percentages of the workforce (Arts 10 and 11 of LA 01.05.2020 and Ministerial Decision οικ.17788/346/8.5.2020).

In the context of a brief legal critique on the award of the state benefit to employees whose employment relations have been suspended, it could be argued that the conditions for the award of this benefit were characterised by lack of consistency, which is normal, up to a certain extent, given the urgency of the situation. In particular, as mentioned above, employees who lost their employment position (either through dismissal or through resignation), from 1 March until the 20 March 2020, were entitled to state benefit. Additionally, for those already receiving unemployment benefits, which were about to expire, a prolongation of two additional months was offered. The rationale of these measures was clearly to offer financial support to employees who have lost their employment position during COVID-19, on the basis of the very limited prospects of finding alternative employment, given the negative financial circumstances. It was also reasonable to award this benefit to those employees who were dismissed or retired until 20 March 2020, since from that date onwards there was a prohibition of dismissals, at least for those entities that have implemented the suspension of employment contracts. However, setting the time limit on the 1 March 2020 for the award of the benefit appears rather arbitrary. Indicatively, we could imagine the case, where an employee lost his/her

[23] For example, if an enterprise affected by COVID-19 opted for suspension of employment contracts, which entered into force on 10 April, the prohibition of dismissals would extend up to 10 July for the entirety of its workforce.

employment position prior to 1 March and, at the same time, did not qualify for the granting of regular unemployment benefit. In fact, this employee would face a very difficult situation, since he/she would not receive any state benefit (i.e. either the ad hoc state benefit of EUR 800 or the regular unemployment benefit), by also having limited prospects of finding an alternative job. This is the reason why we consider that special provisions should also exist for these cases, either through the extension of the ad hoc state benefit or through the granting of the unemployment benefit for some months, without any other conditions.

4.3. OPERATION OF ENTERPRISES THROUGH SAFETY PERSONNEL

In the context of urgent and temporary measures in the Greek labour market adopted in order to combat and limit the spread of coronavirus, and for a period not exceeding six months from 20 March 2020, employers could unilaterally appoint personnel for the secure operation of the business (i.e. operation through safety personnel).[24] The measure was valid until 15 June 2020, when it was substituted by the co-operation mechanism analysed under section 2 above. In particular, the concerned measure could have been utilised by enterprises under the following conditions: First, each employee should have been employed for a minimum period of two weeks within a reference period of one month on a continuous or intermittent basis, and the measure should cover at least 50% of the business staff. Secondly, any employer that resorted to safety personnel should maintain the same number of employees employed at the start of the implementation of the measure. Regarding the interpretation of the term "the same number of employees", for consistency purposes and in the context of systematic interpretation of the provision, it is considered that this term acquires the same meaning as in the case of suspension of employment contracts by affected enterprises, where, as mentioned above, it refers to the same employees with the same terms and conditions of employment.

In light of the research question underlying this contribution, it is underlined that the present measure constituted an exceptional case of job rotation. The system of work organisation through safety personnel did not require the satisfaction of the conditions required for the implementation of the unilateral job rotation, since a relevant decision for business operation through safety personnel lies within the employer's managerial prerogative. However, the measure of safety personnel also guaranteed that the employees would receive at least half of their salary, which might not be taken for granted in the case of a unilateral job rotation under Greek law.

---

24 Article 9 of LA 20.03.2020 and Ministerial Decisions 13564/Δ1.4770/30.3.2020, 14638/Δ1.4991/9.4.2020, 17239/Δ1.5936/2020, as well as Article 31 para 9 of Law 4690/20.

4.4. TRANSFER OF PERSONNEL TO ENTERPRISES WITHIN THE SAME GROUP

In the context of urgent and interim measures in the labour market for dealing with COVID-19 and limiting the spread of it, the employer whose business is severely affected or is under a ban of operation, may transfer staff from a group business to a business of the same group, following a mutual agreement.[25] The group companies that will implement this measure are obliged to maintain, overall, the same number of employees employed prior to the transfer (i.e. the same employees with the same terms and conditions of employment). Although the relevant provisions use the term "transfer", on the basis of the purpose of the legislative provisions, it appears that they refer to the hiring-out of employees within the same group, given that the hiring-out is of a limited duration, whilst the transfer of an employment relationship is permanent.

Regarding the situation of the above measure within the general regime applying to the hiring-out of employees to another undertaking, under Greek law, it is underlined that hiring out normally requires the prior agreement between the concerned undertakings, as well as the consent of the employee.[26] In practice, the hiring-out takes place through a tripartite agreement concluded between the involved parties. Although not entirely clear on the basis of the drafting of the analysed measure, it appears that the hiring-out of personnel between undertakings of the same group, within the context of this urgent measure, may take place through the sole agreement between the concerned enterprises of the group and this has generated relevant academic debate. In particular, according to an expressed view of Greek legal theory, this interpretation leads the provision at stake into a clash with the Greek constitution, given that it violates the core of the employee's autonomy, to the extent that the person of the employer changes (even temporarily) without the agreement of the employee.[27] According to the opposite approach, such an exception is justified due to the urgent circumstances and for the purposes of safeguarding the employment position, whilst the limited duration of the measure guarantees its conformity with the Greek constitution. On a final note, it is clarified that this measure could have been combined with the rest of the measures for affected enterprises (Art 1 para 3, section A.2. of Ministerial Decision 12998/232/28.03.2020).

---

25 Article 10 of LA 20.03.2020 and Ministerial Decisions 13564/Δ1.4770/30.3.2020, 14638/Δ1.4991/9.4.2020 and 17239/Δ1.5936/2020.

26 Georgios Leventis and Costas Papadimitriou, *Individual Labour Law* (DEN 2011) 186 ff (in Greek).

27 See analytically Dimitrios Travlos-Tzanetatos, 'The transfer of personnel within group of undertakings' (Art 10 LA 20.3.2020)' (2020), Labour Law Review Working Paper 2/2020, 1–13 (in Greek).

4.5. UNILATERAL IMPOSITION OF SYSTEM OF REMOTE WORK

Another measure adopted as a response to COVID-19 consisted in the possibility for the introduction of remote work unilaterally by the employer until 30 June 2020 (Art 4 para 2 of LA 11.03.2020 and Article 2 of Ministerial Decision 20788/610/2020). A number of extensions have been adopted with regard to this measure, the most recent of which provide for its extension until 31 May 2021.[28] Employees offering services under a remote work system are entitled to the corresponding salary paid by the employer, but are not entitled to state benefit. It is also worth mentioning that for the affected enterprises the option of remote work organisation could have been combined with the suspension of contracts and operation with security staff. In this sense, the employer could, for example, apply teleworking for certain employees, combined with the operation on security staff organisation for other employees. At the same time, the employer could also suspend a number of employment contracts, provided that the relevant conditions for the lawful imposition of each measure are also satisfied. It appears that this measure might also be combined with the co-operation mechanism, as long as the conditions for the implementation of the latter mechanism are met. Additionally, it was possible for enterprises to agree with their employees whose employment contracts were suspended, to provide remote work for temporary business needs, on the condition that this would concern only up to 10% of the employees being on suspension (Ministerial Decision no. 13564/Δ1.4770/2020).

In a wider context, it should be noted that the main type of remote work is telework,[29] which normally requires the agreement of the parties (i.e. employer and employee) in order to be implemented. Especially in cases where the parties agree to the conversion of a normal employment contract to a telework arrangement, Greek law provides for a three-month trial period, within which each of the parties may unilaterally opt to revert to the previous arrangement by offering a notice period of 15 days to the other party (Art 5 para 2 of law 3846/2010). This provision aims at facilitating the parties to agree on telework by having the option to revert to the previous working

---

[28] Article 4 para 2 of LA 11.03.2020, Art 235 of law 4727/2020, Ministerial Decision 40000/1269/2.10.2020, Ministerial Decisions 20788/610, 26308/768/30.6.2020, 30742/1002/28.7.2020 and 36124/1194/2020, Ministerial Decisions 48690/1476/25-11-2020, 52241/1567/17-12-2020, 3813/102/27-01-2021, 4012/111/27-01-2021, Ministerial Decisions 8689, 8690/199/25.2.2021, 23180/26.4.2021.

[29] It is worth mentioning that one of the first completed studies written in this field in Greek law is the monograph of Costas Papadimitriou, *Computer science, Work, Labour Law* (Sakkoulas 1987) especially 91–104 (in Greek). For an analysis of the current legal status of telework in Greek law see, *inter alia*, Ioannis Koukiadis, *Labour Law, Individual Labour Relations and the Law of Work Flexibility* (Sakkoulas 2017) 304 ff (in Greek). For the issue of working time in telework, see Ioannis Skandalis, *Working Time: Its delineation to contemporary Labour Law* (P.N. Sakkoulas 2017) 74 ff (in Greek).

arrangement, which essentially reduces the reservations of employers and employees towards this form of work.

As it arises from the drafting of this urgent measure, the deviation from the Greek labour law regime applying to normal telework consists in the fact that the prior agreement of the parties is not required for the temporary transition from normal work to telework during the COVID-19 crisis, since the employer might unilaterally implement such a work organisation within the context of the managerial prerogative. However, the interpretation of the urgent measures on telework in light of the wider Greek regime suggests that the rest of rules applying to such a work arrangement continue to apply if the employer might opt for the unilateral imposition of telework. In this regard, a crucial provision is the one stipulating that the cost of telecommunication and the equipment required for telework shall be borne, in principle, by the employer (Art 5 para 3 of law 3846/2010).[30] Thus, employers that utilised this option offered by COVID-19-related urgent labour law measures, should also cater for the provision of the necessary equipment for the performance of telework, as well as cover any related costs.

On a final note, according to empirical studies conducted in the Greek labour market,[31] during the coronavirus period, telework was the tool utilised most by both public and private undertakings for the continuation of their operation with very positive outcomes.

4.6. OTHER MEASURES

A number of other measures have also been adopted as response to COVID-19 in the Greek labour market. The most crucial of these measures are the following:

- A special type of leave (i.e. leave of special purpose) has been introduced for the facilitation of the fulfilment of employees' family obligations arising from the non-operation of educational units (Art 4 para 3 of LA 11.03.2020 and Ministerial Decisions 17239/Δ1.5936/2020, οικ. 17787/5208.5.2020, οικ. 19221/379/19.5.2020). For any four days of leave granted, three of them are considered as special leave, whilst one day is perceived and registered as part of the employee's annual leave. Additionally, two-thirds of the cost corresponding to this leave are covered by the employer and one-third

30 See also Article 7 Framework Agreement on Telework, which was annexed as annex-B to the National General Collective Employment Agreement of 2006–2007 and it is binding for all employers and employees in Greece.

31 For relevant data, see SEPE official website http://www.sepe.gr/gr/research-studies/article/15603201/8-stis-10-ellinikes-etaireies-strafikan-stin-tilergasia-logo-koronoiou/ accessed 19 June 2020.

by the State. Further to the above, Article 35 of law 4690/2020 provides for the possibility for the conclusion of a relevant agreement between the employer and the employee reducing working time by up to 25% (without salary reductions) for the fulfilment of parental obligations, due to the part-time operation of particular educational units. The corresponding reduced working time will be added to another working period, without such additional work being considered as overwork or overtime.

- Possibility for employers to pay the Easter bonus at a later time, i.e. up to 30 June 2020, instead of on 15 April 2020, when it would normally be due (Art 19 of LA 30.03.2020).
- In the field of collective labour law, an additional period for the extension of validity of collective employment agreements has been provided (Art 15 of LA 01.05.2020). In particular, such an additional period of extension of validity was set until 30 June 2020 and covered Collective Agreements and Arbitration Decisions, whose normal three-month extension of validity period expired between 29 February and 30 April 2020, according to Article 9 of Law 1876/1990.[32] Clearly, this provision aimed at preventing the regulatory gap that would arise in cases of expiry of collective employment agreements, due to the impossibility of initiation of negotiations for the conclusion of a new Collective Employment Agreement (CEA) attributed to COVID-19 restrictions on gatherings.

It is noted that the measures referred to in the present section constitute ad hoc legal interventions adopted for the tackling of particular challenges set by the coronavirus pandemic and they do not raise particular interpretative issues, since they introduce exceptional provisions, which do not clash with the generally applicable Greek labour law regime.

5. CONCLUDING REMARKS

As an initial concluding observation regarding the above-mentioned measures, it could be argued that the Greek State was pro-active in adopting responses to COVID-19 within the Greek labour market with a two-fold aim: on the one hand, the measures aimed to inject some flexibility in the labour market, by

---

32 The extension of validity under Greek law refers to a period of three months beginning after the expiry of any collective employment agreement. During such period, the collective employment agreement continues to apply to individual employment relationships normatively, as was the case during its normal operation. The rationale of this concept is to allow the social partners to initiate negotiations, without the existence of a normative gap. For an analysis of the concept of extension of validity under Greek labour law, see Costas Papadimitriou, *Collective Labour Law* (Nomiki Vivliothiki 2019) 148 ff (in Greek).

safeguarding the maintenance of as many working positions as possible, and, on the other, to guarantee a basic level of income by the State for those employees whose employment contracts were suspended. Overall, the combination of different measures appears to have offered an important level of flexibility to enterprises, whilst the loss of working positions was also restricted to a certain extent.

However, a point that negatively affected the implementation of the measures was the lack of compliance characterising some of the enterprises. In particular, the General Confederation of Greek Workers (GSEE) launched a platform called "ANTI-COVID-19 Group of Information and Support for Workers" which has reportedly received a large number of requests and complaints since its launch on 18 March 2020.[33] Most requests and complaints submitted to this platform referred to the non-compliance of employers regarding the granting of the special purpose leave to their employees, and the conversion of full-time contracts to part-time ones or the granting of unpaid leave unilaterally by the employer. Other cases concerned enterprises that remained open despite the ban and requested from employees, who received the state benefit, to provide services without a salary,[34] or the non-adoption of decontamination measures or excessive working time (i.e. over and beyond the maximum working hours set by law) in the supermarket industry.[35] The increased level of lack of compliance might also be attributed to the restricted controls performed by the competent public authorities during this period, due to the lockdown in the public sector.

The following months will be crucial for employment relations in Greece, as in every other country, given that long-term negative financial implications of COVID-19 are anticipated.[36] To this extent, the summer period was a crucial transition period. In order to have a complete view, we should also take into consideration the fact that during the forthcoming months the prohibition of

33 The platform is accessible through this link: ANTI-COVID-19 Group of Information and Support for Workers https://gsee.gr/?page_id=36762 accessed 19 June 2020.

34 Clearly in this case, there was a deception of the State, since the companies declared in false that their employment contracts were suspended in order for employees to receive the state benefit, whilst they continued their operation.

35 Effrosyni Bakirtzi, 'COVID-19 and Labour Law: Greece' (2020) 13 Italian Labour Law e-Journal Special Issue 1 https://doi.org/10.6092/issn.1561-8048/10785 accessed 19 June 2020.

36 Although it is difficult to estimate the extent of coronavirus impact on labour market, a long-term impact is anticipated and this is the reason why the European Centre for the Development of Vocational Training (Cedefop) is designing the second wave of its European skills and jobs survey (ESJS) so as to include questions aimed at discovering whether the coronavirus effects on the EU labour market will be permanent, see CEDEFOP official website https://www.cedefop.europa.eu/en/news-and-press/news/will-coronavirus-have-lasting-labour-market-effects-cedefop-seeks-answers accessed 19 June 2020. For the long-term effects of COVID-19 from a financial perspective, see Iain Begg, 'The economic consequences of Covid-19' (*LSE blog*, 6 April 2020) https://blogs.lse.ac.uk/europpblog/2020/04/06/the-economic-consequences-of-covid-19/ accessed 19 June 2020.

dismissals will no longer apply; thus, a large number of employees will face the risk of job losses.

In light of these parameters, it appears that the competent bodies should carefully design the framework of employment relations in the post-COVID era. Such framework requires the combination of different policies, i.e. policies that will safeguard a certain degree of flexibility for enterprises, while also protecting employment levels,[37] combined with the granting of social support for the categories of employees that will face loss of income and unemployment. The "co-operation" mechanism is an indication of such a multi-dimensional measure; however, this may not be adequate.[38] In this context, the prolongation of particular measures and the careful implementation of additional ones is considered a priority in order to face the far-reaching effects of COVID-19 on the Greek labour market. To this extent, social partners should acquire a more prominent role at the stage of planning the post-COVID employment landscape in Greece in order to ensure that all future measures will be truly suitable to the particularities of each individual sector of activity.

---

37 The safeguarding of jobs is also one of the priorities of the Commission's initiative SURE, see European Commission official website https://ec.europa.eu/info/live-work-travel-eu/health/coronavirus-response/jobs-and-economy-during-coronavirus-pandemic_en accessed 19 June 2020.

38 For a similar approach regarding the positive role of "short-time work" in Germany in safeguarding job positions, which is however combined with questions as to its adequacy to combat the long-term implications of COVID-19 in German labour market, see Arthur Sullivan, 'Short-time work: A vital tool in Germany's economic armoury against coronavirus' *DW* (30 March 2020) https://www.dw.com/en/short-time-work-a-vital-tool-in-germanys-economic-armory-against-coronavirus/a-52952657 accessed 19 June 2020.

A PORTUGUESE APPROACH TO PRIVACY IN COVID-19 TIMES

Through the Keyhole

Maria Raquel GUIMARÃES* and Maria Regina REDINHA**

Time has shown that in periods of crisis the pressure on privacy and on personality rights in general has always increased. The coronavirus pandemic has not been an exception and several problems have emerged during this crisis. Compulsory confinement at home has led to the need for a new division of home "territories" and devices, such as computers and televisions, with the ensuing compression of space, not only physical but also emotional and mental. The impact of these unique events on people's privacy has not yet been the object of a thorough study. In this contribution, the authors intend to discuss some of the issues that confinement has given rise to from a privacy perspective, among family members and housemates, co-workers and employers.

* University of Porto. Professor of Civil Law and Contract Law at the Faculty of Law, University of Porto, Portugal; researcher at CIJE – Centre for Legal and Economic Research/Centro de Investigação Jurídico-Económica (University of Porto, Portugal). rguimaraes@direito.up.pt.

** University of Porto. Professor of Labour Law and Civil Law at the Faculty of Law, University of Porto, Portugal; researcher at CIJE – Centre for Legal and Economic Research/Centro de Investigação Jurídico-Económica (University of Porto, Portugal). redinha@direito.up.pt.

1. PRIVACY IN A CHANGING WORLD

Privacy is not a fossilised concept but a dynamic notion that has been developing over decades in a non-linear way, adjusting to contemporary requirements of a complex global digital world. During the 20th century, it was necessary for the line between public and private, rarely straight and often unclear, to adjust to great milestones, such as two World Wars. What is more, the effect of the development of technology, globalisation and media omnipresence cannot be understated.[1]

In recent decades, the terrorist threat, on the one hand, and the exponential increase in the use of the Internet, on the other hand, with the emergence of social networking, have introduced serious new challenges to the legal framework regarding privacy.[2]

Privacy, as a personality interest, demands multi-level protection at different stages and uses different legal instruments, such as human rights, at the international level. Within the Portuguese legal framework these instruments involve fundamental rights laid down in both constitutional and criminal law. Personality rights, which are designed to protect personality interests in private relations, belong particularly to civil law but also protect individuals in the areas of labour and criminal law.[3] The different layers of protection offered by these

---

1 For a review on the foundations of personality rights, from the Roman *injuria* to the German BGB, see, in the Portuguese literature, Diogo Costa Gonçalves, 'Notas breves sobre a origem dos direitos de personalidade' (2017) II 3 RDC 655, and, in the Italian literature Giorgio Resta, *Dignità, persone, mercati* (Giappichelli 2014) 75.

2 For a European perspective on personality rights and the Internet, see Laura Emilia Weissel, 'Personality Rights and the Internet in Europe' in Ken Oliphant, Zhang Pinghua and Chen Lei (eds), *The Legal Protection of Personality Rights – Chinese and European Perspectives* (Brill 2018) 147. See, also, for a comparative and international perspective, Javier Carrascosa González, 'The Internet – Privacy and rights relating to personality' (2015) 378 Recueil des Cours de l'Académie de droit international 308 ff. On the new jurisdictional problems caused by violations of personality rights through the Internet, see Edina Márton, *Violations of Personality Rights through the Internet: Jurisdictional Issues under European Law* (Nomos 2016) 201. Focusing on the impact of social networking on the right to honour or reputation, see, in Spain, Ramón Herrera de las Heras, *Responsabilidad civil por vulneración del derecho al honor en las redes sociales* (Reus 2017) 9, and on the challenges that big data poses to the current "privacy paradigm", see Bart van der Sloot, *Privacy as virtue. Moving beyond the individual in the Age of Big Data* (Intersentia 2017) 71 ff.

3 The process known as the Constitutionalisation of Civil Law has led some authors to embrace the thesis of personality rights as fundamental rights, merging the two categories of legal tools traditionally used to protect personality interests in different types of relations: between equals, in private relations, and towards the State, in hierarchical ordered relations. See Joaquim de Sousa Ribeiro, 'Os direitos de personalidade como direitos fundamentais' in Nuno Manuel Pinto de Oliveira and Benedita Mac Crorie (eds), *Pessoa, Direito e Direitos: Colóquios 2014/2015* (UM 2017) 271. See also Mafalda Miranda Barbosa and Tomás Prieto Álvarez, *O direito ao livre desenvolvimento da personalidade, Sentido e Limites* (Gestlegal 2020) 42. On the subject of the Constitutionalisation of Civil Law, particularly in Germany after the

legal instruments work in a complementary way, often overlapping in order to protect the various levels of intrusion that affect the interests of the personality.

This intricate set of tools includes a "general personality right", a general clause establishing the right to the free and full development of personality, a foundational right where all the known and unknown, predictable and unpredictable interests of human personality may be involved, based on Article 70 of the Civil Code.[4] This standard allows a permanent update of civil law in the evolving and dynamic context of personality rights, stretching their capacity to face new challenges and unforeseeable crises in a changing world. At the same time, the Code also introduces a special right of personality, expressly protecting the "intimacy of private life", stating that the extent of the protection depends on the nature of the case and the person's condition.[5] This means that the limits of private life (versus public life) depend on the specific circumstances

---

Second World War, and its relevance for the acknowledgment of a general personality right in this country, see Giorgio Resta, *Autonomia privata e diritti della personalità, Il problema dello sfruttamento economico degli attributi della persona in prospettiva comparatistica* (Jovene 2005) 182–190. On the protection of personality in various areas of law, in particular in constitutional law but also criminal law, in addition to civil law, although referring to the protection of "personality rights" in these other areas of law and not personality interests, cf Barbara C. Steininger, 'The Protection of Personality Rights in Comparative Perspective: Basic Questions' in Ken Oliphant, Zhang Pinghua and Chen Lei (eds), *The Legal Protection of Personality Rights – Chinese and European Perspectives* (Brill 2018) 13, 17.

4 The general personality right' is described as a foundational right, source of all the different single personality rights, a radical *jus in se ipsum*, by Orlando de Carvalho, *Teoria geral do direito civil* (FL Fernandes; MR Guimarães; MR Redinha eds, 3rd edn, Coimbra Editora 2012) 202–207. See also Paulo Mota Pinto, *Direitos de personalidade e direitos fundamentais, Estudos* (Gestlegal 2018) 33 ff, 332 ff, 487 ff; Sandra Passinhas, *Propriedade e personalidade no direito civil português* (Livraria Almedina 2017) 218–221. The interpretation of this general clause must take into account rights that are thereby incorporated in civil law. However, the acknowledgment of a general right of personality is not unanimous in Portugal: cf for a system of *numerus apertus* of single personality rights José de Oliveira Ascensão, *Direito civil, Teoria geral, Introdução, As pessoas, Os bens* I (2nd edn, Coimbra Editora 2000) 86–89. For a comparative analysis of general personality right systems versus systems of single personality rights in European countries, see Eva Ondreasova, 'Personality Rights in Different European Legal Systems: Privacy, Dignity, Honour and Reputation' in Ken Oliphant, Zhang Pinghua and Chen Lei (eds), *The Legal Protection of Personality Rights – Chinese and European Perspectives* (Brill 2018) 24, 47–51; Ernst Karner, 'Human Rights and the Protection of Personality Rights in Europe: Comparative Reflections' ibid 87.

5 Art 80 Portuguese Civil Code: *1. Everyone should guard other's intimacy and private life. 2. The extension of reserve is defined according to the nature of the case and the person's condition.* This specific personality right to private life or to privacy is autonomous from other specific personality rights such as the right to life, the right to physical integrity, the right to freedom, the right to one's image, the right to one's word, the right to honour or reputation. The object of each is defined, despite on frequent occasions being jointly called up. For a compilation of Portuguese case law on the right of privacy and other special personality rights see Ana Filipa Morais Antunes, *Comentário aos artigos 70.º a 81.º do Código Civil (Direitos de personalidade)* (Universidade Católica Editora 2012) 74, 217. For an overview of Spanish case law on personality rights and technology see Sandra Gamelia Carballo (ed), *Derecho al honor, intimidad y propria imagen en relación con las nuevas tecnologias* (Sepín 2018) 9.

of each person, circumstances that may vary during their lifetime, constraining the circle of privacy or extending its limits. This also depends on the person's conduct and the extent of the outside world that is allowed to enter their private sphere (subjective elements), but also on objective exterior elements that impose on every individual in a community.[6]

Private life is one of the circles of the vital projection of personal inviolability. Personal life is, however, a narrower concept than privacy as an exclusion zone of the personality that involves not only personal life but every aspect of private life. Traditionally, the area of private life was in essence "a right of reservation" or *riservatezza*, as in Italian classical law: "the person's way of being that excludes others from the knowledge of anything that concerns the person himself or herself".[7]

The latitude of the concept of reserving the privacy of private life is therefore not abstractly determinable, since it varies, even in the workplace, according to the particular position of the subject concerned, namely, the subject's notoriety, his/her public exposure, professional activity, the functions performed, etc., and, ultimately with the boundaries that the person draws for his/her privacy, since the boundary between the public and private spheres is largely defined by the individual.

Time has shown that in periods of crisis the pressure on privacy and on personality rights in general has always increased. The coronavirus pandemic has been no exception and several problems have emerged during this crisis. A particular focus has been put on privacy and data protection issues, namely with regard to COVID-19 mobile device tracing and tracking applications, for their potential for geolocation, contact tracing, hand-in-hand with sensitive health data processing.[8]

---

6 Paulo Mota Pinto, *Direitos de personalidade e direitos fundamentais, Estudos* (Gestlegal 2018) 350, 527–528, 569; Antunes 208–210.

7 Adriano De Cupis, *I Diritti della Personalità* (Giuffrè 1982) 283.

8 See, for all, Giorgio Resta, 'La protezione dei dati personali nel diritto dell'emergenza Covid-19' (2020) 5 Giustizia civile.com http://giustiziacivile.com/pdfpage/2262 accessed 1 July 2020; Laura Bradford, Mateo Aboy and Kathleen Liddell, 'COVID-19 Contact Tracing Apps: A Stress Test for Privacy, the GDPR and Data Protection Regimes' (2020) J Law Biosci Isaa034 https://doi.org/10.1093/jlb/lsaa034 accessed 10 June 2020; Hyunghoon Cho, Daphne Ippolito and Yun William Yu, 'Contact Tracing Mobile Apps for COVID-19: Privacy Considerations and Related Trade-offs' (2020) Cornell University arXiv:2003.11511v2 [cs.CR] https://arxiv.org/abs/2003.11511v2 accessed 10 June 2020; and Maria Antonia Ciocia, 'Geolocalizzazione e norme a tutela della privacy per il contenimento del rischio da COVID-19' in Gianmaria Palmieri (ed), *Oltre La Pandemia. Società, salute, economia e regole nell'era post COVID-19* II (Editoriale Scientifica 2020) 1069. See also the European Parliament resolution of 17 April 2020 on *EU coordinated action to combat the COVID-19 pandemic and its consequences* (2020/2616(RSP)) no 53. In Portugal, The Portuguese National Data Protection Authority (CNPD) has taken a position on a new app (STAYAWAY COVID) designed to track potential contacts with infected persons: CNPD, *Deliberação/2020/277* https://www.cnpd.pt/home/decisoes/Delib/DEL_2020_277.pdf accessed 1 July 2020.

However, several other questions arose from the different COVID-19 national confinement policies such as closure of schools, a limit to the number of people that could meet in public and limited circumstances in which people could leave their homes. Compulsory confinement led to a new division of home "territories" and devices, as computers and televisions, and, inevitably, a compression of space, not only physical but also emotional and mental. The impact of these unique events on people's privacy has not been the object of a thorough study.[9]

Our aim, therefore, is to discuss some of the issues that confinement at home gave rise to from a privacy perspective, among family members or housemates, co-workers, and employers.

2. COHABITATION, FAMILY HOME AND CONFINEMENT

The containment measures dictated by the coronavirus outbreak, reducing people's mobility and social interactions, and imposing a closer and more intimate daily contact between spouses, partners, children, other family members and other people sharing accommodation, changed daily routines and dynamics almost overnight and may even have contributed to a rethinking of the traditional concept of "family".[10]

The legal importance of family members living together in the family home is revealed in Portuguese law through several dispositions designed to protect the stability of this connection established between a family and a house and limiting private autonomy and the parties' freedom of contract when the contractual object is a family home.[11] Article 1673 of the Portuguese

---

More recently the Portuguese Government has issued a disputed proposal of law (Proposal of law no 62/XIV, 14 October) establishing a mandatory app for tracing confirmed cases of COVID-19 for certain professional groups. This proposal was withdrawn due to the lack of support.

9 Several studies have been done on related subjects, such as the report conducted by Athanasios Lapatinas, *The effect of COVID-19 confinement policies on community mobility trends in the EU* (Publications Office of the European Union, 2020) https://publications.jrc.ec.europa.eu/repository/bitstream/JRC120972/jrc120972_covid_techreport_final.pdf accessed 1 July 2020.

10 Guilherme de Oliveira, '"Fique em casa". Notas para uma taxonomia dos "familiares"' (*Observatório Almedina* 7 July 2020) https://observatorio.almedina.net accessed 13 July 2020. The author points out that social isolation has highlighted that meeting socially relevant goals of living together is more important than the legal bonds between individuals, leading to a more "functional" concept of "family".

11 Nuno de Salter Cid, *A proteção da casa da morada de família no direito português* (Livraria Almedina 1996) 155. For the main repercussions on contract law of the ties that link a family to its home, especially concerning sales and lease contracts, see Maria Raquel Guimarães,

Civil Code states that the family residence must be chosen taking into account the demands of the spouses' professional life and the interests of the children. Married partners have the right and the duty to live in the matrimonial home, complying with the reciprocal duty of cohabitation, unless there are "strong reasons" for this not to be the case.[12] This means that marriage restricts freedom to choose the place of residence, the same freedom that is protected through a specific personality right, included in the general clause protecting the general personality right, contained in Article 70 of the Civil Code. With regard to minors, they have their home at the place of residence of the family, chosen by the parents.[13]

Living together is also required for the legal recognition of cohabiting couples or *de facto* couples, as stated by Law 7/2001, 11 May, as these *de facto* couples are required to live in conditions similar to those of spouses for two or more years, in order for the relationship to be recognised as a para-familiar relationship.[14]

If cohabitation or living together is mandatory for family members, it does not follow that the right to privacy cannot be protected *within* the family.

Home is commonly a private place, an ultimate bastion of solitude, a place to disconnect from work and refrain from engaging in work-related electronic communications.[15] However, there is not necessarily a correspondence between home and a private sphere, nor can this private sphere be delimited by "geographical" criteria. Even so, the family residence or home is usually included in the ever-decreasing circle of privacy, as a last stronghold of seclusion from the outside world where the right to be left alone is exerted.[16] This space of privacy is shared among family members. There is a common "private territory" for family members that can be violated through information disclosure, images, invasion or other interferences that involve unauthorised violation of "sacred ground", disturbing each family member's personality right to privacy and

'"Lar, doce lar": Os contratos sobre a habitação familiar, Algumas particularidades de regime' (2020) 2 RED 94 https://cije.up.pt//client/files/0000000001/5-raquel-guimaraes_1610.pdf accessed 1 July 2020.

12 For an exemplification of some of these "strong reasons", see Cid, *A proteção da casa da morada de família no direito português* (Livraria Almedina 1996) 128–129.

13 Art 85 of the Portuguese Civil Code.

14 Law 7/2001, 11 May, DR 2001/109 2797.

15 For the outline of a right to disconnect in the Portuguese legal framework see Francisco Liberal Fernandes, 'Organização do trabalho e tecnologias da informação e da comunicação (Exhausted but unable to disconnect)' (2017) 50 Questões Laborais 7, 11.

16 As mentioned in Paulo Mota Pinto, *Direitos de personalidade e direitos fundamentais, Estudos* (Gestlegal 2018) 528–529, "home life" should be taken for private life, unless proven otherwise, although the *locus* is not the only criterion for defining the scope of privacy and its protection extends to other private places and also public ones. According to Sandra Passinhas, *Propriedade e personalidade no direito civil português* (Livraria Almedina 2017) 116, home is a secure space of privacy and freedom, a shelter and promotes the development of the individual personality.

triggering a legal reaction, as stated in Article 70 no 2 of the Portuguese Civil Code.[17]

In this shared private space, family members have the right to privacy, separate from others family members' privacy. There is a right to privacy *within* matrimony and within the family as there is also private life *outside* marriage and family life.[18] The shared privacy in the bedroom or in the family room does not annihilate each individual's own privacy and the right to its exclusive and distinct protection.

The frontiers of this right to privacy can be difficult to trace in shared living quarters, or when using a family computer or when there is a history of sharing a desk or electronic devices, especially when these are subject to the pressure of intense and constant abnormal use by the other omnipresent family members.[19]

---

17 Art 70 no 2 Portuguese Civil Code: *Irrespective of the civil liability that may arise, the threatened or offended person may apply for measures appropriate to the circumstances of the case, with the purpose of avoiding the occurrence of the threat, or attenuating the effects of an offence already committed.* These measures may include an injunction ordering a *facere* or a *non facere*, namely the seizure of a physical publication or deletion of photographs, videos or texts published online, or preventing an imminent intrusive publication. And they can be combined with compensation for moral damage and collateral patrimonial damage.

18 For further developments on privacy within marriage, see Paulo Mota Pinto, *Direitos de personalidade e direitos fundamentais, Estudos* (Gestlegal 2018) 561; Laura W. Morgen and Lewis B. Reich, 'The Individuals' Right of Privacy in a Marriage' (2010) 23 J Am Acad Matrimonial Law 111; Fan Liying, 'On the Independence of Personalities and Restrictions on the Status of Spouses' in Ken Oliphant, Zhang Pinghua and Chen Lei (eds), *The Legal Protection of Personality Rights – Chinese and European Perspectives* (Brill 2018) 215, 222–224. In general, on the protection of personality rights inside the family, see Elena Bassoli, 'I diritti della personalità nella famiglia' in Filomena Albano et al. (eds), *Le tutele nella famiglia – Nuovi orientamenti legislative e giurisprudenziali* (Giuffrè 2018) 129. On the profound transformation of Portuguese Family Law during the 20th century, its constitutionalisation and deinstitutionalisation, moving the focus from the institution to the individuals and their right to the free development of their personality through family and through marriage, adopting a personalist vision, see Rute Teixeira Pedro, 'A visão personalista da família e a afirmação de direitos individuais no seio de grupo familiar – A emergência de um novo paradigma decorrente do processo de constitucionalização do direito da família' in Nuno Manuel Pinto de Oliveira and Benedita Mac Crorie, *Pessoa, Direito e Direitos: Colóquios 2014/2015* (UM 2017) 335, 341. The author points out that the fact that the individual is a member of a family or a spouse in a marriage does not prevent the recognition and the protection of his/her fundamental rights and personality rights, even though being within a family means the limitation of some of these rights (namely the right to sexual freedom): ibid 347–348.

19 As mentioned in *Directive 2002/58/EC of the European Parliament and of the Council concerning the processing of personal data and the protection of privacy in the electronic communications sector (Directive on privacy and electronic communications)* [2002] OJ L201/37, recital 24, 'terminal equipment of users of electronic communications networks and any information stored on such equipment are part of the private sphere of the users …'. This means that computers, tablets and mobile phones are private devices and that the information stored in these devices is also private, even if the equipment is shared among family members. In this case, however, if information is stored in a single profile or account, in shared files, there is a presumption that it is public among these users, which can be assumed true until it is proved otherwise.

Due to the coronavirus outbreak, the virtual line that divides private and communal spaces inside family homes became a dynamic, diaphanous line requiring constant readjustment. If a living room, a kitchen or a dining room are usually "communal" areas, unlike bedrooms or bathrooms which are mostly reserved for private use, in times of home-schooling or online classes and working from home or teleworking, living areas are converted to offices, demanding working conditions such as silence and concentration.

In spite of this, privacy cannot always be achieved in a common space, transformed into an open-plan office, often distracting and noisy, where telecommuting parents work side by side with young children doing homework or attending an online or TV class. Whatever the case, the exercise of one's right to privacy will most probably interfere with other family members' rights, compressing their scope, limiting *de facto* each one's seclusion. The conflicting rights to privacy in the workspace of different family members working at the same dinner table, the right to privacy in the free moments of another family member, or the right of yet another family member to be left alone will be, in practice, restricted by the particular conditions of the exercise of these rights, specifically by limits of "social suitability" that arise from the fact that no man is an island but a social being, beginning inside a family.[20]

The balance of family members' privacy dictated by very close daily coexistence in the family "headquarters", in "normal" times associated with conserving the unity of family life, must necessarily safeguard the core area of certain personality interests. These restrictions explained by a necessary composition of different personality rights must not be allowed to infringe on an absolute protected core area of privacy, an intimate sphere of secrecy, directly associated with personal dignity, honour and decorum, including secret information on health and sexuality, passwords, intimate journals and correspondence.[21]

3. FROM THE BEDROOM TO THE WORLD

If being in a bedroom creates an expectation of privacy and seclusion, the fact that this bedroom is being broadcast to dozens of classmates during an exam, a class or a webinar, or to co-workers or clients during a meeting, possibly for several hours, changes the legal framework necessary to face possible damage caused by unauthorised images or video recordings.

---

20 About the limits that everyday life imposes on personality rights due to social interaction or "social suitability", see by Orlando de Carvalho, *Teoria geral do direito civil* (FL Fernandes; MR Guimarães; MR Redinha eds, 3rd edn, Coimbra Editora 2012) 204.

21 The right to honour, reputation and decorum is inalienable and cannot be limited even by the holder, operating as a last boundary for other personality rights, as expressly referred to in art 79 no 3 of the Portuguese Civil Code, with regard to the protection of one's image.

The disclosure of unauthorised images or videos recorded during a conference call, revealing the speaker's or attendee's bedroom cannot be regarded as an intrusion into his/her *personal* sphere but as a violation of a larger concentric *private* sphere. Being in one's bedroom taking an exam, attending a class or having a business meeting is *less private* than using the same bedroom for its "normal" purposes, including sleeping, dressing and undressing or simply doing nothing, enjoying a moment of solitude. The implicit invitation to the world to access one's last bastion of solitude when turning on a computer camera inside that room necessarily reduces its "sacred" nature, resulting in a self-limitation of the right by its holder.

At the same time, if the bedroom used in a conference call is the couple's bedroom or a siblings' bedroom, the privacy of these people must also be considered, both in the relation with the "roommate" – since the exposure of a shared bedroom online demands the other's consent –, and also regarding external intrusions, affecting not only one but two different people's personality rights, causing separate moral damage to both of them.

It is a fact that a single back wall of one's home can say a lot about a person. The scenery each person chooses (or not) to frame his/her image, or simply cannot avoid using due to the lack of space, can reveal important information – even personal information – about its owner, his/her tastes, habits, hobbies and, most certainly, wealth and social condition. And even experimenting with broadcasting backgrounds that might work well for remote meetings, such as photos, playing the role of a movie director and avoiding the back wall, can expose or uncover certain traces of personality.

This incursion into another person's home allows a natural voyeurism but also may lead to a type of profiling. The presence of the students in the same classroom or of work colleagues in a shared workspace places them in a neutral and, to some extent, more democratic environment. Opening a virtual window on to our domestic life invites people into our home, a privilege usually enjoyed by only a few and after a certain degree of intimacy and complicity.

Nevertheless, this self-limitation of privacy, which results from the person's use of his/her own camera, can never be taken as a permission for intrusion beyond the strict purposes of the visualisation of that "back scenery" during the same meeting in which it is broadcast. When access to personal information by a third party is a result of an action on the part of the holder of that information, whether it is accidental or involuntary, it is not an offence.[22] The information, however, must not be disclosed. Any recording, publication of images, either

[22] On self-limitation of privacy and its limits see Paulo Mota Pinto, *Direitos de personalidade e direitos fundamentais, Estudos* (Gestlegal 2018) 679, 687–696. As the author points out, this self-limitation of the right to private life needs to be itself limited in time and does not include other uses of the information that were not comprised on the holder's consent. It cannot be taken as a general implicit consent for subsequent interference.

video or photograph, any profiling or any use of information accessed by those means would be considered an affront to the right to privacy, as well as to the person's image and even potentially to his/her right to one's word and character, generating civil and, potentially, in the most severe cases, even criminal liability.[23]

This is not only valid for classmates, co-workers, employers or other parties in a same virtual meeting or class, but also for the platforms and applications that provide the video-meeting services. These digital companies collect personal information about their users, their online experiences and interactions while using the services, possibly without the users' knowledge, and seldom with their consent. Notwithstanding the fact that surveillance and data collection seem to be an inevitable consequence of today's interaction with digital companies – and a challenge to the data protection legal framework –, it is true that the COVID-19 pandemic, forcing people to live their lives online, has shown the gravity of the problem, stressing legal solutions for privacy and data protection.[24]

4. EMPLOYEES' PERSONALITY RIGHTS: OVERVIEW

Since 2003 personality rights have been recognised as such in the Portuguese Labour Code. A separate section (Arts 14–22) is dedicated to the regulation of these rights in the first part of the Labour Code related to the subjects of the employment contract. These Articles embody the growing awareness in the Portuguese legislation of the quality of life in the workplace, and to a certain extent they reflect an ecological approach of the employment contract, which emphasises the personal dimension within the exchange arrangement in the contract. These propositions express the principle that work does not strip

---

23 Additionally the holder can apply for the "measures appropriate to the circumstances of the case", as stated in Art 70 no 2 of Portuguese Civil Code.

24 See Maria Antonia Ciocia, 'Geolocalizzazione e norme a tutela della privacy per il contenimento del rischio da COVID-19' in Gianmaria Palmieri (ed), *Oltre La Pandemia. Società, salute, economia e regole nell'era post COVID-19* II (Editoriale Scientifica 2020) 1071; and Jack M. Balkin, 'The fiduciary model of privacy' (2020) 134 Harv L Rev 11, 13. According to the latter author, the "notice-and-choice models" of privacy – like those of the Portuguese right to private life and the GDPR, based on consent – have been proved inadequate when there are major asymmetries between the parties, not only social, economic and informational, but also power and control asymmetries, as in the relationships with digital companies. Balkin suggests a new "fiduciary model" of privacy. For an extended debate on this model see Lina M. Khan and David E. Pozen, 'A skeptical view of information fiduciaries' (2019) 133 Harv L Rev 497, with references. Other models have been tested, moving beyond the individual privacy paradigm and the consent paradigm, like Bart van der Sloot, *Privacy as virtue. Moving beyond the individual in the Age of Big Data* (Intersentia 2017) 71–143 proposal for an alternative privacy paradigm based on virtue ethics, and Betkier 'Privacy Management Model', based on three requirements: organising, planning and controlling privacy (Marcin Betkier, *Privacy online, law and the effective regulation of online services* (Intersentia 2019) 80 ff).

employees of their personal rights; on the contrary, their attributes of personhood and citizenship are maintained and reinforced in view of the potential conflict within the employment context.[25]

Special protection of the employee's personality rights is therefore recognised by law. Protection that is extended to workers by Article 10 of the Labour Code which includes these rights at the very heart of labour law to be applicable outside the scope of the employment contract to those who are in a situation of economic dependence, and to those employed in public functions (Art 4, Law 35/2014, 20 June).[26]

Unlike the Portuguese Civil Code, the Labour Code does not include a disposition regarding the general right of personality, nor its free development. Instead partial dimensions of the employee's personality are considered and regulated: freedom of expression and opinion; physical and moral integrity; reserve of private life; personal data protection; use of biometric data; confidential nature of medical exams and tests; admissibility of remote surveillance media and confidentiality of messages and access to information.[27]

This catalogue of rights combines unspecific protection against employment harm in the workplace, such as in the provisions regarding freedom of speech or privacy, with the protection made necessary by the use of digital technology, as is the case of biometric data, remote surveillance media and confidentiality of messages and access to information.

The violation of personality rights by the employer is a source of civil liability under Article 483 of the Civil Code and, on the labour level, a due cause for rescission of contract by the employee with compensation (Art 394, Labour Code). The rescission of contract with due cause entitles the employee to compensation for the deliberate breach of his/her legal and contractual guarantees. This compensation covers material and moral damage suffered and is established based on the employee's seniority. The consequences of the infringement of these rights by the co-workers is also a due cause for rescission of the employment contract by the victim, with the right to civil compensation by the employer if he/she is at fault for not maintaining a safe, healthy and appropriate work environment. Moreover, the employee that violates a peer's right commits a disciplinary fault and is guilty of breach of contractual duties and in the most serious cases may even be subject to fair dismissal.[28] He/she is also liable for the moral and patrimonial damage suffered by his/her peer.

---

25 For an overview of employees' personality rights see Maria Regina Redinha, 'Da Protecção da Personalidade no Código do Trabalho' in João Reis, Leal Amado, Liberal Fernandes and Regina Redinha (eds), *Para Jorge Leite – Escritos Jurídico-Laborais* I (Coimbra Editora 2014) 819–854.

26 General Regulation of Work in Public Functions: Law 35/2014, 20 June, DR 2014/117 3220.

27 See arts 15–22 of the Labour Code.

28 Art 394 no 1 c) of the Labour Code.

Outside the autonomous division further protection is granted in the Labour Code to other personality dimensions, including the prohibition of harassment, the right to equality and no discrimination and the freedom of work.

In the Portuguese Labour Procedural Code, a special, simplified and urgent procedure is foreseen for the rapid and effective enforcement of personality rights (Arts 186-D–186-F).

5. PRIVACY PROTECTION OF EMPLOYEES

Privacy is the legal interest protected in Article 16 of the Labour Code. This is a provision aimed at safeguarding the privacy of both workers and employers.[29] The subjective scope of the protection includes the employer and his/her representatives, and the employee. Notwithstanding, the express mention of the extent of protection to both subjects of the employment relationship reflects without true justification the concern for an isometric and levelling view. Indeed, through the employment contract the employer does not enter into a statutory situation different from the one held until then, nor does he/she experience any hetero-limitation of his/her autonomy, contrary to what happens with the employee. The general protection provided by civil law would have been adequate and sufficiently inclusive to safeguard the employer's privacy, because it is not the employee, in a position of legal subordination, who can weaken or violate the counterparty's personality rights.

The right to the intimacy of private life finds its first line of protection in Article 80 of the Civil Code, as was seen before. The provision of Article 16 of the Labour Code deals essentially with the same legal asset: the reserved individual sphere where he/she has absolute control over the exposure and access offered to others.

In methodological terms this means that the labour regulations must necessarily be juxtaposed with the civilian regulations, as they are a particular development or implementation of the latter. There is, therefore, no mutual exclusion or even any erosion of the general civil protection due to the possible "speciality" of labour regulation. The relationship between civil and labour law is one of complementarity and overlap. Its predominance *in casu* will be determined by the amount of protection it is afforded.

---

29 Art 16 Labour Code: *1. Both the employer and the employee must respect each other's personality rights and must, namely, respect the right to privacy. 2. The right to the reserve of private life includes both the access to, as well as the disclosure of aspects concerning the intimate and personal sphere of the parties, namely those regarding family life, love and sexual life, health condition and political and religious beliefs.*

If the violation of privacy occurs outside the scope of the Labour Code protection, the Civil Code will be applicable, due to its general and subsidiary nature.

Thus, if the violation occurs in the workplace and during working time, for example, through the disclosure of elements obtained from the worker's computer, the Labour Code rules will apply, but if there is a violation of privacy through, namely, the practice of stalking by the employer, motivated by extra-contractual conduct and in circumstances external to the work relationship, then the applicable regulation will instead be the Civil Code. However, in terms of sanctions, there may be an overlap when in the labour context the violation can be prevented or the violated right can be partially reinstated by precautionary measures, such as seizures, withdrawal of publications, etc, since in this type of situation the labour protection is complemented by the application of Article 70 no 2 of the Civil Code.

Article 16 no 2 of the Labour Code deals with the delimitation, which is not exhaustive, of the elements that make up the reserve of intimacy which is protected: elements pertaining to personal, family, affective and sexual life, physical and psychological condition, economic status, political and religious beliefs. Here are contemplated the daily personal and family practices and the secrecy sphere of information that the individual, by choice or conviction, intends to keep outside the knowledge of others. Despite not being included in the wording of the norm, sensitive elements of the personal sphere, such as union or social activities, volunteer work or hobbies, for example, are also considered. Also, the access to knowledge of aspects of private life is subject to protection, as well as the dissemination of facts and information concerning the privacy of the employer or worker, whether this knowledge has been accessed lawfully or illegally. The disclosure of facts or information pertaining to the private life of both the employer and the employee constitutes, in itself, a violation of the right of personality regulated under this Article. In other words, alongside a right to the reserve of information that can be obtained within the employment relationship, there is a right to secrecy or silence about the information actually collected.

Furthermore, actions concerning the circle of private life cannot, in principle, be taken into account, directly and immediately, for the assessment of non-compliance under the employment contract, as has been firmly decided in case law.

The right to privacy is a partial waivable right that can exclude the illegality of the harmful act, through the injured party's consent (Art 340 no 1, Civil Code).[30]

---

30 On the borders of waivability in Labour and Employment Law, Guy Davidov, 'Nonwaivability in Labour Law' (2020) OJLS Nonwaivability in Labour Law https://papers.ssrn.com/sol3/papers.cfm?abstract_id=3559244 accessed 27 June 2020.

The waivability, however, is only admissible if there is no harm to human dignity and must be the product of a free and informed expression of consent.

6. TELEWORK

Portugal was the first European country to create a legal provision for telework. In 2003, the Labour Code included telework for the first time as a special employment contract, following the then recent European Framework Agreement on Telework.[31]

According to the Labour Code, Articles 165–171, telework can be agreed as a special employment contract *ab initio* aimed at this form of work or as an agreed transitional arrangement within a pre-existing employment contract. In both cases, written agreement between the parties is required.[32]

Although telework may be a very broad concept covering different types of work, for the purpose of the Labour Code it is defined by the necessary combination of two components: intensive use of information and communication technologies to perform the activity *in obligatio* and the separation of the workplace from the employer's premises.[33]

The evaluation of the intensity of technology follows a qualitative approach that considers the connection between the activity output and the use of information and communication technology and the expertise level required by that use.

Telework employment in Portugal involved a very limited number of employees until the emergency legislation dictated by the COVID-19 pandemic.

Among other exceptional and temporary social and labour regulations, Law Decree 10-A/2020, 13 March,[34] granted permission for the use of telework on the sole command of the employer's or upon an employee's initiative if agreed to by the employer (Art 29 no 1), as long as the activity could be performed

---

31 For the European Framework Agreement on Telework (2002) and for its Implementation Report by the European social partners (2006), see http://resourcecentre.etuc.org/linked_files/documents/Framework%20agreement%20on%20telework%20EN.pdf accessed 27 June 2020.

32 For the Portuguese legal framework of telework, Maria Regina Redinha, 'Cyberspace and Workers' Privacy Protection' in Glória Teixeira and Ana Sofia Carvalho (eds), *Os 10 Anos de Investigação CIJE – Estudos Jurídico-Económicos* (Livraria Almedina 2010) 693, and 'Teletrabalho 2020 ou o encanto de Janos' in Maria do Rosário Palma Ramalho and Teresa Coelho Moreira (eds), *COVID-19 e trabalho: o dia seguinte* (AAFDL 2020) 39, 40 ff.

33 Art 165 Labour Code: *Telework is considered to be work carried out, under legal subordination, usually outside the employer's company and with recourse to information and communication technologies.*

34 Exceptional and Temporary Measures Associated with the Epidemiological Situation of the New Coronavirus – COVID 19, Law Decree 10-A/2020, 13 March, DR 2020/54 22.

under the terms of the definition laid out in Article 165 of the Labour Code. Although this precise provision was revoked during the "state of contingency" by Law Decree 24-A/2020, 29 May,[35] there was an exponential increase in telework in both the private and the public sector highlighting the very many personality rights issues faced by teleworkers, especially when their workplace is also their family home. With the worsening of the pandemic and the return to the "emergency situation", teleworking was made once again mandatory by Law Decree 94-A/2020, 3 November.[36]

If telework is performed at home, inspections by employers should only be carried out with the purpose of monitoring or assessing the work being done or the employer's equipment and these inspections may only be conducted within the limited time frame of the standard working hours.[37]

The Labour Code secures for teleworkers the principle of equitable treatment and of no unfavourable working conditions. Teleworkers therefore enjoy the same general protection accorded to any employee and benefit from all positive measures required to neutralise the specific disadvantages of telework, such as the risk of privacy infringement. Included among the more relevant provisions within this framework are the limitations on the control of the employees' activity through spyware and others means of remote surveillance, such as global positioning systems (Arts 20 and 21 of the Labour Code), or the confidentiality of electronic mail, of other exchanged messages and of internet browsing (Art 22 of the Labour Code).

In the wording of the law there is no mention of the monitoring or surveillance of the immaterial dimensions of the worker's privacy, thus implicitly safeguarding the general statutory provisions offered to any employee, namely data protection, regulation of remote surveillance media and the confidentiality of personal messages and information searched for.

An additional instrument of protection of teleworker's right to privacy is the obligation of information to be fulfilled by the employer at the beginning of the employment relationship and whenever there is a substantial change in the real working conditions (Arts 108 and 109 of the Labour Code). This obligation extends to the use of any tools that could be deemed to invade the employee's reserved sphere, preventing him/her from being subjected to hidden

35 Changes to the Exceptional and Temporary Measures Related to the COVID-19 Disease Pandemic: Law Decree 24-A/2020, 29 May, DR 2020/105 29.

36 Changes to the Exceptional and Temporary Measures Related to the COVID-19 Disease Pandemic: Law Decree 94-A/2020, 3 November, DR 2020/214 168(2).

37 Art 170 Labour Code: *1. The employer must respect the teleworker's privacy and rest periods, as well as the family rest periods, and must provide good psychological and physical work conditions. 2. Whenever telework is performed in the employee's home, visits to the workplace must only be intended to monitor the latter's work and equipment and must only be conducted between 9am and 7pm, with the employee's presence or that of a person designated by the latter.*

observation or surprised by concealed evaluation, in accordance, moreover, with the *López-Ribalda* judgment of the European Court of Human Rights.[38]

7. REDESIGNING PRIVACY IN THE PANDEMIC ENVIRONMENT

Work and privacy are largely antithetic. For decades, private and family life was kept separate from professional life and until the turn of the century labour law offered no orientation in that respect. As might be expected, privacy became relevant in direct proportion to the use of digital technology in the workplace.[39] Today, employees have to be guarded not only against physical disturbances but also against virtual incursions into their vital space and time and if these risks were largely overlooked when there was a limited number of teleworkers, the vast increase in its use caused by the COVID-19 pandemic brought to light the need to broaden the scope of privacy and to compress the employer's rights, particularly when telework is carried out from home.

Even if the employee has a reasonable extended right of privacy recognised by the Labour Code, the overnight transformation of thousands of houses into workplaces, redefined the needs that have to be covered under the concept and widened its personal scope.[40]

As whole families share the same space to live, work and be confined, there is an unavoidable desecration of traditionally private living quarters and intersection of the personal and professional spheres, making it risky to draw a line between them. Among family members, the pandemic has forced an adjustment of the tangent or even overlapped spheres of privacy of each individual, due to the particular conditions dictated by communal living and the omnipresence of others. In the employment relationship the employer's intervention must be kept to a minimum under the strict parameters of the principle of good faith (Art 126 no 1, Labour Code) and the rule of proportionality,[41] to allow the compatibility of his/her right of management with that of the right of privacy of the employee

---

38 *López-Ribalda and Others v Spain* App nos 1874/13 and 8567/13 (ECtHR, 17 October 2019).

39 For the development of the notion of privacy in the labour relationship, Frank Hendrickx, 'Privacy, Data Protection and Measuring Employee Performance. The Triggers of Technology and Smart Work' (2018) 9 (2) ELLJ 9, 100.

40 For another perspective on the same subject, see Michela Bella, 'Risignificare lo spazio domestico ai tempi del COVID-19: tra convivenza e lavoro femminile' in Gianmaria Palmieri (ed), *Oltre La Pandemia. Società, salute, economia e regole nell'era post COVID-19* I (Editoriale Scientifica 2020) 673.

41 The rule of proportionality has been repeatedly affirmed in Portuguese constitutional employment case law, see, e.g. *Acórdão do Tribunal Constitucional* no 632/2008 [2008] DR 6/2009 161–169.

and his/her family members under the criterium of prevalence of personal rights over valued rights stated in Article 335 of the Civil Code.

As the personal and family space may be exposed without the employee's permission or even without him/her being able to prevent or to control the invasion, it is necessary to guarantee that privacy includes even apparent neutral elements collected in the private circle that could be used to profile or discriminate against the employee. Thus, the employer must take preventive action and ensure that the employee is fully informed about the extended features of the working instruments necessary to minimise intrusion (neutral background tools, isolation of working stations, etc.), as it is his/her obligation to create a sound and safe work environment (Art 127 no 1 c) of the Labour Code) in order to avoid liability for breach of lateral duties.

What is more, the notion of infringement of the employee's privacy must be extended so that it includes the privacy of his/her family members or co-habitants, third parties to the employment contract, who may be affected by the employer's or other co-workers' conduct. Home is not only the employee's private territory but the family or other co-habitants' private territory. Thus, if the employee can plead for a compensation and can even terminate the contract with due cause for violation of privacy rights, this should also be possible if the violation is indirect and involves one of the members of the household. This extension can be achieved within the present legal framework through the consideration of such a violation as a breach of the employer's duty of respect as noted in Article 127 no 1 a) of the Labour Code.[42] In fact, the dissociation between the entity that holds the right and the entity that suffers the injury is not strange to labour law, albeit in relation to a completely different field, since the impact of the Coleman judgment of the European Court of Justice.[43]

Since the main issue arising from privacy protection in the employment context is the delimitation of the worker's individual right in relation to the employer's organisational powers, the transparency of the contractual relationship would largely benefit from the existence of rules of good practice and of good governance of work instruments, which could be achieved through the mandatory adoption of a code of conduct within the employer's organisation, as happens, for instance, within the harassment regulation (Art 127 no 1 k) of the Labour Code).

With regard to the protection of privacy in the workplace adapted to the constricting circumstances of the COVID-19 pandemic, we can conclude that

---

42 Compensation and other possible measures dictated by the court to attenuate the effects of the offence may also be imposed on a third party, such as co-worker or a client, if he or she is the perpetrator of the offence, the one who has, for instance, captured or shared a picture or a video without consent.

43 Case C-303/06 *S. Coleman v Attridge Law and Steve Law* [2008] ECR I- 5615.

the Portuguese legal system is not entirely devoid of normative instruments capable of adapting to the health crisis and the future transformations that it may cause in the conformation of the workplace. However, *de lege ferenda*, a redesign of the operative notion of privacy would enable a higher degree of certainty and security in the application of the law.

Additionally, beyond the employment relationship, the general personality right and the right to the "intimacy of private life" – stating that everyone should guard other people's intimacy and private life and appealing to the nature of the case and the person's condition, allow a significant adjustment of privacy protection needs to the current circumstances. Even so, the intensive use of digital technology, the daily exposure of one's private environment, besides one's image, word and character, the inherent compression of the individual's right to solitude and to disconnect and the latent threat of constant surveillance provided by digital companies collecting personal information, suppose an extraordinary test for the legal framework regarding privacy and a considerable task for the interpreter, applying general clauses, standards and open value concepts.

ALTERATION OF THE CONTRACTUAL EQUILIBRIUM DUE TO COVID-19 IN EMPLOYMENT AND CIVIL LAW CONTRACTS UNDER ESTONIAN LAW

Merle ERIKSON and Irene KULL*

Following the spread of COVID-19 to Estonia at the beginning of March 2020, the Government declared an emergency situation from 12 March 2020. For officially and voluntarily closed businesses, staff reductions, reduction of remuneration or working load, the amendment or termination of the employment and other

* Merle Erikson, Professor of Labour Law, School of Law, University of Tartu, Estonia; Irene Kull, Professor of Civil Law, School of Law, University of Tartu, Estonia.

contracts for work or services became one of the legal measures in preventing greater damage. The aim of this contribution is to answer the question under what conditions the affected party may demand amendment of an employment contract and civil law contract – with the example of a contract of mandate – in order to restore the original balance of the obligations, and terminate the contract, in order to assess the level of protection of parties' interests. The comparison of an employment contract and a contract of mandate is based on legal provisions of Estonian law regulating the legal consequences of change of circumstances, which leads to the alteration of balance of contractual obligations in an emergency situation, as was caused by COVID-19.

1. INTRODUCTION

Most of the countries implemented far-reaching bans and restrictions on freedoms in order to deal with the spread of the COVID-19 pandemic. Following the spread of COVID-19 to Estonia at the beginning of March 2020, the Government declared, according to the Estonian Emergency Act,[1] an emergency situation on the evening of 12 March 2020.[2] Emergency measures were valid until 11 May 2020.[3] The overall emergency situation was terminated on 18 May 2020, though certain limitations and special rules continued to stay in force.[4]

---

1 Hädaolukorra seadus (Emergency Act) 2017, https://www.riigiteataja.ee/en/eli/ee/516052020003/consolide/current accessed 25 June 2020. The Emergency Act distinguishes between an emergency and an emergency situation. The Government may declare an emergency situation for resolving an emergency caused by a natural disaster, catastrophe or spread of a communicable disease if it is not possible to resolve the emergency without implementing the management arrangements or measures provided for in an emergency.

2 Declaration of Emergency Situation in the Administrative Territory of the Republic of Estonia, Government order no 76, 2020 https://www.riigiteataja.ee/en/eli/524042020008/consolide accessed 25 June 2020. From 13 March 2020 all schools and other educational establishments, cinemas, theatres, museums, nightclubs, etc. were closed, restrictions were imposed on travelling and temporarily, border checks were established. See Temporary Restoration of Border Checks and Border Control at the Internal Border. Government regulation no 15, 2020 https://www.riigiteataja.ee/en/eli/517032020003/consolide accessed 25 June 2020.

3 From 15 May 2020 the border control between Estonia and Latvia was lifted. From 1 June 2020 the Estonian State border may be crossed for the purposes of entering into Estonia by a person who does not have symptoms of disease and who arrives in Estonia from a Member State of the European Union, Schengen Convention or from the United Kingdom of Great Britain and Northern Ireland. See Imposition of Temporary Restrictions on Crossing the State Border and Establishment of Quarantine upon Crossing the State Border in order to Prevent a New Outbreak of the Coronavirus SARS-CoV-2 Causing the COVID-19 Disease, passed 6 May 2020, entry into force 18 May 2020 https://www.riigiteataja.ee/en/eli/ee/VV/k/530052020001/consolide accessed 25 June 2020.

4 Emergency measures were not very strong in Estonia. Although shopping centres remained to a large extent closed, grocery stores, pharmacies, bank offices, beauty salons, smaller shops, companies providing services and offices remained opened. Restrictions on the Freedom of Movement and on Holding Public Meetings and Public Events as Necessary for Preventing

It should be mentioned that no essential amendments to employment or contract law were introduced due to the crisis.[5] Beside officially closed businesses, a number of others decided on voluntary closure partly for the safety of their employees, but also partly due to the lack of customers. In the situation of forced staff reductions, reduction of remuneration or working load, the amendment or termination of employment or other contracts for work or services became one of the legal measures in preventing greater damage.

The aim of this contribution is to answer the question under what conditions the affected party may demand amendment of an employment contract and civil law contract – with the example of a contract of mandate – in order to restore the original balance of the obligations, and terminate the contract, in order to assess the level of protection of parties' interests. The authors analyse these two types of contracts because the contract of mandate is often concluded in Estonia in lieu of an employment contract. Reasons for choosing a civil law contract instead of an employment contract might be different, such as to pay less tax, avoid payments which are provided by law in cases of leave, for overtime or night work. Also, the workload cannot always be predicted, and the civil law contract provides the desired flexibility.[6] Despite many positive features of civil law contracts, legal differences between employment and civil law contracts became evident in COVID-19 crisis.

The authors of the contribution compare the legal consequences of the alteration of balance of contractual obligations in the emergency situation caused by COVID-19 on the bases of §37 of the Employment Contracts Act (ECA)[7] and §97 of the Law of Obligations Act[8] (LOA).[9] It is common knowledge that the main obligations of the employer are to provide an employee with

---

the Spread of the COVID-19 Disease, passed 16 May 2020, entry into force 18 May 2020 https://www.riigiteataja.ee/en/eli/ee/vv/k/530052020003/consolide accessed 25 June 2020.

5 The amendments were made in the Bankruptcy Act according to which the running of the term of the obligation to file a bankruptcy petition was suspended for the period beginning at the commencement of the emergency situation and ending two months after the termination of the emergency situation on 18 July 2020. Bankruptcy Act (pankrotiseadus) 2003 https://www.riigiteataja.ee/en/eli/519052020005/consolide accessed 25 June 2020.

6 In Estonian labour dispute bodies (labour dispute commissions and courts), the nature of a contract concluded for the performance of work is quite often disputed. The main criterion for distinguishing between contracts is the existence of a relationship of subordination (see, e.g. the Judgment of the Estonian Supreme Court of 20 May 2020 in case no 2-18-6908, para 13).

7 Töölepingu seadus (Employment Contracts Act) 2008 https://www.riigiteataja.ee/en/eli/509052019005/consolide accessed 25 June 2020.

8 In the case of employment relationships, the Employment Contracts Act (TLS) §37 prescribes a specification of the rules for the alteration of balance of contractual obligations provided for in §97 of the VÕS. Seletuskiri töölepingu seaduse eelnõu juurde (The Explanatory Statement of the Draft of the Employment Contracts Act) 2008, 35 www.riigikogu.ee accessed 25 June 2020.

9 Võlaõigusseadus (Law of Obligations Act) 2002 https://www.riigiteataja.ee/en/eli/ee/515012020004/consolide/current accessed 25 June 2020.

work and pay wages for work (§28(1)–(2) ECA). Under §12 of the ECA, an employment contract may be amended only by an agreement between the parties. However, §37 of the ECA gives the employer the opportunity to unilaterally reduce the amount of remuneration. The reduction of wages was one of the main measures used by Estonian employers to survive in the emergency situation established to prevent the spread of COVID-19.[10] As the parties in the employment relationship are not equal and the employee as the weaker party needs protection, then, unlike the general rule of the LOA, the ECA provides the employee with a number of social guarantees that the employer must take into account when reducing wages.

It is important to note that there is no State income protection system in Estonia that could be applied in a situation of economic crisis. However, due to the restrictions implemented to counteract the spread of the COVID-19 disease, a temporary social security measure – the wage compensation – was introduced by the government to protect employees' incomes. Wage compensation was paid by the Unemployment Insurance Fund to employees whose employer's operation had been considerably disrupted by extraordinary circumstances.[11]

The authors start with the emergency situation as a reason for the alteration of balance of contractual obligations, then analyse the possibilities to amend the contract, compare the right to end the contract and finally make conclusions.

2. EMERGENCY SITUATION AS A REASON FOR THE ALTERATION OF BALANCE OF CONTRACTUAL OBLIGATIONS

2.1. EMPLOYMENT CONTRACT

According to §37(1) of the ECA, an employer may unilaterally amend the employment contract, more specifically, reduce wages if the following criteria are met:

1. there are unforeseen economic circumstances beyond the control of the employer; and
2. the employer fails to provide an employee with work to the agreed extent; and
3. payment of the agreed wages is unreasonably burdensome for the employer.

---

[10] It is not yet known how many and what disputes caused the reduction of wages during the emergency situation.

[11] The compensation was paid for the period from 1 March 2020–30 June 2020, but for no more than three calendar months. A similar wage support was paid for January 2021 to entrepreneurs operating in those areas of Estonia where stricter restrictions were established.

As the employer may reduce wages in the short term, these criteria also exist temporarily, because, in the event of a long-term situation, the employer should terminate the employee's employment contract due to economic reasons.

When assessing the employer's ability to amend the employment contract due to the emergency situation established to avoid the spread of COVID-19, the most important criterion is that there must be *unforeseen economic circumstances beyond the control of the employer*. What are the economic circumstances that cannot be foreseen or influenced by the employer? The Explanatory Statement of the Draft of the Employment Contracts Act emphasises that the reasons for amending the employment contract must be objective.[12] Also, only economic circumstances are relevant, not circumstances dependent on the employer's staff or administrative circumstances, or weather conditions.[13]

As mentioned, economic circumstances must first be unforeseeable. This means that the employer could not foresee them when concluding the employment contract. Therefore, there can be no question of seasonal circumstances (for example the reduction of workload in winter).[14] The second requirement is that the economic circumstances cannot be influenced by the employer. Thus, this is not a situation where the employer mitigates its business risk, for example, due to the unsuccessful conclusion of supply or procurement contracts.[15] Rosin explains that economic circumstances beyond the control of the employer include, for example, a significant decrease in orders due to the recession. Since even economists are not able to predict possible periods of recession, it is not reasonable to assume that an employer can envisage it, not to mention influence the recession.[16]

---

12 Seletuskiri töölepingu seaduse eelnõu juurde (The Explanatory Statement of the Draft of the Employment Contracts Act) 2008, 35 www.riigikogu.ee, accessed 25 June 2020.

13 Annika Rosin, 'Töölepingu seaduse §37: kas tööandja võimalus oma äranägemise järgi töötasu vähendada või turvalise paindlikkuse rakendamise positiivne näide?' (Section 37 of the Employment Contracts Act: An Employer's Option to Reduce Pay at its Own Discretion or a Positive Example of the Implementation of Flexicurity?) (2013) 7 Juridica 316, 319.

14 Seletuskiri töölepingu seaduse eelnõu juurde (The Explanatory Statement of the Draft of the Employment Contracts Act) 2008, 35 www.riigikogu.ee, accessed 25 June 2020.

15 See also Egle Käärats et al., *Selgitused töölepingu seaduse juurde/Comments on the Employment Contracts Act. Ministry of Social Affairs* (Juura 2013) 79.

16 Annika Rosin, 'Töölepingu seaduse §37: kas tööandja võimalus oma äranägemise järgi töötasu vähendada või turvalise paindlikkuse rakendamise positiivne näide?' (Section 37 of the Employment Contracts Act: An Employer's Option to Reduce Pay at its Own Discretion or a Positive Example of the Implementation of Flexicurity?) (2013) 7 Juridica 316, 319. Rosin also considers that a factor beyond the control of the employer is, for example, a drastic reduction in orders due to a sudden change in the competitive situation.

As regards the amendment of the employment contract due to the emergency situation established to limit the spread of COVID-19, there was neither significant discussion nor a labour dispute committee in Estonia as to whether the preconditions for reducing wages have been met. In the media, the only guidance given was on the procedure for reducing wages.[17] In the authors' opinion, the emergency situation entailed unforeseen and uncontrollable economic circumstances for employers. As many institutions and companies, as well as borders, were closed due to the emergency situation,[18] many employers were unable to provide employees with work (to the agreed extent). No employer was able to foresee or influence such a situation.

However, the mere existence of unforeseen economic circumstances beyond the control of the employer is not sufficient to amend an employment contract. These circumstances must involve the inability of the employer to provide an employee with work to the agreed extent. As providing the employee with work is the main obligation of the employer, the employer usually has to pay the employee even if the work is not provided.[19] An exception to this general rule may be made in the case of objective economic circumstances prescribed in §37(1) of the ECA. As mentioned before, one of the challenges for employers caused by the emergency situation was their inability to provide work for their employees.

The third important criterion, the existence of which is necessary to amend the employment contract, is that payment of the agreed wages is unreasonably burdensome for the employer. It must, therefore, be assessed whether or not the payment of wages is unreasonably burdensome. According to §7 of the LOA, reasonableness is to be judged by what persons acting in good faith would ordinarily consider to be reasonable in the same situation, taking into account the nature of the obligation, the purpose of the transaction, the usages and practices in the fields of activity or professions involved, etc. From the authors' viewpoint, it cannot be considered reasonable if the continued payment of wages to the agreed extent leads to permanent insolvency of the employer.[20]

---

17 See, for example, 'COVID-19' (Tööelu, 9 April 2020) https://www.tooelu.ee/en/Employee/Working-environment/Hazards-of-the-working-environment/Biological-hazards/COVID-19#kaugtoo, accessed 25 June 2020.

18 Merle Erikson, 'COVID-19 and Labour Law: Estonia' (2020) 13(1) Italian Labour Law e-Journal 1–2.

19 Paragraph §35 of the ECA states that an employer must pay average wages to an employee who is capable of working and ready to do work even if the employee does not work because the employer has not provided him/her with work, has not performed an act required for doing work or has otherwise delayed acceptance of work, unless the employee is at fault in failing to be provided with work.

20 Annika Rosin, 'Töölepingu seaduse §37: kas tööandja võimalus oma äranägemise järgi töötasu vähendada või turvalise paindlikkuse rakendamise positiivne näide?' (Section 37 of the Employment Contracts Act: An Employer's Option to Reduce Pay at its Own Discretion or a Positive Example of the Implementation of Flexicurity?) (2013) 7 Juridica 316, 320.

Hence, the employment contract cannot be amended if the employer is unable to provide the work to the agreed extent due to objective economic circumstances, but at the same time has sufficient financial resources to pay wages and there is no real need to reduce the employee's wages.[21] Following §37(1) of the ECA, therefore, although the economic circumstances have changed, there is no alteration of balance of contractual obligations if the employer is able to continue to pay wages. The ECA protects, first and foremost, the employee's wages, rather than the employer's income.

2.2. CONTRACT OF MANDATE

In accordance with §619 of the LOA, under the contract of mandate, the mandatary undertakes to provide services to the mandator for remuneration, if so agreed. A contract of mandate is widely used in the regulation of legal relations between the legal person and the members of its management body, in the organisation of professional training, providing IT services, etc.

If the contract of mandate was concluded for an unspecified term, both parties have the right to terminate the contract at any time until the mandate is performed (§630(1) and §196(1) LOA). However, if a mandatary wants to terminate the contract concluded on unspecified terms under the general rule described above, the mandatary shall compensate the mandator for any damage caused, if the mandator cannot receive the service or enter into the transaction which is the object of the mandate, in another manner. So, for the mandator, there is no need for a specific legal ground to terminate the contract entered into for an unspecified term before the mandate is performed. Only the mandatary bears the risk that services cannot be obtained in any other manner, and termination may bring the obligation to compensate damages. If the contract is concluded for a fixed period, the right to terminate is limited.[22]

In the emergency situation caused by COVID-19, both parties may be interested in the termination of the contract, regardless of whether it is a fixed-term or an open-ended contract. Specific grounds applicable in emergency situations can be found in §631 of the LOA: both parties have the right to terminate the contract of mandate if it becomes evident that, bearing in mind all the circumstances and the interests of both parties, the party wishing to terminate the contract cannot be expected to continue performance of the

21 See Egle Käärats et al., *Selgitused töölepingu seaduse juurde/Comments on the Employment Contracts Act. Ministry of Social Affairs* (Juura 2013) 79.

22 For example, if a contract of mandate is for the lifetime of one party or for a period longer than five years, the mandatary has the right to terminate the contract once five years have passed from the date of entry into the contract by giving at least six months' advance notice (§630(3) LOA).

obligations until expiry of the term for termination, the term of the contract or until the mandate is performed.

A compelling reason for the extraordinary termination of a contract pursuant to §631 and §196 (1) of the LOA is required.[23] The assessment of a compelling reason depends on the consideration of the interests of the parties by the court. The result of the consideration is also affected by the type of contract. When considering the interests of the parties, an important issue is, among other things, who bears the risk related to the circumstances on which the cancellation is based. The distribution of risk is determined by the contract, in particular its purpose and the relevant laws. Only by way of exception may the termination of long-term contracts be justified by circumstances falling within the sphere of the obligee. In the latter case, termination of the contract may or may not be considered a non-performance of the contract, and the terminating party may, therefore, be liable for damages.[24]

The Supreme Court has clarified that, taking into account the nature of the contract of mandate, the loss of the mandator's trust in the mandatary may give rise to the extraordinary termination of the contract on the basis of §631 of the LOA.[25] In the opinion of the Supreme Court, the loss of the mandator's trust may be caused, among other things, by the lack of loyalty expected from the mandator and by disregarding the mandator's instructions. This concerns in particular, the failure to comply with mandatory safety requirements in an emergency situation. Termination of the contract of mandate may also be due to the end of the need.[26] For example, in connection with restrictions on movement and activity, the need for security or other services may end. Long-term contracts may be terminated by a contracting party both in respect of some of the obligations provided for in the contract, for which there is a

23 LOA §631: "Extraordinary cancellation of contract of mandate. Both parties have the right to cancel both contract of mandate entered into for a specified term and contract of mandate entered into for unspecified term without observing the provisions of §630 of this Act if it becomes evident that, bearing in mind all the circumstances and the interests of both parties, the party wishing to cancel the agreement cannot be expected to continue performance of the contract of mandate until expiry of the term for cancellation or the term of the agreement or until the mandate is performed." LOA §196: "(1) Either party to a long-term contract may cancel the contract with good reason without giving advance notice, in particular if the party cancelling the contract cannot reasonably be expected to continue performing the contract until the due date agreed upon or until expiry of the term for advance notice taking into account all the circumstances and the mutual interests of the parties (extraordinary cancellation)." See also Judgment of the Supreme Court of 14 June 2019 in case no 3-13-481, para 24; of 13 June 2018 in case no 2-16-13032, para 12; of 7 March 2018 in case no 2-16-11889, para 34.

24 Judgment of the Estonian Supreme Court of 17 December 2007 in case no 3-2-1-114-07, para 11; of 9 March 2006 in case no 3-2-1-2-06, para. 18.

25 Judgment of the Estonian Supreme Court of 31 January in case no 3-2-1-180-12, para 13.

26 Judgment of the Estonian Supreme Court of 22 December 2009 in case no 3-2-1-143-09, para 9.

valid reason for termination, and in its entirety, if the contracting party has no legitimate interest in the partial performance of the contract.[27]

In addition, according to §97 of the LOA, the contract may be terminated if a situation of changed circumstances occurs. Paragraph 97 of the LOA defines the change of circumstances as a situation when the circumstances under which a contract is entered into, change after the entry the contract and this results in a material change in the balance of the obligations of the parties. Material change in the balance of the obligations means that the costs of one party for the performance of an obligation increase significantly, or the value of that which is to be received from the other party under the contract decreases significantly.[28]

For the situation of changed circumstances to occur, two criteria have to be fulfilled. First, the circumstances under which a contract is entered into have to change, and second, this change has to bring about a material change in the balance of the obligations of the parties. As for the first criterion, it is in each individual case vital to establish which circumstances can be considered as circumstances under which a contract is entered into. With regard to the global situation caused by the spread of COVID-19, the various national measures taken to hinder the spread of the disease and decrease the rate of new infections could be regarded as a change in circumstances under which a contract is entered into. It can be presumed that the circumstance that forms the basis of the contract is that the economic and social structure nationwide, regionally, and globally continue to operate in a way which the parties are accustomed to. This includes, for example, the presumption that limitations on the freedom of entrepreneurship will be restricted only by providing an adequate time to businesses to adjust to new limitations. The forced closure of all cinemas, nightclubs, theatres, museums and to a large extent, shopping centres,[29] can

---

27 Judgment of the Estonian Supreme Court of 22 December 2009 in case no 3-2-1-143-09, paras 12–13.

28 The Estonian *clausula* or change of circumstances doctrine does not have one specific source, but is rather a mixture of different interpretations of *clausula* doctrines in a number of international private law instruments and German private law. With regard to the definition, the Estonian *clausula* doctrine bears most similarity to the definition of hardship in UPICC Article 6.2.2. as both enable reliance on the *clausula* doctrine not only in situations where the events that change the contractual equilibrium occur after the contract is concluded, but also in cases where the true nature of events become known to the disadvantaged party after the conclusion of the contract. UNIDROIT Principles of International Commercial Contracts 1994 https://www.unidroit.org/instruments/commercial-contracts/unidroit-principles-1994, accessed 25 June 2020. See more in Irene Kull, 'About Grounds for Exemption from Performance under the Draft Estonian Law of Obligations Act. Pacta Sunt Servanda versus Clausula Rebus sic Stantibus' (2001) 6 Juridica International 44–52; Irene Kull, '§97' in Paul Varul, Irene Kull, Villu Kõve, Martin Käerdi, Karin Sein (eds), *Võlaõigusseadus I. Üldosa (§§1-207). Kommenteeritud väljaanne* (Law of Obligations Act I. Commented edition) (Juura 2016), hereinafter "LOA commented edition".

29 Application of Measures of Emergency Situation, order no 77 of the Government of the Republic of Estonia. https://www.riigiteataja.ee/en/eli/508052020004/consolide accessed

presumably be regarded as a change in the circumstance under which contracts have been entered into. However, not all contracts were affected by the measures imposed for the purposes of tackling the spread of COVID-19. The spread of COVID-19 in itself could also be regarded as the change in circumstances under which a contract is concluded. For example, in contracts for providing catering, fitness training, professional training courses or maintenance services, the service provider is obliged to make sure that the risk of infection is kept to a minimum.

The second precondition for the application of §97 of the LOA is that a material alteration in the equilibrium of the obligations of the contracting parties has to occur. In Estonian case law, the threshold of 50% has so far been adopted as an indicative yardstick, which may be revised on the basis of case-by-case analysis, taking into account the specifics of each contract.[30] The material change in the equilibrium of obligations has to occur compared to the time of contracting.

Whereby in the force majeure situation the fulfilment of an obligation is objectively impossible, and the force majeure doctrine provides the debtor with an objection to the obligee's claim, the performance of an obligation is not impossible in case of changed circumstances. The obligor can still perform the contract as agreed upon, although, it is considerably more onerous to him/her.[31] For a number of contractors, the complications caused by COVID-19 or measures taken to restrict its spread, only mean that the fulfilment of their obligations has become materially more onerous or that the value of what they receive from the contract has decreased considerably.

In case of a situation of changed circumstances, a party can only rely on this (i.e. demand amendment or terminate the contract) if all the preconditions stated in §97(2) of the LOA are fulfilled. These preconditions are: (1) at the time of entry into the contract, the injured party could not have reasonably expected that the circumstances might change; (2) the injured party could not influence the change in the circumstances; (3) the risk of a change in the circumstances is not borne by the injured party pursuant to the law or the contract; and (4) the injured party would not have entered into the contract or would have entered into the contract under significantly different terms if the party had known of the change in the circumstances.

---

25 June 2020; Order of the Person in Charge of Emergency Situation for Imposing a Restriction on the Freedom of Movement in Commercial Establishments no 46 https://www.riigiteataja.ee/en/eli/504042020002/consolide accessed 25 June 2020.

30 Judgment of the Estonian Supreme Court of 21 December 2011 in case no 3-2-1-136-11 paras 17, 20. Similar materiality threshold was applied by the Tartu Circuit Court in relation to the market value of a real estate lease in its ruling from 2 April 2018 in civil case no 2-11-45657.

31 Therefore, §97 of the LOA is not applicable in cases where the party is restricted from performing its contractual obligations due to the restrictions prescribed under the emergency situation.

Regarding the unforeseeability criterion, it is reasonable to presume that the spread of COVID-19 and its consequences can be regarded as unforeseeable for contracting parties. Taking into account the mixed and uncertain signals sent by Government officials directly before the establishment of the emergency situation in Estonia, the consequences of the measures imposed might be considered unforeseeable even a short time before they were imposed. Upon deciding whether an aggrieved party bears the risk of changed circumstances, all relevant aspects should be considered. It should be determined whether the contract or the applicable law distributes the risk between the parties *expressis verbis*. If this proves unfruitful, the contract needs to be interpreted using the general tools of interpretation. However, according to Estonian court practice, the obligor should be considered as the bearer of risk in the majority of cases.[32] Therefore, in general, the obligee, in situations where the value of the receivable has diminished, is better positioned to rely on §97 of the LOA than the obligor, who in most instances bears the risk of changed circumstances. In deciding whether the injured party would not have entered into the contract or would have entered into the contract under significantly different terms if the party had known of the change in the circumstances, a reasonable person in a similar situation has to be taken as the objective.[33] Taking into account the severity of the change in circumstances caused by COVID-19, it could be reasonably concluded that in case of contracts affected by COVID-19, that criterion is fulfilled.

3. AMENDMENT OF THE CONTRACT

3.1. POSSIBILITIES TO AMEND THE CONTRACT

3.1.1. Employment contract

As mentioned before, when applying the regulation of §97 of the LOA in employment relationships, there is only one output in §37 of the ECA which gives the employer, as an injured party, the right to reduce wages. As §12 of the ECA generally prohibits the amendment of an employment contract without the consent of the other party, the reduction of wages is one of the few possibilities where an employer can unilaterally amend an employment contract.[34]

---

32 Judgment of the Estonian Supreme Court of 1 December 2011 in case no 3-2-1-136-11 para 22.

33 Irene Kull, '§97' in Paul Varul, Irene Kull, Villu Kõve, Martin Käerdi, Karin Sein (eds), *Võlaõigusseadus I. Üldosa (§§1-207). Kommenteeritud väljaanne* (Law of Obligations Act I. Commented edition) (Juura 2016) 458.

34 ECA §12. Amendment of employment contract. An employment contract may be amended only by agreement between the parties. The ECA also allows the employer to change the

3.1.2. *Contract of mandate*

If the situation of changed circumstances has been established and the preconditions for reliance on it are fulfilled, the aggrieved party may rely on the changed circumstances according to §97(1) and (5) of the LOA. In the case of amendment of mandate contract based on the restrictions caused by COVID-19, the party can, according to §97(4) of the LOA, rely on the changed circumstances also retroactively, to avoid non-performance and the use of legal remedies by the other party. In that case, a court may amend the terms of a contract itself.[35] This allows the parties' claims to be set off against each other.[36] In any case, the court's intervention to the legal relationship may be needed to cure the injustice caused by the changed equilibrium to maintain the contract, if it is reasonable, taking into account the interests of both parties.

3.2. OBLIGATIONS OF THE PARTIES BEFORE AMENDING THE CONTRACT

3.2.1. *Employment contract*

If the employer fulfils the criteria prescribed in §37(1) of the ECA, which gives the right to amend the employment contract, the employer cannot reduce wages at its own discretion. As the reduction of wages concerns the main source of livelihood for the employee as the weaker party in the employment relationship, the legislator has imposed a number of obligations and restrictions on the employer, both before and during the reduction of wages. Reducing wages is an exceptional and extreme measure for the implementation of which the employer must have met the preconditions.

---

organisation of working time; require the employee to work overtime in the event of unforeseen circumstances; and change the content of the agreed work and interrupt or postpone the employee's holiday in the case of an emergency. Мерле Муда, 'Возможнос ти работодателя по одностороннему изменению и прекращению трудового договора как элемент гибкости трудового права в Эстонии' (The Employer's Ability to Unilaterally Amend and Terminate an Employment Contract as an Element of the Flexibility of Labour Law in Estonia), Кантемир Николаевич Гусов (ed), *Международное, российское и зарубежное законодательство о труде и социальном обеспечении: современное состояние (сравнительный анализ). Материалы VII международной научно-практической кон ференции* (International, Russian and Foreign Legislation on Labour and Social Security: Current State (Comparative Analysis). Materials of the VII International Scientific-Practical Conference) (Проспект 2011) p. 296.

35 Judgment of the Estonian Supreme Court of 5 May 2016 in case no 3-2-1-179-15, para 35.

36 Lower courts have ruled that a contract should be amended, and the contractual price reduced due to the changed circumstances. See for example Tartu Circuit Court ruling of 2 April 2018 in case no 2-11-45657.

Under §37(2) of the ECA, before reducing wages, the employer is obliged to offer the employee other work, if possible. The purpose of offering other work is to achieve a situation where the extraordinary circumstances that have arisen for the employer damage the interests of the employee as little as possible.[37] The employee's interests would be least harmed if his/her wages do not become lower. Therefore, an employee should be offered work for which he/she receives similar wages as before.

However, the idea of the legislator is broader. The authors of the ECA from the Ministry of Social Affairs explain that the employee must not only be offered work that matches his/her qualifications and is similar to the agreed work, but also work with lower qualifications and different from the agreed work that the employee can cope with.[38] Such an approach is also supported by the Estonian Supreme Court in cases where the employer is obliged to offer the employee other work in order to avoid redundancy.[39]

In the authors' view, when offering other work, there are different objectives in the case of redundancies and reducing wages. While in the event of redundancy, it is important that the employee retains his/her job and income, in the case of the reduction of wages, it is significant that the wage is reduced as little as possible (or not at all). Thus, in the latter case, it is not necessary to offer the employee other work for which the wage is lower than the wage paid as a result of the reduction of wages. In general, however, the employee has no obligation to accept the other work offered by the employer.

In addition to offering other work, proceeding from §37(4) of the ECA, the employer has another obligation that he/she must fulfil before reducing wages – the employer is required to inform the trustee or, in his/her absence,[40] the employees and consult them.[41] Although §17(1) of the Employees' Trustee Act[42] establishes that the employer must inform and consult a trustee if the

---

37 Seletuskiri töölepingu seaduse eelnõu juurde (The Explanatory Statement of the Draft of the Employment Contracts Act) 2008, 35 www.riigikogu.ee accessed 25 June 2020.

38 Egle Käärats et al, *Selgitused töölepingu seaduse juurde/Comments on the Employment Contracts Act. Ministry of Social Affairs* (Juura 2013) 80.

39 See, for example, the Judgment of the Estonian Supreme Court of 2 February 2012 in case no 3-2-1-152-11; of 21 November 2018 in case no 2-16-708/54.

40 Since trustees have been elected in only 17% of companies, the employer usually communicates with employees instead of them. Jaanika Ait, 'Töötajate kaasamine' (Employee Participation) in Liina Kaldmäe (ed), *Estonian Work Life Survey* 2015, (2017) Series of the Ministry of Social Affairs 1, p. 53.

41 Under §37(4) of the ECA, the employer must provide notice of the reduction of wages no less than fourteen calendar days in advance. The trustee or the employee is obliged to give his/her opinion within seven calendar days as of the receipt of the employer's notice.

42 Töötajate usaldusisiku seadus (Employees' Trustee Act) 2006 https://www.riigiteataja.ee/en/eli/505052017006/consolide accessed 25 June 2020.

employer has at least 30 employees, the employer could also perform these obligations in the event of the reduction of wages, if he/she has fewer than 30 employees.[43] The employee must have the right to know for what reason and to what extent his/her wage is reduced. As the purpose of informing and consulting employees is to minimise the detrimental consequences of the reduction of wages for employees, the employer may make a final decision on reducing wages after the end of consultations.

Third, once employees have been informed and consulted, the employer must comply with the restrictions on the reduction of wages laid down in the ECA. According to §37(1), the employer may reduce the wages to a reasonable extent, but not below the minimum wage, for up to three months over a period of 12 months. Thus, the ECA determines both the extent and the duration of the reduction of wages.

As regards to the reduction of wages to a reasonable extent, the authors consider that the interests of both the employee and the employer must be taken into account when determining the amount of wage to be paid to the employee. It is important for the employee that the wage is reduced as little as possible in order to guarantee an income equivalent to the wage paid so far. On the other hand, the employer has an interest in reducing wages at least to the extent that enables the employer to overcome the financial difficulties. However, under no circumstances may an employee's wage be reduced below the minimum wage. As the average wage in Estonia is about 2.5 times higher than the minimum wage, as a result of reducing wages, the employee's wage may decrease significantly.[44]

In addition to the limit of reducing wages, the employer must also observe the duration of the reduction. As pointed out above, the employer may reduce the wages for up to three months over a period of twelve months. Thus, the duration of the reduction of wages is not related to the calendar year, but wages can be reduced for up to three months over a period of twelve consecutive calendar months. As three months is the maximum period during which wages can be reduced, the legislator has in mind that the wage is reduced for the shortest possible period.[45] There is also no obligation to reduce wages for three

---

43 See also Annika Rosin, 'Töölepingu seaduse §37: kas tööandja võimalus oma äranägemise järgi töötasu vähendada või turvalise paindlikkuse rakendamise positiivne näide?' (Section 37 of the Employment Contracts Act: An Employer's Option to Reduce Pay at its Own Discretion or a Positive Example of the Implementation of Flexicurity?) (2013) 7 Juridica 323.

44 In Estonia, the minimum wage is established by the Government of the Republic and in 2020 this amount is EUR 584 per month. In March 2020, the average gross monthly salary was EUR 1,451. Average Gross Monthly Salary. Statistics Estonia, 27 May 2020 https://www.stat.ee/stat-average-monthly-gross-wages-salaries accessed 25 June 2020.

45 See also Egle Käärats et al., *Selgitused töölepingu seaduse juurde/Comments on the Employment Contracts Act. Ministry of Social Affairs* (Juura 2013) 80.

consecutive months – wages can be reduced by shorter periods, but not more than three months in total.

In conclusion, since the reduction of wages is related to a number of procedural rules and restrictions, the employer cannot act at his/her own discretion in the case of the alteration of balance of contractual obligations. As the law protects the employee, reducing wages must be a well-considered decision.

3.2.2. *Contract of mandate*

Unlike an employment contract, the parties to a mandate contract do not have legal obligations in connection to the amendment of the contract. Paragraph 97 of the LOA sets forth a clear order of preference for the reliance on the *clausula* doctrine, which means that in the first place, the party may demand the amendment of the contract which leads to the conclusion that negotiations should generally precede the claim. At the same time, the LOA does not foresee negotiations between the parties as an obligatory precondition before turning to the courts. There is a possibility that specific obligations will be derived from the general obligation to behave in good faith (§6 LOA).

3.3. RIGHTS OF THE OTHER PARTY IN AMENDING THE CONTRACT

3.3.1. *Employment contract*

Pursuant to §37(3) of the ECA, an employee has the right to refuse to perform work in proportion to the reduction of the wages. The general principle of the employment relationship is that without work, there is no obligation to pay wages, and this principle also applies in reverse: without wages, there is no obligation to work.[46] As the reduction of the workload is one of the preconditions for amending the employment contract in the event of the alteration of balance of contractual obligations, it is logical that the employee cannot be provided with work to the agreed extent and then he/she works less. This is the employee's reaction to the reduction of the wages and this right does not need to be agreed in advance in the employment contract.

---

46 Seletuskiri töölepingu seaduse eelnõu juurde (The Explanatory Statement of the Draft of the Employment Contracts Act) 2008, 35 www.riigikogu.ee, accessed 25 June 2020.

Thus, although the reduction of wages is a decision which worsens the situation of an employee, it also entitles the employee to work less. Working proportionately less means that if the wage of a full-time employee (who works 40 hours per week) is, for example, EUR 2,000 and this is reduced to EUR 1,000, then the employee can also work part-time (20 hours per week).[47]

In order to work less, the consent of the employer is not required, and in the event of the reduction of wages, the employee's working hours must always be shortened. The authors of the contribution are aware that in many cases, when wages were reduced during the emergency situation established to avoid the spread of COVID-19, the working hours of employees were not abridged.[48] Such behaviour is contrary to the ECA and suggests that there was no real reason to reduce wages.

3.3.2. *Contract of mandate*

Pursuant to §6(1) of the LOA, obligees and obligors shall act in good faith in their relations with one another. Paragraph §6(2) of the LOA provides that nothing arising from law, a usage or a transaction shall be applied to an obligation if it is contrary to the principle of good faith. This means that the abuse of rights derived from the law, contract or usages is not allowed. This rule gives judges a remarkably wide discretion in assessing the behaviour of the parties and deciding as to whether or not to apply certain provisions of the LOA or any other legal act, usage or contract.[49]

The extraordinary nature of the COVID-19 pandemic calls for good faith as a tool in the hands of the courts, especially in cases where the amendment of the contract is under discussion, for example, in assessing the right to reduce the remuneration, postpone the performance of obligations, prolong the deadline or make other amendments to the contract. As mentioned above, in most cases, the courts shall not interfere with the content of the contract and shall assess whether the changes proposed by one party allow the original balance between the obligations to be restored, or whether the proposed changes are reasonable. In assessing what is reasonable, the principle of good faith, the nature of the obligation, the purpose of the transaction, the usages and practices in the fields of activity or professions involved and other circumstances shall be taken into account (§7(2) LOA).

---

47 This leads to the difference that if the employee's wage is agreed as a piecework pay (for example, the employee receives EUR 10 for each assembled device), then the employee's wage cannot be reduced, but his or her working time must be shortened.

48 Authors' correspondence with labour law lawyer Ms. Elina Soomets from 11 May 2020 (in possession of the authors).

49 See also Irene Kull, 'Principle of Good Faith and Constitutional Values in Contract Law' (2002) 7 Juridica International 142–148.

3.4. RIGHT OF THE PARTIES TO TERMINATE OR CANCEL THE CONTRACT

3.4.1. Employment contract

Unlike the general principle established in §97(5) of the LOA, in the event of the alteration of balance of contractual obligations, the injured party, i.e. the employer, cannot cancel[50] the employment contract instead of reducing wages. However, such a right is given to an employee, who does not have to agree to reducing wages and may resign.

According to §37(5) of the ECA, if an employer wishes to reduce an employee's wages, the latter has the right to cancel the employment contract, notifying thereof five working days in advance. Upon cancellation of the employment contract, the employee is entitled to compensation to the same extent as in the case of redundancy.[51]

Thus, the legislator has created a special structure for the protection of employees – although the termination of an employment contract is initiated by the employee, he/she receives compensation to the same extent as upon termination of the employment contract by the employer for economic reasons. However, the authors of this contribution assume that employees agree to the reduction of wages instead of cancelling the contract, as the restrictions imposed during the emergency situation to prevent the spread of COVID-19 have led to a recession that makes it difficult to find a new job.

3.4.2. Contract of mandate

Paragraph 97(5) of the LOA foresees that if the amendment of the contract is not possible or if it would be unreasonable for the other party, the aggrieved party may terminate the contract. According to §97(5) of the LOA, for terminating the contract, a situation of changed circumstances must exist and all preconditions have to be established. For the termination of the contract, a unilateral statement without any formal or substantive requirements is sufficient. Termination shall

---

50 Estonian law differentiates termination and cancellation of contract. Termination is ending the contract *ex tunc* and cancellation is ending *ex nunc*. "Termination" is used as a general term.

51 Under §100(1) of the ECA, upon cancellation of an employment contract due to lay-off, an employer is obliged to pay an employee compensation to the extent of one month's average wages of the employee. In addition to the compensation paid by the employer, the employee has the right to receive a benefit from the Estonian Unemployment Insurance Fund – an employee who has been employed by the employer for a period of five to ten years is entitled to one month's benefit; an employee who has been employed by the employer for a period of over ten years is entitled to two months' benefit. Töötuskindlustuse seadus (Unemployment Insurance Act) 2001, §14 https://www.riigiteataja.ee/en/eli/ee/504052020001/consolide, accessed 25 June 2020.

be used during a reasonable period of time after the person becomes aware of the circumstances substantiating the termination (§196 LOA). As a rule, if a party may terminate the contract pursuant to law or the contract, the termination of the contract releases both parties from the performance of their contractual obligations. The rights and obligations which arise from the contract before termination remain valid. Upon termination of a contract, the parties are only required to return that which has been delivered in advance with respect to the time of termination of the contract, except if a person entitled to terminate a contract is no longer interested in the obligations which have already been performed (§196(4) LOA). The only defence available to the other party is the principle of good faith (§6(2) LOA), which provides protection against the abuse of rights provided for in the contract or in the law.

4. CONCLUSION

The above analysis shows that the legal status of a person working on the basis of an employment or contract of mandate in the event of the alteration of balance of contractual obligations is significantly different. As regards the amendment of the employment or civil law contract due to the emergency situation established to limit the spread of COVID-19, there were neither significant discussion nor court cases in Estonia. The emergency situation entailed unforeseen and uncontrollable economic circumstances as a precondition for reducing wages provided for in §37 of the ECA. For civil law contracts, the emergency situation and spread of COVID-19 in itself could be regarded as a change of circumstances under §97 of the LOA. There is a general prohibition to amend employment contracts without the consent of the other party and reduction of wages is one of the few possibilities. In cases of civil law contracts, there are no limits concerning the unilateral amendment of the contract in cases of change of circumstances. Since the reduction of wages is related to a number of procedural rules and restrictions, the employer cannot act at his/her own discretion in the case of the alteration of balance of contractual obligations. In civil law contracts, there are no specific obligations concerning the content of amendments, except the general obligation to behave in good faith. Unlike the general principle established in §97(5) of the LOA, in the event of the alteration of balance of contractual obligations, the affected party, i.e. the employer, cannot cancel the employment contract instead of reducing wages. However, such a right is given to an employee, who does not have to agree to reduced wages and may resign. In conclusion, the law primarily aims to protect both sides of employment relations: to allow the employer to exercise its constitutional right to entrepreneurship – to react quickly to changes in the economic situation; and to protect the employee from possible termination of the employment contract or reduction of remuneration. Using a civil law contract in providing services or work, there are no guarantees except for the general principles which may reduce injustice produced as a result of using rights provided for by law in cases of change of circumstances. The emergency situation established to prevent the spread of COVID-19 clearly highlighted the shortcomings in the regulation of contracts for the performance of work – if contracts of mandate had not been used instead of employment contracts, many workers would have been much more protected during the emergency situation.

THE ITALIAN EDUCATION SYSTEM

A Chronically Ill Patient Facing the Coronavirus Pandemic

Roberta CALVANO*

The author examines the Italian education system during the first six months of the COVID-19 pandemic. Financial difficulties, an overly complex regulatory framework and a general and long-lasting underestimation of education problems by the Italian legislator made it even more difficult to manage the emergency. The pandemic has led to the closure of schools and universities and the transition to distance teaching and learning. During the first semester of the emergency period, the Government adopted several measures by law decrees and executive orders, trying to prevent contagion and to buffer some of the questions. However, a few critical issues seem unsolved and still raise topics of constitutional debate. A slow and cumbersome administration of education together with the problem of the digital divide and the inequalities it reveals, are still apparent. A deep gap in Italian society becoming even deeper – especially in a North-South as well as an Urban-Rural perspective – is the next challenge which politics needs to urgently face in the post-COVID-19 era.

1. DIMENSIONS OF THE PHENOMENON

On 31 January a State of National Emergency was declared by the Italian Government, exercising a power conferred to the cabinet by Article 24, delegated

* Unitelma Sapienza University.

decree no 1/2018. This resolution allowed a six month period of emergency powers, bringing about consequent changes in decision making, and a shifting to mainly governmental acts, with a series of emergency decrees, on a legislative and administrative level, being approved.[1] In the beginning, the measures taken in order to avoid further spread of the disease were, in particular, meant to prevent citizens' circulation and gatherings, by limiting fundamental rights, such as freedom of movement, of assembly, religious rituals, etc. A huge debate soon started in the legal sphere and especially among constitutional law scholars, concerning the sources of the law used,[2] the proportionality of measures taken, and more generally the balancing of the right to collective and individual health and other fundamental rights.[3]

Among these outstanding and unprecedented decisions, these concerning the National Education and University System, and its closure, will be analysed here, as they produced a remarkable impact on a large part of the population and the fulfilment of Articles 33 and 34 of the Italian Constitution (Const.). More broadly this contribution intends to examine the constitutional compatibility of the 2020 anti-COVID-19 measures with the system of principles concerning education, as also laid down in Articles 3, 5, 97, 117.

Italy, being the EU Member State first hit by the pandemic, closed its schools in the first week of March 2020. The Italian Government's decision was soon followed in Europe by Albania, Greece, Czechia and Romania. Most European governments closed their school systems by 16 March 2020.[4] The United Kingdom was the last country to announce such measures, where all the schools closed their doors by 20–23 March.

---

1 See, in this volume, Michele Massa, 'A General and Constitutional Outline of Italy's Efforts Against COVID-19', and for decisions concerning the Constitutional Court's functioning during the emergency, Luca Giacomelli and Elisabetta Lamarque, 'The Italian Constitutional Court and the Pandemic: A National and Comparative Perspective'.

2 Concerning the use of Decrees by the President of the Council of Ministers (DPCM) see Massimo Luciani, Il sistema delle fonti del diritto alla prova dell'emergenza, in Rivista Aic 2/2020, 10 April 2020, https://www.rivistaaic.it/it/rivista/ultimi-contributi-pubblicati/massimo-luciani/il-sistema-delle-fonti-del-diritto-alla-prova-dell-emergenza accessed 15 June 2020; see also the short but illuminating article by Gaetano Silvestri, Covid-19 e Costituzione, in Unicost.eu, Unità per la Costituzione, 4 October 2020, https://www.unicost.eu/covid-19-e-costituzione/ accessed 15 June 2020. On problems of the sources of the law in the emergency see also a monographic number of Osservatorio sulle fonti, 2020, Le fonti normative nella gestione dell'emergenza Covid-19, 4 October 2020, https://www.osservatoriosullefonti.it/archivi/archivio-fascicoli/1544-fascicolo-speciale-2020/file accessed 15 June 2020.

3 Among others, quite relevant is the case of economic freedom, on which see Marcello Cecchetti, 'Le limitazioni alla libertà di iniziativa economica privata durante l'emergenza' in Rivista Aic 4/2020, https://www.rivistaaic.it/it/rivista/ultimi-contributi-pubblicati/marcello-cecchetti/le-limitazioni-alla-liberta-di-iniziativa-economica-privata-durante-l-emergenza accessed 15 June 2020.

4 'How do coronavirus containment measures vary across Europe?' (*Theguardian.com*, 16 March 2020) https://www.theguardian.com/world/2020/mar/12/how-do-coronavirus-containment-measures-vary-across-europe accessed 15 June 2020.

On 18 May after a videoconference meeting of education ministers from all around the EU, it was said that the reopening of schools in 22 European countries had not led to any significant increase in coronavirus infections among children, parents or staff. It is worth recalling France's Education Minister's statement, concerning the fact that "it was more of a risk keeping their children at home than sending them to school now the strict lockdown had ended".[5] Due to the higher severity of the Italian epidemic situation, the Italian government decided to wait.

Nearly 11 million school children attend the National School system in Italy, and 1.5 million are in pre-primary schools.[6] According to data by the Ministry of University and Research 1,759,495 students were enrolled in the Italian University system in 2018/2019 academic year, where 22% of those who first enrolled in the same year chose a degree course taking place in a region other than that of residence, a fact which seems quite relevant in connection with the spread of the disease especially through public transport. These figures show the huge impact which the measures concerning the education system have when combating the spread of contagion.

Notwithstanding the important impact of these decisions concerning teachers, professors, researchers, school and university staff and students, as well as their families, following the containment of the pandemic in June, the legal provisions approved concerning education, were basically the only emergency rules limiting constitutional rights still in force. In the meantime, in other fields economic, social and cultural activities were going "back to normal", even though with different time shifts. In principle, this issue seems to have passed unnoticed, although in the school and university world questions as to the causes of such a different treatment of the education sector have been raised – and the issue has been debated, discussed and criticised.

The main content of the measures concerning education was to lock down schools and universities, so that soon after COVID-19 emergency began, primary, secondary and tertiary school pupils, as well as university students all became distance learning students.[7] As summer approached, a huge question was raised,

---

5 Boffey-K. Willsher, 'Schools reopening has not triggered rise in COVID-19 cases, EU ministers told' (*Theguardian.com*, 18 May 2020) https://www.theguardian.com/world/2020/may/18/french-minister-tells-of-risks-of-missing-school-as-more-pupils-return-covid-19 accessed 15 June 2020. The situation was quite different in the UK, as claimed by Heather Stewart in 'Michael Gove tells councils to "look to their responsibilities" and open schools. The Minister asks local authorities to refuse to allow pupils back on 1 June to "think again".' (*The guardian.com*, 17 May 2020) https://www.theguardian.com/world/2020/may/17/michael-gove-tells-councils-to-look-to-their-responsibilities-and-open-schools accessed 15 June 2020.

6 Relevant data for all countries are published in *Global monitoring of school closures* by Unesco, measuring 1,186,127,211 affected learners, 67.7% of total enrolled learners, 144 country-wide closures, in https://en.unesco.org/covid19/educationresponse accessed 15 June 2020.

7 On the subject, see Stefania Baroncelli, 'La didattica online al tempo del coronavirus: questioni giuridiche legate all'inclusione e alla privacy' in *Osservatorio sulle fonti*, 2020. Available at: http://www.osservato-riosullefonti.it accessed 15 June 2020.

as restaurants, bars and gyms reopened in May, and cinemas and concert halls followed, while e-learning stood as the sole means of access to education for school children until the end of the school year, and university students until mid-September. The Ministry of University and Research left it to each university to establish rules and timing on their own, allowing them to continue "blended" teaching (in presence and online), and a huge effort was made by university professors and researchers as 88% of courses were already online by the end of March.[8] Meanwhile, perhaps because of the more complex nature of the school system, articulated in 20 regions and thousands of schools, the organisation of online teaching in school was more difficult and uneven. And even after the first semester of the pandemic the Ministry of Instruction seemed to be at sea for weeks regarding the management of September reopening. Public statements about splitting classes in alternating groups, online from home and in school, or attending lessons repeated by (the same?) teachers at different times, or sitting in benches surrounded by plexiglass were strongly criticised in the media.[9]

Economic issues were strong enough to push politics to a "stage two", while cultural, educational and more generally human well-being (and even mental health) issues seemed, for a few months, to be not far from a ground zero level in the political debate.

This situation has forced, among other effects, parents to become teachers, more than ever before, being mainly responsible for children's education. One of the most difficult tasks seems to have been providing children with correct and relevant information about COVID-19. In the following discussion several other critical difficulties which emerged within the field of education, will be debated. In particular, this contribution focuses on the following: pre-existing financial, constitutional and legislative issues having a negative impact on managing the emergency in Italy (§2); pros and cons of measures approved by the Italian legislature concerning section 3.1 schools, and section 3.2 universities (§3); as well as issues raised in the context of the online teaching, especially digital divide and safety of those using e-learning platforms (§4).

In discussing the school and COVID-19 topic, a gender issue soon becomes apparent, as a very high percentage of teachers and operators in various capacities in Italian schools are female. According to OECD data, in Italy 78% of teachers and 69% of school managers (82.7% according to another survey using data by the Ministry of Instruction) are female.[10] While women, in particular, in Italy are the main protagonists of the new poverty,[11] for cultural and social reasons it

---

8 Stefania Baroncelli, La didattica online, ibid 441.

9 Rientro a scuola, Azzolina, 'Si pensa al plexiglass tra i banchi' in *Corriere della sera*, 4 June 2020; Il dietrofront di Azzolina, 'Niente gabbie di plexiglas in classe' in *La Repubblica*, 8 June 2020.

10 'La mappa del rapporto di genere in cattedra' in *Tuttoscuola*, 7 March 2019.

11 *Caritas COVID e povertà 2020* report, saying the percentage of new poor rose from 31% in 2019, to 45% in 2020.

is mainly women who have been responsible for managing children e-learning activities, even sacrificing their own working time. Many women have gone back to full-time work in mid-September only when the school system returned to normal functioning. The gender issue is just one of the many topics of discussion concerning how to balance collective health and education, which is not only a right-duty, according to Article 34 Const., but a public interest, related to the construction of an aware citizenship and national unity.

2. PRE-EXISTING DIFFICULTIES OF THE SYSTEM

In September 2019, OECD's *Education at a glance 2019*[12] offered, once again, quite a worrying picture of the Italian education system. Challenges and issues, in particular, concerned: low public funding (expenditure on primary to tertiary institutions as a share of GDP was 3.6%, whereas the OECD average is 5%); EUR 9–10 billion in funding cuts since 2003; widespread early school leaving (14.5%, with peaks of 21% in Sardinia); quite a low number of graduates per year, 28% among 25–34 year-olds, partly because "University fees in Italy are higher than in many other European countries"; school teachers starting salaries still below the OECD average. Finally, it was remarked that "Italy has the lowest share of teachers in the population aged 25–34 years old[13] across OECD countries", having at the same time the largest share of teachers older than 50 (59%). These data suggest that the system is unable not only to offer chances to overcome inequalities and promote the development of schoolchildren's personalities, – fundamental tasks, established in Articles 2 and 3.2 of the Italian Constitution – but also (sometimes) even to fulfil its primary functions.

The situation appears to be the same, or even worse, if one looks at the preschool level. During the school year 2017/2018 there were 13,145 places available within early childhood education operating in the national territory, and 51% only, among the authorised facilities, were public. Public and private facilities together covered an extremely low percentage of what would be needed, a mere 24.7% of the potential users, i.e. children under three years of age.[14]

Comparing the north and the south Italy, the situation looks even more serious, and has been deteriorating over the last few years. A deep north-south gap can be observed, as well as a striking heterogeneity among territories.

---

12 OECD, *Education at a glance 2019*, country notes, https://www.oecd.org/education/education-at-a-glance/ accessed 15 June 2020, Italian sheet, 6.

13 OECD, *Education at a glance 2019*, country notes, Italian sheet, 6.

14 ISTAT (Italian National Institute of Statistics) press release, 6 April 2020. This percentage of coverage of pre-school institutions needed, although slightly increasing, was still below the 33% parameter set in 2002 by the EU for 2010.

While 47 out of 100 pre-school children in Valle d'Aosta, the northernmost Italian region, had education services, in Campania, the most densely populated Mediterranean region, those having access to pre-school facilities were fewer than 9 out of 100 children.

Diagnosis of such a critical situation, despite its complexity, seems to be quite easy, as education is a two-sided problem in the Italian legal order. First of all there is a financial problem, as the public funding of the National School system as well as of the University system was abruptly diminished by the Law 133/2008, at the dawn of the international economic crisis. Later on, the EU financial situation led to the introduction of severe austerity measures, which, since 2011, by decision of the Italian Parliament, are affecting education facilities, including building maintenance and safety, as well as professors, teachers and other education workers' wages.[15] This situation consequently affects students' right to education, set forth in Article 14 of the EU Charter of Fundamental Rights, and in Article 2 of the European Convention on Human Rights.[16] As a result of these legislative decisions, public funding is now commonly considered insufficient and unfairly distributed.[17]

A second, and more intricate issue derives from a complex regulatory framework, worsened even further by the continuous law-making in the crucial field of education. The reason for this phenomenon is in the high numbers of this sector (thousands of teachers, staff, millions of parents), making it a tempting electoral basin for politicians in search of consent.

Since the constitutional reform bill approved in 2001,[18] concerning distribution of powers on a territorial basis, "education" has become a field of: (1) exclusive State law-making power in Articles 33 and 117.2; (2) concurrent State and regional law-making power in Article 117.3; (3) residual regional competence in all that is not included in (1) or (2), or which concerns professional education and training; (4) school autonomy.[19] As a starting point, such a

15 Cuts to education in 2008/2012 were equivalent to 10 billion euros. A hundred-thousand teachers were since then missing to the National School system, according to the Euridice report *Funding on Education in Europe: The impact of the economic crisis*, (2013), https://eacea.ec.europa.eu/national-policies/eurydice/content/funding-education-europe-2000-2012-impact-economic-crisis_en accessed 15 June 2020. The number of teachers in the same years had collapsed in Italy by 11.1% while in Germany it was growing by 13% and in Finland by 12.9%.

16 Protocol to the European Convention for the Protection of Human Rights and Fundamental Freedoms.

17 Adriano Giannola, Gennaro Stornaiuolo, 'Un'analisi delle proposte avanzate sul federalismo differenziato' [2018] *Rivista economica del mezzogiorno* 1–2, 555.

18 Law of constitutional amendment n. 3, 18 October 2001, in Official Journal, n. 248, 24 October 2001.

19 On these questions see Gianpaolo Fontana, 'Art. 33' in Raffaele Bifulco, Alfonso Celotto, Marco Olivetti (eds), *Commentario alla Costituzione*, vol I (Utet 2006), 675; Antonio Iannuzzi, 'Norme generali sull'istruzione e riserva di legge' in *Scritti in onore di Franco Modugno* (Editoriale Scientifica 2011) 1809.

complex distribution of law-making and administrative powers among different levels (in addition to the different statutory discipline concerning five regions with a special status), shows very well how difficult it can be to run the school system.[20] During the pandemic, as in case of every crisis, the problems came to a head, and it can be remarked, with regard to the education, but also in relation to the distribution of health-related powers, that it seems that the constitutional and legislative framework regulating these public services could be improved.[21] While university autonomy was already guaranteed in Article 33.6 Const., school autonomy was first established in Law no 59/1997, a renowned reform bill concerning decentralisation and modernisation of public administration, and then established as a constitutional principle by the constitutional amendment procedure concerning the State-Regions relationship in 2001. Intended to secure a more efficient management of schools, closer to the communities, this reform seems to have been a poisoned chalice for education, as it ended up with a substantial State abdication of its tasks concerning education.[22] Massive cuts to public funding imposed over a decade, combined with a continued complex bureaucracy binding school administrative procedures did the rest. A state of the art of the education system which could not but be explosive at the time of the COVID-19 pandemic.

3. EMERGENCY DECREES AND SCHOOL SYSTEM: IN SEARCH OF A LEGAL FRAMEWORK

(§3.1) News of what was going on in China, concerning the beginning of the pandemic, was considered relevant enough to alarm the National Health System already in January. Yet the education system became involved much later. The first – and the most relevant – decision taken concerned the closure of teaching establishments from 5 March. This measure, clearly impacting the entire education system at all levels, from preschool to University, was prepared by Law Decree no 6, on 23 February 2020 (Art 1, c. 2, letter d, allowing closure "except distance learning activities"),[23] and then implemented in the executive order of

[20] A clear explanation of the contents of the three levels is in judgment of the Italian Constitutional Court 24 June 2009 case no 200/2009, in https://www.cortecostituzionale.it/actionPronuncia.do accessed 15 June 2020.

[21] On these problems, see Giacomo Delledonne and Carlo Padula, 'The Impact of the Pandemic Crisis on the Relations between the State and the Regions in Italy', in this volume.

[22] More on this subject in my books *Scuola e Costituzione tra autonomie e mercato* (Ediesse, 2019) and *La legge e l'Università pubblica. I pincipi costituzionali e il riassetto dell'Università italiana* (Jovene, 2012).

[23] Measure then confirmed and enlarged in Law Decree no 19/2020, converted into Law no 35/2020.

4 March by the president of the Italian Government (DPCM),[24] and entered into force on 10 March. Its validity, at first established until 3 April, was then postponed on a 15-day basis throughout the entire period by other DPCMs, and came to the decision of carrying the school year to the end by continuing teaching online. In the meantime, DPCM of 25 February 2020 had foreseen that "Directors of the schools in which the teaching activity has been suspended due to the health emergency, consulting with the competent collegial bodies, can activate remote teaching methods, for the duration of the suspension, having regard to the specific needs of the pupils with disabilities". In Article 1, letter g DPCM, it was made clear that e-learning was established as the normal method of teaching during the emergency.

Later on, on 8 April, the Law Decree no 22,[25] regarding "School, urgent measures on the regular conclusion and orderly start of the school year and on the conduct of state exams",[26] sets rules that: (1) allow the Ministry of education to adopt executive measures to handle the emergency; (2) fix the deadline of 18 May for school reopening, after which date school activities and final exams rules would have to be adjusted to the situation; (3) derogate the provisions relating to the minimum level of class attendance required and from the rule concerning partial or non-recognition of levels of learning by pupils. The decree then ordered (Art 2.3) that teaching staff had to ensure didactic activities in remote modalities, using available IT tools.

Discussion was raised especially in regard to two articles. Article 1.4 letter b decided on the replacement of the final State exam of the first cycle of education with a final assessment by the class council based on a candidate's paper. The only exam to be held in school would be the "Maturità" (the equivalent of baccalaureate or A levels) (the written part to be replaced with a single interview), being the final State exam of the second cycle of education. The State Examination Committees of the second cycle were composed of internal Commissioners, with an external President. Given the average age of Italian teachers, and the seniority requirements in teaching for Commission Presidents, finding committee chairmen available to conduct examinations in person was difficult, so that university professors were called to offer their collaboration in this role. The decree then established that Ministry acts provide specific arrangements for adjusting the exam to students with disability, with specific learning disabilities, or with special educational needs, taking into account the legislation in force, as well as for students in places of care or hospitals who were unable to leave home.

---

[24] "Decreto del Presidente del Consiglio dei Ministri".

[25] Later converted into Law no 41, 6 June 2020.

[26] Discussed by Enrico Carloni, 'Il diritto all'istruzione al tempo del coronavirus' in *Astrid-Rassegna* (2020) 1.

Later a number of new decrees and administrative orders were issued, dealing with numerous minor issues on a temporary basis. The most interesting aspect involved, in this whole emergency legislative and administrative activity concerning education, seems to be the one concerning e-learning. This subject can be considered particularly relevant from a constitutional law point of view, as online teaching involves fundamental rights to privacy and to health, in addition to the right to education and freedom of teaching set forth in Articles 33–34 of the Italian Constitution.[27] In addition, it should be considered that e-learning raises issues concerning both sides of the teacher-student relationship on a pedagogical plan. The choice and structure of platforms to be used call into question the evolution of the concept of the public function of education.

The discipline that was then established in order to safeguard these fundamental rights and to offer a guideline to allow online schooling to be useful and harmless, especially for the huge number of young people involved, is not easy to determine. Browsing pages and pages of dozens of administrative orders and decrees, nothing seems to have been decided with regard to the choice of a specific ICT platform, as apparently there is no public e-learning network that can be used.[28] No time limit seems to have been set in regard to the duration of video devices, not even in primary schools. Nothing concerning copyright over recorded lessons, nor preference for online streaming, or on protection of school pupils' data transmission to the commercial platforms. All that can be found on official Government websites is a 6 April Mini-guide for distance learning, signed by the Ministry of Education (nothing similar was released for the university e-learning), offering common sense advice to teachers, declaring it would be sent to schools. In addition, the head of department of the Ministry sent a note (no 388, 7 March 2020) explaining general concepts about e-learning, but not considering the Ministry's task to regulate fundamental aspects such as total time online allowed, or which ICT commercial platform should be preferred by schools. No doubt, at the root of this astonishing situation is the provision establishing "school autonomy", set forth in Article 117.3 of the Italian Constitution, apparently being interpreted once again as the legal basis for a

---

27 On which see Marco Benvenuti, 'La scuola è aperta a tutti?' (2018) Federalismi, 4, accessed at https://www.federalismi.it/nv14/articolo-documento.cfm?Artid=37068 and, by the same author 'Un "problema nazionale". Spunti ricostruttivi in tema di "istruzione" e "istruzione e … formazione professionale", tra Stato e Regioni, a partire dalla giurisprudenza costituzionale' (2015) in https://www.federalismi.it/nv14/articolo-documento.cfm?Artid=28434; see also Gianpaolo Fontana, 'La libertà di insegnamento' in Marco Benvenuti and Francesca Angelini (eds), *Le dimensioni costituzionali dell'istruzione* (Jovene 2014) 99.

28 Actually, the situation seems to be more complex according to Maria Chiara Pievatolo, 'Teledidattica: proprietaria e privata o libera e pubblica?' (*Return on academic research*, 8 June 2020) https://www.roars.it/online/teledidattica-proprietaria-e-privata-o-libera-e-pubblica/ accessed 15 June 2020, and https://www.garr.it/it/news-e-eventi/1656-videoconferenza-risorse-garr-per-l-emergenza-covid-19 accessed 15 June 2020.

State's renunciation to play a leading role in regulating education.[29] Once more, autonomy of schools seems to become the source of their misfortune, and in this case the consequences may be quite worrisome. Giving up regulating e-learning in the emergency meant leaving schools managers and personnel in a limbo at best, or seeing them operating as if they were entrepreneurs in a private business for profit, while fundamental rights to instruction, privacy, and health are at stake.

Discussion over this amazing regulatory gap is continuing, as well as that on the reopening, or reclosing, and the manner of organising public exams. Without this omission, it would have been probably easier to overcome a certain reluctance on a part of school teachers to use e-teaching.[30] Meanwhile, an uncertain management of public discourse by the Ministry, and the tendency of Italian politics to argue over small issues, took attention away from the ongoing difficult situation of students' families. The big issue still waiting to be solved was the reopening of schools in September. Article 2 remits to an executive order by the Ministry of Education the power to fix the date of beginning of lessons for the school year 2020/2021.[31] The Ministry takes its decision in agreement with the Conference of Regions, also taking into account the need for recovery of learning.

Parliamentary discussion on conversion as to the Law no 41/2020 of Decree no 22 brought the Italian Senate to a few important amendments concerning State exams.

First of all, in future primary school, descriptive judgments will replace numerical marks, satisfying teachers' requests. The execution of school building interventions has been speeded up: until 31 December 2020, the Mayors and Presidents of the Provinces and Metropolitan Cities were provided with extraordinary powers. Local authorities will, therefore, have one more tool to use to ensure that interventions take place quickly, in time for the start of the next school year. Teachers' recruitment procedures have been changed. The teachers who qualify to participate will no longer take a cross test, but a test with open-ended questions, still on the computer. The test will be different for each class

---

29 In detail in Roberta Calvano, *Scuola e Costituzione, tra autonomia e mercato* (Ediesse ed. 2019).

30 More optimistic is the view by Stefania Baroncelli, 'La didattica online al tempo del coronavirus: questioni giuridiche legate all'inclusione e alla privacy' in *Osservatorio sulle fonti*, 2020 who speaks about 92% of schools being organised for online teaching. The figure cited is referred as declared by a catholic non-profit organisation, Cittadinanzaattiva, but does not seem to have been confirmed by any public authority.

31 Paolo Maci, 'La scuola ai tempi del Covid –19. Una prima lettura del decreto legge n. 22 del 2020' (2020) *BioLaw Journal – Rivista di BioDiritto* 1, 348. According to Paolo Maci this provision represents a violation of a regional power established in Art 117.3 Const., and more generally the decree to have a centralising effect on the powers in the field of education, which should be more clearly justified on an emergency basis.

of competition. The competition notice, which had already been published in the Official Journal at the end of April, will be modified taking into account the innovations introduced during the parliamentary discussion. The tests will take place as soon as epidemiological conditions permit. Trying to offer a long overdue response to the European Court of Justice case law, and especially the famous ruling in the "Mascolo case",[32] on abuse of successive of fixed-term contracts in State schools, it was decided that new contracts have a retroactive effect. The winners of the competition who begin service in 2021/2022, falling within the quota of places destined for the 2020/2021 school year, will be recognised as the legal effect of the contract, from 1 September 2020. The rankings of substitute teachers, a huge and long-standing problem of the Italian school system, will be updated, re-arranged on a local basis, and digitised. This could be a useful simplification to ensure the implementation of the new rules before the next school year, providing relief to the secretariats of the educational institutions, as the Ministry's territorial offices will assign the substitute teachers. Presentation of the applications by candidates will be computerised and the substitutions should then be assigned more quickly.

An amendment to the decree (Art 2, co. 3-ter) then leaves the task of defining the modalities and criteria on the basis of which to provide teaching online and related obligations rendered at a distance by the staff of "Education and Research" facilities to a special collective agreement with trade union associations representing the sector at national level. This regulation will only concern the possible continuation of the emergency period.[31]

Other requests raised by teachers' unions were left unanswered and it took a parliamentary vote of confidence for the decree to be finally approved.[33] It should be remarked that the "School plan 2020–2021" approved with Ministerial Decree on 26 June 2020 seems quite generic in its approach to the reopening of school and facing the problems involved. One of the salient passages of the text appears quite eloquent: "Only with choices adapted to the needs of the reference context and made directly by the subjects who live and govern the territory, in fact, it is possible to respond adequately and promptly to the extreme diversification of training requests from the families, students and students from the entire territorial community. Innovative tools should also be provided to support schools in identifying specific areas to address deficiencies that cannot be overcome with organizational measures within the specific school institution or neighbouring educational institutions through appropriate conventional acts, in relation to the identification of the necessary resources".[34] For instance it can be recalled that the working-training activity program (PCTO, aka

32 Case C-22/13, C-61/13, C-63/13 and C-418/13 *Mascolo and Others*, ECLI:EU:C:2014:2401.

33 A general teachers' strike was declared by their unions on 8 June 2020.

34 School plan 2020–2021, DM 26 June 2020, p. 13.

alternance school-work) was not suspended during the pandemic, ignoring the possible risks and issues it raises concerning the right to health of students.

(§3.2) The emergency measures concerning the University system were less numerous. However, in the silence of the legislator, after the closure, the stopping of research and teaching activities was nonetheless impressive. Law Decree no 22/2020 has just one article concerning universities (Art 7), saying that the electoral procedures for the renewal of the collegiate and monocratic bodies of the universities, to be carried out during these six months, are suspended until the state of emergency continues. Quite oddly, among other urgent decisions made, as an entire world of problems concerning research and teaching during the lockdown has developed, all other decisions were left to universities and their rectors. On this subject it is relevant to recall that DPCM 26 April allowed universities, from 4 May, to restart some of their activities. Examinations, traineeships, research and experimental and/or didactic laboratory activities and exercises could be carried out, the use of libraries in universities was allowed, provided that space and work were organised in such a way as to minimise the risk of proximity and aggregation, and that organisational prevention and protection measures were taken. At the same time, however, the Ministry of University and Research was writing to university deans to allow them to continue exams and teaching online. In June, in an interview with the main Italian newspaper, he announced the general resumption of regular university activities in person from February 2021.[35] No decisions were taken by decree in this field, but letters were written to deans by the Ministry encouraging them to provide "blended teaching", mixing traditional classes with online streaming of the traditional lessons. Quite surprisingly, no reference was made in these letters to the regulations in force, regarding the requirement of online courses, providing rules on lessons duration and their weight in terms of credit points (CFU are doubled for each video lesson compared to a traditional one).[36] It is worth also recalling the consolidated text of legislative decree no 81/2008, concerning workplace safety in the use of video terminals. Article 2 explicitly equates with workers, "the student of education and university institutions and participants in vocational training in which laboratories are used, work equipment in general, chemical, physical and biological agents, including video

---

[35] 'Il ministro dell'Università Manfredi: "Tutti in aula a febbraio"' (*Corriere.it*, 12 June 2020) https://www.corriere.it/sette/politica/20_giugno_12/ministro-dell-universita-manfredi-tutti-aula-febbraio-84f7548a-acb6-11ea-b5f6-e69744c83472.shtml?refresh_ce-cp accessed 15 June 2020.

[36] ANVUR (Italian national Agency for the Evaluation of Universities and Research Institutes), Aims and procedures for the periodic accreditation of telematic courses of study, of universities that provide courses of study in telematic mode, in ww.anvur.org. See also Stefania Baroncelli, 'La didattica online al tempo del coronavirus: questioni giuridiche legate all'inclusione e alla privacy' in *Osservatorio sulle fonti*, 2020 449–450, considers these rules unfit to apply to e-learning by traditional universities during the pandemic.

terminal equipment for periods in which the student is actually applied to the instruments or laboratories concerned". Articles 172–178 set rules applying to work activities involving the use of video terminal equipment, such as time limits, pauses, information about risks to health. Those who organise the activity have to consider neurological and eye health risks, and offer information about posture, physical and mental fatigue, and ergonomic conditions. This regards not only rights of students, but also of professors, especially considering that many of them have taught more courses during the semester.

As an evidence of the relevance and delicacy of the discipline, Article 178 of the decree establishes serious criminal sanctions for those who violate the listed requirements on safety at work.

Teaching and attending courses online raises issues which are also worthy of consideration from other points of view. In a pedagogical perspective, there is a wide international experience and literature concerning e-learning[37] over the last two or three decades. For this reason, thinking that online teaching may simply consist in turning a camera on, while the professor is delivering a lecture, could sound ridiculous, but at the same time, it has to be said, this is exactly what happened in most cases in Italian Universities during the 2020 pandemic.

Notwithstanding the recalled regulatory acts, and the wide experience ranging from Massive Online Open Courses (MOOC) courses to the decades of practice of the 11 online Italian Universities, in 2020 each University has set its own rules of conduct concerning e-learning. It should be remembered that in a number of cases, there was no rule at all, allowing anarchy and the use of commercial platforms with no limit and no apparent consideration for the right to privacy. It is not only a matter of GDPR 2016/679 rules being grossly violated,[38] or even of allowing long hours of online teaching, not considering the impact of the means used, and without adapting the contents of teaching to it. What is more surprising is that, after the summer relief from the pandemic, as figures of the pandemic started rising, universities were going back to the same ruthless lack of rules as if there was no Ministry of University and no problem at all to deal with. All this happens in a University system normally overwhelmed with decrees, regulations and administrative obligations since L. no 240/2010 University reform bill.

---

37 Among others, see Chiara Panciroli (2008), 'For a pedagogical approach to e-learning', *Ricerche Di Pedagogia E Didattica. Journal of Theories and Research in Education*, 3(1). https://doi.org/10.6092/issn.1970-2221/1543 accessed 15 June 2020; Guglielmo Trentin, 'Towards a real sustainability of e-learning. Proceedings of E-learning & sustainability' (2004) (Fondazione ENI Enrico Mattei, Giune 2004) in http://www.altrascuola.article.php?sid=951 accessed 15 June 2020.

38 Even though the Authority for privacy (Garante dei dati personali) in a 26 March decision allowed schools and universities to omit to acquire students' consent to the use of their personal data, many other questions about privacy discipline remained unsolved.

University constitutional autonomy seems to be, in a way that appears to be similar to what happens with school autonomy, the shield behind which a substantial abdication of the State from its tasks is concealed.

4. GOING ONLINE: DIGITAL DIVIDE AND OTHER ISSUES

E-learning is today, and has been in the first phase of the pandemic, a precious and inalienable instrument to guarantee the fundamental right to education throughout the planet.[39]

It is important then to analyse how it was used in the first half of 2020, in light of improving our ability to cope with further crisis which could make e-learning, once again, the only means of teaching. Through "normal" times, e-learning can be very useful for lifelong learning, for students – workers, but it is very clear and widely acknowledged that teaching in person will always be fundamental to the development of the personality of the child, because of the relationship with the teacher and the other pupils, unreplaceable for its psychological evolution.

As to the Italian education system way of coping with the emergency, it has been already recalled, with a quick look at the current legislation, particularly the unified act 81/2008, on safety at work, which specific rules safeguard health of workers using computer display screens on a regular basis. Time limit is set to an amount of at least 20 hours per week (Art 173), i.e. providing workers and students take breaks. School children probably often had an amount of e-learning greater than that duration limit, but there is no reliable official data as to which amount of hours of e-learning was guaranteed. To answer the question on how e-learning was dealt with by schools during the emergency, it is also worth remarking that the Italian law on employee's statute allows video and audio footage of workers, provided that they are informed of the use of such video recordings. Both acts seem to offer quite relevant and useful guidance for a Ministry willing to regulate e-learning, not only, as already said, for University students and professors, but especially for school children and teachers, teaching many hours on a daily basis. Not to mention the question, already recalled, concerning the pedagogical need to adapt teaching to the communication tool used. Despite all this, as mentioned above, no time limit has been established for school e-lessons, nor any indication of caution for subjects involved, considering possible neurological consequences, or even damage to vision as a result of long hours of teaching and attending classes online.

---

39 Before the emergency, the issue was already considered relevant by a few constitutional law scholars, such as Antonio Iannuzzi, 'Diritto all'istruzione e cultura digitale' (2009) in *Informatica e diritto* 134.

A second but equally relevant critical point is to be made in regard to the already mentioned issue of inequalities. In these last few months, this problem has been grossly unveiled by the gap showing among students regarding their access to computer devices. Those who have no access to information technology simply disappear from the sight of their teachers. Long before the pandemic, the issue of digital exclusion has been a subject for discussion among constitutional law scholars.[40] It has long been questioned how deeply this issue affects access to social rights, and there has been much questioning on the possible evolution of instruments of guarantee of classic fundamental rights, such as freedom of speech or right to a fair trial in light of technological evolution. Now that coronavirus changed the lives of billions of people around the globe, inequalities are more evident than ever. In the field of education, this gap may endanger the future of big groups of population throughout the world, especially as the pandemic seems likely to continue. Other global climate and health threats risk making technology essential for the education of millions of people.

Throughout the first semester of the pandemic of 2020, in Italy it has been registered that among school children aged from 6–17 years old, many did not have access to an inadequate IT equipment. The figures are worrying: 12.3% were without a PC/tablet at home, whereas 57.0% shared a PC/tablet with a member of their family. Only 6.1% had their own personal computer.[41]

The Government allocated funds to overcome the difficulties related to this situation. Article 120 of Law Decree no 18/2020 provides special funding in this regard. Eight-five million euros will be invested: 10 million to support existing and new e-learning school platforms, 70 million to finance loans for use of electronic equipment by students, 5 million to train teachers for online teaching. In addition to this, important funding has been invested by the Decree Law no 34, 19 May 2020, in which Articles 236 and 238, increase general funding for university and research, providing scholarships for university students. Article 236 allocates 62 million for university students IT devices and access to platforms and didactic tools.

A further huge problem that should be addressed is the lack of broadband internet access in large areas of the country. The Ministry of Education recently announced that The School Plan, approved by the National Committee for Ultrabroadband, has doubled the funds available to ensure the connection to

---

40 See Oreste Pollicino, Graziella Romeo (eds), *The Internet and Constitutional Law. The protection of fundamental rights and constitutional adjudication in Europe* (Routledge 2016); in Italy, Mimma, Rospi, 'Il diritto di accesso ad Internet come strumento di mobilità sociale e il ruolo del Governo' in Elena Malfatti and Luisa Azzena (eds), *Poteri normativi del Governo ed effettività dei diritti sociali* (Pisa University Press 2017) 285.

41 Istat report 'Spaces in the house and availability of computers for children and teenagers', 6 April 2020, https://www.istat.it/it/files/2020/04/Spazi-casa-disponibilita-computer-ragazzi.pdf accessed 15 June 2020.

81.4% of primary and secondary schools. Over EUR 400 million have already been invested for this purpose, and will be used, on the one hand, to connect more than 32,000 school facilities, and on the other, to provide households with income-related financing for broadband internet access. Hopefully, the timetable for implementing this plan will be speeded up because of the emergency, but still – as previously recalled – the multilevel administrative machine of the educational system seems to react quite slowly to the emergency. As the previous analysis suggests it seems evident, especially in the case of the National School system, that the situation is very difficult to manage. There is a tiresome work in progress, even harder than could be expected due to the difficulty of filling the gaps resulting from previous underfunding and, in some cases, from the actual poor management of the education system by the State. The important effort made with decrees no 22 and 34 will certainly not be able to make up for a delay of decades, but may at least represent an important positive step forward. The constitutional law debate concerning the width of art. 34 Const., is still open, and the COVID-19 emergency will bring new elements to it. It has been recently argued that the fundamental right to education it sets has been limited in the Constitutional Court case law to school activity, excluding the supply of goods, and accordingly a paradigm shift could be detected in this emergency legislation.[42] Actually, recent case law seems to show, on the contrary, an attentive attitude by the Constitutional Court to rights connected and functional to education, as seen in a very important and much-discussed ruling no 275 of 2016,[43] and again in 2020 in ruling no 152. In the recalled 2016 decision, the Constitutional Court noted the primacy of fundamental social rights as compared to the balanced budget principle, in a case concerning the budget of a Region (Abruzzo) not funding adequately public transport for disabled students. More generally, the case law is quite consolidated in safeguarding Article 34, and it can be underlined then, that decision no 7/1967 was not upheld, and the Court has often reaffirmed that the right to school education also implies supply of books/school texts, school meals and public transport to schools are available. Today it can be affirmed then that the picture has completely changed since the 1967 decision.[44]

---

42 A point of view expressed by Lucilla Conte, 'La scuola si è fermata. L'impatto del Covid-19 sui diritti all'istruzione, all'educazione e all'insegnamento' in *La scuola nella democrazia, la democrazia nella scuola* (Editoriale Scientifica 2020), 144.

43 Among others see, Adriana Apostoli, 'I diritti fondamentali "visti" da vicino dal giudice amministrativo Una annotazione a "caldo" della sentenza della Corte costituzionale n. 275 del 2016' (2016) in *Forum costituzionale*, (http://www.forumcostituzionale.it/wordpress/wp-content/uploads/2016/01/nota_275_2016_apostoli.pdf accessed 15 June 2020); and Ines Ciolli, 'I diritti sociali "condizionati" di fronte alla Corte costituzionale' in *Rivista giuridica del lavoro e della previdenza sociale*, 3/2017, 353.

44 This is affirmed in Annamaria Poggi, 'Art 34' in Raffaele Bifulco, Alfonso Celotto, Marco Olivetti (eds), *Commentario alla Costituzione*, vol I (Utet 2006) 705.

After the summer, the pandemic did not come to an end, and soon after school reopened the sudden threat to close down again keeps rising. This seems the most urgent issue to solve while this contribution is being revised. Several EU countries which reopened schools very quickly, before Italy, are now facing a second terrible wave of contagion. The protracted closure of schools in Italy in the first semester, perhaps due to the uniform treatment of all regions, despite their different epidemiological situation, now brings many to consider that new closures, pushed beyond a certain limit could produce serious damage, especially to younger children.

Ultimately, in order to draw a provisional conclusion, it can be useful to recall the Public Higher Education Council's opinion of 18 May 2020. The Council intended to draw the Minister's attention to the need to act promptly, changing some aspects of the general design of the system. These actions need to reduce the minimum number of pupils in each school-based institution and the minimum number of pupils per class, consequently leading to an increase in the number of staff in all school roles (management, teaching, caretakers) so as to ensure the start of the school year in safety for students and staff. Only this kind of measure could have ensured the effective implementation of the necessary recovery and consolidation actions for our pupils.

As to the University system, even though e-learning, in some ways, allowed professors and researchers to do their part, and also to keep several thousands of students safe during the first and hopefully the worst part of the pandemic, now a careful consideration must be made. According to the non-binding guidance by the Ministry letters, Italian Universities planned their current and next semesters only partly online, but changes to this policy seem imminent. In this perspective it could be useful to have more accurate guidelines to the use of digital means of teaching, concerning time limits, video registration and/or streaming, the limits to the use of commercial platforms such as google meet, Microsoft teams, zoom.

As to the role that e-learning can play in the future, it seems necessary to distinguish the acute phase of the emergency, from "normal" times, because they will in any case probably be different from what citizens are used to. Climate change, new pandemics, air pollution problems may create a context where technology can be more and more essential, and even strategic to plan our future. Principles and fundamental rights concerning education, set in the Italian Constitution in Articles 33 and 34 will need again e-learning to be fulfilled, but at the same time, these principles cannot be sacrificed, in my view, to celebrate an uncritical adherence to a new model of online teaching at any cost, disregarding the conditions of context.

It is time for researchers and educators to look more closely at the choices legislators and political actors are making, analysing what kind of assumptions underpin these choices, and what vision of the university and school they advance. This, in the light of all data considered here, has to bring us to attentive reflection and it should probably be recalled now that "critique is essential in times of crisis. It is our job, and our responsibility, not to accept these directives without questioning their impact on the less privileged among us, on the university community as a whole, and on the project of public research and education in which academics are engaged".[45]

[45] Honor Brabazon, 'The academy's neoliberal response to COVID-19: Why faculty should be wary and how we can push back' (*Academic matters*, 29 May 2020). This contribution was updated with reference to phase 1 of the pandemic. The debate continued, but concern remains about the underestimation of the centrality of the education system, and the decentralised management of the emergency in Italy.

PART VII

CORONAVIRUS CHANGING EUROPE

A NEW APPROACH TO THE LEGAL UNDERSTANDING OF "DIRECTNESS" AND "PARTICIPATION" IN THE AFTERMATH OF COVID-19

Ewa Rott-Pietrzyk and Dariusz Szostek*

COVID-19 has caused significant changes in the ways in which societies function. It has affected us on many levels, including in legal matters. Lockdown has forced millions of people to work remotely, which has not only changed their lives but has also influenced the interpretation and application of both public and private law, as well as forcing through changes in the law. In this context, the authors propose a new

* Ewa Rott-Pietrzyk, University of Silesia, Katowice; Dariusz Szostek, University of Opole.

understanding of the terms "directness" and "participation". An analysis of these terms, using various methods of interpretation, indicates that today, "directness" and "participation" should be understood differently, as they are implemented online using electronic means of communication. Many examples from both private and public law prove that there can be no easy return to the traditional, hitherto prevailing understanding of the terms analysed in this contribution. Indeed, there is a wide group of experts who, through various guidelines and recommendations, have indicated the clear need for a new interpretation and understanding of these terms. Against this background, it must be asked whether the COVID-19 crisis has caused a permanent change in the way that directness and participation are understood. This contribution aims to demonstrate the authors' view that the new understanding of "directness" and "participation" has become a fact, and not one currently and typical only applied in the "new normality" of a global pandemic. The authors believe that a new understanding and approach to both notions seems to have become more ingrained and permanent due to the current crisis.

1. INTRODUCTION

It sounds very clichéd right now to say that COVID-19 has had a serious effect on our lives. It has also had a significant impact on the law, on many levels. First, the moves to prevent the effects of the negative phenomena caused by COVID-19 have led to legislative changes[1] being implemented with the use of unusually rapid procedures.[2] Secondly, the need arose to adopt a proper methodology for the interpretation and application of the law. A lockdown was introduced in the majority of the EU Member States, making it virtually impossible for professionals, consumers and general trade to function as usual. Prior to the pandemic, for the binding completion of legal actions (especially those requiring the form of a notarial deed), the physical participation of the parties was necessary, which was forced by the previous interpretation of the terms "directness" and "participation". There is no doubt that COVID-19 imposed the need to rapidly adopt new ways of communicating in various types

---

1 See the legal acts in Poland on this issue, available at the Polish Parliament's official website: http://prawo.sejm.gov.pl/isap.nsf/DocDetails.xsp?id=WDU20200000374 accessed 1 June 2020. Similar laws, or at least laws with a similar purpose, have been adopted in every EU State.

2 Examples, concerning, for instance, the digitisation of courts are presented in a study entitled Bart Krans and others, *Civil Justice and Covid-19 (Septentrio Reports 5 2020)*, https://doi.org/10.7557/sr.2020.5 accessed 26 May 2020 (it includes: Australia, Brazil, Canada, Denmark, England and Wales, France, Germany, Italy, Lithuania, Latvia, the Netherlands, Norway, Poland, Slovenia, Spain), and also: Jeff Galway, Urs Hoffmann-Nowotny (eds), 'Impact of COVID-19 on court Operations & Litigations Practice' (International Bar Association Committee 2020) https://www.lalive.law/wp-content/uploads/2020/05/2020-SGI-IBA_Impact_of_COVID-19_on_court_operations_and_litigation_practice.pdf accessed 1 June 2020.

of social contacts in general,[3] as well as in activities that have legal effects in matters of both private and public law. As a result, this has forced individual legal systems either to change the rules (allowing for "directness" and "online participation"), or to adopt a new interpretation of these concepts. In the private law context, this translates, among other things, into the interpretation of statements of intent (namely, whether a certain legal transaction has been performed at all), the form of performing legal transactions, and the conclusion of agreements in a situation where the traditional and functional private law instruments that had existed to this point, were replaced with new tools from the modern technologies (NewTech) sector. This contribution covers the issue of communication having a legal effect at the level of private law, as well as public law. This analysis is intended to illustrate the need for a different understanding of directness and participation in legal terms.

In the European Union, individual States operate at varying levels of computerisation and digitisation.[4] Various legal regulations in this respect (both private and public law ones) are implemented in the legal systems of the EU Member States, with some of them harmonised at the European level, for instance, the legal acts issued under the New Digital Single Market Strategy.[5] In those European countries with a high degree of computerisation, using digital resources on a grand scale, COVID-19 had less impact on the functioning of the State, administration and judiciary, as well as on citizens as trade participants. In these countries, the use of new technologies is quite natural, so participants in the public and private sectors have become "accustomed to" them. We cannot, therefore, refer to new technologies as a revolutionary tool used for communicating in public channels (e.g. contacts with authorities and courts), or private channels (online legal transactions within the framework of professional, consumer or public trade, also in the form of a notarial deed[6]).

In moderately and poorly computerised countries (such as Poland[7]), the pandemic primarily forces a re-evaluation of the existing policy, of maintaining

---

3 See, e.g. Tiffanie Wen, 'How coronavirus has transformed the way we communicate', from 9 April 2020, https://www.bbc.com/worklife/article/20200408-coronavirus-how-lockdown-helps-those-who-fear-the-phone accessed 1 June 2020.

4 https://digital-competitiveness.eu/wp-content/uploads/ESCP03_Digital-Riser-Ranking_2020-09-14-1.pdf accessed 5 March 2021.

5 See: https://eur-lex.europa.eu/legal-content/EN/TXT/HTML/?uri=LEGISSUM:3102_3&from=PL and: https://ec.europa.eu/info/strategy/priorities-2019-2024/europe-fit-digital-age_en accessed 1 June 2020.

6 This issue has been presented in more depth in two studies: Ewa Rott-Pietrzyk and others, 'Epidemia zachęca do e-aktów notarialnych' (Epidemics increases the popularity of e-notarial deeds), Dziennik Gazeta Prawna, 6 April 2020; Ewa Rott-Pietrzyk and others, 'Czynności notarialne online – podstawy *de lege lata* i uwagi *de lege ferenda*' (Notarial transactions online – *de lege lata* bases *and de lege ferenda* comments), 2020 Forum Prawnicze 4, 38–56.

7 https://www.mckinsey.com/pl/~/media/McKinsey/Locations/Europe%20and%20Middle%20East/Polska/Raporty/Polska%20jako%20cyfrowy%20challenger/Raport-McKinsey_Polska-jako-Cyfrowy-Challenger.ashx accessed 13 June 2020.

the traditional way of performing legal transactions, in favour of NewTech solutions. Furthermore, due to sudden social changes and a change in the way that citizens operate, the pandemic also encourages a different interpretation of the legal provisions relating to the performance of legal transactions. This policy also incorporates new legislation related to COVID-19, which is not always systematically consistent with the existing legal system. The legislative changes introduced in Poland and in other countries, in the first and second quarter of 2020 were twofold. On the one hand, permanent changes were introduced that were not linked to the pandemic threat. On the other hand, changes were made only for the period of the pandemic (temporary changes).

As regards the new approach to "directness" and "participation", the authors believe that introducing piecemeal legislative changes that do not create a coherent, transparent system is not desirable. In addition, the assumption of their purely temporary nature (namely, for the duration of a pandemic) may result in chaos in the legal system in the future, in particular with regard to the methodology of the interpretation and application of the law. The situation as it relates to COVID-19 leads the authors to two main conclusions with regard to the legal systems of moderately or poorly computerised countries. The first one concerns the need to create a coherent legal system, even when rapid legislative changes are required (and to prefer permanent changes in digitisation). The second conclusion concerns the method of interpreting and applying the law in terms of digitisation.

At the legislative level, the changes made with regard to legal acts using new technologies should not be temporary, i.e. with the prospect of returning to the previous status once the pandemic is over. COVID-19 can be the basis for introducing permanent statutory changes. Paradoxically, the phenomenon of a negative nature may therefore contribute to desirable changes in the law of poorly computerised countries as regards the use of new technologies in trade (as well as in the communication between citizens and public administration and the judiciary).

The second conclusion is related to the authors' conviction that, in some countries, the regulations in force allow the existing tools to be used for more intensive computerisation, both in the private and public law, although this would probably involve the adoption of a different methodology of interpreting and applying the law. Above all, however, it would require a willingness to go beyond the literal interpretation of legal regulations in a way that could encourage and enable the use of new technologies. In the case of the Polish legal system, the authors firmly believe that the law *de lege lata* already contains essential tools that open the legal system to performing legal transactions using NewTech (this applies in particular to the form of a notarial deed), assuming that a functional interpretation is adopted. Therefore, the required legislative changes suggested by the authors are not fundamental or revolutionary by nature in relation to the applicable law. The intensified use of new technologies in trade would require only a few changes, of rather a technical nature,[8] classified as in categories of law engineering.

In the presented context, the question arises about understanding the terms "directness" and "participation", in both private and public law regulations. One consequence of the new way in which society functions at every level during a pandemic – in particular, connected with the reduction in direct (physical) contacts between trading participants, along with the simultaneous increase in remote communication and the transfer of many activities to the online world[9] – is the need to establish a new understanding of these terms. Adopting this new understanding would allow for changes in the current practice of performing legal transactions, in particular in terms of fulfilling formal requirements on which the performance and validity of a legal transaction depend. The "new normality" may, therefore, lead to a novel understanding of traditional concepts in law, such as "directness" and "with the participation of" in the national legal systems of the EU Member States and European law.

The aim of the authors is to analyse the interpretation of these terms in order to determine their new meaning in various legal contexts, in which they have so far been understood traditionally. However, the aim is not simply about understanding these terms during the pandemic. The authors' intention is to establish a utilitarian, functional and universal interpretation in similar contexts, for which COVID-19 is only a pretext. The authors modestly hope that the findings made may be relevant even after the pandemic, and may foster the use of new technologies to a much greater extent in countries with poor computerisation and digitisation. This applies, for instance, to Poland, and as the Polish legal system is obviously the closest to the authors, this gives them some insight into the system as internal observers. The authors' proposals will be presented in a broader context, namely taking into account various possible solutions, including those adopted in soft law, which can be used by national legislators, as well as standards of a technical nature.[10]

---

8 Here, the authors use, to some extent, the research and conclusions presented in two studies: Ewa Rott-Pietrzyk and others, 'Epidemia zachęca do e-aktów notarialnych' (Epidemics increases the popularity of e-notarial deeds), Dziennik Gazeta Prawna, 6 April 2020; Ewa Rott-Pietrzyk and others, 'Czynności notarialne online – podstawy *de lege lata* i uwagi *de lege ferenda*' (Notarial transactions online – *de lege lata* bases *and de lege ferenda* comments), 2020 Forum Prawnicze 4, 38-56.

9 This is illustrated by Bart Krans and others, *Civil Justice and Covid-19 (Septentrio Reports 5 2020)*, https://doi.org/10.7557/sr.2020.5 accessed 26 May 2020 and also: Jeff Galway, Urs Hoffmann-Nowotny (eds), 'Impact of COVID-19 on court Operations & Litigations Practice' (International Bar Association Committee 2020) https://www.lalive.law/wp-content/uploads/2020/05/2020-SGI-IBA_Impact_of_COVID-19_on_court_operations_and_litigation_practice.pdf accessed 1 June 2020.

10 For instance, the following norms: ISO/IEC27000, ISO 29115, SP800-63.

In addition, this work is done under the assumption that the proposal for a new approach to "directness" and "participation" using new technologies will not cause any hazard to trade.

2. CHANGE IN THE INTERPRETATION OF THE TERMS "DIRECTNESS" AND "PARTICIPATION"

2.1. INTERPRETATION OF LEGISLATION RELEVANT TO "DIRECTNESS" AND "PARTICIPATION"

2.1.1. General remarks

In a recently prepared study by a wider circle of scholars, including the authors of this work, it was stated that:

> Often in the history of law, including private law, rapid historical changes may cause an impulse to rethink the importance of the legal norms of private law. For example, unsurprisingly, immediately after the Great War, the question arose as to how private law should react to the existing complex situation. The same can be said about the rapid changes that are currently taking place and which are changing the circumstances in which we live so radically. When faced with rapidly changing circumstances, which the legislator did not take into account when drafting the law, an answer is required to the question of whether it is possible, within the framework of the current legal order, to adapt existing legal institutions to the new conditions of social life accordingly.[11]

Importantly, it should also be considered whether such an interpretation ought to be limited exclusively to an emergency situation in which the maintenance of normal interpersonal contacts is extremely restricted? According to the authors' assumptions, the resolution of this dilemma is not limited to the context of the COVID-19 pandemic. On the other hand, a pandemic in poorly computerised countries can speed up the process, which, without such a game-changing factor, would most probably be drawn out over many years. In this context, COVID-19 can actually have a positive effect. There is a good chance that this opportunity will lead to a change in attitudes towards a wider and more ubiquitous use of NewTech. In other words, COVID-19 can contribute to the permanent incorporation of NewTech tools into the tool box, which until now has largely

---

11 Ewa Rott-Pietrzyk and others, 'Czynności notarialne online – podstawy *de lege lata* i uwagi *de lege ferenda*' (Notarial transactions online – *de lege lata* bases *and de lege ferenda* comments), 2020 Forum Prawnicze 4, 43, 44.

been filled by traditional and conservatively presented private law concepts (e.g. *inter praesentes* and *inter absentes* legal acts, the form of a legal transaction, in particular the form of a notarial deed and meeting the requirements of that form).

The interpretation of legal norms is, or at least should be, always contextual.[12] This means it always refers to the spatial, temporal and social reality in which it is performed. The norms have to fulfil their purpose (according to their *ratio legis*), and for this reason, taking a completely abstract approach, it is likely that any potential changes in the law would have to be preceded by an interpretation justifying the departure from a certain practice due to exceptional circumstances (such as COVID-19) leading to actions with legal effect being taken.

Again taking Poland as an example, although the specifics of weaker computerisation can also be applied to other countries, it is worth noting that the current legislation in force has provided a sufficient basis for a new approach to directness already, notwithstanding the current situation caused by COVID-19.[13] The pandemic hazard situation, and its consequences in terms of limiting contacts between trading participants, and social contacts in general, shows only an urgent practical need to construe provisions on the performance of legal transactions, in particular notarial ones, without being exposed to accusations of *contra legem* interpretation.

The concepts of "directness" and "participation" are sufficiently wide that using new technologies should not affect the functions of these terms and the safety of trade. However, so far, they have been understood too narrowly, even though the available technology has allowed for a broader understanding without the need for a teleological reduction. The proposed direction of their interpretation, therefore, corresponds to the *ratio legis* function of the existing provisions on the formal requirements for the effective performance of legal transactions. So it can be said that there is a totally desirable compliance between the results of linguistic and functional interpretation, as well as systemic interpretation. In the case of Poland, the legislative changes that would have to be introduced should therefore be of a more technical nature in terms of using NewTech. Therefore, no fundamental, structural changes are necessary; technical standards would also justify a "new" interpretation of traditional tools and concepts in the field of legal transactions.

---

12 The importance of context is also underlined by Stanley Fish, 'There is No Textualist Position' (2005) 42 San Diego L. Rev. 629 https://digital.sandiego.edu/sdlr/vol42/iss2/8 accessed 1 June 2020.

13 Ewa Rott-Pietrzyk and others, 'Czynności notarialne online – podstawy *de lege lata* i uwagi *de lege ferenda*' (Notarial transactions online – *de lege lata* bases *and de lege ferenda* comments*)*, 2020 Forum Prawnicze 4, 40 ff.

2.1.2. *Interpretation methods (linguistic, systemic and functional interpretation) vs COVID-19*

The choice between the literal meaning of a legal text and a meaning otherwise indicated is the most common interpretative situation.[14] Without going too deeply into the issue of the priority of linguistic interpretation over other methods of interpretation,[15] it should be stated that – in the authors' opinion – the result of applying a linguistic interpretation allows for a broader understanding of the notions of "directness" and "participation".

Taking the dictionary definition, for example, "directness" is interpreted as: without intermediation,[16] in person; and in spatial relations: very close. The understanding of this concept in terms of time is also quite important, as it means: immediately.[17] Meanwhile, "directness" in the sense used in legal regulations so far has most often been understood as "physical participation". This was effectively taking a fairly narrow understanding of the term, i.e. as unity in a specific place at the same time as entities performing a certain legal transaction, for instance parties to a contract concluded in the form of a notarial deed.[18] However, in the dictionary meaning[19] – participation means being in a certain place, but also acting in a certain place (somewhere). Therefore, this does not necessarily mean participation through physical presence in the same geographically defined place. By contrast, "physical" means primarily material, but also recognisable by the senses.[20] In this context, the demarcation line is different from the traditional understanding of the division of legal transactions between present parties (*inter praesentes*) and absent parties (*inter absentes*).

The result of the linguistic interpretation does not, therefore, contradict the interpretation that "directness" and "participation", in modern terms, can occur using NewTech in such a way that both parties operate online at the same time in a way that is accessible to the senses, while also ensuring that the act is recorded (e.g. video registration for notarial transactions). NewTech allows for

---

14 See for example Bernard S. Jackson, *Making Sense in Law* (Deborah Charles Publications 1995) 45.

15 Zygmunt Tobor, *W poszukiwaniu intencji prawodawcy* [Searching the lawmaker's intention] (Wolters Kluwer 2011), 122, referring to the views expressed in doctrine and case law, states that "the application of an interpretation in which the interpreter departs from the linguistic meaning of a provision can be justified only in exceptional circumstances, since the addressees of legal norms are entitled to rely on what they have actually expressed."

16 https://dictionary.cambridge.org/dictionary/english/directly accessed 25 May 2020.

17 https://sjp.pwn.pl/szukaj/bezpośredni.html accessed 25 May 2020.

18 For instance, the sale of a real property (Art 158 of the Polish Civil Code – PCC).

19 https://sjp.pwn.pl/szukaj/obecność%20.html accessed 25 May 2020.

20 Jan Tokarski (ed), *Słownik wyrazów obcych* (PWN 1980) 222, https://dictionary.cambridge.org/dictionary/english/physical accessed 25 May 2020.

remote communication in real-time, with the possibility of directly receiving the image and sound in a way that does not differ from face-to-face contact (depending, obviously, on the strength of internet connections, the quality of software, devices, etc. provided so that the legal transaction can be carried out without any interference). Even if we assume that the result of the linguistic interpretation of a directive is ambiguous, further methods of interpretation are helpful to obtain the result – as suggested by the authors – allowing the terms "directness" and "participation" to be properly understood in the context of new technologies. In the traditional perception of the sequential application of interpretation directives, the failure to achieve a satisfactory result through the application of linguistic interpretation entitles the use of other methods of interpretation.[21]

The principle of the primacy of linguistic interpretation has traditionally been identified with "*interpretatio cessat in claris*", meaning the prohibition of non-linguistic types of interpretation when the application of language rules leads to a clear understanding of the regulation, and interpretation should stop once an unambiguous result has been achieved. This rule, considered in terms of the limits of interpretation,[22] indicates the possibility of applying further methods[23] in situations where there is an ambiguous outcome.[24]

The COVID-19 pandemic not only creates a situational context for legal transactions but also creates a context for thinking differently (namely crossing mental barriers) about the notion of directness, giving it a meaning that would allow it to function under changed circumstances. For this reason, when interpreting the notions of "directness" and "participation", the rules that insist also on referring to non-linguistic elements that constitute the context in which the standards are to operate (functional and teleological rules) are also important, among other things. A functional interpretation allows both the objectives of a certain legal act assumed by the legislator (*ratio iuris*) and the rationale of a certain legal provision (*ratio legis*) to be taken into account. These objectives are either protective by nature (essential objectives) or are seen as instrumental objectives.[25] In teleological rules, these objectives are often referred to by preferring an understanding of phrases oriented towards

---

21 Zygmunt Tobor, 'W poszukiwaniu intencji' 157; Damiano Canale, Giovanni Tuzet, 'On Legal Inferentialism. Toward a Pragmatics of Semantic Content in Legal Interpretation' (2007) 20 Ratio Juris 32, 33.

22 Zygmunt Tobor, 'W poszukiwaniu intencji' 125.

23 Maciej Zieliński, Zbigniew Radwański, 'Wykładnia prawa cywilnego' [Interpretation of Private Law] (2006) 1 Studia Prawa Prywatnego 20.

24 Many discussions and views exist in the doctrine on the acceptability of the use of methods of interpretation other than linguistic interpretation. However, this issue goes beyond the scope of this contribution.

25 Tomasz Gizbert-Studnicki, 'Wykładnia celowościowa' [Purposeful Interpretation] (1985) 3/4 Studia Prawnicze 51 ff.

achieving a certain result. In determining how the objectives are to be achieved, it is necessary to also consider the social relations to which the law applies. The interpreter is obliged to take these into account, but with the assumption of referring to definitely prevalent trends.[26] It has been said that one of the "interpretative guidelines" referring to the values taken into account by the legislator may be a legislative trend that can be detected through the analysis of proposed subsequent amendments presented in subsequent acts in a certain area, as it may indicate the process of approaching the optimal solution by the legislator.[27]

The systemic rules of interpretation, on the other hand, refer to other standards already in force in the legal system. The general message of these rules is to seek such an interpretation that the analysed meaning of a certain phrase is established in such a way as to preserve the coherence of the entire legal system. It is also about compliance with the rules (systemic or branch of law) applicable in a certain legal system. It means that, in the event that a phrase in the text of a provision is considered ambiguous, it is not permitted to assume a meaning that would cause the received norm to be non-compliant with another norm (in particular of a higher order) or a rule of law.[28]

The legislative trends observed in recent months are quite clear as regards the use of NewTech on various levels. The Polish legal system may serve as an example here, as a number of legislative changes have been made[29] with regard to: the admissibility of medical visits online;[30] the adoption of resolutions by collective bodies using means of direct remote communication;[31] online court hearings;[32] the possibility of the Polish Post Office transforming a registered (traditional) letter into an electronic document and delivering it electronically;[33] the activities of local government bodies online, including holding sessions, meetings and assemblies;[34] collegial meetings of public administration bodies containing a real-time transmission of the meeting and multilateral communication in real time.[35]

---

26 Maciej Zieliński, Zbigniew Radwański, 'Wykładnia' 23.

27 Ibid. 23.

28 Ibid. 20.

29 The Act on Specific Solutions related to the Prevention, Counteracting and Control of Covid-19, Other Communicable Diseases and Crisis Situations Caused by Them of 2 March 2020 Journal of Laws of 2020, item 374, as amended, hereafter referred to as the Covid-19 Act.

30 Article 7 item 4 of the Covid-19 Act.

31 Article 14h of the Covid-19 Act.

32 Article 15 zzs of the Covid-19 Act; see also Piotr Rylski, 'Covid-19 and the Civil Justice in Poland' in Bart Krans and others, *Civil Justice and Covid-19 (Septentrio Reports 5 2020)* 43, 44.

33 Article 15 zzu of the Covid-19 Act.

34 Article 15 zzx of the Covid-19 Act.

35 Article 15 zzzi of the Covid-19 Act.

There have been significant systematic changes in other countries as well as within the EU, particularly evident under the new concept of "participation". In the COVID-19 era, participation is also accepted in the form of remote participation, as a result of such measures as a change in the interpretation of constitutional provisions allowing, at least for some MPs or senators, for remote participation in a session meeting and for remote voting within the legislative bodies (the Sejm or Senate). One of the first parliaments to do so was the European Parliament, which held its plenary session of 26 March 2020 completely online, including electronic voting. This is also how the committees of the European Parliament have been proceeding since March. Until now, MPs could only vote while physically present in the Parliament. No other procedure was admissible, mainly because of the narrow understanding of "directness" and "participation".

Another example is the amended interpretation of Article 120 of the Polish Constitution, according to which, for a session meeting to be validly held, the participation of at least half of the MPs is required. During the pandemic, this requirement has been considered met by online participation through electronic means of communication. With regard to this constitutional norm, it has been assumed that there is no need to amend the Constitution itself, and that an amendment to the Rules of Procedure of the Sejm sessions is sufficient.[36] Thus, a broad interpretation of the term "participation" was adopted. In Germany, to enable Bundestag meetings to be held online there was a proposal to amend the Constitution by adding Article 39(3): "The Bundestag will decide on the closing, resumption and *method of* holding sessions" which would allow proceedings to be conducted with simultaneous video and audio transmission.[37]

In particular, it is worth noting that in some EU Member States, including those with a higher degree of computerisation, the legislators reacted immediately also with regard to notarial transactions. Belgium is an example of a country where solutions to facilitate notarial transactions have been adopted, and it has taken a step further down the digitisation road by adopting The Royal Decree on the introduction of the digital Notarial Deed Database[38] (also known as the "NABAN"[39]) making the electronic signing of notarial deeds possible.

36 The admissibility of a remote session of the Sejm or Senate was decided by an amendment to the Rules and Regulations of Sejm Meetings and the Rules and Regulations Senate Meetings, http://www.sejm.gov.pl/prawo/regulamin/regsejm.htm dated 20 May 2020.

37 The analysis of Bundestag online sessions possibilities https://www.bundestag.de/resource/blob/690270/07e7b1aff547a62bbc7477281574de2c/WD-3-084-20-pdf-data.pdf accessed 1 June 2020.

38 In the original languages: '*Koninklijk besluit houdende de invoering van de Notariële Aktebank*'; '*Arrêté royal portant l'introduction de la Banque des actes notariés*'. The Royal Decree was published in the Belgian Official Gazette on 24 March 2020.

39 NABAN aims to create an integrated and secure system in which all notarial deeds are included in a single electronic database. This enables citizens directly to access the notarial deeds to

Additionally, on 10 April 2020, the Belgian Federation of Notaries introduced the possibility for a notary's employee or a trusted person to sign a notarial deed on the basis of a digital power of attorney. This allows notarial deeds to be signed without infringing the measures in place on social distancing during the COVID-19 lockdown.

The outlined examples illustrate how the approach has changed with regard to the notion of "directness" and "participation" during a pandemic in public and private spaces. These examples can be multiplied by referring to COVID-19 regulations adopted in many countries around the world. These changes will have a significant and probably irreversible impact on the interpretation and consistent meaning of the terms "directness" and "participation".

2.2. INTERPRETATION OF "DIRECTNESS" AND "PARTICIPATION" WHILE MAKING STATEMENTS OF INTENT AND IN CONTRACTS: GENERAL COMMENTS

From the perspective of Polish law, the provision relating to the effective filing of a statement of intent (Art 60 of the CCP) and the rules on interpreting a statement of intent and an agreement (Art 65 of the CCP), as well as the rules on filing a statement of intent and on concluding an agreement (Art 61 and Art 66 ff of the CCP), and indeed the general provisions relating to the form of a legal transaction (Art 73 ff of the CCP), do not exclude a new understanding of directness and participation related to the use of new technologies. Neither statutory nor contractual requirements concerning the form of a notarial deed prevent this inclusion (for instance, Art 158 of the CCP). The construction of each traditional concept of private law, in particular making a statement of intent, performing a legal transaction, or entering into a contract, retains its essence when using new technologies. The rules on the interpretation of statements of intent, as provided for in Article 65 of the CCP, remain unchanged.[40] Interpretation directives (subjective and objective[41]) are used both

---

which they are a party. The NABAN will serve as an authentic source for dematerialised (i.e. electronic) documents and will therefore have the same evidential value as traditional paper deeds. Consequently, through the process of this dematerialisation, it will be possible to sign notarial deeds electronically (which is impossible for paper deeds). For details see Olivia Oosterlynck, 'Digital power of attorney soon possible for the signature of notarial deeds', 24 April 2020 https://www.lexgo.be/en/papers/civil-law/property-law/digital-power-of-attorney-soon-possible-for-the-signature-of-notarial-deeds,136159.html.

40 Similar interpretative directives are adopted with varying degrees of detail in other jurisdictions; see more Ewa Rott-Pietrzyk, 'General standards for the interpretation of contracts under the Common European Sales Law' (CESL), (2014) 2 Z. Eur. Priv.r., 376 ff.

41 For more on general interpretative directives see Ewa Rott-Pietrzyk, 'General standards', 380 ff.

to assess whether a statement of intent was made at all, or whether a contract was actually entered into (Art 60 in connection with Art 65 of the CCP) and to determine the scope and meaning of the provisions constituting that statement or contract. The use of a video recording, or other NewTech tools, when concluding a contract does not render these directives useless. However, one of the elements of the context of a legal transaction, for example entering into a contract for the sale of real estate, is subject to change. This element is the method involving the use of new technologies. It does not affect the content of the contract itself, which is subject to interpretation in the context of NewTech according to the interpretative directives adopted in the relevant legal system. It might be argued that, by performing a legal transaction using NewTech, the likelihood of defects in the statement of intent is increased (for instance of an error,[42] threat,[43] or a lack of awareness and freedom[44]). However, such a threat cannot be eliminated even with a more traditional understanding of the terms "directness" and "participation". In addition, every legal system provides for solutions that protect the person making the statement under the influence of defects.[45] Their application will also eliminate the defectiveness of a legal action performed through the use of NewTech tools.

3. CHANGES IN THE APPROACH TO "DIRECTNESS" AND "PARTICIPATION" IN COURT PROCEEDINGS (eHEARINGS)

The COVID-19 pandemic has triggered or increased the number of online court hearings on a global scale in a very short time.[46] Arguments were initially raised in some countries for the inadmissibility of online hearings, including an infringement of the principle of directness of the procedure, digital exclusion and the lack of technological adjustment. During the first two months of the pandemic that narrative changed significantly, and hearings conducted fully online (with a new understanding of "directness" and "participation") have become a reality. There is no place in this contribution for an in-depth analysis of the procedural changes in the legislation in individual countries enabling eHearings. There are many examples of national legal systems where eHearing

42 See Article 84 of the PCC.

43 See Article 83 of the PCC.

44 See Article 82 of the PCC.

45 See Article 88 para 2 of the PCC.

46 More on this issue, with regard to particular countries, see Jeff Galway, Urs Hoffmann-Nowotny (eds), *Impact of COVID-19 on court Operations & Litigations Practice* (International Bar Association Committee 2020).

solutions have been adopted (either before COVID-19 as permanent[47] systemic solutions, or following COVID-19 as temporary solutions[48]) confirming the new approach to "directness" and "participation".

In the context of online court proceedings, it is also worth taking a look at the European soft law, namely the Guidelines on Electronic Evidence in Civil and Administrative Law, adopted by the Council of Europe on 30 January 2019.[49] The Guidelines are to be read together with the Explanatory Memorandum[50] which clarifies the provisions of the Guidelines and reveals the sources used in drawing up the Guidelines. Also noteworthy are the Council of Europe's efforts concerning the guidelines of Online Dispute Resolution (ODR),[51] which affect both evidence and proceedings. The Guidelines are the first international document explaining how courts should handle electronic evidence in civil and administrative proceedings. They were adopted in accordance with the national laws of the Member States of the Council of Europe and the human rights standards established in the case law of the European Court of Human Rights. Electronic evidence related to cloud computing, blockchain, AI algorithms is scarcely explained in the Guidelines or the Explanatory Memorandum. These types of electronic evidence are particularly challenging to courts and legal practitioners. All these types of electronic evidence refer to court digitalisation, but there is still a lack of international standards capable of regulating these questions.[52] This all has to be seen in the context of binding EU law. The increasing need to use electronic evidence in civil and administrative proceedings shows the development of the regulation of EU law in this respect.[53] Namely, the Regulation on Electronic Identification and Trust

---

47 Some countries, such as Germany, Lithuania, the Nordic countries and Slovenia; see in Bart Krans and others, *Civil Justice and Covid-19* (Septentrio Reports 5 2020).

48 For example, in Poland, ibid. As an example in Switzerland: on 16 April 2020, the Swiss government adopted the Ordinance on measures in the field of the judiciary and procedural law relating to COVID-19, https://www.bj.admin.ch/dam/data/bj/aktuell/news/2020/2020-04-16/vo-covid19-justiz-d.pdf see Urs Hoffmann-Nowotny, Sandrine Giroud, Switzerland in Jeff Galway, Urs Hoffmann-Nowotny (eds), *Impact of COVID-19 on court Operations & Litigations Practice* (International Bar Association Committee 2020) 95 ff.

49 Guidelines of the Committee of Ministers of the Council of Europe on electronic evidence in civil and administrative proceedings (Adopted by the Committee of Ministers on 30 January 2019, at the 1335th meeting of the Ministers' Deputies), 30 January 2019, CM(2018)169.

50 Explanatory Memorandum to the Guidelines, https://search.coe.int/cm/Pages/result_details.aspx?ObjectId=0900001680902e0e accessed 2 May 2020. This document explains the Guidelines in detail and delivers some examples of the relevant case law, national laws.

51 See https://www.coe.int/en/web/cdcj/online-dispute-resolution-mechanisms accessed 2 May 2020.

52 Remigijus Jokubauskas, Marek Świerczyński, 'Is revision of the Council of Europe guidelines on electronic evidence already needed?' (2020) 16(1) Utrecht Law Review 13–20, http://doi.org/10.36633/ulr.525.

53 To the extent on detailed information on the digital transformation of the civil justice see two monographs: Maria A. Biasiotti and others, 'Introduction: Opportunities and Challenges

Services for Electronic Transactions in the Internal Single Market (eIDAS)[54] establishes various forms of electronic evidence. It is worth underlining that the eIDAS regulation recognises the fundamental principle that electronic evidence should not be denied legal effect and admissibility as evidence in legal proceedings solely on the grounds that it is in an electronic form.[55] In terms of EU law, the Proposal for the Amendment of Regulation (EC) No 1206/2001 of 28 May 2001 on cooperation between the courts of the Member States in the taking of evidence in civil or commercial matters[56] is also worth taking into consideration. Based on this document, it can be stated that modern communications technology, in particular videoconferencing, which is an important means to simplify and accelerate the taking of evidence, is currently not used to its full potential.

In this context, European law (both binding law and soft law) shows that a different perception of "directness" and "participation" is necessary today, and there is no turning back from it.

4. RECOMMENDATIONS BY THE EUROPEAN LAW INSTITUTE

In Europe, as well as in the scientific community, much attention has been drawn to the need for a new understanding of the term "directness", as well as the possibility of performing activities using NewTech instead of being confined to the traditional understanding of *inter praesentes* activities, which requires the physical presence of parties. Particular attention should be paid to recommendations presented by scholars and experts collaborating within the European Law Institute.[57] They have formulated the ELI Principles for the COVID-19 crisis,[58] Principle 10 of which seems significant in light

for Electronic Evidence' in Maria A. Biasiotti and others (eds), *Handling and Exchanging Electronic Evidence Across Europe* (Cham 2018) 4 ff, and in: Alan Uzelac, Cornelis Hendrik (Remco) van Rhee (eds), *Transformation of Civil Justice, Ius Gentium: Comparative Perspectives on Law and Justice* (Springer International Publishing 2018).

54 Regulation (EU) No 910/2014 of the European Parliament and of the Council of 23 July 2014 on electronic identification and trust services for electronic transactions in the internal market and repealing Directive 1999/93/EC OJ L 257, 2014.

55 In particular, see Article 25(1), 35(1), 41(1), 43(1) of eIDAS.

56 Proposal for a Regulation of the European Parliament and of the Council amending Council Regulation (EC) No 1206/2001 of 28 May 2001 on cooperation between the courts of the Member States in the taking of evidence in civil or commercial matters (COM/2018/378 final).

57 Official page ELI https://www.europeanlawinstitute.eu/ accessed 2 May 2020.

58 https://www.europeanlawinstitute.eu/fileadmin/user_upload/p_eli/Publications/ELI_Principles_for_the_COVID-19_Crisis.pdf accessed 2 May 2020.

of the considered terms (with regard to private law), as well as Principle 5[59] (regarding public law). Principle 10 was entitled: Continuity of Relationships at a Distance. In Clause 1, it introduces the recommendation for national legislators to ensure that contracts can be concluded, management decisions made, and all other legal steps taken at a distance, including notarisation and other participation by notaries.[60] This recommendation is very important for all market sectors in which all notarial transactions play an important role. This applies, for instance, to trading in real estate, exercising corporate rights, or performing certain activities in the field of inheritance law. The ELI recommendations have been formulated in connection with COVID-19 and Principle 10 is aimed at ensuring continuity within the scope of its regulation. However, we accept that these recommendations can be quite valid and applicable, and not only in the context of COVID-19. The pandemic in this case is only a good excuse, a game changer, for introducing or making full use (where *de lege lata* are allowed) of the new rules of the "game" using the NewTech toolbox permanently. In commercial trade, but also in consumer or general trade, it is mainly about the possibility to perform various types of notarial transactions.

We should appreciate the rapid reaction of the ELI in being responsible for its ongoing monitoring of various phenomena of legal importance on the European scale and formulating recommendations or other types of soft law acts. Many of them may influence legislative changes in European Member States (where necessary), and may contribute to a different approach to legal interpretation or a change in awareness of the need to use these or other private law tools.[61] The ELI acts and recommendations, going beyond the awareness of science representatives, can also contribute to overcoming mental barriers and habits that make up the legal culture of a certain country. In the case of digitisation and digitalisation, this is certainly significant.

---

59 Principle 5 JUSTICE SYSTEM "(1) The judiciary should do all that is reasonably practicable to continue to conduct proceedings and trials, particularly though the use of secure video and other remote links where available to the courts […]".

60 Principle 10 CONTINUITY OF RELATIONSHIPS AT A DISTANCE in its (2) sounds: "States should ensure that measures taken due to the COVID-19 outbreak should not prevent the performance of ongoing contracts and other relationships to an extent that is more than necessary and, where possible, should permit performance at a distance."

61 There has been an equally rapid response in the US to ensure continuity in those market sectors where notarial transactions are necessary, both in terms of recommendations and legislative changes in individual states, see Margo H.K. Tank's ongoing study, David Whitaker, Liz Caires, Andrew Grant, 'Coronavirus: US Federal and state governments work quickly to enable remote online notarization and SBA PPP loans to meet global crisis' (DLA Piper 2020) https://www.dlapiper.com/en/us/insights/publications/2020/03/coronavirus-federal-and-state-governments-work-quickly-to-enable-remote-online-notarization/ accessed 20 May 2020.

5. REMOTE IDENTIFICATION WITH THE USE OF NEWTECH AND THE TERMS OF "DIRECTNESS" AND "PARTICIPATION"

5.1. INTRODUCTION: LEGAL ENGINEERING

A change in the understanding of the terms "directness" and "participation", both in the interpretation of the law and in the interpretation of a statement of intent or a contract, should be considered desirable. Not only does it help adapt these concepts to contemporary realities in connection with the COVID-19 pandemic, but above all, because it takes into account social changes (namely the transformation of societies into information societies) and technological changes, which inevitably determine the former. However, the correct use of new technologies in practice, while preserving all the functions of traditional private law institutions, through a new understanding of the terms "directness" and "participation" is no longer so obvious and technically simple.[62] Not all electronic tools allowing the possibility of direct contact can or should be used when performing transactions that are to have legal effects in trade. The issue is much more complicated. It requires taking into account various legal regulations concerning matters such as: the GDPR,[63] the obligation to maintain professional secrecy,[64] cybersecurity,[65] electronic identification, evidence (from electronic document, identification process, authorisation),[66] and the need for authenticity and integrity. In addition, the relevant technical standards applicable to the scope under consideration should also be taken into account.

The technologisation of law is a visible direction that is observed in practice in the science of law, in many cases not forced by circumstances, and is increasingly often in the legislative process. LegalTech,[67] combining IT

---

62 The technical side of the new ways of communicating may also involve a mental barrier for some traders or judges in terms of using NewTech tools; see Bart Krans, Anna Nylund, 'Concluding Remarks on Covid-19 and Civil Justice' in Bart Krans and others, *Civil Justice and Covid-19 (Septentrio Reports 5 2020)* 54 ff.

63 https://eur-lex.europa.eu/eli/reg/2016/679/oj accessed 10 May 2020.

64 Appropriate regulations concerning advocates, attorneys-at-law and others.

65 https://eur-lex.europa.eu/legal-content/EN/TXT/HTML/?uri=CELEX:32016L1148&from=PL accessed 10 May 2020.

66 https://eur-lex.europa.eu/legal-content/EN/TXT/HTML/?uri=CELEX:32014R0910&from=PL accessed 10 May 2020.

67 Sergii Schrebak, 'Integrating Computer Science into Legal Discipline: The Rise of Legal Programming' (2014) 1–33 https://papers.ssrn.com/sol3/papers.cfm?abstract_id=2496094 accessed 22 May 2020; Lawrence Lessig, 'Code is law. On Liberty in Cyberspace, Harvard Magazine' https://harvardmagazine.com/2000/01/code-is-law-html accessed 2 May 2020; Jordan Furlong, 'The evolution of the legal services market' http://www.law21.ca/2012/11/the-evolution-of-the-legal-services-market-stage1/ accessed 17 May 2020 http://www.law21.ca/

and legal knowledge, is already becoming a standard in trade, particularly in economic trade. Currently, many factors, especially in the areas of contract law and corporate law, have become transferred online. Therefore, it is necessary to interpret the provisions concerning such matters as the conclusion of a contract, the conditions of its validity and its execution in the context of using the tools provided by NewTech. COVID-19 has definitely had an intensifying effect on this phenomenon, but it can be assumed that the process will not stop when the pandemic subsides. The behaviour of trade participants acquired or developed during this time will certainly continue.

There is currently a pressing need for legislators to include norms for the use of LegalTech tools in national legal systems. LegalTech norms, as already mentioned, also take the form of soft law, which can change its nature over time. As a result of the solutions adopted by certain legislators, soft law often becomes binding law in particular legal systems,[68] and this is not really a new phenomenon. This can be compared to the process of shaping the *lex mercatoria*, where *lex mercatoria* norms were a response to legal and social phenomena (notwithstanding the legal regulations in force) in view of trading practices and needs (as norms that meet the requirements of trade). Over time, they have become statutory law in many cases.

A similar process is taking place today with regard to technical regulations aimed at the efficient operation of tools within the range of what is known as the LegalTech toolbox.[69] Many behaviours in cyberspace are produced by custom, they evolve into soft law and then into technological norms. Another phenomenon, as pointed out by W. Szpringer,[70] is the interaction of law and technology through a complex system of dependencies and interdependencies, since both law and technology contribute to regulating the behaviour of individuals (namely, the law as a system of orders and prohibitions, and technology as the actual restriction of the freedom of the entity using it).

There is no doubt that, in order to meet the requirements of "directness" and "participation" online, it is necessary to establish appropriate means of electronic communication. Depending on the type of legal transaction (a statement of intent by one party, a contract, a resolution of a collegial body, etc.) and the formal requirements (i.e. the form of the legal transaction), the requirements relating to the means of electronic communication will vary. Certain requirements will, therefore, be applicable to a contract for which neither the

2012/11/the-evolution-of-the-legal-services-market-stage-2/ accessed 17 May 2020 https://www.law21.ca/2012/11/the-evolution-of-the-legal-services-market-stage-3/ accessed 17 May 2020.

68 For example, some national legislators use of the DCFR when drafting new codes.

69 We use here an analogy to the concept of a toolbox within the DCFR regulation.

70 Włodzimierz Szpringer, 'Blockchain jako innowacja systemowa' [Blockchain as a system innovation], (2018) Poltext, 40.

law nor the agreement of the parties provides for formal requirements for its effectiveness, while others will apply to activities requiring secrecy, and others when the data provided are personal data, protected under the GDPR, and still others for regulated activities (namely resulting from sectoral regulations, for instance PSD2[71]). There are also different ways of identifying those who carry out the activities, verifying identity or providing evidence of an activity.

In the real world, when performing a legal action with the physical presence of the parties (face to face), "directness" and "participation" is realistically perceived by many human senses. In the case of "directness" and "participation" online, there is both a technological and an IT component. This involves the risk of external interference (manifested, for example, in the distortion of a statement of intent or a submission by another person), or an interruption in communication, which may result in a defective legal act. The electronic environment is not homogeneous; there are several technological levels, providing different levels of guarantees of authenticity and integrity, as well as guarantees as to the identity of the entities.

5.2. REMOTE IDENTIFICATION OF ENTITIES

Identification in the European Union is stipulated by Regulation (EU) No 910/2014 of the European Parliament and of the Council of 23 June 2014 on electronic identification and trust services for electronic transactions in the internal market and repealing Directive 1999/93/EC (OJ L 257, 25.8.2014)[72] (eIDAS). Article 3 of this regulation contains various types of definition regarding identification, such as: (1) "*electronic identification*" – the process of using personal identification data in electronic form uniquely representing either a natural or legal person, or a natural person representing a legal person; (2) "*electronic identification means*" – a material and/or immaterial unit containing personal identification data and used for authentication for an online service; (3) "*person identification data*" – a set of data enabling the identity of a natural or legal person, or a natural person representing a legal person to be established; (4) "*electronic identification scheme*" – a system for electronic identification under which electronic identification means are issued to natural or legal persons, or natural persons representing legal persons; and finally (5) "*authentication*"[73]

[71] https://eur-lex.europa.eu/legal-content/EN/TXT/HTML/?uri=CELEX:32015L2366&from=PL Directive (EU) 2015/2366 of the European Parliament and of the Council of 25 November 2015 accessed 10 May 2020.
On payment services in the internal market, amending Directives 2002/65/EC, 2009/110/EC and 2013/36/EU and Regulation (EU) No 1093/2010, and repealing Directive 2007/64/EC.

[72] https://eur-lex.europa.eu/legal-content/EN/TXT/?uri=uriserv%3AOJ.L_.2014.257.01.0073.01.ENG accessed 20 May 2020.

[73] Allessio Zaccaria and others, 'EU eIDAS Regulation Commentary' 2020 Nomos, 3 ff.

means an electronic process that enables the electronic identification of a natural or legal person, or the origin and integrity of data in electronic form to be confirmed.

eIDAS is neutral in terms of technology. European and global technological standards are applied in order to execute it.[74] In this contribution, we show examples of technical standards in order to demonstrate that also in technical standards dealing with means of identification with a high level of confidence, "directness" and "participation" can be safely implemented online.

As regards remote identification, it is worth mentioning the technical standard ISO 29115,[75] which sets out four levels of identity authentication. The table below shows how identity can be verified. At LoA2-LoA3 identification levels, namely medium and high ones, it is permissible to verify identity remotely.

Table 1. ISO 29115 identification levels (own study[76])

Level	Description	Identity verification method
LoA1 (low)	Low or no confidence in the declared identity	Own declaration
LoA2 (medium)	Some confidence in the declared identity	Proof of identity through the use of identity information from an authorised source
LoA3 (high)	High confidence in the declared identity	Proof of identity through the use of information from an authorised source and verification
LoA4 (very high)	Very high confidence in the declared identity	Proof of identity through the use of identity information from an authorised source, plus verification and a personal appearance

Source: Compiled by the authors.

ISO 29115 should be considered a guideline for entities implementing methods of electronic identification.

At a global level, the standard SP 800-63,[77] adopted by the National Institute of Standards and Technology at the US Department of Commerce,[78] is relevant to the general framework of determining identity using means of authentication, attestation and assertion in digital systems.[79] It comprises:

- SP 800-63A Enrolment and Identity Proofing;

74 Delegation in Article 30 pt. 4 of eIDAS.
75 https://www.iso.org/standard/45138.html accessed 4 June 2020.
76 Prepared on the basis of standards and private unpublished materials of Michał Tabor, https://www.linkedin.com/in/michaltabor/ accessed 4 June 2020.
77 *Assertion* – a predicate placed in the code. It indicates that the programmer assumes the truthfulness of a certain predicate (certain relations).
78 https://pages.nist.gov/800-63-3/sp800-63b.html accessed 28 May 2020.
79 https://www.nist.gov/tpo/department-commerce accessed 28 May 2020.

- SP 800-63B Authentication and Lifecycle Management;
- SP 800-63C Federation and Assertions.

The standard SP 800-63, like ISO 29115, refers to identification and methods of authenticating identity. It introduces four levels of identity reliability (see Table 2). It is worth noting that for the verification of identity under levels IAL2 and IAL3, online verification of identity is permitted. Al level IAL3, this is done online by a trained employee, namely a real-time remote connection and the transmission of sounds and image, combined with the possibility of verifying this image with an ID photo.

Table 2. 800-63 standard identification levels (own study)

Level	Description	Identity verification method
IAL1 (weak) low confidence	It is not required to associate a certain entity with an identity in the real world	Own declaration
IAL2 (fair) average confidence	Proving and verifying the connection of identity in the real world	Remote or physical verification of identity
IAL3. (strong) high confidence	Proving and verifying the connection of identity in the real world. Confirmation of identity	Physical verification of identity by a trained employee
IAL3 Superior	IAL3 plus biometric pattern	IAL3 requirements plus biometric verification

Source: Compiled by the authors.

Both these standards are, in fact, technical standards, with a significant impact on the application of law, such as the eIDAS Regulation. They allow for online identity verification, for instance by video-verification, also in situations where the "directness" of the contact or the "participation" of the person whose identity is being verified is required for authentication. This is another argument for the necessity of a different, modernised understanding of "directness" and "participation".

5.3. RISKS ASSOCIATED WITH THE NEW APPROACH TO "DIRECTNESS" AND "PARTICIPATION"[80]

Along with the main topic of this contribution, it is worth looking also at the risks associated with using NewTech and the new concept of "directness" and "participation". These risks are not insignificant at all. The context of COVID-19, which has become the starting point for accelerated digitisation,

[80] The risks are so extensive that they have to be studied separately in a separate publication.

has significantly highlighted the risks associated with digitisation and the use of NewTech at various levels. First of all, the social stratification has deepened, with some people having access to modern communication tools and others who are digitally excluded. This exclusion can be observed in many dimensions, network access, skills, proficiency in the use of electronic tools, the quality of the equipment used (e.g. not having modern audio-visual equipment prevents the full use of online services). To a lesser extent, this is also visible in business (in B2B relations), where the risks are relatively small. It could be said that in B2B relations, the need to use NewTech for efficient and continuous operation in times of pandemic outweighs the risks. To a greater extent, however, the risks associated with digital exclusion are revealed through the social aspects, e.g. access to education, information, state institutions and healthcare, or participation in social life, which have been transferred online (e.g. cultural and training events).

The use of new technologies is therefore a major challenge not only in terms of ensuring cybersecurity, the certainty of trading using NewTech, or privacy in a broad sense (not only in terms of GDPR and personal data). This challenge also includes addressing digital exclusion and discrimination. It is also worth noting the voices signalling the possibility of discrimination against people (not only because of access to IT infrastructure, but also because of factors such as skin colour, gender and age[81]). This discrimination can translate into human rights, such as access to courts or access to justice in general. In addition, the pandemic, both in the spring (March, April 2020) and now (October 2020), restricts the possibility of functioning "traditionally", and the fear of infection makes a number of people (especially the elderly) less exposed to the outside world. Without digital skills, they have limited access to various types of services, such as communication with the state administration, services related to health (e.g. video-consultancy or checking the results of examinations in the system), banking services, notarial activities and the aforementioned access to courts.

In the autumn of 2020, there is no longer any doubt that digitisation is necessary and will continue (occupying further areas of human activity). In the context of COVID-19, it is also an important tool for limiting the possibility of contagion. It would therefore be appropriate to take action at both European

81 This subject is addressed, for example, by Eric Showers, Nathan Tindall, Todd Davies, 'Equality of Participation Online Versus Face to Face. An Analysis of the Community Forum Deliberative Methods Demonstration', https://papers.ssrn.com/sol3/cf_dev/AbsByAuth.cfm?per_id=1076975 (accessed 8 October 2020); see also the Report of The European Institute for Gender Equality (EIGE), Gender equality and youth: opportunities and risks of digitalisation, https://op.europa.eu/fr/publication-detail/-/publication/1baab82a-1007-11ea-8c1f-01aa75ed71a1 (accessed 8 October 2020); The focus paper from 29 May 2018 of the European Union Agency For Fundamental Rights, #BigData: Discrimination in data-supported decision making, https://fra.europa.eu/sites/default/files/fra_uploads/fra-2018-focus-big-data_en.pdf (accessed 8 October 2020).

and national level to eliminate discrimination and digital exclusion in areas where online action is necessary. Addressing these risks will make the new approach to directness and participation less of a burden at all levels of human activity, including those of legal significance. This value, if it is developed, would also remain in the post-virus era. Eliminating these risks would mean that the use of new technology would not affect certain essential values, like the right to a fair trial or the right to defence when applied to the activity of courts, for instance. Considering these risks, in order to see the new understanding of directness and participation in terms of permanent change in all important fields of human activity, the quality of the participation and equality while using online platforms has to be guaranteed.

6. ON A FINAL NOTE

The analysis of the current state of the use of NewTech due to COVID-19 leads the authors to the conclusion that the new approach to "directness" and "participation" in a legal sense has undoubtedly become a global fact. As a result of COVID-19 (acting as a kind of "game changer"), there has been a rapid development in the rules of the game as far as communicating on all levels of human activity is concerned. Without this COVID kick, it would likely take years to change these rules, through a slower natural process. However, now that it is here, we believe there is no return to the pre-pandemic status. The only factor that, after the pandemic, might make it difficult to continue the extensive use of NewTech (and to accept a different approach to "directness" and "participation") in relations of legal significance is the human factor, namely human habits, mental barriers, and the belief that what is old and what is known is better than anything new. It is possible that in a few years' time, the developments that we see being applied today to remove doubts about the understanding of the analysed terms (adjusted to the NewTech tools) will themselves be out of date. This is mainly due to the fact that the meaning of these terms will have become quite obvious.

In the context discussed in this contribution, it is worth adding that in the autumn of 2020 the European Commission recognised the need to improve and facilitate electronic trading. As a result, a number of legislative initiatives have emerged. These are reflected, in particular, in the announcement of a revision of the iEIDAS Regulation, and more specifically the Proposal for a Regulation of the European Parliament and of the Council on Markets in Crypto-assets, amending Directive (EU) 2019/1937;[82] as well as the Proposal for a Regulation

82 See: https://ec.europa.eu/finance/docs/law/200924-crypto-assets-proposal_en.pdf (accessed 8 October 2020) COM (2020) 593/3 2020/0265 (COD).

of the European Parliament and of the Council on a pilot regime for market infrastructures based on distributed ledger technology.[83] It can therefore be said that the new approach of "directness" and "participation" has undoubtedly become permanent in the EU, and seems to be permanently secured at least in the short to medium term. In other words, the change in understanding and use of these terms are almost certain to become permanent after the crisis.

83 See: https://ec.europa.eu/finance/docs/law/200924-distributed-ledger-technology-proposal_en.pdf (accessed 8 October 2020) COM (2020) 594/3 2020/0267 (COD).

THE POTENTIAL OF THE COVID-19 CRISIS TO CAUSE LEGAL "DISRUPTION" TO CONTRACTS AND CONTRACT LAW

Christian TWIGG-FLESNER*

This contribution explores whether the COVID-19 crisis has the potential to cause legal disruption to the legal regime for contracts. It first sketches features of the COVID-19 crisis and its effect on the economic and social context of contracts, before setting out a four-step methodology to categorise legal responses to the crisis. It then develops a specific conception of legal disruption, based on Christensen's theory of disruptive technology, which posits that legal disruption occurs once the pre-crisis legal regime for contracts (whether entirely or partially) is displaced by new provisions first targeted at the effects of the crisis. It concludes that the crisis has the potential to cause legal disruption but that this outcome is not inevitable.

---

* University of Warwick. My thanks to Roger Brownsword, Hans Micklitz and the anonymous referee for their comments.

1. SETTING THE SCENE: COVID-19, DISRUPTION AND WHAT IS DIFFERENT

The first half of 2020 was unprecedented in the way the COVID-19 pandemic changed economic and social activities: many businesses were forced to suspend their activities altogether or modify their operations in accordance with social distancing requirements; home-working and home-studying instantly replaced face-to-face activities, and video-conferencing became the alternative to face-to-face meetings. Consumers had to deal with multiple changes at once: many suffered a reduction or complete loss of their income; activities already booked and paid for (such as travel or concerts) were cancelled; and many everyday retail shops had to close for a long period of time. Social activities in cafes, bars and restaurants ceased altogether. Many businesses and consumers have been faced with the economic consequences of the pandemic:[1] for businesses pressures came from preserving their cash-reserves in the face of business disruptions and demands from consumers for refunds; for consumers, recovering prepayments for services which would no longer be provided and having to maintain regular payments for rent, mortgages and loans became challenges. Undoubtedly, the COVID-19 pandemic has caused a huge amount of disruption to daily life.

This contribution focuses on a different kind of disruption: the disruptive effect of the COVID-19 pandemic on law, particularly on contracts and contract law. "Disruption" has become a popular, and perhaps over-used, term in recent times thanks to the impact of digital technology on contract law and other areas of law.[2] In this contribution, I will use the term in quite a specific sense,[3] based on the theory of disruptive technology developed by Clayton Christensen.[4] In his theory, the term "disruption" has a narrower meaning than its ordinary dictionary definition, and I will explain below how this more precise notion of "disruption" can be translated into the contract law sphere to serve as a method for gauging the impact of any new development on existing legal regimes. I will say more about this below, but it is important to stress from the outset that the

---

1 The OECD have described the economic impact as "the most severe economic recession in nearly a century": OECD, 'The world economy on a tightrope' http://www.oecd.org/economic-outlook/june-2020/ accessed 11 June 2020.

2 Christian Twigg-Flesner, 'Disruptive Technology – Disrupted Law? How the Digital Revolution affects (Contract) Law' in Alberto De Franceschi (ed), *European Contract Law and the Digital Single Market* (Intersentia 2016).

3 The "disruption threshold" in my conception of "legal disruption" is ultimately higher than that used by others, e.g., the more complex model developed by Hin-Yan Liu, Matthijs Maas, John Danaher, Luisa Scarcella, Michaela Lexer and Leonard van Rompaey, 'Artificial intelligence and legal disruption: a new model for analysis' (2020) 12 Law, Innovation and Technology 205.

4 Clayton Christensen, *The innovators' dilemma* (Harvard Business Review Press 1997).

mere fact that something new has emerged which requires some kind of change to existing legal regimes does not mean that law has been "disrupted" in the sense that I will use it.

My starting point is a more general one: legal scholars and practitioners are all too familiar with the need to test the application of existing legal regimes to new situations – this much is routine work for lawyers. I use the term "legal regime" in this contribution simply as an umbrella term for legal rules (whether based on legislation, civil codes or case law), regulatory provisions which directly or indirectly relate to contracts, codes of conduct, and enforcement procedures.[5]

Many legal regimes have features which are designed to have a built-in degree of flexibility which facilitates their application in a wide range of circumstances, so it is often a question of how relevant provisions of existing legal regimes should be interpreted and applied to new situations. However, sometimes, a new development is not easily covered by existing legal regimes. This can happen because its underlying principles or concepts, or its substantive provisions, do not cover such a new phenomenon. At this point, lawyers will work out where the gaps or shortcomings in the existing legal regime are, and identify possible ways of addressing these. Usually, this will lead to incremental reforms to the legal regime, perhaps with the addition of a small number of provisions to ensure that existing legal regimes are adapted to cover new developments.

Nowhere has this been more apparent in recent times than the impact of digital technology on new ways of transacting and the debates about how law needs to adapt. Numerous books and articles have been written about the digital revolution and its impact on both commercial and consumer contracts,[6] and some legislation at national, regional and international levels has been adopted.[7] Often, this retains a high degree of coherence with established legal regimes, often by relying on translation tools such as "functional equivalence"[8] and "technological neutrality".[9] Entirely new legal provisions which concern digital contracting specifically have rarely been introduced, and where they have, usually by analogy to established provisions. Whether retaining existing legal rules with

---

5 For present purposes, there is no need to engage with the literature surrounding legal regimes, the rule of law and the political dimension. On this, see e.g. William Hurst, *Ruling before the law* (Cambridge University Press 2018) ch1, esp 19–27.

6 For example, Reiner Schulze and Dirk Staudenmayer, *Digital Revolution – Challenges for Contract Law* (Nomos/Hart 2016); Alberto De Franceschi (ed), *European Contract Law and the Digital Single Market* (Intersentia 2016); Alberto De Franceschi and Reiner Schulze (eds), *Digital Revolution – New Challenges for Law* (Beck/Nomos 2019).

7 For example, chapter 3 of part 1 of the Consumer Rights Act 2015 on digital content (UK) or Directive (EU) 2019/770 on digital content and digital services (EU).

8 I.e., ways of describing how a legal requirement adopted for the physical world can be met by digital technology.

9 These concepts underpin the provisions of the UN Convention on the Use of Electronic Communications in International Contracts 2005, for instance. On "functional equivalence" generally, see David Harvey, *Collisions in the Digital Paradigm* (Hart 2019) 46–63.

little modification or supplementation is the best legal response to the digital revolution may be open to debate, but the steps taken thus far indicate how legal regimes are generally fairly adaptable to unforeseen and novel circumstances.[10]

The same is true of contracts: For many contracts, particularly commercial contracts, parties are expected to, and do, make provision for dealing with unforeseen circumstances which might arise during the lifetime of the contract. This can be done through specific terms dealing with matters such as currency-related price variations, or general terms on force majeure events or hardship affecting one of the parties.[11]

Fundamentally, the COVID-19 crisis could also be regarded as a type of "new development", albeit one of a rather different kind. There is an important difference between the COVID-19 crisis and, say, new technological developments. Many technological developments, including the digital revolution, concern the invention and adoption of new ways of doing things (such as conducting business and consumer transactions), or new objects of legal concern (e.g. the treatment of non-physical assets,[12] such as digitally stored information or data). The difference is that, from the perspective of contract law at least, the COVID-19 pandemic has not presented us with new ways of doing things as such (although lockdowns and social distancing are, of course, new forms of behaviour) but rather has transformed the background context within which contracts are concluded and performed (or rather, no longer performed). In other words, the "new development" in the COVID-19 pandemic is the drastic change to the economic and social context for contracts and contract law. The challenge this has created for contracts and contract law is whether existing legal regimes for contracts provide the tools for managing the impact of this crisis on all kinds of contracts, and, to the extent that they do not, to adjust the legal regime as necessary to mitigate the effects of the COVID-19 crisis. A particular difficulty in this regard has been the need for rapid action, which left little, if any, room for deliberation over the detail of any changes to be introduced. There is one further difference: technological developments tend to be progressive and evolve gradually, albeit at varying pace.[13] The changes prompted by this tend to be long-lasting. The impact of the COVID-19 pandemic is likely to be relatively time-limited in its initial impact, and one would hope that even the aftermath of

---

10 For an excellent discussion of how adaptable contract law is to technological developments, see Eliza Mik, 'The resilience of contract law in light of technological change' in Michael Furmston (ed), *The Future of the Law of Contract* (Routledge 2020).

11 See e.g. International Chamber of Commerce (ICC), 'ICC Force Majeure and Hardship Clauses' https://iccwbo.org/publication/icc-force-majeure-and-hardship-clauses/ accessed 11 June 2020.

12 Chiara Zilioli, 'Crypto-assets: legal characterisation and challenges under private law' (2020) 45 European Law Review 251.

13 Lyria Bennett Moses, 'Recurring Dilemmas: The Law's Race to Keep up with Technological Change' [2007] University of Illinois Journal of Law, Technology and Policy 239.

this pandemic will be relatively short-lived, and the economic and social context will improve significantly.

Despite these differences, the steps which are taken to develop a legal response to the COVID-19 pandemic essentially mirror those that would be taken in respect of other new developments which affect existing legal regimes. However, whilst the particular legal changes prompted by the COVID-19 pandemic are intended to operate for a short period of time, there is a possibility that the legal regimes for contracts (and, indeed, many other areas of law) might be changed, and possibly disrupted, in a lasting way. Whether this outcome is inevitable is the question I seek to explore in this contribution. I will do so in two sections: first, I will chart the four steps of the legal response to the challenges created by the COVID-19 pandemic; secondly, I develop further my particular conception of "disruption" before explaining how contract law might be disrupted by the legal responses to the pandemic and beyond.

2. STEPS FOR DEVELOPING A LEGAL RESPONSE TO THE COVID-19 CRISIS

In this part, I will set out what I regard as the 4 steps in which changes to the legal regime for contracts could be made as a result of the COVID-19 crisis. Before I do so, it is first necessary to explain how a crisis such as the COVID-19 pandemic differs from other new developments.

2.1. FEATURES OF A CRISIS AND RELEVANCE FOR LAW

It is useful to clarify what is meant by "crisis". According to the Oxford English Dictionary, "crisis" can have multiple meanings. In popular usage, it is defined as "A vitally important or decisive stage in the progress of anything; a turning-point; also, a state of affairs in which a decisive change for better or worse is imminent; now applied *esp.* to times of difficulty, insecurity, and suspense in politics or commerce".[14] In this sense, the COVID-19 pandemic is, indeed, a crisis in that it is a decisive stage in the progress of many aspects of daily life and it is certainly a time of difficulty and insecurity, as well as suspense in commerce. In a medical context, "crisis" refers to "the turning-point of a disease for better or worse", or "the point in the progress of a disease when an important development or change takes place which is decisive of recovery or death".[15] In either meanings, a crisis is a defining point in time at which there is a decisive change, where continuity is disrupted and a juncture materialises. The actions taken at this

14 *Oxford English Dictionary* online, entry for "crisis".

15 Ibid.

point may influence the ultimate direction that is taken – it can determine whether a patient will recover or die, or whether a difficult economic situation worsens or is turned around.

Although a crisis can be personal, in that it affects an individual person (e.g. due to an injury), the crisis caused by the COVID-19 pandemic does not merely affect individuals in discrete instances but has a simultaneous collective impact on large numbers of individuals and businesses alike. For present purposes, a crisis can therefore be understood as a severe event which affects a large number of persons (natural and legal) in such a way that it could significantly worsen their position. In particular, it is the effects or consequences of a crisis which are felt – the effects of a crisis constitute a major shift in the general context (rather than the specific context of, say, a particular contract) within which all activities occur, and determines how such activities can be carried out in the changed circumstances created by the crisis.

Understood in this way, it is possible to distinguish a crisis and its effects on the one hand, from novel or unexpected occurrences on the other hand. The latter are essentially of a discrete nature and which do not change the background context against which all activities (including contracts) occur, but instead have a more isolated and less far-reaching effect (although can still be quite dramatic for the parties to particular contracts affected). To this, one might add the occurrence of an unexpected event which affects multiple persons at once, but not on the same scale as a crisis. For instance, the cancellation of the coronation procession for Edward VII or the UK's decision to withdraw from the European Union were both events which affected multiple persons, and the contracts they had concluded,[16] but neither event would truly be described as a crisis. In contrast, the impacts of the First and Second World Wars were far more severe and would both cross the crisis threshold.

This distinction is important in order to explore the implications of a crisis for law and potential changes to be made to the law compared to its pre-crisis form. When it comes to contracts, the discrete impact of unexpected circumstances on a specific contract should be manageable under current legal regimes.[17] The same should be true for multiple contracts affected in a similar way where the unexpected circumstances are such as to impact multiple contracts at once. However, with a crisis, the scale of the circumstances and the consequences which flow from this – whether directly or through action taken by governments in responding to the crisis itself – are such as to severely test the suitability of the current law in providing a suitable means of responding to these consequences.

---

16 See *Krell v Henry* [1903] 2 KB 740; *Herne Bay Steam Boat Co v Hutton* [1903] 2 KB 603 (both on frustration); *Griffith v Brymer* (1903) 19 TLR 434 (mistake).

17 Some elements of current legal regimes may have their origins in earlier periods of crisis, e.g. the first or second world war.

Having considered why a crisis might pose particular challenges for law which do not arise to the same extent as a result of unexpected circumstances of lesser severity, I now turn to set out the steps that might be followed in considering whether, and how, existing law might have to be adapted in order to better manage the consequences of a crisis. When faced with a crisis which affects a huge number of contracts at once, it is possible to identify four steps to determine what the implications for the legal regime for contracts might be: first, the application of existing provisions is tested; secondly, insofar as existing provisions do not provide adequate solutions, or to the extent that those solutions would be unduly burdensome on one or both of the parties, new provisions are introduced; thirdly, provisions intended to have temporary effect have to be unravelled so as to revert to the original legal regime; and finally, a period of reflection to consider whether law reform of a lasting kind is appropriate.

2.2. STEP 1: ESTABLISHING THE LIMITS OF EXISTING LAW

A first step will be to understand the impact of the crisis on contracts and contract law. As explained earlier, a crisis and its consequences significantly alter the context within which all activities, including contracts, take place. Among the consequences of the COVID-19 pandemic are the restriction or outright suspension of economic activity across many industry sectors, restrictions on travel and transport, cancellation of all events and activities involving groups of people, and a significant impact on the income of many individuals because they have been furloughed or lost their job altogether.

These consequences can affect contracts in various ways. The most common types of impact are:

(1) the performance of a contract may no longer be possible at all;
(2) it may still be possible to perform the contract, but doing so would cause hardship, or be very onerous, for one of the parties;
(3) performance would still be possible but the purpose for which one or both parties concluded the contract has gone;
(4) in the case of long-term or subscription contracts, there may be an impact on the ability of either or both parties to fulfil their contractual obligations for some of the contract duration, depending on the length of time the crisis and its consequences subsist;
(5) there will be a delay in performing the contract;
(6) a party may not be able to perform all its obligations in full, e.g. due to limited supplies for multiple contracts;
(7) a party may not have sufficient financial resources to pay for the other party's performance.

In respect of each of these situations (and there will be others), a first step will be to check whether the terms of an affected contract which address unforeseen circumstances and their consequences for that contract provide an answer.[18] Contracts often make specific provision as to what should happen if a contract can no longer be performed as agreed and the parties will respond accordingly. A contract might allocate the specific risk which has materialised to one of the parties.[19] Many standard form contracts will include a force majeure clause and/or a hardship clause, in particular. Such clauses spell out the kinds of events or circumstances triggering their application, often in considerable detail, and stipulate the impact this has on the parties' obligations to perform. Whether the COVID-19 pandemic and its consequences trigger a clause in a particular contract will depend on its wording – if the particular reason which one or both parties seek to rely on is not covered by the wording of the clause, it will not apply, and the parties have to fall back on the relevant rules on the impact of post-formation unforeseen circumstances under the applicable law.

In the absence of a relevant contract term, or where such a term does not cover the particular situation, the rules of the applicable law on post-formation unforeseen circumstances[20] have to be considered to determine, first, if the circumstances which have arisen are such that these rules are engaged, and secondly, what result(s) these rules mandate. The law governing a contract will usually provide rules of some kind or another to come to the aid of the parties to a contract which has been significantly affected by an unforeseen event beyond the control of the parties. However, the scope of such national rules varies. For instance, the doctrine of frustration in English law is quite narrow, and not available for instances of hardship alone.[21] French law on force majeure is only available when performance of a contract has become impossible,[22] although a separate provision on hardship provides an additional basis for dealing with instances when performance is not impossible but would be unduly onerous for one party.[23] Germany has its well-known provision on disruption to the circumstances forming the basis of the contract.[24] Many legal

---

18 For English law, see Hugh Beale and Christian Twigg-Flesner, 'COVID-19 and English Contract Law' in this volume.

19 See e.g., *Salam Air SAOC v Latam Airlines Group SA* [2020] EWHC 2414 (Comm), where the inability to use a dry-leased aircraft due to Coronavirus restrictions did not result in frustration because the risk of "any … occurrence of whatever kind which shall deprive [Salam Air] of the use, possession and enjoyment" had been assumed by the lessee.

20 As between legal systems, these rules differ in both their scope and the type of rule (frustration, force majeure, hardship, disruption to the basis of the bargain, impediment etc), so this generic term is used here.

21 See Hugh Beale and Christian Twigg-Flesner, 'COVID-19 and English Contract Law' in this volume.

22 Article 1218 of the French Civil Code.

23 Article 1195 of the French Civil Code.

24 Article 313 of the German Civil Code (BGB) ("*Störung der Geschäftsgrundlage*").

systems have versions of the principle of *rebus sic stantibus* in a broad sense.[25] Consequences range from termination of the contract, to renegotiation, to temporary suspension of performance (where the impact of the contract is not permanent).

In the context of the COVID-19 pandemic, the application of existing legal regimes in the very different social and economic context which has arisen leads to the key question of whether existing law still works in these new circumstances. Thus, it will have to be examined whether an existing legal regime covers the particular impact of the crisis on each contract *and* that the results the law points to are appropriate in the circumstances. This will inform an assessment of whether an existing legal regime is sufficiently robust/suitable for covering all of the ways in which a contract might be affected, and whether it provides an appropriate solution. It is important to consider both of these aspects separately. Whilst the former is a precondition for the latter, it may be that the results or solutions provided for in law are not appropriate in the circumstances even where the provisions are triggered by the crisis. For instance, the English doctrine of frustration, where it applies, leads to the result that the contract in question is immediately and automatically brought to an end. However, this all-or-nothing approach may not be what either party wants.

In short, this first step will involve testing whether the consequences of the crisis can be resolved adequately through the application of existing legal rules, or whether their application reveals or reinforces shortcomings in the law which necessitate further action. The former result suggests that existing law suffices to deal with the consequences of the crisis and no further specific action is required. The latter, however, will mean that further action is required.

2.3. STEP 2: SPECIFIC STEPS TO MANAGE THE CRISIS

Specifically, with regard to contracts, the question will be whether any changes to the existing legal regime for contracts are required, and if so, which. One can immediately think of a number of points of attack: (1) the conditions for triggering rules on dealing with changed circumstances, i.e. the events and consequences which must occur as well as other conditions such as a lack of foreseeability or absence of risk allocation to one of the contracting parties; (2) the effect of engaging those rules: are the parties automatically discharged from their obligations, are they obliged to renegotiate the contract, or something else?

As noted above, existing legal doctrines dealing with the impact of unforeseen circumstances beyond the control of the parties to a contract are generally well-established features of national contract law, and have been

25 E.g. Croatia: Obligations Act, Articles 369–372; Switzerland: Code of Obligations, Article 119.

deployed for a long time. Of course, elements of these doctrines are undoubtedly open to critique, for example with regard to their scope of application or the consequences for a contract they provide. I pointed out earlier that the extent to which any provision of a legal regime is sufficiently flexible and future-proof can be debated, and this will apply in the same way to the specific legal provisions dealing with the impact of unforeseen circumstances on existing contracts, whether about the interpretation of the relevant provision or the adequacy of the consequences provided for once those provisions have been engaged. In the normal course of things, the features of a particular legal regime tend to be the focus of a steady stream of scholarly writings, and may also occasionally catch the eye of law reform bodies or Parliaments, and law reform proposals might be considered. However, it is rare for reform to legal regimes for contracts to be high-priority issue. Occasionally, a case will come before a court which raises a new question about the way in which the law currently operates, whether that be a question about the scope of the specific elements of the law or questions unresolved by the law as it stands. Sometimes, this might prompt a reform initiative,[26] but more often than not, it ends up as part of the general narrative about the area of law concerned.

This means that there may be existing discussions about potential reforms to the legal regime for contracts in a particular jurisdiction, and the fact that testing the application of the current legal regime to situations affected by the COVID-19 pandemic could prompt a call for such reform debates to be reinvigorated – after all, there may ready-made reform proposals sitting on a metaphorical shelf, waiting to be dusted off and turned into law. However, whilst this may be a tempting response, there are good reasons not to expedite the implementation of existing reform proposals in these circumstances.

Instead, the fact that existing legal regimes are inadequate for the circumstances created by the COVID-19 crisis might make targeted action to address specific issues caused by the crisis more appropriate. Deciding on what course of action to take requires consideration of several questions: first, it must be determined what sort of action is required to address the gaps in the existing legal regime which are causing concern in the context of the crisis, i.e. the substantive changes that are needed in order to ensure that an adequate solution for the impact of the crisis on contracts is provided. It might be feared that such targeted measures could undermine, or even reverse, express risk allocations made under a contract, and affect any insurance cover obtained by

---

26 A good example is the enactment of the Law Reform (Frustrated Contracts) Act 1943 to provide clarity regarding the restitutionary obligations after a contract has been frustrated, partly prompted by the House of Lords decision in *Fibrosa Spolka Akcyjna v Fairbairn Lawson Combe Barbour Ltd* [1943] AC 32. See *Hansard*, vol 128, columns 136–151 for the illuminating second reading debate in the House of Lords.

the contracting parties to cover the risks assumed by them. Furthermore, it might prompt an objection that legal certainty[27] or predictability[28] could be undermined by significantly changing the legal regime which existed when a contract was entered into. It might also affect the potential for parties to reach an amicable and negotiated resolution by renegotiating the terms of the contract in a way that suits their commercial relationship.

Secondly, the appropriate mechanism for introducing such changes needs to be identified. Lawyers might instinctively look at new legal rules, i.e. changes made through legislation. However, this is not necessarily the only available route; for instance, changes could instead be made to codes of conduct operated by trade associations, or by changing regulatory rules, principles or guidance notes, for example in respect of credit agreements. A combination of different mechanisms might be appropriate.[29]

Thirdly, and crucially, a decision will have to be made as to whether such changes are going to be of a temporary nature and be confined to the duration of the crisis, its impacts, and the immediate aftermath (recovery phase), or whether the changes that will be made are going to be unlimited as to duration and therefore remain in place after the crisis and the recovery period has ended. A time-limited response has the advantage that it can be adopted more rapidly and in all likelihood without too many objections, because such changes would be understood to be there to provide an immediate solution to the specifics of the crisis (e.g. impact on tenancies and eviction proceedings). A response which is intended to operate on a permanent basis would require much more careful development and therefore require much more time and care, as its effects would be lasting. However, there may not be any time for more careful development – even if there are existing reform proposals, because these will probably not have been designed with the severe circumstances created by the crisis in mind. Using a crisis as the impetus for pushing through significant reforms to the law, rather than providing a temporary patch for the duration of the crisis, increases the risk that rules drafted under pressure may transpire to be unworkable or so poorly drafted that they create more problems that they solve. So a time-limited response as an immediate reaction would be more appropriate to get through the period of crisis.

---

27 "Legal certainty" has multiple traditions. See John Linarelli, 'Legal Certainty: a common law view and a critique' in Mark Fenwick, Mathias Siems and Stefan Wrbka (eds), *The Shifting Meaning of Legal Certainty in Comparative and Transnational Law* (Bloomsbury 2017).

28 See Roy Goode, 'The Codification of Commercial Law' (1988) 14 Monash University Law Review 135–157, explaining why "predictability" is preferable to "certainty" (at 150).

29 In the UK, for instance, payment holidays in respect of credit agreements and mortgages were introduced by amending Financial Conduct Authority Guidance rather than substantive laws, which has had the unfortunate consequence that obligations on creditors under the Consumer Credit Act 1974 to issue consumer debtors with notices of arrears after two missed instalments still had to be adhered to.

2.4. STEP 3: UNRAVELLING TEMPORARY ADJUSTMENTS

The third step is one which would not normally be relevant when dealing with reforms to the legal regime for contracts in response to new developments such as new technology or business models. It is, however, integral to the way legal regimes are adapted in response to the COVID-19 crisis. Reaching step 3 means that the moment will have come to unravel the temporary changes which were made in response to the crisis. As temporary changes expire or are repealed, the pre-crisis legal regime applies once again. This will usually be done because the context in which those changes were introduced in the first place is no longer acute – for instance, businesses may be able to open up again (even if only in a limited way), so economic, and, eventually, social, activities can resume. There may still be limitations to what is possible for a period of time, but the severe strictness which characterised the lockdowns in many countries will have eased when step 3 becomes relevant.

However, simply stopping the application of temporary measures without any thought given to the immediate aftermath can create new problems. For example, in many countries, moratoria were introduced which allowed debtors under credit agreements a period of time during which no instalments had to be paid ("payment holidays"), and tenants of rental properties were protected from eviction for non-payment of rent.[30] Once these moratoria expire, there will be concerns for those debtors who might still not yet be in a financial position to make regular payments again, and who may suddenly face the prospect of being in default on their repayments and at risk of eviction. This could put a huge amount of pressure on the court system, for instance.

It will therefore be essential to make transitional "recovery" arrangements to prevent the sudden disappearance of the measures which were introduced at the height of the crisis. This could involve a more gradual removal of measures such as moratoria and provision for rescheduling debts and rental payments. It must be recognised that the economic impact on individuals and businesses will not end with the resumption of economic activity but may continue for some time yet (particularly as unemployment might increase once government support schemes expire). It may be that financial support for individuals can be provided through the welfare system to provide some alleviation, but this might not suffice to address the added problem of outstanding payments which have accumulated during the moratorium period.

---

30 See COVID-19 Consumer Law Research Group, 'Consumer law and policy relating to change of circumstances due to the COVID-19 pandemic' (2020) 43 Journal of Consumer Policy 437–450 for a comparative discussion of these.

2.5. STEP 4: REFLECTIONS ON STATE OF THE LAW AND NEED FOR LASTING REFORMS

It may be thought that, once the crisis has subsided and the economic and social context is able to return to conditions comparable to those before the crisis arose, it will be possible to revert to the pre-crisis legal regimes and carry on as before. However, this is not inevitable. Changes were made to the law during the crisis because existing legal rules were found wanting when faced with the rapid and dramatic shift in the economic and social context caused by the steps taken to tackle the crisis. These shortcomings would remain if there was no further consideration of reform after the crisis was over.

Once things have calmed down again, there should be an opportunity for reflecting on the state of the law and whether the shortcomings which were identified should be tackled on a lasting basis. Whilst the urgency of this crisis may have gone, and therefore the need for reform be less pressing, this does not mean that law reform should be put off. Instead, the fact that temporary changes were felt necessary should be a reason for taking a more rigorous look at the law and to think about what changes could be made to reduce the need for temporary interventions, should another severe crisis emerge. One might object that the unusual conditions of a crisis are not a good diagnostic environment for identifying aspects of the law in need of reform because such extreme circumstances are unlikely to arise frequently in the future. There may be some force in this suggestion, but the counter-argument is that the mere fact that we experienced this crisis should provide the impetus for considering reforms to seek a greater extent of future-proofing. This would contribute to increased legal certainty/predictability and thereby allow contracting parties to plan ahead better, particularly with regard to mutual risk allocation under their contracts.

Moreover, the experiences of the crisis might have revealed shortcomings not only in the substantive legal rules, but also in the underlying principles and assumptions on which these rules are based. To use the English common law as an example: it is generally well known for a non-interventionist stance and will not easily interfere in contracts, once concluded.[31] The doctrine of frustration is narrow, and there is generally no basis for intervening in cases of financial hardship.[32] Aside from the nascent recognition of relational contracts,[33] there is no general duty to act in accordance with good faith. Yet, during the crisis, measures were taken which *de facto* compensated for the lack of hardship rules,

---

31 *Prime Sight Limited v Edgar Charles Lavarello* [2013] UKPC 22.

32 *Davies Contractors v Fareham UDC* [1956] AC 696; *Gold Group Properties Ltd v BDW Trading Ltd* [2010] EWHC 323 (TCC).

33 *Bates v Post Office Ltd* [2019] EWHC 606 (QB).

and even the Government sought to exhort contracting parties to act in a way which sounds not far away from what would be expected if there were a general duty to act in good faith.[34] Whilst I do not expect a sudden change of heart in the underlying principles of English contract law,[35] there might nevertheless be renewed interest in reducing the strictness of the law in this regard,[36] even if, in this particular instance, radical reform may be unlikely.

There is, of course, no guarantee that there will be much appetite for law reform once matters have calmed and the crisis has gone. Instead, the daily routine and political priorities will take over,[37] and whatever happened during the period of crisis will remain confined to that context. I doubt, however, that there will not be any long-term effects on contracts and contract law. At the very least, I expect that there will be at least some litigation reaching the courts eventually which will involve questions regarding the substance of existing legal rules and may result in some development or change – particularly in the common law where contract law is still predominantly case-based. I would hope, however, that there will be an effort to consider whether English contract law requires wider reform, not least because there appear to be fewer opportunities for the Court of Appeal and the Supreme Court to consider some of the central aspects of contract law on a regular basis.[38] However, if this does not happen, then the crisis will merely have constituted an interruption to the normal operation of contracts and contract law. If reforms were to be introduced, however, then this could have a disruptive effect. In order to explain what I mean by this, I now turn to elaborate how I use the notion of disruption in the context of law.

3. LEGAL DISRUPTION AND THE COVID-19 CRISIS

I mentioned earlier that the word "disruption" has, perhaps, been overused recently, particularly in the context of how digital technology has disrupted

34 Cabinet Office *Guidance on responsible contractual behaviour in the performance and enforcement of contracts impacted by the COVID-19 emergency* https://www.gov.uk/government/publications/guidance-on-responsible-contractual-behaviour-in-the-performance-and-enforcement-of-contracts-impacted-by-the-COVID-19-emergency accessed 11 June 2020.

35 See further, Hugh Beale and Christian Twigg-Flesner, 'COVID-19 and English Contract Law' in this volume.

36 Vasanti Selvaratnam, 'Good faith: is English law swimming against the international tide?' [2020] Lloyd's Maritime and Commercial Law Quarterly 232.

37 For the UK and EU, there is the difficult issue of the new trading relationship following the UK's withdrawal from the EU, of course.

38 It took for more than two decades for the Supreme Court to be presented with an opportunity to consider the approach to consideration in the Court of Appeal's ruling in *Williams v Roffey Bros.* [1991] 1 QB 1, only for the case to be decided on different grounds: *MWB Business Exchange Centres Ltd v Rock Advertising* [2018] UKSC 24.

business, law and regulation through enabling new digital business models and products.[39] Nevertheless, I regard the notion of "disruption" as a useful guide for determining the effect of reform on any legal regime, including that for contracts. Importantly, not every instance of law reform is disruptive, even if it results in significant changes – something more is required before law reform has a disruptive effect.

I start with the idea of "disruptive technology", developed by Clayton Christensen.[40] His perspective is on the impact of technological developments on incumbent businesses, rather than on legal disruption. He distinguishes between "sustaining technology" and "disruptive technology". In short, sustaining technology results from gradual improvements of established technologies. Businesses involved in making established technologies serve an existing market and customer-base, and adopting sustaining technology allows such businesses to continue to do so. The focus of such businesses is on maintaining their existing customer base and growing that, rather than branching out into other fields.

In contrast, "disruptive technology" is more than just a gradual improvement of existing technology but rather an innovative development. Initially, there may be no demand for such technology, and it may not have the reliability and maturity of established technologies. Among existing customers in established markets, there will be little, if any, interest in this new technology. So how does such technology become "disruptive"? Christensen argues that a new market for innovative technology will emerge, often because such technology appeals to an under-served or altogether new customer base. As new customers adopt and apply this technology, they effectively create a new market. Katyal noted that disruptive technology can "tap unforeseen markets, create products to solve problems consumers don't know they have, and ultimately to change the face of the industry".[41] This can lead to a disruptive effect when innovative technology which initially finds its own market spreads into existing markets for established technologies. Customers in established markets switch to innovative technology, leading to a decline in demand for products based on established technology, eventually pushing established businesses out of their market. Importantly, disruptive technology and the associated market disruption is different from increased competition in established markets by a competitor utilising innovative technology.[42]

This short account of Christensen's theory of disruptive innovation suffices as the basis for the particular notion of disruption I will employ in the context

---

39 Michael J. Copps, 'Disruptive Technology ... Disruptive Regulation' [2005] Michigan State Law Review 309; Roger Brownsword, *Law, Technology and Society* (Routledge 2019) 182–190.

40 Clayton Christensen, *The innovators dilemma* (Harvard Business Review Press 1997).

41 Neal Katyal, 'Disruptive Technologies and the Law' (2014) 102 Georgetown Law Journal 1685.

42 Clayton Christensen, Michael Raynor and Rory McDonald, 'What is Disruptive Innovation?' (2015) Harvard Business Review 44.

of law. In my conception of "legal disruption", there are two interconnected levels of disruption. The first level of legal disruption arises when a new development demands that an adjustment of some kind is made to existing legal regimes. This will be necessary when existing legal regimes are either insufficient to address a new development, or where there are no relevant provisions in such legal regimes at all. In the four-step model developed in the previous section, this will be the case where the outcome of step 1, i.e. the application of existing provisions to the crisis (or any new development for that matter) has revealed that there are gaps or other shortcomings. This will lead to the adoption of new legal provisions within that legal regime to address the gaps/shortcomings thus identified (step 2 in the model above). However, the mere fact that additional provisions are required does not of itself entail a disruptive effect. Often, it is possible to address gaps/shortcomings by modifying existing provisions or by adding new provisions which follow existing patterns by analogy.

For example, the EU recently adopted its Directive on Digital Content and Digital Services (2019/770/EU) which created a conformity requirement for digital content/services which mirrors that already in place for goods.[43] The UK took a similar approach in the Consumer Rights Act 2015.[44] The new provisions extend a familiar approach to a new(ish) development in a way which maintains a high degree of consistency in this area of law. Roger Brownsword characterises such an approach as "coherentism".[45] He argues that a "coherentist" approach is instinctively preferred by lawyers and regulators, because it seeks continuity through ensuring that the legal regime for existing and new products remains coherent. An additional benefit of such an approach is that it also ensures, as much as possible, that legal certainty is maintained.

Such an approach may not always be appropriate. Indeed, as the legal changes introduced during the COVID-19 pandemic show, sometimes a targeted intervention will be necessary which does not necessarily preserve coherence in the way that extensions of existing legal regimes with analogous provisions would. Such targeted interventions can be more tailored to the particular problem which needs to be tackled. In the case of the COVID-19 pandemic, the problem was the changed economic context and the difficulties for borrowers and tenants to keep up their regular instalment payments, for instance. The targeted solution in many countries was the introduction of moratoria on payment obligations.

---

43 Note that the conformity requirement for goods was updated in Directive 2019/771/EU, too. The conformity requirements in both directives are aligned: see Christian Twigg-Flesner, 'Conformity of Goods and Digital Content/Digital Services' in Esther Arroyo Amayuelas and Sergio Cámara Lapuente (eds), *El Derecho privado en el nuevo paradigma digital* (Marcial Pons 2020).

44 See part 1, chapter 3 of the Consumer Rights Act 2015.

45 Roger Brownsword, 'Regulatory Fitness: Fintech, Funny Money, and Smart Contracts' (2019) 20 European Business Organization Law Review 5.

This approach is what Brownsword would call "regulatory instrumentalism".[46] This concept refers to a regulatory approach with a preference for achieving whatever (regulatory) objective is pursued, rather than one which seeks to maintain coherence with existing legal rules and principles.[47] In effect, this is a problem-specific and targeted approach which leaves existing legal regimes mostly unaffected, although it may mean that the way in which this is done will differ considerably from what a coherentist approach might have done.

Crucially, the fact that a targeted approach was chosen will often be indicative of the fact that a coherent development of the law would not have provided an adequate solution to the particular problem. This is where the first level of legal disruption is engaged: the problem-focused development of new legal and regulatory provisions can be disruptive because it does not seek to maintain coherence and consistency with existing legal regimes. However, these new targeted provisions are confined to the specific problem they seek to address without affecting the continued application of existing legal rules to circumstances falling outside the scope of the new rules.

This means that the disruptive effect of the crisis on existing legal regimes at level 1 is limited. If I draw an analogy with Christensen's theory, level 1 disruption can be compared to the creation of a new market for innovative technology which is the first stepping-stone towards the disruption of established markets. At this stage, the fact that a new market for an as-yet underserved customer-base has been created does not yet affect established markets and established businesses. In a similar way, new legal provisions addressing specific new problems or developments are initially confined to this context, and existing legal regimes continue to apply to everything else.

I now turn to explain the second level of disruption. Once this level is engaged, it is possible to speak of true legal disruption. The outcome of level 1 disruption is that there will be parallel legal regimes: the existing legal regime and the specific regime tackling particular problems in a targeted manner. Just as the existence of two separate markets does not constitute disruption in Christensen's theory, level 1 disruption is not yet true legal disruption. According to Christensen, disruption occurs once new technology captures the customer base of established markets and attracts this to the newly created market, resulting in the reduction and eventual disappearance of the established market. In transplanting this to the legal context, I argue that legal disruption occurs when legal rules which were initially confined to a specific identified issue start to be applied beyond their original target. Eventually, this could have

46 See also Edward L. Rubin, 'From Coherence to Effectiveness' in Rob van Gestel, Hans-W. Micklitz and Edward L. Rubin (eds), *Rethinking Legal Scholarship* (Cambridge University Press 2017).

47 Roger Brownsword, 'Regulatory Fitness: Fintech, Funny Money, and Smart Contracts' (2019) 20 European Business Organization Law Review 5.

the effect of eroding the scope of existing legal regimes and result in extending specific rules far beyond their intended target. Such a broadening of the reach of new provisions could be achieved most obviously by clear legislative reform to that effect. However, it can also happen in more subtle ways. Targeted interventions may have employed concepts or principles which differ from those underpinning existing regimes. These concepts or principles may subsequently become the basis for developments in the existing law, or in the regulatory framework which can additionally govern many contracts. In the context of the common law, for instance, it is conceivable that the concepts and principles underpinning new targeted legal rules subsequently influence the way existing legal rules are understood and developed, resulting in a shift in the principles and concepts of existing rules. This development would occur at step 4 of the model outlined above, when law reform is considered because of the experiences gathered during the crisis itself. Where such reform results in provisions initially adopted in the context of a particular crisis becoming a permanent feature of the law, and therefore applicable in circumstances different from the crisis itself, the crisis will have caused legal disruption.

To sum up: legal disruption occurs primarily where changes made to the law, initially adopted to tackle the specific circumstances of a crisis and thus tailored to those circumstances, are subsequently retained and continue to apply after the crisis has faded, and eventually extended to circumstances which are not connected to the crisis. Such legal disruption may occur to legal rules specifically, by changing the doctrinal elements of the law. However, it can also occur in other ways, for example by recognising and deploying new underpinning principles. For instance, Iain Ramsay has argued[48] that the introduction of moratoria and enforcement restriction in respect of consumer credit agreements, combined with existing rules (under the Consumer Credit Act 1974) on rescheduling instalment payments once a debtor has defaulted on their repayment obligations, could be indicative of an emerging principle of "social force majeure".[49] It has even been suggested that the crisis might prompt the emergence of a "societal force majeure" notion which recognises that severe changes in the economic context can affect both suppliers and customers at the same time and that any changes to the legal regime for consumer contracts need to reflect this.[50] Were such emerging principles to be recognised, they could

48 Iain Ramsay, 'Contract Law, social force majeure and adjusting consumer credit contracts' https://creditdebtandinsolvency.wordpress.com/2020/04/18/contract-law-social-force-majeure-and-adjusting-consumer-credit-contracts/ accessed 11 June 2020.

49 Thomas Wilhelmsson "'Social force majeure" – A new concept in Nordic consumer law' (1990) 13 Journal of Consumer Policy 1; Thomas Wilhelmsson, *Critical Studies in Private Law* (Kluwer 1992) 180–216.

50 COVID-19 Consumer Law Research Group, 'Consumer law and policy relating to change of circumstances due to the COVID-19 pandemic' (2020) 43 Journal of Consumer Policy 437–450.

shape the future development of legal regimes in a particular way that would not have occurred otherwise.[51]

4. LEGAL DISRUPTION: WHY IT MATTERS

In the preceding two sections, I have endeavoured to identify the potential for a crisis such as that caused by the COVID-19 pandemic to cause legal disruption, based on a narrow conception of the notion of disruption. My essential point is that a crisis, such as that caused by the COVID-19 pandemic, has the potential to cause legal disruption, but that this is not the inevitable outcome. As long as any changes made to a legal regime are limited to the period of crisis, and its immediate aftermath, it would not be appropriate to speak of legal disruption. At best, this is an *interruption* to an established legal regime without a lasting effect.

Understanding when legal disruption occurs matters for a number of reasons: first, it can provide some reassurance about the appropriateness of short-term, targeted changes in the law to alleviate the impact of a major crisis despite concerns about undermining legal certainty/predictability and contractual risk-allocation. A time-limited change would not cause legal disruption.

Secondly, it helps to identify the point at which long-term effects with a disruptive potential could arise. As explained, this would be the case where lasting reform to a legal regime is undertaken which makes some or all of the temporary changes in that legal regime a permanent feature and is therefore not limited to the period of crisis. It will also be the case where the temporary changes during the crisis are indicative of underpinning principles or assumptions which differ from those which have shaped the legal environment before the crisis arose, and such crisis-inspired principles or assumptions continue to influence the development of the law well beyond the crisis and its aftermath.

Thirdly, it does not regard legal disruption as inherently negative – quite the opposite. My conception of legal disruption is essentially value-neutral, in that it does not ascribe a positive nor a negative view of the occurrence of legal disruption. Rather, it seeks to provide the criteria needed to recognise legal disruption where it occurs. It may be negative if not managed well, but can equally be positive in driving through significant reforms which might be seen as a welcome development.

Fourthly, being able to distinguish legal disruption from incremental legal reform can increase awareness among contracting parties of the significant

---

51 For another example, see Leggatt LJ's reasoning on so-called no-reliance clauses and their relationship with the doctrine of misrepresentation in English Law in *First Tower Trustees Ltd v CDS (Superstores International) Ltd* [2018] EWCA Civ 1396. At paragraph 104, he stresses the legislative policy underpinning the Misrepresentation Act 1967 as the reason why freedom of contract to avoid the application of the Act has been curtailed.

changes which have occurred, and thus support legal certainty/predictability and provide an opportunity for contracting parties to adjust their contract terms in light of the new legal regime.

Finally, legal disruption occurs not simply because additions are made to the legal environment which depart significantly from its existing make-up; as long as these additions are confined to the specific context of a crisis, the general legal environment remains unaffected. Legal disruption happens once the targeted changes made to deal with the crisis become a lasting element of the legal environment and thereby displace the pre-crisis elements.

5. CONCLUSION

The question I have attempted to address in this contribution is whether the COVID-19 pandemic and its consequences should be characterised as having caused disruption to the law. I have argued that when it comes to determining the impact of the crisis on the legal regime for contracts, there is no fundamental difference between a crisis such as the COVID-19 pandemic and any other significant development which requires some kind of adjustment to the legal regime. Indeed, the steps of analysis are broadly the same: test the adequacy of the existing legal environment, consider which changes are required, and, ultimately, decide whether these are temporary or lasting. Legal disruption occurs where changes initially made to address the specific concerns which have arisen in the context of a crisis become lasting changes to the legal environment, and subsequently apply to circumstances not linked to the crisis. Where such changes displace elements of the pre-existing legal environment, legal disruption has occurred.

Does this mean that the COVID-19 pandemic has caused legal disruption? As things stand at the time of finalising this manuscript (March 2021), my answer to this question has to be "not yet". Do I think that, based on what I have said in this contribution, the crisis has the potential for legal disruption? Yes, I do – although I do not regard this as an inevitable outcome. However, were it to be the outcome, even if only in some respects, then I would not necessarily regard this as a bad thing – some legal disruption can ultimately be a positive development of any given legal regime.

I hope this contribution has clarified why the COVID-19 crisis will not invariably lead to legal disruption. At the same time, an analysis of how existing legal regimes for contracts operate in a crisis and the temporary changes that were made should be seen as an indicator that lasting reforms of that legal regime might be necessary even after the crisis has subsided. Whilst such reform may or may not result in legal disruption as I have characterised it, the fact that there could be legal disruption as a long-term outcome of the COVID-19 crisis should not be a reason for resisting such reforms.

RELEVANCE OF THE CONTRACTUAL SOLIDARITY AT THE TIMES OF PANDEMICS

Claudio Scognamiglio*

This contribution aims to outline, in a general perspective, the different possible strategies to respond from the normative point of view to the consequences, direct or indirect, on the contractual relations of the COVID-19 pandemic: a solution entrusted to the jurisprudential law seems appreciable for its elasticity, but the requirements of certainty and predictability appear pre-eminent to be assured only by the legislative intervention.

1. THE FIRST IMPACT OF THE COVID-19 PANDEMIC ON ITALIAN LAW OF CONTRACTS

In the few months that have lapsed since the dramatic health emergency linked to the spread of the COVID-19 pandemic, much research has reflected on its impact on civil law, and in particular on the law of contracts and other obligations.[1]

---

* Tor Vergata University.

[1] See the papers collected in the ebooks published in the context of Giustiziacivile.com: Fabrizio Di Marzio (ed), *Emergenza Covid-19, Speciale n. 1* e *Speciale n. 2, Uniti per l'Italia* (Giuffrè Francis Lefebvre 2020). For a first overview of the opinions of North American scholars, see Katharina Pistor, *Law in the Time of Covid - 19*, 2020, Columbia Law School.

The coordinates of the debate have, therefore, already been set. They begin from the awareness of the absolute exceptionality of the situation that the whole world is now experiencing. Then, questions rise on the identification of the instruments through which we can (try to) face it as to its impact on the execution of contractual relationships and, more generally, on the implementation of obligation.

In this perspective, the strong and evocative appeal to the idea of community as a common commitment and *munus* must be recalled,[2] which has immediately found development in the passionate argument of an author, intended to prefigure "a joint evolution of the system in terms of effectiveness" to be achieved through the contribution of all legal experience: legislator, jurisprudence, doctrine.[3] And the principle, or even the value, of solidarity is also evoked in other contributions, assuming a reinterpretation in the perspective of solidarity of the same concept of the unexpected impossibility of performance.[4] This widens the possibility of application of the general clause of good faith, in the sense of opening up to renegotiation mechanisms of contractual agreements, for example, in the field of rental contracts for real estate for commercial use.[5] Good faith is even considered by some scholars as a criterion for verifying the possible ineffectiveness of the out-of-court exercise of the right during the period of suspension of court activity. In fact, this circumstance deprives the addressee of the out-of-court initiative of others to challenge it in court.[6]

---

2 Fabrizio Di Marzio, 'Comunità. Affrontiamo la nostra prova' in Di Marzio (ed), *Emergenza Covid-19, Speciale n. 1* e *Speciale n. 2, Uniti per l'Italia* (Giuffrè Francis Lefebvre 2020) VII. In French Law, from the perspective of the value of fraternity, Pascal Oudot, *La fraternité, 1789/Covid – 19, La semaine juridique*, 6 July 2020.

3 Francesco Macario, 'Per un diritto dei contratti più solidale in epoca di "coronavirus"' in Di Marzio (ed), *Emergenza Covid-19, Speciale n. 1* e *Speciale n. 2, Uniti per l'Italia* (Giuffrè Francis Lefebvre 2020) n. 1, 207, 212.

4 Antonio De Mauro, 'Pandemia e contratto, Spunti di riflessione in tema di impossibilità sopravvenuta della prestazione' in Di Marzio (ed), *Emergenza Covid-19, Speciale n. 1* e *Speciale n. 2, Uniti per l'Italia* (Giuffrè Francis Lefebvre 2020), n. 1, 227, 229. For a problem reading based on the concept of force majeure, Matthew Jennejohn, Julian Nyarko, Eric Talley, *Covid – 19 as a Force Majeure in Corporate transactions, Columbia Law and Economics Working Paper No 625*, 2020; also published in Katharina Pistor, *Law in the Time of Covid – 19*, 2020, Columbia Law School, 141; Julia Heinich, 'L'incidence de l'épidémie de coronavirus sur les contrats d'affaires: de la force majeure à l'imprévision' in *Récueil Dalloz*, 2020, 611; Christian Twigg-Flesner, 'A Comparative Perspective on Commercial Contracts and the impact of Covid 19 – Change of circumstances, Force Majeure or what?' in Katharina Pistor, *Law in the Time of Covid – 19*, 2020, Columbia Law School, 170.

5 Vincenzo Cuffaro, 'Le locazioni commerciali e gli effetti giuridici della pandemia' in Di Marzio (ed), *Emergenza Covid-19, Speciale n. 1* e *Speciale n. 2, Uniti per l'Italia* (Giuffrè Francis Lefebvre 2020) n. 1, 233, 235. See, for an overviev of French Law, Maxime Ghiglino, 'Coronavirus: exigibilité des loyers commerciaux échus durant la période de fermeture administrative', *Dalloz actualité*, 21 July 2020.

6 Daniele Maffeis, 'Problemi dei contratti nell'emergenza epidemiologica da Covid-19' in Di Marzio (ed), *Emergenza Covid-19, Speciale n. 1* e *Speciale n. 2, Uniti per l'Italia* (Giuffrè Francis Lefebvre 2020) n. 2, 3.

Therefore, it can be said, in order to identify a common denominator of the first reflections on the impact of the pandemic on contract law, that all such impacts are directed towards a reaffirmation of the centrality of the rule of good faith as a general clause. Thus, good faith is capable of empowering the judge to settle the disputes that may have originated from the economic consequences of the health emergency. These consequences are likely to be placed in a much wider temporal dimension than the one that will be proper to the consequences of the health emergency as such. This interpretation of the literature that is being formed on the subject is also confirmed by the contribution of those who, in the framework of an analysis of one of the first interventions of the Italian legislator of the emergency (Art 91 of the Law decree no 18/20, where it introduces a paragraph 6 *bis* to Art 3 of the Law decree no 6/20; see now Art 91 of Act no 27/20[7]) underline the rationale of favouring the adaptation of the performance to the emergency, while avoiding excessive automatism, so as to make it the place where, in a dramatic situation, "the duties of solidarity must prevail over any other interest".[8]

2. SOLIDARITY AS A TECHNIQUE OF RESPONSE TO THE EMERGENCY IN PROGRESS

Moreover, in recent months, the concept of solidarity has been permanent in the discourse of scholars who have reflected on the impact of the regulations dictated by the emergency on the protection of individual liberties. On the one hand, it has been emphasised that the model underlying the normative interventions has reflected "an ethical style and a way of understanding the national interest that leverage, in the final analysis, on the principle of solidarity".[9] On the other hand, there is hope that from the tragedy of the pandemic we can come out

---

7 Article 91 provides that "Compliance with the measures of containment referred to in this decree in always evaluated to the purpose of exclusion, pursuant to and for the purposes of article 1218 and 1223 of the civil code, the debtors liability, also with regard to the application of any disqualification or penalties related to delayed or omitted fulfillment". See, for the legal framework in France, Ricardo Pazos Castro, *'La respuesta del derecho de obligaciones y contratos francés ante la pandemia de Covid – 19'*, *Revista de derecho civil*, 2020, 47–74. See also for an overview of German Law, Constantin Willems, 'Das allgemeine Vertragsrecht in den Zeiten der Coronapandemie' (2020) Zeitschrift fuer das juristische Studium 183–189.

8 Alberto Maria Benedetti, 'Il 'rapporto' obbligatorio al tempo dell'isolamento. Una causa (transitoria) di giustificazione?' in Di Marzio (ed), *Emergenza Covid-19, Speciale n. 1* e *Speciale n. 2, Uniti per l'Italia* (Giuffrè Francis Lefebvre 2020) n. 2, 143, 147.

9 Ilenia Massa Pinto, 'La tremendissima lezione del Covid 19 (anche) ai giuristi' (*Questione Giustizia*, 18 March 2020) http://www.questionegiustizia.it/articolo/la-tremendissima-lezione-del-covid-19-anche-ai-giuristi_18-03-2020.php accessed 18 March 2020.

"rediscovering the reasons for solidarity and living together".[10] The latter extends to the cultural reflection on the tragedy of the present time, not necessarily dwelling on the religious warning that "no one saves himself alone", still placing at the centre the value of solidarity, the lack of which is described, here and now, "first of all as a lack of information".[11]

One can, therefore, certainly agree in the sense that the value of solidarity (which, transposed to the level of poetic language, seems to evoke the "*social catena*", of which one reads in Giacomo Leopardi's *La Ginestra*, and which defends mortals against unholy nature), technically translated into the general clause of good faith or correctness, constitutes a fundamental component of the argumentative instrumentation which must be used by the civil law scholar called upon to face the problems deriving from the impact of the pandemic on contract law. This value is also placed at the centre of the reflections of the civil liability scholar, as a potentially suitable criterion to establish a destination, precisely solidarity, of a share of the compensation due to the victims of torts suffering non-pecuniary losses.[12]

However, the above-mentioned acknowledgement constitutes only the initial moment of the reflection and certainly not its achievement. This observation seems to emerge in a sufficiently clear way from the current debate. In particular, most scholars are aware that the response to the consequences of the pandemic on private law relations cannot be entrusted only to the concretisation of the general clause of good faith by the judge, but requires a multilevel approach. This questions, in the same way, the judge, the legislator and the theoretical jurist. It is enough to consider once again the concluding reflections, of an already mentioned Francesco Macario editorial, which shows the need for a methodological approach such as the one just evoked;[13] or the articulated reconstructive path hypothesised by Alberto Maria Benedetti and Roberto Natoli.[14] The latter, attribute first to the general clause of good faith,

---

10 Gaetano Azzariti, 'I limiti costituzionali della situazione di emergenza provocata dal Covid – 19' (*Questione Giustizia*, 27 March 2020) http://questionegiustizia.it/articolo/i-limiti-costituzionali-della-situazione-d-emergenza-provocata-dal-covid-19_27-03-2020.php accessed 27 March 2020.

11 Paolo Giordano, *Nel contagio* (Einaudi 2020) 23.

12 Marcello Maggiolo, 'Una autentica solidarietà sociale come eredità del coronavirus: per una diversa destinazione dei risarcimenti del danno alla salute' in Marzio (ed), *Emergenza Covid-19, Speciale n. 1* e *Speciale n. 2, Uniti per l'Italia* (Giuffrè Francis Lefebvre 2020) n. 1, 39.

13 Francesco Macario, 'Per un diritto dei contratti più solidale in epoca di "coronavirus"' in Di Marzio (ed), *Emergenza Covid-19, Speciale n. 1* e *Speciale n. 2, Uniti per l'Italia* (Giuffrè Francis Lefebvre 2020) n. 1, 207, 212.

14 Alberto Maria Benedetti, Roberto Natoli, 'Coronavirus, emergenza sanitarie e diritto dei contratti' (*Diritto Bancario*, 25 March 2020) https://www.dirittobancario.it/editoriali/alberto-maria-benedetti-e-roberto-natoli/coronavirus-emergenza-sanitaria-e-diritto-dei-contratti-spunti-un-dibattito accessed 25 March 2020.

the suitability as a source of an obligation of renegotiation, such as to allow the contract to "live its emergency, leaving it then free, after the storm, to resume flowing regularly, in the arrangement originally agreed". Then, they identify, in the area of the general discipline of contracts (through the reference to the exception of non-performance, as a reaction technique in self-protection against the non-performance of the obligation of good faith resulting from the refusal to renegotiate), as well as in a refined extensive reading of the sector regulations contained in Article 9 of Law 192/98, two possible argumentative strategies to respond to the emergency.

But the affirmation of the centrality of the value of solidarity, and of good faith, as a technique of response to the emergency in progress, also cannot be exhaustive from another point of view. One may doubt whether it is just the exceptionality of the moment that requires that solidarity be governed as much as possible by the legislator, rather than, as before, being entrusted to the concretisation by the judge in the individual case at issue.

It is certainly true that Article 41 of the Constitution, stating in paragraph 2, that the private economic initiative "cannot take place in contrast with the social utility or in such a way as to cause damage to security, freedom and human dignity", entrusts the judge with the power to specify, in a single controversial case, these indeterminate concepts, contrary to paragraph 3 of the same provision, attributing to the law the power to determine "the appropriate programs and controls so that public and private economic activity can be directed and coordinated for social purposes". Then, from the point of view of contract law, the debate, which has taken place in recent weeks among the constitutionalists, on the limits within which the state of necessity affects the mechanisms of legal reserve[15] contained in the Constitution, as far as fundamental freedoms are concerned, and can justify a temporary disapplication of the legal reserve, certainly assumes different contents.[16]

3. THE MEDIUM AND LONG-TERM ECONOMIC FALLOUT OF COVID-19: THE ISSUE OF THE STABILITY OF THE JUDICIAL SYSTEM

However, it is also true that the completely exceptional nature of the situation we are living in can be seen from two points of view which cannot be disregarded.

15 In Italian constitutional law, legal reserve means that a particular matter must be ruled by the law and not by an administrative measure.

16 Corrado Caruso, Giorgio Lattanzi, Maria Gabriella Luccioli, Massimo Luciani interviewed by De Stefano, 'La pandemia aggredisce anche il diritto?' (*Giustizia Insieme*, 2 April 2020), https://www.giustiziainsieme.it/it/diritto-dell-emergenza-covid-19/961-la-pandemia-aggredisce-anche-il-diritto accessed 2 April 2020.

First of all, and precisely because of the magnitude of the phenomenon, this is a contingency that affects equally, at this stage, all contractual relations to which both parties are affected, directly or indirectly, by the containment measures. One may think, for example, of the rental contracts of lodgings of university students "off-site". They were often forced to return to their family homes, if only to spend the lockdown period in a less inconvenient way, and they no longer needed to live in the premises of the universities to which they belong, because they took advantage of on-line teaching. Certainly, the rental service is now subjectively unusable for this category of lease, but it is difficult to think of resolving the question through the argument in terms of *causa concreta* which, even in the case of another epidemic –more localised and infinitely less serious in Cuba –, had been used by the Court of Cassation years ago[17] to administer the risk arising from the subjective lack of usability, consistent with the *causa concreta* of the contract, of a package-holiday contract. Here the peculiar reason for the use of the accommodation, in principle, and subject to particularities that can be grasped at the level of the examination of the individual contractual conclusion, seems destined to remain relegated to the level of reasons of the contract and, therefore, the traditional conceptual instrumentation of the contract law doctrine would tend to deny its relevance. However, the mere reaffirmation of the binding nature of the contract for the student away from home, as well as – the polarity of the inverted solution – the termination of the same, would be such as to produce economic effects at first individual, then multiplied by thousands of similar contractual relations, but immediately afterwards also "systemic". It is, therefore, significant in terms of (further) reduction of the purchasing power of the categories concerned, which then require a systemic, and therefore normative, intervention, more than occasioned by the single case of controversy.

A similar discourse can also be made for the medium and long-term economic fallout: here we could exemplify activities that provide catering services. These, even when such service providers are able to eventually continue their operation, will probably have to face not only very serious liquidity problems due to the long period of previous suspension, but also a drastic drop in profitability, if only because of the need to introduce measures of increased security, in terms of so-called social distancing, which will significantly reduce the need for such services. The question does not seem to be solved only individually by renegotiating the terms of individual leases. In fact, in the meantime and

17 Cass. 24 July 2007, 16315. This was a contract to purchase a package tour to Cuba. After the conclusion of the contract, it had emerged that Cuba was, at that time, involved in a dengue epidemic and the tourist wanted to withdraw from the contract, demanding the return of the money paid in advance. His reasoning was that the epidemic would disturb the serenity of the trip and therefore the purpose of the contract, which was to relax.

obviously thinking in general terms, even lessors (those who derive the main part of their income from the civil fruits of their property), will end up in a situation of accentuated economic difficulty. Therefore, from a macro-economic point of view, it will be difficult to think of systematically passing on the cost of the crisis to the class of service providers.

The second of the two aspects mentioned above concerns the plan of the functionality, and of the stability, of the judicial system: a renegotiation of the terms of the contractual relations that would be entrusted only to the concretisation, in the single case of controversy, of the general clause of good faith would result in enormous administrative costs (it has been spoken, in this regard, of the impossibility of carrying out every renegotiation before the judge)[18] and which could not possibly be borne by the State, which is now being called upon to make a financial effort on unprecedented scale. At the same time, it is unfortunately unreasonable to believe that it will always (or even in the majority of cases) be possible to reach an agreement between the parties to the pandemic-stricken contractual relations without going to a court, if the reaching of such an agreement were to be entrusted only to the general evaluation guidelines stemming from the good faith clause.

4. CONCLUSION: WHAT ROLE FOR THE CIVIL LAW SCHOLAR TOWARDS THE COVID-19 PANDEMIC?

Therefore, beyond the unquestionable suggestion of solidarity and good faith – as axiological matrices of the interventions and argumentative strategies that each one of us, in our different roles, is called to develop – the emergency we are experiencing requires above all the intervention of the legislator. The legislation should include the introduction of precise and specific rules, which are easy to administer and able to guarantee a very high rate of predictability of their outcome, so as to circumscribe litigation as much as possible. At this moment, a general discipline of contingencies, implementing the content of the reform project of the Italian Civil Code[19] does not seem a good idea; this would bring to a conclusion the evolution of the traditional reading of the categories of the impossibility occurred and the excessive onerousness occurred.[20] What is

18 Daniele Maffeis, 'Problemi dei contratti nell'emergenza epidemiologica da Covid-19' in Di Marzio (ed), *Emergenza Covid-19, Speciale n. 1* e *Speciale n. 2, Uniti per l'Italia* (Giuffrè Francis Lefebvre 2020) n. 2, 3.

19 Francesco Macario, 'Per un diritto dei contratti più solidale in epoca di "coronavirus"' in Di Marzio (ed), *Emergenza Covid-19, Speciale n. 1* e *Speciale n. 2, Uniti per l'Italia* (Giuffrè Francis Lefebvre 2020) n. 1, 207, 212.

20 Elena Bellisario, 'Covid-19 e alcune risposte immunitarie del diritto privato' (*Giustizia Civile*, 27 April 2020) http://giustiziacivile.com/danno-e-responsabilita/approfondimenti/covid-19-e-alcune-risposte-immunitarie-del-diritto-privato accessed 27 April 2020.

needed is the enactment of a genuine emergency contract law. From this point of view, the first legislative measures, such as those contained in Article 88 of Decree-Law No 18/20, must certainly be welcome, which, as has been noted,[21] prefigures a sort of *ex lege* redetermination of the contents of the contract and in which, as has been pointed out, the awareness of the need to offer "support to economic activities affected by the epidemiological emergency in progress". Here it is advised "to keep the economic flows already acquired, while balancing them (of course) with the allocation of compensatory services",[22] instead of allowing the ordinary mechanisms for the recovery of sums already received, such as to produce, on the macroeconomic level, a particularly negative impact on the recession already underway.

In conclusion, to try to answer the question under which these considerations were developed, it can be said that the role of the civilist in the face of the COVID-19 emergency must be inspired by an attitude of both awareness and humility. Such awareness refers to the enormity of the crisis we are facing and the consequences of it, as well as the contribution that each of us must (try to) make to overcome it. Also, humility, is needed, because not even an argumentative apparatus nourished by the most refined civil dogma can be sufficient to solve the problems that have to be faced, in the absence of a sort of normative New Deal. This should prevent litigation destined to be unleashed as a result of the impact of the pandemic on contract law and should imperatively reallocate the costs and damages suffered by the parties, taking into account the needs of the system as a whole.

21 Antonio De Mauro, 'Pandemia e contratto, Spunti di riflessione in tema di impossibilità sopravvenuta della prestazione' in Di Marzio (ed), *Emergenza Covid-19, Speciale n. 1* e *Speciale n. 2, Uniti per l'Italia* (Giuffrè Francis Lefebvre 2020) n. 1, 229.

22 Fulvio Gigliotti, 'Considerazioni in tema di impossibilità sopravvenuta, per emergenza epidemiologica, di prestazioni dello spettacolo ed assimilate' in Di Marzio (ed), *Emergenza Covid-19, Speciale n. 1* e *Speciale n. 2, Uniti per l'Italia* (Giuffrè Francis Lefebvre 2020) n. 1, 237. "Compensatory services" are services which may bring the same or a similar benefit to the creditor.

LAW AFTER THE COVID-19 PANDEMIC

The Fundamental Binomials

Eduardo VERA-CRUZ PINTO*

The COVID-19 pandemic suspended the world and affected the political, social and economic constructions in which we lived. The law cannot be the same. It is necessary to separate the legal legitimacy to create and apply the rule of law and the political legitimacy to create and apply the law. This implies preparing the critique of the current dominant doctrine about the sources of "Law" based on the fundamental binomials posed by the post-COVID-19 situation. Placing State law in the Rule of Law involves confronting installed powers that violate with impunity fundamental rules of law that protect the human person and his/her dignity, by reforming State institutions and by changing mentalities. This goes through the media and journalists, through the courts, judges and lawyers, through the university and the legal profession schools, through the cult of fear and the risk of freedom, through the debate about the constitution.

1. TELEVISION VERSUS COURTS

In the public debate on "Pandemic Law", the idea that there is a radical opposition between life and freedom has been made concrete in the binomial *collective health* versus *individual freedom*.

* University of Lisbon.

Is there a fundamental legal duty of non-mobility of each person, in full constitutional normality,[1] apart from the legal regime of the state of exception?[2] Or is it just a civic duty of citizenship to be responsible in "taking care of others",[3] without any other censorship than that of the citizen appeal?

Will we go forward to higher levels of legal civility? Will we go back to the legal civility conquered in the past? Or will we return to effective social mechanisms of personal censorship, typical of medieval obscurantism,[4] outside the law and the courts?

Has the history of *the nullum crimen, nulla poena sine lege* rule already been forgotten? In the absence of an express rule that imposes social isolation, State bodies with elected office holders that cannot intervene to guarantee the behaviour of citizens in the sense of isolation, are shifting censorship of these behaviours from the law to the "social agents".[5]

So, those who do not behave in a proper manner are exposed to social censorship, broadcast by the mass media (media alarmism) and legitimised by the "TV station commentators", often faithful to scientific idolatry. They are often identified as bad citizens, socially irresponsible and the target of public disapproval and even physical violence by the "COVID militias".[6]

---

1 Constitutional normality is an expression of the Democratic State of Law that obscures the Democratic State of Law when the Law is exhausted in the word law and thus removes the legal rule from the legal norm. *Sopa de Wuhan: pensamento contemporâneo em tempos de pandemias*, org. Pablo Amadeo (Aspo 2020); Pierre Bourdieu, *Sobre o Estado: cursos no Collège de France (1989–92)* (Companhia das Letras 2009).

2 Bruna Lyra Duque, Adriano Sant'Ana Pedra, 'A harmonização entre os deveres fundamentais de solidariedade e o espaço da liberdade dos particulares no exercício da autonomia privada' (April–June 2016) 95 Revista de Direito Constitucional e Internacional http://www.publicadireito.com.br/artigos/?cod=a1f0cf94512f963e accessed 16 July 2020; Carlos Eduardo Behrmann Rátis Martins, *Introdução ao estudo dos deveres fundamentais* (JusPodivm 2009); Gilmar Ferreira Mendes et al., *Curso de direito constitucional* (2nd edn, Saraiva 2008); José Casalta Nabais, *O dever fundamental de pagar impostos* (Almedina 1998); Caroline Vieira Ruschel, *O dever fundamental de proteção ambiental* (2007) 33 Direito & Justiça 231; Idem *Parceria ambiental: o dever fundamental de proteção ambiental como pressuposto para a concretização do estado de direito ambiental* (Juruá 2010); De Plácido e Silva (updaters Nagib Slaibi Filho, Priscila Pereira Vasques), *Vocabulário Jurídico*, v. I-IV, (Forense 2016); Júlio Pinheiro Faro Homem de Siqueira, *Elementos para uma teoria dos deveres fundamentais: uma perspectiva jurídica.* Revista de Direito Constitucional e Internacional (2016) V. 95, Abr. Jun., 2016.

3 Emmanuel Levinas, 'Mourir pour …' in *Entre nous : Essais sur le penser-à l'autre* (Éditions Grasset 1991) 228–229.

4 James Bridle, *A nova idade das trevas: A tecnologia e o fim do futuro*, trad. port. Érico Assis (Todavia editions 2019).

5 On the non-State see Janice E. Thomson, *Mercenaries, Pirates, and Sovereigns. State-Building and Extraterritorial Violence in Early Modern Europe* (Princeton University Press 1994).

6 We cannot deal here with the difference between strength and violence. John C. Keane, *Reflexiones sobre la violencia* (Alianza 2000); Pierre Hassner, *La violence et la paix : De la bombe atomique au nettoyage ethnique* (Ed. Esprit Paris 1995); John Keane, 'The Long Century of Violence' in *Reflections on Violence* (Verso publisher 1996); Slavoj Zizek, *A Pandemia que Abalou o Mundo* (Relógio d'Água 2020) 65–73.

People who feel targeted and exposed, in defence of their fundamental rights, can address both national and European courts to react against this form of outlaw censorship that violates elementary personality rights, defended by the States, constitutions and European legislation. Bringing the phrase of the miller of Sanssouci up to date, "*there are still judges in Strasbourg.*"

I recall that this is a situation that exposes and worsens the State crisis, precisely when the State is needed the most. The construction of a digital reality by social[7] and communication networks and by TVs and newspapers, created as an alternative to the legal reality (which imposes rights and duties on to the State and a fair judicial process by the competent public authorities) and with claims to replace it, is one of the dangers to the democratic rule of law that the pandemic can aggravate.

In the post-COVID world, judges will be the main actors on the stage of European democracies that defend the rights of their citizens.

2. JOURNALISTS VERSUS JUDGES

If the intrusive digital State concerns us,[8] then companies with digital intrusion means should concern us even more. Televisions (private companies) hire

---

7 Zeynep Tufekci, *Twitter and Tear Gas: How Social Media Changed Protest Forever* (Yale University Press 2017); Emily Parker, *Now I Know Who My Comrades Are: Voices From the Internet Underground* (Sarah Crichton Books/Farrar, Straus and Giroux 2015).

8 François du Bois, 'Private Law in the Age of Rights' in Elspeth Reid and Daniel Visser (eds), *Private Law and Human Rights: Bringing Rights Home in Scotland and South Africa* (Edinburgh University Press 2013); Norberto Bobbio, *Estado, gobierno y sociedad: por una teoría general de la política*, (Editorial Fondo de Cultura Económica 1989); Miguel Calmon Dantas and Vicente Coni, 'Constitucionalismo digital e indignação na sociedade da informação' in *A Transdisciplinaridade e o Direito: Os desafios dos Direitos Humanos na Sociedade da Informação* (4th edn, Evangraf 2017) vol 1, 97–111; Luigi Ferrajoli, 'Il virus mette la globalizzazione con i piedi per terra' in *Il Manifesto*, 17 March 2020 https://ilmanifesto.it/il-virus-mette-laglobalizzazione-con-i-piedi-per-terra/ accessed 17 July 2020; Jaime Cárdenas Garcia, 'Democracia interna en los partidos y democracia participativa' in Revista de Derecho Estasiológico, Ideologia y Militancia, UNAM 146–168 www.juridicas.unam.mx/publica/librev/rev/derestas/cont/1/.../ens8.pdf, 151 accessed 16 July 2020; Maria José Vicentini Jorente and Natalia Nakano, 'Inovação, Tecnologias de Informação e Comunicação e processo disruptivos' (2007) 17(2) Londrina 37; Thomas S. Kuhn, *A estrutura das revoluções científicas* (Beatriz Vianna Boeira e Nelson Boeira tr, 9th edn, Perspectiva 2006); Massimino Daniel de Mello, 'Reflexões sobre democracia líquida e sua fundamentação no plano das teorias democráticas' (2017) 17(2) Revista Jurídica Cesumar – Mestrado: https://doi.org/10.17765/2176-9184.2017v17n2p375-400 accessed 15 July 2020; Antonio Enrique Pérez Luño, *Los derechos humanos en la sociedad tecnológica* (Editorial S.A. 2012); Lenio Luiz Streck, *Hermenêutica jurídica e(m) crise: uma exploração hermenêutica da construção do Direito* (6th edn, Livraria do Advogado 2005); Dennis Redeker, Lex Gill and Urs Gasser, *Towards digital constitutionalism? Mapping attempts to craft an Internet Bill of Rights* (2018) 80 International Communication Gazette 302–319

high-tech companies (more sophisticated than the States) – without adequate supervision[9] and without political responsibility or democratic control – that violate, without censorship and with *"good cause"*, the most elementary rights (personality rights as well as other fundamental rights[10]).

Can this be considered investigative journalism and public service communication? Or is it just a way to make profit by violating rights and breaching duties in the light of an impunity status for "journalists", accepted and guaranteed both socially and by the law and the courts?

We all know the axiological importance of freedom of press and freedom of expression in a democracy.[11] And yet we cannot ignore that the exercise of said freedoms cannot exclude, for instance, the defence of the rights of those who are suspected of having criminal behaviours.

Electronic surveillance companies,[12] personal data merchants[13] (consider the *Cambridge Analytica* scandal[14]) and media companies, in particular

---

https://doi.org/10.1177/1748048518757121 accessed 16 July 2020; Frank La Rue, *Report of the Special Rapporteur on the promotion and protection of the right to freedom of opinion. addendum* (United Nations, Human Rights Council, 1 April 2014); Cass R. Sunstein. *Democracy and the Internet Republic* (Com. Princeton, NJ. Princeton University Press 2001) 224; or (2001) 2 Journal of Law, Technology and Policy available at SSRN: https://ssrn.com/abstract=286293 or http://dx.doi.org/10.2139/ssrn.286293 accessed 16 July 2020; Jan Van Dijk, *The network society* (Sage Publications 2012).

9 Microsoft is trying to solve the difficult point of data journalism with a new tool – Content Insights and Discovery Accelerator (IDA). IDA can analyse hundreds of thousands of documents or long video footage within seconds. Combining artificial intelligence, object vision and optical character recognition (OCR), IDA can analyse pages and extract text, images and other key data. It also helps journalists search long videos, identifying faces or keywords, and provide searchable footage transcript. Cf Jane B. Singer, 'Who are these guys? The online challenge to the notion of journalistic professionalism' (2003) 4(2) Journalism 139–163; Nikki Usher, *Interactive Journalism: Hackers, Data, and Code* (University of Illinois Press 2016); Jochen Spangenberg and Nicolaus Heise, 'News from the crowd: Grassroots and collaborative journalism in the digital age' in Proceedings of the 23rd International Conference on World Wide Web (765–768) ACM (2014); Nic Newman, *Journalism, media and technology trends and prediction 2017* (University of Oxford: Reuters Institute for the Study of Journalism 2017).

10 Daniel Sarmento, *Direitos fundamentais e relações privadas* (Editora Lumen Juris 2004).

11 John C. Keane, 'Journalism and democracy across borders' in Geneva Overholser and Kathleen Hall Jamieson (eds), *The Press* (OUP 2005) 92; Idem 'Liberty of the Press' in *The Media and Democracy* (Polity 1991) 2.

12 Shoshana Zuboff, *The Age of Surveillance Capitalism: The Fight for a Human Future at the New Frontier of Power* (Profile Books 2019); *AA. VV. Tecnopolíticas da vigilância: Perspectivas da margem*, org. Fernanda Bruno, Bruno Cardoso et al. (Boitempo Editorial 2018); *AA. VV. A sociedade de controle: Manipulação e modulação nas redes digitais*, org. Joyce Souza and Rodolfo Avelino (Editora Hedra 2019); Evgeny Morozov, *Big Tech: A ascensão dos dados e a morte da política* (UBU Editora 2018).

13 The data extracted massively and intensively to Internet users, were gathered and processed forming the Big Data used to influence personal behaviour on a planetary scale.
The big global technology companies, taking advantage of the difference in information that exists between those who provide the data and those who own it, use Big Data as market

sovereignty in the time of *Big Other*,[15] make reports using electronic media prohibited for the police themselves to use (without a judge's mandate), in accordance with laws built considering long historical processes of abuse and injustice against the innocent.

In times of intensive and totalitarian communication, such as the case of a pandemic, this type of action has increased.[16] State authorities (police and judicial) take advantage of this "investigation work" of "electronic journalism" to collect elements that they cannot access by investigating, due to having to comply with legal and procedural rules. Fundamental rules of the democratic rule of law are thus circumvented.

We risk having European States with many laws and institutions defending people suspected of committing crimes, and then leaving them completely unprotected when they are considered suspicious by journalists, in media scenarios where their fragility and isolation are complete.

Society in general and the legal community in particular will be more aware of this type of performance of the mass media when, in clear abuse of the status given to research journalism in open and democratic societies, journalists tend to act based on anti-legal arguments such as "those who have not committed crimes should not fear" and "the ends justify the means", violating rights of the data subjects.

---

products that they sell. COVID-19 revealed the extent of this practice and the degree of intrusion and data crossing already achieved (drones, facial recognition technology, infrared scanners, application to classify people by the degree and risk of contagion, etc.). See Marcos Ehrhardt Júnior and Gabriela Buarque Pereira Silva, *Privacidade e proteção de dados pessoais durante a pandemia da COVID-19* https://direitocivilbrasileiro.jusbrasil.com.br/artigos/824478175/privacidade-e-protecao-de-dadospessoais-durante-a-pandemia-da-COVID-19 accessed 5 July 2020.

14 Brittany Kaiser, 'Manipulados: como a Cambridge Analytica e o Facebook invadiram a privacidade de milhões e botaram a democracia em xeque' (Roberta Clapp e Bruno Fiuza tr, Harper Collins 2020); Christopher Wylie, *Mindfuck: Inside Cambridge Analytica's Plot to Break the World* (Profile Books/Penguin Random House 2019); Kris Shaffer, *Data versus Democracy: How Big Data Algorithms Shape Opinions and Alter the Course of History* (Apress 2019); Steven Levy, *Facebook: The Inside Story* (Blue Rider Press 2020); Edward Snowden, *Permanent Record* (Macmillan Publishers 2019).

15 Characterised by new forms of accumulation, new state and business policies and innovative social relations that replace contracts, the rule of law and social trust with the sovereignty of Big Other. Shoshana Zuboff, 'Big Other: capitalismo de vigilância e perspectivas para uma civilização de informação' in *Tecnopolíticas da vigilância: perspectivas da margem* (Heloísa Cardoso Mourão tr, Boitempo 2018) 49.

16 TV renounced plural programming and began to focus its entire broadcast on *Pandemia*, speciality News. Netflix's new series about global outbreaks is eerily timed. The documentary questions our readiness for fast-moving viruses like coronavirus. The fear that results from this way of communicating in a pandemic time fuels the blaming of the other and the acceptance of illegal means to obtain information and evidence about those who are suspected of jeopardising our security. Investigative journalism using computer piracy is more active, taking advantage of the situation.

Judges should be aware of the post-COVID-19 changes in the collective judgment on the subject, critically reviewing the jurisprudence in search of new balances between freedom of information and the right to privacy.

3. FREEDOM VERSUS FEAR

One of the greatest enemies of our freedom, as guaranteed by the law, is fear. COVID-19 reminds us of the political value of fear and its effects on the exercise of freedom.[17]

The situation is even more alarming when the defences against threats – defences which we found in family and in school – are no longer there. The State has been taking the place of family and new social programmers reap the rewards of their work: what is left are isolated, lonely young people, dependent on new chains of solidarity, easily influenced by the MTV model and easily adherent to the social causes in fashion at the moment.

Law researchers need to understand the empirical dimension of risk perception in situations of collective fear induced by the mass media to be able to give an appropriate legal response.[18] The global spread of the "fear of dying" as a result of the pandemic, justified the impact that culturally different views on the world had on State responses to the need for social isolation and domestic confinement, even in the European Union.

When legislating on the pandemic, the world was divided between the social and liberal models, between democrats and authoritarians, and between institutionalists and populists. The defence of freedom is directly related to the way of politically organising our societies by the rule of law, and this requires greater care with education, information and communication and greater demands on those who, in the courts, defend our rights by deciding, with an adequate legal interpretation, the application of the legal norms convened.

---

[17] John T. Jost et al., 'The Politics of Fear: Is There an Ideological Asymmetry in Existential Motivation?' (2017) 35 (4) Social Cognition 324–353; Corey Robin, *Fear: The History of a Political Idea* (OUP 2004); Jean Delumeau, *La peur en Occident, XIVe-XVIIIe siècles* (Ed. Fayard 1978); Barry Buzan, *People, States and Fear: An Agenda for International Security Studies in the Post-Cold War Era* (ECPR Press 1991); Susan Jeffers, *Feel the Fear and Do it Anyway* (Ebury Publishing 1991); Gavin de Becker, *The Gift of Fear* (Bloomsbury Pub Ltd. 2000); Aung San Suu Kyi, 'Freedom from Fear "1991"' in *Freedom from Fear and Other Writings* (Penguin Books Ltd. 1995) 184.

[18] Cass R. Sunstein, *Laws for Fear: Beyond the Precautionary Principle* (Cambridge University Press 2005); Dan M. Kahan, Paul Slovic, Donald Braman and John Gastil, 'Fear of Democracy: A Cultural Evaluation of Sunstein on Risk' (2006) 119 Harvard Law Review; Yale Law School, Public Law Working Paper No. 100, Yale Law & Economics Research Paper No. 317, Available at SSRN: https://ssrn.com/abstract=801964 accessed 8 July 2020, Faculty Scholarship Series, Paper 104 http://digitalcommons.law.yale.edu/fss_papers/104 accessed 8 July 2020; Tomas J. Philipson and Richard A. Posner, *Private Choices and Public Health. The AIDS Epidemic in an economic Perspective* (Harvard University Press 1993) 57–83.

It is important to understand how a citizen's ability to rationalise risk (moving away from an anxious[19] but appealing emotionality[20]), considering the duty of care imposed on social behaviour, is linked to acting out of fear,[21] and what global civil society[22] is willing to accept from States[23] concerning legalised police repression during states of exception that are perpetuated outside constitutional limits. Democracy is in danger from its base, which is individual freedom regulated by law.

Once more, in an age of so many collective dangers and personal anxieties, it is expected that courts are the barrier for those who, having power (whatever it may be), cannot use force to gain advantages, exercise privileges or guarantee impunity. The final word belongs to the judges.

4. JUSTICE VERSUS POLITICS

In a situation where ideas are created and widely spread by those who have access to the communication space, governance moves from elected representatives to the CEOs of companies.

This is already happening. Companies govern through politicians whom they themselves create as market products. Politicians with their own ideas, strong personalities and ideological commitment are held hostage by the entrepreneurs of the various forms of communication. Alternatively, they are forced to fit into the ideas and models defined by the boards of directors of their companies, or they are ostracised.

---

19 Franz Neumann, 'Anxiety and Politics' in *The Democratic and the Authoritarian State: Essays in Political and Legal Theory* (Free Press 1957) 271; Edward Alden and Sheila McNulty, 'Fear and rumour leave America in grip of anxiety' *Financial Times Europe* (11 October 2001) 18; Paul Krugman, 'Fear Itself' *The New York Times* (September 2001); Franz Neumann, 'Anxiety and Politics' in *The Democratic and Authoritarian State. Essays in Political and Legal Theory* (Free Press 1964) 270–300.

20 Antonio R. Damasio et al., 'Subcortical and Cortical Brain Activity During the Feeling of Self-Generated Emotions' (2000) 3 Nature Neuroscience 1049–1056; Gerd Gigerenzer, Peter M. Todd and ABC Research Group, *Simple Heuristics That Make Us Smart* (OUP 1999); George E. Marcus, W. Russell Neuman and Michael B. MacKuen, 'Measuring Emotional Response: Comparing Alternative Approaches to Measurement' (2017) 5(4) Political Science Research and Methods 733–754.

21 Barry Glassner, *The Culture of Fear. Why Americans Are Afraid of the Wrong Things* (Basic Books 1999).

22 John C. Keane, *Global civil society? Contemporary political theory* (Cambridge University Press 2003).

23 Norbert Elias, 'The Fisherman in the Maelstrom' in *Involvement and Detachment* (OUP 1987) 46; Vujadinović-Milinković Dragica, 'Degradation of Everyday Life, Destruction of Society and Civil Society Suppression', paper presented at the University of Bradford, 25–26 March 2000; John Keane, 'Despotism and Democracy. The Origins and Development of the Distinction Between Civil Society and the State, 1750–1850' in John Keane (ed), *Civil Society and the State: New European Perspectives* (Verso Publisher 1988 [1998]) 35–71.

Democratic political parties, especially after the judicial/media intervention that alienated political leading figures for corruption and other crimes, were deprived of the few "institutional" politicians not involved in legal proceedings and were forced to recruit "civil common good servants" for the exercise of political positions.

Political parties ended up in the hands of opportunists created by the mass media. This situation requires deep reform in political parties, namely, to avoid nepotism and the friendship network that made them into employment agencies for incompetents. Closed in on themselves, turned into spokespersons for particular organic interests, incapable of self-criticism, political parties have degraded democratic institutions and the credibility of democracy as a system capable of making legislation for the collective interest and the common good.

Democracy cannot exist without political parties; democracy does not end on election day; democracy needs institutions that inspire the respect of voters; the street matters but it is not the stage of democracy; political parties must have an ideology that serves as a compass for governors and criteria for assessing voter opposition; the public administration must be transparent when acting and recruiting, and corruption must be avoided from the base.

Therefore, it is necessary to undertake, after the reform of the organisation and functioning of political parties, a deep reform of the European Union and its institutions so that politics dominates technocracy, and social values and service to others dominate bureaucracy. That reform is long overdue, and it is vital for our future to be guided by the rule of law and principles that characterise it.

There is only justice by law; there are only laws capable of justice if they look for inspiration in the legal rules (far beyond a mere compatibility with the Constitution); there is peace only if there is justice. The pandemic has shown that the powers of the State can be separated only in constitutional cosmetics. Because, during the pandemic crisis, those powers revealed uniform decisions when only institutional unity was required facing the virus.

The weakness of the judicial system and its governmental dependency was in plain sight when the state of exception ended. The democratic fragility accentuated this dangerous authoritarian drift that submits the judicial to the legislative/executive, in constitutional normality.

Therefore, the basis for the post-COVID-19 State reform must be found in the form and content of legislation, the organic and functional reform of the courts, the recovery of law schools in connection with the courts, and in the creation of conditions for the exercise of the activity of jurisprudents with *auctoritas*. The opportunity for this deep reform was created by the pandemic – and only once this is achieved can State policy be truly guided by law, if that is the desire of society. Judges cannot avoid the responsibility to participate in this task of reforms and of acting, within the judiciary, in line with their functional role in a democracy based on material justice.

5. UNIVERSITIES VERSUS COMPANIES

The European school model (if any), especially the university model, has its bases – organic and thematic – in the North American model instituted and maintained in Europe by governmental and institutional bureaucracy.

The deconstruction of a European identity through teaching and the uncritical imitation of the Anglo-Saxon university model has had catastrophic effects in the defence of the European social model, in linguistic diversity through the right to language and in the defences against populism,[24] racism, and authorised models, such as demagogic advertising. Anglo-Saxon cultural and academic colonialism is more effective than its financial and military version.

The policy changed sides and installed itself in the version of global media capitalism,[25] recruiting at the university that – separated from the European reality – investigates and teaches what is happening in the USA and successfully passes through European and global problems.

Moving, as through a revolving door, between companies, universities and the government, the new political party elites practice what they learned in a school of little pluralism and politically correct thought.[26] Thus, they feed the discourse against institutional politicians, typical of the populist demagogue of assumed authoritarian and nationalist democracies and of those who search that path.[27]

---

24 Jan-Werner Muller, *What Is Populism?* (University of Pennsylvania Press (Hardcover) 2016); John Lukacs, *Democracy and Populism – Fear and Hatred* (Yale University Press 2006); Alain Bihr, *Le spectre de l'extrême droite; les Français dans le miroir du Front national* (Les Editions de l'Atelier – Les Editions Ouvrières 1998); Margaret Canovan, 'Trust the People! Populism and the Two Faces of Democracy' (1999) XLVII Political Studies 2–16.; Cornelius Castoriadis and Roger-Pol Droit, 'Entretien' in Roger-Pol Droit (ed), *La compagnie des contemporains: rencontres avec des penseurs d'aujourd'hui* (Odile Jacob 2002); Annie Collovald, *Le populisme du FN: un dangereux contresens*, Bellecombe-en-Bauges (Ed. du Croquant 2004); Nonna Mayer, *Ces Français qui votent Le Pen* (Flammarion 2002); Aurelien Mondon, 'Nicolas Sarkozy's Legitimisation of the Front National: Background and Perspectives', (2013) 47 Patterns of Prejudice 22–40; Chantal Mouffe, 'The "End of Politics" and the Challenge of Right-Wing Populism' in Francisco Panizza (ed), *Populism and the Mirror of Democracy* (Verso 2005); Josiah Ober, 'The Original Meaning of "Democracy": Capacity to Do Things, not Majority Rule' (2008) 15 Constellations 3–9; Jacques Rancière, *La haine de la démocratie* (La fabrique éditions 2005).

25 Robert Kuttner, *Can Democracy Survive Global Capitalism?* (W. W. Norton & Company 2018).

26 John C. Keane, 'Life after political death: the fate of leaders after leaving high office' in John Kane, Haig Patapan and Paul 't Hart (eds), *Dispersed democratic leadership: origins, dynamics, and implications* (OUP 2009) 279–298; Isabel Hardman, *Why We Get the Wrong Politicians* (Atlantic Books 2019); Christopher H. Achen and Larry M. Bartels, *Democracy for Realists: Why Elections Do Not Produce Responsive Government* (Princeton Studies in Political Behavior Book 4, 2016).

27 On Trumpism and the Slow Down of Democracy in the USA, see Ted Bagley, *The Demolition of Democracy. Has America Lost Its Soul* (Xlibris 2019).

Universities, with their culture of complex and contradictory thinking, as well as strong notions of social, political, scientific and cultural responsibility are a space for dialogue and freedom essential to democracy as well as to a school of politicians with different ideas but committed to the defence – in institutions (not on the streets), through elections (not referenda and rallies of causes, called by social networks[28]) – of freedom, democracy and social justice. Therefore, it is necessary to reopen universities that have been closed by the culture of pandemic fear, and any necessary legislative reforms to enable this should be made. Universities are not companies, nor are they moved by the prospect of their own profit. They are not professional training schools to serve the "labour markets", nor are they schools designed to implement government educational policies. Education is not a product to be bought, nor is that the purpose or content of the legal rule that establishes the "freedom to learn and teach".[29] Studying at a university is everyone's right; not a privilege for anyone who pays.

This is the identity of the European university in the 21st century. Therefore, it is necessary to separate the teaching of law in the universities from the training for legal professions in the professional schools, so that each one contributes to the existence of competent jurists as capable and committed in their professions as in politics and in civic participation for the causes of law and justice.

It is up to the courts to apply university teaching laws pursuant to the university law rule. While being a rather minor and obvious request, it amounts to a vital difference.

6. JURISDICTION VERSUS LEGALISATION

In view of the injustices and inequalities that official politics in democracies cannot effectively combat, new solutions must be found to preserve personal freedom, social cohesion, political pluralism and electoral democracy in Europe.[30]

---

28 Zeynep Tufekci, *Twitter and Tear Gas: How Social Media Changed Protest Forever* (Yale University Press 2017); Emily Parker, *Now I Know Who My Comrades Are: Voices From the Internet Underground* (Sarah Crichton Books/Farrar, Straus and Giroux 2015).

29 Articles 43.º and 74.º of the Constitution of the Portuguese Republic.

30 On the failure of American democracy to combat inequality. Larry M. Bartels, *Unequal Democracy: The Political Economy of the New Gilded Age* (2nd edn, Russell Sage Foundation Co-pub 2016); Virginia Eubanks, *Automating Inequality: How High-Tech Tools Profile, Police, and Punish the Poor* (St. Martin's Press 2018); Cathy O'Neil, *Weapons of Math Destruction: How Big Data Increases Inequality and Threatens Democracy* (Crown/Penguin Random House 2017); Frank Pasquale, *The Black Box Society. The Secret Algorithms That Control Money and Information* (Harvard University Press 2015).

The leading proposal is to build justice by law with political debates for a consensus expressed in law for equal opportunities for all people, no matter what their background and sense of belonging are (the first and most prominent always being that of their common citizenship).

Therefore, the law and its rules (jurisprudential legitimacy – *auctoritas*) guide the law and its norms (political-electoral legitimacy – imperium). This is not the path we are currently following. Academic, political and media discourses have abandoned law and are creating a common pattern in which everything (culture, employment, music, power, etc.) is seen through a racial path.

The model of political organisation of European societies, instead of striving for social cohesion for the political construction of equality,[31] is moving towards that of contracts between racial groups for mere coexistence in State spaces.

The model is going in this direction because the most widespread and progressively accepted means of combating racism is adopting a form of language symmetrical to that used by xenophobes and racists, although democrats claim to be fighting both growing xenophobia and racism. As such, the model is not effective in combating racism and may even increase it.[32]

Radicals are willing to pay that price, while some of us are not. A style of speech based on a set of words and expressions that have a positive meaning, such as "anti-racism", but that are applied in the opposite direction and with political content opposed to what people adhere to will be counter-productive.

This discourse turns out to be a political deception, although there is no absolute moral equivalence between the racist extreme-right discourse and the racist extreme-left discourse. It is a style of speech that wants to be different but is in fact the same as that of racist, xenophobic, populist ideas, with an anti-democratic matrix that is found at the radical extremes of democracies.[33]

---

31 The democratic basis is the political expression of social conflict; non racial/ethnic, religious, national or others. Albert Hirschman, 'Social Conflicts as Pillars of Democratic Market Society' (1994) 22(2) Political Theory 56.

32 On the use made recently by the European racist and xenophobic radical parties already implanted in the election. Pavlos Vasilopoulos et al., 'Fear, Anger, and Voting for the Far Right: Evidence From the November 13, 2015 Paris Terror Attacks' (2018) 14 Political Psychology 6 ff; George E. Marcus et al., 'Applying the Theory of Affective Intelligence to Support for Authoritarian Policies and Parties' (2018) Advances in Political Psychology, supplement, Political Psychology, 40, nº S1, 109–139; Philip E. Converse, 'The Concept of the Normal Vote' in Angus Campbell et al. (eds) *Elections and the Political Order* (Wiley, 1966); Roger Eatwell and Matthew Goodwin, *National Populism: The Revolt Against Liberal Democracy* (Pelican Books 2018); Eric Kaufmann, *Whiteshift: Populism, Immigration and the Future of White Majorities* (Abrams Press 2019).

33 Pavlos Vasilopoulos, George E. Marcus and Martial Foucault, 'Affective Agency: The Rise of Ethno-Nationalist Parties in Europe and the USA' (paper, Annual Meeting of the Midwest Political Science Association, Chicago, IL, April 2019).

Racist radicalism, whatever its racial orientation and influence in the public space, must be constantly combated – in the political, institutional and media space – by democracies in Europe, after the colonial slavery genocide and the Nazi holocaust.

The jurisdiction of European law and the rights of European States need to be defended urgently. The exchange of politics for finance in Europe created the opportunity for the rising of these *causes without a cause*, based on fear, anger[34] and despair.[35] Democracy suffers from a political elite that is not worthy of it, for lack of commitment and courage.

The resurgence of the racialisation of political and cultural discourse in Europe, whatever its intention, can lead to results identical to previous ones. Radical anti-democratic groups or parties (which hide their authoritarian intention in the "political causes") try, on both sides of the political-party spectrum, to gain power through democratic means to impose their ideas using the State (often infiltrating the most voted for parties, changing them from moderates to radicals from the inside – as has been written and analysed).

History has provided various examples of this.[36] Conquering the media space and universities, the radical anti-democratic groups influence ideas to become dominant, take over democratic parties and form elites. From there they easily reach key positions within the State and particularly in the law-making structures, creating laws which, in turn, are implemented with zeal by the militants, who now hold positions in the public administration.

Only the law can prevent this path by giving back to politics what belongs to politics. Only the law allows justice to be reached and only through peace can justice be maintained. The law fights for the equality of all before the law based on dense *criteria* of material justice.

The answer, in Europe, will be the democratic rule of law and not the rule of democratic law, therefore, first of all, social equality through legal equality expressed in the law between equals in citizenship. In the European policies of equality between people (all of them including articles on refugees, emigrants and exiles), the legal maxims are: legalisation through jurisdiction; socialisation instead of racialisation, and; compromised citizenship instead of censorship prohibition.

It is the judges who, in the specific case, must bear this in mind to preserve the democratic possibility under the rule of law.

---

34 Pankaj Mishra, *Age of Anger: A History of the Present* (Ferrar, Strauss and Giroux 2017).

35 Austerity policies in response to the effects of the financial crisis caused by banks was a tragedy in Europe. Pankaj Mishra, *Age of Anger: A History of the Present* (Ferrar, Strauss and Giroux 2017); Eduardo Vera-Cruz Pinto, 'O socialismo espera e desespera por um partido socialista que o queira' in AA. VV. A Austeridade mata? A Austeridade cura? Eduardo Paz Ferreira (ed), Lisbon Law School Editions, (2013) 1459–1482.

36 Frank Biess, *Republik der Angst. Eine andere Geschichte der Bundesrepublik* (Rowohlt Verlag 2019).

7. TRADITIONAL LAWYERS VERSUS ADVOCACY FOR THE FUTURE

Increasingly, forensic professions resort to artificial intelligence[37] in their daily work. Advocacy has radically changed, facing new challenges and ethical problems that are difficult to solve.[38] The advocacy of the future, relocated and facilitated by the use of the algorithm to ensure the promptness of the requested responses and the effectiveness of the solutions, is weakened from the human and social perspective. The liberal professional lawyers with open offices and loyal clients have given space to the big law firms, who identify themselves as service providers.

Lawyers became dependent and salaried workers. Professional orders suffer an identity crisis patent in the tendency to become union associations, limiting their intervention in the social sphere to make the same kind of limited union-style demands. Social responsibility and commitment to justice in the new digital environment are subject to significant distortions.

Interdisciplinary knowledge, such as knowledge of both languages and computers, is required and so is the permanent updating of relevant information (especially in relation to international markets), integration in professional networks of European and international cooperation, horizontal connection in communication networks and information systems, presence in space media audience, knowing how to manage people and heritage, having knowledge of applied behavioural psychology, mastering forensic practices, etc.

However, the most notable challenges lawyers are facing due to the situation created by the pandemic are twofold. On the one hand, the level of professional demands will change (speed, fees, personalised assistance, specialised

---

37 Fabiano Hartmann et al., *Inteligência Artificial E Direito* (Alteridade Editora 2019); Caitlin Mulholland e Ana Frazão (eds), *AA. VV. Inteligência Artificial E Direito – Ética Regulação e Responsabilidade* (Thomson Reuters/Revista dos Tribunais 2019); Paulo Victor Alfeo Reis, *Algoritmos e o Direito* (Almedina 2020); Marcel Leonardi, *Fundamentos De Direito Digital* (Thomson Reuters/Revista dos Tribunais 2019); Allan Rocha de Souza, *Direito Digital: Direito Privado e internet* (2nd edn, Editora Foco 2019).

38 Richard Susskein, *Online Courts and the Future of Justice* (OUP 2019); Idem, *Tomorrow's Lawyers: An Introduction to Your Future* (OUP 2017); Giovani Ravagnani, Bruno Feigelson, Daniel Becker, *O Advogado Do Amanhã – Estudos Em Homenagem Ao Professor Richard Susskind* (Thomson Reuters/Revista dos Tribunais 2019); Marcelo Guedes Nunes, *Jurimetria, Como a Estatística pode reinventar o Direito* (Revista dos Tribunais 2019); Henrique Rocha and Patrícia Peck, *Advocacia Digital* (Thomson Reuters/Revista dos Tribunais 2018); Richard Susskind and Daniel Susskind, *The Future of the Professions: How Technology Will Transform the Work of Human Experts* (OUP 2015); Richard Susskind Obe, *The End of Lawyers?: Rethinking the Nature of Legal Services* (OUP 2010); Stuart Russell, *Human Compatible: Artificial Intelligence and the Problem of Control* (Viking/Penguin Random House 2019); Judea Pearl and Dana Mackenzie, *The Book of Why: The New Science of Cause and Effect* (Basic Books 2018).

knowledge, etc.) in the new collective censorship judgments about the forms of digital exercise of this profession, reflected in the professional (deontological) duties of lawyers. On the other hand, they must learn how to resist - by the applied ethics proper to the identity and essence of "being a lawyer" - technical impositions and technological dependencies in post-COVID professional practice.

All forensic professionals, namely judges, will experience profound changes due to the accelerated anticipation of the future, caused by the COVID-19 pandemic.[39] Lawyers, due to the liberal and competitive nature of the profession, in addition to the instability of the market in which they work, are the professionals who will have to respond with more competence and determination to these changes.

8. CONSTITUTION VERSUS JURISPRUDENCE

Social isolation and withdrawing into homes due to the COVID-19 pandemic necessitated teleworking and forced workers to be "always alert",[40] eventually increasing the exposure of internet users. This is due to the intense and

---

39 David Luban, *Lawyers and Justice: An Ethical Study* (Princeton University Press 1988); Andrew Boon, 'Cause Lawyers and the Alternative Ethical Paradigm: Ideology and Transgression' (2004) 7 Legal Ethics 15 ff; Daniel S. Kleinberger 'Wanted: An Ethos of Personal Responsibility – Why Codes of Ethics and Schools of Law Don't Make for Ethical Lawyers' (1989) 21 Connecticut LR 365; William H. Simon 'The Ideology of Advocacy: Procedural Justice and Professional Ethics' (1978) 29 Wis LR 103; Robert Condlin 'The Moral Failure of Clinical Legal Education' in David Luban (ed), *The Good Lawyer: Lawyer's Roles and Lawyer's Ethics* (Rowman and Allanheld 1983); Donald Nicolson 'Demography, Discrimination And Diversity: Legal Ethics And Social Background' (2005) 12 International Journal of the Legal Profession; Donald Nicolson, 'Making lawyers moral? Ethical codes and moral character' (2005) Legal Studies 601–626; Daniel Markovits, 'Legal Ethics from the Lawyer's Point of View' (2003) 15 Yale Journal of Law & the Humanities 209–293; Eduardo Vera-Cruz Pinto, *Profissões Judiciárias. Regras Éticas e Deveres Deontológicos*, vol I, O Juiz, (AAFDL 2020); Idem, 'O ensino do Direito Romano e o exercício de profissões Judiciárias, nomeadamente da magistratura judicial', (2019) IV 1 Interpretatio Prudentium 13–19; Idem, *O Futuro da Justiça* (Vega 2014); Francisco Pereira Coutinho, 'The Europeanization of portuguese courts' (with Nuno Piçarra) (2012) 4 Silesian Journal of Legal Studies 73–88; António Manuel Hespanha, 'Terão os juízes voltado ao centro do direito?' (2013) LXII 332 Scientia Iuridica 225–254; Margarida Lima Rego, 'Um seguro de responsabilidade civil para os magistrados?' (2013) Novos temas da responsabilidade civil extracontratual das entidades públicas 159–167; AA. VV. Charles Gardner, James J. Alfini et al (eds), *Judicial Conduct and Ethics* (5th edn, LexisNexis 2013); Ross Cranston (ed), *AA. VV. Legal Ethics and Professional Responsability* (Clarendon Press 1996); Robert McPeake (ed), *AA. VV. Professional Ethics* (17th edn, OUP 2016); Sir Fred Phillips, *Ethics of Legal Profession* (Routledge-Cavendish 2014).

40 Jonathan Crary, *24/7. O capitalismo tardio e os fins do sono* (2013/2014) (Nuno Quintas tr, Antígona 2018).

massive use and transfer of activities that have only been conducted in person until now, to the digital. All activities became digital-only, existing solely on the platform.[41]

This new, aggressive and nosy[42] platform capitalism,[43] in addition to its depersonalising effects and intrusion into private life,[44] will force the

---

41 Zoom is a popular choice for video-conferencing meetings and lessons. Unfortunately, hackers have found a way to insert themselves into the meetings and lessons, calling the issue "zoombombing," where meeting organisers have not properly secured the meetings. The complete automation of our daily lives is changing our way of being human. Major technological disruptions have always been met with fear and suspicion. We are especially afraid of the unknown. Now, what is needed is to give programmers the necessary ethical education to prevent technology from determining choices and asking questions. This task is for humans. The organisation of Algorithms using AI by humans is to improve the quality, speed and effectiveness of responses.

42 Yuval Noah Harari, 'The world after coronavirus', *Financial Times*, https://www.ft.com/content/19d90308-6858-11ea-a3c9-1fe6fedcca75 accessed 16 July 2020. The text reflects Harari's technological idolatry that supports a new existentialism that transfers human decisions to machines.

43 Nick Srnicek and Alex Williams, *Inventar el future* (Malpaso 2016); Nick Srnicek, *Platform Capitalism* (Polity Press 2017); Dafna Bearson, Martin Kenny and John Zysman, *New Work and value creation in the platform economy: a taxonomy and preliminary evidence* (Berkeley Roundtable on the International Economy, 2019 – BRIE Working Paper); Michael A. Cusumano, Annabelle Gawer, David B. Yoffie, *The business of platforms: strategy in the age of digital competition, innovation and power* (Harper Business 2019); Harald Gruber, 'Proposals for a digital industrial policy for Europe' (2019) (43)2 Telecommunications Policy 116–127; Antti Hautamaki and Kaisa Oksanen, 'Digital platforms for restructuring the public sector' in Anssi Smedlund, Arto Lindblom and Lasse Miltronen (eds), *Collaborative value cocreation in the platform economy* (Springer 2018); Carlota Perez, 'Structural change and the assimilation of new technologies in the economic and social systems' (1983) 15(5) Futures 357–375; César Rendueles, *Sociofobia: mudança política na era da utopia digital* (Edições Sesc São Paulo 2016); Nick Srnicek, *Platform capitalism* (Polity Press 2017); Amrit Tiwana, *Platform ecosystems: aligning architecture, governance, and strategy* (Morgan Kauffman 2014); UNCTAD, *Information Economy Report 2017: digitalization, trade and development* (United Nations 2017).

44 Despite a set of normative texts that seek to defend it: UN human rights system: Report of the UN Special Rapporteur on the Right to Freedom of Opinion and Expression, A/HRC/23/40: Report of the UN Special Rapporteur on human rights and fundamental freedoms while countering terrorism, A/HRC/13/37; General Assembly Resolution 68/167 European Declarations Conventions, Convention for the Protection of Individuals with regard to Automatic Processing of Personal Data (ETS No. 108). The Data Protection Convention is open to European as well as non-European states. The Convention is currently undergoing a consultation process to modernise it; Convention on Cybercrime (ETS No. 185) Open to non-Council of Europe states; Declaration of the Committee of Ministers on Risks to Fundamental Rights stemming from Digital Tracking and other Surveillance Technologies. See also: 'The rule of law on the Internet and in the wider digital world' Issue paper published by the Council of Europe Commissioner for Human Rights. See also: Global Governance and Surveillance Reform; Five Principles. The five principles were developed by AOL, Apple, Facebook, Google, LinkedIn, Microsoft, Twitter, and Yahoo who are calling on states to endorse and enact the principles which relate to: (1) limiting government's authority to collect users' information; (2) Oversight and accountability; (3) Transparency about government demands; (4) Respecting the free flow of information; (5) Avoiding Conflicts Among Governments.

reorganisation of the model of legislative production that places the Constitution at the top of the normative pyramid. It is the very idea of a formal constitution as a fundamental law that is in crisis, and with it the model of political organisation of European societies as States of law in which law is made exclusively by the State.

The non-retrogression of social rights,[45] the defence of personality and minority rights and the civic duties of social isolation and staying home[46] are implemented and carried out only in a pandemic situation[47] and understood

45 Víctor Abramovich and Christian Courtis, *Los derechos sociales como derechos exigibles* (Trotta 2004); Gustavo Amaral, *Direito, Escassez e Escolha. Critérios Jurídicos para Lidar com a Escassez de Recursos e as Decisões Trágicas* (2nd edn, Lumen Juris 2010); Bobbio Norberto, *A era dos direitos* (Carlos Nelson Coutinho tr, Campus, 1992); Ernst Wolfgang Bockenforde, *Estudios sobre el Estado de Derecho y La Democracia* (Rafael de Agapito Serrano tr, Trotta 2000); José Joaquim Gomes Canotilho, *Direito constitucional e teoria da constituição* (7th edn, 9th reimp, Almedina 2000); Idem, 'O direito constitucional como ciência de direção – o núcleo essencial de prestações sociais ou a localização incerta da socialidade (contributo para a reabilitação da força normativa da "constituição social")' in José Joaquim Gomes Canotilho et al (eds), *Direitos fundamentais sociais* (Saraiva 2010) 11–32; Felipe Derbli, *O princípio da proibição de retrocesso social na Constituição de 1988* (Renovar 2007); Deutch Welle, *Merkel: Coronavirus is Germany's greatest challenge since World War Two* https://www.dw.com/en/merkel-coronavirusis-germanys-greatest-challenge-since-world-war-two/a-52830797 accessed 18 March 2020; Konrad Hesse, *A força normativa da Constituição* (Sergio Antonio Fabris 1991); Samanta Ribeiro Meyer-Pflug and Roberto Senise Lisboa, 'Artigo 1°' in Wagner Balera and Vladmir Oliveira da Silveira (coords) and Mônica Bonetii Couto (org), *Comentários ao Pacto Internacional dos Direito Econômicos, Sociais e Culturais* (Clássica 2013) 27–37; Jorge Reis Novais, *Direitos Sociais. Teoria Jurídica dos Direitos Sociais enquanto Direitos Fundamentais* (Editora Coimbra 2010); Diane Roman, 'L'effectivité des droits fondamentaux dans le secteur de la santé, sous le prisme de l'Union Européenne' in Saulo José Casali (ed), *A Efetividade dos Direitos Fundamentais no Mercosul e na União Européia* (Paginae 2010) 165–200; Boaventura Sousa Santos, *Pela mão de Alice: o social e o político na pós-modernidade* (7th edn, Cortez 1997); Ingo Wolfgang Sarlet, *A eficácia dos direitos fundamentais: uma teoria geral dos direitos fundamentais na perspectiva constitucional* (10th edn, Livraria do advogado 2009).

46 Marco Túlio Cícero, *Dos Deveres* (Martin Claret 2007); Immanuel Kant, *Metafísica dos Costumes, Parte II: Princípios Metafísicos da Doutrina da Virtude* (Artur Mourão tr, Edições 70 2004); Norberto Bobbio, *Direitos e deveres na República: os grandes temas da política e da cidadania* (Daniela Beccaccia Versiani tr, Elsevier 2007); Jorge Miranda, *Manual de Direito Constitucional, Tomo IV, Direitos Fundamentais* (Editora Coimbra 2000) 76 ff; José Carlos Vieira de Andrade, *Os Direitos Fundamentais na Constituição Portuguesa de 1976* (5th edn, Almedina 2016); José Casalta Nabais, *Por uma Liberdade com Responsabilidade: estudos sobre direitos e deveres fundamentais* (Coimbra Editora 2007); Paulo Otero, *Instituições Políticas e Constitucionais*, vol I (Almedina 2007); Adriano Sant'Ana Pedra, 'A importância dos deveres humanos na efetivação de direitos' in Robert Alexy, Narciso Leandro Xavier Baez, Hans Jörg Sandkühler, Paulo Hahn (eds), *Níveis de efetivação de direitos fundamentais civis e sociais: um diálogo Brasil e Alemanha* (UNESCO 2013); Carlos Eduardo Behrmann Rátis Martins, *Introdução ao estudo dos deveres fundamentais* (JusPodivm 2009).

47 Arturo Chimal Arechavala, 'Las políticas públicas frente a las emergências sanitárias a partir de la experiencia mexicana frente a la pandemia de la influenza A (H1N1)' in Ingrid Brena Sesma (ed), *Emergencias sanitárias* (Instituto de Investigaciones Jurídicas/Universidad Nacional Autónoma de México 2013) 137–158; Sueli Gandolfi Dallari, 'Poderes Republicanos

as being *legal*, thus harnessing the protection of the country's legal and constitutional framework. The revision of the dominant theory of formal sources of law is inevitable. The new theoretical topic to be explored in the post-COVID world is whether legal (*ius*) is the source of the law, instead of the law being a source of what is legal (*ius*). It is a legal revolution that, the later it is done, the worse its effects will be on the stability of current societies.

The pandemic reopened old wounds. The only legal answer with a future is to change mentalities and to fight legalistic exclusivism and constitutional totalitarianism by accepting that rule of law cannot be created by *imperium* but by *auctoritas*; that the legitimacy to create, interpret and apply it lies in the experience and socially accepted knowledge of the jurisprudents, and not in the election for positions of political representation; that the legal rule (*regulae iuris*) is based on the similarity of solutions of identical concrete cases (generalisation) and not on the political ideologies that won the election or on the consensus of the parliamentary majorities. This is *ius* and *iustitia*.

The politicism/statehood of the Constitution do not allow for a crisis of politics and the State does not call into question the Constitution and in effect the crisis of constitutionalism. This may be the opportunity to initiate a change in law that puts us in a position where humanity might have a future.

9. CONCLUSION

The way television networks and news channels have been communicating the COVID pandemic to the public has created new forms of censorship in relation to the behaviour of individuals who question the enactment of laws and the courts' jurisprudence; as it is currently being conducted, the journalistic enquiry on potential crimes is hampering the legal principle of presumption of innocence, harming the judge's role as guarantor of the individual/suspect's rights.

The fear of contamination and the state of emergency have created an environment of acceptance towards laws that restrict citizens' personal and political freedoms, without due proportionality. The pandemic environment has created a 'sanitised' democracy that is less attentive and alert to the separation of

e a defesa do direito à saúde. Evolução da proteção do direito à saúde nas Constituições do Brasil' in Sandra Mara Campos Alves, Maria Célia Delduque and Nicolau Dino Neto (eds), *Direito Sanitário em perspectiva*, II (Brasília ESMPU/FIOCRUZ 2013) 21–44; José Casalta Nabais, 'A face oculta dos direitos fundamentais: os deveres e os custos dos direitos' (2002) 3(2) Revista Direito Mackenzie, first page; Leandro Bastos Nunes, *Crimes relacionados à pandemia do coronavirus*. https://www.leandrobastosnunes.com.br/coronavirus-consequencias-noambito-penal-relativasaodescumprimento-das-determinacoes-do-poderpublico/ accessed 17 July 2020; Boaventura de Sousa Santos, *Vírus: tudo o que é sólido se desfaz no ar*, https://www.ces.uc.pt/pt/agenda-noticias/destaques/2020/virus accessed 18 March 2020.

powers, namely between the executive and the judiciary. The use of legalism as a response to political problems has accentuated the institutional arrogance of the parliamentary majorities with prejudice to the social pluralism of our societies. The universities, now understood as businesses, have reduced the law degrees to a professional/technical training directed at the job market with the effect of hampering the legal culture; lawyers, themselves, have moved from being a liberal profession to becoming a subordinate work-force in law firms which has the effect of impairing the universal access to justice.

All of these signs of degradation of the law as an instrument of justice were aggravated by political decisions to combat the pandemic, forcing a radical review in relation to the sources of law.

EPILOGUE

This volume purports to provide an overview of the national and international measures developed to fight the COVID-19 pandemic in Europe, and aims to serve as a "toolbox" for judges and practitioners. By the time the book goes to print, the coronavirus, we are afraid, has not finished its devastating work. Virus mutations were even threatening that worse is still to come. Vaccination, however, is hopefully showing a way out. Developments such as these make it difficult to predict what the future will bring. We have therefore refrained from presenting the reader with a fully-fledged conclusion. Instead, we intend to offer you some ideas of a methodological nature, as well as some acknowledgements.

As regards the methodology: how did our project come into being? The historical background is to be found in the late 20th century, when several working groups of legal academics from various countries emerged. Commissions, such as Ole Lando's Commission on European Contract Law, were created and working groups, such as those begun by Christian von Bar, Giuseppe Gandolfi and Reiner Schulze, among others, came up with drafts for a European Civil Code. By the early years of the current millennium, such projects began to run out of steam. The work was done, the money was spent. This did not mean that the members of the various groups lost touch. On occasions such as New Year, or disasters – as perceived by many – such as Brexit, contacts were again taken up, instigated by academics such as Hugh Beale and Matthias Storme. Likewise, early in 2020, when the pandemic started spreading, the group of former Commission members, now at around 100 members, proposed the idea of turning the negative development of the pandemic into something positive. The idea of a special volume was born. Over the past few months, this project has come to fruition. We will now present the way in which we have approached our task.

One of the first questions posed was: what purpose should the volume have? Two options were raised. The majority of the potential authors considered a classical overview of the law the best option. A minority would have preferred to pursue a more politically-oriented approach. This group came to publish a number of reports.[1] The majority, representing the mainstream, contributed to the present volume.

1 Christine Riefa, 'Coronavirus as a Catalyst to Transform Consumer Policy and Enforcement', (2020) 43 Journal of Consumer Policy 451–461.

Who are these authors? At the outset it must be said that the idea of a special volume on the coronavirus and the law attracted widespread approval. In the end, more than 80 colleagues joined the project. Who would manage the project? Six academics volunteered: Ewoud Hondius (University of Utrecht, Netherlands), Marta Santos Silva (University of Maastricht, Netherlands) – who also served as coordinator –, Andrea Nicolussi (Catholic University of Milan), Pablo Salvador (Universitat Pompeu Fabra, Barcelona), Christiane Wendehorst (University of Vienna, Austria) and Fryderyk Zoll (Jagellonian University, Cracow, Poland). Thus, the Editorial Board was formed. The work consisted of attending weekly Zoom meetings, inviting peer reviewers and performing the various odd jobs which go with the role of editor.

At an early stage, the Editorial Board decided to use double blind peer review in order to maintain the quality of the various chapters. This was an interesting experience. Most authors were happy with the improvements suggested by the peers, but occasionally an author would give the impression that he or she was less used to receiving constructive criticism by anonymous peers.

This project resulted in two publications. The first appeared in digital form, on Intersentia Online, by the end of August 2020. It was made available freely so that it could be used in practice immediately, but also to allow improvements where necessary. The second publication, this time in print and digital formats, is the present volume.

We now arrive at the acknowledgements. First of all, our thanks go out to the authors of the various chapters of this book. We are grateful for their cooperation which has allowed us to witness a form of European intellectual solidarity during a difficult time for everyone.

The same applies to the many (anonymous) peer reviewers. Almost without exception they accepted the not always easy task of judging the quality of the papers submitted. We would thus like to thank: Adriana Almasan, Esther Arroyo, Ewa Baginska, Elena Bargelli, Alfredo Batuecas Caletrío, John Bell, Matteo Bonelli, Roger Brownsword, Gert Brüggemeier, Raquel Carvalho, Rui Cascão, Caroline Cauffman, Olha Cherednychenko, Gregor Christandl, Aurelia Colombi Ciacchi, Cees van Dam, Mariolina Eliantonio, Duncan Fairgrieve, Alberto de Franceschi, Maria Paz García Rubio, Fernando Gómez-Pomar, Michele Graziadei, Thomas Jaeger, Monika Jagielska, Monika Jurcova, Christof Koolen, Bernhard Kresse, Laura Macgregor, Gianclaudio Malgieri, Sebastian Martens, Giuseppe Martinico, José Carlos de Medeiros Nóbrega, Katarzyna Michałowska, Antonio Manuel Morales Moreno, Rodrigo Momberg Uribe, Horatia Muir Watt, Madalena Narciso, Luca Nogler, Pedro del Olmo, Guillermo Palao Moreno, Ekaterina Pannebakker, Agustin Parise, Barbara Pasa, Maria do Céu Patrão Neves, Cándido Paz-Ares, Frans Pennings, Christina Peristeridou, Pascal Pichonnaz, Fabrizio Piraino, Jerzy Pisulinksi, Edoardo Raffiotta, Giovanni di Rosa, Harriet Schelhaas, Reiner Schulze, Pietro Sirena, Hanna Stahyra,

Karl Stöger, Matthias Storme, Radosław Strugała, Eric Tjong Tjin Tai, Stefano Troiano, Carles Vendrell Cervantes, Giuseppe Vettori and Reinhard Zimmermann.

We are grateful as well to the editorial assistants for their support: Wojciech Banczyk (Jagiellonian University, Cracow), Yannic Duller (University of Vienna), Sophia Fida (University of Vienna), Tomás Gabriel García-Micó (Pompeu Fabra University, Barcelona), Ignacio García-Perrote Martínez (Pompeu Fabra University, Barcelona), Henriikka Malmi (Maastricht University), Katarzyna Poludniak-Gierz (Jagiellonian University, Cracow), Giuseppe Portonera (Catholic University of Milan), Carlo Rusconi (Catholic University of Milan), Marielène Wertenbroek (Maastricht University), Francesco Zecchin (Catholic University of Milan) and Laura Zsarnai (Maastricht University).

We are grateful to the publisher, Intersentia, in particular Ann-Christin Maak-Scherpe and Rebecca Moffat, and to the professional proofreaders.

Together with the publisher, we are intending to add to the online version of this publication. Any papers dealing with new developments or cases involving COVID-19 should be sent to Ann-Christin Maak-Scherpe at mail@intersentia.co.uk. Such papers may deal with new developments or with cases involving COVID-19.

We would also like to thank the illustrator of our cover, Fatinha Ramos, and, finally, we acknowledge the generous funding of the project by the Catalan Notaries Guild and the Spanish Property and Mercantile Register Guild in Spain.

Ewoud Hondius
Marta Santos Silva
Andrea Nicolussi
Pablo Salvador Coderch
Christiane Wendehorst
Fryderyk Zoll

EUROPEAN LAW INSTITUTE

ANNEX: ELI PRINCIPLES FOR THE COVID-19 CRISIS

2020

PREAMBLE

The outbreak of COVID-19 has brought immense suffering and death to a considerable number of people around the world. It has impacted fundamentally the functioning of States, their democratic institutions and legal systems. Therefore, it is understandable that governments have and are continuing to resort to exceptional measures in seeking to get control over the spread of COVID-19. These exceptional measures inevitably restrict the fundamental rights of citizens in ways that can be justified only in these extraordinary circumstances. It is in the greatest interest of society that these measures against COVID-19 are imposed and enforced within the framework of established democratic principles, the international legal order and the rule of law.

Therefore, although the spread of COVID-19 justifies limitations on the functioning of institutions such as Parliaments and courts, these limitations must be subject to democratic control, must not be misused and not applied for purposes other than measures related directly to the COVID-19 crisis.

The measures taken by governments such as mandatory quarantine, the closure of borders, restrictions in mobility, are also having a dramatic impact on business, trade and employment. It is essential that the legal measures taken to address the hardship and other difficulties caused by COVID- 19 take into account principles of solidarity and fairness as well as the need for co-ordinated action between States at an international or EU level as appropriate.

In these circumstances, the European Law Institute (ELI), an entirely independent non-profit organisation established to provide practical guidance in relation to European legal development, puts forward a summary of some of the important legal issues that arise in relation to the COVID-19 crisis.

Its summary, made from an independent non-governmental perspective with due consideration of what has been published by other bodies, is set out in 15 principles. These are addressed to all European States (whether or not Member States of the EU), and are intended to guide European States, EU institutions and other bodies with the object of ensuring that everything that is done accords with the rule of law and democratic values.

PRINCIPLE 1: FUNDAMENTAL VALUES, PRINCIPLES AND FREEDOMS

1. Despite the unprecedented situation due to the COVID-19 outbreak the fundamental values, principles and freedoms enshrined not only in primary EU legislative rules, such as the Treaty on European Union (TEU), the Treaty on the Functioning of the European Union (TFEU) and the Charter on Fundamental Rights and Freedoms (CFREU), but also in the European Convention on Human Rights (ECHR) and in the constitutions of States throughout Europe, must be preserved and maintained.
2. States may legitimately restrict particular fundamental principles or freedoms by way of exceptional measures in order to protect human life and health, on condition that such measures are limited to what is strictly necessary and proportionate, are temporary solely for the duration of the crisis and its immediate aftermath and subject to regular scrutiny by Parliaments and the courts.
3. Fundamental principles relating to freedom of expression, access to public information, the freedom of the press and access to justice through the courts should be fully respected.

PRINCIPLE 2: NON-DISCRIMINATION

1. The COVID-19 crisis does not justify any kind of discrimination based on nationality or any of the other criteria and in the situations recognised as unacceptable under anti-discrimination laws in Europe. Any measures taken by States as a response to the COVID-19 crisis must be applied in a non-discriminatory manner and scrutinised for any unintended discriminatory effects.
2. The prohibition of discrimination applies, in particular, to medical assistance and to the supply of goods, services or residential housing that is usually available to the public and may become scarce due to the crisis. Assistance offered for returning home in the COVID-19 crisis, such as State-organised re-patriation flights, should not differentiate between a

Member State's own nationals and others lawfully resident in that State or individuals enjoying a comparable legal status.

PRINCIPLE 3: DEMOCRACY

1. The unprecedented situation due to the COVID-19 outbreak should, in no case and for no reason, legitimise measures that, irrespective of their intention, might result in a repressive or authoritarian course of action, undermine democratic public institutions and/or impede the citizens' entitlement to democratic government, either permanently or temporarily.
2. Parliaments must not be deprived of their powers by the state of emergency, and should, wherever possible, take the most important decisions themselves (through the use of technology, where desirable), which will then be further implemented by governments. Parliaments must in any case be provided with the opportunity to decide when the state of emergency has come to an end, and to review and undo steps taken by the government during the state of emergency.
3. During the COVID-19 crisis, elections should be organised only if there is a guarantee that all requirements for free, equal and democratic election procedures can be observed. If the requirements are not met, then every effort should made to put them in place, but in the meantime elections should be postponed.

PRINCIPLE 4: LAWMAKING

1. Governments must not abuse the crisis by utilising the curtailment of regular Parliamentary debate and processes to promote measures and policies unrelated to the COVID-19 crisis. Ordinary Parliamentary processes and legislation must be used for such measures. The crisis must not be used to adopt emergency laws that may secure privileges for governments in enhancing their powers during the COVID-19 crisis or thereafter in cases unrelated to the COVID-19 crisis.
2. If possible, legislation responding to the COVID-19 crisis that was passed under accelerated or curtailed procedures should be enacted separately and should automatically cease to remain in force at a date when the COVID-19 crisis is over. Where such legislation seems to be useful in the longer term it should be revisited and approved through ordinary procedures.
3. Even in a state of emergency and under accelerated or curtailed procedures, all due efforts must be made to make sure legislation is in conformity with

the constitution, EU law and any other law higher in rank, in particular as far as fundamental rights are concerned. Reasonable efforts must be made to correct deficiencies even during the COVID-19 crisis, duly taking into account the need for stability.

PRINCIPLE 5: JUSTICE SYSTEM

1. The judiciary should do all that is reasonably practicable to continue to conduct proceedings and trials, particularly though the use of secure video and other remote links where available to the courts. In any case, the judicial system should maintain a minimum level of operations to deal with urgent matters, safeguard the rule of law and provide proper remedies to litigants, provided that the right to a fair trial, including the right to defence, is not infringed. The restrictions on the operation of the judiciary must be immediately removed when the COVID-19 emergency permits.
2. States should take appropriate measures to suspend or extend, where necessary, deadlines or time periods (whether fixed by statute or by courts) so that the rights of parties are not prejudiced by the emergency.
3. Measures must be taken to provide appropriate protection for those held in prisons. Where this is not possible, consideration should be given by the appropriate authority to granting temporary release to prisoners who are not considered to be a danger to society and particularly to the elderly and those with serious underlying health conditions.
4. Administrative sanctions and fines imposed on citizens for the violation of COVID-19 emergency legislation must have sufficient foundation in the law and they must be subjected to effective judicial review.

PRINCIPLE 6: PRIVACY AND DATA PROTECTION

1. States should ensure that, in accordance with the General Data Protection Regulation (GDPR), other data protection law, and the CFREU, public authorities and employers are allowed to process personal data (including telecom data) insofar as this is necessary to mitigate the COVID-19 pandemic. However, such processing of personal data should be minimised and the least intrusive solutions should always be preferred, in accordance with the proportionality principle.
2. Processing of particularly sensitive data, such as health data, or particularly intrusive forms of processing, such as the use of geo-tracing and geo-tracking, should be submitted to data protection authorities for approval and the

source code of any applications should be disclosed at least to a broad range of independent non-governmental organisations for scrutiny. Use of such applications should be based on free consent or, if compulsory, on a parliamentary act which clearly sets out the conditions in line with the relevant law. All actions taken by States should follow a pan-European approach, particularly with regard to mobile applications.

3. In any case, data collected on the basis of such extraordinary measures must be either fully anonymised or erased as soon as practicable after the COVID-19 crisis has come to an end, and any software allowing the collection of data must be disabled. This is without prejudice to data being used for research, such as under Article 89 GDPR, with appropriate safeguards.

PRINCIPLE 7: BORDERS AND FREEDOM OF MOVEMENT

1. Borders within the EU should as far as possible remain open for Union citizens and their family members, and every EU Member State must allow its own residents to enter, irrespective of nationality, and should facilitate transit of individuals returning to their homes. Schengen principles as well as bilateral and multilateral agreements should remain in place also for States that are non-EU Member States, but which are party to those agreements.
2. Total closing of borders for individuals enjoying freedom of movement should generally be considered a disproportionate response where less intrusive measures, such as quarantine and testing, are feasible. States may wish to consider restricting mandatory quarantine to cases where:
   a. there is scientific evidence that a person coming from the State to which borders have been closed has a significantly higher risk of being infected than its own population and the Member State imposes the same quarantine on its nationals when returning from the relevant State; or
   b. it is a necessary measure to reduce overall mobility and is accompanied by corresponding restrictions on freedom of movement within the relevant State's own territory.

   In any case, quarantine must be dispensable for urgent cases, including for strong humanitarian reasons.
3. Member States should facilitate the entry and exit of frontier workers and providers of cross- border services, in particular in critical sectors such as health care, care for persons in need, or agriculture.

PRINCIPLE 8: FREE MOVEMENT OF GOODS AND SERVICES

1. EU Member States should take all possible measures so as to avoid obstacles to cross-border movement of goods and services within the EU, prioritising urgent transport services, such as supply of food, medical supplies and other essential goods (eg via 'green lanes'). Bilateral and multilateral agreements dealing with the free movement of goods and services should also remain fully in place under the same conditions with non-EU Member States that are party to those agreements.
2. The COVID-19 crisis does not justify bans on particular goods being exported, or particular services being provided, to other EU Member States if they are to be used within the EU unless allowing the exporting of goods or the provision of services would cause a state of emergency for the relevant State's own population.
3. Member States should not apply quarantine requirements to transport workers whose crossing of borders is required for the application of this Principle, and deny entry to foreign transport workers only if they have been tested positive for or show symptoms of COVID-19. Member States may, however, impose safety conditions, including mandatory health certificates, provided these conditions are science-based, proportionate, applied in a non-discriminatory manner and duly published.

PRINCIPLE 9: EMPLOYMENT AND THE ECONOMY

1. Where businesses or employees suffer economic detriment resulting from measures taken by the State, such as lockdowns, reasonable efforts should be taken to mitigate the negative economic effects by way of State aid, in conformity with EU State aid policy, and preferably based on a joint policy of EU Member States to avoid competition distortion between EU Member States. Particular efforts should be made to minimise loss of employment.
2. States should ensure that they provide employers and employees with sufficient and updated information about COVID-19 contamination. All employees should be provided with the highest standards of health and safety protection appropriate to their work, or if that is not possible be allowed to work from home.
3. A State's decisions concerning the lockdown of particular industries should have a legitimate purpose, be evidence based, reasonable, proportionate and subject to regular scrutiny.

4. States should consider ensuring that businesses receiving public subsidies on an EU or national level re-evaluate their financial planning in the light of the economic disruption expected from the outbreak of COVID-19 and refrain under the present circumstances from payments of dividends, bonuses and other financial contributions to shareholders and management.

PRINCIPLE 10: CONTINUITY OF RELATIONSHIPS AT A DISTANCE

1. States should ensure that contracts can be concluded, management decisions can be made, and all other legal steps can be taken at a distance, including notarisation and other participation by notaries.
2. States should ensure that measures taken due to the COVID-19 outbreak should not prevent the performance of ongoing contracts and other relationships to an extent that is more than necessary and, where possible, should permit performance at a distance.

PRINCIPLE 11: EDUCATION

1. States should make sure that schoolchildren, apprentices, students and all other individuals undergoing programmes of education that are essential for their future career do not suffer any lasting detriment from the COVID-19 crisis, and in particular that solutions are found to provide distance teaching and examinations, so that individuals can graduate without significant delay.
2. In the field of education, particular attention should be paid to measures avoiding discrimination linked to distance teaching, such as by providing extra support to families with poor technical skills or equipment, or to those suffering for other reasons from suboptimal learning environments.

PRINCIPLE 12: MORATORIUM ON REGULAR PAYMENTS

1. In order to mitigate the economic disruption expected from the outbreak of COVID-19, States should provide, if necessary, for a moratorium on some regular payments, particularly on taxes, rents, and loans. Such measure should be based on the general principle that the final maturity date is extended for the duration of the moratorium and that neither the calculation of the amount due, nor that of other taxes or instalments

subsequently due, are in any way increased. Statutory period of limitations should likewise be suspended for the same period.

2. In accordance with their laws and legal systems, States should make special provisions for debt collection and insolvency proceedings to avoid some of the adverse consequences caused by COVID-19 measures on cash flow and liquidity, including a temporary stay on these proceedings and a postponement of the duties of board of directors to alert the insolvency authorities.
3. Furthermore, in conformity with the principle of solidarity, States should favour partial or full release of certain types of matured debts, either on public policy grounds or by mutual consent between the parties.

PRINCIPLE 13: FORCE MAJEURE AND HARDSHIP

1. Where performance of a contract is temporarily or definitively prevented directly or indirectly due to the COVID-19 outbreak or States' decisions taken in relation to the COVID-19 outbreak, States should ensure that existing law on impossibility or *force majeure* applies in an effective way, and provides reasonable solutions. In particular, the contractual allocation of risk in these instances should be evaluated in the light of existing contracts, background legal regimes and the principle of good faith.
2. Where, as a consequence of the COVID-19 crisis and the measures taken during the pandemic, performance has become excessively difficult (hardship principle), including where the cost of performance has risen significantly, States should ensure that, in accordance with the principle of good faith, parties enter into renegotiations even if this has not been provided for in a contract or in existing legislation.
3. In conformity with the principle of solidarity, States should ensure that the consequences of the disruption of contractual relationships, such as the cancellation of travel arrangements, should not be at the sole risk of one party, in particular of a consumer or SME.

PRINCIPLE 14: EXEMPTION FROM LIABILITY FOR SIMPLE NEGLIGENCE

1. Given the urgent and dramatic circumstances in which doctors, healthcare professionals, and other providers in the medical sector have to provide services, States should ensure that these professionals are not held liable for adverse events related to the COVID-19, except in the case of at least gross negligence.

2. The same applies with respect to other professionals and holders of public offices who had to take quick and difficult decisions directly related to the COVID-19 crisis.
3. These exemptions from liability do not apply to the liability of the State, which remains liable pursuant to the existing specific regime of liability.

PRINCIPLE 15: RETURN TO NORMALITY

1. National governments should publish as soon as is practicable plans for an exit from the emergency and, in accordance with the rule of law, a return to normality and the ending of the emergency measures imposed for the crisis.
2. The ending of emergency measures and a return to normality should be monitored by EU institutions.

2021 Supplement

INTRODUCTION TO THE 2021 SUPPLEMENT

After more than a year since its start, the COVID-19 pandemic still generates a lot of legal concerns. The everyday legal issues have evolved to some degree, but new issues have arisen in 2021. With large scale testing and vaccinations, states face new challenges, both in dealing with the proportionality of measures to be taken in where there is a low epidemiological risk and in ensuring the equitable distribution of vaccines. The European Commission published, on 17 March 2021, a strategy for a common path to Europe's safe re-opening, which includes, inter alia, the basis for a Europe-wide Digital Green Certificate. However, important decisions, including which restrictions to lift under which circumstances, remain with the individual States. The same holds true for vaccine rollout within the individual States, including issues of prioritisation. In the same vein as the existing (2020) ELI Principles for the COVID-19 Crisis, the ELI wishes to provide further guidance on these issues by way of supplementing these Principles with two new Principles.

PRINCIPLE 16: PROPORTIONALITY OF MEASURES IN CASES OF LOW EPIDEMIOLOGICAL RISK

1. Restrictions of movement and activities imposed on the population during the COVID-19 crisis must not be imposed on an individual beyond what is necessary and proportionate in the light of the fundamental rights at stake

and the epidemiological risk posed by that individual. This means that restrictions may have to be lifted for an individual if
   a. the epidemiological risk posed by that individual is low, and/or
   b. there are no compelling reasons of public interest to apply the restrictions to all individuals in an equal manner irrespective of the actual risk.

2. An individual poses a low epidemiological risk within the meaning of paragraph (1)(a) where there is, in the light of the facts of the individual case and scientific evidence, sufficient reason to believe that the individual will not spread any variants of the virus currently in circulation. Particular regard must be had to whether that individual
   a. has been vaccinated; or
   b. has, within a defined period in the past, recovered from COVID-19; or
   c. has just been negatively tested.

   Scientific evidence must be regularly evaluated, including having regard to the types of vaccination or testing methods, timespans, and other relevant criteria. Significant changes in scientific evidence should lead to dynamic adjustment of certificates issued.
3. Compelling reasons within the meaning of paragraph (1)(b) may include, in particular, practical difficulties in checking any relevant certificates in the circumstances, a possible demoralising or disturbing effect on other individuals, or a particularly high need for safety.
4. Parties from the private sector should be allowed to restrict sale of goods or provision of services, or any other transaction, to individuals with a low epidemiological risk within the meaning of paragraph (2), provided that this
   a. is within the limits set by applicable law on non-discrimination; and
   b. does not in fact deprive individuals who cannot produce a certificate of low epidemiological risk from goods or services of essential significance.

PRINCIPLE 17: EQUITABLE DISTRIBUTION OF VACCINES

1. The administration of vaccines should comply with the principles of fairness and equality in design and in impact. This means in particular that
   a. The order of priority, during the gradual build-up of vaccination capacities, should be assessed generally according to four criteria:
      i. vulnerability with regard to the acute effects of COVID-19 and its variants;
      ii. higher risk because of lack of access to healthcare;

    iii. a necessarily higher risk of spreading and multiplying factor and/or systematic contact with ill and vulnerable persons, to the extent that vaccination prevents vaccinated persons from spreading the virus;
    iv. systematic contact with ill and vulnerable persons, as well as key individuals for the functioning of the Public State.
  b. Registration for vaccination should be designed and implemented in a non-discriminatory way, avoiding discrimination including any based on disabilities, age, economic or social capacities.
  c. Vaccination should be offered in a safe and non-threatening environment, with appropriately trained staff and under a close monitoring and assessment system which ensures a zero waste approach.
2. Both principles of precaution and efficiency should determine the administration of a second injection, if two injections are needed.
  a. This means in particular that an assessment of risks should determine whether public health imposes a second injection to those already vaccinated with a first injection or whether it is better to have a larger range of people vaccinated with a first injection.
  b. The decision should be documented, transparent and rely on thorough scientific analysis.
3. If COVID-19 variants require vaccinating afresh the principle of precaution and efficiency should be applied, which may mean vaccinating first unvaccinated persons instead of following the principle set out under paragraph 1.
4. Within the EU, procurement and distribution of vaccines should be based on the foundational value of solidarity between EU Member States, which implies setting up coordinated mechanisms between them, including fostering respect of the principles set above. The EU Vaccine Sharing Mechanism is part of this endeavour.
5. As there is a need to ensure wide vaccination across the Globe to hasten the general reduction of the pandemic, EU Member States should find a fair and effective balance between domestic vaccinations and support of the COVAX Facility to share vaccines with all low and middle income countries.

ABOUT THE EDITORS

Ewoud Hondius read law in Leyden and New York (Columbia). He received a doctorate from Leyden and honorary degrees from Edinburgh and Leuven. He is Emeritus Professor of European Private Law at the University of Utrecht. Previously, he was a Visiting Professor in Cambridge, Kyoto, Münster, Paris and Sydney. He has written several books on private and consumer law. He is a membre titulaire of the International Academy of Comparative Law and member of the Royal Netherlands Academy of Sciences.

Marta Santos Silva, PhD in Laws, is Lecturer at the Faculty of Law at Maastricht University, affiliated senior researcher at the Institute for Consumer, Competition & Market at KU Leuven and appointed Member of the Expert Group on Liability and New Technologies of the European Commission. She received the Europa Prize 2008 for notable academic achievements in several Member States of the European Union. She has been working in academic and policy pan-European projects for the harmonisation of European Private Law since 2005 and has a vast international experience in teaching and academic management.

Andrea Nicolussi is Full Professor of Civil Law at the Law Faculty of the Catholic University of Milan, where he teaches comparative private law and family law. His published works focus on unjustified enrichment, contract law and tort law, as well as biolaw and family law. He has taken part in international collaborations such as the Study Group on a European Civil Code and the Eusoco project and was a member of the National Bioethics Committee.

Pablo Salvador Coderch is Emeritus Professor of Civil Law at the University of Pompeu Fabra, Barcelona. Renowned for his work in the field of Private Law, he is a member of the International Academy of Comparative Law, the American Law Institute, the European Law Institute and Academia de Jurisprudència i Legislació de Catalunya.

Christiane Wendehorst is Full Professor of Civil Law at the University of Vienna. She is founding member and President of the European Law Institute (ELI) and chair of the Academy Council of the Austrian Academy of Sciences. She is member of the Academia Europea, the International Academy for Comparative Law, the American Law Institute as well as of the Austrian Bioethics Committee and the Executive Board of the Austrian Jurists' Forum (ÖJT). Prior to moving to Vienna, she held chairs in Göttingen and Greifswald and was Director of the Sino-German Institute of Legal Studies.

Fryderyk Zoll is Full Professor at the Department of Civil Law at the Jagiellonian University and at the European Legal Studies Institute at the University of Osnabrück. He received an honorary doctorate from the University of Ternopil and was honoured with the Private Law Prize at the IX St. Petersburg International Legal Forum (Shortlist, 2019) and the Medal Bene Merentibus Iustitiae (2013). He is a member of the European Law Institute and the international association for the judicial independence and world peace.